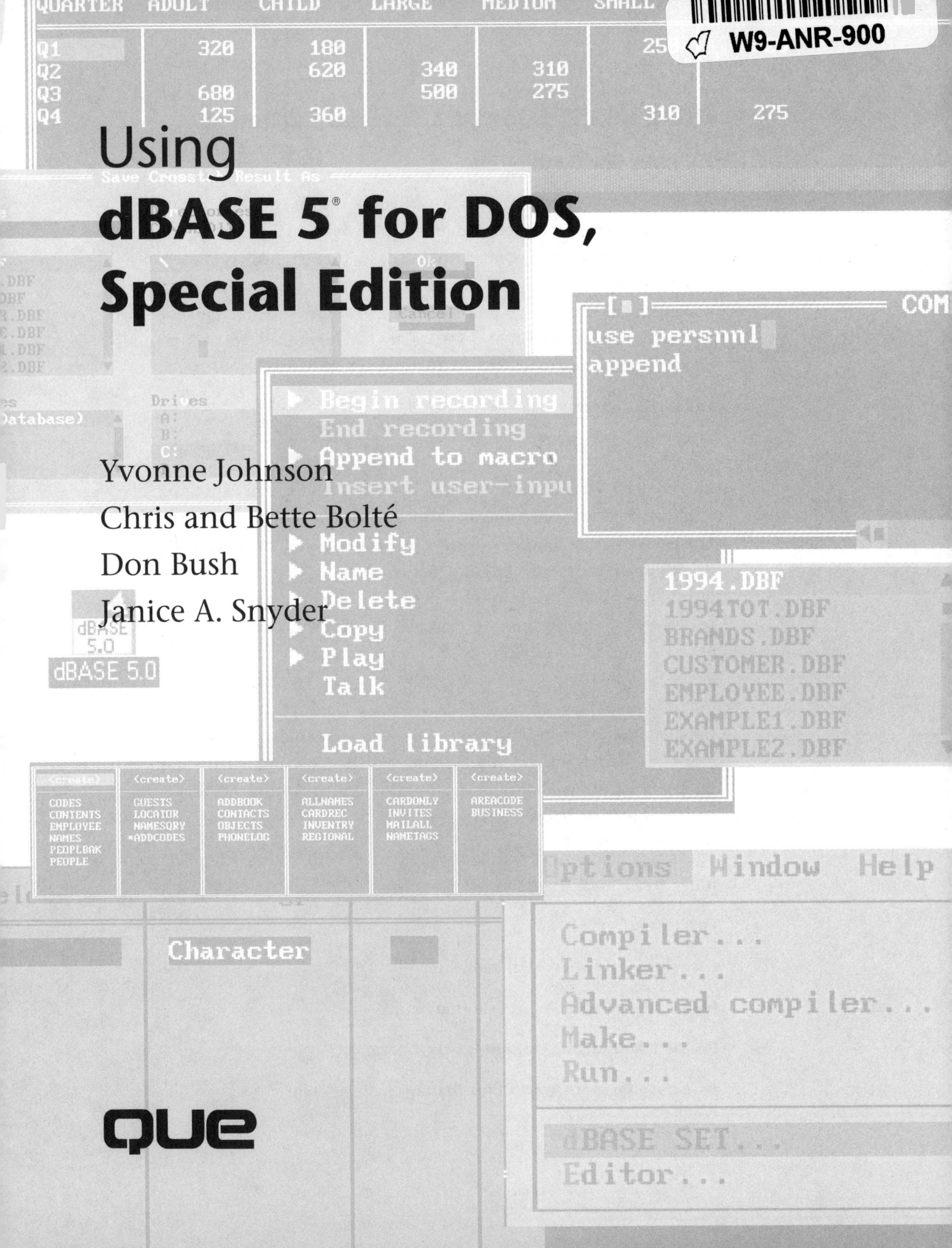
W9-ANR-900
Using
dBASE 5® for DOS,
Special Edition
Yvonne Johnson
Chris and Bette Bolté
Don Bush
Janice A. Snyder
dBASE 5.0
QUE

Using dBASE 5 for DOS, Special Edition

Library of Congress Catalog Number: 94-67605

ISBN: 1-56529-728-8

96 95 94 4 3 2 1

Interpretation of the printing code: The rightmost double-digit number is the year of the book's printing; the rightmost single-digit number, the number of the book's printing. For example, a printing code of 94-1 shows that the first printing of the book occurred in 1994.

Screen reproductions in this book were created with Collage Complete from Inner Media, Inc., Hollis, NH.

Publisher: David P. Ewing

Associate Publisher: Don Roche, Jr.

Managing Editor: Michael Cunningham

Product Marketing Manager: Greg Wiegand

Associate Product Marketing Manager: Stacy Collins

Credits

Publishing Manager
Nancy Stevenson

Acquisitions Editor
Jenny Watson

Acquisitions Coordinator
Deborah Abshier

Product Director
Kathie-Jo Arnoff

Product Development Specialists
Ella Davis
Lisa D. Wagner

Production Editor
Linda Seifert

Copy Editors
Elsa Bethanis
Lisa Gebken
Julie Macnamee
Lynn Northrup
Wendy Ott
Nicole Rodandello
Maureen Schneeberger

Editorial Assistant
Jill Stanley

Technical Editors
Kurt Schroeders
Janice A. Snyder

Technical Specialist
Cari Ohm

Book Designer
Paula Carroll

Cover Designer
Jay Corpus

Imprint Manager
Kelli Widdifield

Production Team
Kim Cofer
Amy Cornwell
Karen Dodson
Chad Dressler
DiMonique Ford
Teresa Forrester
Dennis Clay Hager
Carla Hall
Bob LaRoche
Elizabeth Lewis
Malinda Lowder
Wendy Ott
Beth Rago
Nancy Sears Perry
Dennis Sheehan
Mike Thomas
Tina Trettin
Mary Beth Wakefield
Karen Walsh
Donna Winter
Jody York

Indexer
Charlotte Clapp

Composed in *Stone Serif* and *MCPdigital* by Macmillan Computer Publishing

About the Authors

Yvonne Johnson has been involved in teaching and writing about PCs since they first came into use. For 12 years she owned and operated a successful computer training school. During that time she authored all the training material for the school and wrote several books published by Que and other publishers. After selling the school, she now devotes more of her time to writing, consulting, and programming. Her training and writing background has made her exceptionally well-versed in database, word processing, graphic, spreadsheet, presentation, integrated, and publishing software. She holds a BA degree from Centre College of Kentucky with a major in Education and English. She did her postgraduate work at the University of South Florida.

Chris Bolté has been working with personal and minicomputers for over 15 years. He has written several database applications in network environments, and has experience in dBASE, SQL, ORACLE, and other popular programming languages. He has performed training for software packages designed for various customers, and has written design, maintenance, and user manuals for many different applications. He contributed to *Using dBASE 5 for Windows*, Special Edition, and *Killer dBASE for Windows*, both published by Que books, and to *Inside dBASE for Windows*, published by New Riders Publishing.

Betty Bolté has been an editorial and software training consultant for several years, working in the central Indiana area. She enjoys working with people to help them understand the joys and complexities of computers, without intimidating them with excessive jargon. She writes her own computer training materials, and writes articles and edits other writers' work. She provided technical editing for New Riders Publishing, and contributed to *Using dBASE 5 for Windows*, Special Edition, and *Killer dBASE for Windows*, both published by Que books.

Don Bush is a freelance writer with a background in microwave systems engineering and personal computers. Over the last 10 years, he also has given training classes in programs such as dBASE and Lotus 1-2-3, and he has done consulting projects. He lives with his family in Virginia City, Nevada.

Janice A. Snyder is an independent consultant, specializing in microcomputer software applications. She has worked with databases on mainframes, minicomputers, and PCs for 10 years. As Director of the Administrative Computer Center at Indiana Wesleyan University for three years, she directed the search, acquisition, conversion, and successful implementation of a new administrative software system. She coauthored Que's *Excel 5 for Windows Quick Reference*, revised *1-2-3 Release 5 for Windows Quick Reference* and *Easy 1-2-3 Release 5 for Windows*, and has developed and technical-edited several other Que books. Jan lives in Virginia Beach, Virginia, having recently moved from "Que territory" in Indiana.

Trademark Acknowledgments

Contents at a Glance

Introduction 1

Getting Acquainted with dBASE 5 **9**

1 What's New in dBASE 5 for DOS? 11

2 Getting Started with dBASE 5 25

3 Exploring the New Desktop 33

4 Understanding the Control Center 67

Getting Acquainted

Creating and Using a Database **105**

5 Designing the Structure of a Database 107

6 Adding Records 125

7 Editing and Deleting Records 143

8 Organizing Your Database and Generating a Quick Report 161

Creating/Using Databases

Using More Sophisticated Features **185**

9 Using Queries To Search Databases 187

10 Using Advanced Techniques with Queries 223

11 Creating and Using Input Forms 251

12 Creating Custom Reports 287

13 Designing and Using a Mailmerge Report and Label 323

14 Using Crosstabs 343

15 Using Relational Databases for Complex Situations 359

Using More Features

Programming in dBASE 5 **381**

16 Getting Started with Programming 383

17 Exploring Some Sample Programs 421

18 Creating Custom Applications 477

19 Using the Applications Generator and the Compiler 527

Programming in dBASE 5

Using High-Level Tools 563

20 Programming with SQL 565

21 Creating Objects with UI 605

Using High-Level Tools

Reference Guide 635

22 Using dBASE 5 Commands 637

23 Using Functions 751

24 Using SET Commands To Configure dBASE 5 827

25 Using SQL Commands 879

26 Using UI Properties, Methods, and Commands 899

27 Using System Memory Variables 1041

28 Using Preprocessor Directives 1055

29 Using the System Configuration File 1063

Index 1091

Reference Guide

Contents

Introduction **1**

Who Should Read This Book? 2
What's in This Book? 2

I Getting Acquainted with dBASE 5 — 9

1 What's New in dBASE 5 for DOS? — 11

Upgrading from dBASE IV to dBASE 5 12
Exploring the New Desktop Interface 12
- The New Main Menu Bar 13
- The New Windows in dBASE 5 14
- New Dialog Boxes 18
- Crosstab Expert 19
- Desktop Accessories 19
- Project Manager 19
- New Help System 20

Working with Files 21
Using the New Editor 22
Using the User Interface Language Enhancements 23
From Here... 24

2 Getting Started with dBASE 5 — 25

Starting dBASE 5 from the DOS Prompt 25
- Starting dBASE 5 from Windows 26

Using the Mouse 27
Setting Up the Environment 27
Exiting dBASE 31
From Here... 32

3 Exploring the New Desktop — 33

Looking at the Components of the Desktop 33
Using the Menu Bar 34
Using Dialog Boxes 36
- Pushbuttons 38
- Input Boxes 39
- Check Boxes 39
- Radio Buttons 40
- List Boxes 41
- Spin Boxes 42

Using the Command Window 43
    Entering Commands in the Command Window 43
    Reusing a Previous Command 44
Working with Multiple Windows 45
    Opening a Window 45
    Sizing a Window 47
    Moving a Window 48
    Displaying Several Windows 48
    Listing Open Windows 50
    Closing a Window 51
Using the Control Center 51
    Accessing the Control Center 51
    Returning to the Desktop 52
Working with Files 52
    Creating a New File 52
    Opening an Existing File 53
    Canceling the Open File Dialog Box 55
    Changing Directories 55
    Saving Files 56
    Printing Files 57
    Closing Files 58
Working with Tools 58
    Using the ASCII Chart 59
    Using the Calculator 60
    Using the Calendar 61
Getting Help 62
Shelling to DOS 64
From Here... 65

4 Understanding the Control Center 67

Using the Categories 68
    Creating Files 69
    Opening Files 70
    Modifying Files 72
Using Catalogs 73
    Creating Catalogs 73
    Changing the Catalog 75
    Editing the Description 76
    Adding a File to a Catalog 76
    Removing a File from a Catalog 78
Recording Macros 78
Importing Data 82
Exporting Data 83
Using DOS Utilities 84
    Changing the Drive or Directory 86
    Changing the List of Files Displayed 88
        Sorting the List of Files 89
        Marking and Unmarking Files 90

Performing Operations on Files 91
Deleting Files 92
Copying Files 92
Moving Files 93
Renaming Files 94
Viewing Files 94
Editing Files 95
Password Protecting Files 96
Changing Settings 101
Exiting the Control Center 102
From Here... 103

II Creating and Using a Database 105

5 Designing the Structure of a Database 107

Reviewing Your Manual Database 107
Understanding Database Terminology 108
Records 108
Fields 109
Values 109
Defining Your Database 110
Naming a Field 110
Choosing the Type of Field 110
Using Character Field Types 110
Using Numeric Field Types 111
Using Date Field Types 111
Using Float Field Types 111
Using Logical Field Types 112
Using Memo Field Types 112
Specifying the Field Width 113
Indexing a Field 113
Benefits of Indexing a Field 113
Creating Indexes that Use Multiple Fields 115
Entering Your Database Design into dBASE 5 115
Saving the Database Structure 118
Modifying a Database Structure 121
From Here... 124

6 Adding Records 125

Understanding the Data-Entry Process 126
Adding Records Using the Edit Screen 128
Adding Records from the Browse Screen 130
Editing a Record As You Add It 131
Keeping Track of Records 132
Adding Data to Character, Numeric, and Logical Fields .. 133
Adding Data to Memo Fields 134
Closing the Database 137

Understanding More about the Text Editor 137
Moving Around and Editing in the Text Editor 137
Inserting and Replacing Text 139
Adding and Removing Lines 139
Using Block Commands 139
Inserting Page Breaks 139
Searching and Replacing Text 139
Attaching Text Files 140
Printing Memo Fields 141
Saving and Exiting 141
From Here... 142

7 Editing and Deleting Records 143

Reviewing Your Database 143
Using the Display Screens To Edit Records 144
Using the Edit Screen 145
Using the Browse Screen 145
Locking Fields 146
Changing the Size of a Field 148
Freezing Fields 149
Finding Records 149
Using a Simple Index 150
Using the Go To Menu 152
Using the Search Commands 153
Making Changes 154
Undoing Changes 155
Removing Records 156
Blanking Records 156
Deleting Records 156
Marking Records for Deletion 157
Unmarking Records for Deletion 157
Erasing Marked Records 157
Exiting and Closing the Database 158
From Here... 158

8 Organizing Your Database and Generating a Quick Report 161

Organizing the Records for the Report 161
Understanding Indexes 162
Creating Simple Indexes 163
Creating More Sophisticated Indexes Using Expressions 165
Understanding Expressions 165
Using Functions in Expressions 166
Using Character Functions 166
Using Numeric Functions 167
Combining Data Types in an Index Expression 168
Converting Dates to Strings 168

Converting Numeric Values to Strings 168
Converting Both Dates and Numerics to Strings 169
Using Nesting Functions 169
Using the dBASE 5 Expression Builder 169
Using Indexes 169
Creating Multiple Field Indexes 171
Approximating Dictionary and ASCII Ordering 171
Using Conditional Indexing 172
Searching with Indexes 173
Using Other Options on the Organize Menu 175
Reorganizing the Database by Sorting 176
Generating a Quick Report 178
Using the Default Quick Report Form 179
Choosing Quick Report Printing and Display Options 182
From Here... 184

III Using More Sophisticated Features 185

9 Using Queries To Search Databases 187

Retrieving Data Successfully 188
Creating a Query 189
Understanding the File and View Skeletons 190
Modifying the View Skeleton 191
Renaming a Field 191
Removing a Field 191
Adding a Field 192
Moving a Field 192
Entering Simple Search Values 193
Entering Values in Character Fields 193
Entering Values in Numeric Fields 195
Entering Values in Date Fields 195
Entering Values in Logical Fields 196
Searching in Memo Fields 197
Processing a Query 198
Practicing with a Query 199
Using an Existing Query 200
Saving Query Output as a New Database 200
Using More Complex Search Values 201
Using Relational Operators in Searches 201
Searching with Wild Cards 203
Searching for Embedded Values 203
Searching for Values in a Range 204
Searching for Values that Sound Alike 206
Searching for Records with Multiple Conditions 207
Searching for Values in Multiple Fields 207
Searching for Multiple Values in the Same Field 209
Combining AND and OR Conditions 209

Filtering Records with Condition Boxes 212
- Testing for Deleted Records 212
- Searching for Values in a Memo Field 213

Finding a Specific Record with a Query 215
Creating and Using Calculated Fields 216
- Using Functions in an Expression 218
- Adding More Calculated Fields 220
- Removing Calculated Fields 220

Saving a Query for Repeated Use 221
Creating a New Query from an Existing Query 221
Using a Query with a Report 221
From Here 222

10 Using Advanced Techniques with Queries 223

Performing Summary Calculations with a Query 223
- Combining Summary Operators 225
- Using Conditions with Summary Operators 226
- Using Multiple Summary Operators 227

Grouping Records 227
Using Example Variables in Conditions 229
Indexing Query Output 230
- Specifying an Index for the View 230
- Using Complex Indexes in a Query 231

Sorting Query Output 231
- Sorting on Multiple Fields 233
- Combining Sorts and Searches in the Same Field 235

Updating Values in a Database with a Query 236
- Replacing Values 237
- Adding Records 241
- Marking Records for Deletion 243
- Unmarking Records Marked for Deletion 244
- Saving Update Queries 244

Retrieving Data from Multiple Databases 245
Using the Fastest Query Method 248
- Using Optimized 249
- Using Keep Speedup Indexes 249

From Here... 249

11 Creating and Using Input Forms 251

Creating Forms for Better Data Input 252
- Creating Forms with the Forms Design Screen 253
- Getting Acquainted with the Forms Design Screen 253
- Building a Form from a Blank Work Surface 255

Entering and Editing Text 255
Adding and Removing Fields 256
Moving, Copying, and Sizing Form Elements 257
Modifying the Appearance of a Memo Field 259
Specifying Field Attributes 261
- Using Templates 261
- Using Picture Functions 266

Using Edit Options 269
Editing Allowed 270
Permit Edit If 270
Message 271
Carry Forward 272
Default Value 272
Smallest/Largest Allowed Value 272
Range Must Always Be Met 273
Accept Value When 273
Value Must Always Be Valid 273
Unaccepted Message 274
Modifying Field Attributes 274
Adding Calculated Fields 274
Organizing a Form with Lines and Boxes 275
Adding a Box 276
Adding Lines 277
Deleting a Box and Lines 278
Adding Color to the Form 279
Changing the Colors of a Field 279
Changing the Colors of an Area on the Form 280
Saving a Form and Exiting 281
Creating MulTiple-Page Forms 282
Modifying a Custom Form 283
Using Custom Forms 284
From Here... 285

12 Creating Custom Reports 287

Creating a Report with the Reports Design Screen 288
Getting Acquainted with the Reports Design Screen 288
Choosing Your Method 290
Using Quick Layouts for a Quick Start 290
Using the Columnar Layout 290
Using the Form Layout 290
Using the Mailmerge Layout 291
Designing a Custom Report 291
Setting Margins and Tabs 292
Understanding Bands 292
Page Header Band 293
Report Intro Band 293
Detail Band 293
Report Summary Band 294
Page Footer Band 294
Group Band 294
Adding Fields to Reports 294
Sizing Memo Fields 295
Moving Fields in the Bands 296
Moving a Field within a Band 296
Moving a Field to Another Band 296
Deleting Fields from the Bands 297

Specifying Field Attributes 297
Changing the Width of a Field 297
Using a Template 297
Using Picture Functions 299
Using the Suppress Repeated Values Option 302
Modifying Field Attributes 302
Adding Calculated Fields 302
Using Unnamed Calculated Fields 304
Using Hidden Calculated Fields 304
Adding Fields that Perform Summary Math 305
Grouping Records 307
Adding a Group Band 308
Adding Group Summary Fields 310
Using Only Group Bands in a Report 310
Entering Text 310
Using Styles 311
Adding Page Headers and Page Footers 312
Using Lines and Boxes 313
Saving a Report and Exiting the Reports Design Screen 314
Using a Report 315
Selecting Records for a Report with a Query 315
Viewing the Report on the Screen 315
Printing the Report 315
Using the Destination Menu 316
Using the Control of Printer Menu 317
Using Output Options 318
Using the Page Dimensions Menu 319
Creating and Using Print Forms 320
Using Other Print Menu Options 321
From Here... 321

13 Designing and Using a Mailmerge Report and Label 323

Designing the Mailmerge Report 324
Entering Data in Bands 324
Entering Text and Adding Fields 326
Enhancing the Text 329
Using Calculated Fields 329
Modifying, Moving, and Removing Fields and Text 330
Inserting Page Breaks 330
Saving and Exiting the Report 330
Modifying a Report Design 331
Designing a Label 331
Using the Labels Design Screen 331
Setting the Label Dimensions 332
Choosing a Predefined Size 332
Specifying a Custom Size 333
Entering Text and Adding Fields 335
Modifying, Moving, and Removing Text and Fields 338
Saving the Label Report and Exiting 338

Modifying the Label Design 339
Using Mailmerge and Label Reports 339
Selecting the Records for a Report with Queries 340
Viewing the Report on the Screen 340
Printing the Report 341
From Here... 342

14 Using Crosstabs 343

Understanding a Crosstab 343
Creating Crosstabs 346
Opening a File for a Crosstab 348
More About Columns and Categories in a Crosstab 348
More About Summary Fields in a Crosstab 349
More About the Browse Window 349
Saving a Crosstab 350
Exploring Some Examples 350
Example 1: Finding the Total Cases Sold 351
Example 2: Finding the Average Number of Cases Sold .. 351
Example 3: Finding How Many Cases Sold In a Quarter ... 352
Example 4: Finding the Total of All Brands 352
Example 5: Finding the Total Brands per Region 353
Example 6: Finding the Maximum Cases Sold 354
Example 7: Finding the Gross Sales 354
Example 8:Finding the Cost and Number Sold 356
Creating Reports with Crosstabs 357
From Here... 358

15 Using Relational Databases for Complex Situations 359

Understanding Relational Databases 360
Recognizing Situations Requiring Relational Databases 361
Designing a Relational Database 364
Defining the Data Entities 364
Deciding What To Include in the Databases 365
Determining How Data Is Related 367
Refining the Database Design 369
Creating the Files 370
Creating Catalogs for Relational Databases 371
Using Queries To Set Up Relationships 371
Creating Forms for Relational Databases 374
Creating Reports for Relational Databases 376
From Here... 378

IV Programming in dBASE 5 381

16 Getting Started with Programming 383

Realizing the Benefits of Writing Programs 384
Practicing Good Programming Techniques 384
Using Commands and Functions 388

- Taking Action with Commands 388
- Getting Results with Functions 390
- Controlling Programs with Preprocessing Directives 391

Entering Code 396

Using the Desktop Editor To Enter Code 397
- Navigating the Edit Window 398
- Inserting and Replacing Text 398
- Selecting Text 399
- Deleting Text 399
- Copying and Moving Text 400
- Undoing Changes 400
- Searching and Replacing Text 400
- Saving and Exiting 402

Using the Program Editor To Enter Code 403
- Navigating the Edit Window 404
- Inserting and Replacing Text 404
- Selecting Text 404
- Deleting Text 404
- Copying and Moving Text 405
- Undoing Changes 406
- Search and Replace 406
- Saving and Exiting 406

Using Your Text Editor or Word Processor To Enter Code 406
- Using Your Text Editor 406
- Understanding the Clipboard 407
- Using a Word Processing Program 408

Documenting Programs 409
- Adding a Note on a Line by Itself 409
- Adding a Note to a Command Line 409

Managing Your Project with the Project Manager 410
- Creating a Project 410
- Defining Compile and Link Options for Your Project 411

Compiling a Program 412
- Setting Compiler Options 413
- Using Advanced Compile Options 414

Debugging Programs 415

Developing Programs for Use on a Network 417

From Here... 418

17 Exploring Some Sample Programs 421

Establishing Coding Standards 422

Defining a Memory Variable 424
- Initializing Memory Variables 424
- Making Memory Variables PUBLIC or PRIVATE 428
- Using the Data in Your Memory Variables 429
- Making More of Memory Variables with Arrays 432

Setting the Environment Variables 434
- Saving the Current Environment 435
- Establishing Your Environment 436

Selecting a Data Table ... 437
Indexing a Data Table with the Index Command ... 438
Determining the Menu Structure ... 441
Using Text-Based Menus ... 441
Using dBASE IV Menus ... 442
Using Object-Oriented Menus ... 444
Obtaining Input from the User ... 444
Storing User Input in a Memory Variable ... 444
Showing Prompts and Getting Input with @...SAY...GET ... 445
Using @ To Format the Screen ... 451
Using Objects for Screen Input ... 452
Testing the Input with the IF Command ... 453
IF—A Simple Conditional Command ... 454
Processing in a WHILE Loop ... 455
Providing Output ... 457
Displaying Data on the Screen ... 457
Running a Report with the Report Form Command ... 457
Writing a Program That Uses Preprocessor Directives ... 458
Using the Debugger ... 459
Watching Your Code in the Code Display Window ... 460
Getting Help from the Command Help Window ... 460
Monitoring Your Variables in the Display Window ... 460
Setting Breakpoints in Your Code ... 461
Watching Progress in the Debugger Window ... 462
Seeing What the User Sees ... 462
A Sample Debug Session ... 462
Code for Customer Tracking ... 465
RCUSTFOR.PRG ... 466
RCUSTFOR.DFM ... 469
RCUSTFOR.MNU ... 472
From Here... ... 476

18 Creating Custom Applications 477

Defining the Files in the Applications ... 477
Designing an Application ... 479
Designing an Invoice Application ... 481
Designing an Inventory Application ... 484
Designing Forms for Data Input and Output ... 485
Creating and Modifying Program Files ... 485
Automating the Application with Menus ... 486
Understanding Menus ... 489
Using Menu Bars and Pull-Down Menus ... 490
Using the Define Command ... 490
Using Pop-Up Menus ... 491
Exploring a Sample Menu Program ... 492
Enhancing Pop-Up Menus ... 496
Using Pop-Up Lists ... 497
Creating and Using Windows ... 498

Writing Help Screens 502
Building a Procedure Library 504
Running External Programs 508
Using Keyboard Macros 511
Creating and Using Reports 512
Sorting Your Data Table 513
Indexing Your Data Table 515
Locating What You're Looking For 515
Displaying Your Results 518
A Sample Report Program 520
Moving Your Data Around 524
From Here... 526

19 Using the Applications Generator and the Compiler 527

Building Applications for Other Users 528
Planning Programs for the Applications Generator 528
Getting Started with the Applications Generator 533
Creating the Mailer Application 533
Learning the Work Surface 536
Designing the Menu 536
Using Pull-Down and Pop-Up Menus 539
Generating Code for Your Application 548
Generating Documentation about the Application 549
Running the Mailer Application 551
Learning Additional Capabilities of the Applications Generator 552
Using Advanced Testing with the dBASE Debugger 553
Changing the Applications Generator Code 555
Delivering Executable Code 556
Getting Ready for Linking 556
Getting Your Files Together 557
Building a Compact Executable 558
Building a StandAlone Executable 559
Using Your Application 559
Producing an Application for Distribution 559
From Here... 560

V Using High-Level Tools 563

20 Programming with SQL 565

Understanding SQL 566
Using SQL Two Ways 567
Working with Tables 568
Columns and Rows 568
Data Types 571
Building SQL Statements 573

Dealing with Data ... 574
Retrieving Data with the Select Command ... 574
Adding Data with the Insert Command ... 581
Changing Data with the Update Command ... 582
Deleting Data with the Delete Command ... 583
Controlling Security ... 584
Using SQL Utility Commands ... 587
Converting a Database to a Table ... 587
Importing Data into a Table ... 587
Exporting Data from SQL ... 588
Rolling Back Transactions ... 588
Using SQL in Program Code ... 590
Understanding and Using Cursor Commands ... 590
Declaring Cursors ... 590
Opening a Cursor ... 591
Fetching a Cursor ... 591
Closing a Cursor ... 591
Using UPDATE with DECLARE CURSOR ... 592
Using DELETE with DECLARE CURSOR ... 593
Embedding SQL Code in dBASE Applications ... 594
Recovering from Errors ... 600
Using SQL for Transaction Processing ... 601
From Here... ... 604

21 Creating Objects with UI 605

Creating a New Form ... 605
Using the Form Designer ... 606
Changing Properties Using the Object Inspector ... 608
Using the DEFINE FORM Command ... 609
Adding Objects to the Form ... 612
Adding Field Entry Objects ... 613
Adding Control Objects ... 613
Customizing the Form Objects ... 614
Creating a Menu ... 618
Generate the Default Menu ... 618
Modify a Menu ... 619
Editing the Command Files ... 622
Running the Form ... 633
From Here... ... 634

VI Reference Guide 635

22 Using dBASE 5 Commands 637

Understanding Command Syntax ... 637
Working with Operators ... 639
Operator Types ... 639
Operator Precedence ... 641
dBASE 5 Commands Listed Alphabetically ... 642

23 Using Functions 751

Functions Listed Alphabetically ... 751

24 Using SET Commands To Configure dBASE 5 827

Categorizing the SET Commands ... 828
- Database SET Commands ... 828
- Database Encryption SET Command ... 828
- Date and Time SET Commands ... 829
- General SET Commands ... 829
- Help Message Display SET Commands ... 829
- Memo Field SET Commands ... 829
- Memory SET Commands ... 830
- Network SET Commands ... 830
- Number Display SET Commands ... 830
- Output Redirection Commands ... 830
- Printing SET Commands ... 831
- Program File SET Commands ... 831
- Screen Display SET Commands ... 831
- Sound SET Commands ... 832
- SQL SET Commands ... 832

SET Commands ... 832

25 Using SQL Commands 879

SQL Data Types ... 879
SQL Functions Used in SELECT ... 880
SQL Predicates ... 881
dBASE 5 Functions and Commands in SQL ... 882
SQL Security ... 882
SQL Command Descriptions ... 882

26 Using UI Properties, Methods, and Commands 899

Using Dot Reference Notation ... 899
Properties ... 900
Methods ... 982
Commands ... 987

27 Using System Memory Variables 1041

- _Alignment ... 1041
- _Box ... 1042
- _Clipboard ... 1042
- _Cmdwindow ... 1043
- _Indent ... 1044
- _Lmargin ... 1045
- _Padvance ... 1045
- _Pageno ... 1046
- _Pbpage ... 1046
- _Pcolno ... 1046
- _Pcopies ... 1047

_Pdriver 1047
_Pecode 1047
_Peject 1048
_Pepage 1048
_Pform 1048
_Plength 1049
_Plineno 1049
_Ploffset 1049
_Ppitch 1050
_Pquality 1050
_Pscode 1051
_Psize 1051
_Pspacing 1052
_Pwait 1052
_Rmargin 1052
_Tabs 1053
_Wrap 1053

28 Using Preprocessor Directives 1055

Compiler Basics 1055
Preprocessor Directives 1057
#define 1057
#if...#endif 1058
#ifdef 1059
#ifndef 1060
#include 1060
#undef 1061

29 Using the System Configuration File 1063

Configuration Commands 1065
Memory Allocation Commands 1073
CTMAXSYMS 1073
MVARSIZE 1073
MVMAXBLKS/MVBLKSIZE 1073
RTMAXBLKS/RTBLKSIZE 1074
Managing Memory and Temporary Files 1074
Function Key Assignment Commands 1075
<key label> 1075
SET Commands in CONFIG.DB 1076
Color Setting Commands 1079
Design Surface Programs 1080
PRGAPPLIC 1081
PRGBROWSE 1081
PRGCC 1082
PRGDATA 1082
PRGEDIT 1082
PRGFORM 1082
PRGLABEL 1082
PRGQUERY 1082

Default File Extension Settings 1083
Using the Mouse with dBASE 1086
- Using the Mouse in Work Surfaces 1086
- Control Center 1086
- Menus 1086
- Navigation Line 1087
- Lists 1087
- Data-Entry Boxes 1087
- Error and Warning Boxes 1087
- Help Screens 1087
- Browse Screen 1087
- Edit and Form Screens 1088
- Database Design 1088
- Form, Label, and Report Design 1088
- The Program Editor 1088
- Queries Design 1088
- Applications Generator 1088
- Using the Mouse in Programs 1089

Index **1091**

Introduction

When MS-DOS was introduced for the IBM-PC in 1981, dBASE II database management software already had been providing information solutions for CP/M computer users for several years. Although spreadsheet software, such as VisiCalc, helped to establish the personal computer as a common desktop accessory, dBASE II brought the exciting power of database management to personal computer users. The ability to categorize, store, and report information through dBASE II's English-like commands enabled non-data processing people to take control of their own information needs. Those people who obtained and used dBASE had a "leg up" on those who didn't have access to it. If you could have polled a group of 1978 CP/M computer users for their ideal mix of software, you would have gotten a significant response for WordStar, VisiCalc, and dBASE II.

Many situations have changed in the world of personal computing since the late 1970s. Today's computers are vastly more powerful. The powerful new computers can run thousands of available program packages. MS-DOS has been improved through six major upgrades. dBASE II has evolved through dBASE III, dBASE III PLUS, dBASE IV, dBASE IV 2.0, and dBASE 5. Many competitive products have come (and gone) since 1981, but dBASE is still one of the most popular and widely used database programs.

Que's *Using dBASE 5 for DOS*, Special Edition, is your resource for bridging your information management needs with dBASE 5's features and benefits. Hundreds of thousands of computer users have significantly upgraded their skills by learning from Que's *Using* titles. *Using dBASE 5 for DOS*, Special Edition, represents a commitment to you. The commitment is to present to you the complex, powerful dBASE 5 program in a logical and task-oriented fashion. Using this book, you will understand how to organize your information needs, master the user interface, and ultimately become more productive using dBASE 5.

Who Should Read This Book?

Using dBASE 5 for DOS, Special Edition, is written for both novice and experienced database users. For the novice database user, this book provides tutorial instructions and examples. For the more experienced user, this book provides advanced topics and quick reference to almost every command, function, and feature of dBASE 5.

This book explains the key concepts of dBASE 5 without being highly technical or intimidating. *Using dBASE 5 for DOS*, Special Edition, recognizes that your learning time is limited. This book reflects the important consideration that you need to become productive immediately and then builds on practical skills as you learn intermediate and advanced concepts.

If you are new to dBASE and are learning dBASE 5, this book is ideal for you. The text does not rush database concepts or presuppose that you are familiar with a topic. If you are upgrading to dBASE 5 from an earlier version, you will find the inclusion and treatment of new features to be your fast track for taking advantage of the upgrade. Whether you are a relative beginner or you simply need to brush up on your dBASE skills, you will find this book to be an important addition to your computer library.

What's in This Book?

You can flip quickly through this book to get a feel for its organization. *Using dBASE 5 for DOS*, Special Edition, divides the generous scope of dBASE 5 into six distinct parts. Each part builds on your learning from the preceding part. Each part is designed to provide you with a level of practical capability. You need not proceed to a subsequent part to benefit from the capabilities of dBASE presented in an earlier part. You may, for example, stop reading after Part II to utilize what you learned. You may choose not to proceed to Part III for several weeks or more.

The book contains a detailed Reference Guide that includes programming commands, functions, SET commands, SQL commands, User Interface commands, System Memory Variable commands, Preprocessor Directives, and system configuration commands.

Take a moment to read about each part of the book:

Part I: Getting Acquainted with dBASE 5

Part I first gives upgraders a brief summary of the new features in dBASE 5, then explains the basic features of the dBASE 5 program. The chapters in this section help you form a good foundation for setting up and using the program. The information presented helps you learn dBASE 5's personality and become more comfortable with the application.

Chapter 1, "What's New in dBASE 5 for DOS?" presents the new features that have been added to enhance dBASE 5. This chapter is particularly valuable to you if you are upgrading from dBASE IV Version 2.0 because it gives you an idea of what topics to turn to in the book.

Chapter 2, "Getting Started with dBASE 5," begins your hands-on use of the program by getting your dBASE 5 installation off on the right foot. You learn to start dBASE 5, use the mouse, and set up the dBASE environment.

Chapter 3, "Exploring the New Desktop," takes you on an informational tour of the new dBASE "desktop," the name given to the new design of the screen (user interface). You get acquainted with dBASE's menu system and dialog boxes, the Command Window, and the Control Center. In addition, you learn to work with multiple windows and the new dBASE tools, the calculator and calendar.

Chapter 4, "Understanding the Control Center," gives a more in-depth look at the part of the program that beginner and intermediate users will use most. You learn how to use the panels in the Control Center, how to set up and use catalog, and how to use the DOS utilities. This chapter is very central to a good understanding of dBASE and the efficient use of the program.

Part II: Creating and Using a Database

Part II's chapters are basic and tutorial in nature, helping you to become productive with dBASE 5 right away. With the information presented in this section, you will be able to tap dBASE 5's information management power without having to master more advanced concepts. If you have been intimidated by the scope of fully featured database management programs, Part II demonstrates that you *can* be productive without an extensive investment in learning time.

Chapter 5, "Designing the Structure of a Database," takes you "hands-on" into the design of a database. This chapter introduces and demystifies database terminology. This chapter steps you through the database definition process, the saving of your definition, and the modification of existing definitions. Just as databases are at the core of database management software, this chapter is at the core of your dBASE 5 learning.

Chapter 6, "Adding Records," shows you how to input data in your newly designed database. You become familiar with the Edit and Browse screens and the methods of navigating these screens. You see the dBASE 5 word processor features as you learn about memo-field editing and printing. Finally you learn to close a database.

Chapter 7, "Editing and Deleting Records," demonstrates the distinction between adding new data and editing existing data. You become acquainted with editing techniques such as locking and freezing fields, and you learn ways to undo edits. You learn techniques to locate a desired record from all your data, and finally you learn to mark records for deletion and erase them.

Chapter 8, "Organizing Your Database and Generating a Quick Report," shows you how to print or view data the easy way. It builds on this easy reporting method by showing you how to organize the data with indexes or by sorting, and it demonstrates the proper use of the printer.

Part III: Using More Sophisticated Features

Part III presents more advanced concepts when you are ready to move on from the knowledge you gained in Parts I and II. In Part III, you learn to use the Control Center and the menu system.

Chapter 9, "Using Queries To Search Databases," explains dBASE 5's powerful and user-oriented Query By Example feature. Incorporating queries into your information-searching activities increases your information selectivity significantly. Simple and more complex queries are demonstrated in this chapter.

Chapter 10, "Using Advanced Techniques with Queries," takes the use of queries to their most advanced stages. You learn to perform calculations, use update queries to change data, and retrieve data from multiple databases.

Chapter 11, "Creating and Using Input Forms," shows you how to add polish to your editing screens. This chapter familiarizes you with methods of designing clear, informative editing forms that are easier to use. You learn how to create calculated fields in the form, and how to use picture functions, edit options, and templates to validate the data that is entered in a field in the form.

Chapter 12, "Creating Custom Reports," does for your printed view of database information what Chapter 11 did for your screen view. You use the dBASE report designer to produce professional-quality reports complete with headings and summaries, calculated fields, templates, and picture functions.

Chapter 13, "Designing and Using a Mailmerge Report and Label," enables you to produce versatile form letters and labels in a variety of formats. You learn the special features of the mailmerge report form, and you learn to produce labels ranging from mailing labels to inventory shelf tags.

Chapter 14, "Using Crosstabs," presents the new reporting feature, cross tabulation. You learn to use this powerful feature to tabulate a field in a database from two different aspects.

Chapter 15, "Using Relational Databases for Complex Situations," concentrates on the extensive relational database provisions of dBASE 5. This feature of dBASE 5 is truly one of the most powerful, yet one of the most simple features to use. It increases the effective use of data immensely.

Part IV: Programming in dBASE 5

This part deals with writing, compiling, and debugging your own programs using dBASE 5's extensive programming language. Users who feel confident with the dBASE 5 program, yet have no knowledge of programming, can gain from this section. Users with a programming background will be able to use this section to launch their own applications.

Chapter 16, "Getting Started with Programming," eases you into programming rationale and concepts. In this chapter, you see that you don't have to be an information management specialist to begin programming in the dBASE 5 environment.

Chapter 17, "Exploring Some Sample Programs," helps you to see by example what can be accomplished with dBASE 5's programming language. Many of the sample programs perform tasks that are fairly common, so you should be able to incorporate some of the programming code into your own programs.

Chapter 18, "Creating Custom Applications," introduces you to the fundamentals of creating a custom application. It details the parts of an application and explores the use of macros.

Chapter 19, "Using the Applications Generator and the Compiler," highlights two of the dBASE 5 programmer's most potent tools. You learn how to use the Applications Generator to reduce your program-coding responsibilities while retaining the features of dBASE 5 programs. You see how your applications and code segments can be compiled into secure pseudocode.

Part V: Using High-Level Tools

Part V explores the use of Structured Query Language (SQL) and the new User Interface (UI) commands. As the title suggests, this section requires a high level of expertise.

Chapter 20, "Programming with SQL," introduces dBASE's implementation of Structured Query Language (SQL). SQL promises to be the best solution for the interoperation of data management environments. This chapter prepares you to make practical use of SQL. You even see how to embed SQL code in your dBASE applications.

Chapter 21, "Creating Objects with UI," explores the use of the User Interface commands that create objects for menus, forms, and so on. This new feature lends even more power to the developer's tool box.

Part VI: Reference Guide

Part VI is a rich dBASE 5 reference source. Part VI devotes sections to dot prompt and programming commands, built-in functions, SET commands, SQL commands, UI commands, System Variable commands, and Preprocessor Directives. In addition, the CONFIG.DB file is covered in detail. This complete reference section extends the usefulness of *Using dBASE 5 for DOS*, Special Edition, beyond a learning tool to a reference tool.

Chapter 22, "Using dBASE 5 Commands," lists all the programming commands in alphabetical order and gives the syntax, purpose, and an example for each command.

Chapter 23, "Using Functions," lists all the functions in alphabetical order and gives the syntax, purpose, and an example for each function.

Chapter 24, "Using SET Commands To Configure dBASE 5" lists all the SET commands and gives the syntax, purpose, and an example for each command.

Chapter 25, "Using SQL Commands," lists all SQL commands in alphabetical order and gives the syntax, purpose, and an example of each command.

Chapter 26, "Using UI Properties, Methods, and Commands," is divided into three sections, each organized alphabetically. The first section lists the properties you can use to customize the look of your objects. The second section describes the methods that your object uses to do its job. The last section details the syntax and purpose of each UI command you can use to create objects.

Chapter 27, "Using System Memory Variables," lists commands used with memory variables in alphabetical order and gives the syntax, purpose, and an example of each command.

Chapter 28, "Using Preprocessor Directives," lists all the directives in alphabetical order and gives the syntax, purpose, and an example of each directive.

Chapter 29, "Using the System Configuration File," details the use of the DBSETUP program and the proper way to configure dBASE for effective use on your particular hardware.

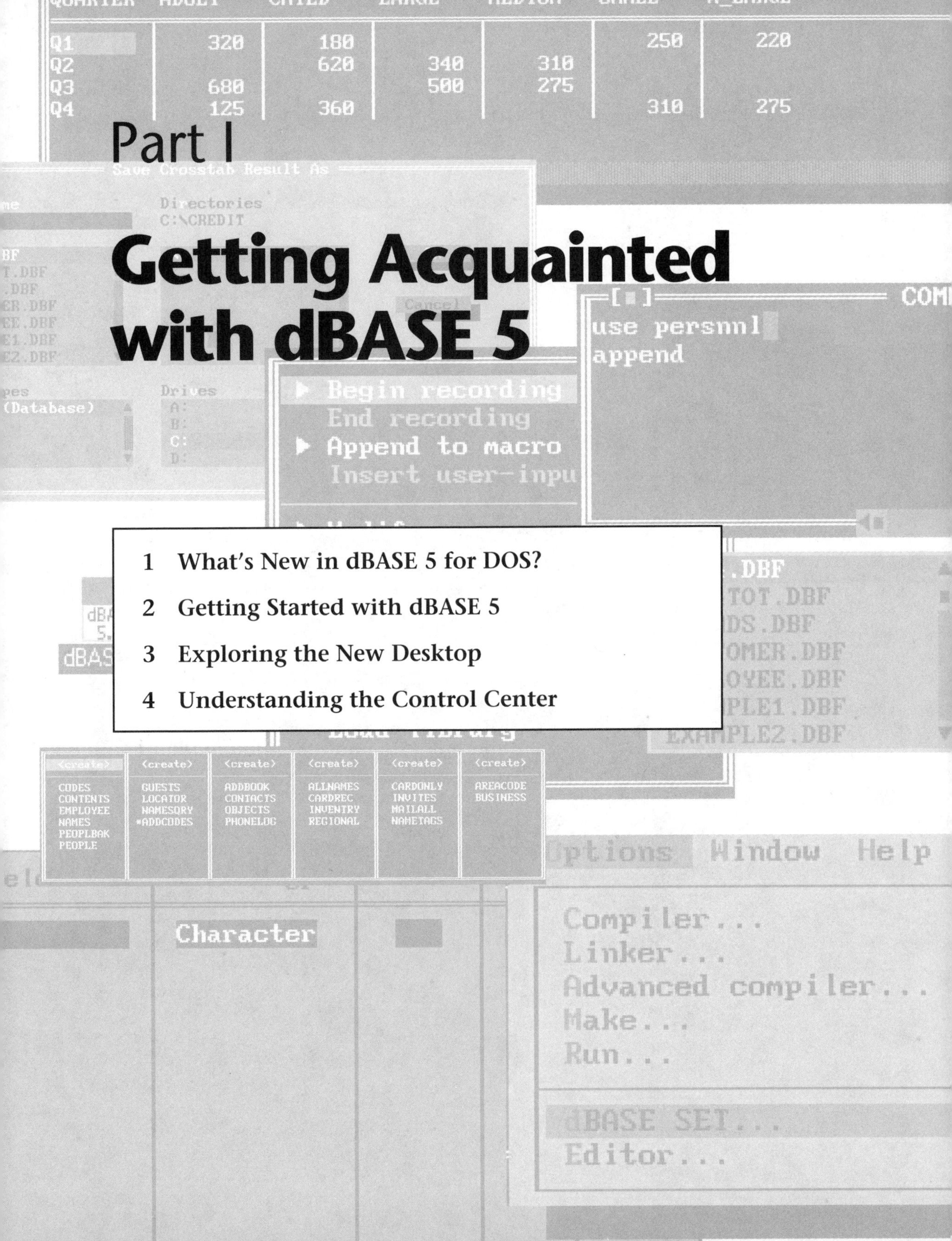

Part I

Getting Acquainted with dBASE 5

1 What's New in dBASE 5 for DOS?

2 Getting Started with dBASE 5

3 Exploring the New Desktop

4 Understanding the Control Center

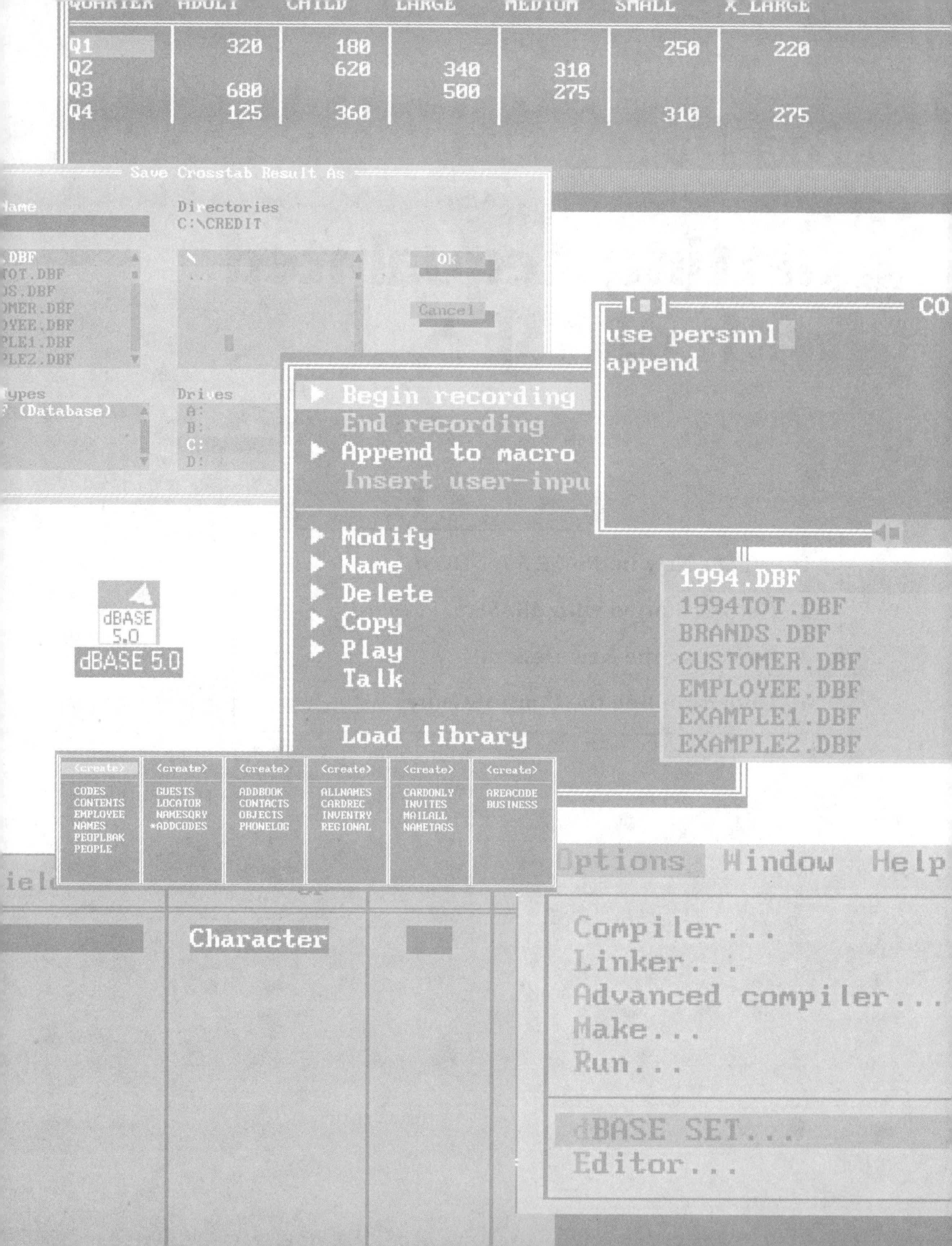

QUARTER ADULT CHILD LARGE MEDIUM SMALL X_LARGE
Q1 320 180 250 220
Q2 620 340 310
Q3 680 500 275
Q4 125 360 310 275
Save Crosstab Result As
Directories
C:\CREDIT
Ok
Cancel
Drives
A:
B:
C:
D:
(Database)
use persnnl
append
Begin recording
End recording
Append to macro
Insert user-inpu
Modify
Name
Delete
Copy
Play
Talk
Load library
1994.DBF
1994TOT.DBF
BRANDS.DBF
CUSTOMER.DBF
EMPLOYEE.DBF
EXAMPLE1.DBF
EXAMPLE2.DBF
dBASE 5.0
dBASE 5.0
<create>
CODES
CONTENTS
EMPLOYEE
NAMES
PEOPLBAK
PEOPLE
<create>
GUESTS
LOCATOR
NAMESQRY
*ADDCODES
<create>
ADDBOOK
CONTACTS
OBJECTS
PHONELOG
<create>
ALLNAMES
CARDREC
INVENTRY
REGIONAL
<create>
CARDONLY
INVITES
MAILALL
NAMETAGS
<create>
AREACODE
BUSINESS
Options Window Help
Character
Compiler...
Linker...
Advanced compiler...
Make...
Run...
dBASE SET...
Editor...

Chapter 1

What's New in dBASE 5 for DOS?

Borland's dBASE 5 for DOS is a major upgrade of the previous release of dBASE. Many impressive new features have been incorporated into this powerful database management system. Upgraders will welcome the new Integrated Development Environment (IDE), called the Developer's Desktop, yet appreciate that all of the design surfaces, including the Control Center, are still available in their original format. You can work in screens you know (and love?) and then progress to the enhanced features at your own speed, without experiencing "new version shock."

New users of dBASE 5 will find the program reasonably easy to learn, simplified by the new main menu bar, windows, dialog boxes, and the new Help system. Application development tools and dBASE 5 programming language enhancements enable programmers to design and implement menu-driven database applications ranging from small and simple needs to large and complex situations.

In this chapter, you learn about the following new features and concepts:

- Upgrading from dBASE IV to dBASE 5
- The new desktop interface
- The new main menu bar
- Desktop accessories
- Project Manager
- Working with files

- New editor
- User interface language enhancements

You get only a glimpse of these new features in this chapter; refer to other chapters in this book for an in-depth explanation. The cross-reference notes in the margins lead you to the pertinent page numbers.

Upgrading from dBASE IV to dBASE 5

Tip
Remember, you will need even more disk space for the files you create, such as database files, index files, programs, report and screen form designs, and so on.

Because dBASE 5 is a fairly large program that contains many new features, you should have at least 14.5M of disk space available during installation of the dBASE 5 system. After installation, dBASE 5 requires 9M of disk space. The more disk space you have available, the better.

In addition to sufficient disk space, dBASE 5 requires at least 4M of memory, although at least 6M is recommended for the best performance. You need an 80386 or higher computer to run dBASE 5.

dBASE 5 for DOS is fully compatible with data, code, and applications from dBASE III PLUS and dBASE IV. When you are migrating from a previous version of dBASE, your existing CONFIG.DB file is not modified or replaced. The SET commands are compatible with dBASE 5, and can be further modified after installation by using DBSETUP or by directly editing CONFIG.DB.

▶ See "Using SET Commands," p. 827

The performance of dBASE 5 has been greatly increased by use of 32-bit DOS extender technology, both in the dBASE system and with user-written dBASE programs. The many new features and enhancements in dBASE 5 make the upgrade well worth the cost and effort.

Exploring the New Desktop Interface

▶ See "Looking at the Components of the Desktop," p. 33

Borland has created a new Desktop Interface, also called the Developer's Desktop, which is a window-like environment where you work with files, set options, and access programming tools. The new desktop, shown in figure 1.1, facilitates your work in dBASE 5 by putting commonly performed tasks a mouse-click away. Following are the basic elements of the desktop:

- Menu bar and menu options
- Command window
- Screen window

- Status bar
- Message line

The Developer's Desktop contains many other elements, which appear when selected from a menu or as a result of other database operations.

The New Main Menu Bar

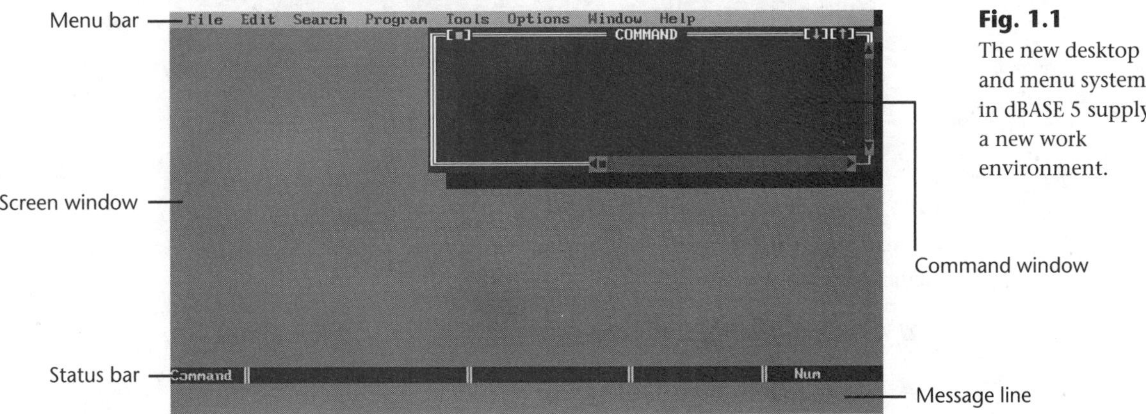

Fig. 1.1
The new desktop and menu system in dBASE 5 supply a new work environment.

Another new item in dBASE 5 is the main menu bar. If you have used Turbo C++ before, you will recognize this as part of the IDE. Listed below are the eight pull-down menus that now are available to you:

- File
- Edit
- Search
- Program
- Tools
- Options
- Window
- Help

You will find the new main menu bar easy to use, especially if you've worked with Turbo C++ or Windows before. You have the option of using the mouse or the keyboard to open the pull-down menus (see fig. 1.2).

▶ See "Using the Menu Bar," p. 34

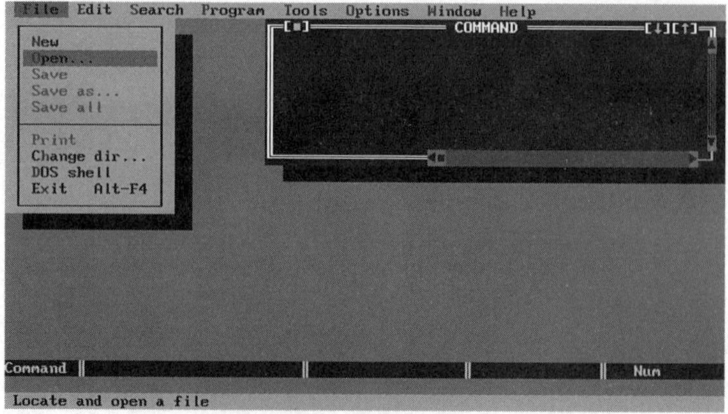

Fig. 1.2
The new pull-down menus are much easier to use in the IDE (Integrated Development Environment).

The New Windows in dBASE 5

There are several types of windows that can appear on the Desktop, including:

- Command window (see fig. 1.3)
- Screen window (see fig. 1.4)
- Edit window (see fig. 1.5)
- Message window (see fig. 1.6)
- Information window (see fig. 1.7)
- Clipboard window (see fig. 1.8)
- Inspector window (see fig. 1.9)
- Add Help window (see fig. 1.10)
- Menu Designer window (see fig. 1.11)
- Project window (see fig. 1.12)

▶ See "Using the Command Window," p. 43

The dot prompt from earlier versions of dBASE has been replaced by the Command window. To execute a command that is visible in the Command window, place the cursor anywhere on that command's line, and then press Enter or double-click. You can edit commands using the Command window's full-screen editing capabilities, and then execute the edited commands in the same way.

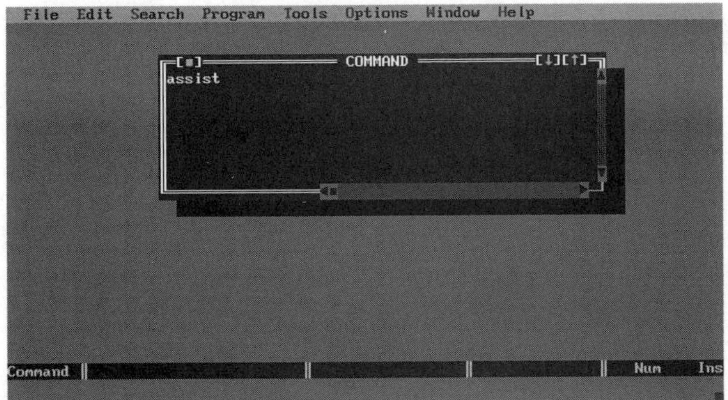

Fig. 1.3
The Command window replaces the old dot prompt by issuing commands typed into the Command window's workspace.

The Screen window and the Command window appear every time you start dBASE 5 if you don't have the statement COMMAND=ASSIST in your CONFIG.DB file. The Screen window is the full-screen window on which you are opening other windows. Output from commands such as DISPLAY and LIST appears in the Screen window rather than cluttering the Command window.

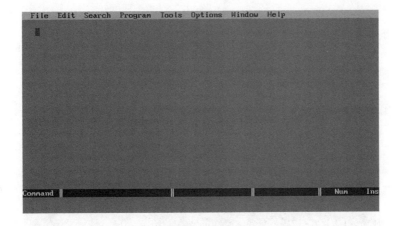

Fig. 1.4
The Screen window displays output from commands you issue in the Command window.

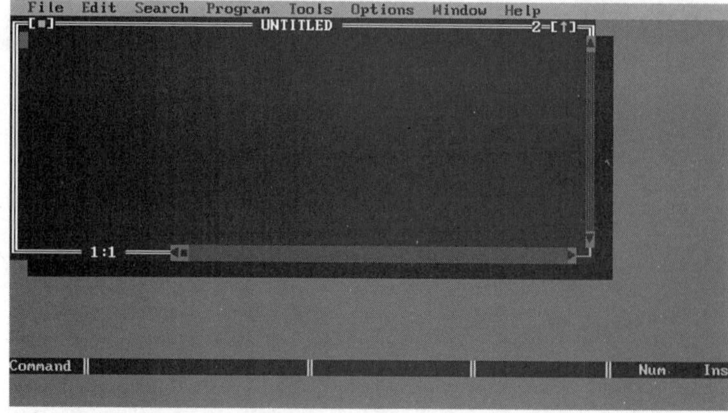

Fig. 1.5
The Edit window appears when you open an ASCII text file or a program file (PRG).

Fig. 1.6
The Message window shows you warning messages or errors, such as compile errors.

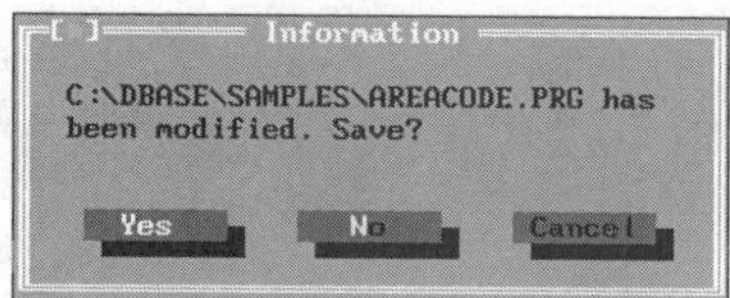

Fig. 1.7
The Information window displays to suggest an action or request confirmation.

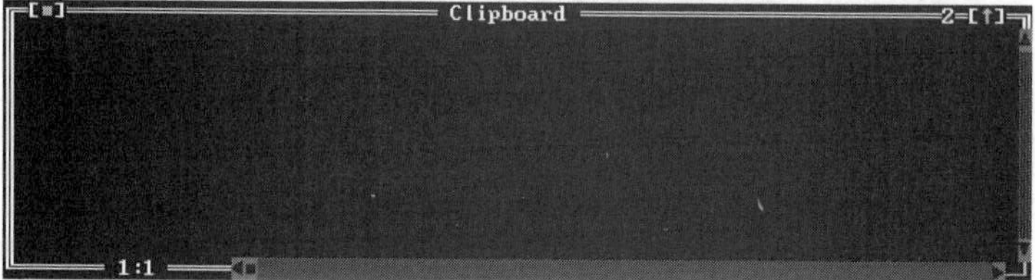

Fig. 1.8
The Clipboard window can display text that you have cut or copied, and pasted to a new position in a file.

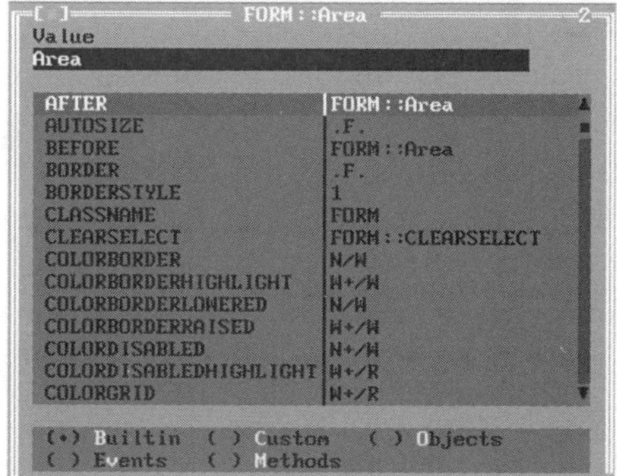

Fig. 1.9
The Inspector window displays a design object's properties and enables you to change them.

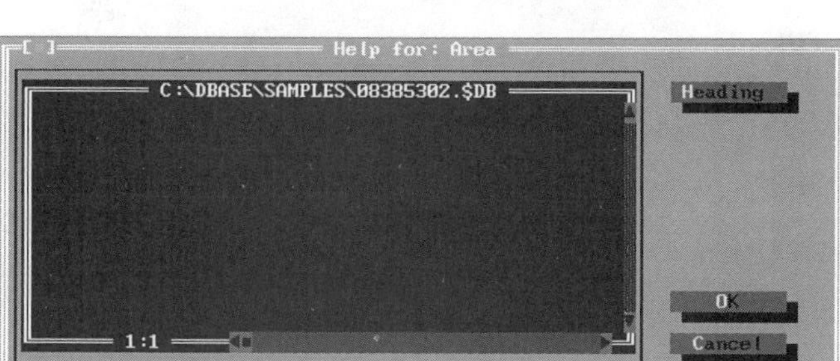

Fig. 1.10
The Add Help window is used to design a help screen for fields on a data entry form.

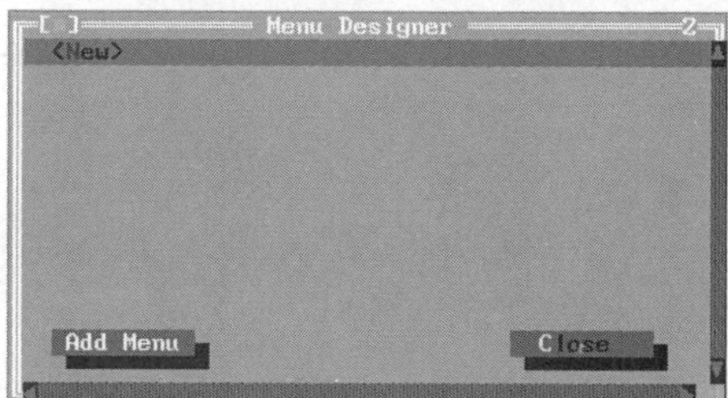

Fig. 1.11
The Menu Designer window is used to create a menu system for an application.

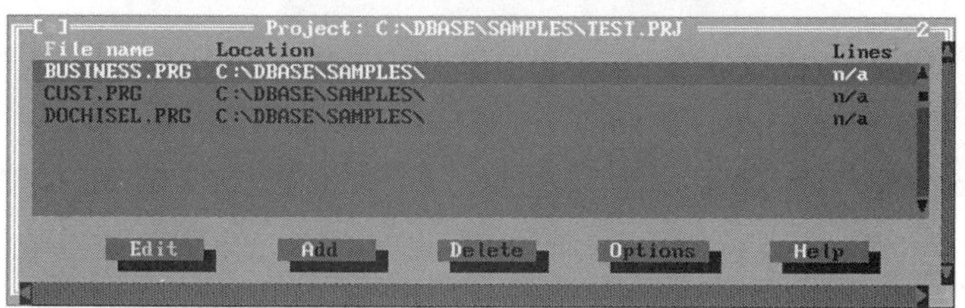

Fig. 1.12
The Project window lets you manipulate the components of a project file.

New Dialog Boxes

► See "Working with Multiple Windows," p. 45

► See "Using Dialog Boxes," p. 36

Dialog boxes are displayed when dBASE 5 requires additional information to continue with an action. For example, the Open File dialog box appears as a result of selecting the **O**pen command from the **F**ile menu. You are expected to provide the drive, directory, and file name for the file you want to open (see fig. 1.13). Different objects are used in the dialog box, depending on the type of information needed. A dialog box can contain one or more of the following objects, some of which are illustrated in figure 1.13 and figure 1.14:

- Input box
- List boxes
- Pushbuttons
- Check boxes
- Spin boxes
- Radio buttons
- Scroll bars

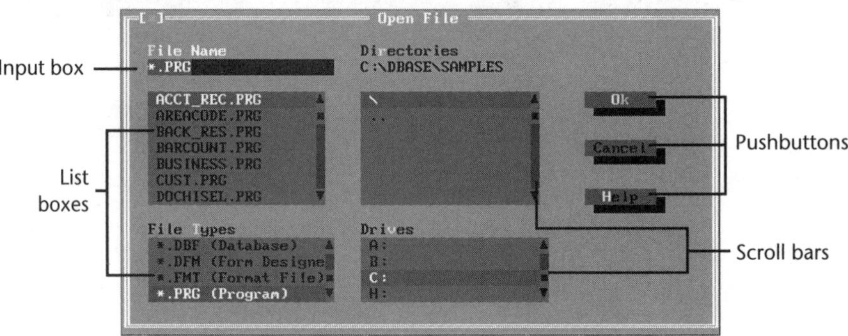

Fig. 1.13
The Open File dialog box provides easy navigation by using list boxes with scroll bars and pushbuttons.

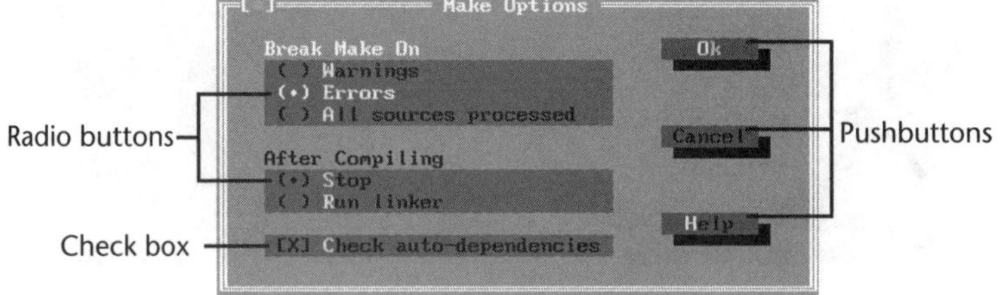

Fig. 1.14
The Make Options dialog box lets you select options with radio buttons and a check box.

By using the mouse to point and click, you can navigate the new dialog boxes very quickly and easily. You also can press Tab or Shift-Tab to move from one area to another, or press Alt and an area's highlighted letter to move to that area.

Crosstab Expert

Cross-tabulation lets you extract data from an existing database file to create a new database file structured in table format, similar to a spreadsheet. The new Cross Tabulation Expert dialog box (see fig. 1.15) helps you create the new crosstab file. The data is grouped into new records, with summary calculations based on fields you specify.

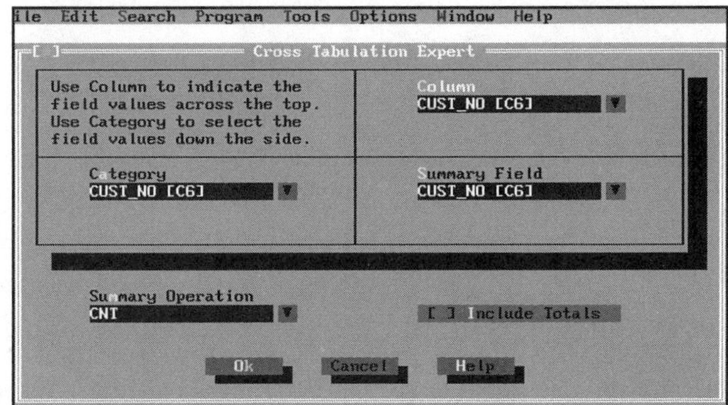

Fig. 1.15
Evaluate your data in crosstab format using the Cross Tabulation Expert dialog box.

Turn to Chapter 14, "Using Crosstabs," for a closer look at this new feature.

Desktop Accessories

Tools to complement the Developer's Desktop include a calendar, a calculator, and an ASCII chart (see fig. 1.16). You can find each of these accessories on the **T**ools menu.

▶ See "Working with Tools," p. 58

You can display these windows while you are working in other windows, and move them around on the desktop to a more convenient spot.

Project Manager

The Project Manager, new in dBASE 5, is used to document the dependencies among associated files. After you define the pieces of your dBASE application, the Project Manager can automatically take care of compiling and linking to create the executable file.

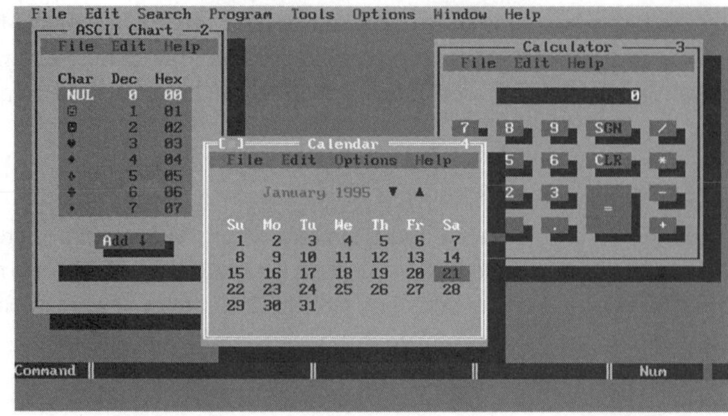

Fig. 1.16
The ASCII chart, calendar, and calculator give you ready access to typical desktop tools.

▶ See "Managing Your Project with the Project Manager," p. 410

You can view your project information in the Project window (refer to fig. 1.12). The management features available in this window:

- Display the files used to create the application
- Add a file to the list
- Edit the list of files
- Delete files from the project list
- Set Options to determine how each file in the project is compiled

New Help System

▶ See "Getting Help," p. 62

dBASE 5 includes an extensive on-line Help system that provides you with valuable assistance with dBASE, covering commands, functions, objects, and general topics (see fig. 1.17).

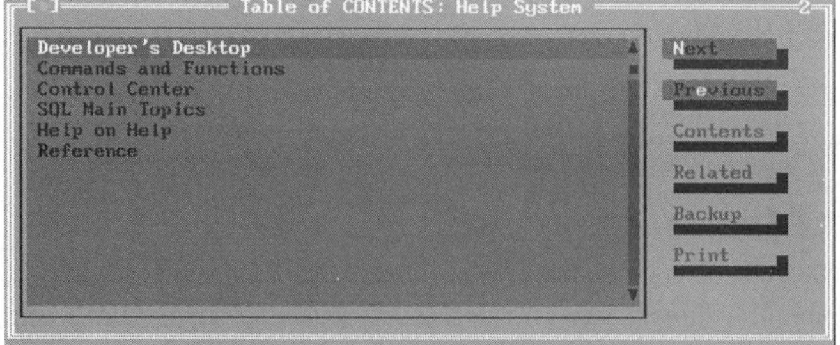

Fig. 1.17
The Help Table of Contents leads you into more detailed help for the topics displayed.

A new feature of the Help system is context-sensitive command help. Click the right mouse button on a line in the Command window or in the new Editor to display help for that command, as shown in figure 1.18.

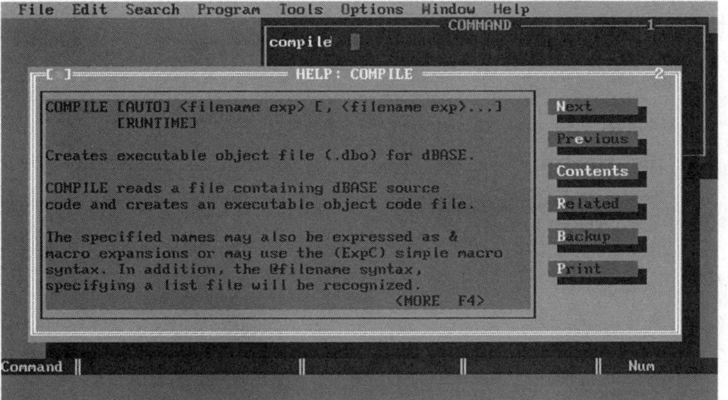

Fig. 1.18
The context-sensitive Help screen for a command in the Command window.

Working with Files

Using the new main menu bar, you can choose the **F**ile menu and select the **O**pen option to open the new Open File dialog box, which is similar to the Open File dialog box in Windows applications (see fig. 1.19). First, specify the type of file that you want to work with. The types listed in the File **T**ypes list box follow:

Extension	Type of File
.	All Files
DFM	Form Design
DBF	Database
FMT	Format
PRG	Program
PRJ	Project
QBE	Query

dBASE 5 supports other file types, many of them selectable from the Open File dialog box. Change the File **T**ypes to `*.*` to display files with all extensions.

You have the option of typing the file name in the **F**ile Name input box or choosing the file name from the list of files in the **F**ile Name list box. You can find files in other directories or drives by changing the selections in the Di**r**ectories or Dri**v**es list boxes.

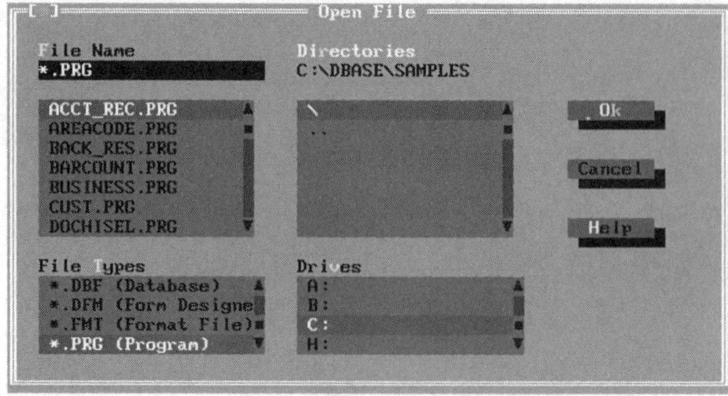

Fig. 1.19
The Open File dialog box is a new way to open files in dBASE 5.

▶ See "Opening Files," p. 70

In addition to opening files using this new method, you also can save files using the **F**ile **S**ave option and print files using the **F**ile **P**rint option. Create a new file by choosing **N**ew from the **F**ile menu. Note that you can still use the Control Center to open, save, and print files.

Using the New Editor

The new desktop editor provided in dBASE 5 (see fig. 1.20) works very much like the DOS text editor. The editor enables you to edit ASCII text files, such as program files (PRG), form design files (DFM), and preprocessor files (DPP).

Note

You must open a file using the Open File dialog box to use the desktop editor. Using MODIFY COMMAND (or selecting a file to modify from a Control Center panel) opens the standard program editor, which was available in previous versions of dBASE. To edit a new file (Untitled) in the new editor, choose the **N**ew option from the **F**ile menu.

An advantage to the new editor is that you can open the same file in more than one window, a benefit when you want to look at one section of code while editing another section of code.

```
 File  Edit  Search  Program  Tools  Options  Window  Help
[■]              C:\DBASE\SAMPLES\AREACODE.PRG              2=[↕]
*******************************************************************************
* PROGRAM NAME: AREACODE.PRG
*               AREACODE DATABASE SCREEN
*               SAMPLE BUSINESS APPLICATION PROGRAM
* LAST CHANGED: 06/20/90 08:00AM
* WRITTEN BY:   Borland International Inc.
*******************************************************************************
*       FILES USED:
*       Database      =  Codes.dbf  (Area code file)
*       Index file    =  Codes.mdx
*         TAG: City   =  city  <= Master
*         TAG: Code   =  code
*       External procedure file = Library.prg
*******************************************************************************
* Main procedure
PROCEDURE Areacode

   * Link to external procedure file of "tool" procedures
   SET PROCEDURE TO Library

   * Set up database environment
   DO Set_env
      1:1
```

Fig. 1.20
Enter source code or edit other ASCII text files using the new desktop editor.

You can move to a specific line number, select a text block, and undo changes. In source code, you can list routines (PROCEDUREs) and select a routine to edit or load. Use the Find dialog box to locate text, or the Replace dialog box to search and replace text.

▶ See "Entering Code," p. 396

The desktop editor works with the new Clipboard, letting you copy or move selected text.

▶ See "Understanding the Clipboard," p. 407

Using the User Interface Language Enhancements

The dBASE 5 language enhancements support *event-driven* programs with UI (User Interface) windows. The term event-driven means that the program waits for the user to perform an *event*, such as clicking the mouse on a pushbutton.

The Form Designer and Menu Designer use UI objects called *controls*. You can create user interfaces for your programs that have multi-file form windows which contain these controls, such as entry fields, pushbuttons, radio buttons, list boxes, and so on. Figure 1.21 shows two of the windows available in the Form Designer, which assist in your design of UI windows.

▶ See "Adding Objects to the Form," p. 612

When you define an object in a form, you also can control the object's *properties*—the behavior and appearance of the object. The Object Inspector shows the properties of the selected object and enables you to make changes without programming.

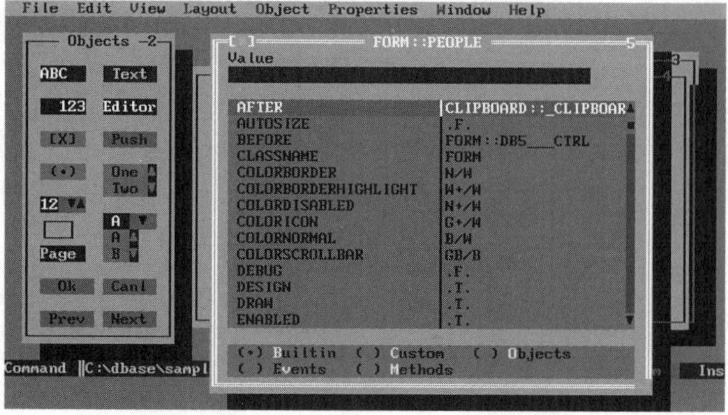

Fig. 1.21
Design forms using the new Object palette and Object Inspector on the Form Designer surface.

Refer to Chapter 26 for a list of UI commands you can use in your programs. The DEFINE command for each object includes the syntax for the properties applicable to the object.

From Here...

The many enhancements in dBASE 5 enable you to create applications that will outshine those you have created before. But before you start programming, think about the basics—laying the groundwork for an effective database application.

Chapter 2

Getting Started with dBASE 5

Now that you have a conceptual foundation of database logic and DOS operation from the preceding chapter, you are ready to begin working with dBASE 5. In this chapter you learn about:

- Starting dBASE 5 from the DOS prompt
- Starting dBASE 5 from Windows
- Using a mouse
- Setting up the environment
- Exiting dBASE

You already should have dBASE 5 installed. After you have completed the default installation process, you should notice the following subdirectories have been created in your dBASE directory: CUA_SAMP, DTL, SAMPLES, and SQLHOME.

Starting dBASE 5 from the DOS Prompt

After you have installed and configured dBASE 5 to meet your needs and specifications, you are ready to start the program and begin working. When you start dBASE 5, a copy of dBASE 5 is taken from the hard disk and placed in the computer's memory. Until the computer has loaded dBASE into memory, you cannot work with it.

Tip
If dBASE 5 is not in the system path, you must change to the dBASE directory by typing **cd \dbase**. Now you can type **dbase** to start the program from its directory.

Starting dBASE 5 is easy. If you followed the suggestions of the Install program and placed the C:\DBASE directory into the system path in the AUTOEXEC.BAT file, just type **dbase** at the system prompt, and press Enter.

Note

You also can change directories after you have started dBASE. The steps for doing this are described in Chapter 5. You may have to change directories from within dBASE if your computer uses a program-access menu or a DOS shell that shields you from using DOS directly.

Now that you have dBASE ready to run, you are going to need to store the data you create. You should create a new subdirectory of the dBASE directory and name it PRACTICE. To set up this directory, be sure you are using the disk drive where the dBASE program is located, and then follow these steps:

► See "Changing the Drive or Directory," p. 86

1. Type **cd \dbase** to change to the dBASE directory.
2. Type **md practice** to create a subdirectory called PRACTICE.
3. Type **cd practice** to change to the PRACTICE subdirectory.

Tip
If you start dBASE from the directory where you want to store your files, dBASE uses this as the default directory.

Now that you are in the subdirectory PRACTICE, you can start dBASE by typing **dbase** and pressing the Enter key.

Starting dBASE 5 from Windows

If you are using Microsoft Windows, you can start dBASE 5 using any of the following methods:

- Start the File Manager program, select the \DBASE directory, and then select the program DBASE.EXE.
- Select **R**un from the **F**ile menu in Program Manager, then type **c:\dbase\dbase.exe** as the program name. (Substitute a different drive letter for c: if you have installed dBASE in another drive, or omit the drive letter if dBASE is installed in the same drive as Windows.)
- Double-click the dBASE 5 program icon (see fig. 2.1). dBASE 5 automatically starts for you.

If you do not see an icon for dBASE 5 in Windows, create a program group by selecting **N**ew from the **F**ile menu. (If DBSETUP found a \WINDOWS directory on your system, it already may have created a dBASE 5 group icon for you.) Choose Program **G**roup and then click OK. Type **dBASE 5.0** in the **D**escription text box. In the **G**roup File text box, type **c:\dbase\dbasedos.grp** and then click OK. The dBASE 5.0 program group is created, which includes icons for dBASE for DOS 5.0, dBINFO, and the dBASE 5.0 Setup Utility.

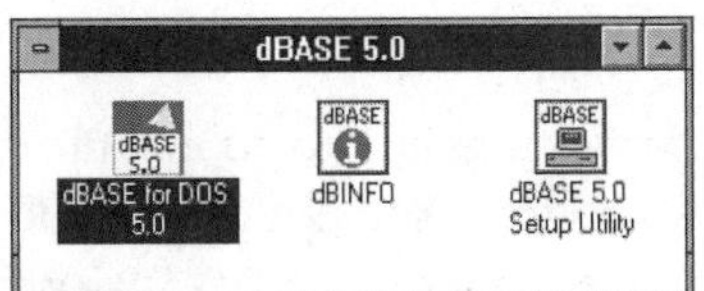

Fig. 2.1
You can double-click the dBASE 5 program icon to start dBASE from Windows.

Using the Mouse

Before you begin using dBASE 5, you need to know a few things about the mouse. When you start dBASE 5, the program automatically checks to see whether a mouse driver is loaded into memory. If you want to use the mouse, be sure you have loaded the mouse driver (usually MOUSE.SYS in your CONFIG.SYS file, or MOUSE.COM or MOUSE.EXE in your AUTOEXEC.BAT file) before running dBASE 5. Consult the instructions that came with the mouse hardware for information on installing the proper driver.

When the mouse is active, dBASE 5 displays a *mouse pointer* on the screen. The mouse pointer is a small rectangle (like a cursor) that can be moved around the screen by moving the mouse. This pointer is used to reposition the cursor or select items on the screen, similar to the way you use the arrow keys in other programs.

If you are unfamiliar with a mouse, you need to understand a few terms. When you are instructed to *click* an item, you should move the mouse pointer on the item, and then press and release the *mouse button*. If you have more than one button, you normally use the left mouse button. To *double-click* an item, press the button twice, very quickly. To *drag* an object with the mouse, hold down the button while moving the mouse.

Tip
If you don't have a mouse, don't worry! Anything you can do with the mouse in dBASE 5 also can be accomplished using the keyboard.

Setting Up the Environment

For dBASE 5 to run properly, you need to make sure two lines are included in your CONFIG.SYS file:

```
FILES = 99
BUFFERS = 15
```

Caution

If you do not set the number of files to FILES = 99, you may see an error message `Too many files are open`. If you encounter a message like this while using dBASE 5, check your CONFIG.SYS file, and change the FILES and BUFFERS statements to match the statements listed previously.

The dBASE 5 environment settings are stored in a file called CONFIG.DB, located in your dBASE 5 directory. You can change the settings in CONFIG.DB, and either save them to CONFIG.DB, or to another file name which can be retrieved when you start dBASE 5. You may want to set different environments for various dBASE applications, especially suited to the needs of the users of the applications. The following listing of settings is found in the default CONFIG.DB file:

```
COLOR OF NORMAL = N+/BG
COLOR OF TITLES = W+/BG
COLOR OF MESSAGES = W/B
COLOR OF BOX = W+/B
COLOR OF INFORMATION = BG+/B
COLOR OF HIGHLIGHT = RG+/W
COLOR OF FIELDS = W+/N
DISPLAY = VGA25
EXCLUSIVE = ON
STATUS = ON
SQLDATABASE = SAMPLES
SQLHOME = C:\DBASE\SQLHOME
```

You can use settings to determine such things as the color of your displays, printer drivers, date formats, whether the beep (bell) sounds on errors, and whether the clock is displayed in the upper-right corner of your screen.

Note

If you create more than one configuration, choose one other than CONFIG.DB when you start dBASE 5 by using the /c parameter with the file name. For example, to start dBASE using a configuration file you named CONFIG.PAY, type the command **dbase /c C:\dbase\config.pay**. If you do not specify a configuration file, dBASE uses the CONFIG.DB file.

Because dBASE 5 looks for the CONFIG.DB file in the current directory on startup, you also can have more than one file named CONFIG.DB, each in a different subdirectory. Starting dBASE from the application's subdirectory that contains its own CONFIG.DB eliminates the need for the /c parameter to specify the file name.

You can edit the CONFIG.DB file by using the desktop editor (see fig. 2.2), the DOS editor, or your word processor (save as an ASCII text file). Or, change the settings by using the menus in the DBSETUP program.

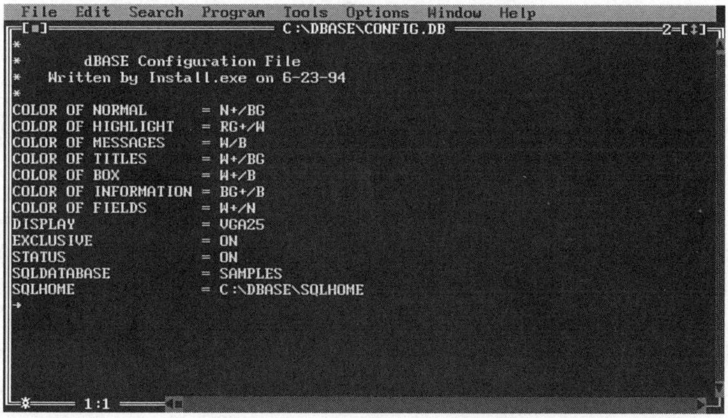

```
File  Edit  Search  Program  Tools  Options  Window  Help
[■]                  C:\DBASE\CONFIG.DB                  2=[↕]
*
*       dBASE Configuration File
*   Written by Install.exe on 6-23-94
*
COLOR OF NORMAL      = N+/BG
COLOR OF HIGHLIGHT   = RG+/W
COLOR OF MESSAGES    = W/B
COLOR OF TITLES      = W+/BG
COLOR OF BOX         = W+/B
COLOR OF INFORMATION = BG+/B
COLOR OF FIELDS      = W+/N
DISPLAY              = VGA25
EXCLUSIVE            = ON
STATUS               = ON
SQLDATABASE          = SAMPLES
SQLHOME              = C:\DBASE\SQLHOME

1:1
```

Fig. 2.2
Edit the CONFIG.DB file to set up the environment for yourself and other users.

Additional environmental commands are used to set up the environment for your application's users. (This environment normally is set through the application's main program file.) The SET commands set up the display and a number of other things that affect the way your application looks and feels to the user. You may want the user to see things differently than you see them when you are working on the program. While you're writing the program, for example, you probably want to see such things as help, a display of the program code being executed, and several other messages dBASE provides.

Tip
Another way to edit the CONFIG.DB file is to use the dBASE 5 program editor. Type **modify command config.db** in the Command window, and press Enter.

When you prepare an application for your users, however, you want it to look as much like a "real" program as possible. You don't want dBASE intruding with its own messages. As part of the housekeeping in your root program module, then, you want to add the following code:

```
SET TALK OFF
SET ECHO OFF
SET SCOREBOARD OFF
SET STATUS OFF
SET HELP OFF
```

SET ECHO displays program code lines as your program executes. SET TALK echoes the results of various commands to the screen. Turn TALK off because you want your application to process the results of your commands and display them the way you want them displayed. (In some cases, you don't display them at all; you simply use the results elsewhere in the program.)

▶ See "Using SET Commands," p. 827

The *scoreboard* (SET SCOREBOARD) is dBASE 5's way of communicating messages to the user when the status bar is off. You can hide these messages in your application by setting the scoreboard to OFF—although these messages are important to you as you develop and test your program. Setting SCOREBOARD OFF, however, does not enable the user to see such things as the `Caps` or `Ins` status displays. Many users want to see these displays. SET STATUS OFF hides the dBASE 5 status bar at the bottom of the screen. Because you provide your own help in your application, setting HELP to OFF prevents dBASE from displaying Help information to users.

▶ See "Setting the Environment Variables," p. 434

The look of your user environment is a good indication of the professionalism of your programming. Remember that although you do most of your environment housekeeping at the start of your application code, you can use the SET commands at any point in your application to modify or customize the work surface, or the way dBASE 5 handles your data. Remember, also, that when you change the SET command within a program, the command remains the way you put it until you change it again. If you want to make a temporary change to an environmental parameter, be sure to do your housekeeping by resetting the parameter to your application's default value when the program returns to the main menu.

dBASE 5 provides access to setting environment variables through the **O**ptions menu on the main menu bar (see fig. 2.3). Choose the **d**BASE SET option.

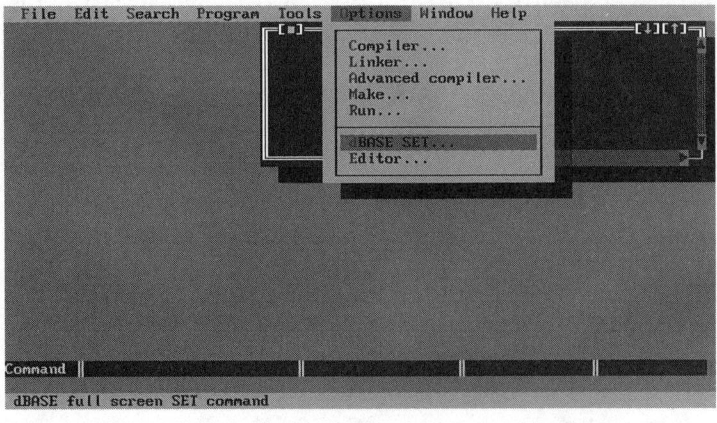

Fig. 2.3
You can use the dBASE SET command to change many environment features in dBASE.

When you choose **d**BASE SET, a screen is displayed, with five menus representing five categories of settings. They are:

- Options
- Display
- Keys
- Disk
- Files

Choosing Options displays the box shown in figure 2.4. Notice you have options for several different items. You can choose where you want the dollar sign to be placed by changing the setting beside Currency sign. You also can choose the number of decimal places, and the date order. By spending some time working with these menus, you can customize your environment settings.

▶ See "General SET Commands," p. 829

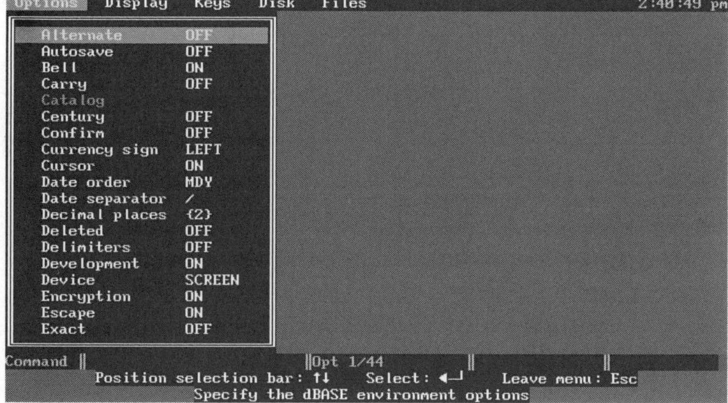

Fig. 2.4
Use the dBASE SET Options menu to configure many different environment variables.

Exiting dBASE

When you tell dBASE you want to exit the program, dBASE asks whether you want to save any information you still have open on the desktop. To quit dBASE, use one of the following methods:

- Open the **F**ile menu and choose E**x**it.
- Press Alt-F4.

From Here...

This chapter focused on how to get started working with dBASE 5. In this chapter you learned to start the dBASE 5 program from either the DOS prompt or Microsoft Windows. Once inside dBASE 5, you can perform actions without a mouse; however, you probably will find the mouse to be a quicker way to move through menus and to design screens and reports. After you become accustomed to the default environment configuration set at installation, you can experiment with other settings you learned about in this chapter.

Now that you know a little about getting started in dBASE 5, you can explore some of the major screen features in the following chapters:

- Chapter 3, "Exploring the New Desktop," to learn to use dBASE menus, dialog boxes, windows, and other tools for productivity. You also learn to manage your files.

- Chapter 4, "Understanding the Control Center," to learn how to use the panels in the Control Center to access many types of files, to create and use a catalog, and to use the DOS utilities.

Chapter 3

Exploring the New Desktop

dBASE 5 now uses a new Desktop, which is a window-like environment where you can develop, run, and debug your dBASE application programs. This chapter discusses the new elements of the Desktop.

- Using the menu bar
- Using dialog boxes
- Using the Command window
- Working with multiple windows
- Accessing the Control Center
- Working with files
- Working with tools
- Getting help

Looking at the Components of the Desktop

dBASE 5 uses a new Desktop that Borland provides as its IDE (Integrated Desktop Environment). The new Desktop is much easier to use, and you are likely to appreciate this new environment once you have learned its features. Figure 3.1 shows the new Desktop.

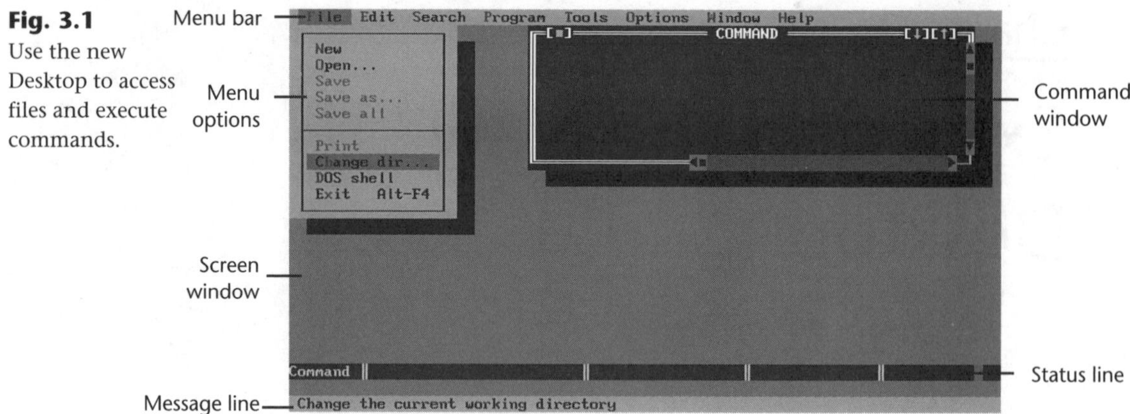

Fig. 3.1 Use the new Desktop to access files and execute commands.

Table 3.1 shows you the major components of the new Desktop.

Table 3.1 Components of the New Desktop

Components of Desktop	Use
Menu bar	Gives you access to the different menus and their options.
Menu options	Performs an action or displays additional options or dialog boxes.
Command window	Accepts dBASE commands (dot prompt replacement), enables editing, and displays a command-line history.
Screen window	Displays command and design surface output.
Status line	Displays different information according to the design surface on which you are working.
Message line	Displays instructions for the item or menu on which you are working.

Using the Menu Bar

The new main menu bar in dBASE 5 gives you a set of eight menus. These menus enable you to work with files, change settings, access tools, and compile and run programs, as described in Table 3.2.

Table 3.2 The New Main Menus

Menu	Description
File menu	Lets you open, save, and print files, change directories, and exit dBASE 5.
Edit menu	Gives you access to the Clipboard, and options to copy and move text.
Search menu	Lets you search and replace text, list routines in a program, and go to a routine or line number.
Program menu	Enables you to compile, link, and run programs.
Tools menu	Gives you access to the new Form Designer, Crosstabs, ASCII Chart, Calendar, and Calculator.
Options menu	Lets you set options to customize Desktop tools and change SET commands.
Window menu	Enables you to access various windows by name or number.
Help menu	Lets you access the on-line Help system.

When you start dBASE 5, the menu bar is visible at the top of the Desktop, but you don't see the menu options until you pull down a menu. The menus can be pulled down only one at a time. You pull down (or open) a menu and select a menu option either with the mouse or the keyboard. You may find using the mouse to be the quickest way to access menus and menu options.

To access a menu using the mouse, move the mouse pointer over a menu name and click the left mouse button. For example, if you want to open a file, first click on **F**ile to open the File menu. To choose a menu option, you also click on it: click on **O**pen. You now see the Open File dialog box. (Click the Cancel button to close the dialog box.) If you have pulled down a menu, and don't want to select an option, click anywhere outside the pull-down menu to close it, or click the right mouse button. You also can click on another menu name to open a different menu.

To access a menu using the keyboard, simultaneously press the Alt key and the emphasized (different color) letter of the menu name. To open a file, for example, hold down Alt while pressing F. Now that you have the **F**ile menu open, you can press the emphasized letter of the option you want to select: you press O to select **O**pen. Alternatively, you can press the down-arrow key until the selection bar highlights the **O**pen option, and then press Enter. To exit the pull-down menu without selecting an option, simply press the Esc key.

You notice in this book that letters which are emphasized on-screen are bolded here to remind you that you can select using the emphasized letters.

Tip
The F10 key can be used to access the last menu in which you performed an action.

You see some options in the pull-down menus that appear to be dimmed. Options that are dimmed are not available for you to use until other criteria have been met. For example, the **C**opy option on the **E**dit menu is dim until you have selected text in an editor window—text on which you can perform Copy. After you select text and use the **C**opy option, the **P**aste option, which had been dim on the **E**dit menu, becomes available because you are ready to paste the text you copied.

Using Dialog Boxes

Tip
You can recognize a menu option that displays a dialog box by the ellipsis (...) next to it.

When dBASE 5 needs more information to perform an option you have selected, a *dialog box* may be opened. When you open the **F**ile menu and choose the **O**pen option, the Open File dialog box is opened, waiting for you to supply information such as the drive, directory, and file name for the file you want to open.

When a dialog box is open you cannot access the menu bar. You can move the dialog box around on the Desktop by dragging its title bar, but you can't resize it as you can resize windows. Note that a dialog box is referred to by the name in its title bar, which resembles the menu option name used to open the dialog box. For example, opening the **F**ile menu and choosing Save **A**s opens the Save As dialog box.

The ways you can move to the various elements in the dialog box are

- Click the mouse pointer on an area.
- Simultaneously press Alt and the emphasized letter of the element.
- Press Tab, or press Shift-Tab.

After you have filled in or selected the required elements in the dialog box, you signal to dBASE to continue with an action by choosing the appropriate pushbutton, often the **O**k pushbutton. (You can choose a pushbutton by clicking it or tabbing to it and pressing Enter.) dBASE closes the dialog box and performs the requested action.

To close a dialog box, thus canceling its action, click the close button in the top-left corner of the dialog box, or press Esc, or if there is a Cancel pushbutton, choose it.

Now you will explore the various elements, or objects, that can be found in a dialog box. A dialog box can contain any combination of these objects. Figures 3.2 and 3.3 illustrate some of the objects.

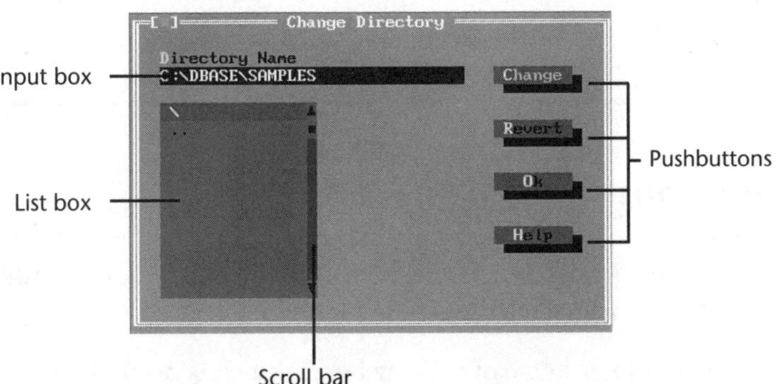

Fig. 3.2
The Change Directory dialog box uses a scroll bar and pushbuttons to give you faster access to your files.

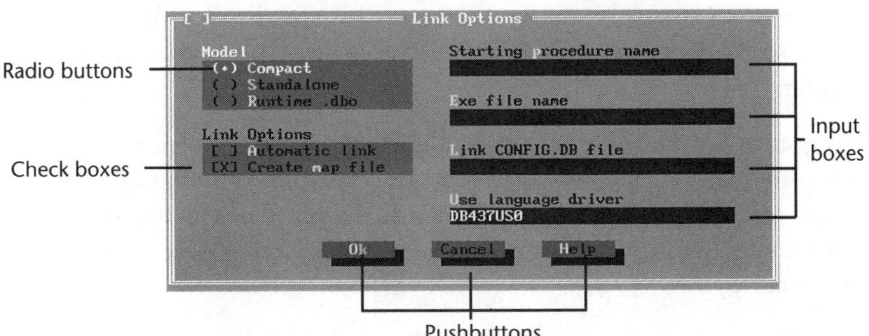

Fig. 3.3
The Link Options dialog box contains check boxes, radio buttons, input boxes, and pushbuttons.

The different components of a dialog box are shown in Table 3.3.

Table 3.3 Elements of the Dialog Box

Element	Description
Pushbutton	Executes an action or displays more options.
Input box	Enables you to type text or numbers.
Check box	Enables you to select one or more options. The check box also toggles on and off. An X in the check box means the option is turned on.

(continues)

Table 3.3 Continued

Element	Description
Radio buttons	Presents a group of option buttons for which only one can be selected.
List box	Displays a list of alternatives from which you can select. Scroll bars enable you to scroll to items when the list is longer than the list box.
Spin box	Enables you to enter a number or to arrow up or down to reach a number.

Pushbuttons

Pushbuttons enable you to take an action, usually after filling in the dialog box. Most dialog boxes contain an Ok pushbutton and a Cancel pushbutton. (You can always cancel by pressing the Esc key.)

In the normal color scheme of a dialog box, the text is black. Text for the area that has *focus* (is highlighted) becomes white—such as when you tab to that area. Likewise, text on a pushbutton has focus—becomes white—when you tab to it. The pushbutton with white text is the one that takes action if you press Enter.

If there is a pushbutton with cyan (aqua blue) text, this is the default pushbutton. Unless you choose another action, the default pushbutton is the action that is carried out when you press Enter. (The button is no longer a default if another button has white text.) Not all dialog boxes have a default pushbutton.

Tip
The emphasized letter on pushbuttons is yellow. Often, the Ok button has a yellow O and a cyan k. Press Alt-O to choose the button or just press Enter.

You can use any one of these methods to choose a button:

- Press the Tab key until the pushbutton you want has focus (the text on the button turns white). Then press Enter to take the action.
- Press the Alt key and then the emphasized (yellow) letter of a pushbutton. The action is taken immediately (you won't have a chance to press Enter or change your mind).
- Click the pushbutton to immediately take the selected action.

Input Boxes

Input boxes, sometimes called *text boxes*, are areas where you can input text. The input box usually has a title or description directly above it telling you the information you need to supply. Figure 3.3 shows a dialog box with more than one input box.

Use basic editing keys while typing text in the input box. These are described in Table 3.4.

Tip
Unless the cursor is in an input box, you can use the emphasized letter alone to choose a pushbutton (or other object), *without* pressing the Alt key.

Table 3.4 Input Box Edit Keys

Key	Description
Backspace	Removes character to the left of the cursor.
Del	Deletes character at the current cursor position.
Home	Places the cursor at the beginning of the text box.
← →	Moves one character to the left or right.

You can toggle the status of Insert mode by pressing the Insert key, enabling you to either insert or type over text in an input box.

Caution

When you are about to enter text in an input box that already contains information (the input box is green, not blue), be careful! If the first key that is pressed is *not* an arrow key, the contents of that input box are deleted. If you intend to edit the existing information, press an arrow key first, and then edit. An alternative is to click the input box at the place you want to edit.

Check Boxes

Check boxes toggle choices on or off. A check box is designated by a pair of brackets [ ] directly to the left of its descriptive text. By clicking on the brackets or text, you place an X in the check box or remove the X. An X in the check box indicates that the option is turned on. Remove the X to turn the option off. Figure 3.4 shows some check boxes in the Find dialog box. Note that the check box and its text are highlighted for the first check box because it was just selected.

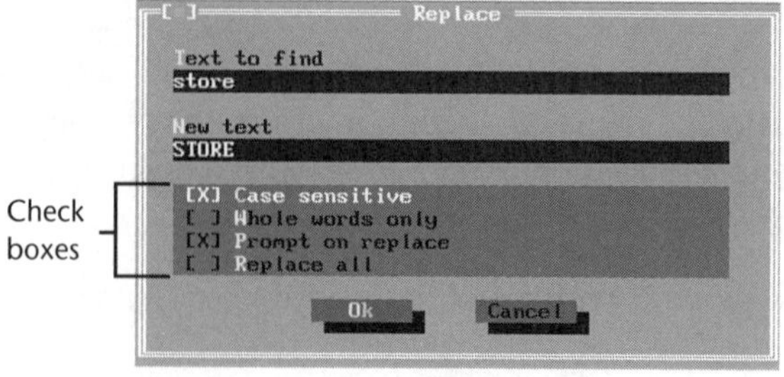

Fig. 3.4
A marked check box in the Replace dialog box tells dBASE to carry out that action for you.

Following are some methods you can use to select a check box:

- Press the emphasized letter of the check box name.
- Click the brackets or text.
- Use the arrow keys to highlight the option (the text becomes white) and press the space bar to toggle it.

Use the same methods to deselect a check box, removing the `X`. A dialog box can have any number of check boxes, and any or none can be selected.

Radio Buttons

Radio buttons present a group of choices; however, only one radio button in the group can be selected. Radio buttons use parentheses () to the left of the text describing each option. When you select a radio button, a dot appears between the parentheses. If the area between the parentheses is blank, the radio button is turned off.

To select a radio button, use any of these methods:

- Press the emphasized letter of the radio button's text.
- Click the parentheses or text.
- Use the arrow keys to highlight the option and press the space bar.

Figure 3.5 shows two sets of radio buttons in the Make Options dialog box.

The only way to change a radio button selection is to select another radio button in the group.

Table 3.6 Scroll Bar Actions

Action	Movement
Click scroll arrow	Scrolls one line of text in direction of arrow that is clicked.
Press and hold down the mouse button on a scroll arrow	Continuously scrolls list until you release mouse button.
Drag scroll box	Scrolls quickly in direction you drag.
Click scroll bar on either end	Scrolls one workspace (list box) of information.

Note

The scroll bars in list boxes are usually vertical scroll bars, to move up and down in the list. Windows such as the Command window, which is discussed in this chapter, have both horizontal and vertical scroll bars. With the horizontal scroll bar, you also can scroll left and right in the window.

You can use any of the following methods to select a list box item:

- Use the scroll bar or direction keys to locate the item, highlight it, and then press Enter.
- Use an alphabetical search by typing the first letter of an item for which you are looking. Continue typing letters you are looking for until you have reached your selection. When you are done, press the Enter key.
- Use the left mouse button to double-click the item you want.

Tip
You can use the keyboard in place of the mouse actions on a scroll bar. To navigate the list box, use Home, End, Page Up, Page Down, ↑, and ↓.

Spin Boxes

Spin boxes are used to enter a number for an option in a dialog box. The current number setting appears in a small text box, with up- and down-arrow buttons at the right side (see fig. 3.7). This text box with its spinner buttons is the spin box. Only numbers (or sometimes dates, as in the Desktop Calendar tool) can be entered in a spin box.

Use one of the following methods to choose a number in a spin box:

- Repeatedly click the up arrow to increment the number, or the down arrow to decrement the number in the box.
- Type a number in the box.

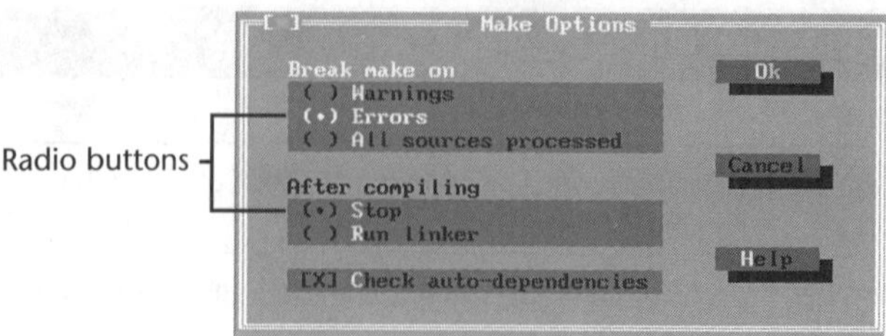

g
b

List Boxes

List boxes display information sequentially in a box, enabling you to select the item you want. List boxes can contain a simple list from which you can make a selection. Or list boxes can contain information that varies based on search criteria in an input box and other list boxes. For example, in the Open File dialog box, selecting a file type from the File **T**ypes list box puts the wild-card criterion (such as *.PRG) in the **F**ile Name input box. All file names that match this wild card and also match the drive and directory in the other list boxes appear in the **F**ile Name list box (below the input box). See figure 3.6. When you select an item in the **F**ile Name list box, the file name appears in the input box and is the file opened when you press **O**k.

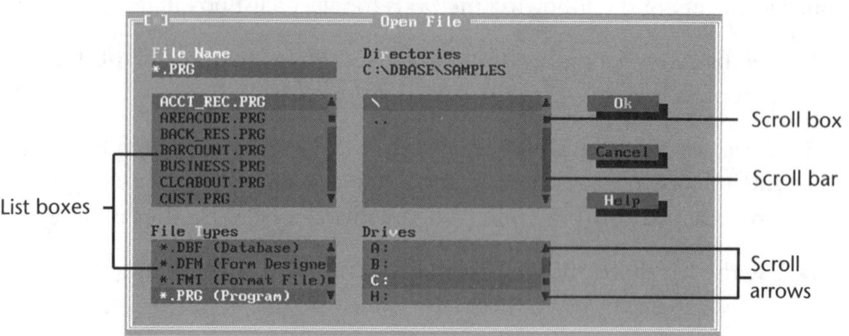

Fig. 3.6
The Open Fil
dialog box
contains four l
boxes with scro
bars.

You see a vertical *scroll bar* in each list box. Scroll bars enable you to see lists that are too long to fit in the size of the box. The parts of the scroll bar are the scroll arrows (located at each end of the scroll bar), the scroll box (used to drag quickly), and the scroll bar itself, as shown in figure 3.6. Each part has a function in viewing the files in the list box, as described in Table 3.6.

- "Spin" to a greater or lesser number by holding down the mouse button with the mouse pointer on an arrow.
- Press the ↑ or ↓ keys on the keyboard to increase or decrease the number in the spin box.

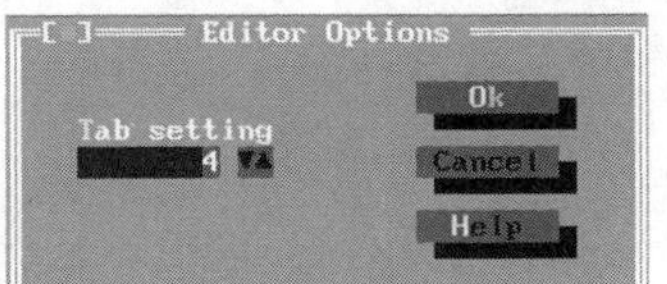

Fig. 3.7
A spin box is used for selecting a number, such as the Tab setting for the Editor.

Using the Command Window

The Command window in dBASE 5 replaces the dot prompt found in previous versions of dBASE. Commands are entered in the Command window, which has full-screen editing capabilities. You can edit commands that you are typing or have previously issued by inserting and deleting text, and even by using copy, cut, and paste.

Another advantage of the new Command window is that the command output is not mingled with the commands themselves; the output for commands like DIR, LIST, DISPLAY, and @SAY, appears in the Screen window, which is the full-screen window on which the Command window (and other windows) is opened (see fig. 3.8).

The Command window already is open when you start dBASE 5. If you closed it during your work session, you can reopen it by one of the following methods:

- From the Desktop, open the **W**indow menu and choose C**o**mmand.
- Press Alt-1. (Windows are numbered; the Command window is always window number 1.)
- If you are working in the Control Center, open the Exit menu and choose Exit to Command Window.

Entering Commands in the Command Window

You can enter commands in the Command window just like you used to at the dBASE IV dot prompt. For example, if you want to see a listing of the current directory, you can type **!DIR** and then press Enter to execute the command.

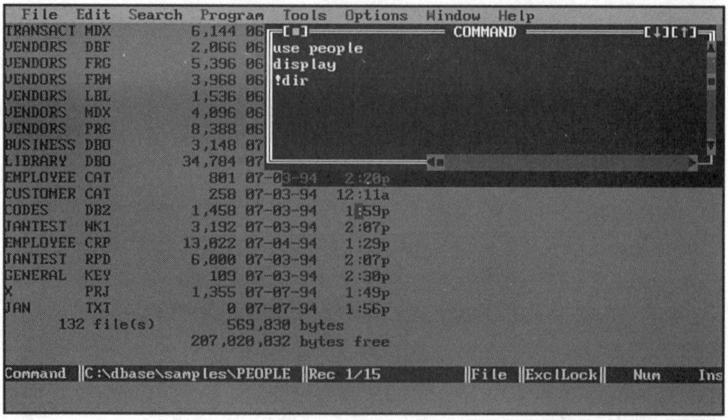

Fig. 3.8
The Command window is used for executing dBASE commands, with output appearing in the Screen window.

▶ See "Using Commands and Functions," p. 388

For a complete list of commands, refer to Part VI, the Reference Guide of this book.

Each command you issue during a session stays in the Command window—as many command lines as memory enables. Scroll bars on the Command window enable you to scroll to areas not currently visible in the window. You also can enlarge the window, to see more commands without scrolling. See the next section, "Working with Multiple Windows," for more information on managing the window itself.

Tip
To get help on a command in the Command window, place the cursor anywhere on the same line as the command, and then right-click or press F1.

Each command line is appended to the end of the list in the Command window. If you use a function key for a command, the command also appears in the Command window. For example, if you press the F2 (Assist) key to go to the Control Center, the `assist` command is added to the Command window (refer to fig. 3.8). When you use full-screen features that remove the Command window from view, such as the Control Center and the Form Designer, the Command window retains its command history.

If the command you enter in the Command window has an error, dBASE displays an error dialog box. Choose **E**dit to return to the line that contains the error or choose **C**ancel to return to the end of the Command window commands. You also can choose **H**elp to get help on the error.

Reusing a Previous Command

The Command window enables you to reissue commands that are in the window. This feature gives you the flexibility to go back and look for a command that you need to use again—especially helpful for commands with complex syntax. Before executing the command again, you can change the arguments—or any other part—by editing the command line. When you execute an edited command, the edited version is appended to the end of the command list in the Command window, and then executed. You do not lose the history of commands you have entered before.

To reissue a command in the Command window, do one of the following:

- Place the cursor anywhere in the command line, and then press Enter.
- Double-click the command line.

Working with Multiple Windows

The Command window and Screen window—the primary windows of the Developer's Desktop—already have been introduced. You can access several more windows on the Desktop. You could, for example, open a program you are coding in an Edit window, open another program for reference in another Edit window, open a third Edit window for writing notes as you work, and open the Clipboard window to view text that you cut or copy. You can have all these windows, along with the Command and Screen windows, visible on your Desktop simultaneously, and switch among them as you work.

Tip
Select a block of commands and copy it to the Clipboard. You can open an Edit window and paste the commands from the Clipboard to the Edit window.

Other actions that can take place in windows are compiling programs, and creating forms and menus. You can arrange the windows on the Desktop and adjust the sizes as required.

▶ See "Understanding the Clipboard," p. 407

Opening a Window

You open the **F**ile menu and choose **O**pen to open existing files in Edit windows. To open a new file in an Edit window, such as one in which you can take notes, open the **F**ile menu and choose **N**ew. The Cl**i**pboard is opened from the **E**dit menu.

Although you can have several windows open at the same time, only one is the active window—the one with its title bar highlighted. The Screen window is an exception; it has no title bar. When it is activated by opening the **W**indow menu and choosing Sc**r**een or by pressing Alt-Space, it temporarily hides the other open windows until a key is pressed.

dBASE 5 numbers the windows you open to facilitate selection from the **W**indow menu or keyboard. The Screen window does not have a number, but the Command window is always window number 1. The List All window (which lists the open windows) is window number 0. Other windows you open are numbered 2 through 9. The window number appears in the top-right corner of the window (see fig. 3.9).

Note

As you open windows, they are given the first available number from 2 to 9. If you open windows 2, 3, and 4, and then close window number 3, the next window you open is assigned number 3. MDI (Multiple Document Interface) forms, such as the Desktop Calculator and Desktop Calendar, also use these numbers. If you have more than nine windows or forms open, the new windows are not assigned a number.

The window number does not show on the active window. Instead, there is a *zoom box* for sizing the window (described in the next section). The active window also has scroll bars (if needed) and a close box, which disappear when another window is activated.

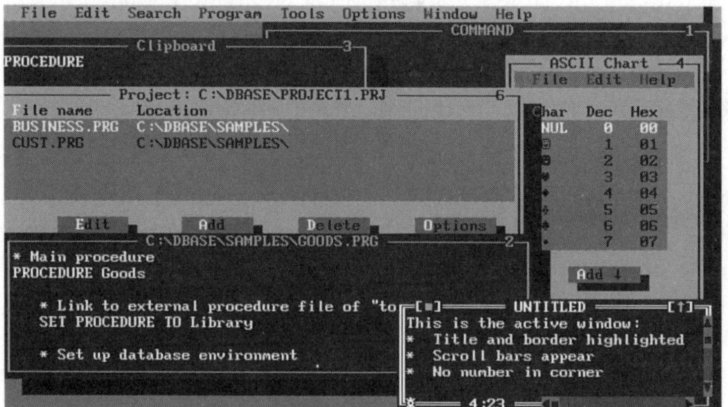

Fig. 3.9
Open windows to help you manage your work in the new Desktop. Opening too many windows can hinder your work!

Choose any of these methods to activate a window:

- Click anywhere on the window you want to activate.
- Click the title bar if the windows are cascaded (stacked).
- Open the **W**indow menu and choose Ne**x**t or press Ctrl-F6 to go to the next numbered window.

- Open the **W**indow menu and choose **L**ist All and select a window from the list.
- Press Alt and the window's number. Alt-4 selects window number 4.

Sizing a Window

You can *size* windows to make them the size you want for the kind of work you are doing in each window. If you are debugging a program and want to see the maximum amount of text, you may want to expand the Edit window to full-screen size. It is easy to shrink the window again, if you want to access other windows on the Desktop. Or maybe you want to resize the Command window, to make it narrower so it doesn't obscure the Screen window, where you are trying to see the output from the commands you are entering. You also can shrink a window to a small icon, to get it out of your way temporarily without closing it.

Use any of the following methods to change a window's size:

- Open the **W**indow menu and choose **S**ize, or press Alt-F8. Press Shift and the arrow key that pertains to the direction you want to size the window. Press Enter when the window is the size you want.
- Drag the resize corner (the lower-right corner of the window) until you have reached the size you want (see fig. 3.10).
- Click the zoom box (located in the top-right corner of the window). See the effects described in Table 3.7.

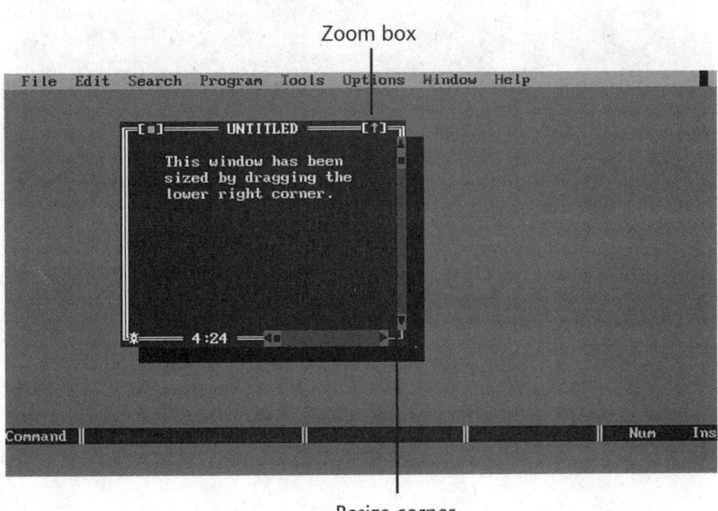

Fig. 3.10
Using the resize corner is a fast way to size a window.

Table 3.7 Using the Elements of a Zoom Box

Element	Effect on a Window
Up arrow	Expands window, usually to full-screen size.
Down arrow	Shrinks window to icon. Click the icon to bring the window back to its original size.
Double arrow	Restores fully expanded window to its previous size.

Moving a Window

During a work session, you could have several windows open, making it necessary to move a window to a different place on the Desktop.

Use either of the following methods to move a window:

- Open the **W**indow menu and choose **M**ove, or press Alt-F7. Then use the arrow keys to move the window where you need it (see fig. 3.11). After you have moved the window, press Enter.
- Drag the title bar until the window is positioned where you desire.

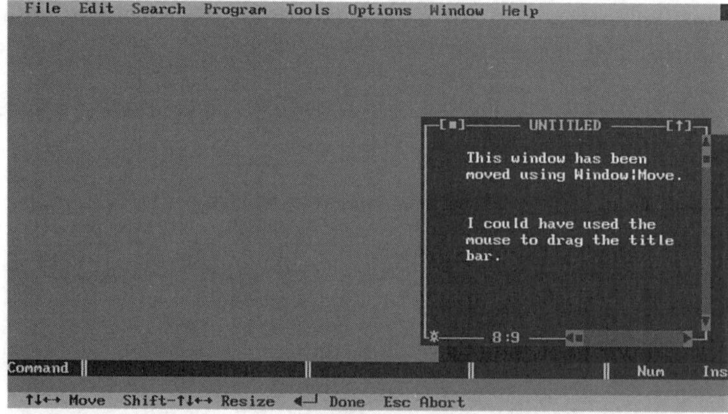

Fig. 3.11
The message line reminds you how to move and size windows on the Desktop.

Tip
You can get a window out of the way by dragging it almost off the edge of the screen, so that much of it seems to disappear.

Displaying Several Windows

After you have opened several windows, you can let dBASE instantly arrange and size them for you by *tiling* or *cascading*. Tiling displays the open windows in somewhat equally sized tiles on the screen (see fig. 3.12). To tile all sizeable windows that are currently open, open the **W**indow menu and choose **T**ile.

Note

The Screen window can't be tiled because it is full-screen and not sizeable. It can be brought to the front by pressing Alt-space bar. If a window isn't sizeable, then it cannot be tiled or cascaded. Other examples are the Desktop Calculator, Calendar, and ASCII Chart. After tiling or cascading windows, these Desktop tools can be opened on top of the other windows by choosing them from the **T**ools menu.

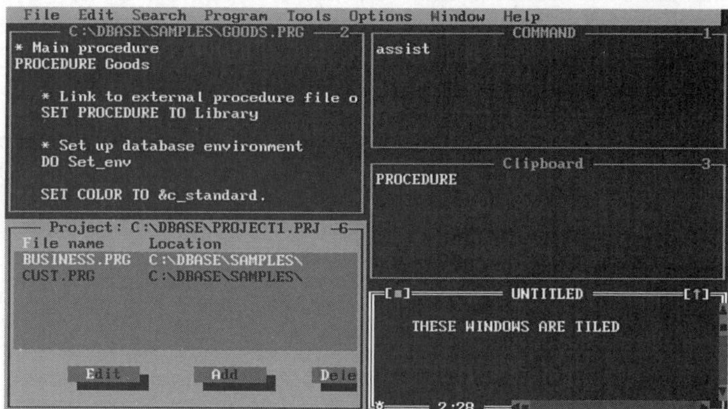

Fig. 3.12
Instantly arrange your windows by tiling them. The window sizes and arrangement may not be ideal.

Cascading stacks the open windows so each of their title bars peek out at the top of the stack. This way you can click a window's title bar to bring it to the top (front) of the stack (see fig. 3.13). The active window is always the one at the top of the cascaded stack. To cascade all sizeable windows that are currently open, open the **W**indow menu and choose C**a**scade.

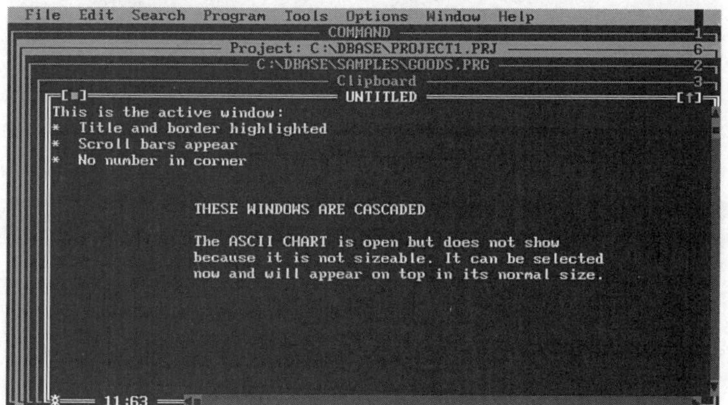

Fig. 3.13
Activate a cascaded window by clicking its title bar.

Listing Open Windows

You have learned in this chapter that open windows are numbered in their top-right corners so you can activate them by number using the keyboard. But what if your windows are overlapping and you can't see the number in the corner of some? You could rearrange your windows, or you could select the window from the **W**indow menu.

Open the **W**indow menu and choose **L**ist All or press Alt-0 (zero) to display a list of the numbered windows and forms that are open (see fig. 3.14). Notice at the right side of the List All Windows window that the type of window is shown, such as EDITOR or FORM.

Choose one of the following ways to activate a window on the list:

- Use the scroll bars to find the window name, and then double-click it.
- Click the number or window name, and then click the **S**elect pushbutton.
- Use the arrow keys to highlight the window name, and then press Enter.

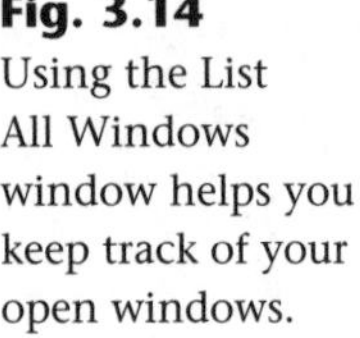

Fig. 3.14
Using the List All Windows window helps you keep track of your open windows.

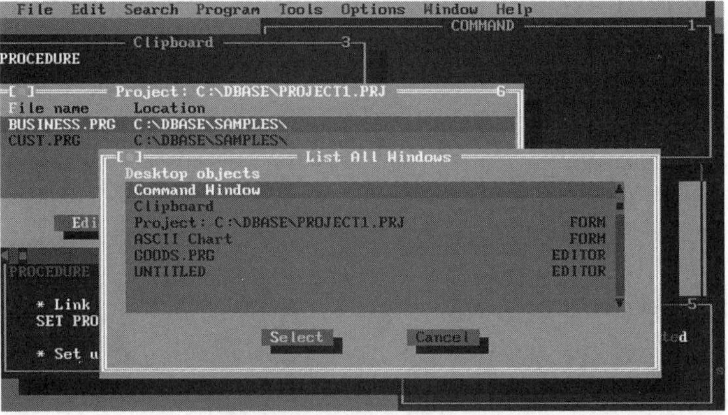

Note

The Screen window is not listed in the List All window. To activate it, open the **Win**dow menu and choose Sc**r**een or press Alt-space bar. The List All window can be used to activate forms, such as the ASCII Chart, that do not appear if you tile or cascade the open windows.

Closing a Window

After you have finished working in a window, you can close it to make free space on the Desktop for other windows you want to open. The window you want to close must be active to use the close box or the **C**lose option. Use any of the following methods to close a window:

- Click the window's Close box, which is located in the top-left corner of the active window.
- Open the **W**indow menu and choose **C**lose, or press Ctrl-F4 to close the active window.
- Open the **W**indow menu and choose Clos**e** All to close all of the open windows.

It is not necessary to close any of the windows before exiting dBASE. You will, however, want to be sure that you have saved each file that you modified, or dBASE prompts you whether you want to save before exiting.

Using the Control Center

dBASE 5 does not display the Control Center initially, as was normal in dBASE IV. You see the Developer's Desktop, which provides the work surfaces and window-like environment that enhance dBASE's capabilities. dBASE 5 still provides the Control Center where you can work on your files and use the same options with which you have become familiar.

Tip
To display the Control Center when dBASE is started, put the line `COMMAND = ASSIST` in the CONFIG.DB file.

Accessing the Control Center

Use any of the following methods to access the Control Center:

- Press the F2 key. You see the word `assist` appear in the Command window, and then the Control Center appears (see fig. 3.15).
- Type the word **assist** in the Command window and then press Enter.
- Open the **W**indow menu and choose Co**n**trol Center from the Desktop menu bar.

Refer to Chapter 4, "Understanding the Control Center," for complete instructions on using the Control Center features.

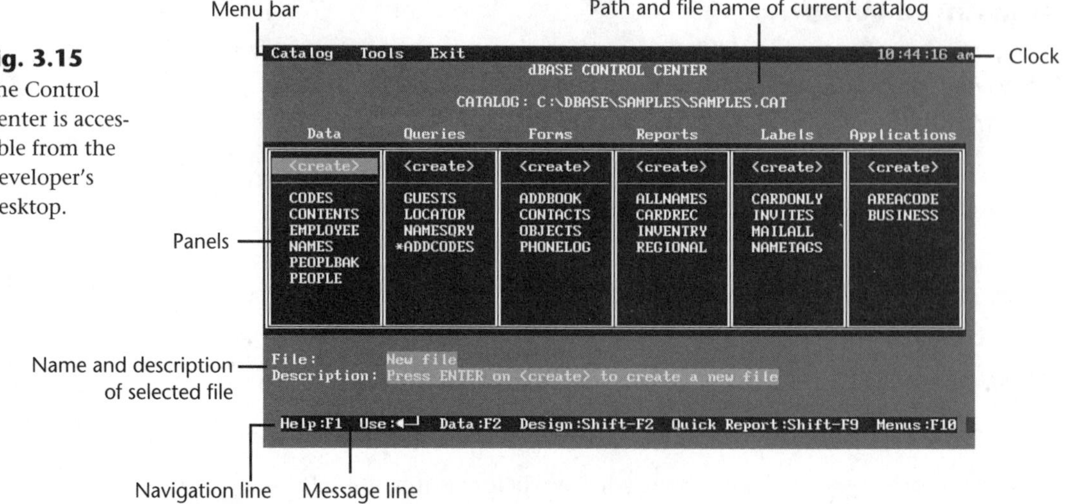

Fig. 3.15
The Control Center is accessible from the Developer's Desktop.

Returning to the Desktop

To return to the Desktop from the Control Center, do one of the following:

1. Open the Exit menu and choose Exit to Command Window.

2. Press Esc. At the prompt box which asks if you want to abandon the operation, choose Yes.

Working with Files

► See "Using the Categories," p. 68

dBASE 5 has new ways of working with files. You still can use the Control Center, including its DOS Utilities for file management, but the Developer's Desktop is even better! It offers new dialog boxes and the capability of opening your files simultaneously in multiple windows, as you learned earlier in this chapter. You can even compile and run your programs, and work with design tools from the Desktop. This section describes working with files, using the options on the Desktop's **F**ile menu (see fig. 3.16).

Creating a New File

When you open the **F**ile menu and choose the **N**ew option, a blank, untitled Edit window is opened on the Desktop (see fig. 3.17). Edit windows are used to edit ASCII files, such as program (PRG) files. You can use editing features in this new window, including copying, cutting, and pasting text. You also can move and resize the window, as discussed previously.

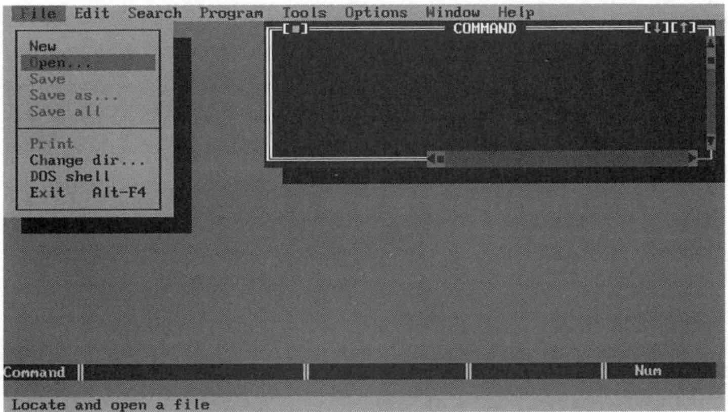

Fig. 3.16
The Desktop's File menu offers new ways to perform several file operations.

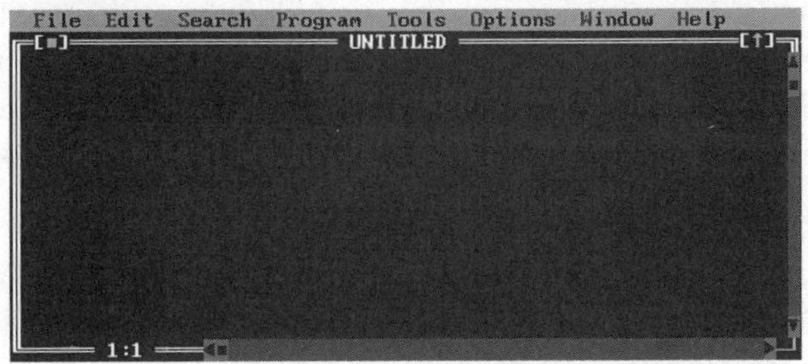

Fig. 3.17
Choosing **N**ew from the **F**ile menu opens an untitled Edit window.

Because the Edit window is a temporary buffer, you must save the contents in a file (see "Saving Files" later in this chapter) if you want to keep the information you have entered. If you try to close the Edit window or compile the program it contains, dBASE prompts you to save it first. You can open several new Edit windows, all named `Untitled` in each title bar, but you must activate and save each one individually.

Tip
Open an Edit window to write yourself notes and reminders while you are working or to store blocks of program code to use later.

Opening an Existing File

In dBASE IV, the Control Center was used to open a file from the appropriate panel. In the Desktop, you use the **F**ile menu to open a file. The Open File dialog box enables you to locate the file name using scrollable list boxes.

Follow these steps to open an existing file:

1. Open the **F**ile menu and choose **O**pen. The Open File dialog box appears, as shown in figure 3.18.

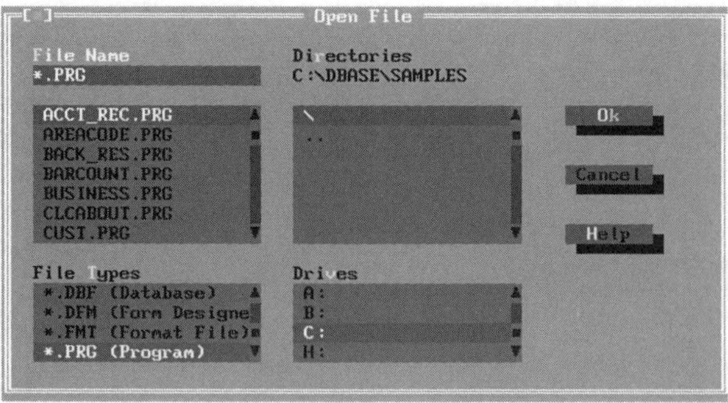

Fig. 3.18
Use the Open File dialog box to access your files in dBASE 5.

Tip
If you already have the correct drive, directory, and file type, double-click the file name in the **F**ile Name list box. The file opens on the Desktop.

2. Use the Dri**v**es list box to choose the correct drive (probably correct already). Use the Di**r**ectories list box to choose the directory where the file is located. If you want to go back a level in the directory tree, double-click the double dot (..) entry in the list box. Use the scroll bars to navigate through the list box. When you have highlighted the correct directory, press Enter, or double-click it, to make its path appear above the list box.

3. Choose the file type you want to open in the File **T**ypes list box. Table 3.8 shows the types of files available. Highlight and press Enter, or double-click the file type.

   The **F**ile Name input box shows your file type selection. The **F**ile Name list box contents change to show only the files which match the selected file type and are in the drive and directory path chosen.

Table 3.8 File Types in the Open File Dialog Box

File Type	Description
.	All Files
*.DBF	Database
*.DFM	Form Design
*.FMT	Format File
*.PRG	Program
*.PRJ	Project
*.QBE	Query

4. Choose the file name from the **F**ile Name list box. Or, if you prefer, type the name in the input box. Choose one of these ways to open the specified file:

   - Double-click its name.
   - Highlight its name and press Enter.
   - Highlight its name and choose **O**k.

The file is opened in the appropriate editor or design surface.

Canceling the Open File Dialog Box

You can cancel your decision to open a file. Use any of the following methods:

- Choose the Cancel button.
- Press the Esc key.
- Click on the Close button (top-left corner).

Changing Directories

In the Open File dialog box, a directory already is selected in the Di**r**ectories list box, the directory from which you started dBASE. If this is not the directory you want to use for this work session, you can change the default directory path.

◄ See "Starting dBASE 5 from the DOS Prompt," p. 25

To change to a new default directory for the session:

► See "Changing the Drive or Directory," p. 86

1. Open the **F**ile menu and choose C**h**ange Dir to display the Change Directory dialog box shown in figure 3.19.

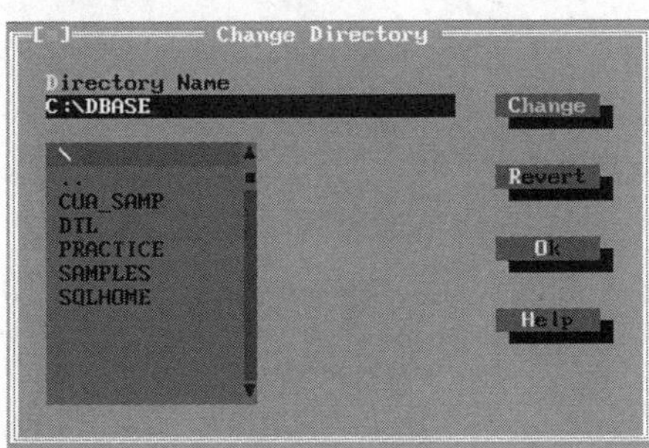

Fig. 3.19
You can use the Change Directory dialog box to change the default directory used to open and save files.

2. Use the list box to choose the directory to which you want to change. If you want to go back a level in the directory tree, choose the double dot (..) entry. If you want to start at the root directory, choose backslash (\) in the list box. Use the scroll bars to navigate through the list box.

3. Choose the **C**hange pushbutton to change to the highlighted directory or double-click the name of the directory. The directory path is displayed in the **D**irectory name input box.

4. Choose **O**k.

Tip
Choose the **R**evert button to return to the same directory that was displayed when you opened the Change Directory dialog box.

dBASE uses the directory you choose for the remainder of the session or until you change the directory again.

Saving Files

You should make a habit of saving your files frequently during a dBASE work session. Saving your files protects your work in case your computer shuts down or locks up for any reason.

If you are making significant changes to a file and don't want to lose your original version, you can open the **F**ile menu and choose the Save **A**s option to save to another file name (see fig. 3.20). dBASE saves your files with the extension of PRG (program file), or you can type in a file name and extension. For example, you could save a text file with the extension TXT.

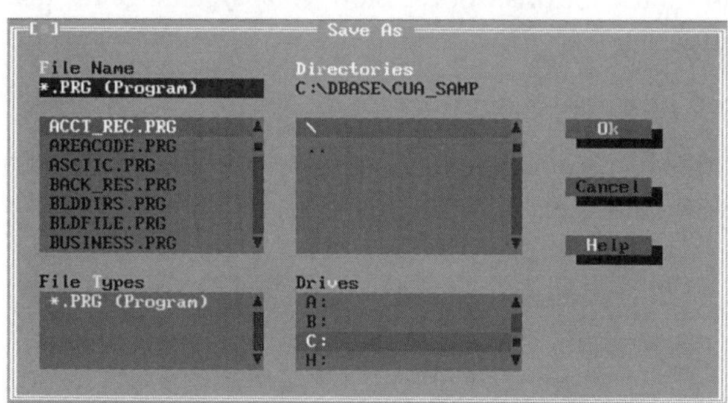

Fig. 3.20
Use the File Save As dialog box to give your new file a name, or to save an existing file to a new name.

The **F**ile menu offers you the following options for saving files:

- Choose **S**ave to save an existing (named) file. No dialog box appears. If you try to use **S**ave on an untitled Edit window, the Save As dialog box appears to prompt you for a name.

- Choose Save **A**s to save the contents of an untitled Edit window or to save the contents of the active Edit window to a name you specify. The Save As dialog box appears.

  Use the Save As dialog box the same way you use the Open File dialog box, choosing the drive and directory to which you want to save the file. Browse file names in the **F**ile Name list box, but do not use one of those names unless you want to overwrite a file! Type a new name for the file in the **F**ile Name input box, and then choose OK.

- Choose Save A**ll** to save all of the files currently open in Edit windows. This option works the same as **S**ave, except it applies to all open Edit windows, not just the active window.

Tip
An asterisk in the lower-left corner of the Edit window indicates that the file in the window has been modified. You must save the file to keep the modifications. The asterisk disappears each time you save the file.

Note

If you select a file name in the Save As dialog box that already exists in the current directory, dBASE presents an Information window to tell you that the file exists. Choose **O**verwrite to save with file name (you lose the data from the previously existing file). Or choose Cancel to avoid overwriting; then, try again. You have to open the **F**ile menu and choose Save **A**s again because the dialog box has closed.

Tip
Press Ctrl-Enter to save a file using the keyboard.

Printing Files

Open the **F**ile menu and choose the **P**rint option to print the contents of an active Edit window. If a window cannot be printed—such as the Project window—the Print option is dimmed (unavailable).

You must save a file before you can print it. If you choose **P**rint with an Untitled Edit window activated, dBASE warns you it can't find Untitled. Cancel, and then open the **F**ile menu and choose Save **A**s. After you name the file by saving it, you can print it.

Note

If you have a problem with the printer output, you can check the commands that were set in the system printer memory variables. Refer to Chapter 27, "Using System Memory Variables," for a complete reference.

If your printer port is properly configured and a printer is attached, dBASE prints the file without further notice—no dialog box. A window displays telling you the file is printing, but there are no pushbuttons enabling you to change your mind and cancel.

On the printout, the file name, current date, and page number appear at the top of each page.

Closing Files

Closing a file in dBASE can be done with the click of the mouse button. All you have to do is click on the close button, which is a little square box located in the upper-left corner of the window. Use the close button to quickly close a window when you are finished using that window.

Note

Be sure you have saved any modifications you have made to the file displayed in the window; otherwise, dBASE prompts you with an Information window (see fig. 3.21). In the Information window, you can choose **Y**es to open the Save As dialog box, choose **N**o to close and lose all modifications since the last save, or choose Cancel to do nothing and return to the Edit window.

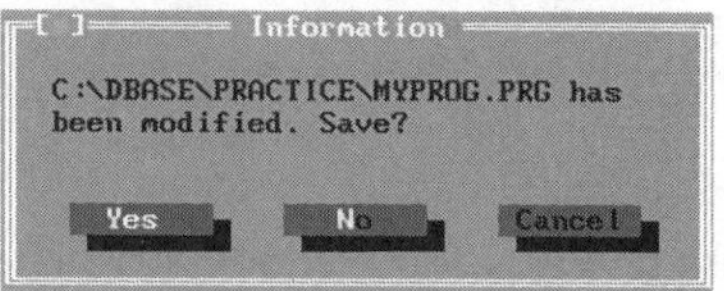

Fig. 3.21
dBASE warns you if you try to close a window without saving your modifications to the file.

You also can open the **W**indow menu and choose the **C**lose option from the Desktop menu bar. Another option, Clos**e** All, closes all the windows on the Desktop. If any of the windows are untitled or modifications have not been saved, the Information window appears as shown in figure 3.21 and described in the Note.

Working with Tools

dBASE 5 has provided three Desktop accessories you can open on the Developer's Desktop and use as needed: the ASCII Chart, the Desktop Calculator, and the Desktop Calendar. You can find the program code for these accessories in the \DBASE\CUA_SAMP directory.

Using the ASCII Chart

You can open the extended ASCII Chart on the Desktop by opening the **T**ools menu and choosing **A**SCII Chart. Use this tool to look up ASCII values in Decimal and Hexadecimal, create strings, and copy characters to the Clipboard, which then can be pasted to an Edit window.

The ASCII Chart can be displayed in two sizes. It is opened in the smaller size. Open the **E**dit menu and choose M**a**ximize to display the larger view of the chart, as shown in figure 3.22. Use the scroll bar to scroll to more values. You can open the **E**dit menu and choose M**i**nimize to reduce the ASCII Chart to its smaller view. Move the chart to a new position by dragging its title bar.

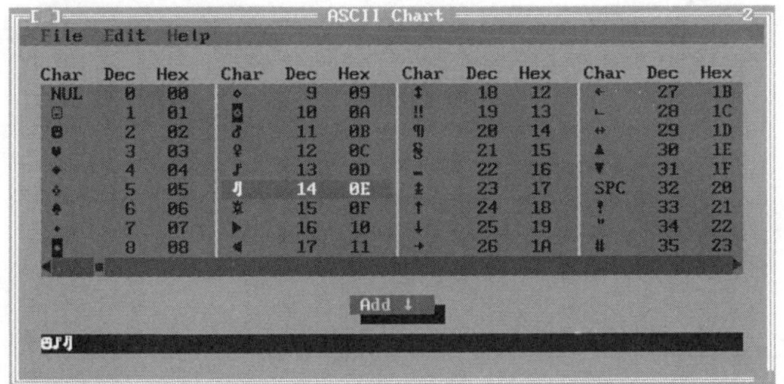

Fig. 3.22
Use the maximized ASCII Chart to copy characters to the Clipboard for use in a program.

To copy characters to the Clipboard, follow these steps:

1. Highlight the character you want to copy.
2. Choose the **A**dd button. The character is placed in the input box below the Add button.
3. Repeat steps 1 and 2 to place as many characters as you want in the input box.
4. Open the **E**dit menu and choose **C**opy. The contents of the input box are copied to the Clipboard.
5. Close the ASCII Chart by clicking the close button (located in the top-left corner of the window) or by opening the **F**ile menu and choosing E**x**it.

   Clicking the close button closes the ASCII Chart but keeps the contents of the input box. If you open the ASCII Chart again, your previous

Tip
You can double-click each character you want to place in the input box, rather than highlighting and choosing the **A**dd button.

selections are in the input box. Opening the **F**ile menu and choosing E**x**it to close the ASCII Chart removes the contents of the input box.

▶ See "Understanding the Clipboard," p. 407

Now that the characters are on the Clipboard, which you can view by opening the **E**dit menu and choosing Cl**i**pboard, they can be pasted into an Edit window.

Using the Calculator

dBASE has included the Desktop Calculator which can perform basic math calculations. The Calculator window cannot be resized, but you can move it by dragging its title bar. To use the calculator, do the following:

1. Open the **T**ools menu and choose **C**alculator. You see the calculator appear, as shown in figure 3.23.

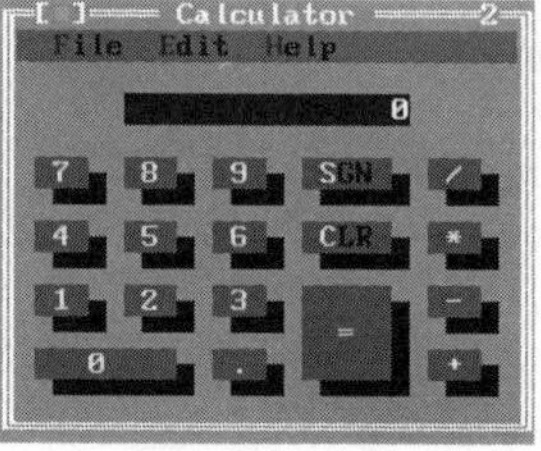

Fig. 3.23
dBASE includes a new calculator you can use on the Desktop.

Tip
You can also use the keyboard to enter numbers and operators in the Desktop Calculator.

2. Enter the first number by clicking the calculator's number keys. The numbers you click appear in the input box.
3. Click an operator (/, *, –, or +).
4. Enter another number.
5. Click the equal sign (=). The result appears in the input box.

You can open the **E**dit menu and choose **C**opy to copy the contents of the input box to the Clipboard. It then can be pasted to other windows.

Use the **S**GN pushbutton on the Calculator to change the sign of the value displayed in the input box from positive to negative or from negative to positive. The Calculator has a **C**LR pushbutton to cancel a single entry. Open the **E**dit menu and choose C**l**ear to cancel the entire calculation and start over.

Close the Calculator window by clicking the close button. The current calculation is retained. If you reopen the Desktop Calculator, the prior value is displayed in the input box. If you had a calculation in progress, you may continue with it. For example, the value displayed is not necessarily the result of the calculation but could be the last value you entered. You have not lost the series of numbers you have already entered; continue with the next operator and other values as needed.

You can close the Desktop Calculator without retaining the calculation by opening the **F**ile menu and choosing E**x**it.

Using the Calendar

The Desktop Calendar provides access to a standard calendar, enabling you to click quickly through the months to locate an important date. Like the other Desktop accessories, you can copy your selection to the Clipboard, from which it can be pasted to other windows. In this case, you are copying the date you have highlighted on the calendar.

To use the Desktop Calendar, open the **T**ools menu and choose Ca**l**endar. The calendar opens, as shown in figure 3.24. You cannot resize the calendar. Move it by dragging its title bar.

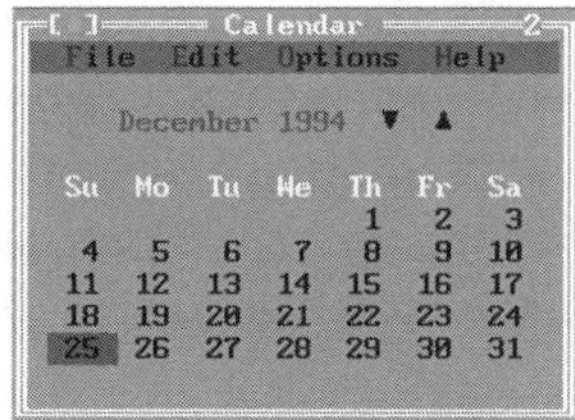

Fig. 3.24 Use the Desktop Calendar for handy reference while you work in dBASE 5.

Table 3.9 shows the operations you can perform using the keyboard and the calendar's menus.

Table 3.9 Desktop Calendar Options

Menu Option	Key	Action
Edit, **C**opy	Ctrl-Ins	Copies the date to the Clipboard.
Edit, **T**oday		Highlights today's date (from system clock).
Edit, **P**revious	Page Up	Pages back one month.
Edit, **N**ext	Page Down	Pages forward one month.

(continues)

Table 3.9 Continued

Menu Option	Key	Action
Edit, **S**et New Date		Enables you to alter today's date to change the point of reference.
	→	Moves to next day.
	←	Moves to previous day.
	↓	Moves to next week.
	↑	Moves to previous week.
Options, **D**ate Format used		Enables you to change the date format in **E**dit, Copy.

When you open the Desktop Calendar, today's date is highlighted. Choose another date by clicking it. Use the mouse to move forward a month at a time by clicking the up arrow (next to the year). Click the down arrow to move back a month.

Close the Calendar window by clicking the close button or by opening the **F**ile menu and choosing E**x**it. If you use the close button, the same date that was highlighted will be highlighted if you reopen the Calendar. If you open the **F**ile menu and choose E**x**it to close the Calendar, the system date is highlighted next time you open the Calendar.

Getting Help

The Desktop Help system enables you to seek help from indexes in the **H**elp menu or very specifically from where you are working—context-sensitive help. You can find valuable information on using commands, functions, UI objects, and general topics. Learn more about the Desktop and the Form Designer!

Open the **H**elp menu and choose the **H**elp Index (or press F1) to display the Table of Contents for the Help system (see fig. 3.25). From this window, you can highlight a topic for which you want more detail, and then choose the **N**ext pushbutton. The table of contents for that topic is displayed. As you keep highlighting a topic and choosing **N**ext, you arrive at a more detailed information window, with `<MORE F4>` in the lower-right corner. At this detail level, you can press F4 to continue reading the help text, or press F3 to go back. The **B**ackup pushbutton takes you backward through each window you have viewed in this session with the Help system. Table 3.10 describes the action of the pushbuttons in the Help System window.

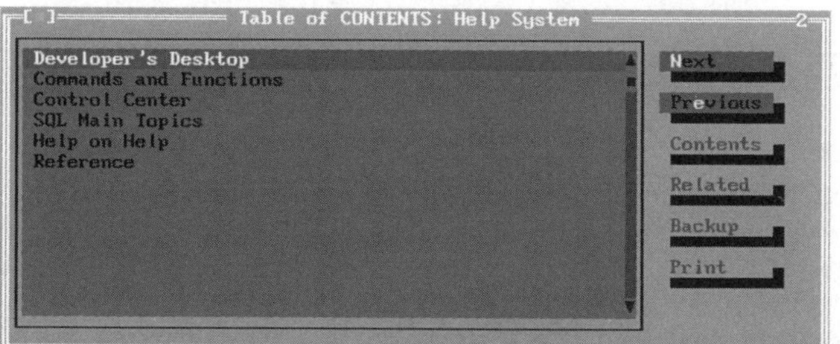

Fig. 3.25
dBASE 5 provides a new Help system. Here is the top index.

Table 3.10 Pushbuttons in the Help System Window

Pushbutton	Action
Next	Moves to the next page of the Table of Contents.
Pr**e**vious	Moves to the previous page of the Table of Contents.
Contents	Returns to the Table of Contents.
Related	Displays related topics (dimmed when none available).
Backup	Backs up through help windows you viewed in this help session.
Print	Prints the current help window's contents.

Another **H**elp menu option is **K**eyboard Help. This option displays the Help system for shortcut keys, cursor keys, and function keys. You also can press Ctrl-F1 to open this Help System window. Press F4 to see the succeeding screens; press F3 to back up. To close a Help System window, press Esc or click the Close button in the top-left corner.

Tip
You can double-click a Table of Contents topic to go to the next level.

You can get quick help for any dBASE command or function by typing the command in the Command window and pressing F1. Typing **help** and the command name or function name also works, such as **help compile** or **help DATE()**. If the command is already in the Command window or in an Edit window, click the right mouse button on the command line. A help window opens, showing the syntax and description of the command. For example, if you right-click the command `use customer` in the Command window, a help window for the USE command is displayed (see fig. 3.26). This Help feature is especially useful when you are writing program code in an Edit window and want to check the arguments for a command without searching through levels of Help windows.

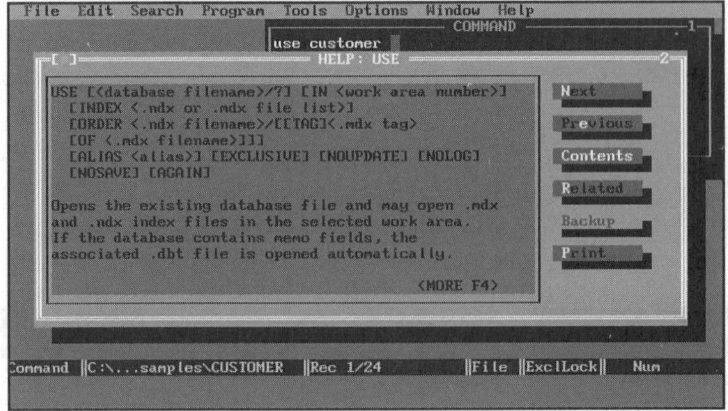

Fig. 3.26
Right-click a command line in the Command window or an Edit window to see help for that command.

If you want to see an explanation of a particular menu option in the Desktop, highlight the menu option (don't click it) and then press F1. Figure 3.27 shows the Help window that opens as a result of highlighting the C**o**mpiler option on the **O**ptions menu and then pressing F1.

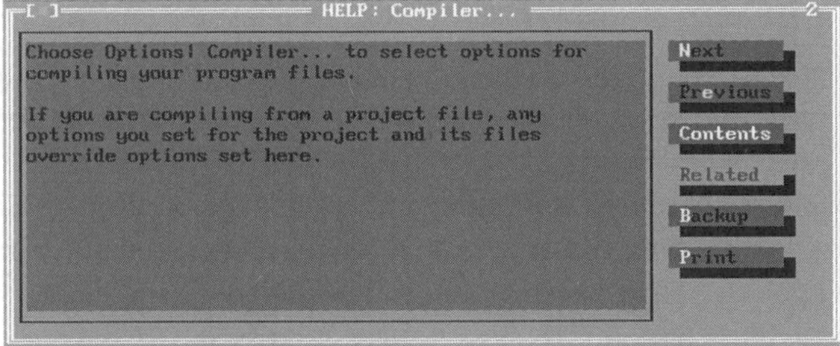

Fig. 3.27
Press F1 for help on a highlighted menu option.

Shelling to DOS

dBASE gives you more flexibility by providing access to DOS temporarily without quitting dBASE. To use this feature, open the **F**ile menu and choose **D**OS Shell. The Desktop clears and you are taken to the DOS prompt (see fig. 3.28). When you are ready to go back to dBASE, just type the word **exit** at the DOS prompt.

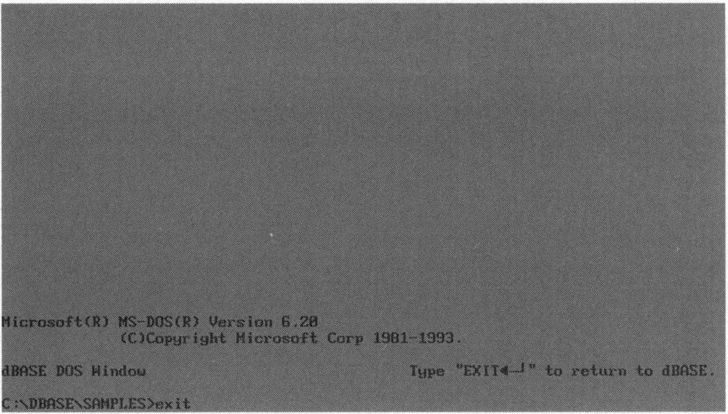
Microsoft(R) MS-DOS(R) Version 6.20
(C)Copyright Microsoft Corp 1981-1993.
dBASE DOS Window
Type "EXIT↵" to return to dBASE.
C:\DBASE\SAMPLES>exit

Fig. 3.28
dBASE lets you shell to DOS. The DOS window reminds you to type exit and press Enter to return to dBASE.

Caution

While you have shelled to DOS, be sure not to install any TSR programs or print files with the DOS print command. These actions can cause memory to be misallocated.

Tip
Open the **E**dit menu and choose **C**opy to copy the contents of a Help window to the Clipboard. You then can open the **E**dit menu and choose **P**aste to put the Clipboard contents in an Edit window.

You may prefer to use the DOS Utilities in the Control Center to execute many DOS commands from menu options.

▶ See "Using DOS Utilities," p. 84

From Here...

In this chapter, you received more in-depth information to help you get around in the new Developer's Desktop. You have become familiar with many of the menu options, dialog boxes, windows, and tools available to you in dBASE 5.

Look at chapters that will complement what you have just learned about working with files and the contents of windows:

- Chapter 4, "Understanding the Control Center," to learn how to use the panels in the Control Center to access many types of files, to create and use a catalog, and to use the DOS utilities.

- Chapter 16, "Getting Started with Programming," to learn about programming technique and the mechanics of entering and modifying your program with the Editor.

Chapter 4

Understanding the Control Center

The Control Center includes a number of components, each of which is intended to organize your database work and assist you in commanding dBASE 5. You learned in Chapter 3 to use the Developer's Desktop which gives you a new alternative for working with files. You also learned to work with the Command window, which replaces the dot prompt of earlier versions of dBASE. The Control Center, a carryover from dBASE IV, looks and acts much the same as before. While you are learning the Developer's Desktop, you still have a familiar way to access your files—the Control Center.

In this chapter, you learn the following about working in the Control Center:

- Using the categories
- Using catalogs
- Recording macros
- Importing and exporting data
- Using DOS utilities
- Performing operations on files
- Password protecting files
- Changing screen settings
- Exiting the Control Center

When you start dBASE 5, the Desktop appears, showing the Screen window and Command window. To access the Control Center, press F2, or open the **W**indow menu and choose Co**n**trol Center.

Using the Categories

The most prominent components of the Control Center are the *panels* that take up the majority of the center of the screen. The panels, sometimes called *categories*, are used to organize and list the different files that make up an application. The Control Center also includes a number of other features to provide information, instructions, and access to commands.

Figure 4.1 shows a list of files that display if you start dBASE 5 from the \DBASE\SAMPLES subdirectory (or changed to that directory within dBASE). Table 4.1 summarizes the role of each panel.

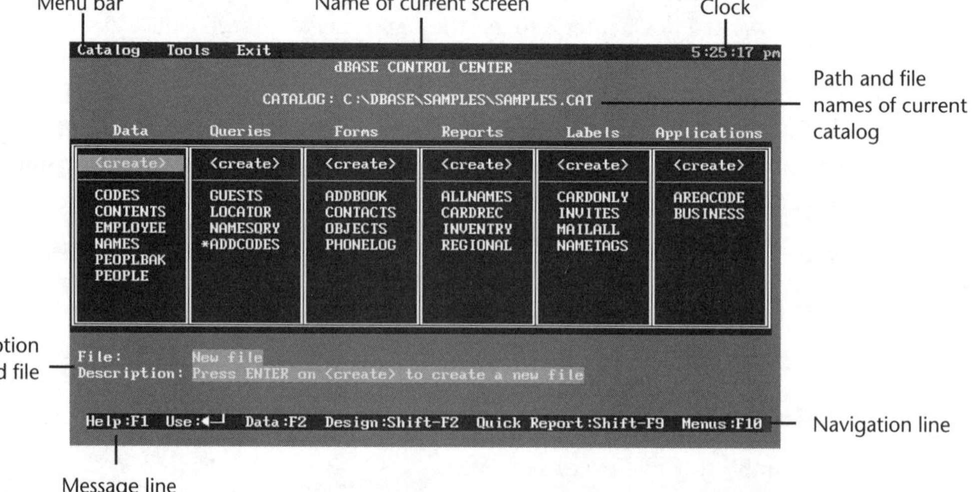

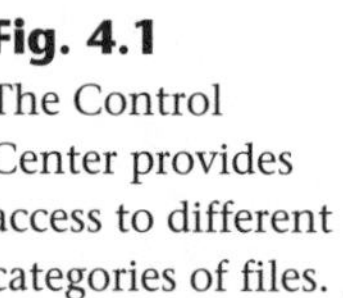

Fig. 4.1
The Control Center provides access to different categories of files.

Panel	Purpose
Data	Lists all the databases associated with the application. Files grouped here have the DBF extension.
Queries	Lists all queries built on one or more of the databases. Files include view queries with QBE extensions and update queries with UPD extensions. Update queries are marked with an asterisk (*) preceding the file name.

Table 4.1 The Role of the Panels in the Control Center

Panel	Purpose
Forms	Lists all the data-entry and editing forms built for a database or query. Source files have the SCR extension.
Reports	Lists all the reports issued for a database or query. Source files have the FRM extension.
Labels	Lists all the label files issued for a database or query. Source files have the LBL extension.
Applications	Lists all the application menu and program files that organize, manipulate, or use any other file. Source files have the APP extension or the PRG extension. Other types of files also are organized here.

Notice that each panel has a horizontal line directly under `<create>`. This line is a guide that shows which files currently are open and which are closed. To run or modify a previously created file, you have to open it first. Opening a file makes the file available to the computer's memory. When you open a file in the Control Center, it appears above the horizontal line in its panel. You can tell at a glance which files are open by looking at which files are above the line.

To select a file in a panel, place the *panel selector* (also called the *cursor*) on that file name and press Enter. You can move the panel selector by clicking with the mouse, by pressing arrow keys, or by pressing Tab or Shift-Tab.

Creating Files

The most common way of adding a file to the Control Center is to create it. You see that each panel includes a `<create>` button immediately below the panel name. Place the panel selector on `<create>` and press Enter (or click with the mouse) to signal that you want to create a file of that specific type.

◀ See "Creating a New File," p. 52

After you activate `<create>`, dBASE 5 displays a design screen specific to that panel. If you select `<create>` in the Data panel, the database design screen is displayed, ready for you to define fields for the new data file (see fig. 4.2). Specify the requirements for the file you are creating and save the file under a name you give it; that name appears on the panel list.

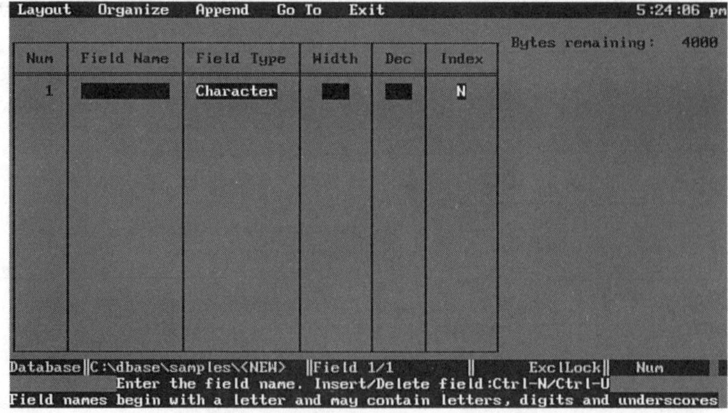

Fig. 4.2
Choosing the `<create>` button in the Data panel displays the database design screen.

> **Note**
>
> All files other than database files depend on or grow out of a database file. When you create any other type of file, you typically have a database file or a view query in use before you create the new file. You get a reminder message to open a database or view file if you try to create a file in the Reports or Labels panels.

Opening Files

◄ See "Opening an Existing File," p. 53

You open most files for the sake of viewing or displaying them, for the purpose of changing their design, or, in the case of certain types of files, for printing them. Two or more of these options are listed in the prompt box that opens when you highlight a file name and press Enter. The options you see depend on the type of file with which you are working. Assume, for example, that you want to open the People database file. Place the panel selector on `PEOPLE` in the Data panel, and press Enter. The prompt box shown in figure 4.3 appears.

> **Note**
>
> The navigation line at the bottom of the Control Center screen provides information about keys you can use while you are operating in the current screen. For example, the navigation line in figure 4.3 suggests:
>
> ```
> Select option and press ENTER, or press first letter of
> desired option.
> ```

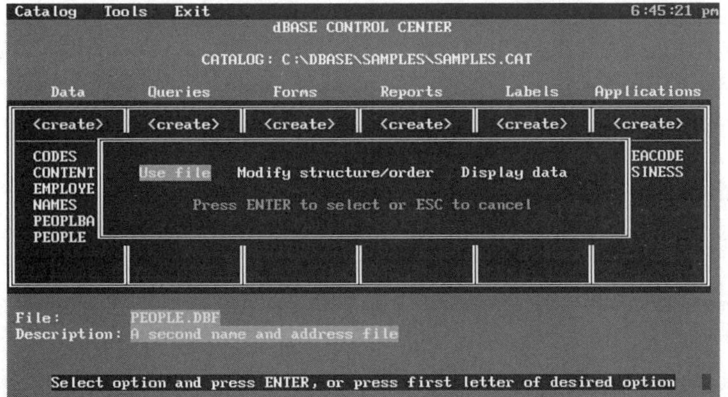

Fig. 4.3
The prompt box for the Data panel.

With the selector on the `Use File` option, press Enter again. By selecting Use File, you open the file and place its name above the panel line in the Data panel (see fig. 4.4).

Note

The prompt box appears only if the INSTRUCT setting is set to ON (the default setting). When INSTRUCT=ON, dBASE provides a good deal of on-screen assistance when you select commands and perform other operations. For help on changing this setting, see Chapter 24.

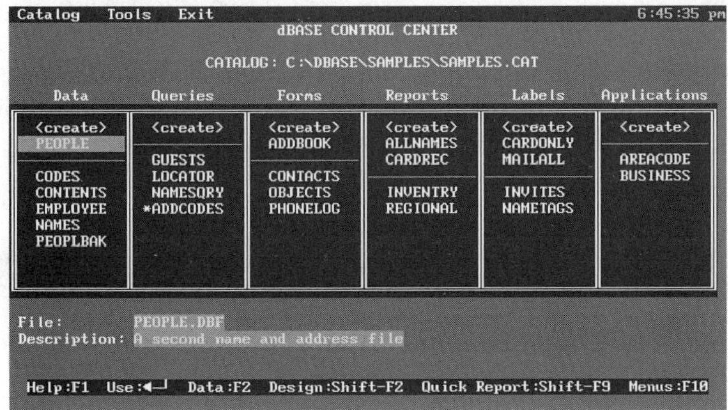

Fig. 4.4
The Use File option opened the PEOPLE database, which is shown above the line in the Data panel.

dBASE 5 "remembers" which files belong with which database. If you open a database file that has other files associated with it, for example, those files are brought above the horizontal lines in their respective panels. The PEOPLE database has associated forms, reports, and labels, as you can see in figure 4.4.

Modifying Files

In the prompt box shown in figure 4.3, the other options, `Modify Structure/Order` and `Display Data` also *open* the data file, but take you to different screens. The Modify Structure/Order option accesses dBASE 5's database design screen; the Display Data option accesses the Edit/Browse screen.

▶ See "Modifying a Database Structure," p. 121

▶ See "Using the Browse Screen," p. 145

These options are pertinent to the Data panel. You also can modify or display files in the other panels. For example, highlight the file `ADDBOOK` in the Forms panel and press Enter. In the prompt box that appears, choose `Modify Layout` (see fig. 4.5) and press Enter. The Forms Design screen appears, which enables you to modify the ADDBOOK form layout.

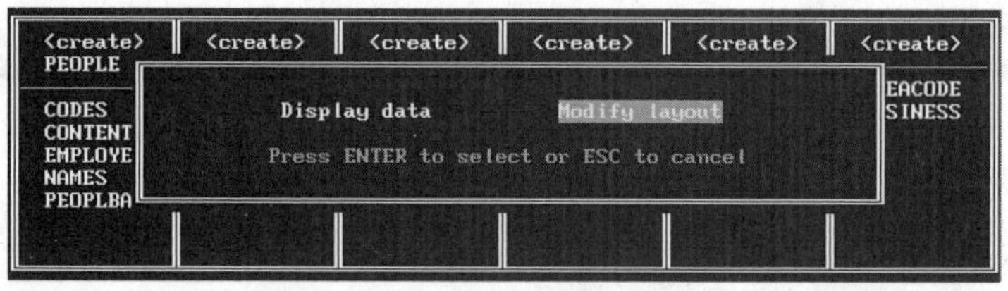

Fig. 4.5
The prompt box for the Forms panel presents the Modify Layout option.

Tip
If you are using a mouse, you can click the key labels on the navigation line rather than pressing those keys.

The navigation line at the bottom of the Control Center screen lists several options and corresponding function keys. The function keys offer shortcuts to accessing files for display, design, or printing purposes. Function keys act as shortcuts, or *hot keys,* for certain menu-based options that appear in prompt boxes. Table 4.2 lists the function keys and the prompt box functions they perform.

Table 4.2 Function-Key Equivalents of Prompt Box Options

Function Key	Prompt Box Option
F2 (Data)	Display Data (works for all panels except Applications)
Shift-F2 (Design)	Modify Structure/Order (Data panel) Modify Query (Queries panel) Modify Layout (Forms, Reports, and Labels panels) Modify Application (Applications panel)
Shift-F9 (Quick Report)	Print Columnar Report (works for all panels except Applications)

Using Catalogs

A *catalog* is a filing structure dBASE uses to keep track of your files. A catalog works like a DOS directory, but is able to cross directory boundaries when organizing the files of an application.

Although in a catalog you can put together files that have nothing in common with one another, you defeat the purpose of a catalog if you do. Files in a catalog belong together logically; the catalog implicitly recognizes the relationship between these files.

Creating Catalogs

If you are starting dBASE 5 fresh and are in a new data directory with no files in it, you must create a catalog to reflect the work you're going to store in this directory. dBASE 5 does not enable you to work in the Control Center without a catalog. So, if you have the proverbial blank slate, dBASE 5 initially assigns a blank catalog named UNTITLED. Every directory you use for the first time with dBASE 5 is set up with an UNTITLED catalog. Assume you are in a directory called PRACTICE, which you want to use for practicing the exercises in this book. If you start dBASE 5 from this directory, you see the screen shown in figure 4.6.

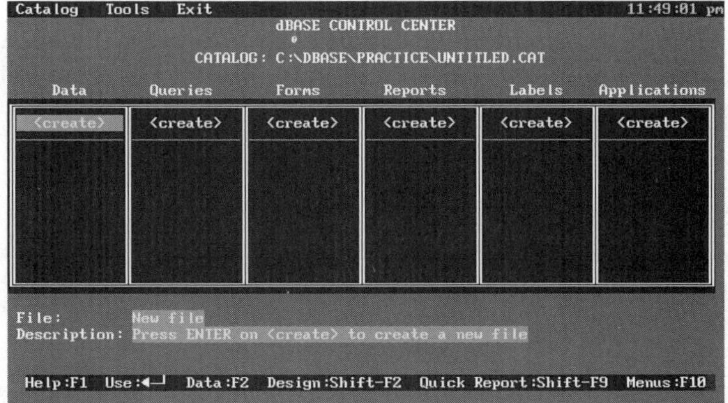

Fig. 4.6
Beginning work in a new directory with an UNTITLED catalog.

Tip
If you have an existing directory you want completely loaded into a catalog, erase all CAT files in that directory and start dBASE from there. The catalog will contain all pertinent files except for PRG and APP.

Unless you have some reason to keep the name UNTITLED, change the catalog name. Follow these steps to change the catalog name from UNTITLED to a name you specify:

1. Press Alt-C to access the Catalog menu (or click the Catalog menu).

2. Press M to select `Modify Catalog Name`. The current catalog is listed after the directory path.

3. Press Backspace to delete the name UNTITLED.CAT, type the new name (in this case PRACTICE, as shown in fig. 4.7), and press Enter. The CAT extension is added automatically.

Catalog names must follow the DOS file-naming rules described later in this chapter. The catalog itself is a file that stores the names and vital statistics of all the member files.

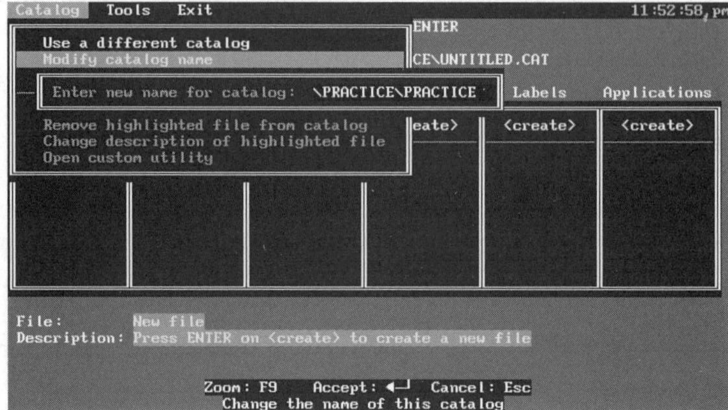

Fig. 4.7 Changing the name of the UNTITLED catalog to PRACTICE.

You may encounter situations in which you want to set up more than one catalog in the same directory (to subdivide a logical set of files into two sub-applications, for example). To create a second catalog for a directory, follow these steps:

1. Open the Catalog menu.
2. Select Use a Different Catalog. A pick list of existing catalogs for this directory appears (see fig. 4.8). Notice that a `<create>` option is in the pick list so you can set up a new catalog.
3. Select `<create>` and press Enter.
4. On the fill-in line, type the name of the new catalog, and then press Enter. dBASE 5 creates the new catalog and changes to that new catalog.

If you have multiple catalogs in a directory, dBASE 5 keeps track of the one you used last and restores that one to the screen the next time you work in that directory. Anytime you change to a new directory, however, dBASE 5 also changes the catalog.

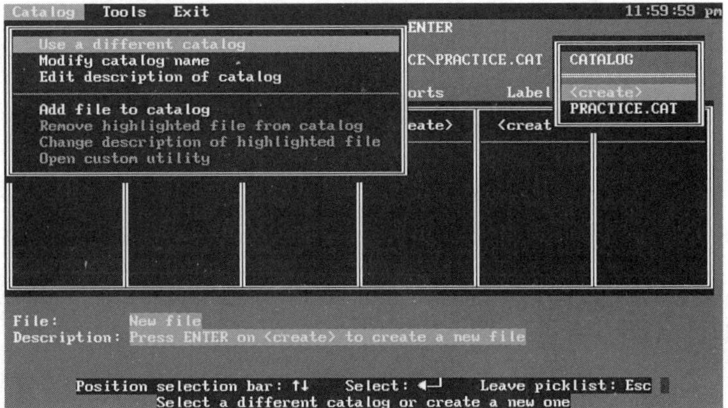

Fig. 4.8
Creating a new catalog in the current directory.

Note

The information about the catalog you last used in a directory is stored in a file called CATALOG.CAT. This file also stores a master list of all the catalogs in the directory. Do not remove this file from your directory.

Changing the Catalog

Assuming you have a number of catalogs on your disk directory, you need to know how to manipulate them. Choosing a catalog is the first step in manipulating catalogs.

When you open Control Center, an active catalog is displayed. If you haven't created one for the current directory, dBASE 5 displays the UNTITLED catalog. If you have created one or more catalogs, dBASE starts with the last catalog you worked with in the preceding work session. You can change to another catalog in the same directory by using the Catalog menu and selecting the Use A Different Catalog option. A pick list with all available catalogs appears (see fig. 4.9). As you move the selector among the catalogs, you can see a description window above the file identification line. Select the catalog you want.

After you select a catalog, that catalog stays in effect until you choose another one. You can activate a catalog from the Command window by issuing the SET CATALOG TO *<name>* command.

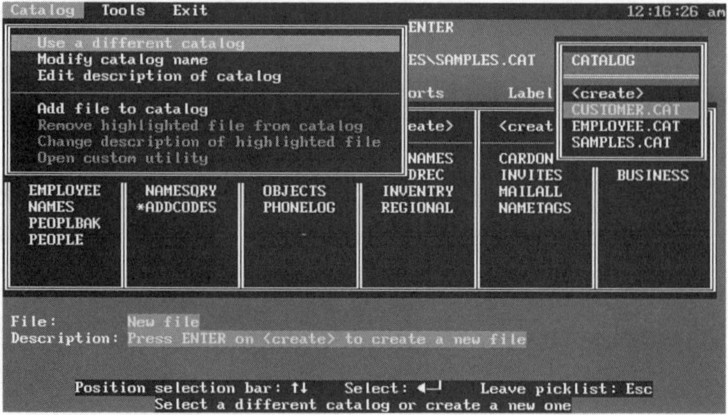

Fig. 4.9
Changing to a different catalog.

Editing the Description

A description can be useful if you use many catalogs (the description appears on-screen, as shown in fig. 4.9, to remind you of the contents of the catalog), but serves no other purpose. From the Catalog menu, choose Edit Description of Catalog to display a window with the current description, if any, of the current catalog (see fig. 4.10). Use the Backspace key to erase the old description, and then type a new description. Press Enter to complete the process.

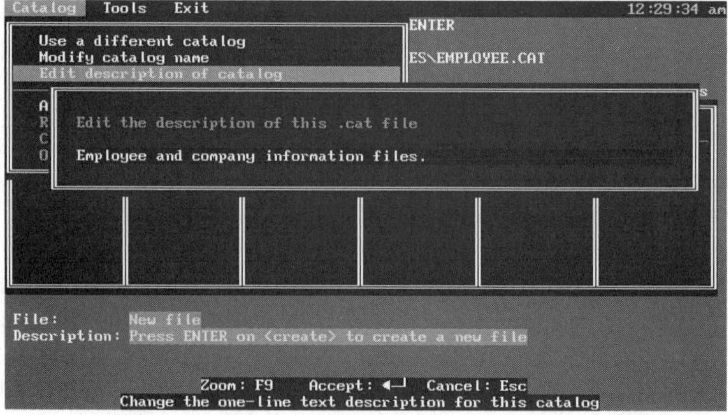

Fig. 4.10
Use Edit Description of Catalog to create a new or more meaningful description.

Adding a File to a Catalog

You may think that putting related files together in the same directory is enough to indicate a relationship. But, remember that a single database can logically serve two or more different applications. You need to set up two catalogs to reflect each of the directories in which the applications reside.

To add a file from another directory to the current catalog, follow these steps:

1. In the Control Center, place the panel selector in the Data panel if you want to add a database file (place the panel selector in another panel if you want to add a file of another type).

2. Press F10 to access the Catalog menu.

3. Select the Add File to Catalog option. A pick list appears, showing files of the type appropriate for the panel you have selected.

4. If the file you want is in another directory, select the `<parent>` option (see fig. 4.11). A list of files in the next higher directory on the tree appears. Child directories of this directory are listed in angle brackets.

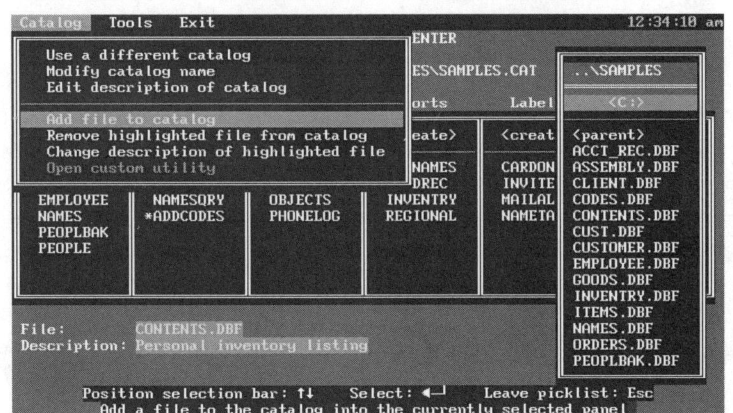

Fig. 4.11
Use the `<parent>` option to change the pick list.

5. If the file you want is in one of the child directories, select it and press Enter. If the file you want is in the PAYROLL directory, for example, select `<PAYROLL>` from the pick list.

   A list of all the database files in that directory appears.

6. Select the database you want to add. That database is added to the Data panel. To add the Client file, for example, select that file from the pick list.

7. If the file you want is on another drive, select the drive identifier (usually `<C:>`) and select the drive you want from the pick list that appears. Continue from step 4.

Note

Do not add files from a floppy disk to a catalog. If you need to add a file from a floppy, be sure to copy that file on your hard disk drive. If you don't, dBASE looks for that file on the floppy disk drive every time you want to use that catalog.

Removing a File from a Catalog

Any file you create with the Control Center is added to the current catalog. If you no longer need a file, you can remove it from the catalog, and optionally remove it from the disk, by using the Remove Highlighted File From Catalog option. You also can press Delete as a shortcut around the menu. This option works only for the current file—the one highlighted by the panel selector. If the selector is located on a `<create>` option, you cannot access this option. You cannot remove a file if it is open (above the horizontal line).

After you activate the Remove Highlighted File From Catalog option, you are asked to verify the decision. If you respond Yes, the file is removed from the catalog and you are asked whether you want to remove the file from disk. If you respond Yes, the file is completely deleted and dBASE keeps no memory of it.

Recording Macros

► See "Using Keyboard Macros," p. 511

Macros record many keystrokes into one easy-to-use keystroke. Whenever you have to perform a task over and over again, you can create a macro for those keystrokes. Then when you want to perform the task, you can "play" the macro and have it carry out the steps automatically.

You record macros from the Control Center. To record a macro, follow these steps:

1. Press Shift-F10 (Macros), and then select Begin Recording.
2. Assign the macro to a function key (F1 through F9) or to a letter key on your keyboard by pressing the key. Assigning a macro to a key gives the macro a name. Use this name to call the macro. If you assign the macro to the F9 key, for example, you can call it by pressing Alt-F9.

3. Perform all the steps you want the macro to do. dBASE 5 records these steps to the macro as you perform them.

4. Press Shift-F10, and then select End Recording.

To play back a recorded macro, press Alt-*function key*, where *function key* is the one you assigned to the macro in step 2 of the preceding instructions. If you assigned the macro to a letter, press Alt-F10; at the prompt type the letter of the macro you want to call.

Using Shift-F10 and Alt-F10 to record and play back macros is the simplest way to use macros. You also can control macro creation and playback by using the Control Center Tools menu and selecting the Macros option. From the Control Center, access the Tools menu, and then select the Macros option. This menu is shown in figure 4.12.

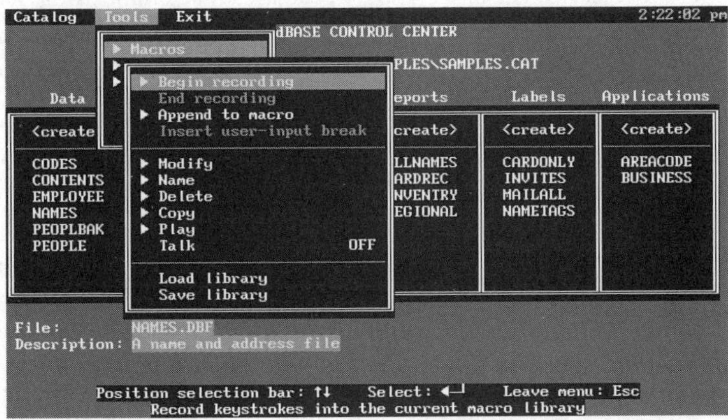

Fig. 4.12
Access the Macros submenu from the Tools menu in the Control Center.

The Macros submenu contains options that enable you to begin recording and to play back the macro. These options work the same way as Shift-F10 and Alt-F10, described in the preceding steps, but they ask you to provide the name for the macro by selecting it from a macro display table (see fig. 4.13). When you first install dBASE, the table is empty. When you select Begin Recording and then press a function key or a letter to name a macro, that position on the macro table is occupied, and you begin recording immediately. As you record a macro, the message line on all screens reads `Recording Macro: Press Shift-F10 E to end.`

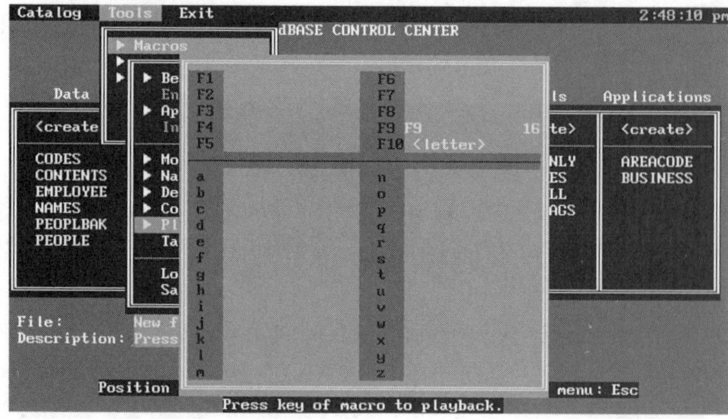

Fig. 4.13
The macro display table lists macros you have assigned to their corresponding keys.

Tip
If the macro is still running too fast, you can slow it down by pressing < (the less-than sign) one or more times while the macro is running. You also can press the > (greater-than sign) to speed up the playback.

dBASE 5 plays back the macro faster than you can follow with your eyes. If you want to slow down the process so you can see what's happening, select the Talk option from the Macros submenu so the setting is ON rather than OFF. When you play back the macro with the Talk setting ON, dBASE 5 reports each macro command on-screen.

The macros you create stay around only for the length of your current work session. If you want to use the macro in subsequent work sessions, you must save it. You use the Save Library option from the Macros submenu for this purpose. When you activate this option, dBASE 5 requests the name of the library in which you want to store the macros (see fig. 4.14). Fill in a regular file name (for example, GENERAL) and press Enter. dBASE 5 saves the macro library under the name you give it and assigns it the extension KEY.

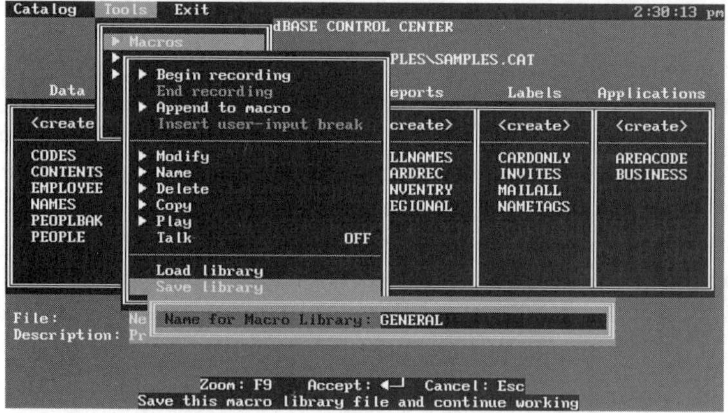

Fig. 4.14
Use the Save Library option to give a name to a macro library.

When you want to use the library in a later work session, activate the Load Library option from the Macros submenu. dBASE 5 displays a pick list of all available libraries in the current directory. Select the library you want and press Enter to bring it to the macro display table. If the library is on another directory or disk, the pick list gives you the option of changing directories.

Tip
When you press a key for the macro you want to use while you are viewing the macro display table, dBASE 5 begins to play back the macro immediately.

Using the Name option on the Macros submenu, you can place a short description of the macro on the macro display table in place of the single letter or function key. If you record the database-backup procedure to a macro with the F9 key, for example, select Name from the Macros submenu, specify the letter of the macro you want to name, and type a more descriptive macro name. The name must be 10 characters or less and cannot contain a space. The next time you use the macro display table, you see the name you assigned, rather than just a letter (see fig. 4.15).

To the right of the macro name in the macro display table you will see a number. This number represents the total number of keystrokes in the macro.

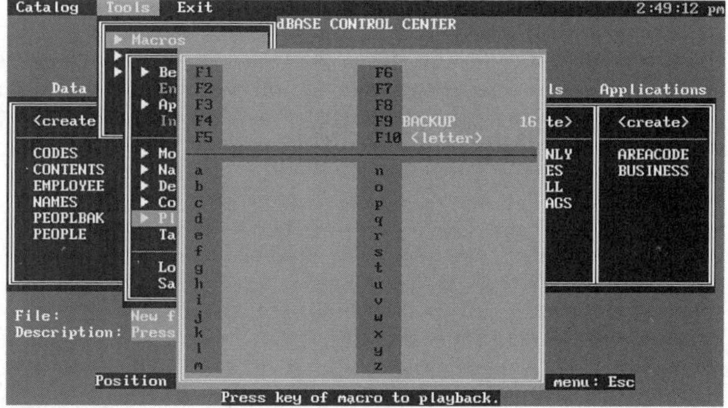

Fig. 4.15
A name has been assigned to the F9 macro.

Other options on the Macros submenu enable you to edit a macro without recording it again. One way to do this is to add or append commands to the end of a current macro. Use the Append to Macro option for this purpose. Select the macro you want to modify, and then carry out the necessary commands. As you perform the commands, they are recorded in the usual way.

Tip
To restore macros that were saved to a macro library, run a program on startup that has the command RESTORE MACROS FROM `<macro file>`.

A more flexible approach to changing a macro is to use the Modify option. This option displays an edit screen in which the individual commands and cursor controls you recorded are listed (see fig. 4.16). You can change any of these commands, add to them, delete them, and more. After you make your changes, press F10 (Menu) to display the Exit menu for the edit screen, save the changes, and return to the Control Center.

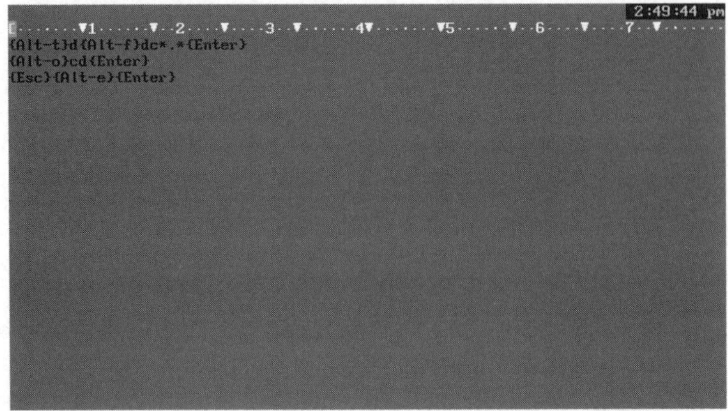

Fig. 4.16
Use the Modify option on the Macros submenu to edit a macro.

Notice that commands and cursor controls in the edit screen are specified by enclosing their names in curly braces {}. The names of the keys are the same as the names on the key caps, with the exception of the arrow keys. To indicate an arrow key, use the following names:

{rightarrow}

{leftarrow}

{uparrow}

{downarrow}

In addition, if you use a booster key such as Shift, Alt, or Ctrl, separate the booster key from the activated key by a hyphen; for example {Ctrl-End}, {Alt-T}, and so on. Letters and words you type to activate menu options and fill-in boxes are not enclosed in braces. They are typed directly.

Importing Data

The Import submenu enables you to import data into dBASE 5 from the following file types: PFS:FILE forms, dBASE II database files, Framework II, Framework III, and Framework IV database and spreadsheet frames, RapidFile data files, and Lotus 1-2-3 spreadsheets, Release 1A or Release 2.

Note

You also can translate an ASCII text file into a dBASE database file, but not from the Control Center. First, create a database with the same fields as the ASCII file. In the database design screen, choose the Append menu, then select Copy Records From Non-dBASE File. Use one of the .txt file options.

▶ See "APPEND FROM," p. 655

To import data using the Control Center, follow these steps:

1. From the Desktop, press F2 to access the Control Center.
2. Open the Tools menu and select Import. The Import submenu displays the following five choices:
   - RapidFile
   - dBASE II
   - Framework (Versions II, III, and IV)
   - Lotus 1-2-3 (Release 1A and Release 2)
   - PFS:FILE

▶ See "IMPORT FROM," p. 702

3. Choose the file type you want to import. Make a more specific choice if another submenu appears.
4. Locate the file in the directory pick list; highlight the file name and press Enter.
5. Enter a description for the new DBF file in the input box. Press Enter.

   dBASE 5 imports the file, giving it the same name, but with a DBF extension. The file is opened (see the Data panel) in the current catalog.

Tip

To import a file from a program that is not on the Import submenu, see if that program can export data to a dBASE DBF file. If so, create the export file, and then open the file in dBASE as you would other dBASE files.

Exporting Data

The Export submenu enables you to translate dBASE 5 data to formats used by several programs. To export data using the Control Center, follow these steps:

1. From the Desktop, press F2 to access the Control Center.
2. Open the Tools menu and select Export. The Export submenu displays the following choices:

- RapidFile
- dBASE II
- Framework (Versions II, III, and IV)
- Lotus 1-2-3 (Release 1A and Release 2)
- VisiCalc
- PFS:FILE
- SYLK - Multiplan
- Text fixed length fields
- Blank delimited
- Character delimited {"}

3. Choose the file type to which you want to export. Make a more specific choice if another submenu appears.

▶ See "Exporting Data from SQL," p. 588

▶ See "EXPORT TO," p. 698

4. Locate the database file in the directory pick list. This is the file that you want to export to another file type. Highlight the file name and press Enter. dBASE 5 translates the file. The new file has the same name, except that the extension is the type you chose.

Note

If the program to which you want to export the dBASE file is not on the Export submenu, check whether your program can import a dBASE DBF file. Another alternative is to export using one of the last three (text) options, and then import the text file in your other program. The following describes the text choices:

Text fixed length files export to a text SDF file. Blank delimited exports to text files where blank spaces are used to separate records. Character delimited text places a special delimiter, such as double quotes, around character fields.

Using DOS Utilities

dBASE 5 gives you easy access to DOS commands and utilities. The menu options discussed in this section include the options you use to manage your disks and files in ways the Control Center panels and options cannot handle. A few of the options *can* be handled by the new Developer's Desktop, as you learned in Chapter 3. Common situations in which you use the options in the DOS Utilities screen are as follows:

- Changing data directories after you start dBASE 5
- Copying files from one disk to another, especially for backup purposes
- Deleting files that are not part of a catalog

◀ See "Working with Files," p. 52

These management options are included on the DOS Utilities submenu. You access this submenu from the Control Center Tools menu, and then press D to select the DOS Utilities option. The DOS Utilities screen with its work surface and menu appears (see fig. 4.17).

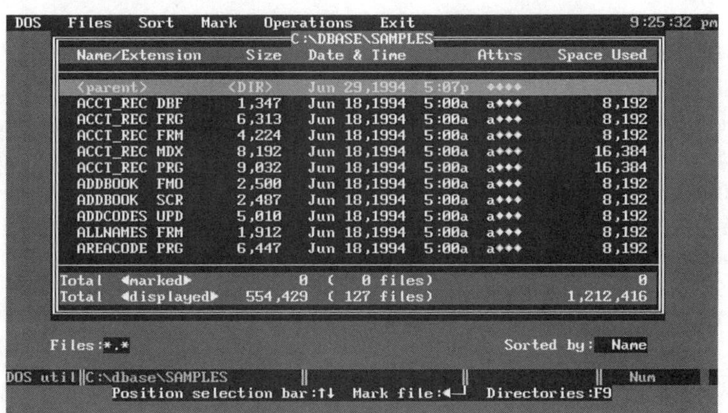

Fig. 4.17
The DOS Utilities screen is one way dBASE helps you manage your files.

The DOS Utilities screen has as its work surface a list of files from the current drive and directory, which is identified in the top center of the work surface. The file list includes, from left to right, the following information on each file:

- The name of each file
- The file extension
- The size of the file
- The date and time the file was last modified
- A list of the file's attributes
- The amount of disk space required for the file

The bottom of the file list reports the total sizes for all files listed and all files marked. Marking files is discussed in the section, "Changing the List of Files Displayed," later in this chapter.

Below the totals' lines, the work surface reports the status of two indicators: `Files` and `Sorted by`. The `Files` indicator specifies which files in the directory are listed—the naming pattern used to list the files. The default naming pattern is *.*, indicating that files with any first name (the first *) and any extension (the second *) are included in the list.

The `Sorted by` indicator specifies the order in which the files appear in the list. The default value is Name, meaning that the files are sorted alphanumerically by letters and numbers in the first name.

Changing the Drive or Directory

The file list in the DOS Utilities screen is controlled through the menu bar and certain function-key shortcuts. From the information in the preceding section, you may have surmised that you can change the file list by changing the directory, the pattern in the `Files` indicator, and the `Sorted by` order. In fact, all are possible; singly or together, these three options control the list and overall arrangement of the files you see.

The most important of the options that affect the file list is the one that changes the directory, because this option determines the list of available files. Earlier in this chapter, you learned that changing the directory is an important step in changing catalogs. dBASE 5 derives its list of available catalogs from the list of files with the CAT extension found in a particular directory. If the catalog you want is in a disk directory different from the current one, you have to change to a new directory before changing the catalog.

You change directories for one of two reasons: to change the default for purposes of establishing a new catalog, and to view another directory for the sake of information. Each of these purposes is served by a different menu on the menu bar.

To change the default directory and, by implication, the catalog, use the DOS menu and the Set Default Drive:Directory option (see fig. 4.18). To view the list of files in the directory to which you changed, use the Files menu and the Change Drive:Directory option (see fig. 4.19).

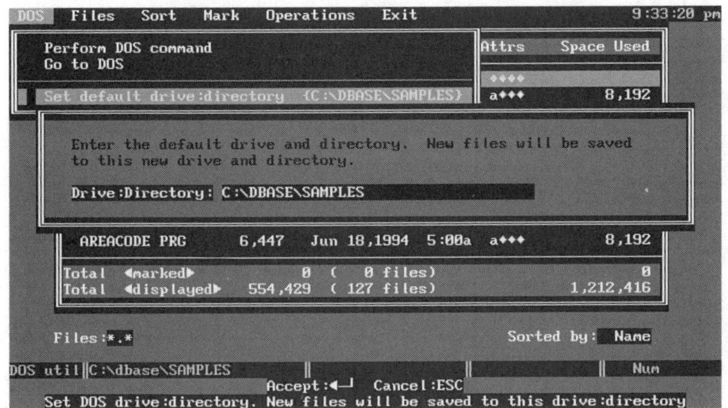

Fig. 4.18
Setting the default drive and directory in the DOS Utilities screen.

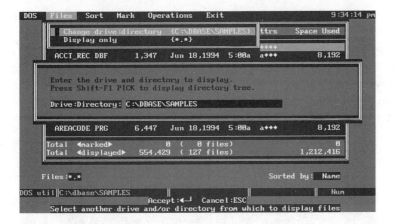

Fig. 4.19
Viewing a different drive and directory.

When you activate either of these options, dBASE 5 presents an input box into which you type the path of the new drive or directory. You can take advantage of several shortcuts in this process. You can generate a pick list consisting of all the directories on a particular drive, arranged in tree fashion. With the tree on-screen, "climb" through it with the selector, highlight the directory you want, and press Enter to select it. Using the mouse, you also can double-click the directory you want.

To generate a pick list, activate the Set Default Drive:Directory option. Instead of typing the new directory in the input box, press Shift-F1 (Pick). dBASE 5 generates a directory tree (see fig. 4.20). If you want to change to the SAMPLES directory, for example, move the selector bar to that branch of the tree and press Enter, or double-click the mouse, to complete the change and return to the DOS Utilities work surface.

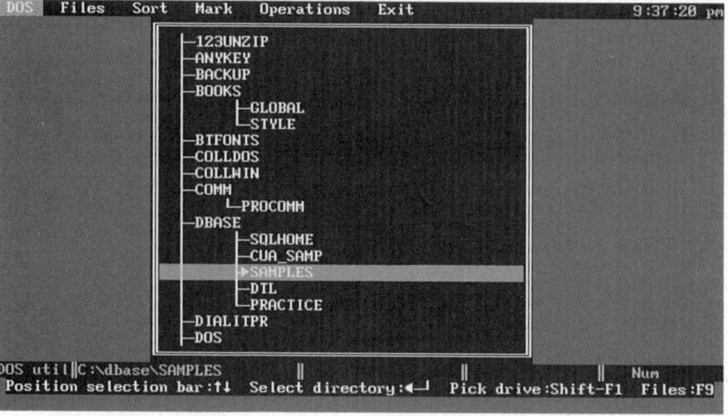

Fig. 4.20
Using the directory-tree pick list to change directories.

Another way to change the directory of the file list is to select the name of a directory in the list. If you are in the DBASE directory and you want to change to the PRACTICE directory, for example, select PRACTICE in the files list (see fig. 4.21). If you want to move backward along the tree, select the `<parent>` directory item in the list. This action takes you back one level in the tree. If the directory you want to move to is not directly adjacent to the current directory, repeat these steps until you find the correct directory.

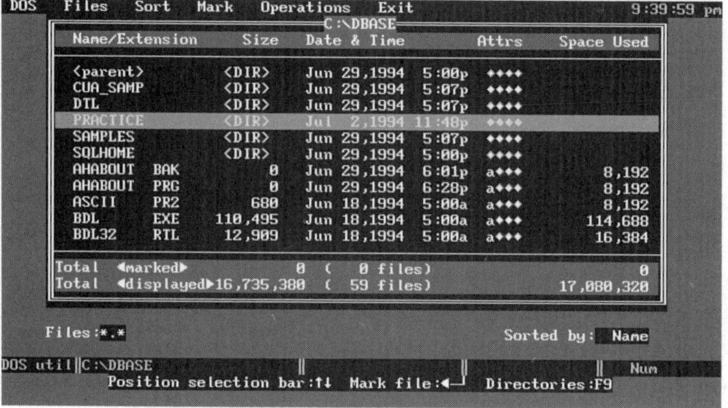

Fig. 4.21
Changing a directory through the file list.

Tip
Instead of activating the menu bar, press F9 (Zoom) from the DOS Utilities screen or click the `Directories:F9` label.

Changing the List of Files Displayed

Changing the directory causes a different list of files to appear on the work surface, but the list still includes all the files in the directory. You may need only a portion of the complete list of files to address a particular question. You can, for example, inspect a list of "foreign" files, say Lotus 1-2-3 Release 2.4 worksheets, with the idea of importing the data into a dBASE 5 file. Because Lotus 1-2-3 Release 2.4 files end with the extension WK1, you can save yourself some search time if you organize all the WK1 files together in the list or restrict the list to just WK1 files.

You can address this problem in two ways: sort the list by extension and move the selector to the items in which you are interested, or extract the WK1 files from the list by filtering out other types of files. Use the Sort menu for the first approach; use the Operations menu for the second.

Sorting the List of Files

Using the Sort menu, you can arrange the list of files according to one of the following file characteristics:

- Name
- Extension
- Date & Time
- Size

By default, the file list you see on-screen is sorted by file name (see fig. 4.22). Use the other sorting options to locate files by some feature you remember about the files. If you forgot the name of a file but remember that you created it last October, for example, you can arrange the list by Date & Time and focus easily on those files that meet your search criterion. To sort files by extension (for example, to locate all the WK1 files), select Extension.

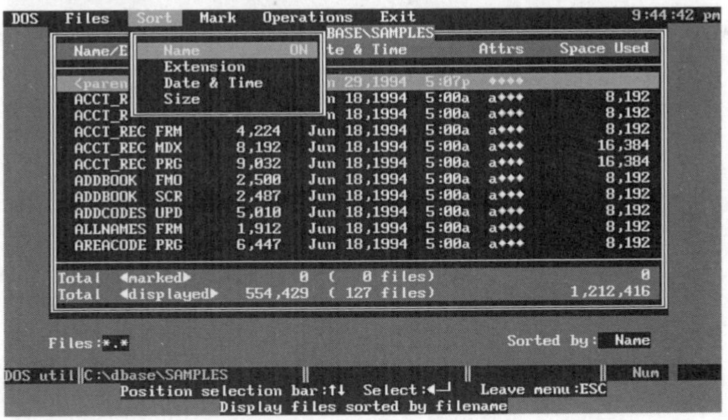

Fig. 4.22
Using the Sort menu provides a quick method of locating your files.

To change the sort order, activate the Sort menu and select the sort option you want. The list of files is reordered immediately.

Marking and Unmarking Files

The DOS Utilities Operations menu lists the filing operations you can perform on single or multiple files in the file list. This menu includes the most common types of filing activities, including deleting files, renaming files, and copying and moving files to other disks or directories.

To carry out a filing operation, start by marking the files on which you want to operate. Do this by moving the cursor to the file you want and pressing Enter. An arrow appears in front of the file to mark it.

If the files you want to mark have a common element in their file names, you can mark them more quickly by using the Files menu to limit the display to only the target files, and then using the Mark menu to mark all the files in the display in a single step.

Suppose you want to mark all the files with the extension WK1. Access the Files menu, and then select Display Only. A fill-in box appears, asking you to indicate the pattern for the files you want (see fig. 4.23). To list only the WK1 files, type ***.WK1**. The leading asterisk indicates that you do not care what the name of the file is, you only care that the file has the WK1 extension. Table 4.3 shows some other patterns you can specify by using the asterisk wild card. The table also includes examples of patterns built by using the question mark (?) wild card. Use the question mark in place of a single character position in the file name or extension.

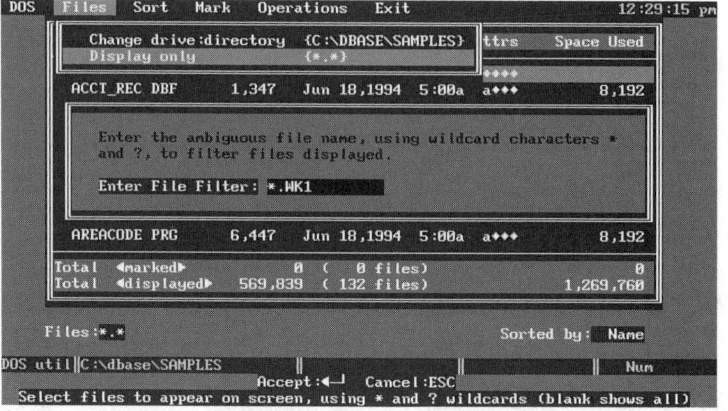

Fig. 4.23
Limiting the file display with the Display Only option.

Table 4.3 Using Wild Cards To Limit File Displays

Pattern	Example of Files Selected
.	All files
*.SCR	All files with the SCR extension
ACCTS.*	All files with the name ACCTS, regardless of extension
ACCT?.DBF	All files with ACCT as the first four positions of the name and any other character (or no character) in the fifth position, and the extension DBF; for example, ACCT.DBF, ACCT2.DBF, and ACCT8.DBF
ACCTS.D??	All files with the name ACCTS, and an extension beginning with the letter D; for example, ACCTS.DBF, ACCTS.DBO, and ACCTS.DOC

Performing Operations on Files

After you mark files (see the previous section), you can perform any of the following file operations:

- Deleting
- Copying
- Moving
- Renaming
- Viewing
- Editing

Tip
To unmark a file, move the selector to individual file and press Enter to remove the arrow. Or, use the Mark menu to Unmark all.

These operations are performed from the Operations menu. From the Control Center, open the Tools menu and choose DOS Utilities to display the DOS Utilities screen.

Before asking for the details of the operation you select, dBASE 5 asks you to specify on which of the following groups you want to operate:

- A single file (the one highlighted by the selector)
- All the marked files
- All the displayed files

After indicating which files you want, the next step is to state the details of the operation you selected from the Operations menu.

Deleting Files

Follow these steps to delete a file from the disk:

1. In the DOS Utilities screen, mark the files(s) you want to delete.
2. Open the Operations menu and choose Delete.
3. Choose whether to delete the single file, marked files, or displayed files. A prompt box appears (see fig. 4.24).

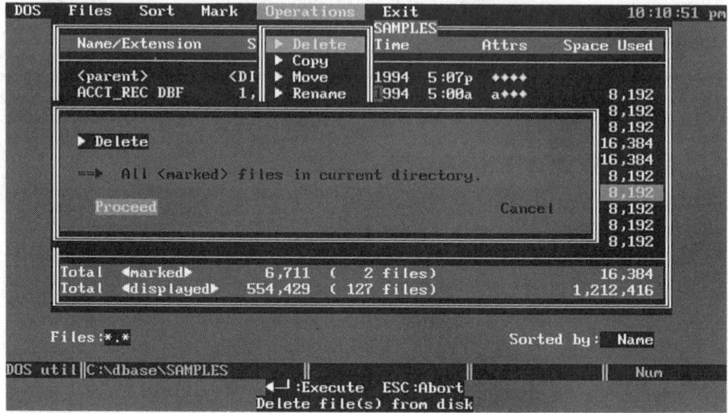

Fig. 4.24
Make sure you have marked the file you want to delete before proceeding.

4. Choose Proceed to delete the file(s), or Cancel (Esc) to avoid the deletion.

Tip
You also can delete a file by opening the Catalog menu and choosing the Remove Highlighted File From Catalog option in the Control Center.

Copying Files

Follow these steps to copy a file to another directory or file name, while keeping the original file:

1. In the DOS Utilities screen, mark the files(s) you want to copy.
2. Open the Operations menu and choose Copy.
3. Choose whether to copy the single file, marked files, or displayed files. A fill-in box appears (see fig. 4.25).
4. Specify a destination drive and directory, and then specify a different file name or file-name pattern. Press Enter after typing each entry.

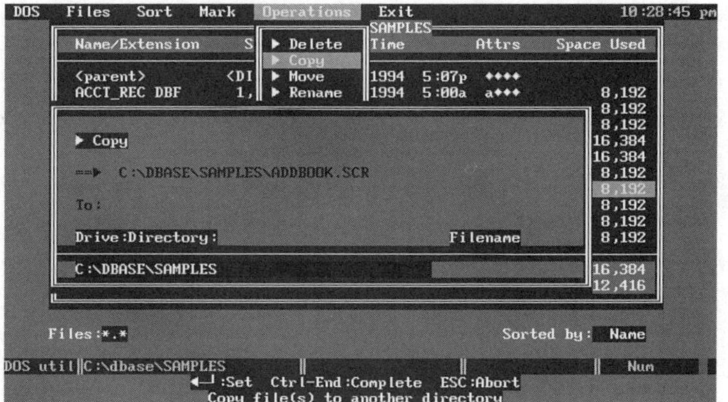

Fig. 4.25
After choosing a file to copy, specify the destination directory and file name.

Note

A file name pattern can include wild cards, as illustrated in table 4.3. For example, you can copy all the marked files to another directory and at the same time give the files a new extension. You can mark old program files, then copy (or move) them to another directory, specifying the file name *.OLD. Each file is copied to the directory, keeping the same file name, except the PRG extension changes to OLD.

5. Press Ctrl-End. The file(s) are copied, and the original file(s) remain in the current directory.

Moving Files

Follow these steps to move a file to another location and delete it from the original location:

1. In the DOS Utilities screen, mark the files(s) you want to move.
2. Open the Operations menu and choose Move.
3. Choose whether to move the single file, marked files, or displayed files. A fill-in box appears.
4. Specify a destination drive and directory.
5. Press Ctrl-End. The file(s) are moved, and the original file(s) are deleted from the current directory.

> **Note**
>
> Make sure you actually have a file marked before you choose to perform an operation on marked files. If you do not, you receive an error message from dBASE reminding you to mark a file.

Renaming Files

You also can rename a file from the DOS Utilities menu, without having to exit to DOS. Follow these steps to rename a file:

1. In the DOS Utilities screen, mark the files(s) you want to rename.
2. Open the Operations menu and choose Rename.
3. Choose whether to rename the single file, marked files, or displayed files. A fill-in box appears (see fig. 4.26).

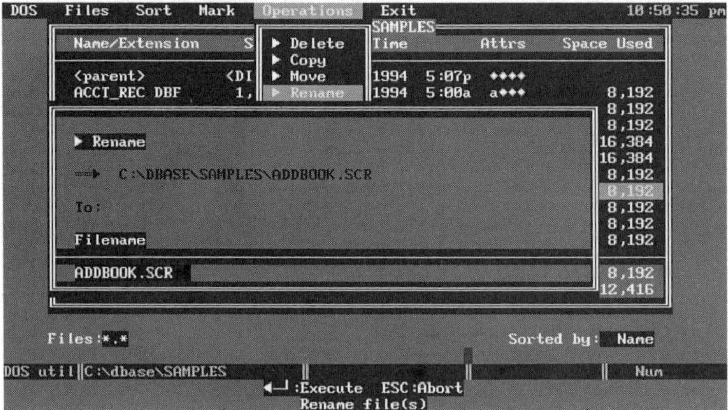

Fig. 4.26
Enter the new name of the file you want to rename.

4. Specify the new file name or file-name pattern.
5. Press Enter to rename the file(s).

Viewing Files

You can view a file's contents before performing any other operation on it. You can use the View option to look at your macro files, program files, or other text files. Follow these steps to view a file:

1. In the DOS Utilities screen, move the selector bar to the file you want to view.

2. Open the Operations menu and choose View. The file is displayed in a view screen (see fig. 4.27).

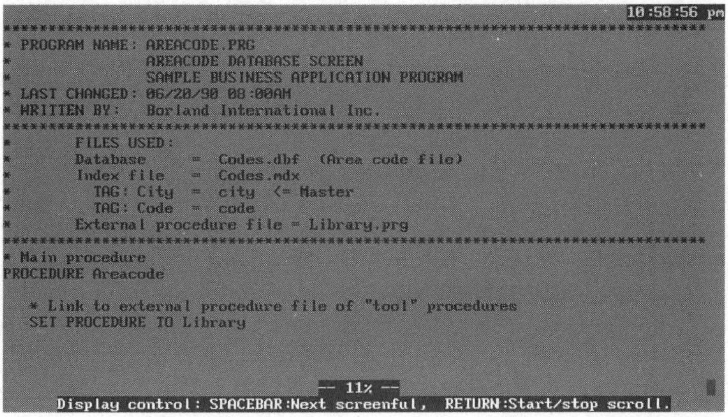

```
                                                                    10:58:56 pm
*****************************************************************************
* PROGRAM NAME: AREACODE.PRG
*               AREACODE DATABASE SCREEN
*               SAMPLE BUSINESS APPLICATION PROGRAM
* LAST CHANGED: 06/20/90 08:00AM
* WRITTEN BY:   Borland International Inc.
*****************************************************************************
*        FILES USED:
*        Database      =  Codes.dbf  (Area code file)
*        Index file    =  Codes.mdx
*          TAG: City   =  city  <= Master
*          TAG: Code   =  code
*        External procedure file = Library.prg
*****************************************************************************
* Main procedure
PROCEDURE Areacode

   * Link to external procedure file of "tool" procedures
   SET PROCEDURE TO Library

                                   -- 11% --
      Display control: SPACEBAR:Next screenful,  RETURN:Start/stop scroll.
```

Fig. 4.27
Using the View option enables you to view the contents of a file.

3. Use the space bar to scroll a screen at a time. Press Esc to exit the view.

Note

If you view a non-text file, the text appears garbled. You may be able to tell whether a file is a text file or a non-text file by examining the file's extension. You can better appreciate the distinctions between file extensions after reading the chapters about programming in Part IV of this book.

Editing Files

You can edit a file you have selected in DOS Utilities, if the file is a text file. Follow these steps to edit a file:

1. In the DOS Utilities screen, move the selector bar to the file you want to edit.

2. Open the Operations menu and choose Edit. The file is opened in the Program editor (see fig. 4.28).

3. Edit as needed. Exit by choosing Exit, and then Save or Abandon.

Caution

Do not try to edit EXE or COM or $$$ files. That can make these and other programs, including dBASE, inoperable.

► See "Using the Program Editor To Enter Code," p. 403

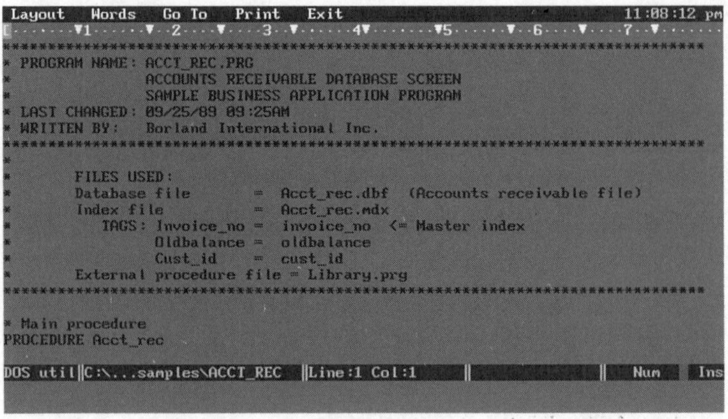

Fig. 4.28
Access the Program editor by choosing Edit in the Operations menu.

Password Protecting Files

▶ See "PROTECT," p. 725

You can restrict access of certain files or fields to those who need the access, preventing unauthorized use. dBASE 5 enables you to create and maintain security for files and fields. After security is established, users must have passwords to start dBASE, and will have access to files and fields only as permitted in the Protect utility. Programmers can use the ACCESS() function in program logic to return the access level of the current user, to restrict access to parts of an application.

To establish security, you must first assign an administrative password. Follow these steps:

1. In the Control Center, open the Tools menu and choose Protect Data. The prompt box informs you that the protect utility permanently assigns passwords to dBASE and your data.

2. Select Proceed. The password screen is displayed as shown in figure 4.29.

3. Type a password in the input box, up to 16 alphanumeric characters. The characters do not show as you type them. Press Enter.

4. Type the password again, to confirm. Press Enter. The Protect screen appears.

The administrative password has now been set. The Protect Data option can only be accessed using this password. You are prompted to use it each time you use the Protect Data option (or the PROTECT command).

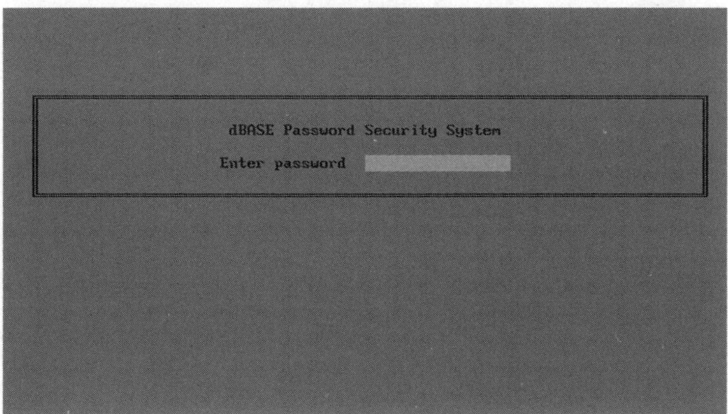

Fig. 4.29
Setting the administrative password to control dBASE security.

Caution

If you forget the password, you cannot retrieve it from the system. Any files protected by the password are unavailable. You should write the password on a piece of paper and keep it in a secure place.

► See "Controlling Security," p. 584

Now that you have assigned or used the administrative password to display the Protect screen, you can set up security by defining user profiles for up to eight access levels (1 has the most privileges, 8 has the least).

On the Protect screen, the Users menu is already open. Set a profile for each user who is to be granted some kind of access to dBASE. Figure 4.30 shows the profile settings for a user. Enter the following:

- Login name (As many as eight alphanumeric characters)
- Password (As many as 16 alphanumeric characters)
- Group name (As many as eight alphanumeric characters)
- Full name (As many as 24 alphanumeric characters)
- Access level (A number from 1 through 8)

Select Store User Profile and press Enter to store this record (until saved on Exit).

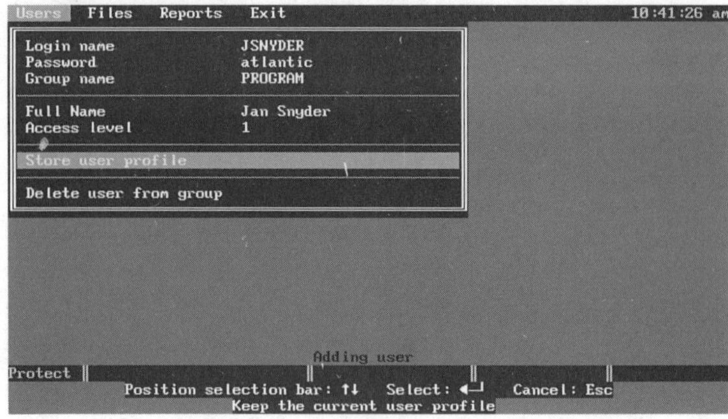

Fig. 4.30 Press Enter to access and set each item of the user profile.

File level access enables you to set a variable scale of privileges to each group member. Based on the access level that you assign each individual user, you can restrict the level of security in a database.

Open the Files menu to define file privileges:

1. Choose New File to display a file pick list. Move the selector to the file you want to protect, and then press Enter.

2. Enter the Group Name for the group of users who are to be assigned access to the file you chose in step 1.

3. Select File Access Privileges to display the File Access Levels submenu (see fig. 4.31). Press Enter to select each area; use the up- or down-arrow key to change the setting. Press the left-arrow key to exit this submenu.

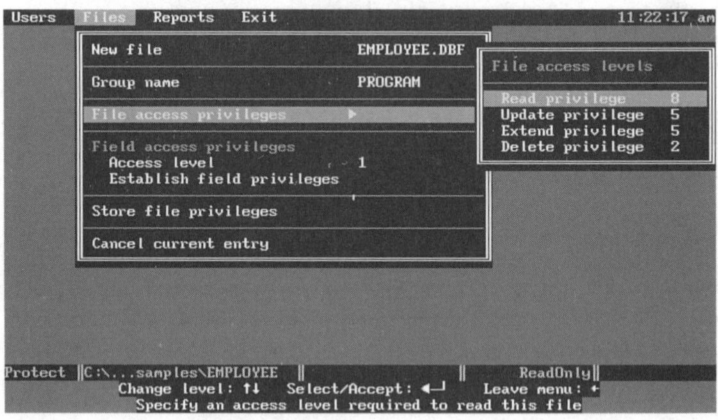

Fig. 4.31 Assigning an access level for each privilege of the file.

An access level of 8 means that any user who has a user profile has the privilege. An access level of 3 indicates that only users with an access level of 1, 2, or 3 could have the privilege.

Following is the meaning of each privilege:

- Read: Can read this file
- Update: Can edit existing records in this file
- Extend: Can add records to this file
- Delete: Can delete records from this file

4. If you want to assign privileges at the field level (optional), choose Access Level, press Enter, and then enter the access level for which you want to define access for fields.

   Select Establish Field Privileges to display a pick list of fields. Move the selector to highlight a field, and then press Enter to cycle among the choices: FULL, R/O (read only), or NONE. Highlight other fields and set privileges for each. Press the left arrow to go back and choose other access levels for which you want to assign field privileges.

5. Select Store File Privileges when you are finished defining access for this file and group. The privilege settings are stored so you can go on to set other files and groups.

Note

The file access you assign does not override a read-only attribute set in DOS.

To see the user profiles you have entered, open the Reports menu and choose User Information. When asked whether to send the report to the printer, choose No. (If you do want to print, choose Yes.) The user settings are displayed in a view screen, as shown in figure 4.32. Press a key to close the view. You also can display file information from the Reports menu, including the file and field privileges that have been set.

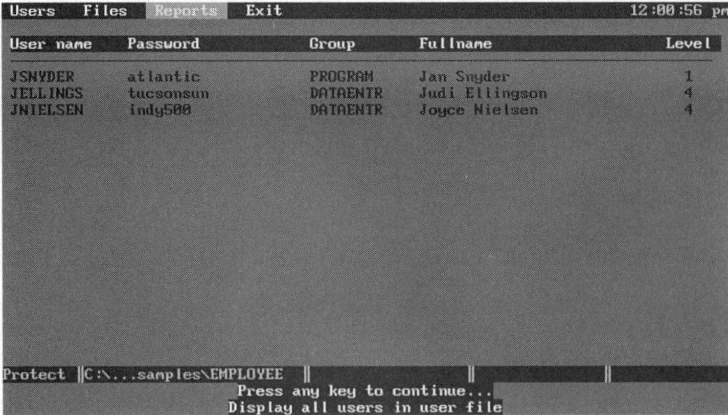

Fig. 4.32
Viewing the user profile settings for password security.

Note

You can edit or delete a user's settings by opening the Users menu and entering the user's Login, Password, and Group name. When asked if you want to edit, choose Yes, and then change the information. If you want to delete the user, highlight Delete User From Group, and then press Enter.

To save the user profile and file privilege settings, open the Exit menu and choose Save (or Abandon if you don't want to save the settings). Choose Exit from the Exit menu to return to the Control Center.

Caution

After you save security set on a file, an encrypted version of the database file is created with a CRP extension. To keep the file secure, delete the DBF version of the file—after copying to a disk and storing it in a safe location. Rename the CRP version with a DBF extension.

To encrypt the index files, reindex them, or create them with an already encrypted database file.

Because security has been established, the next time dBASE is started, a Login screen is presented. Only users who have been set up with a profile in the Protect utility can log in. To log in, enter your group name, user name, and password (see fig. 4.33).

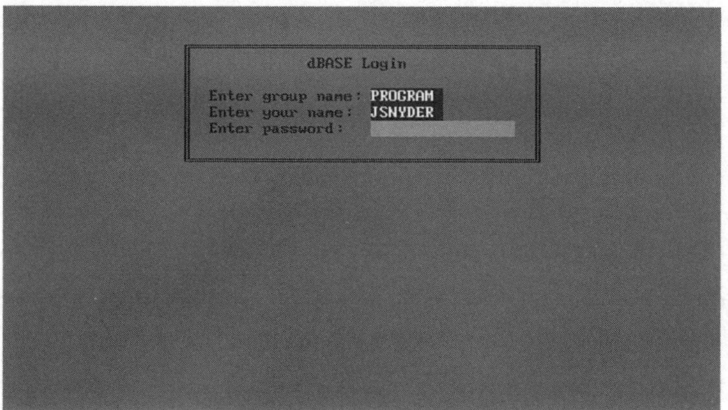

Fig. 4.33
The Login screen for dBASE 5, after password security is set up.

The password does not show when it is typed. Press Enter. The dBASE Desktop opens. Privileges set in the Protect utility screen now are active.

Note

Be sure you really want to use password security before you establish it. The only way to disable security is to rename or delete the DBSYSTEM.DB file. If you do this, none of the encrypted DBF files will be readable. When you want to read the files again, rename the DBSYSTEM.DB file back. Files are then accessible and security is enabled.

Changing Settings

Instead of having to program a different SET command every time you want to change a screen setting, dBASE gives you the opportunity to change some of these settings from the menus. The settings are used only in the current work session; you must edit the CONFIG.DB file to make permanent changes.

◄ See "Setting Up the Environment," p. 27

Because the Control Center, open the Tools menu and choose Settings to display the screen for changing settings. The Options pull-down menu already is open. Use the arrow keys to move the selection bar to the setting you want to change. The message line at the bottom of the screen describes each option that you highlight. Press Enter to cycle through the settings allowed for each option.

Tip
This is just a subset of the temporary settings available. You can have access to more settings from the Developer's Desktop. From the **O**ptions menu choose **d**BASE SET.

You also can use the mouse to toggle the settings. Some options on the menu require you to type in the new setting, such as number of decimal places. Just click on the number of decimal places and type in the new number you want to use.

When you are finished with the Options menu, there is nothing to save, because these are temporary settings for this session. You can press Esc to return to the Control Panel, but let's look at the Display menu first.

The Display menu enables you to change display attributes of the screen—mainly colors. These are the settings you can change:

- Display mode: Changes the number of lines displayed on the screen, depending on the capabilities of your monitor.
- Standard - All: Sets attributes for text and headings onscreen. You also can change the individual items under Standard - All.
- Enhanced - All: Sets attributes for special screen areas, such as boxes, fields, and the status line. You also can change the individual items under Enhanced - All.
- Perimeters of the Screen: Changes the color of the border around the screen.

▶ See "General SET Commands," p. 829

Let's change the color of Normal text, one of the Standard display options. Click on the Normal Text option in the Display menu. The color options are displayed for foreground and background (see fig. 4.34). The default colors for Normal text (on a color monitor) are White Foreground—the text color—on a Cyan Background. Use the arrow keys to move the highlight to a new color in the Foreground column. Use the right arrow to move to the Background column and change its color. You also can make the text blink, but that would not be advisable in most cases. Press Ctrl-End to select the settings. Press Esc to return to the Control Center.

Exiting the Control Center

When you have finished working in the Control Center, you can return to the Desktop, or exit dBASE 5 to return to DOS (or Windows, if you are running dBASE 5 in Windows).

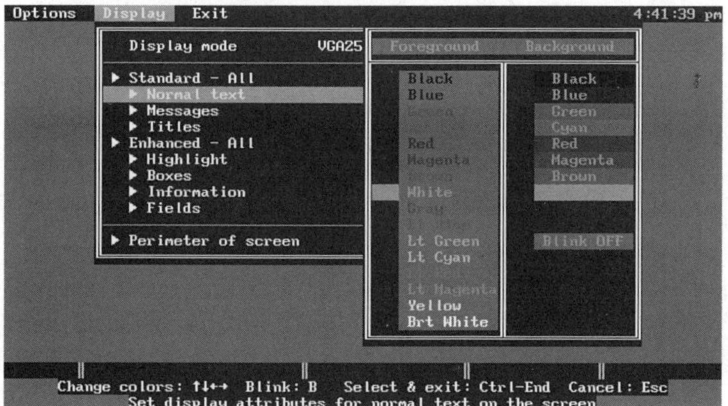

Fig. 4.34
Use the display options to change the color of various parts of your screen.

There are two methods to return to the Desktop:

- Open the Exit menu and choose Exit to Command Window. (The Command window is on the Desktop.)
- Press Esc. dBASE asks if you are sure you want to abandon operation. Choose Yes.

To exit to DOS or Windows:

- Open the Exit menu and choose Quit to DOS.

> **Caution**
>
> Failure to properly exit to DOS (or Windows) could result in critical damage to your dBASE files. Be sure to always exit to DOS. DO NOT just turn off your computer!

From Here...

This chapter has given you a closer look at the many features of the Control Center. You learned how to create and modify files, to access files in the panels, and to organize your applications with catalogs. You also learned to use DOS Utilities to perform several operations on files and to set password security on files.

Now that you know the basics of getting around in dBASE 5, you are ready to move on to creating and using a database in the following chapters:

- Chapter 5, "Designing the Structure of a Database," discusses how to design a database structure.
- Chapter 6, "Adding Records," explains how to enter data in the edit screen or browse screen to create new database records.
- Chapter 9, "Using Queries To Search Databases," shows you how to create queries to selectively extract the data you have entered into the database.
- Chapter 11, "Creating and Using Input Forms," teaches you to create custom forms for more accurate data entry in a more useful design.

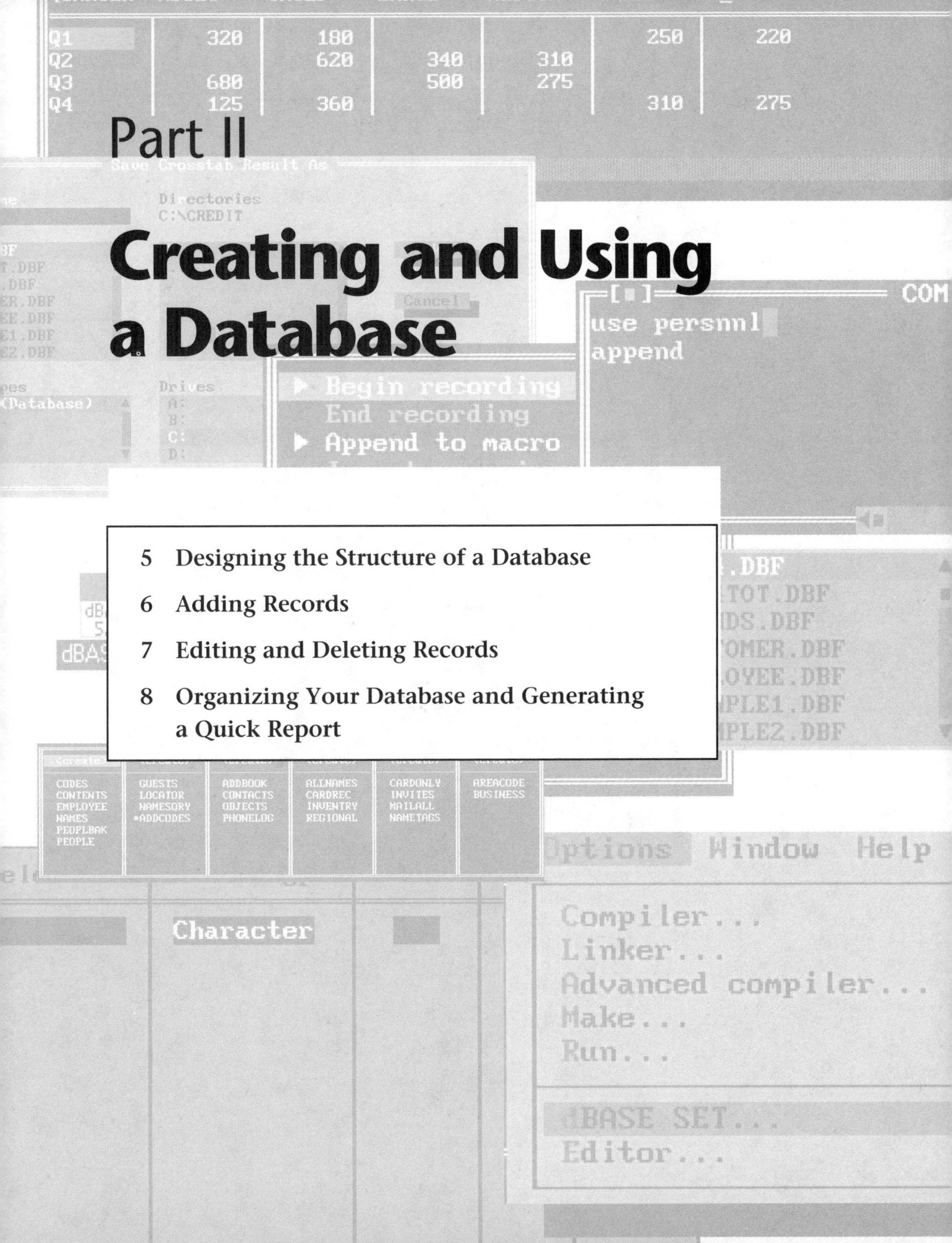

Part II

Creating and Using a Database

5 Designing the Structure of a Database

6 Adding Records

7 Editing and Deleting Records

8 Organizing Your Database and Generating a Quick Report

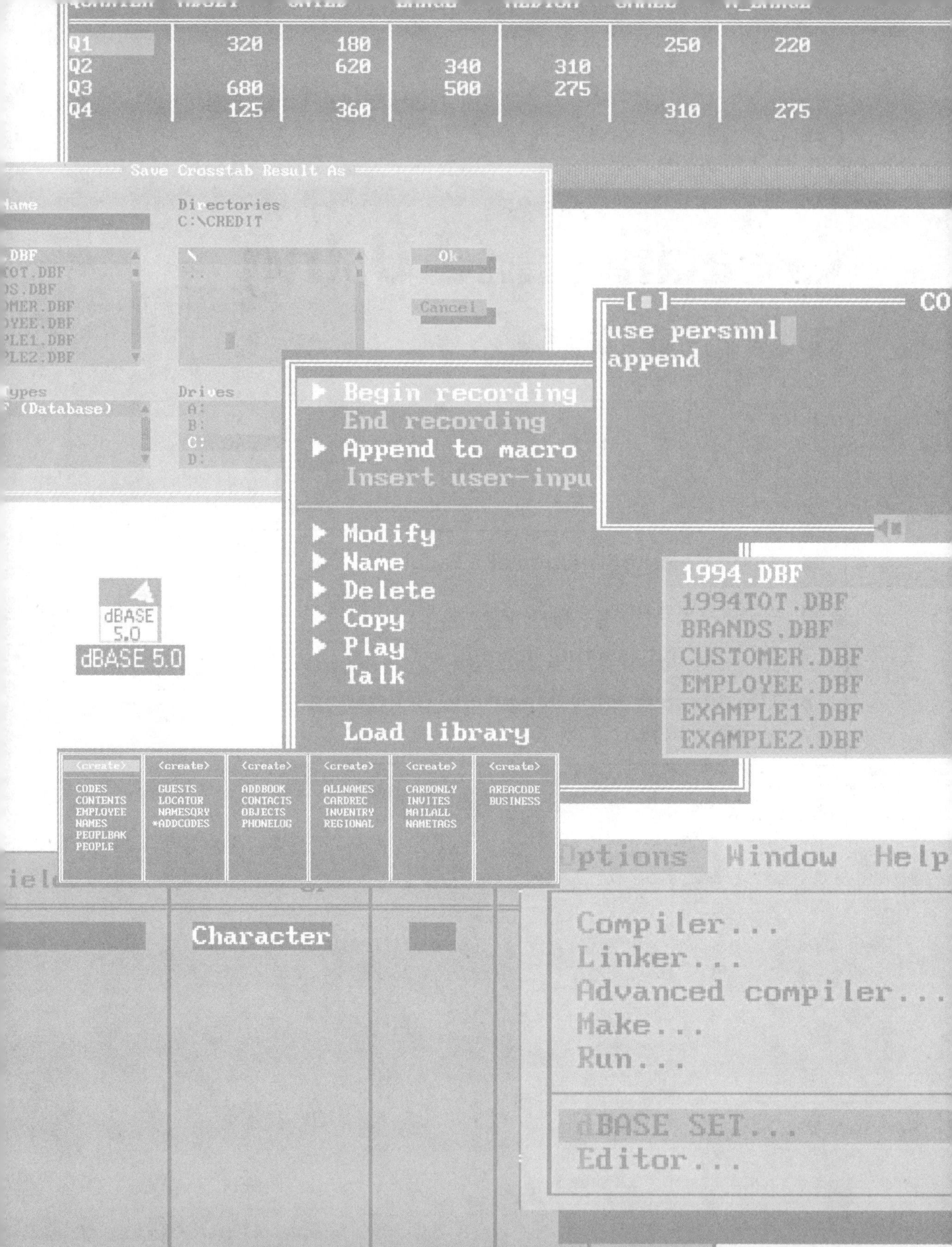

Q1 320 180 250 220
Q2 620 340 310
Q3 680 500 275
Q4 125 360 310 275
Save Crosstab Result As
Directories
C:\CREDIT
Ok
Cancel
Drives
(Database)
use persnnl
append
Begin recording
End recording
Append to macro
Modify
Name
Delete
Copy
Play
Talk
Load library
1994.DBF
1994TOT.DBF
BRANDS.DBF
CUSTOMER.DBF
EMPLOYEE.DBF
EXAMPLE1.DBF
EXAMPLE2.DBF
dBASE 5.0
dBASE 5.0
<create>
CODES
CONTENTS
EMPLOYEE
NAMES
PEOPLBAK
PEOPLE
<create>
GUESTS
LOCATOR
NAMESQRY
*ADDCODES
<create>
ADDBOOK
CONTACTS
OBJECTS
PHONELOG
<create>
ALLNAMES
CARDREC
INVENTRY
REGIONAL
<create>
CARDONLY
INVITES
MAILALL
NAMETAGS
<create>
AREACODE
BUSINESS
Window
Help
Character
Compiler...
Linker...
Advanced compiler...
Make...
Run...
dBASE SET...
Editor...

Chapter 5

Designing the Structure of a Database

In most manual databases, information is kept on forms or cards. For example, inventories often use cards, your Rolodex is a database set up on cards, and your local library started with cards for its book database. Other databases, such as personnel records, telephone survey records, and accounts receivable records, are set up on forms. The forms have blanks for information, and those blanks may or may not be filled out.

In this chapter, you learn how to design a database around the information in your forms or cards. You learn how to design the database structure and how to enter that structure into dBASE 5. In Chapter 6, you learn how to add records to your new database, and in Chapter 7, you learn how to edit and delete records already entered into your database.

Specifically, in this chapter, you learn how to do the following:

- Define a database structure
- Choose field types
- Create simple indexes
- Enter your design into dBASE 5

Reviewing Your Manual Database

If the database you're planning is based on a preexisting manual system, review your manual database before you design your database in dBASE 5. Before the local library starting using computer databases to keep track of books, it had a fully developed card system to do the same job. If you plan to put your employees' records on computer using dBASE 5, make sure that your personnel record-keeping works the way you want *before* you transfer the design to dBASE 5. If you don't, any problems with the manual system are transferred to your dBASE system.

If you don't have a manual system such as an inventory system or Rolodex you're working with, try out your design on paper before you start in dBASE.

Ask yourself how your manual system is working. Are there complaints from the people who use the information? Do the people who use the information, including yourself, have any ideas for improvement? For example, if you're designing an address database, ask yourself if there's any information that you wish you had on your Rolodex but don't. If you're doing a database of invoices for accounts receivable, ask the accountants if they have any ideas. Maybe they want the company contact's phone number next to the contact's name. When you design your database, you can put the phone number immediately after the name. When you learn to use custom entry forms in Chapter 13, you'll be able to design a custom entry form that makes it as easy as possible for the accountants to enter the information.

Now is your chance to right the wrongs of your manual system. No matter how complex your manual system is, rethinking it now will help your dBASE 5 system flow more smoothly, and the data entry go faster. You'll be able to solve problems more effectively and make points with the people using the information, too.

Understanding Database Terminology

As you become acquainted with the dBASE 5 procedures you use to put together a database, you should become comfortable with the terms dBASE 5 uses to describe database structures and values. You encounter these terms in help screens, messages, and command prompts. To take full advantage of what dBASE is telling you, you have to understand dBASE's language.

Records

A *record* is the set of details or facts that describes a single entity in the database. Each card in a Rolodex is a record. In a personnel database, a record consists of all the data on a given employee. A record could be all the information on a form, or if you think of the database as a table, the records are the rows of information. Figure 5.1 shows a portion of a personnel database in a table format, where each personnel record, or row of information, consists of a LASTNAME, FIRSTNAME, Social Security Number, BIRTH_DATE, and HIRE_DATE.

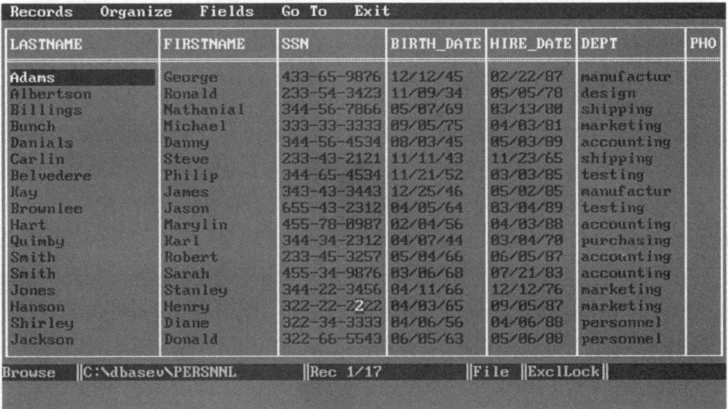

LASTNAME	FIRSTNAME	SSN	BIRTH_DATE	HIRE_DATE	DEPT	PHO
Adams	George	433-65-9876	12/12/45	02/22/87	manufactur	
Albertson	Ronald	233-54-3423	11/09/34	05/05/78	design	
Billings	Nathanial	344-56-7866	05/07/69	03/13/80	shipping	
Bunch	Michael	333-33-3333	09/05/75	04/03/81	marketing	
Danials	Danny	344-56-4534	08/03/45	05/03/09	accounting	
Carlin	Steve	233-43-2121	11/11/43	11/23/65	shipping	
Belvedere	Philip	344-65-4534	11/21/52	03/03/85	testing	
Kay	James	343-43-3443	12/25/46	05/02/85	manufactur	
Brownlee	Jason	655-43-2312	04/05/64	03/04/89	testing	
Hart	Marylin	455-78-0987	02/04/56	04/03/88	accounting	
Quimby	Karl	344-34-2312	04/07/44	03/04/70	purchasing	
Smith	Robert	233-45-3257	05/04/66	06/05/87	accounting	
Smith	Sarah	455-34-9876	03/06/68	07/21/83	accounting	
Jones	Stanley	344-22-3456	04/11/66	12/12/76	marketing	
Hanson	Henry	322-22-2222	04/03/65	09/05/87	marketing	
Shirley	Diane	322-34-3333	04/06/56	04/06/88	personnel	
Jackson	Donald	322-66-5543	06/05/63	05/06/88	personnel	

Fig. 5.1
In a database listed in table format, the rows are the records, and the columns are the fields.

Fields

The columns shown in figure 5.1, with headings like LASTNAME or FIRSTNAME, represent the fields in the database. A *field* is synonymous with a database category. A field is a blank on a form or card. A field stores a particular type of data. In the example in figure 5.1, a field is identified at the top of a column of data and includes all the data in that column. In common usage, saying that a database has five columns—as in the example—is the same as saying that it has five fields in each record.

Values

A *value* is the information in a field—the actual phone number in the phone number blank on a form or the actual name in the name blank of a Rolodex. If the database is listed as a table, with rows for records and columns for fields, a value is an individual item of data at the intersection of a row and a column. In the database in figure 5.1, a value is equivalent to the information that goes in a single slot of the table. To pinpoint a value in the table, you must describe it in terms of the record it belongs to and the field it occupies. It's Nathanial's LASTNAME, Stanley's SSN, or Donald's HIRE_DATE.

Defining Your Database

To define a database in dBASE, you must tell dBASE what fields you want in each record. In terms of a table of data, you must tell dBASE what columns you want for each row of information. In terms of a database where the information comes from a filled-out form, you must tell dBASE what blanks are on the form.

In the following section, you learn the steps of setting up a database by naming and defining fields for your information. Later in the chapter, you actually enter your database design into dBASE 5.

Naming a Field

Tip
When naming fields, use the underscore character (_) instead of the space character.

After you decide what information or data you're going to put into your database, the next step in designing your database is to name the fields. In dBASE, you're limited to 10 characters for the names of fields. In Chapter 11, you learn how you can use longer names for your data input by using custom forms. When you name a field, try to make the name reflect the nature of the information and its description. For instance, a field name for a Social Security Number might be SOCSECNUM or SSN. The name for a field with the number of units in stock might be NUMUNITSTK or UNITSTOCK.

Choosing the Type of Field

Tip
When you name a field, select a name that reminds you of the contents of the field.

A *data type* specifies the kind of data you intend to store in a field. You can use one of three basic data types: character, numeric, or date. Each type confers on its field certain properties that enable dBASE 5 to check the validity of data entered in that field and to do certain kinds of processing on the data. Designating a field as numeric, for example, enables the data in the field to be calculated.

In addition to the three primary field types—character, numeric, and date—dBASE 5 permits three other field types that you use in special circumstances. These field types are the logical, float, and memo.

Using Character Field Types

Character fields accept any type of information. Character fields are limited to 254 characters; these characters can be any letters, symbols, or numbers. Most fields in your database will be character fields.

Character fields are also good for storing numbers that will not be used in calculations, such as ZIP codes, model numbers, or part numbers.

Tip

If your field will have letters and numbers in it, use a character field. A character field will accept numbers, but a numeric field will not accept letters.

Using Numeric Field Types

Numeric fields are for numbers that can be used in calculations. If you have an Age field and later want to calculate the average age of the individuals in your database, use a numeric field.

With a numeric field, you must specify the number of decimal places your numbers will have. Because numeric fields won't accept letters or symbols, using them can help prevent mistakes in data entry.

Using Date Field Types

Date fields are eight characters long. You enter the data into a date field in the format MM/DD/YY. Telling dBASE that your field is a date allows indexing and sorting by month, day, or year without having three separate fields.

Using Float Field Types

The second numeric field type that dBASE 5 permits is the *float* type. The word *float* refers to a floating-point number, which is a number that stores a value to the full precision of the system rather than to a designated number of decimal places.

▶ See "Using Custom Forms for Better Data Input," p. 284

In every respect, a float field is defined in the same way as a numeric field. You still specify the field width and number of decimal places in the same way. The only differences happen internally, with the way the number is stored on disk. Without getting involved in the technical details, you should understand how these differences affect you and your work.

If you store the result of a calculation as a floating-point number, dBASE 5 stores the calculated value to the full precision of the system, even though the number displays only to the limits of the definition. For example, what you see on-screen as `2` may be stored as 2.000000000001. If you perform calculations with this number, you may get results in which 2+2 does not equal exactly 4.

What guidelines should you follow in defining numbers? If you deal with scientific or technical applications that include very large or very small numbers, and you need high levels of precision in all your calculations, set up your numbers in float fields. For just about any other application, set up your numbers in numeric fields.

Using Logical Field Types

A logical field is set up to handle information with only two possible values, either true or false, or yes or no. A *logical* field always has a width of one position and permits only four possible entries: true (T or t), false (F or f), yes (Y or y), or no (N or n). An example of a logical field might be a field that tracks whether a check has cleared in a check register database. The field can have two possible values—either the check has cleared, or it hasn't.

In a logical field, dBASE does not recognize the difference between uppercase and lowercase. Consequently, a Y is the same as a y, and T is the same as t.

You can set up certain categories in more than one way. If the database has a Sex field (which can have one of two possible answers), for example, you can set it up as a character field with a width of one and with possible values *M*(ale) and *F*(emale); alternatively, you can set up a field as a logical field with possible values *T*(rue) and *F*(alse).

What are the advantages of each approach? With a character field, the allowable values are closer to terms the world recognizes as alternatives in the category; *M* means male and *F* means female. With a logical field, someone reading the table of values may not know whether T means male or female. But a logical field has more built-in validity control—dBASE 5 permits only the values true, false, yes, and no. If your finger slips and you press R rather than T, dBASE 5 doesn't accept the entry into a logical field. If you make this typing error with a character field, dBASE 5 records the R as a correct value.

Using Memo Field Types

The *memo* field is a variable-width field that accommodates data larger than 254 characters, or that doesn't fit any particular pattern. The memo field is useful to keep track of miscellaneous details about people in your database—say, Joe's wife's name, Mabel's wedding anniversary, or John's favorite restaurant. It is possible to set up separate fields for spouse names, anniversaries, likes, and dislikes. The problem with this approach is that dBASE 5 creates space for these fields in every record, whether you need to use the fields or not. It is also difficult to know in advance what miscellaneous information you may want in your database.

You could set up a character field to use for stray facts. Because a character field can be as long as 254 positions, such a field can record a whole series of comments. The problem with this solution, however, is that it's the same as setting up separate fields. dBASE 5 sets aside the space for this field for each record in the database, whether you use the field or not.

The perfect solution is to use memo fields. The data you type in the memo field is actually stored in a separate file. dBASE 5 sets up this file automatically whenever you use a memo field. The memo-field file has the same name as the database, but it has the extension DBT rather than DBF. When you open a database file, dBASE 5 automatically opens any associated DBT file.

For a single record, you can store as many as 64,000 bytes of data in a memo field. With such a large capacity, the memo field is perfect for storing notes, comments, or any large blocks of unstructured information.

▶ See "Adding Data to Memo Fields," p. 134

You pay a price for the flexibility of memos. The contents of a memo field are generally hidden from view; they don't appear in a display view of the database. You must specifically request that the memo for a particular record appear, or you can design a "memo window" in a customized data-entry form to reveal the memos automatically.

▶ See "Adding Fields to Reports," p. 294

You're also limited in how you can search for information in a memo. The search process cannot take advantage of the search commands used for searching other types of fields. Even with these limitations, memo fields are useful for keeping all your facts in order.

▶ See "Searching in Memo Fields," p. 197

Specifying the Field Width

The *width* of a field specifies the length of the longest data item that can be stored in the field. The maximum width is determined by the field type. A character field can be as wide as 254 positions and as small as one position. A date field, on the other hand, is always eight positions wide.

For numeric fields, the field width must include the decimal and decimal places. To determine the width, count one position for each digit of the number, one position for each decimal place, and one position for the decimal point. If you want to store 999,999.999 as the largest number in a numeric field, for example, the width of this field is 10; the field has three decimal places. Notice that you don't count a position for the comma.

Tip
If you later find that your field width is insufficient, you can change it easily. See "Modifying a Database Structure" later in this chapter.

Indexing a Field

The index value for a field is probably the simplest part of the field definition: you specify Yes or No for each field. Yes signifies that you want dBASE 5 to maintain an index which, if you choose to use it, displays your records alphabetically, numerically, or chronologically by the values in that field.

Benefits of Indexing a Field

The main purpose of indexing is to organize records in a certain order for review. Indexing on a given field enables dBASE to keep track of the order of the records based on that field. For example, if the name of a field in an address database is LASTNAME, the LASTNAME index enables dBASE to alphabetize the database on the last names in your database. If you print mailing labels from the address database, you can use a ZIPCODE index to list the addresses by ZIP code.

► See "Reorganizing the Database by Sorting," p. 176

Indexing a database on a field rearranges the data for reporting and display purposes, as on the Edit or Browse screens, but doesn't rearrange the database on the disk file. To actually rearrange a database on the disk file, you must sort the database.

Assume that you have to get out a mailing to your customers as cheaply as possible. If you send the mailing bulk rate, you save money on postage. The post office, however, requires bulk mail to be presorted by ZIP code. The problem is organizing the list numerically by ZIP code.

Suppose that you have the following database:

Record #	Name	ZIP Code
1	Jones	25149
2	Smith	31511
3	Jefferson	21691
4	Pauly	31972
5	Richmond	21101

If you organize this database so that the ZIP codes are in numerical order, the database appears on-screen in the following order:

Index #	Record #	Name	ZIP Code
1	5	Richmond	21101
2	3	Jefferson	21691
3	1	Jones	25149
4	2	Smith	31511
5	4	Pauly	31972

A good example of a database with several indexes is the book catalog in a library. The author catalog is the book catalog indexed by author, and it contains an alphabetized list of entries by author, where each entry points to the location of the book on the shelves. The subject catalog is the same book catalog indexed by subject, and it contains an alphabetized list of entries by subject. The title catalog is the book catalog indexed by title.

A dBASE 5 index does the same thing: it provides a list in alphabetical order (or numerical or chronological order) of the records in the database. When you display data by using an index, the records appear rearranged in the Browse and Edit screens; if you look at the status bar, however, you see that the record pointer still refers to the record by its original record number.

dBASE 5 stores index information in an MDX or multiple index file. dBASE 5 also can recognize single index files, or NDX files, generated by earlier versions of dBASE.

The letters *MDX* and *NDX* refer to the file extension assigned to the index. (Indexes are stored on the disk under a file name.) If you work with an MDX index, dBASE 5 stores the index on disk under the same name as the database, but distinguishes the index from the database by assigning the extension MDX. Remember that the database file has the extension DBF.

dBASE 5 uses the MDX file as a repository for all the indexes you need for the database, up to a total of 47. If you need more than one index, you create each separately and supply each a name. dBASE 5 stores each index in the MDX file and references the indexes by the names you assigned. dBASE refers to the name of the index as the *index tag*.

Creating Indexes that Use Multiple Fields

It's also possible to have a single index on several fields. In an address database, you could set up an index that first organized the database according to ZIP code, then within each ZIP code, organized the database according to LASTNAME. The database would then have the information arranged so that all records with the same ZIP code would be arranged alphabetically by LASTNAME within that ZIP code.

▶ See "Creating More Sophisticated Indexes Using Expressions," p. 165

Entering Your Database Design into dBASE 5

Now that you have some idea how to design your database, it is time to enter the design into dBASE 5. In dBASE 5, you create databases with the database design screen (see fig. 5.2). If you are in the Command window, you can access the design screen directly by typing **create** and then pressing the

Enter key. You also can go to the Control Center by pressing F2 or typing **assist**, and then pressing the Enter key.

From the Control Center, you access the design screen by clicking `<create>` with the mouse or by putting the panel selector on the Data panel's `<create>` button and pressing Enter. You also can press Shift-F2 (Design).

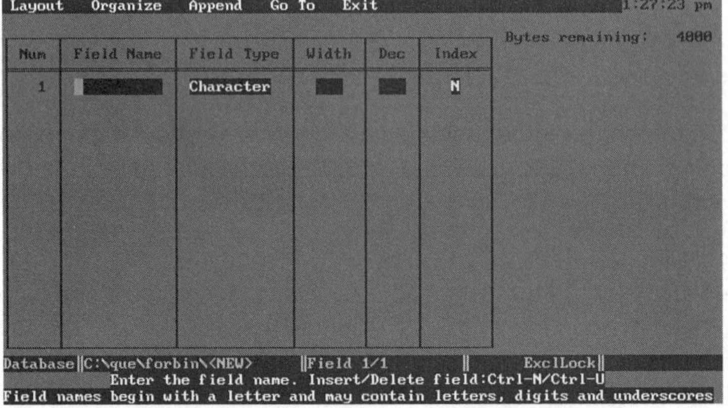

Fig. 5.2
Enter your database design into dBASE 5 by using the database design screen.

> **Note**
>
> The Command window in dBASE 5 replaces the dot prompt of earlier versions. All dBASE commands and functions previously used at the dot prompt are applicable in the Command window.

If you understand dBASE 5's requirements for setting up field definitions, the layout of the database design screen should present no surprises. Its work surface is a simple table format in which columns are designated for the Field Name, Field Type, Width, number of decimal places (Dec), and the Index value.

The rest of the design screen is made up of the menu bar across the top of the screen, the status bar below the work surface, and the navigation and message lines at the bottom of the screen. Notice that the status bar displays the name of the design screen in the first section; the second section indicates by the word `<NEW>` that you are working on a new file—a file that hasn't been named yet. The third section lists the number of the field the selector currently is highlighting and the total number of fields in the structure. At start-up, this section reads `Field 1/1`. The fourth section is blank, and the fifth section lists key indicators, including `Ins` (if the Ins key is pressed) and `Caps` (if the Caps Lock key is pressed).

To define the structure of a new database, you fill out one row on the work surface for each field in the database. You start with the first field (Num 1). When you finish defining the first field, the cursor advances to Num 2.

Follow these steps to enter your design:

1. Start defining a field by typing the name of the field. The field name can be up to 10 characters long. It can be made up of any combination of letters, digits, or the underscore (_) character, as long as the name begins with a letter. The space, however, is an illegal character. If you try to use the space or any other illegal character, dBASE 5 beeps and ignores the character.

2. After you enter the field name, press Enter or Tab to advance to the Field Type column. In this column, notice that dBASE 5 uses the default Character type. If you want the field to be a character type, advance to the Width field by pressing Enter or Tab again. To change the type, press the first letter of the type you want: **N**umeric, **F**loat, **D**ate, **L**ogical, or **M**emo (or **C**haracter to change back to the default). dBASE records that type and advances to the next column. If you forget what the field type choices are, you can press the space bar to cycle through the possibilities. When the correct type appears, press Enter to advance the cursor.

3. Next, if you selected the character, numeric, or float type, you must specify the field width. If you selected date, the cursor automatically records a width of 8 and advances to the Index column. If you selected a logical or memo type, the cursor records fixed widths (1 for logical and 10 for memo) and advances to the Field Name column for the next field.

Note

You can't set an Index for logical or memo fields.

4. The last thing you do is tell dBASE if you want an index of the field. You can index on as many fields as you like (except for logical and memo fields); dBASE generates a separate index for each field. These indexes are simple, single field indexes.

► See "Creating More Sophisticated Indexes Using Expressions," p. 165

The navigation and message lines at the bottom of the screen provide information about your possibilities at the moment. In particular, these lines provide information about the limits you can set on field widths for character and numeric fields, and on the number of decimal places you can set for numeric fields.

A hypothetical personnel database consisting of a number of character, date, and numeric fields is shown in figure 5.3. The design includes two fields of interest: Active, a logical field that records whether the employee is on active assignment or on leave without pay; and Comment, a memo field.

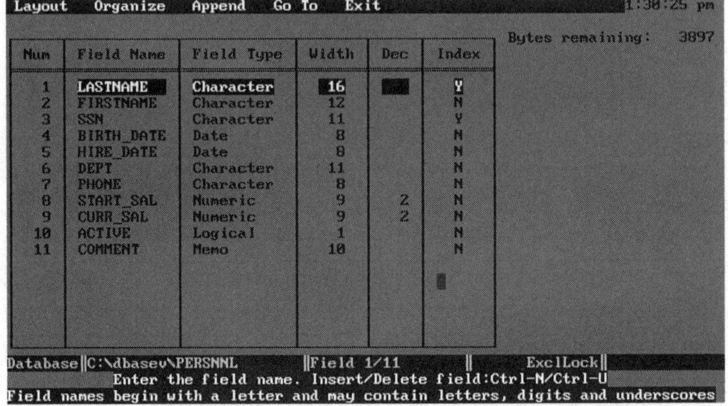

Fig. 5.3
Before you quit, double-check your structure for the proper number of decimals and for indexed fields.

To summarize, a database description calls for the following information about each field in the database:

- Name
- Type
- Width
- Decimal places (for numeric fields only)
- Index value

Saving the Database Structure

After you complete the definition and layout of your database fields, you must save the structure before you can start entering your data. Save the structure from the database design screen by using either the Layout menu or the Exit menu. Each of these menus has a Save command. The Layout menu

Save command saves the structure, but returns to the database design screen. The Exit menu Save command saves the database and returns to the Control Center. In either case, you're asked to provide a name for the new database during the save operation.

Tip
If you want two versions of your design, you can save any design surface with a different name by selecting the Save This File Structure option from the Layout menu.

If you activate the Layout menu, the pull-down menu shown at the top left of figure 5.4 appears. If you then select Save This Database File Structure, a fill-in box that asks for the name of the database appears. Type the file name and press Enter. dBASE saves the database with the name you specify and adds the extension DBF. Remember that the file name cannot be longer than eight characters, not including the extension. After you complete the save, notice that the second section of the status bar shows the new file name.

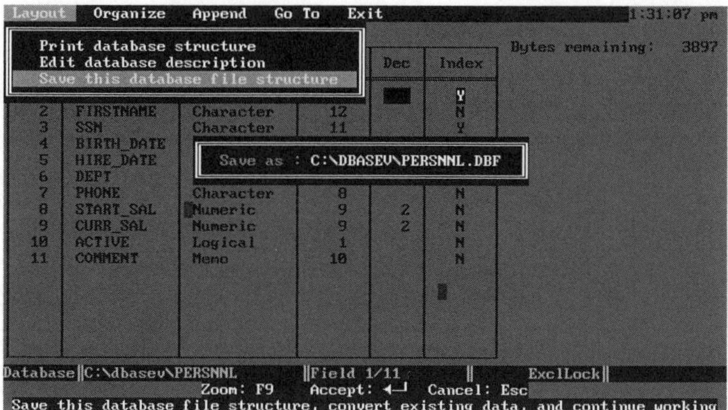

Fig. 5.4
Use either the Layout menu or the Exit menu to save the completed database design.

Note

If you entered the database design screen from the Command window, you already gave your database a name when you used the CREATE command. Also, if you entered from the Command window, you return to the Command window when you exit, not the Control Center.

Caution

If you use Esc to leave the database design screen, your structure is not saved. If you haven't saved the structure and want to, choose No when asked whether you want to abandon this operation. Then save the design using the Layout or Exit menu.

After you save the database structure, you can add data (as explained in Chapter 6), reorganize it (as explained in Chapter 8), or design queries.

▶ See "Adding Records," p. 125

▶ See "Organizing Records for the Report," p. 161

Note

For reference, you may want a paper copy of the structure of the database. A paper copy can help when you need to cite the names of fields or work with the database from the Command window. To generate the printout from the database design screen, use the Layout menu and the Print database structure command. Assuming that the print settings are correct for your printer, select the Begin printing option from the Print menu that appears. The Print menu is discussed in more detail in Chapter 8.

You may find that including a short description of the database is helpful. The description you type appears in the file identification section of the Control Center when you highlight the database file name in the Data panel. You assign the description by using the Layout menu Edit Database Description command. When dBASE presents a fill-in box asking for the description, type the description and press Enter (see fig. 5.5).

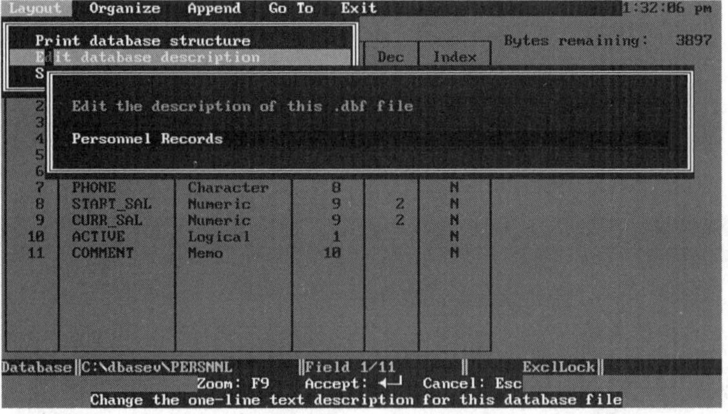

Fig. 5.5
Enter a description for the database file from the Layout menu.

After you finish your work in the database design screen, exit to the Control Center by using the Exit menu. This menu has two options: Save Changes And Exit or Abandon Changes And Exit. You can duplicate the function of the Save Changes And Exit option by pressing Ctrl-End; duplicate the Abandon Changes And Exit option by pressing Esc. If you abandon your work, you lose only the changes you made since the last time you saved the database.

Troubleshooting

I lost my structure design when I left the design screen.

If you use Esc to exit the design screen, dBASE does not save your design. Use the Layout or Exit menu, or type Ctrl-End instead.

When I returned to dBASE, I couldn't find my database design.

Check to make sure that you are in the correct Catalog from the Control Center.

Check also the spelling of your file name. dBASE saves only the first eight letters for a database name. If you typed more letters, those letters won't appear in the name. For example, if you type **PERSONNEL**, only PERSONNE appears.

Another possibility: If you entered the design screen by using the CREATE command from the Command window, you may have typed CREATE STRUCTURE, which saves your database design as the file STRUCTURE.

After saving my design, I decided to change one field from character to numeric. Will that be a problem?

dBASE saves the change with no problems. You must specify the number of decimal places (which can be 0), and you must include the decimal—but not commas—in your field width.

Modifying a Database Structure

After you create a database structure, you may think that the structure is written in stone. With dBASE 5, however, your database can change as the world changes. To make structural changes to a database, reactivate the database design screen. From the Control Center, highlight the database name in the Data panel and press Enter to display the prompt box. Select the Modify Structure/Order option to return to the database design screen (see fig. 5.6). To bypass the prompt box, highlight the database file name in the Control Center and press Shift-F2 (Design).

To modify the structure of a database file with the mouse, double-click the file name in the Data panel, or click on the file name, and then click on the `Design:Shift F2` label in the navigation line.

To reach the design structure screen from the Command window, type **MODIFY STRUCTURE**, followed by a carriage return. At the prompt, type in the name of your database.

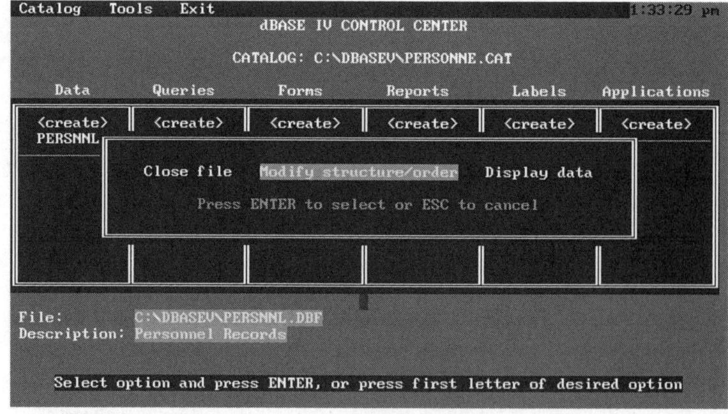

Fig. 5.6 Double-click the file name and select Modify Structure to change your database design.

► See "USE Command," p. 748

Note

If you are working on a network and you do not want anyone trying to access your database while you are modifying it, you can use the USE EXCLUSIVE command before the MODIFY STRUCTURE command from the Command window. Other users will be locked out of the database.

Caution

When modifying a database structure, save the database design periodically. A good rule of thumb is to make all changes in one column and save, and then make all changes in the next column and save. Don't modify two column entries at once for more than one field. In other words, make all your field name changes and save; then make all the changes to the field widths and save. Also, save your design before adding any more records.

When you make changes to a database for which you have already entered some data, be careful about the kinds of changes you make to the structure. Eventually, dBASE 5 pours the data back into the database structure. If you make too many changes or the wrong kinds of changes to your structure when you modify it, the data may no longer "fit" in the structure. If you make a drastic change, such as deleting a field from the structure, all the data that was in that field is lost when you save the structure. Always back up your data before modifying the structure.

To more easily modify the structure of a database that has many fields, use the Go To menu from the database design screen (see fig. 5.7). This menu includes commands to move the selector to the top field in the list, the last field in the list, and to any particular field given its number in the list. Activate the Go To menu in the usual way and then highlight a command.

To delete or insert a blank field, use the commands Ctrl-N and Ctrl-U, respectively, as described at the bottom of the structure design screen. The bottom of the screen is also used for other helpful hints regardless of the menu you are using.

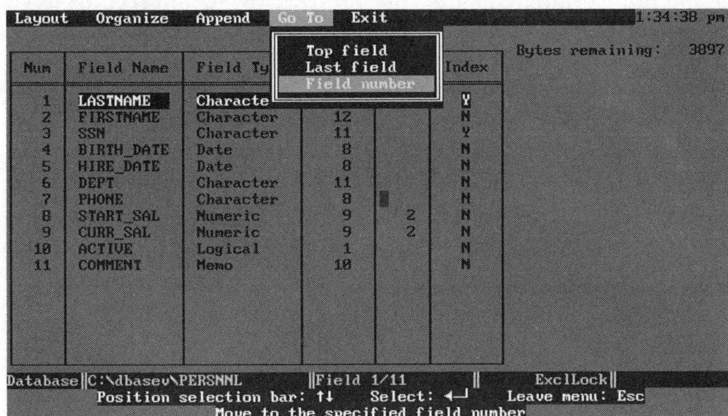

Fig. 5.7 Use the Go To menu to jump to another field in a long database design.

Troubleshooting

I tried to modify the structure and ended up losing all my records. What happened?

Two things may have happened. If you make so many changes that dBASE can't decide in which new fields the old field information goes, you can lose the old information. Another problem occurs if you press Esc while dBASE is modifying the structure and moving the records to the new structure. In that case, you can lose all information in both the old and the new databases.

I want to add to my database design a field containing miscellaneous information that I edit frequently. A character field would do the job, but editing a character field is very awkward. Any ideas?

Use a memo field instead. The dBASE memo text editor has block commands, search commands, and several other features that make it useful for editing character fields that change frequently. Another advantage of the memo field is that it takes up only as much disk space as it needs. Regular character fields take up their entire field width (as many as 254 characters) even if the field is empty.

From Here...

In this chapter, you learned how to design a database structure by specifying fields and their characteristics, as well as how to go back into the design and make changes.

For more information on database structures and fields, refer to the following chapters in this book:

- Chapter 6, "Adding Records," shows you how to add records to your database and use the Edit and Browse screens.
- Chapter 7, "Editing and Deleting Records," shows you how to delete and make changes to the records in your database.
- Chapter 8, "Organizing Your Database and Generating a Quick Report," explains how to prepare a "quick report" for listing information in your database. This chapter also shows you how to generate advanced indexes using dBASE expressions.

Chapter 6

Adding Records

Data entry is obviously an important job, one on which the integrity of the database hinges. During the data-entry process, you begin to learn the meaning of "garbage in/garbage out." If you enter data properly in the beginning, when you later ask questions of the database, you will get reliable answers.

In this chapter, you learn how to add information to the database you designed in Chapter 5. You learn to enter your data into the different types of fields and how to make on-the-go corrections. You now have your toy box (the database), and you are ready to put in the toys (the data). In this case, every toy goes in a special place, a cubbyhole cut exactly to the correct dimensions.

In this chapter, you learn how to do the following:

- Enter data in your database through the Browse and Edit screens
- Move around the screen for on-the-go corrections
- Use the dBASE 5 text editor to enter data in Memo fields

In Chapter 7, you learn how to go back into a database to make changes to the data and clean up any garbage. In Chapter 8, you learn how to organize your database with indexes and how to get the information back out of your database by using dBASE 5's Quick Report. During this process, you'll discover whether you have any "garbage out."

Understanding the Data-Entry Process

You add records to a database in either the Browse or Edit screens.

The Edit screen shows a single record with the fields listed down the left side of the screen. The fields are in the order they were entered when the database structure was designed (see fig. 6.1). The word `Edit` appears at the bottom left of the screen on the status bar.

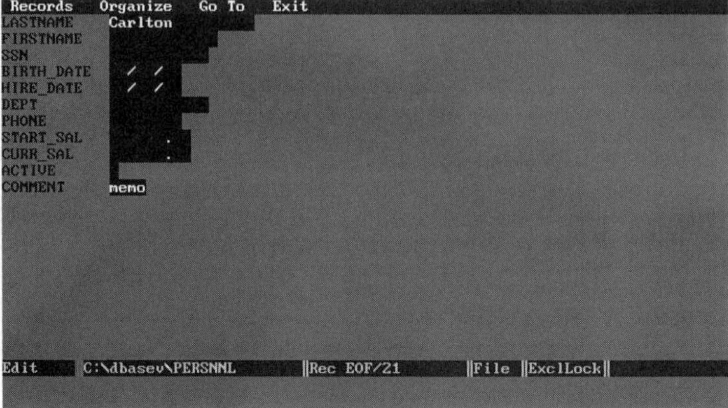

Fig. 6.1
The first records added are in the Edit screen.

The Browse screen displays records across the screen in a table format (see fig. 6.2). Each column in the Browse screen represents a single category (field) in the database; each row represents a complete record of data in the database. The names of the fields are listed across the top row of the Browse screen. The word `Browse` appears on the status bar at the bottom left of the screen.

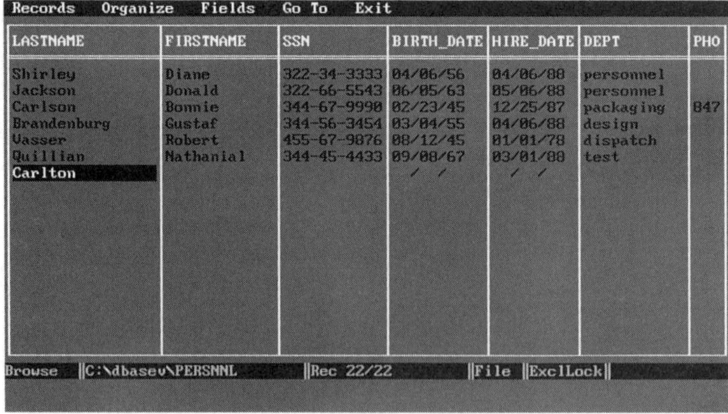

Fig. 6.2
You can see more records—but fewer fields—on the Browse screen.

Note

If no records are in your database, you end up in the Edit screen no matter which of the following procedures you use.

You can reach the Edit and Browse screens in several ways.

From the Command window:

- To reach the Edit screen from the Command window, type **append** and then press Enter (see fig. 6.3). If no database is in use, dBASE 5 asks you for the name of the database. This command takes you to the Edit screen and places you at the bottom of the database on a blank record.

▶ See "APPEND" and "BROWSE," pp. 654 & 659

- To get to the Browse screen from the Command window, type **browse** and then press Enter. Again, if there is no database in use, dBASE asks for the database name.

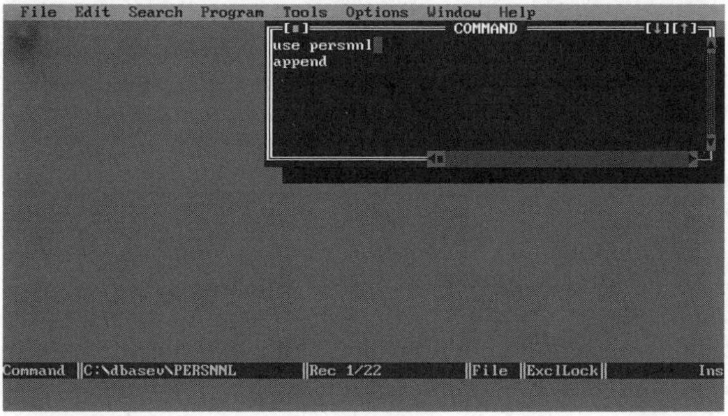

```
File  Edit  Search  Program  Tools  Options  Window  Help
                          [■]========== COMMAND ==========[↓][↑]
                          use persnnl
                          append

Command  ||C:\dbasev\PERSNNL        ||Rec 1/22        ||File  ||ExclLock||        Ins
```

Fig. 6.3
The APPEND command gets you to the Edit screen from the Command window.

From the Control Center:

- To reach the Edit screen from the Control Center, highlight the database name and press F2. If there aren't records added yet, you reach the Edit screen directly. If there are records in the database, pressing F2 takes you to the screen and record you were last using. For example, if you were last looking at record number 4 of the database on the Edit screen, F2 returns you to record number 4 on the Edit screen. If you were last looking at record number 99 on the Browse screen, F2 returns you to record number 99 on the Browse screen. If this is your first

Tip
To reach the Control Center from the Command window, type **assist** and press Enter, or press F2.

viewing and you have records in the database, F2 takes you directly to the Browse screen.

- To reach the Browse screen from the Control Center, double-click on the database name and choose Display Data in the dialog box that appears (see fig. 6.4). You can also reach the dialog box by highlighting the database name and pressing Enter.

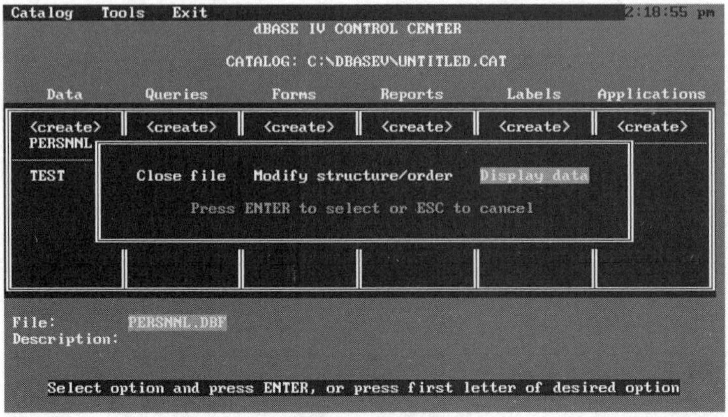

Fig. 6.4
The Display Data choice takes you to the Browse screen if you have records in your database; if you don't, it takes you to the Edit screen.

After you're in either one of the screens, you can switch to the other screen by pressing F2 unless there aren't any records in the database. Then the Browse screen is not accessible, and pressing F2 does not switch screens.

Adding Records Using the Edit Screen

To add records using the Edit screen, call up the Edit screen as described previously. If the fields are blank, begin filling them in. If the fields have information in them, you're looking at a record already in the database. That record is called the *current record*, and whatever field is highlighted is called the *current field*. Either use the Go To menu or press Ctrl-PgDn to reach the bottom of the database. dBASE asks whether you want to add more records (see fig. 6.5). Answer Yes.

You can also jump directly to a blank record by using the Add New Records option on the Records menu (see fig. 6.6).

To add a new record to the database, fill out the current field, advance to the next field, fill it out, and continue in this way until all the fields are filled out. Each field name is followed by a "slot" where you type the value for that field. The slot is as long as the field width you defined for that field.

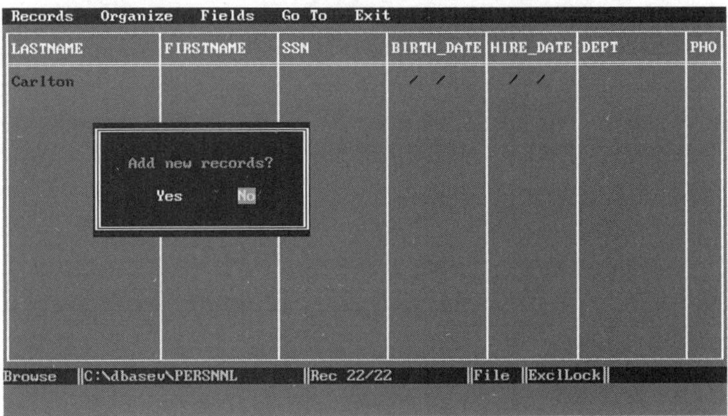

Fig. 6.5
When you reach the end or bottom of the database, dBASE asks if you want to add more records.

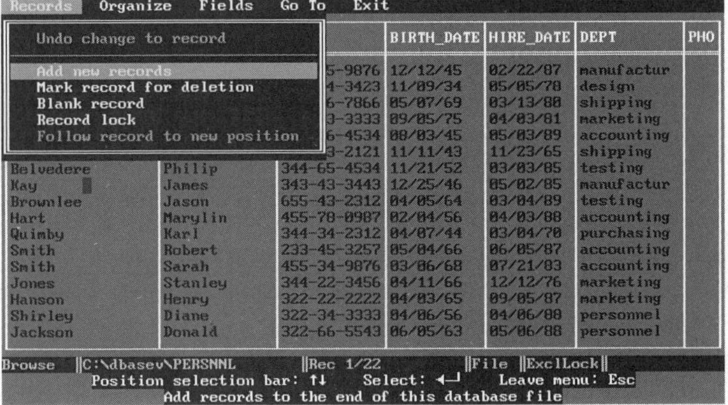

Fig. 6.6
With the Records menu, you can jump immediately to the end of the database file to add new records.

Fill out the record one field at a time. Depending on how much data you enter in the field, one of two things happens. If the data you enter completely fills the field, dBASE 5 beeps and advances the cursor to the next field. If the data doesn't fill the field, you must signal that you finished entering data for that field by pressing Enter. Pressing Enter advances the cursor to the next field. When you fill out the last field, dBASE 5 advances out of the current record, displays a blank form for the next record, and positions the cursor in the first field of that new record.

Note

Consider entering information in indexed character fields in all uppercase letters. In dBASE 5, simple indexes use the ASCII sorting order in which all lowercase letters come after all uppercase letters. In other words, *de la Cruz* will come after *Zambino* even though *d* comes before *Z* in the alphabet.

▶ See "Understanding Indexes," p. 162

Caution

The record you just filled out isn't necessarily added immediately to the disk file. The record is first added to a "record buffer" in the computer's memory. When the buffer is full, dBASE 5 writes all the records in the buffer to disk. For this reason, NEVER TURN OFF YOUR COMPUTER WHILE YOU ARE STILL IN dBASE. You could lose data that you thought you had already entered.

Troubleshooting

I went into my database in the Edit screen. I can't find any records, even though I know I added several, and I can't get to the Browse screen.

The database you have entered is empty. Chances are, you entered a different database than you intended. Exit using Esc and, from the Control Center, double-click the database name again. Watch for databases with similar names.

I highlighted a database name from the Control Center and pressed F2. I ended up in the Edit screen instead of the Browse screen. I repeated this several times, and the same thing happened.

If there are records in a database, pressing F2 will take you to the screen and record you last used. Sometimes this is the Edit screen, and sometimes this is the Browse screen. To reach the other screen, simply press F2 again. If you are in the Edit screen, you will jump immediately to the Browse screen.

Adding Records from the Browse Screen

To add records in the Browse screen, call up the Browse screen as described in the preceding section. The records are listed in rows across the screen. With either the Go To menu or Ctrl-PgDn, move to the bottom of the database. dBASE then asks whether you want to add records. Answer Yes, and then begin typing in the information across the field columns. You also can move down the screen adding information in a given field for each record. Moving down the screen is advantageous if you have a database with a lot of similar information and you want to add that information to every record, then add other information later.

For example, if you build an accounts receivable file and you have a sheet with company names and account numbers but no other information, you may want to move down the Browse screen, adding only the company name and account number. Then return to the top of the database and add other information, such as address and phone contacts.

Another advantage of the Browse screen is that you can review the records above the one you are working on as you go along. You can check previous entries for the correct information, and you also can make sure you aren't duplicating information that you already entered.

The disadvantage of the Browse screen is that you see a limited number of fields on-screen at any one time. dBASE 5, however, includes some commands in the Fields menu that partially compensate for this limitation. These commands enable you to freeze a field on-screen, lock certain fields on the display, and resize fields.

Using the Edit screen is best if you want to add all information to each record as you go along and have no need to review the other records. An example might be entering data from forms filled out by prospective clients. It would be easier to enter all the information from one form, and then go to the next form rather than trying to flip through the forms. In Chapter 11, you learn how to make the data-entry screen match the appearance of your physical form to make the data-entry process even easier.

Tip
Use the Edit screen to add records if your information is coming from filled-out forms. Use the Browse screen to add records if your information is coming from a printed row/column list.

Caution

If you leave the database in the middle of a record using the Esc key, you lose that record information and have to reenter it. To leave without losing the information, either finish the record, press Ctrl-End, or use the Exit menu.

Editing a Record As You Add It

Before you move to the next blank record, you can correct the current record by bringing the cursor back to the item you want to change, erasing the error, and substituting the correction. The way that you move the cursor depends on the display screen you're using. If you are in the Edit screen, use the up- and down-arrow keys to move the cursor to the preceding and following fields. If you are in the Browse screen, use Tab rather than the up-arrow key and Shift-Tab instead of the down-arrow key to move between fields. The Tab and Shift-Tab keys also work in the Edit screen. In either screen, use the left- and right-arrow keys to move the cursor within a field. If you exceed the limits of a field, the left- and right-arrow keys advance the cursor to the adjacent field.

The F3 (Previous) and F4 (Next) keys move you from field to field also.

After you move the cursor to the error, erase it by using the Backspace key (if the cursor is to the right of the error) or the Delete key (if the cursor is

Tip
You also can use the mouse to move the cursor to the field you want to edit by repositioning the mouse pointer and clicking.

directly on the error). To erase the entire value in a field, use the Field menu Blank Field command in the Browse screen.

Note

You also can erase a field partially or totally by using Ctrl-T or Ctrl-Y. These keys erase from the point of the cursor to the right. To erase the entire field, the cursor should be at the left edge of the field.

Depending on the type of error you are correcting, you sometimes can type the correction over the error instead of deleting the error first. To insert new characters in the middle of a string, press the Ins key, position the cursor where the new characters are to be inserted, and type. When you press Ins, the `Ins` indicator appears in the status bar. Pressing Ins a second time turns off the `Ins` indicator and returns dBASE to overwrite mode.

Troubleshooting

I made a mistake entering a date. Can I go back and change it?

No problem. Use the F3 and F4 keys to move from field to field, and just type over the new date. Use the Exit menu when you finish adding records, and the new date is stored in your database.

I tried to change a numeric field, but the number keeps coming out wrong.

If you leave a numeric field using the arrow keys, the new number you entered will be placed next to the old number, and the two together will be entered as the new field value. Make sure that you leave the numeric field by pressing the Enter key after entering the new number.

Keeping Track of Records

dBASE 5 assigns each record in the database a *record number*. Each time you add a new record to the database, dBASE 5 finds the record with the highest number, adds 1 to it, and assigns that number to the new record. The records you add, therefore, are assigned numbers in the order you enter them in the database. dBASE 5 refers to this order as the *natural order* or the *order of entry*. When you display records, they appear in natural order. In Chapter 8, you learn how to use indexes to alter the natural order to arrange and display records in other ways using indexes.

When you first open a database, dBASE 5 automatically positions itself at the first record in the database. This location also is referred to as the *top* of the database. When you add records, dBASE goes to the bottom of the database and steps beyond the last record to an area called the *end of file*, or EOF for short. This area is identified on the status bar when you add records. The third section of the status bar reads `Rec EOF/#`, where # represents the total number of records in the database. The only exception to this notation is the case in which no records are in the database at all; in this case, the status bar reads `Rec None`.

Note

To turn off the beep that dBASE sounds at the end of each record for your current working session, call up the Browse or Edit screens from the Control Center. Activate the Tools menu and select the Settings option. From the Settings menu, select the Bell option and change the setting to OFF by pressing the space bar or Enter, or by clicking with the mouse.

Likewise, if you don't want dBASE 5 to automatically advance to the next field, turn the Confirm setting ON. If you do this, you must always press Enter (or use the mouse or arrow keys) to advance the cursor to the next field.

You also can reach the Settings menu from the Options menu on the Command window screen.

Adding Data to Character, Numeric, and Logical Fields

The type of field you enter data into makes some slight differences in how you enter that data and how it is displayed. In all fields, you enter the data from left to right. In a character field, the data is aligned or justified to the left side of the field. If you do not completely fill the field, you have some trailing blanks to the right of the last character. In some situations, you may want to get rid of those trailing blanks. See Chapter 8, "Organizing Your Database and Generating a Quick Report," for details.

▶ See "Creating More Sophisticated Indexes Using Expressions," p. 165

In a numeric field, the numbers are aligned or justified to the right side of the field. Right justification helps to display columns of numbers, because the numbers line up on their decimal point. When you enter a new number or replace an existing number, however, you type the digits for the number at the left side of the field. If the number contains decimals, the number aligns properly within the field slot when you press the decimal point. If the number doesn't contain decimals, it aligns properly when you press Enter to advance the cursor.

Note

If you go back into a numeric field to make a change, leaving the field with the arrow keys will generate a different result than if you leave the field with the Enter key. Leaving with the arrow keys will put the new digits next to the old digits. Leaving with the Enter key will delete the old digits. Suppose that the old value in a numeric field is 1.00 and you type a 2 at the left side of the field. If you leave the field with the arrow keys, the new value stored in the field would be 21.00. If you type the 2 and then leave by pressing the Enter key, the new value would be 2.00.

dBASE is set up initially to record dates in the form MM/DD/YY. Notice that any date fields in the data-entry form already have the slashes (/) in the field slot to separate the month, day, and year. You do not have to type these slashes when you enter a date. If you don't type the slashes, you must type a leading zero for any month, day, or year less than 10. To enter the date January 1, 1909, for example, you can type **010109** or **1/1/9**. If you type a slash, dBASE takes that as a signal to end one unit and begin the next. If you make an error entering a date so that what you type is not a valid date, dBASE displays the message Invalid date (Press space). Press the space bar and edit the entry to make it a valid date.

Note

For dates in other centuries, you must change the template to reflect the year with four positions rather than two. To change the template, access the Tools menu at the Control Center, select Settings, and then select Century (see fig. 6.7). By default, the Century setting is OFF. When you change the setting to ON by pressing Enter or the space bar, or by clicking the mouse, dBASE displays all date templates as MM/DD/YYYY. You then can enter and display dates with a full century specification.

The situation with logical fields is simpler because your choices are limited to T, F, N, or Y in either uppercase or lowercase letters. Attempting to enter anything else causes dBASE to beep without advancing the cursor, although no error message appears.

Adding Data to Memo Fields

When you view a database with memo fields in Edit or Browse mode, you see only a marker in the field. The marker is simply the word `memo` (lowercase) or `MEMO` (uppercase). The word `memo` (lowercase) indicates that the record has no text in that memo field; `MEMO` (uppercase) indicates that the record does have text in the memo field (see fig. 6.8).

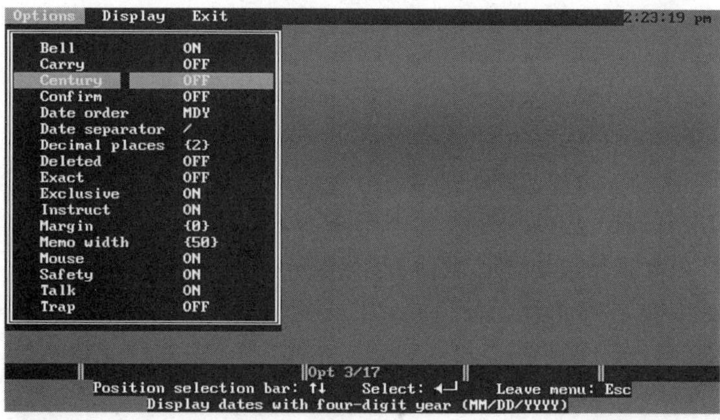

Fig. 6.7
To change the date field format so you can enter century information, use the Tools menu.

Records Organize Fields Go To Exit

BIRTH_DATE	HIRE_DATE	DEPT	PHONE	START_SAL	CURR_SAL	ACTIVE	COMMENT
06/05/63	05/06/88	personnel		.	.		memo
02/23/45	12/25/87	packaging	847-9887	230000.00	.	Y	MEMO
03/04/55	04/06/88	design		.	.		memo
08/12/45	01/01/78	dispatch		.	.		memo
09/08/67	03/01/88	test		.	.		memo
/ /	/ /			.	.		memo

Browse C:\dbasev\PERSNNL Rec 17/22 File ExclLock

Fig. 6.8
The word MEMO (uppercase) indicates there is text in the memo field.

II Creating/Using Databases

The text in the memo field is not visible until you open the memo field. To add text to a memo, you must open the field before you can add text. You can open a memo field in one of four ways:

- Place the cursor on the memo marker and press Ctrl-Home.
- Place the cursor on the memo marker and press F9 (Zoom).
- From the preceding field in the record, press F4 (Next); from the following field press F3 (Previous). These keys advance the cursor and open the memo in one move.
- Double-click on the memo marker with the mouse.

After you open a memo field, the regular display disappears, and dBASE 5 gives you access to its built-in text editor (see fig. 6.9).

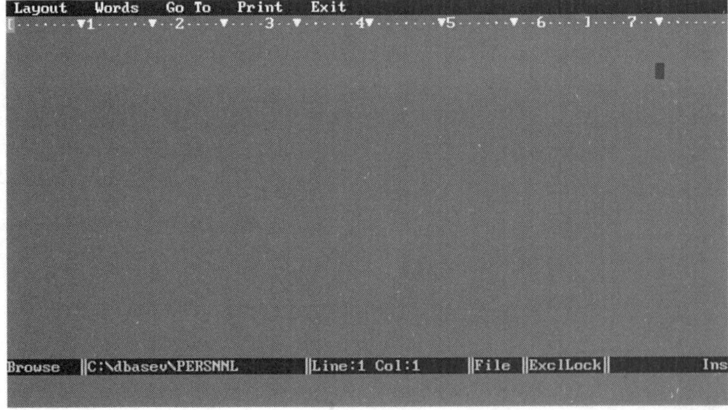

Fig. 6.9
Pressing Ctrl-Home takes you to the dBASE text editor to add text to memo fields.

Tip
To use a text editor other than the one supplied by dBASE, add a WP=PATH for the editor in the CONFIG.DB file.

As you type the text of the memo, dBASE word-wraps it to fit within the margins set by the ruler line, which appears below the text editor's menu bar. The ruler line marks the margins for the memo with the characters [for the left margin and] for the right margin. By default, the left margin is set at 0 and the right margin is set at 65, meaning that dBASE can put up to 65 characters on each line of the memo. Because dBASE 5 word-wraps text, you don't have to press Enter at the end of each line of text. Press Enter only when you want to end a paragraph or override the word-wrapping feature for a particular line.

After you type the memo, save it. When you save the memo, you exit from the text editor and return to the memo marker in the Edit or Browse screen. Save the memo in one of these ways:

- Press Ctrl-End.
- Press F3 (Previous) or F4 (Next). These keys also advance the cursor to the previous or next field in the display screen after leaving the text editor.
- Access the text editor's Exit menu, and then select the Save Changes and Exit option.

If you're writing a long memo, you can save it periodically as you work without exiting the text editor by using the text editor's Layout menu. This menu has only one command: Save This Memo Field.

If you change your mind after entering any new text and don't want to save the memo, press Esc to abandon the memo. Any text entered since the last save is abandoned. You also can access the Exit menu, and then select Abandon Changes and Exit.

For more information on the text editor, such as how to add other text files to memos and how to print memos, see the following section, "Understanding More about the Text Editor."

Closing the Database

When you finish adding records, you can leave the database by pressing Esc or Ctrl-End, or you can use the Exit menu. Using Esc abandons information in the record you're currently on. To save that record, press Ctrl-End or use the Exit menu.

When you return to the Control Center, you can now move to another database by clicking on the name of the one you want to use. If you entered the database from the Command window, you return there.

Understanding More about the Text Editor

The text editor menu bar has pull-down menus that enable you to make adjustments to the format of the text (the Words menu), to move the cursor to a specific word or phrase within the text (the Go To menu), and to print the text (the Print menu). Some of these same commands also are available through hot-key shortcuts. In addition, some key commands have no equivalents on the menus.

Moving Around and Editing in the Text Editor

Table 6.1 lists the possible commands in the text editor. These commands function the same way for all uses of the text editor.

Table 6.1 Word Processing Commands

Function	Menu/Command	Key Command
Delete previous		Ctrl-Backspace word
Delete to end of current word		Ctrl-T
Delete current line	Words/Remove Line	Ctrl-Y
Insert new line	Words/Add Line	Ctrl-N
Insert page break	Words/Insert Page Break	

(continues)

Table 6.1 Word Processing Commands

Function	Menu/Command	Key Command
Go to specific line	GoTo/Go To Line Number	
Search for specific text	GoTo/Forward Search or Backward Search	Shift-F5
Search for next occurrence of text	GoTo/Forward Search	Shift-F4
Search for previous occurrence of text	GoTo/Backward Search	Shift-F3
Replace searched text with specified	GoTo/Replace	Shift-F6
Select text for copy, move, or deletion		F6
Move text		F7
Copy text		F8
Delete block		Delete

In addition to the editing commands, the text editor includes some special cursor-movement keys, listed in Table 6.2.

Table 6.2 Cursor-Movement Keys in the Text Editor

Action	Keys To Press
Move to following word	Ctrl- →
Move to previous word	Ctrl- ←
Move down one screen	PgDn
Move up one screen	PgUp
Move to top of text	Ctrl-PgUp
Move to bottom of text	Ctrl-PgDn
Move to beginning of current line	Home
Move to end of current line	End

You also can use the mouse to reposition the cursor by moving the mouse pointer to the appropriate location and clicking.

Inserting and Replacing Text

As you type, text usually is inserted or squeezed between already existing text. To type over existing text, press the Ins key. The status bar at the bottom of the screen indicates whether the insert key is on or not.

Adding and Removing Lines

To add a line, you can either type in the new line where you want it, with insert on, or you can press enter at the end of the previous line. You also can choose the Add a Line option from the Words menu.

To remove a line, you can use the Delete or Backspace keys to delete the text, or you can choose the Delete a Line option from the Words menu. Be careful, as the command deletes a line, but not a sentence. For instance, a sentence on two lines will be cut in half.

Using Block Commands

To move, delete or, copy a block of text, first highlight the text. You can do this with the mouse by holding down the left button and moving to the end of the block. You can also press F6 at the beginning of the block and press Enter at the end of the block.

After the block is highlighted, press Delete to delete it.

To move the highlighted text, move the cursor to the new location and press F7.

Inserting Page Breaks

To tell the editor to begin a new page at a certain point in the text, insert a page break by opening the Words menu and choosing Insert Page Break. This command is usually used when you're printing a memo and you want certain text to start at the top of a new page.

Searching and Replacing Text

To find text in a document, use the Go To menu. The Go To Line Number command is used mostly in programming but is handy if, for instance, you have been adding comments to a memo field and numbering them.

You can use the Forward Search and Backward Search commands to search forward and backward, respectively, in the memo to look for specific text.

You can find text and automatically replace it with other text. If you wanted to replace every occurrence of the word *better* with the word *superior* in an Employee Review Comment Memo, you can use the Replace command.

With all the search commands, you can control case-sensitivity. To find text with the same capitalization, change the Match Capitalization to Yes. With Match Capitalization set to No, a search for *mike* will find *mike* or *Mike*. With Match Capitalization set to Yes, a search for *mike* will find only *mike*, not *Mike*.

Attaching Text Files

One powerful feature of the dBASE memo editor is the capability to attach documents to the memo field. Suppose that you have a customer database and you want to attach a letter you sent to the customer to the customer's record. First, store the letter from your word processor as a DOS text file. Then enter dBASE and the customer database. Enter the memo field as described earlier. Open the Words menu and choose Write/Read Text File. Give it the name of the file and the text is added to the memo.

Tip
To read a file into your memo, use Ctrl-KR. To write the memo or a highlighted portion of it to a TXT file, use Ctrl-KW.

It's also possible to add the memo text to another file in the same way. Write the file to disk using the same command; then, from the other program (for example, your word processor), open the text file. This option of writing to disk allows you to take memos and format them in more sophisticated word processors than the dBASE text editor (see fig. 6.10). The file is saved with the name you provide, along with the TXT extension.

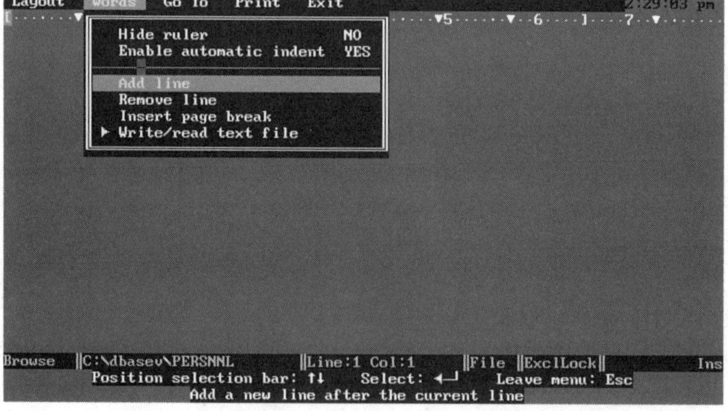

Fig. 6.10
Use the Words menu to write a memo field to disk as a TXT file.

Printing Memo Fields

The Print menu enables you to print a copy of the memo currently on-screen. When you print the memo, the printer stops at the bottom of the text on the last page. To finish printing the last page, you must use the Eject Page Now command (see fig. 6.11).

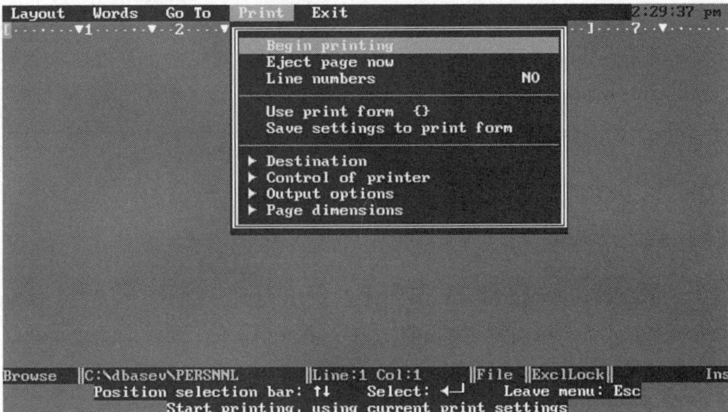

Fig. 6.11
Use the Print menu to print your memo. Don't forget to eject the last page.

> **Note**
>
> Printing to a DOS file is not the same as Writing to a DOS file shown in the Words menu. Printing to a file saves page numbers and margins in the file. To save just the text, use the Write command in the Words menu.

Saving and Exiting

You can save your memo by pressing Ctrl-End or choosing Save from the Layout menu. If you press Esc to leave your memo, you lose any changes you made.

> **Troubleshooting**
>
> *One of my fields is too short for the information I need to enter. What do I do?*
>
> If you haven't entered any data into your database, use the procedures described in Chapter 5, "Designing the Structure of a Database," for modifying your database structure. Read that chapter before you try to modify the structure of your database. If you aren't careful, you could lose information you may have already entered in the database.
>
> (continues)

(continued)

I have entered several records in my database and discovered I need another field in the design. What do I do?

Refer to the section "Modifying a Database Structure" in Chapter 5. You can insert a field into the structure design, and dBASE will add your records automatically to the new design. The new field will be in each record and will be blank. Do not add more than one field at a time if you have data in your database. You could end up losing some of the information.

From Here...

In this chapter, you learned how to use the Edit and Browse screens to add data to your database and make on-the-go corrections. You also learned how to use the dBASE memo text editor to add memos to your database records.

For information relating directly to adding records to a database, you may want to review the following chapters:

- Chapter 7, "Editing and Deleting Records," shows you how to go back into the database and make additions and corrections to the information.
- Chapter 11, "Creating and Using Input Forms," shows you how to make inputting your data easier by designing custom input forms.
- Chapter 19, "Using the Applications Generator and the Compiler," shows you how to set up an easy-to-use menu system to add records to your database.

Chapter 7

Editing and Deleting Records

In the previous two chapters you learned how to design the structure of a database and how to enter data into the database. In this chapter, you learn how to go back into a database and make changes to the records. There are several reasons for doing this. Perhaps the information has changed. An employee may have retired or received a pay raise. Perhaps you have received new address information for a client. Perhaps you have discovered an error on a form you were using to enter data. Regardless of the reason you want to make changes, the ease with which you can edit records is one of the benefits of dBASE 5.

In this chapter, you learn how to:

- View records in the Browse and Edit screens
- Modify the Browse screen display
- Find records in a database
- Edit records in a database
- Remove records in a database

Reviewing Your Database

Now that you have your database set up and at least some of the data entered, you are ready to go back into the database and make changes to the data. Before you do, review your database design to verify that it is as functional as it can be. Are all the fields wide enough? Are there any fields that are too wide? Do you have a field that you originally thought would be a numeric field but may work better as a character field, or vice versa? Do you have enough fields?

Reviewing your database before you make editing changes saves you time later, if the problems you identify can be solved easier by a database structure modification. A simple example is an address field on your client database. You may have discovered that you did not have enough room for suite numbers in the address field when you started entering data. Your first thought was to go back into the database and abbreviate street names, so you would have enough room to add the suite numbers when they occurred. Increasing the width of the address field is another option. You can also add a field to your database for additional address information, and call it SUITENUM or ADDRESS2. Either way, modifying the structure of the database is a better long-term solution than editing the data and trying to squeeze it all in the single address field.

Tip
A second field for address information is better than a longer single address field when the address information must fit on address labels.

If you find that the database structure needs to be changed, review "Modifying the Structure" in Chapter 5. Remember to save your new structure often, preferably after every change, no matter how minor. Otherwise you can lose data in your database.

If you review your database and find that only changes to the values in the fields are required, this chapter shows you the easiest way to edit field data.

Using the Display Screens To Edit Records

You can edit your database in either the Edit screen or the Browse screen. To reach either of the screens from the Control Center, double-click on the database name and choose Display Data from the dialog box. This will take you to the Browse screen shown in figure 7.1. Once in the Browse screen, you can reach the Edit screen by pressing F2.

You can also reach the screens from the Command Window by typing **APPEND** and pressing Enter. If your database is not in use, dBASE 5 asks you for the name. Enter the name in the dialog box and you then jump to the Edit screen.

Once in either screen, you can press F2 to jump to the other screen. Either screen can be used to edit your records.

Records Organize Fields Go To Exit

LASTNAME	FIRSTNAME	SSN	BIRTH_DATE	HIRE_DATE	DEPT	PHO
Ca[illegible]lin	Steve	233-43-2121	11/11/43	11/23/65	shipping	
Smith	Robert	233-45-3257	05/04/66	06/05/87	accounting	
Albertson	Ronald	233-54-3423	11/09/34	05/05/78	design	
Hanson	Henry	322-22-2222	04/03/65	09/05/87	marketing	
Shirley	Diane	322-34-3333	04/06/56	04/06/88	personnel	
Jackson	Donald	322-66-5543	06/05/63	05/06/88	personnel	
Brown	John	322-98-3456	09/04/56	09/03/77	testing	894
Bunch	Michael	333-33-3333	09/05/75	04/03/81	marketing	
Adams	Sarah	342-98-9875	08/09/67	01/04/77	assembly	342
Kay	James	343-43-3443	12/25/46	05/02/85	manufactur	
Jones	Stanley	344-22-3456	04/11/66	12/12/76	marketing	
Quimby	Karl	344-34-2312	04/07/44	03/04/70	purchasing	
Adams	Robert	344-43-4983	07/06/60	01/01/92	testing	432
Quillian	Nathanial	344-45-4433	09/08/67	03/01/88	testing	
Brandenburg	Gustaf	344-56-3454	03/04/55	04/06/88	design	
Danials	Danny	344-56-4534	08/03/45	05/03/89	accounting	
Billings	Nathanial	344-56-7866	05/07/69	03/13/80	shipping	

Browse ||C:\data\PERSNNL ||Rec 17/30 ||File ||ExclLock||

Fig. 7.1
You can use either the Edit screen or the Browse screen, shown here, to edit your database.

Using the Edit Screen

The Edit screen shows one record at a time with the fields listed down the left side of the screen. The Edit screen is useful for editing several fields on each record. Because only one record is shown, it is easier to keep track of which record you are editing (see fig. 7.2).

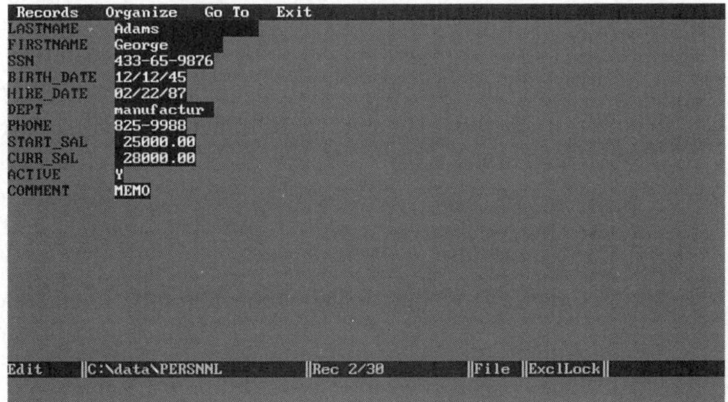

Fig. 7.2
Use the Edit screen if you prefer to edit one record at a time.

Using the Browse Screen

The Browse screen displays the records in a table format, with each record in a row and the fields in columns. Because several records are displayed at one time, the Browse screen is easier to use than the Edit screen when you want to jump from a field in one record to another field in another record. This feature is useful if you are making minor editing changes to various records in your database. If you need to make changes to the same field in several different records, it is easy to move down the screen from record to record in the Browse screen.

If you have more fields in your database than can be displayed on one screen, the other fields will be outside the field of view. You can move the view area and pan across the fields by clicking on the side bars with the mouse cursor, or by using F3 (Previous) and F4 (Next) while the cursor is on the last field visible. dBASE 5 slides the screen to the side as you pan across the fields.

Sometimes you want to see two different fields on-screen at the same time but you can't because they are more than one screen apart. If you want to view two or more fields that are normally separated by more than one screen, the Browse screen has several options with which you can control which fields are displayed.

With these options, you can display the fields on the screen just the way you want them in order to make it as easy as possible to edit.

Locking Fields

As you move across the screen to view the records, the fields at the left side of the screen disappear as fields on the right move into view. If you use one of these fields on the left as a reference to key on, you won't know which record you are editing if the field disappears. For example, if you are referencing the last name of an employee in a personnel database, the LASTNAME field disappears as you move the fields across the screen. In figure 7.3, you can see that the LASTNAME field is not visible at the same time as the memo field. The question is, how do you know which record the memo field belongs to if you can't see the LASTNAME field?

Records Organize Fields Go To Exit

BIRTH_DATE	HIRE_DATE	DEPT	PHONE	START_SAL	CURR_SAL	ACTIVE	COMMENT
11/11/43	11/23/65	shipping		.	.		MEMO
05/04/66	06/05/87	accounting		.	.		memo
11/09/34	05/05/78	design		.	.		memo
04/03/65	09/05/87	marketing		.	.		memo
04/06/56	04/06/88	personnel		.	.		memo
06/05/63	05/06/88	personnel		.	.		memo
09/04/56	09/03/77	testing	894-0923	23000.00	24934.00	Y	memo
09/05/75	04/03/81	marketing		.	.		memo
08/09/67	01/04/77	assembly	342-9856	24564.00	25987.00	Y	memo
12/25/46	05/02/85	manufactur		.	.		memo
04/11/66	12/12/76	marketing		.	.		memo
04/07/44	03/04/70	purchasing		.	.		memo
07/06/60	01/01/92	testing	432-0987	23456.00	24765.00	Y	memo
09/08/67	03/01/88	testing		.	.		memo
03/04/55	04/06/88	design		.	.		memo
08/03/45	05/03/89	accounting		.	.		memo
05/07/69	03/13/88	shipping		.	.		memo

Browse ‖C:\data\PERSNNL ‖Rec 17/30 ‖File ‖ExclLock‖

Fig. 7.3
The LASTNAME field of the personnel database is not visible when viewing fields to the right, such as the memo field.

With dBASE 5, you can "lock" a field so that it stays on the left side of the screen regardless of which fields you are viewing. You can lock as many adjacent fields on the left side of the screen as you need.

Figure 7.4 shows the same display with the LASTNAME field locked so that it always appears at the left edge of the screen as you move across the various fields.

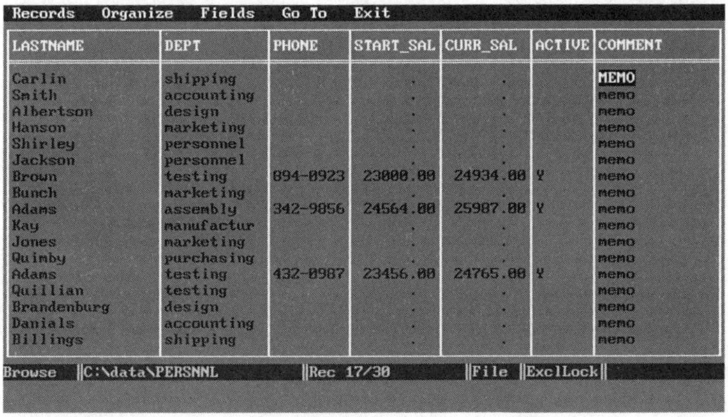

Records Organize Fields Go To Exit

LASTNAME	DEPT	PHONE	START_SAL	CURR_SAL	ACTIVE	COMMENT
Carlin	shipping		.	.		MEMO
Smith	accounting		.	.		memo
Albertson	design		.	.		memo
Hanson	marketing		.	.		memo
Shirley	personnel		.	.		memo
Jackson	personnel		.	.		memo
Brown	testing	894-0923	23000.00	24934.00	Y	memo
Bunch	marketing		.	.		memo
Adams	assembly	342-9856	24564.00	25987.00	Y	memo
Kay	manufactur		.	.		memo
Jones	marketing		.	.		memo
Quimby	purchasing		.	.		memo
Adams	testing	432-0987	23456.00	24765.00	Y	memo
Quillian	testing		.	.		memo
Brandenburg	design		.	.		memo
Danials	accounting		.	.		memo
Billings	shipping		.	.		memo

Browse ‖C:\data\PERSNNL ‖Rec 17/30 ‖File ‖ExclLock‖

Fig. 7.4
Locking the LASTNAME field in the personnel database forces the field to stay on the left of the screen no matter which fields are viewed.

To lock a field, follow these steps:

1. Place the field(s) you want locked on the left of the screen by using the Tab key or F3 and F4 keys.

2. Open the Fields menu and choose Lock Fields on Left (see fig. 7.5).

3. Enter the number of fields you want locked in the dialog box.

From now on, no matter how many fields you have in the database, as you pan across the database, the fields you lock remain on the left side of the screen.

Note

If you lock a field that normally appears in the middle of your database on the Browse screen, you won't be able to see fields to the left of the locked field after locking.

To unlock fields, open the Fields menu, choose Lock Fields on Left, and enter 0 for the number of locked fields.

II

Creating/Using Databases

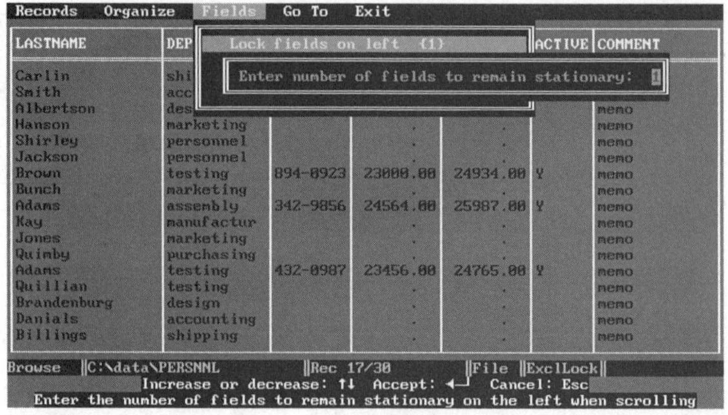

Fig. 7.5
To keep a field visible on the left of the screen, use the Lock Fields on Left command from the Fields menu.

Changing the Size of a Field

Another option you have for modifying the Browse screen is to change the space a field takes up on the screen. For example, if you use the LASTNAME field to know which record you are on, it is possible that you only need the first eight letters of the name to know which employee record you are editing. With dBASE 5, you can shrink the display for the LASTNAME field down to only eight letters and leave the rest of the screen for the fields you must edit.

To change the size of a field, follow these steps:

1. Move the mouse pointer to the right border of the field you want to size.

2. Drag the border (hold mouse button down while moving mouse pointer) to the left or right accordingly.

Or if you don't have a mouse, you can:

1. Move the cursor to the field you want to resize.

2. Open the Fields menu and choose Size Field.

3. With the left- and right-arrow keys, move the borders of the field back and forth to the size you require.

4. Press Enter to set the size for displaying the field.

You also can use the Shift-F7 (Size) keys to change the width of the field.

Note

Changing the size of the field on the Browse screen doesn't change the size of the field in the database itself. If you need to change the field in the database so your data fits better, you must modify the structure. However, if you make a field width in the database structure smaller, you will lose any previously entered information that doesn't fit in the new field size.

◀ See "Modifying a Database Structure," p. 121

Freezing Fields

If you make changes to the same field in many records, you can force the cursor to stay in that field as you move from record to record by "freezing" that field. For example, if you are editing the ZIPCODE field in an address database, you can freeze the ZIPCODE field so that no matter which movement keys you press as you move up and down the screen, the cursor won't leave the ZIPCODE field. Editing a field goes faster when the field is frozen because you can't accidentally move to another field. All the movement keys, such as F3 (Previous) and F4 (Next), move only in the frozen field. If you freeze a field, you are less likely to edit data in the wrong field. And, because you don't have to check which field the cursor is in, data editing is easier and more efficient.

To freeze a field, choose the Freeze Field option from the Fields menu and type in the name of the field you wish to freeze. If you wish to move the cursor out of the frozen field, you must unfreeze the field. To undo the freeze, issue the command a second time and erase the target field.

Just as you can force the cursor to stay in one field by freezing the field, you can keep the cursor in one record in a similar fashion by using the Edit screen rather than the Browse screen to edit. When you are in the Edit screen, you cannot move from a given field in one record to the same field in the next record. Consequently, if you are making changes to several fields in each record, using the Edit screen makes it easier to keep from jumping accidentally to the next record.

Finding Records

After you choose the screen in which to do your editing, the next step is to find the records you want to edit. If the database is small and you're familiar with the records, you can scroll through the database using the Browse screen to find the record to edit. If the database is large, though, simply browsing can become very time-consuming. Then you have several options to speed up the process.

Troubleshooting

I tried to make a field column in the Browse screen smaller, but the size won't go below 10 characters.

The resize process won't narrow a column any more than the width of the field name. If your field name is 10 characters wide, the smallest the field column is displayed is 10 characters wide. Trying to make it smaller deletes the characters from the data shown on the screen but doesn't narrow the column.

I locked a field on the left and now part of my data is gone. What happened?

If you lock a field that sits in the middle of your database, you cannot see any fields to the left of that field. The fields are still there, but they are not visible. For this reason it is important to enter your most important fields first when designing the database structure.

I froze a field and now I want to edit another field but there is no unfreeze command.

To unfreeze a field, use the same command, Freeze Field from the Fields menu, but erase the name of the field to be frozen. You can also just enter the name of the next field to be frozen and that will automatically unfreeze the first field.

Using a Simple Index

When you design your database, you pick one or two of the fields to be key fields. In a personnel database or an address database, the key field is usually the individual's last name. In a simple inventory, the key field can be the part number or the model number.

► See "Reorganizing the Database by Sorting," p. 176

Once you identify a key field, dBASE 5 has the ability to rearrange the records in the order of the key field by creating an index. The index is a list of the record numbers as they would appear if the database was actually reorganized or alphabetized in the order of the key field. For example, a typical index can indicate that the first record in the database, when alphabetized on last name, is record number 32. The second record is number 45, and so on. dBASE 5 can take the index and display the records on the screen in the same order as though they had actually been reorganized.

To display the records in the order of a key field, follow these steps:

1. Open the Organize menu and choose Order Records By Index (see fig. 7.6).

You are shown a list of indexes that matches the key fields you select when you design the database structure. For instance, if you identify LASTNAME as a key field, there is an index listed called LASTNAME.

2. Choose the index you want by double-clicking the index name or moving the cursor and pressing Enter. The records are then displayed in the order of your key field.

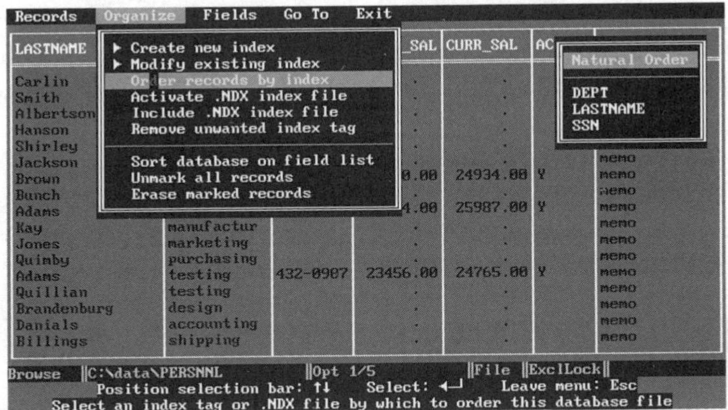

Fig. 7.6
Use the Order Records By Index command to view your database in the order of a key field.

It is much easier to skim your database now when looking for records to edit. To switch back to the natural order that the records were entered originally, select Natural Order from the index list.

Another command that is available when you order records by an index is Follow Record To New Position, in the Records menu. This command controls how the record pointer moves after you make a change to the database that involves a key field. When you order records by an index, dBASE 5 maintains that order throughout any changes you make. If you edit a record and change its key value, the record immediately assumes its proper place in the order based on the new key value. For example, if you found a misspelled name in the LASTNAME field and corrected it, dBASE 5 would automatically move the name to its new position as dictated by the LASTNAME index.

▶ See "Creating Simple Indexes," p. 163

The setting for the Follow Record To New Position command determines whether the screen cursor goes with the new record to its new position, or stays where the record was initially. If the command is set to YES, the cursor moves; if the command is set to NO, the cursor moves to the record that previously followed the changed record. YES is the default setting.

In normal practice, you change the setting to NO if you have to change a whole series of records. If you need to relocate 10 employees from the manufacturing department to 10 other departments, for example, you would order the records by an index on DEPT, do an index search for manufacturing, and then edit the department for each manufacturing entry. When you press the down arrow (in Browse) or PgDn key (in Edit) to move to the next manufacturing record, the record you just changed moves to its new location.

To ensure that the cursor moves to the next manufacturing record, rather than moving with the changed record, you need to change the Follow Record To New Position setting before you start your edits. Access the Records menu, and then select Follow Record To New Position. dBASE changes the setting to the opposite value without prompting you and returns to the work surface.

Using the Go To Menu

Whether or not you use an index, you can jump around the database looking for the records you need. The Go To menu, shown in figure 7.7, has several commands to help you move through the database.

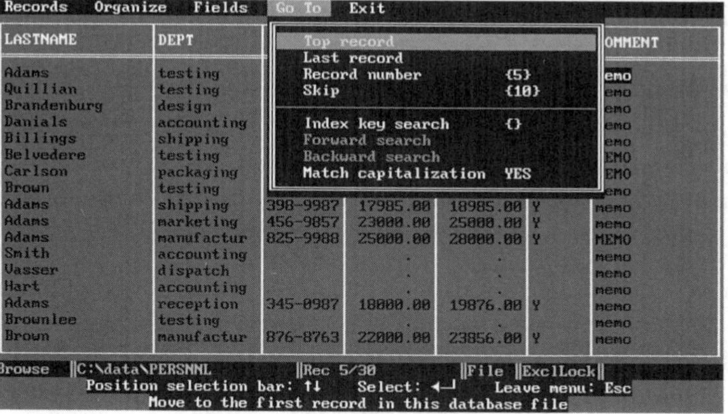

Fig. 7.7
Use the Go To menu to move around the database.

Choosing Top Record from the Go To menu takes you to the very first record in the database. Choosing Last Record takes you to the bottom of the database to the last record.

Choosing Skip will jump down ten records. To change the number of records skipped, choose Skip from the Go To menu, press Enter and in the dialog box that appears, type in the number of records you wish to skip each time.

If you know the record number for the record you're searching for, you can use the Go To Record Number command.

Using the Search Commands

To find records faster, you can also have dBASE 5 search the database for you. If you know the value of a certain field in the record you are looking for, you can ask dBASE 5 to search the database to find the record that has that value in that field.

For example, if you want the record with the value SMITH in the LASTNAME field, using the search commands on the Go To menu will tell dBASE 5 to review all the records in the database until it comes to a record with the value SMITH in the LASTNAME field. dBASE 5 then stops and displays that record at the top of the screen. If it can't find such a record, dBASE 5 displays a `Not Found` message.

To search a database, open the Go To menu and choose the Forward Search command to search from the current record toward the bottom of the database. If dBASE 5 reaches the bottom of the database without finding a match, it starts back at the top.

Use Backward Search to search from the current record toward the top of the database. If dBASE 5 doesn't find a match before reaching the top, it continues the search from the bottom of the database.

To use either Search command, follow these steps:

1. Place the cursor in the field you want to search.
2. Choose the Go To menu.
3. Double-click on either the Forward Search or the Backward Search command.
4. At the Enter Search String: prompt, enter the value you want to find (see fig. 7.8). dBASE 5 finds only exact matches, so you must type the search value exactly as it appears in the database.

You can use wild-card characters in the search string. A *wild card* can be an asterisk (*) or a question mark (?). An asterisk signifies that you don't care what precedes or follows the literal characters in the search string. If you look for New York and you type **New*** as the search string, for example, dBASE finds *New York*, as well as *New Orleans*, *New Brighton*, and any other city beginning with *New*.

The question mark takes the place of a single position in the search string. If you are looking for cities with names of four letters, for example, use the search string **????**. Four question marks limit the search to those cities with four letters. If the first character of the city name is M, for example, modify the search string by typing **M???**.

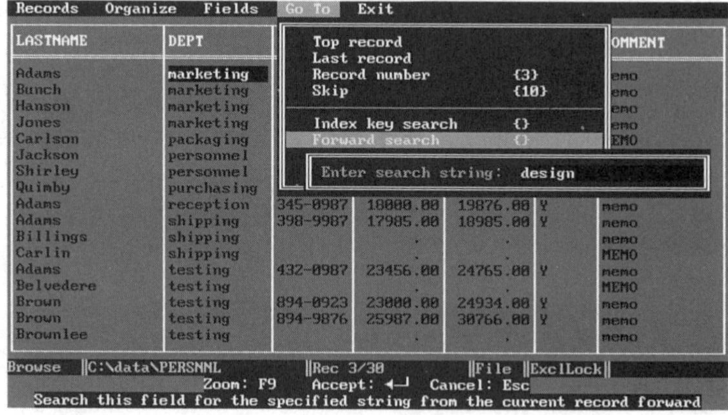

Fig. 7.8
Use the Search commands on the Go To menu to find records with known field values.

If you want the search to match exactly the capitalization as you type it, set the Go To menu command, Match Capitalization, to YES. If you don't care if dBASE 5 finds *smith* or *SMITH* or *Smith*, then set the Match Capitalization command to NO.

▶ See "Using Queries To Search Databases," p. 187

After you find the first occurrence of the field value, you can use the Shift-F3 (Find Previous) and Shift-F4 (Find Next) Keys to move to the next record with a matching field value.

Tip
dBASE 5 enters your search value in the Forward Search and Backward Search slots. You can search forward or backward without retyping the string value.

Note

The Index Key Search command on the Go To menu searches the database in the key field in a manner similar to the Forward and Backward search. It isn't necessary to position the cursor on the key field. With the Index Key Search you can specify multiple fields to search. This command requires an index on multiple fields. For simple, single-field indexes, the Index Key Search offers no advantage over Forward or Backward Search.

Making Changes

After you find the record you want to edit, simply place the cursor on the field to change and type in your changes.

▶ See "Creating Multiple Field Indexes," p. 171

Use the Shift-Tab, Tab, or F3 and F4 keys to move the cursor to the preceding and following fields. In either the Edit or Browse screen, use the left- and right-arrow keys to move the cursor within a field. If you exceed the limits of a field, the left- and right-arrow keys advance the cursor to the adjacent field.

In the Edit screen, PgDn and PgUp will move down and up one record. In the Browse screen, these commands move you down and up one screen.

You can also use the mouse to move the cursor to the field you want to edit by repositioning the mouse pointer and clicking. Clicking the left-most and right-most vertical borders in the Browse screen moves the view area one field to the left or right.

To make changes, you can either type over the information, or first erase it and retype it. Erase old data by using the Backspace key (if the cursor is to the right of the error) or the Delete key (if the cursor is directly on the error). If you want to erase the entire value in a field, open the Fields menu and choose the Blank Field command in the Browse screen.

Note

You can also erase a field partially or totally by using Ctrl-T or Ctrl-Y. These keys erase from the point of the cursor to the right. If you want to erase the entire field, the cursor should be at the left edge of the field.

If you want to insert new characters in the middle of a string, rather than typing over them, press the Ins key, position the cursor where you want to insert the new characters, and type. When you press Ins, the `Ins` indicator appears in the status bar. Pressing Ins a second time turns off the `Ins` indicator and returns dBASE 5 to type-over mode.

Undoing Changes

If you decide that the changes you made to a record are incorrect and you want to restore the original data, undo all the changes you made by opening the Records menu and choosing the Undo Change To Record command.

Caution

You must UNDO changes before you leave the current record. After you leave a record, dBASE 5 records the changes to the record. You can no longer undo the changes, even if you move back to that record again. If this happens, you will have to type the old data back into the record.

Removing Records

You have two options if you need to remove complete records from the database and replace them with new records. You can either blank a record—which blanks all the values in the fields—and fill in new information. Or you can delete a record—which removes it completely from the database—and then later add a new record.

◀ See "Understanding the Data-Entry Process," p. 126

If most of the editing changes that you make are to field values, so that only an occasional record is to be removed completely, blanking records is more convenient than deleting and adding.

If you have many records to remove and many records to add to the database, it's simpler to divide the process into two steps. First delete the records to be removed, as described below under "Deleting Records." When that process is complete, add the new records.

Blanking Records

To blank a record, open the Records menu and choose Blank Record. All field information in that record is removed. You can now type in new information. Blanking a record leaves an *empty* record in the database; it does not *remove* the record from the database. If you want to eliminate the record totally to reflect an employee's resignation, for example, you must delete it.

Note

If you blank a record, the new record with the new information has the same record number as the old record. If you delete a record and then add a new record later, the new record has a new record number and appears in a different position in the database when displayed in natural order.

Deleting Records

Deleting records is a two-step process. First you place a mark on the record, indicating that you want to delete the record. Secondly, you eliminate all the marked records. The second step is called *packing the database*. dBASE 5 has you delete in two steps so that you have the opportunity to reverse your decision and unmark a record. Up until you pack the database, any or all of the records you mark can be unmarked and spared deletion.

Marking Records for Deletion

You can mark a record in one of two ways. You can open the Records menu and choose the Mark Record For Deletion command. This command places a `Del` indicator on the current record; so be sure that you select the correct record before issuing the command. The `Del` indicator appears in the sixth section of the status bar (see fig. 7.9). You also can use the Ctrl-U hot key to mark the record.

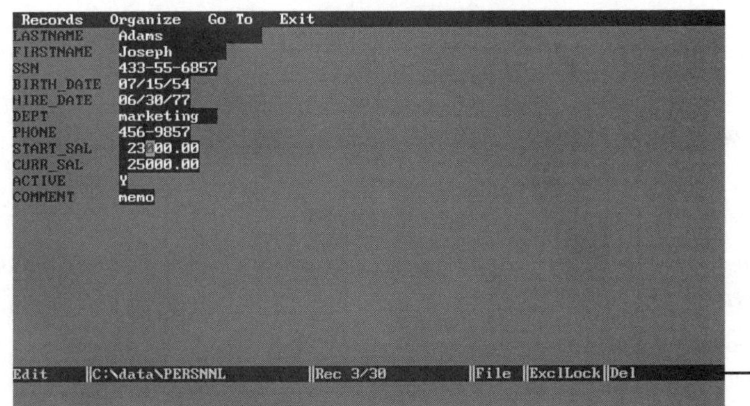

Fig. 7.9
When you mark a record for deletion, `Del` appears on the bottom right of the status bar.

Unmarking Records for Deletion

After you mark a record, you can remove the mark by using the Records menu again. For a record marked for deletion, the menu replaces Mark Record For Deletion with Clear Deletion Mark. Choose Clear Deletion Mark to remove the mark from the current record. You also can remove the deletion mark from a record by pressing Ctrl-U a second time. If you want to remove the marks on all deleted records, open the Organize menu and choose the Unmark All Records command.

Erasing Marked Records

To pack the database and remove all the marked records, open the Organize menu and choose Erase Marked Records.

> **Caution**
>
> Erasing marked records deletes the marked records permanently and renumbers all the records in the database. You cannot recover the deleted records once they've been erased.

Exiting and Closing the Database

When you finish editing the records of your database, choose Exit from the Exit menu to leave. Remember, if you use Esc to leave, any changes to the current record will be abandoned.

To close the database, double-click on the database name in the Control Center and choose Close Database from the dialog box. You can also open another database, and the current database will be closed.

Troubleshooting

After making changes and exiting, I went back into the database and found some of the changes weren't made. What happened?

If you leave the database using Esc, the changes you make to the current record are abandoned. To save the changes, use the Exit menu.

I deleted several records from my database, but when I went back in, the records are still there.

Because Ctrl-U both marks and unmarks records, a possibility is that some records were unmarked inadvertently. Always check for the `Del` indicator on the status bar before erasing marked records. Another possibility is that the records were marked, but not erased. Deleting records involves two steps. First, mark the records by opening the Records menu (or pressing Ctrl-U) and choosing the Mark Record For Deletion command. Then erase the marked records using the Erase Marked Records command from the Organize menu.

I accidentally blanked a record when I tried to blank only a field. What can I do?

Open the Records menu and choose the Undo Change To Record command. This puts all the information back into the record. Do not, however, leave the record before the UNDO, otherwise dBASE 5 saves the blank field values and you won't be able to retrieve the lost information. If this happens, you will have to retype in the lost information—a good reason to have a printout of your database.

From Here...

In this chapter you learned how to enter a database and make editing changes to the field values. You learned how to use a simple index to make it easier to find records and how to remove records by blanking and deleting.

For more information related directly to editing data in your database, refer to the following chapters in this book:

- Chapter 5, "Designing the Structure of a Database," leads you through the design of a database. With proper database design, you can avoid many trips back into the database to edit records.
- Chapter 6, "Adding Records," covers adding records to the database. When numerous records are added and deleted, making it a two-step process can save you time. First delete old records, then add new ones.
- Chapter 9, "Using Queries To Search Databases," shows you how to find records in databases using conditional searches.
- Chapter 18, "Creating Custom Applications," shows you how to create a simple menu system to edit records.

Chapter 8

Organizing Your Database and Generating a Quick Report

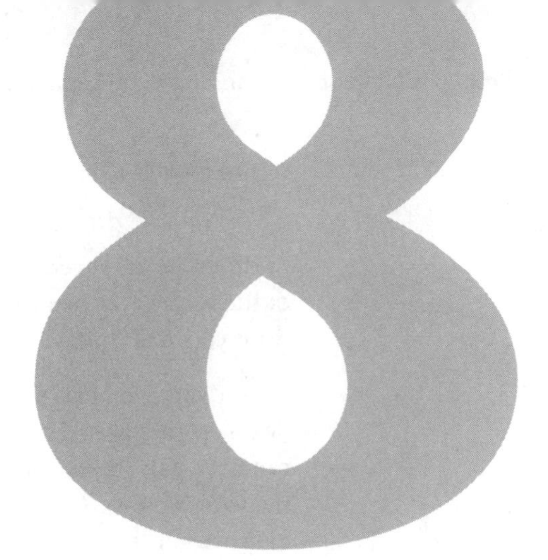

It is seldom that the information fed into a database is in exactly the order you want it to be. Employees don't start at a company in alphabetical order. But having a database ordered in some manner makes finding records easier and makes printouts easier to analyze. Perhaps you would like the names alphabetized, or certain numbers in numerical order. Perhaps you have a video library and you would like a list of your videos alphabetized by title or perhaps by your favorite actors. With your database ordered, records are easy to find, and easy to compare.

In this chapter, you learn how to:

- Organize a database using sorting and indexing
- Print a Quick Report to a printer or to the screen
- Choose your printing options

Organizing the Records for the Report

In dBASE 5 there are two ways to get your data organized the way you want. One way is to rearrange the data itself. Like ordering a deck of cards, each record could be placed in its proper position within the database. Physically rearranging a database is called *sorting*.

Another, more clever way, to organize a database is to simply generate a list of the records in the order they would appear if they were reorganized. Such a list is called an index.

One advantage of an index over sorting is that you can have numerous indexes on the same database. For a video library database, for instance, you can have a list of your videos organized by the title, another list or index with the videos ordered by the starring characters, or another index where the videos are listed by type; all the westerns on one page, all the suspense videos on the next. You can have up to 47 indexes in dBASE 5, so you can order an index in just about any manner you can imagine.

With a dBASE 5 index, you can index a database by alphabetizing on character fields, numeric fields, or date fields. You can alphabetize on one field, then, once that is done, alphabetize on a second or even third field.

For instance, you can order a personnel database by last name, by department, or by the employee's salary. You can also arrange the database by department, and then alphabetize by last name within the department.

You can also order parts of your database; listing for instance, only the employees in a personnel database whose last names start with the letter "B", or perhaps just those that started their employment after a certain date.

Understanding Indexes

Indexes do not actually arrange the records in the database. Instead, dBASE 5 uses an index to display the records in the arranged order on the Browse or Edit screens or in a Quick Report. For example, for a typical personnel database, the LASTNAME index is a list of the records in the order they would be in if the database were reorganized in order of the employees' last names. Records with SMITH in the LASTNAME field would be listed after records with JONES in the LASTNAME field.

In a typical inventory database, the PARTNUM index is a list of parts arranged by part number. The record for the part with a part number of 976 would come immediately after the record for the part with the PARTNUM of 975.

In both of these examples, the field used for the ordering is called the key field or the index key.

The ordering for indexes in dBASE 5 can be either ascending or descending, using the ASCII sort sequence. An ascending order is ordered from A to Z, a descending order, from Z to A.

For the ASCII sort sequence, words with uppercase letters come before words with lowercase letters. In other words, *Zebra* (uppercase Z) would be placed before *animal* (lowercase a) and *animal* would be placed before *zebra* (lowercase z) in an ascending index.

For sorting, in which case the database is completely reorganized and stored to disk in the new order, either the ASCII or the Dictionary sorting sequence can be used. In the Dictionary sorting sequence, words that start with uppercase and lowercase are kept together. *Zebra* and *zebra* would be placed next to each other, and both would appear after *animal*. (*Zebra* would come before *zebra*.)

Note

dBASE 5 indexing, because it uses the ASCII sorting order, places fields starting with numbers before fields starting with letters. In Dictionary sorting, the opposite is true. If the Dictionary sorting sequence for fields with numbers (or numbers and characters) is required, you must sort your database, not index it. See "Reorganizing the Database by Sorting" later in this chapter to learn how to sort and physically rearrange the records.

In dBASE 5, you can have up to 47 indexes. dBASE 5 stores each index in the MDX file and references the indexes by the names you assign. The name of the index is referred to as the *index tag*.

You can index on several fields at the same time. Multiple field indexes are described later in this chapter in the section "Creating Multiple Field Indexes." But, before you can use an index, you must create the index.

Creating Simple Indexes

You can create an index in dBASE 5 in two ways. The first way is to mark a field in the Database design screen. If you change the value of the Index setting to Yes during database design or modification, dBASE 5 creates an index with a tag of the same name as the field name. Figure 8.1 shows the Database design screen. Notice that the LASTNAME, SSN, and DEPT fields are marked Y in the Index column.

Marking a Y in the Index column tells dBASE 5 to create a single field index using that field as the key field.

Layout Organize Append Go To Exit 3:10:55 pm

Bytes remaining: 3897

Num	Field Name	Field Type	Width	Dec	Index
1	LASTNAME	Character	16		Y
2	FIRSTNAME	Character	12		N
3	SSN	Character	11		Y
4	BIRTH_DATE	Date	8		N
5	HIRE_DATE	Date	8		N
6	DEPT	Character	11		N
7	PHONE	Character	8		N
8	START_SAL	Numeric	9	2	N
9	CURR_SAL	Numeric	9	2	N
10	ACTIVE	Logical	1		N
11	COMMENT	Memo	10		N

Database ‖C:\dbasev\PERSNNL ‖Field 1/11 ‖ ExclLock‖
Enter the field name. Insert/Delete field:Ctrl-N/Ctrl-U
Field names begin with a letter and may contain letters, digits and underscores

Fig. 8.1
You can create a single field index by placing a Y in the Index column of the Database Structure Design screen.

Note

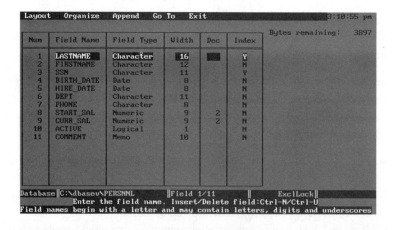

The index that dBASE 5 creates through the Index field in the structure table is *ascending*; that is, the index is organized from the lowest value to the highest value. For character fields, the index also is organized in ASCII sorting sequence.

You also can create an index by opening the Organize menu from the Browse or Edit screens and choosing the Create New Index command (see fig. 8.2).

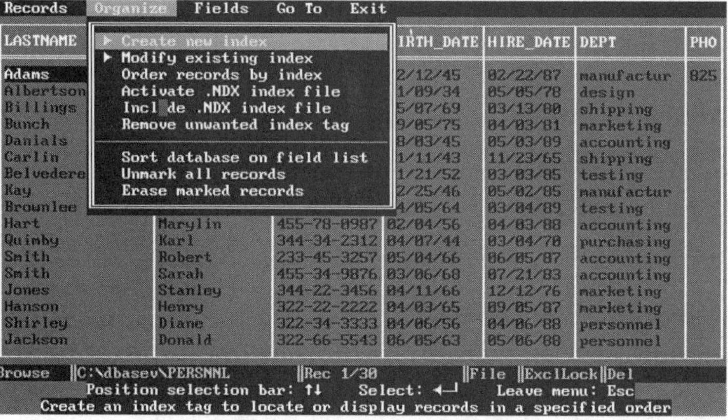

Fig. 8.2
You can create an index from the Organize menu on the Browse or Edit screens.

Follow these steps to create an index from the Organize menu:

1. Open the Organize menu and choose Create New Index.
2. In the submenu that appears, highlight Name of Index and press Enter.

3. Enter the name you want to give the index. For simple indexes, you may want to name the index the same as the key field. For instance, the LASTNAME index orders the personnel database on the LASTNAME field.

4. Highlight Index Expression and press Enter. Enter the expression you want to use. For simple indexes on single fields, the expression is the name of the key field. In the personnel database example, you can type **LASTNAME** to make the LASTNAME field the key field. You can also use more complex expressions to index on multiple fields.

Tip
When you name an index, choose a name that reminds you of the key field(s) used in the index.

Creating More Sophisticated Indexes Using Expressions

dBASE 5 does not limit you to simple indexes on single fields. When you enter the index expression as described previously, you have a wide variety of options in developing an index expression that will best order your data for your purposes.

To build more complex index expressions on multiple fields and characteristics of fields, it is important to understand the use of expressions and functions in dBASE 5. Expressions are used in creating indexes, in creating queries, custom reports, and custom input screens.

All the expressions and functions described in the following sections are just a small sampling of what is available in dBASE 5. These expressions and functions can be used to create more sophisticated indexes that can in turn be used to make more sophisticated reports using the Quick Report described later in this chapter.

Understanding Expressions

An expression in dBASE 5 is simply a statement about the value in a field. For example, the expression LASTNAME means the value in the LASTNAME field. The expression LASTNAME+FIRSTNAME means the value in the LASTNAME field connected directly—or concatenated—to the value in the FIRSTNAME field, including blank spaces. If the value in the LASTNAME field with a field width of eight is Quincy and the value in the FIRSTNAME field for the same record is John, the expression LASTNAME+FIRSTNAME would return the value Quincy(space)(space)John.

▶ See "Searching for Records with Multiple Conditions," p. 207

▶ See "Replacing Values," p. 237

▶ See "Adding Calculated Fields," p. 274

If you used the expression LASTNAME+FIRSTNAME in an index expression, the resulting index would be called a multiple field index and would tell dBASE 5 to first order the database on the LASTNAME, then on the FIRSTNAME. This ordering sequence is similar to the alphabetizing in a phone book.

The expression LASTNAME–FIRSTNAME (minus sign instead of plus sign) would mean the value in the LASTNAME field concatenated to the value in the FIRSTNAME field without spaces. In terms of the preceding example, this expression would return the value **QuincyJohn (space, space)**.

You might use this expression to use an index search where you did not want to be concerned with blank spaces at the end of fields.

▶ See "Adding Calculated Fields," p. 302

Expressions can be mathematical in nature. The expression PRES_SAL – STRT_SAL means the mathematical difference between the value in the PRES_SAL field and the STRT_SAL field. Subtracting the starting salary from the present salary in a sample personnel database would give you the total raises an employee had received. Using such an expression as an index expression would enable you to order a database on employees' raises without actually calculating the actual raises.

Using Functions in Expressions

You can also use functions in your expressions. A function is a programming-like command that tells dBASE to do something to a value. This value may be the value from a field, like Quincy, it may be a variable used in a dBASE program, or it may be a value entered on the screen by a computer operator. Depending on the specific function, the values used may be character values, numeric values, logic values, or date values.

Using Character Functions

An example of a character function useful in index expressions is **LEFT( ).** This function is used in the syntax format:

```
LEFT(<string>/<memo field name>, <number>)
```

This function tells dBASE to take the left number of characters from either a character string or a memo field. For instance, LEFT(LASTNAME,4) means take the left four characters from the value in the field LASTNAME. In our example, this function would produce Quin.

Using this function in an index expression would enable you to order your database on just the left four characters of a given field. Perhaps you had placed a special salesman's sales area code as the first four characters of a memo or comments field in a sample real estate database. By using the LEFT( ) function you could order your database on this code even though the comments field or memo field had other information in it.

The RIGHT( ) function has a similar syntax:

```
RIGHT(<string> / <memo field name> , <number>)
```

This function could be used to order a database on the characters at the end, or on the right, in a character field. Perhaps you have an inventory listing that must be ordered on the bin location of parts which you have coded into the last four characters of the part number. You can use the RIGHT( ) function to order your database on this subsection code.

The **SUBSTR( )** function performs like the RIGHT( ) and the LEFT( ) functions except that it finds characters in the middle of character fields. The SUBSTR( ) syntax is

```
        SUBSTR(<string> / <memo field name>, <start position>,
    [<number of characters>])
```

The <start position> specifies the starting position from which characters are copied. The optional *<number of characters>* specifies how many characters to copy. If *<number of characters>* is omitted, all characters to the end of the input string are copied to the returned value.

Using this function in an index expression would enable you to order your database on middle characters of a field. Perhaps the location code in the inventory database is the middle three numbers rather than the last four. You could use the SUBSTR( ) function to pull these characters and order the database by them.

Two more functions useful in creating index expressions are the UPPER( ) and LOWER( ) functions. The syntax for these functions is:

```
UPPER(<string>)
LOWER(<string>)
```

The UPPER( ) and LOWER( ) functions change all the letters of a string to upper- or lowercase. You can use these functions when you want to order a database as though all the characters in the specified field were capitalized even though they aren't capitalized in the database itself. They can be used to change the ordering of a database from ASCII to Dictionary.

Using Numeric Functions

Many dBASE 5 functions are designed to work on numeric fields rather than character fields. These functions return a numeric result. One example of a numeric function useful in creating an index expression is the INT( ) function. This function has the following syntax:

```
INT(<numeric expression>)
```

INT( ) returns the integer value of a number. The integer value of a number is that number with any digits to the right of the decimal removed. With the

INT( ) function, the number 12.23487 becomes the integer 12. This function might be used where you wanted to order your precious metal inventory by weight categories. Ingots weighing between 12 and 13 ounces, for example, would be listed together, but not necessarily in the order of exact weight.

Combining Data Types in an Index Expression

As mentioned earlier in this chapter, you can *concatenate*, or combine, character fields. If LASTNAME and FIRSTNAME are both character fields, you can use the expression LASTNAME + FIRSTNAME as an index key. Concatenation works only for character fields. You cannot, for example, concatenate a numeric field with a character field, or a date field with a numeric field.

Several dBASE 5 functions enable you to convert numeric and date fields into character strings so you can create index key expressions that mix different data types.

Converting Dates to Strings

To combine a character field with a date field in a single index expression, you must convert the date to a character string using an expression such as the following:

```
DEPT + DTOS(HIRE_DATE)
```

The DTOS( ) function returns a character string in the format YYYYMMDD for the HIRE_DATE value. This string is concatenated to the DEPT character field value. In the example personnel database, an index with this expression would order the database by department, then would list employees within the same department by HIRE_DATE

Converting Numeric Values to Strings

In much the same way that you combine dates and character strings, you can combine character strings and numerics. Rather than the DTOS( ) function, you use the STR( ) function to convert numerics to strings. To do so, index the database with the following expression:

```
DEPT + STR(STRT_SAL)
```

The STR( ) function returns a character string for the STRT_SAL value. A returned string has no numeric value, but is simply a sequence of digits that can be concatenated to the DEPT value. In the example personnel database, an index with this expression would order the database by department, then would list employees within the same department by their starting salaries.

Converting Both Dates and Numerics to Strings

Combining an index on a date type and a numeric type requires you to convert both types to strings using the appropriate functions.

DTOS(Date field) + STR(numeric field)

With an expression similar to this, a product sales inventory database could be ordered on a field with a projected sales date, then on a second field with a projected sales price.

Using Nesting Functions

In dBASE 5 it is possible to nest functions; that is, to take a function of a function. If you needed to concatenate a model number with the first four digits of a price code, you could use the STR( ) function on the price code to generate the character string for the price. Then, to get the left four digits of the price character string, you could use the LEFT( ) function. Such an expression might look like this:

MODEL_NUM + LEFT(STR(PRICE))

Caution

Avoid mismatching function types, such as nesting a numeric function when the outer function requires a character argument.

Tip

Always count your parentheses when using nested functions. There should always be an equal number of left and right parentheses.

Using the dBASE 5 Expression Builder

When entering an index expression you can type in the expression, or you can use the dBASE 5 Expression Builder. When you are prompted for the index expression as described below, rather than typing the expression, press Shift-F1. From the dialog box, pick the field you are using, the operator, and any functions.

▶ See "Replacing Values," p. 237

The use of expressions and functions gives you great flexibility in creating indexes.

Using Indexes

Once you have created an index, you can use it to order your database for viewing in the Browse or Edit screens, or for printing a Quick Report. To use an index, open the Organize menu from the Edit or Browse screens, and choose the Order Records By Index option. dBASE 5 displays a pick list of all the index names—called index tags—in the production index file. Choose an index tag from the list by highlighting it and pressing Enter. As you highlight a tag, the key (or index expression) for that tag is shown to the left of the tag name (see fig. 8.3).

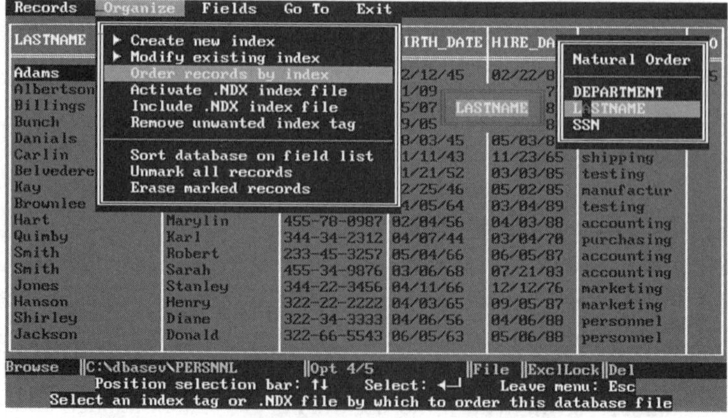

Fig. 8.3 When you highlight your index choice, the index expression appears next to the name.

After you choose an index, dBASE 5 orders the database (see fig. 8.4). If you want to revert to the original order of the database, you can select the Natural Order option at the top of the pick list.

Records Organize Fields Go To Exit

LASTNAME	FIRSTNAME	SSN	BIRTH_DATE	HIRE_DATE	DEPT	PHO
			/ /	/ /		
Adams	George	433-65-9876	12/12/45	02/22/87	manufactur	825
Adams	Joseph	433-55-6857	07/15/54	06/30/77	marketing	456
Adams	Robert	344-43-4983	07/06/60	01/01/92	test	432
Adams	Sarah	342-98-9875	00/09/67	01/04/77	assembly	342
Adams	Sharon	564-98-9843	09/08/66	02/03/89	reception	345
Adams	Kathy	432-23-4567	07/08/71	02/03/90	shipping	398
Albertson	Ronald	233-54-3423	11/09/34	05/05/78	design	
Belvedere	Philip	344-65-4534	11/21/52	03/03/85	testing	
Billings	Nathanial	344-56-7866	05/07/69	03/13/80	shipping	
Brandenburg	Gustaf	344-56-3454	03/04/55	04/06/88	design	
Brown	Robert	344-98-8757	09/07/65	09/05/90	test	894
Brown	John	322-98-3456	09/04/56	09/03/77	test	894
Brown	Daniel	766-98-7856	06/04/67	08/02/88	manufactur	876
Brownlee	Jason	655-43-2312	04/05/64	03/04/89	testing	
Bunch	Michael	333-33-3333	09/05/75	04/03/81	marketing	
Carlin	Steve	233-43-2121	11/11/43	11/23/65	shipping	

Browse C:\dbasev\PERSNNL Rec 22/30 File ExclLock

Fig. 8.4 The personnel database ordered using the LASTNAME index.

After you select an index tag to use, that index stays in effect for any work you do with the database until you select another tag or close the database.

When you close the database, dBASE 5 loses its memory for which index, if any, you set. If you want to reorder the database later, you must select that index tag again from the Organize menu.

In the following section you learn how to use indexes with complex key expressions for specific applications.

Creating Multiple Field Indexes

One of the most common uses of complex index expressions is to create indexes on more than one field.

Suppose that you want to create an index that organizes employees initially by last name, then by first name within last name. In other words, you would like dBASE 5 to first order the records by alphabetizing on the LASTNAME field. Then, for all records with the same last name, you would like these records ordered by alphabetizing on the first name. (This is exactly the way a phone book is ordered.) The index must reference two fields simultaneously, LASTNAME and FIRSTNAME; you can't do that by entering Y in the Index column of the Database design screen as you would for a simple index. To create an index using multiple fields, display the Browse screen, open the Organize menu, and choose the Create New Index command. Name the multiple field index just as you name a single field index.

For the index expression, you must enter a combination of the fields on which you want to order the database. The field names must be combined or *concatenated*. To form an index that first orders a database on LASTNAME, then on FIRSTNAME, type **lastname+firstname**. (You also can type **LASTNAME+FIRSTNAME**.) If necessary, you can concatenate more than two character fields. You can, for example, include the employee's middle initial in the index to organize names in which the last and first names are the same. To include an INITIAL field in the index, use the index expression lastname+firstname+initial.

The key expression to order records in a real estate property database first on AREA, then on AGENT, is area+agent. Using such an index would list the properties grouped together by area; within each area, the properties are grouped together by agent. Such a list would be useful for searching for properties in a given area, then finding out which agent is handling that property.

If the key expression is entered as agent+area, the list would have the properties organized by agent; for each agent, the properties would be grouped by area. Such a list is handy for reviewing each agent's list of properties and the areas in which they are located.

Tip
When you include a field name in an expression, you can type the name in uppercase, lowercase, or any combination of the two.

Approximating Dictionary and ASCII Ordering

When you first create an index expression, you may be perplexed at the results of an alphabetical sort. For example, *BAKER* comes before *abercrombie*. dBASE's default sort order is based on the ASCII character set. ASCII is an acronym for American Standard Code for Information Interchange and refers to a standard way computers store data internally. ASCII order arranges all uppercase letters before lowercase letters, which means uppercase *B* comes before lowercase *a*.

Functions placed within the indexing expression can correct this problem, however. You can convert the field you are indexing to upper- or lowercase before indexing. If you want to order a database on the LASTNAME field and then on the FIRSTNAME field using the dictionary sort order, for example, you can use the following index key expression:

UPPER(LASTNAME + FIRSTNAME)

The actual values of the field in the database do not change when you index with this expression. Rather, dBASE 5 concatenates the LASTNAME and FIRSTNAME fields into one field, converts all characters to uppercase, and then stores that value in the index file as the key for that record. The database appears the same, but the displayed order changes: *abercrombie* comes before *BAKER*. This sort order is the order a dictionary follows when alphabetizing and is easier for the user to comprehend.

Using Conditional Indexing

dBASE 5 enables you to set up an index that selects records to display which meet a given condition. To list only employees in the personnel database example whose last name is Adams, you can create an index that is restricted to just those people using the FOR clause on the Create New Index submenu (see fig. 8.5). Restricting the index has the effect of hiding records that do not meet the condition you specify. When the index is active, you see only the records that meet the condition.

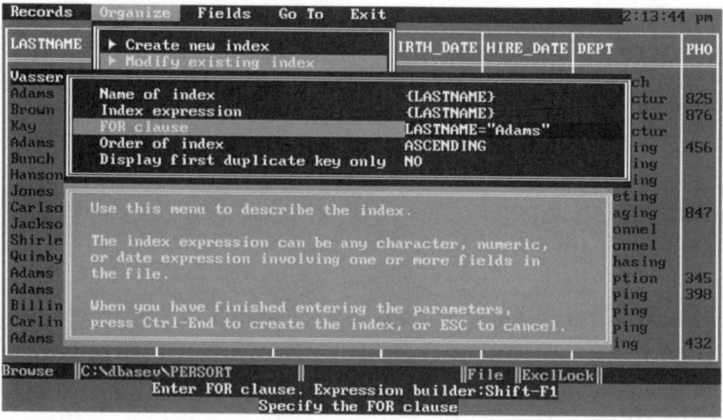

Fig. 8.5
The FOR clause option enables you to select records that match a set condition.

To set up an index condition, open the Organize menu, choose the Create New Index option, and select the FOR clause option in the dialog box.

You set the conditions in the FOR clause option by referencing the name of the field on which you want to set the restriction (in fig. 8.5, the field is LASTNAME), providing a logical operator (in this case, the equal sign), and specifying the condition (in this case, "Adams"). You use quotation marks to enclose the condition only when the field being restricted is a character field. If you work with a numeric field, don't use punctuation around the number condition (START SAL = 25000, for example). If you work with a date field, enclose the date in braces (for example, HIRE_DATE = {01/01/89}).

Searching with Indexes

In Chapter 7, you learned how to search a database for particular field values for the purpose of editing. One of the drawbacks of the search commands on the Go To menu is that they only work on one field at a time. In a personnel file, for instance, you can look for the last name *Smith* or you can look for the first name *Joe*, but you cannot search for *Joe Smith*.

To search for values in multiple fields, such as finding an employee with the name *Joe Smith*, you can use the Index Key Search command on the Go To menu of the Edit and Browse screens.

First create an index on the multiple fields you want to search (if you haven't already done so). To find a match in the FIRSTNAME field and the LASTNAME field, create an index with the key expression lastname+firstname. After you have established the index, order the database on that index by opening the Organize menu and choosing the Order Records By Index command. Once the database is ordered, use the Index Key Search option in the Go To menu to find the records you want. You don't have to locate the cursor in a particular field before you conduct the search. The search process only searches the fields listed in the index key expression. Other fields are ignored.

dBASE 5 searches the database on the index and, if the program finds a matching value, moves the cursor to that record. If more than one record in the database meets the search condition, dBASE 5 moves the record pointer to the first record in the list.

Because the database has been rearranged by the key fields, all the other records that meet the condition are immediately below the first record.

Note

When you enter a search value for a complex index expression, dBASE 5 does a literal search for the value, including blank spaces. Consequently, you must account for the full width of the field in specifying a search expression. To locate the record for Richard Mather, for example, you have to type Mather(*six spaces*)Richard, making sure to follow the last name with enough blanks or spaces—six in this case—to fill out 12 character positions (the field width). To get around this difficulty, index on LASTNAME–FIRSTNAME. Use a minus sign rather than a plus sign between the field names. With this index, you can specify the search value as MatherRichard (no spaces).

Troubleshooting

I try to set up an index in the database design screen but nothing happens.

You cannot index on logical or memo fields. Make sure the field you choose is either a character, date, or numerical field.

I set up an index on multiple fields, but the database is ordered by the wrong field first. Rather than organizing by state, then city, it's organizing by city first.

When you concatenate the fields, the field you want ordered first should appear in the concatenation first. For ordering first on State then City, use STATE+CITY.

When I order my databases by last name, the name "deSimone" is appearing in the wrong place.

The indexing process uses an ASCII order sequence in which all capital letters go before all lowercase letters. A name starting with a capital *Z* comes before a name starting with a lowercase *a*. To move deSimone to the right position, you can try capitalizing the first letter. If that doesn't work, you can use the following expression as the index key expression:

UPPER(LASTNAME+FIRSTNAME)

This key expression will index on the last name and first name as though they were capitalized in the database. It does not actually change the field values to all capitals.

I try to use a FOR condition index, but no records ever match the condition. What is wrong?

The condition must be met perfectly. If the capitalization is different, dBASE 5 won't find matching records. See Chapter 9, "Using Queries To Search Databases," for more information on specifying search conditions.

Using Other Options on the Organize Menu

When you create an index using the Organize menu (see fig. 8.6), you have several options not available when you create an index in the Database Structure design screen.

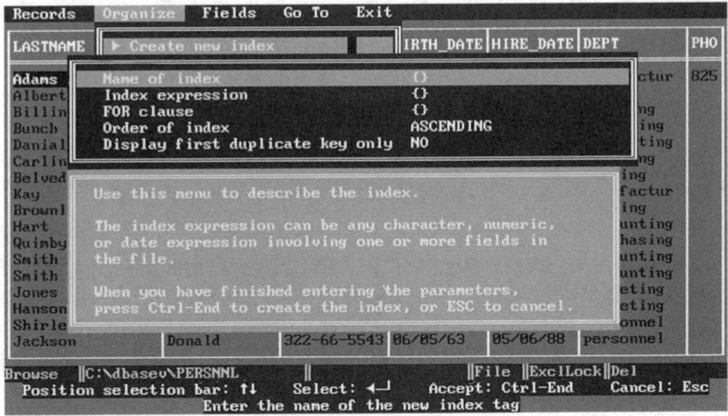

Fig. 8.6
You have several options from which to choose when creating an index.

You can choose the order of the index. You can select ASCENDING (lowest to highest within the range of values), or you can select DESCENDING (highest to lowest within the range of values). In a character field, an ascending index progresses from the letter A to the letter Z.

To put your index in descending order, open the Organize menu, choose Create New Index, highlight the Order Of Index option in the submenu, and press the space bar or Enter to change the setting from ASCENDING to DESCENDING.

The Display First Duplicate Key Only command controls whether records with duplicate index values are displayed. When set to NO, all records with the same value in the key field are displayed. When set to YES, only the first occurrence of the value is displayed. For example, in a personnel database, when the command is set to NO, all employees with the LASTNAME of Brown are displayed. With the command set to YES, only the first Brown in the list is displayed. The other employees with the LASTNAME of Brown are not displayed.

The Organize menu also enables you to delete an index tag or to modify one. To remove a tag, select Remove Unwanted Index Tag; then choose the index from the pick list that appears.

To modify an existing index, open the Organize menu and choose Modify Existing Index. Choose the index you want to modify. Modifying a tag involves the same choices you make when you create a tag.

Reorganizing the Database by Sorting

In previous sections of this chapter, you learned how to use an index to rearrange your records prior to printing your Quick Report. You also learned that such an arrangement uses the ASCII ordering sequence. If the ASCII ordering sequence doesn't do the job for you, you have the option to physically rearrange the records by sorting. When you sort a database, you can use either ASCII or Dictionary ordering sequences.

Dictionary order follows the conventions used in arranging entries in a standard English dictionary; uppercase and lowercase versions of the same letter are considered the same letter. Indexing, on the other hand, uses ASCII order to arrange entries. *ASCII order* sorts uppercase letters (A through Z) before lowercase letters (a through z). In ASCII sequence, for instance, the name *daVinci* is sorted after the name *Zola*.

When sorting, dBASE 5 rearranges the records, assigns the records new numbers, and stores them on disk in a separate database file. After sorting a database, you have two copies of the same data: the original database and the sorted database. You can get rid of the original after the sort, but you have a period of time in which both copies are on disk.

Tip
Before deleting your old, unsorted file, check your new file to make sure the sort performed the way you intended.

Note

When a database is sorted to a new file, the sorted order becomes the new natural order.

In an indexed database, new records are included in the index as they are added (when they appear on-screen), or in a report in their proper place. New records added to a sorted database are added at the bottom of the database, and aren't in their proper place. To move new records to their proper place, you must again sort the database.

Remember, indexing does not physically move records, but only displays them in the indexed order. Sorting moves records into their proper place, and they stay there until the database is again sorted and new record numbers are assigned.

To sort on one or more fields, follow these steps:

1. Open the Organize menu and choose Sort Database On Field List.
2. A screen form appears. Enter the field(s) you want the database sorted on and the type of sort you require (see fig. 8.7). The first field named in the list determines the highest level of the sort; other fields named below it are secondary sorts. You don't have to select the same sort type for each field in the list. You can make one field sort Ascending Dictionary and the next Descending ASCII.
3. When you finish specifying the sort conditions, press Ctrl-End.
4. dBASE 5 asks for the name of the file in which you want to store the sorted records. Type a name and press Enter. If the name is already in use, you are asked to verify that you want to overwrite that file.
5. You are then asked whether you want to supply a description for the file. If you provide a description, it appears on the file identification line of the Control Center whenever you highlight the file in the Data panel.

After you sort the database, the records appear in sorted order when reviewed in the Browse or Edit screen, or when listed in a Quick Report.

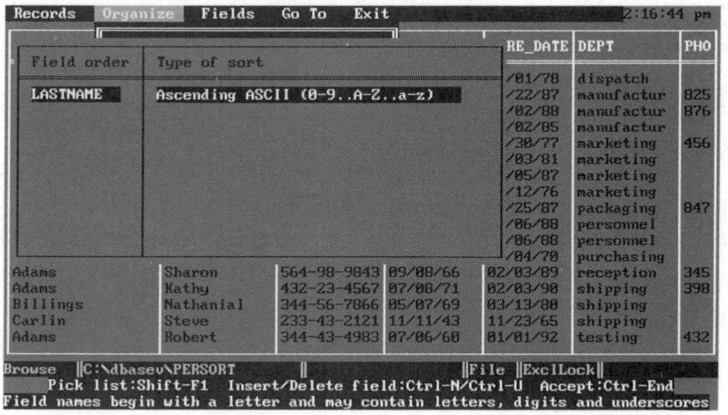

Fig. 8.7
Sorting a database is done from the Organize menu of the Browse or Edit screens.

Note

To select the name of a field in the Sort menu, you can type the name of the field or press Shift-F1 (Pick List) to bring up a list of fields. Highlight the field you want and press Enter to place it. To change the type of sort, press Enter from the Field order column and use the space bar to cycle to the sort order you want. All fields—character, numeric, and date—have the same possibilities. You can't sort on a logical or memo field.

Generating a Quick Report

The purpose of setting up databases, and presumably the reason you design your own, is to keep track of information. Perhaps the information is accounting data such as accounts receivable, accounts payable, and general ledger. Or perhaps the data is the result of a telephone survey, or maybe it is credit card order information for a mail order business. Regardless of the source, it's not always sufficient to simply store the information in the computer. At some time or another, you will want to take that information out of the computer and print it on paper.

A paper printout—perhaps because of our history with the printed word—is often easier to read than a display screen. It is also easier to jump between pages when visually scanning. A paper printout is also easier to fax (for now), easier to store in a file drawer, and easier to review without a computer. Paper printouts make good backups if you make mistakes during the editing process and lose information. Paper printouts are easier to make copies from and easier to share at committee meetings. Paper printouts are easier to make penciled editing changes to, and paper printouts don't fade when the electricity fails. Paper printouts also make better paper airplanes.

Regardless of your reason for needing a paper printout of your database, dBASE 5 provides you with several options. The Quick Report is a quick and easy report format you can use to list the information in your database. Later, in Chapter 12, "Creating Custom Reports," you learn the more advanced techniques for printing the information in your database and for choosing which information to print.

Using the Default Quick Report Form

If you need a quick printout of the database in its natural order, or the order in which the records were entered, you can print the default Quick Report. You can arrange the data for the report using either sorting or indexing. In fact, anytime you have ordered a database on the Browse or Edit screen, the Quick Report will print the data in the same order.

You also will learn how to change the various printing options.

To print a Quick Report, follow these steps:

1. From the Control Panel screen, click the database you wish to use for the report.

2. Press Shift-F9 (Quick Report) or click Quick Report in the navigation line at the bottom of the screen.

3. From the Quick Report menu that appears (see fig. 8.8), choose Begin Printing. Your Quick Report starts printing on the system default printer.

Note

If the last page of your report doesn't print, press Form Feed on your printer or open the Quick Report menu and choose Eject Page Now.

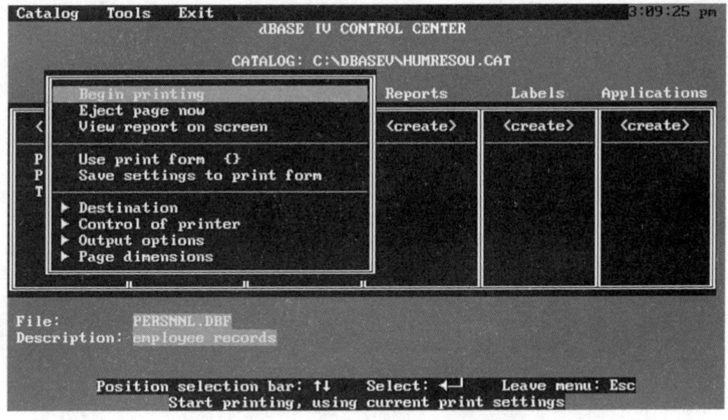

Fig. 8.8
For a Quick Report of your database, press Shift-F9 and choose Begin Printing from the menu.

Note

The Quick Report menu is the same menu you see when you open the Print menu from the Custom Report design screen, as described in Chapter 12.

Tip
For Quick Reports, use a wide carriage printer and the smallest print available.

The Quick Report prints in the simple table format, shown in figure 8.9, with each field name as the head of a column and each record representing a row. It's very similar to the Browse screen, discussed in Chapter 7. In the Quick Report, all numeric fields are totaled, and the total prints at the bottom of the report.

Fig. 8.9
A sample Quick Report.

```
Page No.    1
05/25/94
```

LASTNAME	FIRSTNAME	SSN	HIRE_DATE	DEPT	PHONE
			/ /		
Adams	George	433-65-9876	02/22/87	manufactur	825-9988
Adams	Joseph	433-55-6857	06/30/77	marketing	456-9857
Adams	Kathy	432-23-4567	02/03/90	shipping	398-9987
Adams	Robert	344-43-4983	01/01/92	testing	432-0987
Adams	Sarah	342-98-9875	01/04/77	assembly	342-9856
Adams	Sharon	564-98-9843	02/03/89	reception	345-0987
Albertson	Ronald	233-54-3423	05/05/78	design	
Belvedere	Philip	344-65-4534	03/03/85	testing	
Billings	Nathanial	344-56-7866	03/13/80	shipping	
Brandenburg	Gustaf	344-56-3454	04/06/88	design	
Brown	Daniel	766-98-7856	08/02/88	manufactur	876-8763
Brown	John	322-98-3456	09/03/77	testing	894-0923
Brown	Robert	344-98-8757	09/05/90	testing	894-9876
Brownlee	Jason	655-43-2312	03/04/89	testing	
Bunch	Michael	333-33-3333	04/03/81	marketing	
Carlin	Steve	233-43-2121	11/23/65	shipping	
Carlson	Bonnie	344-67-9990	12/25/87	packaging	847-9887
Danials	Danny	344-56-4534	05/03/89	accounting	
Hanson	Henry	322-22-2222	09/05/87	marketing	
Hart	Marylin	455-78-0987	04/03/88	accounting	
Jackson	Donald	322-66-5543	05/06/88	personnel	
Jones	Stanley	344-22-3456	12/12/76	marketing	
Kay	James	343-43-3443	05/02/85	manufactur	
Quillian	Nathanial	344-45-4433	03/01/88	testing	
Quimby	Karl	344-34-2312	03/04/70	purchasing	
Shirley	Diane	322-34-3333	04/06/88	personnel	
Smith	Robert	233-45-3257	06/05/87	accounting	
Smith	Sarah	455-34-9876	07/21/83	accounting	
Vasser	Robert	455-67-9876	01/01/78	dispatch	

► See "Modifying, Moving, and Removing Fields and Text," p. 330

If your database has more fields than can fit on one width of paper, dBASE 5 folds the columns back so that each record takes up two or three rows at a time, depending on how many fields there are. The names at the top of the columns also fold back, as shown in figure 8.10. You can remove fields so the report will fit on the page by editing the Quick Report layout using the Report design screen.

```
Page No.  1
05/25/94

LASTNAME      FIRSTNAME       SSN          BIRTH_DATE  HIRE_DATE  DEPT
PHONE    START_SAL   CURR_SAL  ACTIVE      COMMENT

                                             / /         / /
            0.00            0.00
Adams          George         433-65-9876  12/12/45    02/22/87   manufactur
825-9988  25000.00    28000.00   Y         skilled in CNC milling machines
Adams          Joseph         433-55-6857  07/15/54    06/30/77   marketing
456-9857  23000.00    25000.00   Y
Adams          Kathy          432-23-4567  07/08/71    02/03/90   shipping
398-9987  17985.00    18985.00   Y
Adams          Robert         344-43-4983  07/06/60    01/01/92   testing
432-0987  23456.00    24765.00   Y
Adams          Sarah          342-98-9875  08/09/67    01/04/77   assembly
342-9856  24564.00    25987.00   Y
Adams          Sharon         564-98-9843  09/08/66    02/03/89   reception
345-0987  18000.00    19876.00   Y
Albertson      Ronald         233-54-3423  11/09/34    05/05/78   design
            0.00            0.00
Belvedere      Philip         344-65-4534  11/21/52    03/03/85   testing
            0.00            0.00           Has three kids graduating from college the same
                                           year

Billings       Nathanial      344-56-7866  05/07/69    03/13/80   shipping
            0.00            0.00
Brandenburg    Gustaf         344-56-3454  03/04/55    04/06/88   design
            0.00            0.00
Brown          Daniel         766-98-7856  06/04/67    08/02/88   manufactur
876-8763  22000.00    23856.00   Y
Brown          John           322-98-3456  09/04/56    09/03/77   testing
894-0923  23000.00    24934.00   Y
Brown          Robert         344-98-8757  09/07/65    09/05/90   testing
894-9876  25987.00    30766.00   Y
Brownlee       Jason          655-43-2312  04/05/64    03/04/89   testing
            0.00            0.00
Bunch          Michael        333-33-3333  09/05/75    04/03/81   marketing
            0.00            0.00
Carlin         Steve          233-43-2121  11/11/43    11/23/65   shipping
            0.00            0.00
Carlson        Bonnie         344-67-9990  02/23/45    12/25/87   packaging
847-9887 230000.00            0.00     Y   Started work month early

Danials        Danny          344-56-4534  08/03/45    05/03/89   accounting
            0.00            0.00
Hanson         Henry          322-22-2222  04/03/65    09/05/87   marketing
            0.00            0.00
Hart           Marylin        455-78-0987  02/04/56    04/03/88   accounting
            0.00            0.00
Jackson        Donald         322-66-5543  06/05/63    05/06/88   personnel
            0.00            0.00

Jones          Stanley        344-22-3456  04/11/66    12/12/76   marketing
            0.00            0.00
Kay            James          343-43-3443  12/25/46    05/02/85   manufactur
            0.00            0.00
Quillian       Nathanial      344-45-4433  09/08/67    03/01/88   testing
            0.00            0.00
Quimby         Karl           344-34-2312  04/07/44    03/04/70   purchasing
            0.00            0.00
Shirley        Diane          322-34-3333  04/06/56    04/06/88   personnel
            0.00            0.00
Smith          Robert         233-45-3257  05/04/66    06/05/87   accounting
            0.00            0.00
Smith          Sarah          455-34-9876  03/06/68    07/21/83   accounting
            0.00            0.00
Vasser         Robert         455-67-9876  08/12/45    01/01/78   dispatch
            0.00            0.00
     432992.00       222169.00
```

Fig. 8.10
If there are too many fields for the Quick Report, the fields fold back on themselves.

Choosing Quick Report Printing and Display Options

There are several options on the Quick Report menu to help you control the printing and display of your report (see fig. 8.11).

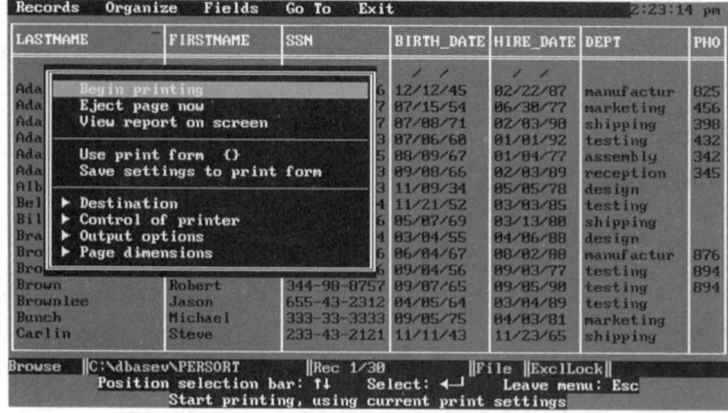

Fig. 8.11
You can access printing and display options for the Quick Report by pressing Shift-F9.

Table 8.1 describes the options on the menu shown in figure 8.11.

Table 8.1 Quick Report Printing and Display Options

Option	Purpose
Begin Printing	Sends the report to the selected destination (printer or file)
Eject Page Now	Use to form-feed paper
View Report On Screen	Prints report to screen
Use Print Form { }	Uses custom printer settings
Save Settings To Print Form	Saves custom printer settings
Destination	Displays a menu to select printer or file as the destination
Control of Printer	Displays a menu to select text quality and page-advance options
Output Options	Displays a menu to select pages to print, starting page number, and number of copies
Page Dimensions	Displays a menu to select page length, offset, and line spacing

With the Use Print Form{ } command, you can print your report in different formats automatically. If you use different printers or different types of paper, you can either change the print options each time you print, or you can save the settings to a print form. Use the Save Settings To Print Form command to save the settings. Give the print form a name that will remind you of the reason for the print form. You can call it LEGAL.PTF if the form is set up to print on legal paper. Once you save it, you can use that print form anytime with the Use Print Form command.

With the Destination command, you can send the report to a file and call it up with a word processor for more advanced formatting such as using fonts or including graphics.

Troubleshooting

When I print out the Quick Report, the fields are scattered all over the paper and don't make any sense to me.

You probably have more fields in the database than dBASE 5 can print across one page of paper. When this happens, the fields are folded back on the page. The first couple of lines are the field names; the next couple of lines are the field values for the first record, and so on. You can either use a wider printer or smaller type. Your other option is to go to Chapter 12 and learn how to create a custom report. Then you can have the fields print out any way you choose.

When I try to print my report, the last page won't come out of my laser printer.

Use the form feed button on the printer or the Eject Page Now option from the Quick Report menu. Either command will tell the printer to eject the last page.

When I printed my report, all the records were in the wrong order.

Check the index expression for the index you specified. You may have inadvertently ordered the database on the wrong field.

My report only included employees with the last name of Quincy. Where are the rest of the records?

Check the index you used for ordering. If it is the one you want, check the FOR Condition for that index and make sure it is blank.

From Here...

In this chapter you learned how to print a Quick Report and how to order the records in your database for displaying and reporting purposes.

For more information on printing your database, refer to the following chapters in this book:

- Chapter 9, "Using Queries To Search Databases," teaches you more sophisticated techniques for indexing and for selecting records to appear in either a Quick Report or a Custom Report.
- Chapter 10, "Using Advanced Techniques with Queries," expands on Chapter 9 and shows even more advanced techniques for selecting records for reporting purposes.
- Chapter 12, "Creating Custom Reports," teaches you how to take complete control of the report printing process. This chapter includes report layout, performing calculations in your report, and choosing fields to appear.
- Chapter 13, "Designing and Using a Mailmerge Report and Label," illustrates how to create letters, reports, and labels that pull information selectively out of the database that you can add to your letter or mailing label.

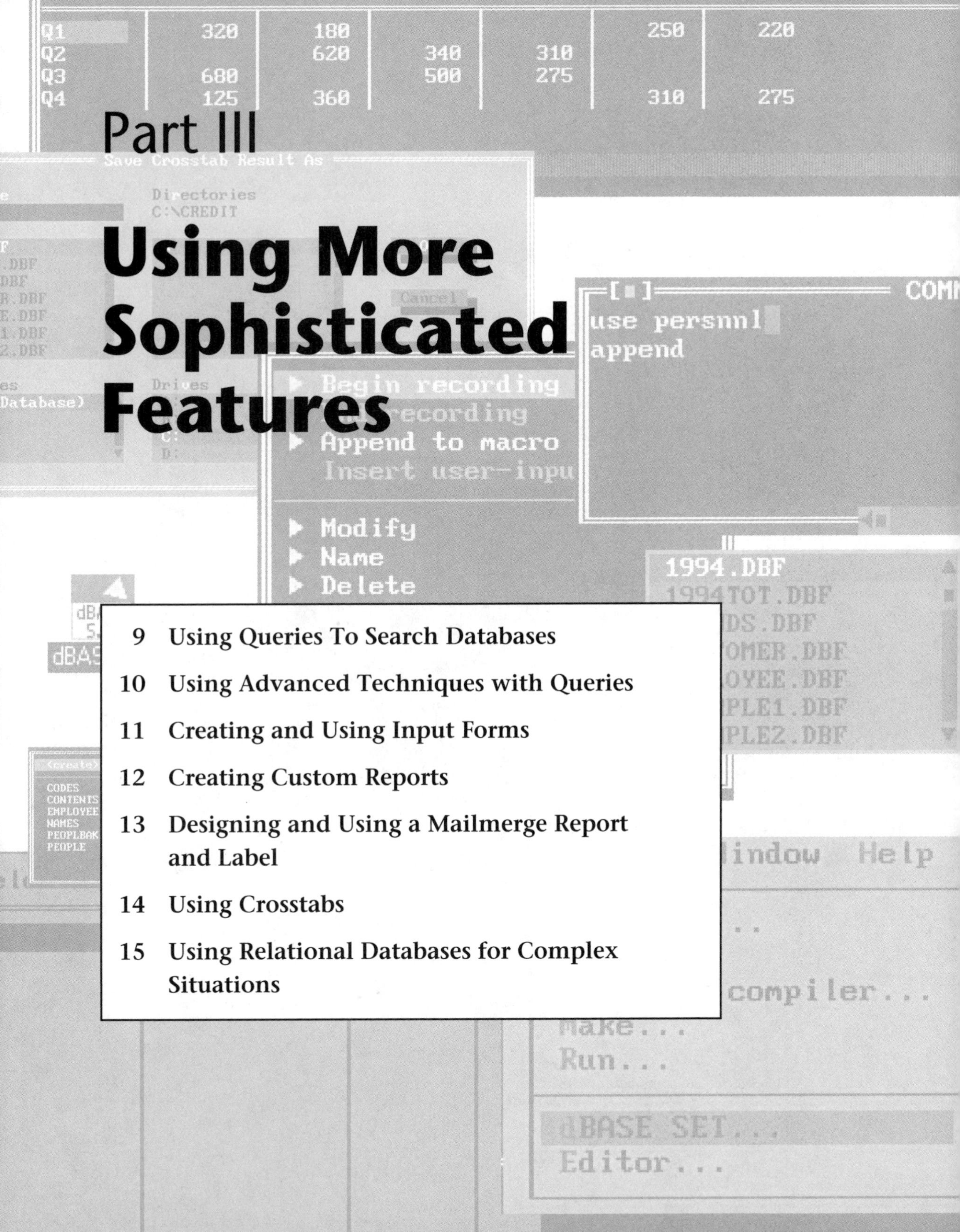

Part III

Using More Sophisticated Features

9 Using Queries To Search Databases

10 Using Advanced Techniques with Queries

11 Creating and Using Input Forms

12 Creating Custom Reports

13 Designing and Using a Mailmerge Report and Label

14 Using Crosstabs

15 Using Relational Databases for Complex Situations

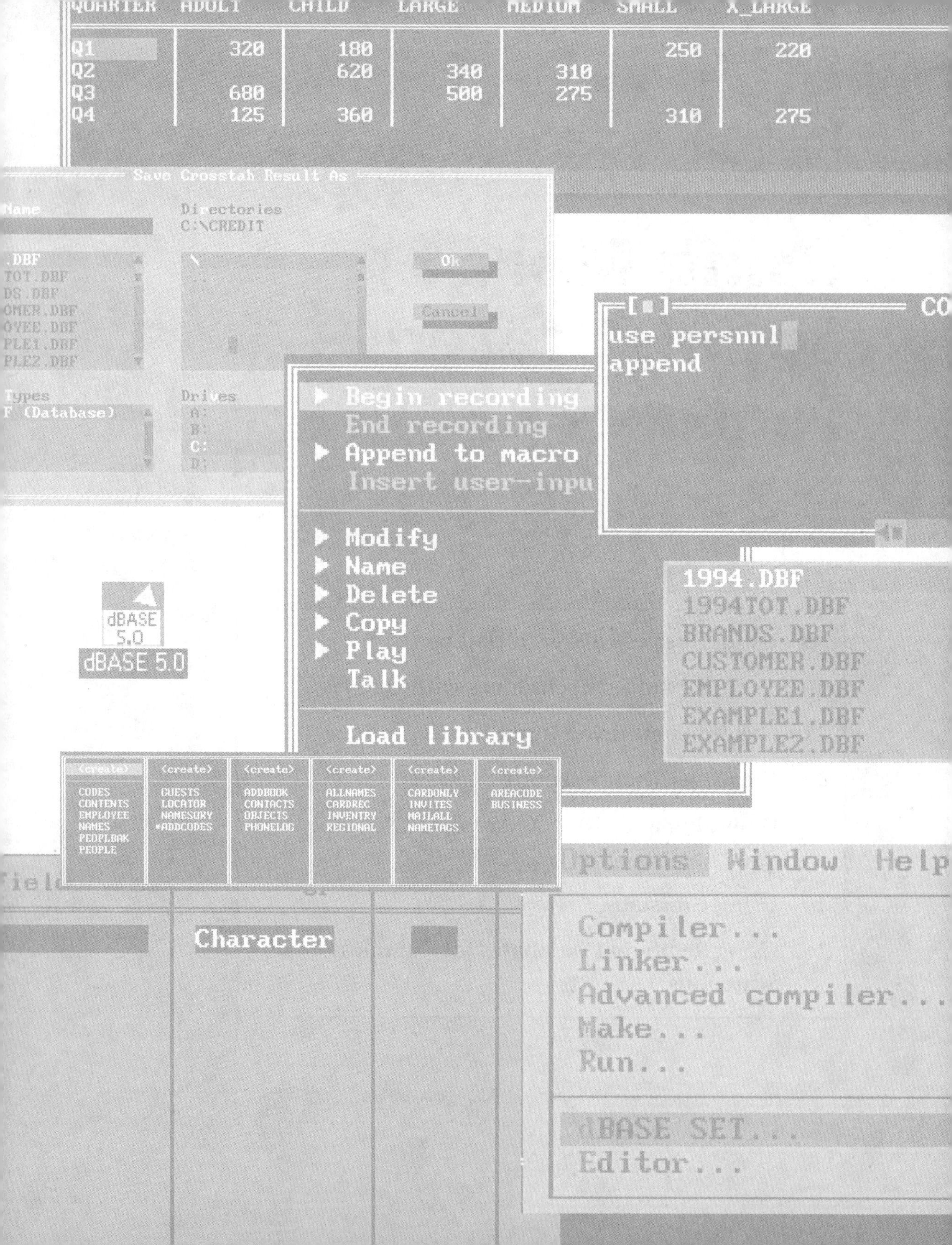

QUARTER ADULT CHILD LARGE MEDIUM SMALL X_LARGE
Q1 320 180 250 220
Q2 620 340 310
Q3 680 500 275
Q4 125 360 310 275
Save Crosstab Result As
Name
Directories
C:\CREDIT
Ok
Cancel
Types
Drives
A:
B:
C:
D:
use persnnl
append
Begin recording
End recording
Append to macro
Modify
Name
Delete
Copy
Play
Talk
Load library
1994.DBF
1994TOT.DBF
BRANDS.DBF
CUSTOMER.DBF
EMPLOYEE.DBF
EXAMPLE1.DBF
EXAMPLE2.DBF
dBASE 5.0
dBASE 5.0
<create>
CODES
CONTENTS
EMPLOYEE
NAMES
PEOPLBAK
PEOPLE
<create>
GUESTS
LOCATOR
NAMESQRY
*ADDCODES
<create>
ADDBOOK
CONTACTS
OBJECTS
PHONELOG
<create>
ALLNAMES
CARDREC
INVENTRY
REGIONAL
<create>
CARDONLY
INVITES
MAILALL
NAMETAGS
<create>
AREACODE
BUSINESS
Window
Character
Compiler...
Linker...
Advanced compiler...
Make...
Run...
Editor...

Chapter 9

Using Queries To Search Databases

In Chapter 7, you learned how to look at the records in a database with the Edit or Browse screen. But even with small databases, you rarely want to look at every record in the database when you need some information. In Chapter 7, you also learned how to search for a record with a particular value. This is useful, but more than likely, you want to look at a subset of the database, not just go to one record at a time.

Using queries, you can have dBASE 5 display a subset of only the records that meet your criteria. For example, in a database of customer information, you can tell dBASE 5 to show you only the records that have a certain zip code or a specific state. If you are interested in looking at only certain fields, you can have dBASE 5 display those fields and no others. When working with large databases, you almost always want dBASE 5 to limit the records and fields that it displays.

The tool you use to limit the display of records and fields is the *"query by example" (QBE)* feature. QBE is a Control Center operation that is accessed from the Queries panel. Using QBE you can refine your searches to be so specific that you can find one unique record out of thousands in the database. QBE also enables you to restructure fields, sort the database, perform calculations, and aggregate data.

This chapter teaches you how to use QBE to limit dBASE 5 searches and data presentations. Chapter 10 teaches you how to use the more advanced QBE features. In this chapter, you learn how to:

- Create, execute, and save view queries
- Enter simple search values

- Enter complex search values
- Use condition boxes in queries
- Save query output as a database
- Use queries to select records for reports

Retrieving Data Successfully

Seldom are database systems used for the sole purpose of storing data. The primary function of a database system is data retrieval. It doesn't matter how well a database is constructed or how much information it contains—if the user does not know how to get the information out of the database, the database is useless.

Because the QBE feature is the dBASE 5 vehicle for retrieving data, it is very important to understand exactly how to use QBE. The QBE feature is used to create a query, which is basically a format for selecting the fields you want to work with and specifying the data that you want to use. A query can be used to select records for viewing, editing, updating, or including in a report. Additionally, the subset of records selected by a query can be saved as a separate database file.

With the Query design work surface, you can construct simple queries to look at your data and then refine them step by step until you see only the records you want in the order you want them. The following examples show some typical criteria that might be used in a query. Notice how the query becomes more and more precise.

- All the houses for sale in the multiple listing database that cost at least $200,000.
- All the houses for sale in the multiple listing database that cost between $200,000 and $300,000.
- All the houses for sale in the multiple listing database that cost between $200,000 and $300,000 and are located on the east side of the city.
- All the houses for sale in the multiple listing database that cost between $200,000 and $300,000, are located on the east side of the city, and have a three-car garage.

- All the houses for sale in the multiple listing database that cost between $200,000 and $300,000, are located on the east side of the city, have a three-car garage, and have at least one acre of land.

Creating a Query

dBASE has two types of queries—*view* queries and *update* queries. View queries are used primarily to select records for reports or to display records on-screen for the purpose of browsing or manually editing. Update queries perform operations on the database that automatically modify existing records. This chapter deals exclusively with view queries.

▶ See "Updating Values in a Database with a Query," p. 236

To explain the use of view queries, this chapter uses a customer database as an example. The structure of this database is shown in figure 9.1. This database is simple, but it serves to explain many facets of the QBE feature.

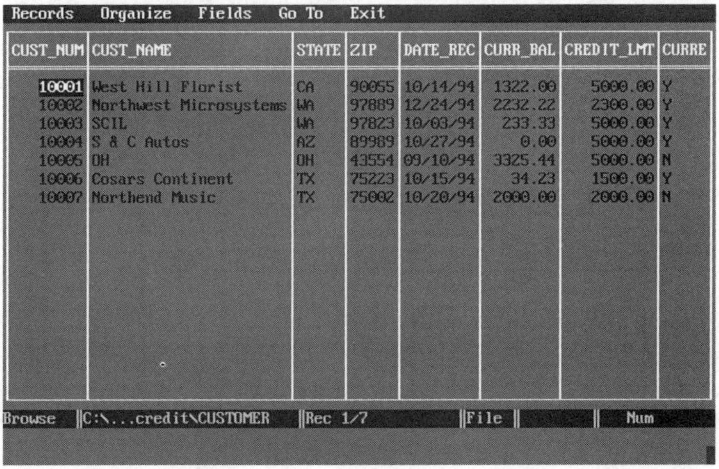

Records Organize Fields Go To Exit

CUST_NUM	CUST_NAME	STATE	ZIP	DATE_REC	CURR_BAL	CREDIT_LMT	CURRE
10001	West Hill Florist	CA	90055	10/14/94	1322.00	5000.00	Y
10002	Northwest Microsystems	WA	97889	12/24/94	2232.22	2300.00	Y
10003	SCIL	WA	97823	10/03/94	233.33	5000.00	Y
10004	S & C Autos	AZ	89989	10/27/94	0.00	5000.00	Y
10005	OH	OH	43554	09/10/94	3325.44	5000.00	N
10006	Cosars Continent	TX	75223	10/15/94	34.23	1500.00	Y
10007	Northend Music	TX	75002	10/20/94	2000.00	2000.00	N

Browse C:\...credit\CUSTOMER Rec 1/7 File Num

Fig. 9.1
The structure of the customer database example showing the field names, types, lengths, decimals, and index status.

The process of creating and using a query is simple and straightforward. From the Control Center, select the database you want to query and make it the active database. Move the highlight to the Queries panel and choose `<create>`. The Query design screen is displayed (see fig. 9.2).

Like other work surfaces in dBASE 5, the Query work surface has a menu bar at the top of the screen. Under the menu bar is the *file skeleton* of the active database (CUSTOMER.DBF in this example). Below the file skeleton is the *view skeleton*. The F3 and F4 keys are used to move back and forth between the two views (F3 moves to the previous skeleton and F4 moves to the next skeleton). At the bottom of the screen are the *status bar* and *navigation line*. Like other work surfaces, messages appear on the bottom line of the screen.

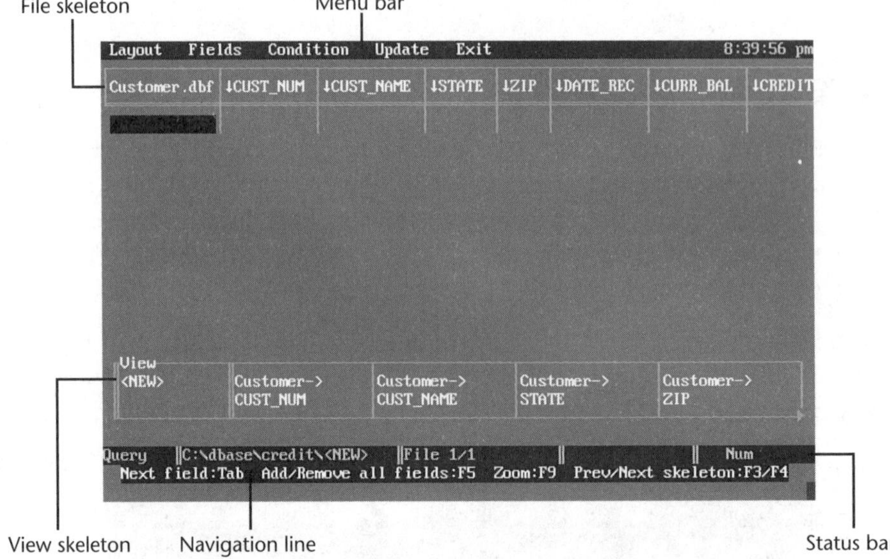

Fig. 9.2
The Query design screen showing the file skeleton and the view skeleton.

Understanding the File and View Skeletons

To create an effective and useful query, you should become familiar with the file and view skeleton areas of the Query design screen. You use these areas to select data and modify the presentation of that data on-screen.

Notice that the file skeleton lists the name of the current database (CUSTOMER.DBF) and the field names (CUST_NUM, CUST_NAME, and so on). You can scroll the file skeleton to the right or left by pressing Tab or Shift-Tab, respectively. Pressing End or Home takes you to the end or the beginning of a skeleton, respectively.

Using a mouse, you can move the highlight to a field on the file skeleton by clicking in the input area under the field name. You can scroll the skeleton to the right by clicking the mouse on the right edge of the screen in the field input area. You can scroll the skeleton to the left by clicking the left arrow next to the file name. This arrow is not displayed unless the skeleton has been scrolled to the right.

Each field name in the file skeleton has a down arrow before the name. This arrow indicates that the field is included in the view skeleton. Under each field name in the file skeleton is an input area. This is the area in which you type the conditions that you want the query to search for in the database.

The view skeleton specifies which fields are displayed when a query is processed and the results are displayed on-screen. Initially, all fields in the view skeleton are the same as those in the file skeleton (in the same order), but you can remove fields from the view skeleton or move them to different locations to change the appearance of the data when the query is processed. Like the file skeleton, the view skeleton may have too many fields to display on the screen at once, but you can scroll to them by using Tab or Shift-Tab.

Using a mouse, you can select a field in the view skeleton by clicking on the line that forms the top of the box that outlines the view skeleton.

Modifying the View Skeleton

The view skeleton can have fields renamed, removed, added, and rearranged to customize the way data is presented when the query is executed.

Tip
To scroll through fields in the view skeleton, click the arrow located on the bottom line of the view skeleton.

Renaming a Field

If you want a field to have a different name in the view skeleton, follow these steps:

1. Move the highlight to the field in the view skeleton that you want to rename.
2. Open the Fields menu and choose Edit Field Name.
3. Type the new name and press Enter.

Removing a Field

To remove a field from the view skeleton, follow these steps:

Tip
To change the name of a field in the view skeleton, move the highlight to the field in the view skeleton, type a new name, and press Enter.

1. Press F4 to move the cursor to the view skeleton area of the Query design screen. The highlight moves to the top border of the first field in the view skeleton.
2. Use Tab and Shift-Tab to move right and left in the view skeleton until the field you want to delete is highlighted.
3. Open the Fields menu and choose Remove Field From View; or press F5 to remove the selected field from the view skeleton. The other fields move left in the skeleton to fill up the space left by the deleted field. The down arrow before the name in the file skeleton is also removed.

Using the mouse, you can remove a field from the view skeleton by clicking that field in the file skeleton and then clicking the down arrow. Alternatively, you can click the field in the view skeleton and then click the `Remove from view:F5` label on the navigation line.

Adding a Field

To add a field to the view skeleton, follow these steps:

1. Press F4 to move the highlight to the file skeleton area of the Query design screen. The field under the database name is highlighted.

2. Press Tab or Shift-Tab to go to the field you want to add to the view skeleton.

3. Open the Fields menu and choose Add Field to View; or press F5. The selected field is added to the view skeleton, and a down arrow appears next to the field name in the file skeleton area of the screen.

4. Because the field is added to the end of the view skeleton, you might want to move it to a new location.

With the mouse, you can add a field to the view skeleton by clicking that field in the file skeleton and then clicking the blank space before the field name (where the down arrow is displayed). Alternatively, you can click the field in the file skeleton and then use the mouse to open the Fields menu and choose Add Field to View.

Moving a Field

You may want to rearrange the order of the fields in the view skeleton so that the most important fields appear on the left or certain fields are displayed next to each other. To move fields in the view skeleton, follow these steps:

1. Press F4 to move the cursor to the view skeleton area of the Query design screen.

2. Move the cursor to the desired field.

3. Press F6 to select that field. To select more than one field to move, use Tab or Shift-Tab to extend the selected fields to the right or left.

4. After you select all the fields you want to move, press Enter.

5. Press F7.

6. Use Tab or Shift-Tab to move the selected fields to their new location.

7. When the fields are where you want them, press Enter.

Troubleshooting

I tried to change the name of a field in the view skeleton by moving the cursor to the field and typing the new field name. I typed "First Name," and when I press Enter, dBASE displayed the message, `Must be a legal field name`.

Field names cannot have spaces in them, even in the view skeleton. Use an underline between the two words and dBASE accepts the field name.

I accidentally removed the first field from the view skeleton. When I pressed F5 to put it back, it was not redisplayed in the view skeleton.

When a field is added to the view skeleton, it is added to the end of the skeleton regardless of where it was originally. The field was added to the view skeleton when you pressed F5, but it evidentally was not visible on the screen. To put the field back in the desired position, move it with F7.

Entering Simple Search Values

When you create a query, you specify the conditions (values) you want dBASE 5 to use to search the database. To specify a query condition, position the cursor in the file skeleton in the field that will contain the condition and type the condition. For example, to see all the records with a credit limit of $5,000, move the cursor to the CREDIT_LMT field in the file skeleton and type **5000**. If you want to see all the records that have Washington in the STATE field, type **"WA"** (including the quotation marks) in the STATE field in the file skeleton.

Note

A search value that is entered in a character field must always be enclosed in quotation marks.

To remove a search value from a field, highlight the input area of the field and press Ctrl-Y. The field blanks out, and that search criterion is removed.

The details of entering search values differ for different field types. The following sections provide details for entering criteria in character fields, numeric fields, date fields, and logical fields.

Entering Values in Character Fields

As noted earlier, when searching for a value in a text field, the value must be enclosed in quotation marks. Figure 9.3 shows an example of a query on a text field. Notice that the value "WA" is entered in the STATE field. This query asks dBASE 5 to present only records that have the value WA in the STATE field. Figure 9.4 shows the view resulting from this query. Every record presented meets this condition.

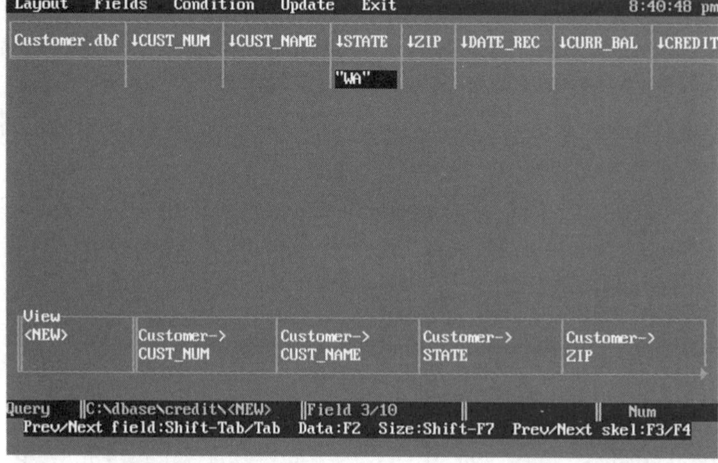

Fig. 9.3
Querying for records with "WA" in the STATE field.

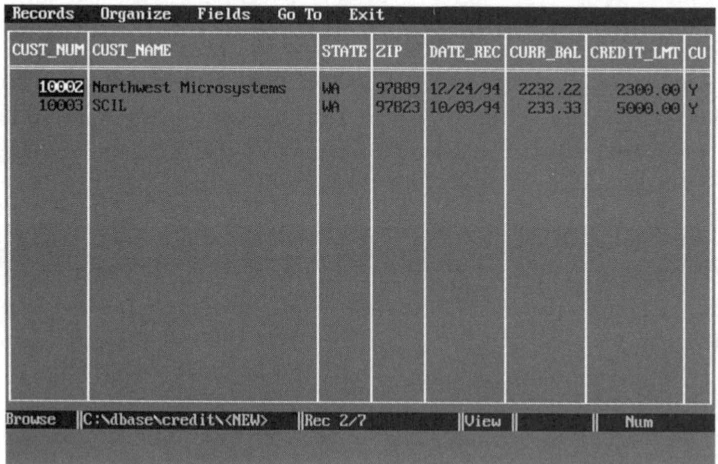

Fig. 9.4
The result of the search for STATE = "WA," a search on a character field.

Searching for all the records in which the value of one field equals the value in another field is also a valid type of search in a character field. For example, you might have a database for employees that has a RES_ST field and an EMP_ST field. The RES_ST field contains the name of the employee's state of residence, and the EMP_ST field contains the name of the state in which the employee works. You could search for all the records of employees who live and work in the same state. The query would look like figure 9.5. Notice that the value EMP_ST is preceded by an equal operator and is not enclosed in quotation marks. It is not necessary to use quotation marks because EMP_ST is a field name and not an actual value in the search field. Remember that dBASE is not case-sensitive, so, as you can see in the figure, it is not necessary to capitalize the field name in the query.

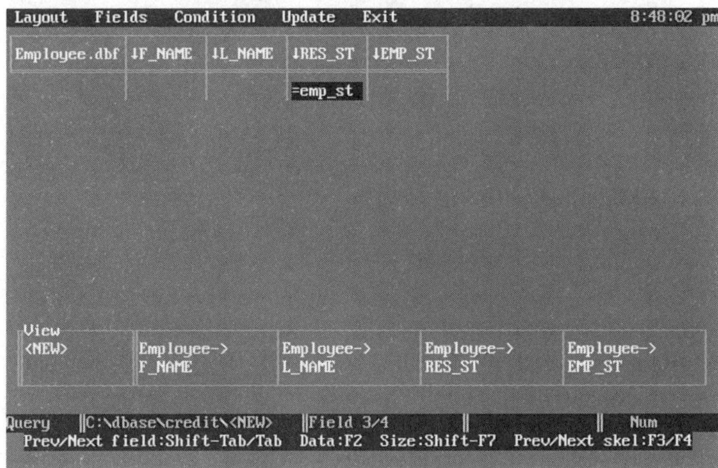

Fig. 9.5
A query that searches for a value equal to the value in another field.

Entering Values in Numeric Fields

Querying a numeric field is a matter of entering the search value below the search field. Figure 9.6 shows a query search for all records with a credit limit of $5,000. Notice that the value is entered without a dollar sign or a comma. No punctuation, except a minus sign for negative values, should be entered with a numeric value. Figure 9.7 shows a view screen of records from the Customer database that meet this criterion.

◄ See "Choosing the Type of Field," p. 110

Field names also can be entered as search conditions in a numeric field. For example, to find out which customers have charged to their credit limit, you would type **=CREDIT_LMT** in the CURR_BAL field. (Note the use of the equal operator when using a field name.)

Entering Values in Date Fields

Unless you use another field name, you must enclose search values entered in a date field in braces ({ }). Figure 9.8 shows a query that will search for all records with a DATE_REC value of October 14, 1994. The result of this search is shown in figure 9.9.

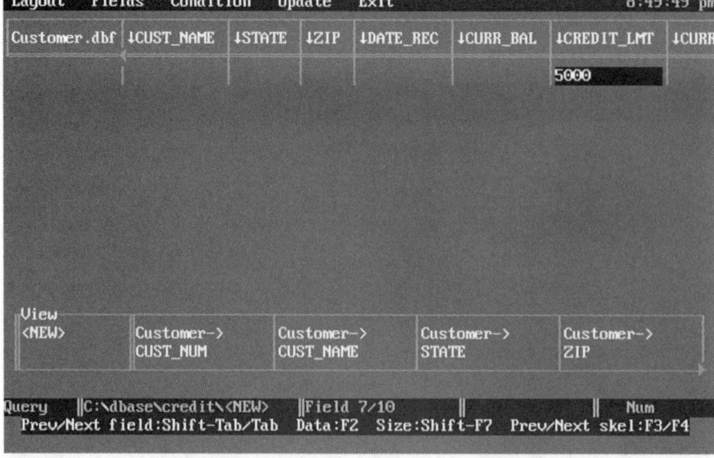

Fig. 9.6
Querying for records with a credit limit of $5,000.

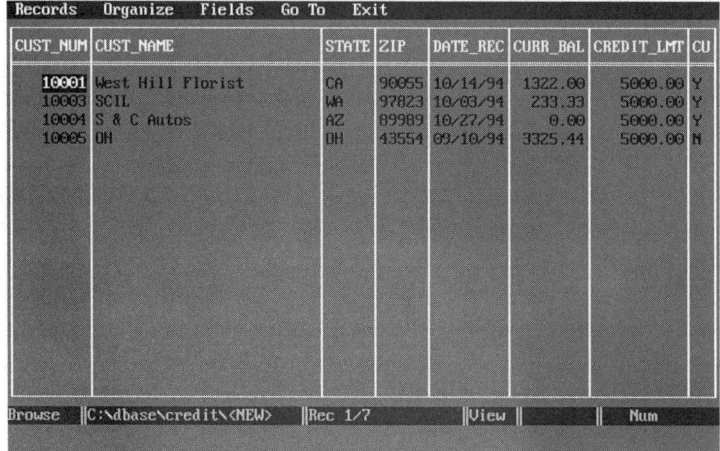

Fig. 9.7
The result of the search on a numeric field showing all records with a credit limit of $5,000.

Entering Values in Logical Fields

Searches in logical fields require that you enter the search value as .T. for True or .F. for False. The periods before and after the logical value tell dBASE that this entry is not just the character T or F, but a logical value. Figure 9.10 shows the specification of a search on the logical field CURRENT; figure 9.11 shows the results of this query. All records selected display "Y" in the CURRENT field. ("Y" for "Yes" is equivalent to "T" for "True.")

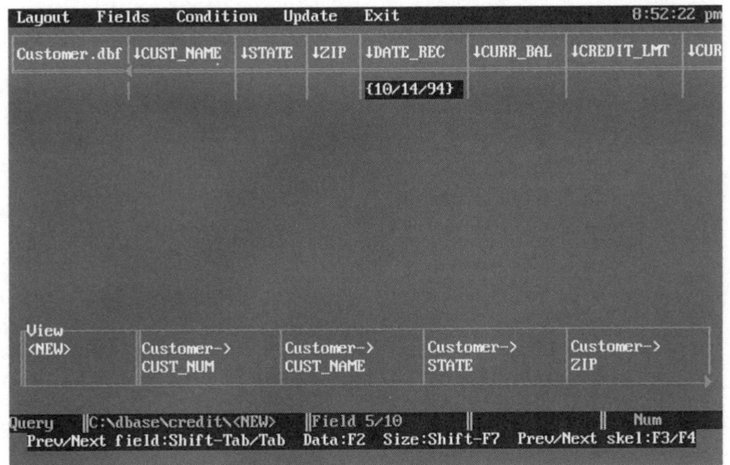

Fig. 9.8
A date field query searching for all records where DATE_REC is equal to 10/14/94.

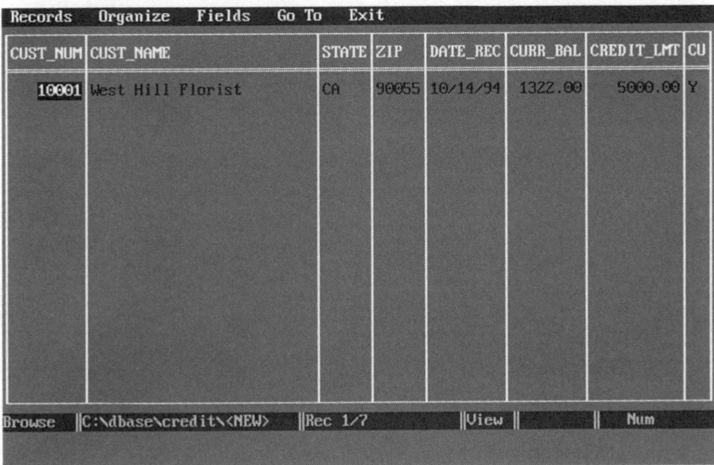

Fig. 9.9
The result of the search on the DATE_REC field showing the only record with a date of 10/14/94.

Searching in Memo Fields

Memo fields provide powerful capabilities, but their unique nature prevents their use in query by example. If you place a search criterion in a memo field in the file skeleton, dBASE rejects your query. The screen displays an error box and the message line displays the message, `Operation with memo field invalid`.

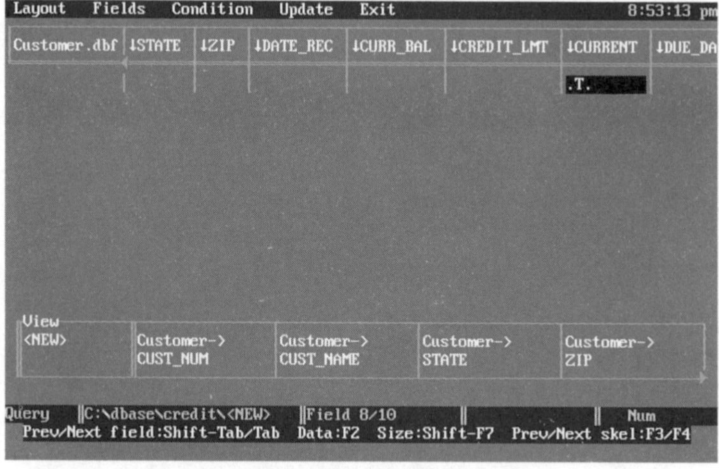

Fig. 9.10
A query on a logical field that searches for all records in which the CURRENT field contains a true value.

Records Organize Fields Go To Exit

CUST_NUM	CUST_NAME	STATE	ZIP	DATE_REC	CURR_BAL	CREDIT_LMT	CU
10001	West Hill Florist	CA	90055	10/14/94	1322.00	5000.00	Y
10002	Northwest Microsystems	WA	97889	12/24/94	2232.22	2300.00	Y
10003	SCIL	WA	97823	10/03/94	233.33	5000.00	Y
10004	S & C Autos	AZ	89989	10/27/94	0.00	5000.00	Y
10006	Cosars Continent	TX	75223	10/15/94	34.23	1500.00	Y

Browse ║C:\dbase\credit\<NEW> ║Rec 1/7 ║View ║ ║ Num

Fig. 9.11
The result of a search on a logical field showing all records that have a true value (Y) in the CURRENT field.

Processing a Query

◄ See "Choosing the Type of Field," p. 110

After you enter the desired value in the search field in the file skeleton, press F2 to execute the query. dBASE 5 searches the database and presents the Browse screen with the records that match the criteria specified in the file skeleton. You can then look at the records or make changes to the data.

If you're using a mouse, click `Data:F2` to execute the query instead of pressing F2.

To return to the Query design screen, open the Exit menu and choose Transfer to Query Design. You can add new conditions or change the conditions in the query and execute the query again.

Troubleshooting

When I press Shift-F2, dBASE displays the message `Cannot go to Browse/Edit or return to previous design screen if errors exist.`

Unfortunately, the dBASE message does not help you by identifying the source of the error. This message is most often caused because quotation marks were not used in a text field. Check all fields for proper syntax when this message occurs. Remember to use braces for date values.

I want to find all the records that have "Y" in the field called MARRIED. I used the query "Y" and dBASE displayed all the records rather than just the records that have a "Y."

The MARRIED field is a logical field, and even though it contains "Y" and "N," you cannot search on these letters. You must use the search criteria .T. or .F. dBASE ignored your erroneous query and displayed all the records.

Tip
As a shortcut, press Shift-F2 to return to the Query design screen from the Browse screen.

Practicing with a Query

To see how a view query works, activate a database from the Control Center. Move the cursor to `<create>` in the Queries panel and press Enter. When the Query design work surface appears, do not enter any conditions in the file skeleton. Press F2 to execute the query. All the records in the database are selected and presented on-screen. The results on the screen are essentially the same as those obtained when you highlight a database name and press F2 from the Control Center. Figure 9.12 shows the data view for the Customer database that results from the default query. Notice the word `View` in the status bar. Press Shift-F2 to return to the Query design screen.

Records Organize Fields Go To Exit

CUST_NUM	CUST_NAME	STATE	ZIP	DATE_REC	CURR_BAL	CREDIT_LMT	CU
10001	West Hill Florist	CA	90055	10/14/94	1322.00	5000.00	Y
10002	Northwest Microsystems	WA	97889	12/24/94	2232.22	2300.00	Y
10003	SCIL	WA	97823	10/03/94	233.33	5000.00	Y
10004	S & C Autos	AZ	89989	10/27/94	0.00	5000.00	Y
10005	OH	OH	43554	09/10/94	3325.44	5000.00	N
10006	Cosars Continent	TX	75223	10/15/94	34.23	1500.00	Y
10007	Northend Music	TX	75002	10/20/94	2000.00	2000.00	N

Browse ║C:\dbase\credit\<NEW> ║Rec 1/7 ║View ║ ║ Num

Fig. 9.12
The view of a database presented by the default query.

Using an Existing Query

Later in this chapter you will learn how to save a query. When a query has been saved, it is listed in the Queries panel in the Control Center. To use an existing query to display data, follow these steps:

1. Highlight the name of the desired query in the Queries panel.
2. Press Enter.
3. Choose Display Data.

If you want to see the query itself on the Query design work surface, follow these steps:

1. Highlight the name of the query in the Queries panel.
2. Press Enter.
3. Choose Modify Query.

Saving Query Output as a New Database

The records that meet the conditions of a query can be saved as a separate database. Creating a new database with a subset of records is useful for disbursing partial information to people who do not need the entire database. For example, the Customer database could be divided into states by querying the database on each state and saving the output as a new database. Then the databases for the states could be given to the account managers.

To save the output of a query to a new database, follow these steps:

1. Enter the value in the search field.
2. Open the Layout menu and choose Write View as Database File.
3. Type a file name and press Enter.
4. Type a description, if desired, and press Enter.

The file is saved in the current directory and added to the catalog. The name of the new file appears in the Data panel of the Control Center.

Using More Complex Search Values

All of the query examples described in the preceding sections look for a value in the database that matches or "equals" the value in the search field. Sometimes this type of search is not adequate. For example, you might want to find a record with any REC_DATE after December 1, 1994. Or you might want to find all the records for any state beginning with the letter A. dBASE 5 is capable of handling these searches as well. It uses relational operators in conjunction with the values to express the condition.

◀ See "Using Catalogs," p. 73

Using Relational Operators in Searches

Table 9.1 lists the relational operators you can use in query searches.

Table 9.1 Relational Operators

Operator	Operator Name	Description
>	Greater than	All records whose field value is greater than the specified search value.
<	Less than	All records whose field value is less than the search value.
=	Equal to	Only records whose field value is equal to the search value.
==	Exactly equal to	This operator is just like the equal operator, but it is used when the Exact match setting has been turned off with a SET command.
<> or #	Not equal to	Records whose field value is not equal to the specified value.
>=	Greater than or equal to	Records whose field value is greater than or equal to the search value.
<=	Less than or equal to	Records whose field value is less than or equal to the search value.
$	Included	Used in character fields, $"AB" means "process records whose field includes the letters AB." See "Searching for Embedded Values" later in this chapter for information on using this operator.
Like	Pattern match	Like the DOS wild-card search, this operator enables wild-card characters.
Sounds like		A soundex match, which often finds words that "sound like" the search value.

Figure 9.13 shows a query for records with a value in the CREDIT_LMT field greater than $2,000.

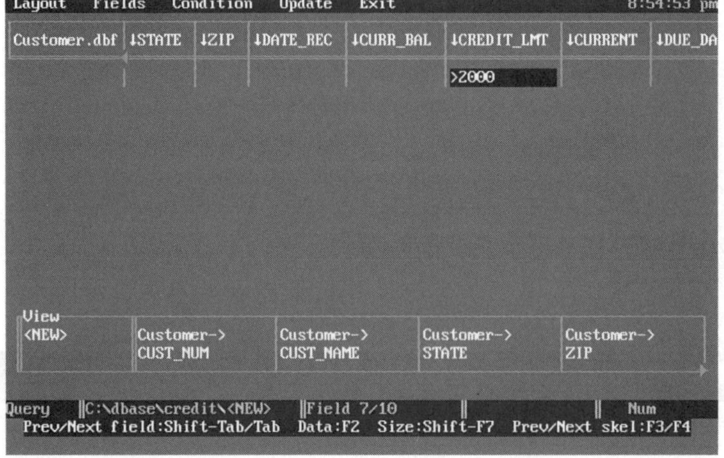

Fig. 9.13
A search that uses a relational operator to find all records with a credit limit of more than $2,000.

Press Shift-F1 to pull up the Expression Builder menu to choose an operator when specifying search criteria. Select a relational operator from the second column (see fig. 9.14) by highlighting it with the mouse or the arrow keys, and then press Enter or click the mouse to include the operator in your expression.

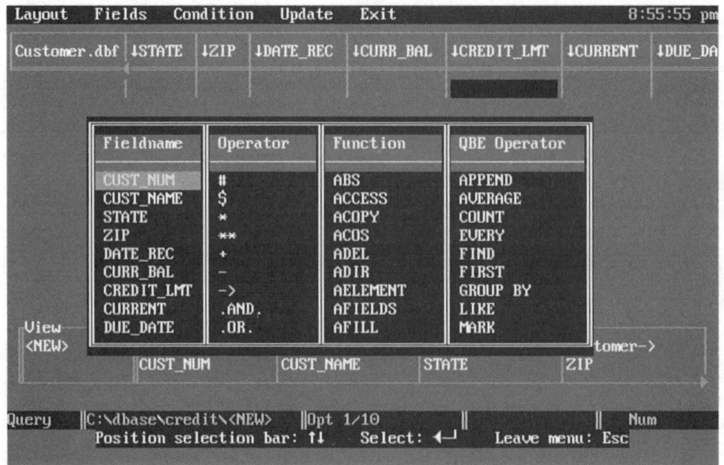

Fig. 9.14
The Expression Builder menu that is displayed by pressing Shift-F1.

Searching with Wild Cards

The like relational operator enables you to find records that have character-field values that match a template you specify using wild cards. dBASE 5 recognizes two wild-card characters—the question mark (?) and the asterisk (*). The question mark stands for any character in the position it holds. The asterisk stands for any characters and any number of characters in the position it holds.

Figure 9.15 shows a search that will find all records that have the character W in the first position of the STATE field. Figure 9.16 shows the result. If you enter **"W*"** without the like operator, the query looks for STATE fields with exactly that string: an uppercase W followed by an asterisk (*). The like operator tells dBASE to interpret the * and ? characters as wild cards.

Note

Because the STATE field has a character width of two, the value like "W?" could also be used in the query. If the STATE field contained the full names of states, the value like "W*" would have to be used.

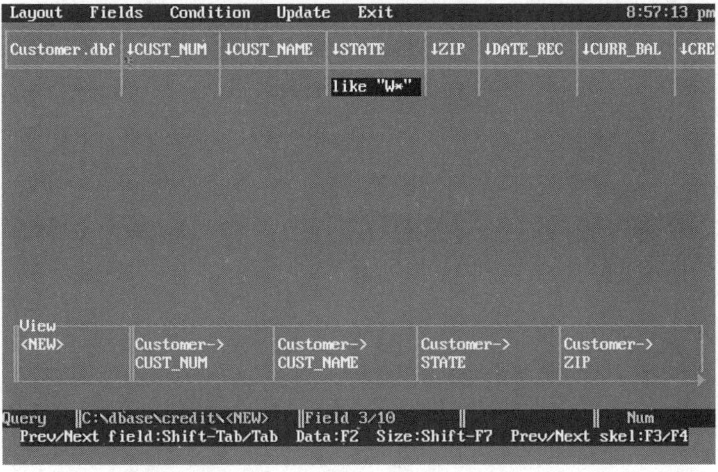

Fig. 9.15
A LIKE search variable with a wild card. This query finds all records with a state that begins with the letter "W."

Searching for Embedded Values

Use the $ relational operator to search for values embedded in a character field. If you want to find all records in the Customer database that have the letters *North* in the CUST_NAME field, for example, type **$"North"** in the CUST_NAME field in the file skeleton, as shown in figure 9.17. The result of this search is shown in figure 9.18. Notice that the search locates any record where the letters *North* appear adjacent to one another in the CUST_NAME field. Notice also that the letter N is capitalized and that the records that match this criterion also show a capital letter N.

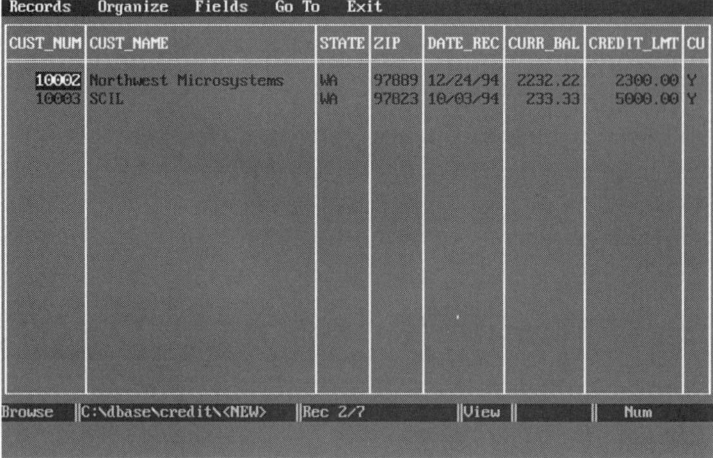

Fig. 9.16
The result of the LIKE search for STATE is like "W*".

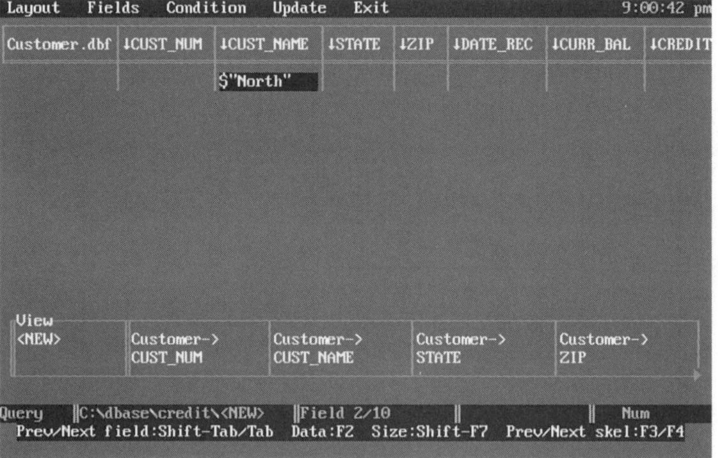

Fig. 9.17
A query that searches for the character "North" embedded in the customer's name.

Searching for Values in a Range

You may want the view screen to display records whose search field value falls between a range of values. In the appropriate field, use a statement that dictates the lower end of the range and a separate statement dictating the higher end of the range. Separate these two statements with a comma. When you press F2 to initiate the query, dBASE searches for records that meet both conditions and fall within your specified range.

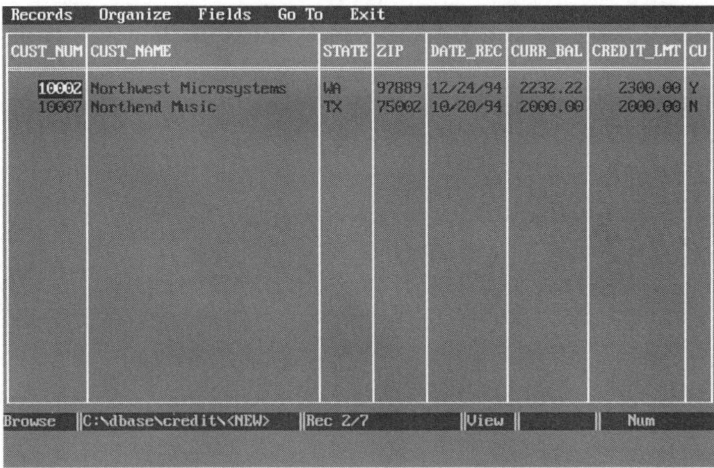

Fig. 9.18 The result of the search for the embedded characters "North."

Figure 9.19 shows the file skeleton with such a range specified in the CURR_BAL field. This query asks for all records between 1,000 and 3,000—those records with values greater than 1,000 and less than 3,000. Figure 9.20 shows the resulting view screen.

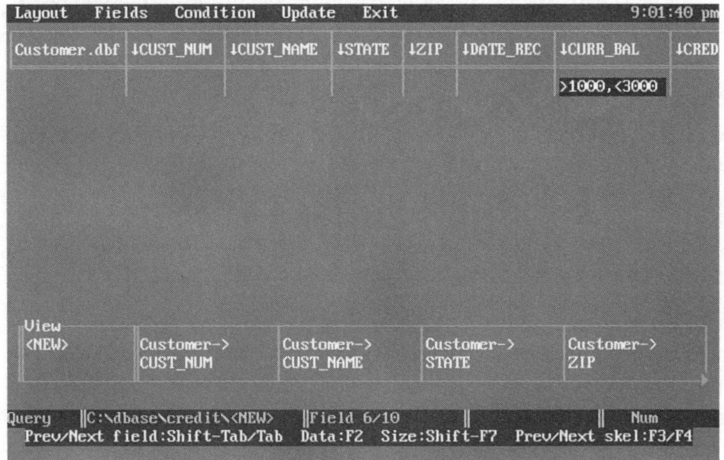

Fig. 9.19 A query that searches for a range of values between 1,000 and 3,000.

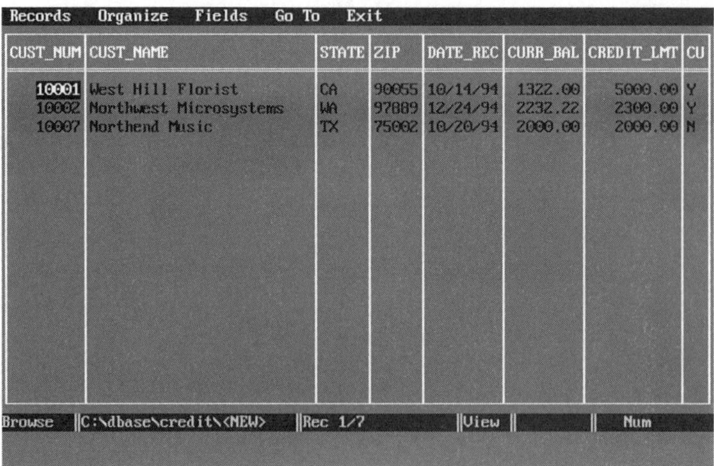

Fig. 9.20
The result of the search for a current balance between 1,000 and 3,000.

Troubleshooting

When I search for values in a range, dBASE displays the message, `No records found.` *I know there are records that fall within the range.*

When you work with a range specification, be sure that the first expression really does form the lower boundary, that the second forms the upper boundary, and that the two together indicate a range. A common mistake is to specify a range like <1000, >3000. This range asks for all records that are less than 1000 and greater than 3000. dBASE 5 cannot find any records that meet these criteria because you are asking it to find a number that has both values simultaneously.

I want to find all the records for the Sales department and the Production department. I used the criteria "Sales","Production" in the DEPT field and got the message, "No records selected." I know there are records. What am I doing wrong?

This is a common error caused by the way we phrase what we want to find. You want to find Sales AND Production, so you tried to put both criteria in the field on the same line. What you really are trying to find is Sales OR Production. You must enter "Sales" on the first line of the DEPT field and "Production" on the next line. See "Searching for Multiple Values in the Same Field" later in this chapter for more information.

Searching for Values that Sound Alike

The "sounds like" relational operator is used to search for values that are not spelled the same but sound alike. For example, the SOUNDS LIKE operator could be used to search for a first name that sounds like *Burt*. The records selected could include those with a first name of *Burt* or *Bert*. Figure 9.21 shows the query that would be used for this example.

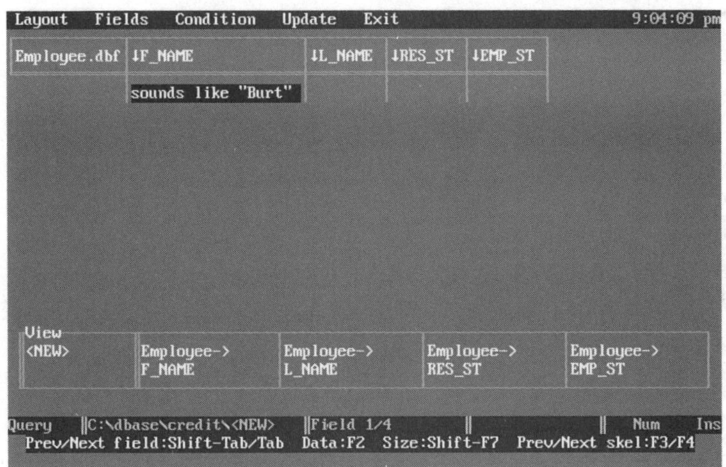

Fig. 9.21
A query that uses the SOUNDS LIKE operator to find values that sound alike.

Searching for Records with Multiple Conditions

dBASE 5 provides several ways to combine searches in a query. You may want to search for more than one value in a field, or you may want to search for records that meet conditions in more than one field. Combining search conditions enables you to further refine your database searches. The following sections explain how to design queries with multiple conditions.

Searching for Values in Multiple Fields

When you want a search to find records that meet search values in two different fields, enter each search value in the appropriate field on the same line in the file skeleton. The query treats values on the same line in the file skeleton as AND searches. dBASE tests each database record to see whether it matches both the first value and the second value. Suppose you want to search the Customer database for all records with WA in the STATE field and with a value in the CURR_BAL field greater than $2,000.

To create this query, follow these steps:

1. Remove any existing conditions or expressions by highlighting them one at a time and pressing Ctrl-Y.

2. Move the cursor to the STATE field and type **"WA"**. Make sure that you include the double quotation marks.

3. Move the cursor to the CURR_BAL field and type **>2000**.

   The Query design screen should look like figure 9.22.

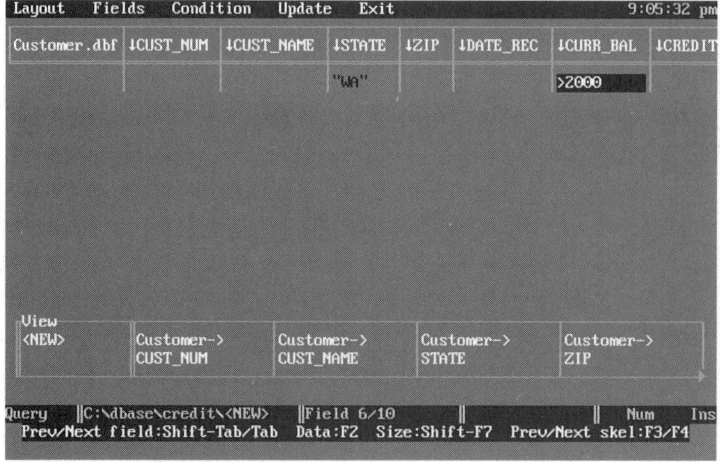

Fig. 9.22
An AND search on two fields. The query finds all records with a state of "WA" that have a current balance greater than $2,000.

4. Press F2 to process the query.

   Figure 9.23 shows the result of this search.

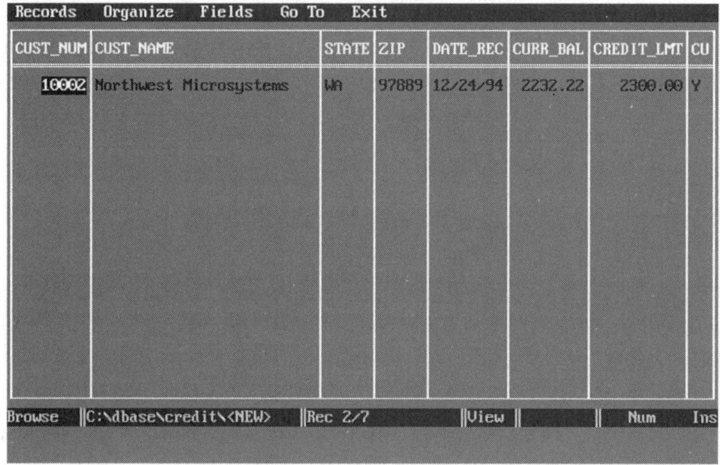

Fig. 9.23
The result of the AND search showing records that meet both conditions.

5. Press Shift-F2 to return to the Query design screen.

You can specify search values in as many of the file skeleton fields as you want because dBASE 5 treats each criterion on the same line as an AND condition. If the first match is made AND the second match is made AND the third match is made, and so on, the record is included in the view screen.

Searching for Multiple Values in the Same Field

Another type of search that is frequently used is the OR search. This search is used to find records that have more than one value in the same field. For example, you may want to search for all the records in Washington, California, and Texas. To search for multiple values in the same field, place the first search value in the appropriate field in the file skeleton. Press the down-arrow key to add another line to the file skeleton. Place the second search value in the field on this second line. Continue adding new lines for each of the desired values. When you place search conditions on different lines in the file skeleton, dBASE treats each condition as an OR condition. (To be included in the selected records, a record can match any one of the values.)

Figure 9.24 shows a query that will find all the records for Washington and Texas. Figure 9.25 shows the result of the query.

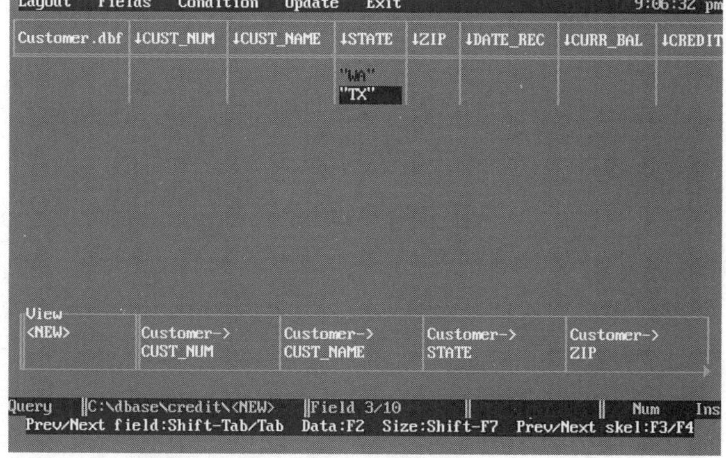

Fig. 9.24
An OR search on the same field. This query finds all records for the state of Washington and for the state of Texas.

Combining AND and OR Conditions

You can combine AND and OR queries. Search values on the same line of the file skeleton are treated as AND queries; values on separate lines are treated as OR queries. Figure 9.26 shows a query that will search for all records that have WA in the STATE field and that have less than $3,000 in the CURR_BAL field; or that have TX in the STATE field and more than $1,000 in the CURR_BAL field. Figure 9.27 shows the resulting view screen.

Records Organize Fields Go To Exit

CUST_NUM	CUST_NAME	STATE	ZIP	DATE_REC	CURR_BAL	CREDIT_LMT	CU
10002	Northwest Microsystems	WA	97889	12/24/94	2232.22	2300.00	Y
10003	SCIL	WA	97823	10/03/94	233.33	5000.00	Y
10006	Cosars Continent	TX	75223	10/15/94	34.23	1500.00	Y
10007	Northend Music	TX	75002	10/20/94	2000.00	2000.00	N

Browse ║C:\dbase\credit\<NEW> ║Rec 2/7 ║View ║ ║ Num Ins

Fig. 9.25
The result of the OR search on the same field showing the records from both states.

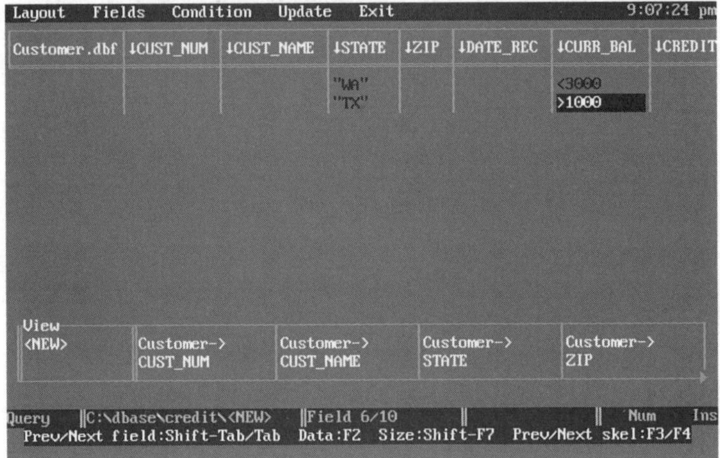

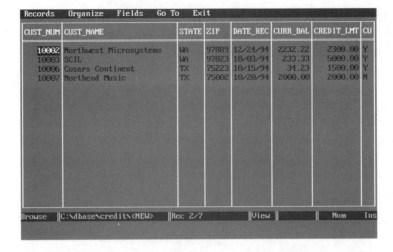

Fig. 9.26
Two AND searches combined with an OR search. This query finds all records for Washington with a current balance less than $3,000 and all records for Texas with a current balance greater than $1,000.

You also can create a query in which you specify OR conditions on different fields. You place the OR conditions on different lines of the file skeleton. Figure 9.28 shows a search for records that have WA in the STATE field or that have more than $1,000 in the CURR_BAL field. Figure 9.29 shows the result of this query.

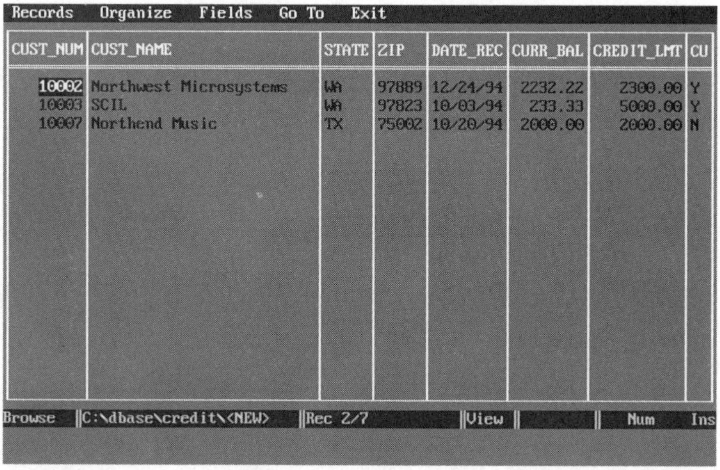

Records Organize Fields Go To Exit

CUST_NUM	CUST_NAME	STATE	ZIP	DATE_REC	CURR_BAL	CREDIT_LMT	CU
10002	Northwest Microsystems	WA	97889	12/24/94	2232.22	2300.00	Y
10003	SCIL	WA	97823	10/03/94	233.33	5000.00	Y
10007	Northend Music	TX	75002	10/20/94	2000.00	2000.00	N

Browse ‖C:\dbase\credit\<NEW> ‖Rec 2/7 ‖View ‖ ‖ Num Ins

Fig. 9.27
The result of the combined AND and OR search.

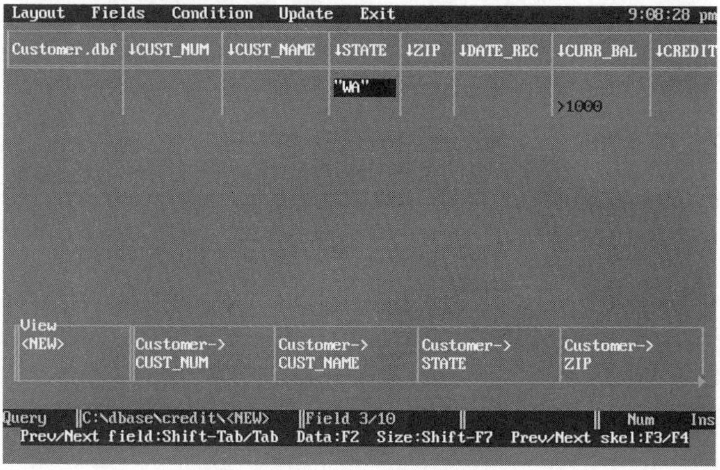

Layout Fields Condition Update Exit 9:08:28 pm

Customer.dbf	↓CUST_NUM	↓CUST_NAME	↓STATE	↓ZIP	↓DATE_REC	↓CURR_BAL	↓CREDIT
			"WA"				
						>1000	

View <NEW> Customer->CUST_NUM Customer->CUST_NAME Customer->STATE Customer->ZIP

Query ‖C:\dbase\credit\<NEW> ‖Field 3/10 ‖ ‖ Num Ins
Prev/Next field:Shift-Tab/Tab Data:F2 Size:Shift-F7 Prev/Next skel:F3/F4

Fig. 9.28
An OR search on two different fields. This query finds all records for the state of Washington and all records (regardless of state) with a current balance less than $1,000.

Queries can become quite complex. Theoretically, you can construct a query with 12 rows of OR conditions, and each query can contain any number of AND conditions. In practice, such a query is very difficult to understand and takes a long time to process on a large database.

Generally, you find yourself using queries with one or two OR conditions and one or two AND conditions. Sometimes, you construct a simple query and then add more AND and OR conditions to refine the search until the view screen contains one or two very specific records.

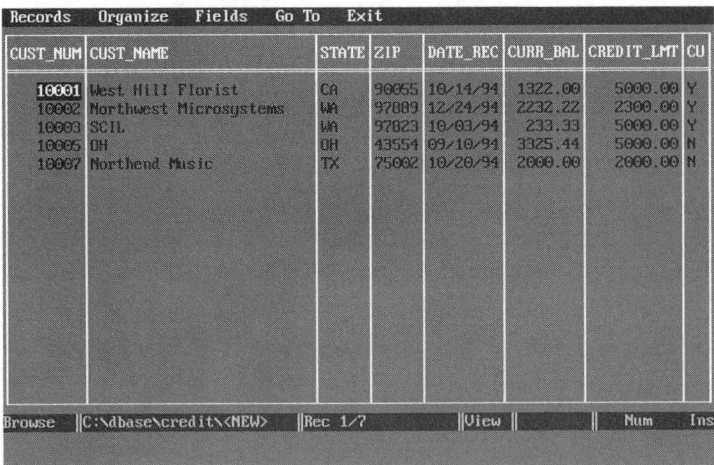

Fig. 9.29 The result of an OR search on two different fields.

Filtering Records with Condition Boxes

Although applying filters to the fields in a file skeleton enables you to search and evaluate your database in a sophisticated manner, occasionally you use the condition box to filter records in the query. The condition box performs two functions that the file skeleton cannot—it searches for deleted records and searches in memo fields. It can also be used to perform the same type of searches that are specified in the file skeleton. For example, to search for all the records of customers in Texas or Washington, you can enter this expression in the condition box:

state="TX" .or. state="WA"

To open and use the condition box from the Query design screen, open the Condition menu and choose Add Condition Box. An empty condition box appears on the Query design screen. The following sections explain how to use the condition box to test whether a record has been marked for deletion and how to search memo fields for particular information.

Testing for Deleted Records

To test for deleted records, follow these steps:

1. Open the Condition menu and choose Add Condition Box.
2. In the condition box, type **deleted( )**. This dBASE function returns TRUE if the record is marked for deletion and FALSE if the record is not

marked for deletion. Figure 9.30 shows the condition box with this expression entered.

3. Press F2.

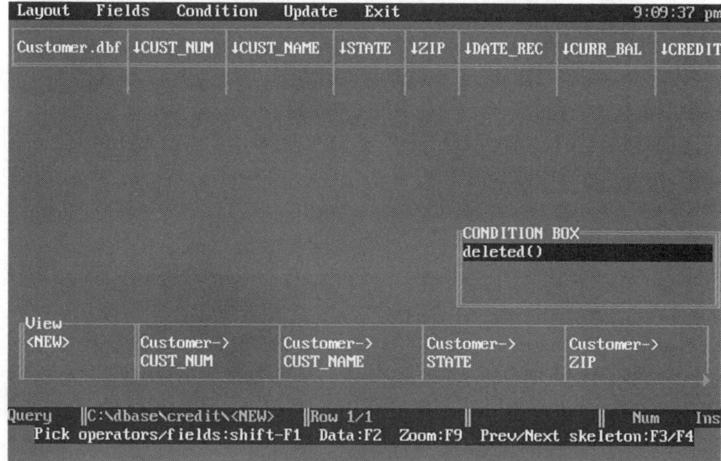

Fig. 9.30
The condition box set up to search for deleted records.

Searching for Values in a Memo Field

As you learned earlier, you cannot enter a value in a memo field input area in a query. To filter records based on values in a memo field, you must use the condition box. If your database has a memo field named COMMENT, for example, and you want to select records in which COMMENT contains the words `Call later`, you add a condition box and enter the value in the condition box.

◀ See "Deleting Records," p. 156

▶ See "Marking Records for Deletion," p. 243

▶ See "Unmarking Records Marked for Deletion," p. 244

To perform this type of search, follow these steps:

1. Open the Condition menu and choose Add Condition Box.

2. In the condition box, type the dBASE expression **"call later" $ comment**. The $ (included in) operator tells dBASE to look at each memo field. If the character string *call later* is in the memo field, the record is placed in the view. Figure 9.31 shows the Query design screen with this condition in place. Note that this is a case-sensitive search; for example, *call LATER* would not be found.

3. Press F2. The view screen shows the records whose memo field contains the string *call later*. To read the memo, place the cursor in the field labeled MEMO and press Ctrl-Home. To exit the memo field, press Ctrl-End.

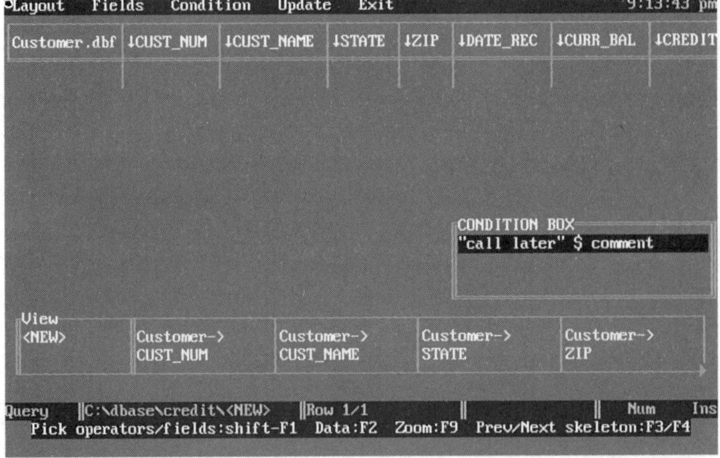

Fig. 9.31
The condition box set up to search for text in a memo field.

> **Note**
>
> To make it easier to type a lengthy condition statement in a condition box, click `Zoom:F9` in the navigation line to expand the size of the box to the width of the screen. If the condition box is not zoomed, a lengthy statement will scroll as it is typed. Click `Zoom:F9` again to shrink the box to its original size.

When you no longer need a condition box, remove it from the screen by choosing Condition, Remove Condition Box. Removing the condition box also deletes the condition.

To hide the condition box and change it into a marker (so that you can see the file skeleton, for example), move the highlight out of the condition box, choose Condition from the menu bar, and choose Show Condition Box NO. When you change the condition box to a marker, the words `CONDITION BOX` appear above the view skeleton to remind you that a condition is in effect. To display the condition box again, choose Condition, Show Condition Box YES.

Unlike the file skeleton, the condition box treats additional lines of conditions as AND conditions. Records must meet all conditions specified. Figure 9.32 shows a condition box that will search for all deleted records with a value of TX in the STATE field.

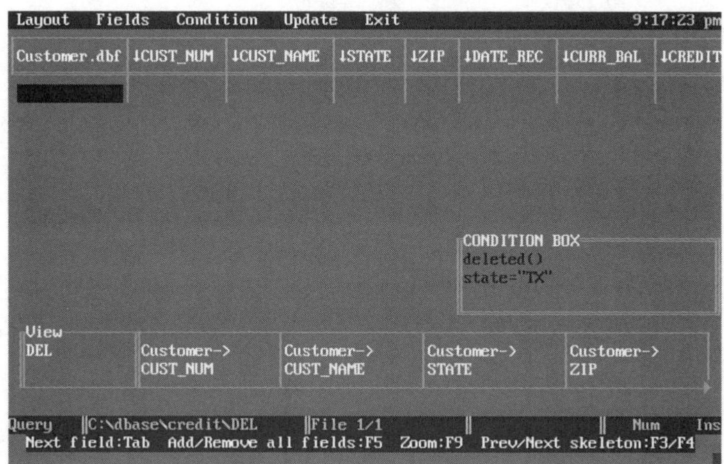

Fig. 9.32
The condition box set up to search for an AND condition—all records for the state of Texas that are marked as deleted.

Finding a Specific Record with a Query

By using the find operator, a query can locate specific records in the database in much the same way as the Forward Search option in the Go To menu. When you use a query to find a record, all the database records are shown in the view screen, with the first record that meets your query conditions highlighted. If you use a query to find a record, you have the advantage of being able to specify a complex condition, whereas a forward search can search only for a single value.

To use queries to find a record, enter the query conditions as you normally do, but also enter the word **find** below the database file name in the file skeleton. Figure 9.33 shows an example of a FIND query that searches for the first record in the Customer database with a current balance value less than $1,000.

Figure 9.34 shows the results of the FIND query. All the records in the database are shown in the view screen; the first record that meets the search criteria is highlighted in the top row. You can see the records that do not meet the search criteria above the top row by pressing the up-arrow key.

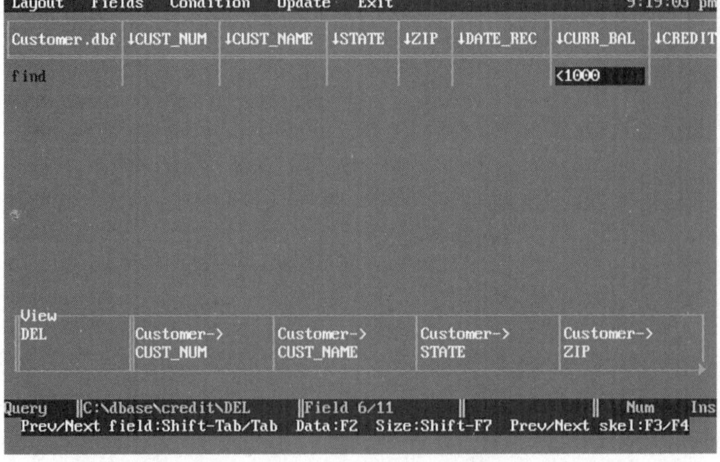

Fig. 9.33
A FIND query that finds all records with a credit balance that is less than $1,000.

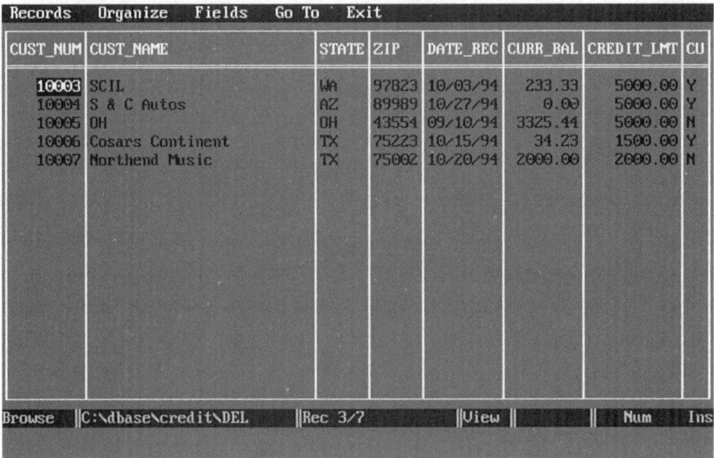

Fig. 9.34
The record in the top row meets the condition of the FIND query.

Creating and Using Calculated Fields

Sometimes the database fields do not provide all the information you need in the view screen. You might need to calculate a value using one or more fields in the file skeleton. For example, in the Customer database you could calculate a customer's remaining balance by subtracting the current balance from the credit limit. When a calculated field is created, it can be added to the view skeleton just like a regular field.

Note

The term *calculated field* may be misleading. A calculated field does not have to perform a mathematical calculation. It simply has to perform some type of operation. When the text field F_NAME is joined with the text field L_NAME, an operation is performed; thus, the expression F_NAME+L_NAME is an expression that can be used to create a calculated field.

To create a calculated field and add it to a view skeleton, follow these steps:

1. From the Query design screen, open the Fields menu and choose Create Calculated Field. A Calculated Fields skeleton is displayed below the active file skeleton.

2. Enter the expression for the field, such as **CREDIT_LMT–CURR_BAL**.

3. To add this calculated field to the view skeleton, press F5 and type a name for the calculated field such as **CRED_REM**. The field is added to the far right side of the view skeleton. You can move the field to another position in the view skeleton as outlined earlier in this chapter.

When a query that has a calculated field is executed, the results of the calculated field are shown on the screen just like a regular field. If changes are made to the fields that are used in the calculation expression, the result is recalculated automatically in the calculated field. In the preceding example, if the credit limit is originally $3,000 and the current balance is $1,000, the value of the calculated field is $2,000. If you change the credit limit to $5,000, the calculated field immediately changes to $4,000. Because a calculated field is a "read-only" field, changes cannot be made manually in the calculated field.

You can use the calculated field to limit searches as if it were a real database field. Move the highlight to the calculated field by pressing F4 and then press the down-arrow key to highlight the box below the calculated field. Enter the search value. Figure 9.35 shows the calculated field CRED_REM with a search value of <1000. Figure 9.36 shows the result of this query. Notice in figure 9.35 that the CRED_REM calculated field was moved to the view skeleton so that you can see it without using the Tab key. Notice also that the field has the code R/O (this stands for Read Only).

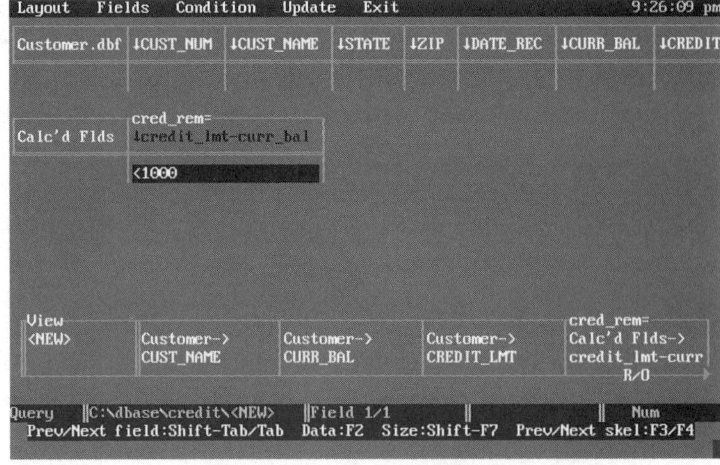

Fig. 9.35
A query based on a calculated field. This query finds all records that have less than $1,000 left for available credit (the credit limit minus the current balance).

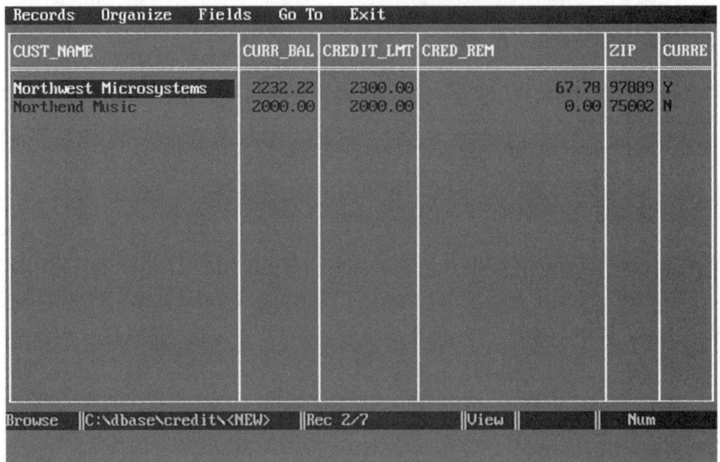

Fig. 9.36
The result of the query using a calculated field.

Using Functions in an Expression

dBASE 5 has almost 200 functions. Many of these functions can be used in expressions to perform a calculation.

Suppose you want to create a field that displays the name of the month for the date that is entered in the DATE_REC field. The CMONTH( ) function will perform this calculation for you. Figure 9.37 shows the query with the calculated field. Figure 9.38 shows the result of the calculation.

Now suppose that the Customer database has an additional date field called CRED_DATE which contains the date that credit was first issued to the customer. If you want to calculate how many years the customer has been buying on credit, the expression would be

INT((DATE( )-CRED_DATE)/365)

This expression subtracts the current system date (the date in the PC's clock/calendar) from the CRED_DATE. The result of this subtraction is expressed in days. The number of days is divided by 365 to calculate the number of years. The INT( ) function truncates the decimal portion of the dividend. Figure 9.39 shows a calculated field with this expression, and the result is shown in Figure 9.40.

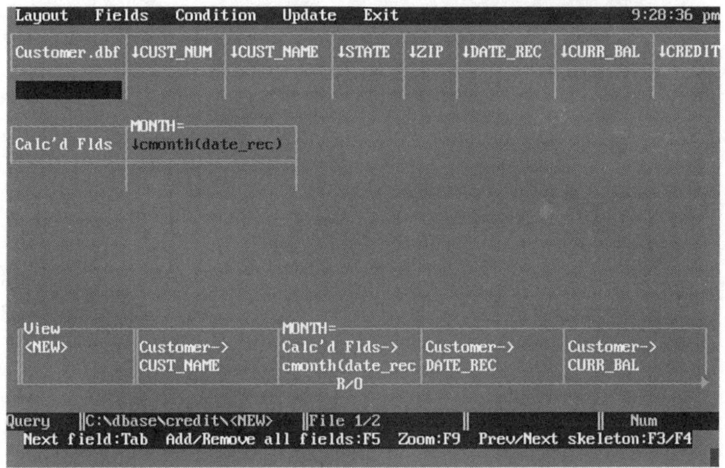

Fig. 9.37
A calculated field that uses a function to convert the numeric representation of the month in the DATE_REC field to the alpha representation of a month (i.e., January, February, and so on).

Records Organize Fields Go To Exit

CUST_NAME	MONTH	DATE_REC	CURR_BAL	CREDIT_LMT	ZIP	CURREN
West Hill Florist	October	10/14/94	1322.00	5000.00	90055	Y
Northwest Microsystems	December	12/24/94	2232.22	2300.00	97889	Y
SCIL	October	10/03/94	233.33	5000.00	97823	Y
S & C Autos	October	10/27/94	0.00	5000.00	89989	Y
OH	September	09/10/94	3325.44	5000.00	43554	N
Cosars Continent	October	10/15/94	34.23	1500.00	75223	Y
Northend Music	October	10/20/94	2000.00	2000.00	75002	N

Browse C:\dbase\credit\<NEW> Rec 1/7 View Num

Fig. 9.38
The result of the calculated field showing the names of the months in the MONTH field.

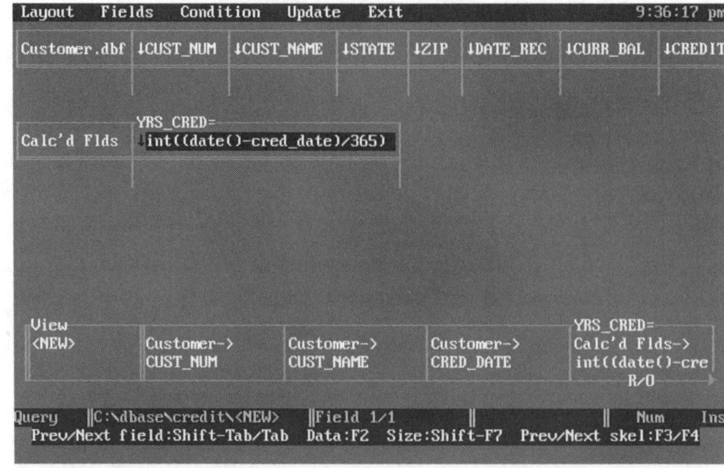

Fig. 9.39
A date function used in a calculated field to determine the number of years that a customer has had credit.

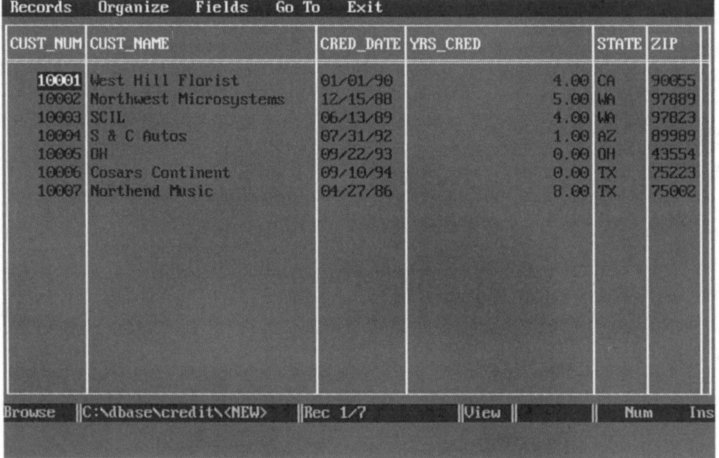

Fig. 9.40
The result of the date function showing only whole years because the INT( ) function truncates the decimal value in the computation.

Adding More Calculated Fields

► See "Replacing Values," p. 237

► See "Adding Calculated Fields," p. 274

Additional calculated fields can be added to the Calculated Field skeleton by following the same steps outlined previously. dBASE has no limit to the number of calculated fields you can add to the skeleton.

Removing Calculated Fields

To remove a calculated field from the Calculated Field skeleton, perform these steps:

1. Highlight the field in the Calculated Field skeleton.

2. Open the Fields menu and choose Delete Calculated Field.

You can remove a calculated field from the view skeleton just like a regular field is removed. Highlight the field in the view skeleton and press F5.

Saving a Query for Repeated Use

After you construct a query that presents only the records you want in the order and format you want them, you may want to save the query for future use. Follow these steps:

▶ See "Grouping Records," p. 227

▶ See "Adding Calculated Fields," p. 274

1. Open the Layout menu and choose Save This Query. dBASE 5 prompts you for a name.

2. Type a file name and press Enter. dBASE appends the extension QBE to the file name and saves the query in the current directory. dBASE also adds the query to the current catalog and to the Queries panel in the Control Center so it is available for use.

Using a query from the Queries panel saves time and effort. If you need to look at a database in a certain way every day or create a daily report using only selected records, create a query that fills your need and save it. Then use the query every day instead of creating the same query every time you need it. If something in the query changes slightly every time you use it, such as the value of a date field, simply modify the query as explained in the next section.

Creating a New Query from an Existing Query

You can save a query and then use it as the basis for other queries. After you save the first query, highlight it in the Queries panel, press Enter, and choose Modify Query. Make changes as necessary and save it with a new name, or save it with its original name. If a new name is used, the new query is added to the catalog; your original query is unaltered.

Using a Query with a Report

It is very simple to use a query to select records for a report. Follow these steps:

1. Highlight the query in the Queries panel.

2. Press Enter.
3. Choose Use View.
4. Highlight the report in the Reports panel.
5. Press Enter.
6. Choose Print Report or Display Data.
7. Choose Current view.

From Here...

This chapter showed you how to retrieve information from your database by using queries. For more information relating to queries, you may want to read the following chapters:

- Chapter 10, "Using Advanced Techniques with Queries," shows you how to use the Query design work surface to create queries that summarize and update information in a database.
- Chapter 23, "Using Functions," lists and explains all the functions available in dBASE. These functions can be used to create calculated fields.

Chapter 10

Using Advanced Techniques with Queries

In Chapter 9, "Using Queries To Search Databases," you learned some very powerful techniques with queries. If you are an average user, those techniques are adequate for about 85 percent of what you do. For some of the more advanced tasks that you must perform, dBASE provides summary calculations, grouping of records, update queries, and queries that can extract data from multiple databases.

In this chapter, the Customer database described in Chapter 9 is used frequently for examples. You may want to review the fields in the database by referring to figure 9.1.

Advanced query techniques that are covered in this chapter include:

- Performing summary math in queries
- Grouping records
- Sorting and indexing the output of a query
- Using update queries
- Linking multiple databases

Performing Summary Calculations with a Query

All the queries discussed thus far have displayed a subset of records. Sometimes, however, you don't want to see every record; you only want to see a calculation that is performed on all of the records. For example, you may not need to see all the records for subscribers to a newsletter, but you may need to know how many subscriptions there are so that you will know how many newsletters to print. You can use a summary operator to total the number of subscriptions in the QTY field. For a database that lists all the equipment for each department in a company, you may want to know the average cost of all the equipment used in the Sales Department. You can use a summary operator to average the cost.

dBASE provides seven summary operators that can be used in a query: SUM, AVG, MIN, MAX, STD, VAR, and CNT. See Table 10.1.

Table 10.1 Summary Operators

Operator	Description
SUM	Adds all the values in the field and returns the total
AVG (or AVERAGE)	Adds all the values in the field, divides by the number of records, and returns the average value in that field
MIN	Returns the smallest value in that field
MAX	Returns the largest value in that field
STD	Calculates standard deviation
CNT (or COUNT)	Counts the number of records that meet the specified conditions
VAR	Calculates population variance

◄ See "Using the Default Quick Report Form," p. 179

► See "Using a Report," p. 315

Note

Summary operators are also called *aggregate operators*. They are used not only in queries, but in the quick report and custom reports.

To summarize a field when performing a query, simply type the operator in the appropriate field in the file skeleton and execute the query. Figure 10.1 shows a query that asks for the average value (AVG) of the values in the CURR_BAL field.

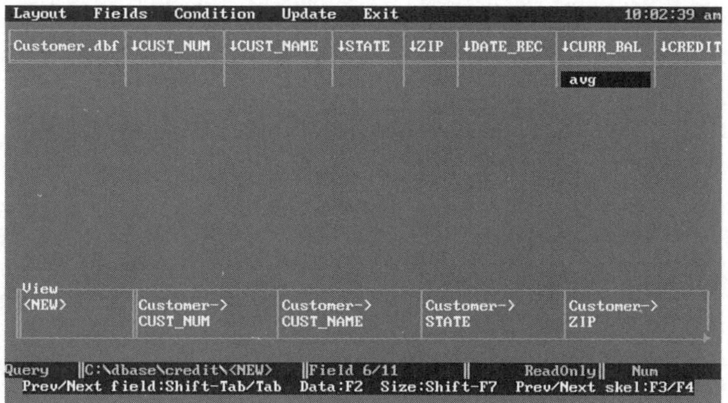

Fig. 10.1
A query that uses the AVG summary operator to find the average amount in the CURR-BAL field.

Figure 10.2 shows the result of this query. The only field that shows a value is the field in which you specify the summary operator. The other fields are blank, which makes sense because dBASE 5 cannot enter anything in the other fields.

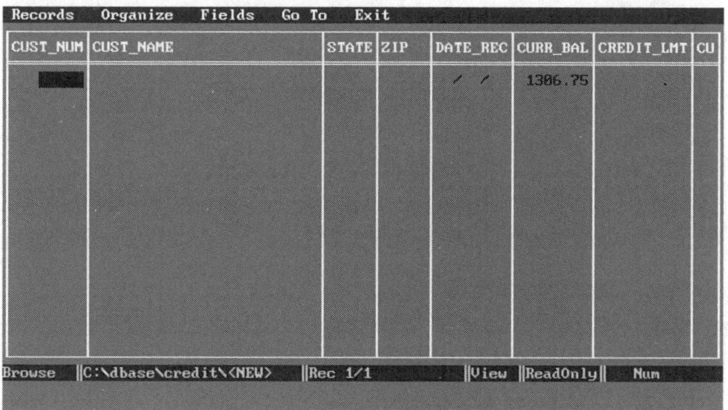

Fig. 10.2
The result of the AVG query shows only the average in the CURR_BAL field and no data in any other fields.

Combining Summary Operators

You can combine summary operators with other conditions if you use the AND relationship. For example, by placing AVG in the CURR_BAL field and "WA" in the STATE field, as shown in figure 10.3, you can find the average value of the CURR_BAL fields for records that also have WA in the STATE field. Notice in figure 10.3 that AVG does not have to be capitalized because dBASE 5 is not case-sensitive, but the quotation marks are necessary. Figure 10.4 shows the result of the query.

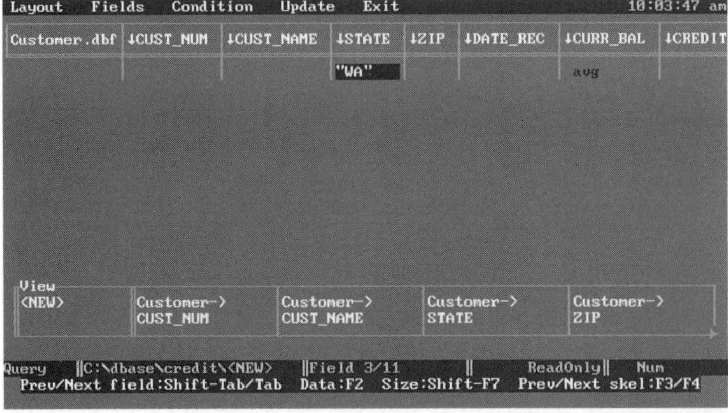

Fig. 10.3
A query that finds the AVG for only those records for the state of Washington.

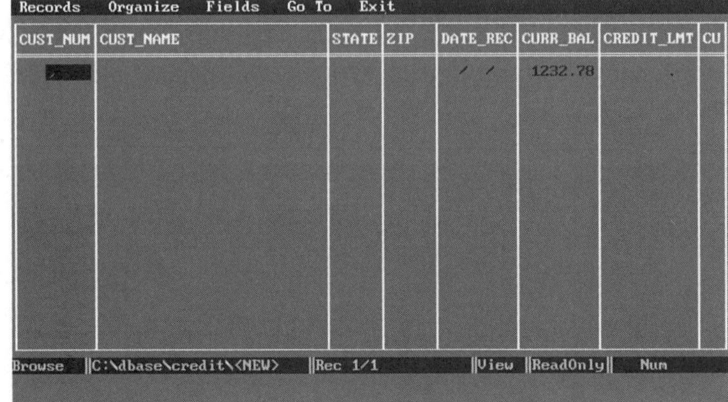

Fig. 10.4
The result of the AVG query for selected records looks just like the result of a query for all records, but the amount is different, of course.

Using Conditions with Summary Operators

In all summary operations, if a condition is specified, the value returned is only for records that meet any specified search condition. If you do not specify a condition, all records are summed, or averaged, and so on.

The word *unique* can be used to define a special condition for a summary operator. If you enter the SUM operator followed by the word *unique*, dBASE will add all of the values in the field that are unique. In other words, if two records have the same value, only one of the values will be included in the sum. Suppose you want to know what the company's credit limit would be like for 10,000 groups that are based on every credit limit now offered. First you would need the total of each unique credit limit now being offered. You could get the answer to this problem by typing **sum unique** in the CREDIT_LMT field in the file skeleton, as shown in figure 10.5.

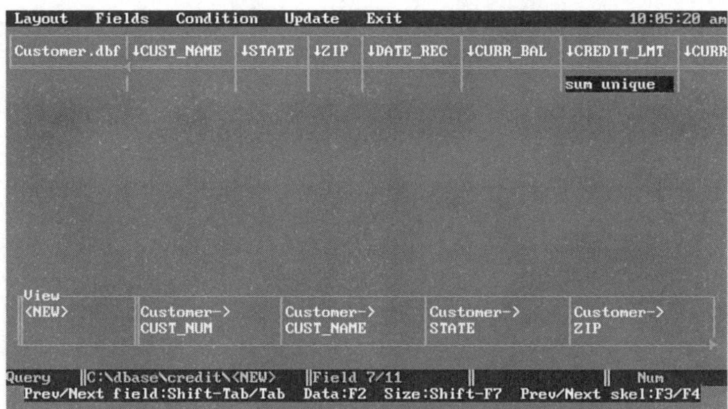

Fig. 10.5
A query that uses the UNIQUE operator to sum the unique credit limit values.

Using Multiple Summary Operators

Multiple summary operators can be used in the same query. For example, you could include the AVG on the CREDIT_LMT field and the SUM on the CURR_BAL field.

> **Troubleshooting**
>
> *When I use a summary operator, the message* `Data type mismatch` *is displayed.*
>
> Not all summary operators can be used in all types of fields. AVG, SUM, STD, and VAR can be used in numeric or float fields. MIN and MAX can be used in numeric, float, character, and date fields. CNT can be used in numeric, float, character, date, and logical fields. No summary operators can be used in a memo field.
>
> Summary operators also cannot be used in update queries or with the FIND operator.

Grouping Records

In the preceding example, only the current balances for one value of the STATE field are averaged. But by using the grouping feature, you can have all the states listed with an average for each state.

To group records for summaries, enter the words **GROUP BY** in the field you want to group. In figure 10.6, for example, the query is constructed so that all records for each state are grouped together and the average of the CURR_BAL field for that group is reported. This operation works most efficiently if you have created an index for the GROUP BY field and have selected Include Indexes from the Fields menu. The result of this grouped query is shown in figure 10.7. If the field that you want to group on is not indexed, you must modify the database structure and index the field, or sort the database and use the sorted file for the query. If a field is not indexed, dBASE has no way to group the records because they are not physically together in the database.

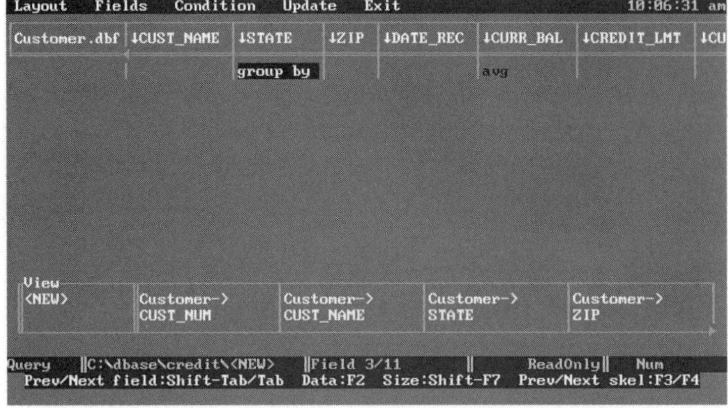

Fig. 10.6
This query groups each state and calculates the average for each.

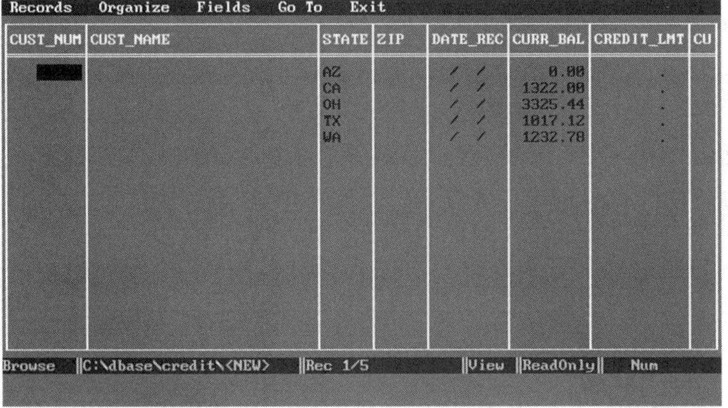

Fig. 10.7
The result of the query lists each state with its corresponding average.

When you add operators (such as AVERAGE or GROUP BY) to the query, click a field in a file skeleton where you will use the operator and then press Shift-F1 to open the Expression Builder menu (see fig. 10.8). Select the operator you want to use and click it to place it in the field. Note, however, that VAR and STD cannot be grouped.

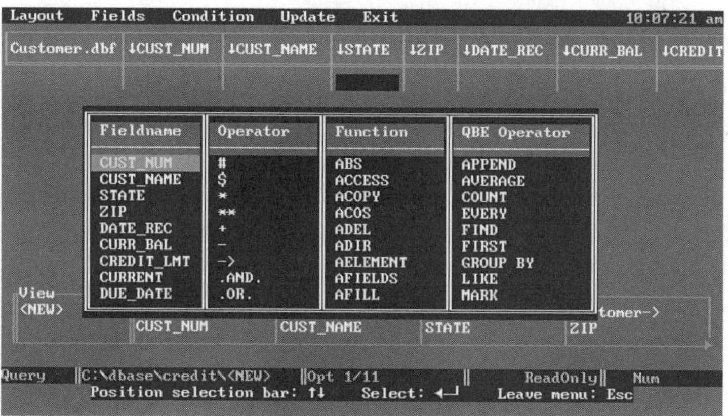

Fig. 10.8
The Expression Builder menu can be used as an aid for selecting the correct field names, operators, and functions.

Using Example Variables in Conditions

Example variables can be used in conditions to compare the value in one field of a record to the value of another field in the same record. In the Customer database you might want to see which records are $1,000 or less under the credit limit. To find this out, you could create an example variable for the CREDIT_LMT field. Suppose you call the variable LIMIT. (The variable can be any word of 10 characters or less.) Then, using the variable, you could enter the condition **>=limit–1000** in the CURR_BAL field. Figure 10.9 shows this condition. To arrive at the same result you could also enter **>=credit_lmt–1000.** Example variable can be used as a shortcut to create shorter field names.

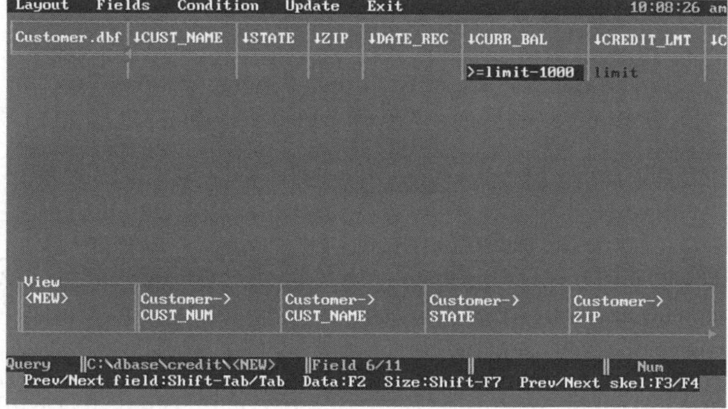

Fig. 10.9
A query that uses an example variable in the condition to find records with a current balance that is 1000 or less under the credit limit.

Indexing Query Output

In all the previous examples, the output of a query has displayed the records in record number order, that is, the order in which they were entered in the database. You may want to see these records in some other specified order. The Query design work surface provides two ways to order the view records: You can sort them, or you can tell the query to use an existing index and present them in indexed order.

Using an index is the best method of organizing the records. The only drawback to using indexes is that you cannot create them "on the fly" in the Query design work surface. If you created the necessary indexes before you enter the Query design work surface, you can access them. If you need an index you haven't created, however, you must return to the Control Center to create the index.

Specifying an Index for the View

To reorganize a view by using an existing index, follow these steps:

1. In the Query design work surface, open the Fields menu.
2. Move the highlight to Include Indexes NO and press Enter. Although you cannot see it because the menu is exited immediately, the NO changes to YES. Now all the indexes you have created for the database are available. When you change Include indexes to YES, symbols are displayed next to each indexed field.

   The symbol indicates the type of index order used:

   Up arrowhead: ascending ASCII.

   Down arrowhead: descending ASCII.

   Pound sign (#): field used in two or more index tags, at least one ascending ASCII and one descending ASCII.
3. Move the cursor to the field on which you want to index the view screen. Open the Fields menu again and choose the option Sort on This Field. Choose the type of sort you want. Note that the type of sort you choose must be the same type you used when you indexed the file. If you choose another type, the query is processed like a sort, and you gain nothing by using indexes.
4. Press F2 to process the sort. The view screen appears (much faster now, particularly if you're working with a large database).

Using Complex Indexes in a Query

You may have created a complex index in the Control Center, such as CUST_NAME+STATE. After you specify Include Indexes, you can use complex indexes in a query. Complex indexes appear in the file skeleton to the far right, after all the database fields. You can use complex index fields for indexing and selecting as if they were regular database fields.

◄ See "Creating Indexes that Use Multiple Fields," p. 115

Sorting Query Output

Sorting the view screen is another way to order the records in a view. But remember, using indexes is the preferred method. In large databases sorting can be slow, and sorting the database also requires additional disk space. Additionally, sorting on more than one field produces a read-only view that cannot be edited.

To sort the output of a query, follow these simple steps:

1. Specify the query conditions that you want in the file skeleton.
2. Move the highlight to the field in the file skeleton that you want to sort.
3. Open the Fields menu and choose Sort on This Field. The Sort Definition menu appears, as shown in figure 10.10.

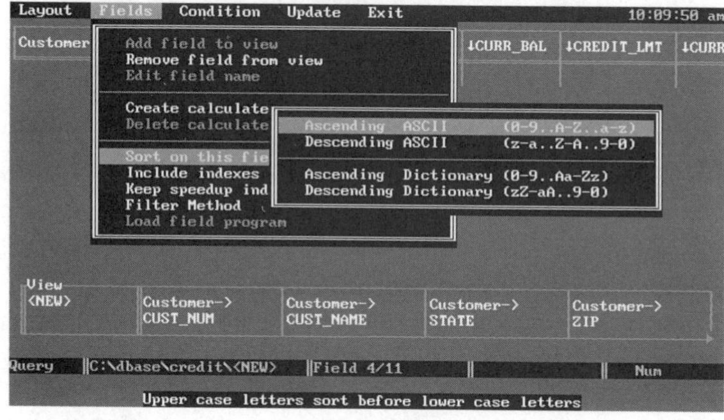

Fig. 10.10
The Sort Definition menu shows the four types of sorts dBASE can perform.

4. Choose the type of sort you want and press Enter to return to the Query design screen. (See Table 10.2 for examples of the various types of sorts.) The type of sort selected is displayed in the field with a numbered sort operator (see Table 10.3). Figure 10.11 shows a query with an Ascending Dictionary sort in the STATE field.

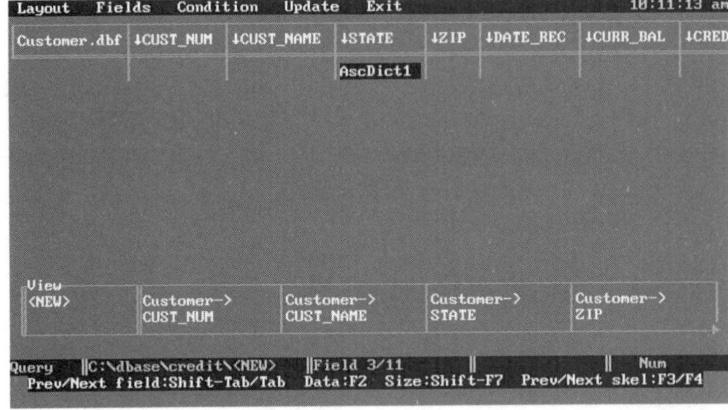

Fig. 10.11
This query lists the states in Ascending Dictionary order.

5. Press F2 to execute the query; figure 10.12 shows the resulting view screen. The records are sorted by the value in the STATE field.

Records Organize Fields Go To Exit

CUST_NUM	CUST_NAME	STATE	ZIP	DATE_REC	CURR_BAL	CREDIT_LMT	CU
10004	S & C Autos	AZ	89989	10/27/94	0.00	5000.00	Y
10001	West Hill Florist	CA	90055	10/14/94	1322.00	5000.00	Y
10005	OH	OH	43554	09/10/94	3325.44	5000.00	N
10006	Cosars Continent	TX	75223	10/15/94	34.23	1500.00	Y
10007	Northend Music	TX	75002	10/20/94	2000.00	2000.00	N
10002	Northwest Microsystems	WA	97889	12/24/94	2232.22	2300.00	Y
10003	SCIL	WA	97823	10/03/94	233.33	5000.00	Y

Browse C:\dbase\credit\<NEW> Rec 1/7 View ReadOnly Num

Fig. 10.12
The STATE field sorted in Ascending Dictionary order.

Tip
You can type the sort operators in the appropriate fields instead of using the menus. If you type the operator yourself, you do not have to include a number. There is an advantage to doing so as you will soon see.

dBASE offers four options for sorting your views. In Ascending ASCII, entries beginning with numbers appear first, then entries beginning with uppercase letters appear, in alphabetical order, followed by entries beginning with lowercase letters. Entries beginning with special characters, such as commas, semicolons, asterisks, and so on, are ordered by where the character appears in the ASCII sequence. (ASCII refers to how characters are stored in a computer.) Descending ASCII is the reverse of Ascending ASCII.

Dictionary sorts treat uppercase and lowercase characters the same. The Ascending Dictionary sort follows the pattern Aa, Bb, Cc, and so on. Descending Dictionary reverses Ascending Dictionary. Table 10.2 shows examples of the four types of sorts dBASE provides.

Table 10.2 Types of dBASE Sorts

Ascending ASCII	Descending ASCII	Ascending Dictionary	Descending Dictionary
8888888888	cccccccccc	8888888888	CCCCCCCCCC
9999999999	bbbbbbbbbb	9999999999	cccccccccc
AAAAAAAAAA	aaaaaaaaaa	AAAAAAAAAA	BBBBBBBBBB
BBBBBBBBBB	CCCCCCCCCC	aaaaaaaaaa	bbbbbbbbbb
CCCCCCCCCC	BBBBBBBBBB	BBBBBBBBBB	AAAAAAAAAA
aaaaaaaaaa	AAAAAAAAAA	bbbbbbbbbb	aaaaaaaaaa
bbbbbbbbbb	9999999999	CCCCCCCCCC	9999999999
cccccccccc	8888888888	cccccccccc	8888888888

The sort operators shown in Table 10.3 can be entered directly or you can use menu options (explained later) to enter the operators.

Table 10.3 Sort Operators

Type of Sort	Operator
Ascending ASCII	Asc
Descending ASCII	Dsc
Ascending Dictionary	AscDict
Descending Dictionary	DscDict

Sorting on Multiple Fields

Sorting on multiple fields is simple. You just have to remember to define the sorts in the order that you want them sorted. If you want to sort on the STATE field first and then on the CUST_NAME field (so that the records appear alphabetized by customer name in each state), for example, define the STATE sort first and the CUST_NAME sort second.

When you define additional sorts, dBASE 5 appends a number to each sort in the file skeleton. The sort process follows this numerical sequence: the lowest number indicates the major sort, the next lowest number is the next sort, and so on. For example, Asc1 is performed before AscDict2.

Tip
Rather than sorting more than one field, use a complex index instead. For example instead of sorting on the STATE field and the CUST_NAME field, use the complex index STATE+CUST_NAME.

Because dBASE assigns the appended sort numbers throughout the query session, you may have a query with a major sort defined as AscDict5, if you specified four sorts previously in the session—even though none of those four sorts are in effect at the time.

When you work with a query repeatedly, dBASE does not enable you to use more than nine different sorts if the sorts are specified by using the menu; dBASE does not accept a 10th sort. If you try to use a 10th sort, the message, `Cannot use a sort priority number higher than nine` appears. If you use all nine sorts, you must save the query, return to the Control Center, select the query you just saved, and return to the Query design work surface. dBASE resets the sort counter, enabling you to continue with more sorts. If you enter your own sorting operators, you don't need to worry about the counter.

Figure 10.13 shows the file skeleton with a major sort by STATE and a secondary sort by CUST_NAME. Figure 10.14 shows the result of this multiple-field sort.

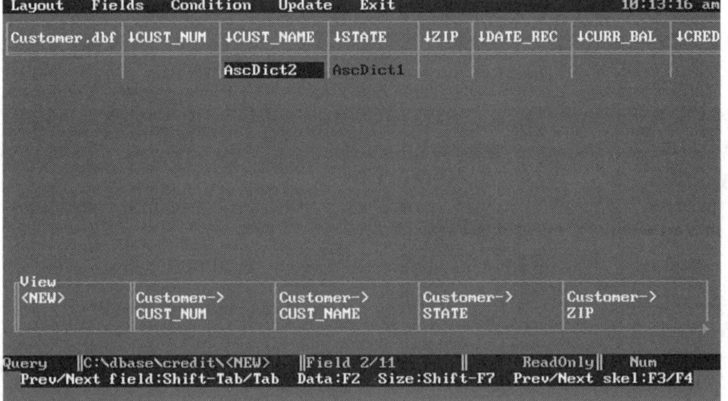

Fig. 10.13
A query that sorts on the STATE field as the primary sort field and then on the CUST_NAME field as the secondary sort field.

Note

If you sort more than one field or select the Dictionary sort, the message `ReadOnly` appears on the status line. The `ReadOnly` message reminds you that you cannot access this database to change values in it.

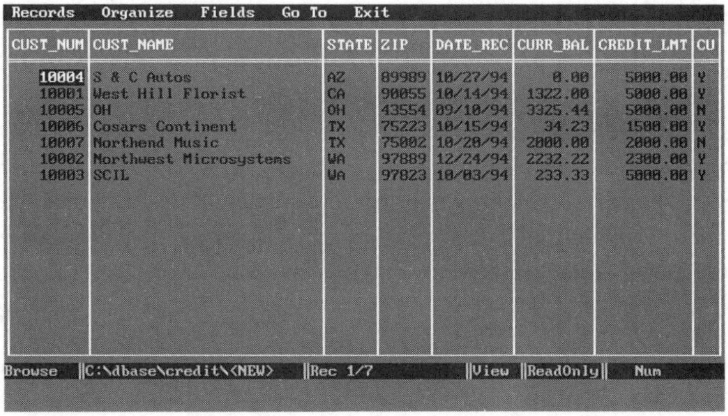

Records Organize Fields Go To Exit

CUST_NUM	CUST_NAME	STATE	ZIP	DATE_REC	CURR_BAL	CREDIT_LMT	CU
10004	S & C Autos	AZ	89989	10/27/94	0.00	5000.00	Y
10001	West Hill Florist	CA	90055	10/14/94	1322.00	5000.00	Y
10005	OH	OH	43554	09/10/94	3325.44	5000.00	N
10006	Cosars Continent	TX	75223	10/15/94	34.23	1500.00	Y
10007	Northend Music	TX	75002	10/20/94	2000.00	2000.00	N
10002	Northwest Microsystems	WA	97889	12/24/94	2232.22	2300.00	Y
10003	SCIL	WA	97823	10/03/94	233.33	5000.00	Y

Browse ║C:\dbase\credit\<NEW> ║Rec 1/7 ║View ║ReadOnly║ Num

Fig. 10.14
The result of the sort on two fields shows that the states are alphabetized and then the customer names are alphabetized within the states.

Troubleshooting

I tried to use GROUP BY in a query, but it will not group the data in the field.

The GROUP BY operator cannot be used alone to group data. It can only be used with a summary operator. To group the data, sort it or use an index.

When I sort on the MFG field, IBM is sorted with the other company names that start with "I."

You are using the Ascending ASCII sort which sorts words with all uppercase letters before words with uppercase and lowercase letters. You should use the Ascending Dictionary sort.

After sorting the database on two fields in a query, I find that I cannot make corrections when the data is displayed on the Browse screen.

This is because sorting on more than one field makes the resulting data Read Only. If this is a problem for you, create a complex index using both fields rather than sorting on the fields.

Combining Sorts and Searches in the Same Field

If you want to sort on a field that will also specify a condition, first enter the search value. Then open the Fields menu and choose Sort on This Field. After you finish defining the sort, the search value and the sort definition appear in the field separated by a comma.

Tip
Remember that you can type the sort operators instead of using the menu.

For example, if you want to sort the records by ZIP, but you want to view only records in which ZIP>"60001", the entry in the file skeleton would be >"60001", Asc1.

Updating Values in a Database with a Query

As you learned in Chapter 9, "Using Queries To Search Databases," dBASE has two types of queries—view queries and update queries. Thus far, the discussion in this book has pertained to only view queries. With an update query, you can replace values in database fields, append records to the database from another database, mark records for deletion, and unmark records previously marked for deletion.

The first two steps for creating an update query are just like the steps for creating a view query:

1. Activate the desired database file in the Data panel of the Control Center.

2. Move the cursor to the Queries panel, highlight `<create>`, and press Enter to display a Query design screen.

3. Open the Update menu and choose Specify Update Operation. The Update Operation menu appears (see fig. 10.15).

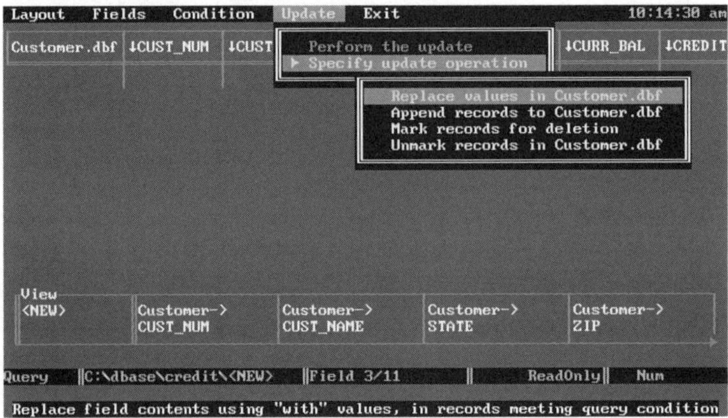

Fig. 10.15 The Update Operation menu shows the four types of updates that dBASE can perform.

4. Depending on the type of update operation you select, follow the instructions in the sections that follow.

You can carry out four update operations: Replace, Append, Mark, and Unmark. The following sections explain how to use an update query for each operation.

Replacing Values

The Replace Values option enables you to replace the values of all or a subset of database records with another value. The replacement value can be any valid dBASE expression. For example, if the CUST_NUM values in the database start at 1 and you decide that you want them to start at 10,000, follow these steps to replace the values in that field:

1. Open the Update Operation menu and choose Replace Values in Customer.dbf. Notice that the option includes the name of the currently active database.

2. Choose Proceed when dBASE tells you that the view skeleton will be deleted. Because update queries do not put data on-screen, you don't need a view skeleton.

   The word `Replace` appears under the name of the database in the file skeleton to remind you that this query is an update query. (This portion of the skeleton is commonly known as the *pothandle*.)

3. Move the highlight to the CUST_NUM field. Type the following:

   with CUST_NUM + 10000

   Figure 10.16 shows the update query with this replacement expression in place. This expression tells dBASE to replace all CUST_NUM values with the old CUST_NUM value plus 10,000.

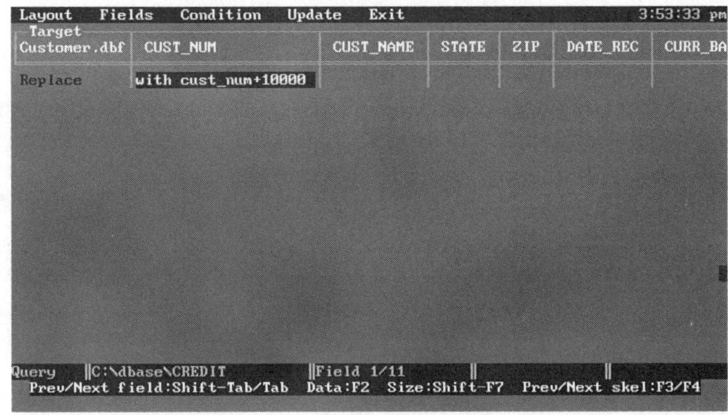

Fig. 10.16 This Replace query adds 10,000 to each customer number.

4. Open the Update menu and choose Perform the Update. When the update is completed, dBASE displays the message `Press any key to continue`; do so to return to the Query design screen.

5. Press F2 to display the database with the CUST_NUM fields changed (see fig. 10.17).

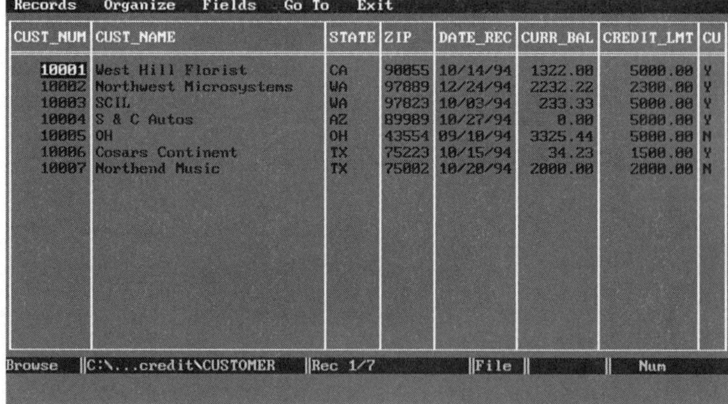

Fig. 10.17
The result of a Replace update shows the new customer numbers.

You can limit the records that are replaced by including search conditions in the update query. If you want to replace CUST_NUM values in records only for the state of WA, for example, type **WA** in the STATE field and type **with CUST_NUM+10,000** in the CUST_NUM field. Only records meeting the specified condition are updated. As with query by example, you also can use AND and OR conditions to limit the replacement.

Functions can also be used in expressions to replace values. Study the following examples shown in figures 10.18 through 10.23.

Figure 10.18 shows a query on the Employee database that uses the substring function to replace the full name in the field with the first letter in the name, thus creating the middle initial. Figure 10.19 shows the results. Although it is not considered good practice to include a period in a middle initial field, if you wanted to do so the expression would look like this:

```
substr(middle,1,1)+"."
```

Figure 10.20 shows a query that will change all the characters entered in a field to uppercase. You might want to do this for a field that has been typed in a variety of ways causing the data to look inconsistent or sort incorrectly.

In figure 10.21, the replace query trims the trailing spaces from the first name field, adds a space, and combines the last name field. Then it changes the entire string to uppercase. The field that is updated with the information has been added to the database and is actually empty for each record, so the update command is really adding information.

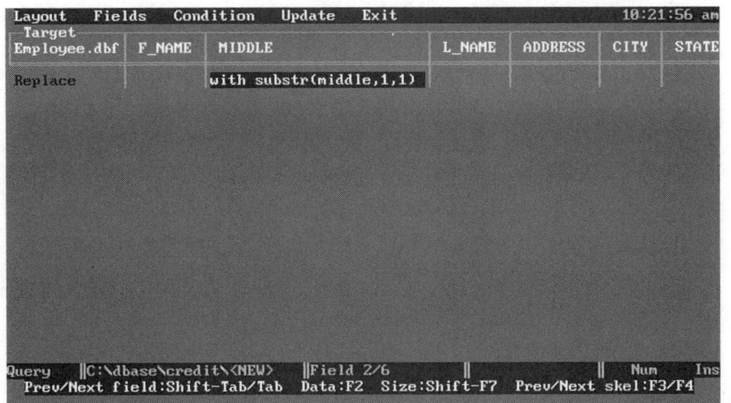

Fig. 10.18
This Replace query uses the substring function to replace the name in the MIDDLE field with the first letter of the name.

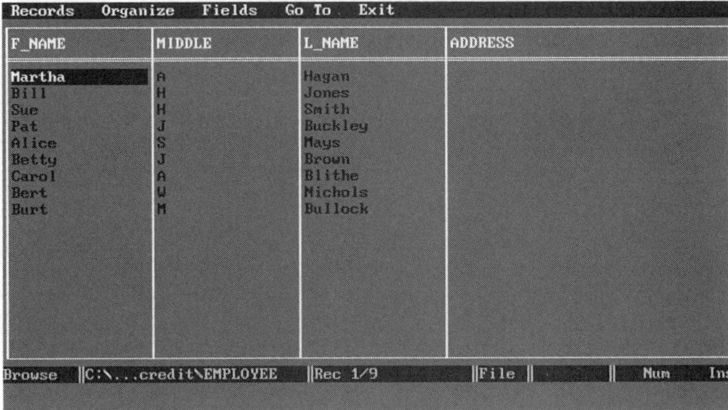

Fig. 10.19
This is the result of the Replace query that changes the full name to an initial.

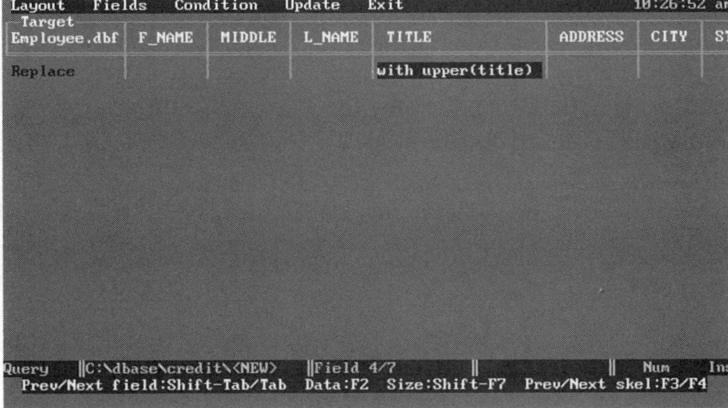

Fig. 10.20
A Replace query that changes all the characters in the TITLE field to uppercase.

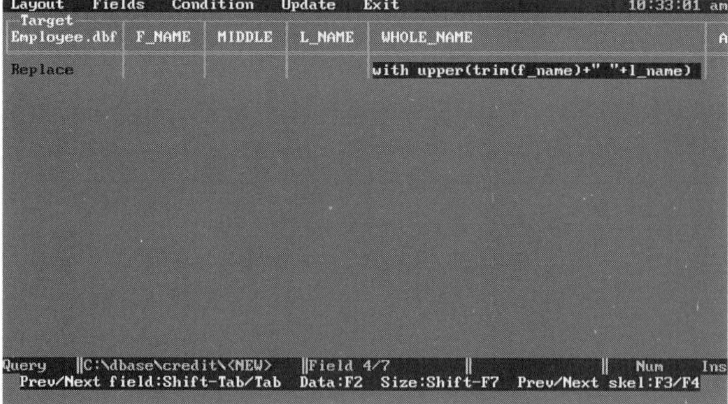

Fig. 10.21 A Replace query that fills the WHOLE_NAME field with the first name plus the last name and then converts it to uppercase.

To delete data in a field, use the condition with " " (see fig. 10.22).

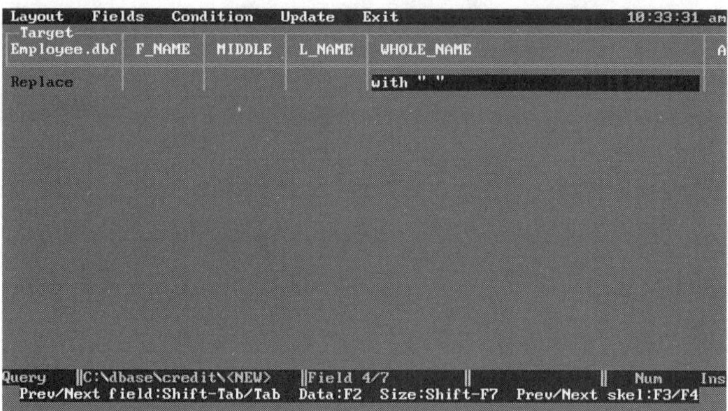

Fig. 10.22 A Replace query that deletes data in the WHOLE_NAME field.

Figure 10.23 combines a character field with a numeric field that is converted to a character field. dBASE cannot combine a character string with a numeric string. Both strings must be the same type before they can be combined. Notice in the query that the blank spaces at the end of the ID character field must be trimmed with the TRIM( ) function and the blank spaces at the beginning of the converted numeric field GRADE must be trimmed with the function LTRIM( ).

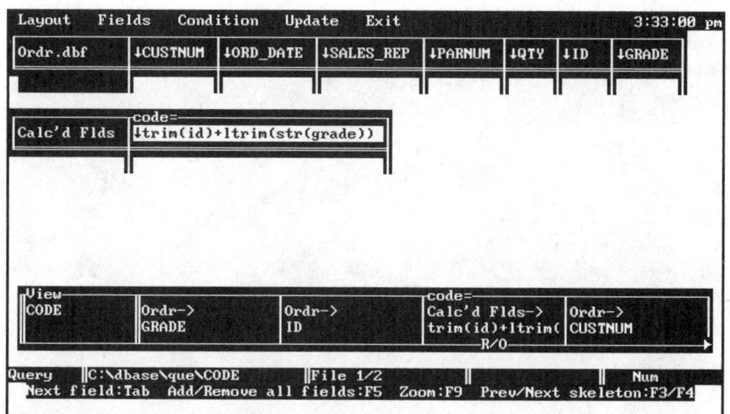

Fig. 10.23
A Replace command that combines a character field with a numeric field.

Adding Records

You can use an update query to add records from one database to another when the structures of the two databases are not identical. (If the databases are identical, you can append records in the Database design screen by choosing Append, Append Records from dBASE File.) Suppose that you want to append records to the Customer database (called the *target database*) from a database named Oldcust (called the *source database*). To use an update query to append records from the Oldcust database, follow these steps:

1. Be sure that both databases are in the current catalog.

2. In the Data panel of the Control Center, select the target database file (in this case, the Customer database). Make the target database file the active database by highlighting it and pressing Enter. If the selection box appears, choose Use File.

3. Highlight `<create>` in the Queries panel and press Enter. A new Query design screen appears with the CUSTOMER.DBF file skeleton in place.

4. Open the Layout menu and choose Add File to Query. When the file list appears, choose the source database (in this case, Oldcust) by highlighting it and pressing Enter. A file skeleton for OLDCUST.DBF is added to the Query design screen (see fig. 10.24).

5. Move to the Customer file skeleton.

6. To start the Append update, open the Update menu and select Specify Update Operation. From the submenu that appears, choose Append Records To Customer.dbf and press Enter.

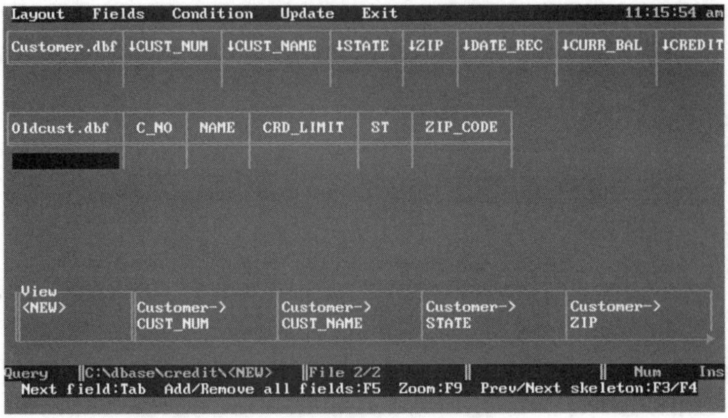

Fig. 10.24
A query that has had a second database added to the query screen.

7. A warning box appears to tell you that changing the view query to an update query deletes the view skeleton. Choose Proceed to continue. Notice that when you return to the Query design screen, the word `Target` appears above the CUSTOMER.DBF file skeleton and the word `Append` appears below the file name.

8. Enter matching variable names in the fields of the two databases so that dBASE will know which fields in the two databases correspond to each other. (Use F3 and F4 to go back and forth between the two skeletons.) For example, type the variable name **NA** in the NAME field of OLDCUST.DBF and in the CUST_NAME field in CUSTOMER.DBF. Even when the field names of the source database and target database are the same, you must tell the query how to match the fields with variables. Figure 10.25 shows the update query with variable pairs in place. The variable pairs tell the query where in the target database to put the data from the source database.

Tip
If the source database file and the target database file are not in the same catalog, and you plan to append from the source database repeatedly, create a new catalog that contains both files.

9. Open the Update menu and choose Perform the Update. dBASE executes the query, adding one record to the target database (CUSTOMER.DBF) for each record in the source database (OLDCUST.DBF). When the update is done, a note box appears with the message `Press any key to continue`. When you press a key, you return to the Query design screen.

10. To see the results of the query, press F2. A display of the database with the appended records appears.

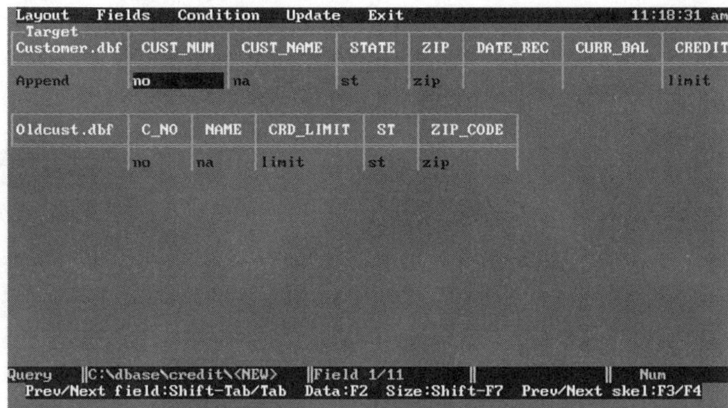

Fig. 10.25
An Append update query with variable pairs entered in the fields that are included in the Append operation.

The Append operation can be used with conditions to add only specific records to a database. If a condition is entered in a field that also contains a variable, the variable name and the condition should be separated with a comma.

Marking Records for Deletion

In Chapter 7, "Editing and Deleting Records," you learned that you can mark a record for deletion by highlighting it in a Browse or Edit window and pressing Ctrl-U. Although this method is fine for marking records occasionally, it is very tedious to mark a large number of records for deletion this way. It is more efficient to use an update query to mark records for deletion because the records can be isolated by a query condition.

To create an update query to mark records for deletion, follow these steps:

1. Open the Update menu and choose Specify Update Operation, Mark Records for Deletion.

2. Choose Proceed when dBASE tells you that the view skeleton will be deleted. The word `Mark` appears under the name of the database in the file skeleton to remind you that this query is an update query.

3. Specify the condition that selects the desired records for marking.

4. Open the Update menu and choose Perform the Update. A message is displayed indicating the number of records to be marked for deletion. Press Enter. When the update is completed, dBASE displays the message `Press any key to continue`; do so to return to the Query design screen.

5. Press F2 to display the database with the records marked for deletion. (When the cursor is on a marked record, the status bar displays `Del` on the right side.)

Note

Remember that marking a record for deletion does not actually delete the record. You must choose Organize, Erase Marked Records in the Browse/Edit screen to eliminate the records and "pack" (compress the size of) the database.

Unmarking Records Marked for Deletion

Similarly, you can unmark records that previously have been marked for deletion with an update query. Follow these steps:

1. Open the Update menu and choose Specify Update Operation.
2. Select Unmark records in filename.dbf. The word `Unmark` appears under the file name in the file skeleton.
3. Specify a condition if desired.
4. Open the Update menu and choose Perform the Update.
5. Press any key.
6. Press F2 to see the data.

Note

Rather than using the menus to specify an update operation for Replace, Append, Mark, or Unmark, you can simply type the desired operation in the input area under the file name in the file skeleton.

Saving Update Queries

Update queries are saved just like view queries, by opening the Layout menu and choosing Save this query. dBASE uses an extension of UPD for update queries. The Queries panel of the Control Center does not display the extensions of query files, but you can differentiate between the two types of queries because an update query has an asterisk beside it.

Retrieving Data from Multiple Databases

▶ See "Using Queries To Set Up Relationships," p. 371

One of the most powerful features of dBASE is its capability to work with multiple database files at once. This ability to relate different files is the reason dBASE is called a relational database management system.

Using the dBASE 5 Query design screen, you can easily link (relate) two or more database files (a maximum of eight). This enables you to have fields from more than one file in your view. For two files to be linked, they must share a common field, as in the following example:

ORDER file	ITEMS file
PARTNUM	PARTNUM
QTYORDER	DESCRIP
CUSTNUM	PRICE

In this case, you could link the two files on the common PARTNUM field.

To link two files with the link-by-pointing method, follow these steps:

1. Make one of the databases the active database.
2. Highlight `<create>` in the Queries panel and press Enter.
3. Open the Layout menu and choose Add File to Query. Highlight the desired file and press Enter.
4. For each database, choose Fields from the menu bar. Highlight Include Indexes NO and press Enter to set the option on YES. Linking takes place more quickly if the common field in the lookup database is indexed.
5. Position the cursor in the common field of the first file skeleton.
6. Open the Layout menu and choose Create Link by Pointing. The link marker, `LINK1`, will appear below the field name in the file skeleton.
7. Press F4. Position the cursor in the common field in the second file skeleton and press Enter. The same link marker will appear in this field, indicating that the link has been made.

8. Select the fields from both databases that you want to see in the view by pressing F5 when the highlight is on the field. (Use F3 and F4 to go to the file skeletons.)

9. Move the fields in the view skeleton if desired.

10. If desired, designate fields to sort the records.

11. Press F2 to execute the query.

Tip
A link marker can be any word with a maximum of ten characters. The marker can be typed by the user in both of the common fields, rather than using the link-by-pointing method.

If you create additional links among files with the pointing method, the number of the link is indicated by the link marker (LINK2, LINK3, and so on). Figure 10.26 shows two databases that are linked on the PART_NUM and PART_NO fields. The figure shows link markers that have been entered by the user. Notice that the markers are not entered in uppercase as the link-by-pointing method enters them. The result of the query is shown in figure 10.27.

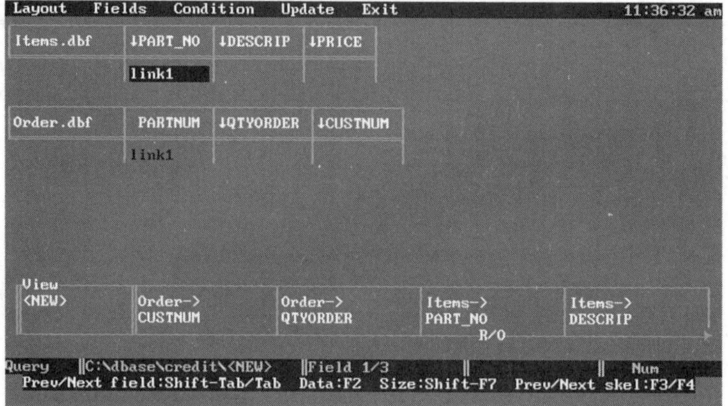

Fig. 10.26
A query that links two databases.

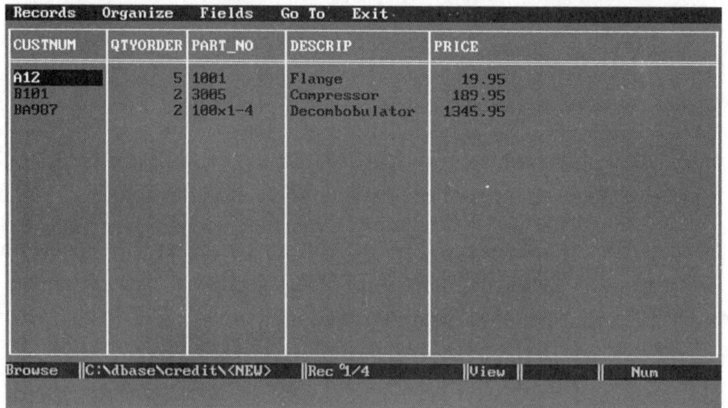

Fig. 10.27
The result of linking two databases shows fields from both databases.

When two files are linked, each record in the *master database* (the database that is listed before the other database) is looked up in the second database. If the second database has one or more matches, all the matches are included in the query output. This is called a *many-to-many relationship*. If you want to see all the records, even the ones that do not have a match in the linked database, you must use the word **every** before the link marker in the master database, as shown in figure 10.28.

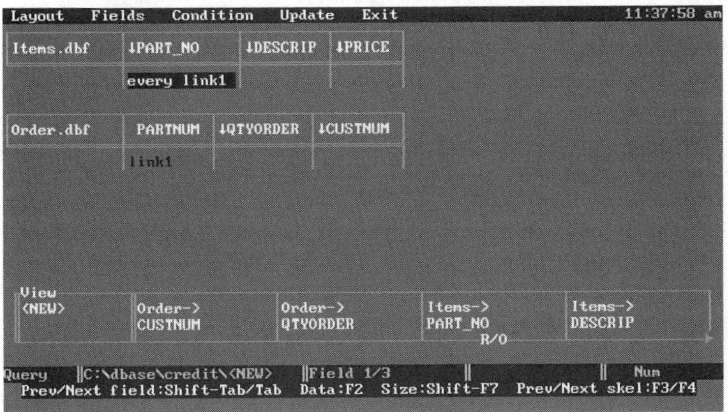

Fig. 10.28
A linking query that will include every record.

If you want only the first record that matches a record in the database to be included in the query output, use the word **first** before the link marker in the lookup database, as shown in figure 10.29.

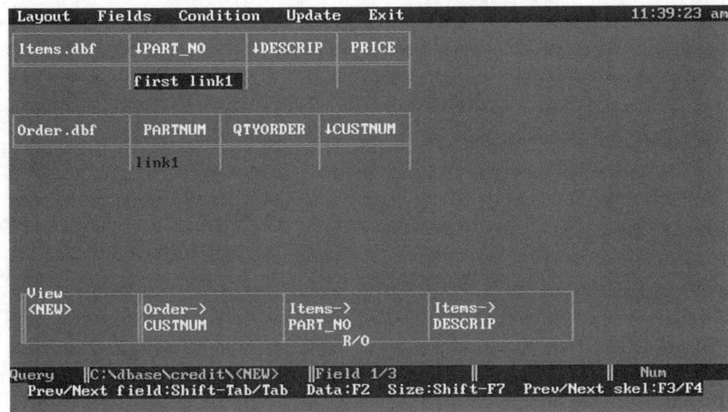

Fig. 10.29
A linking query that includes only the first record in the source database that matches each record in the target database.

Troubleshooting

After I have performed a query, I cannot modify the records.

Any subset of records that is presented on a Browse/Edit screen as a result of a query can be edited unless the query uses a summary operator, or the data in the records come from linked fields in multiple databases. In addition, fields that are "read-only" (such as calculated fields), fields that have been renamed, fields sorted by the Dictionary sort, or multiple sort fields cannot be edited.

I mistakenly replaced data in the database with the Replace update query. How can I get the data back the way it was?

Most Replace queries can be reversed by using another Replace query. For example, if you mistakenly replace the numbers in a field with the number + 100, you can perform another Replace update that subtracts 100 from the number.

Using the Fastest Query Method

dBASE actually uses one of three methods to process a query. Each method is designed to process the query the fastest way for a certain type of condition that is entered in the query. Table 10.4 lists and describes the three methods.

Table 10.4 Query Methods

Method	Description
INDEX...FOR	dBASE creates a new, temporary index based on the condition entered in the query, such as "WA" in the STATE field. The expression used for the index would be FOR state = "WA."
SET FILTER	dBASE filters the records based on the condition in the query. This option is used when the range of records is large.
SET KEY	dBASE uses a key range if the range of records is small and the field on which the range is based is indexed.

You can select the method that you want to use by following these steps in the Query design work surface:

1. Open the Fields menu and choose Filter Method.
2. Press the spacebar to cycle through the choices. Be sure the desired choice is displayed and press Ctrl-End to return to the query screen.

Using Optimized

If you do not select a method of filtering the query, dBASE uses the Optimized option by default. This option automatically selects the fastest method for the conditions in your query. You can relax and let dBASE select the method for you on every query you create.

Using Keep Speedup Indexes

If you use the Index...For filtering method for a query, and you plan to save the query and use it over and over again, it is a good idea to set Keep Speedup Indexes to YES. This option will speed up the execution of subsequent queries because dBASE will save the temporary index that it creates to process the query the first time. Obviously, the time required to re-create the index each time the query is executed is saved. Although speed is gained with this method, disk space is sacrificed.

Tip
If you use the Optimized method, you may still want to set the Keep Speedup Indexes to YES if disk space is not a problem for you. You will gain speed in performance.

From Here...

Now that you have learned more about queries, you may want to begin designing your own custom reports to use with queries. Refer to the following chapters for more information.

- Chapter 12, "Creating Custom Reports," gives you basic information on how to create a columnar, form, and mailmerge report.
- Chapter 13, "Designing and Using a Mailmerge Report and Label," goes into more detail on the mailmerge form and label.
- Chapter 15, "Using Relational Database for Complex Situations," describes the role of queries in setting up relational databases.

Chapter 11

Creating and Using Input Forms

Although you can use dBASE's default data-entry screens to enter, edit, and view data, a custom form makes entering and editing data easier and more accurate. A custom data-entry form also ensures that data is formatted correctly and that the right type of data is entered: characters go into a character field, numbers go into a numeric field, and so on.

You can use a single custom form to input, edit, or view data, or you can design different forms for each of these purposes, changing the formatting and editing options. You can design one form that displays data without allowing any changes, for example, and another that displays only certain parts of a database's information. Another reason users design custom forms is to make the screen input form match the hard copy form from which data is being entered. It's much easier for a user to enter data in fields that are in the same order as those on the hard copy. Jumping around on a hard copy form to find the data that goes in a certain field can cause errors.

In this chapter, you learn how to create a custom form by using the dBASE Forms Design screen. You learn how to place fields on the form and move them around to make the form pleasing to the eye. dBASE provides a wide array of formatting and editing options that give you full control over the data you enter and how that data is displayed on-screen. Custom forms make a huge difference in how easy and productive dBASE can be. With the information in this chapter, you can create elegant and easy-to-use forms for your dBASE systems.

In this chapter, you learn to do the following:

- Create a form with Quick Layout
- Enter field labels and position fields on a form
- Specify field attributes and edit options
- Add and remove regular and calculated fields
- Add and delete lines and boxes
- Enhance a form with color
- Create multipage forms

Creating Forms for Better Data Input

Tip
Don't crowd fields and text on one screen. Two spaciously designed screens are better than one crowded, busy-looking screen.

As you know, the default Edit screen lists all the fields in the database in one column, with the names of each field on the left of each entry area. Using a custom form allows you to place more than one field on a line so that more fields can be seen on the same screen. If not all the fields in the database fit on the same screen, you can use multiple screens.

Because field names are limited to ten characters, field names are not always adequate. On a custom form, you can use any text that you want to use to describe a field. For example, rather than using the field name DOB, you can use Date of Birth. Rather than the logical field name RATE, you can use a question such as *Does this project require a rate?*

In addition to field labels, you can enter text of an instructional or explanatory nature. For example, you can indicate an acceptable range for a field, or list the phone number of the person to call if there is a question about the data in a certain field.

Custom forms also enable you to group data more logically. If you design an order-entry form, for example, you can group customer information in one area, order information in another, and shipping information in a third. You also can use boxes and lines to define the areas more clearly.

The Forms Design screen provides options to create messages to prompt the user and assign colors to emphasize the important data. Templates, picture functions, and editing options provide various kinds of data validation. For example, you can specify a template to use for data entry or to specify an acceptable range of values.

Creating Forms with the Forms Design Screen

To begin the creation of a new form, you must access the Forms Design screen. To access this screen, start from the Control Center and follow these steps:

1. In the Data panel, highlight the database file for which you want to create a custom form, and press Enter. When the selection box appears, choose Use File.

2. Move the cursor to the Forms panel, highlight `<create>`, and press Enter. This action tells the Control Center you want to create a new form for the active database.

   When the Forms Design screen appears, the Layout menu displays, with the Quick Layout option highlighted.

3. Choose from either of the following options:

   - Press Enter if you want to choose Quick Layout and have all the fields and field names placed on the form for you. The form looks exactly like the default Edit screen. You can then modify the form as desired.

   - Press Esc to cancel the Layout pull-down menu. A blank screen is presented. You must place all the fields and enter all the text from scratch.

> **Note**
>
> If the database has many fields, it's easier to build a custom form from scratch than it is to move fields and text around on a form that's been created with the Quick Layout option.

Getting Acquainted with the Forms Design Screen

The Forms Design screen is basically a work table on which you arrange form elements to make a presentable, easy-to-read form you can use to display and enter data (see fig. 11.1). Before you start to create a form, take a quick tour of the Forms Design screen.

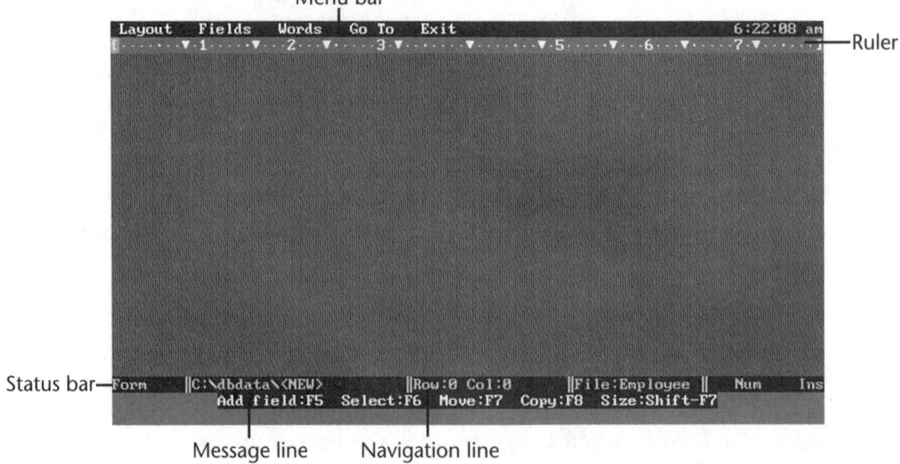

Fig. 11.1
The Forms Design screen is the surface on which fields and text are placed to create a form.

Across the top of the screen is the familiar dBASE menu bar, modified to fit the Forms Design screen functions. Each item on the menu bar contains options that apply to the process of designing and creating forms.

> **Note**
>
> Take a moment to explore the menus available in the design surface screen: Layout, Fields, Words, Go To, and Exit. Pull down each menu and look at the options available. These options are discussed in more detail in the exercises that follow.

Under the menu bar is the ruler. Because the form is used only on-screen and is not printed, the ruler is really provided as a guide for the position of the cursor.

The status bar appears below the work surface, showing information about the form. The far left section of the status bar shows the word `Form` to remind you that you are in the Forms Design screen. The next section shows the name of the current form, with a complete DOS path. If you haven't yet named the current form by saving it, the name of the form is `<NEW>`. The next section of the status bar shows the row and column of the cursor's position. To the right of the `Row:Col:` display is the name of the database file for which you're building this form. The far right section of the status bar shows the state of the Num Lock key, the Caps Lock key, and the Ins key. When any of these keys are in effect, an indicator appears in the far right section of the status bar.

The work surface takes up most of the screen. On the work surface, you add data fields, text, lines, and boxes to make the form readable and usable.

The next-to-last line of the screen is the dBASE navigation line, showing key assignments that perform various tasks. The display on the navigation line changes, depending on what you're doing on the Forms Design work surface. The navigation line always provides appropriate assistance.

As usual, the last line of the screen is the message line, which provides helpful messages about what you are doing at any given time. Error messages also appear here.

Building a Form from a Blank Work Surface

If you decide to start from a blank Forms Design work surface, the first thing you do is add the necessary text and database fields. If you design the form in an orderly fashion, you begin by entering a title for the form. Then you start entering the text for the first field label, and then add the field. As you add more fields, you might reach the point where you want to group certain areas on the form. You draw lines or boxes to visually organize the form. Finally, when all the text and fields are placed on the form, you specify special attributes for certain fields.

Entering and Editing Text

Text can be entered directly on the work surface by moving the cursor to the desired position with the cursor keys or the mouse and typing the text.

After text is added it can be moved, deleted, and edited. Special editing keys are listed in table 11.1.

Table 11.1 Editing Keys

Key	Description
Bksp	Deletes the text to the left of the cursor.
Del	Deletes the text at the cursor position or the field at the cursor position.
Ctrl-N	Inserts a blank line at the cursor position.
Ctrl-T	Deletes the word at the cursor position or the field at the cursor position.
Ctrl-Y	Deletes a line at the cursor position.

(continues)

Table 11.1 Continued

Key	Description
Enter	Moves the cursor to the next line in Overtype mode. Inserts a blank line in Insert mode.
F6	Selects the character at the cursor position. To select a block, move the cursor to the last position and press Enter.
F7	Initiates the move command for selected text. After pressing F7, move the cursor to the upper-left corner of the new position and press Enter.
F8	Initiates the copy command for selected text. After pressing F8, move the cursor to the upper-left corner of the new position and press Enter.
Insert	Toggles between the Insert mode and the Overtype mode. Use the Insert mode to insert text in existing text. Use the Overtype mode to type over existing text.

You can also position text on the screen with the Position option in the Words menu. Select the text to be positioned with F6. From the menu bar, choose Words, Position, and select Left, Center, or Right.

Adding and Removing Fields

Tip
When adding fields to the work surface manually, do not place fields or text in the top row of the Forms Design work surface. Reserve this row for the menu bar. If you put fields or text in the first line, the menus are overwritten.

To add individual fields to the work surface, follow these steps:

1. Position the cursor on the Forms Design work surface where you want the field to appear.

2. Open the Fields menu and choose Add Field, or press F5. A Field List menu appears (see fig. 11.2). The left column of the Field List menu shows all the fields of the active database. The name of the database is at the top of the left column.

   The right column of the menu is titled `CALCULATED`. This column lists fields with values calculated from other database fields or other form fields. When you first create a form, this column is empty, except for the `<create>` option. You learn about calculated fields in the section "Adding Calculated Fields," later in this chapter.

3. Choose the field you want to add by highlighting it and pressing Enter. The selected field is placed on the work surface at the cursor's location.

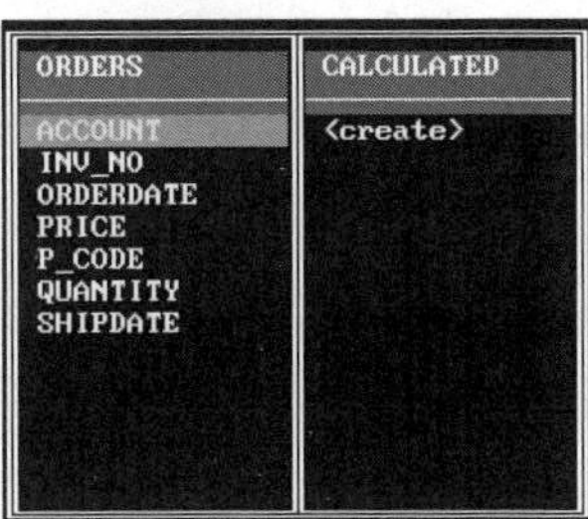

Fig. 11.2
The Field List menu lists all the fields that are available for placement on the form.

To remove a field from the form, move the cursor to the field. Then open the Fields menu and choose Remove Field; or simply press Del. To remove several fields from the form, move the cursor to the first field and press F6. Move the cursor to the last field and press Enter. Then press Del; or open the Fields menu and choose Remove Field.

Moving, Copying, and Sizing Form Elements

To move or copy work-surface elements, such as fields, text, boxes, or lines, begin by selecting the elements to be moved or copied. The technique of selecting elements differs for the different types of elements, but after an element is selected, the moving process is the same.

- *To select a single field:* Place the cursor in the field you want to select, press F6, and complete the selection by pressing Enter.

- *To select multiple fields:* Place the cursor at the beginning of the first field you want to select and press F6. Use the arrow keys to highlight the area that contains all the fields you want to select. As you do this, a *selection highlight* appears, showing you the area selected. When the selection highlight covers the fields you want to select, press Enter to complete the selection.

- *To select a box:* Move the cursor to any location on the box. Press F6 and press Enter.

- *To select text:* Move the cursor to the beginning of the text you want to select. Press F6. Use the arrow keys to move to the end of the text, and press Enter to complete the selection.

- *To select lines:* Lines on the form resemble text more than boxes, so you select them as you would text.

- *To select an area of the form:* This technique works for selecting text, fields, or both. Place the cursor at one corner of the area you want to select and press F6. Move the cursor to the opposite corner of the area you want to select; notice the ghost that shows you what has been selected. When the ghost covers the area you want to select, press Enter to complete the selection.

Tip
If you do not have a mouse, move the selection highlight with the Tab key instead of the arrow keys. It's faster.

You can use the mouse to select fields or text. Position the mouse pointer at the corner of the area to be selected. Hold down the mouse button, drag the mouse over the selection, and then release the button.

Figure 11.3 shows the Forms Design work surface with a selected area.

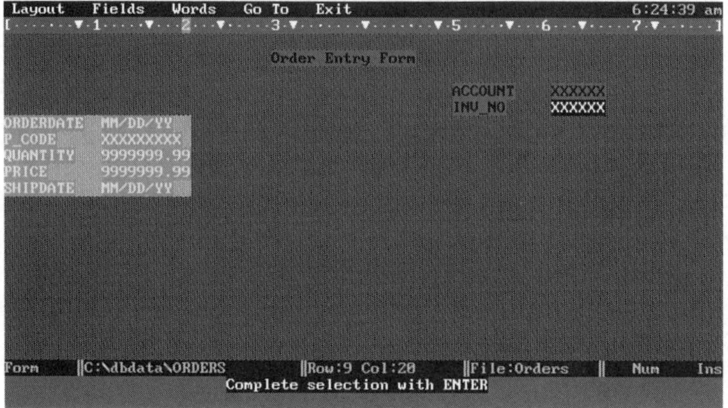

Fig. 11.3
A selected area, ready to be moved or copied.

After you select the area you want to move or copy, the next step is to press F7 to move or F8 to copy. Then use the arrow keys to move the selected area on the work surface. The ghost of the selected area moves to show you where you are moving the area. After you position the ghost where you want it, press Enter to tell dBASE to move or copy the selected area. If the new position of the ghost covers text or fields, dBASE displays the question `Delete covered text and fields?` Choose Yes to place the new area and delete what is under it, or choose No to return to the form to move to a new location and press Enter again. When you're finished, press Esc.

◄ See "Adding Data to Memo Fields," p. 134

To move a block using the mouse, drag the mouse over the block to select it, click `Move:F7` in the navigation line, position the mouse pointer to the new location, and click the mouse button.

With Move and Copy, you can arrange the fields in a pleasing layout. Rearranging fields in this way is particularly handy if you used Quick Layout to place the fields on the work surface.

To change the width of a field, select it as described earlier in this section and press Shift-F7. Now press the left-arrow key to decrease the size of the field, or press the right-arrow key to increase the size. The original size remains on-screen for reference, and a ghost appears to show the modified size. Press Enter when you've resized the field to your satisfaction. If the new size of the field covers text or other fields on-screen, dBASE asks you to confirm that you want to delete the underlying field or text. Changing the size of a field on the form doesn't affect the size of the field in the database.

Use these techniques to move the fields and text on the form until the form design is pleasing and easy to use. Figure 11.4 shows a custom form with descriptive text and well-organized fields.

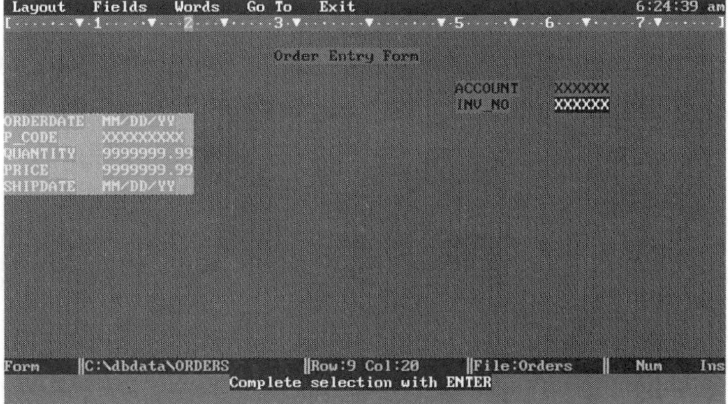

Fig. 11.4
A well-designed custom form has organization and clarity.

Modifying the Appearance of a Memo Field

When you place a memo field on the form—using either the Quick Layout or Add Field option—the memo field appears as a *marker* with the word `MEMO` in it, just as it appears in default data-entry forms. You can leave the memo field this way or display the text of the memo field in a *window* on the screen.

To display a memo field in a window, follow these steps:

1. Move the cursor to the memo-field marker (the word MEMO). Then open the Fields menu and choose Modify Field. Or move the cursor to the memo field and press F5.

2. Move to the Display As option and press Enter. The setting changes from MARKER to WINDOW (see fig. 11.5).

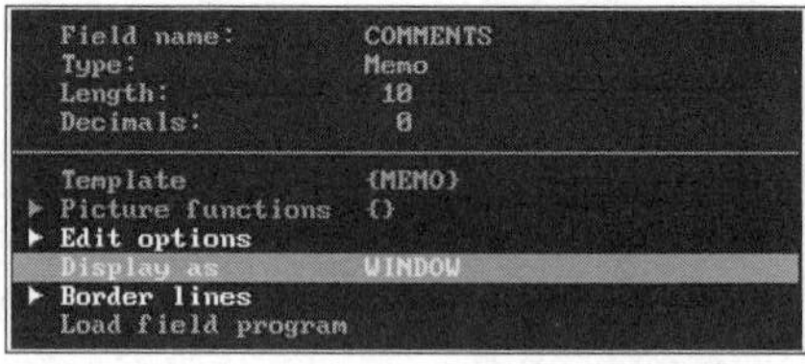

Fig. 11.5 Changing the display of a memo field is accomplished by changing the Display As setting.

3. Notice that the setting changes to WINDOW. Press Ctrl-End to accept the new field configuration.

4. At this point, use either of the following methods to draw the window:

   ■ If the memo field was placed by the Quick Layout, the memo window marker appears on the screen as a box filled with Xs. Press Shift-F7 to resize the window. Use the arrow keys to make the window the size you want, as in figure 11.6. Press Enter to accept the new size.

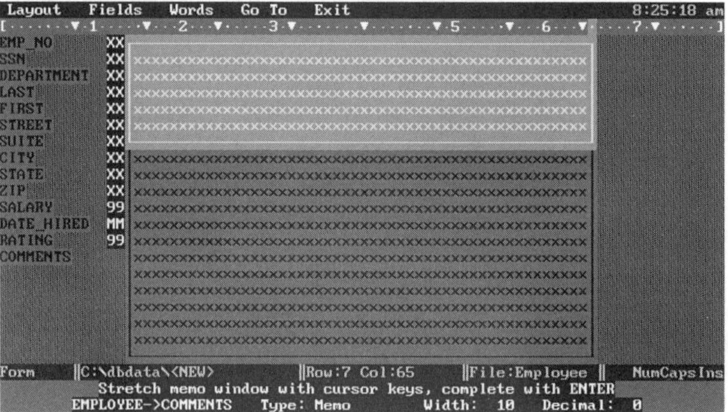

Fig. 11.6 When you resize the memo field window, the new size is highlighted.

   ■ If the memo marker was placed in the form by the user, the size of the window is defined by pressing Enter when the pointer is at the upper-left corner and when the pointer is at the lower-right corner.

5. If necessary, move the memo window to a new location on the form.

To access the memo-field window so that you can enter or edit data, move the cursor to the memo-field window and press Ctrl-Home. The word processor is invoked inside the window. Press Ctrl-End to save any changes and exit. Press Esc to exit without saving the changes.

Note

The size of the window placed on the form does not have to display all the data in the field. When reviewing or editing the memo field, you can press F9 to open the field.

Specifying Field Attributes

For efficient use, databases require accurate data. Although no database system can assure complete accuracy of entered information, dBASE provides some powerful capabilities that help you avoid many garbage-in/garbage-out problems. By using dBASE forms, you can specify limits and conditions for fields to ensure more accurate data entry. You can require that database fields receive information consistent with their field types. You can ensure that a field which must contain only numbers—whether that field is a numeric or character field—gets only numbers from the user. You can set high and low limits on numeric fields, require uppercase or lowercase letters in character fields, and so on.

Tip
Formatting fields with template symbols and picture functions makes data more readable on-screen and easier to use.

dBASE uses *templates, picture functions,* and *edit options* to specify attributes for fields. A field template enables you to specify valid input characters for each position of the field. Picture functions provide editing and validation capabilities that apply to the field as a whole. Edit options enable you to specify a range within which entered data must fall. You also can use edit options to make a field read-only and to set default values for a field.

Using Templates

A *template* enables you to specify character-by-character what type of data can be entered into a data-entry field. You can, for example, tell dBASE you want all characters in a field to be numeric; if the user enters something other than a numeric character, dBASE beeps impolitely and does not accept the entry.

If the field is 10 characters wide, the template for that field should contain 10 symbols, specifying what type of character can be entered in each position.

To specify the template symbols, follow these steps:

1. Place the cursor on the field you want to modify.

2. Open the Fields menu and choose Modify Field.

3. Highlight Template on the Field Definition menu and press Enter. A help screen showing all the template symbols appears (see fig. 11.7). Use the Help screen to assist you in finding the correct symbols for the template you enter in the input field.

Fig. 11.7
The Character Template Symbols screen list, the template symbols, and their uses.

```
Character Template Symbols
  9   Accept digits and signs          Y     Y or N
  #   Accept digits, spaces,           L     T, F, Y, or N
      signs, and periods               X     Any character
  A   Accept alpha characters          !     Convert to uppercase
  N   Accept alpha, digits, and      other   Insert into display.
      underscore                             Store with input data unless
                                             @R function is used.
```

Consider these two template symbols: A specifies that an alphabetic character must be entered at the position; 9 specifies a numeric entry (including a plus or minus sign).

The following table shows some examples of different templates and their editing effects when you apply these symbols to a character field with a width of 5:

Template	Data Entered	Data Displayed	Comment
99999	12345	12345	The template requires numeric characters, so it accepts the entry 12345.
AAAAA	12345	nothing	The template requires alphabetic characters, but only numerics were entered; dBASE rejects all the characters, beeping when the invalid characters are entered.
AAAAA	abcde	abcde	The template requires alphabetic characters, so it accepts the entry abcde.
9A9A9A	abcde	nothing	dBASE rejects the entry because alphabetic characters are in the first position, which accepts only numeric data.

As you can see, the template specifies what type of character can be entered and displayed at each position in the data field. If an invalid character is entered, dBASE beeps and rejects the character.

Note

dBASE rejects the first invalid character entered. If you enter one or more valid characters before typing an invalid one, the valid characters are entered into the field. Be sure to check the data in the field before accepting it.

The template characters you can use for a field differ with the type of field. Template characters for the different types of fields, with their validation effect, are listed in tables 11.2, 11.3, and 11.4.

Table 11.2 Character-Field Template Symbols

Template	Effect
9	Accepts only digits (0 through 9) and signs (+, –). Does not accept a decimal point.
#	Accepts spaces, digits, signs, and a decimal point. Note that you can use the template characters 9 and # for character fields as well as numeric fields.
A	Accepts alphabetic characters only.
N	Accepts alphabetic characters, numeric digits, and the underscore character.
Y	Accepts Y or N for Yes or No.
L	Accepts T, F, Y, or N for True, False, Yes, or No.
X	Accepts any character.
!	Accepts any alphabetic character and changes it to uppercase. Other characters are unaffected.
Other	Displays in the field any other character that you put in the template. When the user enters data into the field, the cursor skips these template characters, which become part of the input data. For example, you can specify a template of (999)999-9999 for phone numbers; users can enter numbers where the 9 template symbols are specified, but the parentheses and dash become part of the data stored for this field. (You can prevent these characters from becoming part of the input data by specifying the R picture function with the template.) These "other" characters are referred to as *literals*; they are placed in the field exactly as you type them in the template.

Table 11.3 Numeric-Field and Float-Field Template Symbols

Template	Effect
9	Accepts only digits (0 through 9) and signs (+, –). Does not accept a decimal point.
#	Accepts spaces, digits, signs, and a decimal point.
Other	Displays literal characters in the field.
.	Specifies the decimal point location.
,	Displays a comma at this position if the number is large enough.
*	Displays leading zeros as asterisks (*). Frequently used for check protection because this symbol fills the left side of the field with asterisks.
$	Displays leading zeros as dollar signs ($). Also used for check protection.

Table 11.4 Logical-Field Template Symbols

Template	Effect
L	Enables T (True), F (False), Y (Yes), or N (No).
Y	Enables only Y (Yes) or N (No).
Other	Displays literal characters in the field.

No template symbols are available for date fields. You can modify the date-field formats by changing the way dBASE displays dates—use the Settings option of the Tools menu on the Control Center. Memo fields also have no template symbols available.

The following table shows some examples of template symbols applied to character fields:

Value Entered	Template	Result	Explanation
123	99,999	123	The comma template symbol has no effect if the number is not large enough to require the comma in this position.

Value Entered	Template	Result	Explanation
12345	99,999	12,345	The comma template symbol takes effect here because the number is large enough to require a comma in that position.
12345	AAAAA	nothing	The A template symbol enables only alphabetic data entry and display. During entry, dBASE beeps and rejects each digit as it is entered; during display, nothing appears.
123ab	999!!	123AB	The 9 template symbol enables digits to be entered or displayed in the first three positions; the last two positions are changed to uppercase letters by the ! template symbol.
12345	NN,NNN	12,345	The N template symbol enables alphabetic and numeric input.
abcde	NN,NNN	ab,cde	The N template symbol enables alphabetic input; the comma literal puts the comma in the specified position.

Template symbols used for numeric data fields are similar, but oriented more toward display of numeric values.

Value Entered	Template	Result	Explanation
123 1234	$9,999 $9,999	$$$123 $1,234	The $ template symbol replaces all leading zeros to the left of the first digit in the field with dollar aligns. The * template symbol has the same effect, replacing leading zeroes with asterisks.
123	999.99	123.00	The **.** (decimal) template symbol determines the decimal position in the field. dBASE fills in positions after the decimal if the value does not have the same or more decimal positions.

Using Picture Functions

Picture functions offer validation and editing control for the field as a whole. You may want all characters entered in a field converted to uppercase. Rather than specify a string of ! template symbols, you can simply specify the ! picture function, which changes all available characters in the field to uppercase. The picture functions differ, depending on the type of data field being defined.

When creating a field, highlight the Picture Functions option on the Field Definition menu and press Enter. The Picture Functions menu appropriate to the type of field you're creating appears. To modify the picture functions for a field, place the cursor in that field and select Fields, Modify field from the menu bar, or press F5. The Picture Functions menu appropriate to the type of field you are modifying appears.

When you select Picture Functions for a character field, the menu shown in figure 11.8 appears. Move the highlight to the picture function you want to apply to the field and press Enter. Pressing Enter toggles the ON/OFF status of that function. If you select Scroll Within Display Width or MulTiple Choice, additional menus display with more options.

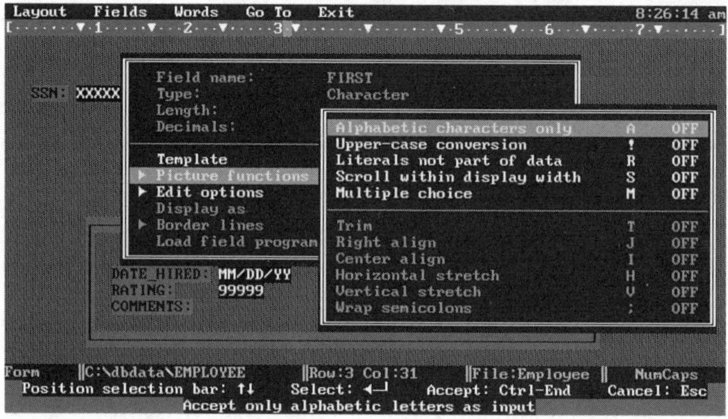

Fig. 11.8
The Picture Functions screen for a character field lists the functions that can be applied at the top of the box. The dimmed options cannot be applied.

Select or toggle the setting for a picture function by clicking the option with the mouse. Click the `Accept: Ctrl-End` label on the navigation line to save your choices.

If you're working with character fields, you can use the picture functions listed in Table 11.5.

Table 11.5 Character-Field Picture Functions

Menu Description	Picture Function	Effect
Alphabetic Characters Only	A	All characters in the field must be alphabetic.
Upper-Case Conversion	!	All characters entered into the field are changed to uppercase. Nonalphabetic characters are not affected.
Literals Not Part of Data	R	Literals are not stored as part of the data. Use this function in conjunction with a template using literal characters. A template such as (999)999-9999, for example, accepts digits in the positions marked by 9 and includes the parentheses and dash in the data put into the database field. If you use the same template and add the R picture function, the data-entry effect is the same, but the parentheses and dash aren't entered into the database.
Scroll Within Display Width	S	Scrolls entry within the display width. Use this function with a character field too wide to fit easily on the form. You can, for example, define a scroll width of 10 for a database field 15 characters wide. On the form, the field is 10 characters wide, but the field scrolls right and left to allow entry of up to 15 characters. When you select this option, you are asked to specify the scroll width.
MulTiple Choice	M	Enables multiple choice for the field. You specify a list of acceptable inputs for this field. When you choose this option, an input box appears in which you list acceptable entries, separated by commas. If you use this function with a STATE field, for example, you can identify as acceptable the entries AL, AK, CA, and so on.

When using a mulTiple-choice field on a form, make a selection by pressing the space bar to scroll through the list; when the desired choice is highlighted, press Enter to select it. Alternatively, enter the first character of the desired choice; dBASE highlights the first choice that starts with that character in the mulTiple-choice list. Pressing the character again causes dBASE to highlight the next choice starting with that letter. When the desired choice is highlighted, press Enter to accept it.

The Picture Functions help screen for character fields is divided by a horizontal line; below this line are six choices not available if you use the field for data entry. These six functions apply to fields that display data, rather than to fields that accept input. Several of these functions apply specifically to the display of memo fields, as shown in Table 11.6.

Table 11.6 Display-Field Picture Functions

Menu Description	Picture Function	Effect
Trim	T	Trims leading and trailing blanks off the value displayed in the field.
Right Align	J	Aligns the value so that the last character is on the right margin of the field.
Center Align	I	Centers the value in the field.
Horizontal Stretch	H	Causes a long character field or the text of a memo field to extend to the left and right margins of the report, rather than be confined to the template width.
Vertical Stretch	V	Causes the field to take up as many lines as necessary (each line as wide as the field template) to print the value.
Wrap Semicolons	;	Starts a new line when a semicolon is encountered in the field.

The picture functions available for numeric fields differ from those available for character fields. Table 11.7 lists the numeric-field picture functions.

Table 11.7 Numeric-Field and Float-Field Picture Functions

Menu Description	Picture Function	Effect
Positive credits followed by CR	C	Displays the characters CR (for credit) after positive numbers; a favorite of accountants.
Negative debits followed by DB	X	Displays the characters DB (for debit) after negative numbers; another accountant special.
Use ( ) around negative numbers	(	Places parentheses around negative numbers.
Show leading zeros	L	Shows leading zeros; otherwise blanks are used.
Blanks for zero values	Z	Puts all blanks in a field that has a zero value. If you don't use this function, a database field that has a value of zero prints zeroes in each place on the field—for example, a field template of 99.9 shows a zero value as 0.0.
Financial format	$	Displays numbers in financial format: a leading dollar sign, commas in the number, and two decimal places. The dollar sign floats, occupying the position to the left of the first digit of the field value.
Exponential format	^	Uses the scientific form of a number: for example, 2.3E4 for 23,000.

Using Edit Options

In addition to using template symbols and picture functions to control data entry and presentation, you can use a series of edit options for each field. Edit options control actions that take place when the user enters the field.

To apply edit options to a form field, place the cursor on the field. Then open the Fields menu and choose Modify Field, or press F5. The Field Definition menu appears. Choose Edit Options from this menu. The Edit Options menu appears (see fig. 11.9). Now choose the options you want to apply to the field. Most edit options require you to provide additional information, although some options are activated simply by turning the setting ON or OFF. The edit options are described in the following paragraphs.

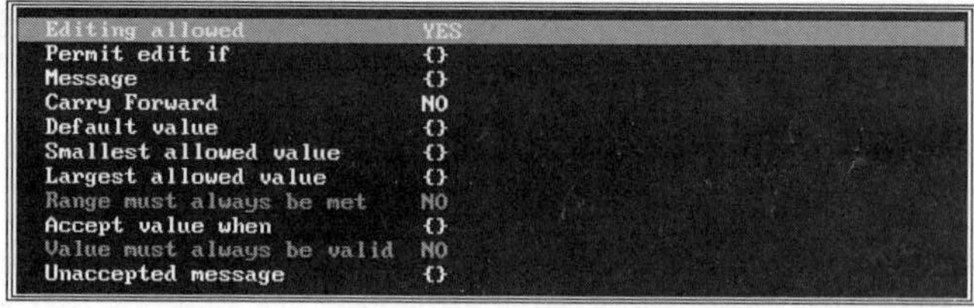

Fig. 11.9
The Edit Options menu lists the special editing conditions and characteristics that can be applied to a field.

Editing Allowed

When a field is placed in a form, the default option for Editing Allowed is YES. If you set Editing Allowed to NO, you cannot enter new data in a field or edit existing data. If the field contains data, the data is displayed, but the cursor will not enter the field when the user accesses the form. These read-only fields are used when the database contains information you want to display but do not want someone to change. To enter data in the field initially, you would have to use a form that did not disallow editing in the field, or you would have to set up a second edit condition that allowed editing only under certain conditions.

Permit Edit If

The Permit Edit If option enables you to set a condition under which a field that does not allow editing can be edited. If the condition is met, the user can enter or change information in the field.

When you choose Permit Edit If, the { } entry field changes to enable you to enter a dBASE expression. Type the dBASE expression that determines whether dBASE is to allow the user to edit the field. You also can press Shift-F1 to display the expression-builder menu for help in creating the expression. An *expression* essentially is a formula that dBASE evaluates to True or False. In this case, if the expression evaluates to True, the user can edit the field's information; if it evaluates to False, the field is skipped.

In a Customer database, for example, you can disallow the user from entering an address if no name is entered, because the customer name is a key information field. For each field, you can select Permit Edit If and enter the expression ISBLANK(CUST_NAME) which means "permit this field to be edited only if the CUST_NAME field is not blank."

Note

When setting up forms that use Permit Edit If fields, remember that the fields in a dBASE form are processed from top to bottom and from left to right on the same line. If you want to permit an edit based on a field in the form, make sure that field is processed before the Permit Edit If field. Consider the CUST_NAME # " " example. If you position the address field containing this condition on the form before the user has the chance to enter something in the CUST_NAME field, the expression always evaluates to False, and the user never can enter anything in the address field.

dBASE expressions can be simple or complex. When you specify a Permit Edit If expression, you are not limited to values in other fields on the form. You can have a field that uses the expression `CDOW(DATE())="Monday"`. (This expression allows entries on Mondays only.) This condition might appear dubious at first, but it might be used for a field in which all current data must be entered on Monday. There might be another field for entering data that is not considered current. This kind of setup could be used to differentiate between current and past-due postings.

Message

The Message option enables you to specify a message (up to 79 characters) that is printed on the 25th line of the form when the cursor is in the associated field. This option enables you to provide context-sensitive help, which is a help message appropriate to the field being edited. Unfortunately, you cannot display a message on the 25th line of the screen for a field that was skipped because of a failed Permit Edit If test.

To add a message to a field, highlight the Message option and press Enter. Now type the message. When you finish typing the message, press Enter to accept the message and return to the Edit Options menu.

Caution

Do not include double quotation marks (" ") in the message you specify for the Message option. dBASE cannot interpret double quotation marks in a message correctly. When you save the form, dBASE reports a compilation error. Although the form is listed in the Forms panel, you can't use the file to view or edit data, but you can modify it and delete the quotation marks.

Carry Forward

When you add a record to a database, dBASE normally presents an input screen with blanks in all the fields. Sometimes, however, you may want a new record to contain a value entered in the preceding record. Set the Carry Forward option to YES to provide this capability.

Tip
All fields on a form can be set to carry the data forward by setting Carry to ON in the Settings menu that is accessed from the Tools menu in the Control Center.

If you're entering data sorted by date, for example, you want to be able to enter the date only when it changes from the preceding record; just set Carry Forward to YES for the date field. The date field for a new record displays the date entered in that field for the preceding record. When the cursor reaches that field, you can press Enter to accept the date. To change the date, simply type the new date. That date is then carried forward to the next record.

Default Value

You can specify a default value for a field by choosing the Default Value option and entering the desired value. When the form appears, the default value appears in the field. You can accept the default value by pressing Enter when the cursor enters the field, or you can change the value simply by typing a new value. The next record that you add, however, again displays the default value.

Suppose that you have an order-entry form with a date field, and you always want today's date to appear in the field when the form is used for data entry. You can have dBASE insert the current date in that field by typing DATE( ) for the Default Value option. When you use the form, the current date appears in the field; you can change the date simply by entering a new date.

You can use any value as a default value, as long as it matches the field type. Character values must be enclosed in double quotation marks (" "). To use the abbreviation for *Washington* as the default in a character field, for example, type "WA" for the Default Value option. If you want a specific date to appear as the default in a date field, type {01/01/93}.

Smallest/Largest Allowed Value

Use the Smallest Allowed Value and Largest Allowed Value options to specify a range of acceptable values for the field. Specifying a range of acceptable values is most useful when used with date or numeric fields, but you can also do so with character fields.

You may have a form with a date field that should accept values for only the year 1993. To set the range of acceptable values, highlight Smallest Value Allowed and type {01/01/93}; highlight Largest Value Allowed and type {12/31/93}—make sure that you include the curly braces. If you enter a date outside this range when you use the form, dBASE beeps and displays the following message:

```
Range is 01/01/93 to 12/31/93 (press SPACE)
```

Although less common, you also can specify ranges of acceptable values for character fields; in the case of character fields, the test is made alphabetically. Suppose that you have a database with a five-character PART_NUM field, and all the part numbers are prefixed with the letters A through D. You can specify the smallest value to be “A0000” and the largest value to be “D9999.” Any value not starting with the letters A, B, C, or D causes an error. dBASE beeps and displays this message on the message line:

```
Range is "A0000" to "D9999" (press SPACE)
```

Range Must Always Be Met

The Range Must Always Be Met option checks to see whether the data falls within the specified range every time you exit the field if this option is set to Yes. Otherwise, data is checked only after it has been changed.

Accept Value When

The Accept Value When option enables you to specify a dBASE expression that tests the value entered in the field. If the value passes the test (the expression evaluates to True), the value is accepted. If the value does not pass the test, the entry is rejected and must be reentered. The Accept Value When option is a powerful tool for making sure that the data going into a database is valid.

Suppose that you have a customer database, for example, and your company has decreed that customer numbers are five characters long. You can define a CUST_NUM field of character type with a length of five. To make sure that the entered customer number is a full five characters long, define an Accept Value When expression of LEN(TRIM(CUST_NUM))=5. That expression says “the length of the CUST_NUM when trailing blanks spaces are trimmed off must be 5.” If you enter A323 in the CUST_NUM field, the expression LEN(TRIM(CUST_NUM)) evaluates to 4, and the value entered is rejected.

Because dBASE expressions can be very complex, you can use the Accept Value When option to perform complex validation tests.

Value Must Always Be Valid

The Value Must Always Be Valid option checks the validity of data every time you exit the field if set to Yes. Otherwise, validity is checked only when data is changed.

Unaccepted Message

Use the Unaccepted Message option in conjunction with the Accept Value When option to specify a message to appear on the 25th line of the screen when the value entered in a field does not pass the Accept Value When expression. The Unaccepted Message option enables you to customize the error message for the field.

For example, if you define an Accept Value When expression of LEN(TRIM(CUST_NUM))=5 (as described in the preceding example), you can define the Unaccepted Message as `Customer Numbers must be exactly five characters long`. If the user enters a customer number less than five characters long, this message appears. You also can use the Unaccepted Message option to give specific directions to the user in the event of a data-entry error. Unaccepted messages can be up to 79 characters long, but do not make the message too long because it will cover the dBASE message "(press SPACE)". Then the user of the form may not know how to recover from the error condition.

You can use the mouse to select Edit options. To toggle Yes/No values, click the option. For options requiring data entry, type in the required information; then click the `Accept` label on the navigation line. To expand the data-entry area for long expressions, click the `Zoom:F9` label, enter the data; then click `Zoom:F9` again to return to the Edit options menu. To open the Expression Builder list, click the `Pick Operators/Fields:Shift-F1` label.

Modifying Field Attributes

◄ See "Performing Summary Calculations with a Query," p. 223

After the templates, picture functions, and edit options have been defined, they can be modified as needed. To modify a field attribute, place the cursor on the field and press F5. Make changes as desired.

Adding Calculated Fields

Special fields can be added to the form to show a calculation that's not represented by a "real" field in the database. These fields are called *calculated fields,* and they are just like calculated fields added to queries. These fields do not actually store data; they only perform and display a calculation on the form.

You may have a Customer database, for example, that includes a field (PURCHDATE) for the date of each customer's last purchase. If you want the form to display how many days from the current date that purchase was made, you can add a calculated field.

To create a calculated field that subtracts the last purchase date from the current date, follow these steps:

1. Position the cursor on the form and type a label for the calculated field such as **Number of days since last purchase:**
2. Position the cursor after the label in the location where the new field will appear.
3. Open the Fields menu and choose Add Field, or press F5. The Field List menu appears.
4. Move the cursor to <create> in the CALCULATED column and press Enter. The Field Definition menu appears.
5. Highlight the Name option, press Enter, and type the field name (**SINCE_LST**, for example).
6. If you want, highlight the Description option, press Enter, and type a description.
7. Highlight the Expression option and press Enter. Type the expression and press Enter. (The expression for the example would be **DATE() - PURCHDATE**.
8. Specify a Template option if you want.
9. Specify a Picture Function if you want.
10. Press Ctrl-End to accept this definition of the calculated field. The Forms design screen reappears, with the calculated field included.

When the form is used to enter or view the records in a database, dBASE calculates the number of days from the last purchase to the current date and displays it in this calculated field.

Organizing a Form with Lines and Boxes

Adding boxes and lines to a form often improves the form's readability and the user's comprehension of the data. Boxes can more clearly define the relationship of groups of information on the form. Lines also can be used to group information, but unlike a box, which is rectangular, lines can be drawn around areas in any shape as shown in figure 11.10.

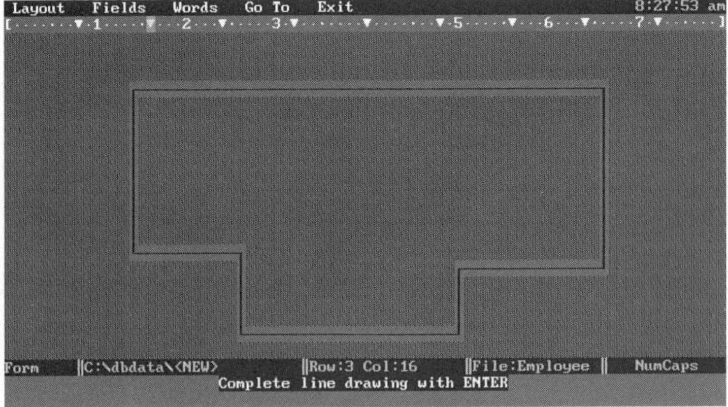

Fig. 11.10
Lines that create an unusual shape on a form can be used to outline special areas on the form.

Adding a Box

To add a box to the form, follow these steps:

1. Open the Layout menu and choose Box. When the Box menu appears, choose the border style you want for the box (see fig. 11.11).

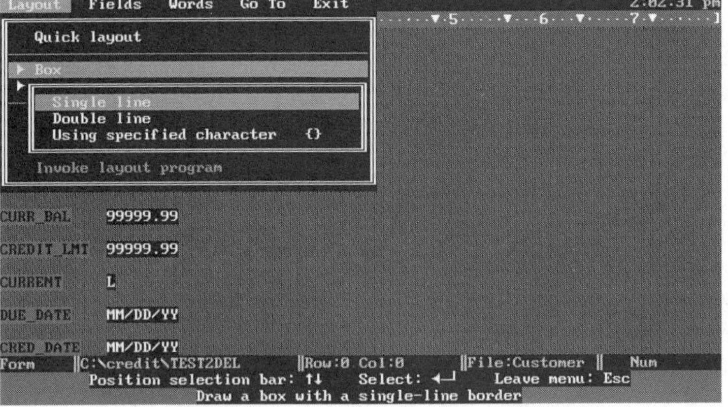

Fig. 11.11
The box border styles options are the same as the Line options.

The Using Specified Character option enables you to specify what character is to be used as the border. If you want a box made out of asterisks, for example, choose Using Specified Character, select it from the list, or type the asterisk and press Enter.

2. When the work surface reappears, use the arrow keys to position the cursor at the upper-left corner of the planned box and press Enter.

3. Use the arrow keys to move the cursor to the lower-right corner of the box. You can see the box change shape as you move to this corner.

As you move the cursor, the box extends over text and fields using the style that you selected. When the box is the correct size and shape, press Enter to accept it.

To position a box using the mouse, first click the location for the upper-left corner of the box. Position the mouse pointer on the location for the lower-right corner of the box, and then click again.

The box in figure 11.12 serves as a border for the title of the form. You can move the box by selecting it (use F6 and Enter, as described earlier in this chapter), pressing F7, and then using the arrow keys to move the box. Only the box moves; any text in the box remains in its original position.

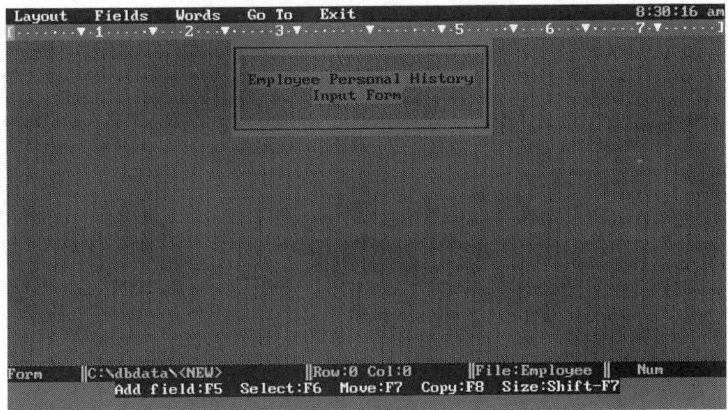

Fig. 11.12
Placing a box around the title of a form gives it a finished look.

To resize a box, select it and press Shift-F7. Use the arrow keys to move the lower-right corner, changing the size of the box. With the F7 and Shift-F7 keys, you can completely change the appearance of the box on the form.

Adding Lines

You may want to use several lines to divide the form into logical parts or create special relationships as shown in figure 11.13.

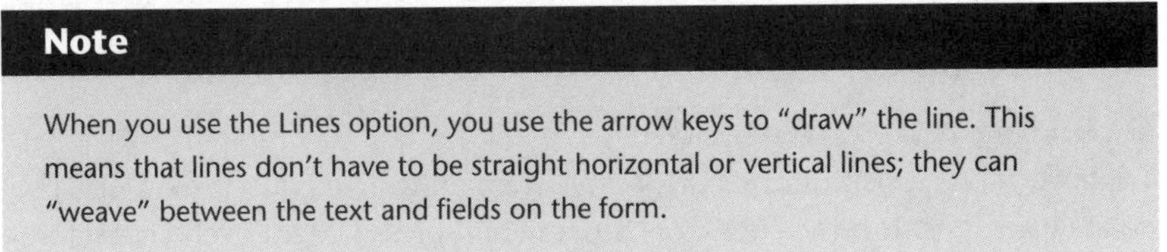
Note

When you use the Lines option, you use the arrow keys to "draw" the line. This means that lines don't have to be straight horizontal or vertical lines; they can "weave" between the text and fields on the form.

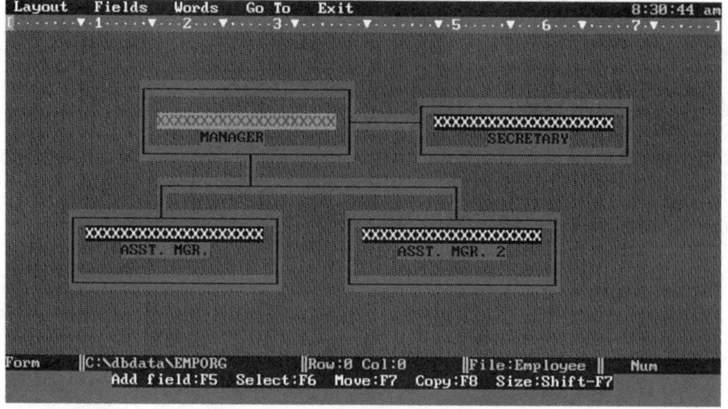

Fig. 11.13
A form that uses lines to show an organizational relationship similar to an organization chart.

To place lines on the form, follow these steps:

1. Open the Layout menu and select Line.

2. Choose Single Line or Double Line from the submenu that appears. To draw the line with characters (asterisks, for example), move the cursor to Using Specified Character and press Enter. A box displays with the acceptable characters. Move the cursor to the one you want and press Enter to return to the form.

3. Move the cursor where you want the line to start and press Enter to start the line-drawing process.

4. Use the left-arrow or right-arrow key to draw the line horizontally. Use the up-arrow or down-arrow key to draw a vertical line. (Lines may intersect, if desired, and if you change the direction of the line from horizontal to vertical or vice versa, dBASE draws a corner.)

5. After you've drawn all the lines, press Enter.

You can use the mouse to draw lines by clicking instead of pressing Enter. Be sure to hold the mouse steady; otherwise, you could end up with some stair-step lines that you have to delete one character at a time. To make your lines straight, use the arrow keys.

Tip
If you do not have a mouse, you can select the line with F6 and then delete it with Del.

Deleting a Box and Lines

To delete a box, position the cursor anywhere on the box and press Del. To delete lines, position the cursor on the line and press Del for each character that makes the line or highlight the line by dragging the mouse over it and pressing Del.

Adding Color to the Form

Using colors on a custom form can make a significant contribution to the readability and usefulness of a form. You can use colors to identify important fields and to draw the user's eye to certain parts of the form.

To apply color to the form, select the area you want to color and then apply the new color to that area. Each row-and-column position on the form has two colors associated with it: a foreground color and a background color. The *foreground* refers to the character displayed in that position; the *background* refers to the area behind the character. The default form has a blue background with a white foreground, which means that the characters (foreground) are white on a field of blue (background). Table 11.8 in the following section shows the available foreground and background colors for a color monitor. You will notice that there are more colors to choose from for the foreground than there are for the background.

Monochrome monitors are much more limited. Monochrome monitors can display white, bright white, or black in the foreground, and white or black in the background. Monochrome monitors also can display an underline on foreground characters.

Changing the Colors of a Field

To change the color of a field, follow these steps:

1. Select the field whose color you want to change by moving the cursor into the field. You do not have to press F6 to add color to a single field.

2. Open the Words menu and choose Display. A menu showing all the foreground and background colors appears. A cursor appears to the left of the last choice in the Foreground column.

3. To see how different foreground and background combinations look, use the up- and down-arrow keys to move the cursor up and down the Foreground column. As you move the cursor, the foreground colors of the Background column change, showing what the field looks like with each color combination.

4. To look at different background colors, press the right-arrow key to move the cursor to the Background column. Then use the up- and down-arrow keys to select different background colors. As you move the cursor, the background colors of the Foreground column change, again showing you what the field looks like with different backgrounds.

5. Press Ctrl-End to accept a combination.
6. Move the cursor off the field to see the result of the color change.

Table 11.8 Colors Available on a Color Monitor

Foreground	Background
Black	Black
Blue	Blue
Green	Green
Cyan	Cyan
Red	Red
Magenta	Magenta
Brown	Brown
White	White
Gray	Blinking
Light Blue	
Light Green	
Light Red	
Light Magenta	
Yellow	
Bright White	

To select display colors with the mouse, click the Words menu and the Display option, and then click the foreground and background colors you want to use. Click the `Select & Exit:Ctrl-End` label in the navigation line to save your choices.

Changing the Colors of an Area on the Form

You may want to change the colors of an area of the screen to draw attention to it or simply to make a more pleasing contrast on-screen. The process is not much different from changing a field's colors.

To change the colors of an area on-screen, follow these steps:

1. Position the cursor on the upper-left corner of the area and press F6. Move the cursor to the lower-right corner of the area and press Enter to accept the selection.
2. Open the Words menu and choose Display. When the color selection menu appears, make select a foreground color and a background color.
3. Press Ctrl-End to accept the color selection.
4. When you return to the Forms design screen, press Esc to remove the highlighting from the selected area.

Note

Some parts of the area may not have the selected background color. Areas of the surface without characters are not affected by the foreground and background colors, so they take the default form background color of blue. You may have to type spaces in these areas to color them.

Thoughtful use of colors can make the form easier to use. If the form contains fields that must be filled to maintain the database's integrity, for example, you can make those fields a different color from other fields. The user of the form then knows that he or she cannot skip that field. (Make sure that the field is not left blank by using a validation check on the field.) A distinct field color visually reminds the user why the field must be filled.

For forms used to view data, add color to emphasize the most important data. You can color an entire area with a different background color and change the field colors to emphasize these areas.

Use some caution when you design with color, however. Too many colors can confuse the screen. As a general rule, don't use more than two colors for the form's background and not more than two other colors for fields' backgrounds.

▶ See "SET Commands," p. 832

Saving a Form and Exiting

After the form is designed, be sure to save it. To save a form, follow these steps:

1. Open the Layout menu and choose Save This Form.

2. The first time you save a form, dBASE asks you for the name of the form. Names must conform to the DOS file-naming conventions: the name can be a maximum of eight characters, have no spaces, and include only digits, characters, and the underscore or hyphen character. Use a name that represents the form in some way.

3. If you already saved the form, the form name box has the name in it. Press Enter to accept the name and save the form. If you want to give the form a new name, enter the new name in the box. This renaming feature is useful if you want to modify a form and save both the original and the modified versions of the form. Give the modified version a new name; the original version remains unchanged.

Tip
As you design a form, save often by pressing Ctrl-Enter. It's frustrating to near the end of the process and lose your work because of a power failure.

To exit the Forms design screen, open the Exit menu. Then choose Save Changes and Exit; or choose Abandon Changes and Exit. (If you haven't saved the form previously, you have to type a name and press Enter if you choose Save Changes and Exit.) When you exit from the Forms Design screen, notice that the new form you just created is listed in the current catalog, ready to be used.

Creating MulTiple-Page Forms

Some database designs have more fields than can fit on one screen. Custom forms are easier to read and use if the data fields are not crowded together on the screen. You can design custom forms with up to 16 pages, although you seldom need more than two or three pages.

To design a custom form with more than one page, simply design the first page of the form, move the cursor to the bottom of the first page, and press PgDn. A second, blank page appears. Follow this same procedure to add subsequent pages. Scroll back to the preceding page by pressing PgUp.

Tip
Remember when designing a form that you cannot leave a blank line at the top of the form design. If you do, it will not be displayed when the form is used.

MulTiple-page forms are useful even when you can fit all database fields on one screen. If your data falls into logical groups, putting those groups on separate pages may make the form easier to use. If you're entering data in a customer-information database, for example, you can use one screen for information about the customer's name, address, and telephone number, and another screen for information about the customer's business and purchasing guidelines.

Note

When you use mulTiple-page forms, consider repeating one or two fields on each page so the user has no doubt about which record is in use. In the customer-information form example, you could include the customer name on each page of the mulTiple-page form. This gives the user a frame of reference when entering data in other fields. The field (or fields) repeated on subsequent screens should be read-only fields. (On the Edit Options menu for the field, set Editing Allowed to NO). As you'll remember, the cursor can't stop on a read-only field.

You can put a field on a form any number of times simply by positioning the cursor where you want the field to appear and choosing Add Field from the Fields menu.

Modifying a Custom Form

To modify a custom form, highlight the name of the form in the Forms panel in the Control Center and press Enter. The menu shown in figure 11.14 displays Choose Modify Layout. Make the desired changes, save the form, and exit the Forms Design screen.

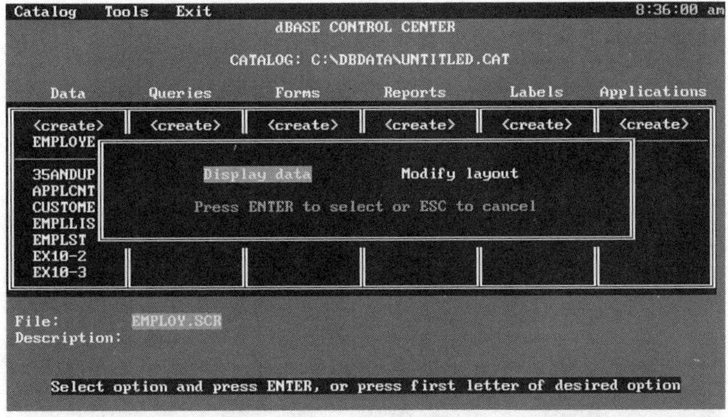

Fig. 11.14 When a form is selected by pressing Enter, this menu displays.

Note

If you set INSTRUCT to OFF (using the Settings option on the Tools menu), you must highlight an existing form and press Shift-F2 to modify that form. With INSTRUCT set to OFF, highlighting a form name and pressing Enter causes dBASE to activate that form, placing it on-screen.

Troubleshooting

I am trying to design a form that has two screens. I want the fields on the second screen to start on the top line of the screen. I "push" the fields off the first screen by inserting blank lines. When I use the form, the fields that should start at the top of the second screen are on the last line of the first screen. What did I do wrong?

I can think of two reasons why this could happen. You may have a blank line at the top of the form, or you may have the ruler displayed. When the ruler is displayed, it takes up a line on the screen and gives you a false sense of where the first line of the form is. Be sure to delete all blank lines at the top of the screen, turn the ruler display off, and then push the fields down as you described.

Why can't I delete spaces in front of a field to move the field to the left?

You can do this if there really are spaces before the field. Spaces are created by pressing the spacebar. They can be deleted. The background of the form which is ruled off like spaces cannot be deleted.

Using Custom Forms

To use a custom form, move the cursor in the Control Center to the Forms panel, highlight the form name you want to use, and press Enter and choose Display Data. The form appears on-screen, showing the information in the first record of the database, if the database contains records. Figure 11.15 shows a completed form in use.

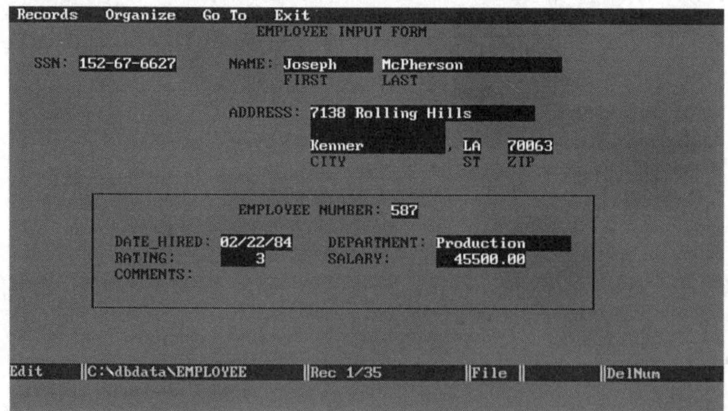

Fig. 11.15
This custom form, displaying a record, is much easier to read than the default form.

All the keystrokes you use on a default form to move from field to field or edit data are the same on a custom form. You can use the dBASE menu bar with a custom form, just as you do with default forms to add records, mark records for deletion, edit existing records, and find the records you want to view or edit. You can switch back and forth between the custom form and the Browse screen with F2.

If a memo field marker or window is used in a custom form, it's accessed the same way that it is in the default form—by pressing Ctrl-Home.

To open the memo window using the mouse, just double-click inside the window. Pull down the word processor menus from the top of the screen by clicking the menu name and option you need. Click the Exit menu and the Save Changes and Exit option, for example, to exit the window and save the information you entered.

◄ See "Adding Data to Memo Fields," p. 134

◄ See "Using the Edit Screen," p. 145

When using a mulTiple-page form, use PgUp and PgDn to move forward and backward through the pages. When you reach the last page, pressing PgDn displays the first page of the next record. Similarly, pressing PgUp while on the first page of a mulTiple-page form displays the last page of the preceding record.

From Here...

Custom forms make dBASE easier to use, for you and for anyone who uses the system you design. This chapter introduced form design, including ways to format, edit, and validate the data entered and displayed on a custom form. Many of the same techniques you learned in this chapter can be applied to creating custom report forms. The following chapters relate to reports:

- Chapter 12, "Creating Custom Reports," describes the process of creating and using a report that contains report bands.

- Chapter 13, "Designing and Using a Mailmerge Report and Label," focuses on the special type of report called a mailmerge. It also discusses the related activity of creating mailing labels.

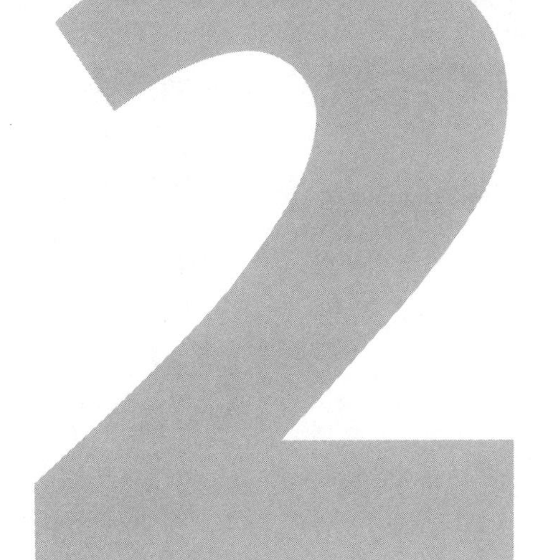

Chapter 12

Creating Custom Reports

Reports are the most visible evidence of a dBASE 5 database application. You may have the most sophisticated database design, wonderful input screens, and a wealth of informative data in the system, but if your reports are difficult to read and understand, your database is less than successful. dBASE 5 offers an extremely sophisticated, easy-to-use feature for creating excellent reports. In this chapter, you move beyond the default quick reports you learned to generate in Part II, and learn to create custom reports using the Reports design screen.

As you'll see, the Reports design screen is very similar to the Forms design screen described in Chapter 11, so learning to use the Reports design screen will be a little easier for you. With the Reports design screen you can create reports simply by placing database fields on-screen, entering text, drawing lines and boxes, and so on. You also can add summary and calculated fields and group records by content. The Reports design screen is a very powerful tool for creating specialized reports.

In this chapter, you learn about the following:

- Using Quick Layout
- Using report bands
- Adding and removing fields
- Specifying field attributes
- Creating calculated fields

- Using summary fields
- Using a custom report

Creating a Report with the Reports Design Screen

As you'll remember, the Quick Report is a columnar report that lists the field names as the columnar headings. Although this report is quite adequate, it could be improved. For example, you might want a simple column report that has more descriptive column headings. With the Reports design screen, you can create just such a report.

To design a custom report, follow these steps:

1. Select the desired database from the Data panel of the Control Center.
2. Move the cursor to the Reports panel, highlight `<create>`, and press Enter.
3. At this point, you have two options:
   - Choose Quick Layout and then the type of report that you want to design, and dBASE places the fields and field labels on the form for you (unless you're designing a mailmerge report).
   - Press Esc and start with a clean slate. If you choose this second option, you have to place the fields and text yourself.

Figure 12.1 shows the Reports design screen as it appears if you press Esc. This surface is like a designer's table, on which you add, edit, and move around the many elements that make up a successful report. The following section takes you on a tour of the Reports design screen.

Getting Acquainted with the Reports Design Screen

At the top of the Reports design screen is the familiar menu bar, which has options that pertain to building a custom report. Below the menu bar is the ruler used to set the margins and tabs for the printed report. The numbers on the ruler represent tens position markers; instead of 10, 20, 30, you see 1, 2, 3. The arrows that point down locate the tabs.

Most of the screen is used to display the report bands. As you can see in figure 12.1, the Reports design work surface has five bands: the Page Header,

Report Intro, Detail, Report Summary, and Page Footer. Below the title of each band is a shaded blank line. Text and fields placed in the blank line of the band print out in specific areas of the report.

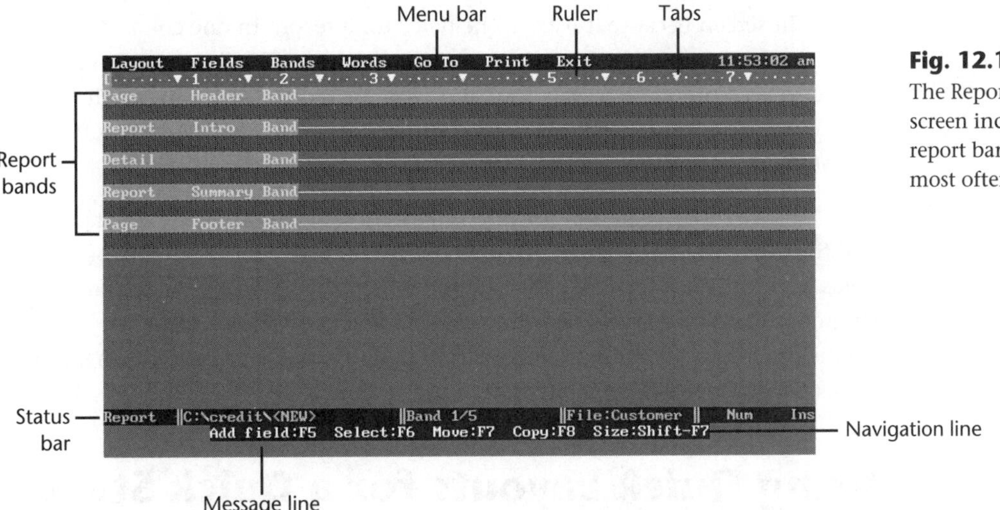

Fig. 12.1
The Reports design screen includes the report bands used most often.

At the bottom of the screen is the standard dBASE 5 status bar, which shows information about the work surface. The far left section of the status bar reads `Report`, indicating that you are in the Reports design screen. The next section shows the name of the report you're designing. If this report is new, the path ends with `<NEW>`. The next section of the status bar relates information about the cursor location. If the cursor is in a band's title bar, this section reads `BAND`, followed by a fraction indicating which band. If the cursor is in the third of five bands, for example, the cursor location is `BAND 3/5`. If the cursor is in the lines of a band, the line and column numbers in that band are shown. The `File:` indicator specifies the currently active database file. The last section of the status bar shows the status of the Num Lock, Caps Lock, and Ins keys. If the `Num`, `Caps`, or `Ins` indicators appear in this section of the status bar, the related key is active. Press that key to deactivate it.

At the bottom of the Reports design screen is the navigation line, which reminds you of the available function keys.

As with other work surfaces in dBASE, the last line is the message line, where dBASE displays messages explaining what actions it expects.

Choosing Your Method

If you opt for the Quick Layout method of designing a report, you can select one of three types of reports: columnar, form, or mailmerge. The columnar report is like the Quick Report or the Browse screen; the form report is similar to an Edit screen because it lists all the fields for a record in one column; the mailmerge report is a free-form type of report where the fields are generally placed to accommodate a letter format. If you use Quick Layout for a columnar report or a form report, dBASE places the fields and field labels for you, but no fields or text are placed if you select the mailmerge type of report.

The Quick Layout can be a benefit or a hindrance, depending on the database and the desired report appearance. If you must remove a large number of fields from the report, change the order in which the fields appear, and reposition or retype field labels, the Quick Layout becomes a quick headache. If, on the other hand, the report you want to design needs very little editing, the Quick Layout method is the method to use.

Using Quick Layouts for a Quick Start

As noted in an earlier set of instructions, when you create a report, the Layout menu is displayed automatically with the Quick Layout option highlighted. At this time, you can select Quick Layout and then select a report type, or you can press Esc. If you press Esc, you can still choose Layout, Quick Layout, and select a report type.

Using the Columnar Layout

Figure 12.2 shows the Reports design screen with a columnar report created with Quick Layout.

Notice that the field names are listed in the Page Header band and the fields are listed in the Detail band. The fields are placed two spaces apart and have the same width as defined in the database structure. All numeric fields are totaled in the Report Summary band. The report that dBASE created is actually the default Quick Report.

Using the Form Layout

Figure 12.3 shows a form layout report created by Quick Layout for the same database. Notice that dBASE places database fields in the Detail band, putting one field on each line of the band. The field labels are placed to the left of each database field.

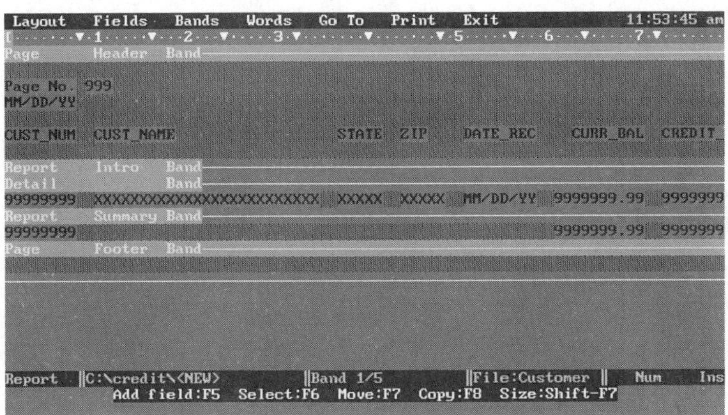

Fig. 12.2
A columnar report created by Quick Layout places all fields horizontally in the Detail band.

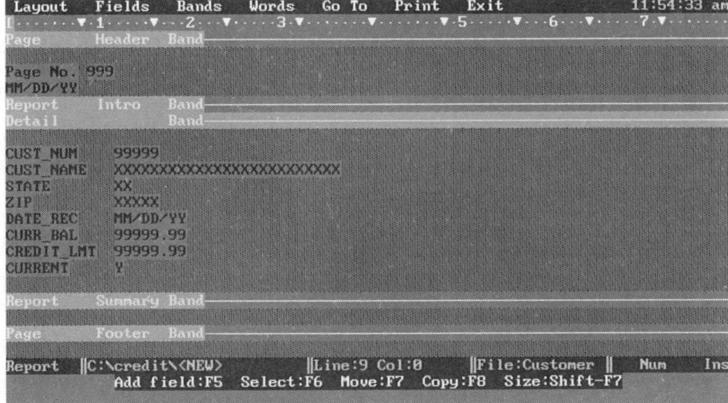

Fig. 12.3
The default form layout report lists all the fields vertically in the Detail band.

Using the Mailmerge Layout

If you select Mailmerge Layout, no fields are placed on the form (see fig. 12.4). Only the report bands are created for you.

Designing a Custom Report

As already discussed, you don't have to use the Quick Layout option to put fields and text in the bands of the work surface; you can add fields one at a time and type the desired text wherever you want it. Because a report is usually created with the intention of printing it, it's important to set the margins for a report before you even begin placing the fields and text in the bands. After you start adding the fields to the report, you must thoroughly understand report bands so that you can place text and fields correctly in order to achieve the desired result.

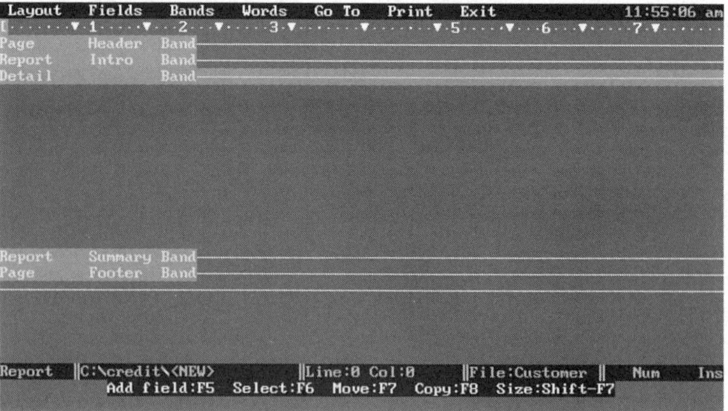

Fig. 12.4
The Mailmerge Layout report does not place fields in the report.

Setting Margins and Tabs

The ruler controls the left and right margins of the report as well as the tab settings. To modify these report settings, choose the Words menu and then select Modify Ruler. The cursor moves into the ruler. Use the left and right arrows to move the cursor left and right along the ruler. (Pressing the space bar is the same as pressing the right arrow.)

The left margin is indicated by a left bracket ([ ) in the ruler; the right margin, by a right bracket ( ]). Reset the margins by moving to the desired margin position on the ruler and typing a left or right bracket.

To set a new tab, place the cursor at the desired location and type an exclamation mark. A triangle that's pointing down appears to represent the tab. To remove a tab, place the cursor on the down-facing arrow and press Del or move to the right of the tab and press Backspace.

After you modify the ruler, press Enter to return to the Reports design work surface.

Note

As the cursor moves in the work surface, a highlight moves on the ruler so that you can always see in what column the cursor is located.

Understanding Bands

You can think of report bands simply as sections of a report. Each band performs a particular function. The amount of space that each band uses in a report is determined by the number of lines in the band.

Page Header Band

The Page Header band prints at the top of every page in the report. This band usually does not contain a field from the database; it can contain the title of the report, a predefined field such as a date or time, a page number, column headings, and so on.

> **Note**
>
> If a field is included in the Page Header band, the contents of the field for the current record print. Usually, the record that's current at the time the page header prints is the first record that appears in the detail band for that page of the report.

The Page Header band can be suppressed on the first page of the report if a Report Intro band is included in the report.

Report Intro Band

The contents of the Report Intro band prints only on the first page of the report, after the Page Header band. The text in this band can be isolated on a single page such as a report title page by inserting a page break after the text. To insert a page break, move the cursor to the last line in the Report Intro band, and then open the Words menu and choose Insert Page Break.

If you create a title page for a report in the manner described above, you wouldn't want the page header information to print on that page. To suppress the Page Header band on the title page, choose Bands and select NO for Page Heading in Report Intro.

> **Note**
>
> The Report Intro band usually doesn't include a field from the database, either. If it does, however, the contents of the field are taken from the first record processed in the report.

Detail Band

The Detail band is actually the body of a report, and it prints once for each record in the database. Think of the Detail band as a processing loop. Everything in the Detail band (including blank lines) prints for each record until all the records are processed.

Report Summary Band

The Report Summary band prints at the end of the report after the last record prints in the Detail band. Use the Report Summary band to summarize data printed in the Detail band. This summary can include totals and averages of numeric fields or counts of how many records were printed.

Page Footer Band

The Page Footer band prints at the bottom of each page of the report. This band is good for printing page numbers, the date, the time, a copyright notice, and so on. This band can contain summary fields to calculate page totals.

Tip
The Detail band isn't the correct place to type column headings. If you type column headings in the Detail band, they are repeated for every record.

> **Note**
>
> If you use summary fields in the Page Footer band, you must reset the fields to zero after each page. See "Adding Fields that Perform Summary Math" later in this chapter.

Group Band

dBASE doesn't automatically insert the Group band in a report because it isn't used in every report. If you want to use a Group band, you must add it yourself by using the Bands menu. (See "Grouping Records" later in this chapter.)

The Group band enables you to group records together for processing. This is usually done for the purpose of subtotaling records in the group. For example, you might group equipment records by department name and show a subtotal for the cost of equipment in each department.

Adding Fields to Reports

When adding fields to a report, take care to add the fields in the correct band. Most fields are placed in the Detail band.

To add a field to the report using the field's default width and appearance, follow these steps:

1. Place the cursor where you want to insert a field.

2. Open the Fields menu and choose Add Field; or press F5. The field selection box appears (see fig. 12.5). All the fields in the database appear in the far left column of the field selection box where the name of the database is used as a heading. Choose a database field to add to the report by highlighting it and pressing Enter.

You use the columns labeled Calculated, Predefined, and Summary to create specialized fields. These fields are covered later in this chapter.

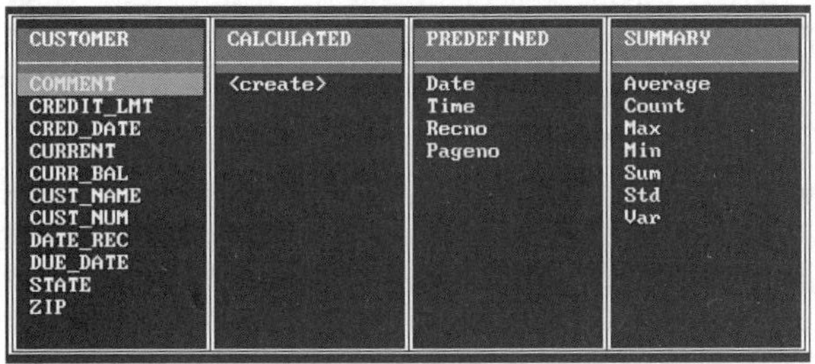

Fig. 12.5
The field selection box lists all fields that can be placed in the report.

3. After you select the field, the field format box appears (see fig. 12.6). This box presents information about the field (its name, type, length, and number of decimal places), along with options to alter the field's appearance on the report. Choose the default values by pressing Ctrl-End. The formatting options are covered later in this section in "Specifying Field Attributes."

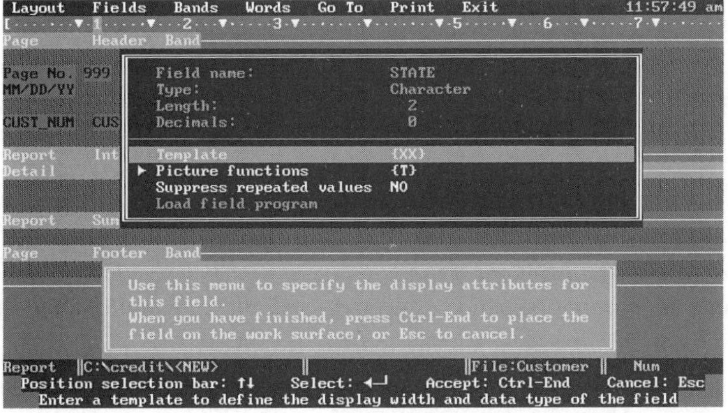

Fig. 12.6
The field format box can be used to alter the field's appearance.

To place a field on the work surface by using the mouse, just click the location to position the cursor, click Add field:F5 in the navigation line or open the Fields menu and choose Add Field. Pick fields from the field selection box by double-clicking the field name.

Tip
You can also display the field selection box by double-clicking the report at the location where you want the field to be placed.

Sizing Memo Fields

When a memo field is placed in a report, it should have vertical stretch turned on, and the field width should be reduced to fit in the available space on the report. For example, if the width of the memo field is decreased to 15 spaces and vertical stretch is on, when the record prints it uses as many lines as it needs (vertically) to print the contents of the field.

To size a memo field, first select the field with F6 and Enter. Then press Shift-F7 and change the width with the arrow keys.

Moving Fields in the Bands

◀ See "Using Picture Functions," p. 266

After you add fields to the bands of the Reports design work surface, you may want to move them to make your report more readable. You can move a field anywhere in the band or from one band to another.

Moving a Field within a Band

To move a field within a band, follow these steps:

1. Position the cursor on the field you want to move.
2. Press F6 and Enter.
3. Press F7.
4. Using the arrow keys, position the cursor in the band at the new location and press Enter. If you move the field on top of another field or some text, dBASE asks whether you want to delete the covered field or text. If you reply Yes, the old field is deleted and replaced by the moved field. If you reply No, the move does not occur, and all fields remain in their original positions.
5. Press Esc to deselect the field.

Moving a Field to Another Band

To move fields from one band to another, you follow a slightly different procedure:

1. Select the field you want to move by pressing F6 and Enter.
2. Use the arrow keys to move the cursor to the band into which you want to move the field.
3. Press F7. A ghost of the field appears at the cursor location. Use the arrow keys to place the ghost at the new field's location.
4. Press Enter to complete the move.
5. Press Esc to deselect the field.

To move a field with the mouse, select it by dragging the mouse over the field area; then release the mouse button. Click the new location to reposition the cursor; then double-click the `Move:F7` label in the navigation line.

Deleting Fields from the Bands

Deleting a field is even simpler than moving one. Simply place the cursor on the field and press Del. The field disappears from the band.

Specifying Field Attributes

Various field attributes can be controlled for the purpose of a report. For example, you can change the field width, add a template, or add a picture function. Good use of template symbols and picture functions can turn an acceptable report into an excellent one. Well-presented data creates a professional-looking report that is easier to read and understand.

Changing the Width of a Field

Changing the width of a field—its length on the report, not the width of the field in the database's structure—is simple. Move the cursor to the field you want to change and press Shift-F7. The entire field is highlighted. Press the arrow keys to make the field larger or smaller. The highlight shrinks or grows as you reduce or enlarge the field's length, although the Xs that mark the size of the original field remain until you press Enter to accept the new size. If you decide not to resize the field, cancel the action by pressing Esc rather than Enter.

To resize a field with the mouse, click the field, click the `Size:Shift-F7` label in the navigation line, move the mouse pointer to resize the field, then click again.

Using a Template

A *template* is a string of formatting symbols, one for each position in a field. The *template symbol* controls what's displayed in a particular position in the field. You use a template to alter the presentation of the field on the report.

◀ See "Specifying Field Attributes," p. 261

To specify a template for a field, position the cursor on the field and press F5. Choose the Template option in the field format box. The braces surrounding the default template disappear, and you can edit the template. After the template characters are entered, press Ctrl-End.

If you add symbols that increase the length of the field (such as commas or decimal places), the field automatically increases in size. This increase may cause other fields on the line to shift to the right to accommodate the larger field.

Table 12.1 lists the template symbols you can use for numeric fields in a dBASE 5 report.

Table 12.1 Template Symbols for Numeric Fields

Symbol	Function
9	Presents only digits, or a positive (+) or negative (–) sign.
#	Presents only digits, spaces, and the positive or negative signs.
.	Specifies the decimal point location in the field.
,	Displays a comma at this location if the number is large enough to require it.
*	Displays leading zeros as asterisks. Placed to the left of the first numeric template symbol, this symbol causes * to appear in all positions to the left of the first digit printed. For example, *999 prints the value 1 as **1.
$	Displays the same as the *, except that a dollar sign is used rather than an asterisk.
Other	Any other character you type in the template is inserted into the display. Use this feature to insert dashes or slashes into a numeric field.

The best way to learn how to use template symbols is to look at examples and use the samples as the basis for new templates. The following table shows several useful examples of templates in a nine-character field:

Data Value	Template	Report Presentation
12345.67	99,999.99	12,345.67
12.34	*99.99	****12.34
12.34	$99,999.99	$$$$12.34
5551212	999-9999	555-1212

With character fields, you use a different set of template symbols. Table 12.2 lists the template symbols you use in a dBASE 5 report for character fields.

Table 12.2 Template Symbols for Character Fields

Symbol	Function
9	Displays digits and signs.
#	Displays digits, signs, spaces, and periods.
A	Displays alphabetic characters only.
N	Displays alphabetic characters, digits, and the underscore.
X	Displays any character.
!	Converts the database value to uppercase in this position.
Other	Any other character you type in the template is inserted into the display at this position.

Again, some examples of the use of the character template symbols are helpful:

Data Value	Template	Report Presentation
abcdefg	!!!!!!!	ABCDEFG
abcdefg	!AAAAAA	Abcdefg
555443333	999-99-9999	555-44-3333

Using Picture Functions

You also can alter the presentation of data in a Report field by using the Picture Functions option from the field format box. Using this option is similar to using template symbols, except that a picture function applies to the entire field, and a template symbol applies to only a single position in the field.

To modify a field's presentation by using the picture method, position the cursor on the field and press F5. Choose Picture Functions from the field format box. Depending on the type of field you're changing, you see either the Character Picture Function menu (see fig. 12.7) or the Numeric Picture Function menu (see fig. 12.8).

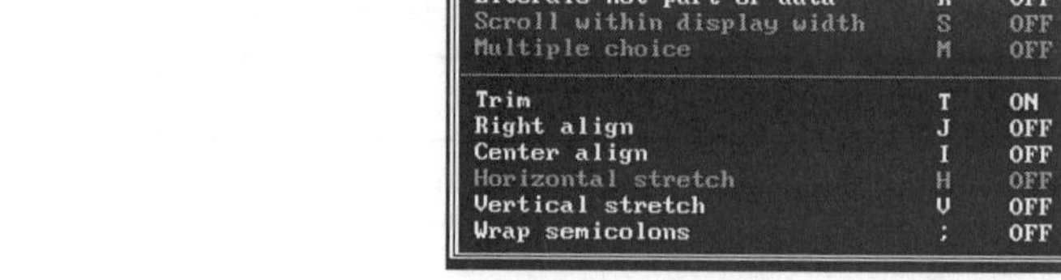

Fig. 12.7 The Character Picture Function menu for a character field shows available options.

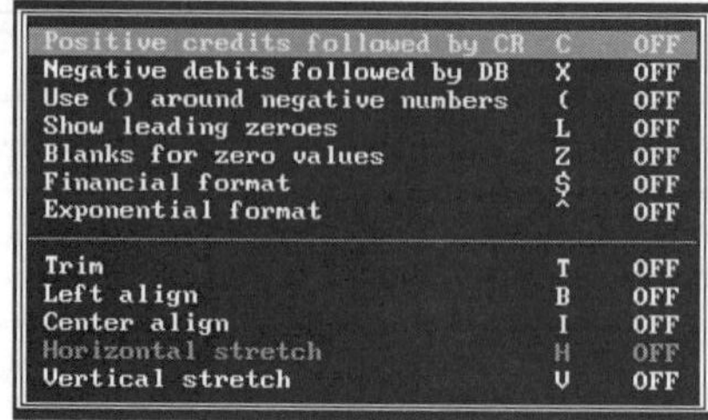

Fig. 12.8 The Numeric Picture Function menu for a numeric field lists formats and attributes for numbers.

To apply a picture function, highlight the function you want to apply to the field and press Enter. The function setting changes from OFF to ON. Press Enter again to change the setting back to OFF. When all functions are set, press Ctrl-End.

Picture functions apply to the entire field. If you select the Upper-Case Conversion function, for example, all characters in the field are converted to uppercase, regardless of their position. Compare this to using a template, in which you place the uppercase conversion character (!) in each position where you want the conversion to occur. Table 12.3 describes the character picture functions.

Table 12.3 Character Picture Functions

Function	Description
Alphabetic Characters Only	Displays alphabetic characters only.
Upper-Case Conversion	Converts all characters to uppercase (numbers are unaffected).
Literals Not Part Of Data	Literal characters in a field consist of nontemplate symbols that you want to appear in a field, such as the hyphen (-) in a phone number field that contains the string 999-9999. If you set Literals Not Part Of Data to OFF, the literal character is counted as one of the characters in the database field. If you set Literals Not Part Of Data to ON, the literal is inserted in the value but is not counted as one of the characters in the field.

Function	Description
Scroll Within Display Width	Causes data to scroll in a field than has a width that is less than the actual width of the field.
Multiple Choice	Enables you to select among different choices for a field entry.
Trim	Removes leading-edge blanks from a value. If the database value has leading-edge blanks, this option causes the field to be left-justified in the report field because the option strips those blanks off.
Right Align	Moves the value to the right of the field.
Center Align	Centers the value in the field. Because dBASE defaults to left alignment for character fields, there is no option for left alignment.
Horizontal Stretch	Used for mailmerge reports, this option causes a long field or text from a memo field to extend to the left and right margins of the report, rather than be confined to the template width.
Vertical Stretch	Used for column or form reports, this option causes the field to take up as many lines as necessary—each line as wide as the field—to print the value. If you have a database character field length of 25, for example, you can specify a field width of 5 and toggle Vertical Stretch ON. If the field is completely full, dBASE uses five lines to print the field.
Wrap Semicolons	Tells dBASE to start a new line when the program encounters a semicolon in the database value for this field.

Numeric picture functions also apply to the entire field. They enable you to bracket negative numbers with parentheses, use a dollar sign, suppress printing when the field has a value of zero, or print `CR` or `DB` for positive and negative numbers in true accounting fashion.

You can select more than one picture function for a field. If you want a field in financial format (a leading dollar sign, commas, and two decimal places) with a DB following negative numbers, for example, toggle Financial Format and Negative Debits Followed By DB to ON. Then define a template to place commas and decimals in the field. An important caution: putting DB or CR after a field does not increase the field's length on the Reports design surface. The DB and CR overwrite anything that usually prints in the three spaces to the right of the field. If you use these picture functions, make sure that you leave space for them to the right of the field.

Use the mouse to select options from the Picture Functions menu. Just click the option you want to use to toggle the ON/OFF settings, and then click the `Accept:Ctrl-End` label on the navigation line to save your settings.

Using the Suppress Repeated Values Option

Reports often have fields with values that repeat line after line, making the reports "busier" than necessary. A report of sales by customer number, for example, may have the Customer Number field in the Detail band. If the report is sorted on that field, the report could show many detail lines, each with the same customer number. To make the report easier to read, you could use the Suppress Repeated Values option on the Customer Number field.

When you use the Suppress Repeated Values option on a field, the field prints out only when the value of that field differs from the value of the field in the previous line. In other words, the first record in a set of repeating records prints the field content. So, in the preceding example, the customer number field prints out only when the customer number changes. This arrangement makes the report much easier to understand.

Modifying Field Attributes

Field attributes can be modified at any time. In fact, when you design a report, you may change the fields many times. To change the size of a field that's been resized already, simply position the cursor on the field and press Shift-F7 again. Then move the left or right arrow to resize and press Enter.

To change a template or picture function, position the cursor on the field and press F5. Select Template or Picture functions, make the desired changes, and press Ctrl-End.

Adding Calculated Fields

◀ See "Adding Calculated Fields," p. 274

Many times a report needs a field that performs a calculation. To create a field that performs a calculation, you must specify an expression. This expression can use the fields from the database, constants, functions, and any valid operation (such as adding, subtracting, multiplying, and so on). For example, you might want to subtract a field called CURR_BAL from a field called CREDIT_LMT. The expression for the calculated field would be CREDIT_LMT –CURR_BAL. The result of the calculated field shows how much available credit is left.

To add a calculated field, follow these steps:

1. Place the cursor in the band of the work surface where you want the calculated field to appear and press F5. The Add Field selection box appears (see fig. 12.9).

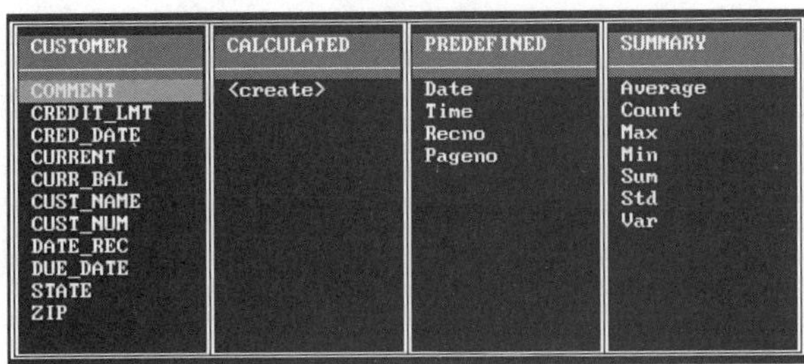

Fig. 12.9
The Add Field selection box is displayed when you press F5.

2. Move the highlight to the `<create>` option in the Calculated column and press Enter. The Field Definition menu displays (see fig. 12.10).

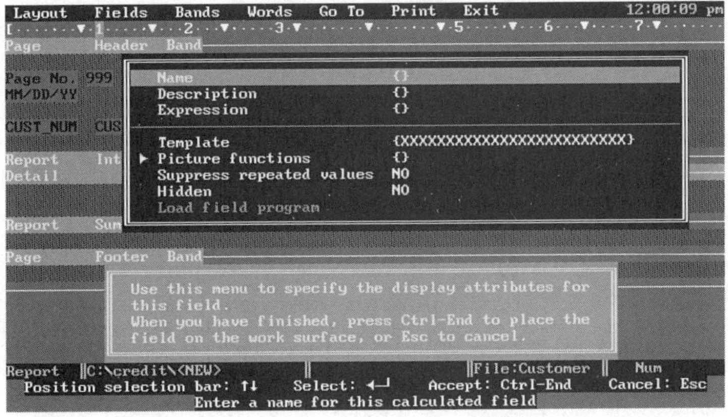

Fig. 12.10
The Field Definition menu enables you to name and describe the field as well as define the expression.

3. With the highlight on Name, press Enter and type the name. Press Enter and move the highlight to Description. Press Enter and type a description. Press Enter.

4. Move the highlight to the Expression option and press Enter. Type the desired expression and press Enter.

5. Use the Template and Picture Functions menu selections to format the field as desired. When you finish with the Template menu and/or the Picture Functions menu, press Ctrl-End.

6. Press Ctrl-End to finish the process and place the field.

> **Note**
>
> The expression for a calculated field cannot exceed 255 characters.

The expression for a calculated field can include functions as well as arithmetic operations (such as adding, subtracting, multiplying, and so on). For example, you may have a numeric field called RESULT that has five decimal places, and you want to round the values in the field to two decimal places. The round function can be used in the expression like this:

ROUND(RESULT,2).

Calculated fields aren't limited to numeric fields. Character fields can use expressions to concatenate fields like RATE+CODE or pull out substrings from the field like SUBSTR(CODE,5,3). The expression IF(ISBLANK(CONVICTED), "No record on file") prints the string ("No record on file") if the CONVICTED field is blank.

Using Unnamed Calculated Fields

An unnamed calculated field is created just like a named calculated field, except the field isn't given a name. This type of calculated field cannot be referenced in the expression of any other calculated field, and it is calculated after all other types of calculated fields.

Sometimes it's necessary to use unnamed fields in a report simply because of the location of the field. Calculation in a report proceeds from top to bottom and left to right. If FIELDA must be calculated before FIELDB, FIELDA must be placed to the left of FIELDB so the calculation will take place correctly. If the fields can't be moved, FIELDA could be an unnamed field. This forces the calculation of FIELDA after FIELDB. Remember, though, that FIELDA cannot be referenced by any other field if it's an unnamed field.

◄ See "Understanding Expressions," p. 165

◄ See "Using Functions in Expressions," p. 166

Using Hidden Calculated Fields

A hidden calculated field does not appear in the report. Unlike the unnamed calculated field, it has a name and it can be referenced by other calculated fields. To make a calculated field hidden, set Hidden to YES (see fig. 12.11).

You might use a hidden field to calculate a total for each record (like QTY*COST), and then add a summary field that displays in the Report Summary band and sums the totals for all records.

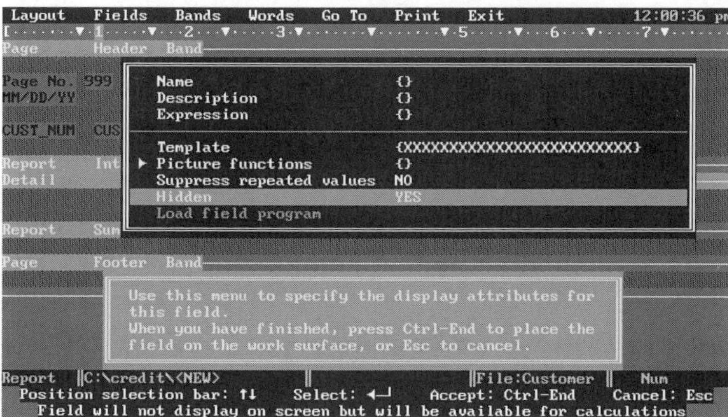

Fig. 12.11 Setting Hidden to YES for a calculated field keeps the field from printing.

Troubleshooting

My calculated fields do not yield the correct results.

Check all calculated fields to be sure they do not reference another calculated field that comes after the field in question. After would be to the right or below. Also be sure that unnamed calculated fields are used correctly. Unnamed fields are calculated after all other fields regardless of location.

I "inherited" a report that has a calculated field. The calculated field seems to include a hidden field. I need to edit the hidden field and change the expression, but I cannot find it on the report. How can I edit this hidden field?

You do not have to "find" the hidden field on the report to edit it. Position the cursor anywhere and press F5. The name of the calculated field is listed in the second column (Calculated) of the Add Field Selection box. Move the highlight to the field name and press Enter. The Field Definition menu displays. (Notice that Hidden is set to YES.) Highlight Expression and press Enter. Edit the expression and press Ctrl-End.

Adding Fields that Perform Summary Math

Summary fields can be used in the Report Summary band that prints at the end of the report to total fields, perform averages, count the number of records in the report, and so on.

To add a Summary field to the report, move the cursor into the Report Summary band, position the cursor where you want the field to appear, and follow these steps:

1. Open the Fields menu and choose Add Field; or press F5. The right column of the field selection box (refer to fig. 12.9) lists the seven types of Summary fields available. Six of these types calculate a value based on a numeric field in the report. In each case, only values printed on the report are summarized.

2. Choose the type of Summary field you want by highlighting it and pressing Enter. The types of Summary fields are described in table 12.4. The Summary Field Description menu appears (see fig. 12.12).

3. Give the Summary field a name and a description.

   Notice that the Operation option on the Summary Field Description menu is set to the Summary field type you choose in step 2.

Tip
Don't use a dBASE 5 reserved word, such as *Count* or *Sum*, for the field name.

4. Highlight the Field to Summarize On option and press Enter. A pop-up menu showing all the fields in the current view appears. Choose the field you want to summarize by highlighting it with the arrow keys and pressing Enter. (Nonnumeric fields appear dimmed in the selection box because you cannot choose them.)

   If you're using a mouse, double-click a field name from the pop-up fields list to select a field to summarize.

5. The Reset Every option enables you to define when you want to reset the Summary field to zero. You may want to reset summary fields for reports only once, at the beginning of the report. In this case, the <REPORT> default is acceptable. You may want to reset a Summary field on each page. To change the setting, highlight Reset Every and press Enter to display the resetting options; then choose the PAGE setting.

6. Use the Template and Picture Functions options to format the appearance of the Summary field as desired. When finished with the Template and/or Picture Functions menu, press Ctrl-End.

7. Press Ctrl-End to place the field and return to the Reports design screen.

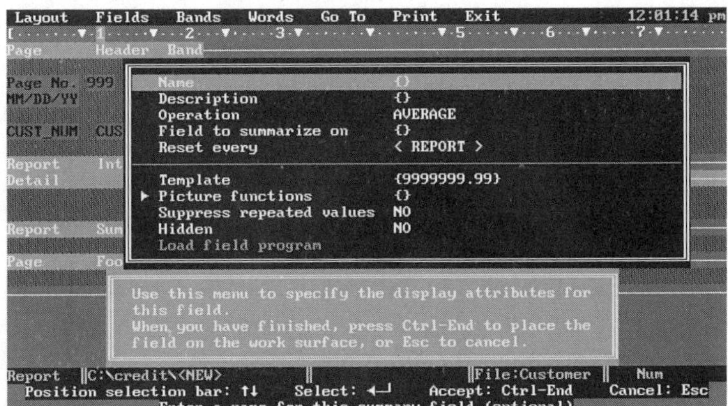

Fig.12.12
The Summary Field Description menu defines the summary field.

Table 12.4 Summary Field Types

Field	Description
Average	Calculates and displays the average value for the chosen numeric field
Max	Prints the highest value reported for a numeric field
Min	Prints the lowest value reported for the numeric field
Sum	Sums all the values for a particular field
Std	Prints the standard deviation of all values reported for the numeric field (standard deviation is a statistical measurement)
Var	Prints the variation (another statistical measurement) of all values reported for the numeric field
Count	Prints how many records are processed in the report

Grouping Records

When you print a report, dBASE 5 processes and prints the records one after another. If the database isn't indexed or sorted, the records appear in the order that they were entered. If you use an index or a sorted database, the records appear in the indexed or sorted order. Although using an indexed field or a sorted database causes records to be grouped, it does allow for any kind of break between groups or summary calculations for each group. To provide this kind of formatting and calculating, dBASE uses the Group band.

Tip
Long reports without groups can be difficult to read. Use the Record Count option to insert a blank line after a specified number of Detail band records are printed.

The Group band can group data by record count (such as 15 records in a group), by a field, or by an expression, like SUBSTR(ZIP,1,3).

◀ See "Indexing a Field," p. 113

◀ See "Organizing the Records for the Report," p. 161

◀ See "Sorting Query Output," p. 231

◀ See "Indexing Query Output," p. 230

When you're grouping records, first decide how you want to group the data. The most common way to group data is by a field. You might group on a field called CITY, or LAST_NAME, or ZIP. If you group on a field, the field must be indexed, or the database must be sorted on that field. Sometimes, you may want to group records on more than one field. For example, you might want to group by CITY and then by LAST_NAME. You can accomplish this grouping of data by using two Group bands and sorting on both fields (or by using a complex index that uses both fields).

Adding a Group Band

When you add a Group band to the report, dBASE actually adds two bands—the Group Intro band and the Group Summary band. These bands work in conjunction with the Detail band; they don't replace the Detail band. The Group Intro band prints before the Detail band for each group, and the Summary band prints after the Detail band for each group. When a new value in the grouping field is encountered, the Group Intro band prints again, followed by the Detail band, and then the Group Summary band. This process continues until all the groups are printed.

The Group Intro band usually contains text that refers to the group, such as field headings for the fields included in the Detail band or a statement that identifies the group and contains the field used for the group (see fig. 12.13).

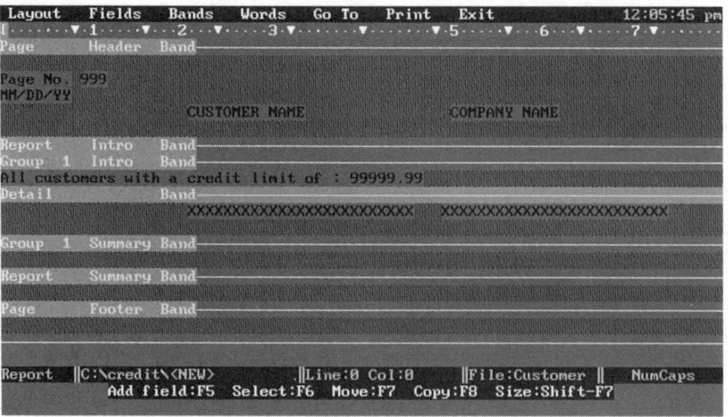

Fig. 12.13
A Group Intro band prints at the beginning of every group.

The Group Summary band may contain one or more blank lines to create a break between the groups, summary text that refers to the group, or summary fields (see fig. 12.14).

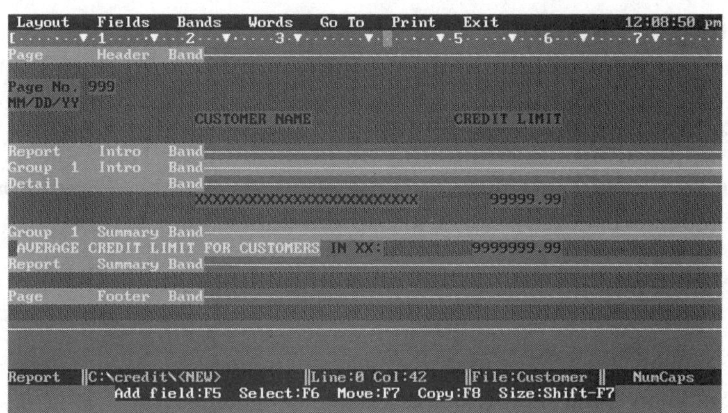

Fig. 12.14
A Group Summary band prints at the end of every group.

To add a group band, follow these steps:

1. Move the cursor to the Report Intro band border.
2. Open the Bands menu and choose Add a Group Band.
3. Select Field value, Expression, or Record Count.
4. Select the field you want to group on if you chose Field value (in Step 3); type the expression and press Enter if you chose Expression (in Step 3); or type the number of records and press Enter if you chose Record Count (in Step 3).

To add text or fields in the Group Intro band or the Group Summary band, insert one or more blank lines (use Ctrl-N), type the desired text, and add the desired field.

Troubleshooting

My report is grouped on the DEPT field. Even though the field is indexed, the report creates two different groups for Sales and sales.

Lowercase letters and uppercase letters are sorted separately, not together. Update the records in the database with an expression like UPPER(DEPT), and try the report again. If you don't want the department field to display in all capital letters, use a field template. You can also index the field using UPPER in an expression.

When I try to add a Group band, the menu option is dimmed.

You do not have your cursor positioned in the correct band. Move the cursor to the Report Intro band and open the Bands menu. You can also position the cursor in the Page Header band.

Adding Group Summary Fields

You can add summary fields in the Group Summary band just as you can in the Report Summary band. To add fields to the Group Summary band, follow these steps:

1. Place the cursor at the desired position on line 0 of the desired Group Summary band. Type any text that you want.
2. Open the Fields menu and choose Add Field; or press F5. The Field List appears.
3. Highlight the type of summary field you want to put in the Group Summary band and press Enter.
4. Give the field a name (and description, if desired).
5. Highlight Field to Summarize On and press Enter. Type the name of the field and press Enter.
6. Choose the Reset Every option and enter the desired reset value. Usually, this is the name of the field on which you are grouping. You'll rarely want a Group Summary field to reset on anything but the group expression.
7. Press Ctrl-End.

Using Only Group Bands in a Report

Although it is unusual to create a report that doesn't print record information in the detail band, it's possible to do so, and most likely would be done when only a group summary is required in the report. Figure 12.15 shows a simple report that groups on the NAME field and displays a summary for each group that prints the name and the total of the QTY field for the group. Figure 12.16 shows the output of the report.

Entering Text

Adding text to the Reports design screen is simple. You move the cursor to the desired location and start typing. To add a line, place the cursor in the line *above* where you want the new line, choose Words from the menu and select Add line. If you only have one line in a band, you cannot insert a line above it by using Add Line. To add a line at the top of the band, turn Insert on, place the cursor at the beginning of the top line of the band, and press Enter. A new blank line appears. To delete a line, position the cursor on the line. Then open the Words menu and choose Remove Line, or press Ctrl-Y.

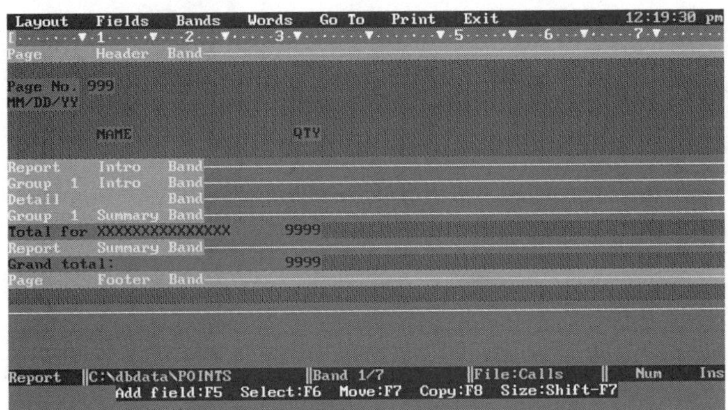

Fig. 12.15
This report does not print record information in the Detail band. It prints only summary information.

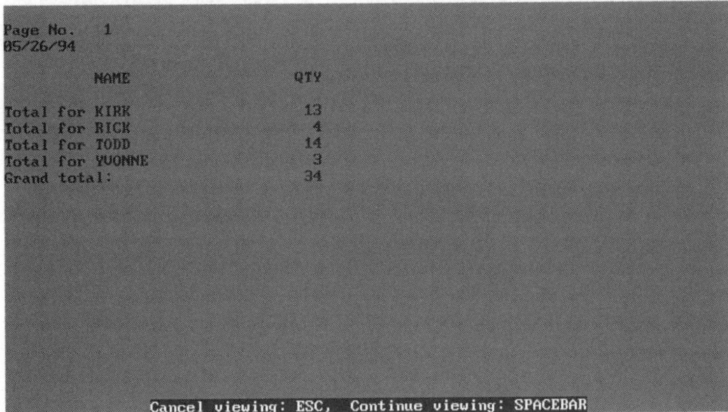

Fig. 12.16
The results of the report that uses no Detail band uses only the Group and Report Summary bands.

Using Styles

Reports are easier to read if certain parts of the text are emphasized. For example, column headings can be underlined and summary totals can be printed in bold. dBASE 5 provides six different print styles for text: plain, boldface, underline, italic, superscript, and subscript. Fonts can also be applied to text if you have set them up in the CONFIG.DB file.

To apply a style to text or field values, follow these steps:

1. Move the cursor to the first position and press F6.
2. Move the cursor to the last position and press Enter.
3. Open the Words menu and choose Style.
4. Highlight the desired style or font (if any have been set up) and press Enter to turn it ON (or OFF if you want to remove it).

Note

You cannot apply styles to text or fields across bands. You must apply the styles in one band at a time.

Adding Page Headers and Page Footers

The Page Header and Page Footer bands appear at the top and bottom of each report page. If you include a Report Intro band and a Report Summary band, the Page Header and Page Footer bands print before and after the Intro and Summary bands.

Page headers and page footers are used to include information you want to appear on every page of the report. At the top of each page you may want to include the title of the report and a date and time stamp so that the reader doesn't have to turn back to the first page to determine this information. You also may want to put column headers in the Page Header band so that they print at the top of each page.

To add text in a page header, follow these steps:

1. Place the cursor in the Page Header band or Page Footer band. Press Ctrl-N; or open the Words menu and choose Add Line. Repeat this step to add as many blank lines as you want.

2. Type the text you want. Use the alignment options in the Words menu to center, left align, or right align text.

3. Place predefined fields as you choose by pressing F5 and selecting the fields. The predefined fields are described in Table 12.5.

Tip
You can add blank lines by turning on the INS mode and pressing Enter. Be careful though—you might split a line in two accidentally.

Table 12.5 Predefined Fields

Variable	Description
Date	Prints the date when the report is printed, in the format MM/DD/YY.
Time	Prints the time when the report is printed, in the format HH:MM:SS.
Recno	Prints the record number of the database record being printed. Although this predefined variable isn't useful in the Page Header or Page Footer band, you may want to use it in the Detail band.
Pageno	Prints the current page number of the report.

Troubleshooting

When the title of my report is centered, it disappears from the screen.

The default width of the report is 255 columns. Unless you change that width, a short title disappears off-screen to the right. Scroll to the right to see the title properly centered on the 255-column-wide report. If you want the report to be fewer than 255 columns wide, change the right margin on the ruler as discussed in "Setting Margins and Tabs," earlier in this chapter.

The title of my report prints on the top of every page. I want it to print on the first page only.

You have the title in the Page Header band. Place the title in the Report Intro band.

I have placed the DATE field in the report but I do not like the format of the predefined field. How can I change the format so the date looks like this: January 10, 1995?

Instead of using the predefined DATE field, use a calculated field with this expression: MDY(date( )).

Using Lines and Boxes

Lines and boxes help organize a report or call attention to certain parts of the report. Boxes and lines are added to and deleted from reports in the same way that they are in forms.

◄ See "Organizing a Form with Lines and Boxes," p. 275

To add a box to the report, follow these steps:

1. Open the Layout menu and choose Box. When the Box menu appears, choose the border style you want for the box.

   The Using Specified Character option enables you to specify what character is to be used as the border. If you want a box made out of asterisks, for example, choose Using Specified Character, type *, and press Enter.

2. When the work surface reappears, use the arrow keys to position the cursor at the upper-left corner of the planned box, and press Enter.

3. Use the arrow keys to move the cursor to the lower-right corner of the box. The border of the box is made with the style or special character you designated. You can see the box change shape as you move to this corner. As you move the cursor, the box extends over text and fields. When the box is the correct size and shape, press Enter to accept it.

To position a box using the mouse, first click the location for the upper-left corner of the box. Position the mouse pointer on the location for the lower-right corner of the box, and then click again.

To place lines on the report, follow these steps:

1. Open the Layout menu and choose Line.
2. Choose Single Line or Double Line from the submenu that appears. To draw the line with characters (asterisks, for example), select Using Specified Character and type the character you want to use.
3. Move the cursor where you want the line to start and press Enter to start the line-drawing process.
4. Use the left-arrow key or right-arrow key to draw the line horizontally. Use the up-arrow or down-arrow key to draw a vertical line. (Lines may intersect if desired, and if you change the direction of the line from horizontal to vertical or vice versa, dBASE draws a corner.)
5. After you draw all the lines, press Enter.

◄ See "Adding a Box," p. 276

◄ See "Adding Lines," p. 277

You also can draw lines with the mouse. After selecting the type of line from the Layout menu, move the mouse pointer to the location where you want the line to begin. Drag the mouse to the location where you want the line to end, and then release the mouse button. Click the mouse to end line drawing.

To delete a box, position the cursor anywhere on the box and press Del. Lines can be deleted with the Del key a character at a time, or they can be selected with F6 and deleted with the Del key.

Saving a Report and Exiting the Reports Design Screen

To save and exit the Reports design screen, choose Exit, Save Changes and Exit. If the report hasn't been saved before, dBASE prompts you for a name. Type the name and press Enter.

Save a report often while you are designing it by pressing Ctrl-Enter. To save the report and continue working on it, open the Layout menu and choose Save This Report.

Using a Report

A report can be run against an "original" database or a sorted version of the original. It can be run against a view of a database (a subset of a database that's selected with a query), or against a database that's been created by writing a query to a file. When a report is used, the output of the report is either sent to the screen or to a printer.

Tip
Save yourself time when you have to create similar reports by creating and saving the first report and then saving the report with a different name.

When you use reports that use Group bands, remember that the database must have the proper index active or the database must be sorted on the field that the report groups on. If more than one field is grouped on, the database must be sorted by the fields in the order of the groups or a complex index that matches the order of the groups must be activated.

Selecting Records for a Report with a Query

If you don't want to run the report against all the records in a database, you can use a query to select the desired records. First, create the query and save it. Then follow these steps to use the query with the report:

◄ See "Creating a Query," p. 189

◄ See "Saving a Query for Repeated Use," p. 221

1. Select the query from the Queries panel making it the active query.
2. Highlight the report in the Reports panel and press Enter.
3. Choose Print Report.
4. Choose Current View.
5. The Print menu is displayed. Make the desired selections from this menu. (See "Viewing the Report on the Screen" and "Printing the Report" in this section.)

Viewing the Report on the Screen

You can view the report on the screen by choosing the Print menu, and then selecting View Report On Screen. Use this option to review a report quickly to check its format, or just to see information.

To stop the report from displaying on-screen, press Esc. If Esc does not interrupt the display, change the set command for Escape to ON. Set commands are accessed by choosing Tools in the Control Center and then choosing Settings.

Tip
Make it a practice to view a report before printing it.

Printing the Report

You can print your report directly from the Reports design screen by using the Print menu. You also can print from the Control Center by highlighting the name of the report in the Reports panel and pressing Enter. In both cases, dBASE 5 displays the Print menu (see fig. 12.17). The Print Menu options control all aspects of printing the report.

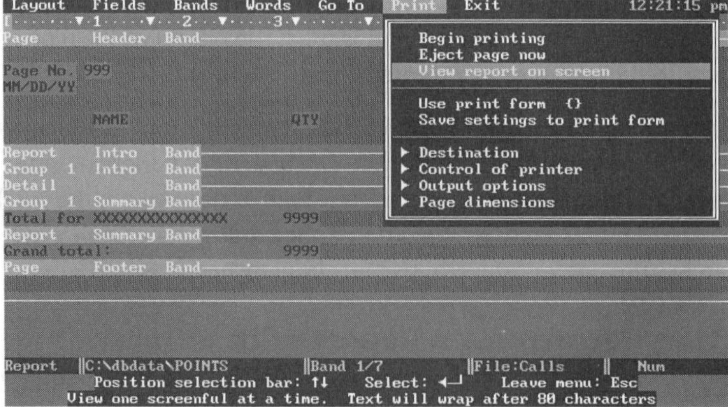

Fig. 12.17
The Print menu controls the output and the setup of the printer.

Using the Destination Menu

If you choose Destination from the Print menu, the Destination menu appears (see fig. 12.18). Initially, the default setting in the Write To option is PRINTER. When you print with this setting selected, the report is sent to the printer currently defined. If you want to create a DOS file instead of a printed report, press Enter to change the Write To setting to DOS FILE. A default file name with an extension of PRT displays in the Name of DOS File option. If you want to use a different name, you can change the name.

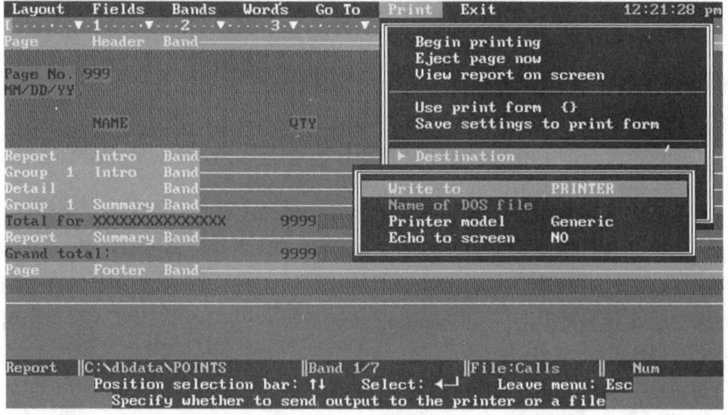

Fig. 12.18
The Print Destination menu determines the kind of output.

You also can tell dBASE 5 that you're using a different type of printer than the one you defined when you installed dBASE 5. To do so, highlight the Printer Model option in the Destination menu. Press Enter to cycle through the printer drivers defined during installation. To print the report to the screen at the same time the report is sent to the specified destination, highlight the Echo To Screen option and press Enter to change the setting from NO to YES.

Using the Control of Printer Menu

You can control how the printer prints the report with the Control of Printer option on the Print menu. When you choose this option, the Printer Control menu appears (see fig. 12.19). You use options on this menu to customize the report.

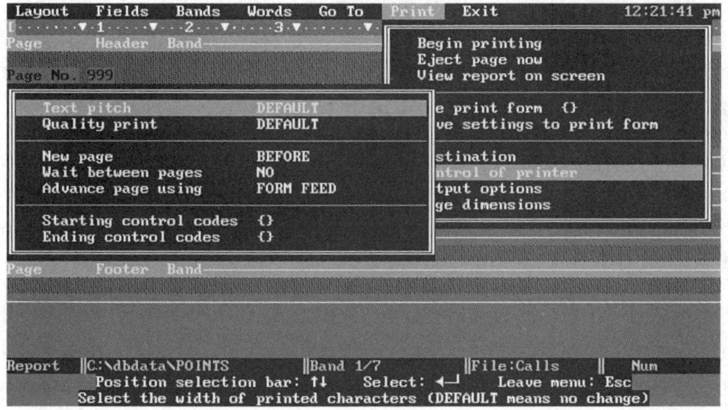

Fig. 12.19
The Printer Control menu determines pitch, print quality, and other options.

The Text Pitch option defines the number of characters per inch that the printer uses for the report. Press Enter to cycle through the available pitches, which are a function of the printer driver selected from the Destination menu. ELITE (12 characters per inch), PICA (10 characters per inch), and CONDENSED (which varies by printer type, but usually is 15 to 18 characters per inch) generally are available settings for this option. The DEFAULT selection, though a function of the printer type, is usually 10 characters per inch.

Tip
Do not set Quality print on YES in the Control of Printer options if you are using a laser printer. An error will occur.

The Quality Print option defines whether the report is to be printed in the standard print or a higher-quality print. If you're using a typical dot-matrix printer, the printer passes over a line of print one time for standard print and twice for quality. Standard print is faster and generally acceptable for draft purposes. You can change the Quality Print option to YES when you want the report to look better. Quality print also is called *letter quality* or *near-letter quality* in printer manuals. As with text pitch, the availability of quality print depends on the printer. Most laser printers use quality print exclusively.

Some printers default to standard print, and others default to quality print. For this reason, you have three choices: DEFAULT, YES, and NO. You can specify NO to override the quality print on a printer that defaults to quality.

The New Page option on the Printer Control menu tells dBASE 5 when to move the paper to the top of a new page. Press Enter to cycle through the choices. BEFORE moves the paper to a new page at the start of the report. BOTH issues a page eject before the report starts and when it's done. NONE causes no page ejects, either before or after the report is printed. AFTER causes the printer to go to a new page only when the report is completed.

The Wait Between Pages option has two choices. If you're printing a report on individual sheets of paper that must be fed into the printer manually, choose YES. dBASE 5 pauses at the end of each page and waits until you tell it to continue printing. For continuous-feed computer paper, choose NO so that the report prints from start to finish without pausing.

The Advance Page Using option tells dBASE 5 whether to send a form-feed command to the printer or to send a series of line-feed commands when the report has to go to the top of a new page. Some older printers cannot handle form-feeds; in these cases, press Enter to select the LINE FEED setting.

The Starting Control Codes and Ending Control Codes options enable you to enter strings of codes that the printer understands and uses to modify its actions. Although you may not need this capability, it does exist; codes are great for selecting fonts. Refer to your printer manual for a list of the codes the printer understands, and be sure the printer is set up to receive the codes. If you type the code incorrectly, the code will print on the report instead of having the desired effect.

Using Output Options

If you choose Output Options from the Print menu, the Output Options menu appears (see fig. 12.20). You use the four options on this menu to control specifics about the report you are printing.

- The Begin On Page option enables you to begin printing a report on a page other than 1. Notice that page 1 is the default setting for this option. You can enter a page number as high as 32767.

- The End After Page option is the opposite of the first option. You can specify which page of the report is the last page printed. The default for this option is 32767. If your report is fewer than 32,767 pages (and let's hope that it is), this setting simply means the report will continue to print through the last page.

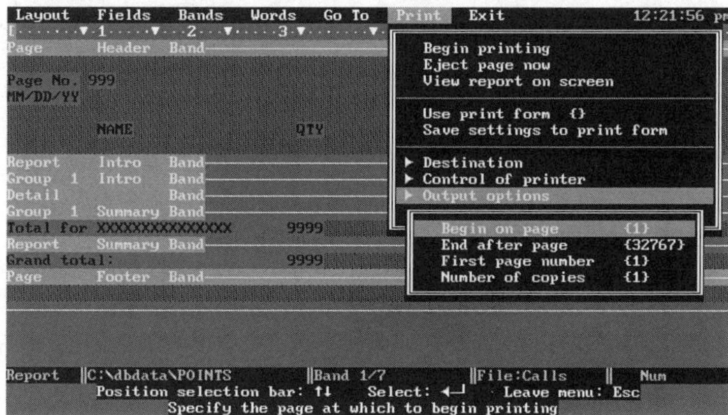

Fig. 12.20
The Output Options menu determines the beginning and ending page, the number of copies printed, and the beginning page number.

- The First Page Number option tells dBASE 5 what page number to use when it starts numbering pages. If you used the Begin On Page option to start printing the report at page 50, you can use the First page number option to start the page numbering at 50. If the first page of the report is actually the beginning of a section in a report that's put together from other sources, you can use this option to give page 1 a different number consistent with the numbering in the larger report.

- The Number Of Copies option specifies how many times the report is to print. If the number of copies is more than one, dBASE prints the complete report first and then prints it again. This means that the pages of each copy are collated.

Using the Page Dimensions Menu

You can alter the dimensions of the printed page by using the Page dimensions option from the Print menu. When you select this option, the Page Dimensions menu appears (see fig. 12.21).

- The Page Size option defines the dimensions of the paper. The options include the standard 8.5 x 11 and legal size, as well as special sizes called A4, B5, and Executive.

- The Length of Page option defines how long the page is in terms of lines. A standard 8 1/2-by-11-inch page has 66 lines. If you use non-standard-sized paper, remember that the printer prints six lines per inch. Use the Length of Page option to set the page length accordingly.

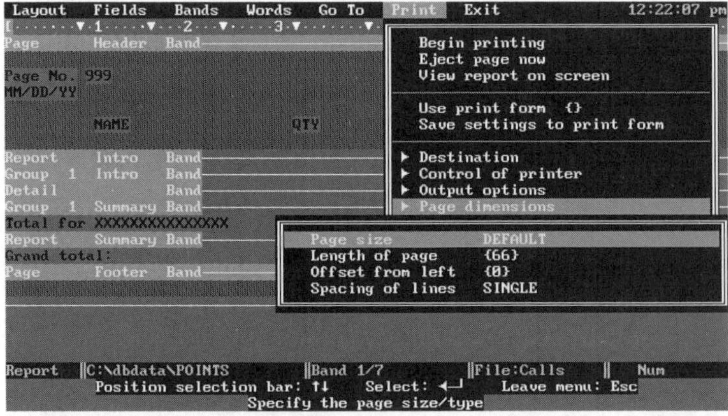

Fig. 12.21
The Page Dimensions menu sets the paper size, page length, left offset, and spacing.

- For the Offset from Left option, specify an integer that represents the number of inches of extra margin added to the left edge of the page. Setting a left offset is helpful, for example, when you print the report on paper that has holes punched on the left edge. Without modifying the design of the report, you can add an extra half or three-quarters of an inch to clear the punch holes.

- The Spacing of Lines option has three settings. Cycle through the settings by pressing Enter or clicking the mouse. You can choose SINGLE, DOUBLE, or TRIPLE spacing.

Creating and Using Print Forms

After you specify the desired printer settings, you can save them to a print form with the Save settings to print form option on the Print menu. A *print form* contains all the specifications you made for a report: the destination, page dimensions, and other settings made in the Print menu. When you choose Save settings to print form, dBASE 5 asks for a print file name. The default file name is the report name with the extension PRF.

After you save print settings, you can reestablish them for this or any other report by using the Use Print Form option from the Print menu. After you select this option, type the name of the print form that stores the specifications you want to use; dBASE 5 reads those settings from the file and uses them. You can use a print form for any report you create, not just the report for which you originally set the specifications. Note that when you save your report design, the print form you selected is automatically associated with the report as the default print form.

Using Other Print Menu Options

After all the preparation you've done, you're ready to print the report. In practice, you may find that you seldom change the output options (Destination, Control Of Printer, and so on). The first option you select from the Print menu may be Begin Printing. When you choose Begin Printing, dBASE 5 sends the report to the printer (or to the DOS file, if you made that specification), using the current default settings or the settings in the retrieved print form. If you want the printer to go to a new page before printing the report, choose Eject page now, and then select Begin Printing.

From Here...

This chapter explored most of the capabilities of dBASE 5 report designing, but additional specialized reports are discussed in these chapters:

- Chapter 13, "Designing and Using a Mailmerge Report and Label," discusses the special report features that apply to this type of report, such as word wrap and page breaks.
- Chapter 14, "Using Crosstabs," reveals the power of the new reporting feature, Cross Tabulation.
- Chapter 15, "Using Relational Databases for Complex Situations," gives real-life examples that use relational databases to manipulate data in an efficient way.

Chapter 13

Designing and Using a Mailmerge Report and Label

In Chapter 12 you learned all about creating custom reports—how to place text, lines, boxes, and fields in a report; how to use Report bands; and how to print the report for selected records. The same principles that you learned in Chapter 12 can be applied to creating the mailmerge report and the label report. Even though the mailmerge form and label report are similar to the columnar and forms layout, they are different enough to deserve special attention.

For many dBASE 5 users, mail merging is their primary task. The dBASE 5 *Mailmerge feature* lets you write a standard letter and then "plug" information from a database into the letter at specified locations. The Label feature, just like mailmerging in theory, allows you to create a label and "plug in" name and address information from a database.

In this chapter, you learn how to do the following:

- Create a mailmerge report
- Create a label
- Merge the report and label with a database

Designing the Mailmerge Report

To design a mailmerge report, you follow the same steps that you would to create any type of custom report:

1. Select the desired database from the Data panel of the Control Center.
2. Move the cursor to the Reports panel, highlight `<create>`, and press Enter.
3. Choose Quick Layout.
4. Choose Mailmerge Layout.

The mailmerge Reports design screen has all five bands, as shown in figure 13.1.

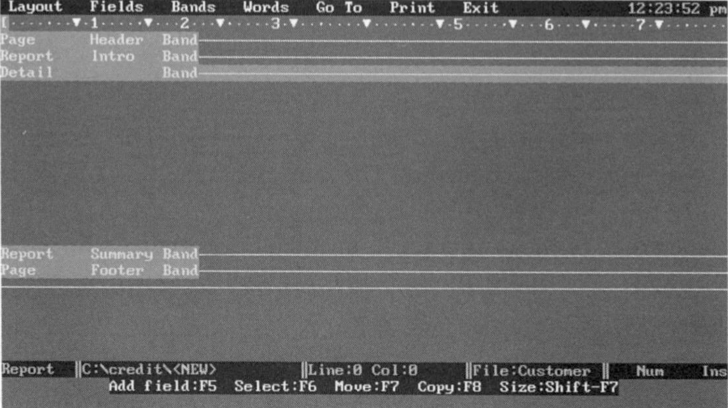

Fig. 13.1
The Reports design screen for a mailmerge report has all five Report bands.

Entering Data in Bands

In figure 13.1, the Page Header, Report Intro, Report Summary, and Page Footer bands have no blank lines in them, but the Detail Band has many blank lines. Normally, the Detail Band is the only band used in a mailmerge report. You might use the Report Intro or Report Summary band in a mailmerge report, but it is very unlikely that you will use the Page Header or Page Footer bands unless the mailmerge letter has more than one page.

Note

Sometimes users place blank lines in the Page Header to increase the top margin when the letter prints. This causes a problem, however, if the letter has more than one page, because the second page should not start as low on the page as the first page (which generally prints on letterhead). If the mailmerge letter is more than one page long, place the extra blank lines at the top of the Detail Band instead of in the Page Header Band.

The mailmerge letter itself is entered in its entirety in the Detail Band. The Report Intro or Report Summary bands could be used to print out information about the mailmerge report. For example, the Report Intro band could contain text like this: "Sales Promo letter sent 01/01/95 to all customers in the CUSTOMER database." Rather than using the Report Intro Band for this text, you could put it in the Report Summary Band and include a summary math field that counts the number of letters that went out in the mailing. For example, the text might read: "Sales Promo letter sent 01/01/95 to XXXXXX customers in the CUSTOMER database." The XXXXXX represents a calculated field that counts the records processed.

◄ See "Understanding Bands," p. 292

When a mailmerge layout is created by dBASE 5, certain settings in the Bands menu are different from the settings used for standard report versions. The options Begin Band on New Page and Word Wrap Band are both set to YES (see fig. 13.2). The Begin band on New Page option causes a new page to be generated for each record processed. The word-wrap option lets you type in the Detail band just as you would if you were using a word processing program. When the cursor gets to the right margin, it automatically returns to the left margin of the next line.

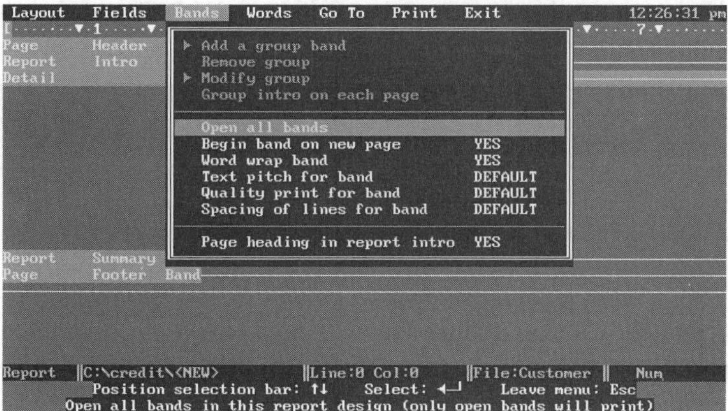

Fig. 13.2
When mailmerge layout is used to create a report, the Begin Band on New Page and Word Wrap Band are set to YES by default.

The Bands menu contains the following options:

Text Pitch for Band

Quality Print for Band

Spacing of Lines for Band

Although these options are set to the printer's default, you can change these options. You may want to set the Text Pitch for Band option to Pica, Elite, or Condensed, for example, to force the printer to print in a different pitch. You can set the Quality Print for Band option to YES so that if your printer has a letter-quality print mode, the document prints in letter quality. The Spacing of Lines for Band option can be changed to SINGLE, DOUBLE, or TRIPLE.

You can cycle through available options in the Bands menu by clicking the menu item. Click on Text Pitch for Band, for example, to select from Pica, Elite, or Condensed type.

Entering Text and Adding Fields

Before you start typing information in the Detail Band, set the margins for the paper you will be using. From the Words menu, select Modify ruler. Use the right-arrow key to move the cursor to the appropriate column for the right margin, press the right bracket ( ]), and press Enter. The appropriate column for the right margin is determined by the pitch that you select. If you select Pica, allow 10 characters per inch. If you select Elite, allow 12 characters per inch. Therefore, if you want one-inch margins on a standard sheet of paper (8 1/2" x 11"), set the right margin on 65 for Pica or on 78 for Elite.

When entering text, place the cursor in the Detail Band and begin typing. The first line of a standard business letter usually contains the date. You can type the date or use the predefined date field by pressing F5 and choosing Date in the PREDEFINED panel.

Note

If you use the predefined date field, the date on which the letters are actually printed will be used. If you want to print the letters immediately but mail them in a week, you might want to type the date instead of using the predefined field.

After typing the date, press Enter four times to place the cursor in the standard position for the inside address. On the first line of the inside address, place the fields that make up the name. For example, you might place the fields like this (notice the spacing and punctuation included):

TITLE FNAME MI. LNAME, SUBTITLE

to get this result:

Mr. John A. Smith, Jr.

Note

When a database structure is designed for a mailing list, at least three fields require punctuation. These fields hold a person's title (Mr., Mrs., Miss, or Dr.) a person's middle initial, and a person's subtitle (Jr., Sr., or III). If the punctuation is not included in the field itself, then it must be included in the mailmerge report. This can cause two problems. First, if the field is blank, the report still prints the punctuation. If the contents of the field do not require punctuation, like Miss or III, the punctuation still prints. A simple solution to the problem is to include the punctuation in the database field, however, experienced database designers do not consider this a good practice because it takes up extra space on the disk. A better solution to the problem is to include the punctuation in the report by using calculated fields. See "Using Calculated Fields" later in this section.

To place a field, press F5 and choose the desired field from the list of fields. Specify a template and/or a picture function if desired. Press Ctrl-End when finished. See "Specifying Field Attributes" in Chapter 12 for more information about templates and picture functions.

On the next line of the inside address, place the company name field, if such a field exists in the database. Don't worry if some records have a company name and some do not. dBASE 5 automatically eliminates the line if the field is blank for any given record.

On the following lines place the address field(s). Finally, on the last line of the inside address, place the city, state, and ZIP code fields. Be sure to space between the fields and use a comma after the city field.

The standard business letter format requires one blank line between the inside address and the salutation. On the salutation line, enter the desired text and fields:

◄ See "Adding Fields to Reports," p. 294

Dear TITLE LNAME:

Note

Some database designers create a separate field just for the salutation. It's a wise decision if you use a mixed method of addressing people in the list. If you want to address some people by their first names or a nickname and others more formally by their title and last name, you must use a separate field for the salutation. Since informal salutations use a comma and formal salutations use a colon, the punctuation should be included in the salutation field, not in the report.

After the salutation, leave one blank line and then type the text of the letter, placing fields in the body of the letter as needed. As you type the body of the letter and add a field to the text, remember to leave proper spacing between the text and the field.

Finish the letter with the signature block. Figure 13.3 shows a typical mailmerge report design, and figure 13.4 shows the result.

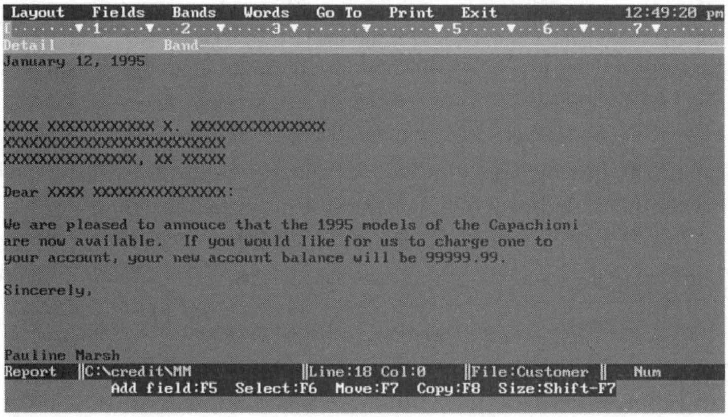

Fig. 13.3
A typical mailmerge report design showing the placement of the fields in the Detail band.

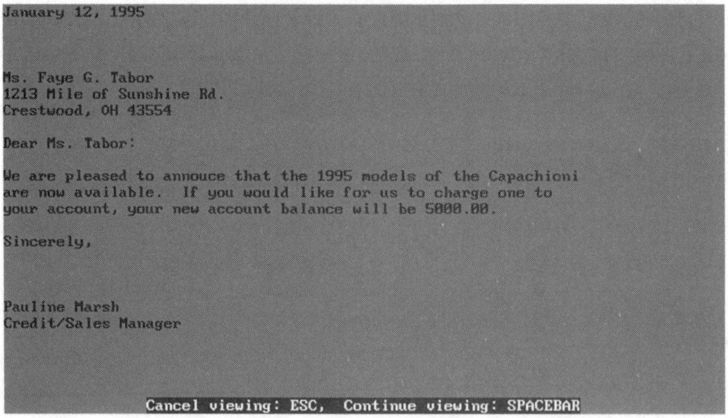

```
Layout   Fields   Bands   Words   Go To   Print   Exit              12:49:20 pm
Detail          Band
January 12, 1995


XXXX XXXXXXXXXXX X. XXXXXXXXXXXXXXX
XXXXXXXXXXXXXXXXXXXXXXXXX
XXXXXXXXXXXXXXX, XX XXXXX

Dear XXXX XXXXXXXXXXXXXXX:

We are pleased to annouce that the 1995 models of the Capachioni
are now available.  If you would like for us to charge one to
your account, your new account balance will be 99999.99.

Sincerely,



Pauline Marsh
Report  ║C:\credit\MM          ║Line:18 Col:0    ║File:Customer ║   Num
             Add field:F5  Select:F6  Move:F7  Copy:F8  Size:Shift-F7
```

Fig. 13.4
The result of the mailmerge report showing the actual contents of the fields.

```
January 12, 1995


Ms. Faye G. Tabor
1213 Mile of Sunshine Rd.
Crestwood, OH 43554

Dear Ms. Tabor:

We are pleased to annouce that the 1995 models of the Capachioni
are now available.  If you would like for us to charge one to
your account, your new account balance will be 5000.00.

Sincerely,



Pauline Marsh
Credit/Sales Manager



                 Cancel viewing: ESC,  Continue viewing: SPACEBAR
```

Enhancing the Text

Remember that you can apply styles like bold and underline to text to emphasize it. You can also draw lines and boxes to organize the data in the report.

Note

Remember to use the shortcut keys Ctrl-Y to delete a line and Ctrl-N to insert a line.

Tip
When the letter is finished, check to see if you added the correct fields. When you move the cursor to a field, the name and other specific information about the field is shown in the Status Line.

Using Calculated Fields

Calculated fields can be created and used in mailmerge reports the same way that they are used in other reports. The numeric field in figure 13.4, for example, is a calculated field that adds the price of the new sale item (called the Capachioni) to the field that contains the person's current balance. The expression for the calculated field might look like this: 1250+CURR_BAL.

As mentioned earlier, calculated fields also can be used to work around a problem that can pop up if a field requires punctuation in the report. The problem is that the report will print the punctuation even if the field is empty. Figure 13.5, for example, shows that the field prints the first name, a period, and the last name.

```
January 12, 1995


Mr. John . Jones
5912 Hollywood Blvd.
East Marsh, CA 90055

Dear Mr. Jones:

We are pleased to annouce that the 1995 models of the Capachioni
are now available.  If you would like for us to charge one to
your account, your new account balance will be 5000.00.

Sincerely,



Pauline Marsh
Credit/Sales Manager



             Cancel viewing: ESC,  Continue viewing: SPACEBAR
```

Fig. 13.5
An example of a report that includes unnecessary punctuation.

To avoid this problem, create a calculated field for the middle initial field (MI) that uses this expression: IIF(MI<>" ", MI+"."+" ", " "). This expression says that if the middle initial field is not blank, print the middle initial field followed by a period and a space. The "else" part of the function simply inserts a space if the field is empty. To ensure proper spacing with this

◄ See "Adding Fields that Perform Summary Math," p. 305

calculated middle initial field, the last name field must be immediately to the right of the calculated field with no spaces between the two fields.

Modifying, Moving, and Removing Fields and Text

After a field has been placed in a mailmerge report, it can be modified, moved, or removed just as it can in a columnar or form layout report. To modify a field, place the cursor on the field and press F5. Make the desired modifications (such as template and picture functions), and press Ctrl-End. Text is modified by inserting text or typing over text. Use the Insert key to toggle between the insert and overstrike modes.

To move text, fields, or text and fields, place the cursor on the first character and press F6. Place the cursor on the last character (unless you want to move only one field, then leave the cursor where it is), and press Enter. Press F7, place the cursor in the new location, and press Enter.

To delete a field, place the cursor on the field and press the Delete key. To delete more than one field or a field and text, place the cursor on the first character and press F6. Move the cursor to the last character and press Enter, and then press the Delete key. dBASE 5 displays the message: `Perform block deletion`. Choose Yes to delete.

Inserting Page Breaks

Page breaks are inserted in text to create multipage letters. To insert a page break, position the cursor on the line that should begin the new page. Open the Words menu and choose Insert Page Break. The page break is a dashed line that extends across the width of the band. To delete a page break, position the cursor on the dashed line and press Del.

Saving and Exiting the Report

After you have a good start on the creation of the mailmerge document, be sure to save it. From the Layout menu, select Save Report, type the desired name of the report, and press Enter. The report is saved to the disk, and the report remains on the screen for more editing. Save the report often while you are creating it. After the report has been saved for the last time, exit the report by choosing Exit, Abandon Changes, and Exit. If changes have not been saved, this option will display a message that asks whether you want to abandon changes. If you choose Yes, the program returns to the Control Center, where you see the name of your report design in the Reports panel. If you choose No, you can save the changes and then exit the report.

Modifying a Report Design

To modify a mailmerge report, highlight the name of the report in the Reports panel, and press Shift-F2 or press Enter and choose Modify Layout. Make the necessary changes, save the report, and exit to the Control Center.

Designing a Label

The Labels panel in the Control Center is used to create label or envelope reports. The most commonly used envelope sizes are #7 (for personal use) and #10 (for business use). Labels are available in all shapes and sizes for computerized printing. For example, you can buy labels on continuous paper that work in a pin-feed printer (a printer that pulls paper through by the pinholes at the edges of the paper). Sheets of labels for pinfeed printers are available with one, two, or three columns of labels per sheet. Labels also are available for laser printers. Perhaps the most commonly used size of labels is the 15/16-inch high by 3 1/2-inches wide label. dBASE uses this size as a default but has many other common sizes available. In addition to the common sizes provided, dBASE alwo provides an option to specify a custom size.

Using the Labels Design Screen

You start creating your label design in the Control Center by selecting the database from the Data panel and making it the current database. Then you move the cursor to the Labels panel of the Control Center and choose <create>. The Labels design screen appears, as shown in figure 13.6. You create your label designs on the work surface of this screen.

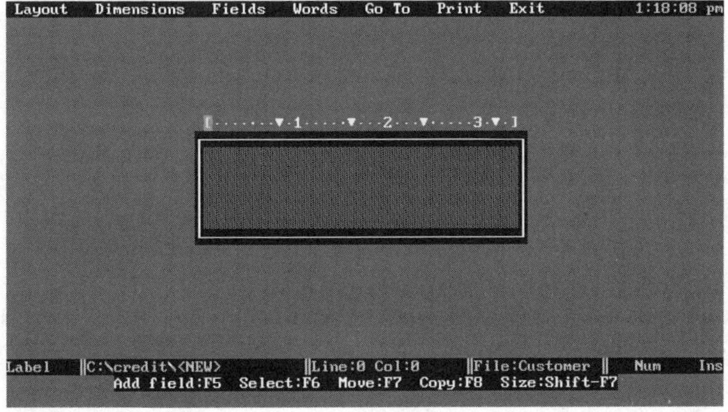

Fig. 13.6
Unlike the Reports design screen, the Labels design screen has no report bands.

The Labels design work surface is like the Reports design work surface, but much smaller because a mailing label is much smaller than the page on which a report is printed. The Labels design screen has no report bands, and the menu bar is slightly different. The Bands option is not included, but another option called Dimensions is added.

Setting the Label Dimensions

The Dimensions menu shown in figure 13.7 lets you define the sizes and types of labels that dBASE 5 prints. This menu is divided into two parts: predefined sizes and other options. The Predefined size option is a set of common label sizes and page formats; the other options let you design custom-sized labels.

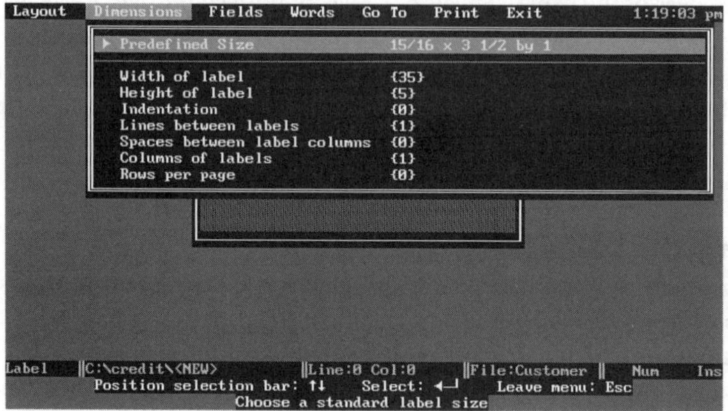

Fig. 13.7
The Dimensions menu shows the current options for the default label size.

Just as you create reports with the Report design work surface, you create labels by placing fields on the Labels design work surface. You can format these fields in different ways, move them around to position them in the most readable arrangement, and add whatever text you want.

Choosing a Predefined Size

Choosing Predefined size from the Dimensions menu opens a size menu (see fig. 13.8). The sizes listed in this menu are commonly used label sizes. Choose a size by highlighting it and pressing Enter. When the Labels design screen reappears, notice that the Label work surface is adjusted to the correct size for your selected format.

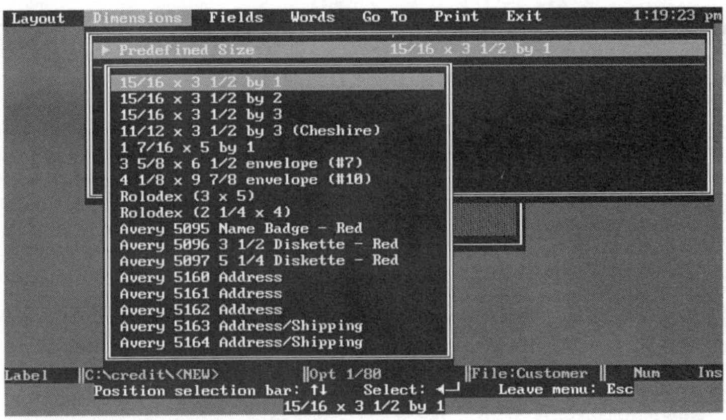

Fig. 13.8 The Dimension predefined size menu has options for Cheshire lables, envelopes, Rolodex cards, and various Avery labels.

You can use the mouse to select a label format. Click on the Dimensions menu label, Predefined Size, and then the size option you want.

Specifying a Custom Size

Below the Predefined size option on the Dimensions menu is a series of options for creating custom-sized labels. Figure 13.9 shows these options (and several other useful measurements) on a sheet of mailing labels.

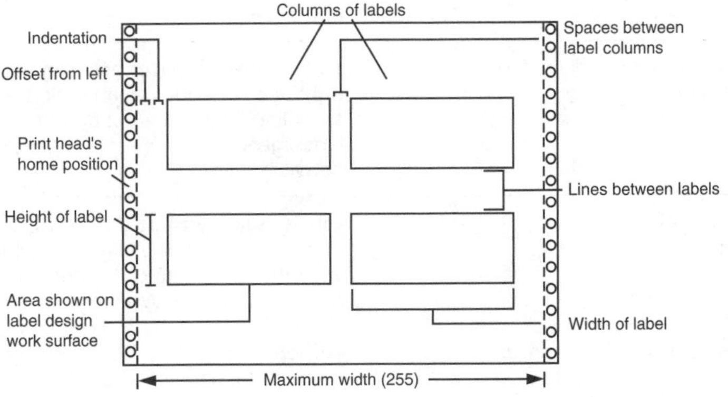

Fig. 13.9 Label design and printing options.

Table 13.1 describes the options that are available for custom size labels.

Table 13.1 Custom Size Label Options

Option	Default	Description
Width of label	35	The number of characters on the label surface from the left edge to the right edge. The equivalent value in inches depends on the pitch you select in the Print menu. If you use Pica type, which is 10 characters per inch, 35 characters would equal 3 1/2 inches. If your printer is set for a different pitch, adjust this number. If your printer is set for 12 characters per inch, for example, it can print 42 characters on a 3 1/2-inch-wide label.
Height of label	5	The number of rows in the label, from top to bottom. Most printers use a spacing of 6 lines per inch; if your printer is set for a different figure, recalculate how many lines print on the label.
Indentation	0	The number of characters from the left margin where the first character begins printing.
Lines between labels	1	The number of lines between the bottom of one label and the top of the next.
Spaces between label columns	0	The number of spaces between the right and left edges of labels on the same line. This value is 2 or 3 because labels generally have some space between them.
Columns of labels	1	Labels usually are laid out with 1, 2, or 3 columns on each sheet. As with any dimension, you can change this setting for custom applications.
Rows per page	0	This option specifies the number of rows on the page of labels.

If you have a label format that isn't on dBASE's list of predefined sizes, you have to change the dimensions on the Dimensions menu to create the new format. Choose Dimensions from the menu bar and change each of the applicable options.

Note

Creating a custom label design often requires some trial and error, no matter how carefully you measure the label sheet. Remember, too, that the alignment of the label sheet in the printer is critical. Aligning the sheet also may require some experimentation. When you print labels, you can print sample labels (one line of labels). You can use this option to align the paper correctly before starting to print a whole run of labels.

You can use the custom options to customize the way your labels print, and to create a report that lists database information in columns—a feat impossible to accomplish with the Reports design screen. Figure 13.10 shows an example of a two-column report created with the Labels design screen. This report shows database records listed side by side, which is a more condensed way to present the data.

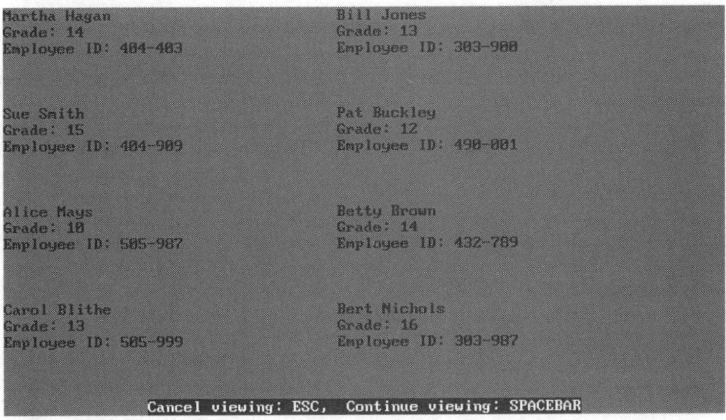

Fig. 13.10
A two-column report created with the Labels design screen.

Entering Text and Adding Fields

As a rule, very little text is used on a label. However, if text is required, it is added by typing the text in the desired location. Here's an example of a label that might require text. Suppose you have a mailing list of high schools, and you want to send the football coach a letter about your new videotape called "Developing the Passing Quarterback." The database does not have a field that lists the name of the football coach, so the label must have the text "Attention: Football Coach" on the line under the name of the high school.

To place a field from your database on the Labels design work surface, follow these steps:

1. Move the cursor to the place where you want the field to print on the label. The status line at the bottom of the Labels design screen identifies the row and column position of the cursor.

2. Press F5.

3. From the list of fields displayed, choose the desired field. Change the template for the field and specify picture functions if desired. (See "Specifying Field Attributes" in Chapter 12 for more information about templates and picture functions.) Press Ctrl-End.

To use the mouse to position fields on the label design screen, click on the spot where you want to place a field. Click the Fields menu label in the menu bar and then click Add Field. From the fields list, select a field to add by clicking the field name and then click again to accept your choice. To accept the template, click the `Accept:Ctrl-End` key label in the navigation line.

When the fields for an address label are placed, they will resemble the configuration of the inside address used in the mailmerge letter. Figure 13.11 shows a label that has all the fields placed. If you could see the field names, the label design would look like this:

HS_NAME

Attention: Football Coach

ADDRESS1

ADDRESS2

CITY, STATE ZIP

Figure 13.12 shows the result of the label report.

In figure 13.12, dBASE 5 uses the full length of each field—whether the value in that field actually needs the full length. As a result, the line with the CITY, STATE, and ZIP fields looks awkward because there is so much blank space between the end of the city name and the start of the state abbreviation. dBASE provides a way for you to eliminate this extra space.

When placing multiple fields on the same line, press the Spacebar between the fields to allow the right amount of space between the fields. This causes dBASE to trim the actual data in the field and place only the number of spaces that you have typed between the fields. Figure 13.13 shows the same label design used in figure 15.11, with spaces typed between the CITY, STATE, and ZIP fields; figure 13.11 shows a shaded area between these fields. Figure 13.14 shows the result of the new design. The last line of the label now looks much more professional.

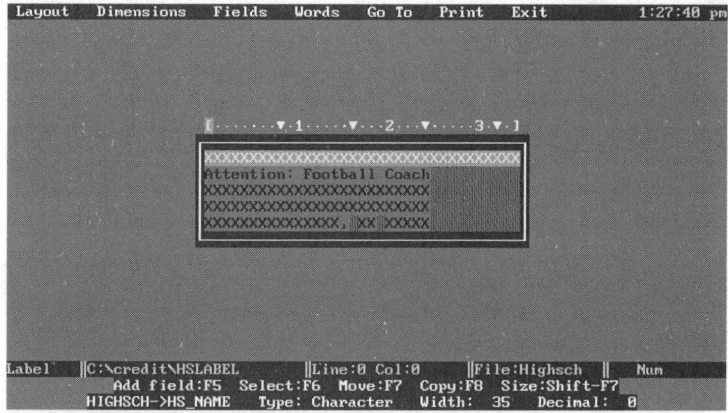

Fig. 13.11 A completed label design with all the fields placed appropriately.

```
DuPont Manual High School
Attention: Football Coach
101 High School Road
Louisville,        KY 40213

Brentwood Christian Acadey
Attention: Football Coach
101 Franklin Rd.
Brentwood,         TN 37027

Thomas Jefferson High School
Attention: Football Coach
1212 Jefferson Ave.
Chicago,           IL 60601

PS 129
Attention: Football Coach
1213 103rd St. N.
New York,          NY 10001

          Cancel viewing: ESC,  Continue viewing: SPACEBAR
```

Fig. 13.12 The result of the label design.

Note

You can place any of the four types of predefined fields: Date, Time, Recno (the record number of the field being printed), and Pageno (the page number currently being printed). Any predefined fields you add appear on each label on the sheet because the Label design is for one label.

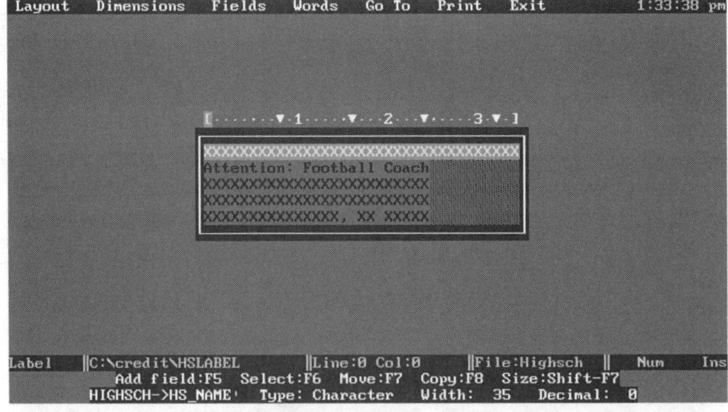

Fig. 13.13
An improved label design that creates more professional looking spacing between the fields.

```
DuPont Manual High School
Attention: Football Coach
101 High School Road
Louisville, KY 40213

Brentwood Christian Acadey
Attention: Football Coach
101 Franklin Rd.
Brentwood, TN 37027

Thomas Jefferson High School
Attention: Football Coach
1212 Jefferson Ave.
Chicago, IL 60601

PS 129
Attention: Football Coach
1213 103rd St. N.
New York, NY 10001

Cancel viewing: ESC, Continue viewing: SPACEBAR
```

Fig. 13.14
The result of the improved design.

Modifying, Moving, and Removing Text and Fields

Modifying, moving, and removing fields on the Labels design screen use the same procedures as in the Reports design screen. These techniques are outlined in detail in Chapter 12.

Saving the Label Report and Exiting

Saving the label format is the same as saving information produced on other work surfaces. From the menu bar, choose Layout and Save the Label Design. The file is saved to the disk and remains on the screen for editing. As with all your work, you should save the file several times as your design progresses.

Tip
To save the design and continue working, press Ctrl-Enter.

To exit the Labels design screen, choose Exit, Abandon Changes and Exit. If you choose Save Changes and Exit from the Exit menu, dBASE asks whether you want to abandon any changes that you made since the last time you saved the file. Choose Yes to return to the Control Center, where you see the name of your label design in the Labels panel. Choose No if you want to save the file again before exiting.

Modifying the Label Design

To modify the label design, highlight the label name in the Labels panel of the Control Center and press Enter. In the selection box that appears, choose Modify layout. You also can highlight the label name and press Shift-F2. You will return to the Labels design screen with your design ready for modification. Make the desired modifications; save the file, and exit.

To modify a label format from the Control Center with the mouse, click the file name in the Labels panel, and then click the `Design: Shift-F2` key label in the navigation line.

> **Troubleshooting**
>
> *When I try to create a label, I get this message, Warning: no predefined label definitions found. Press any key to continue. When I press a key, I can continue to design a report but the Dimension menu no longer lists all the size options.*
>
> The label dimensions are kept in a file called DBASEDOS.INI which is located in the dBASE installed directory. Evidentally, this file has been deleted. Try reinstalling the program.
>
> *When I print my mailmerge report with the database, the letters run together. The second letter starts on the same page as the first letter, and so on.*
>
> Check the setting Begin Band on New Page in the Bands menu. This option should be set to Yes. If you used the Mailmerge Layout to create the report, the Begin Band on New Page option is set on Yes by default. If you created the mailmerge report "from scratch," the Begin Band on New Page option is set on No.

Using Mailmerge and Label Reports

Mailmerge reports and labels can be run against a complete database or records selected by a query. In the case of mailing labels, the labels are usually run in zip code order to facilitate bulk mailing or a presorted first class mailing. To run a mailmerge or label by a certain field order, the field must be indexed and that index must be active, or you must sort the database on that field and then run the reports against the sorted database file.

Tip

When running labels in zip code order, don't forget to run mailmerge letters in the same order so letters match up with labels.

Selecting the Records for a Report with Queries

You can use queries to limit the database records that are processed by the mailmerge or label report. For example, you can use a query to limit the labels to records that have a specific state in the STATE field or to a range of ZIP codes. The following steps show you how to use a query to print a mailmerge or label report:

1. Move the highlight to the Queries panel and highlight the desired query. Press Enter and choose Use View. (This step assumes that the query has already by created and saved. For information on creating and saving queries, see Chapter 9, "Using Queries To Search Databases.")
2. Highlight the desired mailmerge report in the Reports panel or the desired label report in the Labels panel, and press Enter.
3. From the selection box that appears, choose Print Report or Print Label.
4. Select Current View to use the active query.
5. The print menu is displayed (see fig. 13.15). Make the desired selections from this menu.

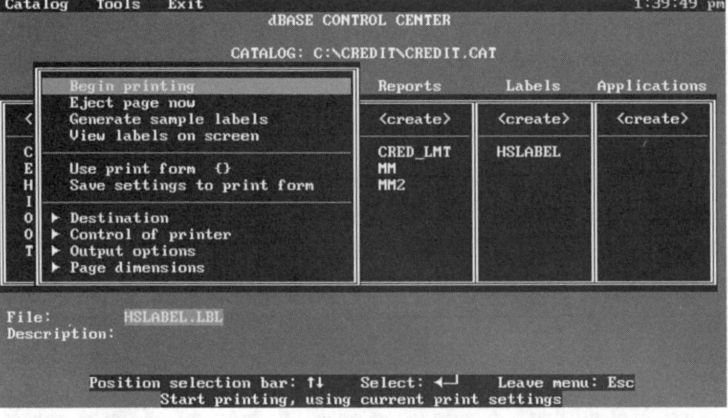

Fig. 13.15
The print menu provides an on-screen preview, controls the printer and output options, and determines the destination of the report.

Viewing the Report on the Screen

Viewing the on-screen report is an excellent way to test the report before printing. You can view a report from the design screen by choosing Print from the menu bar and then selecting View Report on-screen or View Labels on-screen. By viewing the on-screen report, you can find errors and make corrections before printing.

Viewing labels on-screen will not help you see if the labels line up and print correctly on the label sheet. To make sure that the labels print correctly, select the Generate Sample Labels option from the Print menu. To test labels with this feature, follow these steps:

1. Load the label sheet in the printer. If using a pinfeed printer, position the top of the label sheet so that the first line prints in the first row of the labels. Because every printer is different, you probably will have to guess the first time. Make sure that the left edge of the labels is at the 0 column mark on the printer.

2. Choose Generate Sample Labels from the Print menu. dBASE prints one row of labels. Adjust the paper in the printer if the sample labels didn't print correctly.

3. Choose Generate Sample Labels again to see whether your adjustment is accurate. Continue adjusting and generating sample labels until the labels print correctly.

Printing the Report

After you complete the report design and test it on the screen, you can return to the Control Center to print the report with the desired records in the selected database.

To print your mailmerge or label report, follow these steps:

1. Make the correct database current by highlighting it in the Data panel of the Control Center, pressing Enter, and choosing Use File from the options presented.

2. If you're using a query to limit the label output, make the query active by highlighting it in the Queries panel and pressing Enter.

3. Highlight the mailmerge report in the Reports panel or the label report in the Labels panel and press Enter.

4. From the options presented, choose Print Report or Print Label; the Print screen then appears.

5. Make changes in the print menu as desired. (See "Printing the Report" in Chapter 12, "Creating Custom Reports.")

6. Choose Print Report or Print Label.

From Here...

The columnar, form, mailmerge, and label layout reports give dBASE a robust reporting capability that can satisfy most of the users' needs. Another dimension has been added to reporting by the new feature called crosstabs. Although this is not a report feature, it can be used to create a database on which a report can be run. The crosstab database gives dBASE 5 a very unique added dimension.

- Chapter 14, "Using Crosstabs," explains another type of report that can be generated with dBASE 5. This powerful report type helps you consolidate data in way that regular reports cannot.

- Chapter 17, "Exploring Some Sample Programs," includes an example of a program that runs a report.

Chapter 14

Using Crosstabs

The crosstabs feature is a powerful new addition to dBASE 5. This feature lets you analyze database information in a spreadsheet fashion. Databases contain long lists of data that can be difficult to interpret, while spreadsheets categorize data in a way that makes it easier to recognize trends.

In this chapter, you learn how to do the following:

- Create a crosstab
- Navigate a crosstab
- Save a crosstab as a database
- Create reports with crosstab databases

Understanding a Crosstab

Creating a crosstab is best explained with an example. Table 14.1 shows the structure of the BRANDS database which will be used in this chapter to create crosstabs.

Table 14.1 Structure of the BRANDS Database

Field	Type	Length	Dec	Index
YEAR	Character	4		N
QUARTER	Character	2		N
BRAND	Character	15		Y
SIZE	Character	10		Y

(continues)

Table 14.1 Continued

Field	Type	Length	Dec	Index
REGION	Character	5		Y
COST	Numeric	5	0	N
CASES_SOLD	Numeric	5	0	N

The data in the database is shown in Table 14.2. The database contains the name of a product, the number of cases sold in each region for each size in each quarter, and the cost of a case.

Table 14.2 Data in the BRANDS Database

YEAR	QUARTER	BRAND	SIZE	REGION	COST	CASES_SOLD
1994	Q1	Remko	Small	South	300	250
1994	Q2	Remko	Medium	South	360	310
1994	Q3	Remko	Large	South	420	500
1994	Q4	Remko	X-Large	South	480	275
1994	Q1	Remko	X-Large	North	480	220
1994	Q2	Remko	Large	North	420	340
1994	Q3	Remko	Medium	North	360	275
1994	Q4	Remko	Small	North	300	310
1994	Q1	Aristocrat	Adult	East	190	320
1994	Q2	Aristocrat	Child	East	110	280
1994	Q3	Aristocrat	Adult	West	190	230
1994	Q4	Aristocrat	Child	West	110	360
1994	Q1	Aristocrat	Child	North	110	180
1994	Q2	Aristocrat	Child	South	110	340
1994	Q3	Aristocrat	Adult	East	190	450
1994	Q4	Aristocrat	Adult	West	190	125

YEAR	QUARTER	BRAND	SIZE	REGION	COST	CASES_SOLD
1993	Q1	Remko	Small	East	300	320
1993	Q2	Remko	Medium	East	360	390
1993	Q3	Remko	Large	East	420	280
1993	Q4	Remko	X-Large	East	480	100
1993	Q1	Remko	Small	North	300	180
1993	Q2	Remko	X-Large	North	480	140
1993	Q3	Remko	Small	North	300	230
1993	Q4	Remko	Large	North	420	260
1993	Q1	Aristocrat	Adult	East	190	290
1993	Q2	Aristocrat	Adult	East	190	135
1993	Q3	Aristocrat	Child	East	110	165
1993	Q4	Aristocrat	Child	East	110	185
1993	Q1	Aristocrat	Child	West	110	195
1993	Q2	Aristocrat	Adult	West	190	230
1993	Q3	Aristocrat	Adult	West	190	240
1993	Q4	Aristocrat	Child	West	110	260

The organization of data in the database makes it difficult to compare the sales for each product in each region or to see what the average sale per quarter is. With the crosstabs feature you can perform calculations that are related to two aspects of a database and see these kinds of relationships. For example, a crosstab can create a table that lists the sizes across the top and the quarters down the side, and tabulates the number of cases sold per quarter for each size. The crosstab table is shown in figure 14.1.

In addition, a crosstab can include totals in the table. The previous example would look like figure 14.2 if totals were included.

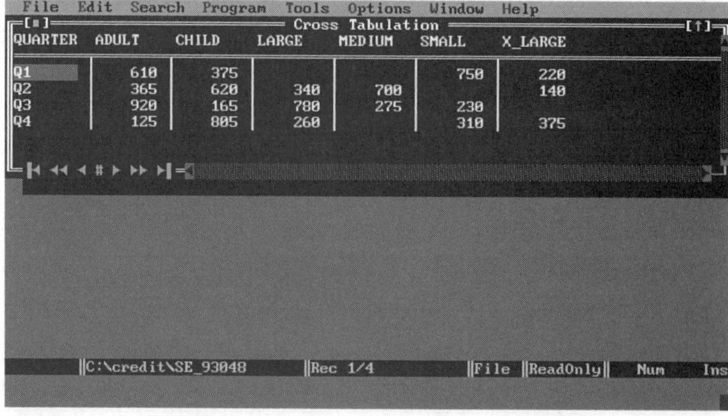

Fig. 14.1
A crosstab table showing the breakdown of sizes sold by quarter.

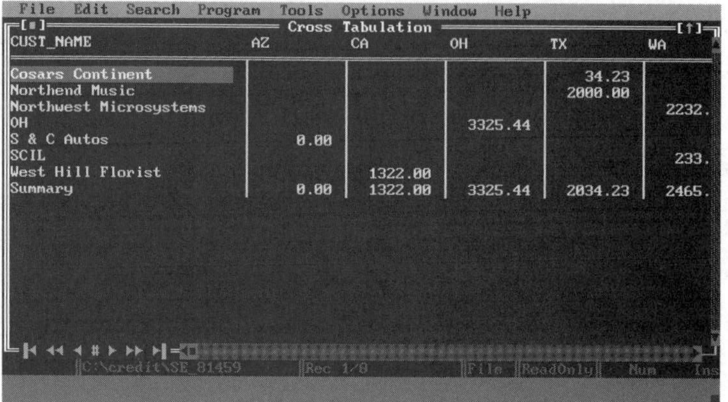

Fig. 14.2
A crosstab showing the breakdown of sizes sold by quarter with totals included.

Creating Crosstabs

A crosstab is created on the Desktop interface using the Crosstab Expert. To create a crosstab, go to the Desktop and follow these steps:

1. Open the **T**ools menu and choose Cross **T**abulation. If no database is currently open, dBASE 5 displays the Open DBF File dialog box as shown in figure 14.3. The directory that is displayed is the default directory. All DBF files in the default directory are displayed in the file list box.

◄ See "Using Dialog Boxes," p. 36

2. Type the name of the desired file or select the name from the list box and choose OK. The Crosstab Expert dialog box is displayed as shown in figure 14.4. (When selecting a file from the list box, you may have to

scroll the list to bring the file that you want into view. If the file that you want is located in another directory, change the directory in the directory list box, and then select the file from the file list box.)

3. Select the field that will create the columns of the table. dBASE 5 will list the unique contents of this field as column headings in alphanumeric order.

4. Select the field that will create the categories. dBASE 5 will list the unique contents of this field as row headings in alphanumeric order.

5. Select the field that will be used to summarize the data.

6. Select the summary operation that should be used by the summary field selected in Step 5.

7. Select Include Totals if desired.

8. Choose OK. While the cross tabulation is taking place, dBASE 5 displays a small window that says, `Working: Computing Cross Tabulation`. When the calculation is finished, dBASE 5 displays the table in a Browse window (see figs. 14.1 and 14.2).

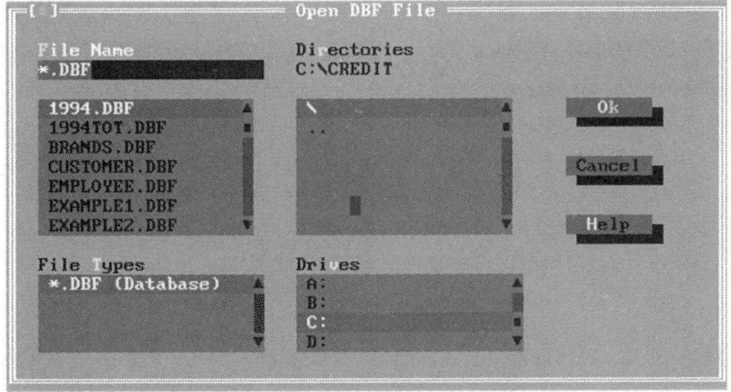

Fig. 14.3
The Open DBF File dialog box lists the files in the current directory.

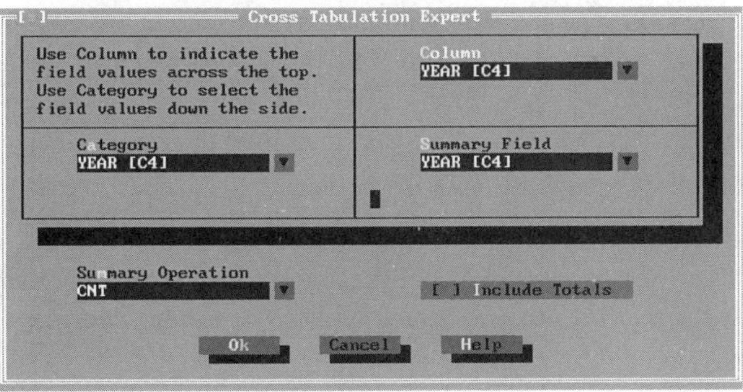

Fig. 14.4
The Crosstab Expert dialog box contains drop-down lists for the Column, Category, Summary Field, and Summary Operation.

Opening a File for a Crosstab

The steps for creating a crosstab assume that no database file is currently in use, but this is rarely the case. You may have been using a file in the Control Center and then decided to exit to the Desktop to create a crosstab. Exiting the Control Center does not close the database that you were using. When you create a crosstab, dBASE will assume that you want to use the database that you were using in the Control Center, and the Open DBF File dialog box will not be presented. If this is not the file you want to use, you must exit the crosstab Browse window and open the appropriate database.

Forewarned is forearmed—so consider yourself forewarned. Three strategies can be used to prevent this problem. Before returning to the Desktop, highlight the database that you want to use with the crosstabs feature in the Data panel and press Enter. Then choose Use File. When you return to the Desktop and choose Tools and Cross Tabulation, dBASE 5 will use the desired database file. Or, when you return to the Desktop, type this command in the Command window: **Close databases**. When you choose Tools and Cross Tabulation, the Open DBF File dialog box will appear, and you can select the desired file. A third strategy is to type the following command in the Command window: **Use dbname** (the name of the file you want to use). This command not only opens the named database, but it also closes the current database.

Note

After you have created a cross-tabulated table, the database file used for the table remains open. If you want to create a crosstab for a different database, use the command Close databases before creating the next crosstab or the Use dbname command.

More About Columns and Categories in a Crosstab

When the Crosstab Expert dialog box is first displayed, the Columns, Categories, and Summary Field options all display the name of the first field in the database. The field type and length are displayed in square brackets beside the field name. To choose a different field, tab to the option and press the Down arrow (or Up arrow) to scroll the choices. You can also begin typing the field name; dBASE 5 will display the correct field name when enough letters have been typed to identify the field.

To choose a field with the mouse, click the arrow to the right of the option to display a list box. Double-click the desired field name. If the field name is not visible, use the scroll bar to scroll the list, and then double-click the desired field name.

When specifying the field for the columns in a crosstab table, keep in mind that dBASE 5 will truncate any value in the field that is more than ten characters long. If the value contains blanks or special characters, the blanks or characters are replaced by an underline.

If you choose a numerical field for the columns, the values in the field are preceded by the letter "F." If you choose a logical field, the headings "True" and "False" are used. You cannot specify a memo field for columns.

For categories, dBASE limits the number of characters to 100; blanks or special characters are displayed as is. Any type of field can be specified as a category except a memo field.

More About Summary Fields in a Crosstab

Summary fields can use the following summary calculations: AVG, CNT, MAX, MIN, and SUM. The type of field specified as the summary field determines the summary calculations that can be used. If the field is a numeric or float field, all of the summary calculations are available for use. If the summary field is a logical or character field, only the CNT, MAX, and MIN calculations are available.

◄ See "Adding Fields that Perform Summary Math," p. 305

More About the Browse Window

The Browse window has a button in the upper-left corner and one in the upper-right corner. Like any window in dBASE, the button in the upper-left corner closes the window when you press Esc or click the button with the mouse pointer. The button in the upper-right corner is called the resizing button and resizes the window when clicked. The number of the window is displayed just to the left of the resizing button (if the window is not selected). When the window is selected, the sizing button is over the number.

A navigation bar in the lower-left corner of the window can be used with the mouse to scroll through the records. The arrow on the left of the bar takes you to the first record. Conversely, the last arrow on the right takes you to the last record in the database. The double arrows on the left take you to the previous screen of records, and the double arrows on the right take you to the next screen of records. The single arrow to the left of the number sign (#) takes you to the previous record, and the single arrow on the right of the number sign takes you to the next record.

◄ See "Working with Multiple Windows, p. 45

Saving a Crosstab

Unfortunately, saving a crosstab is not like saving a query. You cannot save the format of the crosstab and use it over and over again as you can with a query. The data displayed in the Browse window can be saved to a DBF file. This file can be used just like a regular database file: it has a structure, it can be added to a catalog and be queried, reports and forms can be created for it; and so on.

To save the crosstab table, click the button in the upper-left corner of the window border or press Esc. dBASE 5 displays the message: `Do you want to save the Cross Tabulation result?` Choose Yes. The Save Crosstab Result As dialog box is displayed, as shown in figure 14.5. Make certain that you select the desired directory in the dialog box, type a name for the file, and press Enter (or click OK). The file will save to disk, and you will return to the Desktop.

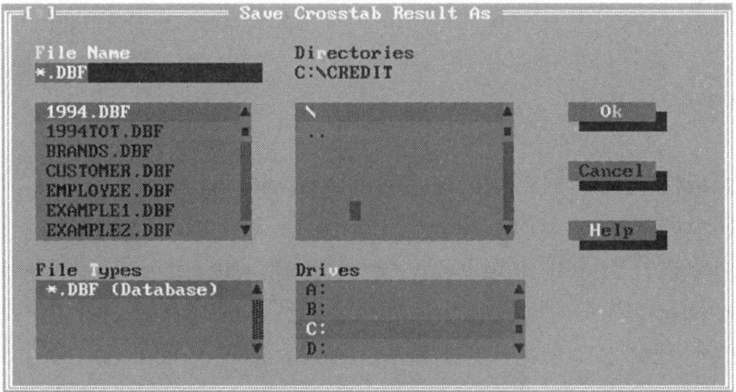

Fig. 14.5
The Save Crosstab Result As dialog box list the names of databases in the current directory.

Note

If you choose No for the prompt, `Do you want to save the Cross Tabulation result`, dBASE displays the message: `Closing the cross tabulation results database`. Press Enter to choose OK or click the OK button with the mouse. You will then return to the Desktop.

Exploring Some Examples

Crosstabs can be difficult to learn. If you study the examples in this section, it might be easier for you to create a crosstab with your own data. Each example asks a question that can be answered by creating a crosstab. Take another look at the data in the BRANDS database to familiarize yourself with the file before looking at the first example.

Example 1: Finding the Total Cases Sold

How many cases of each size of product were sold in 1993 and 1994?

Create a crosstab that uses the following options:

Column: SIZE

Category: YEAR

Summary Field: CASES_SOLD

Summary Operation: SUM

The resulting crosstab is shown in figure 14.6.

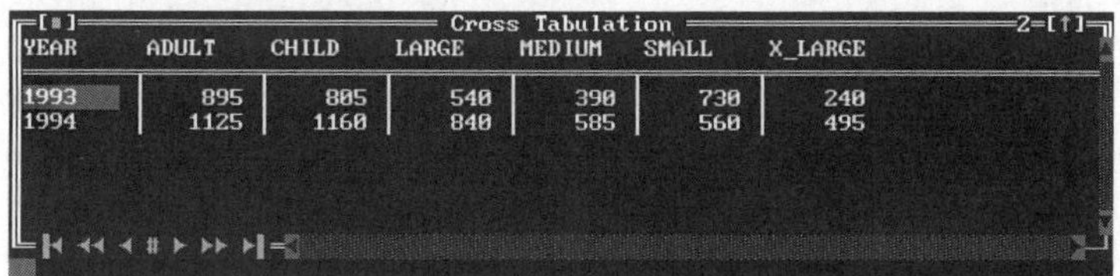

Cross Tabulation

YEAR	ADULT	CHILD	LARGE	MEDIUM	SMALL	X_LARGE
1993	895	805	540	390	730	240
1994	1125	1160	840	585	560	495

Fig. 14.6
The crosstab table for Example 1 shows the number of cases sold for each size in each year.

Example 2: Finding the Average Number of Cases Sold

What is the average number of cases of each size of product sold for each quarter of 1993 and 1994?

Create a crosstab that uses the following options:

Column: SIZE

Category: QUARTER

Summary Field: CASES_SOLD

Summary Operation: AVG

The resulting crosstab is shown in figure 14.7.

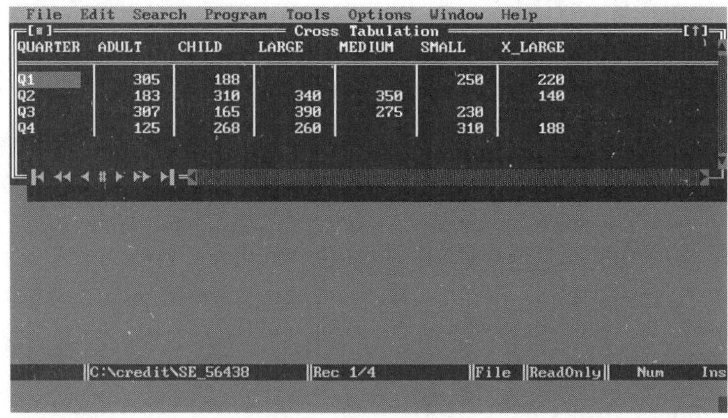

QUARTER	ADULT	CHILD	LARGE	MEDIUM	SMALL	X_LARGE
Q1	305	188			250	220
Q2	183	310	340	350		140
Q3	307	165	390	275	230	
Q4	125	268	260		310	188

Fig. 14.7 The crosstab table for Example 2 shows the average number of sizes sold broken down by quarters.

Example 3: Finding How Many Cases Sold in a Quarter

How many cases of each size of product were sold in each quarter of 1994?

◀ See "Using Queries to Search Databases," p. 187

◀ See "Using Advanced Techniques with Queries," p. 223

This is a trick question. You cannot create a crosstab that looks at three aspects of the data (size, year, and quarter), but you can query the database on the year, write the query output to a database file, and then create a crosstab from the resulting database.

Create a crosstab that uses the following options:

Column: SIZE

Category: QUARTER

Summary Field: CASES_SOLD

Summary Operation: SUM

The resulting crosstab is shown in figure 14.8.

Example 4: Finding the Total of All Brands

How many cases of all brands and sizes were sold in 1993 and 1994 in each region?

Create a crosstab that uses the following options:

Column: REGION

Category: YEAR

Summary Field: CASES_SOLD

Summary Operation: SUM

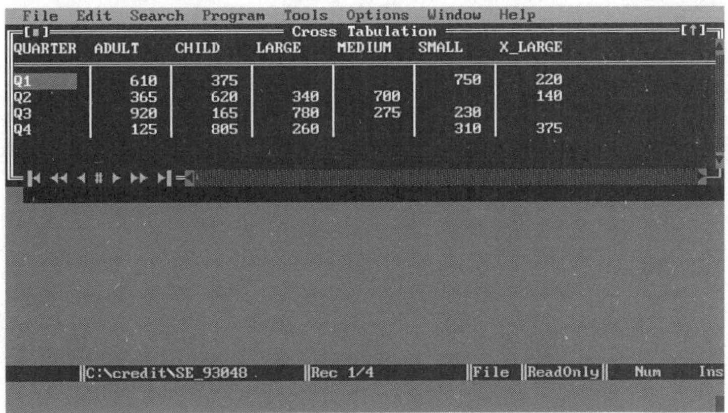

Fig. 14.8
The crosstab table for Example 3 shows the total number of sizes sold broken down by quarter.

The resulting crosstab is shown in figure 14.9.

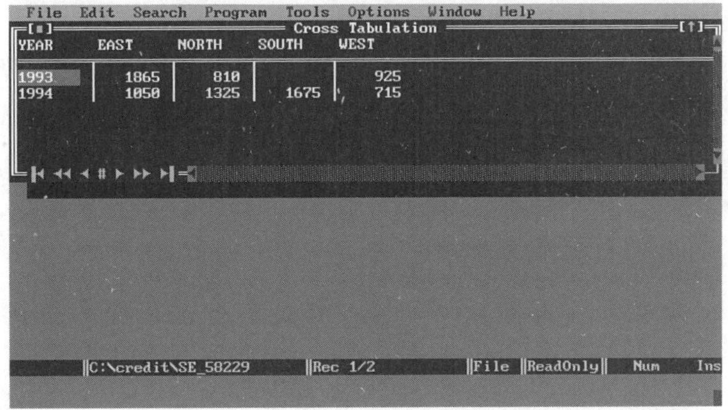

Fig. 14.9
The crosstab table for Example 4 shows the number sold in each region broken down by year.

Example 5: Finding the Total Brands per Region

How many cases were sold for each brand in each region?

Create a crosstab that uses the following options:

Column: REGION

Category: BRAND

Summary Field: CASES_SOLD

Summary Operation: SUM

The resulting crosstab is shown in figure 14.10.

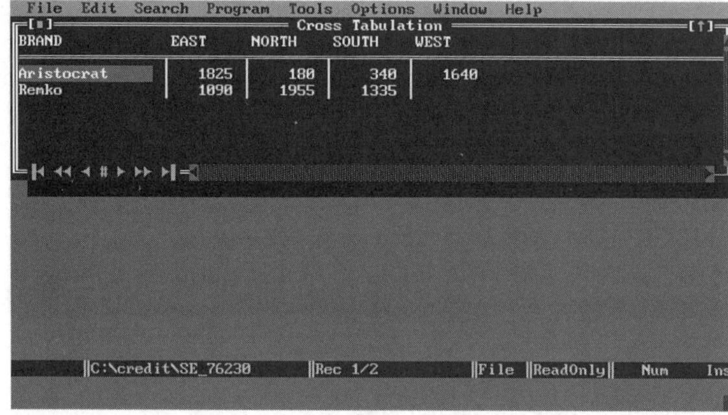

Fig. 14.10
The crosstab table for Example 5 shows how many cases were sold for each brand in each region.

Example 6: Finding the Maximum Cases Sold

Over the two-year period, which region sold the most of which size in any one quarter?

Create a crosstab that uses the following options:

Column: REGION

Category: SIZE

Summary Field: CASES_SOLD

Summary Operation: MAX

The resulting crosstab is shown in figure 14.11.

Example 7: Finding the Gross Sales

How much money was taken in for each brand in each region in 1994?

As in Example 3, this crosstab cannot be created without first querying the database. To find out how much money was taken in for each brand, you must add a calculated field to the query that multiplies the cost of a case (COST) times the number of cases sold (CASES_SOLD). In the example, the calculated field is called TOTAL. The query must be written to a database, and the resulting database can be used to create the crosstab.

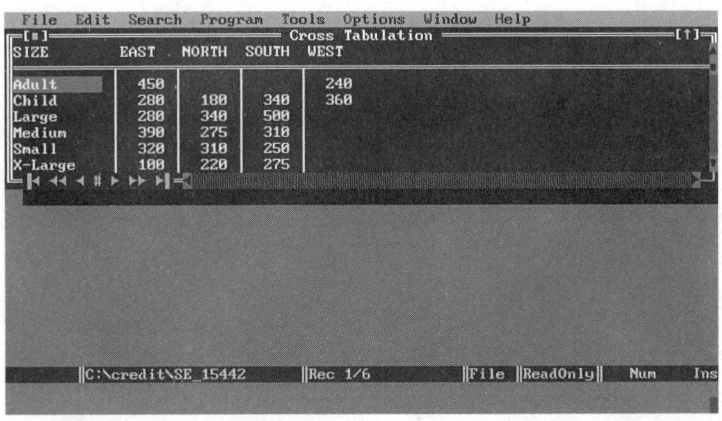

Fig. 14.11
The crosstab table for Example 6 shows the highest number of cases sold in each region for each size.

After querying the database with the calculated field, create a crosstab that uses the following options:

Column: REGION

Category: BRAND

Summary Field: TOTAL

Summary Operation: SUM

The resulting crosstab is shown in figure 14.12. Figure 14.13 shows the same crosstab table with totals included.

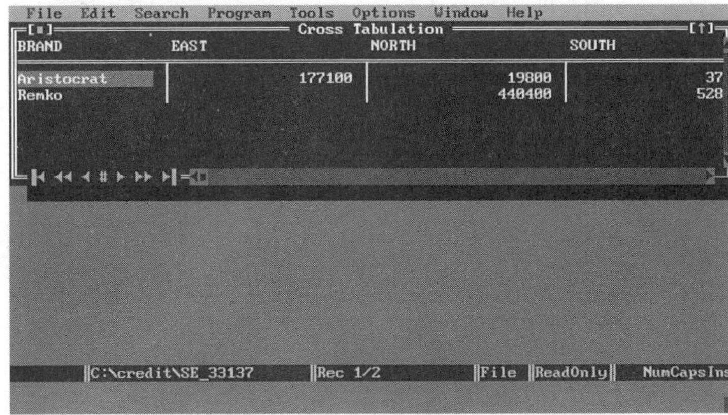

Fig. 14.12
The crosstab table for Example 7 shows the total sold for each brand in each region in 1994.

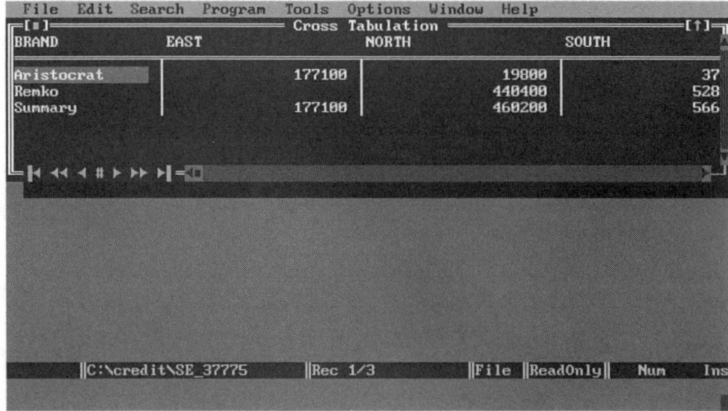

Fig. 14.13 The crosstab table for Example 7 including totals for each brand in each region.

Example 8: Finding the Cost and Number Sold

How much does each size cost and how many were sold of each size?

Create a crosstab that uses the following options:

Column: COST

Category: SIZE

Summary Field: CASES_SOLD

Summary Operation: SUM

The resulting crosstab is shown in figure 14.14. Notice that the column headings begin with "F" because COST is a numeric field. After you save the crosstab as a database file, you can change these field names, but remember that a field name cannot start with a number.

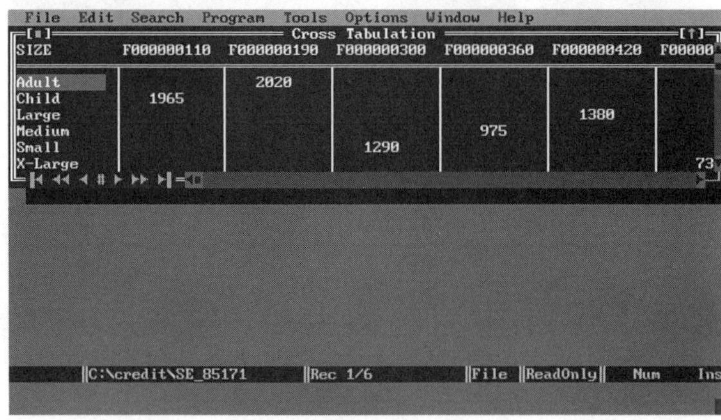

Fig. 14.14 The crosstab table for Example 8 shows the number sold and the total cost for the number sold.

Creating Reports with Crosstabs

The crosstab table itself is closer to a report than a database, but the crosstab is saved as a database file, not a report file. To print a report, therefore, you must use the crosstab database file as you would any other database. To get a quick report, display the data in the file and press Shift-F9. If you want to rearrange the columns or create some calculated fields, use the Reports design screen with the database. The columnar layout is the best type of report to use with a crosstab database.

For example, look again at figure 14.10. The regions are listed in alphabetical order. If you want the regions to be listed in the order North, South, East, and West, use the Reports design screen and move the fields so they are placed in the desired order (see figs. 14.15 and 14.16).

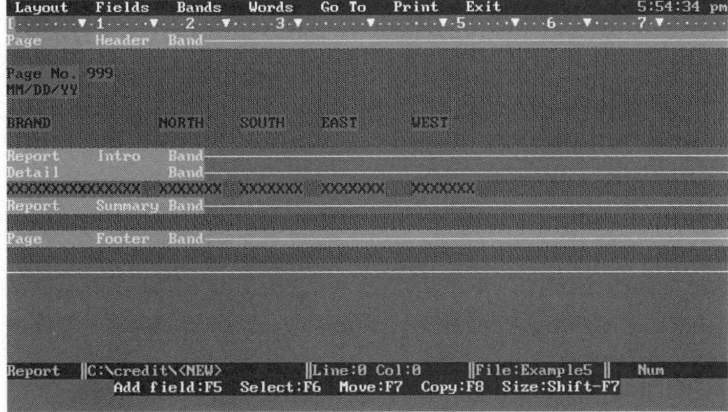

Fig. 14.15
The Reports design screen shows the revised report with a new order of fields.

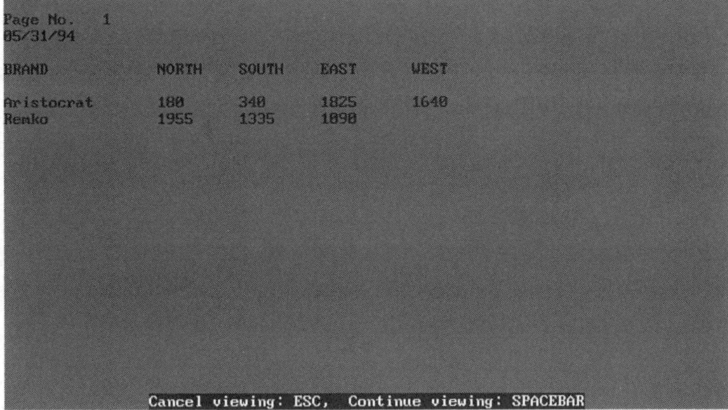

Fig. 14.16
The result of the revised report list shows the data in the new order.

◀ See "Generating a Quick Report," p. 178

◀ See "Creating Custom Reports," p. 287

Note

The Group Band is usually not used with crosstab databases because only unique values are listed in the row headings. It would not make sense in most cases to group on the calculations in a column.

Troubleshooting

I have tried to create the same crosstab table several times. When I try to select a field for the column heading, sometimes the field is listed in the drop-down menu and sometimes it isn't.

At first glance this might sound like a program bug, but I doubt that it is. I have never seen this happen. I think you have two databases that have almost the same fields, and you are using the wrong database. This is easy to do. Remember, after creating a crosstab for one database, if you want to create a second crosstab for a different database, you must use the appropriate table.

When I try to type the name of the field in the Column or Category box, the Crosstab Expert dialog box disappears.

You probably pressed the spacebar accidentally (field names cannot have spaces). The spacebar exits the dialog box without a warning.

From Here...

You might want to review all the chapters that pertain to queries and reports—two areas that indirectly relate to crosstabs.

- Chapter 8, "Organizing Your Database and Generating a Quick Report," gives you basic information about using the default report form, printing the report, and viewing the report on-screen.

- Chapter 9, "Using Queries To Search Databases," explains simple queries.

- Chapter 10, "Using Advanced Techniques with Queries," covers advanced query techniques including adding calculated fields, sorting, using update queries, and linking databases with queries.

- Chapter 12, "Creating Custom Reports," covers all aspects of creating a custom report, including Quick Layout, report bands, calculated fields, and summary fields.

Chaper 15

Using Relational Databases for Complex Situations

Although you may work with database projects that require only one database, most dBASE applications require two, three, or more databases to represent the different types of data in the application. dBASE 5 can create sophisticated database applications with multiple databases and tie those databases together in productive ways.

In this chapter, you learn the essentials of working with multiple-file databases. Defining the databases and how they work together is the most important aspect of creating these applications. The first part of this chapter discusses the theory of relational databases in simple terms. When you finish this section, you won't be an expert, but you will know enough to design and develop good relational database systems.

The real strength of dBASE is its capability to create complex databases and database relationships; this chapter gives you the tools to make full use of these capabilities.

The following topics are covered in this chapter:

- Defining a relational database system, including the files and their relationships
- Testing the databases to make sure the file structures and relations work the way you want them to work
- Techniques of reporting on relational databases

Understanding Relational Databases

Relational database systems are models of how data in the "real world" falls together. If you analyze a real-world example you will be able to see exactly how a relational database system should be created. Let's look at a common example involving sales. A retailer's operation has information about each inventory part, each customer, and each order. Each of these logical groups of information can be called a *data entity*. In a database system developed for this company, each entity would have its own database file to hold its specific information. The customer database would contain fields for the customer's name, address, phone number, and probably a unique customer number. The order database would most likely contain fields for the unique customer number, a quantity, a part number, an invoice number, and a date. The inventory database would contain fields for the number on hand, the part number, the cost, and the retail price.

The *relational* aspect of this system comes into play because a relationship exists between the data entities, and you want the database to represent those relationships. In this example, a relationship exists between the customer and the orders: a customer places each order. Similarly, a relationship exists between the order database and the inventory database: each order is for some part in inventory. Figure 15.1 shows the data entities and the relationships between them.

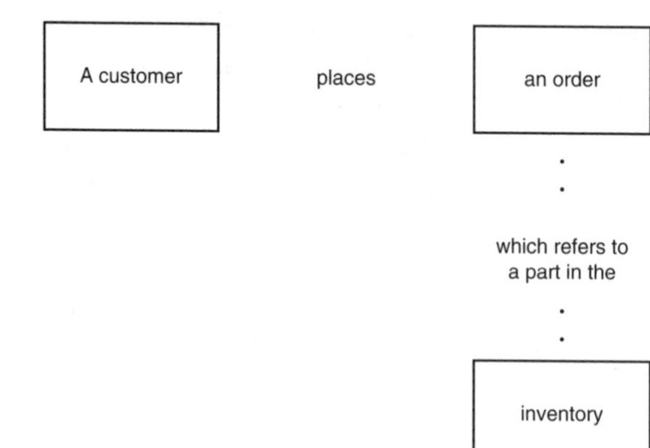

Fig. 15.1
A graphical representation of related databases.

A relational database system can relate two or more database files to each other, enabling you to draw information from all files based on these relationships. For example, when entering an order in the Order database, the customer number could retrieve and display the customer's name and address from the Customer database, but the customer's name and address would not be stored physically (in fields) in the Order database. The part number also could retrieve and display the retail cost from the Inventory database. This is the relational aspect of dBASE; you relate two files based on a field common to both files.

Less experienced database designers tend to handle these types of situations in one of two ways: they create databases that include redundant fields or they create one big database with all the possible fields included. For example, an experienced database designer might include the name and address fields in both the Customer database and the Order database, or the designer might create only one database that includes the fields for the customer information and the order information. Either way, there is duplication of data. The duplication is fairly obvious in the first example. You would have to enter the customer information in the Customer database and the same information in the order database. In the second example, you may be thinking there aren't any duplications of data because all the fields are included only once in each record. However, every time you enter an order for the same customer, you will have to type the customer's name and address. What if the customer orders ten items (thus creating ten records)? You will have to type the name and address ten times. By creating a unique field that is common to both databases, you can link the databases and eliminate the duplication of data.

By eliminating the necessity to key duplicate information in two or more databases, relational databases make your system more consistent and reliable. Because you have no duplication, a relational database system saves disk space and reduces the effort required for data entry and editing.

Recognizing Situations Requiring Relational Databases

Now let's look at a class registration example. This could apply to high school or college registration or to continuing education for employees. Take a look at the following categories of information and see if you can group the categories into logical entities and decide what additional categories would be needed to relate the entities. Keep in mind that a student can register for more than one class, and you want to be able to report on all the classes taken by one individual as well as report on the roster for each class.

Student's Name

Student's Address

Student's Phone Number

Name of Class

Date of Class

Location of Class

Class Instructor

Cost of Class

Instructor's Address

Instructor's Phone Number

This example would have four logical entities: a database that lists the complete student population, a database that lists the class registrations, a database that lists all the classes available, and a database that lists the complete instructor population. New categories would include a unique student number (probably the Social Security number), a unique identifier for each class, and a unique number for each instructor (again, probably the Social Security number). The relationship of these databases is shown in figure 15.2.

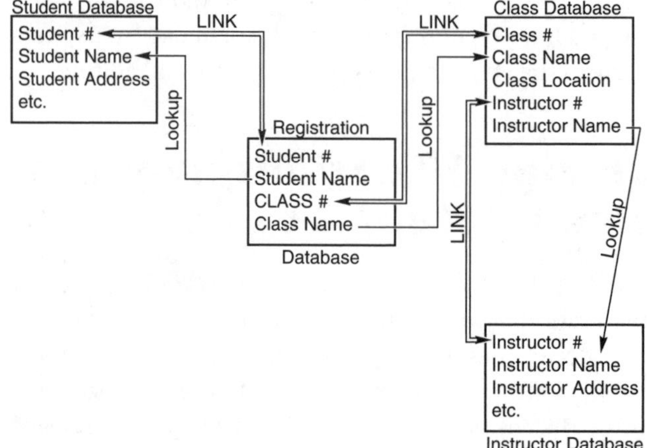

Fig. 15.2
The relationship of the class registration databases.

Notice that the student's name appears in the Registration database, but it is actually retrieved from the Student database. The same kind of relationship exists between the Registration database and the Class database. The class name in the Registration database is retrieved from the Class database. From this one example you can see that a database can be linked to more than one other database. Notice that the same type of relationship exists between the Class database and the Instructor database.

Now, consider this example. You want to create a database system for employee benefits. You need the following categories of information:

Employee Name

Employee Address

Employee Phone Number

Date of Birth

Age

Employee Department

Date Hired

Current Salary

Number of Dependents

Life Insurance Coverage Amount

Cost of Life Insurance (based on age)

Hospitalization Coverage Amount

Cost of Hospitalization (based on number of dependents)

Figure 15.3 shows the logical entities and their relationship.

If you study the relationships in this model, you will see the same type of linking and lookup functions as in the previous example. In fact, all systems are basically the same. They vary only in the number of entities in the system and the number of linking and lookup fields.

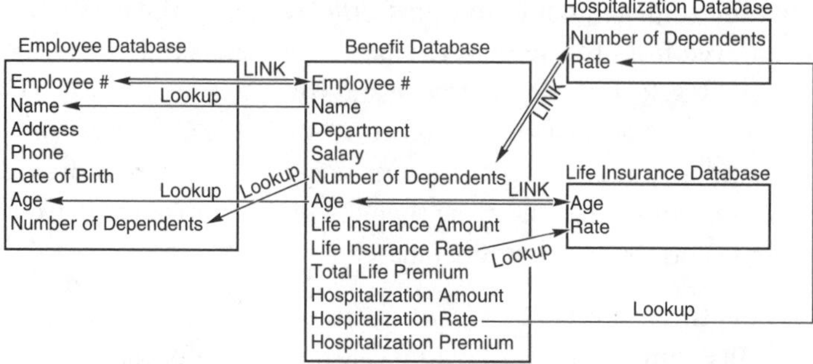

Fig. 15.3 The databases for employee benefits and their relationships.

Note

An interesting and more complex relationship could be established in the class registration model by adding the instructor's name to the Registration database as a lookup field. The Registration database would have to use the Class # field to lookup the Instructor # in the Class database and then the Class database would lookup the instructor's name (based on the Instructor #) in the Instructor database.

Designing a Relational Database

Earlier in this book you learned to design a database file structure and enter data in the file. You actually designed a system with only one file. Designing, defining, and creating a multiple-file, relational database isn't much different, but it requires more thought at the beginning and more testing along the way to ensure the results you want. You must ensure that the fields necessary to define the relation exist in the related database files. The next sections explain the steps you take to design a relational database:

1. Define the data entities for the system.
2. Decide which databases and fields to include in the system.
3. Determine how the data is related.
4. Refine the database design.

◀ See "Defining Your Database," p. 110

◀ See "Designing the Structure of a Database," p. 107

Defining the Data Entities

When designing a relational database system in dBASE, start as you do when designing a single-file system, with a clear idea of the output you need from the system. Pattern your system after the way data flows in the real-world system for which you are designing the relational database system. You might begin by thinking about the way in which you want the system to present the results of data inquiries and the kinds of reports and screen output that will be produced. By looking at the output you need from the system, you can identify information you need in the databases.

Deciding What To Include in the Databases

When you start to design a database, don't worry about the relationships that may exist; concentrate only on the data the system needs. After you design the individual database structures, you can easily define the relationships and how to implement them in dBASE. In this chapter you will design a relational system for the first example—the Sales (cutomer/order/inventory) system. Tables 15.1 through 15.3 show the three databases for the example system and the data you need. (Note that the field names given in the first column are descriptive, not "valid" field names that you would type in the file structure.)

Table 15.1 Structure for the Customer Database

Field name	Type	Width	Dec	Index
Customer Name	Character	25		Y
Address 1	Character	25		N
Address 2	Character	25		N
City	Character	15		N
State	Character	2		Y
ZIP Code	Character	9		Y
Phone	Character	10		N
Contact	Character	10		N
Credit limit	Numeric	8	2	N
Preferred Customer	Logical	1		N

Table 15.2 Structure for the Inventory Database

Field name	Type	Width	Dec	Index
Part Number	Character	15		Y
Description	Character	25		N
Supplier	Character	25		Y
Qty On Hand	Numeric	5	0	N
Reorder point	Numeric	5	0	N
Price	Numeric	8	2	N
Cost	Numeric	8	2	N
Auto Reorder?	Logical	1		N

Table 15.3 Structure for the Order Database

Field name	Type	Width	Dec	Index
Customer Name	Character	25		Y
Address 1	Character	25		N
Address 2	Character	25		N
City	Character	15		N
State	Character	2		Y
ZIP Code	Character	9		Y
Phone	Character	10		N
Order Date	Date	8		N
Invoice Number	Character	10		Y
Part Number	Character	15		Y
Quantity	Numeric	8	0	N
Price	Numeric	8	2	N

Tip
When thinking about the fields that should be included in each database, remember to consider the information that you need from database fields in reports.

After you have listed all the fields that you need in each database, the duplication of data should be quite clear. After you are sure that the database design incorporates the information you need to generate the reports and query screens, you are ready to figure out the relationships between the database files. The next step is to define fields that can be used to link the databases and eliminate the duplication of fields.

Determining How Data Is Related

Computer system designers have long relied on graphical techniques (that is, scribblings on paper) to define computer systems. This section describes a graphical technique for figuring out the relationships you should include in the dBASE system you are designing.

First, draw a small box and put into it the name of one of the databases—for example, the CUSTOMER database. If you think about how CUSTOMER relates to other databases in the dBASE system, you know that a relationship exists between the customers and the orders of the company: customers place orders. Draw another box to the left of the CUSTOMER box and name it ORDERS. Now draw a diamond between the two boxes (diamonds represent a relation) and draw lines between the boxes and the diamond. Figure 15.4 shows the diagram.

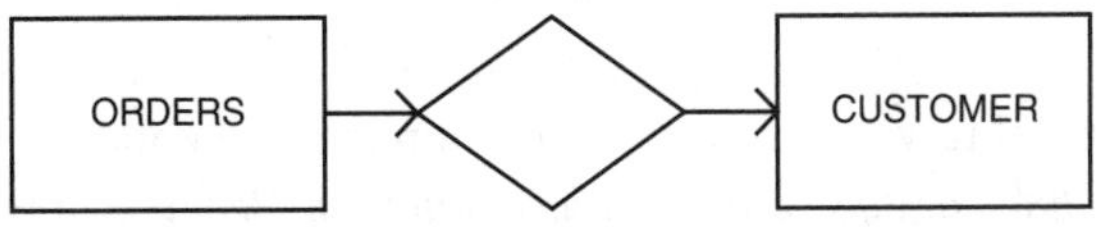

Fig. 15.4
The relationship between the ORDERS database and the CUSTOMER database.

You should give the relationship a name, for the sake of clarity (in this example, the relationship can be called *is placed by*; that is, ORDERS are placed by CUSTOMER). You also should define how you want to implement this relationship; in other words, how you want to define the relationship to dBASE.

dBASE relates databases through a common field. Each database on either side of the relation must have a field that contains the same information. In the *controlling* database, you tell dBASE what the field is. In the *controlled* database, you can give the field a different name (although the field must be of the same data type and size), but the database must be indexed on that field if the relationship is to work.

In this example, the common information between the ORDERS and CUSTOMER databases is the customer's name. If the ORDERS database has the customer's name, dBASE can relate each record in ORDERS with the proper record in CUSTOMER, providing you with access to CUSTOMER fields (such as the address, city, and state). You can use the NAME field in both ORDERS and CUSTOMER to relate the two databases. However, the NAME field isn't quite adequate for linking because the entries in this field would not necessarily be unique.

Instead of storing the entire customer's name in the ORDERS database, replace the long NAME field in the ORDERS database with a shorter field in which you store a customer number; name this field CUST_NUM. Then modify the CUSTOMER database to add a CUST_NUM field, making sure that you index on that field.

dBASE uses the two CUST_NUM fields to match records in the ORDERS database to the customer information in the CUSTOMER database. Wherever possible, use this technique to reduce redundant storage of large fields and to decrease the possibility of mistakes. Errors when entering a one to six digit customer number are much less likely than when entering up to 25 characters of a customer name. Now the database diagram looks like figure 15.5.

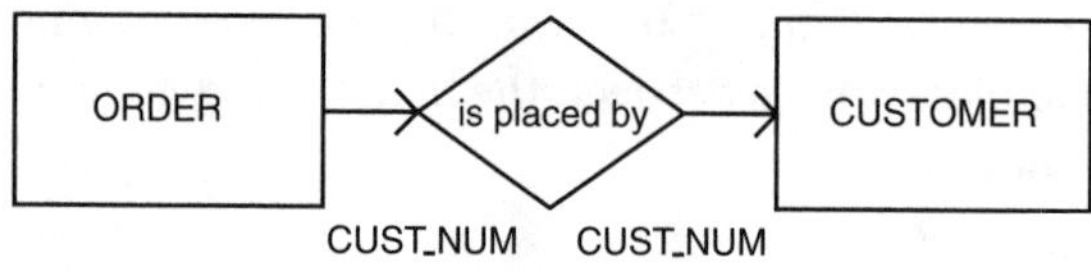

Fig. 15.5
The ORDERS and CUSTOMER databases related by a common field.

Tip
Make sure that your diagram makes a note of the need to index that field.

Concepts essential to your understanding of relational databases are the concepts of *controlling database* and *controlled database*. When you use a relation in a dBASE database to access data in different files, one database file is the controlling database; the other is the controlled database. If you print a report from the ORDERS database using the CUST_NUM relation to get information about the customer from the CUSTOMER database, ORDERS is the controlling database and CUSTOMER is the controlled database. Because dBASE ties a record in CUSTOMER to a record in ORDERS, ORDERS controls which record is accessed in the CUSTOMER database. The controlled database must be indexed on the related field (in this case, CUSTOMER must be indexed on the CUST_NUM field).

Figure 15.6 shows the relationship that the INVENTRY database has to the system. This diagram is called an *entity-relation diagram*. The diagram presents the entities (the database files) and the relationships (the way they are tied together) in a graphical, easy-to-understand format.

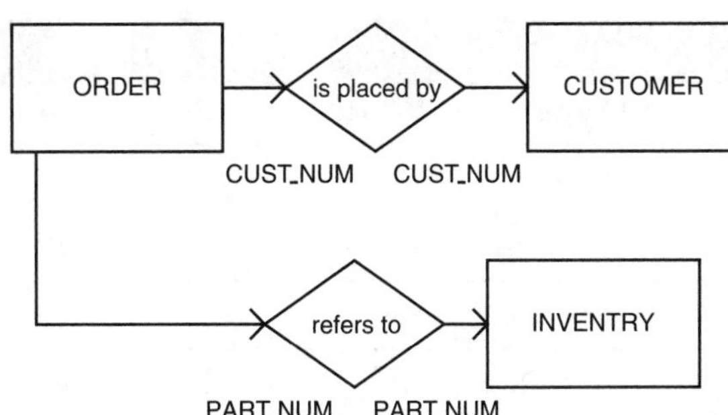

Fig. 15.6
A completed entity-relation diagram.

Refining the Database Design

After you have created the entity-relation diagram for your system, you can refine the database structures to include the necessary relational fields. Tables 15.4 through 15.6 show the refined structures of the three files. (Again, the field names given in the first columns are descriptive, *not* valid field names.)

Table 15.4 Refined Structure for CUSTOMER Database

Field Name	Type	Width	Dec	Index
Customer Number	Numeric	6	0	Y
Customer Name	Character	25		Y
Address 1	Character	25		N
Address 2	Character	25		N
City	Character	15		N
State	Character	2		Y
ZIP Code	Character	9		Y
Phone	Character	10		N
Contact	Character	10		N
Credit limit	Numeric	8	2	N
Preferred Customer	Logical	1		N

Table 15.5 Refined Structure for INVENTRY Database

Field Name	Type	Width	Dec	Index
Part Number	Character	15		Y
Description	Character	25		N
Supplier	Character	25		Y
Qty On Hand	Numeric	5	0	N
Reorder point	Numeric	5	0	N
Price	Numeric	8	2	N
Cost	Numeric	8	2	N
Auto Reorder?	Logical	1		N

Table 15.6 Refined Structure for ORDERS Database

Field Name	Type	Width	Dec	Index
Customer Number	Numeric	6	0	Y
Order Date	Date	8		N
Invoice Number	Character	10		Y
Part Number	Character	15		Y
Quantity	Numeric	5	0	N

Note the inventory database was named INVENTRY to meet the DOS restriction of eight-character file names. The databases are refined by adding a CUST_NUM (Customer Number) field in the CUTOMER.DBF file and replacing the customer information in ORDERS.DBF file with the same CUST_NUM field.

Now the relational database design is complete. You know what data the files must contain, what indexes must be created, and how to relate the database files together. The next step is to transfer the paper design into dBASE.

Creating the Files

After you define the database system on paper, you must create the files in dBASE. Doing so is no different from defining single-file databases; in fact, the process simply involves defining single-file databases one at a time until all the related databases are complete.

Entering data in related databases is also the same as entering data in single-file databases. Remember, though, that the data you enter in the common, relational field must be identical in both databases or dBASE won't be able to look up the correct record. It is advisable to print a report that can be used as a reference when entering data. For example, print the CUSTOMER database so that you can refer to the CUSTNAME when entering CUST_NUM in the ORDERS database.

Note

You should not enter all the records in the databases immediately. Enter only a few test records in each database.

Creating Catalogs for Relational Databases

After you create the databases and add a few test records, you should create a catalog that contains the related files. As you create queries, forms, and reports, these files will be added to the catalog automatically.

In this example, only three database files are related; all three are required for the queries and reports of the chapter. In real dBASE 5 systems, however, you may have other databases that relate to one or more of these databases. For example, you may have a Supplier database that relates to the Inventory database and a SalesRep database that relates to the Order database. You can create a different catalog to include the Inventory and Supplier databases and another catalog to include the Orders and the SalesRep databases. Remember, a file can be added to as many different categories as you want.

◀ See "Using Catalogs," p. 73

Using Queries To Set Up Relationships

After the databases are created and added to a catalog, you must "tell" dBASE 5 how these databases are related. You do this with a query. Queries are the key to creating relational systems.

When creating a query, place the databases in the query (the controlling database first), and then relate them by linking the proper fields in the file skeletons and including the desired fields in the view skeleton. (See Chapters 9 and 10 for a detailed explanation of file skeletons and linking databases through queries.)

> **Note**
>
> You can't link databases on logical or memo fields. Logical fields obviously do not have enough unique values for linking records, and memo fields are just not designed for linking.

Figure 15.7 shows the relationship between ORDERS and CUSTOMER. All the fields in both databases are included in the view skeleton, but this isn't mandatory. Instead of creating one query that includes all the fields, you can create several different queries that include different fields. These different queries are used for different kinds of forms or reports. The way you handle queries is a personal preference. If you like to create forms and reports using Quick Layout, it's better to use a query that has the exact fields that you want in the form or report included in the view skeleton. Otherwise, all the fields will be included in the form or report and you will have more deleting and moving to do when editing the form. Figure 15.8 shows the output of the query shown in Figure 15.7.

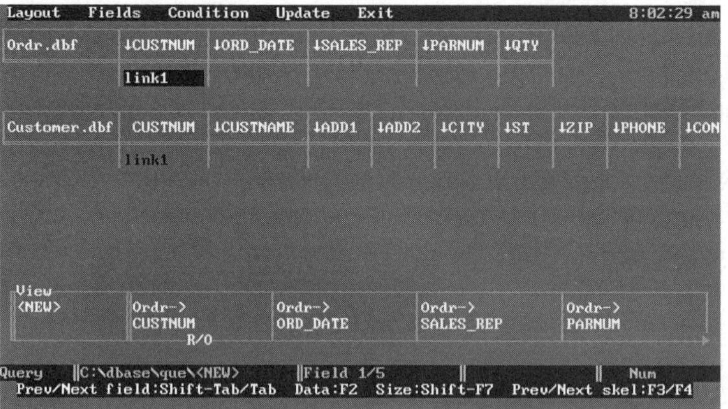

Fig. 15.7
The query that creates the relationship between ORDERS and CUSTOMER.

Notice that the linking field is marked as R/O (Read Only). To make the field available for editing, place the cursor on the field in the view skeleton and press F8.

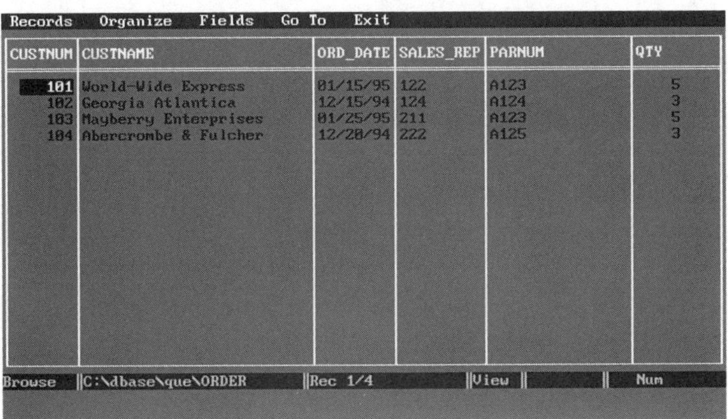

Fig. 15.8
The output of the query shown in figure 15.7.

After you set up the query properly, you can test the relational aspects of the database system from the Query design screen and make changes as necessary. When you are confident that the query ties the databases together properly, you can save the query and use it later to create forms and reports for the relational database system.

Additional database files can be added to the query and linked to the other databases as needed. Figure 15.9 shows a query for the three databases, ORDERS, CUSTOMER, and INVENTRY, and figure 15.10 shows the output.

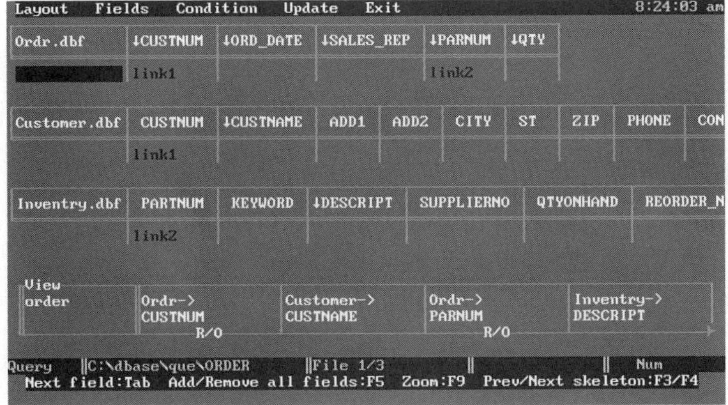

Fig. 15.9
A query that relates three databases.

◄ See "Sorting Query Output," p. 231

◄ See "Indexing Query Output," p. 230

You can add sorts or indexes to a query for a relational database system just as you can for a single-database query. You can sort on any field present in the view skeleton. This would let you present the view sorted on CUST_NAME, for example.

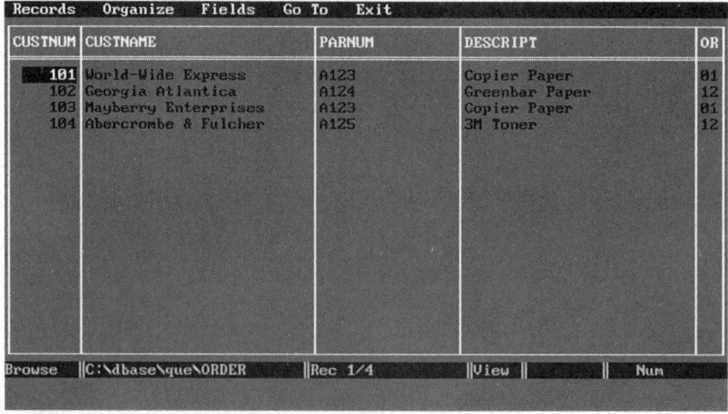

Fig. 15.10
The output of the query relating three databases.

Creating Forms for Relational Databases

Forms for relational databases are created just like forms for single database files, with one exception. The query that links the database files must be in use when a form is created. The query tells dBASE what fields from each database to make available to the form. Figure 15.11 shows the list of fields that are available to create a form for order information. Notice that the list of field names includes fields that are in CUSTOMER, ORDERS, and INVENTRY.

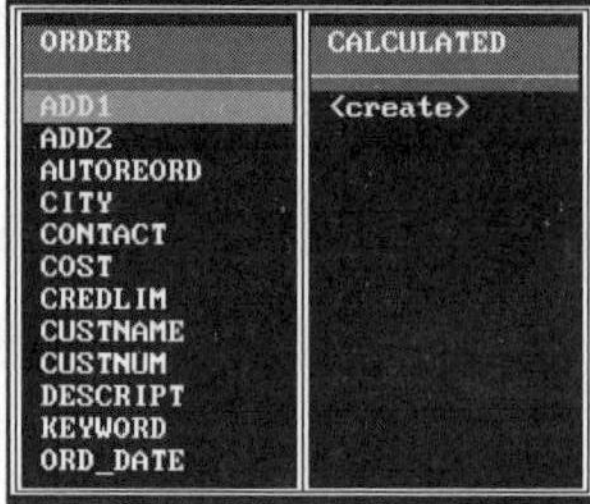

Fig. 15.11
The list of fields available in a relational database system.

Unlike forms that are created for single-file systems, forms created for multiple-file, related systems can't be used to add or delete records. They can only be used to edit records.

The completed form for the relational database system is shown in figure 15.12. Notice that the form contains the CUSTNAME field. This field provides data validation for the customer number. Remember that the CUST_NUM retrieves the customer's name from the CUSTOMER database. If the wrong name is displayed, you know you have entered the wrong number.

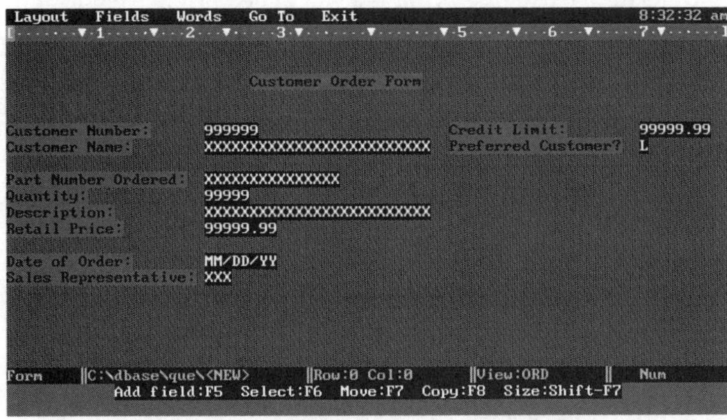

Fig. 15.12
A form that can be used to edit data in a relational system.

When using a lookup field (like CUSTNAME), you must decide whether the field should be available for editing. When data is changed in a lookup field, the changes are passed back to the original database. Consider the following example: You enter a customer number, the customer name is retrieved, and you notice that the name is misspelled. Do you want to be able to correct the spelling? Your immediate answer to this question is probably, "Of course I do!" But the question is like a two-edged sword. What if the name isn't spelled incorrectly, but the user accidentally makes an entry in the field that causes the name to be misspelled. If the error goes uncorrected, then the name will be changed in the CUSTOMER database to the incorrect entry.

When designing a form, you can control the editing of a lookup field with the Edit options. Place the cursor on the field and press F5. Choose Edit options and Editing allowed, YES or NO.

Note

Because linking fields are marked as Read Only in a query, these fields won't be available for editing in the form even if the Edit options are changed to Editing Allowed YES. To make a linking field editable, remove the Read Only marking in the query form as described earlier in this chapter.

Creating Reports for Relational Databases

Reports for relational database systems are designed just like reports for single-file databases. Before designing a report for related databases, however, you must use the query that relates the databases. As in the case of designing a form, dBASE must have some way to know what fields should be made available in the Reports design screen.

Figure 15.13 shows the list of fields available to create a form for the Sales model. Notice that the list of field names includes fields from the CUSTOMER, ORDERS, and INVENTRY database files. Figure 15.14 shows a completed report that would be used as a printed invoice.

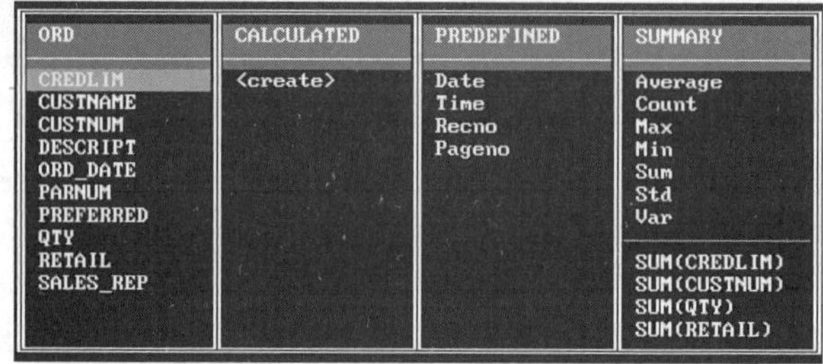

Fig. 15.13
Fields from linked databases available in a report.

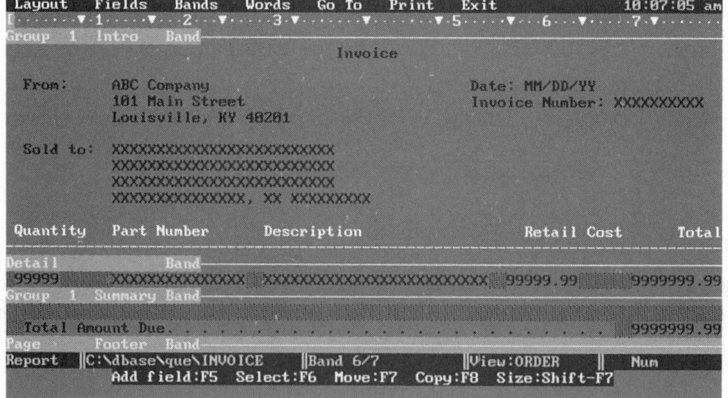

Fig. 15.14
A completed report form for linked databases used as an invoice.

Note

Remember that calculated, predefined, and summary fields can be used in a report for a relational system in the same way that they are used in reports for single-file systems.

```
                              Invoice
 From:    ABC Company                            Date: 11/25/94
          101 Main Street                        Invoice Number: 120001995A

          Louisville, KY 40201

 Sold to: Mayberry Enterprises
          3434 Mayberry Way
          Mayberry, NC

Quantity  Part Number     Description                 Retail Cost      Total
--------------------------------------------------------------------------------
    5     A123            Copier Paper                  32.95         164.75
    4     A124            Greenbar Paper                17.95          71.80

 Total Amount Due. . . . . . . . . . . . . . . . . . . . . . . .       236.55

              Cancel viewing: ESC,  Continue viewing: SPACEBAR
```

Fig. 15.15 Results of the report when it is run against the linked databases.

Figure 15.15 shows the results of the report. The report does not use any of the following bands: Report Intro, Page Header, Report Summary, or Page Footer. The Group band groups on the INV_NO field that must be sorted in the query show the relationship of the three databases. The Group Intro band has the following settings:

Group intro on each page YES

Begin band on new page YES

Word wrap band YES

The Group Intro band is repeated on each page and each group starts on a new page so that each group of records for the same invoice number will be printed on a separate page as a separate invoice. The word wrap is turned on so that dBASE will eliminate empty fields (like ADD2) from the form and print fields without trailing spaces.

The Detail band prints the following fields: QTY, PARNUM, DESCRIP, RETAIL, and EXT. The EXT field is a calculated field with the expression QTY*RETAIL. The Group Summary band prints the grand total of the invoice with a summary field called GRANDTOT. The GRANDTOT field summarizes on the calculated field called EXT.

Note

You could also add a calculated field to the Report Summary band of this report to compute the tax due. For a 7% sales tax, the expression for the TAX field would be GRANDTOT*.07. The GRANDTOT field would no longer appear on the form. It would only be used to compute the tax and the total with tax. A new calculated field would have to be added to the Report Summary band that adds TAX to GRANDTOT field.

Troubleshooting

I have a field that does not let me make changes. I have changed the Edit Options to allow editing, but it still does not let me edit the field.

The field must be a linking field. Change the field in the query that links the databases so it is not Read Only by pressing F8 on the field.

I have linked two databases and want to create a form for editing. When I press F5 to place a field, I see that some of the fields that I want are not in the list.

Go back to the query that relates the databases and add the missing fields to the View Skeleton by pressing F5. Save the query again.

From Here...

This chapter is the capstone of what you can do with dBASE if you have no background in programming or have no desire to become a programmer. You can sharpen your skills by reviewing Chapters 23 and 24 in Part VI, the Reference Guide. If you are interested in programming, the following chapters will provide the information you need in this area:

- Chapter 16, "Getting Started with Programming." This chapter introduces the basic steps in dBASE language programming.

- Chapter 17, "Exploring Some Sample Programs." This chapter expands your knowledge of programming by providing documented examples.

- Chapter 18, "Creating Custom Applications." In this chapter you learn to use basic procedures for creating a complete application that uses dBASE programs to create menus, reports, forms, and so on.

- Chapter 19, "Using the Applications Generator and the Compiler." This chapter shows you how to use dBASE's Application Generator to automate the process of creating custom applications.

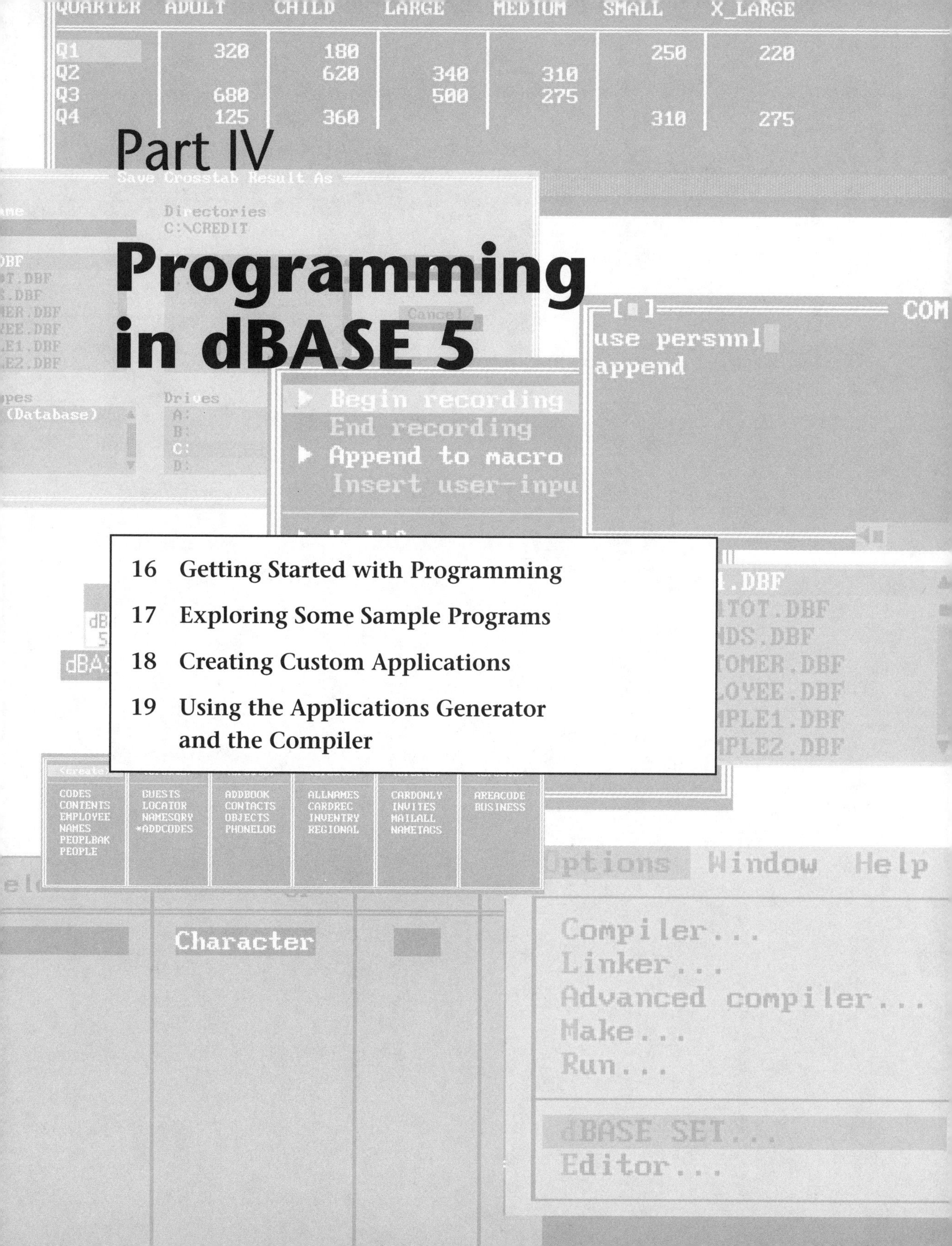

Part IV

Programming in dBASE 5

16 Getting Started with Programming

17 Exploring Some Sample Programs

18 Creating Custom Applications

19 Using the Applications Generator and the Compiler

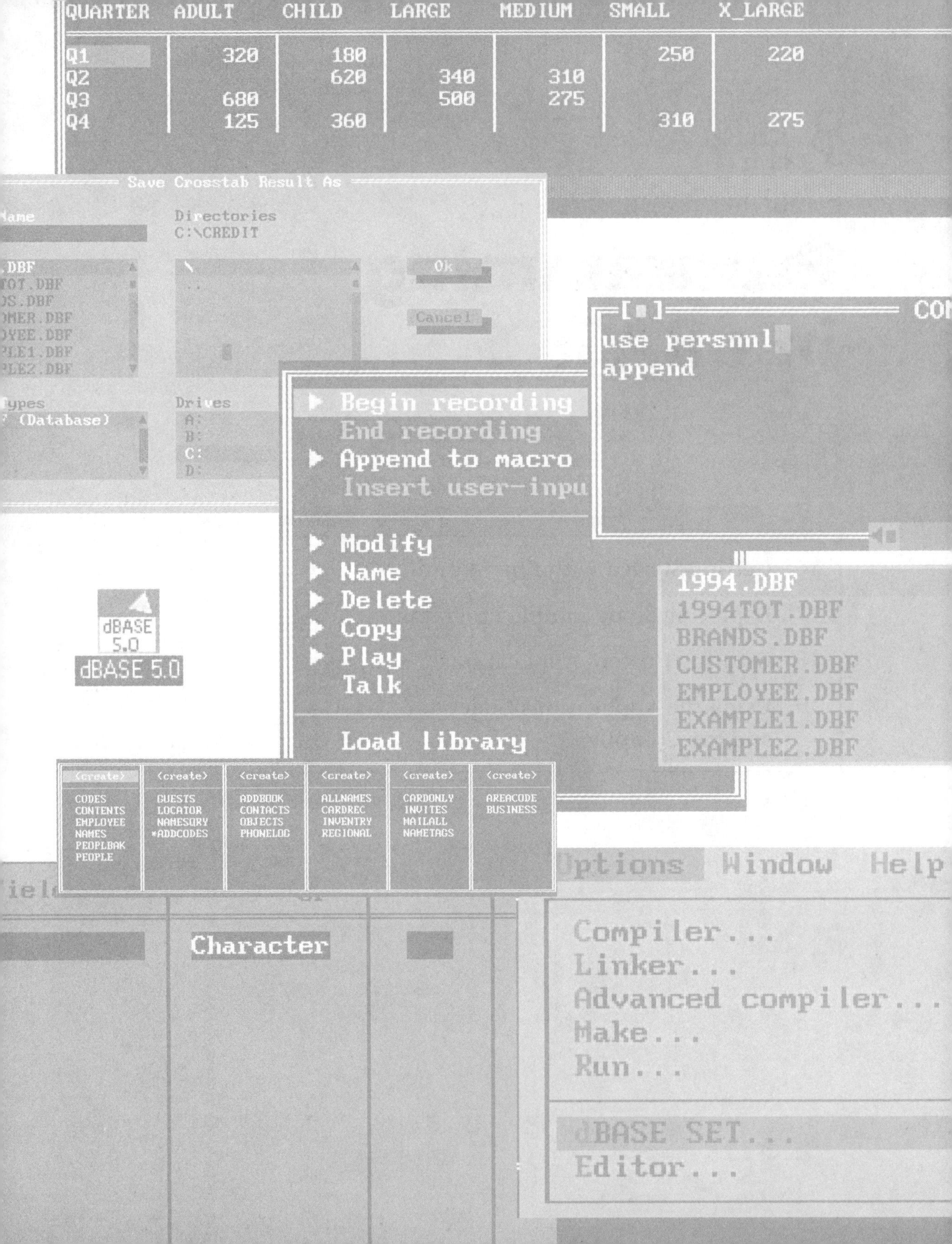

QUARTER ADULT CHILD LARGE MEDIUM SMALL X_LARGE
Q1 320 180 250 220
Q2 620 340 310
Q3 680 500 275
Q4 125 360 310 275
Save Crosstab Result As
Directories
C:\CREDIT
Ok
Cancel
Drives
A:
B:
C:
D:
(Database)
use persnnl
append
Begin recording
End recording
Append to macro
Modify
Name
Delete
Copy
Play
Talk
Load library
1994.DBF
1994TOT.DBF
BRANDS.DBF
CUSTOMER.DBF
EMPLOYEE.DBF
EXAMPLE1.DBF
EXAMPLE2.DBF
dBASE 5.0
dBASE 5.0
<create>
CODES
CONTENTS
EMPLOYEE
NAMES
PEOPLBAK
PEOPLE
<create>
GUESTS
LOCATOR
NAMESQRY
*ADDCODES
<create>
ADDBOOK
CONTACTS
OBJECTS
PHONELOG
<create>
ALLNAMES
CARDREC
INVENTRY
REGIONAL
<create>
CARDONLY
INVITES
MAILALL
NAMETAGS
<create>
AREACODE
BUSINESS
Window
Help
Character
Compiler...
Linker...
Advanced compiler...
Make...
Run...
dBASE SET...
Editor...

Chapter 16

Getting Started with Programming

Now that you have spent some time exploring the dBASE 5 Desktop and Control Center and the various ways you can use dBASE 5 as an ad hoc database management system, you are ready to dig into the real power of the program. This power is hidden behind front ends, such as the Control Center, automatic screen, report and label generators, and the Applications Generator. But to control and manipulate the power of dBASE 5, you need to learn a bit about programming and the dBASE language.

You can use the programming tools in dBASE 5 in two ways. The first is to fine-tune applications, reports, screens, and labels created by the automatic programming features. The second is to create your own applications. The next few chapters explore both methods, and also scratch the surface of the Applications Generator and the SQL commands available with dBASE 5. Before you get too involved in the details, however, you learn the answers to a few basic questions about programming in general and dBASE 5 command programming in particular.

In this chapter you learn the basics of programming using dBASE 5. Specifically, you learn how to:

- Use commands and functions
- Use the built-in editor
- Debug programs
- Compile a program
- Document a program

Realizing the Benefits of Writing Programs

Many users find that they can use the Control Center to do everything they want to do with a database. The Control Center is an improvement over its predecessor, the Assistant. You can do just so much, however, from a structured set of menus that allow you to execute only one command at a time. Writing your own database applications is much more efficient. When you have a repetitive task to perform, such as accounting, customer maintenance, or inventory control, you do not need to perform the task one step at a time from the Control Center.

Among high-level programming languages for data manipulation purposes, dBASE is the most popular. What that means to you, as a future dBASE application developer, is that you have in dBASE 5 all the power of a "real" programming language like C or Pascal, along with a comprehensive toolbox of commands and functions designed for use in a database environment.

Automating your database processes by writing applications is the natural next step after you become comfortable with the Control Center and, perhaps, the Applications Generator. Before you start the programming process, however, you need to develop a programming frame of mind. When you develop an application, you need to think a little differently than when you work from the Control Center.

When you work from the Control Center, you perform each step as you need it. For example, you set up your database and enter data. Then you query it, write a report, or print labels. There are, however, some elements you cannot do automatically. You cannot make repeated similar queries without entering the whole query over and over again. You cannot automatically use the results of one query to formulate the next. In short, you must perform every step, one step at a time, manually. And to repeat the same steps with different data, you must start all over again.

Practicing Good Programming Techniques

When you write a program, you should think in terms of just two things: tasks and data. *Tasks* are those functions you want the program to perform, and *data* is the information you need to give to, and get from, the program.

When you think of tasks as they apply to your application, you need to break them down into individual actions that, together, make up the task. The smaller and more independent you can make those actions, the more smoothly your tasks (and, therefore, your application) will flow. This technique is called *structured programming*, and the individual actions are called *program modules*. An alternative technique, *object-oriented programming*, will be discussed in later chapters.

Note

It's a good practice to write the tasks down as a statement: "The program shall..." These statements form a top-level requirement for your program that can be reviewed by the end-user.

Good programmers view a total application as a large task composed of several smaller tasks, which are made up of program modules. These modules are, in turn, broken up into program segments called *procedures*. As you progress from the largest task to the smallest module, you progress from the general to the specific.

For example, think through an accounting program. An accounting program keeps track of cash receipts and expenditures. That's the big picture. You can break down the function of the program into two broad tasks: keeping track of money coming in, and keeping track of money going out. Each of those tasks breaks down further. Keeping track of money coming in, for example, may include keeping track of cash sales, accounts receivable (money owed to you), and money paid against receivables.

Keeping track of money going out may break down into cash outlays (petty cash), credit purchases (accounts payable), and cash payments on credit purchases. Other tasks may include keeping track of sales taxes collected and paid, payroll, interest charged and paid, and many other accounting tasks. Each of those individual tasks must be programmed as a single module, designed to do one thing and one thing only. When the program needs to perform that particular task, it calls the module. In a dBASE language program, each of those modules, if created correctly, is a single program file with the file extension PRG.

To simplify the creation of program modules, you can build a library of procedures. Procedures are program fragments that do a particular thing, such as calculate the interest on a loan. When you want a module to perform that calculation, you can direct it to use the procedure, instead of writing new code within the module to perform the calculation. That way, no matter how many times the program must calculate loan interest, you write the code only once.

This kind of programming has three benefits:

- Writing the program takes less time
- The program code is shorter
- The program runs faster

When you plan a program, you follow this top-down approach by creating a cascading series of PRG files. The first file generally carries the name of your application. If you call your accounting program dAccount, for example, your top module is named DACCOUNT.PRG. DACCOUNT.PRG can display a Welcome screen, perform some type of security tasks if you want to make sure that the user is authorized to use the accounting system, or perform other general start-up tasks. Then your top module can start the next module, which usually presents some type of main menu.

Depending on how you create your menu system, the second module probably presents the screen that you return to, whenever your program completes a task. When you make a menu selection from this main work surface, you actually move down the tree to the program module that performs the task you select.

If you choose to work on accounts receivable, for example, you can make that selection from your main menu or work surface. In all probability, because a number of smaller tasks, or *subtasks*, come under the general heading of accounts receivable, the module invoked by your selection presents another work surface or menu with choices that relate to only accounts receivable. When you select a task from this second work surface, you go one more level down the tree and select a module that performs the specific accounts receivable task you want.

How you display these choices is up to you. With dBASE 5, you have a variety of menu types that enable you to create custom work surfaces. You can use a very simple box menu with numbered selections, or you can go up a step and add a bar menu. If you really want a nice screen, you can build a desktop menu with selections across the top of your screen, each of which can "drop down" bar menus for subtasks. No matter how you choose to present your application, the menu choices you create are used to invoke a module you design to perform that single function, and no more.

Note

Remember, when you plan your application, start with the big picture and progress to the specific. Never let a single module perform more than one task, and make sure that all modules return to the work surface when they have finished their respective tasks. Your program then will operate in an orderly manner in which modules execute and then complete themselves, leaving nothing hanging to come back and disrupt the program later. You move from a central point to a task and back again.

Many years ago, a bright entrepreneur wrote a college thesis. His theory was that an air freight company which sent all its planes out from a central point each evening to all of the cities in North America, picked up freight, and returned to the central point where the freight was redistributed and sent to its destination, can operate more smoothly and economically than one that tried to go point to point. No one agreed with the thesis, because the method of the day was to route freight from shipping city to receiving city directly. "No," the entrepreneur said. "That causes too much redundancy in shipping routes and too many chances to lose packages." The result of that thesis was Federal Express, one of today's largest and most efficient freight companies.

Writing dBASE programs is similar to shipping via Federal Express. You must always work from a central module in your program, and always return to that module. The main module can do two things. First, it can route the user to the module that performs the task the user wants performed. Second, it can clean up after the user by clearing memory variables, closing databases, and performing other housekeeping functions. This cleanup ensures that when the user makes the next menu choice, all the data is ready for use, and only the required files are open. Without housekeeping and logical routing of your program flow, you risk losing or corrupting data; and, you create situations in which you could lock up the computer in program nightmares, such as endless loops.

Tip

As you write each module of your program, run it to check for problems. See the "Debugging Programs" section later in this chapter for more information.

A couple of situations exist in which you would not, in all probability, generate program code from scratch: when you want to modify older dBASE programs to take advantage of increased functionality in dBASE 5; and when you want to tweak (modify and enhance) dBASE 5 code created by the Applications Generator or other automated processes, such as automatic report generation.

▶ See "Changing the Applications Generator Code," p. 555

In the first case, although you can use much of what you generate with dBASE III Plus (and virtually all of what you generate using versions of dBASE IV), you may find that you want to redesign many of your modules to get the full benefit of new features in the later releases. Even with dBASE 5 code generated by the Applications Generator, you discover that in many ways you can improve on the generated code to increase execution speed and improve the looks of your application. The Applications Generator, however, is a great way to create the bulk of your application, after which you can do the fine-tuning.

Using Commands and Functions

Tip
The Command window accepts any command line that you can enter at the dot prompt in any previous version of dBASE.

Now that you have a better understanding of the benefits of writing a dBASE 5 program, you can begin to write command lines in the Command window. The fundamental building blocks of dBASE 5 programming are fields, variables, commands, and functions.

Fields from your data tables are thoroughly covered in previous chapters. Variables are simply names for locations in the computer memory for storing values.

Taking Action with Commands

Commands cause an action to occur. They do something; they tell the program flow to change, or they manipulate data directly. Some frequently used commands are listed in Table 16.1.

Table 16.1 Common Commands

Command	Purpose
DO	Executes another program module
GO	Takes you to a specific record number
USE	Tells dBASE 5 to open a database and go to the first record
SAVE	Saves data to special files
SKIP	Moves pointer to a different record in the data table
STORE	Puts information in memory variables
WAIT	Pauses execution of your program

These are commands; they implement a direct action. Two of the more important actions performed by dBASE 5 commands—program flow control and program data control—tend to be confusing.

Commands for program flow control are among the things that can make dBASE 5 programs more powerful than the Control Center. Program flow commands tell the program where to go next in its execution. Remember that a program works by executing the commands you give it, one at a time. The program executes the first command, then the second, and so on. The program cannot back up, go to another module, or make a decision unless you give the program a command to interrupt its linear flow and do something else. Those commands that tell your program to "do something else" are called *program flow commands.*

Several of the program flow commands serve to break your code into blocks. These commands have a statement to start the block and another to end or close the block. These commands are listed in Table 16.2.

Table 16.2 Flow Control Commands Requiring End Statements

Start Block	End Block
DO CASE	ENDCASE
DO WHILE	ENDDO
FOR	ENDFOR or NEXT
IF	ENDIF
PRINTJOB	ENDPRINTJOB
SCAN	ENDSCAN

Tip
To enhance the readability and the traceability of your code, indent the code in each block several spaces from the code preceding or following it. The offset gives a visual indication of a flow change.

For example, when you use the condition command IF, you must use ENDIF at the end of the code string involved, as follows:

```
IF <memvar1> = 0
     ? <memvar2>
     USE <database>
     LOCATE FOR <field1>=<memvar2>
     DO <otherpgm>
ENDIF
```

If the condition *<memvar1>* = 0 is true, the next lines of code perform their actions: displaying another memory variable, opening a database, going to the first record, and locating the record that contains the contents of the second variable in the field named *<field1>*. Then your program executes another module, *<otherpgm>*.

The compiler checks for matched begin and end block statements. If it does not find the correct ending for each block, it reports the error in a window. The compiler attempts to determine where it thinks the missing end command is. However, because a failure to close a block puts the rest of your code in that block, the compiler may point to the end of file.

Note

If you write a loop with a condition that can never be false, you can create an "infinite loop" in your program. Be sure that you do not SET ESCAPE OFF, so that you can exit your program if this error occurs. If SET ESCAPE is OFF, the only way to exit an infinite loop is to reboot the system. See the section "Setting Up the Environment" in Chapter 17.

Notice the command DO *<otherpgm>*. This command sends the program off to execute another module (*otherpgm*). The example is a dual example of program flow control. The first instance of flow control is the use of the IF command. The program either executes the commands between IF and ENDIF or it doesn't, depending on whether the IF condition is met. The second example of program flow control is the DO command. The program departs from the linear execution of commands and moves processing to a completely different module.

Unlike the flow control commands, *program data control commands* deal strictly with data. These commands have nothing to do with the way the program executes. They relate to databases, memory variables, and other types of data used by your program.

An example of this type of command is the STORE command. When you use STORE *<value>* TO *<memvar>*, you place data (*value*) in a memory variable (*memvar*) for subsequent use. This command has nothing to do with the order in which other commands are executed. It deals with data only. This command is equivalent to *<memvar>=<value>*.

Getting Results with Functions

Functions are much different. They also perform actions, but they do it differently from commands. Functions always perform their task and return a result. You can spot a function by the presence of two parentheses as part of the function name. Between the parentheses is the object on which the function operates. With certain functions, you put nothing between the parentheses. In such cases, the object is predetermined by the function itself.

Several kinds of functions exist, generally grouped by task. Some of these include functions for operating on text strings or for converting data from one type to another, such as converting dates to character data. Some functions manipulate numbers. Some functions, such as DATE( ), simply return a system or program variable and don't operate on anything. The function DATE( ) returns the system date. If you want to store the system date in a memory variable called *Today*, you can use the STORE command and the DATE( ) function as follows:

```
STORE DATE( ) TO Today
```

A simpler way to assign the value to a variable is to use the equal sign, as follows:

```
Today = DATE( )
```

If you prefer to use the date as text, add the Date-to-Character function, DTOC( ), to change the date to a character type. In the example that follows, dBASE 5 stores the result in a new memory variable called *Today1*. Notice that you can *nest*, or *embed*, one function inside another:

```
Today1 = DTOC(DATE( ))
```

To sum up simply, commands cause some type of program execution or data flow control; functions act directly on data and return a result you can use in your program.

By combining commands and functions, your program generates the results you are looking for. Nesting of commands and functions is a powerful way of managing and manipulating your database applications to generate reports, organize information, and improve your user's productivity.

Controlling Programs with Preprocessing Directives

Sometimes you want to write your program so that portions of the code aren't compiled and executed. For instance, while working on your program, you can include certain debugging code to simplify locating errors, but once the program is finished, those sections of code are no longer needed for the execution. To make your program run faster and cleaner, you turn off the debug routines. The easiest way to do this is to use *preprocessing directives*, which are sometimes referred to as *compiler directives*. The directives dBASE 5 uses are listed in Table 16.3.

Table 16.3 Preprocessing Directives dBASE 5 Supports

Directive	Purpose
#define	Creates a preprocessor macro (a name) and optionally associates it with code or with a value
#undef	Releases a preprocessor macro name previously defined with #define
#if	Controls conditional compilation of commands
#ifndef	Controls conditional compilation of code based on whether a preprocessor macro is defined—the #ifndef condition is true if the macro isn't defined
#ifdef	Controls conditional compilation of code based on the definition of a preprocessor macro
#else	Specifies a block of commands that is compiled only if the associated #ifdef or #if *<condition>* is false
#elif	Combination of #else and #if that is evaluated only if the #ifdef or #if statement is false
#endif	Associated with #if to close processing loop
#include	Inserts contents of *<filename>* into the current file at the location of the #include statement

You can use directives to define preprocessor *macros* that apply a name to any constant value or to a set of instructions, allowing you to simplify your code or set up a condition for testing. Conditional compilation allows you to compile portions of your code and test the conditions you've defined. Directives also allow you to put code or a set of preprocessor macro definitions into an individual file, and then incorporate that file (using #include) in each source file that uses the code or the macro definitions.

Preprocessor directives are statements you can write into your code which instruct the compiler how to compile the code. A directive starts with a number sign (#) and is usually entered in lowercase letters, though you can use uppercase if preferred. The # character can be preceded by spaces, but the directive is limited to 1,024 characters. Preprocessor directives can be nested up to 32 levels, giving you further control over how the compiler handles the different sections of your program code.

Note

Compiler directives can be made extremely complex by using already defined macros in a macro definition.

As you compile your program, the preprocessor looks through your program searching for preprocessor directives. It then expands any macros you define using the #define directive, includes any text from files that you specify using the #include directive, retains any source code you mark for compilation, and ignores any code you mark to skip during this compilation. The preprocessor creates an intermediate source file (with a DPP extension) where it writes the preprocessed code; and, then dBASE 5 compiles it into an object file, and deletes the intermediate file on completion.

Conditional compilation is used most often when you debug a program or when you write code to be used on two different platforms (DOS and UNIX, for instance). When debugging your program, you can compile the part of your code that works. You can test for whether a preprocessor macro you define as DEBUG is *not* defined. If it is defined, the code doesn't compile; but if it's not defined, the code compiles. When compiling your program, you set the preprocessor to ignore or to compile code by either defining or not defining DEBUG:

```
#ifndef DEBUG
*code you don't want to compile if DEBUG is defined
#endif
```

When writing code for two different platforms, say UNIX and DOS, you can define two sets of code for the definition of the main menu, depending on which platform the code is being compiled. You write one PRG file as a central base for the code containing both procedures. When you compile the code, you define the operating system directive which tells the compiler to compile UNIX and ignore the DOS-specific procedures.

If you want to include a file in your program, use the #include directive. This file can contain dBASE 5 code or preprocessor statements or both. You can apply a set of #define statements to a source file, for instance. By putting related #define statements in a single file, you can use #include to insert these #defines in every source file that needs them, saving you from putting all your #define statements in every source file of your program.

For example, you can put #define statements into a file; then, at the beginning of each source file that needs those #define statements, you simply enter an #include statement, such as:

```
#include "Mydefs.h"
```

If you must change any of the #define statements, simply change the definition in "Mydefs.h," and after recompiling, all your source files with the #include "Mydefs.h" statement use the changed definition.

Be careful, though, in using these directives. You can inadvertently change all the macros in an include file by including several include files in one file. For instance, if one include file contains another include file, it's possible you can include both of them in one source file. You don't want to do this; so to avoid accidentally changing your macros, use the #ifndef and #define in each of the include files to control whether the macros get defined.

The code you can use in each include file can look something like this:

```
#ifndef _THIS_H_FILE
    #define _THIS_H_FILE
... && all your defines
#endif
```

In this example, which is the first time your include file is included in the current file, _THIS_H_FILE is defined. The next time the same include file is included, if at all, #ifndef _THIS_H_FILE will be false, and the #defines aren't executed.

Tip
Preprocessor macros have no memory overhead, so you can make unlimited use of them to define constants instead of using memory variables. This reduces your memory variable count.

The #define directive allows you to associate names with code or text in order to ensure your source code is more readable. This also allows you to assign descriptive names to your constants. Naming your constants makes your code more readable; and, if the value of a constant changes, the name allows you to change only the definition of the constant and not every occurrence of it. Once you've assigned a name to your macro, define the text string that replaces it, then the preprocessor replaces all occurrences of the macro it encounters with your defined text string.

The syntax for a #define directive is:

```
#define <macro name>[(<parameter list>)][<macro expression>[(<parameter list>)]]
```

where the *<macro name>* is one you choose. The *<macro expression>* is text you indicate for replacing the *<macro name>*, and the *<parameter list>* contains parameter names that can be used as arguments for a function. Nesting macros allows you to define one macro, then use that definition in subsequent macros.

If you want to reuse a previously defined macro, use #undef <*macro name*> to release the name, then use #def to create a new definition.

The #if directive is used to conditionally compile specified blocks of code. When the #if statement returns a true value, the preprocessor includes the associated block of commands, defined by a #if statement at the start of the block, until it finds a #elif, #else, or #endif statement. If the #if statement is false, the associated block is ignored.

Syntax for using the #if statement is

```
#if <condition>
     <commands>
[[#elif <condition>
     <commands>]/
[#else
     <commands>]]
#endif
```

where <*commands*> is any series of dBASE 5 statements, preprocessor statements, or both; and, <*condition*> is any logical expression using preprocessor macros you define which bring back either a true or false value. The condition can use any of the customary relational, logical, or mathematical operators, such as AND, OR, NOT, (), =, < >, +, /, *. The only exceptions are the substring comparison operator ($) and the exponentiation operator (^), neither of which can be used in the <*condition*> string.

Only one #else or #elif statement can be used with each #if statement. The code within a block of commands set off by #else or #elif is only compiled if the associated #if <*condition*> is false.

Note

Remember to close the conditional directive statements (#if..#elif/#else...#endif) the same as you close any IF command.

The #ifdef directive is used to conditionally compile blocks of code depending on if you define a preprocessor macro. This directive has the opposite result of #ifndef because if the macro is defined, the #ifdef statement compiles the block of code specified. If the #ifdef statement is false, the block of code is not compiled, and the #else and #elif statements act the same as they do in the #if and #ifndef statements.

The syntax for using #ifdef is

```
#ifdef <macro name>
     <commands>
[[#elif <condition>
     <commands>]/
[#else
     <commands>]]
#endif
```

The same rules apply for using the #ifdef statement as for the preceding #if statement.

Using preprocessor directives can seem a bit confusing at first, but you get the hang of it pretty quickly once you realize they are basically the same as any other programming commands, just more specific and exclusive. Their power comes from the ability they give you in programming for more than one situation at a time. This increases your efficiency as a programmer.

Troubleshooting

How do I determine which of my blocks is closed?

Using the preceding indentation method of coding simplifies the process of finding missing block end statements. For blocks that are deeply nested and span several pages, it's useful to print the code (preferably on fanfold paper). You can then use a pen to connect each block starting command with its matching block end command, starting from the innermost block. None of your lines should cross each other.

There are no compile errors, but my program does nothing.

The compiler does not check for block closure on preprocessor directives. If you define a macro, *<macroname>*, and then start a #ifndef *<macroname>* block, the compiler doesn't see the rest of your program. Be sure to match beginning and ending block statements.

Entering Code

There are three ways for you to write and edit your dBASE 5 code:

- You can use any ASCII text editor (or any word processor that features an option to save ASCII text files, sometimes simply called *DOS text files*).

- You can use the built-in program editor.
- You can use the file viewer.

The benefit of the program editor or the file viewer, at least for beginners, is that you can easily write your code, compile it, run it, and debug it without ever leaving dBASE 5. Each of these methods is discussed in the sections that follow.

Using the Desktop Editor To Enter Code

Before you can use the Desktop Editor, shown in figure 16.1, you need to have a program, some text, or an untitled file open on the Desktop. Open the **F**ile menu and choose **O**pen. Next, select the desired program or text file, then choose **M**odify to open it. Alternatively, **O**pen the **F**ile menu and choose **N**ew to open a new file. The next step is to begin typing. It's that easy.

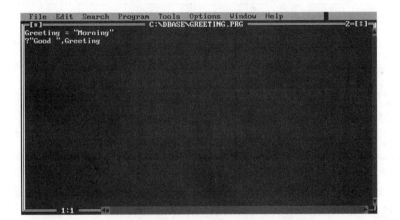

Fig. 16.1 The Desktop Editor.

> **Caution**
>
> The Desktop Editor doesn't allow you to save changes to DBF records. Editing other binary files, such as an executable (EXE) or object file, can result in data loss or corruption if invalid changes are saved.

Tip
Open the **W**indow menu and choose **L**ist All to select any currently open file to edit.

Navigating the Edit Window

Getting around inside either the program editor or the Desktop Editor is much like getting around inside your favorite word processing package. Specific commands help you travel from line to line and word to word quickly. Many of these, shown in Table 16.4, may even look familiar.

Table 16.4 Cursor Movement Keys in the Desktop Editor

Action	Keystrokes	Alternate
Character left	Left arrow	Ctrl-S
Character right	Right arrow	Ctrl-D
Word left	Ctrl-Left arrow	Ctrl-A
Word right	Ctrl-Right arrow	Ctrl-F
Line up	Up arrow	Ctrl-E
Line down	Down arrow	Ctrl-X
Page up	PgUp	Ctrl-R
Page down	PgDown	Ctrl-C
Beginning of line	Home	
End of line	End	
Top of file	Ctrl-PgUp	
Bottom of file	Ctrl-PgDn	

To jump to a specific line number within your file, open the **S**earch menu and choose **G**o to Line Number; or press Alt-G. The Go To Line dialog box appears where you can enter the line number you want to jump to. If you choose a line number that is greater than the number of lines in your file, the Editor presents an Error box that warns you that the value must not be greater than the last line number. Choose OK and try again.

Inserting and Replacing Text

To insert text into previously typed text, position your cursor where the new text is to be entered. Be sure that you are in Insert mode before typing. The Insert key is a toggle switch that turns on insert/turns off overstrike, or turns off insert/turns on overstrike.

Selecting Text

You can select text in increments of a character at a time to hundreds of lines of text. In the Desktop Editor, you can use the keyboard to select by holding down *Shift* while using the arrow keys to move the highlighting to the end of the desired block, as described in Table 16.5.

You can use your mouse to ease this process. Position the mouse cursor at the beginning of the block of text, press and hold down the mouse button, and drag to extend the highlighting to include all of the text you want to select. Once your text is selected, you can cut, paste, insert, delete, or copy it.

Table 16.5 Selecting Text Blocks in the Desktop Editor

Action	Keystrokes
Left one character	Shift-Left arrow
Right one character	Shift-Right arrow
End of line	Shift-End
Beginning of line	Shift-Home
Same column next line	Shift-Down arrow
Same column previous line	Shift-Up arrow
One page down	Shift-PgDn
One page up	Shift-PgUp
Left one word	Shift-Ctrl-Left arrow
Right one word	Shift-Ctrl-Right arrow
End of file	Shift-Ctrl-End
Beginning of file	Shift-Ctrl-Home

Deleting Text

To delete text, select the desired block and then press Delete. You can also use the menu options by opening the **E**dit menu and choosing C**l**ear; or type Alt-E, then L as another shortcut. To delete single characters, position your cursor on the character and press Delete.

Copying and Moving Text

To duplicate a block of text, you actually need to do two things: copy and paste. To copy the text within a window or into a different window:

1. Highlight the block of text you want to copy.
2. Open the **E**dit menu and choose **C**opy; or press Ctrl-Ins. The text block is copied to the dBASE Clipboard and remains selected there.
3. Position the cursor where you want the block copied to, whether within the current window or a new one.
4. Open the **E**dit menu and choose **P**aste; or press Shift-Ins. The text block appears after the cursor location.

Moving text is very similar to copying it, but you use cut instead of copy. To move a desired text block,

1. Highlight the block of text you want to move.
2. Open the **E**dit menu and choose Cu**t**; or press Shift-Del. The text block is moved to the dBASE Clipboard and remains highlighted there.
3. Position the cursor where you want the text block to appear, either in the current window or a different one.
4. Open the **E**dit menu and choose **P**aste; or press Shift-Ins.

Undoing Changes

Oops! You didn't mean to do that? Choose **E**dit, **U**ndo to cancel your last change. This restores the file in the active window to the way it appeared before your last edit or cursor movement.

Searching and Replacing Text

Using search and replace in the Desktop Editor is like using the same features in your favorite text editor. Those features, like search and replace, only work on the active window's contents. To begin, choose **S**earch, Find to find a given text string or code; or, choose **S**earch, **R**eplace to find and replace a given text string or code with a new one.

You have several options from which to choose. **C**ase Sensitive allows you to tell dBASE 5 to distinguish between uppercase and lowercase. The **W**hole Words Only option ensures that dBASE 5 searches for whole words or partial words, depending on which way you toggle it. For example, you can search on the word "state." If **W**hole Words Only isn't selected, dBASE 5 may find "statement," "understated," and other parts of words containing the same spelling. You can also choose to have dBASE 5 **P**rompt On Replace if you are doing a Search, Replace. This allows you to verify the action before it occurs.

To Find text, do the following:

1. Open the **S**earch menu and choose **F**ind. The Find dialog box appears, as shown in figure 16.2.

2. Enter the text string you want to find. The history list shows you text for which you previously searched.

3. Select the **C**ase sensitive and/or **W**hole Words Only check boxes if desired.

4. Choose **O**K to begin the search.

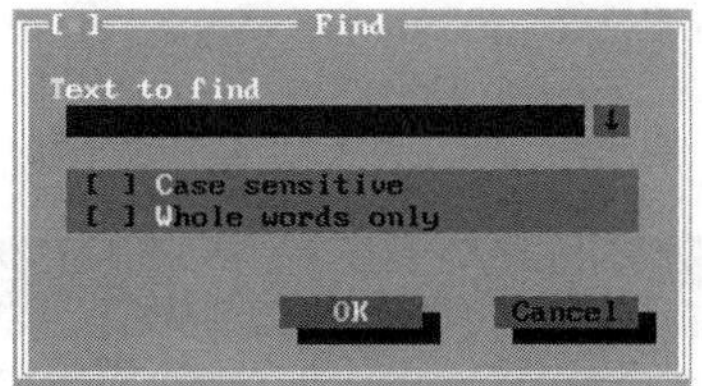

Fig. 16.2
The Find dialog box.

To look for another occurrence of this text string, choose **S**earch again; or press Ctrl-L. The previous Find settings remain in effect for subsequent searches.

To Replace text, follow these simple steps:

1. Open the **S**earch menu and choose **R**eplace. The Replace dialog box appears, as shown in figure 16.3.

2. Enter the text string you want to find. In the **T**ext to Find input box, the history list shows you text you previously searched for.

3. Enter the text you want to put in its place in the **N**ew Text input box. A history list shows previous replacement text, if any.

4. Choose appropriate options, including whether you want dBASE 5 to prompt you before replacing text.

5. Choose **O**K to begin search and replace.

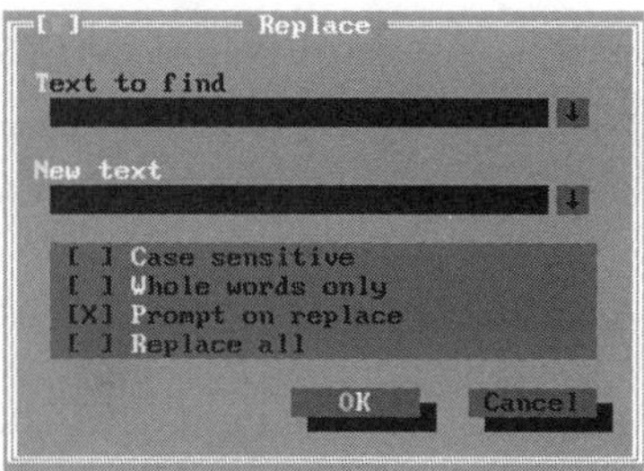

Fig. 16.3
The Replace dialog box.

Choose **R**eplace All to have the Editor replace all occurrences without asking you each time. Once the Editor finds the first occurrence of the text you specify in the preceding steps, if you marked the **P**rompt on replace option, the Editor asks if you want to replace the old text with the new. Choose **Y**es and the Editor replaces it, and then prompts you again when it finds the next occurrence.

You may also use the Search command to locate certain types of codes as Table 16.6 indicates.

Table 16.6 How To Locate Types of Code

Menu Option	Key(s)	Description
Pr**e**vious routine	Alt-B	Goes to the previous routine in the current source program
Ne**x**t routine	Ctrl-B	Goes to the next routine in the current source program
Loa**d** routine	Ctrl-O	Opens other program file referenced at cursor position
List routines	Alt-R	Displays a list of functions and procedures from which you can select and go to

Saving and Exiting

To close your current work file, choose **W**indow **C**lose; press Ctrl-F4; or click the close button at the top left of the active edit window. If you change anything in your file, you are prompted to save your changes or cancel the operation.

As with any computer file, you need to save your changes frequently to prevent accidental loss of information. Be sure to save frequently during the programming process by choosing **F**ile **S**ave to save your document, or **F**ile Save **A**s to save the current document with a new name. If you choose **F**ile **S**ave when creating a new file, dBASE 5 displays the Save File As dialog box, using the default file type *.PRG.

The Save File As dialog box appears if this is the first time you save this file, or if you chose the Save File As option. If a file exists with the same name, you get a message from dBASE 5. You can either overwrite the existing file, or click Cancel and start over to enter a different file name.

When you work with several different files at once, you can choose **F**ile Save A**l**l to save all modified files. This works the same as **F**ile **S**ave, but saves the contents of all the files, not just the file in the active Edit window. If no Edit windows are open, this menu option is dimmed, indicating it is not available.

To Exit the Desktop editor, click the **C**lose button at the top-left corner of the window. If the file wasn't saved before, you are prompted for a file name. If the file was saved, the file on disk is replaced. To exit without saving, press Esc. You are asked if you want to save any changes, and are given three choices: Yes, No, or Cancel. Choose **N**o to exit without saving.

Using the Program Editor To Enter Code

You can use the Program Editor (see fig. 16.4) to modify any ASCII file: program (PRG), screen (FMT), or text (TXT). Type the following command format in the Command window:

MODIFY COMMAND <*filename*>

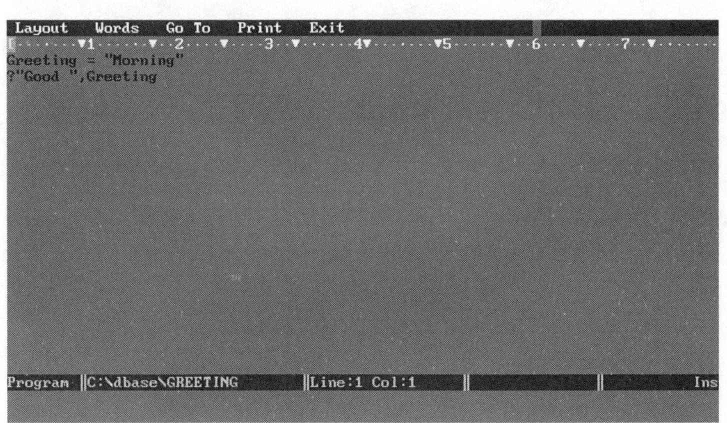

Fig. 16.4
The Program Editor is a basic DOS editor.

When you don't specify a file extension, dBASE 5 assumes PRG, the default extension for programs. You can also start the program editor from the Control Center. Select the file to be modified from the Applications panel by double-clicking on it, or use the arrow keys and select by pressing Enter. Select Modify Application and the Program Editor starts with the file loaded.

Navigating the Edit Window

Getting around inside the program editor is much like getting around inside your favorite word processing application. Specific commands help you travel from line to line and word to word quickly. Refer to Table 16.4 for these commands.

To jump to a specific line number within your file, open the **S**earch menu and choose **G**o to Line Number; or press Alt-G. The Go To Line dialog box appears where you can enter the line number to which you want to jump. If you choose a line number that is greater than the number of lines in your file, the Editor puts you at the last line in the file.

Inserting and Replacing Text

To insert text into previously typed text, position your cursor where the new text is to be entered. Be sure that you are in Insert mode before typing. The Insert key is a toggle switch that turns on insert/turns off overstrike, or turns off insert/turns on overstrike.

Selecting Text

In the Program Editor, press F6 to turn on SELECT; then move the cursor to highlight the block, and complete your selection with a carriage return. You can only select one block in a window at one time. Once you select your text, you can cut, paste, insert, delete, or copy it.

You can use your mouse to ease this process. Position the mouse cursor at the beginning of the block of text, press and hold down the mouse button, and drag to extend the highlighting to include all of the text you want to select. Once your text is selected, you can cut, paste, insert, delete, or copy it.

Deleting Text

You can undoubtedly make mistakes as you enter your code, so it is important for you to know the fastest ways of deleting text. Check Table 16.7 for hints on how to do this efficiently in the program editor.

Table 16.7 Keystrokes for Deleting Text in the Program Editor

Action	Keystrokes	Alternate
Delete character	Del	
Delete character to left	Backspace	
Delete previous word	Ctrl-Backspace	
Delete line	Ctrl-Y	
Delete to end of word	Ctrl-T	
Insert mode on/off	Ins	Ctrl-V
Delete selected block	Del	

Copying and Moving Text

To duplicate a block of text, you actually need to do two things: copy and paste. To copy the text within a window or into a different window:

1. Select (F6) the block of text you want to copy, and press Enter.
2. Press F8. The text block is copied to a temporary buffer.
3. Position the cursor where you want the block copied to within the current window.
4. Press F8 again. The text block appears after the cursor location.

Moving text is very similar to copying it, but you use cut instead of copy. To move a desired text block,

1. Highlight (F6) the block of text you want to move, and press Enter.
2. Press F7. The text block is moved to a temporary buffer.
3. Position the cursor where you want the text block to appear in the current window.
4. Press F7 again. The text appears after the cursor location.

Undoing Changes

Unfortunately, the program editor provides no means for undeleting or undoing mistakes you made, except to abort the editing session. This allows you to start over with the previously saved version of the program.

Search and Replace

To use the Search and Replace feature, choose Go To. You are given three options. You can search forward or backward, or replace. Select what you want to do; then enter the search string for the initial search, and enter a replacement string if you are replacing text. The editor locates the first occurrence of the search string. If you are replacing, the editor prompts to Replace:R, Replace all:H, Skip:S, or Cancel:Esc.

Search and Replace wraps from the end to the beginning of your file to continue its task.

Saving and Exiting

To save your file, press Ctrl-End or Ctrl-W to save your work and exit the program editor. You can abandon any changes you made by pressing Esc, which dumps you out of the editor.

Using Your Text Editor or Word Processor To Enter Code

Sometimes it is easier and faster to write your program using the text editor or word processor you use most often. As long as your word processor can generate an ASCII file, you can write your code using the word processor, then execute the code from within dBASE.

Using Your Text Editor

You can use your favorite text editor in one of two ways. The first is to start and use it outside of dBASE 5 just as if you didn't own dBASE. That's the more difficult of the two ways, because you have to quit dBASE 5, edit the file, and then reload dBASE. The other way is to SET EDIT from the Command window, inside a program, or in the CONFIG.DB file. The syntax is

```
SET EDITOR TO [<full path name and suffix>]
```

indicating the path for locating your word processing system. Your application can then specify which type of editors are used for various memo fields within the program.

To change the name of the word-wrap (memo field) editor, enter

```
SET WP TO [<full path name and suffix>]
```

thus allowing you (and your user) to utilize a different word processing editor for entering text into data table memo fields.

You can also change the default editor from the main menu. Choose **O**ptions, **d**BASE Set, Files and enter the path and suffix in the appropriate field for the program editor and the Memo editor.

The program editor checks the compiled (DBO) program file before execution to ensure that it is the most recent version of your program; your text editor doesn't do this for you. Therefore, be sure that SET DEVELOPMENT is set to ON (the default setting) before you start to make changes with your text editor. This ensures that dBASE 5 checks the relative date and time stamps on PRG and DBO files and recompiles if you changed the PRG file since the last compile.

You can use your own editor if you have experience with it. Be aware, however, that dBASE 5 occupies a great deal of memory, allowing for less low DOS memory for word processing programs. Your text editor can simply require too much memory to be used from within dBASE 5. For beginners, the dBASE 5 program editor is more than adequate.

Understanding the Clipboard

The Clipboard is a special kind of window that holds text temporarily, allowing you to copy (paste) it to a different location. Copying text can be done within a window or to an entirely different one. This special window works in the background, where you won't notice it unless you want to. To see what is on the Clipboard, choose **E**dit, Cl**i**pboard. The Clipboard window appears on the Desktop, as shown in figure 16.5, so that you can copy, cut, and paste the text. Table 16.8 lists the key combinations for these tasks.

```
Clipboard
do case testvar
  case testvar=1
     exitvar=2
#ifdef oranges
  case testvar=2
     exitvar=1
#endif
endcase
? "testvar:",testvar,"exitvar",exitvar,"Tvar",tvar2,tvar3
     10:1
```

Fig. 16.5
Text copied or cut from within an editor appears on the Clipboard.

Table 16.8 Using the Clipboard

Action	Keystroke	Alternate
Copy to Clipboard	Ctrl-Ins	
Cut to Clipboard	Shift-Del	Ctrl-K Y
Paste from Clipboard	Shift-Ins	

Tip
Save the text on the Clipboard by selecting the Clipboard window and choosing **F**ile Save **A**s.

The Clipboard retains the text saved there until you cut or copy another block of text, select all the text on the Clipboard and choose **E**dit C**l**ear, or exit from dBASE.

Using a Word Processing Program

As mentioned previously, it's a little more complicated to enter your code into dBASE 5 if you wrote it using your word processing program. But there are advantages to using a package with which you are familiar.

One of the primary benefits of using your favorite word processor is that you can use all the features of the software to copy, move, and paste code wherever you want it. You can do this faster in this environment because you know the ins and outs of the package and the shortcuts that speed up your work.

Because you can save your document in your word processor, you may feel more comfortable using it to write your code. You can also save your code in dBASE 5; but, you may prefer the comforting reassurance of the familiarity of word processing.

You already know how to use the Search and Replace commands and other tools that make writing your code easier. You can use the Search command to check for ENDIF and other closing commands to ensure your loops are closed, thus saving you debugging time later.

After you finish writing the code, outlining everything that it's intended to do, and double-checking for obvious syntax errors and typing errors, you need to save your document in ASCII format. Some word processors offer many choices for the kind of ASCII text you can select. Select either straight ASCII or DOS text to ensure that dBASE 5 can incorporate your carefully prepared code into its programming conventions.

Troubleshooting

I can't retrieve my word processing document into dBASE's editor. What can I do?

If the editor or compiler can't recognize your file, you are probably not using an ASCII editor. Check the word processor for other file formats in which it can save files. These are usually listed under a Save As choice. If your word processor doesn't have any valid ASCII choices, try selecting Print to Disk with an ASCII printer as the driver and the desired file name as the target.

Documenting Programs

When you write a program, be sure to insert comments into your program file. These comments explain what the code does. Although the code you write requires no explanation now, your comments are an invaluable guide when you return to modify the code several months from now. If someone else must modify your code, your comments are essential to that person.

Adding a Note on a Line by Itself

To place a lengthy comment in your code, you can put it on a line by itself. To do this, start the line with an asterisk (*). This tells the program to ignore the characters on that line and proceed.

Adding a Note to a Command Line

To add a comment after a command, use a double ampersand (&&). This type of comment may reside on the same line as a program statement.

The following program shows examples of both ways to add a note:

```
* This program is used to search for a record
USE Maillist                  && Open the data table
SET ORDER TO TAG Customer     && Set the index tag
SEEK "John Smith"             && Search for John Smith
RETURN                        && Return to calling program
```

The first line of the program starts with an asterisk; this line reminds you of the purpose of the program code. Double ampersands (&&) follow commands on subsequent lines. Whether you use an asterisk and a whole line, or && and a partial line, dBASE 5 ignores comments.

Managing Your Project with the Project Manager

Each application you write will most likely contain more than one file, for example program files, format files, and menu files. dBASE 5 provides an easy and efficient way to keep all of the related files together with the Project Manager. You use the Project Manager to define a project and specify the relationships between each of the pieces of the application. After the project is set up, the Project Manager automatically compiles and links the files together based on your specifications.

Creating a Project

The Project Manager is used to create a project and to view the files associated with a defined project at any time. Figure 16.6 shows the Project Manager window in which you can view your application's related files. The Project Manager also allows you to set global or local compile and link options for all files in the project or specific files, respectively.

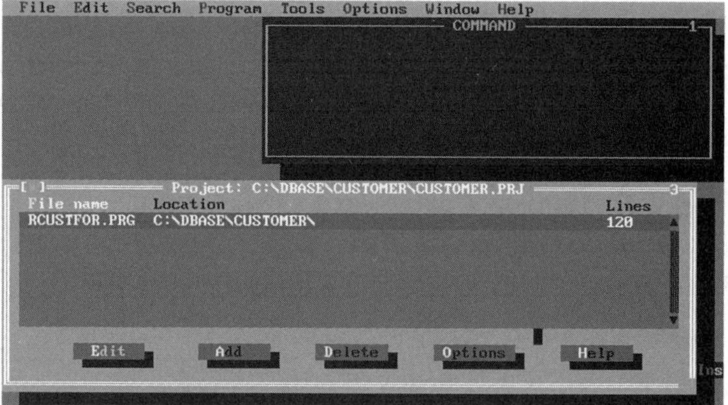

Fig. 16.6
The Project Manager lets you see the files that are used by your application.

Creating a project requires four steps:

- Open the project file by opening the **W**indow menu and choosing **P**roject Manager. The most recently opened project file is highlighted in the window. Choose **E**dit to modify the file.
- If desired, use **A**dd to attach new source files to the selected project file.
- If desired, specify the project file options for include files, compiling, and linking by selecting the **O**ptions button.

- Create the executable file by selecting **P**rogram and choosing **C**ompile from the dBASE menu.

Another way to open or create a new file for the project is to open the **F**ile menu and choose **O**pen, then type in the name of the PRJ file or a new name to create a new file. If the file exists, dBASE opens it; if the file doesn't exist, dBASE creates one. If you want to save the file in a different directory, specify the full path name for the file when you name it.

You can delete a file from the project by highlighting the file to be deleted and selecting **D**elete from the Project Manager window.

Defining Compile and Link Options for Your Project

If you just want to specify the options for one file, highlight the file then select the **O**ptions button. A dialog box appears as shown in Figure 16.7. You can specify a directory for all include files and a directory where you want dBASE to store files. You can also choose to Define Preprocessor **S**ymbols, **E**xclude from Link the highlighted project file, or enter a new command to act as a **R**eplacement Command for Compile.

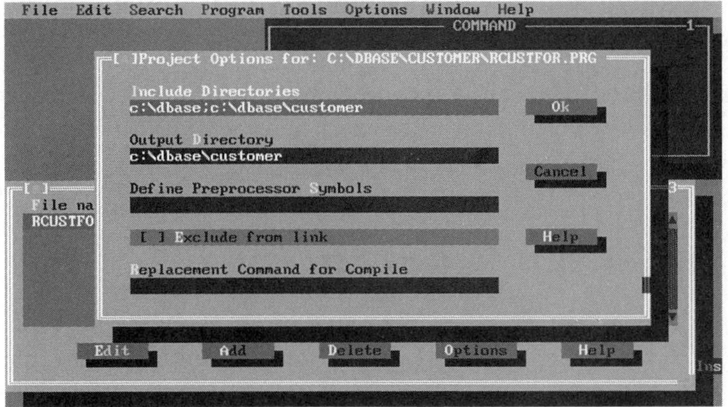

Fig. 16.7
You control how your project files relate to each other.

You have control over how your project is compiled and linked. Select **O**ptions and choose **M**ake from the dBASE menu and a dialog box appears with several options, as shown in figure 16.8. The first section on the dialog box is for Break make on radio buttons, which allow you to stop the project from being linked and compiled. The first radio button (**W**arnings) stops the process if a warning is generated by the compiler. The second radio button

(**E**rrors) will halt the make process only if a file in the project contains errors. Your last choice is to have the process stopped after **A**ll Sources Processed is completed.

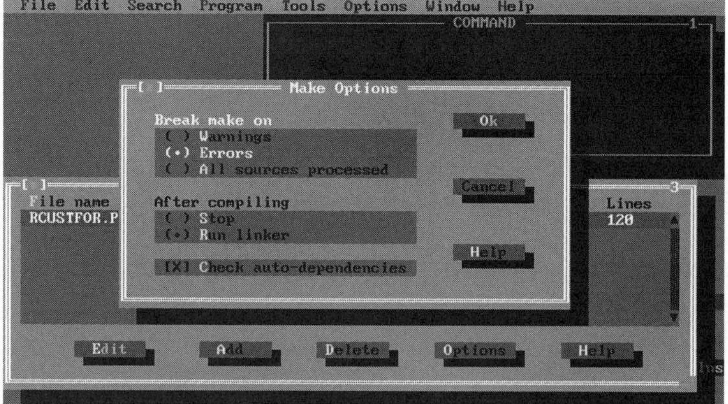

Fig. 16.8
Control how dBASE makes your project through the **O**ptions **M**ake window.

The next section of the dialog box, After compiling, includes radio buttons to indicate which actions are performed after compiling. You can either choose **S**top to create the object files and halt the project's make process, or choose **R**un Linker to have dBASE create an executable (DBO) file for your project.

dBASE defaults to **C**heck auto-dependencies whenever a project is made. You can turn this off if you don't want to check for every DBO file with a PRG file or other source file within the project list.

Compiling a Program

Compiling your program is the ultimate test of whether you write your code correctly. If you find an error, though, you join the ranks of tens of thousands of programmers debugging their code. Most programs have some error in them when they are first run.

You can compile and test each module as you write it, saving you debugging time later. Waiting to start the debugging process until after all your modules have been written and strung together makes it more difficult to pinpoint any errors. Also, if you plan to use one module more than once in your program, debugging the module before you insert it throughout a lengthy program makes the debugging process simpler.

▶ See "COMPILE," p. 667

The syntax for using the COMPILE command is

```
COMPILE [AUTO] <progname> [,<progname>...] [RUNTIME]
```

The file you want to compile is inserted where *<progname>* appears in the above syntax. You need to include a path for any file that isn't resident in the default directory or on a path set with the SET PATH command. You can also use & macro expansions to indicate a program file name, or use the (ExpC) simple macro syntax. Other ways you can identify which program to compile are to use the *@filename* syntax to specify a list file, or to use wildcard characters.

When you request that dBASE 5 run a program file, it checks the dates on the files to see if your source code was modified since the last object file was created. If the source code is later, dBASE 5 compiles the source and a new DBO file is created. The object code is then executed. The COMPILE command creates object code from your dBASE 5 program without having to execute the code immediately. You can enter a list of file names on the COMPILE command line in order to compile several separate programs simultaneously.

Some examples of how to compile using different file name conventions follow:

COMPILE myprog1

COMPILE @progset.lst

PGNAME = "myprog.prg"

COMPILE (PGNAME)

COMPILE myprog1, myprog2

Setting Compiler Options

Compiler options allow you to tailor your compilation process. Open the **O**ptions menu and choose **C**ompiler; this opens the Compile Options dialog box (see fig. 16.9). The first option performs the same as the [AUTO] option on the command line. The compiler checks the dates of the PRG file and the DBO file. If the PRG file is dated earlier than the DBO file, COMPILE will skip compiling that file. If the PRG was modified since the last DBO was created, COMPILE creates a new DBO file.

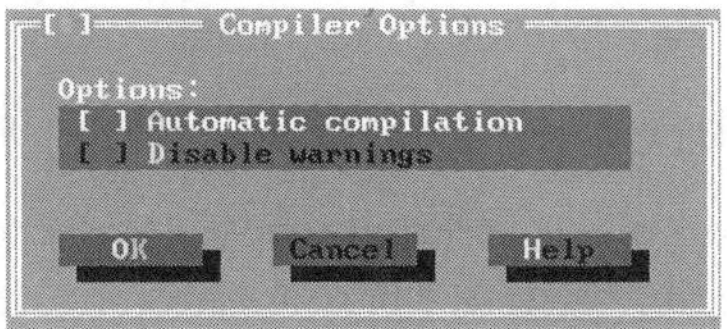

Fig. 16.9
The Compiler Options dialog box.

The second field disables the display of warnings by the compiler. The compiler always displays error messages. In a development environment, it's a good idea to always look at all errors and warnings that the compiler generates. If you use some function that you know produces a warning, you can turn off the warnings to provide a clearer indication of the error messages.

Using Advanced Compile Options

The desktop provides the capability of enhancing the operation of the compiler with several options. Open the **O**ptions menu and choose Advanced Compiler to bring up the Advanced Compiler Options dialog box, shown in figure 16.10. The values input to this screen are stored and are available even if you exit the program and restart it.

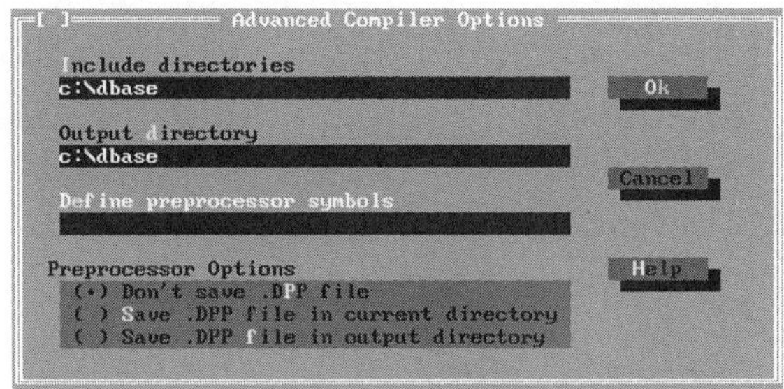

Fig. 16.10
Advanced Compile Options extend your file location options.

If you store your #include files in a separate directory than your main program code, you can direct the compiler to search in directories other than the current default to find #include files. In the Include directories field, enter the subdirectories to be searched. Each subdirectory should be separated by semicolons, up to a maximum of 254 characters.

If you store your executable file (compiled program code) in a different directory than your code, type the directory name into the Output directory field. The object modules are directed to this directory when compiling is complete. The linker checks the validity of the directory before trying to write to it.

If you use preprocessor directives to segment your code, you can define any required preprocessor macros in this window. Type the symbol definitions into the Define preprocessor symbols field. These directives can also be entered in the Command window before the COMPILE command.

When the compiler reads your source code, it creates a preprocessed copy of the file. This file contains only those lines of code that weren't bypassed by the #ifdef, #ifndef, or #if preprocessor directives. The final fields in the window determine whether or not the compiler saves the file after preprocessing into a preprocessor file (DPP). Comments are not removed from this file, but inactive code based on the value of the preprocessor symbols is removed. This file can be examined if your code is not working to determine if some of the code that you thought was executing was excluded. You can direct the file to the default directory or to the output directory if you decide to save it.

Debugging Programs

Debugging (finding and fixing program flaws) your programs can be the most frustrating of programming activities. Because it's among the most important, however, take a moment to learn a few debugging tips. You can debug easily or with difficulty.

▶ See "Using the Debugger," p. 459

Do not run an application for the first time immediately when the total application is finished. Each module needs to be tested and debugged individually. That way, when the application is complete, the only bugs you find are most likely the result of interaction between modules.

Tip
To run your program, type DO *<programname>* in the Command window, or use your mouse to choose **P**rogram **R**un.

When you start the debugging process, your first step is to attempt to run the program. Assuming that your code is not perfect, at some point in compiling or executing your program you can experience an anomaly, ranging from a screen that you don't like, to a total disruption of program execution. If you simply have a wrong screen or incorrect menu text, go back to the program module and correct the error. The next time you execute the module, dBASE 5 compares the file creation times on the compiled and uncompiled files and recompiles if the source code (PRG file) is newer than the existing compiled version.

When you run a dBASE 5 program, dBASE automatically compiles the PRG file. *Compiling* makes your program run faster and smoother. If you made a syntax or spelling error, the compiler helps you by spotting the error and stopping the compilation. Now you have a chance to fix the error and continue.

Tip
The Debugger makes inserting break points easier and allows you to follow your code execution.

If the program goes astray without any real indication of why, however, your debugging skills are brought into play. Failing to close off a command is one of the most common bugs in dBASE programming. The compiler generally catches such failures. When a bug is caught by the compiler, you can fix it and proceed. But when you have a bug that the compiler didn't catch, you have to find the bug. One of the best ways to find a bug is with break points. A *break point* is a pause placed in a program that causes the program to stop executing.

Suppose that you have a program which seems to execute perfectly, except that when you look for the data in the data table, you find it isn't there. You know that you saved the information, but you cannot figure out why your program didn't properly append the new record to your data table. You do know roughly where in your program the saving and appending was supposed to take place; so you place SUSPEND commands at several points in your code around the place where you suspect the problem lies.

▶ See "SUSPEND," p. 745

SUSPEND stops execution of the program at a break point and activates open objects. While the program is suspended, you can enter commands in the Command window. This allows you to check and change things like the status of files, memory variables, and SET commands. This is your chance to correct your program to make it work the way you intended.

▶ See "RESUME," p. 735

If you suspend, you can look at the appropriate memory variables and data tables to see what has happened up to this point in the program. Suppose that you check the memory variables and find everything correct, so you run the program again. This time, when you get to the first SUSPEND, you enter RESUME in the Command window and the program continues to execute until it reaches the next break point. You suspend again and check the data tables. This time you find that the data is not where it's supposed to be, so you return to the program code and examine what happened between the two break points.

Tip
A suspended program remains in memory, thus reducing the amount of available memory for your session, until you issue a CANCEL, RESUME, or QUIT command.

The program remains suspended until you give it a CANCEL, RESUME, or QUIT command in the Command window. CANCEL cancels all files called with DO, including those that are suspended. QUIT cancels the same as the CANCEL command, but also exits you from dBASE 5. If you edit your PRG file while it is suspended, cancel and compile to make sure that dBASE 5 recognizes the changes.

You suspect that you accidentally used the wrong memory variable when appending the data table. So you move the break points to either side of where you think the error is, and run the two tests again—this time with the break points closer together. You narrow the area of possible trouble down to a few instructions. When you run the program and check the variables, you find that your suspicion is correct. You repair the offending command, remove the break points, and run the module again. This time it executes correctly. You have debugged your code using break points.

Developing Programs for Use on a Network

Although this book does not go into detail about network applications, it is important to know about some of the issues you can encounter if you begin developing multi-user (network) programs.

▶ See "Using dBASE 5 Commands," p. 637

▶ See "Using Functions," p. 751

▶ See "Using Set Commands," p. 827

Concurrency control refers to the management of a data table record when more than one user wants access to it at the same time. Suppose that user A reads, or browses, a record in a data table on a local area network. User B, unaware that user A is browsing the record, accesses it and makes a change. User A, unaware of the change made, decides to make a change as well. The first change to hit the record is made and the second change overwrites it. Neither user ever knows which change is made.

The way dBASE 5 prevents this problem is by exercising concurrency control in the form of *record locking*. If the record is locked when user B makes the change, user A is informed that the change can't be made because the record is locked. You can lock records when they're actually being changed (written to) and leave them unlocked during reading or browsing. That way, anyone can browse a record, but only one user can update it at a time.

Tip
dBASE 5 handles most record-locking tasks automatically, and now allows up to 4,096 locks per data table.

The second issue, *data integrity*, concerns the number and correctness of data table records. As a rule, having more than one copy of a data table record is unwise because you never know which one is accurate. When you perform certain *relational functions* (procedures that use two or more data tables to produce a combined, or result, *dataset*), however, you create a second copy of some records. In this situation, dBASE 5 prevents data integrity problems by building a *virtual result dataset*, a temporary data table in which the data exists in memory only for the time that you use it. If you alter a record in the result, you must update the original data table or lose the change. When the procedure is over, you have no chance to keep several copies of the record and risk future confusion.

Another data integrity problem occurs during transaction processing. *Transaction processing* is a procedure that allows users to update records one at a time. Each update, whether it is to an entire record (such as adding a record to a data table) or simply to a field in a record (such as changing an address or phone number in a personnel record), is considered a single transaction. (The opposite of transaction processing is *batch processing*, in which hundreds of records are added to a data table at one time.) If the process is interrupted (by a power failure, for example) during transaction processing, only part of the record may be correct. In dBASE 5 multi-user databases (and single-user databases, as well), you can control the update process through BEGIN TRANSACTION...END TRANSACTION and ROLLBACK commands.

When you use the BEGIN TRANSACTION command, you automatically create a transaction log. This log contains every action that occurs until the program encounters the END TRANSACTION command. If your update is interrupted, you can use the ROLLBACK command to backtrack to the point just before the aborted transaction began, based on the information in the transaction log. This system reduces the probability of your database being corrupted because of a hardware or software failure during a database update.

From Here...

You now know how to use the different editors to write code, how to compile your program, and how to fix errors. You also learned the importance of documenting what your program does for future reference by you or someone else. If you would like to learn more about programming techniques, you may want to review the following chapters:

- Chapter 5, "Designing the Structure of a Database," reviews the basics of creating your own database.
- Chapter 17, "Exploring Some Sample Programs," provides examples of code that are written for dBASE 5 applications.
- Chapter 18, "Creating Custom Applications," tells how to modify the dBASE 5 setting to generate a specialized database for a specific purpose.
- Chapter 19, "Using the Applications Generator and the Compiler," addresses issues related to issuing commands to the Application Generator to create an application.

- Chapter 20, "Programming with SQL," uses the Structured Query Language to write programs.
- Chapter 21, "Creating Objects with UI," addresses the object-oriented approach to programming.

Chapter 17

Exploring Some Sample Programs

Now that you've explored some of the building blocks of an application like top-down program structure, program modules, commands, and functions, look at how to write programs for different intents and purposes.

This chapter examines an operational program to see how to index a specific data table, print a report, accept user input, and test the input using the conditional command IF. You learn how to manipulate your data using INDEX, @...SAY, @...GET, memory variables, and WHILE loops. You look at writing a program that uses preprocessor directives to control how it is compiled, and how to use dBASE's debugger to "fix" any problems. One of the major enhancements to the dBASE language in dBASE 5 is the addition of objects which provide a cleaner user interface. You look at a program that uses objects for the user interface.

In this chapter, you explore programs and procedures that

- Print a report
- Obtain user input
- Display prompts to the user
- Test user input with conditionals
- Use preprocessor directives

For this chapter, the task is to create a customer tracking system. The fields that are tracked are used to create the CUSTOMER data table:

Field Name	Type	Width
ctCustId	CHARACTER	5
ctCompany	CHARACTER	30
ctAddrLn1	CHARACTER	30
ctAddrLn2	CHARACTER	30
ctCity	CHARACTER	30
ctState	CHARACTER	2
ctZipCode	CHARACTER	10
ctPhone	CHARACTER	15
ctFax	CHARACTER	15

Establishing Coding Standards

Your program is made up of statements containing dBASE commands, dBASE functions, data table fields, and memory variables. To make your program more easily read and maintained, you should establish some standard practices for naming, code appearance, and comments. Standards ensure that all the modules in your program look similar and have similar levels of documentation, regardless of which member of your development team produced the code. Some of the things you should address in your standards are:

- Names of modules
- Names of variables
- Names of fields
- Use of capitalization
- Use of spacing
- Use of comments

Tip
You can use the long name capability of memory variables and procedures to make your code more readable.

Your standards are driven by constraints of the language. The dBASE language enables both upper- and lowercase letters to be used anywhere on the line. Any number of spaces can be used to separate words and commands. Field names are limited to 10 characters. File names are limited by DOS to eight characters. Memory variables and procedure names are unlimited, but only the first 10 characters of memory variables and the first nine characters of procedure names are significant. Memory variables in dBASE can be of any data type, and can even change type in a program. The maximum length of any command line, including the spaces, is 4,096 characters.

Caution

If you create two variables or procedures with long names, make sure the names are unique in the first 10 characters, otherwise you could change a value unexpectedly. For example, if you have a sequence

```
clMyFirstBigVariable = 23

clMyFirstBinaryVariable = 1
```

the value of `clMyFirstBigVariable` also has been changed to 1, because dBASE only sees `clMyFirstB` as the name for both variables.

Using the same case for all of your code doesn't make the code easy to read. Indiscrimate use of capitalization also can make your code less readable. If comments are not placed in the code, your program can be very difficult to maintain in the future. With these constraints in mind, you can establish your standards. The standards used in this chapter are:

- All dBASE commands and functions appear in all capital letters.
- Memory variables do not change data type in the program.
- All memory variable names are descriptive of their scope, type, and content. The format for the variable is *<type>*[*<scope>*]*<content name>*. The *<type>* is a single character indicating the type of data: *c* for character, *l* for logical, *d* for date, or *n* for numeric. The *<scope>* is *l* for local or *g* for global. The *<content name>* is mixed upper- and lowercase with the first letter of each word in the name uppercase. For example: *clTempName*.
- The field names follow the same rules as the memory variables. The *<scope>* always is *t* for table. The *<type>* also can be *f* for floating point or *m* for memo.
- Forms are named with a type of r.
- Menus are named with a type of u.

- Blocks of code are indented five characters.
- Continuation lines are indented three characters.

Tip
Indenting the code for loops and subroutines makes your code easier to read.

Defining a Memory Variable

Memory variables are among the most useful elements of the dBASE language. Memory variables give you "boxes" to hold bits of data temporarily until you need them again. *Memory variables* are temporary storage places for any type of data you can put in a data table field, except for memos. You can have as many as 15,000 memory variables (if your available memory permits), but the default is 500. With good programming practice, 500 should be more than enough for most applications. The name of a memory variable can be as long as you want, but dBASE only looks at the first 10 characters.

Tip
Memory variables are typed only by storing something in them. This makes it very easy to accidentally change the data type. A good programming practice is to make sure that your memory variables never change data type in your code.

To use a memory variable, you must *initialize* it by storing some type of data in it. You can manipulate data in the memory variable, make the memory variable usable by other program modules, or make the memory variable usable only by the program module that initialized it. When you're finished with it, you remove the memory variable.

In processing variable names in statements, dBASE looks first for a data table field, and then for a memory variable. If you have a memory variable with the same name as a field in your data table, you can direct dBASE to use the memory variable by preceding the name with M->, for example. M->cDate refers to the memory variable cDate. Careful naming and use of capitalization can make your code almost self-documenting and avoid problems with duplicate names. All memory variable names must be unique in the first 10 characters.

Initializing Memory Variables

Initializing memory variables is a simple matter of placing a particular type of data in them. Because you can put four types of data in memory variables (character, numeric, date, and logical), you have four types of memory variables. You can initialize memory variables in two ways. First, you can use the STORE command. To create a memory variable called *clName* that contains the name *John Smith*, use the following command:

```
STORE "John Smith" TO clName
```

You also can use the equal sign (=) as an assignment statement to initialize a memory variable. To create the same memory variable created in the previous example, using less code and thus creating a cleaner program, enter the following:

```
clName = "John Smith"
```

STORE can be used to initialize a list of memory variables, whereas the equal sign method can only initialize one variable at a time. When you are writing program code, practice using only one of these methods and then stick to it. You produce more consistent code, which is easier to read, modify, and troubleshoot later on—especially if someone else needs to modify your code.

When you initialize character-type memory variables, place the text assigned to the variable in quotation marks. Using the same technique, you can use numbers as text in a memory variable, as in the following example:

```
clHouseNum = "123"
```

In this example, the number 123 is treated as character-type data rather than as a numeric value.

When you initialize a memory variable that later is to accept character values, you can initialize it by storing a character value in it or by storing blank spaces in it.

Note

Remember this important, though subtle, point: The contents of any memory variable are treated as data—even blank spaces and the number zero are considered data. Just because a memory variable seems "empty" does not mean that the memory variable has no contents. Because some sort of value—even a space—is required to initialize a memory variable, all active memory variables always contain a value.

You can insert blank spaces into a memory variable in two ways. One way is simply to type the number of blank spaces you need between the quotation marks. To store 20 blank spaces in the memory variable *clAccept,* for example, you could enter the following:

```
clAccept = "                    "
```

As you can see, you cannot easily tell at a glance exactly how many spaces appear between the quotation marks. A more efficient way to store 20 spaces in the memory variable is to use the SPACE( ) function. Between the parentheses following SPACE, type a number indicating the number of places you want your memory variable to hold. To create the same memory variable used in the previous examples, enter the following:

```
clAccept = SPACE(20)
```

To initialize a numeric-type memory variable, simply assign it a numeric value, remembering to omit quotation marks, which would convert your numeric value to character data. To store the number 100.05 in the memory variable *nlCost*, enter the following:

```
nlCost = 100.05
```

You can initialize a numeric memory variable to any number. Most of the time, however, you use an initial value of zero. Remember, initializing simply means that you are opening the memory variable by putting a value in it. That value can be an actual value that you are about to use, or it can be an "empty" value (zero or spaces) that prepares the memory variable for future use. You cannot refer to a memory variable in your program unless it first has been initialized.

When you initialize a memory variable to accept numbers, initialize the memory variable to zero. You can use the following command:

```
nlCost = 0
```

Even though you can later use the memory variable to hold a value with two decimal places, for example, you still initialize the memory variable with zero and no decimal places. When you accept the variable (using an @...GET command), you use PICTURE to format the value for the correct number of decimal places. Examine the following code:

```
nlCost = 0
@ 10,15 SAY "Enter the cost: " GET nlCost PICTURE "9999.99"
READ
@ 15,15 SAY "The cost that you entered is " + nlCost
```

Although this code initializes *nlCost* to 0, PICTURE formats the variable so you can enter any value from 0 to 9999.99. The 9s are important because they tell dBASE to accept numbers only, not characters. The "+" connects, or *concatenates*, two or more character strings together to create one character string. The limit on concatenation of character strings is 254 total characters.

Date memory variables are initialized a bit differently from other memory variables. You have three methods for initializing a memory variable for a date: you can store the contents of a date field in a memory variable; use braces ({ and }); or use the character-to-date function, CTOD( ).

Storing an existing date field in a memory variable is a straightforward operation. If the date field in the data table is called *dtStrtDate*, for example, enter the following:

```
dlStartDate = dtStrtDate
```

The memory variable *dlStartDate* is a date-type memory variable.

If you want to enter the date as a literal character string, however, you can use the following command:

```
dlDate = {10/15/99}
```

In this case, *dlDate* is initialized to contain the date October 15, 1999. In the same way that you stored blank spaces to initialize a character memory variable, you can use the braces to store a blank date to initialize a date variable:

```
dlDate = {}_
```

The third way to initialize a date memory variable is to initialize another type of memory variable and then convert it to a date variable. To convert a character memory variable to a date variable, use CTOD( ), the character-to-date function. To convert *clDate* (a character variable) to *dlStartDate* (a new date variable), enter the following:

```
dlStartDate = CTOD(clDate)
```

In addition to character, numeric, and date, dBASE 5 has one more type of memory variable: *logical*. Logical memory variables have only two possible values: .T. (true) or .F. (false). When you use a logical memory variable to receive input from a user (perhaps as a response to a Yes or No question), however, you don't want to force your user to type .T. or .F.—the simpler, more user-friendly response is Y and N. Fortunately, dBASE accepts .Y. as a substitute for .T., and .N. for .F.. You can, therefore, use Y and N for T and F, as long as you modify the string to become .Y. or .N. before saving it to the logical memory variable. The string becomes .T. or .F. when in the logical memory variable. The tracking program uses logical memory variables to determine if the user is finished with the application. If so, the *llDone* value is true; if not the *llDone* value is false, as in the following segment:

```
llDone=.f.
```

You can create many memory variables at once—but, don't use that fact as an excuse to become sloppy or inefficient in your programming. Use as many memory variables as you need for a program module, but when you are finished with a memory variable, clear it from memory.

To clear a memory variable, use the RELEASE command. The syntax for RELEASE follows:

```
RELEASE <memvar list>/[ALL [LIKE/EXCEPT<skeleton>]]
```

Notice that RELEASE enables you to clear memory variables in a variety of ways. You can release specific memory variables—for example, to clear *mFirstName* and *mLastName*, enter the following:

```
RELEASE clFirstName, clLastName
```

Using options of the RELEASE command, you can clear groups of memory variables that match certain criteria. To clear all memory variables that start with cl (for example, *clFirstName* and *clLastName*), enter the following:

```
RELEASE ALL LIKE cl*
```

To release all memory variables, enter this command:

```
RELEASE ALL
```

Caution

Be cautious with the ALL option. You can accidentally clear memory variables that you still need.

The RELEASE ALL EXCEPT syntax enables you to select those memory variables which you want to remain active.

Making Memory Variables PUBLIC or PRIVATE

Memory variables may be *public* or *private*. Public memory variables are available for use by any program module within your application. Remember, when you put a value into a public memory variable, that value remains until you change it. If you reinitialize the memory variable, perhaps from another module, you wipe out the contents and replace them with the initialization value.

Private memory variables are used only by the module in which they were initialized or by modules called by the module that initialized the private memory variable. When you exit a module, you automatically "hide" from use by other program modules all PRIVATE memory variables initialized by that module. If you return to the module in which you were using the private memory variable, the memory variable becomes active again and contains the same data it held when you exited from the module.

An easy way to remember the difference between public and private variables is to think of public variables as *global* (available to the entire application) and private variables as *local* (available only to the current program module).

You can declare memory variables private or public with the PRIVATE or PUBLIC commands, both of which you can use in two different ways. With the first method, you declare memory variables by name—for example, PUBLIC memvar1, memvar2, memvar3.

In the second method, you use a *skeleton* to declare as public or private all memory variables that fit a certain pattern. `PUBLIC ALL LIKE clF*`, for example, makes public all memory variables that start with the letters clF. The command `PRIVATE ALL LIKE ??????01` makes private all memory variables whose names consist of six characters followed by the number 01, such as *nlCost01*, *llGood01*, or *clSell01*.

In general, the limitations on memory variable size and contents are the same as the similar limitations on field type and size within a data table. Remember to initialize memory variables to the same data type as the data you put in them.

Note

Memo fields cannot be stored into memory variables.

Using the Data in Your Memory Variables

After you get data into your memory variable, you can use, manipulate, and change it. One of the best uses for memory variables is as data-type converters. Sometimes the format of the data in your data table is not the format needed for reports or calculations. To solve this problem, you can use the functions provided in dBASE to change or convert the data into the format you need. You can use memory variables to store the converted value and perform your reports or calculations.

You can use several functions to manipulate data in memory variables. These functions range from functions like STUFF( ), which enable you to modify a character string, to those like CTOD( ), which enable you to change the data type from one kind (character) to another (date). You also can use math functions, which enable you to perform a calculation on the contents of a memory variable.

In fact, you can use most functions to manipulate the data in a memory variable just as you can use functions to alter raw data. Some functions, however, achieve their greatest usefulness when used with memory variables. Following is a list of some of those functions. For more complete information on these functions, including syntax, refer to Part VI, "Reference Guide," later in this book.

ASC( )	DMY( )	LTRIM( )	STR( )
AT( )	DOW( )	MDY()	STUFF( )
CDOW( )	DTOC( )	MONTH( )	SUBSTR( )
CHR( )	DTOS( )	RAT( )	TIME( )
CMONTH( )	LEFT( )	REPLICATE( )	TRANSFORM( )
CTOD( )	LEN( )	RIGHT( )	TYPE( )
DATE( )	LIKE( )	RTRIM( )	UPPER( )
DAY( )	LOOKUP( )	SOUNDEX( )	VAL( )
DIFFERENCE( )	LOWER( )	SPACE( )	YEAR( )

Several mathematical functions can be used on numbers or the contents of numeric memory variables. Remember that a function returns a value equal to the results of the function performed on the value within the parentheses. You discovered an easy use of functions when you used the CTOD( ) function to change a character string into a date string for the purpose of initializing a date memory variable. Another useful function pair is STR( ) and VAL( ).

You can use STR( ) to change the contents of a numeric memory variable to a character string. VAL( ) performs the opposite function, turning a character string into a number. Suppose that you want to accept the character "1" and use it as the number 1. Character "1" is stored in the memory variable *clAnswer*. You want to store the contents of *clAnswer* in the memory variable *nlChoice*, and make *nlChoice* a numeric memory variable. To do this, you can enter the following:

```
nlChoice = VAL(clAnswer)
```

This example is typical of the way you can use functions to modify the data in memory variables.

A more sophisticated use of memory variables for data handling is *string manipulation*. When you capture a string of characters in a memory variable, the string sometimes is not set up exactly the way you need it to be. It may have too many characters, unneeded spaces, or have letters in the wrong order. For example:

```
clTestCharge = 00-0000-00-0000-000
clTestCharge = STUFF(clTestCharge, 1, 2, '06')
nlHyphLoc = AT(-, clTaskId)
clTestCharge = STUFF(clTestCharge, 9, 2, SUBSTR(clTaskId, nlHyphLoc+1, 2))
clTestCharge = STUFF(clTestCharge, 12, 4, RIGHT(clTaskId, 4))
clTestCharge = STUFF(clTestCharge, 17, 3, '000')
```

The code segment above takes the contents of the variable *clTaskId* and inserts portions of it into the *clTestCharge* variable. The format for the *clTestId* is 9999-99-9999. The format for the *clTestCharge* variable is 99-9999-99-9999-999.

The STUFF( ), RIGHT( ), and SUBSTR( ) functions enable you to modify the character strings stored in the *clTestCharge* memory variable. You can use AT( ) to locate a specific character in a field or memory variable. The code segment uses AT( ) to locate the hyphen (-) that separates the first and second sections in *clTaskId.*

SUBSTR( ) enables you to capture a specified number of characters in a field or memory variable from a given starting position of the field or memory variable. In the code segment, you capture the substring which starts at character 6 and is 2 characters long. The STUFF( ) command is then used to insert it into *clTestCharge* starting at character 9. You can do the same thing from a data table field rather than from a memory variable.

RIGHT( ) enables you to capture the characters from the right end of the string for the length requested. In the code segment, the right 4 characters from *clTaskId* are inserted starting at character 12 in *clTaskCharge.* Notice that the functions can be nested to reduce the use of temporary variables.

Two other functions, LTRIM( ) and RTRIM( ), frequently are used to manipulate data in memory variables. These functions remove unwanted blank spaces preceding or following the value. LTRIM( ) removes extra spaces from the left side of a character string. RTRIM( ), or simply TRIM( ), removes all trailing spaces (those on the right). Figure 17.1 shows examples of LTRIM( ) and RTRIM( ).

When you run this program, you see the original character string ("John") does not equal each of the character strings with the inserted space. When the character string with the space is trimmed, however, it does equal the original character string.

Fig. 17.1
Use LTRIM( ) and RTRIM( ) to strip off unwanted characters.

```
* Program showing the benefit of LTRIM() and RTRIM()
SET EXACT OFF
mVar1 = "John"
mVar2 = "John "
mVar3 = " John"
mVar4 = " John "
* Test RTRIM(), "John" = "John "
? '"John" = "John " '
?? mVar1 = mVar2      && If EXACT is ON, returns .T.
? '"John" = RTRIM("John ") '
?? mVar1 = RTRIM(mVar2)
* Test LTRIM(), "John" = " John"
? '"John" = " John" '
?? mVar1 = mVar3
? '"John" = LTRIM(" John") '
?? mVar1 = LTRIM(mVar3)
* Test LTRIM() and RTRIM(), "John" = " John "
? '"John" = " John " '
?? mVar1 = mVar4
? '"John" = LTRIM(RTRIM(" John ")) '
?? mVar1 = LTRIM(RTRIM(mVar4))
```

Making More of Memory Variables with Arrays

You can use memory variables far more efficiently if you want to store a large number of values that are, in some way, related. You want to keep these values together, and you want to avoid using up a lot of memory space by initializing a large number of memory variables.

To do this, you use variable arrays. *Arrays* are like cubbyholes into which you stick values. All the cubbyholes are in the same array, so you deal with the array only. You can handle the data in the cubbyholes as discrete data, however, following all the same rules as memory variables. Each cubbyhole is called an *array element*. The advantage is that you can use a DO loop to initialize all the values, since each value is identified by subscripts on the array name. This provides a means for writing tighter code rather than using 40 separate variable names.

If you want to use 40 different memory variables, all of which hold data relating to the Maillist program, for example, you can build an array that looks like figure 17.2.

The array in figure 17.2 is a *two-dimensional array*, which means that the array has both length and width greater than one element. In this case, the length is 10 elements and the width is four. If the width was only one element, the array would be one-dimensional. From the standpoint of how you use arrays, very little difference exists between the two.

Initializing an array is simple. Use DECLARE to name the array and indicate its *matrix structure* (the number of rows and columns). The syntax of the DECLARE command is

```
DECLARE array[R,C]
```

In this syntax, *array* is the name of the array, *R* is the number of rows, and *C* is the number of columns. The elements of an array can be any data type. You can, in fact, have all the various data types present in a single array. When you store data in an element of an array, you set the data type for that element. The array as a whole, however, has no assigned data type.

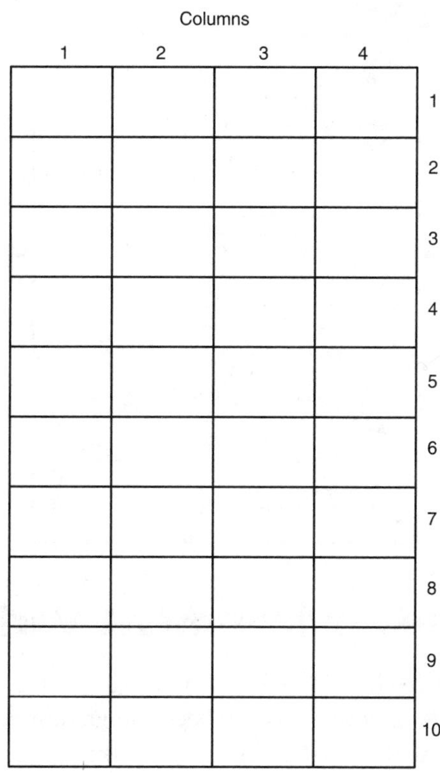

Fig. 17.2
Use arrays to keep related information together for quicker access.

You use STORE to place data in an array in the same way you place data in a memory variable, except that you must give the coordinates of the element into which you want to store the information. If you want to store the contents of the fields in the Maillist data table in an array called *maillist*, you can do it as shown in figure 17.3.

The program in figure 17.3 uses COPY TO ARRAY to assign the field names to the first column of the array. The program then uses a DO loop to assign the second column of the array with field names. When *xcount* equals FLDCOUNT( ), the DO loop ends. All fields from the current record have been assigned to the second column of the array, and another DO loop starts. This loop is used to display the contents of the entire array on-screen, one row at a time. After the entire array has been displayed, the data table is closed, and the program ends.

Fig. 17.3
This program uses COPY TO ARRAY to assign field names.

```
PROCEDURE fldarray
   *
   * Declare and initialize variables
   *
   PRIVATE xcount
   STORE 1 TO xcount
   *
   * Open table and create the array
   *
   USE maillist ORDER customer
   DECLARE maillist[2,FLDCOUNT()]
   *
   * Fill in the first column of array with values
   * from current record
   *
   COPY TO ARRAY maillist NEXT 1
   *
   * Fill in second column of array with field names.
   * Using UPPER,LOWER & SUBSTR functions to store values
   * in proper capitalization.
   *
   DO WHILE xcount <= FLDCOUNT()
      STORE UPPER(SUBSTR(FIELD(xcount),1,1)) + ;
            LOWER(SUBSTR(FIELD(xcount),2)) ;
            TO maillist[2,xcount]
      STORE xcount + 1 TO xcount
   ENDDO
   * Print out contents of the array on a fresh screen
   *
   CLEAR
   STORE 1 TO xcount
   DO WHILE xcount <= FLDCOUNT()
      ?  maillist[2,xcount] AT 5
      ?? maillist[1,xcount] AT 40
      STORE xcount + 1 TO xcount
   ENDDO
   *
   * Close the table and release array and variable
   *
   CLOSE DATABASES
   RELEASE maillist, xcount
RETURN
```

Setting the Environment Variables

▶ See "Using Functions," p. 751

You must consider two environments when using dBASE 5. The first is the environment you set for yourself as you begin programming and which was created when you installed dBASE 5. The second is the one you set for your users. Start by configuring your own environment. For the most part, your environment is determined by the CONFIG.DB file. This file is a simple ASCII file containing commands that determine the configuration of dBASE 5 at start-up. A typical CONFIG.DB file looks like this:

```
*** Please align tabs for columns, = starts second column, && starts third
column. BELL   = OFF
CLOCK  = ON
COLOR OF NORMAL   = N+/BG     && Gray on cyan
COLOR OF TITLES   = W+/BG     && Bright white on cyan
COLOR OF MESSAGES = W/B && White on blue
COLOR OF BOX   = W+/B    && Bright white on blue
COLOR OF INFORMATION    = BG+/B     && Bright cyan on blue
COLOR OF HIGHLIGHT      = RG+/W     && Bright yellow on white
COLOR OF FIELDS   = W/N && Bright white on gray
```

These commands determine such things as the color of your displays, whether the beep (bell) sounds on errors, and whether the clock is displayed in the upper-right corner of your screen. (For more on CONFIG.DB, see the "Reference Guide" later in this book.)

Saving the Current Environment

The other group of environmental commands is used to set up the environment for your application's users (this environment normally is set through the application's main program file). The SET commands set up the display and a number of other things that affect the way your application looks and feels to the user. You may want the user to see things differently from the way you see them when you are working on the program. While you're writing the program, for example, you probably want to see such things as help, a display of the program code being executed, and several other messages dBASE provides. If you don't save the current settings and restore them when your program completes, you can interfere with the operation of other dBASE programs. For this reason, you should include a routine at the beginning of your program that stores the current state of all of the environment settings that you will change in your program. The SAVESETS procedure from the code for our Customer Tracking System stores all the current settings in an array with the name of the environment variable.

```
PROCEDURE SaveSets
*-----------------------------------------------------------
* TITLE:  SaveSets
* ABSTRACT:  This procedure saves the current value of the
* system SET commands that are changed in the program.
*-----------------------------------------------------------
    PUBLIC ARRAY cgSetArray[2,8]
    PRIVATE clFormRun
*-----------------------------------------------------------
* Row 1 of the array is the environment condition being
* stored. Row 2 of the array is the status of the condition.
* Start by storing the name of all the conditions.
*-----------------------------------------------------------
    cgSetArray[1,1] = "SCOREBOARD"
    cgSetArray[1,2] = "STATUS"
```

```
    cgSetArray[1,3] = "HELP"
    cgSetArray[1,4] = "TALK"
    cgSetArray[1,5] = "ECHO"
    cgSetArray[1,6] = "ESCAPE"
    cqSetArray[1,7] = "PRINT"
    cgSetArray[1,8] = "PROCEDURE"

    FOR nlIndex = 1 TO 8       && Index for each condition

    * Get the current setting and store it in row 2 of the array
       cgSetArray[2,nlIndex] = SET(cgSetArray[1,nlIndex])
        SET &cgSetArray[1,nlIndex] OFF    && Set new value

    NEXT    && End of nlIndex for cgSetArray

*-------------------------------------------
*-- Make sure that FormRun.dbo file is active
*-------------------------------------------
    cgSetArray[2,8] = SET(cgSetArray[1,8])
    clFormRun = HOME() + 'FORMRUN.DBO'
    SET &cgSetArray[1,8] TO &clFormRun

RETURN   && End of procedure SaveSets
```

Establishing Your Environment

When you prepare an application for your users, you want it to look as much like a "real" program as possible. You don't want dBASE intruding with its own messages. The code in SAVESETS also sets the environment to the condition desired for your program. Using the macro substitution function & enables the routine to be written as a FOR...NEXT loop to SET each environment condition.

SET ECHO displays program code lines as your program executes. SET TALK echoes the results of various commands to the screen. You want to turn TALK OFF because you want your application to process the results of your commands and display them the way you want them displayed. (In some cases, you don't display them at all; you simply use the results elsewhere in your program.)

▶ See "Writing Help Screens," p. 502

The *scoreboard* (SET SCOREBOARD) is dBASE 5's way of communicating messages to the user when the status bar is off. You can hide these messages in your application by setting the scoreboard to OFF—although these messages are important to you as you develop and test your program. Setting SCOREBOARD OFF, however, does not enable the user to see such things as the Caps or Ins status. Many users want to see this information and there is no dBASE function that returns the status of these keys. SET STATUS OFF hides the dBASE 5 status bar at the bottom of the screen.

When you design your own application in dBASE, you should create your own help screens associated with the data input fields of the program. Your users may need assistance in what the application is looking for in each of the fields. For example, if you have a user identification number that needs to be entered, and the user doesn't know what you're asking for (company badge number, Social Security number, birthday, and so on), having a help screen associated with the field enables the user to find out helpful information. dBASE, on the other hand, can't help the user in this situation, so you need to SET HELP OFF to be sure that the user gets access to your help screens, not dBASE's.

Another environmental setting, SET PRINT OFF, is the default setting and can be used to reset output back to the screen if a program runs after a subprogram aborts that was printing. SET PRINT ON directs the output to the printer.

The look of your user environment is a good indication of the professionalism of your programming. Remember that although you do most of your environment housekeeping at the start of your application, you can use the SET commands at any point in your application to modify or customize the work surface or the way dBASE 5 handles your data. Remember, also, that when you change a SET command within a program, the command remains the way you set it until you change it again. If you want to make a temporary change to an environmental parameter, be sure to do your housekeeping by resetting the parameter to your application's default value when the program returns to the main menu.

Selecting a Data Table

Now that you have established your environment, and know how to store temporary values, your program needs to know where the permanent data is stored. The USE command does exactly what the name implies: it tells dBASE to use a specific data table for whatever commands and procedures follow. The syntax for the USE command follows:

```
USE <data table name> [INDEX <index name>] ¦ [ORDER <tag name>]
```

Notice that when you want to use a data table but want to incorporate the indexed version, use the syntax which includes the INDEX or ORDER command, but not both.

Tip
Use either GOTO TOP or GO TOP to ensure the pointer is positioned at the first record of the index for the data table.

Two examples of the USE command can be seen in the section of code shown here:

```
* If the index file does not exist, create it
IF .NOT. FILE ('CUSTOMER.MDX')
     USE Customer  && Open data table with no index
     INDEX ON ctCustID TAG ctCustID
     INDEX ON ctCompany TAG ctCompany
ENDIF
USE Customer ORDER ctCustID   && Open with index
GO TOP
```

This example shows the GO TOP command, which jumps your pointer to the first record in the data table. It also shows the syntax for using INDEX, which is covered next.

Indexing a Data Table with the Index Command

INDEX creates a second file that tells the dBASE record pointer to move from record to record in a certain order. In other words, INDEX creates a "road map" to locations in your data table, based on your instructions. INDEX enables you to order your data based on the contents of a combination of one or more fields and functions. In the case of INDEX, that combination is called the *key expression*. The file containing the road map is called the *index file*, or just the *index*.

The complete syntax for the INDEX command follows:

```
INDEX ON <key expression> TO <.NDX filename>/
   TAG <tag name> [OF <.MDX filename>]
     [FOR <condition>][UNIQUE] [DESCENDING]
```

Note

INDEX ON enables you to set a condition on the records being indexed. Using FOR enables you to create an index that orders only specific records of your data table.

Tip
The key expression can be as simple as a single field in your data table, or a complex combination of several fields and functions. Create indexes that match the order in which you want to search or report on your data.

An index file is a listing of information dBASE needs to access, in a specified order, the records in a data table file. When you use an index, record access is remarkably fast because the record pointer does not have to travel through the entire data table until it reaches the sought-after record. Instead, dBASE refers to the index, which tells the record pointer where to go. The record pointer then can jump directly to the selected record.

When you use the INDEX ON...TO command, the index file, which carries the file extension NDX, is called a *single-index* file because it contains only the information for indexing on a single key expression. When you update a data table file by adding or deleting records, the index file is updated automatically if it is open. If the NDX file is not open when changes are made, you must reindex. Although you normally do not use NDX files, you should be aware of them, because if you modify older dBASE programs you may encounter NDX files.

If you are going to maintain more than one index on your data table, you have another, more efficient choice than NDX files, the *multiple-index* file. This file, which carries the extension MDX, contains information for several indexes, on different key fields, for the same data table. When writing dBASE 5 programs, use MDX files rather than the less efficient NDX files.

You create a tag index with the INDEX ON...TAG command or by entering Y in the Index column of the data table structure. The first time you create the index, dBASE builds the file automatically and assigns it the same name as the data table file, but with the extension MDX rather than DBF. This file is called the *production MDX file* because it is opened whenever the data table is opened. Each index you create in an MDX file contains a *tag*, a name by which the index is referenced. In the production MDX file, all tags are updated whenever the data table is changed, whether the tag is active or not.

One MDX file can contain up to 47 tags. If you need more than 47 tags (a rare case, indeed), you can create a different MDX file and add tags to the new file. This file is not updated unless it is open when you update the data table. To create an index in the production MDX file, use the following command:

```
INDEX ON <expression> TAG <tagname>
```

To create a new MDX file, you can use a command such as the following:

```
INDEX ON <expression> TAG <tagname> OF <new .MDX file>
```

You specify the new name of the MDX file by typing the new name in your INDEX command line, following the keyword OF. As long as a data table is open and you use legitimate fields when you add tags to a multiple-index file, that file continues to be associated with the data table.

You need to learn two other important keywords. The first, UNIQUE, tells dBASE that you want INDEX to ignore duplicate key fields. The second keyword, DESCENDING, tells dBASE 5 to build the index in descending order rather than the default ascending order.

To begin exploring INDEX, consider the structure of the data table called Customer described at the beginning of the chapter:

Tip

Although MDX files can contain 47 different indexes, using too many indexes slows down data table operations. Also, the tags in each MDX file can refer to only one data table. You can't use one MDX file for all your tables!

Field Name	Type	Width
ctCustId	CHARACTER	5
ctCompany	CHARACTER	30
ctAddrLn1	CHARACTER	30
ctAddrLn2	CHARACTER	30
ctCity	CHARACTER	30
ctState	CHARACTER	2
ctZipCode	CHARACTER	10
ctPhone	CHARACTER	15
ctFax	CHARACTER	15

Although you don't normally use a single-index file, you should know how one is created. To create a single index called STATES.NDX using State as the key field, enter the code shown below:

```
USE Customer
INDEX ON ctState TO States
```

As mentioned earlier, you use multiple-index (MDX) files rather than single-index (NDX) files in your dBASE 5 programming. The advantage is that multiple-index files can contain many different indexes, each referred to by a tag, while only using one DOS file handle. You create three tags for the same data table in a multiple-index file with the following code. Use Customer, Contact, and State+City as the key fields:

```
USE Customer
INDEX ON ctCustId TAG ctCustId
INDEX ON ctCompany TAG ctCompany
INDEX ON  ctState+ctCity TAG xtRegion
```

Tip
Linking two fields with an INDEX ON...TAG command tells dBASE to index on the first field, then on the second.

This code creates an index with the name CUSTOMER.MDX, containing the three tags specified. Notice that you can link two fields into one TAG, as shown in the fourth line of the code.

You can decide to start an alternative MDX file with a tag for ZIP codes and to call the alternative index PROSPALT.MDX. To start this alternative file, use the following command:

```
INDEX ON ctZip TAG ctZip OF Prospalt
```

Multiple-index files offer other benefits besides ease of use and efficiency. When you use the production MDX files, every time you update the data table by adding or deleting records, you automatically update all the associated indexes.

Troubleshooting

I search many different data tables for a certain field. Can I create a file of index tags to use whenever I need to index on a particular field?

Unlike a procedure library, where you can store different procedures to be called from any program, index tags are specific to each data table. After you've indexed a data table using a specific field, the selected records are remembered. However, you can't use the index tags of one data table to create an index of a second data table. MDX files are tied to individual data tables, so you cannot put the indexes from more than one data table into them.

Determining the Menu Structure

Now that you have the data table set up, the next thing to address is what order the user accesses the capabilities of your program. A system of menus is the easiest user interface to guide the user through the capabilities of your system. There are three different ways to develop a menu system in dBASE 5:

- Text-based
- MENU, BAR, POPUP, and PAD commands
- Menu objects

Using Text-Based Menus

▶ See "Using dBASE 5 Commands," p. 637

The ?, @, @...SAY, and @...SAY...GET commands provide a simple form on the screen with a title and user prompt. These capabilities have been in the dBASE language since before dBASE III. The @*<row>*,*<column>* command enables you to place the cursor at a specific location on the screen or printed page. This doesn't provide the slick interface that today's users expect from a program, but you may see it if you are called on to maintain older code.
A menu written with these commands looks similar to the following code:

```
CLEAR
nlAnswer = -1
@ 3, 15 SAY "Main Menu"
@ 5, 5 SAY "0. Exit"
```

```
@ 7, 5 SAY "1. Add Record"
@ 9, 5 SAY "2. Delete Record"
@ 11, 5 SAY "3. Reports"
@ 13, 5 SAY "Type the number of your selection" GET nlAnswer
READ
```

The user then types in the number from the menu to select an option. This method is not very robust, and takes much coding to handle extraneous input the user can type. An IF block then is used to route the user to the correct procedure.

Using dBASE IV Menus

▶ See "Using the Applications Generator and the Compiler," p. 527

▶ See "Using dBASE 5 Commands," p. 637

With the advent of dBASE IV, the capability of easily generating bar, pull-down, and pop-up menus was added to the language. This system is used by the code generator built into the Applications Generator. Each of these commands is covered in detail in the reference section. The following commands are used for horizontal menus:

```
DEFINE MENU <menu name> [MESSAGE <message text>]
DEFINE PAD <pad name> OF <menu name> PROMPT <prompt text>
    [AT <row>, <col>][MESSAGE <message text>]
ON SELECTION PAD <pad name> OF <menu name> [<command>]
ACTIVATE MENU <menu name> [PAD <pad name>]
```

The DEFINE MENU command creates a bar on the top of the screen with an optional message centered at the bottom of the screen. A separate DEFINE PAD command is used to place a choice in the bar menu. The text of the choice that appears in the bar is the prompt text, which was padded with one space at either end. The message for a PAD overwrites the message for the MENU. The PAD( ) function tells which pad the user selected and can be combined with a DO CASE block to select the appropriate procedure.

Vertical menus are created with a similar set of commands:

```
DEFINE POPUP <popup name> FROM <row1>, <col1>[TO <row2>, <col2>]
   [PROMPT FIELD <field name>/PROMPT FILES [LIKE <skeleton>]/
   PROMPT STRUCTURE][MESSAGE <message text>]
DEFINE BAR <line number> OF <popup name> PROMPT <prompt text>
   [MESSAGE <message text>][SKIP [FOR <condition>]]
ON SELECTION POPUP <popup name> /ALL [<command>]
ACTIVATE POPUP <popup name>
```

Pull-down menus are created by simply having the pop-up menu positioned directly below the choices on the bar menu. The code segment shown in figure 17.4 creates a pop-up menu, activates it, and branches to a subroutine to handle the choice the user makes off the screen. The resulting menu is shown in figure 17.5.

```
CLEAR
DEFINE POPUP MainMenu FROM 3,20 TO 10,46 MESSAGE "Select the
➥system to access"
DEFINE BAR 1 OF MainMenu PROMPT "CHARGE TRACKING SYSTEM" SKIP
DEFINE BAR 2 OF MainMenu PROMPT "Exit"
DEFINE BAR 3 OF MainMenu PROMPT "Proposal Tracking"
DEFINE BAR 4 OF MainMenu PROMPT "Charge Tracking"
DEFINE BAR 5 OF MainMenu PROMPT "System Management";
     SKIP FOR .NOT. ((ngAccess = 9) .OR. (ngAccess = 19))
ON SELECTION POPUP MainMenu DO MenChoice
ACTIVATE POPUP MainMenu
RETURN

PROCEDURE MenChoice
DO CASE
     CASE BAR() = 2
     DEACTIVATE POPUP
     lgDone=.t.
   CASE BAR() = 3
     SET PROCEDURE TO RFPSys
     DO RFPSys
   CASE BAR() = 4
     DO ChrgMain
   CASE BAR() = 5
     DO MSecure
ENDCASE
RETURN
```

Fig. 17.4 Use BAR and POPUP commands to design a menu.

Fig. 17.5 You can design menus to simplify use of your applications.

The menu provides the user with a highlight bar that can be moved from choice to choice. The user presses the Enter key to make a selection. In this example, you can see that when the user selects an option from the menu, the program branches to the MenChoice subroutine. The subroutine uses the BAR( ) function to determine which selection was made by the user and then uses a DO CASE statement to route to the appropriate subroutine. For example, if the user selects "Proposal Tracking" the BAR( ) function returns a value of 3 and the program changes the default procedure file and does the subroutine RFPSys.

The SKIP command enables the choice to be shown on the menu, but dims it so the user cannot select it. Likewise, the SKIP FOR command only enables selection of the item when the FOR condition is false, acting like the SKIP when the condition is true.

Code must still be added to this menu system to handle the case of the user pressing the Escape key. Even if SET ESCAPE OFF is added, the Escape key still exits the menu.

Tip
Use the READKEY( ) function to determine which key the user pressed to exit your routine.

Using Object-Oriented Menus

The main addition to the language with dBASE 5 is the object extension for the user interface. You can now create forms which have menus as associated objects. This is the code generated by the Form Designer. An example of the complete code for the Customer Tracking System is shown at the end of this chapter. After you have created a FORM with the DEFINE FORM command, you add a menu to it using the following commands:

```
DEFINE MENUBAR <menu bar name>
DEFINE MENU <menu name> OF <menu bar identifier>
DEFINE MENUITEM <menu item name> OF <menu identifier>
```

With all the additional properties and methods available for each object, the code to generate object menus can be longer than the code required for similar menus using the techniques described in the previous sections. The code generated is better behaved, more easily maintained, and more easily reused. The user interface is also easier for the user to navigate through. These are the primary reasons for moving to object-oriented coding.

Obtaining Input from the User

Database systems need someone to enter the required information. There are many different ways of accepting input from a user: simple "yes-no" questions on the screen, menu choices, or more complex data-entry screens. The menu screens already have been covered, so now look at getting more complex data from the user.

dBASE can accept user input five ways: ACCEPT, INPUT, WAIT, @...SAY...GET, and through UI objects. ACCEPT, INPUT, and WAIT can only accept input into a memory variable. GET can accept data into either a memory variable, or directly into a field in your data table. UI objects can accept and display any kind of data.

Storing User Input in a Memory Variable

ACCEPT and INPUT are virtually the same, except that ACCEPT can accept only character information, whereas INPUT can accept any data type.

These commands are still in the language primarily to maintain compatibility with earlier releases of dBASE. They are not recommended for use in coding modern applications. These commands are not nearly as flexible as @...SAY...GET, because neither ACCEPT nor INPUT enables you to position the prompt where you want it on-screen. The screen location of the prompt is determined by whatever else is on the screen at the time. After you clear the screen, for example, the prompt appears at the upper left corner of the screen. The syntax of the two commands follows:

```
ACCEPT/INPUT [<prompt>] TO <memvar>
```

The most common use of the INPUT is to ask the user for a selection of yes/no or simple numbers.

```
INPUT '  Do you want to continue? (Y/N)  ' to MChoice
clear
```

Tip
ACCEPT and INPUT are commands left from the early days of dBASE and are not recommended for use in new code.

WAIT is similar to ACCEPT/INPUT, except that WAIT accepts one character only and does not require Enter to be pressed, whereas ACCEPT/INPUT accepts more than one character and waits for Enter to be pressed. After the user presses one character, WAIT resumes the program. You may find WAIT useful for multiple-choice questions. The syntax for WAIT is as follows:

```
WAIT [<prompt>] [TO <memvar>]
```

A typical example of how wait is used in a program is for confirmation that the user has finished reading the screen. To tell the system to wait until the user has read the message, use the following command:

```
WAIT "Report completed, Press any key to continue"
```

If you don't specify a prompt, dBASE provides the default prompt, `Press any key to continue`. This is necessary to keep the user from staring at a screen and not knowing what to do to continue using the application.

Showing Prompts and Getting Input with @...SAY...GET

The @...SAY...GET construct is rather complex in that it has many options. To begin with, you need to understand that the basic purpose of the variants of the @ command—whose most common variant is @...SAY...GET—is to enable you to place a prompt at any location on the screen and then accept user keystrokes in response to the prompt. The Forms tool in the Control Center generates format files containing @...SAY...GET commands.

By using the command options, you can open a window wherever you like on-screen, capture the result of some operation and display it at a location on-screen of your choosing, or print a message anywhere on-screen. The syntax of the @...SAY...GET command follows:

```
@ <row>,<col> [SAY <expression>
      [PICTURE <expC>] [FUNCTION <function list>]]
   [GET <variable> [[OPEN] WINDOW <window name>]
      [PICTURE <expC>] [FUNCTION <function list>]
      [RANGE [REQUIRED] [<low>],[<high>]]
      [VALID [REQUIRED] <condition> [ERROR <expC>]]
      [WHEN <condition>] [DEFAULT <expression>]
      [MESSAGE <expC>]]
   [COLOR [<standard>] [,<enhanced>]]
```

Upcoming examples show other @ command options. The major uses, however, are covered in the preceding syntax.

An interpretation of the most common use of the command is

```
@ screen location SAY a prompt for the user
   GET the user's input
```

If you want your user to add to or modify records in a data table, you need to write a more complex set of instructions. The procedure shown in figure 17.6, used in a cost-tracking program, is a short example of such a routine.

Fig. 17.6
Using @...SAY to get user input to add a record to a database.

```
PROCEDURE AddTask
* Add record to Task data table for charge tracking system
*
clTestTask = SPACE(12)     && Initialize memory variables
clTestCharge = SPACE(19)
clWrongAns = '  '
llStayIn = .T.
* Keep asking for more until user doesn't leave blank or
➥presses escape
DO WHILE llStayIn .AND. (clTestTask = SPACE(12) .OR.
➥LEN(clTestTask) = 0)
    CLEAR
    @1,25 SAY "ADD NEW CHARGE NUMBER/TASK"
    @7,5 SAY "Enter the task number:    "  GET clTestTask
    ➥PICTURE "9999-99-9999"
    READ
    nlExitKey = READKEY()
 * Check for escape key
    IF nlExitKey = 12 .OR. nlExitKey = 268
       llStayIn = .F.
    ENDIF
    IF llStayIn
 * By default the charge number is for Company 6 and
 * uses the same last digits as the task number
       clTestCharge = STUFF(clTestCharge, 1, 2, '06')
       clTestCharge = STUFF(clTestCharge, 9, 2,
       ➥SUBSTR(clTestTask, 6, 2))
```

Fig. 17.6
Continued


```
clTestCharge = STUFF(clTestCharge, 12, 4, RIGHT(clTestTask,
➥4))

clTestCharge = STUFF(clTestCharge, 17, 3, '000')
       @9,5 SAY "Enter the charge number: " GET clTestCharge
       ➥PICTURE "99-9999-99-9999-999"
       READ
       nlExitKey = Readkey()
* Check for escape
        IF nlExitKEY = 12 .OR. nlExitKEY = 268
           llStayIn = .F.
       ENDIF
    ENDIF     && End if stayin is true
ENDDO
IF llStayIn
    SELECT 1     && Open the charge # data table with all
    ➥indexes for update
    USE DOCHARG INDEX DOCGDO,DOCGCO
   GOTO TOP
* Check for duplicate entry
    IF .NOT. EOF()
       LOCATE FOR DO_NO = '&clTestTask' .AND. Charge_No =
       ➥'&clTestCharge'
    ENDIF
* If no duplicate, insert a blank record in the data base
    IF EOF() .AND. .NOT. FOUND()
       APPEND BLANK
    ELSE     && If duplicate found
       llStayIn = .F.
       @14,5 SAY "That charge number already exists for this
       ➥DO'
       ACCEPT "Press enter to continue" to clWrongAns
    ENDIF
ENDIF
IF llStayIn     && Insert values into new record
    REPLACE DO_No WITH clTestTask
    REPLACE Charge_no WITH clTestCharge
    CLEAR
    DO DOChgAdd     && Display data to user
    READ
   nlExitKey = READKEY()     && Allow to reject or accept
    IF nlExitKey = 12 .OR. nlExitKey = 268
       DELETE     && If rejected delete the inserted record
       llStayIn = .F.
    ENDIF
ENDIF
USE
RETURN
```

Tip

Be careful with @...SAY...GET and READ. If you use the SET FORMAT TO command or SAVE on any GETs, you could get unexpected results when you issue the READ.

This program sets up a loop to continue prompting the user for a task number until the Escape key is pressed or something is typed into the field. The @...SAY and @...SAY...GET commands provide a simple form on the screen with a title and user prompt. If data is entered, it is put into the standard format for a charge number based on the delivery order number. Notice that the STUFF( ) command is used to change the middle of the string variable *clTestCharge*. The format for the command is:

```
STUFF(<variable>,<starting position>,<length>,<new contents>)
```

In this case, the dummy string inserted into *clTestCharge* is modified by inserting information from the user's input of delivery order number. The proposed charge number then is presented to the user on a second input form to enable modification from the default. Each request for input is followed by a check for the Escape key. The table of delivery order and charge numbers is opened and checked for a duplicate entry. If there is no match, a blank record is added to the data table. The new data is inserted into the new record using the REPLACE command. The user then is presented the record for verification. If Escape is pressed, the record is deleted, otherwise the record is left in the data table. Finally, the data table is closed and the routine returns to the calling program.

After you get the user's response, you must read it to a memory variable that you previously have initialized to accept the data. The @...SAY...GET command is used most often in a screen format file. An example of this is shown in figure 17.6, where the user is prompted to provide the delivery order number and the charge number. The variables are initialized at the top of the subroutine to contain spaces for the length of the desired input.

Roughly translated, this code means the following:

1. Store 12 spaces in a memory variable called *clTestTask*.
2. On the first line of the screen, 25 characters from the left edge, print the phrase ADD NEW CHARGE NUMBER/DO.
3. On the seventh line of the screen, 25 characters from the left edge, print the phrase Enter the DO number:.
4. Display the current contents of *clTestTask* with a format of four numbers, a hyphen, two numbers, a hyphen, and four numbers.
5. Read the entry to the memory variable *clTestCharge*.

Notice that the command syntax mentions PICTURE. PICTURE is a keyword that enables you to force certain types of data as the acceptable response.

Any time you have a GET, a block of spaces opens on-screen. The size of that block, in characters, is determined by the type of data it is expected to accept. If it is accepting data for a numeric memory variable, the space is as many as 20 characters wide. If it is accepting character data, it is the size of the string to which the memory variable was initialized.

By using a PICTURE template, you can determine what the GET accepts. You can, for example, force all characters to be uppercase by filling the template with exclamation marks (!). Table 17.1 shows the various kinds of PICTURE templates available.

Table 17.1 Picture Templates

Template	Description
!	Converts to all uppercase
#	Enables numbers only (including blanks, periods, and signs)
$	Displays the SET CURRENCY string rather than leading zeros
*	Displays * rather than leading zeros
,	Displays digits to the left of the comma
.	Specifies decimal location
9	Enables numbers only (including signs)
A	Enables letters only
L	Enables logical data only
N	Enables letters, numbers, and underscores
X	Enables any character
Y	Enables only Y or N; converts lowercase to uppercase; converts to .T. or .F. in the memory variable for storage

You also have FORMAT functions available that, when used with the PICTURE keyword or the TRANSFORM( ) function, change the data you input to a different format. Table 17.2 shows the formats available. Note that the formats closely follow the PICTURE templates—and in some cases, such as !, with no difference. If you place a lowercase character in a GET field using PICTURE or FORMAT !, dBASE changes the response to all uppercase characters.

Table 17.2 FORMAT Options for @...SAY...GET

Option	Description
!	Enables any characters; converts letters to uppercase
^	Shows number in scientific notation
$	Displays numbers as currency ($*nnn.nn*)
(	Encloses negative numbers in parentheses
A	Enables alpha characters only
B	Aligns numeric data to the left side of a field (@...SAY only)
C	Displays CR after a positive number for accounting applications
D	Uses the SET DATE format in effect for dates
E	Uses the European date format
I	Centers text in the field
J	Aligns text to the right side of a field
L	Displays leading zeros
M	Enables a list of choices for a GET
R	Displays literals but doesn't enter them
S<*n*>	Limits the width in characters of a field to *n* and scrolls within the field if the data is too big to fit
T	Trims leading and trailing blanks
X	Opposite of C; displays DB after a negative number
Z	Displays zero numeric value as a blank string

The various keyword options available in @...SAY...GET give the command its power. Using the COLOR option enables you to set different colors to highlight your prompt (SAY) and the response field (GET). Standard color is used for the prompt, and enhanced color is used for the response. Your selections override the settings for the rest of your program for the prompt and the response. You can embed a preset default response in the GET field by using the DEFAULT keyword option. You can test for an acceptable response by specifying an expression that defines a valid response with the VALID keyword and displays your own custom error message (ERROR) if the condition is not met.

If you want to display a message when your program reads the GET statement, you can use the MESSAGE option with any valid character expression. The message then appears centered, on the bottom line of the screen. The WINDOW option enables you to open an editing window on the contents of a memo field. You can specify a range of acceptable numbers with RANGE if your GET memory variable is the numeric data type.

The WHEN keyword is an extremely useful option. WHEN enables you to control when the user can respond. You use WHEN to set a condition that must be met before input is accepted. If the expression that defines the condition returns a logical true (.T.), the GET enables a response. If not, the cursor skips to the next available GET field. Therefore, you can read a response to an earlier GET, test it with an expression, and—based on the results of the test—direct the cursor to the next desired field.

When you use @...SAY...GET to design a data input form, you can use the commands CREATE/MODIFY SCREEN to build your screen. These commands build the @...SAY...GET statements for you.

Using @ To Format the Screen

Now you can explore four other uses for @: @...CLEAR, @...FILL, @...TO, and @...SCROLL. The first, @...CLEAR, is a safe way to clear a screen without clearing any data. The syntax for @...CLEAR is:

```
@ <row1>, <col1> CLEAR [TO <row2>, <col2>]
```

If you want to clear the entire screen without affecting any of the data or memory variables, for example, use the following command:

```
@ 0,0 CLEAR
```

or

```
CLEAR
```

The cost-tracking program performs this action at the end of most procedures, as you can see at the end of the master program (refer to fig. 17.1).

Rather than clearing the entire screen, however, you also can clear only a portion of the screen. To clear only the upper half of the screen, use this command:

```
@ 0,0 CLEAR TO 12,0
```

You can clear only the section of the screen used to display a message after the user has finished reviewing the message, as seen in the following code segment:

```
IF SEEK(mName)
    DO SomePrgm
ELSE
   clDummy = " "
      @ 20,10 SAY "Record not found." GET clDummy
      READ         && READ , pauses program and waits for key press
      @ 20,10 CLEAR TO 20,26
ENDIF
```

The @...FILL command works exactly the same way, except that it fills the designated area with the color of your choice. The syntax for the @...FILL command follows:

```
@ <row1>, <col1> FILL TO <row2>, <col2>
      [COLOR <color attribute>]
```

You may find the @...FILL command especially useful for highlighting important information on the screen.

The @...TO command draws a box with a double-line or single-line border, starting with its upper-left corner at coordinates specified in *<row1, col1>* and its lower-right corner at coordinates *<row2, col2>*, as shown in the following syntax:

```
@ <row1, col1> TO <row2>, <col2>
[DOUBLE/PANEL/<border definition string>]
[COLOR <color attribute>]
```

You use the PANEL keyword to present a solid border with highlight in reverse video.

The @...SCROLL command enables you to move the contents of a certain region of the screen left, right, up, or down by a specified number of characters. The syntax for the @...SCROLL command follows:

```
@ <row1>, <col1> TO <row2>, <col2>
      SCROLL [UP/DOWN/LEFT/RIGHT][BY <expN>][WRAP]
```

If you want to move the section from row 10 to row 15 up three lines, for example, you use the following command:

```
@ 10,79 TO 15,79 SCROLL UP BY 3
```

Using Objects for Screen Input

With dBASE 5 you can now create form windows that have many different types of data-entry objects. An example of the use of the forms object is shown in the program at the end of the chapter.

Troubleshooting

All of my prompts are appearing on my printer rather than on the screen. What's going on?

When you generate a report to the printer you occasionally use SET PRINT ON. If you didn't reset this command, then all output appears on the printer. To fix the problem, locate every place you used SET PRINT ON in the program being executed and be sure there is a matching SET PRINT OFF. Another way is to use SET PRINT OFF at the beginning of each procedure that generates screen output. This handles either a forgotten SET PRINT OFF or a program error that exited to a higher routine before the SET PRINT OFF was executed.

Testing the Input with the IF Command

You learned earlier that dBASE evaluates your program code one statement or command at a time, from start to finish. Sometimes, however, you want the program to go off in a different direction, depending on the results of a particular command's execution. This decision-making function and subsequent program flow control are the province of the *conditional commands*. Conditional commands determine the real usefulness of a programming language—and dBASE 5 is rich with conditionals.

Before you discover the conditional commands, you need to understand what they do and how they do it. Conditionals help you make decisions. The simplest conditional, IF, enables you to make a decision based on two options, much as the word *if* does in everyday life. Consider the statement, "IF it rains, we will stay inside." The other choice, not staying inside, obviously proceeds from the alternative: it is not raining. You have two choices only: you can stay in or go out. That approach also works if one choice is very specific; the alternative is everything else. In the rain example, suppose that it snows. You still don't have to stay inside, because it is not raining.

You don't have many choices with IF, but you can string many IFs together: IF it rains, we will stay inside; IF it snows, we will go skiing; IF the sun shines, we will go outside; IF the wind blows, we will go sailing; and so on. DO CASE, a dBASE command, makes such multi-condition situations much simpler.

Suppose that you have all these choices, but what you really want to do is lay on the beach. You cannot do that unless it's warm and the sun is shining.

Perhaps you know that the sun is out, but you will not go to the beach unless the temperature reaches 80 degrees. You could check the thermometer, and IF it is 80 degrees, off you go. Suppose you check at 7 a.m. and find, not surprisingly, that the temperature is only 60 degrees. Is that the end of your beach plans for the whole day?

What you need is a conditional that enables you to check periodically until the temperature reaches 80 degrees, when you can head for the water. In dBASE, that conditional command is DO WHILE. You can use DO WHILE to execute the same block of code over and over until some predetermined condition is met.

IF—A Simple Conditional Command

IF provides a way for you to specify one or two possible conditions, let your program test for them, and then continue program execution based on the results of the test. The syntax for the IF command follows:

```
IF <condition>
   <commands>
[ELSE
   <commands>]
ENDIF
```

The IF command has two levels. In simple terms, the IF command says, "IF *x* occurs, do something; otherwise (ELSE), do something different." You always must close off the command with ENDIF. Notice the way IF statements are structured:

```
IF x
    Do something
ELSE
    Do something different
ENDIF
```

You have two ways to write an IF construct. The first is to put your conditions in the first line. If the conditions are met, dBASE executes the code between the IF and the ENDIF. If the conditions are not met, dBASE "falls through" those instructions without executing them and begins executing program instructions after the ENDIF.

Sometimes, however, you want to have two distinct choices of code to execute before continuing with the rest of your program. To do this, you can *nest* your IF constructs. Nesting is a technique that enables you to execute an IF command and then, if conditions warrant, execute another from inside the first IF construct (before the ENDIF is reached).

You might say, for example, "IF it doesn't rain, we will go out. ELSE, IF you find a good TV show, we will watch it. IF a good TV show is not on, then rest." Now if it rains, you have another decision to make—whether a good show is on TV. Observe how this example is structured in dBASE programming:

```
IF it doesn't rain
     Go out
ELSE
     IF good TV show
       Watch it
     ELSE
       Rest
     ENDIF
ENDIF
```

When you nest IF constructs, you must use the ELSE clause. The other reason for using the ELSE clause is to keep code modules separate and self-contained.

If you choose not to use the ELSE clause, when the IF command tests for your condition and doesn't find it, the program skips all the code within the construct and continues after the ENDIF. If you use the ELSE clause, and the IF condition is not met, the program starts executing at the ELSE. When that block of code is completed, program execution continues after ENDIF. IF is really that simple.

The subroutine in figure 17.6 uses these commands to determine whether to add a new record to the data table, as shown in the following code segment:

```
IF EOF() .AND. .NOT. FOUND()
     APPEND BLANK
ELSE       && If duplicate found
     StayIn=.F.
     @14,5 SAY "That charge number already exists for this DO'
     ACCEPT "Press enter to continue" to WrongAns
ENDIF
```

Processing in a WHILE Loop

At times, you may want to reexecute a block of code over and over until some specified event causes execution to stop or changes program flow. The broad description of this activity is *looping*. In dBASE 5, two commands help you execute program loops: DO WHILE and its subcommand, LOOP. Depending on how you use DO WHILE, you may or may not use both these commands. Look at the following syntax of DO WHILE:

```
DO WHILE <condition>
   <commands>
     [LOOP]
     [EXIT]
ENDDO
```

The DO WHILE command is fairly simple to use. First, you set up a condition that dBASE can test. If that condition is true, then dBASE executes the commands after the DO WHILE statement. When ENDDO is reached, dBASE loops back to the DO WHILE statement and tests the condition. If the condition still is true, then the commands are executed again. If the condition then is false, however, execution of the program continues with the line following ENDDO.

The LOOP command's syntax is, simply, LOOP. In DO WHILE, you may choose to use LOOP to go back to the DO WHILE condition test before you reach the ENDDO statement. LOOP normally is used in an IF construct so that, if a condition is met, the looping starts again, ignoring the commands after LOOP and before ENDDO.

You also can use EXIT. EXIT enables the program to break out of the loop even if the condition supplied with DO WHILE is true. EXIT causes the program to continue with the line after ENDDO.

The procedure in figure 17.6 uses a DO WHILE loop at the top of the procedure to force the user to make an input before continuing to the next input field. The procedure checks to see if the user entered data or pressed the Escape key to exit the routine.

You sometimes can use the SCAN command rather than a DO WHILE construct, enabling you to perform some operation on record after record. This approach enables you, for example, to set up a filter so only records that meet a condition are used.

```
SCAN [<scope>] [FOR <condition>] [WHILE <condition>]
   [<commands>]
     [LOOP]
     [EXIT]
ENDSCAN
```

Note

Avoid excessive use of LOOP and EXIT because they can make a program harder to follow. If you do use these statements, be sure to include comments as shown in these examples.

Providing Output

The final step in your program implementation is to display the information to the user. This information may be required on the screen or on the printer.

◀ See "Creating Custom Reports," p. 287

◀ See "Using the Default Quick Report Form," p. 179

Most programs need to generate some form of printed output for review and, in many cases, dissemination. There are many considerations to formatting the report's layout. What information must be included? In what format? How much detail is necessary for the report to be useful? The first step is to set up the environments for creating the report, then you design the report format using any of the methods described earlier in this book. Once you begin writing your program, you then can use the REPORT FORM command to generate the report based on the current data table.

Displaying Data on the Screen

Individual records are displayed on the screen using the same forms that were used for data input. To see more records, the BROWSE capability of dBASE can be used. The program at the end of the chapter shows two uses of browse to display the data in different index order to the user. A separate BROWSE object has been created to contain the table data while it is being browsed. You also can use the reports developed in the command center by directing their output to the screen with the REPORT FORM command.

Running a Report with the Report Form Command

After your report format is created, your environment variables set, and the data tables indexed to access the information you wish to include in the resulting report, it's time to enter the code to enable your user to generate the desired report. The sample code shown here displays a report on the printer:

```
REPORT FORM PrPhone TO PRINTER
```

This program prints a list of the phone list using the requested report format PrPhone using the REPORT FORM command. This command tells dBASE to send the data to the designated report format. You already set up some of the formatting instructions (layout, and so on) when you designed your report, so those instructions are not included in the program. The printer setup commands are stored in the PRF file and need to be activated with SET _PFORM = <*filename.PRF*> if they are different than the normal setup. To display the report on the screen, omit the TO PRINTER command after the REPORT FORM command.

Writing a Program That Uses Preprocessor Directives

You learned about writing code to control the compiling process in Chapter 16, "Getting Started with Programming." Now look at how the section of a procedure in figure 17.7 was modified to be compiled for two different printers. The memory variable *ctrlseq* has been set up to send the setup commands to the printer. Not all users have a laser printer though, so two different copies of the executable are created, one that resets an HP LaserJet and one that resets an Epson dot-matrix. Prior to compiling this routine, the PRT_TYPE variable is set to either "HP" or "EP." If the variable is not set, the #ifndef directive determines this and the #define directive is executed to set PRT_TYPE to HP.

Fig. 17.7
You can control how your code is compiled by using preprocessor directives.

```
PROCEDURE CRDUMP
* CRDUMP.PRG
* This program dumps all the data tables to the printer
* AUTHOR: Chris Bolte          DATE: JUN 89
CLOSE ALL
CLEAR
SELECT 1
ctrlseq=""
* Check to see if the print_type variable has been defined.
* If it has not, set it to be HP
#ifndef prt_type
 #define prt_type HP
#endif
* Using the value of the print_type variable, set the ctrlseq
* to the correct one for the selected printer
#if prt_type = "HP"
  ctrlseq=chr(27)+"E"+chr(27)+"&l0O"+chr(27)+"(10U"+chr(27)+
  ➥"(s0p10h12vsb3T"
#elif prt_type = "EP"
  ctrlseq=chr(27)+"@"
#endif
SET Device to print
@1,1 say ctrlseq
```

You can use preprocessor directives to check for printer setup. The main advantage of preprocessor directives is that if the critera in the #if statements are not met, the code is not included in the resulting executable, unlike the IF statement where the code is always included. This reduces the size of your executable. By combining the #if and #include you can include or exclude large blocks of code for different customers. This enables you to use the same base code, but customize it for your various clients.

Using the Debugger

When you have a problem with your program, dBASE 5 has a powerful tool to help. The Debugger enables you to monitor your program and the variables in it while it is running. Start the Debugger from the Command window by typing `DEBUG` *<program>* rather than `DO` *<program>*. This recompiles your program and brings up the Debugger screen shown in figure 17.8 with the source code for your program loaded in the code display window. A highlight bar indicates the first executable line that the Debugger found in the code. The Debugger uses six different windows to display data for you to track your program.

- Command Help window
- Debugger window
- Code Display window
- Display window
- Breakpoints window
- User window

```
 C:\DBASE\CUSTOMER\CADO2.PRG
  3 * Bugs added to demonstrate d          ---- Debug Commands ----
  4 *                               B       - Change Breakpoint entries
  5     PARAMETERS clTestTask,clS   D       - Change Display entries
  6     clTestTask = SPACE(12)      E       - Edit program file
  7     llStayIn = .T.              L       - Continue from given line
  8 * Keep asking for more until    [n]N    - As 'S' but on same or above level
  9     DO WHILE llStayIn .AND. (   P       - Show program traceback info
 10         CLEAR                   Q       - Quit debugger
 11         @1,25 SAY "ADD NEW CH   R       - Run until interrupt or error
 12         @7,5 SAY "Enter the D   [n]S    - Execute next statement
 13         READ                    U       - Suspend & go to command window
                                    CTRL-L  - Continue from selected line
 DISPLAY                            CTRL-T  - Toggle breakpoint on selected line
                          :         [n]←┘   - Repeat last step or next
                          :         [n]↑    - Show previous line
                          :         [n]↓    - Show next line
                          :         F1      - Toggle Command Help On/Off
                                    F9      - Show user screen
 DEBUGGER
Work Area: 1      Database file:              Program file: cado2.prg
Record:  0        Master Index:               Procedure:    CADO2
ACTION:                                       Current line: 5

Stopped for step.
```

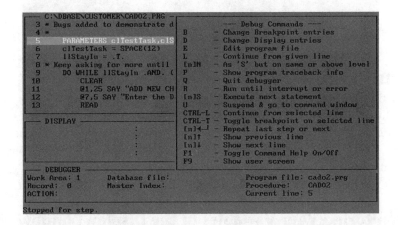

Fig. 17.8
The Debugger provides multiple windows to step through your code and find errors.

Note

The PROCEDURE line is not considered to be executable because it just provides dBASE with a pointer to the start of a routine.

Watching Your Code in the Code Display Window

A copy of your program is loaded into the code display window. A highlight bar shows the current line that is being examined. You can use the cursor control keys, including Page Up and Page Down to move the highlight. As soon as you enter the first command key after starting the Debugger, the Help window disappears, leaving you with a full-screen width for the code display window as shown in figure 17.9. You also can enter a number and then press either the Up arrow or the Down arrow to go that many lines forward or backward in the procedure. If you press Ctrl-L, the line that is highlighted becomes the next step that executes.

```
── C:\DBASE\CUSTOMER\CADO2.PRG ──────────────────────────────────────
 4 *
 5     PARAMETERS clTestTask,clStayIn
 6     clTestTask = SPACE(12)      && Initialize memory variables
 7 •   llStayIn = .T.
 8 * Keep asking for more until user doesn't leave blank or presses escape
 9     DO WHILE llStayIn .AND. (clTestTask = SACE(12) .OR. LEN(clTestTask) =
10         CLEAR
11         @1,25 SAY "ADD NEW CHARGE NUMBER/DO"
12         @7,5 SAY "Enter the DO number:   "  GET clTestTask PICTURE "9999-
13         READ
14         nlExitKey=READKEY()

── DISPLAY ──────────────────────────     ── BREAKPOINTS ──────────
                   :                        1:
                   :                        2:
                   :                        3:
                   :                        4:

── DEBUGGER ─────────────────────────────────────────────────────────
Work Area: 1       Database file:             Program file: cado2.prg
Record:  0         Master Index:              Procedure:    CADO2
ACTION:                                       Current line: 5

Stopped for step.
```

Fig. 17.9
The Help window disappears when not needed, leaving the full screen width for your code.

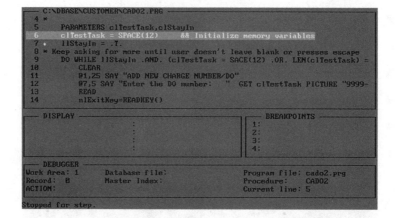

Getting Help from the Command Help Window

When the Debugger is first started, the Command Help window is displayed on the right side of the screen as shown in figure 17.8. This window gives a brief listing of all the available commands in the Debugger and their functions. As soon as you type any action into the Debugger window, the Command Help window closes, revealing the Breakpoint window under it. The Command Help window can be reopened at any time by pressing F1.

Monitoring Your Variables in the Display Window

The Debugger enables you to set up to 10 different variables to watch while your program executes. Press D from the Debugger window to enter the Display window shown in figure 17.10. Type the name of the variable or field that you want to monitor. Initially, the Display window indicates that the variable does not exist. This is as expected, because memory variables do not exist until they are initialized, and fields do not exist until the data table is open. Good selections for variables to monitor depend on the program; usually the variables that control conditionals or loops are excellent candidates.

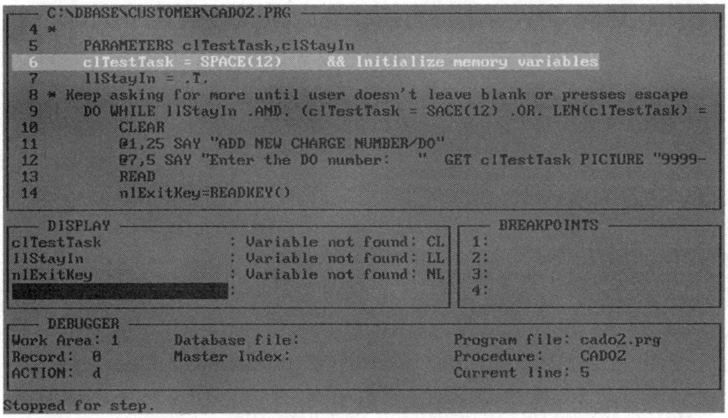

```
C:\DBASE\CUSTOMER\CADO2.PRG
 4 *
 5      PARAMETERS clTestTask,clStayIn
 6         clTestTask = SPACE(12)      && Initialize memory variables
 7         llStayIn = .T.
 8 * Keep asking for more until user doesn't leave blank or presses escape
 9      DO WHILE llStayIn .AND. (clTestTask = SACE(12) .OR. LEN(clTestTask) =
10          CLEAR
11          @1,25 SAY "ADD NEW CHARGE NUMBER/DO"
12          @7,5 SAY "Enter the DO number:   "  GET clTestTask PICTURE "9999-
13          READ
14          nlExitKey=READKEY()

DISPLAY                                              BREAKPOINTS
clTestTask              : Variable not found: CL      1:
llStayIn                : Variable not found: LL      2:
nlExitKey               : Variable not found: NL      3:
                        :                             4:

DEBUGGER
Work Area: 1      Database file:           Program file: cado2.prg
Record:  0        Master Index:            Procedure:    CADO2
ACTION:  d                                 Current line: 5

Stopped for step.
```

Fig. 17.10
You can watch what your variables are doing in the Display window.

Setting Breakpoints in Your Code

Using the cursor keys, you can scroll through the procedure in the code display window. To stop the procedure at a specific line, you set a *breakpoint* in your code. Scroll down to the line and press Ctrl-T. A new breakpoint is inserted into the Breakpoint window, to stop the program when the LINE( )=<*selected line*> and PROG( )=<*current procedure*>. The format for the breakpoint is the same as the conditional clause in a FOR or IF statement. You also can create breakpoints that are based on the value of variables or fields by entering the desired conditions in the Breakpoint window. Press B to enter the Breakpoint window and then scroll down to a blank line. Enter the conditions that you want to be true when the program stops. Examples of both types of breakpoints are shown in figure 17.11. To clear a line breakpoint, use the Ctrl-T again on the same line, or enter the Breakpoint window and delete the line that contains the breakpoint to be eliminated. Up to 10 different breakpoints can be entered at one time.

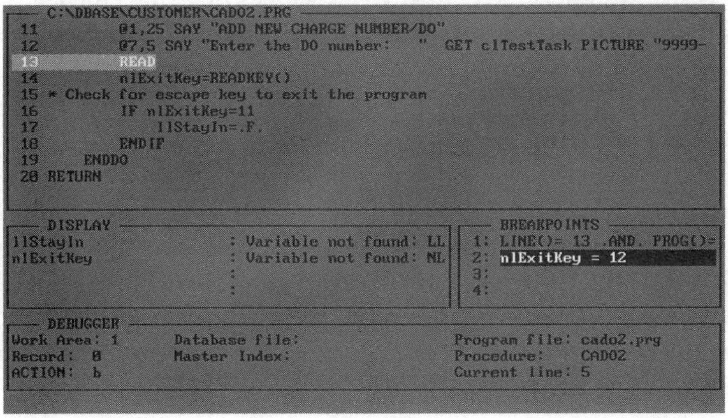

```
C:\DBASE\CUSTOMER\CADO2.PRG
11          @1,25 SAY "ADD NEW CHARGE NUMBER/DO"
12          @7,5 SAY "Enter the DO number:   "  GET clTestTask PICTURE "9999-
13          READ
14          nlExitKey=READKEY()
15 * Check for escape key to exit the program
16          IF nlExitKey=11
17              llStayIn=.F.
18          ENDIF
19      ENDDO
20 RETURN

DISPLAY                                              BREAKPOINTS
llStayIn                : Variable not found: LL      1: LINE()= 13 .AND. PROG()=
nlExitKey               : Variable not found: NL      2: nlExitKey = 12
                        :                             3:
                        :                             4:

DEBUGGER
Work Area: 1      Database file:           Program file: cado2.prg
Record:  0        Master Index:            Procedure:    CADO2
ACTION:  b                                 Current line: 5
```

Fig. 17.11
Breakpoints create places for the debugger to stop the program.

Watching Progress in the Debugger Window

The Debugger window shows the current status of your debug session. The status is displayed for each of the following environments:

- Work Area—Which of the 225 possible work areas is current
- Data table file—What data table file currently is open
- Program file—Which program file is open
- Procedure file—Which procedure in the program file is being executed
- Record—The current record pointer in the data table file
- Master Index—The currently active index file
- ACTION—The current action you are performing

ACTION is the entry point for all of your commands to the Debugger. While the cursor is on the ACTION field, you can enter one of the commands, or use the cursor keys to scroll through the procedure in the code display window. Several of the commands are affected by scrolling through the procedure. Ctrl-L sets the current line to the next executing line. Press U to suspend execution and return to the Command window. This enables you to set the value of memory variables to match what you want them to be at that point in the code. From the Command window, type RESUME to return to the Debugger. Press R to run the program at full speed, or S to step through the program. Whenever user input is required, the Debugger switches to the User screen to enable you to provide the expected input. The scroll bar moves down the code display screen as the code executes.

Seeing What the User Sees

The User screen shows exactly what your user sees while the program is running. You can switch back and forth from the Debugger to the user screen using the F9 key.

A Sample Debug Session

Part of the procedure shown in figure 17.6 has been broken out into a separate procedure to accept the delivery order number and return it with a flag to stay in or exit. During the modification, some bugs crept in to demonstrate how to use the Debugger. The new routine is shown in figure 17.12. This routine compiles without error. However, when you run it using DO CADO2, you get an error: `Invalid or unknown function`. Now you need to start the debug process.

```
PROCEDURE CADO2
* Add record to delivery order data table for charge tracking
➥system
* Bugs added to demonstrate debugger
*
    PARAMETERS clTestTask, llStayIn
    clTestTask = SPACE(12)     && Initialize memory variables
    llStayIn =. T.
* Keep asking for more until user doesn't leave blank or
➥presses escape
    DO WHILE llStayIn .AND. (clTestTask = SACE(12) .OR.
    ➥LEN(clTestTask) = 0)
       CLEAR
       @1,25 SAY "ADD NEW CHARGE NUMBER/DO"
       @7,5 SAY "Enter the DO number:    "  GET clTestTask
       ➥PICTURE "9999-99-9999"
       READ
       nlExitKey=READKEY()
* Check for escape key to exit the program
       IF nlExitKey=11
           llStayIn=.F.
       ENDIF
     ENDDO
RETURN
```

Fig. 17.12 Locating bugs with the Debugger makes debugging easy.

Let's walk through it together. Some of the steps that are shown are used to demonstrate the different methods of moving through your code. Debugging your own program may take fewer steps, or be even more complex.

1. Select CANCEL from the Error window, type **DEBUG CADO2** in the Command window, and press Enter.

2. Press D to enter the Display window. Several variables are used in control statements and you want to observe each of these. The three variables to watch are *clTestTask, nlExitKey,* and *llStayIn.* Type each variable name on a separate line and press Enter or the down arrow to move to the next line.

3. Press Escape to return to the Debugger window. Scroll down to the READ command. Press Ctrl-T to insert a breakpoint at that line.

4. Press B to enter the Breakpoint window.

5. Press the down arrow to go to the next blank line and type **nlExitKey = 12**. This stops the program whenever the value of *nlExitKey* is 12. Press Escape to return to the Debugger window.

6. Press R to run the program until an error occurs. The program stops on line 10 and the `Invalid or unknown function` message appears on the status line at the bottom of the screen. The contents of the Display window now show the current contents of *clTestTask* and *llStayIn*. *nlExitKey* still shows as Variable not found, because it has not yet been initialized.

7. Press E to edit the procedure. A warning comes up on the status line that the object file no longer matches the source. Press the space bar to clear the warning. The program editor is opened with your procedure loaded and the cursor placed at the line where the error was detected. Correct the error, in this case the 'P' was left out of the word SPACE. Press Alt-E, S to save the changes.

8. The debugger still is working with the original object file, so you now have a choice to make. If the changes made were not major, you can continue to execute the program to detect other errors. If the changes make a major difference in how the code operates, you need to get out of the debugger by typing **Q** to recompile the code and by typing **DEBUG CADO2** in the Command window again. In this case the correction was to the outer DO loop. Additional errors can occur in the loop and you can step through to watch the variables change.

9. Type **2S** to execute the next two steps of the program. These lines set up the user screen for input.

10. Type **R** to run to the next breakpoint. The cursor now is positioned on the READ line. The status line shows that you are stopped at breakpoint 1.

11. Press S to execute the READ. The Debugger opens the User screen to accept input for the program.

12. To test the exit handler, press Escape. The Debugger screen reappears, with the cursor on the line after the READ.

13. Press S to load the key pressed value into *nlExitKey*. The Display window now shows that the value of *nlExitKey* is 12. However, the IF statement tests for a value of 11. This has to be corrected. Press E to edit the procedure as you did in step 7. Once in the program editor, change the 11 to a 12 in the IF*nlExitKey* = 11 statement.

14. To continue testing your exit handling routine, because the Debugger still works with the original program file, not the one you just modified, you need to reset the value of *nlExitKey* to the value that is being tested. Press U to suspend the program. The Debugger exits to the Command window.

15. Type **nlExitKey = 11**. This sets the value of the *nlExitKey* to the value expected in your IF loop.

16. Type **RESUME** to return to the Debugger. The Debugger screen reappears with the cursor still at the same line in the code.

17. Press S to step through the code. The program now goes into the IF loop. Because you have set the value of *nlExitKey* to 11, the second breakpoint does not execute. If you had left the value 12, each line would have generated a breakpoint as long as the value of *nlExitKey* remained 12.

18. Press B to enter the Breakpoint window. Scroll down to the second breakpoint and use the Backspace key to delete the breakpoint, then press Enter to accept the change. Press Escape to return to the Debugger window.

19. Press S again and the value of *llStayIn* in the Display window changes from T to F.

20. Press S seven more times and you can watch the routine step through the exit procedure. When the program ends, the Debugger closes and returns to the Command window.

21. Restart the debug cycle to check that all the bugs have been found and fixed.

As you gain experience in writing and debugging programs, the debugging process becomes easier. The Debugger helps you learn to correct problems by locating obvious ones for you. However, some subtle bugs slip by the Debugger. You learn to recognize and correct some potential problems before you even finish writing a procedure.

Code for Customer Tracking

The code for the Customer Tracking system is broken into three modules. The RCUSTFOR.PRG file contains the code for all the procedures accessed from the menu. The RCUSTFOR.DFM file contains the definition of the form. The RCUSTFOR.MNU contains the code for the definition of the menu.

RCUSTFOR.PRG

This routine is the main program for executing the form and receiving the user input. In addition to the main procedure, the file includes the procedures for handling events from the menu and form, and the procedures for saving and restoring the environment. The preprocessor directive #define is used to include the menu definition statements in the final executable. The SaveSets procedure is called at the beginning to save the environment settings and SET the conditions for the program. The preprocessor directive #include is used to bring in all the code for the form definition. A BROWSE object is created for displaying reports on the screen. The form is executed with the ReadModal( ) method. All user input is handled by the form object until the user exits the form. The Action property indicates how the user exited the form and enables you to take action on the OK button from the form, in this case, close the data table. Finally, the CleanUp procedure is called to restore the environment.

The procedure PrPhones uses the REPORT FORM command to send formatted output to the printer.

The CustReport and IDReport procedures each use the BROWSE object to display information on the screen. The order of the data is changed by using the SET ORDER TO command to select the correct index tag. The TEXT property of the BROWSE object is changed in each routine to change the title of the Browse window on the screen. The ReadModal( ) method is used to help the user move around the report.

The SaveSets and CleanUp procedures use the array *cgSetArray* to store the environment variables. This uses only one memory variable to store all the environment settings, and enables the use of the FOR...NEXT loop to rapidly save and restore the settings.

```
*-----------------------------------------------------------
* TITLE: Customer Information System
* ABSTRACT: Allows display, input, and reports on customers
*-----------------------------------------------------------
     PRIVATE lVoid, clOldProc, clFormRun, clDispMode, clNewMode

     #define Menus Yes
    DO SaveSets   && Save current SET values and turn off

    * Bring in the code for the main form description
    #include "rCustFor.DFM"
```

```
    *------------------------------------------------------
    * Create a browse object for display of data on the screen.
    *------------------------------------------------------
    DEFINE BROWSE cfBrowse;
       PROPERTY;
       LEFT      1,;
       TOP       8,;
       WIDTH     78,;
       HEIGHT    10,;
       MODIFY    .F.,;
       VISIBLE       .T.,;
       STATUSMESSAGE    "Scroll through the customer list"

    rCustFor.Action = .F.  && Set .T. by OKHAND before closing
    lVoid = rCustFor.ReadModal()   && Open the form and get input

    IF rCustFor.Action     && Allows for action on OK select
       USE    && Close the data table
    ENDIF     && End of IF rCustFor.Action

    RELEASE rCustFor          && Release the form and object ref.

    DO CleanUp  && Restore the environment

RETURN         && EOP: rCustFor

PROCEDURE PrPhones      && iPrPhones.ONCLICK
*---------------------------------------------
* TITLE:  Print Phones
* ABSTRACT:  Prints a phone list from the data
* table.  This handles the OnClick event from
* the iPrPhone item in the File,Reports menu.
*---------------------------------------------
   SET ORDER TO ctCompany
   REPORT FORM PhonList TO PRINT
RETURN

PROCEDURE CustReport     && iCompName.ONCLICK
*-----------------------------------------------------------------
* NAME: Customer Report
* ABSTRACT:  ONCLICK - Event handler for iCompName
* Displays a report in a browse window on the screen
* in company name order.
*-----------------------------------------------------------------
    SET ORDER TO ctCompany
    cfBrowse.Text = "Customers by Company Name"
    lvoid = cfBrowse.ReadModal()
RETURN

PROCEDURE IDReport     && iCustID.ONCLICK
*-----------------------------------------------------------------
* NAME: Customer ID report
* ABSTRACT:  ONCLICK - Event handler for iCustID
* Displays a browse window on the screen with the records in
* Customer ID order.
*-----------------------------------------------------------------
```

```
SET ORDER TO ctCustID
    cfBrowse.Text = "Customers by ID number"
    lvoid = cfBrowse.ReadModal()
RETURN

PROCEDURE SaveSets
*-----------------------------------------------------------
* TITLE:  SaveSets
* ABSTRACT:  This procedure saves the current value of the
* system SET commands that are changed in the program.
*-----------------------------------------------------------
   PUBLIC ARRAY cgSetArray[2,8]
   PRIVATE clFormRun
*-----------------------------------------------------------
* Row 1 of the array is the environment condition being
* stored. Row 2 of the array is the status of the condition.
* Start by storing the name of all the conditions.
*-----------------------------------------------------------
   cgSetArray[1,1] = "SCOREBOARD"
   cgSetArray[1,2] = "STATUS"
   cgSetArray[1,3] = "HELP"
   cgSetArray[1,4] = "TALK"
   cgSetArray[1,5] = "ECHO"
   cgSetArray[1,6] = "ESCAPE"
   cgSetArray[1,7] = "PRINT"
   cgSetArray[1,8] = "PROCEDURE"

   FOR nlIndex = 1 TO 7    && Index for each condition

    * Get the current setting and store it in row 2 of the array
      cgSetArray[2,nlIndex] = SET(cgSetArray[1,nlIndex])
      SET &cgSetArray[1,nlIndex] OFF     && Set new value

    NEXT    && End of nlIndex for cgSetArray

*-------------------------------------------
*-- Make sure that FormRun.dbo file is active
*-------------------------------------------
   cgSetArray[2,8] = SET(cgSetArray[1,8])
   clFormRun = HOME() + 'FORMRUN.DBO'
    SET &cgSetArray[1,8] TO &clFormRun

RETURN   && End of procedure SaveSets

PROCEDURE CleanUp
*-----------------------------------------------------
* TITLE:  CleanUp
* ABSTRACT:  This procedure restores the saved value of the
* system SET commands that were changed in the program.
*-----------------------------------------------------
    FOR nlIndex = 1 TO 7   && Index for the array

* Check to make sure the array entry is not blank
      IF .NOT. ISBLANK( cgSetArray[1,nlIndex] )
* If not blank, set to original value
         SET &cgSetArray[1,nlIndex] &cgSetArray[2,nlIndex]
```

```
        ENDIF   && End of check for not blank

    NEXT   && End of Index for array

    IF .NOT. ISBLANK( cgSetArray[2,8] )
           SET PROCEDURE TO &cgSetArray[2,8]
    ENDIF

RETURN
```

RCUSTFOR.DFM

This file contains all of the commands to define the form used for user input and data display. The line continuation character ; is used to enhance the readability of the code. First, the form is named and sized with the DEFINE FORM command. The default data table, CUSTOMER.DBF, is opened with no index active. Next, the preprocessor directive #include is used to bring in all the menu definition commands. The #ifdef...#endif preprocessor directives around the #include enables you to exclude the menus for the form from your executable simply by not defining the Menus macro name. The TEXT objects define the labels placed beside the entry fields. The TEXT property of the TEXT objects defines what appears on the screen. The ENTRYFIELD objects are set to help the user enter data into your form. Each ENTRYFIELD is tied to a specific field in the data table with the DATALINK property. The location of each object on the form is determined by the objects LEFT, TOP, and WIDTH properties. Finally, the PUSHBUTTON objects are defined. Each PUSHBUTTON has an ONCLICK property that refers to one of the procedures in the RCUSTFOR.PRG file.

```
*------------------------------------------------------------
* rCustFor.DFM
* TITLE:  Form Definition File
* ABSTRACT:  Define a full screen form to use for the main menu.
* Use the continuation character ; to format the commands
* for easier readability.
*------------------------------------------------------------
DEFINE FORM rCustFor ;
   PROPERTY ;
      HEIGHT            22,;
      LEFT              0,;
      TEXT              "Customer Information",;
      TOP               0,;
      WIDTH             80

rCustFor.CURRMAST = "CUSTOMER"     && Name of Master alias for form

USE CUSTOMER.DBF   && Open the data table

* Bring in the menu definition commands
```

```
#ifdef Menus
    #include "rCustFor.MNU"
#endif

* Label for the ID field on the form
DEFINE TEXT cfLblID OF M->rCustFor ;
   PROPERTY ;
      LEFT               1,;
      TEXT               "Customer ID",;
      TOP                1,;
      WIDTH            11

* Customer ID data entry field.
DEFINE ENTRYFIELD cfCustId OF M->rCustFor ;
   PROPERTY ;
      DATALINK           "CUSTOMER->CTCUSTID",;
      LEFT               18,;
      PICTURE            "XXXXX",;
      TOP                1,;
      WIDTH              5

DEFINE TEXT cfLblComp OF M->rCustFor ;
   PROPERTY ;
      LEFT               1,;
      TEXT               "Company",;
      TOP                2,;
      WIDTH              7

DEFINE ENTRYFIELD cfCompany OF M->rCustFor ;
   PROPERTY ;
      DATALINK           "CUSTOMER->CTCOMPANY",;
      LEFT               18,;
      PICTURE            "XXXXXXXXXXXXXXXXXXXXXXXXXXXXXX",;
      TOP                2,;
      WIDTH              30

DEFINE TEXT cfLblAddr OF M->rCustFor ;
   PROPERTY ;
      LEFT               1,;
      TEXT               "Address",;
      TOP                3,;
      WIDTH              7

DEFINE ENTRYFIELD cfAddr1 OF M->rCustFor ;
   PROPERTY ;
      DATALINK           "CUSTOMER->CTADDRLN1",;
      LEFT               18,;
      PICTURE            "XXXXXXXXXXXXXXXXXXXXXXXXXXXXXX",;
      TOP                3,;
      WIDTH              30

DEFINE ENTRYFIELD cfAddr2 OF M->rCustFor ;
   PROPERTY ;
      DATALINK           "CUSTOMER->CTADDRLN2",;
      LEFT               18,;
      PICTURE            "XXXXXXXXXXXXXXXXXXXXXXXXXXXXXX",;
```

```
      TOP              4,;
      WIDTH            30

DEFINE TEXT cfLblCity OF M->rCustFor ;
   PROPERTY ;
      LEFT             1,;
      TEXT             "City",;
      TOP              5,;
      WIDTH            4

DEFINE ENTRYFIELD cfCity OF M->rCustFor ;
   PROPERTY ;
      DATALINK         "CUSTOMER->CTCITY",;
      LEFT             18,;
      PICTURE          "XXXXXXXXXXXXXXXXXXXXXXXXXXXXXX",;
      TOP              5,;
      WIDTH            30

DEFINE ENTRYFIELD cfState OF M->rCustFor ;
   PROPERTY ;
      DATALINK         "CUSTOMER->CTSTATE",;
      LEFT             50,;
      PICTURE          "!XX",;
      TOP              5,;
      WIDTH            2

DEFINE ENTRYFIELD cfZipCode OF M->rCustFor ;
   PROPERTY ;
      DATALINK         "CUSTOMER->CTZIPCODE",;
      LEFT             55,;
      PICTURE          "XXXXXXXXXX",;
      TOP              5,;
      WIDTH            10

DEFINE TEXT cfLblPhon OF M->rCustFor ;
   PROPERTY ;
      LEFT             1,;
      TEXT             "Phone",;
      TOP              7,;
      WIDTH            7

DEFINE ENTRYFIELD cfPhone OF M->rCustFor ;
   PROPERTY ;
      DATALINK         "CUSTOMER->CTPHONE",;
      LEFT             18,;
      PICTURE          "XXXXXXXXXXXXXXX",;
      TOP              7,;
      WIDTH            15

DEFINE TEXT cfLblFax OF M->rCustFor ;
   PROPERTY ;
      LEFT             40,;
      TEXT             "FAX",;
      TOP              7,;
      WIDTH            5
```

```
DEFINE ENTRYFIELD cfFax OF M->rCustFor ;
   PROPERTY ;
      DATALINK          "CUSTOMER->CTFAX",;
      LEFT              45,;
      PICTURE           "XXXXXXXXXXXXXXX",;
      TOP               7,;
      WIDTH             15

DEFINE PUSHBUTTON bfOK OF M->rCustFor ;
   PROPERTY ;
      LEFT              1,;
      ONCLICK           OKHand,;
      TEXT              "&Ok",;
      TOP               17,;
      WIDTH             10

rCustFor.bfOK.Procfile = "OKHAND.PRG," + HOME() + "FORMRUN.DBO"

DEFINE PUSHBUTTON bfCancel OF M->rCustFor ;
   PROPERTY ;
      LEFT              11,;
      ONCLICK           CanHand,;
      TEXT              "Cancel",;
      TOP               17,;
      WIDTH             10

rCustFor.bfCancel.Procfile = "CANHAND.PRG," + HOME() +
"FORMRUN.DBO"

DEFINE PUSHBUTTON bfPrev OF M->rCustFor ;
   PROPERTY ;
      LEFT              21,;
      ONCLICK           PrevHand,;
      TEXT              "&Prev",;
      TOP               17,;
      WIDTH             10

rCustFor.bfPrev.Procfile = "PREVHAND.PRG," + HOME() + "FORMRUN.DBO"

DEFINE PUSHBUTTON bfNext OF M->rCustFor ;
   PROPERTY ;
      LEFT              32,;
      ONCLICK           SkipHand,;
      TEXT              "&Next",;
      TOP               17,;
      WIDTH             10

rCustFor.bfNext.Procfile = "SKIPHAND.PRG," + HOME() + "FORMRUN.DBO"
```

RCUSTFOR.MNU

This file contains all the commands to set up the menu for the form. The main menu, a bar menu that appears at the top of the form window, is set up with the DEFINE MENUBAR command. Each choice on the bar menu is created using the DEFINE MENU command to create a pull-down menu system. The TEXT property shows the choice that appears on the menu. The & character is used to indicate which letter in the TEXT can be used as a hot key to select the choice from the menu. Individual choices on the pull-down menus are created with the DEFINE MENUITEM command. Each MENUITEM has an ONCLICK property that refers to an event handling procedure, either in the RCUSTFOR.PRG or in the library of procedures delivered with dBASE 5. The HOME( ) function is used to indicate the source directory for dBASE. The STATUSMESSAGE property provides a one-line help message at the bottom of the screen.

```
*-----------------------------------------------------
* rCustFor.MNU
* TITLE: Main Menu Definition File
* ABSTRACT: This is the main bar menu for the customer
* information form.
*-----------------------------------------------------
DEFINE MENUBAR MenuBar1 OF rCustFor

DEFINE MENU uMBFile OF rCustFor.MenuBar1;
   PROPERTY ;
      STATUSMESSAGE "File operations",;
      TEXT "&File"

DEFINE MENUITEM ifExit OF rCustFor.MenuBar1.uMBFile;
   PROPERTY ;
      ONCLICK  MDExit,;
      PROCFILE "MDExit.PRG," + HOME() + "FORMRUN.DBO",;
      SHORTCUT "Ctrl-F4",;
      STATUSMESSAGE "Close the form",;
      TEXT "E&xit"

DEFINE MENU uReports OF rCustFor.MenuBar1.uMBFile;
   PROPERTY ;
      STATUSMESSAGE "Select and generate reports from the data table",;
      TEXT "&Reports"

DEFINE MENUITEM iCompName OF rCustFor.MenuBar1.uMBFile.uReports;
   PROPERTY ;
      ONCLICK  CustReport,;
      STATUSMESSAGE "Report by company name",;
      TEXT "&Customer list"

DEFINE MENUITEM iCustId OF rCustFor.MenuBar1.uMBFile.uReports;
   PROPERTY ;
      ONCLICK  IDReport,;
      STATUSMESSAGE "Customer list by ID number",;
      TEXT "Customer &Id list"

DEFINE MENUITEM iPrPhone OF rCustFor.MenuBar1.uMBFile.uReports;
   PROPERTY ;
      ONCLICK  PrPhones,;
```

```
        STATUSMESSAGE "Phone list by Company",;
        TEXT "Print &Phone List"

DEFINE MENU uMBSrch OF rCustFor.MenuBar1;
    PROPERTY ;
        STATUSMESSAGE "Search for specific records",;
        TEXT "&Search"

DEFINE MENUITEM iGoTop OF rCustFor.MenuBar1.uMBSrch;
    PROPERTY ;
        ENABLED .t.,;
        ONCLICK  MDGoTop,;
        PROCFILE "MDGoTop.PRG," + HOME() + "FORMRUN.DBO",;
        SHORTCUT "Ctrl-Pgup",;
        STATUSMESSAGE "Move to the first record in the table",;
        TEXT "&Top Record"

DEFINE MENUITEM iGoBtm OF rCustFor.MenuBar1.uMBSrch;
    PROPERTY ;
        ENABLED .T.,;
        ONCLICK  MDGoBtm,;
        PROCFILE "MDGoBtm.PRG," + HOME() + "FORMRUN.DBO",;
        SHORTCUT "Ctrl-Pgdn",;
        STATUSMESSAGE "Move to the last record in the table",;
        TEXT "&Last Record"

DEFINE MENUITEM iGoRecNo OF rCustFor.MenuBar1.uMBSrch;
    PROPERTY ;
        ENABLED .T.,;
        ONCLICK  MDGoRNbr,;
        PROCFILE "MDGoRNbr.PRG," + HOME() + "FORMRUN.DBO",;
        STATUSMESSAGE "Move to the specified record",;
        TEXT "&Record number..."

DEFINE MENUITEM iSkip OF rCustFor.MenuBar1.uMBSrch;
    PROPERTY ;
        ENABLED .T.,;
        ONCLICK  MDSkip,;
        PROCFILE "MDSkip.PRG," + HOME() + "FORMRUN.DBO",;
        STATUSMESSAGE "Move by skipping the specified number of records",;
        TEXT "S&kip..."

DEFINE MENUITEM iLine1 OF rCustFor.MenuBar1.uMBSrch;
    PROPERTY ;
        SEPARATOR .T.

DEFINE MENUITEM iIndex OF rCustFor.MenuBar1.uMBSrch;
    PROPERTY ;
        ENABLED .T.,;
        ONCLICK  MDIdxKey,;
        PROCFILE "MDIdxKey.PRG," + HOME() + "FORMRUN.DBO",;
        STATUSMESSAGE "Use an index to search for the specified value",;
        TEXT "&Index key..."
```

```
DEFINE MENUITEM iLine2 OF rCustFor.MenuBar1.uMBSrch;
   PROPERTY ;
      SEPARATOR .T.

DEFINE MENUITEM iForward OF rCustFor.MenuBar1.uMBSrch;
   PROPERTY ;
      ENABLED .T.,;
      ONCLICK  MDFwd,;
      PROCFILE "MDFwd.PRG," + HOME() + "FORMRUN.DBO",;
      STATUSMESSAGE "Search this field for the specified value from the current
record forward",;
      TEXT "&Forward..."

DEFINE MENUITEM iBackwrd OF rCustFor.MenuBar1.uMBSrch;
   PROPERTY ;
      ENABLED .T.,;
      ONCLICK  MDFwd,;
      PROCFILE "MDFwd.PRG," + HOME() + "FORMRUN.DBO",;
      STATUSMESSAGE "Search this field for the specified value from the current
record backward",;
      TEXT "&Backward..."

DEFINE MENUITEM iMtchCap OF rCustFor.MenuBar1.uMBSrch;
   PROPERTY ;
      ENABLED .T.,;
      ONCLICK  MDCS,;
      PROCFILE "MDCS.PRG," + HOME() + "FORMRUN.DBO",;
      STATUSMESSAGE "Case sensitive search",;
      TEXT "&Match capitalization"

DEFINE MENU uMBOrg OF rCustFor.MenuBar1;
   PROPERTY ;
      STATUSMESSAGE "Order records by index",;
      TEXT "&Organize"

DEFINE MENUITEM iOrder OF rCustFor.MenuBar1.uMBOrg;
   PROPERTY ;
      ENABLED .T.,;
      ONCLICK  MDOrder,;
      PROCFILE "MDOrder.PRG," + HOME() + "FORMRUN.DBO",;
      STATUSMESSAGE "Select an index tag by which to order this table",;
      TEXT "&Order records..."

DEFINE MENU uMBHelp OF rCustFor.MenuBar1;
   PROPERTY ;
      STATUSMESSAGE "Get help",;
      TEXT "&Help"

DEFINE MENUITEM iHlpIndx OF rCustFor.MenuBar1.uMBHelp;
   PROPERTY ;
      STATUSMESSAGE "Show index for dBASE on-line help",;
      TEXT "&Help index"

DEFINE MENUITEM iHlpKeys OF rCustFor.MenuBar1.uMBHelp;
   PROPERTY ;
      STATUSMESSAGE "Show keystroke help for the developer's desktop",;
```

```
      TEXT "&Keyboard help"

DEFINE MENUITEM iHlpObj OF rCustFor.MenuBar1.uMBHelp;
   PROPERTY ;
      ONCLICK  HelpObj,;
      PROCFILE "MENUEDIT.PRG,C:\DBASE\IDELIB.DBO",;
      STATUSMESSAGE "Get help for the current object",;
      TEXT "A&ctive field"

DEFINE MENUITEM iLine1 OF rCustFor.MenuBar1.uMBHelp;
   PROPERTY ;
      SEPARATOR .T.

DEFINE MENUITEM iHlpAbt OF rCustFor.MenuBar1.uMBHelp;
   PROPERTY ;
      STATUSMESSAGE "Get information about this form",;
      TEXT "&About"
```

From Here...

You've now explored the ins and outs of writing a program that prints a report, obtains keyboard data from the user during execution, and displays text prompts to the user. You've also seen how you can use preprocessor directives to control how your program compiles depending on certain preset conditions. To learn more about programming in dBASE, you may want to check out the following chapters.

- Chapter 19, "Using the Applications Generator and the Compiler," explains how to make your programming job easier.

- Chapter 20, "Programming with SQL," introduces you to using the powerful English-like syntax of Structured Query Language commands and functions.

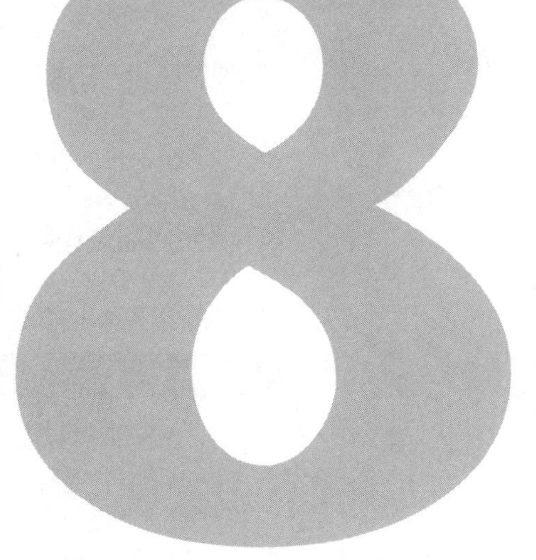

Chapter 18

Creating Custom Applications

Now that you learned the basics of programming technique, and explored some typical programs, you are ready to design your own application. As detailed in the previous chapters, you need to spend some time designing your application before you create your databases or procedures. This design process involves determining what you want the application to do. A good starting point is actually the end result—what you need to print or display on the screen. You use the information from your report and screen designs to determine what fields you need in your database. During this design process, you determine how all your files will interact.

In this chapter you explore ways to do the following:

- Use menus in your program
- Design your own windows
- Write your own help screens
- Build a procedure library
- Design and print reports

Defining the Files in the Applications

dBASE 5 has several file types it uses to execute your commands. Some of the things you probably ask it to do deal with programming, data storage, indexing, memos, report generation, screen generation, label generation, queries, and macros. To avoid confusion and to make these tasks easy to track, dBASE 5 assigns a default extension to each type of file you create. Naturally, the extension does not define a type of file, rather it identifies itself as a certain kind of file. This makes locating the file easier. For example, if you want to create a database, dBASE adds DBF to the end of the name you enter, thus identifying it as a database file.

Note

It's possible that you may want to use a different extension; you must be careful about making this decision. Changing the conventions used within your database makes it difficult to use, particularly if you want to export the file to another database, or if someone unfamiliar with your programming style needs to modify what you create. If you do decide to change the conventions, be sure to document the newly defined extensions for your records.

Table 18.1 identifies some of the more common file types that dBASE recognizes. dBASE looks at the extension in order to find files to associate with your requests. For instance, if you want to modify a format file, you ask dBASE to show you a list of all files with the extension FMT. This makes finding a given type of file easy and fast.

Table 18.1 Conventional File Types That dBASE Recognizes

Extension	File Type
CAT	Catalog of related files
DBF	Database file
DBO	Compiled program code
DBT	Database memo files
FMO	Compiled format files
FMT	Format source code files
FRG	Report form source code
FRM	Report forms
FRO	Compiled report forms
LBG	Label source code
LBL	Label files
LBO	Compiled label files

Extension	File Type
MDX	Multiple-index files
MEM	Memory files
NDX	Index files (dBASE III Plus)
PRG	Program source
QBE	Query files
QBO	Compiled query files
SCR	Screen form files
TXT	Text files
VUE	View files (dBASE III Plus)

Source code files, those with the extensions PRG, FRG, or FMT, contain ASCII program code enabling you to edit these files as needed, using either your favorite ASCII editor, the file viewer editor, or program editor. However, compiled (object) code files, with extensions such as DBO, FMO, or LBO, were converted into more efficient machine language and therefore cannot be edited or viewed.

You can manipulate the file types using any of several commands within dBASE 5. CREATE builds a new data table (DBF). If you need to change the organization of the data table structure, you can use the MODIFY STRUCTURE command. Or you can use the MODIFY COMMAND command to build a new program (PRG) file or change one you created earlier. The other source code files can be modified in the same manner. You can also generate a report form using dBASE's automatic features and then modify to fine-tune the report manually. For more information on CREATE and MODIFY see Chapter 22.

◄ See "Working with Files," p. 52

Designing an Application

Defining the data table is the first step in writing an application, but it's not the first step in the design process. As with any programming process, the first thing you must do is decide the outcome of the program, that is, what can the program accomplish? Some applications simply produce financial reports, others create class registration systems for college students, and others may generate invoices on the first day of each month. What is your application's job?

Figure 18.1 identifies the six-step process you can follow to write your application. As you can see, the first step is to define the job to be done by the application; then define the data tables to be used. All database applications are primarily data storage systems. You use the surrounding application only to add to the data, to edit the data, or to manipulate it into reports, labels, or other forms of output. After defining your data tables, you can start writing the actual code, beginning with the data tables and proceeding with program and reporting functions. When everything else is complete, you can begin the debug and test phase.

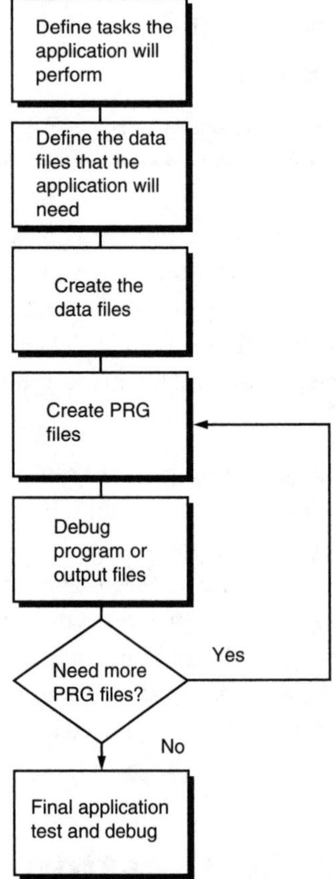

Fig. 18.1
Following this six-step process makes writing applications easier to manage.

You can do the second step of the process, creating the data tables necessary for your application, in one of two ways. Your choice depends on the uses you have for the data in the database.

Designing an Invoice Application

One possible use for a dBASE application is to track expenses for your company. A subsystem of this can track invoices. The main output of this system is a printed invoice similar to the one shown in figure 18.2.

Invoice #

Name:
Address:

Phone:

Qty	Item Description	Price each	Sub Total
		Total	

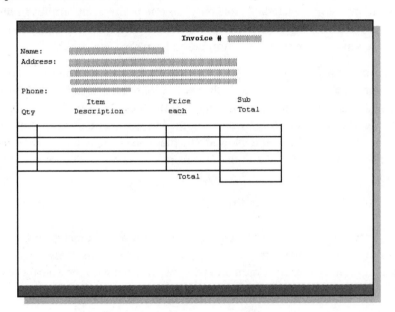

Fig. 18.2
Having the form on paper helps with the design.

There is certain information you need to have in order to accurately invoice your customers. The following are some of the fields you can use:

Company Name

Contact Name

Address Line 1

Address Line 2

City, State, ZIP Code

Phone Number, Extension

Fax Number

Customer Type

Current Balance

You can also determine some of the relationships between the fields by looking at the form. For each invoice, you can have multiple items. This is called a many-to-one relationship. There are two ways to code this in a database.

You can put a certain number of fields in each record for items, but this limits you to only that many items before creating a new invoice. A more efficient method is to create a separate data table for the items and relate it to the invoice table by the invoice number. This is called *normalizing* your database, to insure that each data table only has one-to-one relationships in the records. Likewise, each company can have more than one invoice, so you want to separate the company information from the invoice.

You can group all of your files for this application together. You should do this both at the DOS level and in dBASE. To group the files at the DOS level, create a separate subdirectory to contain all the files, for example INVOICES. Change to this subdirectory by opening the **F**ile menu and choosing the C**h**ange Directory command. Now all the files you create will be in their own directory. To group the files in dBASE, create a separate Catalog for the application. In the Command window, type:

SET CATALOG TO INVOICES

Press Enter and select **Y**es in the dialog box to create a new catalog. Enter the description of the catalog in the pop-up window that appears. Press Enter and the prompt returns to the Command window. You will see a message on-screen that `File catalog is empty`, which it should be since you just created it!

All files that are created are now added to the catalog INVOICES.

◀ See "Defining Your Database," p. 110

To convert this list of required data to a database file, you must decide what kind of information to store in each field. The quantity, price, total, and balance fields are the only fields that require Numeric field types. Although ZIP codes, phone numbers, and invoice numbers are usually totally numeric, they are stored in character fields because they aren't used for calculations. Invoice paid is a logical field, because it only requires a yes/no value. All the other fields are character fields. Use the CREATE command to create the following data tables. Additional fields are added to handle tax exempt companies, charged taxes, and discounts for certain clients. The field names selected should be descriptive of the contents. The naming convention used here shows *<data type><scope><contents name>*. The data type can be "c" for character, "n" for numeric, "l" for logical, or "d" for date. Because these are all field names in tables, the scope is t" for table. For memory variables, the scope could also be "g" for global or "l" for local. The contents name should be as descriptive as possible. By using capital letters at the beginning of words in your names, you can eliminate the requirement for underscores (_) between parts of the name. You should also make sure that none of your names is a *reserved* word in dBASE. Reserved words are ones used as commands in dBASE; for example, ORDER.

Tip
Remember to save your work frequently as you develop your database.

CUSTOMER

ctCompId	CHARACTER	5	
ctCompany	CHARACTER	50	
ctContact	CHARACTER	50	
ctAddress1	CHARACTER	50	
ctAddress	CHARACTER	50	
ctCity	CHARACTER	30	
ctState	CHARACTER	2	
ctCountry	CHARACTER	10	
ctZipCode	CHARACTER	10	
ctPhone	CHARACTER	15	
ctFax	CHARACTER	15	
ctTaxId	CHARACTER	15	
ntNormDisc	NUMERIC	10	3
ntBalance	NUMERIC	10	2

SALES

ctCompId	CHARACTER	5	
ctInvNum	CHARACTER	8	
dtInvDate	DATE		
ntInvTot	NUMERIC	10	2
ltInvPaid	LOGICAL		
ctInvPayBy	CHARACTER	5	
dtInvDue	DATE		
ntInvDis	NUMERIC	10	3
ntInvTax	NUMERIC	10	2

ITEMS

ctInvNum	CHARACTER	8	
ctItemDes	CHARACTER	30	
ntItemQty	NUMERIC	7	
ntItemPric	NUMERIC	10	2

If you need to modify your data table after saving it, you can use the MODIFY STRUCTURE command. Any modifications need to be done before adding data; because if you modify the structure when there is data in the table, you can lose data.

> **Caution**
>
> You must have exclusive access to a data table to modify the structure. If you have SHARE installed or you are on a network, you will get an error if you try to modify the structure and the EXCLUSIVE property is not ON. Use SET EXCLUSIVE ON before you use a file in which you are going to modify the structure.

Designing an Inventory Application

Another common use for database applications is to track inventory. Looking at the previous example, you can see that the item description is a long field that has to be typed in often. Creating a data table of all your items in stock makes this task simpler. You assign a separate number to each item and input the description of the item into the table. Then the invoice system can be modified to accept the item number instead of the item description.

You need one additional table to track the inventory.

STOCK

ctItemId	CHARACTER	14	
ctItemDesc	CHARACTER	30	
ntOnHand	NUMERIC	7	
ntOnOrder	NUMERIC	7	
ctSupplier	CHARACTER	5	
ntItemPric	NUMERIC	10	2
ntItemCost	NUMERIC	10	2

You need to modify two of the existing tables to handle both invoices and inventory. The ITEMS table needs to refer to ITEM_ID instead of ITEM_DESC; and the SALES table needs to get a field that indicates whether it is an invoice or an order. The ITEM_PRICE field appears in both the STOCK and the ITEM tables to allow selection of the normal price or a sale price.

SALES			
ltOrder	LOGICAL	1	
ctCompId	CHARACTER	5	
ctInvNum	CHARACTER	8	
dtInvDate	DATE	8	
ntInvTot	NUMERIC	10	2
ntInvPaid	LOGICAL	1	
ctInvPayBy	CHARACTER	5	
dtInvDue	DATE	8	
ntInvDisc	NUMERIC	10	3
ntInvTax	NUMERIC	10	2
ITEMS			
ctInvNum	CHARACTER	8	
ctItemId	CHARACTER	30	
ntItemQty	NUMERIC	7	
ntItemPric	NUMERIC	10	2

You need to consider how you want to access the data in your tables at this point. While you create the tables, dBASE 5 offers you the choice of flagging any field in the table as an index field. If you set this flag to true, dBASE 5 creates an entry in the multiple index file (MDX) for the data table for the selected field. This allows you to order your reports based on this field.

Designing Forms for Data Input and Output

Once you create the data tables, you can use them to create your data input screens, output screens, and output reports. Creating reports (FRM) and forms (FMT) at this point allows you to call them when you write your programs.

Creating and Modifying Program Files

You have the power to create and modify your data tables, reports, and forms. Now you can start on program files. You're not done with the database files completely, however. After you finish with the basics of writing a small program, you return to data tables to manipulate the data in several interesting ways.

You have two ways to perform dBASE commands. One way is to enter your commands interactively from the Command window. The other is to create a program file which contains all the commands to execute.

When you write your commands interactively, you cannot do certain commands. The program flow commands that return you to different points in your program, for example, don't work in the Command window because dBASE 5 processes these commands one at a time. In addition, if you perform repetitive tasks (such as opening a data table and searching for records), you must type the same commands over and over again.

Tip
Remember to comment your code throughout the development process. This makes it easier to modify later, and makes it easier for someone else to understand.

When you put your commands into a program, you preserve them in a listing called a *program file*, also called a *PRG file* because of its file extension. From this file, dBASE reads the commands one at a time and processes them. You can use the program flow commands that alter the flow of the program; you can also perform tasks over and over again simply by using the program you create.

Note

Certain dBASE commands aren't intended to be used within a program and are not supported by the Compiler; for example, CREATE QUERY and MODIFY STRUCTURE. You normally don't want your users to change your database structures, queries, forms, or reports. Save those commands for your own use from the Command window.

Automating the Application with Menus

Now that your data tables are defined, you need to provide a logical method for your users to get data in and out of the data table. The best way to do this is to offer a menu system. Besides the organization of the data itself, the menu system—or user interface—is probably the most important aspect of your application. In dBASE 5, you have two vital tools to help you develop your user interface: menus and windows.

dBASE 5 uses four basic types of menu: horizontal-bar, pull-down, pop-up, and list. Whichever type you select, you need to design the flow of your program carefully. The following are rules of thumb for menu design:

- Never switch between menus on the same level. Provide only menu choices that offer a submenu of that choice or return you to the next higher menu. Switching between menus on the same level produces "spaghetti" code, which can cause endless loops that prevent a user from exiting the menu choice.

- Always provide an escape so that users can return to a higher-level menu if they get into trouble. The escape can be a RETURN TO MAIN MENU command or QUIT TO DOS command, depending on the level of the menu in the overall menu hierarchy. Be sure to close off all files, memory variables, and databases so that you can make this selection.

- Plan your menu hierarchy to flow naturally from one function to the next; the hierarchy should reflect the way users work with the application.

- Keep your main menu selections as broad as possible, based on the main purposes of the application.

- Offer a submenu that provides utilities such as backups, database packing, and reindexing.

Figure 18.3 shows the generic block diagram of a typical menu system.

The diagram in figure 18.3 shows three levels of menus. First is a top-level menu (or main menu), with three choices. Each of the three main choices offers a submenu, or second-level menu, and each second-level submenu offers additional third-level menus. Each second-level submenu includes an n choice and a final choice that returns you to the main menu. The n choice is the escape. Each third-level submenu also has an escape to the second-level submenu or the main menu. Following the rule of thumb for menu design, none of the choices within a given level sends you to another choice within that level.

The window, the second tool for developing your user interface, enables you to carry out different activities in confined portions of the screen. You can use windows; for example, to list data or supply help messages.

A window is like a small screen on your large screen—it is treated as an entity separate from the screen around it. You can carry out operations in a window without affecting another window or the original dBASE screen.

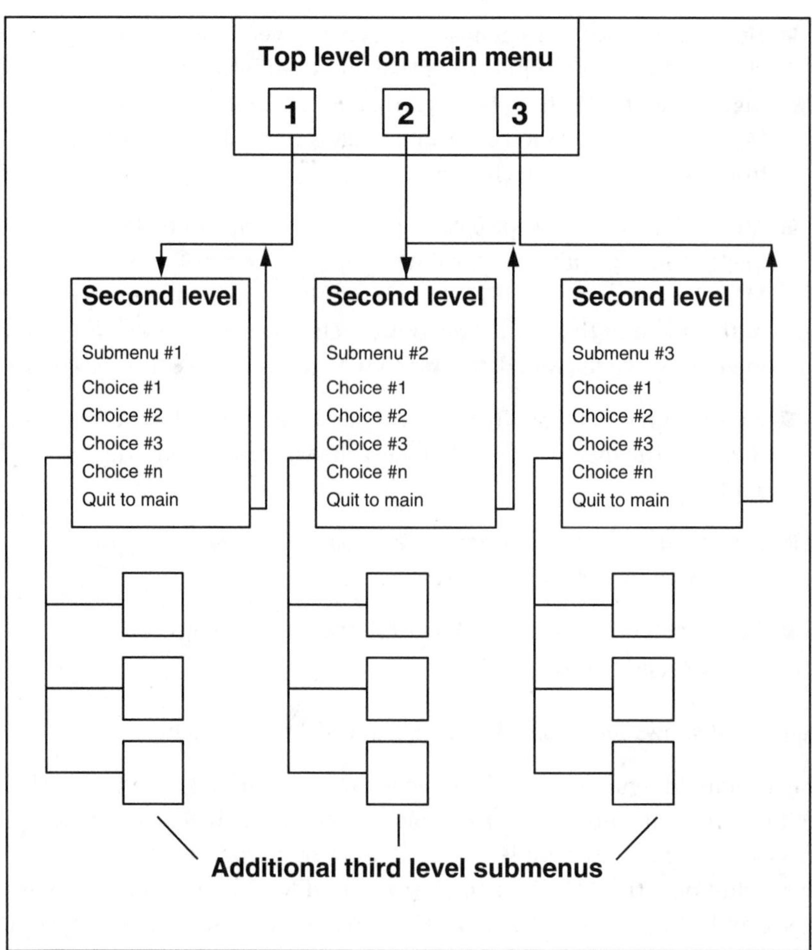

Fig. 18.3
Typical hierarchical menu flow.

► See "APPEND FROM ARRAY," p. 656

Memory variables often are used for storing data before you place the data into the data table. An *array* is a way to create a memory variable that has slots for storing many memory variables. An array is similar to a data table in memory. Therefore, the command APPEND FROM ARRAY can place all the information contained in an array into the data table. One row in the array becomes one record in the data table.

When you write a program, you find that you can use some code over and over again. You can write code to place error messages on-screen. The same error message can occur during different parts of the program. The error message `Record not found`, for example, may appear when dBASE 5 searches a data table and can't find a record.

You can place such an error message in a separate procedure. When an error message occurs, the correct procedure is run from the procedure file. Procedure files perform a function similar to that of the DO CASE...ENDCASE commands. You use procedures when you create menus.

Functions are common in dBASE programming. LTRIM() and RTRIM(), for example, trim blank spaces from the left or right of a character string, and MAX() determines the maximum value. In addition, dBASE allows you to create your own functions, called user-defined functions, or UDFs. You can use dBASE commands, for example, to create a UDF to center text on-screen.

With the RUN command, you can access DOS programs and run them from inside dBASE. DOS's BACKUP and RESTORE commands, for example, enable you to back up and restore data from a hard disk.

For more information on these functions and commands see Chapters 22 and 23.

Finally, a keyboard macro allows you to assign multiple keystrokes to a key so that you or the application user can perform a task simply by pressing a preassigned key.

Understanding Menus

The four types of menus used in dBASE are bar menus, pull-down menus, pop-up menus, and lists. Each type is easy to create and use.

The bar menu is similar to most Windows applications, or dBASE 5's main screen. Menu choices appear across the top of the screen, and you make selections by moving along the list and pressing Enter. The dBASE menu bar may contain your top-level, or main menu, choices.

Pop-up menus are vertical menus that you can use for main menus, but they are more commonly secondary menus that "pop up" on-screen.

A pull-down menu is really just a combination of a bar and pop-up menu. When you move to an option on the bar menu, a pop-up menu appears below the option on the bar menu. You then choose tasks from the pulled-down menu.

The list enables you to create a menu of existing data items. You can use data from a data table to create a list menu.

Using Menu Bars and Pull-Down Menus

Tip
Each menu choice should start with a different letter so the user can select each item by the first letter.

Before learning about menu bars and pull-down menus, you need to be aware of menu design concepts, including the menu hierarchy—the system for grouping menus and submenus.

The first step in grouping your menus involves designing the menu contents. You can list on a piece of paper all the functions your application performs. Collect those functions into logical groups, with each function calling another menu or executing a single program module (PRG file). After you complete this step, draw your menus with the individual choices that execute your plan. Make sure that you include escape choices, top menu choices for utilities, and a way to exit from the program and return to DOS.

Tip
Enhance your program by defining the pads of your main menu in the order in which you want the highlight bar to access them.

Certain commands are unique to dBASE menus. The following are the steps and commands involved in building and using a bar menu:

1. Name the menu. (DEFINE MENU)
2. Name the menu prompts. (DEFINE PAD)
3. Designate the action to take when the user selects a choice. (ON SELECTION PAD, ON PAD, ON MENU, ON EXIT PAD, ON EXIT MENU, or SHOW MENU)
4. Open the menu. (ACTIVATE MENU)
5. Close the menu. (DEACTIVATE MENU)

A *pad* is a bar menu choice that has four elements: a pad name, a user prompt, a set of location coordinates, and an optional message that appears on the lower line of the screen in the dBASE message area.

Using the Define Command

The following are syntax diagrams for commands used to define menus and pads:

```
DEFINE MENU <menu name> [MESSAGE <expC>]
```

and

```
DEFINE PAD <pad name> OF <menu name> PROMPT
<expC> [AT <row>,<col>] [MESSAGE <expC>]
```

The character expression after MESSAGE is the first level of help for your users. The contents of the character expression is displayed at the bottom of the screen when the menu is activated or a pad is highlighted.

After you name the top menu and define its pads, define the action to take if the user selects a particular pad. You have three choices of action available:

you can execute an application module, have the user press Enter to activate a pop-up submenu, or have the submenu pop up automatically when the user moves the highlight bar to the top menu choice. The last two choices create a pull-down menu.

The following commands correspond to each method, beginning with ON SELECTION PAD:

▶ See "ON SELECTION PAD," p. 721

```
ON SELECTION PAD <padname> OF <menuname> [<command>]
```

This command allows the user to move the highlight to the pad and, when the user presses Enter, execute the program code. The code can be a program in a PRG file or in a procedure library file.

The next example calls a submenu when the user moves the highlight bar to a pad and presses Enter:

```
ON SELECTION PAD <padname> OF <menuname> ACTIVATE POPUP <nextmenu>
```

Finally, the following example creates a menu that doesn't require the user to press Enter. You use ON PAD instead of ON SELECTION PAD for this purpose:

▶ See "ON PAD," p. 718

```
ON PAD <pad name> OF <menu name> ACTIVATE POPUP <nextmenu>
```

To use the menu created in this example, execute the ACTIVATE MENU command. Because you need to name the menu and the optional opening position of the highlight bar, use the following syntax:

▶ See "ACTIVATE MENU," p. 652

```
ACTIVATE MENU <menu name> [PAD <pad name>]
```

When you finish using a menu, remember to put the menu away and close open files and memory variables. The following command closes a bar menu:

```
DEACTIVATE MENU
```

Using Pop-Up Menus

Pop-up menus can appear on-screen at any time; however, they normally appear when you make a menu choice from a top-level menu. The pop-up menu is defined much differently from the menu bar. With pop-up menus, you define the appearance of the menu using various menu commands; then you use DO CASE to define the actions to take when you make a selection. Use the following steps and commands to build pop-up menus:

- To name the menu use DEFINE POPUP.
- To define each menu bar use DEFINE BAR.

- To define the actions each selection will invoke use ON SELECTION POPUP and DO CASE.
- To open the menu use ACTIVATE POPUP.
- To close the menu use DEACTIVATE POPUP.

A *bar* is a pop-up menu choice that has three elements: the line number in the pop-up menu, the user prompt, and an optional message.

The syntax for defining a pop-up menu follows:

```
DEFINE POPUP <popup name> FROM <row1>,<col1>
   [TO <row2>,<col2>] [PROMPT [FIELD <field name>]
   /[FILES [LIKE <skeleton>]]/STRUCTURE]
   [MESSAGE  <expC>]
```

To define each choice available in the pop-up menu, use the following syntax:

```
DEFINE BAR <line number> OF <popup name>
   PROMPT <expC> [MESSAGE <expC>]
      [SKIP [FOR <condition>]]
```

To define a task to perform, use this syntax:

```
ON SELECTION POPUP <popup name>/ALL [BLANK] [<command>]
```

Tip
Popups created using the FILES [LIKE *<skeleton>*] syntax are not modifiable by the user.

To make a selection, move the highlight bar to the desired choice and press Enter, or press the first character of the selection. After you make the choice, the DO CASE command uses the number of the bar (as you define it with the DEFINE BAR statement) as follows:

```
CASE BAR() = n
      DO <next-program>
```

The BAR() function returns the number you assign to the bar in the DEFINE BAR statement. You also can invoke the next level of pop-up menu by using the ACTIVATE POPUP command instead of the DO command. Make sure that you don't try to activate a pop-up menu before you define it and its bars. The BARPROMPT() function allows you to use the bar text in your code. You can use this to get field or file names from a pop-up list. See Chapter 22 for more information about the various menu commands.

Exploring a Sample Menu Program

The next two program listings show the code needed to create and use a bar menu, pull-down menu, and pop-up menu. Each example is a working menu system. The options on the submenus, however, lack the code necessary to make the options work; when an option is selected, the message `This Choice Is Not Installed` appears.

The first listing creates a bar menu with pull-down submenus. Note that the pull-down menu is actually a pop-up menu placed directly below the corresponding option on the bar menu (see fig. 18.4).

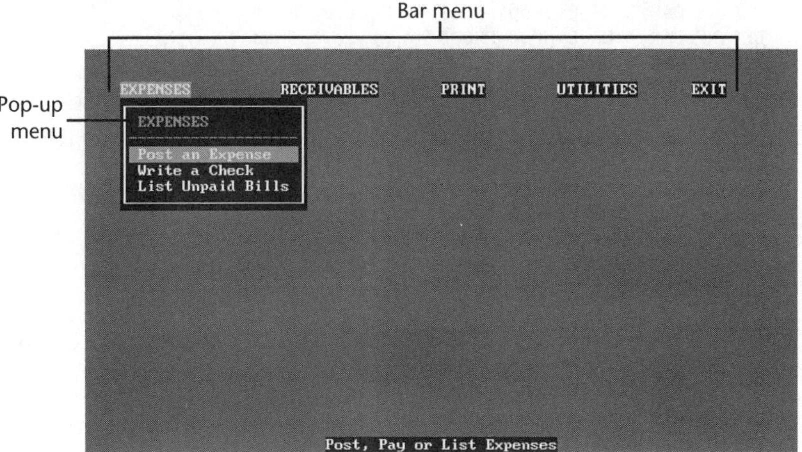

Fig. 18.4
This menu is a result of the sample menu program.

```
* General housekeeping commands

clLine = REPLICATE('-',25)

* Define the main bar menu
DEFINE MENU MainMenu
   DEFINE PAD pmExp OF MainMenu PROMPT "EXPENSES" AT 2,4 ;
      MESSAGE "Post, Pay or List Expenses"
   DEFINE PAD pmRcv OF MainMenu PROMPT "RECEIVABLES" AT 2,22 ;
      MESSAGE "Post, Receive or List Receivables"
   DEFINE PAD pmPrnt OF MainMenu PROMPT "PRINT" AT 2,40 ;
      MESSAGE "Print Utilities, Print Invoices"
   DEFINE PAD pmUtils OF MainMenu PROMPT "UTILITIES" AT 2,53 ;
      MESSAGE "Application and System Utilities"
   DEFINE PAD pmGetOut OF MainMenu PROMPT "EXIT" AT 2,68 ;
      MESSAGE "Close Files, Exit the Application"

*The next section defines the actions to be taken when a selection
is made from *the bar menu. In each case, except Exit, a pull down
menu will be shown.
   ON PAD pmExp OF MainMenu ACTIVATE POPUP ExpPop
   ON PAD pmRcv OF MainMenu ACTIVATE POPUP RcvPop
   ON PAD pmPrnt OF MainMenu ACTIVATE POPUP PrntPop
   ON PAD pmUtils OF MainMenu ACTIVATE POPUP UtilPop
   ON SELECTION PAD pmGetOut OF MainMenu DO Esc
```

```
*When you select Exit, the escape procedure is executed. Notice
that you must use *ON SELECTION PAD rather than ON PAD before a DO
command. The next step is to *define the pull-down menus. Even
though the menus appear on-screen as a pull-down *menu, remember
that each pull-down is created using a pop-up menu placed below
*its corresponding selection on the bar menu.
 DEFINE POPUP ExpPop FROM 3,4 TO 9,24     && EXPENSES selection
   DEFINE BAR 1 OF ExpPop PROMPT " EXPENSES" SKIP
   DEFINE BAR 2 OF ExpPop PROMPT clLine SKIP
   DEFINE BAR 3 OF ExpPop PROMPT " Post an Expense"
   DEFINE BAR 4 OF ExpPop PROMPT " Write a Check"
   DEFINE BAR 5 OF ExpPop PROMPT " List Unpaid Bills"
      ON SELECTION POPUP ExpPop DO ExpProc

DEFINE POPUP RcvPop FROM 3,22 TO 9,42    && RECEIVABLES selection
   DEFINE BAR 1 OF RcvPop PROMPT " RECEIVABLES" SKIP
   DEFINE BAR 2 OF RcvPop PROMPT clLine SKIP
   DEFINE BAR 3 OF RcvPop PROMPT " Post Sales"
   DEFINE BAR 4 OF RcvPop PROMPT " Receive a Payment"
   DEFINE BAR 5 OF RcvPop PROMPT " List Receivables"
      ON SELECTION POPUP RcvPop DO ExpProc

DEFINE POPUP PrntPop FROM 3,40 TO 8,60   && PRINT selection
   DEFINE BAR 1 OF PrntPop PROMPT " PRINT" SKIP
   DEFINE BAR 2 OF PrntPop PROMPT clLine SKIP
   DEFINE BAR 3 OF PrntPop PROMPT " Print Utilities"
   DEFINE BAR 4 OF PrntPop PROMPT " Print Invoices"
      ON SELECTION POPUP PrntPop DO ExpProc

DEFINE POPUP UtilPop FROM 3,53 TO 8,78  && UTILITIES selection
   DEFINE BAR 1 OF UtilPop PROMPT " UTILITIES" SKIP
   DEFINE BAR 2 OF UtilPop PROMPT clLine SKIP
   DEFINE BAR 3 OF UtilPop PROMPT " Application Utilities"
   DEFINE BAR 4 OF UtilPop PROMPT " System Utilities"
      ON SELECTION POPUP UtilPop DO ExpProc

ACTIVATE MENU MainMenu PAD pmExp       && Activate the bar menu
RETURN

PROCEDURE SaveSetUp
PUBLIC glTalk, glEcho, glStatus, glHelp
glTalk = SET(TALK)
glEcho = SET(ECHO)
glStatus = SET(STATUS)
glHelp = SET(Help)
CLEAR
SET TALK OFF
SET ECHO OFF
SET STATUS OFF
SET HELP OFF
RETURN
*The next procedure, Esc, quits the application and returns to DOS
when Exit is *selected from the bar menu.
PROCEDURE Esc
DEACTIVATE MENU
QUIT
RETURN
```

```
*The ExpProc procedure is called by each of the pop-up menus. This
is only done *for demonstration purposes. In a normal program, each
pop-up menu would call a *separate procedure. Notice, in this
procedure, that all of the options have been *deactivated.
PROCEDURE ExpProc

DO CASE
   CASE BAR() = 3
      @ 21,25 SAY "This Choice Is Not Installed"
      WAIT
      @ 21,0 CLEAR
   CASE BAR() = 4
      @ 21,25 SAY "This Choice Is Not Installed"
      WAIT
      @ 21,0 CLEAR
   CASE BAR() = 5
      @ 21,25 SAY "This Choice Is Not Installed"
      WAIT
      @ 21,0 CLEAR
ENDCASE
RETURN                 && Return from the procedure
```

The first procedure called in the listing performs general housekeeping tasks such as clearing the screen, shutting off extraneous display to the screen, and shutting off the status bar. Next, 25 hyphens are stored in a memory variable, *clLine*, which creates a dividing line in the menus.

The bar menu is defined next, and has five selections: EXPENSES, RECEIVABLES, PRINT, UTILITIES, and EXIT. Each option is placed in the third row of the screen, at column positions 4, 22, 40, 53, and 68, respectively. Each menu selection displays a different message at the bottom of the screen.

Four ON PAD commands and one ON SELECTION PAD command direct the flow of the program, based on the option the user selects. Notice that the ON PAD commands activate a pop-up menu as soon as the user selects the bar menu option. When EXIT is chosen on the bar menu, ON SELECTION PAD requires that the user press Enter to select this option. When EXIT is chosen, a procedure called *esc* is executed.

Tip
To invoke a procedure or program from the top-level bar menu, use ON SELECTION PAD.

The four pop-up menus are defined next, with DEFINE POPUP commands. Along with the definition of the menu itself, each selection from the pop-up menus is defined with the DEFINE BAR commands. After each menu and its associated selections is an ON SELECTION POPUP command. This command redirects program flow according to the way each menu is designed to call a different part of the application.

The EXPENSES menu, for example, can redirect flow to a program that handles your accounts payable, whereas the RECEIVABLES menu can redirect program flow to a different program—one that manages your accounts receivable. Each ON SELECTION POPUP statement for each pop-up menu redirects the program to another procedure or program file. For demonstration purposes, each ON SELECTION POPUP command redirects the program flow to one procedure: ExpProc.

▶ See "SKIP," p. 743

In each pop-up menu definition, two DEFINE BAR commands contain the SKIP option. SKIP causes the cursor to skip these bars when the user presses the arrow keys to move through the menu. This option indicates bars that are menu text, not menu options.

The first skipped item is the pop-up menu title; the title EXPENSES is skipped, for example. The second is the divider line: *clLine*. This line is simply cosmetic—it separates the menu title from the options. Even though this line was initialized with 25 hyphens, only the number of hyphens needed to fill the menu is displayed.

The ACTIVATE MENU command actually displays the main menu on-screen. The option PAD pmExp appears in this command. This option is included so that the selection EXPENSES is always the selection first highlighted. If the command contained PAD pmPrnt, then the PRINT option of the main menu is the first option highlighted.

At the end of the program is procedure code. Two procedures are included here: Esc and ExpProc. The procedure Esc is activated when you select EXIT from the bar menu; ExpProc is activated by any other bar menu selection. Although procedures are used for actions in this example, separate PRG files can easily be called from each menu choice.

Enhancing Pop-Up Menus

Tip
SKIP is also handy for controlling access to different menu options.

A few tricks can help you enhance the look of your pop-up menus. One trick is to insert blank lines (bars) between choices for aesthetic reasons when your submenu has only a few choices. You insert blank lines by skipping a number in the <line number> modifier of the DEFINE BAR command. Don't forget that you insert lines when you write your CASE statements; if you create menu selections on bars 1, 3, 5, and so on, remember to test only on those lines (not on all lines in the range, i.e. 1, 2, 3, 4, 5) in your DO CASE construct. Use `BAR() = 1`, `BAR() = 3`, `BAR() = 5`, and so on.

You also can insert lines that aren't menu choices but are dividers between groups of selections in a long menu, as you do with the memory variable *clLine*. Instead of just using this memory variable once however, use it in different bar locations to separate commands.

A second trick allows you to skip a noneffective menu selection; for example, you can skip a menu choice that browses an empty database. The keyword SKIP, along with a FOR condition enables you to avoid selecting that choice. The FOR RECCOUNT() = 0 expression, for example, tests for an empty database. The actual program line looks something like the following:

```
DEFINE BAR 3 OF PopMenu PROMPT "Display records"
     SKIP FOR RECCOUNT() = 0
```

dBASE 5 enables you to specify a command to be executed when the user moves to and away from bars in a pop-up menu. The syntax of the ON EXIT POPUP command is as follows:

```
ON EXIT POPUP <popup name> [<command>]
```

See Chapter 22 for more information on these commands.

Using Pop-Up Lists

Pop-up menus contain fixed information—text you define with the PROMPT keyword. Lists, however, are pop-ups that contain information you want to put into them, usually called *variable data*. Examples of variable data include lists of data table contents, results of a DIR listing, or results of a listing of active fields in a database. The following listing uses a pop-up menu to show the contents of the Customer database.

```
*The following code fragment demonstrates a pop-up menu for listing
the contents *of a field of the Customer database. By using the
pop-up, you can scroll through *the database.
* Perform housekeeping commands

CLEAR ALL
CLEAR

* Test for a color display and set colors
?IF ISCOLOR()
         SET COLOR OF BOX TO r/w
         SET COLOR OF MESSAGES TO w/r
         SET COLOR OF HIGHLIGHT TO w/r
ENDIF
USE Customer     && open database
* Define list pop-up using the field ctCompany. Display a message
* at the bottom of the screen to tell user how to exit the list.
DEFINE POPUP Fields FROM 2,5 TO 10,50 PROMPT FIELD ctCompany ;
      MESSAGE "Press Esc to close the list"
* When the user makes a selection from the list, redirect
* the program to the procedure DispField
      ON SELECTION POPUP Fields DO DispField
ACTIVATE POPUP Fields
CLEAR ALL
```

```
PROCEDURE DispField
   STORE PROMPT() TO clSelection    && retrieve selection

   @ 12,10 SAY "The field you selected is: "+clSelection
   WAIT
RETURN
```

In this program, you see that some of the housekeeping is done first: the screen is cleared, and then special colors are set (for a color monitor). Next, the Customer database is opened.

The DEFINE POPUP command creates the pop-up menu, but the prompt is set to the Company field in the database. When the ACTIVATE POPUP command is executed, a pop-up window appears on-screen, listing all the contents of the Company field. Use the arrow keys to scroll through the list of companies.

The ON SELECTION POPUP command redirects the program flow to the procedure DispField after the user makes a selection from the list. When DispField is executed, the selection PROMPT() is stored in the memory variable *clSelection*. The procedure simply prints the selection on-screen. You can, however, use the selection as the basis of a SEEK command to find the selected record.

Control is returned from the procedure back to the main part of the program. The pop-up list appears again, and the user can make another selection. If the user presses Esc, the pop-up is deactivated and the data table is closed.

Creating and Using Windows

Windows are much more than simple on-screen graphic elements. When designed and used properly, windows provide an additional work surface for actions performed by you or by the application. An example of a window for your own actions is one that pops up with context-sensitive help after you press F1. A window that lists data table contents in response to a query you make, is a window used for the application's actions. In both cases, the action takes place inside the window. If you write your application cleverly, you can open additional windows with additional actions going on within them. You can use up to 20 windows on one screen to display your output, menus, and messages.

You create a window by following these steps:

► See "DEFINE WINDOW," p. 687

1. Define and name the window using the DEFINE WINDOW command. This command uses the following syntax:

```
DEFINE WINDOW <window-name>
   FROM <row1>,<col1>
   TO <row2>,<col2>
   [DOUBLE/PANEL/NONE/<border definition string>]
   [COLOR [<standard>]
   [,<enhanced>] [,<frame>]]
```

The DEFINE WINDOW command allows you to describe the window location, size, colors, and name.

2. Activate the window with the ACTIVATE WINDOW command.

   After you define and name a window, you can invoke it at any time with the ACTIVATE WINDOW *<window-name>* command. Remember, if you use the same name in two window definitions, your system keeps only the last one you define.

▶ See "ACTIVATE WINDOW," p. 653

3. Inside the window, write the code for the actions you want to occur. As long as you didn't use DEACTIVATE WINDOW on the window or activate another window on top of it, all the program steps you write between the ACTIVATE WINDOW and DEACTIVATE WINDOW commands execute inside the window.

4. Close the window with the DEACTIVATE WINDOW command. Make sure that you close all open files, data tables, and memory variables before you close the active window.

You are ready to make a window to list the contents of your Customer data table, as shown in the following example:

```
DEFINE WINDOW Sample FROM 3,5 TO 10,70
     USE Customer
     ACTIVATE WINDOW Sample
     DISPLAY ALL
     USE
     DEACTIVATE WINDOW Sample
CLEAR WINDOWS
```

After the window is activated, all commands and actions take place in the window. Remember that text positioned with @...SAY...GET is placed relative to the window, not the entire screen.

The SCAN command enables you to perform almost the same function as DO WHILE .NOT. EOF( ) and SKIP, but with less code. SCAN uses the following syntax:

```
SCAN [<scope>] [FOR <condition>][WHILE <condition>]
   [<commands>]
   [LOOP]
   [EXIT]
ENDSCAN
```

You don't need the LOCATE and CONTINUE (or SKIP) commands with SCAN, as you do with DO...WHILE.

The following listing demonstrates a simple dBASE 5 window.

The following program fragments illustrate the use of windows to browse part of a database record by record.

```
CLEAR ALL                            && Housekeeping
*  Now define the window in which your information will appear
DEFINE WINDOW Browser FROM 5,0 TO 12,79 DOUBLE COLOR W+/R,N/RB
ACTIVATE WINDOW Browser              && Open the window
CLEAR                                && Clear the window
@ 0,35 SAY "TELEPHONE LIST"          && Give it a title

clRespons = " "                      && Initialize the memory
                                     && variable
USE Customer                         && Open the database

SCAN WHILE .NOT. clRespons $ "Qq"    && Scan the database record
                                     && by record until the end
                                     && or the user says to quit
DISPLAY cfCustomer, cfContact,       && Display the parts
cfPhone OFF
                                     && of the record you
                                     && want
?                                    && Add a couple of blank lines
?                                    && and prompt the user for a
                                     && response that you read into
                                     && the memvar clRespons

WAIT "Press Q to Quit, Return For Next Name" TO clRespons
CLEAR                                && Clear in preparation for
                                     && the next record if Q was
                                     && not selected
ENDSCAN                              && Close off the SCAN command
USE                                  && Close the database
RELEASE clRespons                    && release the memvar
DEACTIVATE WINDOW Browser            && Close the window
RELEASE WINDOW
QUIT                                 && Return to DOS
```

There is a new operation in the listing. Look at the following line of code:

```
SCAN WHILE .NOT. clRespons $ "Qq"
```

This line uses the $ argument. The dollar symbol here is the relational operator used for substring comparison. It indicates that you are going to compare the contents of the memory variable *clRespons* with the characters that come next. In this case, the next characters are Q and *q*. If the Q or the *q* is the same as the character stored in *mrespons*, a logical true (.T.) is returned. The line allows you to scan so long as you don't type Q or *q*. A rough translation of this code follows:

```
SCAN as long as it is .NOT. true that clRespons contains Q or q
```

Windows have many uses in dBASE 5 applications. One use is to create pop-up error messages using the ON ERROR command. When your program suffers an error, you simply activate the window you defined earlier as your error window, attach appropriate text messages to the error, and then display the text in the error window. You then prompt for a keystroke to clear the window, read the keystroke, deactivate the window, and take appropriate action to correct the error.

Remember, from the time you open a window to the time you close it, programming steps that appear are executed within that window. The window is a small version of the display and should be treated as such.

You also can use a window to pop up part of a program for user action. If, for example, you want to prompt the user for a response based on some event in your application, you can put that routine into a window. When the event occurs, the window pops up requesting user input and the user responds. At the completion of the action, the application collects the response and closes the window. Using the pop-up window gives your application a professional look and clearly focuses the user's attention on the required action. Such pop-up windows are called *dialog boxes*. One of the best uses for a dialog box is providing your user with help on the various fields in your data table.

You also can design windows to accept user input into a memo field. Because memo fields are actually 10-character pointers to text in a memo file (FILENAME.DBT), you can enable the user to use the dBASE text editor (or whatever external editor you have designated) to add or edit memos or notes to data table records. To perform this action, you use a special version of the @...SAY...GET command. First, you define a window. Next, you use the following command to open the window and accept user input:

```
@ <x>,<y> [SAY <"message"> [GET <memofield-name> [OPEN]
   WINDOW <window-name>]]
```

This command selects the window you designate in <*window-name*> and, when you press Ctrl-Home or F9, opens the window in the text editor mode. You then can type any message you want or edit the existing message. When you press Ctrl-End, the memo is saved to the DBT file and is available whenever you display the contents of that memo field. If you add the keyword OPEN before WINDOW in this command, the window is opened at once and then replaced with the editing window when you press Ctrl-Home.

You also can use windows to isolate and highlight activities within your application. When an important event takes place, such as an error message or a dialog between user and program, you can place the event in a window to call the user's attention to it. This can be done to cover confusing displays (without having to delete them), or to switch program execution temporarily to the immediate work at hand. After the event passes and the required user input is collected, you can easily return to normal program execution by closing the window.

Writing Help Screens

While dBASE 5 provides extensive help on the internal commands and functions, it doesn't provide information on your specific application. You must design screens to describe to your users what information is required on the input screens. To provide context sensitive help on every field, the best method is to create a help data table. The data table has two fields:

HelpName CHARACTER 10
HelpText MEMO

Use the ON KEY command to define the procedure to be executed when the user presses F1. Before each block of GETs, you assign a value to a parameter that is passed to the help procedure. The help procedure searches the data table for a HelpName that matches the parameter and displays the associated memo field. The following code fragment shows how this is done:

```
***************************************************************
* PROGRAM:  GET_DATA                                          *
* ABSTRACT:  This program asks the user for input and         *
* handles the help request by accessing a help data table.    *
***************************************************************
*
**  First do the housekeeping ****
*
DO SaveSets
CLOSE DATABASES
*
*** Done with housekeeping, Select an area for help
SELECT 10
*
*   Open the help data base and set up the window
*
USE HelpDb ORDER FieldName
DEFINE WINDOW HELPVIEW FROM 7,7 to 18,60 DOUBLE
*
*   Set the F1 key to be the Help key, and VARREAD() provides
*     the key name that identifies the help screen.
```

```
*
ON KEY LABEL F1 DO HelpScreen
*
*  Start prompting the user for input
*
SELECT 1
clHelpId = "FILEID"     && Help can be for memory variables
clFileNam = "           "
CLEAR
@1,1 SAY "Enter the name of the file: " GET clFileNam
READ
*   :                   && Normally validate input
*   :                   && this example works as is
*   :
USE (clFileNam)         && Help can also be for data tables
APPEND BLANK
clHelpId = "COMPANY"    && Change to different help
@3,1 SAY "Enter the company number: " GET CompanyId
@4,1 SAY "Company: " GET Company_NM
@5,1 SAY "Address: " GET Address1
@6,10 GET Address2
READ
*   :
*   :                   && More routines to be done
*   :
CLOSE DATABASES
RETURN

**************************************************************
* PROCEDURE:  HelpScreen                                     *
* ABSTRACT:  This program displays the help screen required  *
*  based on the input parameter.                             *
**************************************************************
PROCEDURE HelpScreen
SELECT HelpDb               && Assumes database opened in main
ACTIVATE WINDOW HELPVIEW    && Open the window for display
CLEAR                       && Clear and display the memo field
DISPLAY HelpText OFF FOR FieldName = VARREAD()
WAIT                        && Let user read before closing
DEACTIVATE WINDOW HELPVIEW && Close the window and go back
RETURN
```

Troubleshooting

When I activate my window, it doesn't appear where I want it. Why?

Check to make sure you've used different names for each window definition utilized in your application. If you used the same name in two different window definitions, your system keeps only the last one that the application executes, causing your window to appear in a different location than you intend.

Building a Procedure Library

When you write application code, you may find that you repeatedly use the same bits of code. Sometimes you reuse the fragments within the same application; sometimes you use them in several applications. You can preserve frequently used bits of code and reuse them at will by creating a *procedure library*.

▶ See "DO," p. 695

You can use the DO command to run chunks of code exactly as if they are separate programs. In earlier examples, you took pieces of code you wanted to run from within a program module and treated them as procedures. But you also can hold many different procedures in a completely separate file, called a *procedure file*. You can simultaneously access procedures in any or all of three ways:

- Use the SYSPROC = <*filename*> command in your CONFIG.DB file to specify a procedure file to be used with dBASE.
- Use the SET PROCEDURE TO <*filename*> command to specify a procedure file for use by your application.
- Use the SET LIBRARY TO <*filename*> command to access a procedure library file for routines you intend to use with various dBASE 5 applications.

These commands tell your program where to look for procedures. Use the DO command to execute the procedures, just as you run an external program module. See Chapters 22 and 23 for more information on these commands.

Tip
SYSPROC can't be closed, so you don't have to worry about opening and closing the file each time you need to use it.

In dBASE 5, all programs are treated as procedures, including the active program module. After you identify the locations of the usable modules or procedures, dBASE knows exactly where to look to run them. dBASE looks for procedures in the following order: SYSPROC, then SET PROCEDURE, then SET LIBRARY. You can close a procedure file by using SET PROCEDURE TO without a procedure file name. You can open and close procedure libraries as you need them, instead of leaving them open all the time. Because you can have only a single procedure file open at once, you gain the use of other files if you open and close them as needed.

The following is the general format of a procedure file:

```
* Procedure library file Procfile.PRC
*
PROCEDURE Proc1
<code for Proc1>
```

```
RETURN
PROCEDURE Proc2
<code for Proc2>
RETURN
PROCEDURE Procn
<code for Procn>
RETURN
```

You always start a procedure with `PROCEDURE <procedure name>` and end with `RETURN`. The PROCEDURE command identifies the procedure, and the RETURN command returns control of program execution to the program that called the procedure. The number of procedures you can have in an open procedure file is limited by memory. You can have as many as 963 procedures in a single file.

Another interesting use for a procedure is to simulate the creation of custom commands. Although you cannot execute a procedure the same way you execute a command, you can program the equivalent of a custom command and execute it with DO *<procedure name>*. When you use a procedure, however, you can carry information to it from the module that executes it, modify the information in your procedure, and then pass the information back to the calling module. This flow of information is called *passing parameters*, and dBASE 5 provides several ways to perform this activity.

Note

Storing a value in a public memory variable and then using it later within the procedure isn't an efficient way to pass parameters.

You can pass parameters from the DO command to the procedure in a two-step process: identification and initialization. You can pass parameters using memory variables, but this isn't the best method. You still use memory variables, however, when you perform your two-step process. No matter how you pass information between programs or procedures, you still need a temporary "holding tank" for the data.

▶ See "PARAMETERS," p. 722

In step one, you identify the parameters you need in a procedure to avoid having to hard-code variables in a program module. Suppose you have a program module you want to reuse throughout your application, but the module uses different data at different points in the application. You have two choices: hard-code the memory variables in the procedure and duplicate the procedure with different information for each of the uses to which you plan to put it, or set up memory variables as parameters and pass the information to them when you use DO to run the procedure.

When you know the memory variables you want to use as parameters, you can initialize them in a slightly different way. Make PARAMETERS the first command in the procedure to be called. This command assigns the parameter names you specify in memory variables as part of the DO command that calls the procedure. Then use DO *<procedure name>* [WITH *<parameters>*]. The parameters you use with the WITH keyword can be any memory variables and need not have the same names as the parameters you specify in the PARAMETERS command. dBASE 5 supports two different ways of passing the parameters, by reference or by value. If you just put the variable name in the WITH list, the variable is passed by reference. In this case any changes made to the value of the parameter in the called procedure will be passed back to the calling procedure. If you place the variable name in parentheses in your WITH list, only the value of the variable is passed to the called procedure. Any changes made to the value in the called procedure will not have any effect on the value in the calling procedure. The PARAMETERS command uses the following syntax:

```
PARAMETERS <parameter list>
```

► See "PUBLIC," p. 726

► See "PRIVATE ALL," p. 724

The list can contain up to 50 different memory variables or array elements. Arrays and memory variables are treated differently. A PUBLIC array element is always treated as if it is passed by value. Any changes made in the called procedure do not affect the value outside the procedure. A public memory variable, however, is changed if it's passed by reference as a parameter to a procedure. Parameters passed to the procedure become private memory variables within the procedure, and are released when you complete the procedure and use RETURN to return to the program module that called it. To insure that you do not accidentally change a public memory variable, you can use PRIVATE in your procedure to define local names for your variables. To avoid confusion, you can use parameter names different from the names of the public memory variables that created the parameters. Although you use different names for the memory variables and the parameters, the parameters are created in the procedure in the order in which you pass them using the WITH keyword in the DO command. Your code appears as follows:

```
DO procedure1 WITH memvar1, memvar2, memvar3
PROCEDURE procedure1
   PARAMETERS parm1, parm2, parm3
   <procedure-code>
RETURN
```

In this example, *memvar1* becomes *parm1*, *memvar2* becomes *parm2*, and so on. Upon the execution of the RETURN command, *parm1*, *parm2*, and *parm3* are released because they are actually private memory variables. Whenever you need the data stored in one of the parameters within the procedure, store it to a memvar to avoid altering the original value of the passed variable. The following short program shows the effects of passing parameters:

```
***
* Test for parameter passing
****
PUBLIC ARRAY cpArray1[2,3]
PUBLIC cpMyVar
*** First do all the housekeeping
clEcho = SET("ECHO")        &Store the old value
clStat = SET("STATUS")      &Store the old value
clTalk = SET("TALK")        &Store the old value
SET ECHO OFF        &Don't show commands
SET STATUS OFF      &Remove status bar and clear screen
SET TALK OFF        &Don't show values changed
** Initialize all the variables
nlArg1 = 1
nlArg2 = 2
cpMyVar = "Yes"
cpArray1[1,2] = "Hi"
*
*** Show the initial values on the screen.
? "nlArg1 = ", nlArg1, "     nlArg2 = ", nlArg2
? "cpMyVar = ", cpMyVar, "cpArray1 = ", cpArray1[1,2]
*** Call the procedure with a public array element, a public
*    memory variable, a local memory variable, and
*    a local memory variable passed by value
*
DO ParmTest WITH cpArray1[1,2], cpMyVar, nlArg1, (nlArg2)
*
* Display the values after the procedure call
*
? "Back in Main routine"
? "nlArg1 = ", nlArg1, "     nlArg2 = ", nlArg2
? "cpMyVar = ", cpMyVar, "cpArray1 = ", cpArray1[1,2]
WAIT
*** Return all settings to original values
SET ECHO &clEcho
SET STATUS &clStat
SET TALK &clTalk
RETURN

PROCEDURE ParmTest
*
* Procedure to change the values passed in
*
PARAMETERS lVar1, lVar2, lVar3, lVar4
lVar1 = "Now"       & Set the public array element
lVar2 = "Wow"       & Set the public memory variable
lVar3 = 10 & Set the local memroy variable
lVar4 = 20 & Set the local memory variable passed by value
*
* Show the new values on the screen
*
? "In Procedure ParmTest"
? "nlArg1 = ", lVar3, "     nlArg2 = ", lVar4
? "cpMyVar = ", lVar2, "cpArray1 = ", lVar1
RETURN
```

The output from this program is shown in figure 18.5. With the first screen display, the values shown are 1, 2, Yes, and Hi. Inside the called procedure, the values are 10, 20, Wow, and Now. Upon return from the procedure, the values are 10, 2, Wow, and Hi. The values of the array element clArray1[1,2] and clVar2 which were passed by value are unchanged from the values they had before the call to the procedure.

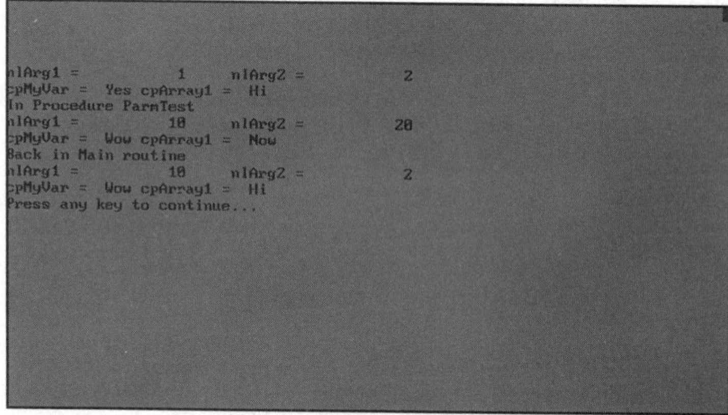

Fig. 18.5
Output of a program that uses passing of PUBLIC and PRIVATE parameters.

► See "PCOUNT()," p. 806

To keep track of the number of parameters that are passed, use the PCOUNT( ) function. For example, if after executing the procedure in the preceding code, you include the command ?PCOUNT( ), the number 4 would be returned, indicating that four parameters are passed to the procedure. PCOUNT() can be used to check whether any or all of the parameters required by the procedure were passed. You can use this for error handling and to provide procedures with optional parameters in the list.

Running External Programs

You can include non-dBASE language programs in your applications in three ways: by using the RUN command or the RUN() function to run an external program from within the dBASE code, or by using LOAD and then CALL on assembly language modules—a method that requires knowledge of other programming languages.

When you use RUN to run an external program, especially a DOS command, make sure that COMMAND.COM is in the current DOS path or verify that you used COMSPEC in your AUTOEXEC.BAT file. When you leave your dBASE 5 application to run the DOS command (by using RUN), your computer's operating system must know where to look for the command processor. If you ignore this requirement, you get an error message. When you issue the RUN command with a DOS command, your application leaves dBASE, executes the DOS command, and returns to the dBASE application. It appears to the user that the activity was carried out by the dBASE application. For example, from the Command window, type the following command:

```
RUN DIR
```

This command displays a DOS directory of the current subdirectory. This is different from the dBASE DIR command, which doesn't display all files by default—only database files and related database information.

The RUN command also executes an external program. Make sure, however, that you have the memory to run the program and your dBASE application. The memory does not have to cover all the dBASE application, the runtime, and the external program, because most of dBASE departs from your system's memory when you use the RUN command.

Enough of dBASE remains in memory, however, so that when you finish using the external program, your system can return automatically to the point in your application where you left off. Your system needs enough memory to hold some of dBASE, some of the program you are executing, and COMMAND.COM. Not only does this mean you need sufficient memory, but it also means that when you run a DOS command, dBASE must be able to find COMMAND.COM.

Note

A shorthand notation for RUN is the exclamation point (!). For example, instead of using this command:

```
RUN <program-name/DOS-commands>
```

you can use this command:

```
! <program-name/DOS-commands>
```

Both commands yield the same result.

If the program you want to run uses a considerable amount of memory, you can use the RUN() function instead of the RUN command. This function can temporarily reduce the size of dBASE, leaving more room for your other program to run. The syntax of the function follows:

```
RUN([<expL1>,]<expC>[,<expL2>])
```

The expression `<expC>` is a character expression containing your program name. Place quotes around the program name (to indicate it is a character string not a value) and path, or use a character type variable that contains this information.

The expressions `<expL1>` and `<expL2>` are optional logical expressions. If the first expression is false (.F.) or not specified, dBASE loads the operating system command processor and then your program. When you exit your program, a completion code (usually 0) is returned to dBASE. If you don't want the operating system to load, set the first expression to true (.T.). Without COMMAND.COM, you will lose the ability to search the DOS path and to process batch command files. If you set the *<expL1>* to true, you must remember to include the full path for the command you want to execute. To reduce the amount of memory used by dBASE, set the second logical expression to true (.T.). Otherwise, your program must fit in available memory while dBASE is running.

Remember that RUN() is a function, not a command, so it must be used with a command, such as the ? command. The following example runs the program named MYPROG.EXE, which is located in the \DOS subdirectory on drive C:

```
nlResult = RUN(.T.,"C:\DOS\MYPROG.EXE",.T.)
```

Caution

Do not use RUN or RUN() to execute memory-resident programs, such as screen savers and device drivers. Remember that PRINT also has a memory resident portion and must be loaded before dBASE to use it with RUN.

dBASE loads most of itself into extended memory, leaving more low DOS memory available for running external programs. Therefore, you don't need to use the RUN() function, depending on the amount of extended memory you have.

▶ See "CALL," p. 663

Another way to use external programs is with the CALL construct. You can write a program module in C, assembly language, or any other language that can generate a binary with no stack segment, and execute it from within your dBASE application by following three rules:

- You must have the code module in *binary* format with no stack segment, or in a file with a BIN extension (you don't need to include the extension in your CALL statement).

- You pass parameters in the form of a character expression, a memory variable, or an element of an array. The data type doesn't matter, except for memo types, which aren't allowed.

- You must use LOAD to place the module into memory before you can call it. You can have up to 16 such modules, of up to 64K each, in memory at one time.

▶ See "LOAD," p. 709

When do you use RUN and CALL? Each has slightly different uses, depending on the application. RUN takes excellent advantage of small third-party programs or utilities that can enhance your application. By using other programs, you don't have to write the program yourself. Also, your application can take advantage of data in another application, or it can enable the user to switch back and forth between applications. You can allow your users to execute Lotus 1-2-3 from within your dBASE application.

▶ See "RUN," p. 738

CALL has a different benefit. Often you need to perform some function for which dBASE is not designed, such as using communications or controlling I/O ports. If you program in assembly language, however, you can build excellent routines for managing these low-level computer functions. You can include advanced features in your dBASE 5 applications by coding them in assembly language, compiling them to a binary file, and then calling them from your dBASE application. An example is delivered with dBASE 5 in the SAMPLES subdirectory.

Using Keyboard Macros

You can use *keyboard macros* to store small, useful routines and execute them from the keyboard or from within a program module. (Don't confuse the keyboard macro with the macro substitution operator, &.)

◀ See "Recording Macros," p. 78

Three commands are associated with keyboard macros: SAVE MACRO, RESTORE MACRO, and PLAY MACRO. If you do not require the macros to be accessible to more than one program, you can also directly load the keyboard buffer with the KEYBOARD command.

When do you use a keyboard macro? Suppose you have a series of keystrokes you want to save and reuse from time to time. Perhaps you want to enable the user to press a function key to execute these keystrokes, or you want to include the keystrokes in a program module as a subroutine. By recording the keystrokes, saving them to a macro associated with a function key, and then saving the macro to a macro file, you can reuse the keystrokes whenever you want.

You create a keyboard macro through the Control Center by accessing the Tools menu and selecting Macro. When you invoke the choice, you are asked to name the macro. You see a menu of name choices starting with F1 (Alt-F1). If you choose F10 (Alt-F10), you can add any letter of the alphabet to the function key. For example, you can choose Alt-F10-A (hold down Alt and F10 and then press A). You can have up to 35 keyboard macros (F1 through F9 plus the 26 letters of the alphabet). You can save your macros to a single file with a KEY file extension by using the SAVE MACRO command. You then can reload them into memory with the RESTORE MACRO command, and use them in your application code with the PLAY MACRO command.

After you name the macro, and until you press Shift-F10-E, every keystroke you make is put in the macro. Shift-F10-E ends the macro-recording process. At this point, your macro is in memory but isn't permanently saved. As long as you stay in dBASE, the macro is available.

If you want to save the macro permanently, use SAVE MACRO, which saves all the macro definitions currently in memory to whatever file you name. You also can save up to 36 macros by using different files when you use SAVE MACRO. To activate a particular set of macros, you simply use RESTORE MACRO on the file that contains the macros you want. You can invoke the macro by pressing Alt and the appropriate function key or by inserting PLAY MACRO in your program code.

If you do not want to save the commands as a separate file, you can put them in a string for the KEYBOARD command:

```
KEYBOARD <expC> [CLEAR]
```

This command executes faster than the `PLAY MACRO` command because no files have to be loaded from the disk. The *<expC>* is limited to 20 characters unless you set the typeahead buffer larger using `SET TYPEAHEAD <expN>`. *<expN>* can range from 0 to 32,000, enough for some fairly long macros.

Creating and Using Reports

► See "REPORT FORM," p. 732

You learned to create custom reports in Chapter 12. You can use these reports in your program by opening the data tables and queries required and then using the REPORT FORM command.

```
REPORT FORM <report name> [TO[PRINT][FILE]]
```

Occasionally, your reports can be too complex to design with the report generator. You can write programs that provide output to the screen, printer, or a file in the exact format that you desire. Using SET PRINT ON/OFF and @...SAY... you can direct the output to the printer. You can decide not to have the printer tied up while the report is generating, if your calculations between lines are going to take a long time. You can use SET ALTERNATE TO *<filename>* to direct the output to a temporary file. Use SET ALTERNATE ON/OFF to redirect the output to the temporary file. When the report completes, print the file. If you have installed PRINT prior to entering dBASE, you can use the DOS PRINT command, otherwise use TYPE *<filename>* >LPT1.

▶ See "SET ALTERNATE TO," p. 833

```
! PRINT <filename>
```

Sorting Your Data Table

By default, your records are ordered in the sequence of entry. This may not be the order desired in your report. You can use two methods to control the order of your data. The first way to control data order, with SORT, physically changes the order of the data and stores it in a new database with the natural record order based on the sort order. The second method, using INDEX, produces a virtual (nonphysical) ordering of data. Both have their uses, although INDEX is the more useful of the two.

When you use SORT, dBASE must copy the rearranged data to a new data table. The data in the original data table is not altered. You receive an error message for attempting an "illegal" sort if you try to make SORT alter data in the original data table with commands such as the following:

Tip
Sorting requires making a copy of all or some of the data table, which eats up disk space. Indexing, rather than sorting, uses a minimal amount of disk space, and is processed much quicker.

```
USE Mydata
SORT ON Field1 TO Mydata
```

You can only use the SORT command after you open the data table with USE. The syntax for the SORT command follows:

```
SORT TO <filename> ON <field1> [/A] [/C] [/D]
      [,<field2> [/A] [/C] [/D] ...] [ASCENDING]/
      [DESCENDING] [<scope>] [FOR <condition>]
   [WHILE <condition>]
```

In this syntax, /A sorts in ascending order, /C sorts by uppercase and lowercase, and /D sorts in descending order. The syntax of the SORT command can include *<scope>*, FOR, and WHILE. FOR and WHILE both require *conditions*. You see these modifiers in many dBASE commands.

IV

Programming in dBASE 5

When you specify a *<scope>*, you actually specify the number of records for a command to act on. The default scope is the entire file. If you want to sort only the next 15 records from the data table Mydata by using the Name field as the key, for example, enter the following:

```
USE Mydata
SORT TO SortData ON Name NEXT 15
```

In this example, the <scope> is NEXT. NEXT sets the scope to a fixed number of records indicated by the number following NEXT (15 in the example). Other scopes include the following:

ALL	All records from the beginning of the data table to the end of the data table
REST	All records from the current record to the end of the data table
RECORD *x*	Only a single record, where *x* is the record number

In a way, FOR and WHILE are like a *<scope>*, in that you specify the records to act on. FOR and WHILE use conditions, but each chooses records a different way.

FOR starts at the beginning of the *<scope>* or file if no scope is specified, searches the entire *<scope>*, and chooses only the records that match the condition.

WHILE starts at the current record pointer location and searches only while the condition is true. The first record that doesn't meet the condition stops the search and selection of records.

In working with your Customer data table; for example, suppose that you want a command to operate on the customers only in the state of Ohio. You want to store them in alphabetical order by customer name. To store these names in a new data table called OHIO.DBF, use the following code:

```
USE Customer
SORT ON Company TO Ohio /A FOR State="OH"
USE Ohio
LIST
```

This code creates a data table called OHIO.DBF with the same structure as CUSTOMER.DBF but containing only the Ohio customers, arranged alphabetically in customer name order.

The WHILE scope limits the execution of a command to a specified duration. To specify that you want the command to continue as long as the records show a Balance field of less than $50,000, for example, use the scope `WHILE Balance < 50000`.

Indexing Your Data Table

INDEX creates a second file that tells the dBASE 5 record pointer to move from record to record in a certain order. In other words, INDEX creates a "road map" to locations in your data table, based on your instructions. Like SORT, INDEX enables you to order your data based on the contents of a selected field. In the case of INDEX, that field is called the *key field*. The file containing the road map is called the *index file*, or just the *index*.

◀ See "Understanding Indexs," p. 162

The syntax for the INDEX command follows:

```
INDEX ON <key expression> TO <.NDX filename>/
     TAG <tag name> [OF <.MDX filename>]
   [FOR <condition>][UNIQUE] [DESCENDING]
```

Locating What You're Looking For

Now that you understand how to put files in order, you're ready to explore how to get information from a data table. The first search command is LOCATE, which uses the following syntax:

▶ See "LOCATE," p. 709

```
LOCATE [FOR <condition>] [<scope>]
   [WHILE <condition>]
```

LOCATE searches through a data table to find a record that matches the specified *<condition>*. When you issue the command, LOCATE begins with the first record in the data table and skips from record to record until it finds a record that matches the condition. You can use FOR and WHILE with LOCATE to further restrict the condition.

The use of the scope is exactly the same as with SORT. One useful aspect of LOCATE, in fact, is its use of a search scope. Using LOCATE, you can search the Customer data table for a company called *Widgets Unlimited* in Indiana. After opening the Customer data table with USE Customer, use the following command:

▶ See "SORT TO," p. 743

```
LOCATE FOR Company = "Widgets Unlimited" .AND. ;
State = "IN"
```

Notice the Boolean operator AND with the periods on either side. You can find Widgets Unlimited in Indiana while ignoring the companies in Colorado and California.

Tip

When you use LOCATE with FOR or WHILE in a large database file, verify that index tags exist for appropriate fields. dBASE uses index tags—even if not currently active— to speed up record searches.

Note

Boolean mathematics uses logical functions, thus the Boolean operators are AND, NOT, OR, and () for grouping. The first three listed must be surrounded by periods, for example ".AND.".

SEEK and FIND, the two other search commands, take advantage of indexed files. SEEK evaluates an expression and returns a logical true if it can locate the expression. The result of the evaluation must be in the contents of the active index tag in at least one record in the active data table; otherwise, dBASE returns a logical false. SEEK looks for the expression only in the active index tag. The SEEK() function does the same thing as seek, but also returns a result, as shown in the following segment of code.

```
* Code fragment demonstrating SEEK()
USE Customer                    && Open the data table
INDEX ON Company TAG CoIndex    && Build a tag index
IF SEEK("Widgets Unlimited")    && Did you find it?
     DISPLAY Contact            && Display the contents of the
Contact field
                                && for that record
ENDIF                           && Close off the command
USE                             && Close the data table
```

▶ See "SEEK," p. 740

▶ See "FIND," p. 698

SEEK looks for the contents of the key field only, which in this case is Company. If an entry exists in the Company field somewhere in the data table for Widgets Unlimited, dBASE finds it. However, dBASE finds only the first occurrence. To find additional listings for Widgets Unlimited, you need to do a bit of *looping* and use the conditional command DO WHILE, which is covered later in this chapter.

FIND is the other search mechanism you can use with indexed files. Like SEEK, FIND is very fast and has the same single-field, first-occurrence, no-scope limitations. FIND, however, doesn't evaluate an expression and then go into the data table to see whether it can find the expression. FIND looks for the first occurrence of a *literal* (a text string or number) and then returns the data itself, instead of a logical true or false indication.

FIND can search for the partial contents of a field and return the entire contents, or it can return the contents of other fields—the same way the example using SEEK returned the Contact after it located the proper record. In both instances, the command's biggest benefit is its capability to locate a record rapidly and move the record pointer so that you can manipulate the contents of other fields in the record.

SEEK works well with memory variables; it works much better than FIND. FIND works with literal strings, whereas SEEK uses a string in quotation marks. To search for the name *Smith* in the Lastname field, for example, issue this command:

```
FIND Smith
```

or

```
SEEK "Smith"
```

The problem with FIND comes up when "Smith" is stored in a memory variable. Consider the following examples:

Example A	**Example B**
STORE "Smith" TO cust	STORE "Smith" TO cust
FIND cust	SEEK cust

In both examples, the memory variable *cust* contains the string Smith. When FIND is executed in example A, dBASE looks for the literal string *cust* rather than the assigned *Smith*. Nothing is found, unless someone's last name is *Cust*. In example B, SEEK uses the contents of *cust*, which is *Smith*, and the correct record is found. To get the same results from the FIND, you must use the MACRO function:

```
FIND &cust
```

If you use a multiple-index file, you must activate the index tag so that when you use SEEK or FIND, dBASE knows which key field to use. dBASE has a mechanism for indicating which index or key to use—the SET ORDER command. In the multiple-index example shown in Chapter 17, you created an MDX file with tags for Customer and Contact. The segment of code is shown below to refresh your memory:

▶ See "SET ORDER TO," p. 865

```
* Code fragment illustrating the use of .MDX files
*
USE Customer
INDEX ON Customer TAG Customer
INDEX ON Contact TAG Contact
INDEX ON City TAG City
USE
```

Now, if you want to use SEEK to determine whether an entry for *Joe Jones* exists, you use the index based on the Contact field as the key. You need to put the Contact field in use to control the order of the data table.

In other words, you want your data table to appear to be in Contact order. Use the following commands:

```
* Code fragment illustrating SEEK with .MDX file
*
USE Customer ORDER TAG Contact     && Open the data table using the
                                   && Customer.MDX multiple-index
                                      file
                                   && Establish Contact as the tag
                                   && which determines the index
                                      and key
IF SEEK("Joe Jones")               && If you find the record....
     DISPLAY                       && Display it
ENDIF                              && Close off the command
USE                                && Close the data table and
                                      index
```

SET ORDER is required any time you open a data table with a multiple-index file. You also use SET ORDER if you don't want the data table indexed, yet you want to leave the multiple-index file open. Issuing the command SET ORDER TO without specifying a value deactivates all indexes and allows the records to be accessed in their natural order. A data table is said to be in natural order when the records are listed in the order in which they were entered.

You have opened data tables with the USE command throughout this chapter. But you have not yet tried an important option available with USE. The complete syntax for USE follows:

```
USE [<data table filename>/?] [IN <work area number>]
   [INDEX <.NDX or .MDX file list>]
   [ORDER <.NDX filename>/[[TAG]<.MDX tag>
   [OF <.MDX filename>]]]
   [ALIAS <alias>] [EXCLUSIVE] [NOUPDATE] [NOLOG]
        [NOSAVE] [AGAIN]
```

When the topic of multiple data tables is covered, you learn that you can open several (as many as 255) data tables at one time and place them in separate work areas. You use the IN keyword to indicate in which work area you want to open your database. You also can use the SELECT # command (where # is the number or letter of the desired work area) before you open the data table, in which case you don't need the IN keyword.

Displaying Your Results

After you use LOCATE, SEEK, or FIND to position the record pointer, you can do something with the data in the record. You can perform further manipulations with the contents of one or more fields. You can also display the contents of one or more fields. You have three ways to do that. You can use the question mark (?), the DISPLAY command, or @...SAY. All three work in roughly the same way. Any parameter not in quotation marks is considered a field name or a memory variable. The display shows the contents of the field or the memory variable. If the modifier is enclosed in quotation marks, it's considered to be a literal and is displayed verbatim—word for word. You can display several items by separating them with commas. The following code shows an example using ? and DISPLAY.

```
* Code fragment demonstrating two ways to display data
USE Customer ORDER TAG Company      && Open Customer
                                    && Select the Company index tag
? Company, Contact                  && Print the contents of the
                                       fields
                                    && Company and Contact
DISPLAY Company, Contact OFF        && Display the contents
                                    && of the fields Company and
                                    && Contact, OFF shuts off the
                                       display
                                    && record number
USE                                 && close Customer
```

In most cases, if all you want to do is display the contents of a record, using ? is the easiest method. If you also want the record number, use DISPLAY.

You can use ? to get the results of a function. If you type *? TIME()*, for example, dBASE responds with the system time.

If you need to send the contents of a field to a printer, however, using DISPLAY is easier. The syntax for DISPLAY follows:

▶ See "DISPLAY/LIST," p. 690

```
DISPLAY [[FIELDS] <expression list>] [OFF]
   [<scope>] [FOR <condition>]
   [WHILE <condition>] [TO PRINTER/TO FILE <filename>]
```

You get the advantage of scope as well as the capability to send the field contents to the printer or a file. The default scope for *DISPLAY* is the current record. On the other hand, ? displays only the data on the screen—a quick and dirty way to get a display if that's all you need.

For formatted reports, @...SAY gives you the most power. You can position text and values precisely in any location on a line or page. The general format is:

```
@,<row>,<col> SAY <expression>[PICTURE <expC>][FUNCTION<function
list>]
```

For screen displays, ROW has a range from 0 to 24, and COL has a range of 0 to 79. On printer output, the row and column ranges depend on the font you choose for the report. An additional constraint on printer output is that the column numbers must constantly increase for a given row and the row numbers must constantly increase for a page.

DISPLAY and ? have a relative called LIST. You encountered LIST when you explored data table structures earlier in this chapter. LIST is very much like DISPLAY, both in syntax and usage, with two exceptions: LIST does not stop when it fills a screen with data, and the default scope for LIST is the entire file. LIST works well with long lists, and DISPLAY with single or few items.

Because you can use LIST to send the list to a file or printer, LIST is good for dumping large amounts of data. LIST also is very proficient in creating simple reports without any fancy formatting. Use DISPLAY to print a heading line and then find a record; and use LIST to send all or some selected records to the printer. LIST prints the field names on the first line and then each record, making a columnar report.

A Sample Report Program

The following procedure, CREMPCHG, is used to print a report on all employees and the number of hours they propose to work on different projects. Memory variables are used to track the line number and page number in the report. This is an easy way to make sure that the output is printed on the line you want. You control when the line number is incremented and by how much. By tracking the line number you can also handle different sizes of paper before incrementing the page number. The second procedure, CROUTPUT, is called by CREMPCHG to determine where to send the output and initialize the output device.

Note

In a multiuser environment, you don't want to hard-code your filenames so that users can generate the same report file at the same time. When using temporary filenames in your program, set it to equal the user ID of the person using the program. For example, if your user ID is stored in a memory variable *logname*, the code to create a total data file would look like this:

```
TOTAL ON Period TO (logname)
USE (logname)
```

This allows you to eliminate the need for hard-coding a temporary name into the program, thus freeing up that filename for another purpose.

```
PROCEDURE CREMPCHG
* CREMPCHG.PRG
* This program prints a report for each employee of the charge
* numbers that hours have been proposed on for the period.
* AUTHOR:  Chris Bolte                DATE:  May 94
*
```

```
* Perform housekeeping
*
PUBLIC PerStart,PerEnd,ThisFY,ThisPer
SET DEVICE TO SCREEN
SET TALK OFF
CLOSE DATABASES
PageCnt = 1            && Initialize variables Page 1, line 0
LineCnt = 0
Done = .F.
Outchoice = 'O'
Outdevice = SPACE(7)
LastPost = DATE()
EndDay = DATE()
*
*  For very long reports, it is sometimes useful to find out
*  how long they take to create.  This gets the start time.
*
StrtTim = Time()
StartVal = VAL(SUBSTR(StrtTim,1,2))*3600 + VAL
➥(SUBSTR(StrtTim,4,2))*60 +;
         VAL(SUBSTR(StrtTim,6,2))   && Convert to seconds
*
MaxLines = 20        && Start with maxlines for screen, 20
*
*  Ask the user what output device, 80 column report
*
DO CROutput WITH OutChoice, OutDevice, MaxLines, Done, 80
*
*  The user may have decided not to generate the report,
*  so check to see that we are not done already
*
IF .NOT. Done
  SET DEVICE TO SCREEN  && Output on screen
  CLEAR                 && Tell the user what is happening
  @1,1 SAY "Employee hours report being generated"
*
* This report is generated from three data tables:
*  Employees, Proposals, and Charge numbers
*
  USE NAMES ORDER EmpName IN 2
  USE Proposal ORDER EmpName IN 1
  USE DOCHARG Index DOCGDO IN 3
  SELECT Names      && Report for each employee
  SCAN
    TestNa = TRIM(Names->EmpLast)
    TestIn = LEFT(Names->EmpFirst,1)
    SELECT Proposal  && Get the proposals this employee is in
    SET FILTER TO EmpLast = Testna .and. EmpInit = TestIn .AND.;
         Period = ThisPer .AND. FiscalYear = ThisFY
    GO TOP
    LineCnt = 1     && Start at the top of the page
    IF .NOT. (Outchoice $ 'sS')  && Keep user informed on progress
       Set device to screen
       @6,6 SAY "Processing : " + EmpLast + Names->EmpNo
    ELSE
       CLEAR
    ENDIF
```

```
    SET DEVICE TO &Outdevice   && Route output to selected device
*   First we print a header on the page.
    @LineCnt,5 SAY "Employee report for " + TestIn + '. ' + TestNa;
        +'  '+Names->EmpNo
    LineCnt = 3
    @LineCnt,1 SAY "Charge Number      Proposed     Period   FY DO"
    LineCnt = 4
    @LineCnt,22 SAY "Hours"
    LineCnt = 5
*  Now display the information on the charge number.  Each
*  field is displayed under the right column in the heading
    SCAN
       @LineCnt,1 SAY charge_No
       @LineCnt,22 SAY prop_Hours
       @LineCnt,35 SAY Period
       @LineCnt,42 SAY Fiscalyear
*   Use the LOOKUP function to find the project number from
*   the DOCHARG table matching the charge number in the
*   proposal data table
       @LineCnt,48 SAY ;
        LOOKUP(doCHARG->DO_NO,CHARGE_NO,DOCHARG->CHARGE_NO)
       LineCnt = LineCnt+1       && Increment the line count
       IF LineCnt >= MaxLines    && If over the lines per page
          LineCnt = 1              && Reset to top of page
          PageCnt = PageCnt+1      && Increment page count
          IF OutChoice $ 'Ss'    && Pause for screen output
             WAIT "Press return to see next page"
             CLEAR
          ELSE
             EJECT                  && Form feed for printer output
          ENDIF            && End if screen
       ENDIF          && End if over lines per page
       LOOP           && Get next charge number
    ENDSCAN           && Display next line
    SELECT Names        && Select the employee data table
    LOOP            && Get the next name
  ENDSCAN           && Do the next employee
  EndTim = Time()    && Get the time of finish
  EndVal = VAL(SUBSTR(EndTim,1,2))*3600 +
VAL(SUBSTR(EndTim,4,2))*60 +;
        VAL(SUBSTR(EndTim,6,2))  && Convert to seconds
  TotTime = (EndVal-StartVal)/60   && Total time in minutes
  LineCnt = LineCnt+3            && Add to bottom of report
  @LineCnt,50 SAY TotTime PICTURE "9999.99"
  @LineCnt,60 SAY "Minutes total"
ENDIF
SET DEVICE TO SCREEN  && Make sure all output shows on screen
CLOSE ALL
RETURN
```

The procedure CREmpChg called the procedure CROutput at the beginning. CROutput determines the output device and proper control sequences based on user input. Parameters are passed to indicate to CROutput how long the lines on the report will be and to provide return variables for the control sequences.

```
PROCEDURE CROUTPUT
* CROUTPUT.PRG
* This file selects the output device given a choice
* of Screen, HP LaserJet II, Epson FX-86, or disk file.
* Outchoice stores one character device flag
* Outdevice stores  Screen, FILE, or Printer
*
* AUTHOR:  Chris Bolte   DATE:  MAY 94
PARAMETERS OutChoice,OutDevice,MaxLines,Done,Width
CLEAR
OutChoice = 'o'      && Set Outchoice so WHILE fails
Done = .F.           && Not
OutDevice = 'SCREEN'
*
*  Begin the main loop. Ask for user's choice until valid.
*
DO WHILE .NOT. (OutChoice $ "sShHeEfFxX")
 ACCEPT ;
 "Output to (S)creen, (H)P, (E)pson, (F)ile, or exit (X)? ";
        TO OutChoice
ENDDO
IF OutChoice $ "xX"        && Return to calling routine
 Done = .T.
ENDIF
CtrlSeq = CHR(27) + 'E'         && Reset command for HP
IF .NOT. Done
 DO CASE
  CASE OutChoice $ "Ss"    && Screen output
   OutDevice = "SCREEN"
   Maxlines = 20
  CASE OutChoice $ "eE"    && Epson dot-matrix printer
   OutDevice = "PRINTER"
   IF Width>80             && if more than 80 character line
    CtrlSeq = CHR(15)        && Use small font
   ELSE                    && otherwise
    CtrlSeq = CHR(18)        && use large font
   ENDIF
   MaxLines = 60             && 60 line page on dot-matrix
  CASE OutChoice $ "hH"    && HP Laserjet
   OutDevice = "PRINTER"
   IF Width <= 80            && Up to 80 use Courier Portrait
    CtrlSeq = CtrlSeq + CHR(27) + "&l6d0O" + CHR(27) + "(10U" ;
        + CHR(27) + "(s0p10h12vsb3T"
    MaxLines = 60            && 60 lines per page
   ENDIF
   IF Width > 80             && Width>80 use Lineprinter Landscape
    CtrlSeq = CtrlSeq + CHR(27)+"&l8d1O"+CHR(27)+"(11U";
            +CHR(27)+"(s0p16.6h8.5vsbT"
    MaxLines=50             && 50 lines per page
   ENDIF
  CASE OutChoice $ "fF"     && Output to disk file, get name
   ACCEPT "File name: " to OutDevice
   MaxLines = 60              && Format for 60 line pages
   OutDevice = "TO "+OutDevice
 ENDCASE
```

```
  IF OutChoice $ 'eEhH'      && for printers
    SET DEVICE TO PRINT        && send reset command
    @0,0 SAY ctrlseq
    SET MARGIN TO 0
    SET DEVICE TO SCREEN
  ENDIF
ENDIF
RETURN
```

Linking three different data tables is not always easy, so this example shows you how you can program the capability into your applications.

Moving Your Data Around

Four commands—IMPORT, EXPORT, COPY TO, and APPEND FROM—allow you to translate files of dissimilar types of data. These commands enable you to adapt data entered into dBASE for use by other programs or adapt data from other programs for use by dBASE.

IMPORT enables you to accept data from PFS:File, Framework, Rapidfile, Lotus 1-2-3, and dBASE II files. EXPORT allows you to send dBASE data to Lotus 1-2-3, PFS:File, Framework, Rapidfile, or dBASE II files. COPY enables you to transfer data to dBASE II, comma-delimited, VisiCalc, Framework, Rapidfile, Standard Data Format, Multiplan, and Lotus 1-2-3 files.

Using any of these commands is relatively straightforward. To translate records from the Customer database to a 1-2-3 worksheet, for example, use the following code:

```
USE Customer              && Opens Customer
COPY TO Customer TYPE WKS && Copies records to a WKS file
```

You can use one final command set to manipulate the data table. The set consists of four commands—DELETE, RECALL, PACK, and ZAP—with the first three commands often used together. For more information on these commands see Chapter 22.

When you use DELETE, you don't actually delete anything. The DELETE command marks a record for deletion. You can unmark it any time. As long as you merely mark the record for deletion, it remains in the data table and associated indexes. Deletions become permanent when you use the PACK command.

◄ See "Deleting Records," p. 156

You can use DELETE on all or some of the records in a data table. You use DELETE to mark individual records when the dBASE record pointer is at the record you want to dispose of. You also can use a scope with DELETE to eliminate a range or group of records meeting specified criteria. If you want to mark all records in a data table for deletion, you can use DELETE ALL To actually remove all the records, but ZAP is faster.

When you list a data table, deleted records still appear, but an asterisk (*) appears before records marked for deletion. If you don't want deleted records to appear when you list a data table, use the command SET DELETED ON. This command acts as a filter, displaying only those records that aren't marked for deletion. To view deleted records again, use the command SET DELETED OFF.

Tip
Before PACK or ZAP will work, you must have sole access to the data table, by using the USE EXCLUSIVE command. Be sure your indexes are open or PACK reorders the records without updating your index files.

After you delete records, you can RECALL the records or PACK the data table. You use RECALL just as you use DELETE. If you use DELETE NEXT 5 to mark the next five records as deleted, then you can reposition the record pointer and use RECALL NEXT 5. The deletion marks on the five records are removed. To remove records from the data table permanently, you must use DELETE to mark the records and then use PACK. The command PACK appears on a line by itself following the marking process.

Another way to empty a data table is to use ZAP, which does the same thing as DELETE ALL and PACK but in a different way—and much faster. Don't use ZAP unless you are certain that you want to empty the specified data table. When you use ZAP, all associated indexes are updated appropriately.

ZAP follows the setting of SET SAFETY. If you have issued the command SET SAFETY ON (the default setting) and then type *ZAP* to clear the contents of the data table, you are prompted with `Are you sure?`, to which you may answer Yes or No. If SET SAFETY is OFF, however, using the ZAP command clears the data table without giving you a chance to change your mind.

▶ See "SET SAFETY," p. 871

Now that you know how to create a data table and manipulate the data in it, your next task is to learn how to use the data in more than one data table at a time. When you use multiple data tables, you're using the *relational* capabilities of dBASE 5.

Troubleshooting

My reports have the data in the right place on the page, but on separate pages.

When using @<*row*>,<*col*>SAY, if you try to print further up or to the left of the current position, dBASE issues a page feed command to your printer. Go back over your code to be sure you ordered your print commands from left to right and from top to bottom on the page.

From Here...

Now you've looked at how to use menus and windows in your program to customize your application and make it easier for the user to input data. You've learned to write help screens to assist your users as they work with your application. You've learned how to build a procedure library and design and print reports specific to your application. To fine-tune your application, you may want to check out the following chapters:

- Chapter 12, "Creating Custom Reports," tells you how to tailor your report to suit your specific needs.
- Chapter 15, "Using Relational Databases for Complex Situations," covers topics relating to designing applications.
- Chapter 19, "Using the Applications Generator and the Compiler" shows you how you can write your program in less time by having dBASE write it for you.
- Chapter 21, "Creating Objects with UI" shows you how to use dBASE objects to make your application professional, efficient, and easily modifiable, not to mention easy for the user to work with.
- Chapter 24, "Using SET Commands To Configure dBASE 5," tells you how to use each of the SET commands in your application.

Chapter 19

Using the Applications Generator and the Compiler

You have seen in previous chapters that building a dBASE 5 application involves more than manipulating the data table. Your application must include such vital elements as error trapping, testing user input, housekeeping, and maintaining data integrity. You also must provide program documentation so that users and technical support people can figure out what to do if something goes wrong. All this extra work takes time and experience. One of the best ways to reduce the time involved and to increase your experience in developing applications is to use the dBASE 5 Applications Generator.

In this chapter, you learn:

- How to use the dBASE 5 Applications Generator
- Types of applications you can develop from scratch
- How to polish your applications
- How to customize your applications by adding code
- More about using the dBASE 5 debugger
- How to compile your applications and prepare them for distribution

Building Applications for Other Users

You need to consider two important factors when you build programs for other users. First, you won't always be around to support the application, so the application must work cleanly (be bug-free) and be understood easily by its users. Second, many users on occasion can misuse the program, so the application must be designed to prevent misuse and to keep the user from damaging data.

The Applications Generator, or *Ap Gen*, enables you to build complex, well-documented dBASE code. You work with the Ap Gen through a pull-down menu system similar to the Control Center. Unlike the dBASE III Plus Ap Gen, dBASE 5 includes the generator as part of the main dBASE 5 program, which means that you don't need to invoke an external program. New users draw great benefit from using the dBASE 5 Ap Gen. The generator is a state-of-the-art program that considers housekeeping, error tracking, and other nuances that separate the amateur applications from the professional ones.

As professional and advanced as the Ap Gen is, however, remember that the more complex the application is, the more potential there is for error. Also, the types of errors you encounter are tougher to find. Syntax errors are common in programmer-generated code, but rare in machine-generated code. Also rare are open-ended constructs, such as DO WHILE or IF, which need commands to close them off. You can use all your debugging tools to find errors. Fortunately, dBASE has an excellent set of debugging tools to help you locate them.

Another benefit of using the Applications Generator is the substantial time you save when coding complex, but repetitive and common, sections of the application. Code for a complex set of menus can run to hundreds of lines and take days to write, check, and document. The Applications Generator allows you to produce the code in a few hours or so, and leaves time to add the polish that marks the professional application. In other words, you can use the Applications Generator to do your "grunt work" even if you are an experienced dBASE 5 user.

Tip
Thorough planning before you start coding your program can save you time and headaches.

Planning Programs for the Applications Generator

Preplanning takes on a whole new meaning when you work through a series of pull-down menus. The Ap Gen doesn't make it convenient for you to check your code along the way and test it module by module, as you do when you develop an application manually. Certainly, you can generate, test, modify, and test again, but you limit the need for that if you take time to plan before you start.

The first step is to plan the data flow, the program flow, and the menu structure with great care. You can build program modules before you run the Ap Gen. Some of the modules can be report forms, label forms, special help windows, and other external or special modules you learn about later. You need these modules because your application uses them and the Ap Gen asks you about them as you design the structure of your application. Building your application only to find that you need to make another report is frustrating.

Equally important is the layout of your data tables. Examine your application and decide how many and what kind of data tables you need. Keep the user input in mind and create the data tables in advance. The Ap Gen uses your data tables exactly as you tell it to, including whatever relational operations you've defined to exist among multiple data tables. As you progress, you learn how to take advantage of most of dBASE 5's features from within the Applications Generator.

Follow a special order when you plan your application. If you plan according to this order without backing out to build some missing piece, your plan develops smoothly. In general terms, you need to prepare the following items, in order, before you start building your application with the Ap Gen:

- Reports
- Labels
- Data input forms
- Databases
- Indexes

You may think that by putting reports and labels before databases, the list is backward. When you develop a system, however, you must determine what reports you need first. From the information you include in the reports, you can tell what fields you need in a database or databases.

The order in which the Applications Generator expects you to develop your application is different from the order in which you plan the application. Plan your order according to the following steps:

1. Prepare the files you need to use during the application generation process.
2. Start the Applications Generator.
3. Create the welcome screen.
4. Create the main menu.
5. Create each of the submenus.
6. Create other objects, such as lists or batches.
7. Attach the actions of each object or menu to its object.
8. Generate the menus.
9. Generate the documentation.
10. Generate the application code.
11. Print the documentation.
12. Add any outside modifications to the program and insert them in the PRG files created by the Ap Gen. (Do not include those additional modules you add from within the Ap Gen process by using the Embed Code option.)
13. Run the application and debug.

Tip
Ap Gen can make the overall debugging job easier by eliminating hard-to-find errors.

In simple terms, then, you prepare external files, build the menu system, designate the actions of the menu choices, add your modifications, and debug. By using the Applications Generator, you can cut your coding time by 70 to 80 percent. Remember, however, that you can spend about 60 percent of your time writing and debugging 95 percent of your application. The last 5 percent of your program can consume 40 percent of the total time it takes you to produce a finished program. When you get the application written and it works, for the most part, you still have a good way to go before you finish the job.

Let's look at how you could create a Mailer application. You can use this as part of the invoice application discussed in Chapter 18. This application enables you to input, edit, and delete records for a mailing list, as well as print a report and mailing labels. You see the report that is used, the labels, the screen form, and how each is created. Finally, after you see the report, labels, and screen format, you see the data table and index to use for this application. The application design follows the design order listed previously.

The data tables to be used with this application are the INVOICE and INVENTORY database files described in Chapter 18.

◄ See "Designing an Invoice Application" and "Designing an Inventory Application," pp. 481 & 484

To create the CUSTOMER data table, and for each table necessary for the application, in the Command window, type the CREATE command followed by the data table name, as shown in the following:

CREATE CUSTOMER

► See "CREATE/ MODIFY APPLICATION," p. 675

When creating the database structure, specify *Y* in the Index column for the COMPANY field to create an index tag for this field.

Before using the Applications Generator, you need to design your report and label formats and your data-entry screen form. (Refer to Chapters 8, 12, and 13 for specific details on designing and creating reports and labels.)

The report for the Mailer application is a simple columnar report. The fields displayed in the report are COMP_ID, COMPANY, CONTACT, ADDRESS1, ADDRESS2, CITY, STATE, ZIP, PHONE, and FAX. Figure 19.1 shows the report format used.

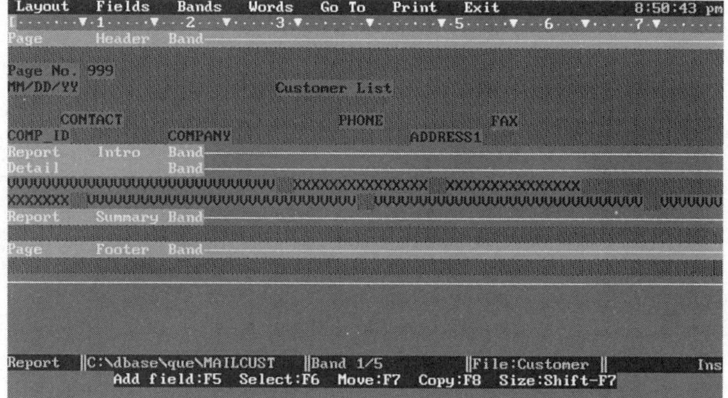

Fig. 19.1
Reports can be used to display any information from the database.

When you are ready to create a report, you can use the Quick Layouts option from the Layout menu. In the report, you add an extra line to the Detail band, and move the CONTACT, PHONE, and FAX fields to the new line. Delete the BALANCE, TAX, and NORM_DISC fields. Center the report heading, Customer List, at the top of the report. To create the report from the Command window, type the following:

► See "CREATE/ MODIFY REPORT," p. 676

CREATE REPORT MAILCUST

Tip
A shortcut for creating a label is to highlight the field, then press F5.

The labels you create are *1-up* labels (only one label across). The label is made up of the following fields:

COMPANY

ADDRESS1

ADDRESS2

CITY, STATE ZIP

CONTACT

► See "CREATE/ MODIFY LABEL," p. 675

Type **ATTN:** as text. When creating the label, use the Add Field option from the Fields menu. This option enables you to place each field on the label. To create the labels, use the following command:

CREATE LABEL MAILLBLS

You can create a form to add, edit, and browse the data in the data table. The form you create looks like the one shown in figure 19.2.

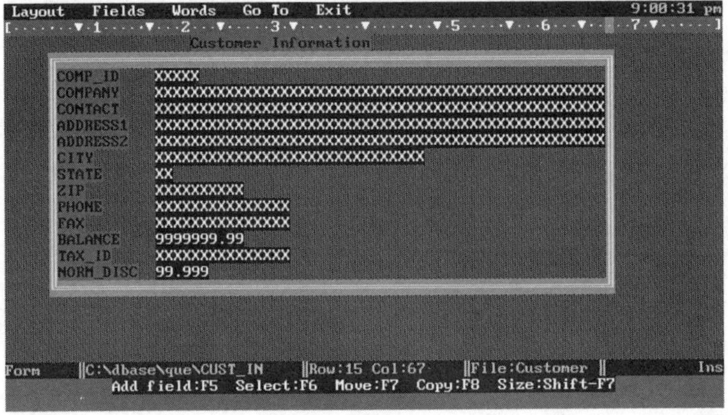

Fig. 19.2
Forms enable you to easily add to, edit, or browse a data table.

As with the report, you can use Quick Layouts from the Fields menu to place the fields on-screen. Move the fields down the screen by inserting blank lines. Center the fields by selecting the fields and titles with F6 and selecting Words, Position, Center from the menu. Draw a box around the fields from row 4, column 20, to row 15, column 60. Finally, add the text on-screen by typing at rows 2, 18, and 19, and then centering the text. You can create the screen format by typing the following:

CREATE SCREEN CUST_IN

When you finish creating and saving the screen form, you are ready to use the Applications Generator.

▶ See "CREATE/ MODIFY SCREEN," p. 677

Troubleshooting

I've generated an application using Ap Gen, and made some minor modifications to the code during debug, but now I've been told I need to add some capabilities to the application. How should I do this?

After you've modified the program, you don't want to regenerate the code using Ap Gen. You can make as many additions to the code as you want, as long as you do so manually. See "Changing the Application Generator Code" later in this chapter for more information on how to do this.

You could also generate the new section as a separate piece of code and call it from within the original application code.

Getting Started with the Applications Generator

Now that you planned your application and created the files you need in advance, you need to start the Applications Generator. You can start the Ap Gen from the Control Center or the Command window. From the Control Center, move to the last panel, Applications. You can select `<create>` under that panel; or, if you want to modify an existing application, select that application. The other way to select the Ap Gen is to use the command CREATE APPLICATION (or MODIFY APPLICATION if you want to work on an existing application).

Creating the Mailer Application

From the Command window, type the following command:

CREATE APPLICATION MAILER

In response to your command, you see the Application Definition screen (see fig. 19.3).

You use this screen to enter basic information about your application. First, you must name your application. The name you choose needs to be the same one you used to open the Ap Gen. Second, you must give your top menu a name and specify an opening database. The choice of whether to fill in the remaining fields is up to you. The entries you can make are shown in the following list:

Application name: *MAILER*

Description: *Mail list manager*

Main menu type: *BAR*

Main menu name: *MAINMENU*

Database/view: *CUSTOMER.DBF*

Set INDEX to: *(blank)*

ORDER: *COMPANY*

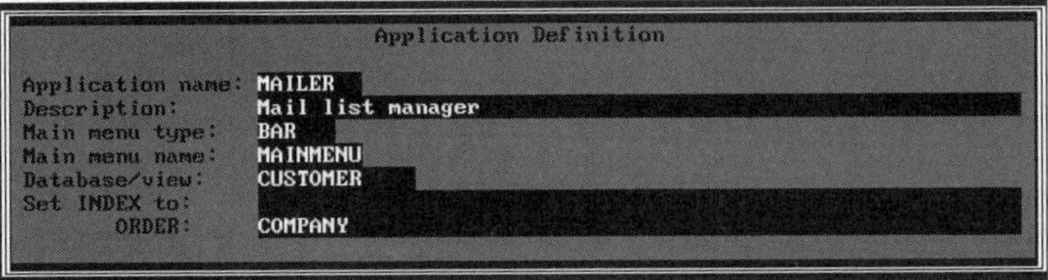

Fig. 19.3
Define your application using the Application Definition screen.

Because you are using the default multiple-index file, you can leave Set INDEX to: blank.

> **Caution**
>
> The Set INDEX to field is usually left blank because this field is only used to set NDX files. In dBASE 5, most indexing is done with MDX files, so entering data in this field can cause unwanted results. If you see error messages that are confusing to you, check this field to be sure it is blank.

You can use the mouse to select options in the Application Definition screen. Select the menu type by clicking on the input field to cycle through available menu types. To select a Database/view or Index file, press Shift-F1 in the appropriate input field to display a pick list, then click on the desired item to select it.

Note

If you press Shift-F1 to select a database or view, the file may not appear in the pick list if it's not in the current catalog. Make sure that the files you use with your application are in the current catalog.

After you fill in the Application Definition screen, save it by pressing Ctrl-End, or by clicking Accept at the bottom of the screen.

After you fill in the opening screen and save it, you see the work surface, which looks like the one shown in figure 19.4. You can change any of the information from the previous screen, using the Application menu choices Name And Describe and Modify Application Environment.

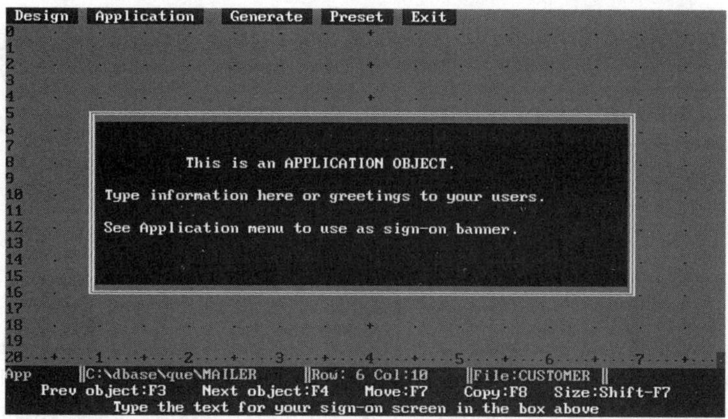

Fig. 19.4 The Application Generator opens with its own default welcome screen that you can modify.

Notice the large box on the work surface. You can use that box as a welcome screen for your application. First, you need to remove the existing text. Press Ctrl-Y and a line is deleted each time it is pressed; the remaining lines scroll up to fill the blanked line. You then can enter any text you want for your opening screen. Edit the box so that it looks like the one in figure 19.5.

Fig. 19.5 The Welcome screen can say anything you want it to say.

This figure represents what dBASE 5 calls an *application object.* Anything you create or use in the Applications Generator that becomes part of your finished program is an application object. Objects can be anything from a welcome screen, such as this, to a menu or a batch procedure.

Learning the Work Surface

Tip
Pressing F7 on some objects, such as a pop-up menu, causes dBASE to ask if you want to move the object or just the item selected.

You need to know a few rules for moving around in the work surface. First, you can move an object around the work surface by pressing F7 and using your arrow keys. When you have the object positioned where you want it, press Enter. You also can change the vertical and horizontal size of an object by pressing Shift-F7, and then using your arrow keys to make the box larger or smaller in either direction. Finally, press F10 or Alt and the first letter of a menu choice to display the menu bar. If you run into trouble and need help, press F1.

Note

The choices along the top menu bar change as you enter the menu from different points in your application-generating process. As you select different objects, the menu changes to display the one used last for that particular object.

You also can use the mouse to access menu options. Click the menu name in the menu bar, and then click the option to select it. For example, click Application, then Display Sign-on Banner, and then Yes to choose that option. To close a menu, click outside the menu area. This may take you to another menu which had been previously opened from another object. Clicking outside of all objects clears all open menus from the screen.

Although several objects may be on the screen at the same time, only the highlighted one is current and affected by your commands.

Tip
Remember to frequently save your work in progress. Press F10 for the menu, select the Application menu, and then select Save Current Application Definition.

Note

Remember that each application object is complete with its own MDI menu, or main menu, depending on the type of object and its associated properties. Be sure you are using the correct menu for the object you want to work with.

Designing the Menu

You can set up the welcome box so that it appears each time you start the application. You can do this in three steps:

1. Press F10 to invoke the menu and select the Application menu.

2. Select Display Sign-On Banner.

3. From the dialog box, select Yes.

Each time you start the application, this welcome box appears on-screen and identifies for the user the chosen application.

You can now create the application's main menu. The main menu is created from the Ap Gen's Design menu, shown in figure 19.6.

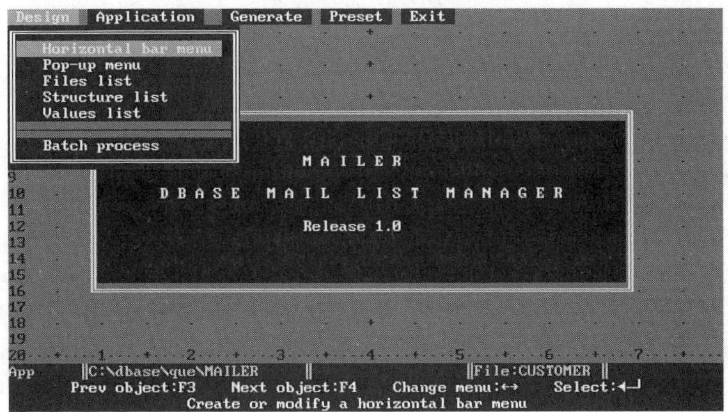

Fig. 19.6
The Application Generator's Design menu lets you create a unique set of menus to suit your needs.

This menu allows you to design horizontal bar menus, pop-up menus, file lists, structure lists, values lists, and batch processes. To create the main menu, follow these steps:

1. From the Design menu, select Horizontal Bar Menu.

2. When a list box appears on-screen, select `<create>`.

3. Fill in the menu dialog box that appears, as shown in figure 19.7. Press Ctrl-End when complete.

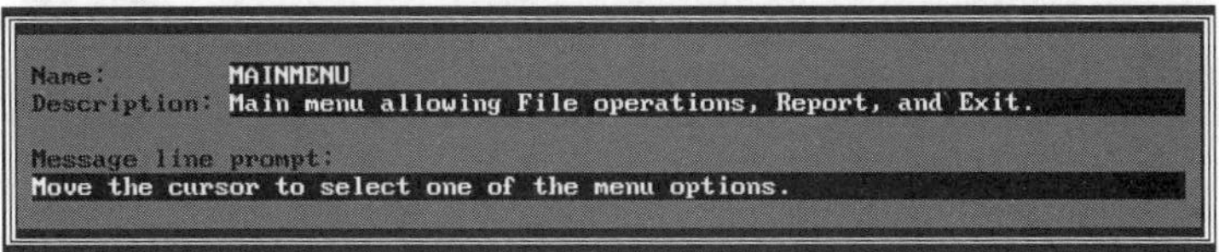

Fig. 19.7
The Menu dialog box allows you to name your menu.

After you save the information in the dialog box, a double-line box appears across the top of your screen. This box is the bar menu in which you can place the top menu choices.

At this point, you are just creating a graphic. Menus created from this Ap Gen choice are incapable of doing anything at this moment. You attach actions to them later. When you add text to the menu, you first must press F5. Pressing F5 enables you to type menu items in the menu. These are the pads for your menu. To add your menu choices to the top menu bar, follow these steps:

1. With the cursor in the menu box, press F5, type **FILES**, and press F5 again.

2. Move the cursor to column 30, press F5, type **REPORTS**, and press F5 again.

3. Move the cursor to column 60, press F5, type **EXIT**, and press F5 one final time.

Figure 19.8 shows the top menu of the Mailer application that uses the database you created earlier. Three choices are available in this example: FILES, which allows the user to add, delete, and change data table records in the Customer data table; REPORTS, which enables the user to print or display the associated reports for the application; and EXIT, which lets the user exit to the Command window or to DOS.

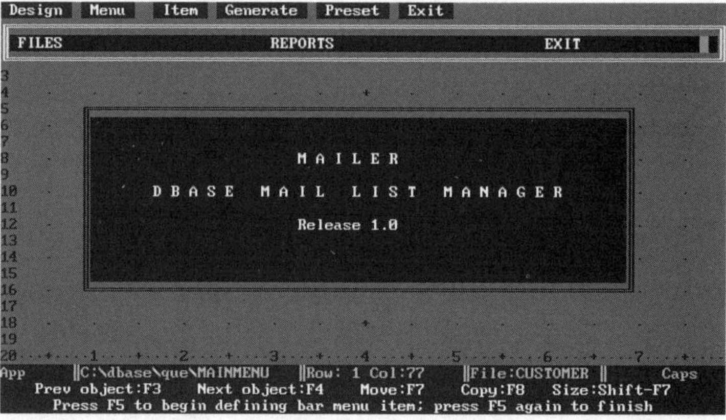

Fig. 19.8
Ap Gen displays the menu the way your user sees it.

To save the work you have done on the menu, press F10, select Menu, and then select the Save Current Menu option.

Using Pull-Down and Pop-Up Menus

Now that you have built your top menu, you need to build the pull-down menus from which the user selects one of several choices along the bar menu. Do you remember the difference between pull-down and pop-up menus that was discussed in Chapter 18? dBASE 5's Applications Generator treats all vertical moving bar menus as pop-ups. If the pop-up is invoked by a horizontal bar menu, it's treated in the application as a pull-down menu. Consequently, the menus in this exercise are treated as pull-down menus. To create pull-down menus, however, you select Pop-up Menu. Again, you create a cosmetic screen at this point. Actions are attached later.

Tip

In DOS, your file names—including the menu names—may only be 8 characters long.

You need to create two pop-up menus and name them according to the items they are attached to on the main menu; the pop-up menus are named Receiver, Expenses, Print, and Utility. While Exit is an option on your menu, you don't need to create a pop-up menu unless you want to for aesthetic reasons. To create the Receiver menu, follow these steps:

1. Select Pop-up Menu from the Design menu. Select `<create>`.

2. When the pop-up information box appears on-screen, fill in the blanks with the information shown in figure 19.9.

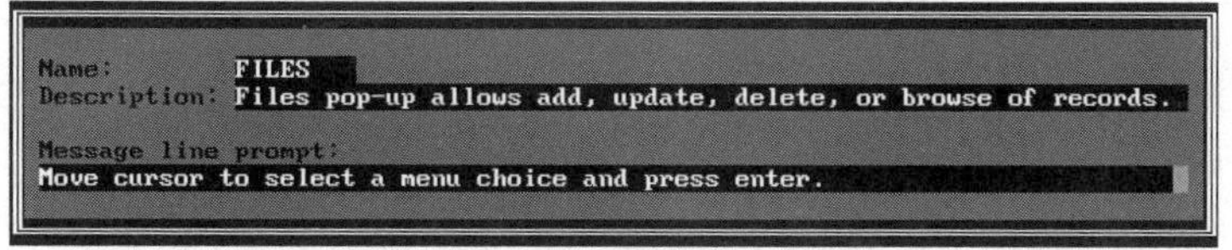

Fig. 19.9
You use the menu dialog box to name your pop-up menus.

3. Save your work. An empty pop-up menu box now appears on-screen.

4. Type the following menu options, pressing Enter after each:

   Add a Record

   Delete a Record

   Modify a Record

   Browse all Records

5. Press Shift-F7 to size the menu box. Press the up-arrow key four times, and then press Enter.

6. Press F7 to move the menu. Choose Entire Frame from the menu that appears.

7. Use the cursor keys to move the menu to row 2, column 0, and then press Enter. The completed menu is shown in figure 19.10.

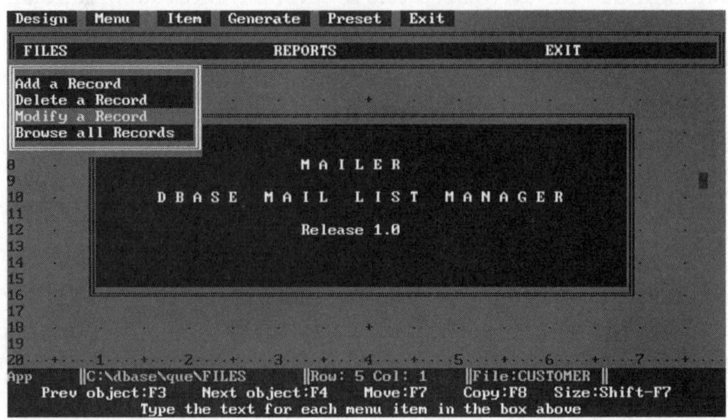

Fig. 19.10
When Ap Gen displays your completed menu, check it for accuracy and aesthetics.

8. Choose Menu. Choose Save Current Menu, and then select Put Away Current Menu.

To create the Reports menu, repeat the previous steps using the following lines in step 4. Position this menu at 2,29 in step 7:

Customer List

Mailing Labels

Tip
Save and put away objects that you aren't using. This frees memory for dBASE 5 to use on other objects.

You now attach the pop-ups to the main bar menu. To attach a pop-up menu to the main menu, make sure that the bar menu is in view. Highlight the menu option to which you attach the pop-up. Make sure that you have the Main menu on-screen. If you have no menus on-screen, open the Design menu, select Horizontal Bar Menu, and then from the list box select MAINMENU. If all your menus are displayed, you can put away the pop-up menus. To do so, make one of the pop-up menus the current object. Then select Menu, and select the Put Away Current Menu option.

To attach the pop-ups, perform the following steps:

1. With the main menu on-screen, make the bar menu the current object by selecting it. Move the cursor until FILES is highlighted.

2. Invoke the dBASE Ap Gen top menu bar, and choose Menu.

3. Select Attach Pull-Down Menus. (Remember, pop-up menus can be used as pull-down menus.) You are asked whether you want the menu that you attach to carry the top menu's attributes and drop automatically. Answering Yes causes the pull-down to appear when you select the Main menu option. Answering No means that the user must select with Enter to pull down the menu. Select Yes.

4. Select Item from the menu. This menu, seen in figure 19.11, lets you assign specific actions to the selected item on the menu, in this case FILES. Menu items shown with an arrow beside them have submenus with additional choices. The last choice on the menu, Assign message line prompt, allows you to override the default one line help message that appears when the menu is selected. You can enter a line that is specific to this menu item, providing more context-sensitive help.

   The Write help text choice allows you to provide even more help for your users. This menu choice opens the text editor to allow you to write one or more screens of information. The help text you enter is displayed when the user places the cursor on the item and presses F1.

   Three of the choices allow you to directly affect the data table when the user selects the item, by changing the default data table, changing the record position, or changing the active index. You can set up a separate window for operations selected after this item using the Define logical window.

   The Bypass item on condition allows you to enter a condition when the item isn't selectable to the user. This can be useful for an application that has a multi-level access control set up, where certain choices are only available for administrators, or for adding labels to your menu.

   The Embed code option allows you to insert code before or after the item selection which dBASE 5 includes in the generated application. You can use this to initialize memory variables or perform other tasks that are required to make your application perform. The most used choice is Change action, which allows you to assign a specific action to the menu item.

5. Select Change Action and the menu shown in figure 19.12 are displayed. The choices on this menu provide access to most of the dBASE 5 commands that operate on the data table or the screen. The text of the menu choice includes the associated dBASE 5 command in uppercase

Tip

Make all of your Change actions "do" dBASE programs. This ensures that the user can change his or her own code as often as desired, and the code won't disappear during a regeneration by Ap Gen.

on the right side of the menu. Using this menu, you can allow your user to perform any operation dBASE is capable of supporting. More complex options are available under the Run program selection, which allows you to add in blocks of code, call dBASE procedures, run DOS programs, or batch files.

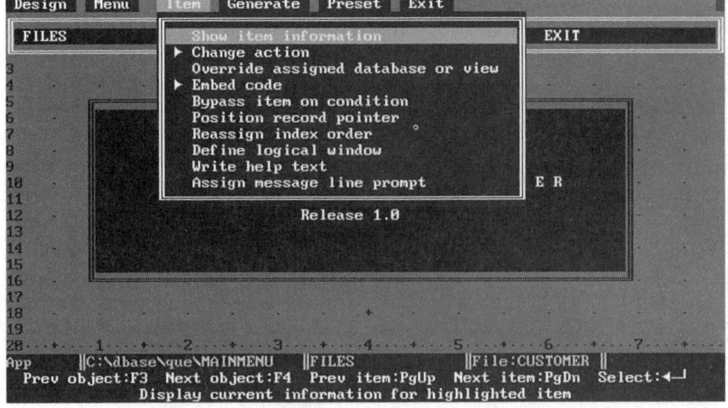

Fig. 19.11 The Item menu allows you to assign special functions to your menu choices.

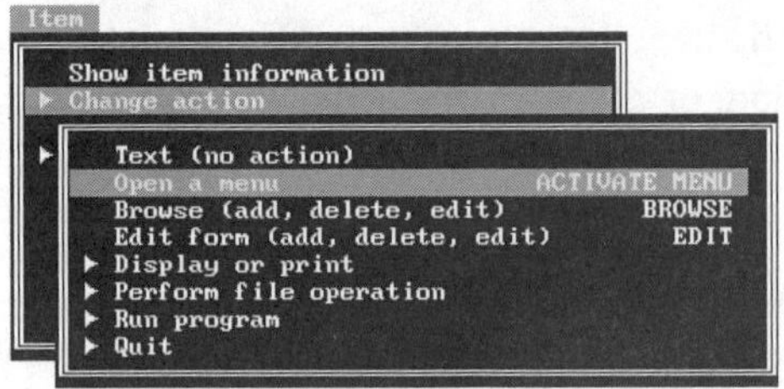

Fig. 19.12 The Change Action menu allows you to assign dBASE commands to your menu items.

6. Select Open A Menu. A form appears on-screen so that you can specify which menu to activate. Fill in the form with the following, and press Ctrl-End when finished:

   Menu type: **POP-UP**

   Menu name: **FILES**

   Select the menu type, and then exit from the Applications Generator menu.

Note

The pick list of available menu files will not include any application objects on the surface which have not been saved.

7. Move to Reports, the next choice on the menu. Repeat steps 2 through 5 for each pad, substituting the appropriate pop-up menu for Files when specifying the pop-up menu name.
8. When you are finished, move to the Exit choice on the main menu.
9. Open the Item menu and select Change Action. From the Change Action submenu, select Quit. You can have your application quit to DOS or return to the Command window.
10. Select Return To Calling Program, read the message that appears, and then select OK.
11. While the Ap Gen's menu is still active, select Menu; then select Save Current Menu to save the changes made to the MAINMENU bar menu.
12. From Menu, select Put Away Current Menu.
13. From the Application menu, select Save Current Application Definition to save the latest changes to the application.

Tip
You can move to the next menu item without having to exit the Item menu by pressing the PgDn key. PgUp moves to previous item. The status bar displays the filename of the current item and open database.

At this point in your application, the only things that work are the pull-down menus. The choices on those menus, however, are not activated; that's the next step. You must attach actions to each of the pull-down menu's options. Work on the Files menu first, and then the other menus.

To attach actions to the pull-down menu options for the Files menu, follow these steps:

1. Open the Design menu, select Pop-up Menus, and from the list of menus, select the Files menu. The Files menu appears on your work surface.
2. Select Add a Record, the first choice on the menu.
3. Open the Items menu and select Change Action.
4. Select Edit Form (Add, Delete, Edit). Because your first Files menu choice is Add a Record, use Edit Form in the Append mode to begin adding records.
5. A form appears on-screen so that you can customize Edit Form (see fig. 19.13). Fill out the form as shown in the figure, using the format file CUST_IN.

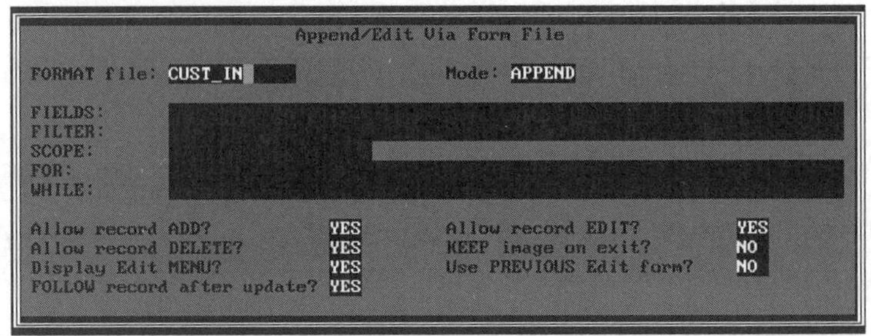

Fig. 19.13
Select your choices to allow the user to edit and append records.

6. After you fill out the form, as shown in figure 19.13, save your changes, then exit the Item menu.

7. Select Delete A Record, the second choice on the menu.

8. Open the Items menu and select Change Action.

9. Select Edit Form (Add, Delete, Edit). Because your Files menu choice is Delete A Record, use Edit Form in the Edit mode to begin deleting records.

10. A form appears on-screen so that you can customize Edit Form (see fig. 19.14). Fill out the form as shown in the figure, using the format file CUST_IN, and only allowing for deletion from the database.

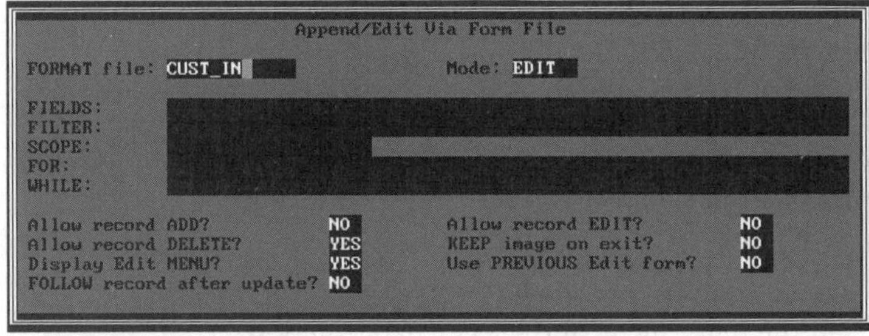

Fig. 19.14
Select your options to allow your user to delete records.

11. After you fill out the form, as shown in figure 19.14, save your changes, then exit the Items menu.

12. Select Modify A Record, the third choice on the menu.

13. Open the Items menu and select Change Action.

14. Select Edit Form (Add, Delete, Edit). Because your Files menu choice is Modify A Record, use Edit Form in the Edit mode to begin editing records.

15. A form appears on-screen so that you can customize Edit Form (see fig. 19.15). Fill out the form as shown in the figure, using the format file CUST_IN, and only allowing for editing to the database.

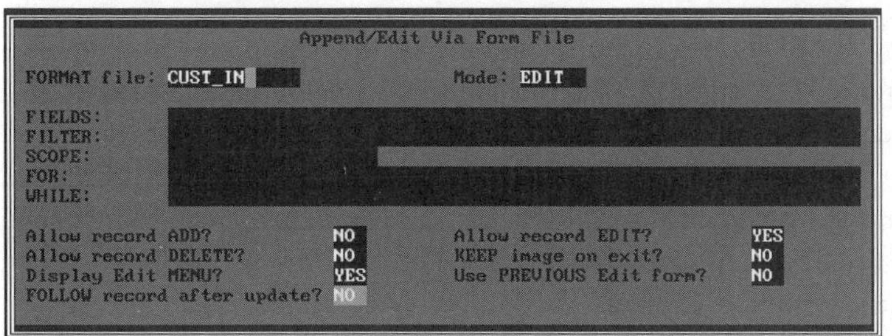
Append/Edit Via Form File

FORMAT file: CUST_IN Mode: EDIT

FIELDS:
FILTER:
SCOPE:
FOR:
WHILE:

Allow record ADD? NO Allow record EDIT? YES
Allow record DELETE? NO KEEP image on exit? NO
Display Edit MENU? YES Use PREVIOUS Edit form? NO
FOLLOW record after update? NO

Fig. 19.15
Select the choices that only allow the user to edit records.

16. After you fill out the form, as shown in figure 19.15, save your changes, and then exit.

17. Select Browse All Records, the fourth choice on the menu.

18. Open the Items menu and select Change Action.

19. Select Browse (Add, Delete, Edit). Because your Files menu choice is Browse All Records, you use Browse to view your records in either a column format or form format.

20. A form appears on-screen so that you can customize the Browse form (see fig. 19.16). Fill out the form as shown in the figure, using the format file CUST_IN, and not allowing addition, deletion, or editing to the database.

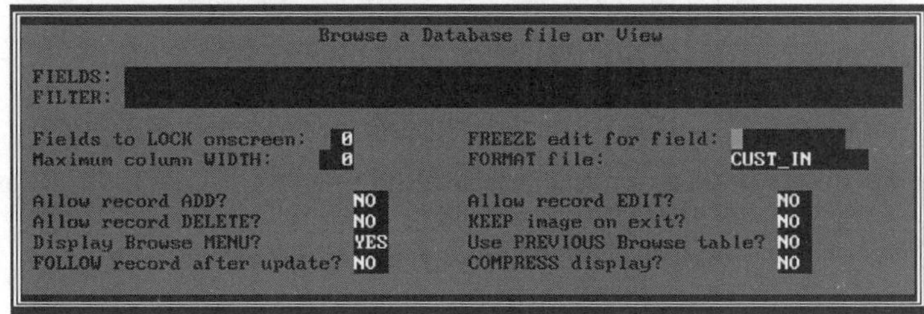
Browse a Database file or View

FIELDS:
FILTER:

Fields to LOCK onscreen: 0 FREEZE edit for field:
Maximum column WIDTH: 0 FORMAT file: CUST_IN

Allow record ADD? NO Allow record EDIT? NO
Allow record DELETE? NO KEEP image on exit? NO
Display Browse MENU? YES Use PREVIOUS Browse table? NO
FOLLOW record after update? NO COMPRESS display? NO

Fig. 19.16
Select choices that prevent the user from adding, deleting, or editing records in your database.

21. After you fill out the form, as shown in figure 19.16, save your changes.

22. Choose Menu and then select the option Save Current Menu. All changes to the Files menu are saved. Finally, select Put Away Current Menu.

At this point, you have created a welcome screen, top menu bar, and two pull-down menus. You attached both pull-down menus (Files and Reports) to your menu bar, which you named MAINMENU. You also selected actions for the choices in your Files pull-down menus.

Now you add choices to the second menu, the Reports menu. You see a slight difference here, although the basic procedure is the same. Because the Ap Gen doesn't create report forms, you did that yourself earlier. Now, you use those two forms; one form is the customer listing report (MAILCUST) and the other is the mail label form (MAILLBLS). Although you can run these forms from the Command window with the Report Form or Label Form commands, you use them here instead.

Before you can add actions to the options on the Reports menu, you must display the Reports menu. To display the menu, press F10, select the Design menu, and select Pop-up Menu. From the list of menus, select Reports and then press Enter.

To attach actions to the options of the Reports menu, you go through the same basic procedure with Reports as you did with Files. Now, however, you use the Display Or Print option on the Change Action choice of the Item menu (you used Browse for the Files submenu you just created). When you select Display Or Print, you see a menu like the one shown in figure 19.17.

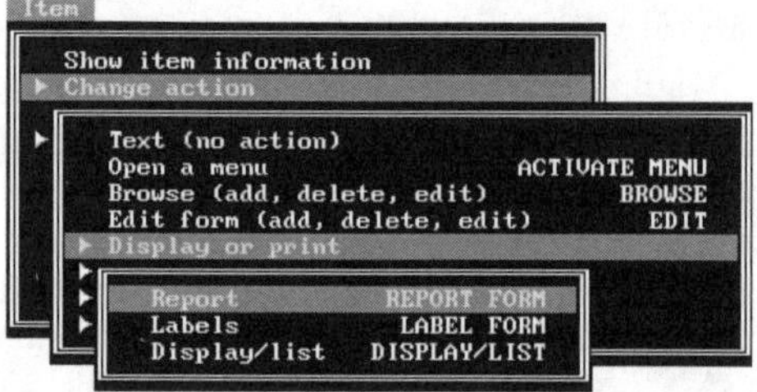

Fig. 19.17 The Display Or Print menu allows you to display reports, labels, or data.

To attach the report and mailing labels to the options, follow these steps:

1. Select Customer List, the first choice on the menu.
2. Open the Items menu and select Change Action.
3. Select Display Or Print. From the Display Or Print menu, select Report.
4. A form appears on-screen so that you can specify the report to print and the options for the report (see fig. 19.18). Fill out the form as shown in the figure. The default of a Plain heading format stops the dBASE date and page number from printing on each page.

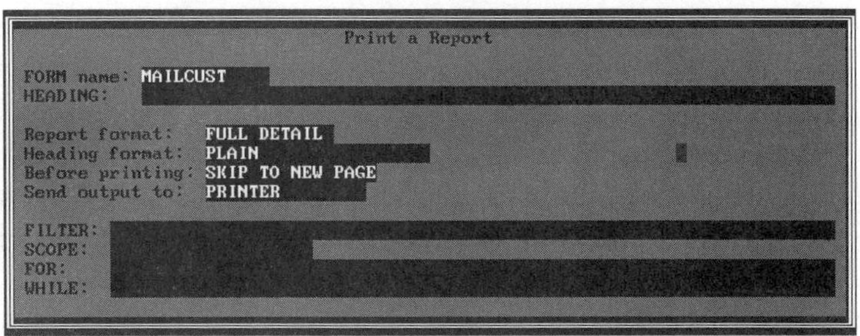
Print a Report

FORM name: MAILCUST
HEADING:

Report format: FULL DETAIL
Heading format: PLAIN
Before printing: SKIP TO NEW PAGE
Send output to: PRINTER

FILTER:
SCOPE:
FOR:
WHILE:

Fig. 19.18
Use this form to determine where your output appears.

5. After you fill out the form, as shown in figure 19.18, save your changes and then exit.

6. Select Print Labels, the second choice on the menu.

7. Open the Items menu and select Change Action.

8. Select Display Or Print. From the Display Or Print menu, select Labels.

9. A form appears on-screen so that you can specify the labels to print and the options for the labels (see fig. 19.19). Fill out the form as shown in the figure.

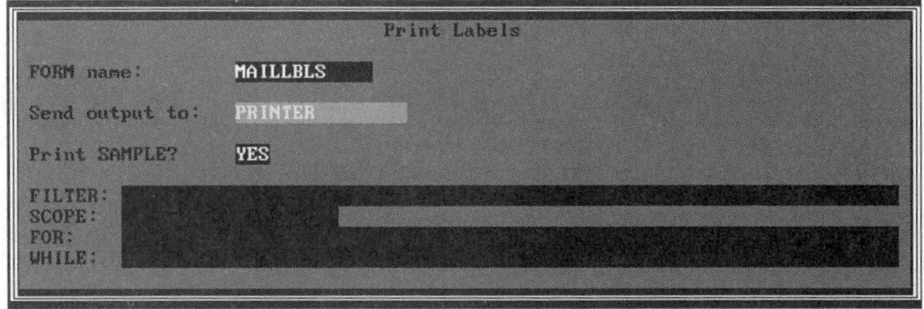
Print Labels

FORM name: MAILLBLS

Send output to: PRINTER

Print SAMPLE? YES

FILTER:
SCOPE:
FOR:
WHILE:

Fig. 19.19
Use this form to determine which label file to use.

10. After you fill out the form, as shown in figure 19.19, save your changes.

11. Choose Menu and then select the option Save Current Menu. All changes to the Files menu are saved. Finally, select Put Away Current Menu.

You have gone through all the steps required to design a simple application. Before you can use the application, however, you must generate the actual program code. The next section describes generating code for your application.

Generating Code for Your Application

Many of the choices on the Applications Generator menus have dBASE 5 commands written next to them in uppercase letters. The Applications Generator uses these commands to build the code for the choices you make. After you are familiar with the dBASE language, you can anticipate the ways in which the Ap Gen uses these commands. That knowledge may help you get the most out of the Ap Gen. As you develop your application, keep track of enhancements suggested by the structure and flow of your application and the commands used by the Ap Gen. As you continue to polish your program, you can insert small refinements into the code. Later in this chapter, you learn how to perform simple enhancements to Applications Generator code.

After you build your application, you get to make basic changes. Some of these changes include the dBASE environment, sign-on defaults, and display options. You set up these changes with the Preset menu any time during the development of your application.

The Preset menu enables you to make changes in four areas: Sign-On Defaults, Display Options, Environment Settings, and Application Drive/Path. These options allow you to change the sign-on defaults (information in the welcome box), the colors on the screen, the options in the environment (Set commands), and the drive and path used for the application.

After all changes are made and you are ready to generate code, save all changes made to the application. To save, press F10, select the Application menu, and then select the option Save Current Application Definition. Next, generate program code by following these steps:

1. If the Sign-On screen isn't selected, press F10. Open the Generate menu.

2. Select the option Select Template. You are asked for a template name. The following names can be used:

DOCUMENT.GEN	Used to generate program documentation
MENU.GEN	Used to generate an application
QUICKAPP.GEN	Used to generate a single-menu application

   When you generate the application, use MENU.GEN. When generating documentation, use the file DOCUMENT.GEN. When your application has only a single menu, use QUICKAPP.GEN. If you create an application that uses layers of menus, as does Mailer, you must use MENU.GEN as the template. You must set the template before choosing Begin Generation from the Generate menu.

3. Select the option Begin Generation.

   The hard disk begins working, and you see many messages on-screen in the status line as dBASE creates each procedure. After a few minutes, you see the message: `Generation is complete. Press any key.`

4. Press Enter.

5. Choose the Exit menu.

6. Select Save All Changes And Exit. dBASE returns to the Command window or the Control Center, depending on where you were when you invoked the Applications Generator.

When program generation is finished, you have two program files: the main menu file (MAINMENU.PRG), and the rest of the application (MAILER.PRG). Several other non-program files also are created at the same time, which dBASE 5 uses to generate your final application.

The two program files are full of procedures; each function of the application is created as a procedure. The application then calls each procedure when you make a selection from the menu.

This process differs from the way many programmers write dBASE programs. When writing a program without the aid of the Applications Generator, a programmer probably would create a separate program file for each function. Doing so makes testing and debugging easy. With only two files of procedures, however, the program is faster.

Generating Documentation about the Application

With the Applications Generator, you not only can generate program code, but you also can generate documentation about the application. This documentation isn't something that can be given to a user to learn how to use the application. Rather, it is documentation about the aspects of the application which is used by a programmer to maintain the code. The following is an excerpt from a documentation file that was created for the Mailer application:

```
Display Application Sign-On Banner: Yes

Screen Image:
0         10        20        30        40        50        60        70
>....+....|....+....|....+....|....+....|....+....|....+....|....+....|....+.
00:
01:
02:
03:
04:
```

```
05:
#============================================================#
06:           "  "
07:           "  "
08:           "                    M A I L E R  "
09:           "  "
10:           "         d B A S E M A I L   L I S T   M A N A G E R  "
11:           "  "
12:           "                    Release 1.0 "
13:           "  "
14:           "  "
15:           "  "
16:
#============================================================#
17:
18:
19:
20:
21:
22:
23:
24:
>.....+....¦....+....¦....+....¦....+....¦....+....¦....+....¦....+....¦.....+.
Main Menu to Open after Sign-On: MAINMENU.BAR
Sets for Application:
--------
   Bell         ON
   Carry        OFF
   Centry       OFF
   Confirm      OFF
   Delimiters   OFF
   Display Size 25 lines
   Drive
   Escape       ON
   Path
   Safety       ON
Starting Colors for Application:
-------
   Color Settings:
      Text             : W+/B
      Heading          : W/B
      Highlight        : GR+/BG
Page: 2  Date: 6-1-94  5:38p
   Box             : GR+/BG
   Messages        : W+/N
   Information     : B/W
   Fields          : N/BG
Database/View: CUSTOMER
Index File(s): CUSTOMER
Index Order: COMPANY
============================================================
Menu/Picklist definitions follow:
-----------
Page: 3  Date: 6-1-94
Layout Report for Horizontal Bar Menu: MAINMENU
-----------
```

The excerpt generates specifics about the application: menus, what appears on-screen, databases and index, and the purpose of each menu option. This documentation is helpful for creating user documentation.

To create program documentation, open the Generate menu and choose Select Template. Type **DOCUMENT.GEN**. Save your input, then select Begin Generating and press Enter. Ap Gen creates an ASCII text file MAILER.DOC that contains the application documentation.

Running the Mailer Application

After you create the application and generate the code, you can run the application easily. You can start the application in one of three ways: from the DOS prompt as you start dBASE, from the Control Center, or from the Command window.

To start the application from DOS, change to the directory that contains the application, type **DBASE MAILER**, and press Enter. dBASE loads into memory, and in turn, loads and executes Mailer.

To run the application from the dBASE 5 Control Center, move the pointer to the Applications panel in the right column of the Control Center screen. Highlight MAILER, and press Enter. You are asked whether you want to Run Application or Modify Application. Select Run Application.

To start the application from the dBASE 5 Command window, type **DO MAILER** and press Enter.

When you select Exit, you return to one of two screens. You return to the Command window if you started from DOS or from the Command window. If you started from the Control Center, however, you return to the Control Center.

Troubleshooting

I get lost in all the different menus that pop up on the screen as I click different objects. How can I tell which menu to use for which object?

An easy way to be sure of which object you are working with is to check the status bar for the file name and item name. Additionally, the menus you see are associated with only the object you have selected, therefore, merely selecting another object brings up a different menu.

Learning Additional Capabilities of the Applications Generator

Now that you've seen how the Ap Gen speeds up your coding tasks and how it speeds up the program execution, you need to see what else it can do. You've created menus and attached the tasks to be performed by each. There are five additional capabilities available in the Applications Generator:

- Batch process
- File list
- Structure list
- Values list (all values accessed through the Design menu)
- Quick Applications Generator

The *batch process* enables you to directly program several functions, which your application performs on its own without user intervention. Even though the user can initiate the batch process by making a menu selection, the various components or activities contained in the batch execute under program control.

An example of a batch process is a Maintenance menu that gives you the options of Copy the Data Table, Pack the Data Table, and Reindex the Data Table. Another option on the menu can be Perform All. Each of the menu options performs a dBASE command. Perform All, however, calls a batch process that copies, packs, and reindexes the data table all at once.

Creating a batch process is similar to creating a pop-up menu. You enter the process names as you do menu items, you attach actions to the process names, and you attach the batch process to a menu option. Activating the batch process is no different from activating any menu option.

Tip
The files pick list, used to allow users to select a file, is created from the file names in a given directory on your disk.

The *files list* allows you to tell users what they can do, and then provides the users with a list of files from which they select. A good example of this process is a reports menu that enables the user to select to print a report, and then offers a list of available reports.

The *structure list* takes the files list a step further by allowing users to select for use specific fields within a data table. For example, perhaps you offer users a menu choice for browsing a data table. You can also let them select which fields they want in the display. With practice, you can even add program code that enables them to index one of the selected fields to show the browse display, in order, based on a particular key field.

Taking this progression of lists another step further, you can use the *values list* to narrow the scope of the file search. This step is achieved by assigning values, or a range of values, for the data table in use. The purpose behind these lists is to give the user a way to narrow the scope of a data table under scrutiny.

Tip
To create a simple one-menu application that enables users to work with a single database, select Generate Quick Application from the Application menu.

Using Advanced Testing with the dBASE Debugger

Earlier in this book, you learned several simple ways to debug your application. For longer, more complex applications, debugging your code is a more formidable task. Your sample mail list application created with the Applications Generator, for example, is well over 1,000 lines of code. If you make changes to the program code created by the Applications Generator, your application can misbehave when you first run it. To prevent this problem, you need to use the debugging tools included in the dBASE 5 debugger.

The *debugger* is a full-screen program that you access in one of three ways. The first time you run your program code, dBASE 5 compiles the source code into dBASE 5 object code. If your program hits a serious snag, such as a syntax error or open construct (an IF without an ENDIF, for example) during the compile process, you normally receive an error box.

◄ See "Using the Debugger," p. 459

► See "DEBUG," p. 681

Note

You aren't wrong if you use the Applications Generator to generate application code. Earlier in this chapter, you were encouraged to use the Ap Gen to create code, and that encouragement bears repeating. Most professional programmers use code generators of one type or another to get the bulk of their code written quickly and with minimal errors. Using a code generator, however, doesn't guarantee error-free code. Rather, the types of errors you end up with can involve technically valid code (no syntax errors), but may not be the code you intend to use; therefore, your application can produce unwanted results.

Running the program code a step at a time is where early application planning pays off. If you carefully plan your application, you know exactly what is supposed to happen as it executes. Admittedly, you can have a few surprises if you don't write all the code involved (code that is created by the Applications Generator), but you still have a good idea of the general program flow. When the debugger starts running your application, it continues

◄ See "Using the Program Editor To Enter Code," p. 403

► See "TYPE," p. 747

until it makes an error. You then stop program execution, insert breakpoints by using the breakpoint window in the debugger, and execute again. At this point, the debugging resembles the elementary debugging you did earlier in this book; however, it gets more complex. You can execute one of two options to trace the wanderings of your program's procedures: single-step through the program and observe the results of executing each line of code, or trace procedure calls.

Tip
The NUMBER command option numbers the program lines in the printout of your program code. This makes it easier to refer to and modify.

When you trace procedure calls, you find many of your tougher problems—problems that make your program suddenly perform a task it shouldn't perform. Another problem is finding data you didn't expect in a location where it doesn't belong. Both problems are symptoms of an incorrect procedure call or faulty program loop. By stepping through the application one instruction at a time and tracing execution, you get closer to locating and solving the problem. By using the Trace command, P, you get a list of what calls what. Before you attempt your first debugging session on a large application, make sure that you have a printout of all the codes the Applications Generator creates. You can print program code by using the Print menu from the program editor screen, or by using the TYPE command from the Command window. To print the MAILER.PRG and MAINMENU.PRG files, for example, use the following commands:

```
TYPE MAILER.PRG TO PRINTER NUMBER

TYPE MAINMENU.PRG TO PRINTER NUMBER
```

Tip
When you add your own modifications to the application, don't forget the program documentation.

dBASE has added many useful comments to the code listing. This feature is called *program documentation* and is crucial if future users must determine what you and the Applications Generator did when you wrote the code. (Do not confuse this with the documentation you can generate when you create the program.)

With the program listing in front of you, plan the locations for your breakpoints, the correct procedure calls, and proper program execution. Run the program—or single-step it—and observe the results. As you get closer to the specific incorrect command or commands, watch your program listing and the edit window of the debugger. Because you can edit your code and re-execute it from inside the debugger, you can try modifications and test them to see whether they give you the results you expect. The debugger numbers each line of code, so you can back up or jump ahead to any point in your application to begin execution. Any time you forget a debugger command, press F1 for Help.

Changing the Applications Generator Code

Although the Applications Generator helps you perform the basic steps involved in creating your application, at times you can make minor changes in your program code. Because the Ap Gen generates dBASE program files (PRG files), you can edit the program the same way you would edit dBASE programs you wrote yourself—by using the dBASE program editor.

Caution

Regenerating code produced by the Ap Gen erases any modifications you may have made. Be sure you do not have the Ap Gen regenerate code which you edited, unless you want to start over from the pre-edited version of the code.

For the MAILER application, dBASE creates two program files: MAILER.PRG and MAINMENU.PRG. To edit either of these files, use the MODIFY COMMAND statement from the Command window to invoke the program editor (as described in Chapter 16) or choose File Open from the main menu. To edit the MAINMENU file, for example, type the following command:

MODIFY COMMAND MAINMENU.PRG

The program code appears on-screen.

Caution

Be careful when making changes to generated code. If you change even one element in a line of code, such as an index tag name or variable name, that element can reappear elsewhere in the program. Your alteration can then affect how other sections or modules of the program perform.

You may want to "borrow" sections of code from the generated code to include in the programs that you write yourself. Some programmers, for example, use the Applications Generator to design a menu structure, then they delete everything else from the code and add their own modules to be executed when various menu items are selected.

Troubleshooting

When editing the code generated by Ap Gen, I can't find the routines that are called. Why not?

Remember that Ap Gen creates two procedure files, MAILER.PRG and MAINMENU.PRG. The menu definitions are in the MAILER.PRG, but the actions are in the MAINMENU.PRG. Use the file editor to open both of the procedures at the same time and switch between them. You can use the Search option to find the procedure you need. If it's not in the first procedure, select the other window and press Ctrl-L to search again using the same string.

Delivering Executable Code

Tip
Because executable files are unreadable, they also are unchangeable. This feature prevents users from getting inside your complicated application to make changes or to accidentally wipe out data.

Now that your application is finished and debugged, you can distribute it. You can distribute a dBASE 5 application several different ways. The easiest way—if all your users have copies of dBASE 5, or if you are on a local area network with dBASE 5 shared among several users—is to distribute the compiled versions of your code. These versions include the reports, labels, format, and program files. The files are *object code files*, which means that dBASE 5 stripped out the comments and unnecessary spaces, parsed the commands, and produced a binary file that dBASE runs directly. Although, in this case, dBASE is an interpreter (your application files must be interpreted—they cannot run by themselves), files executed in this manner run faster than source code files and have the benefit of being unreadable by your users.

With dBASE 5 for DOS, you also can generate executables directly from your applications. First you compile all of your procedures, screens, reports, and labels. This is made easy by creating a project file that contains all the procedures in your application. Select the first procedure file and then select Window/Project manager. This allows you to create a project (PRJ) file. Add each of your procedures, screens, reports, and labels into the project window using the Add option. Set up your environment using the Options menu. You can set the Linker options to generate a compact version, a stand-alone version, or a RunTime version of your application.

Getting Ready for Linking

Before you can use linking, you need to prepare your application. You also must follow several rules when you use any type of executable application. If you don't follow the rules, your application won't run correctly, no matter how well you debug it. Start out by making sure that you have built your application to run consistently from the correct directories. When you use an application with full copies of dBASE 5, you most likely installed it. When you install the application, you can customize it to operate in preselected subdirectories. If you do, how do your users know where to put the application when they receive it in the mail? To prevent such a problem, you must always produce an installation program. That program, often just a simple DOS batch file, creates the proper subdirectories and copies programs, any resource or run-time libraries, indexes, and data files to their proper places.

With dBASE IV, a separate product, RUNTIME, was required to deliver executable applications to users who did not have a copy of dBASE IV. In dBASE 5, a true compiler and linker are provided. Three different modes of operation are provided with the linker: RUNTIME, Compact, and StandAlone. The link for RUNTIME in dBASE 5 is only used for checking to see if any of the commands or functions that are disallowed in executables have been used. It does not actually perform the link or generate an executable. The Compact version of the linker links together all the compiled versions of the procedures, screens, reports, and labels. It does not link in the run-time libraries (RTL) or resource (RES) files. To distribute a Compact version, you must also distribute the RTL and RES files required by the application. If you are distributing more than one dBASE application, this method allows you to send out smaller executables which all use the same copy of the run-time libraries and resource files. The StandAlone version links the run-time libraries and resource files into the executable. The resulting executable is larger than the compact version, but requires no additional files except the data tables and indexes.

Note

Don't create an application that runs from the root directory. Instead, always create a special subdirectory to keep these files separate from any other files on your user's hard drive.

Tip

When you are testing your application, turn off the DOS PATH by using SET PATH at the DOS prompt. This ensures that all of your files are in the right directory.

Another rule you need to follow scrupulously concerns debugging. Before you attempt to link your application for distribution, make sure that the application is completely debugged. If you don't, users who don't have access to you may not know how to handle your application's "quirks."

Getting Your Files Together

You have to make sure that all the files required by your application are together. Make sure that all program, report, label, and format files referenced in the application are together in the same directory. The best way to ensure this is to create a subdirectory just for preparing executable versions of your applications.

dBASE 5 has the additional capability of combining your files into a project. Select **W**indow, **P**roject Window to open the project window. Select Add to add files to your project. The file selection window allows you to include files from any directory into your project. With a project file active, you can use **P**rogram, **M**ake to build the entire application.

You need to distribute some other files with your application; and, when you initially write your application, you need to avoid using some dBASE commands. The following commands aren't supported in executable applications:

ASSIST	COMPILE	CREATE/MODIFY FILE
CREATE/MODIFY LABEL	DEBUG	HELP
CREATE/MODIFY QUERY	HISTORY	SET DEBUG
RESUME	SET DOHISTORY	CREATE/MODIFY SCREEN
HISTORY	SET INSTRUCT	CREATE/MODIFY
CREATE/MODIFY VIEW	MENU DRIVEN SET	CREATE/MODIFY REPORT
MODIFY COMMAND/FILE	SET SQL	SET STEP
SET TRAP	SUSPEND	SET ECHO
CREATE/MODIFY STRUCTURE	SET HISTORY	LIST/DISPLAY HISTORY

You cannot start a command line with the macro substitution character (&). When your application is complete, you place the application, the appropriate data files and indexes, and any RTL or RES files onto your distribution disk. As pointed out earlier, you should include a batch file for installing your application.

Building a Compact Executable

With the project window open and selected, open the Options menu, choose Linker and click the Compact button. Select OK to save the options. Open the Select menu and choose Build to create the application. The Build option combines the Make and Link options. The Make option executes the Compile option on each file in your project file. The executable that is created is an EXE file, but it requires access to the DBASE32.RTL run-time library to execute. This file must be on your distribution disk and in the current directory or path. You must also include all the data tables. Depending on the code, you may also require one or more resource files, DBASE.RES, DBASE1.RES, DBASE2.RES, DBASE3.RES.

Caution

Linking puts additional demands on your system. Make sure you have enough RAM and disk space to accomplish your task.

Building a StandAlone Executable

With the project window open and selected, select Options|Linker options and click on the StandAlone button. Select OK to save the options. Select Program|Build to create the application. The Build option combines the Make and Link options. The Make option executes the Compile option on each file in your project file. The executable that is created is an EXE file that doesn't require any additional library or procedure files to execute. You must still include the data tables on your distribution disk, however.

Using Your Application

Starting the application is easy. Change to the directory that contains the files you just generated—for example \DBASE\MAILER. When you check your directory, you can see that you have these files:

MAILER.DBO

CUSTOMER.DBF

CUSTOMER.MDX

To start the Mailer application, type the following command and press Enter:

MAILER

The application operates just as if you started it from dBASE 5.

Producing an Application for Distribution

If you produce an application for distribution, copy the files onto master distribution disks, create an installation program and place it on the distribution disks. As a final predistribution test, install and run your application from the distribution disks. If all goes well and the application installs and runs correctly, use that set of disks as masters for duplicating and producing distribution sets for your users. The master disks you create are called *gold disks*. From the gold set, you can make another set that you actually use in the physical duplication of the production disks for distribution. This working set is called the *silver set*. Put the gold set in a safe place. Use DISKCOPY or XCOPY/S when creating complete copies of your disks for distribution.

Never use the DOS COPY command when copying complete disks, since any subdirectories can be missed during the copy operation.

Make sure that you create adequate documentation for your application. Solid documentation gives users a source from which to learn about the application, how to install and use it, and what to do if they get lost.

One final word about distribution: you need to establish a release-numbering system so that you know what release of your application users have. The release numbers change as you add enhancements or fix the inevitable bugs that crop up. You never want to lose track of which set of disks has bugs on it and which set has the bugs fixed.

Troubleshooting

I just got a panic call from a user who can't access the files necessary to use the application delivered to him. What happened?

You may have forgotten to turn off the DOS path command, thus the application is looking for the directory you used to develop the application on your system. You'll need to change the path the executable searches for and reship the application to the user. If all the files shipped, you may be able to tell him what directories need to be added to his path.

From Here...

- Chapter 16, "Getting Started with Programming," is a refresher of the basic skills necessary for programming in dBASE. This chapter also teaches you how to use the new compiler, and how to use the power of the new Debugger tool.
- Chapter 17, "Exploring Some Sample Programs," shows you how programs are coded to perform different tasks. This chapter walks you through how to code using dBASE 5's new features to obtain user input, test the input, and communicate with the user.
- Chapter 18, "Creating Custom Applications," helps you define the pieces of your program using a procedure library, menus, and macros to ensure that your application does what you expect.

- Chapter 21, "Creating Objects with UI," teaches you how to write programs using dBASE 5's newest feature, object-oriented code, which allows you to write event-driven program code—code which is more versatile and reusable than linear code.
- Chapter 22, "Using dBASE 5 Commands," details the syntax and individual purpose for commands used in programs written in dBASE.

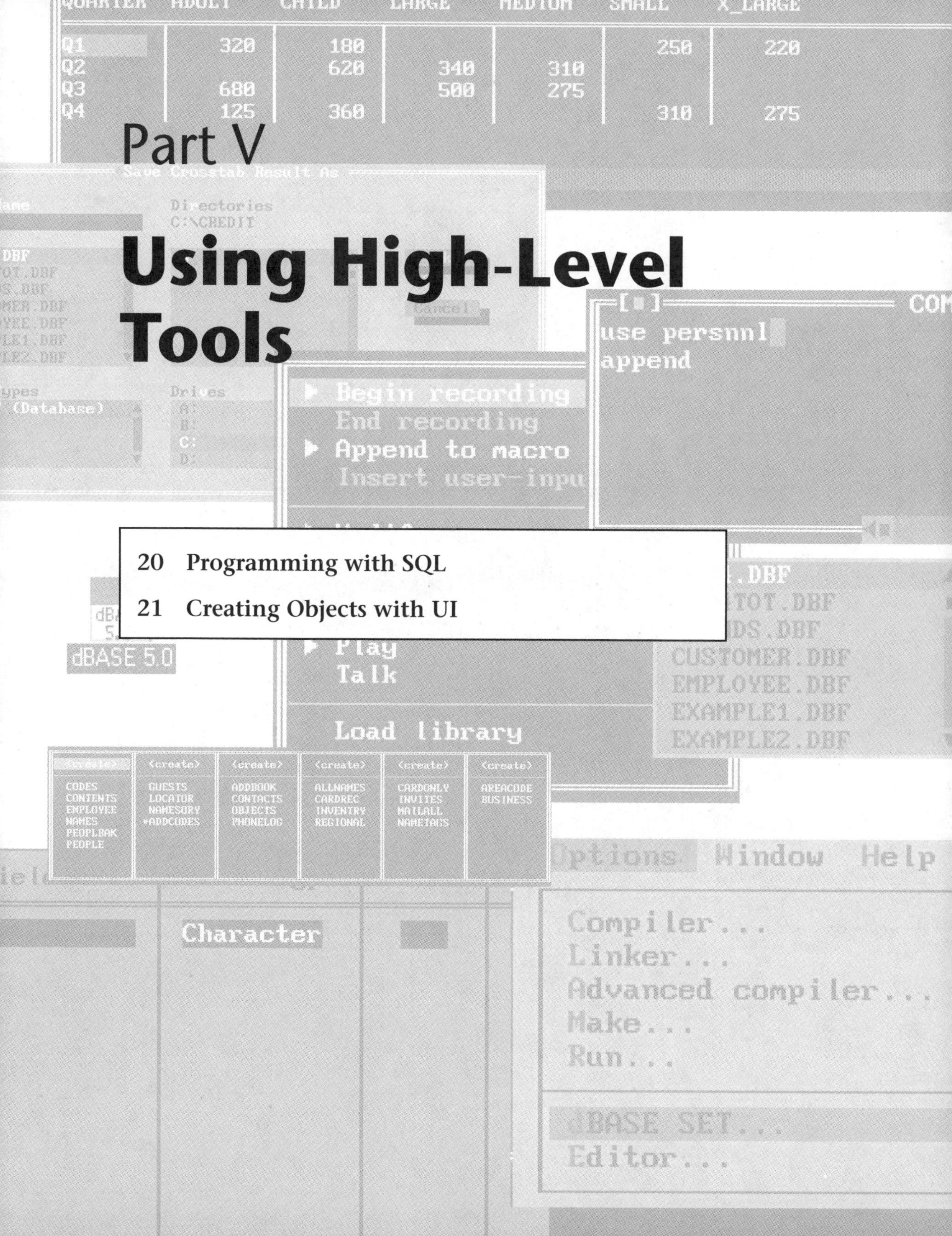

Part V

Using High-Level Tools

20 Programming with SQL

21 Creating Objects with UI

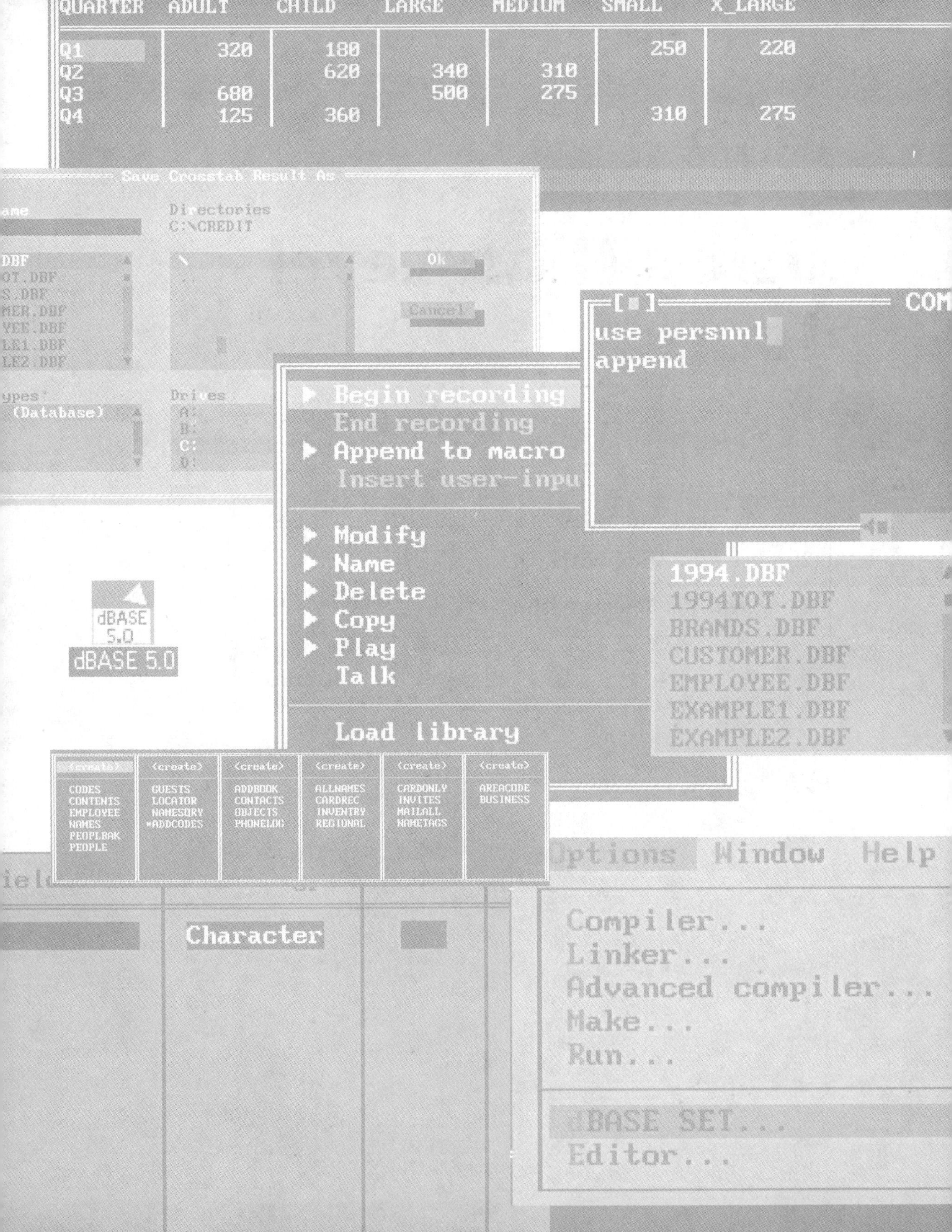

QUARTER ADULT CHILD LARGE MEDIUM SMALL X_LARGE
Q1 320 180 250 220
Q2 620 340 310
Q3 680 500 275
Q4 125 360 310 275
Save Crosstab Result As
Directories
C:\CREDIT
Ok
Cancel
Drives
(Database)
use persnnl
append
Begin recording
End recording
Append to macro
Modify
Name
Delete
Copy
Play
Talk
Load library
1994.DBF
1994TOT.DBF
BRANDS.DBF
CUSTOMER.DBF
EMPLOYEE.DBF
EXAMPLE1.DBF
EXAMPLE2.DBF
dBASE 5.0
dBASE 5.0
CODES
CONTENTS
EMPLOYEE
NAMES
PEOPLBAK
PEOPLE
GUESTS
LOCATOR
NAMESQRY
*ADDCODES
ADDBOOK
CONTACTS
OBJECTS
PHONELOG
ALLNAMES
CARDREC
INVENTRY
REGIONAL
CARDONLY
INVITES
MAILALL
NAMETAGS
AREACODE
BUSINESS
Window
Help
Character
Compiler...
Linker...
Advanced compiler...
Make...
Run...
dBASE SET...
Editor...

Chapter 20

Programming with SQL

dBASE 5 includes the powerful data-handling capabilities of dBASE Structured Query Language (SQL—pronounced "sequel"). Before you dig too deeply into dBASE SQL, you need to understand some of the basics of this excellent database management facility. This chapter begins with a discussion of SQL as a database management tool. First you learn what advantages SQL has over native dBASE databases. Then you learn about the structure of dBASE SQL databases and data tables.

You get an introduction on how to use SQL in dBASE 5, both interactively and from within your dBASE 5 applications. Next, you take a tour of the SQL command syntax, which includes fewer than 30 commands. After you understand SQL structure and commands, you are ready to delve deeper into SQL as an adjunct to your dBASE 5 application development tasks. Finally, you learn about the power of dBASE SQL as a multiuser, transaction-oriented database management tool in conjunction with the powerful dBASE procedural language. Specifically, this chapter teaches you to:

- Use SQL to simplify your programming
- Work with tables
- Insert, Delete, and Modify data
- Use SQL in Program Code
- Embed SQL Code
- Recover from errors

Understanding SQL

SQL is a *nonprocedural language*, which means that you cannot write a SQL program with looping constructs, conditionals, and other program-flow structures. SQL is designed to do just one task: manage data. The language is used to create databases, place data in them, modify the data, and retrieve data from the database. SQL also provides controls on the use of the data, methods for browsing the database, and a few data-handling utilities. While dBASE 5 includes a SQL module, dBASE did not invent the language. A former IBM employee, Dr. E.F. Codd, created this powerful query language. Currently, SQL is used in many different database programs. (To learn more about SQL, read *SQL and Relational Basics* by Fabian Pascal.)

For a data-handling language like SQL to be useful, you must be able to use it interactively or from within an application. The language must have the capability to merge data from several sources and it must work well in a multiuser environment. Most importantly, the data-handling language must be specialized (optimized) for data handling only. The language also must coexist comfortably with a procedural language (like dBASE 5) so that full applications can be built. The combination of dBASE and SQL fulfills all these requirements.

Because SQL is designed strictly as a data-handling language, it greatly simplifies the management of data. Data retrieval processes that take many lines of code in dBASE take only a single statement in SQL. Admittedly, the data management statements in SQL are far more complex than those in dBASE. Even given that complexity, however, SQL statements are simpler and more straightforward than the many lines of code and iterative processes required to extract groups of records from a dBASE database. SQL uses a combination of statements, verbs, predicates, and clauses to build a single SQL command. If that sounds like the tools for building a sentence in English, you have picked up on one of SQL's strengths. When you read a SQL command, it sounds like a plain English sentence. This English-like structure adds to SQL's ease of use.

When you compare the ways SQL and dBASE manage data, you see some differences and some similarities. The two are similar—though not identical—in the way they store data. SQL and dBASE are quite different, however, in the commands they use to retrieve data. Because of this, certain commands in the dBASE language cannot coexist with SQL. In a program that includes SQL, or from the SQL prompt, you cannot use these "disallowed" dBASE commands. For a complete list of allowed commands, refer to the dBASE 5 manual.

Using SQL Two Ways

You can use dBASE SQL interactively in SQL mode from the Command window, or you can create special program files with the file extension PRS instead of the regular dBASE PRG extension. PRS files can contain both SQL and dBASE 5 commands as long as you don't use any disallowed commands. You must designate a SQLHOME directory path, however, in your CONFIG.DB file. The easiest way to set up a SQL path in CONFIG.DB is to use DBSETUP. You must use SET SQL ON in the Command window to get into SQL mode, and you cannot use SQL commands while in dBASE mode—the regular dBASE Command window (see fig. 20.1). You enter SQL commands the same way you do dBASE commands. SET SQL OFF returns you to dBASE mode.

Tip
"SQL" appears at the lower-left corner of the status bar when in SQL mode; "Command" appears when in dBASE mode.

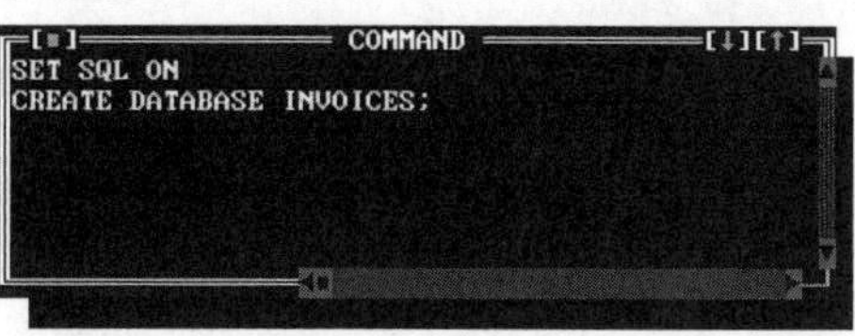

Fig. 20.1
dBASE SQL uses the same window as the Command window, just in a different mode.

Caution

Be careful when entering SQL commands interactively. In dBASE, you can break the command string with a semicolon (;) to continue to the next line; doing the same thing in SQL terminates the command. Pressing Enter executes the command. When writing code non-interactively, you can continue the SQL command to the next line by pressing the Enter key. The semicolon is used to indicate the end of the command string.

SQL commands often are several lines long. Good programming practice actually dictates that you break certain commands, such as SELECT, for each new clause to improve readability as you scan your code. The following is an example of such a command:

```
SELECT Companid, Invoicedat
   FROM Invoices
   WHERE Invoicedat = CTOD("03/05/94");
```

Notice that the FROM and WHERE clauses are indented to improve readability further and that the whole command ends with a semicolon.

Tip
Because of the length of many SQL command strings, it is easiest to write SQL code from within program files, then execute them.

Working with Tables

In dBASE 5, SQL follows most of the same conventions that IBM's DB2 follows. To maintain compatibility with these and other industry-standard SQL databases, dBASE SQL must follow certain guidelines in two important areas. The first area is the syntax of the language, which you learn more about later in this chapter. The second area is the structure of databases and tables.

Note

In the syntax examples throughout the remainder of this chapter, any information shown in brackets ([ ]) is an optional entry, depending on the situation described. For example, INSERT INTO *<table name>*[(*<column list>*)] requires an entry for the *<table name>* but not for the *<column list>*,

dBASE terminology and SQL terminology are quite different. When you speak of a data table in dBASE, you mean a single collection of data, stored in tabular form. When you speak of a database in SQL, you refer to a collection of data tables and a data dictionary that describes the tables, their contents, and the database structure. In dBASE 5, dBASE SQL uses all these concepts and all this terminology, except that data dictionaries in dBASE SQL are called *catalogs*.

Columns and Rows

Another terminology difference is in the way you refer to fields and records. In a dBASE database, the data is laid out in tables, just as in the SQL database. A few differences exist in the structure of the two tables, but you can consider them much the same. The records of the dBASE database are the rows of the table, and the fields are the columns. SQL keeps the terminology simple. Rows are rows and columns are columns. The relationships, however, are the same: SQL rows are the same as dBASE records, and SQL columns are the same as dBASE fields.

You may have heard implications that much more is involved in gaining access to SQL data than to dBASE data. That's both true and not true. It is true that you must open the database before you can use a table. But after you open the database, access to any table within the database is automatic with the execution of any of the data manipulation statements. When you build an application with dBASE SQL, you generally start with CREATE DATABASE and then use CREATE TABLE to create all the tables you need in that application.

The database and its associated tables reside in a single subdirectory whose name is the same as the name of the database. After the database is open, any table you create is included automatically in the database. At the same time, the database's catalog is updated. Don't confuse the SQL catalog with the dBASE catalog; they are very different.

Table 20.1 lists the five commands you can use to manipulate your database. To work with the tables within a database, use the commands listed in Table 20.2.

Table 20.1 SQL Database Manipulation Commands

Command	Description
CREATE DATABASE	Creates a database directory and associated files
SHOW DATABASE	Lists databases
START DATABASE	Opens a database
STOP DATABASE	Closes a database
DROP DATABASE	Deletes a database and all its associated files and tables

Table 20.2 dBASE SQL Table Manipulation Commands

Command	Description
CREATE TABLE	Creates a new table
ALTER TABLE	Adds a column to an existing table
CREATE VIEW	Creates a result table
CREATE SYNONYM	Defines an alias for a table or view
CREATE INDEX	Creates an index for a table or view
DROP TABLE	Deletes a table
DROP VIEW	Deletes a view
DROP SYNONYM	Deletes a synonym, but leaves the table
DROP INDEX	Deletes an index

When you use SQL for the first time, you must begin by creating a database with the CREATE DATABASE command. This command uses the following syntax:

```
CREATE DATABASE [<path>]<database name>;
```

When you create a database, dBASE 5 builds under the dBASE directory a subdirectory with the database name as its name. In that directory are several files. Table 20.3 shows an example of the table files making up a SQL database.

Caution

Specifying the path when you create a database is not necessary; dBASE creates the database as a subdirectory with the database name. However, if you don't specify the full path and a user starts the application under a different subdirectory, dBASE will make an *empty* copy of the database in that subdirectory.

Table 20.3 System Files Added by SQL

Table	Description
SYSAUTH.DBF	The table of authorized table users
SYSCOLAU.DBF	The table of authorized column users and their UPDATE privileges
SYSCOLS.DBF	The table of column names for all tables in this database
SYSIDXS.DBF	The table of all indexes in this database
SYSKEYS.DBF	The table of index keys for this database
SYSSYNS.DBF	The table of synonyms used in this database
SYSTABLS.DBF	The table of tables in this database
SYSTIME.MEM	A memory variable file associated with SYSTIMES.DBF
SYSTIMES.DBF	The table of creation dates/times for all the tables in this database for use in a multiuser environment
SYSVDEPS.DBF	The table of tables for which a view is defined
SYSVIEWS.DBF	The table of views

The catalog does not contain any actual user-created tables; it contains only those tables created and maintained by dBASE 5. When you look at the directory containing the catalog for a given database, you also see all the associated tables in that directory.

Data Types

Creating a SQL table (CREATE TABLE) is a bit more complex than creating a database. The CREATE TABLE command uses the following syntax:

```
CREATE TABLE <table name>
   (<column name> <data type>
   [,<column name> <data type>...]);
```

You must list each of the columns you want in the new data table, and you must give each column a name and a size. If you intend to import data from one or more columns of another data table into your new table, you must give one of the columns in the new table the same name, data type, and size as the source column in the source table. The data types you can use are shown in Table 20.4.

Table 20.4 CREATE TABLE Data Types

Type	Description
SMALLINT	Integer with 6 or fewer digits
INTEGER	Integer with up to 11 digits
FLOAT (x,y)	A signed floating point number with *x* total digits and *y* decimal places
DECIMAL (x,y)	A signed fixed decimal number with *x* total digits and *y* decimal places
NUMERIC (x,y)	A signed fixed decimal number with *x* total digits and *y* decimal places, whose precision is set using SET PRECISION
CHAR (n)	A character string containing up to *n* characters
LOGICAL	A logical true (.T.) or false (.F.)
DATE	A date in the format specified by SET DATE and SET CENTURY

The preceding data types have certain size restrictions. The CHAR type can have a maximum size of 254 characters. When specifying digits and decimal places for the FLOAT and NUMERIC, keep in mind that x may range from

1 to 20, and y from 0 to 18. DECIMAL type uses an x that ranges 1 to 19, and y from 0 to 18.

Tip
When deciding values for x and y, remember that x represents the total number of digits in the field, and y is the number of decimal places.

When you use dBASE 5 in dBASE mode, you create relationships between databases with the SET RELATION TO command and a few other commands that allow you to build up a view of the databases involved. This is a crude, but effective, relational operation. With dBASE, this process takes several lines of code. With SQL, this process takes only one command. With SQL, the view capability is truly relational, and such issues as data integrity are handled automatically. The data tables in Table 20.5 are referenced throughout the remainder of this chapter.

Table 20.5 Data Tables

Table Name	Column Name
INVOICES	INVOICENUM COMPANYID INVOICEDAT INVOICEAMT AMOUNTPD DATEPD
ITEMSOLD	INVOICENUM ITEMNUMBER QUANTITY SALEPRICE DISCOUNT
COMPANY	COMPANYID COMPANY CONTACTNAM STREET CITY STATE ZIP BALANCE
STOCK	ITEMNUMBER DESCRIPTION ON_HAND ON_ORDER COST SALEPRICE

The following example of a VIEW connects two tables (INVOICES.DBF and ITEMSOLD.DBF) by using the linking column Invoicenum. Both the Invoices table and the Itemsold table have the same column, Invoicenum, and contain the same information in that field.

```
CREATE VIEW Invoice
(Invoicenum, Companyid, Invoiceamt, Amountpd, Itemnumber, Quantity)
AS SELECT Invoices.Invoicenum, Companyid, Invoiceamt, Amountpd,
➥Itemnumber, Quantity
FROM Invoices, Itemsold
WHERE Invoices.Invoicenum = Itemsold.Invoicenum;
```

You must create the relationship between the two data tables by setting the linking columns as equal to one another (Invoices.Invoicenum = Itemsold.Invoicenum). The view has six fields: Invoicenum, Companyid, Invoiceamt, Amountpd, Itemnumber, and Quantity. When you use a common field name, you must indicate both table name and column name, separated by a period (.). You also need to tell dBASE SQL which tables you are using by listing them in the FROM clause, separated by a comma (,).

Remember that views are not real tables. You can use CREATE VIEW to create a view of a single table. The purpose is to build a temporary table that is a subset of a real table. They don't exist except as a set of instructions in the SYSVIEWS.DBF table in the database's catalog. When you use a view, dBASE SQL temporarily creates the basis of the view as a virtual table in your computer's memory. If you query the view by using the SELECT statement, dBASE SQL uses those instructions to retrieve the information you requested, and then displays or stores it to whatever file or real table you choose. After you close the database by issuing the STOP command, the view and its description are gone. When you restart the database, however, you can still access the previously created view by issuing the SELECT command.

Tip
When field names are unique between tables being referenced, you do not need to specify which table to use.

Building SQL Statements

SQL commands use a combination of commands and clauses called *statements* and *predicates*, respectively. Experienced SQL users sometimes refer to commands as *verbs*. The predicate is a special condition that modifies another clause, usually a WHERE clause. Typical predicates are BETWEEN, IN, and FOR. In simple terms, a SQL statement has the following structure:

```
VERB <object>
CLAUSE1 PREDICATE
CLAUSE2
CLAUSEn...;
```

This structure appears in the CREATE VIEW example in the preceding section. In this statement, the verb is CREATE VIEW, and its object is Invoice. The first clause is the AS SELECT clause, whose objects are Invoices.Invoicenum, Companyid, Invoiceamt, Amountpd, Itemnumber, Quantity. Next is the FROM clause, followed by the WHERE clause, each with its own objects. All SQL statements are built in this manner, either with or without one or more clauses attached.

Dealing with Data

After the tables are built, four SQL commands deal specifically with the manipulation of data in tables: SELECT, INSERT, UPDATE, and DELETE. These commands put data into, get data out of, delete data from, or change data in a data table. The first and potentially most complex of these commands is SELECT.

Retrieving Data with the Select Command

SQL as a query language owes most of its power to the SELECT command. SELECT, with its clauses and predicates, is the way that you can go to one or more tables of virtually any size or complexity and extract only the particular rows or parts of rows you want. SELECT appears quite simple at first, but it can become complex as you put more demands on it. The two biggest advantages of SQL as a query language—power and the simplicity of the English language-like syntax—are embodied in SELECT. The syntax of the SELECT command follows:

```
SELECT <clause>
[INTO <clause>]
FROM <clause>
[WHERE <clause>]
[GROUP BY <clause>]
[HAVING [NOT] <clause> [AND/OR [NOT] <clause>]]
[UNION <SELECT command...>];
[ORDER BY <clause>/FOR UPDATE OF <clause>]
[SAVE TO TEMP <clause>];
```

The simplest form of SELECT is this: SELECT *<column list>* FROM *<table list>*. Using the Invoices table, you can get a listing of the companies and invoice amounts this way:

```
SELECT Companyid, invoiceamt
FROM Invoices;
```

To see all the columns in all the rows, use a wildcard:

```
SELECT *
FROM Invoices;
```

To restrict the search even further, dBASE SQL allows you to use WHERE clauses that specify certain conditions. Figure 20.2 shows the syntax for a WHERE clause and the results of such a search.

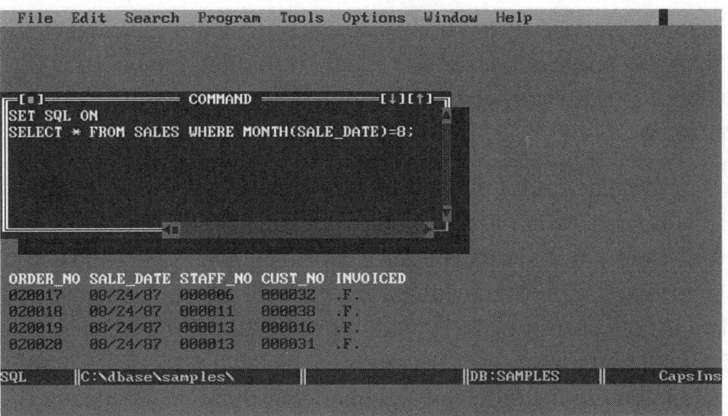

Fig. 20.2
The WHERE clause allows you to narrow the scope of your wildcard search.

The WHERE clause is similar to using the FOR keyword in regular dBASE programming. As with FOR, you can use comparison operators like =, >, and < to set up conditions. You can use the Boolean operators AND, OR, and NOT. (You don't need the periods on either side of the operator as you do in regular dBASE programming.) Most dBASE functions available with FOR in dBASE can be used in a SQL WHERE clause. You also can use five special functions in dBASE SQL that allow you to work with sets of data instead of single values. These *aggregate* functions are as follows:

AVG( )	Average the values in a numeric column
COUNT( )	Count selected rows
MAX( )	Maximum value in a column
MIN( )	Minimum value in a column
SUM( )	Total of values in a numeric column

Like dBASE functions, these SQL functions return a value that you can use as part of your SQL statement or save to a temporary location (memory variable), using the INTO clause. When used with the SELECT statement, SQL functions also can be used to perform a function and return a value. If you want to know the number of companies in the Invoices table, for example, you can use SELECT with DISTINCT and the aggregate function COUNT( ):

```
SELECT DISTINCT COUNT(Companyid)
FROM Invoices;
```

This statement selects only the first occurrence of each company, and the COUNT( ) function returns a number representing how many times SELECT found such an entry in the Invoices table.

Tip
Add conditions to the scope of your SQL statement to narrow the scope of your search and speed the return of the desired result.

As you can see, the trick is to build your SQL statement by adding conditions that narrow the scope of your search. These conditions enable you to group rows (GROUP), order rows (ORDER), and perform several other very specific manipulations.

The first of these modifiers that allows you to perform specific manipulations is DISTINCT. As shown in the previous example, DISTINCT enables you to avoid duplication in the rows you select with SELECT. Suppose that you have several contacts at a particular company in a table called Company. You want to build a list of companies, but you don't want the same company mentioned several times (once for each entry in the table if you have multiple contacts). If you use the following command, every row is displayed:

```
SELECT Companynm
FROM Company;0
```

If you use this command, however, you see only the first occurrence of each entry:

```
SELECT DISTINCT Companynm
FROM Company;
```

No matter how many entries (rows) you have for XYZ Corporation, the listing generated by the SQL statement above shows only the first one. You may use DISTINCT only once in any query, even if the statement uses nested queries. When you use nested queries, you must apply DISTINCT to only the first column mentioned in the statement.

You can format your selected information further with GROUP or ORDER or with the UNION clause. These clauses enable you to perform some of the same tasks you can perform with indexes or relational functions from a single, although complex, SELECT command.

The GROUP BY clause allows you to collect all the rows that have some column in common. You can use the GROUP BY clause with the Invoice table, for example, to group all the records that have the same company; no matter what the natural order of the table, all the same company rows are together. This has the effect of showing the contacts in each company together. You also can use the GROUP BY clause to bring together all of the companies in each city or state.

You can add a bit more selection to the GROUP BY clause by including the HAVING clause. HAVING is somewhat like WHERE in SQL or FOR in dBASE, except that you use HAVING specifically with GROUP BY. The usual structure is this: GROUP BY *<column>* HAVING *<condition>*. To collect all companies in

Indianapolis, for example, you group by city those rows having zip codes starting with 462, as in the following SQL statement:

```
SELECT Companynm, Contactname
FROM Company
GROUP BY City HAVING Zip LIKE "462%";
```

This statement gives you a list of all the rows in the Company table showing the company and contact, collected by city for all entries in the 462+ zip code area. You can use a partial match (just the first part of the zip code) by using the LIKE clause.

If you also want to show the entries in alphabetical order by company, you can insert *ORDER BY Company* before the GROUP BY CLAUSE. Your command would read as follows:

```
SELECT Companynm, Contactnam
FROM Company
GROUP BY Companynm
GROUP BY City HAVING Zip LIKE "462%";
```

You can, of course, use ORDER BY on more than one column. To group the Indianapolis companies and then list their contacts in alphabetical order, use this command:

```
SELECT Companynm, Contactname
FROM Company
ORDER BY Companynm, Contactnam
GROUP BY City HAVING Zip LIKE "462%";
```

You can order by ascending or descending order, but naturally you cannot do both in the same statement.

To get information in your virtual result table without using a legitimate join (you learn about SQL *joins* later in this section), use the UNION clause. Unlike other relational commands, UNION does not require a linking column with the same name in each table being used. It does, however, require the same data type and the same column size.

In a UNION clause, you do not see any relationships between the data attached to the column on which you build your UNION. In other words, simply because two tables yield the same state names from a UNION of the tables, doesn't necessarily mean that the companies in those states are the same. In a relational operation, it is assumed that the columns in each table are the same and that, when the relation is complete, the two tables line up side by side, row to row. If you did a UNION of SELECTS on two different tables—Invoices and Company, for example—you can get a list of all the cities or companies represented, even if the two tables have no records in common. To use UNION, all you need to do is perform a series of SELECT statements with each complete statement separated by UNION, as follows:

```
SELECT <column1>
FROM <table1>
UNION
SELECT <column2>
FROM <table2>
UNION
SELECT <column_n>
FROM <table_n>;
```

Earlier in this chapter, you discovered a SQL structure called a *predicate*. The three simplest predicates used with SELECT are BETWEEN, IN, and LIKE. BETWEEN simply means that you narrow the scope of your query to all the values *between* two independent variables. In other words, you can test a column for all of the entries BETWEEN *x* and *y*. The resulting table contains only those rows that meet the criteria. IN enables you to do the same thing, but in this case you test for all of the entries in a column which fit IN a list that makes part of the clause. You use IN with the WHERE clause for tasks like the following:

```
SELECT Description, Itemnumber
FROM Stock
WHERE SUBSTR(description,1,6) IN ("Widget", "Wazzit");
```

This statement gives you a list of all of the stock items with a description of either Widget or Wazzit associated with it.

You can use the LIKE predicate with the WHERE clause to create a skeleton (including the wildcards _ and %) that allows you to use SELECT based on partial entries. You can do the same thing to a certain extent simply by using the first portion of a character string. If you want to strip a string out of the inside of a column's contents, you have to use the LIKE predicate and wildcards. The benefit of this approach is that you can be quite specific about which characters must be in the string and which are represented by wildcard characters.

To increase your ability to accurately hit the data you want, you need to learn about joins. *Joins* are the hallmark of relational database management systems. Joins take advantage of all the benefits of the relational algebra that is the foundation of relational database management system theory. The ability to perform complex multiple-table (multitable) queries depends upon the database's capability to perform joins properly. Ironically, SQL has no join command. In SQL, joins are simply actions that certain SQL commands perform when they act on multiple tables. In order to understand how to use multitable joins, you also need to understand how to nest queries within a SELECT statement.

Nested queries within a SELECT statement are called *subqueries*. With dBASE SQL, you actually have a choice of using joins or subqueries. For every statement containing subqueries, you can build a statement by using joins that perform the same task. The decision of which to use depends on the complexity of the query.

Tip

Subqueries are easier to construct and more efficient to execute than joins when you have a very complex query to process.

An example of a fairly simple join appears in a CREATE VIEW example earlier in this chapter, and appears here for your reference:

```
CREATE VIEW Invoice
(Invoicenum, Companyid, Invoiceamt, Amountpd, Itemnumber, Quantity)
AS SELECT Invoices.Invoicenum, Companyid, Invoiceamt, Amountpd,
Itemnumber, Quantity
FROM Invoices, Itemsold
WHERE Invoices.Invoicenum = Itemsold.Invoicenum;
```

You connect the column name with the table name in the SELECT clause and list the tables in the FROM clause. Finally, you must have the linking column (in this case, the invoice number column) that is the same in both tables. In this example, the Invoicenum column was used to join the Invoices table with the Itemsold table. The virtual result table built in the join contains all the data in both smaller tables. Called a *natural join,* this excludes all rows from the result table that don't meet the WHERE clause's condition. Another kind of join is called a *forced join*. Forced joins do not use a WHERE condition and a linking column; every row in one table is joined to every row in the other.

Caution

Forced joins generate a table with as many records as the product of the record counts in each table. For example, A 50-record table joined to a 100-record table generates 500 records. This can exceed disk space and RAM limits on your system, possibly causing application failure.

In complex multitable queries that create joins, you can use any of the techniques available for simple queries. You can build several conditions into your query or use functions to narrow your selection criteria. You also can join as many tables (within reason) as you want. Remember, however, that dBASE has to optimize the query; the more complex you make the query, the longer it takes to optimize and execute.

Subqueries really are quite simple. Your *outer* query is your SELECT statement. To limit the records retrieved by the SELECT statement, you can use a WHERE clause to match a column with the results of a second SELECT statement. This second SELECT statement is the *inner* query, and appears inside parentheses. An example of the syntax for subqueries is shown in figure 20.3.

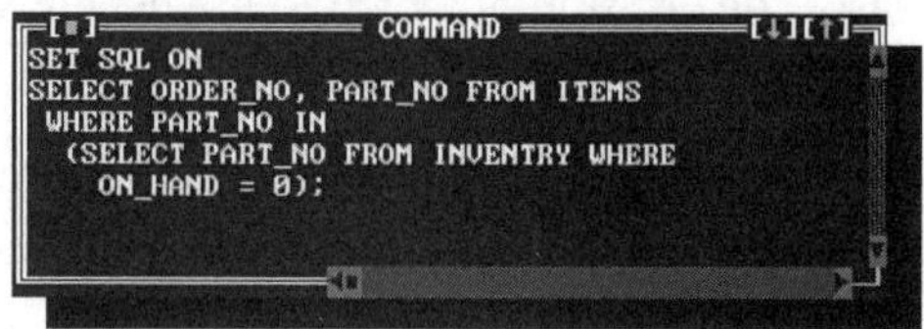

Fig. 20.3
Subqueries are nested inside SELECT statements to restrict your search results.

dBASE SQL has two kinds of subqueries: *simple subqueries* and *correlated subqueries*. Simple subqueries work like simple algebraic statements. You (and dBASE SQL) evaluate them from the inside out, starting with the subquery nested the deepest in the total statement.

Tip
Make your query as lean as possible to allow dBASE to optimize it quickly and efficiently.

After evaluating the deepest subquery, dBASE 5 uses the rows that result to evaluate the next query, and so on. dBASE starts with a fairly large result table and shrinks the table as dBASE whittles away at the available rows, until dBASE reaches the outermost outer query. At that point you have your final result table, which may have only one or two rows in it. Logically speaking, you have the potential for the most complex queries if your tables are large and you have several of them involved in the query.

Keep one caveat in mind when you are nesting queries. Make sure that the WHERE clause, which makes up an outer query, can handle the results the inner query returns. Because the clause often must handle several rows, be sure that you use an appropriate predicate or clause capable of accepting more than one row. As far as syntax is concerned, using a nested SELECT statement as an inner query is no different from using a SELECT statement as a stand-alone query.

Remember that each time dBASE SQL evaluates a nested query, it returns rows in a result table just as if that query were by itself. In turn, the next level of the query must deal with that result table. The process is similar to performing a simple query, saving the results in a view, and then performing another query on the view. The difference is that using subqueries is far more efficient and elegant.

The second type of subquery, the correlated subquery, is a bit more complicated. Whereas the simple subquery produces a result table independent of any outer query, the correlated subquery uses values returned by an outer query. The difference between this and a simple subquery is subtle, but important; the outer query must return values for all the rows that the inner query uses. The inner query then is evaluated for each value. This doesn't mean that the rule of evaluating the inner query first is violated. It means that the total query statement must be performed several times, once for each set of outer query results. The actual last step in the overall query is to correlate the information in the outer query with the information in the inner query to obtain a final result table.

Note

No single format dictates the steps you perform to build a simple or correlated subquery. You must examine the steps your query performs as it evaluates the nested queries and build your query in a logical fashion. A well-structured query yields the best performance.

Keep in mind that anything you can do with subqueries you can do with joins. With a join, you perform a simple query with no nesting. You produce that query by using several tables and then save the results of the query to a result table. When you use joins as an alternative to subqueries, you often need Boolean operators (AND, OR, NOT) to perform the same query. Using nested subqueries, however, is more efficient for dBASE SQL to evaluate and it results in better performance, especially with large tables.

If your inner and outer queries are directed at the same table, you need to assign aliases to keep the queries separate. When you do this, dBASE SQL treats the table as two separate tables. You can use the CREATE SYNONYM statement for this task.

Adding Data with the Insert Command

The INSERT statement enables you to add data to an existing table. INSERT is similar to the dBASE APPEND command, but you do not get a data input screen with INSERT. You must build the statement like any other SQL statement.

Tip
Remember to use quotation marks if your literal is a character string, otherwise the character string is treated as a variable value.

INSERT has two basic syntax diagrams. With the first syntax diagram, you can add a row with specific values in each column. Those values can be any legitimate dBASE value, including strings, numbers, dates, or the contents of memory variables. Using memory variables, you can produce a data input screen for your users and then use INSERT to put the contents of the memory variables you use in the screen to capture user input. When you insert a literal, remember that dates start out as character strings and must be converted to date format with curly braces—for example, {05/01/93}. If you use INSERT to insert dates from date memory variables, however, they are already in the date data types and require no conversion.

The syntax for using INSERT follows:

```
INSERT INTO <table name> [(<column list>)]
   VALUES (<value list>);
```

To use INSERT in this manner, state the *<table name>* of the table for which you intend to insert data. Then list the names of each column where you want to put new values. (You do not need to list columns that remain empty or unchanged.) Finally, list the values that go into the columns in the same order in which you listed the columns. Remember that essentially, you are appending a row onto the data table. In this format, you supply each of the values that go into each column of this new row.

You can use INSERT another way to add rows to a table. If you want to copy the contents of certain rows of a table onto another table (thus appending rows that are only partially filled to the second table), you can use the second form of INSERT. The main use for this second method is to create a second table that you eventually join to the first. In this case, you probably want at least one column in the new table that is identical to a column in the old table. You eventually use that as the linking column in the join.

A similar use might be in an application in which you update one table from user input and several others from the original table. Don't confuse this use of update, however, with the UPDATE command. In this context, updating means appending entire rows to the table. The syntax for the second use of INSERT follows:

```
INSERT INTO <table name> [(<column list>)]
   <SELECT command>;
```

In this case, in place of the VALUES clause, you have a variation on the SELECT command used as a clause. That means you can use SELECT to gather rows from a source table to insert into the target table. All the rules that apply to the stand-alone use of SELECT apply here as well. Make sure that the columns in your column list match the corresponding columns returned as a result of the SELECT statement.

Changing Data with the Update Command

If you want to change the information in an existing row of a table, you need the UPDATE command. UPDATE enables you to specify a row and columns within that row and then change the data in those locations. The syntax for the UPDATE command follows:

```
UPDATE <table name>/<view name>
   SET <column name> = <new value>
   [,<column name> = <new value>...]
   [<WHERE clause>];
```

Use the WHERE clause to locate the correct row; use the SET clause to change the values in one or more columns. You can use this form of UPDATE interactively or from within a program. You can use the second form of UPDATE, however, only in a program. The syntax of the alternative form of UPDATE follows:

```
UPDATE <table name>
   SET <column name> = <new value>
   [,<column name> = <new value>...]
   WHERE CURRENT OF <SQL cursor name>;
```

This use of UPDATE requires an understanding of cursors, explained later in this chapter. For now, be aware that in this alternative UPDATE, the WHERE clause is replaced by the WHERE CURRENT OF clause to locate the correct row. In simple terms, WHERE CURRENT OF tells SQL to go to the row where a pointer currently is located. The pointer, called a *cursor*, is similar in purpose to the dBASE record pointer. All else about this form of UPDATE is the same as in the other form of the command. Remember that you can use this form only from within a program file.

Deleting Data with the Delete Command

The last of the data-handling commands in dBASE SQL is DELETE. DELETE enables you to remove a row from a data table. In one very dangerous case, DELETE actually allows you to remove all the rows from the table. Unlike the dBASE DELETE command, the SQL version actually removes the data in a single step. You are not required to pack the database (using PACK) to erase information physically.

Caution

Be careful when you use the SQL DELETE command. You get a warning box that tells you that your actions are irrevocable, but if you use DELETE without specifying the row to DELETE, you erase all the rows in the table. In other words, if you leave out the WHERE clause, DELETE wipes out all your data.

Like UPDATE, DELETE has two forms. The first is for use interactively or from within a program. The second is for use in program files only. The syntax for both forms follows:

Form 1:

```
DELETE FROM <table name> [<alias name>]
   [<WHERE clause>];
```

Form 2:

```
DELETE FROM <table name>
   WHERE CURRENT OF <SQL cursor name>;
```

Notice that the second form—program file use only—uses the same WHERE CURRENT OF clause as the UPDATE command. The reason is that both commands act on a full row of a table. When you specify that row, your specification must point dBASE SQL to one and only one row. Using a cursor in an embedded procedure is the most precise way to do that. The one-row rule has two exceptions: using UPDATE to update more than one row in an identical manner, and using DELETE to delete more than one row at a time.

In those two cases, the only way to indicate the desired rows is with the WHERE clause.

Troubleshooting

When I enter the wildcard %, I get back a lot of extra data that doesn't apply to what I was searching for. Why?

You need to double-check your code to be sure that the wildcard is being used correctly. Wildcards are very powerful and, when incorrectly used, retrieve more than you want. For example, if you want to find all zip codes in your data table that start with a 4, but you enter %4%, you get a long list. Be sure you only place a percent sign where you want it —representing unknown characters. Also, try narrowing your search using more of the beginning characters in the search string. This helps to limit the resulting data. You may also use the underscore (_) as a single character wildcard to help limit your selections.

Controlling Security

Before you learn about embedding SQL in dBASE applications, you need to know about two other classes of commands. These two classes of commands provide data access security and utilities to simplify your use of SQL with other, non-SQL data.

Security, from the perspective of dBASE 5, is the process by which users gain access, first to dBASE 5, and then to various SQL databases and tables. The first layer of security in dBASE 5 is the general-access security determined by the PROTECT command/utility. PROTECT, when used from the Command window or the SQL Command window, invokes a full-screen utility that allows you to set a variety of security constraints. Among these constraints are file access, generalized access to dBASE 5, and a set of user IDs and passwords.

Tip
To get the most from the security available with dBASE SQL, be sure that at least the minimum dBASE 5 security has been established using PROTECT.

Minimum security consists of assigning IDs to all users who require SQL privileges. The use of PROTECT usually is reserved for the database administrator (DBA). If the DBA has not assigned an ID to a dBASE 5 user and security has been applied to the SQL tables, that user has no access to files in the SQL application.

When the DBA uses PROTECT to set up a security environment, dBASE 5 makes encrypted entries in two environmental files: DBSYSTEM.DB and DBSYSTEM.SQL. After a user is past the login process for dBASE 5 and into the SQL application, all access to SQL tables is governed by the use of two security commands in SQL. The commands, GRANT and REVOKE, are used by the DBA, either interactively or from within an application. The syntax for GRANT, the first of these commands, follows:

```
GRANT ALL [PRVILEGES]/<privilege list> ON
[TABLE] <table list> TO PUBLIC/<user list>
[WITH GRANT OPTION];
```

The first thing you notice about GRANT is the need for a privilege list unless you are granting all privileges. The privilege list is a subset of the following list:

ALTER	Use the ALTER command
DELETE	Use the DELETE command
INDEX	Create an index for a table
INSERT	Use the INSERT command to add rows to a table
SELECT	Use the SELECT command
UPDATE	Use the UPDATE command

Be careful about how you use these privileges in a program; you can restrict a user from performing tasks built into the application that the user is running. In most cases, you need a routine in the application that lets the DBA assign privilege levels to various users, consistent with the way the application is written. In an accounting application, for example, you can give a certain class of user the capability to browse salary data, but not to modify the tables that go into creating it. You use GRANT to give that group of users the capability to use SELECT but not to use ALTER, DELETE, UPDATE, or INSERT on any of the tables involved.

Tip
After you've established all file rights, make a backup copy of DBSYSTEM.DB and DBSYSTEM.SQL files to guard against accidental deletion.

Even though the commands to perform those processes can be available to the users through a menu system, attempts to execute the menu choices are futile unless the user has the proper privilege level.

If you use the PUBLIC keyword, all the selected privileges are assigned to all users. GRANT has a special clause that enables users to grant privileges to other users as long as the PUBLIC keyword is not used. The WITH GRANT OPTION clause allows any user to grant his or her privileges to any other user. The granting user cannot grant privileges he or she doesn't have, of course, but within those guidelines, WITH GRANT OPTION enables users to pass privileges on to other users. When the granting user loses a privilege, the users to whom the user has granted the privilege lose it as well. Remember, you must use the same user IDs in the TO clause as appear in the user lists produced by PROTECT.

If you can grant user privileges in dBASE SQL, you also can revoke them. The REVOKE command is exactly the opposite of the GRANT command in that it takes away the privileges assigned by GRANT. In fact, the syntax for REVOKE is essentially the same, as follows:

```
REVOKE ALL [PRVILEGES]/<privileges list>
   ON [TABLE] <table list>
   FROM PUBLIC/<user list>;
```

Again, be careful how you use this command so that you avoid revoking some of the privileges needed by a user of an application, while leaving other privileges in such a way that the user can perform only part of a preprogrammed process.

When you build an application for a local area network (LAN) accessed by many users, you may want to build security into the application even though the LAN has security capabilities. The reason for this is that users can have application-specific knowledge or requirements that have nothing at all to do with their needs on the LAN.

Security is most useful for simply keeping users out of areas they have no need to use or are not trained to use. The idea that security is necessary only if you want to keep intruders out is just partially correct. Most damage to or loss of data is caused by well-meaning users who simply don't belong in areas of the application for which they are not trained. The judicious use of security measures can help keep those users within the boundaries you or the DBA deem appropriate.

Using SQL Utility Commands

You can use six utility commands to deal with non-SQL data and to keep your application running smoothly. Those commands are DBCHECK, DBDEFINE, LOAD, RUNSTATS, ROLLBACK, and UNLOAD. Of these, three commands—DBDEFINE, LOAD, and UNLOAD—are data-specific; the others deal with tables in the catalog.

▶ See "DBCHECK," p. 885

Converting a Database to a Table

DBDEFINE enables you to take a dBASE 5 database and convert it to a SQL table. The syntax for the DBDEFINE command follows:

▶ See "DBDEFINE," p. 886

```
DBDEFINE [<filename>];
```

As you can see, the file name is optional, meaning that you can use the DBDEFINE command alone to convert all the DBF files in the current database to SQL tables. Keep in mind, however, that any DBF file you want to convert to a SQL file must be in the directory that contains the database to which the table is to be attached. When you use DBDEFINE on a dBASE database, you convert it to a SQL table and update the catalog in the active SQL database. The DBF filename extension does not change, but the format of the file does. Because of the file structure of dBASE data files, the changes are not extensive. Both files, in fact, are the same size. The first byte of the file header, however, is different.

dBASE 5 and dBASE SQL can read the SQL table. To use the dBASE database with dBASE SQL commands, however, you must convert it to a SQL table and ensure that you have the proper entries in the SQL catalog. Another benefit of DBDEFINE is that it converts all production index files (MDX) to the appropriate SQL indexes automatically.

Tip

DBDEFINE automatically converts all production index files (MDX) to the appropriate SQL indexes.

Importing Data into a Table

LOAD enables you to bring data from a non-SQL file into a dBASE SQL table, including dBASE database files from any level of dBASE. The use of the command follows the same file formats as the dBASE APPEND FROM command. If you don't specify a file type, LOAD assumes that the type is dBASE.
The syntax for the LOAD command follows:

```
LOAD DATA FROM [path]<filename>
   INTO TABLE <table name>
      [[TYPE] SDF/DIF/WKS/SYLK/FW2/RPD/dBASEII/
      DELIMITED [WITH BLANK/WITH <delimiter>]];
```

Unlike DBDEFINE, LOAD does not care where the source data is located, as long as you specify the exact path to it. Again, unlike DBDEFINE, the data in the source file is not altered. In other words, DBDEFINE converts the file format of a dBASE 5 database to a SQL table and updates the catalog. LOAD takes non-SQL data and copies it to an existing SQL table, in the process converting it to a format acceptable by that table.

Exporting Data from SQL

▶ See "GRANT," p. 889

▶ See "REVOKE," p. 891

If REVOKE is the opposite of GRANT in the security commands, UNLOAD is the opposite of LOAD in the utilities. Using UNLOAD on SQL data puts it into another, non-SQL format, in a destination file of your choosing. The syntax for the REVOKE command follows:

```
UNLOAD DATA TO [path]<filename>
   FROM TABLE <table name>
      [[TYPE] SDF/DIF/WKS/SYLK/FW2/RPD/dBASEII
      /DELIMITED [WITH BLANK/WITH<delimiter>]];
```

Notice that LOAD and UNLOAD allow you to work with delimited data ASCII files, which can be very useful for importing and exporting data from mainframes or databases that are not directly supported.

Rolling Back Transactions

▶ See "ROLLBACK," p. 892

ROLLBACK is a very special command that can mean the difference between data integrity and the potential for corrupting data in one or more tables. You always use ROLLBACK with the dBASE command BEGIN TRANSACTION. The syntax for ROLLBACK follows:

```
ROLLBACK [WORK];
```

The optional WORK keyword is for compatibility with other SQL syntaxes that require it—IBM DB2 SQL, for example.

The idea behind the ROLLBACK command is that in transaction processing (covered later under "Using SQL for Transaction Processing"), you set up a transaction consisting of a series of commands or processes without actually executing the commands. When the transaction is ready to complete, you can give the user an opportunity to change any information. When the transaction is ready to perform, you commit it, which means that you perform all the tasks in the transaction at the same time. The actual transaction takes a very short time. Only during the transaction are any tables used in the transaction open. When the transaction is complete, all data is updated, and the application awaits the next transaction.

If the transaction is interrupted by a failure of some sort, however, you need a way to ensure that the processes in it are not partially complete. If you had a transaction that, upon completion, updated several tables with new data, and that transaction was terminated prematurely, some tables are updated and some are not. The result can be a discrepancy between tables that should be in agreement. In an accounting application, for example, such a situation can result in an out-of-balance condition. ROLLBACK is the dBASE 5 SQL solution.

ROLLBACK wipes out all of the actions appearing between the dBASE BEGIN TRANSACTION and END TRANSACTION commands that immediately precede and follow the transaction. If you use ROLLBACK on a transaction, you take all the data tables involved back to the state that they were in prior to beginning the transaction. The best way to use ROLLBACK is to place it in a procedure called by the dBASE ON ERROR or ON ESCAPE commands.

The following SQL commands cannot be used between BEGIN TRANSACTION and END TRANSACTION in a dBASE transaction:

ALTER

CREATE

DBCHECK

DBDEFINE

GRANT

REVOKE

DROP

This doesn't mean that you cannot use these commands just before BEGIN TRANSACTION. Actions of these commands, however, cannot be undone by ROLLBACK in the event of an error.

Now that you understand the basics of dBASE SQL and the use of the various SQL commands (with a few exceptions), you are ready to progress to the use of SQL within dBASE 5 programs and applications. A few SQL commands were not yet covered. Those commands are specific to embedded SQL, which is the next subject.

Using SQL in Program Code

You need to know a few things before you discover techniques for using embedded SQL. First, you learn about the special SQL commands that you use only when you embed SQL code in dBASE code. Next, you are introduced to the rules and techniques basic to producing dBASE applications that use SQL to handle the data. You then discover transaction processing techniques, and finally you learn about using dBASE SQL and transaction techniques in a multiuser environment.

Understanding and Using Cursor Commands

The concept of SQL cursors is a bit tricky unless you remember two things: First, the *cursor* really is a row pointer that works in much the same way as the dBASE record pointer. Second, cursors work only on result tables. In other words, you cannot use DECLARE CURSOR for a real SQL table; you must use DECLARE CURSOR for the result of a query. Four SQL statements are associated with dBASE SQL cursors:

- DECLARE CURSOR—Defines a cursor.
- OPEN—Executes an embedded SELECT.
- FETCH INTO—Moves the cursor and transfers row values to memory variables.
- CLOSE—Closes the cursor.

The following sections explain how you use each of these commands.

Declaring Cursors

Tip
DECLARE CURSOR defines the action to take place when the cursor is opened with OPEN, but does not execute an action.

The first step in using a cursor is understanding the DECLARE CURSOR statement. DECLARE CURSOR does two things: it names a row pointer called a cursor; and it defines a result table to be generated with the cursor located before the first row. The cursor is before the first row (or at the end, if the result table is empty) because the FETCH command always advances the cursor one row. The statement uses an embedded SELECT statement to generate the result table. The syntax for the DECLARE CURSOR statement follows:

```
DECLARE <cursor name> CURSOR
FOR <SELECT command>
[FOR UPDATE OF<column list>|<ORDER BY clause>];
```

You can use the DECLARE CURSOR command in a variety of ways, one of which is to set the stage for updating a table with UPDATE. As you see, using cursors and embedding commands in dBASE 5 applications can improve your application's data handling. Cursors also are important because they offer the only easy way to collect the values of multiple rows and return them to your dBASE application's memory variables. Later in this chapter, under "Using Cursors," you see how all four of the cursor statements produce useful data from a SQL table.

Opening a Cursor

The OPEN statement actually executes the process defined by the DECLARE CURSOR statement. The syntax is fairly simple:

```
OPEN <cursor name>;
```

When you issue the OPEN command, all the steps you set up in the DECLARE CURSOR statement associated with the OPEN command execute. The SELECT command creates the result table, and the cursor is positioned just ahead of the first row in the result table. You then are ready to begin collecting data and storing it in memory variables using the FETCH command.

Fetching a Cursor

FETCH performs two functions: the first is positioning the cursor, and the second is collecting and storing the data in the row to which the cursor is pointing. FETCH always moves the cursor ahead one row in the result table. When the cursor comes to rest on that row, it collects the data and stores it in memory variables. The memory variables must have the same names as the column names, perhaps with an *m* in front of the memory variables to keep them visually separate from column names.

▶ See "FETCH," p. 888

You must have the same number of memory variables as you have columns in the SELECT clause. The column contents are stored in the memory variables in the order in which you list the columns in the SELECT clause. In other words, the first column after SELECT goes into the first memory variable, the second column into the second memory variable, and so on.

After you store the values of the columns in the row to which the cursor is pointing, you can use that data elsewhere in the application. When you reissue the FETCH, the cursor moves ahead to the next row and performs the same set of tasks. The syntax of the FETCH command follows:

```
FETCH <cursor name>
   INTO <memory variable list>;
```

Closing a Cursor

The last of the cursor-handling commands is CLOSE. Its purpose is to close the cursor and release any associated memory. If you open the cursor again with OPEN, however, you reexecute the same SELECT statement that the cursor executed originally. This action produces a new result table.

The syntax for the CLOSE command follows:

```
CLOSE <SQL cursor name>;
```

Using UPDATE with DECLARE CURSOR

► See "UPDATE," p. 897

The first technique for embedding SQL processes within a cursor command is using UPDATE with DECLARE CURSOR. In this case, UPDATE is embedded within the DECLARE CURSOR command. Later in this procedure, you use UPDATE in the form of UPDATE WHERE CURRENT OF. Remember the second form of the UPDATE command? You use this form with DECLARE CURSOR...FOR UPDATE OF. To refresh your memory, the following is the second form of the UPDATE command:

```
UPDATE <table name>
   SET <column name> = <new value>
   [,<column name> = <new value>...]
   WHERE CURRENT OF <SQL cursor name>;
```

The following example shows how you can use these two commands in an application:

```
DECLARE Cursorname CURSOR FOR
SELECT Column1, Column2, Column3
FROM Tablename
FOR UPDATE OF Column3;
OPEN Cursorname;
FETCH Cursorname INTO Mcolumn1, Mcolumn2, Mcolumn3;
DO WHILE SQLCODE = 0
DO Procedure WITH Mcolumn1, Mcolumn2, Mcolumn3
UPDATE Tablename
WHERE CURRENT OF Cursorname;
FETCH Cursorname INTO Mcolumn1, Mcolumn2, Mcolumn3;
ENDDO
CLOSE Cursorname;
```

First, you create the cursor, give it a name, create the result table with SELECT, and designate the column (Column3, in this case) on which you eventually perform an UPDATE. Next, use OPEN to open the cursor. Doing so executes the SELECT specified in the DECLARE CURSOR statement. After you open the cursor, get the data in the first row and put it into the appropriate memory variables. You use the FETCH command for this, placing it inside a dBASE DO WHILE construct so that you can continue to loop through the table until the cursor is at the end. At that point, your dBASE procedure can signal the DO WHILE that there are no more rows to scan.

After this process is complete, use DO to perform a dBASE procedure that uses the memory variables you filled with the FETCH. During that dBASE procedure or after it, you perform the UPDATE, an action which you indicated in the DECLARE CURSOR statement. The UPDATE uses the data in the memory variables (which, presumably, you change in the dBASE procedure) to put updated information back into the columns at the cursor location, which hasn't moved because of the WHERE CURRENT OF clause in the UPDATE statement. Finally, you use CLOSE to close the cursor when you loop through all the rows in the affected table and pass beyond the DO WHILE.

Using DELETE with DECLARE CURSOR

In the preceding example, you saw how UPDATE can be used with DECLARE CURSOR to update a row in a table, based on some action in a dBASE 5 procedure. The UPDATE was part of the DECLARE CURSOR statement, as well as a separate statement later on. In the case of DELETE, however, the DELETE isn't part of the DECLARE CURSOR statement. To DELETE the row where the cursor is pointing, you just use the form of the DELETE statement that contains the WHERE CURRENT OF clause, as in the following syntax:

► See "DELETE FROM," p. 886

```
DELETE FROM <table name>
   WHERE CURRENT OF <SQL cursor name>;
```

Caution

Be careful when you use this command. Be sure that you did everything you need to do with the row to which the cursor is pointing. When you execute the DELETE using the above syntax, that row is irretrievably lost.

You also can use the INSERT statement as part of a procedure, but it has no special relationship to the cursor because INSERT adds a row to a table. The new row is appended to the table regardless of where the cursor is pointing.

The following is the general pattern for using cursors:

```
DECLARE CURSOR
OPEN
FETCH
...... dBASE Processing
CLOSE
```

You can embed certain SQL processes in SQL cursor commands to help narrow the range of data in your result table. You also can use UPDATE and DELETE to update and delete data in a SQL table.

Remember, the more you manipulate your data with SQL, the more efficient your application. As a rule of thumb, you should handle all data within tables with the dBASE SQL commands whenever possible. After you remove selected data from the table, you can use dBASE commands. By following this two-part method, you take advantage of the relative strengths of the two languages: dBASE for program control and operating on selected data, and SQL for manipulating tables and selecting data for use by dBASE.

Troubleshooting

I deleted a year's worth of data using the DELETE command in SQL. Is there any way to retrieve it?

Unfortunately, dBASE doesn't allow you to undelete or undo a DELETE. However, if you back up your files periodically (nightly if you're entering a lot of data) you can fall back on those files. If you haven't been backing up your files, you may need to use a separate utility package to undelete the data.

Embedding SQL Code in dBASE Applications

Now that you are familiar with using SQL as part of a procedure, you are ready to take the final step. In the examples, you saw simple cases of the use of SQL and dBASE commands together. You learned that you handle the data with SQL and the program execution with dBASE. You learned about the SQL cursor and how it enables you to deal with subsets of an entire table. Now you can put this theory into practice.

The following pages show sample code for retrieving information, adding information, and updating and deleting rows. Rather than include all the menus and other surrounding code, this example simply shows the individual procedures for each of these processes.

The following section of code, BIGAPP.PRS, is a sample procedure that demonstrates how to insert rows, update rows, and delete rows, among other common manipulations of data tables. To run this procedure, type DO BigApp in the Command window. Since compound expressions are not valid in LIKE clauses an intermediate STORE is used to concatenate wildcards prior to issuing the LIKE in the DECLARE BigSeek used in each procedure.

```
PROCEDURE bigapp
   STORE SET("SCOREBOARD") TO x_SetScore
```

```
    STORE SET("TALK")        TO x_SetTalk
    SET SCOREBOARD OFF
    SET TALK        OFF
    CLEAR
    DEFINE POPUP bigapp FROM 6,30
    DEFINE BAR 1 OF bigapp PROMPT "Query"
    DEFINE BAR 2 OF bigapp PROMPT "Append"
    DEFINE BAR 3 OF bigapp PROMPT "Update"
    DEFINE BAR 4 OF bigapp PROMPT "Delete"
    DEFINE BAR 5 OF bigapp PROMPT "Exit"
    ON SELECTION BAR 1 OF bigapp DO BigQuery
    ON SELECTION BAR 2 OF bigapp DO BigAppend
    ON SELECTION BAR 3 OF bigapp DO BigUpdate
    ON SELECTION BAR 4 OF bigapp DO BigDelete
    ON SELECTION BAR 5 OF bigapp DEACTVATE POPUP
    START DATABASE sales;  && Open database containing company table
    ACTVATE POPUP bigapp
    STOP DATABASE;
    RELEASE  POPUP bigapp
    SET SCOREBOARD &x_SetScore
    SET TALK       &x_SetTalk
RETURN
```

V

Using High-Level Tools

The next procedure, BigQuery, allows query only. It asks the user for the company that will be the subject of the search. After the user's input is captured, the RTRIM and LTRIM functions strip out leading and trailing spaces before doing a wildcard search. Embedding the user response with wild cards permits the user to enter any portion of the company name under search. The LIKE predicate will then find all rows in which the com column contains the fragment entered by the user. The result table will contain all company names that either start with or contain the fragment.

The FETCH command is used here to store the column or field values into memory variables. In this case, the memory variables: `m_com`, `m_con &` and `m_tl1` correspond to the columns specified in the SELECT portion of the DECLARE CURSOR command. The order that the memory variables are listed in the FETCH command determines what field values are stored to them. In this case com (company) is stored to `m_com`, `con` (contact) to `m_con`, and `tl1` (telephone) to `m_tl1`. The variable names don't need to be similar to field names but it is good programming practice.

```
PROCEDURE BigQuery
   STORE SPACE(30) TO m_comp, m_con, m_com
   START DATABASE sales;
   CLEAR
   @ 5,5 SAY "Enter all or part of the company name: " GET m_comp
   READ
   STORE "%" + RTRIM(LTRIM(m_comp)) + "%" TO m_comp
   DECLARE BigSeekQ CURSOR FOR
   SELECT con, com
```

```
    FROM company
    WHERE com LIKE m_comp ;
    OPEN  BigSeekQ;
    FETCH BigSeekQ INTO m_con, m_com;  && Try to get first match.
    IF SqlCode <> 0                    && Check for matches.
       @  8,20 SAY "         No matches found            "
       @ 10,20 SAY "Press any key to return to main menu..."
       READ
    ENDIF
    *
    * Loop while fetch is successful and the user does not press
      ➥Escape.
    *
    DO WHILE SqlCode = 0 .AND. LASTKEY() <> 27
       CLEAR
       @  0, 0 SAY "Here is an entry of the company: " + m_comp
       @  3, 2 SAY "Company. . . .   " + m_com
       @  4, 2 SAY "Contact. . . .   " + m_con
       @  7, 0 SAY "Press ESC to cancel or SPACE to keep
                   ➥searching..."
       READ
       FETCH BigSeekQ INTO m_con, m_com; && Skip to next record
    ENDDO
    CLOSE BigSeekQ;
    CLEAR
 RETURN
```

BigAppend lets you append rows to the company table using the SQL INSERT command. Note the User Defined Function (UDF) used for getting user responses to Yes/No questions.

```
PROCEDURE BigAppend
   STORE .F.        TO m_response       && Initialize variables
   START DATABASE sales;
   CLEAR
   STORE dialogYN("Are you sure you want to add a record?") TO
m_response
   DO WHILE m_response
      STORE SPACE(30)  TO m_con, m_com, m_ad1, m_cit
      STORE SPACE(02)  TO m_sta
      STORE SPACE(10)  TO m_zip
      @  1, 2 SAY "Enter the following"
      @  3, 2 SAY "Company. . . .   " GET m_com ;
             VALID REQUIRED .NOT. ISBLANK(m_com)
      @  4, 2 SAY "Contact. . . .   " GET m_con
      @  5, 2 SAY "Address line 1   " GET m_ad1
      @  7, 2 SAY "City . . . . .   " GET m_cit
      @  8, 2 SAY "State. . . . .   " GET m_sta
      @  9, 2 SAY "Zip. . . . . .   " GET m_zip
      READ
      IF .NOT. ISBLANK(m_com)
        INSERT INTO company
            (companynm, contactnam, street, city, state, zip)
        VALUES (m_com, m_con, m_ad1, m_cit, m_sta, m_zip);
      ENDIF
```

```
        STORE dialogYN("Do you want to add another record?")
        ➥TO m_response
        CLEAR
     ENDDO
  RETURN
```

BigUpdate lets you update a row, and locates rows like BigQuery, then allows the user to update the phone number column.

```
  PROCEDURE BigUpdate
     STORE .F.        TO m_response
     STORE SPACE(30) TO m_comp, m_com, m_con, m_name
     START DATABASE sales;
     CLEAR
     @ 5,5 SAY "Enter all or part of the company name: " GET m_comp
     READ
     STORE "%" + RTRIM(LTRIM(m_comp)) + "%" TO m_comp
     DECLARE BigSeekU CURSOR FOR
        SELECT companynm, contactnam
           FROM company
           WHERE companynm LIKE m_comp;
     OPEN  BigSeekU;
     FETCH BigSeekU INTO m_com, m_con;  && Try to get first match.
     IF SqlCode <> 0                    && Check for matches.
        @  8,20 SAY "         No matches found              "
        @ 10,20 SAY "Press any key to return to main menu..."
        READ
     ENDIF
     DO WHILE SqlCode = 0 .AND. (.NOT. m_response)
        * repeat until last fetch is unsuccessful or m_response is
          ➥True
        CLEAR
        @  0, 0 SAY "Here is an entry of the company: " + m_comp
        @  3, 2 SAY "Company. . . .   " + m_com
        @  4, 2 SAY "Contact. . . .   " + m_con
        STORE dialogYN("Do you want to update this contact name?")
        ➥TO m_response
        IF .NOT. m_response
          FETCH BigSeekU INTO m_com, m_con;  && Skip to next record
        ENDIF
     ENDDO
     CLOSE BigSeekU;
     IF m_response
        @ 7,0 SAY "Enter the new contact name: " GET m_name
        READ
        UPDATE BigList
           SET contactnam = m_name
           WHERE companynm = m_com AND contactnam = m_con;
     ENDIF
     CLEAR
  RETURN
```

BigDelete allows users to delete rows from the company table. It uses much of the same code that is in the BigUpdate procedure.

```
PROCEDURE BigDelete
   STORE .F.        TO m_response
   STORE SPACE(30) TO m_comp, m_com, m_con
   START DATABASE sales;
   CLEAR
   @ 5,5 SAY "Enter all or part of the company name: " GET m_comp
   READ
   STORE "%" + RTRIM(LTRIM(m_comp)) + "%" TO m_comp
   DECLARE BigSeekD CURSOR FOR
      SELECT contactnam, companynm
         FROM company
         WHERE companynm LIKE m_comp;
   OPEN  BigSeekD;
   FETCH BigSeekD INTO m_con, m_com;  && Try to get first match.
   IF SqlCode <> 0                    && Check for matches.
      @  8,20 SAY "          No matches found               "
      @ 10,20 SAY "Press any key to return to main menu..."
      READ
   ENDIF
   *
   * Repeat until last fetch is unsuccessful or m_response is True
   *
   DO WHILE SqlCode = 0 .AND. (.NOT. m_response)
      CLEAR
      @  0, 0 SAY "Here is an entry of the company: " + m_comp
      @  3, 2 SAY "Company. . . .    " + m_com
      @  4, 2 SAY "Contact. . . .    " + m_con
      * Double check if user wants to delete record.
      STORE IIF(dialogYN("Do you want to Delete this row?"), ;
            dialogYN("Are you sure?"),.F.) TO m_response
      IF .NOT. m_response
        FETCH BigSeekD INTO m_con, m_com;  && Skip to next record
      ENDIF
   ENDDO
   CLOSE BigSeekD;
   IF m_response
      DELETE FROM company
          WHERE companynm = m_com AND contactnam = m_con;
   ENDIF
   CLEAR
RETURN
```

DialogYN is a UDF used to get a Yes or No response from the user. It requires a character string that appears above the Yes/No menu and it returns a logical value.

```
FUNCTION dialogYN
   PARAMETERS p_message
   PRVATE x_dialogYN
   PRVATE c_messages
   STORE .F.            TO x_dialogYN
   DEFINE   WINDOW dialogYN FROM 7,15 TO 13,65 DOUBLE
   ACTVATE WINDOW dialogYN
   @ 1, 2 SAY p_message
   DEFINE      MENU       dialogYN  ;
```

```
    MESSAGE "Select option and press ENTER, or press first letter of
    ➥desired option"
    DEFINE       PAD no  OF dialogYN PROMPT "No"  AT 3, 27
    DEFINE       PAD yes OF dialogYN PROMPT "Yes" AT 3, 13
    ON SELECTION PAD no  OF dialogYN DO dialogYN2 WITH PAD()
    ON SELECTION PAD yes OF dialogYN DO dialogYN2 WITH PAD()
    ON KEY LABEL N                   DO dialogYN2 WITH "NO"
    ON KEY LABEL Y                   DO dialogYN2 WITH "YES"
    ACTVATE      MENU       dialogYN
    ON KEY LABEL N
    ON KEY LABEL Y
    DEACTVATE    WINDOW     dialogYN
    RELEASE      MENUS      dialogYN
    RELEASE      WINDOWS    dialogYN
    RELEASE p_message
 RETURN (x_dialogYN)
 PROCEDURE dialogYN2
    *- case structure for exit menu
    PARAMETERS p_pad
    STORE (p_pad = "YES")  TO x_dialogYN
    RELEASE p_pad
    DEACTVATE MENU
 RETURN
```

If you choose to duplicate this application, either you need to re-create the Sales database by using CREATE on it and its accompanying catalog tables, or you need to substitute whatever database you do create in the example code.

The compiler for dBASE SQL does not know how to use multiple databases, unless you create them separately and then handle the multiple databases and their tables individually. When you distribute your application, remember that you need to build the correct directories for each database you use and then place the appropriate data and catalog tables in them. Be sure to distribute the catalog tables with your application.

Another aspect of distributing your application is that dBASE 5 optimizes queries, based on the entries in the catalog tables. The optimization is performed at compile time. Therefore, you must recompile your application from time to time.

You can use multiple databases, but you need to attempt to put all your tables into a single database. If you cannot, one way to keep information straight is to treat each process as a separate transaction. dBASE SQL, however, cannot work with tables in multiple databases within a single query. Whereas multitable joins are quite simple, multiple database joins are impossible in SQL, even though dBASE 5 native code is capable of managing distributed databases.

Recovering from Errors

The preceding example did not include error trapping or other niceties that make the difference between a professional application and one that is just thrown together. In your applications, however, be sure to include appropriate help screens and error messages as well as ways to recover from errors. The example did not include those additions for the sake of clarity while demonstrating the use of SQL embedded in dBASE programs. The ability to include error trapping and recovery is enhanced if you treat your application as a series of transactions. Remember that when you encounter an error that aborts a transaction, you can recover from it and put your data back in order with the ROLLBACK command.

Before you get to transactions, however, you need to understand a bit about how you might build an error recovery routine. As you learned at the beginning of Part 5, you must organize your application in terms of the modules required by the various choices in your menus. Later on, you learned about procedure libraries, and the preceding example demonstrated how you can create a procedure file with individual procedures for querying, appending to, deleting from, and updating a SQL table.

◄ See "Building a Procedure Library," p. 504

When you create a procedure library for your application, be sure to include a procedure for error recovery. Putting the error recovery procedure in the library is a better choice than trying to include it in each program module. Be careful, though. You must ensure that the procedure file is open whenever you perform a programming task. Otherwise, an error causes a second error because the recovery procedure cannot be found. In this case, the results are quite unpredictable. Finally, you need to allow for graceful recovery from errors on the part of your users, hardware or software failure, and intentional aborts through the Esc key.

In general, good error recovery requires that you stop program execution (the error usually does that for you), notify the user of the error and its nature, and offer a graceful recovery that does not jeopardize your application's data. Several kinds of errors can occur. Some you can trap; others, such as hardware failures, you cannot.

When you work with multiple data tables on a multiuser system, you really must use transaction-processing techniques to be able to recover from a hardware failure. Rolling back the transaction is the only way to put several related tables in balance after an interruption during an UPDATE or INSERT.

Errors that occur because the user made an incorrect entry are a bit easier to deal with. The first step in minimizing those errors is to ensure that you confine the acceptable input into a user field to the data type and value range appropriate for the module and table in use. You can do that with a combination of picture templates and the RANGE and VALID keywords in the @...SAY...GET construct. These also allow you to trap a user error and execute an error-recovery procedure. The errors you encounter in user input situations are called *soft errors*. They rarely require anything more than an error message and automatic return to the input field for another try.

Hard errors, however, require careful consideration and carefully prepared recovery techniques. You need to notify the user of the recovery's success or failure. Often, your user has nobody to turn to when an error occurs, and must figure out from the computer screen what happened.

Tip
After you've told the user an error occurs, be sure to provide a way out—either automatically or by user's actions.

In addition, you must avoid forward references to database objects in your programs when you use SQL to manage your data. You must define all database objects at the beginning of any program module that contains SQL commands. Unlike dBASE, dBASE SQL cannot look ahead.

Finally, you cannot create two SQL objects with the same name. This can seem like not much of a problem, but if you use a conditional, such as IF, and you attempt to create the same object in both the IF and the ELSE portions of the construct, the dBASE compiler responds with an error. You get the error even though you know that only one of the objects can ever exist at any one time because the IF forces a choice. The compiler, however, doesn't know that; it only knows that you tried to create two objects with the same name, and thus it reports an error.

Using SQL for Transaction Processing

You heard about transaction processing and now you're ready to dig into this technique for maintaining data integrity and concurrent control. As you learned earlier, when you use transaction processing, the only time the data table is locked is between the BEGIN TRANSACTION and END TRANSACTION commands. The following SQL commands are *not allowed* in transactions:

ALTER

CREATE

DBCHECK

DBDEFINE

DROP

GRANT

REVOKE

In general, you can insert almost any data-handling procedure in a transaction construct. The following rules apply:

- Place everything that prepares for the data handling—including the ON ERROR or ON ESCAPE commands—before the BEGIN TRANSACTION command.
- Before you start the actual transaction, insert a command that tells the transaction how many times to try before giving up.
- Put everything that has anything to do with access to a database and data tables inside the transaction construct.
- Place in memory variables any data that you need after the database is closed, and then work on it after the transaction ends.
- Stop the database (STOP DATABASE) before you exit the transaction.

Caution

Using the STOP DATABASE command before exiting the transaction is allowed, however all changes made during the transaction are committed.

One of the rules says that you need to specify a number of retries before the transaction code begins. To do this, you use the SET REPROCESS command. SET REPROCESS dictates the number of times dBASE attempts to get data from a table.

In any multiuser environment, a variety of things can stop your application from accessing data. Another user can be using the table, the network can be overloaded, or an error can occur. By setting the number of retries (reprocesses), you tell dBASE that you want it to attempt a reasonable number of times to complete the transaction. The result of all of those retries failing is called a *timeout*. Placing the SET REPROCESS command just outside the transaction construct tells dBASE to retry the transaction however many times you designate.

The following sample code shows the update procedure as a transaction.

BigUp2 lets you update a row. It is similar to the BigUpdate routine in BigApp and may be used in its place. This version includes transaction processing.

```
PROCEDURE BigUp2
   STORE .F.        TO m_response
   STORE SPACE(30) TO m_comp, m_com, m_con, m_name
   START DATABASE sales;
   CLEAR
   @ 5,5 SAY "Enter all or part of the company name: " GET m_comp
   READ
   STORE "%" + RTRIM(LTRIM(m_comp)) + "%" TO m_comp
   DECLARE BigSeekU CURSOR FOR
      SELECT companynm, contactnam
         FROM company
         WHERE companynm LIKE m_comp;
   OPEN  BigSeekU;
   FETCH BigSeekU INTO m_com, m_con;  && Try to get first match.
   IF SqlCode <> 0                    && Check for matches.
      @  8,20 SAY "         No matches found              "
      @ 10,20 SAY "Press any key to return to main menu..."
      READ
   ENDIF
   DO WHILE SqlCode = 0 .AND. (.NOT. m_response)
      * repeat until last fetch is unsuccessful or m_response
        ➥is True
      CLEAR
      @  0, 0 SAY "Here is an entry of the company: " + m_comp
      @  3, 2 SAY "Company. . . .    " + m_com
      @  4, 2 SAY "Contact. . . .    " + m_con
      STORE dialogYN("Do you want to update this contact name?")
      ➥TO m_response
      IF .NOT. m_response
        FETCH BigSeekU INTO m_com, m_con;  && Skip to next record
      ENDIF
   ENDDO
   CLOSE BigSeekU;
   STOP DATABASE;   && Unlock all tables while user is doing data
                    ➥entry
   IF m_response
      @ 7,0 SAY "Enter the new contact name: " GET m_name
      READ
      START DATABASE sales;
      BEGIN TRANSACTION   && Start keeping transaction log
      UPDATE company
         SET contactnam = m_name
         WHERE companynm = m_com AND contactnam = m_con;
      END TRANSACTION  && Update successful, erase transaction log
      STOP DATABASE;
   ENDIF
   CLEAR
RETURN
```

The main thing to notice about this rewrite of the procedure is that the data tables are open for significantly less time than they are in the Bigapp procedure file. In the original example, the database and its tables are open for the entire procedure. If a user is slow to enter the new phone number, the table is locked and unavailable for use by other users on a network.

In this latest example, the tables are locked only while the user acknowledges that the correct row is found (or dBASE 5 continues the search). From that point on, all operations on the data table are carried out by the program at program speed. Another point to notice is that the database must be started and stopped outside of the transaction construct. In order to limit the time that you have control of the database, place these commands immediately before and after the transaction. This example can be overzealous for the sake of illustration. With two transactions so close together, the database can be left open for both; it doesn't have to be closed between the transactions.

Note that this example does not have an error-handling procedure. If you try this program without such a procedure, you get another error, as you learned earlier. The location and commands for the error control are indicated in the example as comments.

From Here...

▶ See "SQL Set Commands," p. 832

You've seen how to program using dBASE language and now SQL. You learned to simplify your program, work with tables, manipulate data, and recover from errors. You saw how SQL trims a good deal of fat from your code, making it faster and more easily compatible with other database packages. You are well on your way to becoming a better programmer.

- Chapter 24, "Using SET Commands To Configure dBASE 5," shows you how to tailor your program's environment to create a professional application.

- Chapter 25, "Using SQL Commands," explains each SQL command's purpose and syntax.

- Chapter 27, "Using System Memory Variables," explains the purpose and syntax for using *<memvar>*.

Chapter 21

Creating Objects with UI

Earlier versions of dBASE allowed you to develop forms using the MODIFY SCREEN and @ commands. While these are still available in dBASE 5, an object-oriented form design capability has been added. All of the properties and commands required to create and modify forms are now directly available within your programs. You can use any text editor to develop your program and include UI objects. This can be useful if you don't have direct access to dBASE while coding. A graphic design tool, the Form Designer, has also been added to dBASE 5 to help you design forms, and it writes the code for you.

In this chapter you learn the basics of how to create a user interface (UI) using dBASE UI objects. You learn how to:

- Create a new form
- Modify the properties of objects
- Add objects to the form
- Create a menu

Creating a New Form

You normally design a form as part of an overall project. For this chapter, the task is to create a customer tracking system. The first step is to determine the fields that will be tracked. These fields are then used to create the CUSTOMER data table:

◄ See "Defining Your Database," p. 110

Table 21.1 Fields Used To Create Data Tables

FIELD_NAME	TYPE	LENGTH	INDEX
COMP_ID	CHARACTER	5	Y
COMPANY	CHARACTER	30	
C_ADDR1	CHARACTER	30	
C_ADDR2	CHARACTER	30	
C_CITY	CHARACTER	30	
C_STATE	CHARACTER	2	
C_ZIP	CHARACTER	10	
C_PHONE	CHARACTER	15	
C_FAX	CHARACTER	15	

Now you need to design the form so you can input data into this table.

Using the Form Designer

While you can design and code your forms in an editor, this doesn't allow you to see what you are producing. The Form Designer lets you position and size all the objects on your form. You can also use the Form Designer to write most of the code, and then use a text editor to modify the generated code. In this chapter, the use of the Form Designer will be covered and the generated code will be examined to show how the forms are implemented in code. The following steps explain how to use the Form Designer.

1. Open the **T**ools menu and choose **F**orm Designer. This opens the Open DFM File window shown in figure 21.1. All available Form Designer files, which have a default extension of DFM, are shown in the file list. To modify an existing form, you can select the disk, directory, and file you want to modify.

Tip
Form names must be at least two characters long.

2. To create a new file, type the new name, for example CUST_IN, in the file field.

3. Click on OK or press ENTER.

4. An Information window appears telling you that the file does not exist and asks if you want to create a new file. Click OK.

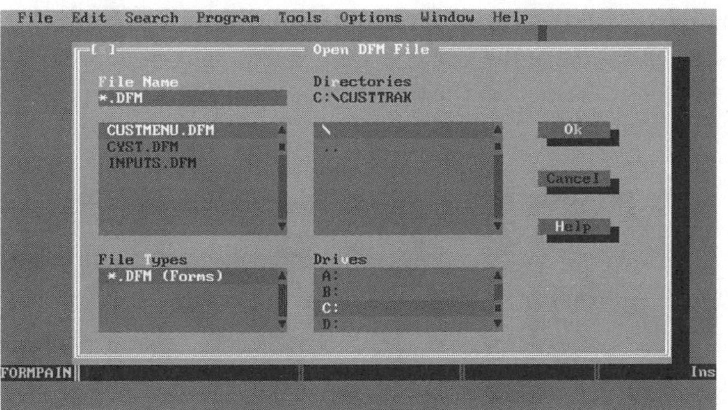

Fig. 21.1
Select any DFM file from the selection area to open a form file.

5. The Form Designer desktop is now on-screen as shown in figure 21.2, with the Form window containing your blank form, and the Object window containing icons for the various objects that can be added to your form.

6. To save the blank form, open the **F**ile menu and choose **S**ave. The Saving Form window briefly appears indicating the full path and file name that is being saved. The Form Designer saves the commands required to generate the form exactly as it is on the screen to a text file named the same as the form with a DFM extension. An additional file to control the display and actions of the form is also created and saved. This file has the same name as the form and a PRG extension.

Tip
If you opened a data table with USE or CREATE commands, a third window showing the table fields is also displayed.

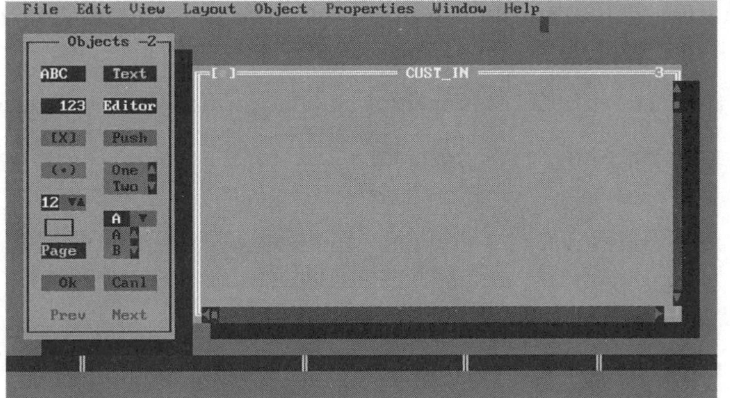

Fig. 21.2
The Form Designer provides a menu and two windows to aid in designing your form.

Changing Properties Using the Object Inspector

▶ See "Left," p. 947

To see the properties of the CUST_IN form object, right-click the form, select **W**indow, Object **i**nspector. The Object Inspector window is displayed as shown in figure 21.3.

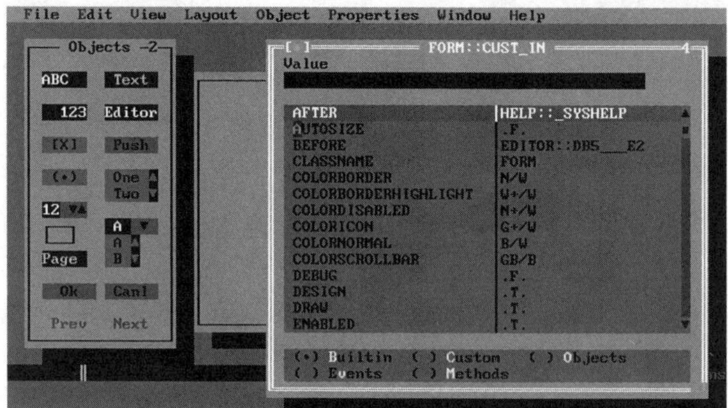

Fig. 21.3
You can change properties using the Object Inspector.

The properties are shown in alphabetical order for the object listed in the title line, in this case FORM::CUST_IN. Most of the values are set to their defaults (see Chapter 26 for UI property defaults). Use the scroll bar on the right to go down the list to the LEFT property. You can see that it shows 21.

To change the value of any of the properties, select the property by double-clicking on it. The cursor is placed in the value field so you can edit the property value. The value field is an example of a SCROLLBOX object. You can directly type in the desired value, use the scroll bar to select a value, or use the up and down arrows to increment or decrement the value.

1. Double-click the LEFT property. The value 21 shows in the value field.
2. Click twice on the up arrow in the scroll bar. The value is increased to 23.
3. Press Enter to save the new value. In the background, you will see the Form window is immediately repositioned to the new location.
4. Click the close box in the upper-left corner of the window to close the Object Inspector.

At this point you can examine the code that has already been created. Open the **F**ile menu and choose Sa**v**e, Exit (or press Alt-F4). The Saving Form window appears briefly, and the Form Designer, Objects, and Form window all close.

Using the DEFINE FORM Command

Open the **F**ile menu and choose **O**pen. Select File **T**ype *.DFM. All the Form Designer form files are now shown in the file list. Select CUST_IN.DFM. The code shown in Listing 21.1 is now shown in the program editor window.

Listing 21.1 The Form Designer Saves Object Code

```
*.......................................................
* C:\CUSTTRAK\CUST_IN.DFM
*   08/02/94  21:13:48
*.......................................................

DEFINE FORM CUST_IN ;
   PROPERTY ;
     HEIGHT            16,;
     LEFT              23,;
     TEXT              "CUST_IN",;
     TOP               3,;
     WIDTH             55

CUST_IN.DISPMODE          = "VGA25"
CUST_IN.MODALFORM         = .T.       && .T. ReadModal(), .F. Open()
CUST_IN.NFLDPLC           = 1         && Last field # placed on form
CUST_IN.NLEFT             = 1         && Next column to place an
object
CUST_IN.NOBJCTR           = 0         && Next number for object
naming
CUST_IN.NTOP              = 1         && Next row to place an object
CUST_IN.SETDISP           = .T.
CUST_IN.SETDISP           = .T.       && .T. change display mode, .F.
maintain display mode
CUST_IN.DISPMODE          = "VGA25"  && Default display mode

*...........................................................
```

This is the code written by the Form Designer to create the blank form on the screen. The FORM object CUST_IN is created using the DEFINE FORM command. The properties that are set are based on the size and location of the form window that was shown on the screen. The properties are:

- The HEIGHT property indicates the number of lines the form window occupies on the screen.
- The LEFT property shows the number of the character column from the left edge of the screen to the left edge of the form window. Remember, the leftmost column on the screen is number 0.

- The TEXT property is the title of the form window.
- The TOP property shows the line number of the top of the form window. Remember that the top line of the screen is number 0.
- The WIDTH property is the width in characters of the form window.

If you modify the code here, the changes will be reflected when you go back into the Form Designer to work on this form. For example, change TOP to 2 and LEFT to 25. This will move the top-left corner of the window up and two spaces to the right. Save the file by selecting **F**ile, **S**ave, and exit the program editor by clicking on the close button in the upper left.

The second file that was created is the program file used to display the form. You also can access this file with the Program Editor. Open the **F**ile menu and choose **O**pen, then choose CUST_IN.PRG from the file list. The code in Listing 21.2 is shown in the Program Editor window.

Tip
Using the #include preprocessor directive allows you to divide your code into smaller, more manageable files.

Listing 21.2 Use Dot Reference Notation To Change Properties.

```
* dBASE 5.0 DFM DRIVER - Do not remove this line
PROCEDURE CUST_IN     && Main program
*------------------------------------------------------------
* NAME
*    C:\CUSTTRAK\CUST_IN.PRG - Main program for form.
*
*------------------------------------------------------------
     PRIVATE lTalk, lVoid, cOldProc, cFormRun, cDispMode, cNewMode
     IF SET( 'TALK' ) = 'ON'
          SET TALK OFF
          lTalk = .T.
     ELSE
          lTalk = .F.
     ENDIF

     *------------------------------------------
     *-- Make sure that FormRun.dbo file is active
     *------------------------------------------
     cOldProc = SET( 'PROCEDURE' )
     cFormRun = HOME() + 'FORMRUN.DBO'
     SET PROCEDURE TO &cFormRun

     #include "CUST_IN.DFM"

     IF TYPE("CUST_IN.SetDisp") = "L" .AND.TYPE("CUST_IN.DispMode")= "C"
        IF CUST_IN.SetDisp
              cDispMode = SET('DISPLAY')
              cNewMode = CUST_IN.DispMode
              SET DISPLAY TO &cNewMode
```

```
        ENDIF
ENDIF

 *------------------------------------------
 *-- If ModalForm is missing from .DFM set it
 *------------------------------------------
 IF TYPE( 'CUST_IN.ModalForm' ) # 'L'
       CUST_IN.ModalForm = .T.  && Assume modal form if not set
 ENDIF

 *----------------------------------
 *-- Open the form based on ModalForm
 *----------------------------------
 IF CUST_IN.ModalForm

       *----------------------------------
       *-- Use Readmodal() to open the form
       *----------------------------------
       CUST_IN.Action = .F. && Set .T. by OKHAND before closing
       lVoid = CUST_IN.ReadModal()

       IF CUST_IN.Action
             *------------------------------------------
             *-- Place code here to process OK pushbutton
             *------------------------------------------
       ENDIF

       IF TYPE("CUST_IN.SetDisp") = "L"
             IF CUST_IN.SetDisp
                   SET DISPLAY TO &cDispMode
             ENDIF
        ENDIF

       RELEASE CUST_IN      && Release the form and object ref.

 ELSE

       *-----------------------------
       *-- Use Open() to open the form
       *-----------------------------
       lVoid = CUST_IN.Open()

       *-----------------------------------------
       *-- Make the form release itself when closed
       *-- Comment out the RELEASE command to keep
       *-- the form defined when closed.
       *-----------------------------------------
       RELEASE CUST_IN

 ENDIF

 IF .NOT. ISBLANK( m->cOldProc )
       SET PROCEDURE TO &cOldProc
 ENDIF
```

(continues)

Listing 21.2 Continued

```
          IF lTalk
               SET TALK ON
          ENDIF

     RETURN
     *-- EOP: C:\CUSTTRAK\CUST_IN.PRG
```

This file shows several good examples for using forms in your programs.

- A header section provides information on the file name and the purpose of the procedure.
- The existing state of the TALK setting is saved so it can be restored at the end of the procedure.
- The commands to create the form are brought into the file using the #include "CUST_IN.DFM" preprocessor directive.
- The ACTION property of the form is modified using dot reference notation. The syntax for dot reference notation is `<object name>.<member name>`, where member name is any property, method, or object associated with the object *<object name>*. This allows you to directly access any method, property, or contained object of an object.
- The form is displayed using the READMODAL( ) method of the form object. This is the default mode of generation of the Form Designer, and can be changed from the Form Designer Properties Options menu.

Exit the program editor by clicking on the close button in the upper-left corner.

Adding Objects to the Form

Type USE in the Command window to close any open data tables. Open the **T**ools menu and choose **F**orm Designer to start the Form Designer again. This time double-click the CUST_IN form from the file menu and the Form Designer comes up with your form loaded. So far your form is only a blank window on the screen. To make it useful, you need to add objects for descriptive text, fields, and menus.

Adding Field Entry Objects

You can associate the form with any data table using the file menu. Select **F**ile, **U**se different table. The Open DBF File window appears to let you select from any data table. Select CUSTOMER.DBF by double-clicking it. A window with the fields in the CUSTOMER data table is added to the Form Designer window. You can add and place the individual fields on the screen using the Add button at the bottom of the data table window. When you click Add, two objects are added to your form, a text object showing the name of the field, and an Entry Field object for the field data.

To quickly add all the fields to the form, open the **L**ayout menu and choose **Q**uick Layout. A selection window appears so you can select the way the fields are placed on the form.

- Vertical places all the field names on the left and the entry field for the data aligned starting in column 13. Each field occupies one line, with no blank lines.
- Top labels places all the fields on the form with as many fields as will fit on each line. The field names are above each entry field. A blank line is placed between the line of EntryFields and the next line of field labels.
- Left labels is similar to the vertical layout. All the field names are to the left of the field name, but an additional blank line is placed between each line.

Click the **V**ertical radio button. Click **O**K and all of the fields from the CUSTOMER data table are added to the form in the Vertical format.

Adding Control Objects

All of the fields required to update your data table are now shown on the form. To make the form useful, you need to add a way for the user to accept or reject the information on the screen. The best way is to add pushbuttons to your form. Objects are available from the Object Palette in the Object window or from the Object choice on the menu.

▶ See "DEFINE PUSHBUTTON," p. 1026

1. Click the Object window to make it active and click the OK button; or select **O**bject, **P**ushbutton and click **O**K. An OK pushbutton object is added to your form.
2. Click the CANCEL button object on the Object Palette. A CANCEL pushbutton is added to your form under the OK push button.

Your form is now fully functional. Open the **F**ile menu and choose **S**ave.

Customizing the Form Objects

Using the mouse or the Object Inspector, you can change the properties of all of the objects in your form. To open the object inspector on a specific object, you place the cursor on the object and right-click. The Object Inspector window will display the properties for the selected object. Right-clicking on a part of the form with no objects will open the Object Inspector with the form properties.

> **Note**
>
> You can resize the entire form by selecting the lower-right corner and dragging it to the desired size. You can also place the form anywhere on the screen by clicking on the top line and dragging the window to a new location.

To select one of the objects on the form, click the object and it will be highlighted. You can then use the mouse to drag the object to a new location. You can also drag the lower-right corner to resize the object.

▶ See "DEFINE ENTRYFIELD," p. 1005

You may want to restrict the choices that the user has for some of the fields. By default, all of the fields are entered into the form as entry field objects. To change the field type:

1. Click the C_STATE entry field, the empty field beside the C_STATE text object, to select it.

2. Press Ctrl-Delete to delete the object.

▶ See "DEFINE COMBOBOX," p. 996

3. Click the Object window to make it the active window.

4. Click the ComboBox object. On the Object Palette, the ComboBox appears as a single choice A, with a down arrow beside it and a list below it (A, B) with a scroll bar (see fig. 21.4).

5. Click the field and drag it up to where the C_STATE entry field was deleted.

6. Drag the right edge to make the value field only two characters wide.

▶ See "DataLink," p. 922

7. With the mouse in the Combobox, right-click to enter the Object Inspector.

8. Scroll down to the DATALINK property and double-click it.

▶ See "DataSource," p. 923

9. Type CUSTOMER->C_STATE in the value field and press ENTER. This sets the field that will store the value from the form.

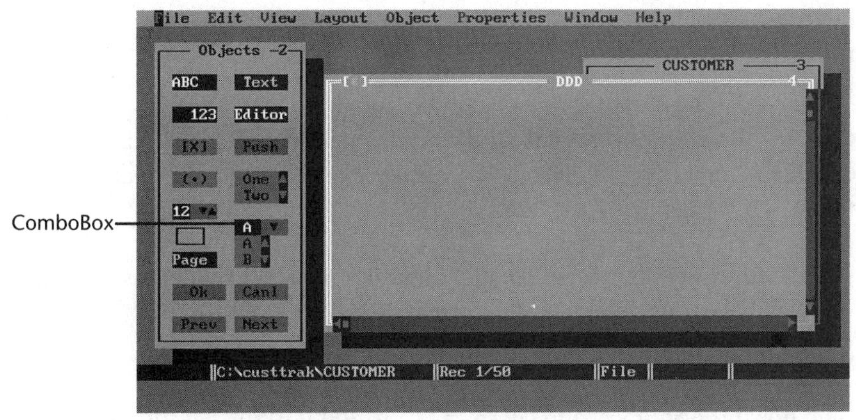

Fig. 21.4
A ComboBox appears below the last field.

10. Double-click the DATASOURCE property and type:

    STRING VA,IN,OH,PA,MD,KY,WV

    This creates a selection list for the field and ties a permanent limit directly into the form. To have a dynamic list, you can use an array that gets filled with the valid values in your program. To do this, set the DATASOURCE to ARRAY VALID_STATES. You would then load your valid state codes into the array VALID_STATES in your program. Other alternatives are shown in Chapter 24.

11. Select the STYLE property. By default, the value is 1, which allows the users to type in numbers or select from the list.

12. Change the value to 2 to restrict the user to picking off the list and press Enter.

▶ See "Style," p. 974

You can click the close box to close the Object Inspector, but because the form is visible behind it, you can make a selection on it.

▶ See "DEFINE TEXT," p. 1037

1. Click the COMP_ID text object and drag it to the top-left corner of the form.

2. Right-click the COMP_ID text object. This opens the Object Inspector on the properties for that object.

3. Scroll down to the TEXT property (or type text) and double-click it to let you change the value.

4. Type in **&Identifier**. Press return to store the value in the property. Using the '&' in front of a letter in the text value sets the letter as

▶ See "Text," p. 976

pickletter value that allows the field to be selected with ALT-<*pickletter*> when the form is executed. The field automatically resizes to handle the text entered.

5. Click the form window to make it the active window and change the COMPANY text to be &*Company name* using the same method. Change the C_ADDR1 text to be &Address.

Because the Address text object sufficiently identifies the block of address fields, you can delete the remaining field labels.

1. Select the C_ADDR2 text object.
2. Hold down the Shift key and click C_CITY to add it to the selection.
3. Add C_STATE and C_ZIP to the selection also using Shift-Click.
4. Press Ctrl-Delete to delete the objects from the form.

To relocate the identifier field and modify it, follow these steps:

1. Click the COMP_ID field and drag it to one space right of the end of the text Identifier.

► See "StatusMessage," p. 973

2. Right-click to display the Object Inspector for the COMP_ID entry field object.
3. Scroll down and double-click the STATUSMESSAGE property. Text entered in the value field here will be displayed on the status line when the form is executed and the cursor is in the COMP_ID entry field.
4. Type:

   Enter the identification number of the company

5. Press return to save the text as the value of STATUSMESSAGE. Other properties that can be changed are shown in Chapter 22.

To rearrange the rest of the fields, follow these steps:

1. Click and drag the C_STATE and C_ZIP entry fields to the end of the line with C_City.
2. You may need to resize the form to be able to see all the fields. Click and drag the lower-right corner of the form until all fields are visible.

3. Click and drag the C_PHONE and C_FAX numbers so they are on one line below the address. You may change the text displayed for these fields using the Object Inspector.

4. Click and drag each of the pushbutton objects so that they are in a single row below the PHONE and FAX numbers.

If you want to have a title at the top of your window, follow these steps:

1. To allow room at the top of the form for a title, select all the fields by opening the **E**dit menu and choosing **S**elect.

2. Click any object and drag all the objects down two lines.

3. Click the Objects window and double-click the text object in the Object Palette. A new text object is placed below the row of pushbuttons.

4. Drag the object to the top of the form.

5. Right-click to modify the properties.

6. Select COLORNORMAL and change it to N/W to have the title appear as gray on white.

7. Select the TEXT property and change it to CUSTOMER COMPANY INFORMATION as a title for your form.

8. To save the form, open the **F**ile menu and choose **S**ave.

► See "ColorNormal," p. 917

Tip
Select a field and use **L**ayout, **A**dd Help to add field-sensitive help to your form.

Your form will now appear similar to the form shown in figure 21.5.

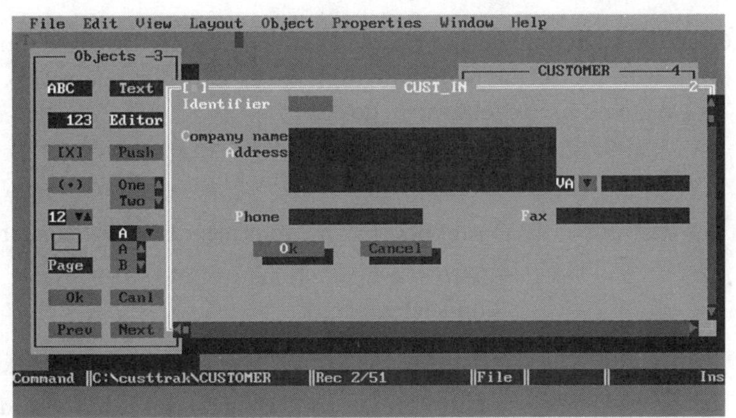

Fig. 21.5
Design your form for a professional appearance.

Troubleshooting

I clicked on an object in the object selector, but nothing appeared on my form.

The Form Designer inserts objects below the last placed object on the form. If the last object placed on the form was at the bottom of the form window, the next object placed is off the screen. You need to enlarge your window so you can see the new object.

Creating a Menu

Now that you have a data entry and display form, you need a way to let the user select an action to perform. The Form Designer also provides access to the Menu Designer. The Menu Designer creates pull-down style menus. All menu objects are associated with a form.

Generate the Default Menu

One of the fastest ways to add a menu to your form is to use the default menu. To use the default menu, follow these steps:

1. With your form loaded in the Form Designer, select **P**roperties, **G**eneration.

2. Click the **C**reate default menu for form check box in the Generation options window.

3. Click OK to save the options.

4. Open the **L**ayout menu and choose **C**reate. The Menu Designer window opens with the default bar menu displayed as shown in figure 21.6. This menu offers the following choices:

Files	**E**xit (Alt-F4) exits the form
Records	**A**dd new records adds records to the data table.
	Set/Clear deletion mark (Ctrl-U) deletes or undeletes records
Search	**T**op Record Ctrl-PgUp goes to the first record.
	Last Record Ctrl-PgDn goes to the last record.
	Record number goes to a specific record.
	S**k**ip skips a certain number of records.
	Index key changes the index being used.

Forward sets the search direction forward.

Backward sets the search direction backward.

Match capitalization determines whether search pays attention to the case of the search string

Organize — **O**rder records creates new indexes

Help — **H**elp index displays the main help menu.

Keyboard help gives help on the keyboard keys.

A**c**tive field displays help on the current field.

About displays information on the application.

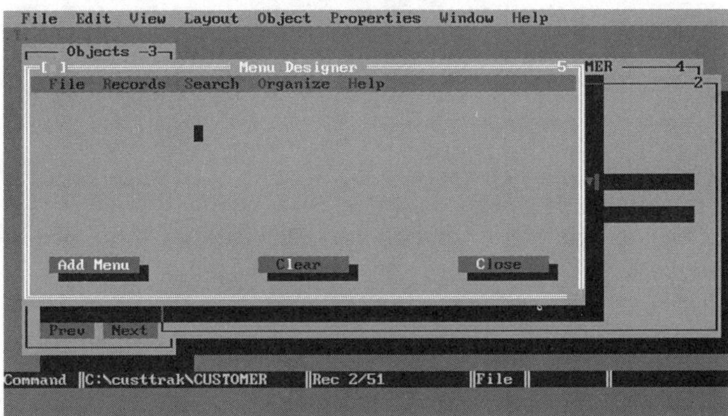

Fig. 21.6
The default menu speeds menu design.

This menu provides most of the options that you would need for an application. Each menu choice has a pull-down menu that can be seen by clicking on the menu choice. Each of the pull-down menus has the choice <*New*>. Don't delete this choice or you won't be able to add choices to the pull-down menus.

Modify a Menu

To add a choice on the bar menu, click the Add Menu button. The Menu Inspector window opens with <*&New*> loaded into the **T**ext field as shown in figure 21.7. Type **&Print** to add a print choice to the main menu. Select the St**a**tus Line Message field to change the message that appears at the bottom of the screen when the Print choice is selected on the menu bar then type:

"Print a report from the data table

The procedure file name is already loaded with the name of the procedure file for the form. If you want to associate the selection of this menu choice with an event handler, the OnClick field allows you to enter the name of the event handler. Click on OK to save the new pad for the bar menu and see the new menu with the additional choice.

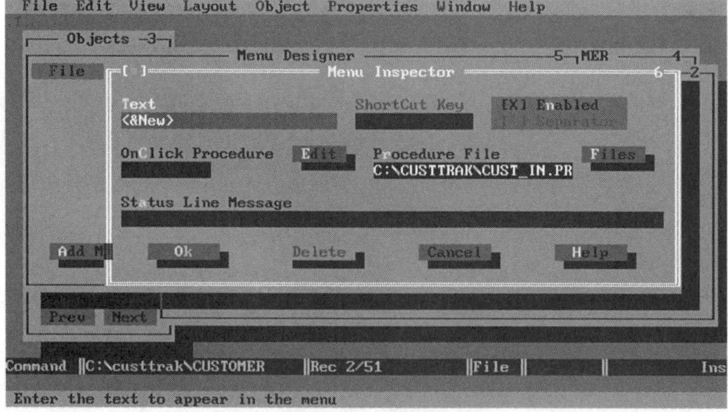

Fig. 21.7 The Menu Inspector lets you set the properties for the menu items in your application.

Click Print to open the pull-down menu. This brings up the Edit Menu window as shown in figure 21.8 with a choice to **E**dit the Menu or O**p**en the Menu. Select O**p**en the Menu and click OK and the pull-down menu for Print is displayed with one entry, <**N**ew>.

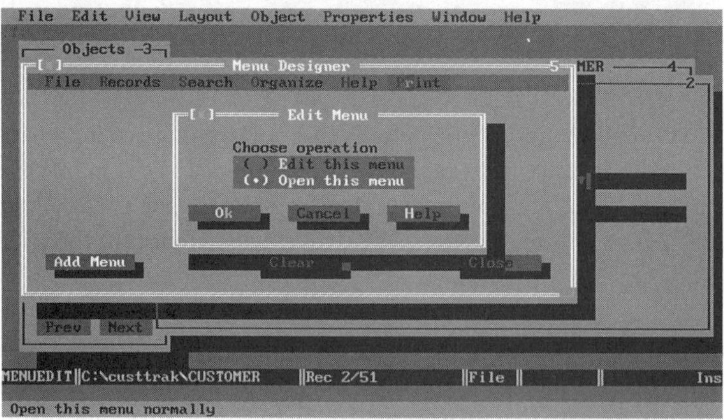

Fig. 21.8 The Edit Menu window allows you to change or open a menu file.

1. To add a choice to a pull-down menu, click the <New> choice on the menu. The Select Action window as shown in figure 21.9 is opened which allows you to add an item or a submenu to a pull-down menu.

2. Select Add new **i**tem to this menu and click **O**K to open the Menu Inspector window. The **T**ext field will be loaded with the choice from the menu, in this case <&New>.

3. Type the new menu choice, &Customer ID list, into the Text field.

4. Click on the On**C**lick field and type in the name of the event handler, CIDLIST. This is a procedure that you write to execute when the user selects the Customer ID List choice off the Print menu.

5. Click the Edit button to create the CIDLIST procedure. The Program Editor is started with the procedure header, title, and return statement already inserted and the cursor positioned where the first command line would go.

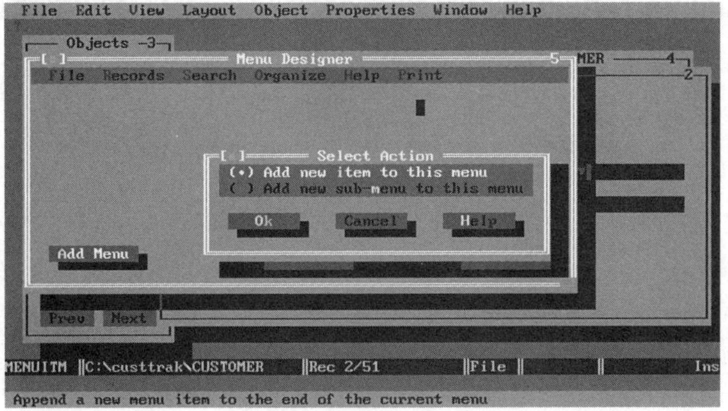

Fig. 21.9 The Select Action window lets you choose between adding a menu item or a sub-menu to an existing menu.

Type in the commands necessary to generate the report:

```
PROCEDURE CIDLIST      && dbMItem1.ONCLICK
*-----------------------------------------------------------------
* NAME
*   ONCLICK - Event handler for dbMItem1
*
*-----------------------------------------------------------------
    SET ORDER TO CUST_ID
    LIST OFF TO PRINT
RETURN
```

Click the Close box to close the Program Editor window and click Yes when prompted to save your changes. Select the St**a**tus Line Message field and type the description, **Customers sorted by ID number**. Click OK to save the menu choice.

Tip
The selected window's bar menu is accessed whenever you use Alt-key combinations. If the Create File window is active, Alt-F takes you to the Create File menu, not the Form Designer menu.

To save the form as modified and exit the Form Designer, select **F**ile, Sa**v**e and Exit from the Form Designer menu.

Editing the Command Files

The Form Designer has now created three different files, CUST_IN.PRG, CUST_IN.DFM, and CUST_IN.MNU. The PRG file contains all the commands used to run the form and any event handlers you wrote as shown in Listing 21.3. The DFM file contains the form setup and display commands as shown in Listing 21.4. The MNU file contains all the code necessary to generate the menus as shown in Listing 21.5.

Listing 21.3 The PRG File Provides Event and Form Control

```
* dBASE 5.0 DFM DRIVER - Do not remove this line
PROCEDURE CUST_IN     && Main program
*-------------------------------------------------------------------
* NAME
*   C:\CUSTTRAK\CUST_IN.PRG - Main program for form.
*
*-------------------------------------------------------------------
     PRIVATE lTalk, lVoid, cOldProc, cFormRun, cDispMode, cNewMode
     IF SET( 'TALK' ) = 'ON'
           SET TALK OFF
           lTalk = .T.
     ELSE
           lTalk = .F.
     ENDIF

     *--------------------------------------------
     *-- Make sure that FormRun.dbo file is active
     *--------------------------------------------
     cOldProc = SET( 'PROCEDURE' )
     cFormRun = HOME() + 'FORMRUN.DBO'
     SET PROCEDURE TO &cFormRun

    #include "CUST_IN.DFM"

     IF TYPE("CUST_IN.SetDisp") = "L" .AND.TYPE("CUST_IN.DispMode")= "C"
           IF CUST_IN.SetDisp
                 cDispMode = SET('DISPLAY')
                 cNewMode = CUST_IN.DispMode
                 SET DISPLAY TO &cNewMode
           ENDIF
     ENDIF

     *--------------------------------------------
     *-- If ModalForm is missing from .DFM set it
     *--------------------------------------------
     IF TYPE( 'CUST_IN.ModalForm' ) # 'L'
```

```
        CUST_IN.ModalForm = .T.  && Assume modal form if not set
    ENDIF

    *----------------------------------
    *-- Open the form based on ModalForm
    *----------------------------------
    IF CUST_IN.ModalForm

        *----------------------------------
        *-- Use Readmodal() to open the form
        *----------------------------------
        CUST_IN.Action = .F. && Set .T. by OKHAND before closing
        lVoid = CUST_IN.ReadModal()

        IF CUST_IN.Action
            *------------------------------------------
            *-- Place code here to process OK pushbutton
            *------------------------------------------
        ENDIF

        IF TYPE("CUST_IN.SetDisp") = "L"
            IF CUST_IN.SetDisp
                SET DISPLAY TO &cDispMode
            ENDIF
        ENDIF

        RELEASE CUST_IN      && Release the form and object ref.

     ELSE

        *-----------------------------
        *-- Use Open() to open the form
        *-----------------------------
        lVoid = CUST_IN.Open()

        *-----------------------------------------
        *-- Make the form release itself when closed
        *-- Comment out the RELEASE command to keep
        *-- the form defined when closed.
        *-----------------------------------------
        RELEASE CUST_IN

    ENDIF

    IF .NOT. ISBLANK( m->cOldProc )
        SET PROCEDURE TO &cOldProc
    ENDIF

    IF lTalk
        SET TALK ON
    ENDIF

RETURN
*-- EOP: C:\CUSTTRAK\CUST_IN.PRG
```

(continues)

Listing 21.3 Continued

```
PROCEDURE CIDLIST     && DBMITEM1.ONCLICK
*-----------------------------------------------------------------
* NAME
*   ONCLICK - Event handler for DBMITEM1
*
*-----------------------------------------------------------------
     SET ORDER TO Comp_Id
     LIST OFF TO PRINT
RETURN


PROCEDURE HelpObj
*------------------------------------------------------------
* NAME
*   HelpObj
*
* DESCRIPTION
*   Displays help for the currently selected object, if any
*
*------------------------------------------------------------
   DO HelpDspy WITH Form.ActiveControl()
RETURN
```

The CUST_IN.PRG file is broken into two procedures, the main CUST_IN procedure and CIDLIST which handles the Print report. CUST_IN contains three blocks of code. The first block, starting with PRIVATE lTalk and ending with ENDIF, saves the current status of the TALK environment setting and turns it OFF. As mentioned earlier, the #include preprocessor directive has been used to bring in the code from CUST_IN.DFM. This allows the code for the form design to be placed in a separate file and then brought in where it is needed. The second block of code starts after #include and ends before the IF lTalk. This is the block which actually displays the form, using the READMODAL( ) method. The OPEN( ) method could also be used, and this choice can be selected in the Form Designer. Open the **P**roperties menu and choose **G**eneration, O**p**en.

The CUST_IN.Action property allows you to program an action to be taken if the user presses OK to exit your form. The Rlease( ) clears the form from the screen. The last block resets TALK to its original value.

Listing 21.4 The DFM File Contains Form Display Objects

```
*.......................................................
* C:\CUSTTRAK\CUST_IN.DFM
*   08/03/94  00:08:30
*.......................................................
*  Define the form that the user will see
DEFINE FORM CUST_IN ;
  PROPERTY ;
     HEIGHT          16,;
     LEFT            17,;
     TEXT            "CUST_IN",;
     TOP             3,;
     WIDTH           62

CUST_IN.CURRMAST   = "CUSTOMER"     && Name of Master alias for form
CUST_IN.MODALFORM = .T.            && .T. ReadModal(), .F. Open()
CUST_IN.NEXTDBF    = "2"            && Next available work area
CUST_IN.NFLDPLC    = 10             && Last field # placed on form
CUST_IN.NLEFT      = 1              && Next column to place an object
CUST_IN.NOBJCTR    = 3              && Next number for object naming
CUST_IN.NTOP       = 13             && Next row to place an object
CUST_IN.SETDISP    = .T.            && .T. change display mode, .F.
maintain display mode
CUST_IN.DISPMODE   = "VGA25"        && Default display mode

*............................................................

*-----------------------------------------------------------------
*-- Set up file structure. This techinique uses a MenuBar object with
*-- menu items for each DBF file the form uses as a linked list.  The
*-- Menubar is attached to the form as a custom property.  This way
*-- the list of files does not conflict with other memory variables.
*-----------------------------------------------------------------
CUST_IN.FileList = FileList
RELEASE FileList

*-----------------------------------------------------------------
*-- If the Master database is already open, get the record number,
*-- close the databases, and re-open on the record number.
*-----------------------------------------------------------------
SELECT 1
PRIVATE nCUSTOMER , fCUSTOMER
IF FileRoot( DBF() ) == 'CUSTOMER' .AND. .NOT. EOF()
   nCUSTOMER = RECNO()
   fCUSTOMER = SET( 'FILTER' )
ELSE
   nCUSTOMER = 0
   fCUSTOMER = ''
ENDIF

CLOSE DATABASE
USE CUSTOMER.DBF ALIAS CUSTOMER
IF nCUSTOMER > 0
   GO nCUSTOMER
```

(continues)

Listing 21.4 Continued

```
   IF .NOT. ISBLANK( fCUSTOMER )
       SET FILTER TO &fCUSTOMER
   ENDIF
ENDIF

*-------------------------------------------------------
*-- Define the menu that represents the master database
*-------------------------------------------------------
DEFINE MENU File1 OF CUST_IN.FileList ;
   PROPERTY ;
       Text        DBF() , ;
       StatusMessage   [Master] ;
   CUSTOM ;
       FileAlias   ALIAS() , ;
       ErrorDBF    .F.

#include "CUST_IN.MNU"

DEFINE TEXT CFDNAME1 OF M->CUST_IN ;
  PROPERTY ;
     LEFT             1,;
     TEXT             "&Identifier",;
     TOP              0,;
     WIDTH            11

DEFINE ENTRYFIELD COMP_ID001 OF M->CUST_IN ;
  PROPERTY ;
     DATALINK         "CUSTOMER->COMP_ID",;
     LEFT             13,;
     PICTURE          "XXXXX",;
     TOP              0,;
     WIDTH            5

DEFINE TEXT CFDNAME2 OF M->CUST_IN ;
  PROPERTY ;
     LEFT             1,;
     TEXT             "&Company name",;
     TOP              2,;
     WIDTH            13

DEFINE ENTRYFIELD COMPANY002 OF M->CUST_IN ;
  PROPERTY ;
     DATALINK         "CUSTOMER->COMPANY",;
     LEFT             13,;
     PICTURE          "XXXXXXXXXXXXXXXXXXXXXXXXXXXXXX",;
     TOP              2,;
     WIDTH            30

DEFINE TEXT CFDNAME3 OF M->CUST_IN ;
  PROPERTY ;
     LEFT             6,;
     TEXT             "&Address",;
     TOP              3,;
     WIDTH            8
```

```
DEFINE ENTRYFIELD C_ADDR1003 OF M->CUST_IN ;
  PROPERTY ;
     DATALINK          "CUSTOMER->C_ADDR1",;
     LEFT              13,;
     PICTURE           "XXXXXXXXXXXXXXXXXXXXXXXXXXXXXX",;
     TOP               3,;
     WIDTH             30

DEFINE ENTRYFIELD C_ADDR2004 OF M->CUST_IN ;
  PROPERTY ;
     DATALINK          "CUSTOMER->C_ADDR2",;
     LEFT              13,;
     PICTURE           "XXXXXXXXXXXXXXXXXXXXXXXXXXXXXX",;
     TOP               4,;
     WIDTH             30

DEFINE ENTRYFIELD C_CITY005 OF M->CUST_IN ;
  PROPERTY ;
     DATALINK          "CUSTOMER->C_CITY",;
     LEFT              13,;
     PICTURE           "XXXXXXXXXXXXXXXXXXXXXXXXXXXXXX",;
     TOP               5,;
     WIDTH             30

DEFINE ENTRYFIELD C_ZIP007 OF M->CUST_IN ;
  PROPERTY ;
     DATALINK          "CUSTOMER->C_ZIP",;
     LEFT              48,;
     PICTURE           "XXXXXXXXXX",;
     TOP               5,;
     WIDTH             10

DEFINE TEXT CFDNAME8 OF M->CUST_IN ;
  PROPERTY ;
     LEFT              7,;
     TEXT              "&Phone",;
     TOP               7,;
     WIDTH             6

DEFINE ENTRYFIELD PHONE008 OF M->CUST_IN ;
  PROPERTY ;
     DATALINK          "CUSTOMER->PHONE",;
     LEFT              13,;
     PICTURE           "XXXXXXXXXXXXXXX",;
     TOP               7,;
     WIDTH             15

DEFINE TEXT CFDNAME9 OF M->CUST_IN ;
  PROPERTY ;
     LEFT              39,;
     TEXT              "&Fax",;
     TOP               7,;
     WIDTH             4
```

(continues)

Listing 21.4 Continued

```
DEFINE ENTRYFIELD FAX009 OF M->CUST_IN ;
  PROPERTY ;
     DATALINK          "CUSTOMER->FAX",;
     LEFT              43,;
     PICTURE           "XXXXXXXXXXXXXXX",;
     TOP               7,;
     WIDTH             15

DEFINE COMBOBOX CMNAME1 OF M->CUST_IN ;
  PROPERTY ;
     DATALINK          "customer->c_state",;
     DATASOURCE        "string VA,IN,OH,PA,MD,KY,WV",;
     LEFT              43,;
     STYLE             2,;
     TOP               5,;
     WIDTH             5

DEFINE PUSHBUTTON BTOK OF M->CUST_IN ;
  PROPERTY ;
     LEFT              8,;
     ONCLICK           OKHand,;
     TEXT              "&Ok",;
     TOP               9,;
     WIDTH             10

CUST_IN.BTOK.Procfile      = "OKHAND.PRG," + HOME() + "FORMRUN.DBO"

DEFINE PUSHBUTTON BTCANCEL OF M->CUST_IN ;
  PROPERTY ;
     LEFT              20,;
     ONCLICK           CanHand,;
     TEXT              "Cancel",;
     TOP               9,;
     WIDTH             10

CUST_IN.BTCANCEL.Procfile = "CANHAND.PRG," + HOME() + "FORMRUN.DBO"
```

The form and all the objects contained within it are defined in the CUST_IN.DFM file. The first command defines the form, its position relative to the active window, its size, and the text that will appear as the form window title. The continuation character ; is used to break the command across several lines to make it easier to read. The dot reference notation is used to establish the values of several of the properties, as noted in the comments.

A top level menubar is created to store the master data table reference information. The handle for this menubar is stored in a custom property of the form and the variable name is released to allow it to be used by your program. This keeps the data tables used by your form tightly associated with the form object.

The #include command is used to bring the form menu description in from the CUST_IN.MNU file. This method allows you to break your code into managable file segments. The defined menus could also be used in other forms since the definitions are separated from the form file.

The remaining paragraphs are the commands for displaying the text and fields on the form. Each paragraph is one command, broken down to make the code easy to read. The properties that are different from the defaults are specifically set in each command. As a minimum this includes the location and size of the text or field.

The entryfields require the DATALINK property to show what data table field or memory variable they are accepting input for and displaying. The scrollbox has an additional property, DATASOURCE, which indicates the location of the possible valid responses that is displayed in the scrolled list.

For the pushbuttons defined at the end of the listing, the procedure that will be run when the button is pressed is set using the ONCLICK property. The PROCFILE property sets the name of the procedure file that contains procedure indicated by ONCLICK.

Listing 21.5 The MNU File Contains the Menu Commands

```
* CUST_IN.MNU
* 08/03/94  00:08:32

DEFINE MENUBAR MenuBar1 OF CUST_IN

DEFINE MENU DBMBAR1 OF CUST_IN.MenuBar1;
  PROPERTY ;
     STATUSMESSAGE "File operations",;
     TEXT "&File"

DEFINE MENUITEM DBMITEM1 OF CUST_IN.MenuBar1.DBMBAR1;
  PROPERTY ;
     ONCLICK  MDExit,;
     PROCFILE "MDExit.PRG," + HOME() + "FORMRUN.DBO",;
     SHORTCUT "Ctrl-F4",;
     STATUSMESSAGE "Close the form",;
     TEXT "E&xit"

DEFINE MENU DBMBAR2 OF CUST_IN.MenuBar1;
  PROPERTY ;
     STATUSMESSAGE "Record operations",;
     TEXT "&Records"

DEFINE MENUITEM DBMITEM1 OF CUST_IN.MenuBar1.DBMBAR2;
  PROPERTY ;
     ONCLICK  MDAdd,;
```

(continues)

Listing 21.5 Continued

```
      PROCFILE "MDAdd.PRG," + HOME() + "FORMRUN.DBO",;
      STATUSMESSAGE "Add a record to the end of this table",;
      TEXT "&Add new record"

DEFINE MENUITEM DBMITEM2 OF CUST_IN.MenuBar1.DBMBAR2;
  PROPERTY ;
      ONCLICK  MDDelete,;
      PROCFILE "MDDelete.PRG," + HOME() + "FORMRUN.DBO",;
      SHORTCUT "Ctrl-U",;
      STATUSMESSAGE "Toggle deletion mark for the current record",;
      TEXT "&Set/Clear deletion mark"

DEFINE MENU DBMBAR3 OF CUST_IN.MenuBar1;
  PROPERTY ;
      STATUSMESSAGE "Search for specific records",;
      TEXT "&Search"

DEFINE MENUITEM DBMITEM1 OF CUST_IN.MenuBar1.DBMBAR3;
  PROPERTY ;
      ONCLICK  MDGoTop,;
      PROCFILE "MDGoTop.PRG," + HOME() + "FORMRUN.DBO",;
      SHORTCUT "Ctrl-Pgup",;
      STATUSMESSAGE "Move to the first record in the table",;
      TEXT "&Top Record"

DEFINE MENUITEM DBMITEM2 OF CUST_IN.MenuBar1.DBMBAR3;
  PROPERTY ;
      ONCLICK  MDGoBtm,;
      PROCFILE "MDGoBtm.PRG," + HOME() + "FORMRUN.DBO",;
      SHORTCUT "Ctrl-Pgdn",;
      STATUSMESSAGE "Move to the last record in the table",;
      TEXT "&Last Record"

DEFINE MENUITEM DBMITEM3 OF CUST_IN.MenuBar1.DBMBAR3;
  PROPERTY ;
      ONCLICK  MDGoRNbr,;
      PROCFILE "MDGoRNbr.PRG," + HOME() + "FORMRUN.DBO",;
      STATUSMESSAGE "Move to the specified record",;
      TEXT "&Record number..."

DEFINE MENUITEM DBMITEM4 OF CUST_IN.MenuBar1.DBMBAR3;
  PROPERTY ;
      ONCLICK  MDSkip,;
      PROCFILE "MDSkip.PRG," + HOME() + "FORMRUN.DBO",;
      STATUSMESSAGE "Move by skipping the specified number of records",;
      TEXT "S&kip..."

DEFINE MENUITEM DBMITEM5 OF CUST_IN.MenuBar1.DBMBAR3;
  PROPERTY ;
      SEPARATOR .T.

DEFINE MENUITEM DBMITEM6 OF CUST_IN.MenuBar1.DBMBAR3;
  PROPERTY ;
      ONCLICK  MDIdxKey,;
      PROCFILE "MDIdxKey.PRG," + HOME() + "FORMRUN.DBO",;
```

```
      STATUSMESSAGE "Use an index to search for the specified value",;
      TEXT "&Index key..."

DEFINE MENUITEM DBMITEM6A OF CUST_IN.MenuBar1.DBMBAR3;
  PROPERTY ;
      SEPARATOR .T.

DEFINE MENUITEM DBMITEM7 OF CUST_IN.MenuBar1.DBMBAR3;
  PROPERTY ;
      ONCLICK  MDFwd,;
      PROCFILE "MDFwd.PRG," + HOME() + "FORMRUN.DBO",;
      STATUSMESSAGE "Search this field for the specified value from the
                     ➥current record forward",;
      TEXT "&Forward..."

DEFINE MENUITEM DBMITEM8 OF CUST_IN.MenuBar1.DBMBAR3;
  PROPERTY ;
      ONCLICK  MDFwd,;
      PROCFILE "MDFwd.PRG," + HOME() + "FORMRUN.DBO",;
      STATUSMESSAGE "Search this field for the specified value from the
                    ➥current record backward",;
      TEXT "&Backward..."

DEFINE MENUITEM DBMITEM9 OF CUST_IN.MenuBar1.DBMBAR3;
  PROPERTY ;
      ONCLICK  MDCS,;
      PROCFILE "MDCS.PRG," + HOME() + "FORMRUN.DBO",;
      STATUSMESSAGE "Case sensitive search",;
      TEXT "&Match capitalization"

DEFINE MENU DBMBAR4 OF CUST_IN.MenuBar1;
  PROPERTY ;
      STATUSMESSAGE "Order records by index",;
      TEXT "&Organize"

DEFINE MENUITEM DBMITEM1 OF CUST_IN.MenuBar1.DBMBAR4;
  PROPERTY ;
      ONCLICK  MDOrder,;
      PROCFILE "MDOrder.PRG," + HOME() + "FORMRUN.DBO",;
      STATUSMESSAGE "Select an index tag by which to order this table",;
      TEXT "&Order records..."

DEFINE MENU DBMBAR5 OF CUST_IN.MenuBar1;
  PROPERTY ;
      STATUSMESSAGE "Get help",;
      TEXT "&Help"

DEFINE MENUITEM DBMITEM1 OF CUST_IN.MenuBar1.DBMBAR5;
  PROPERTY ;
      STATUSMESSAGE "Show index for dBASE on-line help",;
      TEXT "&Help index"

DEFINE MENUITEM DBMITEM2 OF CUST_IN.MenuBar1.DBMBAR5;
  PROPERTY ;
      STATUSMESSAGE "Show keystroke help for the developer's desktop",;
      TEXT "&Keyboard help"
```

(continues)

Listing 21.5 Continued

```
DEFINE MENUITEM DBMITEM3 OF CUST_IN.MenuBar1.DBMBAR5;
  PROPERTY ;
     ONCLICK  HelpObj,;
     PROCFILE "MENUEDIT.PRG,C:\DBASE\IDELIB.DBO",;
     STATUSMESSAGE "Get help for the current object",;
     TEXT "A&ctive field"

DEFINE MENUITEM DBMBAR1 OF CUST_IN.MenuBar1.DBMBAR5;
  PROPERTY ;
     SEPARATOR .T.

DEFINE MENUITEM DBMITEM4 OF CUST_IN.MenuBar1.DBMBAR5;
  PROPERTY ;
     STATUSMESSAGE "Get information about this form",;
     TEXT "&About"

DEFINE MENU DBMBAR6 OF CUST_IN.MenuBar1;
  PROPERTY ;
     STATUSMESSAGE "Print a report from the data table",;
     TEXT "&Print"

DEFINE MENUITEM DBMITEM1 OF CUST_IN.MenuBar1.DBMBAR6;
  PROPERTY ;
     ONCLICK  CIDLIST,;
     STATUSMESSAGE "Customers sorted by ID number",;
     TEXT "&Customer ID list"
```

The CUST_IN.MNU file contains all the commands to set up the main bar menu and all the pull-down menus associated with it. The OF clause on the DEFINE MENUBAR command is used to attach the menubar as a component of the form. The DEFINE MENU commands define each of the choices on the menubar. The choice that is displayed is set using the TEXT property. Each of the pull-down menus is defined by the choices set with the DEFINE MENU commands. The names given to the menus and menuitems are arbitrary. The names shown here are the generic names (for example dbmItem1 of dbmBar1) assigned by the Form Designer. When writing your own code you may use any valid dBASE variable name. For example, you may want to change the last two commands to have the names more descriptive of the choice:

▶ See "OnClick," p. 956

```
DEFINE MENU mcPrint OF CUST_IN.MenuBar1;
  PROPERTY ;
     STATUSMESSAGE "Print a report from the data table",;
     TEXT "&Print"

DEFINE MENUITEM miCustList OF CUST_IN.MenuBar1.mcPrint;
  PROPERTY ;
     ONCLICK  CIDLIST,;
     STATUSMESSAGE "Customers sorted by ID number",;
     TEXT "&Customer ID list"
```

Each pad on the menu bar is created with a DEFINE MENU...OF command. Using the dot reference notation, the OF clause associates the pad with the object MENUBAR1 which is a member of the object CUST_IN. Each item in a pull-down menu is created using the DEFINE MENUITEM...OF command. The dot reference notation is used two levels deep, to associate the menu items with the appropriate pull-down menu, for example CUST_IN.MENUBAR1.DBMBAR1. The OnClick property is used to indicate which procedure in the procedure file to run when the user clicks on the menu choice. The order of the DEFINE commands determines the order of appearance in the menu bar and in the pull-down menus.

The push buttons use an OnClick property that refers to standard event handlers provided by dBASE. The entries in the DFM file are in the order that they will be accessed by the user using the Enter key or the Tab key.

Running the Form

Because the form is simply a dBASE program, you can execute it the same way you do any other dBASE program. The easiest way is to type DO CUST_IN in the command window. This will check for the Object file and if is does not exist or is dated earlier than the CUST_IN.PRG file, dBASE will invoke the compiler. If you modify the DFM or MNU files, you must invoke the compiler manually by typing COMPILE CUST_IN to ensure that you have the lastest version included in your executable file.

The entire form is run from the CUST_IN.PRG file using the ReadModal( ) method, displaying the form shown in figure 21.10.

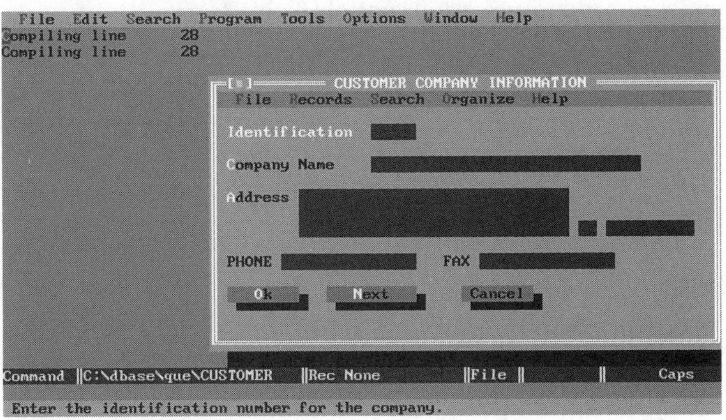

Fig. 21.10
The final form has all fields and its own menu.

Troubleshooting
Why doesn't the cursor go through my fields in order?
While using the Form Designer, use the BEFORE and AFTER properties in the Object Inspector to determine in what order the fields will appear. When editing the code, the order is determined by the order of the DEFINE statements in the procedure file.

From Here...

In this chapter you learned how to use the Form Designer and the Menu Designer to create objects to make your application easier to use. You were introduced to the uses of properties and methods to call procedures and modify the appearance of your objects. To find out more about working with UI objects, you might want to review the following chapters:

- Chapter 16, "Getting Started with Programming," is a refresher course in good programming practice and basic programming standards.
- Chapter 18, "Creating Custom Applications," shows you how to tailor an application to meet your needs, and those of your user.
- Chapter 19, "Using the Applications Generator and the Compiler," details how to have dBASE write your code for you to save you time and debugging.
- Chapter 26, "Using UI Properties, Methods, and Commands," provides in-depth syntax and descriptions of how to use each property, method, and command to create and control UI objects.

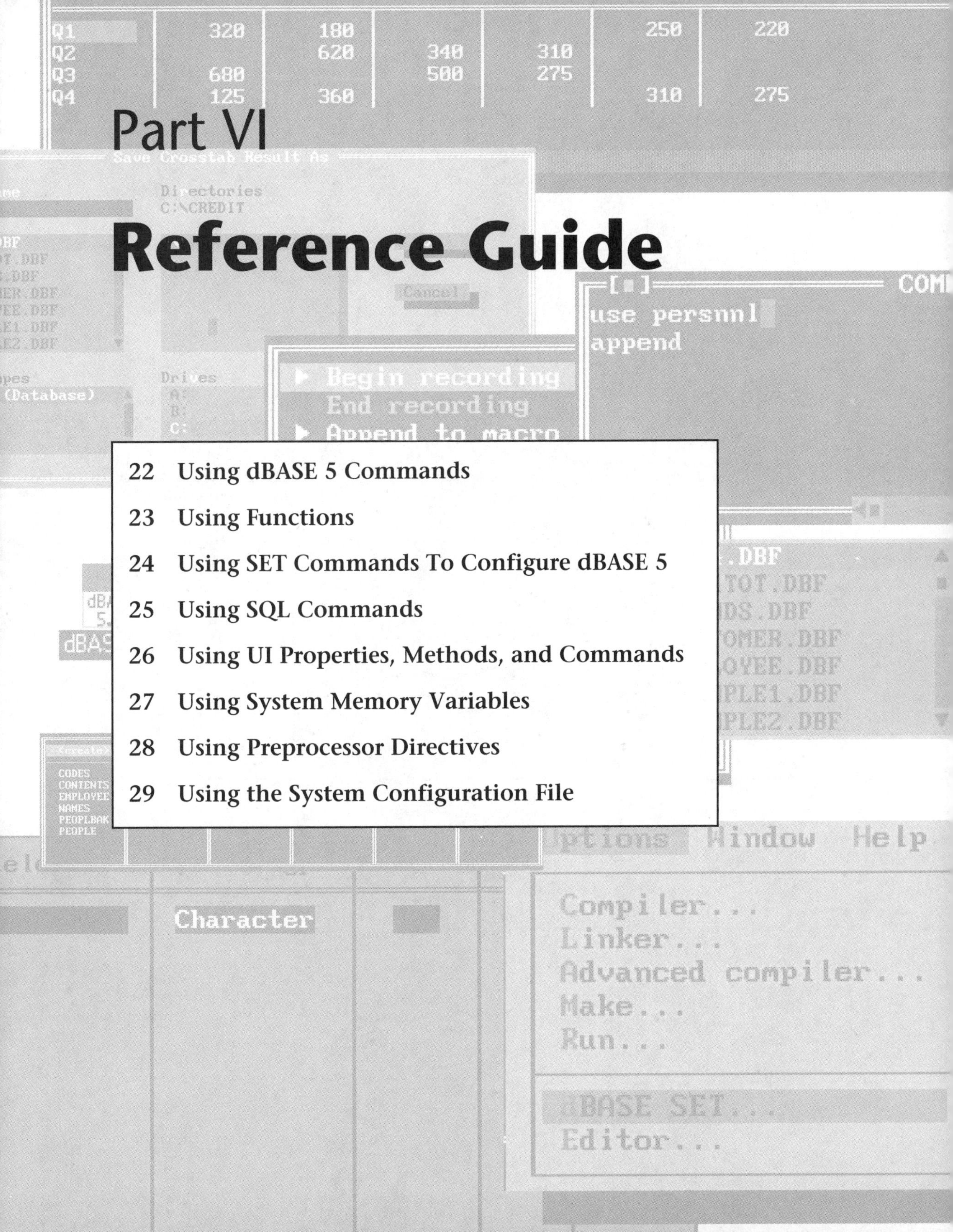

Part VI

Reference Guide

22 Using dBASE 5 Commands

23 Using Functions

24 Using SET Commands To Configure dBASE 5

25 Using SQL Commands

26 Using UI Properties, Methods, and Commands

27 Using System Memory Variables

28 Using Preprocessor Directives

29 Using the System Configuration File

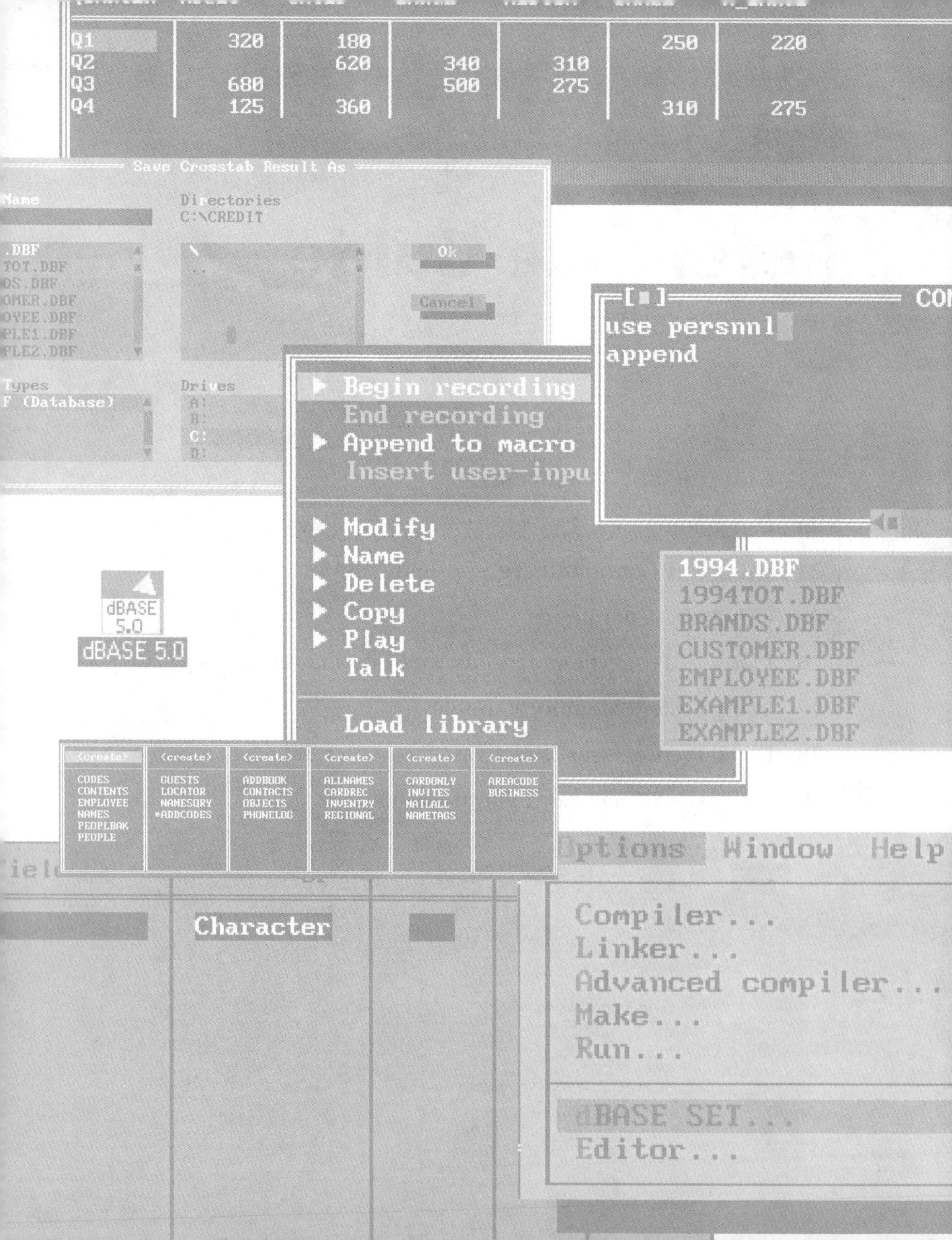

Q1 320 180 250 220
Q2 620 340 310
Q3 680 500 275
Q4 125 360 310 275
Save Crosstab Result As
Name
Directories
C:\CREDIT
.DBF
TOT.DBF
OS.DBF
OMER.DBF
OYEE.DBF
PLE1.DBF
PLE2.DBF
Ok
Cancel
Types
F (Database)
Drives
A:
B:
C:
D:
use persnnl
append
Begin recording
End recording
Append to macro
Insert user-inpu
Modify
Name
Delete
Copy
Play
Talk
Load library
1994.DBF
1994TOT.DBF
BRANDS.DBF
CUSTOMER.DBF
EMPLOYEE.DBF
EXAMPLE1.DBF
EXAMPLE2.DBF
dBASE 5.0
dBASE 5.0
<create>
CODES
CONTENTS
EMPLOYEE
NAMES
PEOPLBAK
PEOPLE
<create>
GUESTS
LOCATOR
NAMESQRY
*ADDCODES
<create>
ADDBOOK
CONTACTS
OBJECTS
PHONELOG
<create>
ALLNAMES
CARDREC
INVENTRY
REGIONAL
<create>
CARDONLY
INVITES
MAILALL
NAMETAGS
<create>
AREACODE
BUSINESS
Options Window Help
Character
Compiler...
Linker...
Advanced compiler...
Make...
Run...
dBASE SET...
Editor...

Chapter 22

Using dBASE 5 Commands

The dBASE 5 commands enable you to duplicate many of the functions of the Control Center. Some commands are used in programs you can write yourself using the dBASE 5 programming language. This powerful language enables you to create simple, short programs or complex applications.

Understanding Command Syntax

As with any language, you must follow certain rules when you enter dBASE commands. Each command has its own *syntax*, or rules governing how you type in the command. When you fail to follow proper command syntax, commands don't work properly, and you may receive a "syntax error" message on your screen.

In this Reference Guide, commands are shown with their available *options* enclosed in brackets ([ ]). Options are command parts that you may or may not use, depending on what you want the command to do. Some bracketed options have several *parameters*, which are shown in italic type, between angle brackets (< >). The italic word inside the angle brackets is not meant to be typed—it stands for a value you must supply. For example, where a syntax diagram shows *<filename.EXT>*, you would type a valid file name and extension.

The LIST command, for example, has the following syntax:

```
LIST [FIELDS <field list>] [OFF] [<scope>]
   [FOR <condition>] [WHILE <condition>]
   [TO PRINTER/TO FILE <filename>]
```

That may look a bit confusing at first glance, but if you separate the command into its various components, it becomes a bit easier to understand. Throughout this Reference Guide, you will see examples that help you understand the command syntax. Table 22.1 shows how to break down each section of the syntax for the LIST command.

Table 22.1 Breakdown of LIST Syntax

Command Item	Description
LIST	The LIST command (sometimes called a "verb"), which enables you to list the contents of a data table.
[FIELDS <*field list*>]	The FIELDS option. If you want to list only a few of the fields in a data table, specify those fields after you type FIELDS. For example, you could specify FIELDS Lastname, Firstname, City.
[OFF]	The OFF option. This prevents the printing of record numbers.
[<*scope*>]	The <*scope*> option. This enables you to limit the range of records to include on the list. You could list only the next 25 records by using a scope of NEXT 25.
[FOR <*condition*>]	The FOR option. This is similar to a scope but enables you to list only those records that meet the <*condition*>. For example, FOR CITY = "Newcastle" would restrict the list to records whose CITY field contained "Newcastle."
[WHILE <*condition*>]	The WHILE option. This will continue adding records to the list until the <*condition*> is no longer true. WHILE RECNO( ) < 100 would list only those records whose record numbers are under 100.
[TO PRINTER/TO	The TO PRINTER and TO FILE options.
FILE <*filename*>]	The slash indicates that you can choose from either portion of the command. TO PRINTER prints the list; TO FILE CITYLIST.TXT sends the list to the indicated file.

Note in all the examples that the brackets and slashes are not in the actual command. The following example combines many of the options of the LIST command:

```
LIST FIELDS LASTNAME, CITY, ZIPCODE FOR ZIPCODE < 90000 ;
   TO PRINTER
```

This command prints a list to the printer of the Lastname, City, and ZIPcode fields for those records whose ZIP Code value is less than 90,000.

Note

Some command examples in this book are too long to fit on one line. They are shown with a semicolon (;) at the end of the first line to indicate that the command continues on the next line. The LIST FIELDS example illustrates this practice.

This Reference Guide contains examples for every dBASE 5 command but does not show every possible variation of options. A little experimentation in your Command window will show you how each command is used. Take the time to try out the examples, and you will discover that command programming is not as complicated as it looks. Be sure to read Part IV of this book to learn about programming in dBASE 5.

Working with Operators

Several different types of operators are available for mathematical, relational, or logical operations or for controlling string values.

Operator Types

dBASE 5 uses four types of operators: mathematical, relational, logical, and string. Mathematical operators are used to perform simple math on numbers. Relational operators are used to define the relationship of one variable to another, such as less than or greater than. Logical operators are used on logical (true or false) variables. String operators are used to combine two or more character variables into one character variable.

The following is a list of the mathematical operators:

Operator	Description
+	Addition, unary positive
–	Subtraction, unary negative
*	Multiplication
/	Division
** or ^	Exponential
( )	Parentheses for grouping

The following is a list of the relational operators:

Operator	Description
>	Greater than
<	Less than
=	Equal to
<=	Less than or equal to
=>	Greater than or equal to
< > or #	Not equal to
$	Substring comparison

Note

The $ symbol used for substring comparison is usually in a statement such as *<expression 1>* $ *<expression 2>*. Think of this statement as meaning "Is expression 1 contained in expression 2?"

The following is a list of the logical operators:

Operator	Description
.AND.	Logical AND
.OR.	Logical OR
.NOT.	Logical NOT
=	Equal to
< > or #	Not equal to
( )	Parentheses used for grouping

The logical operators are used for expressions that result in a true or false logical data type. The results of a logical expression can be shown in a Boolean table, where 0 = false and 1 = true:

A	B	AND	OR
0	0	.F.	.F.
0	1	.F.	.T.
1	0	.F.	.T.
1	1	.T.	.T.

The following is a list of the string operators:

Operator	Description
+	Trailing spaces are left intact when strings are joined
–	The first expression's trailing spaces are moved to the end of the second expression's string
( )	Parentheses used for grouping

Operator Precedence

The set of rules governing the order in which an operation is performed is called the *order of precedence*. For mathematical operations, the order of precedence is as follows:

1. Expressions contained in parentheses
2. Unary positive (+) and unary negative (–) signs
3. Exponential
4. Multiplication and division
5. Addition and subtraction

The order of precedence can have an unanticipated effect on the result of a mathematical equation. For example, the result of the following equation is 14, not 20:

2 + 3 * 4

The result is 14 because the order of precedence rules that multiplication must be performed before addition. (According to the rules, the equation works like this: 4 * 3 = 12, then 2 + 12 = 14.) Parentheses can ensure the desired result: (2 + 3) * 4 = 20.

The order of precedence for logical (Boolean) operators is as follows (note that the logical operators are surrounded by periods):

1. .NOT.
2. .AND.
3. .OR.

As with mathematical operators, parentheses in logical operations ensure the desired (and anticipated) result.

If you have several types of operators in a complex expression, the order of precedence is as follows:

1. Mathematical or string operation
2. Relational operations
3. Logical operations

For operations with the same precedence level, the calculation is performed from left to right.

dBASE 5 Commands Listed Alphabetically

In this section commands are listed alphabetically, and examples and other information are shown for each command.

*/&&

Syntax

```
*/&& (program comment)
```

Purpose: Places a comment or nonexecutable text in the program. You use comments to document the function of a command or a series of commands. Documenting, or *commenting,* your program helps you keep track of what each part of your program is intended to accomplish and helps others understand what the program is doing (or will do) at any point. Comments appear in many of the code examples in this book.

The * must be the first nonspace character on the line; otherwise, dBASE interprets the character as a multiplication symbol. For example, if you enter

```
USE Clients * use the clients database
```

you receive an error message. Use && to add comments to a line that contains a command. Any characters in the rest of the line following * or && are ignored when the program is run or compiled.

Example

```
* This is an example of a comment. Notice that the asterisk
* character is the first nonspace character on the line.
USE CLIENTS         && these are comments that are ignored
```

?/??

Syntax

```
?/?? [<expression 1>
      [PICTURE <character expression>]
      [FUNCTION <function list>]
      [AT <numeric value>]
      [STYLE <font number>]]
  [,][<expression 2> ...]
```

Purpose: Sends the *<expression>* to the screen or to the printer if you use SET PRINTER ON. Use ? to print the expression on a new line; use ?? to print the expression at the current position. The comma (,) option delays printing the expression until dBASE encounters a ?/?? command that does not end with the trailing comma. You can use the trailing-comma technique to print complex expressions that are longer than the available 1024-character command line.

Use the PICTURE, FUNCTION, AT, and STYLE options to format the appearance of the output on the printer. The PICTURE commands are shown in the @...SAY...GET command.

In addition to the values listed in @...SAY...GET commands, the FUNCTION command has three possible values:

V *<number>*	Causes expressions that are displayed in a column to be *<number>* characters wide. You can use this option to print the contents of a memo field; for example, a *<number>* of 0 causes the memo field to be printed as it was stored in the memo editor.
H *<number>*	Is used in conjunction with the system variable _wrap set to true. This arrangement causes word wrapping to be controlled by the _lmargin and _rmargin system variables. This value is used only with memo fields.
;	Causes the text to wrap when a semicolon (;) is found in the text. The semicolon is not printed.

When an expression may not fill in the PICTURE template, you can use four other functions to format the text:

@B	Left-justifies data in the template
@I	Centers the data in the template
@J	Right-justifies data in the template
@T	Used with the other functions. Trims off blank spaces before the text is aligned with one of the other functions.

You can use two other functions for numbers:

$	Displays the floating currency symbol before or after the amount, depending on the SET CURRENCY parameter
L	Displays leading zeros to fill out the field width

The AT *<numeric value>* specifies the starting column number of the expression.

The STYLE option displays the text with various text attributes:

B	Bold
I	Italic
U	Underline
R	Raised (superscript)
L	Lowered (subscript)

To use STYLE to specify the typeface (font) to use for printing, use the numbers 1 through 5, which correspond to the user-defined fonts specified in the CONFIG.DB file. You can make lines overstrike each other by setting the _wrap system memory variable to false.

Example

```
?  "Column 1"
?? "Column 2" AT 10
?? "Column 3" AT 30
* Now print some text and numbers under each column
? "Corn" AT 0 PICTURE "@L !!!!!!!!"
?? 12.33        PICTURE "@$ 99.99"    AT 10
?? "per case"   PICTURE "@I !!!!!!!!" AT 30
? "Tamalies"    PICTURE "@J !!!!!!!!"
?? 1.19         PICTURE "@L 99.99"    AT 10
?? "per can"    PICTURE "@R !!!!!!!!" AT 30
?
```

???

Syntax

```
??? <character expression>
```

Purpose: Sends characters directly to the printer without using any installed printer driver. This command is used most often to send printer control codes.

> **Note**
>
> Use the ?/?? command with the STYLE option to change the printed appearance of an individual item—for example, to print one line in a different font. Use the ??? command to change the printed appearance of larger sections of text. You can use the _pscode and _pecode system variables to set the principal font to use for the printed document.

Example

```
* Send LaserJet reset code
??? "{ESC}E"
```

Syntax

```
@ <row>,<col>
  [SAY <expression>
  [PICTURE <expC>][FUNCTION <function list>]]
  [GET <variable>
    [[OPEN] WINDOW <window name>]
    [PICTURE <expC]
    [FUNCTION <function list>]
    [RANGE [REQUIRED][<low>,][,][,<high>]]
    [VALID [REQUIRED]<condition>[ERROR <expC>]]
    [WHEN <condition>]
    [DEFAULT <expression>]
    [MESSAGE <expC>]]
  [COLOR [<standard>][,<enhanced>]]
```

Purpose: Enables exact positioning and formatting of output text and data, and data input fields. This command can be used to create custom dBASE IV style forms for screens, windows, and the printer. It does not change the location of UI objects. The SET DEVICE command determines whether the output is directed to a printer or to the screen. The *<row>* and *<column>* parameters determine the starting position of the output. @ commands are not stored in files opened with SET ALTERNATE.

The row and column values are relative to the upper-left corner of the screen, or the upper-left corner of the active window, or the top of the page. The *<row>* value can range from 0 to the maximum number of lines on the display or from 0 to 32,767 for a printer if you used SET DEVICE TO PRINT. The *<column>* value can range from 0 to 79 on-screen and from 0 to 255 for a printer. (Your printer may not be able to print all 255 characters on one line.)

Note

If you used SET STATUS ON, the status line appears on line 22. The SET SCOREBOARD ON command reserves line 0. To use lines 0 and 22, set these parameters to OFF, unless you are using a DISPLAY setting that allows more than 25 lines—for example, VGA50.

If you use only the *<row>* and *<column>* parameters, the cursor is positioned for output by other commands which do not allow positioning, such as ?/?? and ACCEPT. All text to the right on the line will be erased. With SET DEVICE TO PRINT, specifying a row number lower than the current row will cause a page feed.

The SAY option shows the information on-screen but doesn't allow it to be changed. Use the GET option to display the information and make it available for editing. You can use multiple @...GET commands to show all information on-screen and then use the READ command to enable full-screen editing mode.

Example

```
* Show two fields on the screen, and then READ the data
firstname = SPACE(10)
lastname = SPACE(10)
@ 12,10 SAY "First Name " GET firstname
@ 13,10 SAY " Last Name " GET lastname
READ
```

The @...SAY...GET command has many available options. You usually can combine these options to determine exactly how the information will be shown and to control the type of information that the user can enter. @...SAY...GET options are shown here.

COLOR	Defines the colors to be used for the variable areas. The *<standard>* color is used for SAY commands, and the *<enhanced>* color is used for GET commands. See the SET COLOR command for color values. You can use the default colors by not specifying the colors.

DEFAULT	Places the preset value in the variable area during APPEND operation. The user can press the Enter key to accept the value or type another value. The default value type must match the variable type used in the GET expression.
ERROR	Displays the *<character string>* if the user inputs a value that doesn't meet the requirements specified with VALID. If no ERROR clause is used, the default error message is `Editing condition is not satisfied`.
FUNCTION	Similar to the PICTURE option, but FUNCTION applies to the entire data item, whereas PICTURE is used for only a portion of the entry.
MESSAGE	Displays a help message when the cursor is placed on the entry field. If SET STATUS is ON, the message will be shown at the bottom center of the screen. If SET STATUS is OFF, you can set the position of the message with the SET MESSAGE...AT command.
OPEN WINDOW	Enables you to open and close the *<window name>* as a default window name.
PICTURE	Restricts the input data to certain types of data and formats the data. The *<character expression>* can include a function, such as @! to force all uppercase characters. The @ symbol indicates that the format should apply to the entire width of the input variable. (See the table of PICTURE functions following these option descriptions.)
RANGE	Defines the lowest and highest value allowed in the input field. You define ranges for character, numeric, and date values for fields of their respective data type. You can use the REQUIRED option to ensure that the contents are checked to be in the range whether or not the user changes the data.
VALID	Provides a condition that must be met before data is accepted. If the input data does not meet the *<condition>*, an Editing condition not satisfied message or ERROR *<message>* appears. You can use the REQUIRED option to force a validity check every time you enter the field, whether the data is changed or

not. Other data on the form may have changed and made the data invalid.

WHEN Prevents the user from placing the cursor on the input field when the *<condition>* is false. If the *<condition>* is false, the input field is skipped.

WINDOW Opens a separate editing window if the variable is a memo field. The window enables you to edit memo fields in a window instead of using the full screen. The *<window name>* must be the name of a previously defined window. The *<row>* and *<column>* parameters of the @ command specify the relative positions in the editing window.

Table 22.2 lists the format functions for the FORMAT and PICTURE parameters.

Table 22.2 Format Functions for FORMAT and PICTURE

Function	Action
!	Allows any character but converts it to uppercase
^	Shows numbers in scientific notation
$	Shows numbers in currency format
(	Puts negative numbers in parentheses
A	Allows alphabetic characters only
B	Left-justifies text (for @...SAY command only)
C	Displays "CR" (credit) after any positive number
D	Uses current date format (set with SET DATE)
E	Uses European date format
I	Centers text (for @...SAY command only)
J	Right-justifies text (for @...SAY only)
L	Displays leading zeros
M	Allows a list of choices for the GET input variable
R	Displays the allowable characters in the input field but doesn't save them with the input data

Function	Action
S <*number*>	Limits field width to <*number*> characters. The field data is scrolled horizontally as needed. Must be a positive number, without a space, such as "S20".
T	Trims leading and trailing blanks from a field
X	Displays "DB" (debit) after a negative number
Z	Displays zeros as a blank string, rather than as zero characters (0)

Some functions can be used together, and some are for specific field types only.

Templates are used to format a single character in the input field. Table 22.3 shows the various available template symbols.

When you use a picture template for a decimal number, make sure that you include a decimal point in the template. You also need at least one digit to the left of the decimal point and another position for the sign (+ or –). To allow positive or negative numbers from 0 to 99.99, for example, use the template 999.99 to allow for the plus or minus sign.

Table 22.3 Template Symbols

Template	Description
!	Converts letters to uppercase characters; allows other characters, such as numbers or punctuation
#	Allows only numbers, blanks, and signs (+ or –)
$	Displays the SET CURRENCY string in place of leading zeros
*	Displays asterisks in place of leading zeros
,	Displays commas if digits appear to the left of the comma position
.	Sets decimal point position
9	Allows only numbers for character data, or numbers and signs (+ or –) for numeric data
A	Allows letters only

(continues)

Table 22.3 Continued

Template	Description
N	Allows alphabetic or numeric characters, including the underscore; no spaces or punctuation
L	Allows only logical data entries (Y/N, .T./.F.)
X	Allows any character
Y	Allows logical Y/y/N/n; converts to uppercase (Y/N)

@...CLEAR

Syntax

```
@ <row 1>, <col 1> CLEAR [TO <row 2>, <col 2>]
```

Purpose: Clears part of the current screen or active window. The specified row and column are relative to the upper-left corner of the active screen or window. If you don't specify the TO row and column, the active screen or window is cleared to the lower right corner. You can only use this command with non-UI screens and windows like those created in previous versions of dBASE. It is ignored by dBASE 5's UI objects.

Example

```
* Clear all of row 12
@ 12,0
* Clear a portion of row 15
@ 15,20 CLEAR TO 15,60
* Clear a rectangular area
@ 10,0 CLEAR TO 15,79
```

@...FILL TO

Syntax

```
@ <row 1>, <col 1> FILL TO [<row 2>, <col 2>]
   [COLOR <color attribute>]
```

Purpose: Changes the color of an area of the screen. The *<row1>, <col1>* parameters are the upper-left corner of the active screen or window. The color attributes are the same values used in SET COLOR. Any text in the FILL area is not erased. However, if you don't specify a COLOR the color is set to black on black (N/N) which makes the text invisible. You can only use this command with non-UI screens and windows like those created in previous versions of dBASE. It is ignored by dBASE 5's UI objects.

Example

```
* Place a white background and red foreground
* in the center of the screen
@ 8,20 FILL TO 12,60 COLOR R/W
```

@...GET

See @.

@...SAY

See @.

@...SCROLL

Syntax

```
@ <row-1>,<col-1> TO <row-2>,<col-2> SCROLL
[UP/DOWN/LEFT/RIGHT] [BY <expN>] [WRAP]
```

Purpose: Shifts the contents of areas on the screen. Use this technique to shift a block up, down, left, or right on the display. You can only use this command with non-UI screens and windows like those created in previous versions of dBASE. It is ignored by dBASE 5's UI objects.

Example

```
* Move a block of text to the right 3 spaces.
@ 3,3 TO 5,10 SCROLL RIGHT BY 3
```

Tip

If the Esc key is pressed when the program is using ACCEPT to collec input, the program might be terminated. You can use the SET ESCAPE OFF command before the ACCEPT command to prevent program termination.

@...TO

Syntax

```
@ <row 1>, <col 1> TO <row 2>, <col 2>
   [DOUBLE / PANEL / <border definition string>]
   [COLOR <color attribute>]
```

Purpose: Draws a box on-screen with a single-line border. Specify DOUBLE to get a double-lined box; PANEL to display a solid, highlighted border; or *<border definition string>* to use any characters you specify as the border. The *<border definition string>* follows the rules of the SET BORDER command. The COLOR codes follow the rules of the SET COLOR command.

You can draw a horizontal line by specifying the same row coordinates, or a vertical line by specifying the same column coordinates.

You can only use this command with non-UI screens and windows like those created in previous versions of dBASE. It is ignored by dBASE 5's UI objects.

Example

```
* Draw a double-line box in the center of the screen
* Make the color of the box Red/White
@ 8,20 TO 12,60 DOUBLE COLOR R/W
```

ACCEPT

Syntax

```
ACCEPT [<prompt>] TO <memory variable>
```

Purpose: Asks the user for an answer to a question and creates a character-type variable from the user entry. The *<prompt>* can be a character string ("Enter your name") or a memory variable. The user can enter as many as 254 characters. If you don't use a prompt, dBASE places a question mark on-screen in the spot where the user enters the data. A better option is the @ command.

The ACCEPT command is used in dBASE command files or programs. If you need to ask the user for a numeric variable, you can use the INPUT command or convert the ACCEPT character memory variable to a numeric data type.

Example

```
* Ask the user's name
* Store it as the username memory variable
@ 10,0          && clear the line
ACCEPT "Please Enter your User ID" TO username
```

ACTIVATE MENU

Syntax

```
ACTIVATE MENU <menu name> [PAD <pad name>]
```

Purpose: Activates a menu that was defined with the DEFINE MENU command and displays the menu on-screen. The PAD option highlights the specified pad name. Only one menu can be active at one time; all others are suspended temporarily until the current menu is deactivated.

You can only use this command with non-UI screens and windows like those created in previous versions of dBASE. It is ignored by dBASE 5's UI objects.

Example

```
* Activate the mainprog menu,
* highlighting the Print choice as default
ACTIVATE MENU mainprog PAD print
```

ACTIVATE POPUP

Syntax

```
ACTIVATE POPUP <popup name>
```

Purpose: Activates a previously defined pop-up menu on-screen. (Pop-ups already must have been defined with the DEFINE POPUP command.) Only one pop-up menu can be active at a time, but previously activated pop-ups remain on-screen until they are deactivated.

You can only use this command with non-UI screens and windows like those created in previous versions of dBASE. It is ignored by dBASE 5's UI objects.

Example

```
* Activate the pop3b popup
ACTIVATE POPUP pop3b
```

ACTIVATE SCREEN

Syntax

```
ACTIVATE SCREEN
```

Purpose: Enables access to the entire screen rather than to the currently active window. Windows and pop-up menus remain on-screen, but the user can overwrite the window or pop-up area. When you deactivate the screen by activating a window, the pop-ups and windows are reactivated.

You can only use this command with non-UI screens and windows like those created in previous versions of dBASE. It is ignored by dBASE 5's UI objects.

Example

```
* Restore access to the whole screen
ACTIVATE SCREEN
```

ACTIVATE WINDOW

Syntax

```
ACTIVATE WINDOW <window name list> / ALL
```

Purpose: Activates and displays windows from memory. You direct all screen output to the window, not the full screen. Windows are created with the CREATE/MODIFY WINDOW command. The ALL option enables you to restore all of the windows in memory. The windows are displayed in the order they are defined.

You can only use this command with non-UI screens and windows like those created in previous versions of dBASE. It is ignored by dBASE 5's UI objects.

Example

```
* Activate the help_05 window just to see how it looks
ACTIVATE WINDOW help_05
```

APPEND

Syntax

```
APPEND [BLANK]/[NOORGANIZE]
```

Purpose: Used to add records to the current database. APPEND displays all the fields of the current record, and you can add data to each field. If you have more than one screenful of fields, use the PgUp and PgDn keys to move from one screen to another. After you enter data in the last field, pressing Enter adds a new record. The PgDn key also adds new records to the database. You can use Ctrl-End to complete a record. Pressing Esc cancels any changes to the current record.

While you are entering data, you can use the PgUp key to display the preceding record. You can use the PgDn key to display the next screenful of fields if you have too many fields for one screen, or use PgUp to see the previous screenful of fields. If you are at the end of the database, you can use the PgDn key to add another blank record.

If the database contains a memo field, move the cursor to the memo field and then use Ctrl-Home or F9 to enter the dBASE 5 editor for the memo field. After you enter the desired text, use Ctrl-End to save the information or press Esc to cancel any changes to the memo information. Use the NOORGANIZE option to prevent the user from accessing the ORGANIZE menu so they can't change indexes.

Examples

```
USE CUSTOMER             && open the database
SET FORMAT TO customer   && open custom data entry screen
APPEND                   && add a record, entering data
```

The BLANK option adds a blank record at the end of the database but does not show the field on-screen for entry. This option usually is used in programs that read values or memory variables from the screen. The following example illustrates the use of APPEND BLANK:

```
* Read two fields from the screen
* adding the information to the STATES database.
* Structure of STATES database
```

```
* Field Name   Type         Length    Dec
* STATE        Character    2
* ZIP          Numeric      5         0
*
* Set up database and memory variables
USE STATES
mstate = SPACE(2)        && character variable
mzip = 0                 && numeric variable
* Read values from screen
@10,15 SAY "STATE " GET mstate PICTURE "!!"
@11,15 SAY " ZIP  " GET mzip PICTURE "99999"
READ
* Store variables to database
APPEND BLANK
REPLACE STATE WITH mstate, ZIP with mzip
```

APPEND FROM

Syntax

```
APPEND FROM <filename>
   [[TYPE] <file type>] [REINDEX]
   [FOR <condition>]
```

Purpose: Copies any or all of the data from one file into the currently active database, adding the new records at the end of the target database. Also used to import data from nondatabase-type files.

This command has two main functions: to add the records from one database into another and to import data from nondatabase files, such as a Lotus 1-2-3 Version 1A worksheet (WKS) file. (Use the IMPORT command to convert WK1 files.) The list of valid types is shown in Table 22.4 (DBMEMO3 is not valid with APPEND FROM).

For you to use APPEND FROM to add data from another database, both databases must have similar structures, but they don't have to be identical. Only data from the same named fields is added to the target database.

After you add the new records to your file, dBASE 5 updates your indexes if you use the REINDEX option, saving you from having to issue a separate command to update your index files.

Examples

If you have two customer databases and want to combine them into one database, you can use the following code:

```
USE CUST2                && second database
APPEND FROM CUST1        && Adds CUST1 data to
                         && CUST2 database
```

The following code appends a database from a comma-delimited (non-database) file:

```
APPEND FROM ORDERS.TXT TYPE DELIMITED
```

APPEND FROM ARRAY

Syntax

```
APPEND FROM ARRAY <array name> [REINDEX]
   [FOR <condition>]
```

Purpose: Used to add records to a database file from a memory array. Memory array variables are stored like rows and columns of data in a spreadsheet. The first column of data in the first row is called data element [1,1], the second column is called [1,2], and so on. The [1,1] array element is entered into the first database field, the [1,2] array element is entered into the second database field, and so on.

If more array elements than fields are in the database, the excess elements are ignored. The [2,1] array element is entered into the next record's first database. The array types and database field types must match.

After you add the new records to your file, dBASE 5 updates your indexes if you use the REINDEX option.

Example

If you have a three-element array and five array values, you can enter the following:

```
DECLARE PARTNUM[5,3]        && sizes the array
...                         && array values assigned
USE PARTS
APPEND FROM ARRAY PARTNUM   && Adds 5 records to database
```

APPEND MEMO

Syntax

```
APPEND MEMO <memo field name>
   FROM <filename>
   [OVERWRITE]
```

Purpose: Imports text from a text or binary file into the memo field of the current record.

You must specify the name of the target memo field. If you don't specify the OVERWRITE parameter, data is added to existing memo data. If you use OVERWRITE, the data replaces existing memo data.

This command is ignored by UI Browse objects.

Example

```
* Add text to the NOTES memo field
USE CLIENT          && the NOTES field is a memo type
GOTO 48             && position to record number 48
* Append the text to existing memo data
APPEND MEMO NOTES FROM SMITH.TXT
```

ASSIST

Syntax

```
ASSIST
```

Purpose: Accesses the Control Center from the Command window. You also can use the command in a program, but you may not want to enable a user to access other files and functions. From the Control Center, you can exit back to the Command window by pressing the Esc key and answering Yes in the dialog box. You also can press Alt-E to open the Exit menu and then choose the Exit to Command Window option.

AVERAGE

Syntax

```
AVERAGE [<numeric expression list>]
   [<scope>]
   [FOR <condition>]
   [WHILE <condition>]
   [TO <memory variable list> / TO ARRAY <array name>]
```

Purpose: Calculates the arithmetic mean of a series of numeric expressions. All records are used to calculate the average unless you use a scope, FOR, or WHILE. The average is displayed on-screen unless you use TO or TO ARRAY to store the average in a specified memory variable or array.

You can use the AVERAGE command to calculate the average of series of data variables.

Note

You may want to exclude records whose numeric fields are BLANK by using the FOR option, as in

```
AVERAGE cost FOR .NOT. ISBLANK (cost).
```

Example

```
* Find the average of two data variables,
* storing the result
* in the COST_AVG and SEE_AVG memvars
USE STOCKS
AVERAGE COST, SELL TO COST_AVG, SELL_AVG
```

BEGIN...END TRANSACTION

Syntax

```
BEGIN TRANSACTION [<path name>]
   <transaction commands>
END TRANSACTION
```

Purpose: Defines the beginning and ending points of a series of commands that are part of a single transaction. With transaction processing, you can make sure that the entire process is completed properly. If the transaction doesn't complete properly, you can change the data back to its original form by using the ROLLBACK command.

During transaction processing, a transaction log file is created in the current directory or under the specified *<path name>*. On a standalone system, the file is called TRANSLOG.LOG. On a network system, the file is called *<computer name>*.LOG, where *<computer name>* is the network name of the computer that started the transaction.

You can use two functions, COMPLETED( ) and ROLLBACK( ), to test whether the transaction or rollback completed without errors. If COMPLETED( ) is true, the transaction completed properly. If ROLLBACK( ) is true, the ROLLBACK command completed properly.

Example

```
* Update the database with transaction processing
* Set up a transaction error trap program
ON ERROR DO trantrap
BEGIN TRANSACTION
USE SALES ORDER TAG SALES
   DO update1          && a program that changes data
   DO update2          && another program
END TRANSACTION
IF ROLLBACK()
   @ 22,20 SAY "Data restored to original state."
ELSE
   @ 22,20 SAY "Transaction rollback unsuccessful."
   @ 23,20 SAY "Restore data from a current backup."
ENDIF
ON ERROR               && clear transaction error trap
RETURN
* This is the trantrap procedure
PROCEDURE TRANTRAP
@ 20,20 SAY "Error occurred during transaction."
@ 21,20 SAY "Removing changes from data files."
ROLLBACK               && roll back the changes
RETURN
```

BLANK

Syntax

```
BLANK [FIELDS <field-list>/LIKE/EXCEPT <skeleton>] [REINDEX]
[<scope>] [FOR <condition>] [WHILE <condition>]
```

Purpose: Fills records or fields with blanks. Using the BLANK command, you can blank an entire record, a set of records, or just selected fields in records. Fields that are designated as read-only cannot be blanked.

After records have been changed, indexes are updated if you use the REINDEX option.

Example

```
* Blank the NAME field in records where the city is Chicago
BLANK FIELDS NAME FOR CITY="Chicago"
```

BROWSE

Syntax

```
BROWSE
   [NOINIT]
   [NOFOLLOW]
   [NOAPPEND]
   [NOMENU]
   [NOEDIT]
   [NODELETE]
   [NOCLEAR]
   [NOORGANIZE]
   [COMPRESS]
   [FORMAT]
   [LOCK <number>]
   [WIDTH <number>]
   [FREEZE <field name>]
   [WINDOW <window name>]
   [[FIELDS <field name1> /R /<column width>]
      /<calculated field name 1> = <expression 1>
      [,<field name2>[/R ][/<column width>]
      /<calculated field name 2> = <expression 2>] ...]
```

Purpose: Enables you to view and edit records in your database. (If a database is not currently in use, dBASE 5 will ask for the database.) Fields are shown in the order of the structure of the database, unless you specify the fields you want by using the FIELDS option or specify FORMAT. You can scroll through records with the PgUp and PgDn keys. You can use the left- and right-arrow keys to view fields that are not displayed on-screen.

While in BROWSE mode, you can add records (unless the NOAPPEND option is used) by moving to the last record and pressing the down-arrow key, or pressing Ctrl-PgDn. dBASE 5 asks whether you want to add records to the database. To say that you do, press Y. You can press the F10 key to activate the BROWSE menu bar, unless the NOMENU option is specified. You can change to the EDIT mode by pressing the F2 key.

If the database file is protected, you can read and edit only those fields allowed by your access level.

Options for BROWSE are described in Table 22.4.

Table 22.4 BROWSE Options

Option	Description
NOINIT	Uses the command line options you specified with the previous BROWSE command
NOFOLLOW	When you are using an indexed file and the index is active, this option doesn't reposition the record if you make a change to a field that is part of the index. If you omit this command, a change to an index field in a record will cause the screen to redisplay.
NOAPPEND	Prevents you from appending records to the database if you move past the last record
NOMENU	Prevents the display of the menu bar
NOEDIT	Prevents you from changing any field
NODELETE	Prevents you from deleting records
NOCLEAR	Keeps the BROWSE table on-screen when you finish browsing. Omitting this option clears the screen after you exit BROWSE.
NOORGANIZE	Prevents use of the Organize menu
COMPRESS	Displays two more lines on-screen by placing the column headings at the top line and not displaying a line separating the headings and data.
FORMAT	Uses the active screen format (FMT) file. The fields still are placed on the same row, but the formatting options specified by the @...GET commands are used (@...SAY commands are ignored). Any fields specified by the FIELDS option are ignored; fields are displayed according to the specification of the format file. This allows use of the validation clauses in the @ command.
LOCK *<number>*	Enables you to specify the number of fields that will not move when you use the arrow keys to move other fields to the display. Use the F3 or F4 key to scroll left or right, respectively. The LOCK option is ignored if you are in EDIT mode.

Option	Description
WIDTH <*number*>	Limits the width of any fields to the value you specify. While you edit a field, the data scrolls in the field when you use the arrow keys. Memo fields always show a width of 4. If you set the width of a numeric field to 5 and the numeric field is eight characters wide, the field data is displayed as asterisks.
FREEZE <*fieldname*>	Enables you to edit only the field specified. All other fields are displayed. If you switch to EDIT mode, FREEZE is disabled.
WINDOW <*window name*>	Enables you to use a window definition to determine the area that will be used by the BROWSE command. The window is closed automatically when you exit BROWSE.
FIELDS ...	Specifies the fields that you want to be displayed during the BROWSE. The /R option to FIELDS enables you to designate a field as read-only. Use <*column width*> to limit the width of a field.

Examples

With the FIELDS option, you can construct calculated fields, as in this example:

```
BROWSE FIELDS COST = QUANTITY*UNIT_PRICE
```

COST will be used as the column heading. Each field can have a column width assigned to it; for example, the code

```
BROWSE FIELDS LASTNAME/8
```

causes the Lastname field to be shortened to eight characters.

```
USE CUSTOMERS                  && open the database
* Look only at the specified fields, allowing editing of data:
* Limit the company field to 10 characters,
* other fields to 20 characters
* Don't allow changing the credit limit field
* Don't allow deleting or adding records
BROWSE NODELETE NOAPPEND FIELDS LASTNAME, COMPANY/10,;
   CRED_LIM /R, SALESMAN WIDTH 20
```

CALCULATE

Syntax

```
CALCULATE [<scope>] <option list>
   [FOR <condition>]
   [WHILE <condition>]
   [TO <memory variable list> /TO ARRAY <array name>]
```

Purpose: Computes various financial and statistical functions from the data fields in your database. The functions available as <*option list*> are shown in Table 22.5.

You can limit the set of figures used to obtain the average by specifying a FOR or WHILE <*condition*>. The calculated values are displayed on-screen (if SET TALK is in its default setting, ON) or stored in the memory variable or array if you use the TO/TO ARRAY option.

Example

```
* Determine the average cost and show the number of items
USE STOCKS
CALCULATE AVG(COST), CNT() TO COST_AVG, NUM_RECS
```

Table 22.5 CALCULATE Options

Option	Action
AVG(<*numeric expression*>)	Calculates the arithmetic average of the values in the numeric field
CNT( )	Counts the number of records that meet the FOR <*condition*>
MAX(<*expression*>)	Returns the largest value in the database field. The database field can be a numeric, date, or character field.
MIN(<*expression*>)	Returns the smallest value in the database field. The database field can be a numeric, date, or character field.
NPV(<*rate*>, <*flows*>, <*initial*>)	Calculates the net present value of the database field. The <*rate*> is the discount rate as a decimal number, as in .10 for 10%. The <*flows*> are a series of signed periodic cash flow values. The <*initial*> parameter is the initial investment.
STD(<*expression*>)	Calculates the standard deviation of the values in the database field. The standard deviation is the square root of the variance.
SUM(<*numeric expression*>)	Returns the sum of the values in the database field for the records specified by the FOR <*condition*>
VAR(<*numeric expression*>)	Determines the population variance of the values in the database field

CALL

Syntax

```
CALL <module name> [WITH <expression list>]
```

Purpose: Executes a binary file program module that has been loaded into memory with the LOAD command. Such files are generally assembly language programs that perform some special function. You can load as many as 16 binary program files at once, and each file can be as many as 64K long.

Some binary program files require an *<expression list>* of variables to be passed to and from the program. The data supplied in the *<expression list>* must be in the form expected by the called program.

Example

```
* Call the FINDFILE.BIN assembly language program
* The BIN file has been previously loaded with LOAD.
filename = "CUSTOMER.INF"     && find this file
foundfile = 0                 && will be 1 if file found
CALL findfile WITH filename, foundfile
IF foundfile = 1
   ? "Found the file!"
ELSE
   ? "Didn't find the file!"
ENDIF
```

CANCEL

Syntax

```
CANCEL
```

Purpose: Stops the currently executing program, closes all program files, and returns you to the Command window. (Procedure files are not closed.) Use this command to stop everything when you test and debug your programs.

Example

```
* Ask whether OK to cancel program
answer = .F.
@ 24,25 SAY "Cancel program? (Y/N) " ;
GET answer PICTURE "Y"
READ
IF answer
   CLOSE PROCEDURE      && needed because CANCEL
                        && doesn't close procedure
   CANCEL
ENDIF
```

CHANGE/EDIT

Syntax

```
CHANGE/EDIT
   [NOINIT]
   [NOFOLLOW]
   [NOAPPEND]
   [NOMENU]
   [NOEDIT]
   [NODELETE]
   [NOCLEAR]
   [NOORGANIZE]
   [<record number>]
   [FIELDS <field list>]
   [<scope>]
   [FOR <condition>]
   [WHILE <condition>]
```

Purpose: Enables you to edit and change the contents of records in the current database or view. CHANGE and EDIT commands are identical. If you don't use FOR, WHILE, or a scope, all records are accessible with the PgUp and PgDn keys.

You can change between BROWSE and EDIT mode by using the F2 key, unless the FOR, WHILE, or *<scope>* option is specified.

You can use the arrow keys to move from field to field in the record. You can use the PgUp and PgDn keys to move to the preceding record or the next record. You can use Ctrl-End to save all changes and Esc to save all changes except those changes made to the current record. Use Ctrl-Home (or F9) to edit a memo field, and press Ctrl-Home again when you have finished with the memo field.

If you use PgDn when you are at the last record, you can append records to the database, unless you use the NOAPPEND option. If you are using dBASE 5 on a network, the current record is LOCKED when you make a change, along with any related records, but the EDIT/CHANGE command is active.

Options for the CHANGE and EDIT commands are described in Table 22.6.

Table 22.6 CHANGE/EDIT Options

Option	Description
NOINIT	Uses the command line options that you specified with the previous CHANGE/EDIT command
NOFOLLOW	When you use an indexed file, this option doesn't reposition the record if you make a change to a field that is part of the index. If you omit this command, a change to an index field in a record causes the screen to redisplay.
NOAPPEND	Prevents you from appending records to the database if you move past the last record
NOMENU	Prevents the display of the menu bar
NOEDIT	Prevents you from making changes to any field
NODELETE	Prevents you from deleting records
NOCLEAR	Keeps the CHANGE/EDIT form on-screen when you finish editing. Omitting this option clears the screen after you exit.
NOORGANIZE	Prevents use of the Organize menu
<record number>	Enables you to edit a specific record, rather than the current record
FIELDS *<field list>*	Enables you to specify which fields will be edited or changed
<scope>	Enables you to specify the number of records used. NEXT 12 would limit you to the next 12 records.
FOR *<condition>*	Enables changes only to those records that meet the condition. FOR STATE = "CA" would permit changes to records whose two-character STATE field contains "CA".
WHILE *<condition>*	Is similar to FOR *<condition>* but begins with the current record and continues as long as the condition is true. WHILE COST < 1000 enables you to edit or change records until a record is found that has a COST of 1000 or more.

Example

```
* Go to record 15, edit the indicated fields
* in the record
* Don't allow appending or deleting records
USE INVOICE              && open the database
GOTO 15                  && goto record 15
EDIT NOAPPEND NODELETE FIELDS CUSTOMER, ITEM, QUANTITY, COST
```

CLEAR

Syntax

```
CLEAR [ALL/FIELDS/GETS/MEMORY/MENUS/
   POPUPS/TYPEAHEAD/WINDOWS/SCREENS]
```

Purpose: Clears the current screen or window and releases any active GET statements. You can specify only one CLEAR action per command.

The ALL option closes all open databases and their associated index, format, and memo files. ALL also releases all memory variables and closes any active catalog file. The FIELDS option releases the field list you set with SET FIELDS. The GETS option clears any open @...GET statements.

The MEMORY option releases any memory variables and performs the same function as RELEASE ALL used at the Command window. The MENUS option clears all user menus from the screen and erases them from memory. The POPUPS option does the same for pop-up menus. The TYPEAHEAD option clears any pending keystrokes in the keyboard buffer. The WINDOWS option clears all windows from the screen and deletes them from memory. CLEAR SCREEN clears all screen memory variables.

You can only use this command with non-UI screens and windows like those created in previous versions of dBASE. It is ignored by dBASE 5's UI objects.

Example

```
* Clear any waiting keystrokes
CLEAR TYPEAHEAD
* Clear the current SET FIELDS list
CLEAR FIELDS
```

CLOSE

Syntax

```
CLOSE ALL
CLOSE ALTERNATE
CLOSE DATABASES
CLOSE FORMAT
CLOSE INDEXES
CLOSE PRINTER
CLOSE PROCEDURE
```

Purpose: Closes any open files. Closing database files with CLOSE DATABASES also closes the database's index, memo, and format files. Properly closing a file ensures that the data is written to disk. The CLOSE ALL command closes all types of files, and returns you to work area 1.

Example

```
CLOSE ALL              && close all files
CLOSE PROCEDURE        && close the procedure file
CLOSE DATABASES        && close DBF DBT NDX MDX FMT files
USE IN 1               && closes DBF in area 1 without
                       && selecting area 1
```

COMPILE

Syntax

```
COMPILE [AUTO] <filename> [,<filename>...] [RUNTIME]
```

Purpose: Reads one or more dBASE 5 programs *<filename>*, and compiles them into executable object code files. The RUNTIME option lists as errors any commands not allowed by the dBASE 5 executable version or compiler. The [AUTO] option makes dBASE check the dates of all the object files used by your program and recompile those whose date is earlier than its source.

When you run a program from the Command window, you use DO *<PRG filename>*; dBASE 5 then compiles the program into an OBJ Code file and runs the program. The COMPILE command compiles the program file without running the program. During the compilation process, the preprocessor directives are processed, each command line in the program is checked for proper syntax, and errors are reported. You should recompile programs created in earlier versions of dBASE 5 before running them under dBASE 5.

The COMPILE command optimizes the object code at the time it is invoked. Constant expressions will be combined and stored in their simplest form. With SET EXACT OFF, IF "ABCDE"="ABC" is stored as IF .F. regardless of what EXACT is set to at runtime.

Caution

Make sure that all your program files have different file names. If you have a CUSTLIST.PRG and CUSTLIST.PRC file, compiling one will overwrite the OBJ Code of the other.

Example

```
* Compile the MAINPROG.PRG program
* (This command is usually used from the Command window,
* not from within programs)
COMPILE mainprog
```

CONTINUE

Syntax

```
CONTINUE
```

Purpose: Searches for the next record that matches the condition specified by the most recent LOCATE command. The LOCATE command finds the first record in the database that matches a specified condition. You then can determine whether that record is the record you want. If it is not, use CONTINUE to look for the next match. You can repeat the CONTINUE command until the end of the LOCATE scope or the end of the file, using the FOUND( ) function to determine if you have found the data you were looking for.

Example

```
SET ESCAPE OFF
USE members
LOCATE FOR date < {04/01/93}
DO WHILE .NOT. EOF() .AND. LASTKEY() <> 27   && Let   user escape
   mYes = .F.
   @ 10, 10 SAY firstname + lastname
   @ 14, 10 SAY "Delete this record? Y/N:"
   @ 14, 35 GET mYes PICTURE "Y"
   READ
   IF mYes
      DELETE
   ENDIF
   CONTINUE
ENDDO
```

CONVERT

Syntax

```
CONVERT [TO <numeric value>]
```

Purpose: Adds to the database a special field for holding information about whether a record currently is locked while being used by another user. The added field, called _dBASElock, is a character field with a default length of 16.

TO *<numeric value>* changes the field length. Allowable lengths are 8 through 24.

The _dBASElock field has space for the following values:

Count	A two-byte hexadecimal number used by CHANGE( ).
Time	A three-byte hexadecimal number containing the time the lock was placed on the record.
Date	A three-byte hexadecimal number containing the date the lock was placed on the record.

Name	A 0- to 16-character representation of the log-in name of the user who is using the record.

Every time a record is changed, the count value increases. You can use the CHANGE( ) function to determine whether the record has been changed. Repositioning the record pointer with the GOTO command sets CHANGE( ) to false, unless another user has made a change to the record. The LKSYS( ) function retrieves the _dBASElock information.

Example

```
* Change a single-user DBF file to a multiuser file
USE CUSTOMER EXCLUSIVE
CONVERT
```

COPY

See COPY TO

COPY FILE

Syntax

```
COPY FILE <filename> TO <filename>
```

Purpose: Is similar to the COPY command in MS-DOS. COPY FILE creates a duplicate of any file. Specify the complete file name and extension for each file to copy. Prompts you to verify you want to overwrite an existing file if SET SAFETY is ON.

Use COPY TO to copy data tables and associated memos and indexes.

Example

```
* Convert a QBE file to
* a program
COPY FILE QTRSALES.QBE TO QTRSALES.PRG
```

COPY INDEXES

Syntax

```
COPY INDEXES <NDX file list>
   [TO <MDX filename>]
```

Purpose: Transforms a list of single-index (NDX) files into index tags contained in a single multiple-index (MDX) file. This capability converts dBASE III index files into MDX files. The TO option enables you to specify the name of the MDX file; if the name is not specified, the files are placed in the current MDX file. If the MDX file does not exist, it is created. The NDX files must be in use before you use the COPY INDEXES command.

Example

```
* Copy the old index files into the MEMBERS.MDX file
USE MEMBERS INDEX LASTNAME, CITY, MEMNUM
COPY INDEXES LASTNAME, CITY, MEMNUM
* Make the MDX file active, closing old index files
CLOSE INDEXES         && production won't be closed
```

COPY MEMO

Syntax

```
COPY MEMO <memo field name> TO <filename>
   [ADDITIVE]
```

Purpose: Copies the information from the memo field of the current record to a file. The ADDITIVE option adds the data to the *<filename>* if it exists; otherwise, the file name is overwritten. If the file name exists, it can be overwritten with SET SAFETY OFF. If you used SET SAFETY ON, dBASE 5 prompts you for verification before overwriting the file.

Example

```
USE CLIENTS                 && open the database
GOTO 12                     && record 12
* Copy record 12's NOTES memo data to the
* CLIENT.TXT file, adding to existing data
COPY MEMO NOTES TO CLIENTS.TXT ADDITIVE
```

COPY STRUCTURE

Syntax

```
COPY STRUCTURE TO <filename>
   [FIELDS <field list>] [WITH PRODUCTION]
```

Purpose: Copies the structure of the current database to a new DBF file but does not copy any data. This action creates an empty database (and associated memo file if needed) from the current database. Use the FIELDS option to specify a list of fields; otherwise, the command affects all the fields in the current database. If PROTECT currently is in use, only those fields authorized to the current user are copied to the new file. To also make a copy of all the index tag expressions in the production MDX file, use the WITH PRODUCTION option.

Example

```
* Create a new database structure from the CLIENTS list
USE CLIENTS
COPY STRUCTURE TO REGION10
```

COPY TAG

Syntax

```
COPY TAG <tag name> [OF <MDX filename>] TO <NDX filename>
```

Purpose: Converts dBASE 5 multiple-index files (MDX) into single-index (NDX) files. You can use COPY TAG to convert dBASE 5 indexes into dBASE III indexes. To use the command, you must have a database active. Only one index tag can be created at a time.

Example

```
* Create a LASTNAME.NDX file from the current database
* The MEMBERS database has an MDX file called MEMBERS.MDX
* There are two index tag fields in
* MEMBERS: LASTNAME and CITY,
* so two COPY TAG commands are needed to create the
* MEMLAST.NDX and MEMCITY.NDX index files
USE MEMBERS
COPY TAG LASTNAME TO MEMLAST
COPY TAG CITY TO MEMCITY
```

COPY TO

Syntax

```
COPY TO <filename>
   [[TYPE] <file type>]
   [FIELDS <field list>]
   [<scope>]
   [FOR <condition>]
   [WHILE <condition>]
   [WITH PRODUCTION]
```

Purpose: Copies all or part of the currently active database into a new file. COPY TO also exports data for use by other programs. All records are copied, including records that were marked for deletion. (Use SET DELETED ON to prevent copying of records marked for deletion.) You can limit the records being copied by using a scope or by using the FOR and WHILE options. If you need only some of the fields in the new file, use the FIELDS option. The WITH PRODUCTION option copies the production index if you are creating a dBASE 5 file.

The TYPE option enables you to copy to non-dBASE 5 file formats. Table 22.7 lists the options and the file types they create.

Table 22.7 TYPE <*file type*> Options

Option	Description
DELIMITED	Comma-separated ASCII file. All fields are separated by commas, and character field data is surrounded by double quotes. Each record is placed on a separate line. Most programs have an option that lets them import comma-delimited files. Creates a TXT file.
DELIMITED WITH <*delimiter*>	Similar to a delimited file, but character fields are surrounded by the character you specify in <*delimiter*>. Creates a TXT file.
DELIMITED WITH BLANK	A delimited file in which character fields are separated by a space character. Creates a TXT file.
SDF	System Data Format ASCII file. A fixed-length file in which each field has the width of the record in the DBF file. A character field of 10 characters will always have 10 characters in it, even if any or all of the positions are blank. Creates a TXT file.
DBASEII	Exports data into a dBASE II (DB2) file. You need to rename the file with a DBF file extension before the file can be used in dBASE II.
DBMEMO3	Exports a dBASE 5 database that contains a memo field into database (DBF) and memo (DBT) files usable by dBASE III. You must use this option to export to dBASE III a dBASE 5 database that has a memo field. Note that dBASE 5 can use and modify dBASE III DBF/DBT files, but you need to use COPY...DB3MEMO to make dBASE 5 files usable by dBASE III.
RPD	RapidFile RPD file format.
FW2	Framework II (FW2) database format.
SYLK	A Multiplan spreadsheet formula file. Each record is converted to a Multiplan row, and fields are converted to columns in the row. The database field names are used as the headings for each column in the spreadsheet file.
DIF	VisiCalc Version 1 (DIF) format. Each record is converted to a VisiCalc row, and fields are converted to columns in the row. The database field names are used as the headings for each column in the spreadsheet file.
WKS	Lotus 1-2-3 release 1A (WKS) format. Each record is converted to a row, and fields are converted to columns in the row. The database field names are used as the headings for each column in the spreadsheet file.

When specifying a file name, do not use the single letters A through J, or M. You can specify a file name such as AA, or other double-letter combinations.

You can use indirect file names as the *<filename>*, which is much faster than using macro substitution file names. If fields in the database were protected with PROTECT, only those fields for which the user has privileges are copied to the new file.

Example

```
USE CUSTOMERS                   && open the database
* Create a WKS file with these fields
COPY TO CUSTOMER TYPE WKS FIELDS COMPANY, CRED_AMT,;
  PAST_DUE
* Create a delimited text file for records
* whose PAST_DUE field is greater than 1000
outfile = "PASTDUE"             && use indirect reference
COPY TO (outfile) TYPE DELIMITED FOR PAST_DUE > 1000
```

COPY TO...STRUCTURE EXTENDED

Syntax

```
COPY TO <filename> STRUCTURE EXTENDED
```

Purpose: Creates a database file containing five fields with information about the structure of the currently active database file: FIELD_NAME, FIELD_TYPE, FIELD_LEN, FIELD_DEC, and FIELD_IDX. This command enables you to create or modify database file structures from within applications without accessing the full-screen interactive process invoked by MODIFY STRUCTURE. The files created are not compatible with versions of dBASE prior to dBASE IV.

Example

```
* Create a structure database from the current database
USE Customer
COPY TO Custstru STRUCTURE EXTENDED
```

COPY TO ARRAY

Syntax

```
COPY TO ARRAY <array name> [FIELDS <field list>]
   [<scope>]
   [FOR <condition>]
   [WHILE <condition>]
```

Purpose: Takes the contents of one or more records from the current database and fills an existing array. The array must already have been created with DECLARE. Make sure that the array is big enough to hold the data from the database.

Field data from the first record is stored in the first column of the array; the second data field is stored in the second column, and so on. The next record is stored in the next row of the array. The array is filled within any restrictions you impose with scope, FOR, or WHILE, until all array elements are filled. The data types of the array elements are the same as the data types in the fields you specify.

Example

```
* Fill up the CUST_ARRAY array with data from
* the customer data file
USE CUSTOMER
DECLARE CUST_ARRAY[RECCOUNT(), 3]    && make the array
COPY TO ARRAY CUST_ARRAY FIELDS CUST_NUM, PAYMENT, PAYDATE
```

COUNT

Syntax

```
COUNT [TO <memory variable>]
   [<scope>]
   [FOR <condition>]
   [WHILE <condition>]
```

Purpose: Counts the number of records in the database that meet the scope, FOR, or WHILE condition. The count can be stored in a memory variable with the TO option. In a network, the database is locked for the user until the count is completed. If you are on a network and used SET LOCK OFF, the database is not locked, but you may not get an accurate count if another user also is using the database.

Example

```
* Find the number of stocks that cost more than $50/share
USE STOCKS
COUNT FOR COST > 50 TO counter
? "Items found: ", counter
```

CREATE

Syntax

```
CREATE <filename>
```

Purpose: Creates a new database file structure for use in programming.

Example

```
CREATE Sales
```

CREATE FROM

Syntax

```
CREATE <filename> FROM <structure extended file>
```

Purpose: Creates a database file from the structure specified in the parameter *<structure extended file>*. CREATE FROM can be used to create databases with a structure defined by the user. When the database file is created, it becomes the active file in the current work area. If the structure extended file has a Y in the FIELD_IDX field, a production MDX file is created for the new database.

Example

```
* Copy structure of Customer database and create
* a Client database with same structure
USE Customer
COPY TO Custstru STRUCTURE EXTENDED
CREATE Client FROM Custstru
```

CREATE/MODIFY APPLICATION

Syntax

```
CREATE APPLICATION <filename>/?
MODIFY APPLICATION <filename>/?
```

Purpose: Starts the dBASE 5 Applications Generator. The Applications Generator creates or modifies the programming code for a complete application, including all the code required for accessing data, printing reports, displaying menus, responding to user selections, and so on. You also can start the Applications Generator from the Control Center.

Example

```
* Create the Payables application
* (This command is normally used
* at the Command window, not in programs)
CREATE APPLICATION payables
```

CREATE/MODIFY LABEL

Syntax

```
CREATE LABEL <filename>
```

Purpose: Causes the labels design screen to appear. You then can design new label formats that are stored in the label (LBL) file. The label file is added to the current catalog. The labels design screen is interactive, just like the Control Center.

After you create the label, save it and then use LABEL FORM to print the database data in the label format. When you create labels, dBASE 5 also creates an LBG file that contains the program commands for printing the label. You can look at or change this file with MODIFY COMMAND *<label filename>*. Changes you make to the LBG file, however, are not reflected in the LBL file.

Example

```
USE CUSTLIST
CREATE LABEL Custmail
```

CREATE/MODIFY QUERY

Syntax

```
CREATE/MODIFY QUERY <filename>/?
```

Purpose: Accesses the queries design screen to create a new query or modify an existing query. A query extracts records that meet the defined query conditions. You also can use a query to modify records in your database. If you use the ? parameter, dBASE 5 shows you a list of available queries. On this list, you can highlight the query you want to use and then press Enter. The query is added to the current catalog.

See Chapter 9 for information on how to use the queries design screen.

Example

```
* Modify the FINDCUST query
* (This command is normally used at the
* Command window, not in a program)
MODIFY QUERY FINDCUST
```

CREATE/MODIFY REPORT

Syntax

```
CREATE REPORT <filename>/?
MODIFY REPORT <filename>/?
```

Purpose: Brings up the dBASE 5 Reports design screen, which enables you to create or modify report forms (FRM files). The Reports design screen enables you to make simple or complex reports based on the active database and any related databases. If you have a catalog open and you have SET CATALOG ON, the report form is added to the catalog. If you use the ? parameter instead of the *<filename>*, dBASE 5 shows a list of all report form files in the current drive/directory. You also can access the Reports design screen from the dBASE 5 Control Center.

After you save the report form file, a generated report form (FRG) file is created. This file contains the dBASE 5 commands required to print the report. You can use MODIFY COMMAND or a text editor to change the FRG file, but changes you make to the FRG file do not affect the FRM file.

Note

When you use dBASE 5 to modify a report form created in dBASE III, the form is saved in a dBASE 5 format and is no longer usable in dBASE III. The dBASE III report is saved in its original form with an FR3 extension.

Example

```
* Change the report form
MODIFY REPORT sales
```

CREATE/MODIFY SCREEN

Syntax

```
CREATE/MODIFY SCREEN <filename>/?
```

Purpose: Accesses the Forms design screen to create custom screen forms that specify the placement of text and data input fields. CREATE creates a new screen. MODIFY changes existing screen files. Use the ? parameter to choose from a list of screens. See Chapter 7 for more information on screen creation.

Example

```
* Change the INV_EDIT screen format
* (This command is normally used at the
* Command window, not within programs)
MODIFY SCREEN INV_EDIT
```

CREATE/MODIFY STRUCTURE

Syntax

```
CREATE <filename>
MODIFY STRUCTURE
```

Purpose: Takes you to the database file design screen to create a file or to modify the structure of the existing file. You specify the field names, types, lengths, and the presence of an MDX tag for each field in your database. The database file is created in the current drive and directory, unless you specify another drive or directory. If a catalog is active, the created database is added to the current catalog. The *<filename>* parameter can be an indirect file name.

The structure of all database files is shown in Table 22.8.

Table 22.8 Database Structure

Item	Description
FIELD NAME	The name of the field, as many as 10 characters long. Use letters, numbers, and the underline (_) character. Spaces and other punctuation marks are not allowed, and the first character of the field name must be a letter. Press Enter to finish the field name.
TYPE	The type of field, specified by the first letter of the allowed types. Field types are Character, Numeric (Binary Coded Decimal), Floating point numeric, Logical (.T./.F., Y/N), Date, and Memo. You also can press the space bar until the desired field type is displayed. Press Enter to finish.
WIDTH	The width of the field. For character fields, the width is the maximum number (as many as 254) of characters allowed in the field. Numeric fields can be as many as 20 digits, including the decimal point and sign.
DECIMAL PLACES	For numeric fields, the number of decimal places allowed.
MEMO	A memo field. Memo fields show as memo on-screen (when the associated memo DBT file is empty) or as MEMO if the DBT file has data.
LOGICAL	One-character fields that hold a T (true) or F (false), or Y (Yes) or N (No).
DATE	A date field, normally displayed as MM/DD/YY. If SET CENTURY is ON, dates display as MM/DD/YYYY.
INDEX TAG	If set to Yes or true, a tag is added to the production MDX file, and a production index file is created and updated.

A database can have as many as 255 fields, with as many as 4,000 bytes per record. A record size counter is shown on-screen. Instructions and error messages appear at the bottom of the screen. The pull-down menus at the top of the screen also can be used.

When you use the MODIFY STRUCTURE command, you should change names and insert or delete fields in two separate operations, or some data may be lost. You can convert field types from one type to another, but be sure to keep a backup copy of your database until you are sure that the data was converted properly. A backup copy of the database (named <*database*>.DBK) is kept automatically by dBASE 5, but the copy is overwritten with the next MODIFY STRUCTURE command.

If you are a network user, the database file must not be in use by others when you use the MODIFY STRUCTURE command. Make sure you have exclusive use of the data file by using SET EXCLUSIVE ON before USE or by including the EXCLUSIVE option in your USE command.

CREATE STRUCTURE EXTENDED

Syntax

```
CREATE STRUCTURE EXTENDED <database name>[<.ext>][IN <alias>]
```

or

```
CREATE <database name>[<.ext>][IN <alias>]STRUCTURE EXTENDED
```

Purpose: Creates an empty database consisting of five fields: Field_Name which consists of a ten character field for storing the names of the fields in your database; Field_Type is a field indicating the type of field named in the field_name column; Field_Len specifies the number of characters which can be entered in the field; Field_Dec determines the number of decimal places; and Field_Idx is a logical value which specifies whether or not to create an index. You can use the structure extended database to store the field names and sizes for any data table. You can then use the CREATE FROM command to create a new copy of the data table during program execution.

Example

```
SET TALK OFF
SET ECHO OFF
CREATE Workers STRUCTURE EXTENDED
APPEND BLANK
REPLACE Field_Name WITH "ctEmpId"
REPLACE Field_Type WITH "C"
REPLACE Field_Len WITH 5
REPLACE Field_Idx WITH "Y"
APPEND BLANK
REPLACE Field_Name WITH "ctLastName"
REPLACE Field_Type WITH "C"
REPLACE Field_Len WITH 20
REPLACE Field_Idx WITH "Y"
USE
CREATE Employees FROM Workers
```

CREATE/MODIFY VIEW

Syntax

```
CREATE VIEW <view filename> /? FROM ENVIRONMENT
MODIFY VIEW <filename>
```

Purpose: Builds (CREATE) or changes (MODIFY) a QBE file. Use the ? parameter to choose from a list of QBE and VUE files in the current catalog.

The VUE file contains information about all open database files, indexes, and work areas; relations between open database files; the current work area number; active field lists; open format (FMT) files; and any filter conditions that are in effect. Use SET VIEW TO to activate a QBE or VUE file. Creates a VUE file which is compatible with the dBASE III PLUS requirements as long as the dBASE III PLUS limits are not exceeded by your dBASE for DOS environment.

FROM ENVIRONMENT creates a VUE file from the dBASE 5 environment.

Example

```
* Create the ADDITEMS view for dBASE III users
CREATE VIEW ADDITEMS FROM ENVIRONMENT
* Create QBE file
CREATE VIEW Augsales
```

DEACTIVATE MENU

Syntax

```
DEACTIVATE MENU
```

Purpose: Deactivates the active menu bar and removes it from the screen, but keeps the menu bar in memory for later use. Because this command always acts on the current menu, you don't need to specify a menu name. DEACTIVATE MENU returns program control to the line following ACTIVATE MENU.

You can only use this command with non-UI screens and windows like those created in previous versions of dBASE. It is ignored by dBASE 5's UI objects.

Example

```
* Deactivate the current menu
DEACTIVATE MENU
```

DEACTIVATE POPUP

Syntax

```
DEACTIVATE POPUP
```

Purpose: Removes the current pop-up from the screen but leaves the pop-up in memory for later use. Any text that was concealed by the pop-up is redisplayed. This command can be used in a program only because a pop-up must be on-screen for it to be deactivated. Program control is returned to the line following ACTIVATE POPUP.

You can only use this command with non-UI screens and windows like those created in previous versions of dBASE. It is ignored by dBASE 5's UI objects.

Example

```
* Deactivate the current pop-up
DEACTIVATE POPUP
```

DEACTIVATE WINDOW

Syntax

```
DEACTIVATE WINDOW <window name list> / ALL
```

Purpose: Clears the windows from the screen but does not delete them from memory. You can redisplay the windows with the ACTIVATE WINDOW command. Any text that was "behind" the window is redisplayed. You can specify a *<window name list>* or use ALL to clear all windows from the screen.

You can only use this command with non-UI screens and windows like those created in previous versions of dBASE. It is ignored by dBASE 5's UI objects.

Example

```
* Clear these two previously loaded windows
DEACTIVATE WINDOW EDIT_WIN, HELP_WIN
```

DEBUG

Syntax

```
DEBUG <filename> / <procedure name> [WITH <parameter list>]
```

Purpose: Starts the dBASE 5 program debugger so that you can see the commands as they execute. You can edit the program or procedure, display the values of expressions, and set breakpoints or stopping points for the program.

The debugger divides the screen into four windows: an edit window, a debug window, a breakpoint window, and a display window.

Example

```
* Debug the CUSTEDIT program
* (The command is normally used from
* the Command window, not in programs)
DEBUG custedit
```

DECLARE

Syntax

```
DECLARE <array name 1>
      [{<number of rows>,} <number of columns>]
   {,<array name 2>
      [{<number of rows>,} <number of columns>]
...}
```

Purpose: Creates one- or two-dimensional arrays of memory variables. Because brackets are part of the command syntax, braces are used in this syntax to show optional items. Note that an entry in brackets ([ ]) is required in an array definition, as in DECLARE readings[20,3]. Array names can contain as many as 10 characters and can contain letters, numbers, or underscores (_), but the names *must* start with a letter. If only one number is specified, the array is one-dimensional. The maximum size of an array (number of rows multiplied by the number of columns) is 65,535. Use PUBLIC ARRAY to declare public arrays.

Example

```
* Create a two-dimensional parts array and a one-dimensional costs
array
DECLARE arr_parts[100,2]
DECLARE arr_cost[100]
```

DEFINE BAR

Syntax

```
DEFINE BAR <line number> OF <pop-up name>
   PROMPT <character expression>
   [MESSAGE <character expression>]
   [SKIP [FOR <condition>]]
```

Purpose: Defines a single option (bar) in a pop-up menu. One DEFINE BAR command is needed for each choice in the pop-up. The *<line number>* specifies where the pop-up bar appears. If the line number exceeds the number of lines available in the pop-up window, the user can scroll choices in the pop-up to reach the option.

PROMPT specifies the text to appear on the bar. Any specified line of text that exceeds the width of the bar is truncated to fit. A minimum of one bar is needed for each pop-up.

MESSAGE enables you to display a message, usually on the last line of the screen (message placement can be changed with the SET MESSAGE AT command). MESSAGE normally provides additional information about the pop-up choice (such as a description) and is limited to 79 characters. The SKIP option displays the bar and its text but prevents the user from selecting the option. SKIP FOR displays the bar at all times but allows its selection only if the *<condition>* is met.

You can only use this command with non-UI screens and windows like those created in previous versions of dBASE. It is ignored by dBASE 5's UI objects.

Example

```
* Define two pop-up bars
DEFINE BAR 12 OF PRINTBAR PROMPT "Choice 1"
DEFINE BAR 13 OF PRINTBAR PROMPT "Choice 2"
* Redefine the second choice so that it can't be selected
bar13 = .F.
DEFINE BAR 13 OF PRINTBAR PROMPT "Choice 2";
   SKIP FOR .NOT. bar13
```

DEFINE BOX FROM

Syntax

```
DEFINE BOX FROM <print column> TO <print column>
      HEIGHT <number of rows>
   [AT LINE <print line>]
   [SINGLE/DOUBLE/<border definition string>]
```

Purpose: Defines the size and style of a box to be printed around lines of text. The left and right edges of the box are defined by the FROM...TO parameters. The HEIGHT parameter specifies the height of the box. Use AT LINE to specify the beginning line number for the top edge of the box; if you don't use AT LINE, the current print line is used.

The box can be made up of single or double lines (SINGLE or DOUBLE), or the characters specified in the *<border definition string>*, which follows the rules of the SET BORDER command.

The _BOX system variable must be set to true for the box to be printed. You use the ?/?? command to specify which text to print in the box.

This command is ignored by dBASE 5 UI objects.

Example

```
* Print a box around the title block
STORE .T. TO_box
CLEAR
DEFINE BOX FROM 20 TO 79 HEIGHT 6 DOUBLE
? &&blank line
? "SALES REPORT" AT 42
? DTOC(DATE())   AT 42
?
?
?
```

DEFINE BROWSE

See Chapter 26, "Using UI Properties, Methods, and Commands."

DEFINE CHECKBOX

See Chapter 26, "Using UI Properties, Methods, and Commands."

VI

Reference Guide

DEFINE COMBOBOX

See Chapter 26, "Using UI Properties, Methods, and Commands."

DEFINE EDITOR

See Chapter 26, "Using UI Properties, Methods, and Commands."

DEFINE ENTRYFIELD

See Chapter 26, "Using UI Properties, Methods, and Commands."

DEFINE FIELD

See Chapter 26, "Using UI Properties, Methods, and Commands."

DEFINE FIELDLIST

See Chapter 26, "Using UI Properties, Methods, and Commands."

DEFINE FORM

See Chapter 26, "Using UI Properties, Methods, and Commands."

DEFINE LISTBOX

See Chapter 26, "Using UI Properties, Methods, and Commands."

DEFINE MENU

Syntax

```
DEFINE MENU <menu name> [MESSAGE <character text>]
```

Purpose: Used with the DEFINE PAD command to create a menu bar. Using DEFINE MENU is the first step in creating a menu bar. The command assigns a name to the menu bar. The optional MESSAGE parameter displays a message of as many as 79 characters at the bottom of the screen. Any message assigned by the DEFINE PAD command overwrites the MENU message, unless you relocate the message with the SET MESSAGE AT command.

You can only use this command with non-UI screens and windows like those created in previous versions of dBASE. It is ignored by dBASE 5's UI objects.

Example

```
* Define the MAINMENU menu bar
DEFINE MENU mainmenu
```

DEFINE MENU...OF

See Chapter 26, "Using UI Properties, Methods, and Commands."

DEFINE MENUBAR

See Chapter 26, "Using UI Properties, Methods, and Commands."

DEFINE MENUITEM

See Chapter 26, "Using UI Properties, Methods, and Commands."

DEFINE OBJECT

See Chapter 26, "Using UI Properties, Methods, and Commands."

DEFINE PAD

Syntax

```
DEFINE PAD <pad name> OF <menu name>
PROMPT <character expression>
   [AT <row>, <col>]
   [MESSAGE <character expression>]
```

Purpose: Defines a single pad of a menu. A *pad* is a choice that is selected from the menu. Use DEFINE PAD to specify all of the pads of a menu. You must use the DEFINE MENU command to define the menu name before you define the pad for that menu.

The PROMPT text is displayed inside the menu pad. Each prompt gets one blank space added to the prompt text. The line AT *<row>*, *<column>* defines the starting location of the prompt text; if this information is not specified, the text is displayed in the upper left corner of the screen. You may need to use the SET SCOREBOARD OFF command to prevent the scoreboard from overwriting any pad text on the first line (line 0) of the screen.

When the menu is displayed on-screen, the left- and right-arrow keys are used to move from one pad prompt to another. For each pad, an optional MESSAGE can be displayed at the bottom of the screen; the message can be as many as 79 characters long.

You can only use this command with non-UI screens and windows like those created in previous versions of dBASE. It is ignored by dBASE 5's UI objects.

Example

```
* Define a menu
DEFINE MENU print
* Define the four pads of the print menu
DEFINE PAD print1 OF print PROMPT "to printer 1"
DEFINE PAD print2 OF print PROMPT "to printer 2"
DEFINE PAD screen OF print PROMPT "to screen"
DEFINE PAD file OF print PROMPT "to file"
```

DEFINE PAGEBREAK

See Chapter 26, "Using UI Properties, Methods, and Commands."

DEFINE POPUP

Syntax

```
DEFINE POPUP <pop-up name> FROM <row 1>, <col 1>
     [TO <row 2>, <col 2>]
   [PROMPT FIELD <fieldname>]
      / PROMPT FILES [LIKE <skeleton>
      / PROMPT STRUCTURE]
      [MESSAGE <character expression>]
```

Purpose: Defines a pop-up menu that contains special fields, messages, and a border. The *<pop-up name>* is the name used when you activate the pop-up or use the ON SELECTION POPUP command. The FROM and TO values are coordinates defining the upper-left and lower-right corners of the pop-up window. The pop-up menu covers any text on-screen within those coordinates. When the pop-up is deactivated, the hidden text is redisplayed.

If you omit the TO coordinates, dBASE 5 automatically sizes the pop-up for the longest field and maximum number of lines: the last column will be 79, and the bottom line number will be the line above the status bar. If the status bar was turned off with SET STATUS OFF, the number of the last line will be one line less than the maximum number of lines on-screen. The minimum window size is 1 row and 1 column. Any prompt lines that don't fit in the pop-up window can be scrolled as the user moves the cursor through the choices.

Use PROMPT FIELD, PROMPT FILES, or PROMPT STRUCTURE if you don't want to use the DEFINE BAR command to create the menu choices for your pop-up menu. PROMPT FIELD places the contents of the named field for each record in the database in the pop-up window (memo fields are not displayed). The PROMPT FILES command displays the catalog file name in the pop-up window. (The LIKE parameter displays only those catalog files that match the *<skeleton>*.) The PROMPT STRUCTURE option displays the fields of the database, or the fields defined by the SET FIELDS list if you used SET FIELDS TO.

The MESSAGE text appears centered at the bottom of the screen, overwriting any other text in that position, including any SET MESSAGE TO text.

You can only use this command with non-UI screens and windows like those created in previous versions of dBASE. It is ignored by dBASE 5's UI objects.

Example

```
* Define the popups
DEFINE POPUP edit_pop from 3,4 TO 10,10
DEFINE POPUP show_pop from 3,15 TO 12,23 PROMPT FILES
DEFINE POPUP prnt_pop from 3,30 TO 8,41;
MESSAGE "Choose a print option"
```

DEFINE PUSHBUTTON

See Chapter 26, "Using UI Properties, Methods, and Commands."

DEFINE RADIOBUTTON

See Chapter 26, "Using UI Properties, Methods, and Commands."

DEFINE RECTANGLE

See Chapter 26, "Using UI Properties, Methods, and Commands."

DEFINE SPINBOX

See Chapter 26, "Using UI Properties, Methods, and Commands."

DEFINE TEXT

See Chapter 26, "Using UI Properties, Methods, and Commands."

DEFINE WINDOW

Syntax

```
DEFINE WINDOW <window name> FROM <row 1>, <col 1>
      TO <row 2>, <col 2>
   [DOUBLE/PANEL/NONE/<border definition string>]
   [COLOR [<standard>] [, <enhanced>] [,<frame>]]
```

Purpose: Defines a window's name, placement, borders, and screen colors. The FROM parameter determines the upper-left corner of the window; the TO parameter sets the lower-right corner. The default border is a single-line box; you can specify DOUBLE for a double-line box or NONE for no lines around the border. The *<border definition string>* follows the rules of the SET BORDER command.

The COLOR option enables you to specify the foreground and background colors used for standard and enhanced characters, and the foreground and background colors used for the frame. Colors are specified in the same way they are with SET COLOR TO. Windows you create with the DEFINE WINDOW command are displayed with the ACTIVATE WINDOW command.

You can only use this command with non-UI screens and windows like those created in previous versions of dBASE. It is ignored by dBASE 5's UI objects.

Example

```
* Define a double-line window
DEFINE WINDOW edit_win FROM 3,10 TO 12,70 DOUBLE
```

DELETE

Syntax

```
DELETE
   [<scope>]
   [FOR <condition>]
   [WHILE <condition>]
```

Purpose: Marks records for deletion in the current database. The records are not removed from the database until you use the PACK command. Records marked for deletion can be unmarked with the RECALL command (see RECALL).

The DISPLAY and LIST commands show marked records with an asterisk (*) in the first column. If the status bar is on-screen (SET STATUS ON), Del is displayed on the status bar to indicate marked records. Use Ctrl-U to mark or recall records when in BROWSE or EDIT. To mark groups of records for deletion, use the scope, FOR *<condition>*, or WHILE *<condition>*. If SET DELETED is ON, deleted records will not display.

Note

DELETE only marks records for deletion. To delete files, use the ERASE command.

Example

```
* Remove all inactive customers
* (Make sure that the date is set correctly!)
USE CUSTOMERS EXCLUSIVE      && open the database
* Mark all records whose last order was more than
* one year ago
DELETE FOR YEAR(Last_ord) < Year(Date())
* Recall customers with no order date, since
* these are probably new customers
RECALL FOR ISBLANK(Last_ord)
* Permanently delete marked records
PACK
```

DELETE FILE

Syntax

```
DELETE FILE <filename> / ?
```

Purpose: Removes a file from disk. These commands are equivalent to the DELETE or ERASE commands in MS-DOS. The *<filename>* parameter must include the file extension. The ? parameter shows you a menu of files. If you erase a database (DBF) file, you also may need to erase the associated memo (DBT) and multiple-index (MDX) files. You cannot use wild cards (*, ?) with the ERASE/DELETE command. The *<filename>* must be closed before you can delete it.

Example

```
* Delete the CUSTTEMP.DBF file and its memo file
ERASE CUSTTEMP.DBF        && assumes file is not in use
ERASE CUSTTEMP.DBT        && delete the memo file
ERASE CUSTTEMP.MDX        && and the multiple-index file
* Remove temporary database
DELETE FILE TEMP.DBF
```

DELETE TAG

Syntax

```
DELETE TAG
   <tag name 1> [OF <MDX filename>]
   [,<tag name 2> [OF <MDX filename>]
   ...]
```

Purpose: Removes index tags from multiple-index (MDX) files if you specify tag names. If you specify index file names, the specified indexes are deleted but not closed. This command enables you to remove from the MDX file any index tags that will not be needed. This may speed up operations that move through the database, such as DISPLAY or LIST.

You also can use DELETE TAG if you are approaching the limit of 47 tags per single MDX file.

You can specify more than one index tag name to be deleted from the MDX file. If you delete all index tags from an MDX file, the MDX file also is deleted.

Example

```
* Remove the CITY tag from the MEMBER.MDX file
USE MEMBER
DELETE TAG CITY
```

DEXPORT

Syntax

```
DEXPORT SCREEN/REPORT/LABEL <filename> [TO <BNL filename>]
```

Purpose: Creates a Binary Named List (BNL) file from a screen, report, or label design file that can be used with the DGEN( ) function to generate dBASE code. dBASE 5 uses the following file extensions for BNL files:

Screens	SNL
Reports	FNL
Labels	LNL

Example

```
DEXPORT SCREEN MYFORM.SCR TO MYFORM
genok=DGEN("FORM.GEN", "MYFORM.SNL")
```

DIRECTORY/DIR

Syntax

```
DIRECTORY/DIR
   [[ON] <drive>:]
   [[LIKE] [<path>] <skeleton>]
```

Purpose: Shows a list of files that match the optional *<skeleton>*; this command is similar to the DOS DIR command. If you don't specify a file skeleton, only database files are listed. For database files, the file name, number of records, file size (in bytes), and amount of remaining space on the disk are shown. A DIR listing of other files shows only the file names. (The file information may not be current unless SET AUTOSAVE is ON. See SET AUTOSAVE.)

Example

```
DIR                 && show all DBF files in current directory
DIR *.FMT           && show only the format files in
                    && current directory
DIR CL*             && show only DBF files starting with CL
DIR D:\DBASE4\DATA  && show DBF files in D:\DBASE4\DATA\
```

DISPLAY/LIST

Syntax

```
DISPLAY/LIST [[FIELDS] <expression list>][OFF]
  [<scope>][FOR <condition>] [WHILE <condition>]
  [TO PRINTER/TO FILE <filename>]
```

Purpose: Shows the contents of the current database on-screen. The DISPLAY command shows only the current record unless a scope is specified. DISPLAY produces a pause at each screenful of data; LIST scrolls all data until the command is completed. You can pause the LIST display by pressing Ctrl-S; press any key to continue. You can press the Esc key to abort LIST or DISPLAY unless you used SET ESCAPE OFF, in which case the Esc key is ignored (see SET ESCAPE OFF).

All fields are displayed unless you used the FIELDS option to specify the desired fields. If the combined width of the fields is wider than your display, the rest of the field information is displayed on subsequent screen lines. If the memo field is empty, memo is displayed. If the memo field has data, MEMO is displayed. You can use the SET MEMOWIDTH command to limit the width of the memo field when displayed (see SET MEMOWIDTH).

You can limit the number of records listed with the scope, FOR, or WHILE options. Use TO PRINTER to print the list; use TO FILE *<filename>* to place the list in a file. The record numbers are displayed unless you use the OFF option.

The field names are shown at the top of the list if SET HEADING is ON (see SET HEADING ON).

Example

```
* Display all records of the ORDERS file that show
* orders on back order (SHIPDATE date field is blank).
* Suppress record numbers from the display.
* All fields will be shown.
USE ORDERS
DISPLAY OFF FOR ISBLANK(SHIPDATE)
* Repeat command, sending list to the printer
* but showing only ITEM, QUANTITY, and SHIPDATE fields
DISPLAY OFF FIELDS ITEM, QUANTITY, SHIPDATE ;
   FOR ISBLANK (shipdate) TO PRINTER
```

DISPLAY/LIST FILES

Syntax

```
DISPLAY/LIST FILES [LIKE <skeleton>]
   [TO PRINTER/TO FILE <filename>]
```

Purpose: Shows a list of all files matching the file name shown in *<skeleton>*. DISPLAY/LIST FILES is similar to the DIR command, except that DISPLAY/LIST FILES also enables you to send the files to the printer or to a disk file. The *<skeleton>* parameter specifies a set of files, such as *.PRG for all PRG files, or CUST*.DBF for all database files starting with "CUST". If you don't specify a file extension, only dBASE 5 database (DBF) files are displayed. The DISPLAY FILES command is similar to LIST FILES, except that the former pauses at each screenful of data.

The file name, the number of records (if a DBF file), and the date and time the file was last updated are shown. The total file size and number of files, along with the remaining unused space on the disk, are shown at the end of the list.

Example

```
* Examples of LIST
LIST FILES     && same as DIR; shows all database files
* Show all format files, one screenful at a time
DISPLAY FILES LIKE *.FMT
* Show all index files (NDX or MDX), plus any file whose
* extension ends with "DX"
LIST FILES LIKE *.?DX
* Create a file containing a list of all DBF files
LIST FILES TO FILE DBFLIST.TXT
```

DISPLAY/LIST HISTORY

Syntax

```
DISPLAY/LIST HISTORY
   [LAST <number>]
   [TO PRINTER/TO FILE <filename>]
```

Purpose: Ignored by dBASE 5. The Command window eliminated the need for a command history. This command will not generate an error, but produces no output. To output the history to a file or the printer, select the text in the Command window. Open the **E**dit menu and choose **C**opy to copy the text to the Clipboard. Open the **F**ile menu and choose **N**ew to open a new file. Use the **E**dit menu and **P**aste to copy the selected commands to the file. Open the **F**ile menu and choose **P**rint to print the file.

DISPLAY/LIST MEMORY

Syntax

```
DISPLAY MEMORY [TO PRINTER / TO FILE <filename>]
LIST MEMORY [TO PRINTER / TO FILE <filename>]
```

Purpose: Shows on-screen the names, contents, and other information of all memory variables. DISPLAY pauses at each screenful of the display, LIST continues until all memory variables are displayed (or until you press the Esc key). You can send the memory variables to the printer with TO PRINTER or to a file with TO FILE <*filename*>.

The LIST/DISPLAY MEMORY command shows the following information: variable name, values, whether the memory variable is public or private, the program that created the memory variable, the number of memory variables used, and the number available.

You can use this command to show the contents of memory variables at various moments during program execution. You also can store the data in a file for viewing at a later time when troubleshooting a program.

Example

```
* Store the contents of memvars in a file
Name = "Wayne Ash"
City = "Auburn"
Sales = 1625.22
cWhen = "Before changes"
LIST MEMORY TO FILE BEFORE.TXT
Name = "Greg Thorsell"
City = "Roseville"
Sales = 448.28
cWhen = "After changes"
LIST MEMORY TO FILE AFTER.TXT
```

DISPLAY/LIST STATUS

Syntax

```
DISPLAY/LIST STATUS [TO PRINTER/TO FILE <filename>]
```

Purpose: Gives you detailed information about the current status of your dBASE 5 session. DISPLAY pauses with each screenful of data; LIST scrolls to the end of the status listing without pausing. You can send the information to the printer with TO PRINTER or to a file with TO FILE *<filename>*. You will find this command very useful when you debug programs.

The status report includes information on each open database file: the current work area number, database drive/path/file name, read-only status, open index files (NDX and MDX), file names of memo files, filter formulas, database relations, and format files. You also see the current file search path, the default disk drive, print destination, any loaded binary program modules, the currently selected work area, printer left-margin setting, and the current procedures file. Also listed are the reprocess and refresh count, settings for devices, currency symbols, delimiter symbols, the number of open files, ON command settings, most SET command settings, and function key assignments. If low-level files are being used, information about these files also is displayed. (See the section, "Using Functions," elsewhere in this Reference Guide for a list of low-level file functions.)

Example

```
* Save the current status to a file for later viewing
LIST STATUS TO FILE STATUS01.TXT
```

DISPLAY/LIST STRUCTURE

Syntax

```
DISPLAY/LIST STRUCTURE
   [IN <alias>]
   [TO PRINTER/TO FILE <filename>]
```

Purpose: Shows the structure of the database. The DISPLAY command produces a pause at each screenful of data; LIST scrolls all data until the end of the structure is reached. You can pause the LIST display with Ctrl-S and then press any key to continue. The Esc key aborts the LIST or DISPLAY, unless you used SET ESCAPE OFF, in which case Esc is ignored (see SET ESCAPE OFF).

The following information is shown: the database file name, number of records, date and time of the last change, complete information on each field (field name, type, size, index tags), and the total number of bytes per record. The size of one record is the sum of all field widths plus one. The extra byte indicates whether the record is marked for deletion (see DELETE).

Normally, the structure of the database in the current work area is displayed. Use the IN <*alias*> option to specify a database in another work area. Use the TO PRINTER option to send the database structure list to the printer. The TO FILE option places the database structure in the specified <*filename*>.

Example

```
* Display the DBF structure on-screen,
* pausing at each screenful
USE CLIENTS
DISPLAY STRUCTURE
* Send the DBF structure to the printer
LIST STRUCTURE TO PRINTER    && don't want pause when printing
* Store the DBF structure in a text file
* (great for database documentation)
LIST STRUCTURE TO FILE CLIENTS.TXT
```

DISPLAY/LIST USERS

Syntax

```
DISPLAY USERS
LIST USERS
```

Purpose: Shows a list of network users who are logged on. The DISPLAY command produces a pause after each screenful of user names; the LIST command scrolls through the list until it reaches the end. If two users log in under the same name, that name appears only once on the list.

Example

```
* Show list of current users
@ 12,10 SAY "Current User List"
DISPLAY USERS
```

DO

Syntax

```
DO <program filename> / <procedure name>
   [WITH <parameter list>]
```

Purpose: Runs a program file or procedure. The DO command compiles the program specified in *<program filename>* (if the program is not compiled already), saves it as a DBO file, and then runs the DBO file. The compiled program runs faster than an equivalent, non-compiled program run in dBASE III and earlier versions which performed line-by-line execution.

WITH *<parameter list>* enables you to pass parameter variables to a procedure. The procedure must have a PARAMETERS statement, and the types of variables used in the DO and PARAMETERS command must match. You can use the DO command at the Command window or from a program file.

Example

```
* Run the CENTER MESSAGE procedure, passing the message
* text as the first parameter and the line number as
* the second.
cMESSAGE = "Please wait while data is accessed..."
DO CENTER WITH MESSAGE, 12
* This is the Center procedure, which does the actual work
* This is contained in the procedure file
PROCEDURE Center
PARAMETERS cMessage, line_num
* Figure out where the starting point should be
* The ABS function makes sure that it is positive
startpos = INT (ABS((80-LEN(message))/2))
@line_num, startpos SAY message
RETURN
```

DO CASE...ENDCASE

Syntax

```
DO CASE
   CASE <condition>
      <commands>
   [CASE <condition>
      <commands>]
   ...
   [OTHERWISE
      <commands>]
ENDCASE
```

Purpose: Performs actions based on the available alternatives. The first match for a condition is the one accessed by the program, even if other CASE *<conditions>* could have been applied. The OTHERWISE action is used if none of the CASE *<conditions>* are true. (For more information about DO CASE, see the example for IF.)

Example

```
* Ask the user to choose items 1-4 or Q (Quit)
* DO the program that matches the choice
DO WHILE .T.              && loop to get choice
   answer = " "
   @ 12,15 SAY "Please enter your choice (1/2/3/4/Q) ";
      GET answer PICTURE "!"
   READ
   * Run the selected program
   DO CASE
      CASE answer = "1"
         DO program1
      CASE answer = "2"
         DO program2
      CASE answer = "3"
         DO program3
      CASE answer = "4"
         DO program4
      CASE answer = "Q"
         EXIT      && exits DO loop
      OTHERWISE
         @ 13,15 SAY "Please choose 1-2-3-4 or Q to quit"
   ENDCASE
ENDDO
```

DO WHILE...ENDDO

Syntax

```
DO WHILE <condition>
   <commands>
   [LOOP]
   [EXIT]
ENDDO
```

Purpose: Repeats a series of commands as long as the *<condition>* is true or until an EXIT command is executed. The LOOP option enables you to restart the loop at any point. The FOR/ENDFOR and SCAN/ENDSCAN commands also run a series of commands while processing a series of records (see FOR and SCAN).

Example

```
* Ask a question, and allow only the desired answer
answer = " "
DO WHILE .NOT. answer $ "YN"
   * Ask the question. Note that the question includes
   * the desired answers
   @ 23,15 SAY "Edit another record? (Y/N)";
   GET answer PICTURE "!"
   READ
   DO CASE
      CASE answer = "Y"
```

```
            DO editrec          && editing procedure
         CASE answer = "N"
            EXIT                && exit DO loop
      ENDCASE
   ENDDO
   RETURN
```

EDIT

See CHANGE

EJECT

Syntax

```
EJECT
```

Purpose: Sends a form-feed character to the printer (or line-feeds if _padvance = "LINEFEEDS"), advancing the paper to the top of the next page (top of form). The EJECT command sets the prow( ) and pcol( ) values to zero.

Tip
Make sure that you position the paper in your printer correctly. If you use a dot-matrix printer and continuous (fanfold) paper, position the paper so that the perforated edge is above the print head and then turn on the printer.

Example

```
* Print contents of memory variables
LIST MEMORY TO PRINT
* Send a form-feed
EJECT
```

EJECT PAGE

Syntax

```
EJECT PAGE
```

Purpose: Tells the ON PAGE handler to advance the paper to the next page by sending the correct number of line feed commands to the printer. EJECT PAGE also performs any other functions defined by the ON PAGE command, such as printing page headers or footers. This command increases the page number system variable (*_pageno*) and sets the _plineno and _pcolno variables to zero.

Example

```
* Send a page eject, using the page handler
* previously defined with ON PAGE
EJECT PAGE
```

ERASE/DELETE FILE

See DELETE FILE.

EXPORT TO

Syntax

```
EXPORT TO <filename>
   [TYPE] PFS/DBASEII/FW2/FW3/FW4/RPD/WK1/WKS
   [FIELD <field list>]
   [<scope>]
   [FOR <condition>]
   [WHILE <condition>]
```

Purpose: Creates files that other programs can use. PFS:File, dBASE II, Framework, Lotus 1-2-3, and RapidFile file types are supported. For other file types, use the COPY command (see COPY). If an index is in use, the records are exported in index order.

If the *<filename>* already exists, it is overwritten without warning unless you used SET SAFETY ON. You can specify individual fields with the FIELD option. You can export parts of the database by using the scope, FOR, or WHILE options.

Example

```
* Export the indicated fields to a RapidFile database
* Use the order specified by the CL_ZIP (Client ZIP
* Code) index
USE CLIENTS ORDER CL_ZIP
EXPORT TO CLIENTS TYPE RPD FIELDS CUSTOMER, CITY,;
   STATE, ZIP_CODE
```

FIND

Syntax

```
FIND <literal key>
```

Purpose: Finds the first record in an indexed file that matches the *<literal key>*. The index key type must match the literal key type. FIND is a fast way to get to a specific record because it looks up the record in the index file instead of looking at each record's data. FIND is similar to SEEK. FIND can search only for a character or numeric string; SEEK can search for an expression.

FIND and SEEK use an index (NDX) or multiple-index (MDX) file. In a multiple-index file, the controlling or master index matches the literal key. You can specify a specific index tag or file by using the SET ORDER TO command (see SEEK, SET ORDER TO).

FIND looks in the master index for an exact match of the literal key, unless you used SET EXACT OFF. (See the following example.) FIND ignores records marked for deletion if you used SET DELETED ON. Any records not part of the SET FILTER command also are ignored.

SET NEAR ON gets the record that is the nearest match for the literal key in case an exact match is not found. With SET NEAR OFF, an unsuccessful FIND results in the placement of the record pointer at EOF( ).

Note that with the FIND command, you don't need to use quotes around the literal key as you do with the SEEK command.

Example

```
* Find a record where CITY="FORT WORTH"
USE CLIENT ORDER CITY
SET EXACT ON
FIND FORT WORTH    && finds only "FORT WORTH"
SET EXACT OFF
FIND FORT          && will find "FORT WORTH", or
                   && "FORT MYERS", or "FORT COLLINS", and so on.
* Equivalent SEEK command, note quotes in command
SEEK "FORT"        && Finds first occurrence of FORT
```

FOR...ENDFOR/NEXT

Syntax

```
FOR <memN> = <starting expN> TO <ending expN> [STEP <step expN>]
  <commands>
  [EXIT]
  [LOOP]
ENDFOR¦NEXT
```

Purpose: Creates a loop to be executed a set number of times. The *<memN>* is assigned the value of *<starting expN>* at the beginning of the loop. All commands in the loop are executed with this value of *<memN>*. The ENDFOR, NEXT, or LOOP command will send the program back to the FOR line. *<memN>* will be incremented by *<step expN>*. The default for *<step expN>* is 1. The resulting *<memN>* is checked against the *<ending expN>*. If *<memN>* is less than or equal to *<ending expN>* the loop is executed again. If *<memN>* is greater than the *<ending expN>* or the EXIT command is used, the program jumps to the line following ENDFOR. The value of *<memN>* can be checked after the loop.

Example

```
DEFINE MYARRAY[5,3]
FOR I = 1 TO 5
    MYARRAY [I,1] = "EMPTY"
    MYARRAY[I,2] = .F.
    MYARRAY[I,3] = 0
ENDFOR
```

FUNCTION

Syntax

```
FUNCTION <procedure name>
```

Purpose: Inserted to indicate a user-defined function (UDF). UDFs perform processes that may not be available among the existing dBASE 5 functions. Functions can be stored in the currently executing file, a procedure file, or any other object code file.

> **Note**
>
> In every DBO file, dBASE 5 maintains a list of functions. You may want to keep all functions in one file to eliminate possible duplicate function definitions.

Example

```
* Function to compute the total cost of an item
* less any discount
FUNCTION tot_cost
PARAMETERS listprice, quantity, discount
* extended cost
ext_cost = (listprice * quantity)
* Determine a discount amount
disc_amt = 0
IF PCOUNT() > 2        && a third parameter was passed
   disc_amt = ext_cost * discount
ENDIF
* total cost including discount
total_cost = ext_cost - disc_amt
* Return the total cost value
RETURN(total_cost)
```

GO/GOTO

Syntax

```
GO/GOTO BOTTOM/TOP [IN <alias>]
```

or

```
GO/GOTO [RECORD] <record number> [IN <alias>]
```

or

```
<record number> [IN <alias>]
```

Purpose: Positions the record pointer on a specific record in a database. BOTTOM and TOP are used to go to the last and first record. If an index is active, TOP goes to the first record according to the index, which may not be record number 1. BOTTOM goes to the end of the database, according to the index. You can go to a specific record number with the RECORD option.

The short version of the command is to simply specify a *<record number>* parameter. The IN *<alias>* option enables you to position the record pointer in another work area. You can use the numbers 1 through 40 or the letters A through J as the *<alias>*, or you can use the file alias specified in the USE command.

Example

```
SELECT 1                          && work area 1
USE INVOICE                       && open the database
GOTO 12                           && to record 12
SELECT 2                          && work area 2
USE CLIENTS ORDER COMPANY         && open database with an index
* If CLIENTS contains 4 records
* indexed on LASTNAME Field
* Record #         LASTNAME
*     1            Appleby
*     4            Duncan
*     5            Jones
*     3            Smith
*     2            Zimmerman
GOTO BOTTOM                      && positions to record 2
* Go to a specific record in another work area
recpoint = 32
GOTO recpoint IN INVOICE         && record # 32 in INVOICE.DBF
```

HELP

Syntax

```
HELP <dBASE 5 keyword or command>
```

Purpose: Enables you to get help on any dBASE 5 command. If you specify a dBASE 5 keyword or command, you are given information about that command. Issuing the HELP command without a keyword brings you to the main Help menu. You also can press the F1 key to access the Help menu.

Press Esc when you want to exit Help and close the Help window. If you are working in the Desktop environment, you may click on one of the other windows to type commands in a different window while keeping the Help window open.

IF...ENDIF

Syntax

```
IF <condition>
   <commands>
ELSE
   <commands>
ENDIF
```

Purpose: Executes a command or series of commands, depending on whether the given <*condition*> is true or false. You can use the IF command only in a program, not at the Command window. You can nest several IF statements together, but in some cases CASE can accomplish the same effect and is easier to understand.

Example

```
* Add a discount to the purchase if more than $1000
IF purchase > 1000
   discount = .10             && 10% discount
ELSE
   discount = .02             && 2% discount
ENDIF
* alternative if more than two choices available
* Note that as soon as a condition is true, the discount
* is applied. If the purchase is $700, only the 5% discount
* is used, even though 700 < 5000
DO CASE
   CASE purchase < 500
      discount = 0
   CASE purchase < 1000
      discount = .05
   CASE purchase < 5000
      discount = .10
   OTHERWISE
      discount = .15
END CASE
```

IMPORT FROM

Syntax

```
IMPORT FROM <filename> [TYPE] PFS/DBASEII/FW2/FW3/FW4/
  RPD/WK1/WKS
```

Purpose: Imports data from non-dBASE 5 files to create a dBASE 5 database. IMPORT creates dBASE 5 files from dBASE II, Framework, RapidFile, PFS:File, and Lotus 1-2-3 files. You must specify the complete file name, including the extension, for each type of file. If you are importing from a dBASE II file, you need to rename the dBASE II file something other than <*filename*>.DBF, such as <*filename*>.DB2. The new dBASE 5 file is called <*filename*>.DBF.

A maximum of 521 fields can be created in the dBASE 5 file, with as many as 254 characters per field with a maximum of 4,000 bytes per record. If you import data from a PFS:File database, IMPORT creates the dBASE 5 database (DBF), format file (FMT), and compiled format file (FMO), with the same file name but with their respective extensions.

Example

```
* Import data from a Lotus 1-2-3 release 2.x WK1 file
IMPORT FROM SALES.WK1 TYPE WK1
```

INDEX ON

Syntax

```
INDEX [ON <key expression>] [TO <NDX filename>]
   [UNIQUE]
```

or

```
INDEX [ON <key expression>]
   [TAG <tag name>] [OF <MDX filename>]
   [FOR <condition>] [DESCENDING] [UNIQUE]
```

Purpose: Creates an index to a database to enable fast access to desired records. Indexing does not rearrange the records in the database; it creates a file containing a sorted order of record pointers to the database.

You can directly index on any type of field except logical or memo fields. You may need to convert one type of data to another if your *<key expression>* includes multiple fields or to index on memo and logical fields. The resulting index file is stored in the current drive/directory unless you specify otherwise. If the index file already exists, you are asked whether you want to overwrite the existing file, unless you specified SET SAFETY OFF.

If you use the INDEX command without options or keywords, dBASE prompts you for the index expression. The TAG option enables you to specify the name of the MDX file; if you don't use the TAG option, dBASE creates an NDX file.

You can use the FOR option to create an index of only the records matching the condition specified with FOR. The UNIQUE option creates an index of just the unique records, rather than all the records. Indexing is done in ascending order, unless you use the DESCENDING option.

Use FOR as an alternative to SET FILTER TO. FOR gives you much faster operation because the condition is evaluated only if the record is changed. If you use SET FILTER TO, the condition is evaluated every time you move the record pointer. The FOR option may not always be useful if you need to create multiple INDEX...FOR commands every time you want to work with just part of the database.

Note

You can use numeric fields in an index expression. If you use several numeric fields as part of the index, however, the index is based on the sum of the values. You should use an index expression that converts the numbers to character strings, as shown in the following example.

If the indexes are not current, use the REINDEX command.

Example

```
* Index on FIRSTNAME + LASTNAME
USE CLIENTS
INDEX ON FIRSTNAME + LASTNAME TAG NAMES
* Index only records where the state is Texas
INDEX ON STATE TAG TEX FOR STATE="TX"
* index on Sales calls and Sales
INDEX ON STR(TotalCalls)+STR(TotalSale)
```

INPUT

Syntax

```
INPUT [<prompt>] TO <memory variable>
```

Purpose: Asks the user to enter characters from the keyboard, which are assigned to the *<memory variable>*. The type of *<memory variable>* created depends on the type of data entered. If the user enters characters, a character variable is created. Numeric entry creates a numeric variable. Date entry creates a date variable. (With a date entry, you must tell the user to use curly braces [{ }] around the date value.) If the memory variable already exists, the new data replaces the old variable data. This command is for compatibility and its functions can be done better using @...SAY...GET.

Example

```
* Ask the user for a number, then verify that
* it is a number
INPUT "Enter a number " TO numval
DO CASE
   CASE TYPE(numval) = "C"       && convert it
      ? "That was a character!"
      numval = val(numval)
   CASE TYPE(numval) = "D"
      numval = dow(numval)
      ? "That was a date! Here's the day number: "
      ?? numval
   CASE TYPE(numval) = "F"
```

```
        ? "That was a floating point number!"
    CASE TYPE(numval) = "U"
        ? "You didn't enter anything!"
ENDCASE
*
* This way, you control what the user enters
numval = 0
@ 5,5 SAY "Enter a number";
        GET numval
READ
```

INSERT

Syntax

```
INSERT [BEFORE] [BLANK]/[NORGANIZE]
```

Purpose: Creates a new blank record. INSERT is similar to the APPEND command, except that records are placed at the current record location, rather than at the end of the database. If the current pointer location is record 48, INSERT creates a new record number 49, with the old record 49 renumbered as record 50. All succeeding records will be renumbered: record 50 is now record 51, 51 becomes 52, and so on.

When a new record is inserted, the empty record is displayed on-screen, and you can enter data. If a format file is active, it displays the record on-screen. Now you can enter data only into the new record; you cannot move to another record. If the record has a memo field, move the cursor to the memo field and press Ctrl-Home to add memo data. After typing your memo data, press Ctrl-End to save the memo data or Esc to escape without saving the memo data. You can use the F1 key to display the various editing keys.

Using the BLANK option creates the record at the current position, but the empty record is not displayed on-screen for editing. Use BROWSE, CHANGE, EDIT, or REPLACE to edit the new record. The BEFORE option creates a record just before the current record. If the current record is record number 84, for example, INSERT BEFORE creates a new record 84.

If you want to have data from the preceding record placed in the new record's fields, use the SET CARRY ON command before the INSERT command (see SET CARRY ON). If you are on a network, you must have exclusive use of the database file before you can use the INSERT command.

The NORGANIZE option prevents using the Organize menu.

Note

The INSERT command usually isn't needed if your files are indexed because an index makes a record appear to be in a position other than its physical record location in the database file. Because INSERT requires records to be physically moved in the database file to make room for the insertion, this command should be avoided when working with large database files.

Example

```
* Insert a record just before record number 59
USE INVOICE
GOTO 59
INSERT BEFORE
```

JOIN WITH

Syntax

```
JOIN WITH <alias> TO <filename>
   FOR <condition>
   [FIELDS <field list>]
```

Purpose: Creates a new database file by combining the records and fields from two open databases. Specify the entire drive and directory along with the file name if you want the new database to be placed in a specific drive and directory.

The FIELDS option specifies the fields to be used from each database. If the two source databases have the same field name, you must precede the field name with the alias name, such as CLIENT->STATE. You can join fields of any type (except memo) to the new database. If you forget to exclude memo field types, you will get an error message. You can use the SET FIELDS command before JOIN as an alternative to the FIELD option.

If you want to extract only part of the source database records, use the FOR *<condition>* option.

During the JOIN operation, the record pointer is positioned on the first record in the active database. Then the second database is scanned to see whether it meets the FOR *<condition>*. If the condition is true, a record is added to the new file. The data from all fields (or the fields specified by the FIELDS option or SET FIELDS TO) is added to the new database. After all records from the second database are scanned, the record pointer in the active file is set to the second record. This process continues until the join is complete.

If either of the files is large, the JOIN operation can take a long time. The JOIN command also can create very large files: if the two databases each have 200 records, for example, and the condition is always true, you end up with 40,000 records (200*200).

To build a relationship between two files, use the SET RELATION command instead of the slow, disk-intensive JOIN command.

Example

```
* Extract all past due accounts (date in PASTDUE
* field older than 30 days) from the SALES database
* into a new OVERDUE.DBF
* Make sure that the CUST_ID field data matches for
* each JOIN operation
USE SALES IN 2
SELECT 1           && work area 1 (active area during JOIN)
USE CUSTOMER
SET FIELDS TO A->CUST_ID, B->PASTDUE, B->LASTPAY
SET TALK ON        && to see the current record number during JOIN
* Perform the JOIN command for the <condition>
JOIN WITH SALES TO OVERDUE FOR ;
   SALES->PASTDUE < DATE()-30 .AND. ;
   CUSTOMER->CUST_ID = SALES->CUST_ID
```

KEYBOARD

Syntax

```
KEYBOARD <character expression> [CLEAR]
```

Purpose: Places a series of characters into the keyboard buffer. dBASE 5 then reads the characters as if the user had typed them. You can place characters into the keyboard buffer up to the limit of the typeahead buffer. The default is 20 characters, unless you use the SET TYPEAHEAD TO command to change the typeahead buffer value. You can use this command to write very large macros and send them to the keyboard.

You can place any of the 255 IBM characters (ASCII values 1 through 255) in the keyboard buffer. You also can use the CHR( ) function, key labels ("{TAB}", "{ALT}", etc.), and numeric ASCII values ({[89]}).

The CLEAR option clears the keyboard buffer. Use CLEAR if you want to clear out, in anticipation of the next keyboard input, any characters the user typed.

Example

```
* Place the user name in the keyboard buffer
* so that it is input in the next keyboard input command
username = "JASON"
KEYBOARD username CLEAR
```

LABEL FORM

Syntax

```
LABEL FORM <label filename> / ?
   [<scope>]
   [FOR <condition>]
   [WHILE <condition>]
   [SAMPLE]
   [TO PRINTER / TO FILE <filename>]
```

Purpose: Uses the *<label filename>* created or modified with the CREATE/MODIFY LABEL command. All data in the current database is displayed, printed, or sent to a file, based on the design of the label. You can limit the number of labels printed by using a scope, FOR, or WHILE clause. Any active filter (SET FILTER TO/SET KEY TO) also limits the labels to be created.

If any indexes are active, they determine the order of the printed labels. If the LBL file was created in dBASE III, the dBASE III label engine prints the labels. For labels created with dBASE IV and above, the LABEL FORM command compiles the label definition into a label object (LBO) file and then processes the labels. A new LBO file is created only if the date and time of the LBG are later than any existing LBO file (unless you used SET DEVELOPMENT OFF).

The SAMPLE option prints a test label on the printer to make sure that the labels are aligned properly. A single row of labels is printed, and a message is displayed asking whether you want more test labels. If the labels did not align properly, adjust the label blanks in the printer, answer Y, and try again until the samples align properly.

The TO FILE option sends the label output to a disk file in the label format. The text file contains any printer codes required by your printer so that you can print labels later by sending this file directly to your printer. The ? option shows you a list of label files from which you can choose.

Example

```
* Print some mailing labels. Use SAMPLE to align the labels
USE MAILLIST ORDER ZIPCODE
LABEL FORM AV6062 SAMPLE TO PRINT
```

LIST

See DISPLAY/LIST.

LIST FILES

See DISPLAY/LIST FILES.

LIST HISTORY

See DISPLAY/LIST HISTORY.

LIST MEMORY

See DISPLAY/LIST MEMORY.

LIST STATUS

See DISPLAY/LIST STATUS.

LIST STRUCTURE

See DISPLAY/LIST STRUCTURE.

LIST USERS

See DISPLAY/LIST USERS.

LOAD

Syntax

```
LOAD <binary filename>
```

Purpose: Loads binary program files into memory. The binary files usually used with this command are assembly language programs that perform low-level functions not available among the dBASE 5 or MS-DOS commands. You can load as many as 16 binary files in memory at one time, and each binary file can be as many as 64K in size. The LIST/DISPLAY STATUS command shows you which binary files currently are loaded. After loading, binary files are accessed with the CALL command (see CALL).

Example

```
* Load binary file DOSCALLS.BIN
LOAD DOSCALLS
```

LOCATE

Syntax

```
LOCATE [FOR] <condition> [<scope>]
   [WHILE <condition>]
```

Purpose: Searches the current database file for the record that matches the <condition>. This operation is a sequential search of the file and therefore can be quite slow compared to an indexed SEEK or FIND. If a match is not found, the record pointer will hold at the end of the file. After a match is found, use the CONTINUE command to look for the next match (see CONTINUE). You can use the WHILE option to restrict LOCATE.

When a match is found, the pointer is positioned at the matching record number, and FOUND( ) is true (see FOUND).

Example

```
* Find the first record that contains "Merger talks" in
* the NOTES memo field. This will be a slow search.
USE WORKDATA
* show number of records
? RECCOUNT()
* show record numbers during LOCATE command
SET TALK ON
LOCATE FOR UPPER(NOTES) = "MERGER TALKS"
* and the results are these:
IF FOUND()
   ? "Found record number ", RECNO()
ELSE
   ? "No match found"
ENDIF
```

LOGOUT

Syntax

```
LOGOUT
```

Purpose: Logs out the current user and establishes a new log-in screen when used with the PROTECT command. The current user is immediately logged out; dBASE 5 then prompts for a new group name, log-in name, and password. The LOGOUT command closes all open databases and their associated files. LOGOUT does not log you out of the network.

Example

```
* Logoff current user and get new user name
LOGOUT
```

MODIFY APPLICATION

See CREATE/MODIFY APPLICATION.

MODIFY COMMAND

Syntax

```
MODIFY COMMAND <filename>
   [WINDOW <window name>]
```

Purpose: Activates the dBASE 5 program editor and enables you to edit command files (programs) and format files. The program editor also is available from the Control Center. You can use the optional WINDOW parameter to edit the file in a window (<*window name*>) rather than the one in the active window (if any) or on the full screen (if no window is active). Programs can be any size up to the limit of available disk space. Each text line can be as many as 1,024 characters long. After you issue the MODIFY COMMAND command, a menu offering various editing commands specific to program files appears at the top of the screen.

To use your own word processor to edit files from within dBASE 5, specify the name of the file that starts up your word processor with the TEDIT command in the CONFIG.DB file.

Example

```
* Edit the CUSTEDIT.PRG program
* (This command is normally used at the
* Command window, not in programs)
MODIFY COMMAND custedit
```

MODIFY FILE

Syntax

```
MODIFY FILE <filename>
   [WINDOW <window name>]
```

Purpose: Activates the dBASE 5 text editor and enables you to edit text files. The text editor also is available from the Control Center. You can use the optional WINDOW parameter to edit the file in a window (*<window name>*) rather than the one in the active window (if any) or on the full screen (if no window is active). Files can be any size up to the limit of available disk space. Each text line can be as many as 1,024 characters long. After you issue the MODIFY FILE command, a menu offering various editing commands specific to text files appears at the top of the screen.

To use your own word processor to edit files from within dBASE 5, specify the name of the file that starts up your word processor with the TEDIT command in the CONFIG.DB file.

Example

```
* Edit the CONFIG.DB file
* (This command is normally used at the
* Command window, not in programs)
MODIFY FILE CONFIG.DB
```

MODIFY LABEL

Syntax

```
MODIFY LABEL <filename>
```

Purpose: Enables you to make changes to an existing label file. Any changes to the label file cause a new label program (LBG) file to be created from the changed label definition. You can use the MODIFY COMMAND *<label filename>* command to change the format of the label. Any changes you make to the LBG file, however, are not reflected in the LBL file.

Example

```
USE PARTS
MODIFY LABEL BINLABEL
```

MODIFY QUERY

See CREATE/MODIFY QUERY.

MODIFY SCREEN

Syntax

```
MODIFY SCREEN
```

See CHANGE/MODIFY SCREEN.

MODIFY STRUCTURE

Syntax

```
MODIFY STRUCTURE
```

Purpose: Enables you to change the structure of the current database (see CREATE/MODIFY STRUCTURE).

Example

```
* Change structure of database
USE CLIENTS EXCLUSIVE
MODIFY STRUCTURE
```

MODIFY VIEW

See CREATE/MODIFY VIEW.

MOVE WINDOW

Syntax

```
MOVE WINDOW <window name>
   TO <row>, <column> / BY <delta row>, <delta column>
```

Purpose: Moves a window to a new screen location. You can move a window by specifying a new location with the TO option, or you can use the BY option to move it relative to its current position. If the window does not fit in its new location, an error message is shown, and the window is not moved. You can use a negative amount to move a window up or to the left of its current position.

You can only use this command with non-UI screens and windows like those created in previous versions of dBASE. It is ignored by dBASE 5's UI objects.

Example

```
* Move the window
MOVE WINDOW edit_win TO 12,3
* Move a window two rows and three columns
* from current position
MOVE WINDOW edit_win BY 2,3
* Move window up two rows, left 5 rows
MOVE WINDOW edit_win BY -2,-5
```

NOTE

Syntax

```
NOTE/* <text>
```

or

```
[<command>] && <text>
```

Purpose: Indicates comments or nonexecutable text or lines in a program. (See */&&.)

ON BAR

Syntax

```
ON BAR  <bar number> OF <pop-up name>  [<command>]
```

Purpose: Executes a command when a bar is highlighted in a pop-up menu. The command can be any valid dBASE command except those used to control program flow, such as IF, ELSE, or DO WHILE loops.

You can only use this command with non-UI screens and windows like those created in previous versions of dBASE. It is ignored by dBASE 5's UI objects.

Example

```
ON BAR ONE OF mypop DO progone
```

ON ERROR/ESCAPE/KEY

Syntax

```
ON ERROR <command>
ON ESCAPE <command>
ON KEY [LABEL <key label name>] [<command>]
```

Purpose: Specifies an action to take if an error occurs (ON ERROR), the Esc key is pressed (ON ESCAPE), or a key is pressed (ON KEY). These commands usually are placed at the beginning of the program (although they can be placed anywhere) to change the actions to take.

These commands set a trap that waits for the condition to occur; when it does, the *<command>* is executed. If the specified *<command>* is DO followed by the name of another program, the commands in that program are executed. If the subprogram contains RETURN, execution of the main program picks up at the line following the statement that sprang the trap. You can cancel the trap by using this command without specifying any action to take (*<command>*), as in ON ERROR.

The ON ERROR command traps only dBASE 5 errors, not errors at the operating-system level (such as the drive not ready error in MS-DOS). ON ERROR usually is used to trap programming errors. Table 22.9 shows the *<key label names>* for the keys that can spring the ON KEY trap. Use ONKEY with no keyname to reset all the keys to their defaults.

Table 22.9 Key Label Names

Key	Name
F1 to F10	F1, F2, F3...
Ctrl-F1 to Ctrl-F10	CTRL-F1, CTRL-F2, CTRL-F3...
Shift-F1 to Shift-F9	SHIFT-F1, SHIFT-F2, SHIFT-F3...
Alt-0 to Alt-9	ALT-0, ALT-1, ALT-2...
Alt-A to Alt-Z	ALT-A, ALT-B, ALT-C...
Ctrl-A to Ctrl-Z	CTRL-A, CTRL-B, CTRL-C...
Left arrow	LEFTARROW
Right arrow	RIGHTARROW
Up arrow	UPARROW
Down arrow	DNARROW
Home	HOME
End	END
PgUp	PGUP
PgDn	PGDN
Del	DEL

Key	Name
Backspace	BACKSPACE
Ctrl-<*left arrow*>	CTRL-LEFTARROW
Ctrl-<*right arrow*>	CTRL-RIGHTARROW
Ctrl-End	CTRL-END
Ctrl-Home	CTRL-HOME
Ctrl-PgUp	CTRL-PGUP
Ctrl-PgDn	CTRL-PGDN
Ins	INS
TAB	TAB
Back-Tab (Shift-Tab)	BACKTAB
Return/Enter	CTRL-M (on most keyboards)

Example

```
* Set up error trapping
ON ERROR DO err_trap
* This error trapping program (ERR_TRAP.PRG) or
* procedure code (PROCEDURE ERR_TRAP)
* saves various program information
PROCEDURE ERR_TRAP
LIST STATUS TO status.err
LIST MEMORY TO memory.err
* Close everything
CLOSE ALL
* Print a message
@ 24,0          && clears a line
@ 24,5 say "Error found. Program status saved. Contact programmer."
WAIT " "        && wait for keystroke before quitting
QUIT
RETURN

ON KEY LABEL BACKTAB DO BackMsg
@ 3,5 SAY "Enter Number" GET ctEnum
@ 4,5 SAY "Enter Name" GET ctName
READ
RETURN

PROCEDURE BackMsg
@ 5,10 SAY "Not Allowed"
RETURN
```

ON EXIT BAR

Syntax

```
ON EXIT BAR <bar number> OF <pop-up name>  [<command>]
```

Purpose: Executes a command when a bar in a pop-up menu is exited. The command can be any valid dBASE command except those used to control program flow, such as IF, ELSE, or DO WHILE loops. To execute the same command when any bar in the pop-up is exited, use the ON EXIT POPUP command.

You can only use this command with non-UI screens and windows like those created in previous versions of dBASE. It is ignored by dBASE 5's UI objects.

Example

```
* When user exits 2nd bar of Mypop pop-up,
* run the Myprint program
ON EXIT BAR 2 OF Mypop DO Myprint
```

ON EXIT MENU

Syntax

```
ON EXIT MENU <menu name> [<command>]
```

Purpose: Executes a command when the user exits pads of a menu that do not have an ON EXIT PAD statement associated with them. The command can be any valid dBASE command except those used to control program flow, such as IF, ELSE, or DO WHILE loops. You may disable a previously assigned command by omitting the *<command>* in the ON EXIT MENU statement.

You can only use this command with non-UI screens and windows like those created in previous versions of dBASE. It is ignored by dBASE 5's UI objects.

Example

```
* When user exits the Opening menu,
* run the Startup program
ON EXIT MENU Opening DO Startup
```

ON EXIT PAD

Syntax

```
ON EXIT PAD <pad name> OF <menu name> [<command>]
```

Purpose: Executes a command when a pad in a menu is exited. The command can be any valid dBASE command except those used to control program flow, such as IF, ELSE, or DO WHILE loops. Use the ON EXIT MENU statement to execute the same commands when exiting all pads in the menu.

You can only use this command with non-UI screens and windows like those created in previous versions of dBASE. It is ignored by dBASE 5's UI objects.

Example

```
* When the Filepad menu pad is exited,
* run the Myprint program
ON EXIT PAD Filepad OF Mymenu DO Myprint
```

ON EXIT POPUP

Syntax

```
ON EXIT POPUP <pop-up name> [<command>]
```

Purpose: Executes a command when the user exits a bar in a pop-up that does not have an ON EXIT BAR statement associated with it. The command can be any valid dBASE command except those used to control program flow, such as IF, ELSE, or DO WHILE loops. To disable a previously assigned command, you may omit the *<command>* from the ON EXIT POPUP statement.

Example

```
* Run the Mylist program when exiting
* bar of the Mypop pop-up
ON EXIT POPUP Mypop DO Mylist
```

ON MENU

Syntax

```
ON MENU <menu name> [<command>]
```

Purpose: Executes a command when a user highlights pads in a menu that do not have an ON PAD statement associated with them. The command can be any valid dBASE command except those used to control program flow, such as IF, ELSE, or DO WHILE loops. To disable a previously assigned command, you may omit the *<command>* from the ON MENU statement.

You can only use this command with non-UI screens and windows like those created in previous versions of dBASE. It is ignored by dBASE 5's UI objects.

Example

```
* Run the Mylist program when pad is
* highlighted in Mymenu
ON MENU Mymenu DO Mylist
```

ON MOUSE

Syntax

```
ON MOUSE <command>
```

Purpose: The ON MOUSE command is used to detect when the user clicks the left mouse button. The specified command is executed after the button is released.

ON MOUSE is not active in: screens where the internal dBASE 5 menu system is active; user-defined menu pads; BROWSE screens; dBASE 5 design surfaces for data, forms, report or labels; the Applications Generator screen; and inside @...GET areas of a screen form. However, ON MOUSE will work on the left and right borders of user-defined menus. Note that SET MOUSE must be set to ON for mouse detection to occur.

You can only use this command with non-UI screens and windows like those created in previous versions of dBASE. It is ignored by dBASE 5's UI objects.

Example

```
* When user clicks mouse button,
* clear the screen
SET MOUSE ON
ON MOUSE @ 1,1 CLEAR
```

ON PAD

Syntax

```
ON PAD <pad name> OF <menu name> [<command>]
```

Purpose: Executes a command when a menu pad is highlighted. When the cursor is placed on the pad of the menu bar, the specified dBASE command is executed. The menus that appear in the dBASE 5 Control Center are pop-up menus. When you move the cursor left and right along the menu options (pads) at the top of the screen, the pop-up menus are displayed. The pop-up menu is enabled with the ACTIVATE POPUP command. Use the ON MENU command to execute the same command for every pad on the menu.

You can only use this command with non-UI screens and windows like those created in previous versions of dBASE. It is ignored by dBASE 5's UI objects.

Example

```
* When Start pad is highlighted in Mymenu,
* run the Startup program
ON PAD Start OF Mymenu DO Startup
```

ON PAGE

Syntax

```
ON PAGE [AT LINE <number> <command>]
```

Purpose: Specifies a command program (page handler) to be executed when the print job comes to the specified line *<number>*. (The *<command>* program also is run when the EJECT PAGE command is executed.) The _plineno system variable keeps track of the current printed line number. When this value equals the *<number>* specified after AT LINE, the *<command>* is executed.

The *<command>*, or page handler, typically is a procedure that prints a footer or header on each page before the print job can continue. See the PRINTJOB...ENDPRINTJOB command for an example of the ON PAGE command.

Example

```
* Before starting report program, set up page handling
* Page break occurs at line 60
* NEW_PAGE is a procedure that does page headings
ON PAGE AT LINE 60 DO New_page
```

ON POPUP

Syntax

```
ON POPUP <popup name> [<command>]
```

Purpose: Executes a command when a user highlights a bar in a pop-up menu that does not have an ON BAR statement associated with it. The command can be any valid dBASE command except those used to control program flow, such as IF, ELSE, or DO WHILE loops. To disable a previously specified command, you may omit the *<command>* from the ON POPUP statement.

You can only use this command with non-UI screens and windows like those created in previous versions of dBASE. It is ignored by dBASE 5's UI objects.

Example

```
* When bar is highlighted in Mypop,
* run the Showme program
ON POPUP Mypop DO Showme
```

ON READERROR

Syntax

```
ON READERROR <command>
```

Purpose: Specifies the commands to be executed if an error occurs during full-screen editing. These errors include basic errors (such as invalid dates) or user-defined errors (such as input that fails a VALID condition).

The <*command*> usually is specified as DO <*command file*>, which recovers from the error or shows a help message for the user. You can reset READERROR by issuing ON READERROR without specifying a <*command*>.

Example

```
* Activate error trapping for the editing program
ON READERROR DO Edit_err
DO EditData          && editing program
ON READERROR         && disable error trapping
```

ON SELECTION BAR

Syntax

```
ON SELECTION BAR <bar number> OF <pop-up name> [<command>]
```

Purpose: Executes a command when a bar is selected or activated. The command can be any valid dBASE command except those used to control program flow, such as IF, ELSE, or DO WHILE loops.

You can only use this command with non-UI screens and windows like those created in previous versions of dBASE. It is ignored by dBASE 5's UI objects.

Example

```
* When bar 3 is selected in Mypop,
* run the Mycount program
ON SELECTION BAR 3 DO Mycount
```

ON SELECTION MENU

Syntax

```
ON SELECTION MENU <menu name> [<command>]
```

Purpose: Executes a command when a user selects or activates pads of a menu that do not have an ON SELECTION PAD statement associated with them. The command can be any valid dBASE command except those used to control program flow, such as IF, ELSE, or DO WHILE loops. To disable a previously assigned command, you may omit the <*command*> from the ON SELECTION MENU statement.

You can only use this command with non-UI screens and windows like those created in previous versions of dBASE. It is ignored by dBASE 5's UI objects.

Example

```
* When a menu pad is selected in Mymenu,
* run the Showme program
ON SELECTION MENU Myname DO Showme
```

ON SELECTION PAD

Syntax

```
ON SELECTION PAD <pad name> OF <menu name>
   [<command>]
```

Purpose: Executes a command when a menu pad is selected or activated. The command can be any valid dBASE command except those used to control program flow, such as IF, ELSE, or DO WHILE loops. To execute the same commands for every pad on the menu, use the ON SELECTION MENU command.

You can only use this command with non-UI screens and windows like those created in previous versions of dBASE. It is ignored by dBASE 5's UI objects.

Example

```
* List some database fields to the printer
* when the pad is selected
ON SELECTION PAD print_pad OF showdata ;
LIST NAME, ADDRESS, CITY TO PRINTER FOR STATE = "AZ"
```

ON SELECTION POPUP

Syntax

```
ON SELECTION POPUP <pop-up name> [<command>]
```

Purpose: Executes a command when a bar that does not have an ON SELECTION BAR statement associated with it is selected in a pop-up menu. The command can be any valid dBASE command except those used to control program flow, such as IF, ELSE, or DO WHILE loops. To disable a previously assigned command, you may omit the *<command>* from the ON SELECTION POPUP statement.

You can only use this command with non-UI screens and windows like those created in previous versions of dBASE. It is ignored by dBASE 5's UI objects.

Example

```
* Show a list of database files
* when the pop-up is chosen
ON SELECTION POPUP DirList DIR
```

PACK

Syntax

```
PACK
```

Purpose: Removes any records that are marked for deletion in the current database. If any indexes are open, the database is automatically reindexed.

The DELETE command marks records for deletion. The records are not actually deleted from the file, however, until you use the PACK command. You can unmark a record with the RECALL command if you do so before you use PACK (*see DELETE, RECALL*).

If any NDX indexes are associated with the file, make sure that they are activated with the USE...INDEX *<index names>* command or the SET INDEX TO command to ensure that the indexes are kept up-to-date. (MDX files are updated automatically.) If the files are not active during the PACK command, you may have problems accessing the data. A quick REINDEX, however, cures that problem.

Note

In a multiuser environment, you must have opened the database file with the EXCLUSIVE option in order to PACK it.

Example

```
* Remove deleted records, reindex
* CLIENTS.MDX is the multiple-index file
USE CLIENTS EXCLUSIVE
PACK
```

PARAMETERS

Syntax

```
PARAMETERS <parameter list>
```

Purpose: Assigns local variable names to a list of variables passed from a calling program. This command usually is used in procedures or functions because variables that are public are available to called programs. The local variables are released when the procedure or function is completed. The variables in the *<parameter list>* can be changed and returned to the calling program. A limit of 10 literals and 50 variables can be passed. See examples under PROCEDURE and FUNCTION.

PLAY MACRO

Syntax

```
PLAY MACRO <macro name>
```

Purpose: Plays back the macro commands assigned to *<macro name>* that are contained in the current macro library. Use the RESTORE MACROS command to load a macro library file. Macros are identified by their macro key, which is assigned when the macro is created. You can assign macro keys as Alt-F1 through Alt-F9, or Alt-F10 followed by a letter (A through Z). Each macro library file can contain as many as 35 unique macros. (See KEYBOARD.)

Example

```
* Load a macro file, play the DATA_IN macro
RESTORE MACROS FROM DATAMAC
PLAY MACRO DATA_IN
```

PRINTJOB...ENDPRINTJOB

Syntax

```
PRINTJOB
      <commands>
ENDPRINTJOB
```

Purpose: Sends a series of programming commands to the printer as part of a print job. Any print job-related settings (such as _pbpage, the beginning printer page) or commands (such as ON PAGE), should be included as part of the print job. See "Using System Variables" elsewhere in this for information about print job-related settings. The PRINTJOB command sends the codes set in _pscodes. The ENDPRINTJOB command sends the codes set in _pecodes.

The PRINTJOB...ENDPRINTJOB command can be used in a program only, not from the Command window. Print jobs cannot be nested; only one print job can be active at a time.

Example

```
* Print a quick list of the inventory
USE INVENTRY ORDER INVENTRY
_peject = "AFTER"        && eject the last page
SET PRINT ON
PRINTJOB
* At the end of the page, do the
* pagehead program or procedure
ON PAGE AT LINE _plength-1 do pagehead
SCAN
   * print the field information for each record
   ? item_num, item_name, instock, backorder
ENDSCAN
ENDPRINTJOB
SET PRINT OFF
RETURN
* end of program fragment
*
* This is the pagehead procedure
PROCEDURE pagehead
```

```
EJECT PAGE
? "Run Date", DATE(), TIME(), "Page " AT 65, ;
     _pageno PICTURE "999" AT 70
?
?
RETURN
* End of pagehead procedure
```

PRIVATE/PRIVATE ALL

Syntax

```
PRIVATE ALL [LIKE / EXCEPT <skeleton>]
PRIVATE <memory variable list>
```

Purpose: Creates a local memory variable that can be different from a memory variable with the same name if that memory variable was created in a higher-level program. You can use PRIVATE on a single memory variable or on a list of memory variables. A *<skeleton>* enables you to specify memory variables with similar names. The skeleton "sum*", for example, could be used to make private all memory variables that start with sum.

The public availability of memory variables becomes important when one program executes another, as often occurs in common structured programming (see Part V).

Example

```
* Declare some memvars as private
PRIVATE ALL LIKE b_*
PRIVATE username
* These are all private variables
b_item1 = "Hard disk"
b_item2 = "Monitor"
b_item3 = 155.33
username = "Jason"
```

PROCEDURE

Syntax

```
PROCEDURE <procedure name>
```

Purpose: Marks the beginning of a subroutine. Most frequently used procedures are short subroutines that perform actions which can be used by many calling programs. You can store procedures in the file currently executing or combine them with other procedures in a procedure file. The SET PROCEDURE and SET LIBRARY commands enable procedure files.

Procedures can have parameters passed through them. Parameters can be explicitly passed with a DO...WITH command, or they can be implied with public variables. You can have as many as 963 procedures per file. All procedure code segments must start with PROCEDURE and end with RETURN. Procedure names are as many as nine characters long and can contain letters, numbers, or underscores (_). (Actually, procedure names are of unlimited length, but only the first nine characters are used by dBASE.)

Procedures execute faster than separate files because they are preloaded into memory.

Example

```
* Procedure to center a message at the indicated line
PROCEDURE center
PARAMETERS message, line_num   && passed from calling program
*
* Figure out where the starting point should be
* The ABS function makes sure that it is positive
startpos = INT(ABS((80-LEN(message))/2))
@ line_num, startpos SAY message
RETURN
* end of center procedure
```

PROTECT

Syntax

```
PROTECT
```

Purpose: Creates and maintains security for dBASE 5 files. This menu-driven process is issued by the database administrator. When you issue the PROTECT command, you are asked for the administrator password. (If a password does not exist, you create one at this time.)

> **Caution**
>
> The administrator password is important. You cannot access the security system without supplying the password. You can change the password only if you enter the correct password when you invoke PROTECT. If you forget the password, you cannot retrieve it from the system, and any files protected by the password are unavailable. You should write the password down on paper, but keep the paper in a secure area (under lock and key—not taped to the computer).

The following list describes the three types of database protection:

- *Log-in security*. Prevents access to dBASE 5 by unauthorized persons.

- *Field and file security.* Can prevent access to certain fields in a database or certain files.
- *Data encryption.* Encrypts dBASE 5 files so that they cannot be read.

PUBLIC

Syntax

```
PUBLIC <memory variable list> / ARRAY
<array name 1> [{<number of rows>,} <number of columns>]
{, <array name 2> [{<number of rows>,} <number of columns>]...}
```

> **Note**
>
> Because brackets are used as part of the required syntax, braces ({ }) denote optional parameters.

Purpose: Makes selected memory variables available to all programs. Note that if you use array names, you should use brackets for the number of array elements, as in my_array[4,12]. You must declare a variable as public before you can assign a value to it. Memory variables created from the Command window are made public automatically. Memory variables created by a program file are normally private, unless you first declare them as public.

If you declared a memory variable public, subprograms can change the values, and the changed values are kept for the main program. Public variables start as logical type variables until you assign a value to them. You can use the LIST/DISPLAY MEMORY command to show whether a memory variable is public or private.

Example

```
* Declare some memvars as public
PUBLIC item1, item2
? TYPE(item1)    && returns "L" for Logical type
item1 = "Wayne"
item2 = 4920
? TYPE(item1), TYPE(item2)  && returns "C" and "N"
                            && (Character, Numeric)
```

QUIT

Syntax

```
QUIT [WITH <expN>]
```

Purpose: Ends the current dBASE 5 session. Any open files are closed, and you are returned to the DOS prompt (or your menuing system). The optional

WITH clause specifies a value to be returned by dBASE to the calling program or operating system.

> **Caution**
>
> Using QUIT or the menu choice for Exit is the only way that you should exit dBASE 5. If you just turn off your computer or press the reset button, any open data or other files may be damaged, resulting in data loss.

Example

```
* Ask user whether it's OK to QUIT to DOS prompt
answer = .F.
   @ 24,15 SAY "Quit to DOS Prompt?";
      GET ANSWER picture "Y"
   READ
IF ANSWER
   QUIT
ENDIF
```

READ

Syntax

```
READ [SAVE]
```

Purpose: Enables you to enter data in a field or memory variable. READ usually is used in dBASE 5 programs to enable full-screen editing or input of record data or multiple memory variables. Several @...GET commands are used to position the input areas on-screen; then the READ command enables you to enter data in fields by typing in those input areas.

The READ command clears the effects of all @...GET commands after completion, unless you use the SAVE option. If you use the SAVE option, make sure that you use the CLEAR GETS command before you do another series of @...GET commands. You also should close any screen format (FMT) files before using the READ command; otherwise, the format file will be activated.

Example

```
* Asks for user input and stores data to variables
mName = SPACE(20)
mAddress = SPACE(20)
llAns = .F.
@ 11,20 SAY "Name...: " GET mName
@ 12,20 SAY "Address: " GET mAddress
@ 15,20 SAY "Is data correct? " GET llAns
DO WHILE .NOT. llAns
  READ SAVE
ENDDO
CLEAR GETS
@ 18,20 SAY "Add another?" GET llAns
READ
```

RECALL

Syntax

```
RECALL
   [<scope>]
   [FOR <condition>]
   [WHILE <condition>]
```

Purpose: Unmarks records that were marked for deletion with the DELETE command (see DELETE). Only the current record is recalled, unless you specify a scope, FOR, or WHILE clause. You can recall a specific record by using a scope of RECORD <n>, where n is the record number, if DELETED is SET ON.

> **Caution**
>
> After the ZAP or PACK commands are used, the records cannot be recalled by dBASE 5.
>
> Be careful if you are using a scope, FOR, or WHILE. You can test your condition or scope by using the LIST/DISPLAY commands (with SET DELETED OFF) to show those records that match the condition. Look carefully at the displayed records to ensure that you are not recalling the wrong records.

Note that SET DELETED must be set to OFF for RECALL to work, unless you specify the record to recall using GOTO or RECALL RECORD *<record number>*.

Example

```
* Recall the current record
USE INVOICE
GOTO 44
RECALL
* An alternative
USE INVOICE
RECALL RECORD 44
* Recall all records
RECALL ALL
```

REINDEX

Syntax

```
REINDEX
```

Purpose: Rebuilds all the single-index (NDX) and multiple-index (MDX) files open in the current work area. The tags inside the production MDX file also are updated. If any indexes were created with the UNIQUE option, the rebuilt index still is unique, even if you have SET UNIQUE OFF. In a network, you must have exclusive use of the database file before you can use the REINDEX command. Indexes automatically are updated (if active) during a PACK command.

Example

```
* Update the index file
USE INVENTORY INDEX INVINDEX EXCLUSIVE
REINDEX
```

RELEASE

Syntax

```
RELEASE <memory variable list>
RELEASE ALL [LIKE/EXCEPT <skeleton>]
RELEASE MODULES [<module name list>]
   /MENUS [<menu name list>]
   /POPUPS [<pop-up name list>]
   /SCREENS [<screen name list>]
   /WINDOWS [<window name list>]
```

Purpose: Removes memory variables or program modules, menus, pop-ups, screens, or windows. This command enables the memory space used by the variables or modules to be used for other purposes. You can specify a list of specific memory variables (ITEM1, ITEM2), or a skeleton (ITEM*).

In a subprogram, RELEASE ALL deletes all memory variables created in the subprogram or any of its subprograms. Memory variables of higher-level programs are not affected. Using the RELEASE ALL command at the Command window deletes all memory variables except system variables.

RELEASE MODULES removes specified program modules (which were loaded into memory with the LOAD command) from memory; do not specify the BIN file-name extension. RELEASE MENUS removes the listed menus from the screen and memory, along with any ON SELECTION and ON PAD commands associated with the listed menus. RELEASE POPUPS, RELEASE SCREENS, and RELEASE WINDOWS do the same thing to pop-ups, screens, and windows, respectively.

> **Caution**
>
> Use the memory variable skeleton pattern carefully. If you use a line like RELEASE ALL LIKE HMEM*, you might delete some needed memory variables. Assign memory variables carefully, or let the end of a subprogram release any private memory variables when it finishes.

Example

```
* Declare some variables as public
PUBLIC qmem1, qmem2, qmem10, username
STORE 0 to qmem1, qmem2, qmem10
username = "Elizabeth"
* release the qmem1, qmem2, and username variables
* but not the qmem10 variable
RELEASE qmem1, qmem2
RELEASE username
```

RELEASE SCREENS

Syntax

```
RELEASE SCREENS <screen name list>
```

Purpose: Removes a screen from memory. The screen must have been saved previously with the SAVE SCREEN command.

Example

```
* Release the edit_scrn screen
RELEASE SCREEN edit_scrn
```

RENAME

Syntax

```
RENAME <old filename> TO <new filename>
```

Purpose: Changes the name of a file from *<old filename>* to *<new filename>*. The complete file name must be specified in both parameters. This command is similar to the RENAME command in MS-DOS.

Note

When renaming a database file, you can use the MODIFY STRUCTURE command to save the file with the new name. Using the MODIFY STRUCTURE command also saves any associated files with the new name.

Example

```
* Rename a program file
RENAME CLIENT.PRG TO DATAENT.PRG
```

REPLACE

Syntax

```
REPLACE <field> WITH <expression> [ADDITIVE]
   [, <field> WITH <expression> [ADDITIVE] ...]
   [<scope>] [REINDEX]
   [FOR <condition>]
   [WHILE <condition>]
```

Purpose: Replaces the contents of the specified field in the current database with the *<expression>*. Only the current record's data is replaced, unless you specify a scope, FOR, or WHILE. The *<fieldname>* and the *<expression>* must be the same type of data. When you put memo data into a character field, the memo data is truncated (shortened) to fit the width of the field. The ADDITIVE option adds the *<expression>* to the data in a memo field. The REINDEX option updates the index file after all the replacements are made.

If the replaced field is part of the active index, the record moves to its new position in the file, which can cause problems if you use a scope, FOR, or WHILE. If you use REPLACE ALL, the REPLACE starts with the first record, according to the index. Because the field changed was part of the index, the record pointer moved past some records.

Suppose that you want to replace a Customer ID field with "CN" plus the old customer ID. You would use a REPLACE ALL command, and the first record would be changed. The record then moves to a new position in the index. The next REPLACE works on the record after the first record's new position; the command will not work on the record that previously followed the first record. To prevent this problem, use SET ORDER TO to place the database in its record number (natural) order before using REPLACE. After the REPLACE is finished, you can use SET ORDER TO *<tag name>* to reactivate the index order.

The REPLACE command starts at the current record position. If you are at the end of the file, no data is replaced unless you specify a scope, FOR, or WHILE.

Example

```
* Replace data in the current record
USE ORDERS
GOTO 58
* Puts current date in SHIPDATE field
REPLACE SHIPDATE WITH DATE()
* Change all STATE fields in the database to uppercase
USE CUSTOMER
REPLACE ALL STATE WITH UPPER(STATE)
```

REPLACE FROM ARRAY

Syntax

```
REPLACE FROM ARRAY <array name>
   [FIELDS <field list>]
   [<scope>]
   [FOR <condition>]
   [WHILE <condition>]
   [REINDEX]
```

Purpose: Places data from an array into the fields of the current database. *Arrays* are groups of variables arranged like records in a database. A column in an array is similar in function to a field in a database. Rows of arrays are like records in a database. The REPLACE FROM ARRAY command takes a row of array data and places it in the current record. The data from the first array element is placed into the first field of the database, the second array element into the second field, and so on until there are no more array elements or database fields.

If a SET FIELDS statement is active, those fields are used by the REPLACE FROM ARRAY command. You also can use the FIELDS option to specify which database fields should be replaced with array elements.

Array elements are placed into the fields in the order specified by the FIELDS option. If you specify scope, FOR, or WHILE, the database fields that meet the condition are replaced by array elements until all of the array elements are used. If additional array elements are available, additional records are used that meet the condition specified with scope, FOR, or WHILE. The REINDEX option updates the index file after all the replacements are made.

Example

Replace the indicated fields with values from the READDATA[ ] array. Each row of the array has four elements: meter readings 1-4, all numeric. The target fields in the READINGS database are also numeric fields.

```
DECLARE ReadData[10,4]
ReadData[1,1] = 0
:
:
USE READINGS
* Make sure there's a value in the first array element
* indicating that there are reading values in the rest of
* that element row
IF ReadData[1,1] <> 0
   APPEND BLANK
   REPLACE FROM ARRAY readdata
ENDIF
```

REPORT FORM

Syntax

```
REPORT FORM <report form filename>/?
   [PLAIN]
   [HEADING <character expression>]
   [NOEJECT]
   [SUMMARY]
   [<scope>]
   [FOR <condition>]
```

```
[WHILE <condition>]
[TO PRINTER/TO FILE <filename>]
```

Purpose: Prints data from the current database or view, using the report form created by the CREATE/MODIFY REPORT command. The report can be sent to the screen, to the printer (with TO PRINTER), or to a file (with TO FILE <*filename*>). The report form (FRM) file is converted to the form program file (FRG) and then compiled to the form object file (FRO). The FRO file is run to print the report.

The ? option shows a list of reports that can be selected. The PLAIN option prints the report with headers or footers printed only on the first page. The HEADING option specifies an extra heading to be printed on each page. NOEJECT cancels the first form feed so that the report starts printing on the current page. The SUMMARY option prints only the subtotals and totals of the report.

Use a scope, TO, or WHILE to limit the report to part of the database. In a network environment, the database file is locked for exclusive use by the report form. If another user used the FLOCK( ) or RLOCK( ) parameters, dBASE 5 displays the message File is in use by another when you try to print. If you receive this message, you can copy the database to a temporary file and run the report from that file, or just SET LOCK OFF.

Example

```
* Print a report of the customers in Nevada
USE CUSTOMERS ORDER CUSTOMERS
REPORT FORM custlist FOR STATE = "NV" TO PRINTER
```

RESET

Syntax

```
RESET [IN <alias>]
```

Purpose: Removes the integrity tag from a file. The integrity tag indicates that a file was a part of a BEGIN TRANSACTION. The integrity tag normally stays with the file until the END TRANSACTION or ROLLBACK command completes successfully, or until the RESET command is used. This command affects the current database unless you use the IN <*alias*> option.

> **Caution**
>
> This command should not be used in a program file. It should be used in the Command window to correct an unusual situation or during the development of a program.

Example

```
RESET IN 2          && reset work area 2
```

RESTORE FROM

Syntax

```
RESTORE FROM <filename>
   [ADDITIVE]
```

Purpose: Retrieves saved memory variables and arrays from a memory variable file. This command can be used to save needed memory variables from one dBASE 5 session for use in another. The ADDITIVE option adds the saved memory variables to any existing memory variables; without ADDITIVE, all existing memory variables are cleared before the saved memory variables are loaded. You can load as many as 15,000 memory variables at one time. (You can adjust that number by modifying your CONFIG.DB file.)

The restored variables are declared as private variable types, unless you declare the memory variables public before using the RESTORE with the ADDITIVE option. Memory variables are saved to a memory file through the SAVE command.

Example

```
* Create some memvars
STORE 0 to qmem1, qmem2,     && private variables
PUBLIC username              && declare it public
username = "Elizabeth"       && give it a value
LIST MEMORY                  && show them on screen
SAVE TO SAVEMEM              && save them to the memory file
RELEASE ALL                  && clear all memvars
RESTORE FROM SAVEMEM         && load them from disk
* Show the restored memvars, note that all are private
LIST MEMORY
```

RESTORE MACROS

Syntax

```
RESTORE MACROS FROM <macro library file>
```

Purpose: Restores or loads macros from the specified macro library file (KEY). Macro library files are created from the Control Center and saved with the SAVE MACROS command. The library file contains macro keystrokes assigned to the macro key. If the macro library contains a macro key that was loaded previously from another macro library, the old macro command is overwritten by the new one.

Example

```
* Load a macro file, play the DATA_IN macro
RESTORE MACROS FROM DATAMAC
PLAY MACRO DATA_IN
```

RESTORE SCREEN FROM

Syntax

```
RESTORE SCREEN FROM <screen name>
```

Purpose: Displays a screen that was saved with a SAVE SCREEN command. The RELEASE SCREEN command removes the screen from memory.

You can only use this command with non-UI screens and windows like those created in previous versions of dBASE. It is ignored by dBASE 5's UI objects.

Example

```
* Restore the screens
RESTORE SCREEN FROM OLDSCRN
```

RESTORE WINDOW

Syntax

```
RESTORE WINDOW <window name list> /ALL FROM <filename>
```

Purpose: Restores specific window definitions from a disk file that was created using the SAVE WINDOWS command. Use the ALL parameter to restore all of the window definitions from the disk file. If the window definition already exists in memory, it is overwritten with the definition from the disk file.

You can only use this command with non-UI screens and windows like those created in previous versions of dBASE. It is ignored by dBASE 5's UI objects.

Example

```
* Save the current windows
SAVE WINDOWS ALL TO wind042
CLEAR                      && clear the screen
@ 15,20 say "Updating user file, please wait"
DO userupdt                && updating program
CLEAR
RESTORE WINDOW ALL FROM wind042
```

RESUME

Syntax

```
RESUME
```

Purpose: Resumes the execution of a program that was stopped with the SUSPEND command. You usually use RESUME during program debugging. You may want to use the CLEAR command to clear the screen before you use RESUME to restart the program. If you used the ROLLBACK command while the program was suspended, the RESUME command restarts the program with the command that appears after the END TRANSACTION statement in the program. (RESUME is used from the Command window only, not in programs.)

Example

```
RESUME
```

RETRY

Syntax

```
RETRY
```

Purpose: Reexecutes a command that caused an error. Using the RETRY command with the ON ERROR command can help you determine which command caused an error. You also can find the error with the ERROR( ) function, correct the error, and then use RETRY to repeat the command that caused the error.

Example

```
* Recover from a printer error. This code fragment is
* part of the ERR_TRAP.PRG program called by the
* ON ERROR DO ERR_TRAP command, and contains code that
* traps many different kinds of errors
*
err_found = ERROR()
DO CASE
   CASE err_found = 126
      ? "Printer not connected or turned on."
   CASE err_found = 127
      ? "Not a valid VIEW file"
   * CASE statements for other errors
ENDCASE
? "Please correct the error; then press a key."
WAIT ""              && wait for the user to press a key
RETRY
RETURN
```

RETURN

Syntax

```
RETURN [<expression> / TO MASTER / TO <procedure name>]
```

Purpose: Returns control to the calling program, to the Control Center, or to the Command window. In the calling program, the command following the calling command (DO *<program>*) is executed next.

In a FUNCTION, the RETURN command returns the computed value of the user-defined function. If you want RETURN to return you to the master (main) program, use TO MASTER. Use TO *<procedure name>* to return control to an active procedure.

You must put a RETURN command at the end of a procedure. At the end of a program, RETURN happens automatically, even if you do not include RETURN in the code.

RETURN releases any private memory variables that were defined in the called program, but it does not release public memory variables. RETURN also clears any ERROR( ) value.

Example

```
* Ask user whether it's OK to cancel out of
* current subprogram
answer = .F.
   @ 24,20 SAY "Cancel this subprogram? (Y/N) " ;
      GET answer PICTURE "Y"
   READ
* return to calling program; otherwise continue
IF answer
   RETURN
ENDIF
```

ROLLBACK

Syntax

```
ROLLBACK [<database filename>]
```

Purpose: Restores the database and index files to the state they were in before the transaction started and then stops the transaction. Any transaction commands not yet executed are ignored, and the program continues, starting with the command following the END TRANSACTION statement. The ROLLBACK command helps to ensure that a series of commands (the transaction) is completed properly. If an error prevents the transaction from completing, you can use the ROLLBACK command to put the data back in its original state, as if the transaction had never begun.

When the ROLLBACK command successfully completes, the ROLLBACK( ) function is set to true. The ROLLBACK can fail if a record's pre- and post-transactional contents are inconsistent or if the transaction log file is unreadable.

See the BEGIN TRANSACTION example for a sample ROLLBACK process.

> **Caution**
>
> ROLLBACK cannot be used in dBASE IV Versions 1.5 or 2.0 with a transaction log file from Versions 1.0 or 1.1. Be sure that the transaction log file was created with the current version.

RUN

Syntax

```
RUN / ! <DOS command>
```

Purpose: Performs a DOS command within a dBASE 5 program or at the DOS prompt. You must have enough memory available to load the COMMAND.COM file (the DOS command processor), or the message Insufficient memory is displayed. You can pass any variables to the DOS command by using macro substitution, as shown in the example.

If you run a program that will use a considerable amount of memory, use the RUN( ) function, described in the "Using Functions" section elsewhere in this "dBASE 5 Reference Guide."

Example

```
* Reset the DOS time to noon
time = "12:00"
RUN TIME &time
* Run the DBINFO program
RUN DBINFO C:
```

SAVE

See SAVE TO.

SAVE MACROS TO

Syntax

```
SAVE MACROS TO <macro library file>
```

Purpose: Saves the currently defined macros in a disk file. You then can use RESTORE MACROS to load the macros during another dBASE 5 session. You can create macros and assign them to macro keys from the Tools menu in the Control Center or by pressing Alt-T from the ASSIST screen.

If the macro library file already exists, you are asked for permission to overwrite the old macro library file (unless you specified SET SAFETY OFF).

Example

```
* Save the currently defined macros
SAVE MACROS TO datamac
```

SAVE SCREEN TO

Syntax

```
SAVE SCREEN TO <screen name>
```

Purpose: Saves the current screen image to memory. You then can clear the screen and recall the screen with the RESTORE SCREEN command.

You can only use this command with non-UI screens and windows like those created in previous versions of dBASE. It is ignored by dBASE 5's UI objects.

Example

```
* Save the current screen
SAVE SCREEN TO scrn012
CLEAR
@ 12,15 say "Please wait while database is updated"
DO DATAUPDT    && program to update the database
* Redisplay the screen
RESTORE SCREEN FROM scrn012
RELEASE SCREEN scrn012   && Good idea to free up memory
```

SAVE TO

Syntax

```
SAVE TO <filename> [ALL LIKE/EXCEPT <skeleton>]
```

Purpose: Saves all or some of the memory and array variables to a disk file so that they can be restored later in the current session (with the RESTORE command) or during another dBASE 5 session. The memory file usually has the extension MEM and is stored on the current drive/directory unless you specify otherwise. All memory and array variables are stored, unless you use the ALL LIKE or EXCEPT options.

See RESTORE for an example of using SAVE TO.

SAVE WINDOW

Syntax

```
SAVE WINDOW <window name list> / ALL TO <filename>
```

Purpose: Saves window definitions to a disk file. The window definitions can be restored from disk with the RESTORE WINDOW command. (See RESTORE WINDOW.)

You can only use this command with non-UI screens and windows like those created in previous versions of dBASE. It is ignored by dBASE 5's UI objects.

Example

```
* Save current window definitions
SAVE WINDOW ALL TO WINDFILE
```

SCAN...ENDSCAN

Syntax

```
SCAN [<scope>]
   [FOR <condition>]
   [WHILE <condition>]
      [<commands>]
      [LOOP]
      [EXIT]
ENDSCAN
```

Purpose: Performs the commands in the SCAN...ENDSCAN construct for all active records in the current database. This construct is an alternative to the DO WHILE command. You can scan only some records by using a scope, FOR, or WHILE. The LOOP command in SCAN...ENDSCAN goes to the beginning of the command sequence. The EXIT command terminates the SCAN and executes the command after ENDSCAN to be executed. SCAN executes faster than equivalent DO WHILE .NOT. EOF( )/SKIP/ENDDO.

Example

```
* Look for unentered zip codes
* If found, do the procedure to determine
* the correct zip code
USE CUSTOMER
SCAN FOR ISBLANK(zipcode)
   DO find_zip    && procedure to determine zip code
ENDSCAN
*
* equivalent code
USE CUSTOMER
DO WHILE .NOT. EOF()
   IF ZIPCODE = 0
      DO find_zip
   ENDIF
   SKIP
ENDDO
```

SEEK

Syntax

```
SEEK <expression>
```

Purpose: Searches for a record in the current database whose indexed key is equal to *<expression>*. The SEEK command searches quickly because it uses the current index to look for data instead of searching through every record.

The expression specified can be a memory variable but must be of the same data type as the key index field. An exact match must be found for the SEEK to be successful, unless you used SET EXACT OFF. Records marked for deletion are ignored if SET DELETED is ON. Also records are excluded according to any SET FILTER command (see SET DELETED, SET FILTER).

If the search is successful, FOUND( ) is set to true (.T.), and the record pointer is positioned on the found record. If the search is unsuccessful, FOUND( ) is false (.F.), and the record pointer is positioned at the end of the file (EOF). If you specified SET NEAR ON, an unsuccessful SEEK causes the record pointer to land on the nearest match.

Example

```
* Find the record with the closest match
* to "Tabasco" in the ITEMS database
* The index key is UPPER(ITEM_NAME)
USE ITEMS ORDER INAME
* Allow for something close
SET EXACT OFF
SEEK "TABASCO"
An alternative procedure:
SET NEAR ON
searchfor = "Tabasco"
SEEK UPPER(searchfor)
* and the results are these:
IF FOUND()                  && found a match
   ? "Found record number ", recno()
ELSE
   IF EOF()                 && not even a close match found
      ? "No match found, at end of file"
   ELSE                     && found a close match
      ? "Closest match is record ", recno()
   ENDIF
ENDIF
```

SELECT

Syntax

```
SELECT <work area/alias>
```

Purpose: Selects a database work area or database as the active database. Work area 1 (or A) always starts as the active area. You can have as many as 225 work areas active, designated by the numbers 1 through 225. You can designate the first 10 work areas by the letters A through J. The maximum areas defaults to 40, but can be set in CONFIG.DB with the MAXWORKAREAS setting.

A work area consists of the active database plus any associated indexes, queries, or format files. You can specify the current work area by the number, letter, or alias associated with the file. You also can use a variable as an explicit expression, such as <*thisone*>, if the variable *thisone* equals 1.

In addition, you can use a numeric expression as the work area, as shown in the example.

Example

```
* Display the number of records in each open database
counter = 1
FOR Counter = 1 to 40
   IF ""<>DBF(Counter)          && test for an open database
   SELECT counter
      * Show work area number, database name, # of records
      ? counter, DBF(), reccount()
   ENDIF
NEXT
```

SET

See Chapter 24, "Using SET Commands To Configure dBASE"

SHOW MENU

Syntax

```
SHOW MENU <menu name> [PAD <pad name>]
```

Purpose: Displays a menu bar without activating it. During your development work on a program, you can use this command to display menus without activating them so that you can see how the menu will appear. When you have displayed a menu this way, you cannot use the arrow keys to move through the menu pads.

You can only use this command with non-UI screens and windows like those created in previous versions of dBASE. It is ignored by dBASE 5's UI objects.

Example

```
* Show the menu bar, just so you can look at it
SHOW MENU main_menu
```

SHOW POPUP

Syntax

```
SHOW POPUP <pop-up name>
```

Purpose: Displays a pop-up bar without activating it. During your development work on a program, you can use this command to display pop-ups without activating them so that you can see how the pop-up will appear. When you have displayed a pop-up this way, you cannot use the arrow keys to move through the options, and no messages are displayed.

You can only use this command with non-UI screens and windows like those created in previous versions of dBASE. It is ignored by dBASE 5's UI objects.

Example

```
* Show the pop-up, just to see how it looks
SHOP POPUP edit_pop
```

SKIP

Syntax

```
SKIP [<number value>] [IN <alias>]
```

Purpose: Moves the record pointer in the database file. A positive *<number value>* moves the pointer forward in the database, and a negative value moves the pointer backward. If the database is indexed, SKIP moves forward or backward according to the index. Any filter set with SET FILTER is observed. You cannot skip past the beginning or end of the file. Use the IN option to skip records in a different work area.

Example

```
* Move forward 5 records
SKIP 5
* Move back 2 records
SKIP -2
```

SORT TO

Syntax

```
SORT TO <filename> ON <field1> [/A] [/C] [/D]
   [, <field2> [/A] [/C] [/D] ...]
      [ASCENDING] / [DESCENDING]
   [<scope>]
   [FOR <condition>]
   [WHILE <condition>]
```

Purpose: Creates a new database from the current database, with the data in the new database sorted by the order of the specified fields. Sorting is done in ascending order (/A) unless you specify descending with /D. You can add the /C option to ascending (/A /C) or descending (/D /C) sorts to specify that dBASE 5 ignore uppercase or lowercase characters. The /A or /D option is required for each field used in the sort. The ASCENDING or DESCENDING options affect all fields that do not have a /A or /D parameter. You can use a scope, FOR, or WHILE to extract a selected part of a database.

The SORT command works much like the INDEX command, but SORT creates a separate database file, and INDEX creates an index file for the current database. Using the SORT command reorders the data in the new database according to the sort fields. The INDEX command does not actually reorder the data; it enables you to work with the data as if it had been reordered. SORT also works with individual fields, not field expressions.

Example

```
* Sort the customer file by last, first, and company names
* into a TEMPCUST.DBF file. Extract only those records
* where the TOTALBUY field is > 10,000.
USE CUSTOMER
SORT TO TEMPCUST ON LASTNAME, FIRSTNAME, COMPANY ;
      FOR TOTALBUY > 10000
```

STORE

Syntax

```
STORE <expression> TO <memory variable list> /
   <array element list>
<memory variable>/<array element> = <expression>
```

Purpose: Stores values in memory variables or arrays. The STORE command enables you to assign a single value to many memory variables. The alternative syntax stores one value in one variable. The *<expression>* used determines the type of memory variable created. If the memory variable already exists, it is overwritten with the new value.

Memory variables can contain letters, numbers, or underscores but must start with a letter. Memory variables can be as many as 10 characters long. You should not use the single letters A through J, and M, because database aliases may use these letters. Memory variables with the same names as database fields are permitted, but they can cause confusion in some situations and should be avoided. If you need a memory variable with the same name as a database field, indicate the memory variable name using the M-> indicator, as M->ctQty.

Example

```
* These two commands are equivalent
STORE "Christine" to username
username = "Christine"
```

SUM

Syntax

```
SUM [<numeric expression list>]
   [TO <memory variable list> / TO ARRAY <array name>]
   [<scope>]
   [FOR <condition>]
   [WHILE <condition>]
```

Purpose: Calculates the sum of a numeric expression and stores the sum in a memory variable or array if you specify TO; otherwise, the sum is displayed on-screen. All numeric fields are summed unless you specify a *<numeric field list>*. All records are used unless you specify a scope, FOR, or WHILE.

Example

```
* Determine the total sales and commissions for January 1993
USE STOCK
SUM SALES, COMM TO sales_sum, comm_sum ;
   FOR SELLDATE >= {1/1/93} .AND. SELLDATE <= {1/31/93}
```

SUSPEND

Syntax

```
SUSPEND
```

Purpose: Stops the current program and returns you to the Command window. When you are at the Command window, you can perform any Command window command and then use RESUME to restart the program where you left off, or use CANCEL to cancel all programs. You can use SUSPEND during debugging.

While your program is suspended, you can start other programs with the DO command. Be careful, however, not to start too many programs or to restart the current program. Memory variables created at the Command window while a program is suspended are private to the suspended program.

> **Caution**
>
> If you find that changes you're making in your program files aren't taking effect, you may be trying to perform operations on a suspended program. DBOs stay open when you're suspended, so they can't be overwritten by the compiler with a new version.

Example

```
* Suspend the program
SUSPEND
```

TEXT...ENDTEXT

Syntax

```
TEXT
        <text>
ENDTEXT
```

Purpose: Sends blocks of *<text>* to the screen. Use this command to print quick blocks of messages to the screen without worrying about specific placement of the text. You can use this command only in program files.

Example

```
* Display some text on the screen
TEXT
The Monthly Status report has been selected.
Please make sure that the printer is ready
and that the proper paper is loaded.
Press a key when you are ready to start the report.
ENDTEXT
```

TOTAL ON

Syntax

```
TOTAL ON <key field> TO <filename>
   [FIELDS <fields list>]
   [<scope>]
   [FOR <condition>]
   [WHILE <condition>]
```

Purpose: Totals the numeric fields of the current database and then creates a second database that contains the total of the fields in the current database. One record is created for each group of records that have the same *<key field>* data. The structure of the TO database is the same as that of the current database, except for any memo fields. If the FIELDS option is used, only those fields in *<fields list>* will be totalled.

The numeric field size must be large enough to hold the sum of all the numeric data. If a field is not large enough, asterisks are placed in that field in the created database. You can use the MODIFY STRUCTURE command to increase the size of the fields in the source database.

Example

```
* Summarize the sales of all stock items into a summary DBF
* Extract only 1991 sales
* The primary index is based on the Stock Number field
USE SALES ORDER STOCK_NUM
TOTAL ON STOCK_NUM TO SALES92 FOR YEAR(SELL_DATE) = 1992
```

TYPE

Syntax

```
TYPE <filename> [TO PRINTER / TO FILE <filename>] [NUMBER]
```

Purpose: Displays the contents of an ASCII text file. The text file usually is displayed on-screen, but it can be sent to the printer with TO PRINTER or to a file with TO FILE <*filename*>. The NUMBER option prints line numbers for each line. If you used SET HEADING ON, the SET HEADING TO page heading is printed on each page. Page numbers are displayed on the right side of the page.

Example

```
* Send the contents of a short help text file to screen
* This could be an alternative to the TEXT/ENDTEXT command
* Make sure the text file is not longer than a screen,
* or part of the file will be scrolled off the screen
TYPE help042.TXT
```

UNLOCK

Syntax

```
UNLOCK [ALL/IN <alias>]
```

Purpose: Releases the record and file locks that were placed on a database so that other users can modify the data. When a user is changing a record on a network, that record is *locked* so that other users cannot change the data. Other users can look at the record. (Entire files can be locked with the FLOCK( ) function.) The UNLOCK command unlocks the record or file lock for the current work area, another work area (the IN <*alias*> option), or all databases (the ALL option). Any files that are related to the file you unlock are unlocked also.

Example

```
* Increase the price on record 15
USE PARTS
GOTO 15              && get to record 15
IF RLOCK()
   REPLACE cost with cost * 1.1
   UNLOCK
ENDIF
```

UPDATE ON

Syntax

```
UPDATE ON <key field> FROM <alias>
   REPLACE <fieldname 1> WITH <expression 1>
   [, <fieldname 2> WITH <expression 2> ...]
   [RANDOM] [REINDEX]
```

Purpose: Takes data from another database into the fields of the current database. The key field matches data from different databases having that field in common. If the target (current) database has several records with a matching key field, only the first record receives the values from the source database.

Both databases must have current indexes that match the key field. If you use RANDOM, only the target (current) database needs to have an index that matches the current field. You do not need to specify the key field name as one of the field names to be replaced, although such a specification is allowed. To take data from the source database, you must use the work area as part of the *<expression>*, as shown in the example. The REINDEX option updates the index file after all the replacements are made.

Example

```
* Update data in the ORDERS database
* from the TEMPORDR database
* The key field is the customer number; the total cost
* is taken from the TEMPORDR database and used to
* update the ORDERS year-to-date values in the ORDERS
* database. The current date is placed in
* the LASTDATE field.
USE ORDERS ORDER CUST_NUM
USE TEMPORDA ORDER CUST_NUM IN 2
UPDATE ON CUST_NUM FROM TEMPORDR ;
  REPLACE YEARSALES WITH YEARSALES + ;
  TEMPORDR->SELLPRICE * TEMPORDR->QUANTITY;
  YEARQTY WITH YEARQTY + TEMPORD->QTY, LASTDATE WITH DATE()
```

USE

Syntax

```
USE [<database filename>/?] [IN <work area number>]
   [[INDEX <.ndx or .mdx file list>]
   [ORDER <.ndx filename>/[TAG] <.mdx tag>
   [OF <.mdx filename>]]
   [ALIAS <alias>] [EXCLUSIVE] [NOUPDATE]] [NOLOG]
      [NOSAVE] [AGAIN]
```

Purpose: Opens a database file (and an associated memo file, if the database has a memo field). USE can open MDX and NDX index files optionally. When you use USE without any options, it closes the database file and associated index and memo files in the current work area. USE ? displays a list of the databases in the current catalog, if CATALOG is ON, or of all databases in the current directory.

The <*database filename*> can be a specific file name, such as CLIENTS, or an indirect reference for a file name, such as (currdata). The IN option enables you to specify the work area number (1 through 255). The area number does not have to be the current area.

The INDEX option enables you to open any associated index files (NDX) or multiple-index files (MDX). The multiple-index file contains fields that were defined as index tags. Each tag is similar to an NDX file, but the tag index pointers are contained in one MDX file. An MDX file can have as many as 47 index tags, but the MDX file uses only one DOS *file handle*. (DOS allows only a certain number of files to be open at any one time. The maximum number of file handles available is specified by the FILES parameter in your CONFIG.SYS file. For you to use dBASE 5, your CONFIG.SYS file should specify FILES = 99 or more.)

The ORDER option determines which index sets the order of the database. This controlling index then is used for order by any SEEK or FIND commands. The ORDER...OF parameter specifies the name of the MDX file. ORDER TAG LASTNAME OF CLIENTS, for example, indicates using the tag LASTNAME that is part of the CLIENTS.MDX file. If you have multiple indexes active, you can use the SET ORDER command to change the controlling index. The ALIAS option specifies the database alias that can be used in other commands. If an ALIAS is not specified, the database file name is assigned as the alias.

The EXCLUSIVE option is used in networks to indicate that only the current user has access to the database, so that the file is not shared by other users on the network. In a non-network environment, the database is opened as EXCLUSIVE automatically, and the EXCLUSIVE option is ignored. The NOUPDATE option makes the database file read-only so that you cannot make any changes to it.

The NOLOG command can be used to open or close files during a transaction without them being part of the transaction log file. NOSAVE opens a database file as a temporary file, which is erased when you close it. Using the AGAIN command, you can open the same database file in more than one work area.

Example

```
* Open the CLIENTS database in work area 1 and
* LETTERS database in work area 2, using the
* ZIP index tag
USE CLIENTS IN 1 ORDER ZIP
USE LETTERS IN 2 ORDER ZIP
```

WAIT

Syntax

```
WAIT [<prompt>] [TO <memory variable>]
```

Purpose: Pauses the currently running program until a key is pressed. You can store the keystroke in the *<memory variable>*, but you instead may want to use @ SAY..GET and READ. You can specify your own message with the *<prompt>* or use the default "Press any key to continue" by not specifying a *<prompt>*.

Example

```
* Wait for the printer to be set up
? "Please make sure the printer is ready, then"
WAIT          && use the default message
```

ZAP

Syntax

```
ZAP
```

Purpose: Removes all records from the current database. This command is the same as a DELETE ALL and PACK command used together but removes the records more quickly. If SET SAFETY ON was enabled (the default), dBASE 5 asks for verification before the file is cleared. If you respond Yes, the file is cleared of all data, but the structure of the file is retained. Any associated index files are reindexed, and any associated memo file is emptied also. On a network, you must have exclusive use of the database before you can use the ZAP command.

> **Caution**
>
> The ZAP command erases all data in a database file. Make sure that you have current backups of the data before you use this command. After ZAP is used on a database, dBASE 5 cannot recover the data that had been marked for deletion.

Example

```
* Clear out the CUSTTEMP database
USE CUSTTEMP
ZAP
```

Chapter 23

Using Functions

Functions give dBASE the capability to perform many different operations. You can use functions to convert from character information to numeric and vice versa, for example, or to select specific information from a character string. Some functions return a true or false answer, performing a test on information. Still other functions enable you to perform mathematical functions.

Many functions require arguments—information you provide so that the function can be performed. A few functions, however, require no arguments. The VERSION( ) function, for example, returns the version of the operating system, without requiring an argument. All functions must be referenced indirectly with a command, even if the command is the question mark (?), which simply places the result of the function on-screen.

Functions Listed Alphabetically

In this section functions are listed alphabetically, and examples and other information are shown for each function. New and enhanced functions are identified with an icon.

Syntax

```
&<memory variable>[.]
```

Purpose: The macro substitution function. The contents of the character memory variable, such as &Username, are placed inside the variable expression. The indirect reference (*<memory variable>*) provides similar capabilities and works faster. The optional period is required if the macro is part of an expression.

Example

```
Name = "Christine"
@ 10, 20 SAY "There are several &names here"
* There are several Christines here
* These two statements will display the same message
@ 12,20 SAY "Current user is &name."
@ 13,20 SAY "Current user is " + name"
FilName = "Customer"
USE FilName    && Opens FILNAME.DBF
USE &FilName   && Opens CUSTOMER.DBF
```

( )

Syntax

```
(<Memory Variable>)
```

Purpose: Parentheses can be used to perform two different functions, grouping and indirect referencing. In this explanation they are being used for indirect referencing. In all versions of dBASE after dBASE III Plus, file names can be represented by any valid dBASE expression. Because of this new feature in the dBASE language there is now a need, in some cases, to force dBASE into understanding that the expression is not a name. Indirect referencing is the name given to the process of identifying an expression as an expression and not a title or name of a field or memory variable.

Example

```
cFileName = "Customer"

The following example would try to open a file called cFileName
USE cFileName

To clarify that cFileName is not a title or label, but an
➥expression, use
Indirect Referencing

USE (cFileName)

If dBASE can figure out that what you are specifying IS an
➥expression, then
Indirect Referencing is optional.  The following example opens a
file called Cust1

cFileName = "Cust"
cFileID   = "1"
USE cFileName + cFileID
```

ABS( )

Syntax

```
ABS(<numeric expression>)
```

Purpose: Returns the absolute value of the *<numeric expression>* or the positive value of the *<numeric expression>*. You can use the ABS function to determine the number of days between two dates, without worrying about getting a negative value.

Example

```
? ABS(1433)                       && returns 1433
? ABS(-792)                       && returns 792
? ABS(-392) > 300                 && returns .T. (392 > 300)
? ABS({11/25/91} - {12/04/91})    && returns 9
```

ACCESS( )

Syntax

```
ACCESS()
```

Purpose: Returns the current user's access level. You then can use the level with the PROTECT command to limit user access to certain fields or databases. Only if the DBSYSTEM.DB file is accessed by dBASE 5 when the program is started will the log-in screen be shown. If a user has an access level of 0, that user cannot access encrypted databases. In a nonnetworked system, ACCESS( ) returns a 0.

Example

```
@ 12,15 SAY "Your access level is " + STR(ACCESS())
```

ACOPY( )

Syntax

```
ACOPY(<source array name>,<target array name>[,<starting element expN>,
   <elements expN>[,<target element expN>[,<copy mode expN>]]])
```

Purpose: Copies elements from a specified source array to a specified target array, and returns the number of elements copied. If the specified target array has not yet been declared, dBASE creates a target array to fit the incoming elements. This function overwrites existing data in the target array, regardless of data type resident in the target array. The syntax of the function consists of two basic components: *<source array name>* which is the array that provides the elements to copy; and *<target array name>* which is the destination of the copied elements.

The next parameters are optional. The parameter *<starting element expN>* indicates the element number of the first element in the array to be copied (see AELEMENT( )). If you do not use *<starting element expN>*, the entire array is copied. To set any of the optional parameters, there can't be any null arguments in the sequence before the parameter being set. ACOPY(A,B,,3) is illegal.

The *<elements ExpN>* parameter has two different functions depending on the value of *<copy mode expN>*. If *<copy mode expN>* is negative, zero, or left off, *<elements expN>* is the number of elements to copy from the source array to the target array. If *<copy mode expN>* is a positive integer, *<elements expN>* is the element number (see AELEMENT( )) of the last element that will be copied in matrix mode. The *<target element expN>* enables you to specify which element to begin copying to. Without it, the elements begin filling the array from the first position.

If the target array has not yet been declared, this value must be ≥ 1 value but is treated as 1 by dBASE. The last parameter is *<copy mode expN>* which controls how the elements from the source array are copied to the target array. The default copy order when *<copy mode>* is zero decimal is to copy the elements in a linear fashion across the array. If *<copy mode expN>* is a nonzero whole number, ACOPY( ) does a matrix copy in which it copies a rectangular area bounded by the values entered in the *<starting element expN>* and *<elements expN>*. The bracketed elements are copied into a rectangle the same size and shape as the rectangle in the source array.

When copying from one array to another, if the target array isn't large enough to contain all of the incoming information, it only stores as much as possible.

Example

```
USE Invoicer
DECLARE BigArray[6,5]    &&Declare array with 6 rows and 5 columns
COPY TO ARRAY BigArray   &&Fill array with first 5 fields of first 6
                         ➥records
:
:
Copycat = ACopy(BigArray, SubArray, AELEMENT(BigArray,2,2),;
   AELEMENT (BigArray,3,3),1,1)    &&Acopy contents of first array
to second array
? Copycat                && Returns the number of elements copied
4
```

ACOS( )

Syntax

```
ACOS(<cosine value>)
```

Purpose: Returns the angle size in radians for any given *<cosine value>*. The *<cosine value>* must be from –1 to +1. Use SET DECIMALS and SET PRECISION to fix the number of decimal places and accuracy returned.

Example

```
? ACOS(.224)        && returns 1.34
```

ADEL( )

Syntax

```
ADEL( <array name>, <position expN>[,<row/col expN>])
```

Purpose: Deletes entries from an array element, row, or column. The remaining values in the array are moved to fill the spaces emptied by the deletion. No change is made to the dimensions of the array.

For one-dimensional arrays, the *<position expN>* is the element number that will be deleted. All other entries in the array will be shifted one element number lower to fill the gap in the array. The values of the entries at the end of the array that are vacated by the shift are set to false (.F.).

For two-dimensional arrays, the *<position expN>* is the row or column number that will be deleted. The third parameter is only allowed for two-dimensional arrays. If *<row/col expN>* is 1 or left out, all elements from the row indicated by *<position expN>* are deleted. All the following rows are moved up one row to fill the deleted space. If *<row/col expN>* is 2, all elements from the column indicated by *<position expN>* are deleted. All the following columns are moved left one column to fill the deleted space. In either case, the values for the entries vacated are set to false (.F.).

Example

```
DECLARE BigArray[4,5]            && Declare a two-dimensional array
:
:
USE STOCK                        && Use a data table
:
:
COPY TO ARRAY BigArray           && Load the array from the table
:
:
NumDel = ADEL(BigArray,3,2)      && Delete column 3
?NumDel                          && Show the number of entries deleted.
```

ADIR( )

Syntax

```
ADIR(<array name>[,<filename skeleton expC>[,<DOS file attribute
expC>]])
```

Purpose: Stores five characteristics of specified DOS files to an array. These characteristics are name, size, date stamp, time stamp, and DOS attributes. The value returned is the number of files which matched the specifications set by the parameters. The *<filename skeleton expC>* parameter enables you to control the file name pattern that the function tries to match. This parameter accepts a quoted string and defaults to "*.*". The default pulls all files that are neither system nor hidden and not directories.

You can further control the search by using the *<DOS file attribute expC>*. Choose either D, H, S, or V to indicate Directories, Hidden files, System files, or Volume labels, respectively, to expand the focus of the function. For example, to add the hidden files that match the other search criteria to the list normally retrieved, use "H" for *<DOS file attribute expC>* in the above syntax.

ADIR( ) automatically sets the rows of the array to fit the number of files found. If the array does not exist, it will be created. If the array exists, it will be resized to five columns and the number of rows required by the file specification. Columns are fixed at five and contain file characteristics information as shown in Table 23.1.

Table 23.1 ADIR( ) Array Structure

Column 1	Column 2	Column 3	Column 4	Column 5
File name	Size	Date	Time	DOS attribute
(character)	(numeric)	(date)	(character)	(character)

The fifth column of the array may contain one of the following attributes:

Attribute	Meaning
A.....	Archive (Read/Write) file
....D.	Directory
.H....	Hidden file
..R...	Read-only file

Attribute	Meaning
...S..	System file
.....V	Volume label
......	No attributes

Example

```
NumDIRs = ADIR(DIRLIST, "c:\", "D") && list all directories in the
                                       ➥root
```

AELEMENT( )

Syntax

```
AELEMENT(<array name>,<subscript1 expN>[,<subscript2 expN>])
```

Purpose: Returns the sequence number of a specified element in an array. This is particularly useful with ASCAN( ), ACOPY( ), and other functions which require the element number as a parameter. The numbering in arrays is left to right, then drop down one row and continue counting.

When specifying the desired element location in the function syntax, *<subscript1 expN>* is the first number of the element, and *<subscript2 expN>* is the second. The inverse of this function is ASUBSCRIPT which returns the element's subscript numbers after you've specified the element number.

Example

```
DECLARE aManager[6]     && One-dimensional array
DECLARE aEmployee[5,6]&& Two-dimensional array
? AELEMENT(aManager,3)
3
? AELEMENT(aEmployee,3,3)
15                      && two rows of six, plus three into third row
```

AFIELDS( )

Syntax

```
AFIELDS(<array name>)
```

Purpose: Stores the four characteristics of the fields in an existing table structure (field name, field type, field length, and number of decimal places) to an array. The function automatically sizes the array to fit the incoming field information from the table, but columns are always set at four. Table 23.2 shows the column headings for the AFIELDS( ) function. The function value is the number of fields in the table open in the current work area. If no data table is open in the current work area, the value returned is 0.

Table 23.2 Column Headings for the AFIELDS( ) Function

Column 1	Column 2	Column 3	Column 4
Field name	Field type	Field length	Decimal places
(character)	(character)	(numeric)	(numeric)
	C = Character		
	D = Date		
	L = Logical		
	M = Memo		
	N = Numeric		
	F = Float		
	B = Binary		
	G = General		

Example

```
USE Stock
FieldCat=AFIELDS(StockFlds)        && get all field characteristics
RecLen=0
* determine length of all character fields
For LoopVar = 1 TO FieldCat
     IF (Stock.Flds[LoopVar,2]="C")&& IF a character field
       RecLen=RecLen + StockFlds[LoopVar,3]     && Add to length
     ENDIF
NEXT
```

AFILL( )

Syntax

```
AFILL(<array name>,<exp>[,<start expN>[,<count expN>[,<fill mode
expN>]]])
```

Purpose: Used to fill a specific element or elements in an array with a set value. *<array name>* indicates a one- or two-dimensional array to "fill," while *<exp>* refers to the expression to be placed into the array. By default, the function starts filling from the first element in the array. To change this, set *<start expN>* to the element where you want to start the fill operation.

The *<count expN>* parameter provides one of two different indicators based on the value of the *<fill mode expN>*. If *<fill mode expN>* is 0, not a whole number, or left off, the fill is done sequentially through the array for *<count expN>*

elements. If *<fill mode expN>* is a nonzero whole number, the fill is done to a rectangular block of elements in the array starting at *<start expN>* and ending at *<count expN>*.

The value returned is the number of array elements filled.

Example

```
DECLARE aStock[4,5]    && Create an array, all values .F.
OnHand=AFILL(aStock,0) && Set all of array to 0
* Now set one column to the default stock item
Descript=AFILL(aStock,Dummy,2,AELEMENT(aStock,4,2),1)
```

AGROW( )

Syntax

```
AGROW(<array name>,<expN>)
```

Purpose: Increases the size of an array by adding a single element, row, or column. The value returned is the number of elements added. To add a single element to a one-dimensional array, or to add a row to a two-dimensional array, set *<expN>* to 1.

To add a column to an array, set *<expN>* to 2. A one-dimensional array then becomes a two-dimensional array. A two-dimensional array shifts all resident values to make room for the new column and then attaches the new elements with a logical value of .F. at the end of the array.

The values for *<expN>* can only be a 1 or a 2. Any other number causes an error message `Invalid function argument`.

Example

```
DECLARE aManager[6,4]
AGROW(aManager,1)&& adds a new row to the array, containing a value
of .F.
* making the dimensions [7,4]
AGROW(aManager,2)&& adds a new column to right side of the array
                 && containing a value of .F. making the dimensions
[7,5]
```

AINS( )

Syntax

```
AINS(<array name>,<position expN>[expN2])
```

Purpose: Places a new element into an array at the specified location. Because AINS does not change the size of the array, the existing values are shifted down, with the last element, row, or column being discarded.

Example

```
DECLARE aTopSales[5,2]      && Top salesmen and amount
:
:
FOR LoopVar = 1 TO 5
     IF TotalSales > aTopSales[Loopvar,2]
* If this salesman sold more, bump everyone in array down
          Ins_Ok=AINS(aTopSales,Loopvar)
          aTopSales[Loopvar,1]=Salesman
          aTopSales[Loopvar,2]=TotalSales
     ENDIF
NEXT
```

ALEN( )

Syntax

```
ALEN(<array name>[,<expN>])
```

Purpose: Counts the number of elements, rows, and columns in a designated array and returns the value. This may come in handy when writing reusable routines you are copying or otherwise working with. You must indicate whether you want to know the rows or elements, or the columns in an array. To do this, set *<expN>* to 0 or leave out for elements, 1 for rows (which means the first number of the subscript), or 2 for columns (which indicates the second subscript).

Example

```
PROCEDURE CheckTop
* This procedure takes a two-dimensional array as
* a parameter and checks the passed in value to
* see if it is larger than the values already in the
* array. If it is, the values in the array are bumped
* down.
PARAMETER AnArray, TopVal, TopPerform
* Use the ALEN function to find number of rows in array
FOR LoopVar = 1 TO ALEN(AnArray,1)
     IF TopVal > AnArray[Loopvar,2]
* If this performer did more, bump everyone in array down
          Ins_Ok=AINS(AnArray,Loopvar)
          AnArray[Loopvar,1]=TopPerform
          AnArray[Loopvar,2]=TopVal
     ENDIF
NEXT
RETURN
```

ALIAS( )

Syntax

```
ALIAS ([<alias>])
```

Purpose: Returns the alias name of the current work area or of the work area specified as the optional *<alias>*. The *<alias>* can be a number between 1 and the value set in CONFIG.DB for MAXWORKAREAS. The default maximum is 40. The *<alias>* can also be a character string that equates to A through J or the defined alias for the data table.

Example

```
SELECT 3                      && work area 3
USE CLIENTS                   && open a database
SELECT 1                      && work area 1
USE ORDERS
* Alias for current work area (1)
? ALIAS()                     && returns "ORDERS"
* Alias for work area 3
? ALIAS(3)                    && returns "CLIENTS"
?ALIAS("C")                   && Returns "CLIENTS"
```

ARESIZE( )

Syntax

```
ARESIZE(<array name>,<new rows expN>,[,<new cols expN>,<retain values expN>])
```

Purpose: Changes the size of the array by adding or subtracting rows and columns, allowing for retention of the resident values if desired. Specify the number of rows in the array with a positive, nonzero number in the *<new rows expN>* parameter. You can create an array as small as one element. To reset the number of columns, set *<new cols expN>* equal to the new number of desired columns, which can be 0 but nothing less than zero. Ignoring this option tells ARESIZE( ) to change the number of rows, but leave the number of columns the same.

To have the current values of the remaining elements retained, set *<retain values expN>* equal to any nonzero value. If *<retain values expN>* is 0 or left blank, the array elements are filled sequentially from the existing array values, changing the mapping of values to element numbers. It returns the number of elements in the new array.

Example

```
? ARESIZE(MyArray,2,1,2) && retains values
? ARESIZE(MyArray,3,2)   && 3 rows, 2 columns, doesn't retain values
```

ASC( )

Syntax

```
ASC(<character expression>)
```

Purpose: Returns the ASCII code of the first character of the *<character expression>*, which can be a character string or a string variable.

Example

```
? ASC("A")          && returns 65
Stockloc = 55C12
? ASC(Stockloc)     && returns 53, since ASC("5") = 53
```

ASCAN( )

Syntax

```
ASCAN(<array name>,<exp>[,<starting element expN>[,<elements expN>
   [,<scan mode expN>]]])
```

Purpose: Performs a search on a specified array for a specified search string. Returns a 1 if the search is found, 0 if not found. *<exp>* is the expression for the scan to look for, *<starting element expN>* indicates the address of the array element to start from. Omitting this parameter causes the scan to begin at the first element in the array. *<elements expN>* determines the number of elements to be scanned. If you want to scan the entire array, omit this parameter.

To specify how the array is scanned, set *<scan mode expN>* equal to 0 or leave blank to perform a linear scan. Set it to any nonzero value to have the scan do a matrix scan, where it searches through a rectangular area for the desired value. The bounds for the matrix scan are determined by the values entered in *<starting element expN>* and *<elements expN>*.

Example

```
DECLARE aActions[10,2]          && Action item list with priority
:
:
NewTask = "Groceries"
ActItem=1
ActPri=2
IF ASCAN(aActions,NewTask)=0     && Check for new task in list
     EmptyRow=ASCAN(aActions,.F.)&& Empty rows are false
     IF EmptyRow <> 0            && There was a blank row
          aActions[EmptyRow,ActItem]=NewTask
          aActions[EmptyRow,ActPri]=1
     ENDIF
ENDIF
```

ASIN( )

Syntax

```
ASIN(<sine value>)
```

Purpose: Returns the angle size in radians for the *<sine value>*. The *<sine value>* must be from –1 to +1. Use SET DECIMALS and SET PRECISION to fix the number of decimal places and accuracy returned.

Example

```
? ASIN(.492)        && returns 0.51
```

ASORT( )

Syntax

```
ASORT(<array name>,[,<starting element expN>[,<elements expN>
   [<sort order expN>]]])
```

Purpose: Sorts the designated array by elements if one-dimensional or by rows if two-dimensional. Returns a value of 1 if successful, 0 if it failed. To specify which element to start with, set *<starting element expN>* equal to the number of the element. When sorting a one-dimensional array, *<elements expN>* indicates the number of elements to sort. When sorting a two-dimensional array, it indicates the number of rows to sort. Omitting this option causes the sort to be done on rows beginning with the value of *<starting element expN>*. Sorting rows moves the entire row to a new location.

Sometimes you may need to change from the default sorting order of ascending. To do so, set *<sort order expN>* to 1, to switch to descending order. Be sure that all elements to be sorted contain the same data type, or you may get unexpected and undesired results.

Example

```
?ASORT(aData,6,3)     && begins sorting with
 *element 6 and sorts three rows of numbers
```

ASUBSCRIPT( )

Syntax

```
ASUBSCRIPT(<array name>,<element expN>, <subscript expN>)
```

Purpose: Reports back to you what the subscripts are for the location of a specific element in an array. Enter the element number in *<element expN>*, then enter the subscript number desired—either a 1 or 2 depending on whether you want a return value for the row or column subscript, respectively. Remember that one-dimensional arrays have element numbers and subscripts that are identical. Therefore, use this function to determine subscripts for two-dimensional arrays to get the most out of the function.

Example

```
DECLARE aActions[10,3]

?ASUBSCRIPT(aActions,7,1)      && Returns 3 for row
?ASUBSCRIPT(aActions,7,2)      && Returns 1 for column
```

AT( )

Syntax

```
AT(<character string1>,<character string2>/
   <memo field name> [,<numeric expression>])
```

Purpose: Looks for *<character string 1>* (the substring) in *<character string 2>* (the source string) or in the *<memo field>*. If *<character string 1>* is found, the starting position number is returned. If *<character string 1>* is not found, or if it is longer than the source string or memo field, then 0 is returned. The optional *<numeric expression>* specifies which occurrence of the substring is sought. For example, if you want to find the second occurrence of the substring, you specify 2 for the *<numeric expression>*. To search a string beginning with the rightmost position of the string, use the RAT( ) function.

Example

```
* Look for "beans"
Lookfor = "BEANS"
Lookin = "String Beans"
* Force Lookin uppercase for exact match
? AT(Lookfor, upper(Lookin))        && prints 8
? AT("BEANS", "STRING BEANS")       && prints 8
```

ATAN( )

Syntax

```
ATAN(<tangent value>)
```

Purpose: Returns the angle size in radians for the *<tangent value>*. The *<tangent value>* must be between –p/2 and +p/2. Use SET DECIMALS and SET PRECISION to fix the number of decimal places and accuracy returned.

Example

```
? ATAN(1.00)          && returns 0.79
```

ATN2( )

Syntax

```
ATN2(<sine angle>, <cosine angle>)
```

Purpose: Returns the angle size in radians for the <*sine*> and <*cosine*> of the same angle. The <*sine*> and <*cosine*> values must be between –p/2 and +p/2. Use SET DECIMALS and SET PRECISION to fix the number of decimal places and accuracy returned.

Example

```
? ATN2(.50, .80)          && returns 0.56
```

BAR( )

Syntax

```
BAR()
```

Purpose: Returns the number of the most recently selected bar from a pop-up menu. This function returns a 0 if there is no active pop-up menu, no pop-up menus have been defined, or the Esc key was used to deactivate the active pop-up menu. This function only works with pop-up menus that were created using the DEFINE POP-UP command. Menus created using DEFINE MENUITEM do not respond to this function.

Example

```
* Determine which bar was pressed
* The pop-up menu was previously defined
@ 12,15 SAY "You selected bar number " + STR(BAR())
```

BARCOUNT( )

Syntax

```
BARCOUNT([<pop-up name>])
```

Purpose: Returns the number bars in the active pop-up menu or a specified pop-up menu. If you do not specify a <*pop-up name*>, the currently active pop-up is used. This function only works with the DEFINE POP-UP style menus, not with DEFINE MENUITEM menus.

Example

```
* Displays the number of bars in pop-up
* The pop-up menu named "TOPMENU" was previously defined
@ 12,10 SAY "There are " + STR(BARCOUNT("TOPMENU")) +;
   " menu items available."
```

BARPROMPT( )

Syntax

```
BARPROMPT(<bar number> [,<pop-up name>])
```

Purpose: Returns the text that is displayed in a specified bar of a pop-up menu, or if no pop-up is specified, the currently active pop-up. The pop-up menu and prompts must have been previously defined. This function only works with the DEFINE POP-UP style menus, not with DEFINE MENUITEM menus.

Example

```
* Display the prompt from the third bar of the "MAILING" pop-up
@ 18,10 SAY "Select the "  +  BARPROMPT(3,"MAILING") + " option."
```

BOF( )

Syntax

```
BOF([<alias>])
```

Purpose: If BOF is true, the record pointer is at the beginning of the file. The optional *<alias>* can be used to indicate an active database in another work area. This function is used often to make sure that the record pointer is not moved past the beginning of the file.

Example

```
* If record pointer is not at beginning of the file,
* move to previous record
USE ORDERS ORDER ORDNUM      && the ORDNUM index is active
GOTO 12                      && go to record 12
IF .NOT. BOF()
   SKIP -1
ENDIF
```

CALL( )

Syntax

```
CALL(<binary filename> [,<expression list>])
```

Purpose: Executes a binary program module, such as those written in assembly language or C. The module first must be loaded with the LOAD command before it can be executed. The *<expression list>* is an option list of values that is expected by the program module, in the same way a procedure expects parameters. Up to seven expressions can be passed to the module. Only one value (the first expression) is returned to dBASE 5 after the module has finished.

Example

```
* The "MONTYPE" binary module determines the type of monitor
LOAD MONTYPE              && loads the module
@ 12,15 SAY "Current monitor is " + CALL(MONTYPE, VIDCARD)
```

CATALOG( )

Syntax

```
CATALOG()
```

Purpose: Returns the drive letter and name of the catalog file currently in use.

Example

```
SET CATALOG TO SAMPLES
? CATALOG()
C:SAMPLES.CAT
```

CDOW( )

Syntax

```
CDOW(<date variable>)
```

Purpose: Returns the day name for the *<date variable>*, which can be a date-type memory variable, field, or any function that returns a date-type variable.

Example

```
* On what day were you born?
Whatdate = {}          && makes an empty date variable
@ 12,15 SAY "What is your birthday? " ;
   GET Whatdate PICTURE "@D"
READ
@ 13,15 SAY "You were born on a " + CDOW(Whatdate)
```

CEILING( )

Syntax

```
CEILING(<numeric expression>)
```

Purpose: Returns the smallest integer that is greater than or equal to the *<numeric expression>*.

Example

```
?CEILING(14.0001)      && returns 15
```

CERROR( )

Syntax

```
CERROR()
```

Purpose: Returns the number of the last compiler error message. The *dBASE 5 Language Reference* manual contains a list of all compiler error messages.

Example

```
* Compile a dBASE 5 program
* Ask user for program name
Progname = SPACE(20)
@ 12,15 SAY "Enter program to compile " ;
   GET prog_name PICTURE "@!"
READ
* Make sure that file exists
IF FILE(Prog_name)          && file does exist
   @ 13,15 SAY "Compiling program, please wait."
   * If an error occurs, print error number and message
   ON ERROR ? ERROR(), MESSAGE()
   * Compile the program
   COMPILE Prog_name
   * Set up normal error-trapping procedure
   ON ERROR DO errtrap
   * Determine whether a compiling error occurred
   IF CERROR() > 0
      @ 20,15 SAY "Your program did not compile."
   ELSE
      @ 20,15 SAY "Program compiled OK."
   ENDIF
ELSE                        && the program doesn't exist
   @ 13,15 SAY "That program doesn't exist."
ENDIF
```

CHANGE( )

Syntax

```
CHANGE([<alias>])
```

Purpose: Returns a logical true (.T.) if another user has changed a record since it was read from the database. Only databases that have been converted to network database files with the CONVERT command can use the CHANGE( ) function. You can force the CHANGE( ) value to false by using a GOTO RECNO( ) command or any command that repositions the record pointer. Use the optional *<alias>* parameter to check the CHANGE( ) in another work area.

Example

```
IF CHANGE()
   @ 12,15 SAY "Record has been changed."
ELSE
   @ 12,15 SAY "Record has not been changed."
ENDIF
```

CHR( )

Syntax

```
CHR(<numeric expression>)
```

Purpose: Converts a *<numeric expression>* to a character expression. You can use this function to send control characters (escape sequences) or to send a line-drawing character to your printer. Use a number from 0 to 255. Note that some printers may not be able to print line-drawing characters.

Example

```
SET PRINT ON            && send "?" output to printer
SET PRINT OFF           && sets output back to screen
* Beeps the speaker and prints the message
? CHR(7) + "Printer at top of form"
```

CMONTH( )

Syntax

```
CMONTH(<date variable>)
```

Purpose: Returns the month name for the *<date variable>*, which can be a date-type memory variable, field, or function.

Example

```
* What month is that?
Whatmonth = {}          && makes an empty date variable
@ 15,15 SAY "Enter any date " ;
   GET Whatmonth PICTURE "@D"
READ
@ 16,15 SAY "The month name is " + CMONTH(Whatmonth)
```

COL( )

Syntax

```
COL()
```

Purpose: Returns the current column position of the cursor. For the @ command, the $ can be used to provide the same value.

Example

```
* Place a message at the current column position
@ 12,col() SAY "Please wait."
@ 13,$ SAY "Wait some more!"
```

COMPLETED( )

Syntax

```
COMPLETED()
```

Purpose: Returns a logical true (.T.) if the BEGIN...END TRANSACTION was completed properly. COMPLETED( ) is set to false with the BEGIN TRANSACTION command and set to true with the END TRANSACTION command. COMPLETED( ) often is used with the ROLLBACK( ) function.

Example

```
* Determine whether the transaction completed properly
IF COMPLETED()
   @ 22,30 SAY "Transaction completed OK."
ELSE
   @ 22,30 SAY "Warning! Transaction did not complete!"
ENDIF
```

COS( )

Syntax

```
COS(<radian angle>)
```

Purpose: Returns the cosine value of the *<radian angle>*. Use SET DECIMALS and SET PRECISION to fix the number of decimal places and accuracy returned.

Example

```
? COS(.822)        && returns 0.68
```

CTOD( )

Syntax

```
CTOD(<character expression>)
```

Purpose: Converts a *<character expression>* to a date variable. (Remember this function as an abbreviation of "Character TO Date.") The *<character expression>* is formatted as MM/DD/YY, unless you have changed the date format with SET DATE and SET CENTURY. A year in the twentieth century is assumed if you specify only two characters as "yy".

An alternative is to use braces ({ }) to convert character text to a date format.

Example

```
Birthdate = "05/06/78"
Datetype = CTOD(Birthdate) && converts to date variable
Datetype = {05/06/78}      && alternative
```

DATE( )

Syntax

```
DATE()
```

Purpose: Returns the current system date in the form MM/DD/YY. You can change the format of the date by using the SET CENTURY, SET DATE, or SET MARK command. The current date is whatever date DOS understands the current date to be, as set by the DOS DATE command or your computer's automatic clock/calendar. If the date is not correct, you must change it at the DOS prompt or by using a RUN DATE command at the dBASE 5 Command window. You can add or subtract values from the DATE( ) value.

Example

```
* Make sure that the date is current
IF DATE() = {1/1/80}    && wrong system date
   RUN DATE             && run DOS DATE command
ENDIF
* Determine next payment due date
Duedate = DATE() + 30   && adds 30 days to the current date
```

DAY( )

Syntax

```
DAY(<date variable>)
```

Purpose: Returns the numeric value of the day of the month of the *<date variable>*, which can be a memory variable, date field, or any function that returns a date-type variable.

> **Note**
>
> DAY( ) returns the day number of the month. DOW( ) returns the day number of the week.

Example

```
* Extract the day of the month number
Duedate = {1/31/92}
? DAY(Duedate)           && returns 31
```

DBF( )

Syntax

```
DBF([<alias>])
```

Purpose: Returns the name of the database in the current work area or in the work area specified by the optional *<alias>*. If no database is open, a null string is returned.

Example

```
CLOSE ALL           && close all databases
IF "" = DBF()       && if no database in use, open CUSTOMER.DBF
   USE CUSTOMER
ENDIF
```

DELETED( )

Syntax

```
DELETED([<alias>])
```

Purpose: Returns a logical true (.T.) if the current record has been marked for deletion; otherwise, DELETED( ) returns a logical false (.F.). The current work area is used, unless you specify another work area with the *<alias>* option.

Example

```
* Say whether or not current record
* is marked for deletion
IF DELETED()
   ? "Record marked for deletion."
ELSE
   ? "Record not deleted."
ENDIF
```

DESCENDING( )

Syntax

```
DESCENDING([[<multiple index file>,] <numeric expression>
   [,<alias>]])
```

Purpose: Returns a true (.T.) value if the specified MDX tag was created using the DESCENDING option, or false (.F.) if it was not. The *<numeric expression>* specifies the tag number, and the optional *<multiple index file>* and *<alias>* expressions specify the index and database files if other than the current files.

Example

```
USE CUSTOMER
INDEX ON CITY TAG REVCITY DESCENDING
? TAGNO("REVCITY")
   6
? DESCENDING(6)
.T.
```

DGEN( )

Syntax

```
DGEN(<character expression>[,<character expression>])
```

Purpose: Runs the dBASE 5 Template Language interpreter from within dBASE to create dBASE programs from template (GEN) files. The first *<character expression>* is the name of the GEN file, and the optional second expression provides an argument to pass to the template program. Returns –1 for failure and 0 for success.

Example

```
* Create a program from ENTERDAT.SCR screen form
DEXPORT SCREEN ENTERDAT
APROGRAM=DGEN("FORM.GEN","ENTERDAT.SNL")
```

DIFFERENCE( )

Syntax

```
DIFFERENCE(<char 1>, <char 2>)
```

Purpose: Determines the difference between two character strings by converting the strings to a SOUNDEX( ) code (*see SOUNDEX*) and then subtracting the two values. A number from 0 to 4 is returned, with 4 representing a close match. If the strings have no letters in common, 0 is returned. One letter in common returns 1.

Example

```
* Compare the difference between two strings
?DIFFERENCE("SMITH", "SMYTHE")          && returns 4
?DIFFERENCE("SMITH", "JONES")           && returns 2
?DIFFERENCE("Janssen", "Jones")         && returns 3
String1 = "Fred"
String2 = "Frank"
?DIFFERENCE(String1, String2)           && returns 2
```

DISKSPACE( )

Syntax

```
DISKSPACE()
```

Purpose: Returns the number of bytes available on the current drive. You can use this information to find out, for example, if there is enough room on the disk to copy the current database.

Example

```
PROCEDURE SPACEON_A
PARAMETER Space_ok        && returned to caller
* Make sure that there is enough room on A: for the file
* If Space_ok is true, there's enough room
USE ORDERS
* Determine approximate file size.
Filesize = (RECCOUNT() * RECSIZE()) + 512
* Determine available space on A:
SET DEFAULT TO A:
Spaceon = DISKSPACE()
SET DEFAULT TO C:
IF Spaceon < Filesize
   ? "Not enough room on the A: drive"
   Space_ok = .F.
ELSE
   Space_ok = .T.
ENDIF
RETURN                    && back to calling program
```

DMY( )

Syntax

```
DMY(<date variable>)
```

Purpose: Converts the *<date variable>* to the form *dd monthname yy*. If SET CENTURY is ON, the year value is converted to YYYY. The *<date variable>* can be a date-type memory variable, a date field, or any function that returns a date-type variable.

Example

```
Pastdue = {4/1/93}
? DMY(Pastdue)            && returns "1 April 93"
SET CENTURY ON
? DMY({11/25/51})         && returns "25 November 1951"
```

DOW( )

Syntax

```
DOW(<date variable>)
```

Purpose: Returns a number corresponding to the day of the week, with Sunday as day number 1, Monday as day number 2, and so on. The *<date variable>* can be a date memory variable, field, or any function that returns a date variable.

Example

```
?DOW({10/31/92})          && returns 7 (Saturday)
```

DTOC( )

Syntax

```
DTOC(<date variable>)
```

Purpose: Converts a date-type variable into a character string. (Remember this function as an abbreviation of "Date TO Character.")

Example

```
Date1 = "01/03/80"        && character variable
Date2 = CTOD(Date1)       && converted to date variable
Date3 = DTOC(Date2)       && back to character variable
```

DTOR( )

Syntax

```
DTOR(<angle degrees>)
```

Purpose: Converts *<angle degrees>* to radians. If the angle has minutes' or seconds' values, convert them to decimal fractions before using DTOR( ).

Example

```
? DTOR(60.525)      && returns 1.06
```

DTOS( )

Syntax

```
DTOS(<date variable>)
```

Purpose: Converts the *<date variable>* into a string variable. The date is converted to a YYYYMMDD character string, even if you have used SET CENTURY or SET DATE to change the date to another form. This function is useful if you want to have an index that includes a date variable.

Example

```
* Set up an index of back ordered parts
* Backdate is a date field
* Partnum is a character field
USE ORDERS
INDEX ON DTOS(backdate)+partnum TAG BACKORDR
```

EOF( )

Syntax

```
EOF(<alias>)
```

Purpose: Returns a logical true (.T.) if the record pointer is at the end of a file; otherwise, returns a logical false (.F.). When EOF( ) is true, the current record number is RECCOUNT( ) + 1 (the dBASE pseudo record). The current work area is used unless you specify the optional *<alias>*. A logical false is also returned if no database is in use in the current or specified work area.

Example

```
USE ORDERS
GO BOTTOM
? EOF()        && returns .F.
SKIP 1
? EOF()        && returns .T.
```

ERROR( )

Syntax

```
ERROR()
```

Purpose: Returns the error number of the last ON ERROR condition. You need to use the ON ERROR command to trap errors. When an error occurs, you can use the RETRY command to try the command again or RETURN to return to the calling program. The *dBASE 5 Language Reference* manual contains a list of all error codes and messages.

Example

```
PROCEDURE Err_trap
PARAMETER fatal, errorcnt
* This is the error-trapping procedure, which was
* enabled with an "ON ERROR DO Err_trap" command
* Fatal = if error is catastrophic, cancel the program
DO CASE
   CASE ERROR() = 125
      @ 22,20 say "Printer not ready, please correct."
      Fatal = .F.              && not a fatal error
   CASE ERROR() = 21
      @ 22,20 SAY "Out of memory, program cancel"
      Fatal = .T.
   * Other CASE statements to handle other errors
```

```
END CASE
* Determine whether a fatal error occurred
IF Fatal                        && Fatal is .T.
   CANCEL                       && Fatal error, cancel program
ELSE                            && Fatal is .F.
   RETRY                        && Try same command again
ENDIF
RETURN
```

EVALUATE( )

Syntax

```
EVALUATE(<VARIABLE>)
```

Purpose: Returns the value of the dBASE expression passed in as a string. The string may be passed in as a memory variable, an array element, a data table field, or directly as a character string. The contents of the string can be a number, a logical value, a function, or a memory variable. If the string is a number or logical value, the value of the number is returned. If the string is a function, the function is executed and the value is returned. If the string is a memory variable, the content of the memory variable is returned.

Example

```
DECLARE Array aCommand[2,2]
REPLACE fCommand WITH 12345 && A database field
aCommand[1,1]=mCommand
mCommand=MEMORY(3)
?EVALUATE(fCommand)          && Returns a number
12345
?EVALUATE(aCommand[1,1])     && Returns the contents of mCommand
MEMORY(3)
?EVALUATE(mCommand)          && Returns result of MEMORY(3) function
9860
```

EXP( )

Syntax

```
EXP(<numeric expression>)
```

Purpose: Returns the value *x* from the equation $y = e^x$. The returned value is always a real number, with SET DECIMALS determining the accuracy of the displayed answer.

Example

```
SET DECIMALS TO 4
? EXP(12)          && returns 162754.7914
```

FCLOSE( )

Syntax

```
FCLOSE(<file handle>)
```

Purpose: Closes a low-level file, previously opened with a FCREATE( ) or FOPEN( ). CLOSE ALL and CLEAR ALL also closes any open low level files. Returns logical .T. if successful and .F. if the close failed.

Example

```
MyFile = FCREATE("Temp.TMP","RW")
OkVal = FCLOSE(MyFile)
```

FCREATE( )

Syntax

```
FCREATE(<filename>[,<privilege>])
```

Purpose: Creates a low-level file and returns the file handle number. The following privileges are available:

R	Read only
W	Write only
A	Append only
RW or WR	Read and write
AR or RA	Read and append

Example

```
MyFile = FCREATE("TEMP.TMP","RW")
```

FDATE( )

Syntax

```
FDATE(<character expression>)
```

Purpose: Returns the date that a file was last modified. The *<character expression>* contains the file name. The FDATE( ) function does not support wild-card characters for the file name. Modify DATE FORMAT with SET DATE, SET MARK, SET CENTURY.

Example

```
? FDATE("C:\DOS\MYTEXT.TXT")
02/22/93
```

FEOF( )

Syntax

```
FEOF(<file handle>)
```

Purpose: Returns true (.T.) if the file pointer is at the end of a file.

Example

```
IF FEOF(MyFile)
   ?"That's All Folks!"
ENDIF
```

FERROR( )

Syntax

```
FERROR( )
```

Purpose: Returns the operating system error number of the last low-level file I/O operation. Returns zero if successful or never executed, or if I/O was intercepted by dBASE and does not reach the operating system.

Example

```
IF FERROR() <> 0
   ?"There is a problem"
ENDIF
```

FFLUSH( )

Syntax

```
FFLUSH(<file handle>)
```

Purpose: Writes the system buffer of a low-level file to disk. Returns .T. if there was not an error, otherwise .F.

Example

```
?FFLUSH(MyFile)
```

FGETS( )

Syntax

```
FGETS(<file handle>[,<bytes to read>][,<end of line character>])
```

Purpose: Reads a character string from a low-level file.

Example

```
MyString = FGETS(MyFile)
```

FIELD( )

Syntax

```
FIELD(<numeric expression> [,<alias>])
```

Purpose: Returns the name of the specified field in the current database. The returned field name is all uppercase characters. The *<number expression>* refers to the field number as shown with LIST/DISPLAY STRUCTURE. If the field number is not defined in the database structure or is not a number from 1 to 521, a null string ("") is returned. The current work area is assumed unless you specify the *<alias>* of a database open in another work area.

Example

```
* Structure of NAMES.DBF is:
* NAME
* ADDRESS
* CITY
* STATE
USE <names>
FOR FlCount = 1 TO FLDCOUNT()
  ? FIELD(FlCount)
```

FILE( )

Syntax

```
FILE("<filename>")
```

Purpose: Determines whether the *<filename>* exists. The *<filename>* must include the complete file name and extension, plus the drive/directory name if needed, and must be enclosed in quotation marks. FILE( ) uses dBASE's PATH when searching for the existence of the file.

Example

```
* Check for the memory file that contains the check number
* If found, load the Checknum variable
* If not found, start with check number 100
IF FILE("CHECKNUM.MEM")
   RESTORE FROM CHECKNUM ADDITIVE
ELSE
   Checknum = 100
   * Create the Checknum.mem memory file
   SAVE TO CHECKNUM ALL LIKE Checknum
ENDIF
```

FIXED( )

Syntax

```
FIXED(<numeric expression>)
```

Purpose: Transforms long, real floating-point numbers into binary-coded decimal (BCD) numbers. You may lose some accuracy of the number during the translation. The allowable range is from .9 x 10^{308} to .1 x 10^{-307}.

Example

```
SET DECIMALS TO 5
Afloat = PI()              && Floating point
Bfixed = FIXED(Afloat)     && BCD
```

FKLABEL( )

Syntax

```
FKLABEL(<numeric value>)
```

Purpose: Returns the name of the function key denoted by the *<numeric value>*. See the SET FUNCTION command for a list of all programmable function keys. The *<numeric value>* can be from 1 to 28.

Example

```
? FKLABEL(8)          && returns "F9"
```

FKMAX( )

Syntax

```
FKMAX()
```

Purpose: Returns the number of programmable function keys available in dBASE 5. The F2 through F10 keys, Shift-F1 through Shift-F10, and Ctrl-F1 through Ctrl-F10 are available for use by dBASE 5. F1 is reserved for the Help key, and F11 and F12 are not available.

Example

```
? FKMAX()             && returns 28
```

FLDCOUNT( )

Syntax

```
FLDCOUNT([<alias>])
```

Purpose: Returns the number of fields in the structure of the specified database file. If no alias is specified, the function returns the number of fields in the database in use in the current work area. If no database is in use, FLDCOUNT( ) returns 0.

Example

```
USE CUSTOMER IN 2
? FLDCOUNT(2)
12
```

FLDLIST( )

Syntax

```
FLDLIST([<numeric expression>])
```

Purpose: Returns the list of fields by a SET FIELDS TO command. The optional *<numeric expression>* specifies which field in the list to return.

Example

```
USE Mylist
SET FIELDS TO Name, City, State
? FLDLIST(2)          Returns MYLIST->CITY
```

FLOAT( )

Syntax

```
FLOAT(<numeric expression>)
```

Purpose: Converts binary-coded decimal (BCD) numbers to long, real, floating-point numbers.

Example

```
Afixed = 14.2254
?FLOAT(Afixed)
```

FLOCK( )

Syntax

```
FLOCK([<alias>])
```

Purpose: Locks the database to prevent multiple users from updating the same file. If the database is successfully locked, a logical true (.T.) is returned. If the database is not being used in a network, a logical false (.F.) is returned. All records are locked in the database, which is useful for operations that need to work on the entire file. To lock individual records, use RLOCK( ). Although other users can't change the data, they can have read-only access to the database. Any database that has been related to the current database also is locked. Use the optional *<alias>* to check the file-locking status of a database in another work area. The files remain locked until you use the UNLOCK command or close the databases. You can use the RETRY command if the command fails.

Example

```
IF FLOCK()
   @ 12,15 SAY "Database is locked, please wait"
ENDIF
```

FLOOR( )

Syntax

```
FLOOR(<numeric expression>)
```

Purpose: Returns the largest integer that is less than or equal to the *<numeric expression>*.

Example

```
?FLOOR(18.839)            && returns 18
```

FOPEN( )

Syntax

```
FOPEN(<filename>[,<privilege>])
```

Purpose: Opens an existing low-level file and sets the specified privilege level.

Example

```
MyFile = FOPEN("TEMP.TMP","RW")
```

FOR( )

Syntax

```
FOR([[<multiple index file>,]<numeric expression>[,<alias>]])
```

Purpose: Returns a true (.T.) value if the specified MDX tag was created using the FOR clause to make a conditional index, or false (.F.) if it was not. The *<numeric expression>* specifies the tag number, and the optional *<multiple index file>* and *<alias>* expressions specify the index and database files if other than the current files.

Example

```
USE CUSTOMER
INDEX ON CITY TAG ZIPCITY FOR ZIP > "44559"
? TAGNO("ZIPCITY")
7
? FOR(7)
.T.
```

FOUND( )

Syntax

```
FOUND([<alias>])
```

Purpose: Returns a logical true (.T.) if the desired record was found with the FIND, LOCATE, SEEK, CONTINUE, LOOKUP( ), or SEEK( ) command. Each work area has one FOUND( ); use the *<alias>* option to determine if a record was found in another work area. When SET NEAR is ON, FOUND( ) returns a true (.T.) only if an exact match is found, but the record pointer is moved to the nearest match.

Example

```
USE INVENTRY ORDER PARTNUM
SEEK "WIDGETS"
IF FOUND()
   @ 12,15 SAY "Found record number " + RECNO()
ELSE
   @ 12,15 SAY "Couldn't find it."
ENDIF
```

FPUTS( )

Syntax

```
FPUTS(<file handle>,<character expression>[,<number of
    characters to write>][,<end of line character>])
```

Purpose: Writes a character string to a low-level file. Returns 0 if failed, or the number of characters written if successful.

Example

```
?FPUTS(MyFile,"This is a temporary file")
```

FREAD( )

Syntax

```
FREAD(<file handle>,<number of bytes to read>)
```

Purpose: Reads a specified number of bytes from a low-level file.

Example

```
NewString = FREAD(MyFile,24)
```

FSEEK( )

Syntax

```
FSEEK(<file handle>,<number of bytes to move>[,<start
    position>])
```

Purpose: Moves the file pointer in a low-level file. Returns byte number in file.

Example

```
NewPoint = FSEEK(MyFile,-5)
```

FSIZE( )

Syntax

```
FSIZE(<character expression>)
```

Purpose: Returns the size in bytes of the specified file. The *<character expression>* contains the file name, which cannot contain wild-card characters.

Example

```
? FSIZE("C:\DOS\MYTEXT.TXT")
12800
```

FTIME( )

Syntax

```
FTIME(<character expression>)
```

Purpose: Returns the time that the specified file was last modified. The *<character expression>* contains the file name and cannot include wild-card characters.

Example

```
? FTIME("C:\DOS\MYTEXT.TXT")
11:13:09
```

FV( )

Syntax

```
FV(<payment>,<rate>,<periods>)
```

Purpose: Calculates the future value based on equal regular deposits (*<payment>*) into an investment yielding a fixed interest rate (*<rate>*) over a number of time periods (*<periods>*). The *<payment>* can be negative or positive. The *<rate>* is the interest rate per period; if the interest rate is yearly, the *<rate>* is the yearly interest rate divided by 12. The *<period>* is the number of payments. The result of the FV function is the total deposits plus the generated (and compounded) interest.

Note

Make sure that you enter the interest value as a decimal number: 14 percent interest should be entered as 0.14. The interest rate should be the interest rate per period: if you are making monthly payments at 14 percent interest, the interest rate is 0.14 / 12.

Example

```
* determine total of all payments
* (principal plus interest paid)
Monthpay = 320.44          && monthly payment
Numperiod = 36             && three year loan (36 months)
Int_rate = 0.1433 / 12     && monthly interest rate
Total_pay = FV(Monthpay, Int_rate, Numperiod)
? Total_pay                && returns 14307.62
```

FWRITE( )

Syntax

```
FWRITE(<file handle>,<character expression>
   [,<number of bytes>])
```

Purpose: Writes characters to a low-level file. Returns number of characters written or 0.

Example

```
CharsWrit = FWRITE(MyFile,"Another Test")
```

GETENV( )

Syntax

```
GETENV(<"DOS environmental variable name">)
```

Purpose: Returns the contents of a DOS environmental system variable such as PATH. You can see the current system variables with the RUN SET command at the Command window. Your DOS operating system manual contains a list of environmental variables. You also can set environmental variables at the DOS prompt with the SET command. The *<DOS environmental variable name>* must be a character string enclosed in quotation marks.

Example

```
* Get the COMSPEC variable
Comspec = GETENV("COMSPEC")
* Will return "C:\COMMAND.COM" on most nonnetworked systems
```

HOME( )

Syntax

```
HOME()
```

Purpose: Returns the directory path from which dBASE 5 was run.

Example

```
? HOME()
C:\DBASE\
```

ID( )

Syntax

```
ID()
```

Purpose: Returns the name of the current user on a multiuser system.

Example

```
mString="The current user is: "
? mString + ID()
The current user is: Johnson
```

IIF( )

Syntax

```
IIF(<condition>, <expression 1>, <expression 2>)
```

Purpose: The immediate IF function, a shortcut to the IF...ENDIF command. If the *<condition>* evaluates to a logical true (.T.), *<expression 1>* is returned. If the *<condition>* evaluates to a logical false (.F.), *<expression 2>* is returned. The two expressions must be the same type: character, numeric, logical, or date.

Example

```
* Determine whether the item is on back order
* {} indicates a blank date
@ 12,15 SAY IIF(ISBLANK(Backdate), "Order completed.",;
   "Items on back order.")
* Equivalent to:
IF ISBLANK(Backdate)
   Message = "Order completed."
ELSE
   Message = "Items on back order."
ENDIF
@ 12,15 SAY message
```

INKEY( )

Syntax

```
INKEY([<number of seconds to wait>])
```

Purpose: Returns an integer value that represents the last key pressed by the user. It does not wait for a keystroke, and the program continues. If no key has been pressed, a value of 0 is returned. You can use the INKEY function in a DO WHILE loop to wait for a key. The optional *<number of seconds to wait>* causes the program to delay for that number of seconds. A value of 0 causes an infinite wait for the user to press a key.

If the keyboard buffer contains characters that have not been processed, INKEY( ) returns the value of the first character in the buffer. You can use CLEAR TYPEAHEAD to clear the keyboard buffer.

Table 23.3 shows values returned by the INKEY function.

Table 23.3 Values Returned by INKEY

Key	Name	Decimal Value	Key	Decimal Value
Ctrl-A	Ctrl-left arrow	1	Shift-F2	-21
Ctrl-B	End	2	Shift-F3	-22
Ctrl-C	PgDn	3	Shift-F4	-23
Ctrl-D	Right arrow	4	Shift-F5	-24
Ctrl-E	Up arrow	5	Shift-F6	-25
Ctrl-F	Ctrl-right arrow	6	Shift-F7	-26
Ctrl-G	Del	7	Shift-F8	-27
Ctrl-H		8	Shift-F9	-28
Ctrl-I	Tab	9	Alt-a	-435
Ctrl-J		10	Alt-b	-434
Ctrl-K		11	Alt-c	-433
Ctrl-L		12	Alt-d	-432
Ctrl-M		13	Alt-e	-431
Ctrl-N		14	Alt-f	-430

Key	Name	Decimal Value	Key	Decimal Value
Ctrl-O		15	Alt-g	-429
Ctrl-P		16	Alt-h	-428
Ctrl-Q		17	Alt-i	-427
Ctrl-R	PgUp	18	Alt-j	-426
Ctrl-S	Left arrow	19	Alt-k	-425
Ctrl-T		20	Alt-l	-424
Ctrl-U		21	Alt-m	-423
Ctrl-V	Ins	22	Alt-n	-422
Ctrl-W	Ctrl-End	23	Alt-o	-421
Ctrl-X	Down arrow	24	Alt-p	-420
Ctrl-Y		25	Alt-q	-419
Ctrl-Z	Home	26	Alt-r	-418
Esc	Ctrl-[	27	Alt-s	-417
F1	Ctrl-\	28	Alt-t	-416
Ctrl-]	Ctrl-Home	29	Alt-u	-415
Ctrl-^	Ctrl-PgDn	30	Alt-v	-414
Ctrl-PgUp		31	Alt-w	-413
Space bar		32	Alt-x	-412
Backspace		127	Alt-y	-411
Backtab	Shift-Tab	-400	Alt-z	-410
Ctrl-Backspace		-401	Alt-1	-451
Ctrl-Enter		-402	Alt-2	-450
F2		-1	Alt-3	-449
F3		-2	Alt-4	-448
F4		-3	Alt-5	-447
F5		-4	Alt-6	-446

(continues)

Table 23.3 Continued

Key	Name	Decimal Value	Key	Decimal Value
F6		-5	Alt-7	-445
F7		-6	Alt-8	-444
F8		-7	Alt-9	-443
F9		-8	Alt-0	-452
F10		-9	Ctrl-0	-404
Ctrl-F1		-10	Ctrl-1	-404
Ctrl-F2		-11	Ctrl-2	-404
Ctrl-F3		-12	Ctrl-3	-404
Ctrl-F4		-13	Ctrl-4	-404
Ctrl-F5		-14	Ctrl-5	-404
Ctrl-F6		-15	Ctrl-6	30
Ctrl-F7		-16	Ctrl-7	-404
Ctrl-F8		-17	Ctrl-8	-404
Ctrl-F9		-18	Ctrl-9	-404
Ctrl-F10		-19	Ctrl-A	-403
Shift-F1		-20		

Note: Alt-key values are used by Macro Handler only.

Example

```
* Wait for the user to press any key before continuing
@ 24,20 SAY "Press a key to continue"
KeyVal = INKEY(0)
```

INSPECT( )

Syntax

INSPECT(<*object reference*>)

Purpose: Accesses the UI Object Inspector dialog box for any designated UI object. This function displays a modeless dialog box containing the specified values for the associated object. Displaying the box will not affect your program's performance or execution.

Be sure to include the full object reference chain in *<object reference>* to ensure you open the desired object. If the value given INSPECT( ) is not a valid object reference, an *Invalid function argument* error appears on-screen.

Example

```
? INSPECT(GrtgForm.Guest)
```

INT( )

Syntax

```
INT(<numeric expression>)
```

Purpose: Truncates the *<numeric expression>* to an integer. All decimal places in the number are discarded.

Example

```
? INT(49.293)            && returns 49
```

ISALPHA( )

Syntax

```
ISALPHA(<string>)
```

Purpose: Tests whether the first character of *<string>* is alphabetic. A logical true (.T.) is returned if the first character is alphabetic. A logical false (.F.) is returned if the first character is not alphabetic.

Example

```
?ISALPHA("Tom")                 && returns true
?ISALPHA("100 Forest Lane")     && returns false
```

ISBLANK( )

Syntax

```
ISBLANK(<expression>)
```

Purpose: Tests an expression to see if it contains a blank value. Returns true (.T.) if the expression is blank; returns false (.F.) if it is not blank.

Example

```
? ISBLANK(" ")
.T.
? ISBLANK("Carl")
.F.
```

ISCOLOR( )

Syntax

```
ISCOLOR()
```

Purpose: Returns a logical true (.T.) if a color video adapter card is installed in your system. You then can use COLOR statements that are appropriate for your monitor/card setup.

Example

```
* Test for presence of color display
IF ISCOLOR()
   SET COLOR TO W/B, N/G
ENDIF
```

ISLOWER( )

Syntax

```
ISLOWER(<string>)
```

Purpose: Determines whether the first character of the *<string>* is a lowercase character. A logical true (.T.) is returned if the first character is lowercase; a logical false (.F.) is returned if the first character is uppercase or a numeric character.

Example

```
? ISLOWER("Thomas Hardy")          && returns false
? ISLOWER("corn on the cob")       && returns true
? ISLOWER("4129 Creek Road")       && returns false
```

ISMARKED( )

Syntax

```
ISMARKED([<alias>])
```

Purpose: Returns a logical true (.T.) if dBASE 5 has placed a marker in the database file indicating that the file is in a state of change. Otherwise, a logical false (.F.) is returned. Use the optional *<alias>* to specify another active work area. Use ISMARKED( ) after a BEGIN TRANSACTION has been established.

Example

```
IF ISMARKED()
   @ 12,15 SAY "Record has been changed."
ENDIF
```

ISMOUSE( )

Syntax

```
ISMOUSE()
```

Purpose: Returns true (.T.) if a mouse driver has been installed, or false (.F.) if no mouse driver is currently active.

Example

```
* Determine if mouse is being used and display appropriate
* message
@18,10 SAY IIF(ISMOUSE(),'CLICK THE MOUSE','USE ARROW &;
    ENTER')
```

ISUPPER( )

Syntax

```
ISUPPER(<string>)
```

Purpose: Determines whether the first character of the *<string>* is uppercase. If it is, true (.T.) is returned. If the first character is lowercase or a numeric character, then false (.F.) is returned. See also ISLOWER( ).

Example

```
? ISUPPER("Wuthering Heights")      && returns true
? ISUPPER("cocker spaniel")         && returns false
? ISUPPER("12 cases")               && returns false
```

KEY( )

Syntax

```
KEY( [<character expression>,] <numeric expression>
   [,<alias>])
```

Purpose: Returns the expression used to create the index. If multiple indexes are active, the *<numeric expression>* is the index number. The current database is used unless an *<alias>* is specified. If there is not an active index, a null string ("") is returned. Use this function and TAG( ) to create UDFs to dynamically change MDYs and tags with the SET ORDER command.

Example

```
USE CUSTOMER INDEX Cust_id, Cust_name
* Cust_id index = Custid
* Cust_name index = UPPER(Custname)
? KEY(2)            && returns "UPPER(Custname)"
```

KEYMATCH( )

Syntax

```
KEYMATCH(<expression> [,<index number> [,<work area>]])
```

Purpose: Returns true (.T.) if the *<expression>* is found in the index keys of the specified index. The *<index number>* is the position of the index in the list of indexes, which can be determined by using the DISPLAY STATUS command or the TAGNO( ) function.

Example

```
* Ask user to enter a last name, then check to
* see if that data exists in the first index key
USE CUSTOMER INDEX LASTNAME
mName=SPACE(20)
@ 5,10 SAY "Last name: " GET mName
READ
IF KEYMATCH(mName,1)
    SEEK mNAME
    EDIT
ELSE
    @ 18,10 SAY "Record added to file."
    APPEND BLANK
    REPLACE LASTNAME WITH mName
ENDIF
```

LASTKEY( )

Syntax

```
LASTKEY()
```

Purpose: Returns the ASCII value of the last key used to exit a full-screen command. Values returned are the same as for INKEY( ) (refer to Table 23.3). Returns a value of –100 for a mouse click.

Example

```
* Wait for user to press F10 key
DO WHILE .NOT. LASTKEY() = 27 & ESCAPE KEY
   @ 24,20 SAY "Press F10 when ready"
   READ
    IF LASTKEY() = -9 & F10 key
         DO ENTRDATA
    ENDIF
ENDDO
```

LDRIVER( )

Syntax

```
LDRIVER()
```

Purpose: Returns the value of the global language driver included in the CONFIG.DB file for dBASE.

Example

```
? LDRIVER()
DB437US0
```

LEFT( )

Syntax

```
LEFT(<string>/<memo field name>,<number>)
```

Purpose: Returns the left *<number>* characters of the character string or of the contents of the memo field. (There is a 254-character limit.) If the *<number>* is 0, a null string is returned; if the *<number>* is greater than the length of the string, the entire string is returned.

Example

```
* Will return "The whole truth"
? LEFT("The whole truth and nothing but",15)
```

LEN( )

Syntax

```
LEN(<string> / <memo field name>)
```

Purpose: Returns the length of the *<string>* or the number of characters in the specified memo field. The length of the entire string, including any spaces, is returned. Use the TRIM( ) function to trim off trailing spaces.

Example

```
* The string has four trailing spaces
?LEN("1495 Arcadia    ")              && returns 16
?LEN(TRIM("1495 Arcadia    ")         && returns 12
Item_desc = "New Hebrides"
?LEN(Item_desc)                       && returns 12
```

LIKE( )

Syntax

```
LIKE(<search pattern>, <string>)
```

Purpose: Compares the *<search pattern>* with the *<string>* and returns a logical true (.T.) if the pattern is found in the string. The search pattern usually contains a wild card—the asterisk (*), which stands for any number of characters, or the question mark (?), which stands for any character in that position.

Example

```
? LIKE("Smith*","Smithereens")        && returns .T.
? LIKE("*son", "Johnson")             && returns .T.
? LIKE("Smith","Smythe")              && returns .F.
? LIKE("J?n", "Jan")                  && returns .T.
```

LINENO( )

Syntax

```
LINENO()
```

Purpose: Returns the line number of the next command in a program that will be executed. Used during debugging to set break points in your program or with the command ONERROR to execute a program such as the line of code in the following example.

Example

```
* In the error-trapping procedure,
* what line number caused the error
@ 24,1 SAY "Error at command before line # " +;
   STR(LINENO())
```

LKSYS( )

Syntax

```
LKSYS(<n>)
```

Purpose: Returns information about when a record was locked or updated and who performed the action. Values of *<n>* are shown in Table 23.4.

Table 23.4 Values for *<n>* in LKSYS

Value	Meaning
0	Time when lock was placed
1	Date when locked was placed
2	Log-in name of user who locked the record
3	Time of the last update or lock
4	Date of the last update or lock
5	Log-in name of the user who last updated or locked the record or database

The database must have been changed previously with the CONVERT command to create a hidden field containing the user name and other information (see CONVERT). A null string is returned if the database was not converted.

Example

```
* Display data and time a record
* was locked.
? "Record was locked " + LKSYS(4) + " " + LKSYS(3)
```

LOCK( )

See RLOCK.

LOG( )

Syntax

```
LOG(<numeric variable>)
```

Purpose: Returns the natural logarithm of the *<numeric variable>*. The logarithm is x, where *<numeric variable>* = e^x. The logarithmic value returned is a type F (floating-point) number.

Example

```
?LOG(2.33)                  && returns 0.85
```

LOG10( )

Syntax

```
LOG10(<numeric variable>)
```

Purpose: Returns the base 10 logarithm of the *<numeric variable>*. The LOG10 function returns y, where *<numeric variable>*=10^y.

Example

```
? LOG10(3)                  && returns 0.48
```

LOOKUP( )

Syntax

```
LOOKUP(<return field>, <look-for expression>,
   <look-in field>)
```

Purpose: Looks at the *<look-in field>* for the *<look-for expression>*. If the expression is found, LOOKUP returns the *<return field>* value. Use this function to return a value from a record when searching a database.

Example

```
* Using LOOKUP() function
USE PARTS ORDER Partname       && part name index is active
* Find the "Brake Pads" record, return number on back order
? LOOKUP(backordr, "Brake Pads", Partname)
```

LOWER( )

Syntax

```
LOWER(<string>)
```

Purpose: Changes the <*string*> to all lowercase characters. To use text from a memo field, first use the MLINE( ) function (see MLINE( )).

Example

```
Bankname = "FIRST TRUST BANK"
? LOWER(Bankname)          && returns "first trust bank"
? LOWER("Acme Painting")   && returns "acme painting"
```

LTRIM( )

Syntax

```
LTRIM(<string>)
```

Purpose: Removes leading blanks from the <*string*>. This is useful in conjunction with the LEN( ) function to determine the number of characters in a character field.

Example

```
* There are two spaces at the beginning of the string
* in quotes,
* below Item_desc = "  Playing cards"
? LTRIM(Item_desc)        && returns "Playing Cards" without
                          && spaces at beginning
? LEN(LTRIM(Item_desc))   && returns 13
```

LUPDATE( )

Syntax

```
LUPDATE([<alias>])
```

Purpose: Returns the date that the database was last changed. If no database is in use, a blank date is returned. The current work area is assumed unless you specify the <*alias*> of a database open in another work area.

Example

```
* Determine whether the inventory database
* was updated today
USE INVENTRY
IF LUPDATE < DATE()
   ? "Inventory database not updated today"
ENDIF
```

MAX( )

Syntax

```
MAX(<expression 1>, <expression 2>)
```

Purpose: Returns the greater value of the two expressions, which can be numeric, date, or character types. The greater number, or the later date, is returned.

Example

```
? MAX(15,33)                     && returns 33
? MAX("Oranges", "Apples")       && returns "Oranges"
                                 && (greater ASCII value)
? MAX({07/04/92}, {01/25/92})    && returns date type
                                 && 07/04/92
```

MCOL( )

Syntax

```
MCOL()
```

Purpose: Returns the current screen column location of the mouse pointer. If no mouse driver is active (for example, if ISMOUSE( )=.F.), then MCOL( ) returns a value of 0. Remember that the first column is column number 0.

Example

```
* Determine if mouse pointer is on left half of screen.
IF MCOL() < 40
    @ 19,10 SAY "Please move the mouse pointer to the right."
ENDIF
```

MDX( )

Syntax

```
MDX(<numeric expression> [,<alias>])
```

Purpose: Returns the name of the multiple-index (MDX) file indicated by the *<numeric expression>*. The current database is used, unless the optional *<alias>* parameter is specified. If no MDX file is active, or if no MDX files are associated with the database, a null string ("") is returned.

Example

```
* PARTS.DBF has a PARTS.MDX multiple-index file
USE PARTS
? MDX(1)               && returns "PARTS.MDX"
```

MDY( )

Syntax

```
MDY(<date variable>)
```

Purpose: Converts a *<date variable>* to the form "month, day, year." The "month" is the full name of the month, "day" is the two-digit day value, and "year" is the two-digit year value. If you have used SET CENTURY ON, four digits will be displayed as the year.

Example

```
Date1 = {10/10/75}
SET CENTURY OFF
? MDY(Date1)           && returns "October 10, 75"
SET CENTURY ON
? MDY(Date1)           && returns "October 10, 1975"
```

MEMLINES( )

Syntax

```
MEMLINES(<memo field name>)
```

Purpose: Returns the number of word-wrapped lines in the *<memo field name>* of the current database.

Example

```
USE CLIENTS
GOTO 43
IF MEMLINES("Notes") > 0
   ? "No comments found in the Notes memo field"
ELSE
   ? "Total lines in Notes memo field is " + ;
      STR(MEMLINES("Notes"))
ENDIF
```

MEMORY( )

Syntax

```
MEMORY([<expN>])
```

Purpose: Returns the amount of system RAM (in kilobytes) that is available in or used by certain memory areas. *<expN>* can be from 0 to 7.

The following optional arguments may be used. The results returned depend on the argument used.

Argument	Returns
0	Approximate amount of available memory. This is the sum of the values returned by MEMORY(3) and MEMORY(6).
1	Amount of memory in the heap.
2	Amount of low DOS memory (in the 640K area) that is available for loading bin files.
3	Amount of unallocated extended memory.
4	Total amount of virtual and extended memory managed by the Virtual Memory Manager (VMM).
5	Amount of extended memory managed by VMM.
6	Amount of memory that dBASE buffer manager is currently using.
7	Size of swap file, if VMM created one.
8	Largest contiguous block of memory.

Example

```
* Display extended memory unallocated
? MEMORY(3)
* Display low DOS memory available
? Memory(2)
```

MENU( )

Syntax

```
MENU()
```

Purpose: Returns the name of the active menu. If no menu is active, then a null string ("") is returned.

Example

```
@ 12,15 SAY "Last menu selected was " + MENU()
```

MESSAGE( )

Syntax

```
MESSAGE()
```

Purpose: Returns the error message of the last error. The *dBASE 5 Language Reference* contains a list of all the error messages on a single-user system. The *Networking with dBASE 5* manual contains a list of network error messages.

Example

```
* In the error-trapping procedure
@ 23,1 SAY "Last error " + STR(ERROR())
@ 24,1 SAY "Error msg  " + MESSAGE()
```

MIN( )

Syntax

```
MIN(<expression 1>, <expression 2>)
```

Purpose: Returns the smaller value of the two expressions, which can be numeric, date, or character types. The smaller number, or the earlier date, is returned.

Example

```
? MIN(15,33)                       && returns 15
? MIN("Oranges", "Apples")         && returns "Apples"
                                   && (lowest ASCII value)
? MIN({07/04/92}, {01/25/92})      && returns date type 1/25/92
```

MLINE( )

Syntax

```
MLINE(<memo field name>, <numeric expression>)
```

Purpose: Extracts the *<numeric expression>* line number from the *<memo field>* in the current database.

Example

```
* Extract the first and last line of the Notes memo field
USE CLIENTS
GOTO 18
? "First line is " + MLINE("Notes",1)
? "Last line is " + MLINE("Notes",MEMLINES("Notes"))
```

MOD( )

Syntax

```
MOD(<numeric expression 1>, <numeric expression 2>)
```

Purpose: Returns the remainder of dividing *<numeric expression 1>* by *<numeric expression 2>*. This can be useful when converting units where division leaves a remainder.

Example

```
? MOD(13, 4)        && returns 1
```

MONTH( )

Syntax

```
MONTH(<date variable>)
```

Purpose: Returns the month number of the *<date variable>*, which can be a date memory variable, a date field, or a function that returns a date-type variable.

Example

```
Date2 = {7/4/91}
? MONTH(date2)      && returns 7
```

MROW( )

Syntax

```
MROW()
```

Purpose: Returns the current row number of the mouse pointer. If no mouse driver is active (for example, if ISMOUSE( )=.F.), then MROW( ) returns a value of 0. Remember that the first row is row number 0.

Example

```
* Determine if mouse pointer is on top half of screen.
IF MROW() < 12
    @ 19,10 SAY "Please move the mouse pointer down."
ENDIF
```

NDX( )

Syntax

```
NDX(<numeric expression> [,<alias>])
```

Purpose: Returns the name of the index (NDX) file for the current database or the index file for the optional *<alias>* database. The index can be specified with the USE...INDEX command or with the SET INDEX TO command. If no index is associated with the *<numeric expression>* that indicates the index number, a null string is returned.

Example

```
USE MEMBERS INDEX Name, City, Memnum
? NDX(2)            && returns "CITY.NDX"
```

NETWORK( )

Syntax

```
NETWORK()
```

Purpose: Returns a logical true (.T.) if the system is connected to a workstation. If not, a logical false (.F.) is returned.

Example

```
* Do some file or record locking command
* if running on a network
IF NETWORK()
   * file or record locking commands
ENDIF
```

ORDER( )

Syntax

```
ORDER([<alias>])
```

Purpose: Returns the name of the primary-order index (NDX) file or multiple-index (MDX) tag. The index file name, but not its extension, is returned in uppercase characters. The current database is used, unless you specify the optional *<alias>*.

Example

```
USE CLIENTS
SET INDEX TO Lastname, Company, City
? ORDER()     && returns "LASTNAME", the primary index
SET ORDER TO 2
? ORDER()     && returns "COMPANY", now the primary index
```

OS( )

Syntax

```
OS()
```

Purpose: Returns the name of the operating system installed on your computer.

Example

```
* If your computer's operating system is DOS 3.3
? OS()                  && returns "DOS 3.30"
```

PAD( )

Syntax

```
PAD()
```

Purpose: Returns the name of the last pad selected from the active menu. You select a menu pad by highlighting the desired pad and pressing the Enter key. The menu pad name is not cleared by the DEACTIVATE MENU or DEACTIVATE POPUP command. This function only works with the DEFINE POP-UP style menus, not with DEFINE MENUITEM menus.

Example

```
@ 12,15 SAY "Last pad selected was " + PAD()
```

PADPROMPT( )

Syntax

```
PADPROMPT(<pad name> [,<menu name>])
```

Purpose: Returns the text appearing in a specified pad of a menu. If you do not specify a *<menu name>*, the currently active menu is used. The menu and pad must have been defined previously. This function only works with the DEFINE POP-UP style menus, not with DEFINE MENUITEM menus.

Example

```
* Display the prompt that appears in the PAD1 prompt of
   the TOPMENU menu
@ 19,10 SAY "Select the " + PADPROMPT("PAD1","TOPMENU") + "option."
```

PAYMENT( )

Syntax

```
PAYMENT(<principal>,<rate>,<periods>)
```

Purpose: Returns the payment required, given the *<principal>*, *<rate>*, and *<periods>*. The *<principal>* can be a positive or negative value and is the principal value of the loan. The *<rate>* is the interest rate per *<periods>*; if the interest rate is a yearly value, you need to divide the annual interest rate by 12. The *<periods>* parameter represents the number of payment periods of the loan.

Note

Make sure you enter the interest value as a decimal number: 14 percent interest should be entered as 0.14. The interest rate should be the interest rate per period: if you are making monthly payments at 14 percent interest, the interest rate is 0.14/12.

Example

```
* Determines payment for a loan
Prin_bal = 250000            && loan amount
Num_pays = 360               && 30 year loan (360 months)
Int_rate = 0.1175/12         && monthly interest rate
Monthpay = PAYMENT(Prin_bal, Int_rate, Num_pay)
? Monthpay                   && returns 2523.52
```

PCOL( )

Syntax

```
PCOL()
```

Purpose: Returns the current column position (relative to _ploffset) of the printer. In @...SAY and @...GET commands, you can use the dollar symbol ($) to get the column position for the screen or the printer, whereas PCOL( ) is used only with the printer.

Example

```
@ 20,15 SAY "Current printing column is " + STR(PCOL())
@ 21,$ + 5 SAY "End of test."
```

PCOUNT( )

Syntax

```
PCOUNT()
```

Purpose: Returns the number of parameters that are passed to a procedure or user-defined function.

Example

```
* Short Procedure file
PROCEDURE ADDRESS
PARAMETERS P1,P2
MYADD=P1+" "+P2
? MYADD
? PCOUNT()
RETURN
* End procedure file, now execute it
DO ADDRESS WITH "Dallas, TX","75299"
Dallas, TX 75299     && Output generated
2                    && Output generated
```

PI( )

Syntax

```
PI()
```

Purpose: Returns 3.14159 as the p value. Use SET DECIMALS and SET PRECISION to change the accuracy of the displayed value.

Example

```
? PI()          && returns 3.1416, with SET DECIMALS TO 4
```

POPUP( )

Syntax

```
POPUP()
```

Purpose: Returns the name of the currently active pop-up menu. If no pop-up menu is defined or active, a null string ("") is returned. This function only works with the DEFINE POP-UP style menus, not with DEFINE MENUITEM menus.

Example

```
? 12,15 SAY "Current pop-up menu name is " + POPUP()
```

PRINTSTATUS( )

Syntax

```
PRINTSTATUS()
```

Purpose: Returns a logical true (.T.) if the printer is on-line and ready.

Caution

Some printers will not support this command, and networked printers or printers with a printer buffer may return an inaccurate response.

Example

```
IF .NOT. PRINTSTATUS()
   @ 15,20 SAY "Please make sure printer is ready."
ENDIF
```

PROGRAM( )

Syntax

```
PROGRAM()
```

Purpose: Returns the name of the program or procedure that was running when an error occurred. Can be used during debugging a program in conjunction with the Breakpoint window. The program name returned does not include its file-name extension.

Example

```
* Simple error trapping
ON ERROR ? "Error ", ERROR(), " in ", ;
   PROGRAM(), "at line", LINENO()
```

PROMPT( )

Syntax

```
PROMPT()
```

Purpose: Returns the character string associated with the last selected pop-up or menu option. If no pop-ups or menus are in memory (even if they have been deactivated), or if the Esc key was used to exit a pop-up or menu, a null string ("") is returned. This function only works with the DEFINE POP-UP style menus, not with DEFINE MENUITEM menus.

Example

```
* Prompt for files in pick list
* Check for Escape key
M_PROMPT = PROMPT()
IF LASTKEY()#27.OR. .NOT. ISBLANK(M_PROMPT)
    M_FILE = TRIM(PROMPT())
    USE (M_FILE)
ENDIF
RELEASE POPUP <name>
```

PROW( )

Syntax

```
PROW()
```

Purpose: Returns the current printing row on the printer. The printing row is set to 0 after an EJECT command.

Example

```
* Eject paper to top of form before continuing
IF PROW() <> 0
   EJECT
ENDIF
```

PV( )

Syntax

```
PV(<payment>, <rate>, <periods>)
```

Purpose: Returns the present value of equal regular *<payments>* at a constant interest *<rate>* for the *<periods>*. If the interest is compounded daily, use a *<rate>* of the annual interest rate divided by 365. If the interest is compounded monthly, use a *<rate>* of the annual interest rate divided by 12.

Note

Make sure that you enter the interest value as a decimal number: 14 percent interest should be entered as 0.14. The interest rate should be the interest rate per period: if you are making monthly payments at 14 percent interest, the interest rate is 0.14/12.

Example

```
* How much has been saved over five years?
Monthpay = 150          && amount saved each month
Int_rate = 0.0822/12    && annual interest compounded monthly
Num_pays = 60           && five years (60 months)
Amt_saved = PV(Monthpay, Int_rate, Num_pays)
? Amt_saved             && returns 7359.49
```

RAND( )

Syntax

```
RAND([<numeric expression>])
```

Purpose: Returns a random number. The optional *<numeric expression>* is the random number seed used to generate the number. If the *<numeric expression>* is a negative number, the seed is taken from the system clock. A seed value of 100001 is the default value. The number returned is from 0 to 0.999999.

Example

```
* Returns first random number, based on a seed of 14
? RAND(14)
* Compute the next random number using the same seed
? RAND()
```

RAT( )

Syntax

```
RAT(<character string1>,<character string2>/
   <memo field name> [,<numeric expression>]
```

Purpose: This function operates like the AT( ) function, used to find one string inside another, except that the RAT( ) function begins searching the source string from the right end of the string (the last character of the string). The function looks for *<character string 1>* (the substring) in *<character string 2>* (the source string) or in the *<memo field>*. If *<character string 1>* is found, the starting position number is returned. If *<character string 1>* is not found, or if it is longer than the source string or memo field, then 0 is returned. The optional *<numeric expression>* specifies which occurrence of the substring is sought. If you want to find the second occurrence of the substring, for example, you would specify 2 for the *<numeric expression>*.

Example

```
* Look for 2nd occurrence of "BEANS"
? RAT("BEANS", "STRING BEANS AND WAX BEANS") && prints 22
```

READKEY( )

Syntax

```
READKEY()
```

Purpose: Returns an integer value for the key used to exit a full-screen command. The value returned is different if data was changed on the screen. Table 23.5 shows the values returned.

Table 23.5 Values Returned by READKEY

Data Changed	# Change	Key Pressed
0	256	Ctrl-S, left arrow, Ctrl-H
(none)	256	Backspace
1	257	Ctrl-D, right arrow, Ctrl-L
2	258	Ctrl-A, Ctrl, left arrow
3	259	Ctrl-F, Ctrl, right arrow
4	260	Ctrl-E, up arrow, Ctrl-K
5	261	Ctrl-J, down arrow, Ctrl-X
6	262	Ctrl-R, PgUp
7	263	Ctrl-C, PgDn
12	(none)	Ctrl-Q, Esc
(none)	270	Ctrl-W, Ctrl-End
15	271	Enter, Ctrl-M (fill last record)
16	(none)	Enter, Ctrl-M (at beginning of record in APPEND)
33	289	Ctrl-Home
34	290	Ctrl-PgUp
35	291	Ctrl-PgDn
36	292	F1 (Help function key)

Example

```
* Save the data only if changed
* This saves time over saving unchanged data
DO inputdata                    && data input routine
IF READKEY() >= 256
   DO savedata                  && save data routine
ENDIF
```

RECCOUNT( )

Syntax

```
RECCOUNT([<alias>])
```

Purpose: Returns the number of records in the database. All records are included, even those excluded by a SET FILTER or SET DELETED ON command. The current database is used, unless you specify the optional *<alias>* of another active database.

Example

```
* CLIENTS.DBF has 138 records
USE CLIENTS
? RECCOUNT()          && returns 138
```

RECNO( )

Syntax

```
RECNO([<alias>])
```

Purpose: Returns the current record number of the database in the current work area or in another open database specified by *<alias>*. If a database is empty, or the current record pointer is at BOF( ), RECNO( ) returns 1. If no database is in use, RECNO( ) returns 0. If the current record pointer is at EOF( ), RECNO ( ) returns RECCOUNT( ) + 1.

Example

```
* ORDERS.DBF has 382 records
USE ORDERS
? RECCOUNT()          && returns 382
GOTO 322
? RECNO()             && returns 322
GOTO BOTTOM
? RECNO()             && returns 382
SKIP 1
? RECNO()             && returns 383
```

RECSIZE( )

Syntax

```
RECSIZE([<alias>])
```

Purpose: Returns the size in bytes of one record of the current database, or of an open database in another area if you use the *<alias>* option.

Example

```
USE ORDERS
? RECSIZE()          && returns size of one record
```

REPLICATE( )

Syntax

```
REPLICATE(<string>, <number of times to repeat>)
```

Purpose: Repeats the *<string>* the specified number of times. This function is useful for drawing lines in reports or for creating simple bar charts based on numeric variables.

Example

```
? REPLICATE("E",4)             && returns "EEEE"
* These are values corresponding to test scores
Grade_a = 3
Grade_b = 10
Grade_c = 15
Grade_d = 8
Grade_f = 2
?"A = " + REPLICATE("A",grade_a)
?"B = " + REPLICATE("B",grade_b)
?"C = " + REPLICATE("C",grade_c)
?"D = " + REPLICATE("D",grade_d)
?"F = " + REPLICATE("F",grade_f)
```

This example displays the following on-screen:

```
A = AAA
B = BBBBBBBBBB
C = CCCCCCCCCCCCCCC
D = DDDDDDDD
F = FF
```

RIGHT( )

Syntax

```
RIGHT(<string> / <variable> , <number>)
```

Purpose: Returns the *<number>* of characters from the string, counting from the last character of the string. You may want to use the TRIM( ) function to remove any trailing spaces.

Example

```
* There are four spaces at the end of "Lunch    "
? RIGHT ("Out to Lunch    ",9)        && returns "Lunch    "
? RIGHT (TRIM("Out to Lunch    "),5)  && returns "Lunch"
```

RLOCK( )

Syntax

```
RLOCK([<character string list of record numbers>, <alias>]/
    [<alias>])
```

Purpose: Used to lock multiple records, where the *<character string list of record numbers>* indicates the records to be locked. The LOCK( ) function is exactly like RLOCK( ). The records in the current database are locked, unless you specify another work area with the optional *<alias>* parameter. The maximum number of records that can be locked is limited only by system memory. After a record is locked, other users can access the record information only in read-only mode.

When all the records are locked successfully, a logical true (.T.) is returned. If the record locking is unsuccessful, a logical false (.F.) is returned. Records are unlocked when you use the UNLOCK command, when the database is closed, or when you quit dBASE 5.

Example

```
* Lock record 15 of the CLIENTS.DBF database
USE CLIENTS
IF RLOCK("15")
   @ 12,15 SAY "Record 15 is locked."
ELSE
   @ 12,15 SAY "Couldn't lock record 15."
ENDIF
```

ROLLBACK( )

Syntax

```
ROLLBACK()
```

Purpose: Returns a logical true (.T.) if the ROLLBACK command was successful. A logical false (.F.) is returned if the ROLLBACK was unsuccessful. You must use BEGIN TRANSACTION before using the ROLLBACK( ) function.

Example

```
* Rollback the transaction if not completed
IF .NOT. COMPLETED()
   ROLLBACK
   IF ROLLBACK()
      @ 22,30 SAY "Transaction rolled back OK."
   ELSE
      @ 22,20 SAY "Transaction rollback failed."
      @ 23,20 SAY "Restore data from backup!"
   ENDIF
ENDIF
```

ROUND( )

Syntax

```
ROUND(<numeric expression>, <number of decimal places>)
```

Purpose: Rounds the *<numeric expression>* to the specified *<number of decimal places>*. If you specify a negative number of decimal places, the number is rounded to whole numbers of 10 * *x*, where *x* is the negative *<number of decimal places>*.

Example

```
SET DECIMAL TO 2
?ROUND(14.3972,1)         && returns 14.4
?ROUND(14.3972,0)         && returns 14
?ROUND(14.3972,-1)        && returns 10
```

ROW( )

Syntax

```
ROW()
```

Purpose: Returns the current row number of the cursor.

Example

```
* Print a message at the current row
@ ROW(), 35 SAY "Please wait."
```

RTOD( )

Syntax

```
RTOD(<radian value>)
```

Purpose: Converts the *<radian value>* to degrees.

Example

```
? RTOD(3.22)         && returns 184.49
```

RTRIM/TRIM( )

Syntax

```
RTRIM/TRIM(<string>)
```

Purpose: Removes trailing blanks from the *<string>*. RTRIM( ) and TRIM( ) are equivalent. These commands are useful for removing excess spaces from data fields.

Example

```
* There are five spaces at the end of each string
? RTRIM("Pinion Rings     ")  && returns "Pinion Rings"
Username = "Cathy Hill     "
? TRIM(Username)              && returns "Cathy Hill"
```

RUN( )

Syntax

```
RUN([<logical expression>,]<character expression>
    [,<logical expression>])
```

Purpose: Run a DOS command or other external program from within dBASE 5. Returns a completion code from the program or operating system. The *<character expression>* is the program name. The first optional *<logical expression>* is to be set true (.T.) if the command or program name is to be passed directly to the operating system. Otherwise, a copy of the operating system's command interpreter (COMMAND.COM) is loaded. If the second optional *<logical expression>* is true (.T.), dBASE 5 is rolled out of memory to make room for the program being run. The amount of memory used by dBASE 5 is reduced to as little as 10K in this case.

> **Caution**
>
> The DOS commands PRINT and ASSIGN are TSR programs. Do not load any TSR program from within dBASE.

Example

```
? RUN(.T.,"C:\ACCESS\ACCESS.COM",.T.)
0
```

SEEK( )

Syntax

```
SEEK(<expression> [,<alias>])
```

Purpose: Searches the currently active database (or another opened database by using *<alias>*) for the *<expression>*. If the *<expression>* is found, a logical true (.T.) is returned; if not found, a logical false (.F.) is returned. An index tag or active index file is required.

Example

```
USE CUSTOMERS INDEX Cust_id
* Look for customer id SM1002
IF SEEK("SM1002")
   @ 12,15 SAY "Found the customer!"
ELSE
   @ 12,15 SAY "Didn't find the customer!"
ENDIF
* This does the same thing, but moves to the found record
USE CUSTOMERS ORDER cust_id
SEEK "SM1002"
@12,15 say IIF(FOUND(),'FOUND IT','NOT FOUND')
```

SELECT( )

Syntax

```
SELECT([<alias>])
```

Purpose: Returns the number of the next available work area, or the work area corresponding to the alias specified. dBASE 5 enables up to the number of work areas set by MAXWORKAREAS in CONFIG.DB, which defaults to 40.

Example

```
CLOSE ALL
USE MYLIST ORDER STREET
USE ADDRESS IN 2 ORDER STREET
? SELECT()
3
? SELECT("ADDRESS")
2
```

SET( )

Syntax

```
SET("<character expression>")
```

Purpose: Returns the status of a SET command, where *<character expression>* is one of the valid SET keywords, surrounded by quotation marks. See Chapter 24, "Using SET Commands To Configure dBASE" for the valid SET keywords.

Example

```
* Make sure that database encryption is set on
mEncrypt = SET("eNCRYPTION")     && Get current setting
SET ENCRYPTION ON                && Turn on encryption
SET ENCRYPTION &mEncrypt         && Reset
```

SIGN( )

Syntax

```
SIGN(<numeric expression>)
```

Purpose: Returns a number for the sign of the *<numeric expression>*. If *<numeric expression>* is negative, a –1 is returned; if it is positive, a 1 is returned; if it is zero, a 0 is returned.

Example

```
? SIGN(13)              && returns 1
? SIGN(-14.22)          && returns -1
? SIGN(0)               && returns 0
```

SIN( )

Syntax

```
SIN(<angle value in radians>)
```

Purpose: Returns the sine of the *<angle value in radians>*. The value returned is a type F (floating-point) number and varies from –1 to +1. Use SET DECIMALS and SET PRECISION to change the accuracy of the displayed value.

Example

```
? SIN(PI()/2)        && returns 1
```

SOUNDEX( )

Syntax

```
SOUNDEX(<string>)
```

Purpose: Converts a *<string>* to a four-digit code indicating its phonetic value. The following logic is followed by SOUNDEX in dBASE 5:

- The code's first character is the first character of the string.
- All occurrences of the letters *a, e, h, i, o, u, w,* and *y,* are removed from the string, except for the first character of the string.
- The remaining letters are assigned a number, as follows:

  1 = b, f, p, v

  2 = c, g, j, k, q, s, x, z

3 = d, t

4 = l

5 = m, n

6 = r

- Excess repeating letters, as the second *e* in *teeth*, are dropped (the first *e* in *teeth* is retained).
- The code is in the form *letter digit digit digit*, with trailing zeros added if the code has fewer than three digits. Any digits after *letter digit digit digit* are dropped.
- Code conversion stops at the first nonalphabetic character.
- Leading blanks are skipped.
- If the first nonblank character is nonalphabetic, a 0000 code is returned.

The result is a sound-alike code that can be used for searching.

Example

```
? SOUNDEX("Smithsonian")   && returns S532
* Set up a soundex index
USE FOODDATA
INDEX ON SOUNDEX(Item_name) TAG FSOUND
SEEK SOUNDEX("Beens")      && will find Item_name "Beans"
```

SPACE( )

Syntax

```
SPACE(<number>)
```

Purpose: Creates a character string with the specified *<number>* of space characters.

Example

```
? SPACE(8)          && returns 8 space characters
? LEN(SPACE(10))    && returns 10
MVA = SPACE(10)     && initializes a memory variable to 10 spaces
```

SQRT( )

Syntax

```
SQRT(<numeric expression>)
```

Purpose: Returns the square root of the *<numeric expression>*. The returned value is always a type F (floating-point) value, even if the *<numeric expression>* is a type F or N. The SET DECIMALS value determines how many decimals are displayed by the result of this function.

Example

```
? SQRT(16)                && returns 4
SET DECIMALS TO 4
? SQRT (2)                && returns 1.4142
```

STR( )

Syntax

```
STR(<numeric expression>[,<length>] [,<decimals>]
```

Purpose: Converts a number to a character string, with a default *<length>* of 10 characters and no *<decimals>*. The *<length>* value includes the decimal point, if any. If you specify fewer decimal places than are in the numeric expression, the value is rounded off to the number of *<decimals>*. If you specify a *<length>* smaller than the number of digits to the left of the decimal, asterisks are returned in place of the number.

Example

```
Number1 = 1423.8374
? STR(Number1)            && returns "1424"
? STR(Number1,7,2)        && returns "1423.84"
```

STUFF( )

Syntax

```
STUFF(<char 1>,<number 1>,<number 2>,<char 2>)
```

Purpose: Replaces part of the *<char 1>* string with the *<char 2>* string. The *<number 1>* is used as the starting point for the replacement. The *<number 2>* value is used to determine the number of characters in the *<char 2>* string to replace in the *<char 1>* string. STUFF( ) does not work in memo fields.

Example

```
* Change all phone numbers in CUSTOMER
* from "xxx xxxx" to "xxx-xxxx
USE CUSTOMER
REPLACE ALL PHONE WITH STUFF(PHONE,4,"-")
```

SUBSTR( )

Syntax

```
SUBSTR(<string>/<memo field name>,<start position>,
   [<number of characters>])
```

Purpose: Extracts part of the *<string>*. The extracted string starts with the character at *<start position>* and continues for the *<number of characters>*. The starting position number must be a positive number.

Example

```
Note_name = "Do Re Mi Fa Sol La Ti Do"
? SUBSTR(Note_name, 7,2)      && returns "Mi"
```

TAG( )

Syntax

```
TAG([<.MDX filename>,] <numeric expression> [,<alias>])
```

Purpose: Returns the name of the multiple-index (MDX) tag for the index specified by the *<numeric expression>*. The current database is used, unless you use the optional *<alias>* parameter to indicate another open database. If there is no tag name, a null string ("") is returned.

Example

```
* The inventory database has the following fields tagged
* Part_num, Part_name, Last_ord, Supplier
* The index tags are contained in the INVENTRY.MDX file
USE INVENTRY
? TAG(3)           && returns "Last_ord"
```

TAGCOUNT( )

Syntax

```
TAGCOUNT([<multiple index file>[,<alias>]])
```

Purpose: Returns the number of indexes that are currently active. If a multiple-index file is not specified, the number of active indexes in the current work area or work area specified by the alias are returned, including any active NDX files.

Example

```
USE CUSTOMER IN 2
? TAGCOUNT(2)
6
```

TAGNO( )

Syntax

```
TAGNO(<index tag or NDX file>[,<MDX file>[,<alias>]])
```

Purpose: Returns the index number for the specified index tag or NDX file order. If you do not specify an alias, the function assumes the currently active work area.

Example

```
USE CUSTOMER ORDER ZIP
?TAGNO("ZIP")
4
```

TAN( )

Syntax

```
TAN(<angle size in radians>)
```

Purpose: Returns the tangent of the *<angle size in radians>*. Use SET DECIMALS and SET PRECISION to change the accuracy of the displayed value.

Example

```
? TAN(PI())                && returns 0
```

TIME( )

Syntax

```
TIME([<expression>])
```

Purpose: Converts the system time into a character string in the format HH:MM:SS. If a valid expression is specified, the character string displays hundredths of seconds, in the format HH:MM:SS:hh. The time is always returned in a 24-hour format. If you need to use the system time in a mathematical calculation, use SUBSTR( ) and VAL( ).

Note

The system time must be set properly for this function to return the current time.

Example

```
* If the current time is 1:44:00 PM
? TIME()        && returns the character string "13:44:00"
```

TRANSFORM( )

Syntax

```
TRANSFORM(<variable expression>, <PICTURE format>)
```

Purpose: Applies a PICTURE format to a variable without requiring that you use an @...SAY command. The TRANSFORM( ) function always returns a character-type variable for any variable used. See the @...SAY command in Chapter 22, "Using dBASE 5 Commands," for complete details of the PICTURE parameters.

Example

```
Unitcost = 4882.33
? TRANSFORM(unitcost, "@$ C")
* Results in "$4,882.33 CR"
```

TRIM( )

Syntax

```
TRIM(<string>)
```

Purpose: Removes trailing spaces; see RTRIM( ).

TYPE( )

Syntax

```
TYPE(<variable name>)
```

Purpose: Determines the type of the *<variable name>*. The variable name must be a character string. Possible types are as follows:

Type	Meaning
C	Character
N	Numeric
L	Logical
M	Memo
D	Date
F	Floating-point number
U	Undefined

Example

```
* Has a user logged in yet?
IF TYPE("user") = "U"
   DO Loguser          && no user logged in, do log-in program
ENDIF
Logdate = DATE()
? TYPE("Logdate")      && returns "D"
Counter = 12
? TYPE("Counter")      && returns "N"
mVar = "Counter"
? TYPE(mVar)           && Returns N
? TYPE("mVar")         && Returns C
```

UNIQUE( )

Syntax

```
UNIQUE([[<character expression>,]<numeric expression>
   [,<alias>]])
```

Purpose: Returns a true (.T.) value if the specified index tag was created using the UNIQUE option to eliminate duplicate records, or false (.F.) if it was not. The *<numeric expression>* specifies the index number, and the optional *<character expression>* and *<alias>* expressions specify the index and database files if other than the current files.

Example

```
USE CUSTOMER INDEX ON ADDRESS1 TO ADDRINDX UNIQUE
? TAGNO("ADDRINDX")
   8
? UNIQUE(8)
.T.
```

UPPER( )

Syntax

```
UPPER(<string/variable>)
```

Purpose: Converts all characters in the *<string/variable>* to uppercase. You must use the MLINE( ) function to extract data from memo fields and then use UPPER( ) to uppercase the variable.

Example

```
* Convert all the LASTNAME field data to uppercase
USE CLIENTS
REPLACE ALL LASTNAME WITH UPPER(LASTNAME)
```

USER( )

Syntax

```
USER()
```

Purpose: Returns the name of the logged-in user on a protected system. A null string ("") is returned if the database is not protected.

Example

```
IF .NOT. ISBLANK(USER())
   @ 20,20 SAY "Current user is " + USER()
ELSE
   @20,20 SAY 'NOT LOGGED IN'ENDIF
```

VAL( )

Syntax

```
VAL(<character expression>)
```

Purpose: Converts character-type data made up of numerals into numeric data. If the *<character expression>* includes a non-number character, 0 is returned. The number of decimals displayed is determined by the SET DECIMAL value. Text is converted from left to right until a non-number character or blank is encountered.

Example

```
Thisaddr = "4933 Magnolia Street"
? VAL(Thisaddr) + 2     && returns the number 4935 (4933+2)
Thisaddr = "PO Box 1085"
? VAL(Thisaddr)         && returns 0
```

VARREAD( )

Syntax

```
VARREAD()
```

Purpose: In conjunction with @..SAY..GET commands used with full-screen editing, this function returns the name of the field currently being edited. The field name is returned as all uppercase characters. Use the ON KEY command to set up a help screen.

Example

```
* Set up the F1 key as the help key
* Showhelp is the help screen procedure
ON KEY LABEL F1 DO showhelp
DO Scrn_input            && screen input program
* Program continues... *
*
*
* The showhelp procedure
```

```
PROCEDURE Showhelp
* Shows help based on the field being edited
CLEAR TYPEAHEAD              && clear any keystrokes in the buffer
DO CASE
   CASE VARREAD() = "CONTACT"
      @ 24,10 SAY "Enter customer contact name"
   CASE VARREAD() = "ADDRESS"
      @ 24,10 SAY "Enter business address"
   OTHERWISE                 && any other field
      @ 24,10 SAY "Enter value"
ENDCASE
RETURN
```

VERSION( )

Syntax

```
VERSION()
```

Purpose: Returns the dBASE 5 version number, which can be useful for dBASE applications that are not downward compatible.

Example

```
* If you are using dBASE version 2.0
? VERSION()                && returns "dBASE 5 2.0"
```

WINDOW( )

Syntax

```
WINDOW()
```

Purpose: Returns the name of the currently active window. This works only on windows defined with the DEFINE WINDOW command, not with the DEFINE FORM command.

Example

```
ACTIVATE WINDOW DATAENT
? "The current window is: " + WINDOW()
The current window is: DATAENT
```

YEAR( )

Syntax

```
YEAR(<date variable>)
```

Purpose: Returns the year as a numeric value from the *<date variable>*, which can be a date memory variable, a date field, or a function that returns a date-type variable.

Example

```
* If the current date is 1/3/93
? YEAR(DATE())      && returns 1993
```

Chapter 24

Using SET Commands To Configure dBASE 5

The SET commands enable you to change many of the default characteristics of dBASE 5. You can specify screen colors, for example, or the type of display you're using. Other SET commands enable you to change the format of the date, change the number of decimals to display, change the current disk drive and directory, and program the function keys to perform dBASE 5 operations.

To access the various SET commands, type **SET** at the Command window or you can use Tools, Settings from the Control Center. Each of the SET options also can be used in your program with any of the various SET...TO commands covered in this section.

When you change any of the SET options at the Command window or Control Center, those changes affect only the current dBASE 5 session. When you exit dBASE 5, the options revert to their defaults. To make permanent changes to the SET options, you must change the CONFIG.DB file (see Chapter 29, "Using the System Configuration File").

The SET( ) function returns the settings of many of the SET commands (see Chapter 23, "Using Functions").

In the section "SET Commands," the SET commands are grouped alphabetically. The default value is shown in uppercase letters, and optional values are shown in lowercase letters.

> **Note**
>
> The actions of the SET commands also can be performed through the Tools, Settings screen in the Control Center.

Categorizing the SET Commands

How often have you thought of a restaurant that serves food you like, but you cannot remember the name of the restaurant so that you can make reservations? You may find that this happens with the SET commands. You know what you want the command to do, but you can't remember exactly which SET command you need.

This section lists the SET commands by category. For example, you may want a SET command to change a network setting. Look under the category "Network SET Commands." When you find the command that you want, look for the syntax in the alphabetical listing in the "SET Commands" section.

Database SET Commands

This group of commands affects the current database by limiting the records being accessed, setting up multiple file relations, setting the accuracy of string comparisons, and other functions.

SET DELETED	SET KEY TO
SET EXACT	SET NEAR
SET FIELDS	SET ORDER TO
SET FIELDS TO	SET RELATION TO
SET FIELDS TO ALL	SET SKIP TO
SET FILTER TO	SET UNIQUE
SET INDEX TO	SET VIEW TO

Database Encryption SET Command

This command determines whether a copied file is created as an encrypted file. Be careful with this command; if you forget your log-in name, the database cannot be unencrypted.

SET ENCRYPTION

Date and Time SET Commands

This group of commands controls the displayed format of dates and times.

SET CENTURY	SET DATE
SET CLOCK	SET MARK TO
SET CLOCK TO	

General SET Commands

These commands are used to change the environment while you are using dBASE 5. You can set up a catalog, change the default drive and directory, assign function keys, change the default editor, control whether commands are stored in the history file, and set the path to be used to access files.

SET	SET DIRECTORY TO
SET CATALOG ON	SET EDITOR
SET CATALOG TO	SET FULLPATH
SET CUAENTER	SET FUNCTION
SET DEFAULT TO	SET WP

Help Message Display SET Commands

These two commands are used to determine how help messages are displayed if incorrect commands are entered, or to control the display of program code as the program is generated by dBASE 5.

SET HELP

SET INSTRUCT

Memo Field SET Commands

These commands affect memo field storage in dBASE 5 memo files or the width of memo field output.

SET BLOCKSIZE TO

SET MEMOWIDTH

SET WINDOW OF MEMO TO

SET WP

Memory SET Commands

These commands are used to optimize memo and index performance.

SET BLOCKSIZE TO

SET IBLOCK TO

SET MBLOCK TO

Network SET Commands

This series of SET commands is used on network installations. These commands enable you to set the exclusive use of a database, lock tables during certain operations, and set the reprocess and refresh rates.

SET EXCLUSIVE

SET LOCK

SET REFRESH TO

SET REPROCESS TO

Number Display SET Commands

These commands affect how numeric variables appear on-screen. You can set the number of decimal points, the precision used in mathematical calculations, and the thousands separator character.

SET CURRENCY

SET CURRENCY TO

SET DECIMALS TO

SET FIXED

SET POINT TO

SET PRECISION TO

SET SEPARATOR TO

Output Redirection Commands

These commands are used to capture screen output and save it in a text file on disk.

SET ALTERNATE

SET ALTERNATE TO

SET DEVICE TO FILE

Printing SET Commands

These SET commands are used with commands that send data to the printer. You can route screen display commands to the printer, set the margins, turn the printed output on and off, or specify a printer port.

SET DEVICE TO PRINTER

SET MARGIN TO

SET PRINTER

SET PRINTER TO

Program File SET Commands

This series of commands is used while you create, use, or debug program files. A program file contains a series of dBASE 5 commands. You can specify the current procedure file, determine whether commands and the settings of variables will be echoed to the screen, enable or prevent access to the design mode, and change various program debugging settings.

SET DEBUG	SET LIBRARY TO
SET DESIGN	SET PROCEDURE TO
SET DEVELOPMENT	SET STEP
SET ECHO	SET TRAP
SET ESCAPE	SET TYPEAHEAD TO

Screen Display SET Commands

This series of SET commands controls the appearance of the screen. You can set screen colors, choose the characters used for menu borders, control whether the cursor is displayed, specify the field delimiters, choose screen format files, control screen message display, and control other settings.

SET BORDER TO	SET DELIMITERS
SET COLOR	SET DELIMITERS TO
SET COLOR OF NORMAL	SET DEVICE TO SCREEN
SET COLOR TO	SET DISPLAY TO
SET CONSOLE	SET FORMAT TO
SET CURSOR	SET HEADINGS

SET INTENSITY
SET MESSAGE TO
SET ODOMETER TO
SET SCOREBOARD
SET SPACE
SET STATUS
SET TALK

Sound SET Commands

These commands control the sound of the bell or turn it on or off. Single tones of any frequency and duration (with a minimum duration of one second) can be specified with these commands.

SET BELL

SET BELL TO

SQL SET Commands

These two commands control the display of SQL queries.

SET PAUSE

SET SQL

SET Commands

In this section, commands are listed alphabetically, and examples and other information are shown for each command. The default value is shown in uppercase letters, and optional values are shown in lowercase letters.

SET

Syntax

```
SET
```

Purpose: Opens the full-screen form for setting or displaying value of dBASE parameters.

SET ALTERNATE

Syntax

```
SET ALTERNATE on/OFF
```

Purpose: Starts (SET ALTERNATE ON) and stops (SET ALTERNATE OFF) the recording to the alternate file of screen output through the ?, ??, LIST, or DISPLAY commands, and keyboard input. The alternate file is specified by the SET ALTERNATE TO command. Using the OFF parameter file does not close the output file; you can add to the currently open file by using the SET ALTERNATE ON command. See the SET ALTERNATE TO command for an example.

SET ALTERNATE TO

Syntax

```
SET ALTERNATE TO [<filename> [ADDITIVE]]
```

Purpose: Creates the text file *<filename>*, which contains the recorded output. The file name has a default extension of TXT and is created in the current directory unless you specify otherwise. The ADDITIVE option enables you to add data to an existing file. If the *<filename>* exists and ADDITIVE is not used, it is overwritten. Use SET ALTERNATE TO or CLOSE ALTERNATE to close the output file. To stop recording screen output in the text file temporarily, use SET ALTERNATE OFF. When you want to resume sending output to the file, use SET ALTERNATE ON.

Any text or data displayed on-screen is also stored in the alternate file. Only @...SAY, EDIT, BROWSE, and APPEND operations are not stored in the alternate file. You can use the ? and ?? commands to store text in a file, along with such other commands as REPORT FORM and LIST. Use the ?? command at the beginning of output recording to eliminate a blank line at the top of the file. The ? command first outputs a carriage return and line feed, which causes a blank line if ? is the first command after the SET ALTERNATE command is used.

Example

```
* Store the contents of certain records
* to a text file
USE Orders ORDER PartNum
SET HEADINGS ON          && field names at top of listSET ALTERNATE
TO BackOrdr.Txt
SET ALTERNATE ON
?? SPACE(20) + "BACKORDERD ITEMS _ " + DTOC(DATE())
?                          && a blank line
* List all back-ordered items older than 30 days
LIST PartNum, PartName, OnHand, BackOrd, BackDate ;
   FOR BackDate < DATE() - 30
SET ALTERNATE OFF
SET ALTERNATE TO
```

SET AUTOSAVE

Syntax

```
SET AUTOSAVE on/OFF
```

Purpose: Determines whether each record is saved to disk immediately or is stored in a disk buffer. SET AUTOSAVE ON saves each record immediately; SET AUTOSAVE OFF stores data in the disk buffer until the buffer is full, and then updates the records on disk. The default setting is OFF.

Example

```
* Turn on AUTOSAVE
* Note: will drastically slow database operations on
* networks with full file commands like replace
SET AUTOSAVE ON
```

SET BELL

Syntax

```
SET BELL ON/off
```

Purpose: Controls whether the bell is sounded when you arrive at the end of a field or when an error occurs. The bell normally is on and has a frequency of 512 hertz and 2 clock ticks (each clock tick is about 0.0549 seconds). You can change the frequency and duration of the bell with the SET BELL TO command. You can sound the bell in your program with a ?CHR(7) command as long as your console is on.

Example

See SET BELL TO for an example.

SET BELL TO

Syntax

```
SET BELL TO [<frequency>, <duration>]
```

Purpose: Sets the frequency (pitch) and duration (length) of the bell. The frequency range is from 19 to 10,000 cycles per second (hertz). For low-pitched sounds, use a frequency between 20 and 550. For a high pitch, use a value from 550 to 5,500. Frequencies above 5,500 may not be audible to all users. The duration can be between 2 and 19 ticks; each tick is about 0.0549 seconds. The bell sounds when the cursor encounters the end of a data entry field or when an error occurs (if SET BELL is ON). Use SET BELL TO without parameters to return to the default values.

Note

You may want to choose a less strident sound for data-entry purposes and a more forceful sound for your error-trapping routines. Some people find the end-of-field bell used with data-entry screens annoying.

Example

```
SET BELL TO 1000, 5
SET BELL ON                && enable the bell
?CHR(7)                    && sound bell
SET BELL OFF               && disable the bell
RETURN
```

SET BLOCKSIZE TO

Syntax

SET BLOCKSIZE TO <*number of 512-byte blocks*>

Purpose: Changes the default block size of the memo fields and multiple-index files. To remain compatible with dBASE III files, the default size is one 512-byte block. A memo field file and index file use up file space in groups of *blocksize*. Larger blocksize values enable faster string manipulation, (for example, searching for data in a memo), but may slow down other I/O processing. Smaller values cause slower string manipulation, but also can offer better performance. To set the block size separately for index files or memo files, use the SET IBLOCK TO or SET MBLOCK TO commands.

Example

```
SET BLOCKSIZE TO 2
```

SET BORDER TO

Syntax

SET BORDER TO [SINGLE/double/panel/none/
<*border definition string*>]

Purpose: Changes the default border of pop-ups, windows, and @...SAY and @...TO commands from a single line to other border types. SINGLE is the default value. Use DOUBLE for double lines, and PANEL for block-character boxes using ASCII character 219 (_). The <*border definition string*> contains values for the eight side and corner positions in a box. Eight values may be specified in the <*border definition string*>. Indicate default values by inserting commas with no values or omitting trailing defaults and the separating commas.

VI

Reference Guide

You can only use this command with non-UI screens and windows like those created in previous versions of dBASE. It is ignored by dBASE 5's UI objects.

Table 24.1 shows the order and positions used for the eight side and corner positions on the border.

Table 24.1 Border Positions

Border number	Position
1	Top line
2	Bottom line
3	Left line
4	Right line
5	Top left corner
6	Top right corner
7	Bottom left corner
8	Bottom right corner

Example

```
SET BORDERS TO ,,179,179,213,184,212,190
```

In the example, border positions 1 and 2 use the default values.

SET CARRY

Syntax

```
SET CARRY on/OFF
```

Purpose: Determines whether data fields are brought forward to new records when you use the APPEND and INSERT commands. A new record normally contains blank fields. With SET CARRY ON, field data from the previous record is placed in the new, blank record. You can use the SET CARRY TO command to determine which fields in the record are carried forward. (See SET CARRY TO.)

Example

```
* Turn on carry during data input routine
SET CARRY ON
DO Data_In            && data input routine
SET CARRY OFF         && reset to default
```

SET CARRY TO

Syntax

```
SET CARRY TO [<field list> [ADDITIVE]]
```

Purpose: Specifies which fields will be carried forward to new records if you used the SET CARRY ON command. The ADDITIVE option adds the <*field list*> to the previous SET CARRY field list. If you need to specify all fields after you use a <*field list*>, use the SET CARRY TO command without a list of fields. SET CARRY TO will turn on SET CARRY without having to issue a separate command.

Example

```
* Add records, assume that Areacode and ZIPcode
* fields are the same as the previous record
USE Customer
SET CARRY TO AreaCode, ZipCode
APPEND
SET CARRY OFF
```

SET CATALOG ON

Syntax

```
SET CATALOG on/OFF
```

Purpose: Determines whether files that you use or create are added to the current catalog. SET CATALOG ON adds these files to the current catalog (set with SET CATALOG TO); SET CATALOG OFF does not add files to the current catalog.

Example

```
* Don't add new files to current catalog
SET CATALOG OFF
```

SET CATALOG TO

Syntax

```
SET CATALOG TO [<filename> / ?]
```

Purpose: Determines the <*filename*> of the active catalog file, which is assumed to have a CAT file name extension and is stored in the current directory. The SET CATALOG TO command automatically performs a SET CATALOG ON command. Use the ? parameter to select the catalog from a list in commands such as USE, MODIFY SCREEN, and so on.

The master catalog file, CATALOG.CAT, contains a list of the other catalogs. The catalog files are standard DBF files with the file structure shown in Table 24.2.

To close a catalog, use the SET CATALOG TO command without parameters.

Table 24.2 Catalog File Structure

Field	Field Name	Type	Width	Description
1	Path	Character	70	Drive and directory name.
2	File_Name	Character	12	File name, including extension.
3	Alias	Character	8	Alias file name.
4	Type	Character	3	The default file extension of the type of file.
5	Title	Character	80	An optional description of the catalog. If SET TITLE is ON, you are prompted for a description each time you create or add a new file.
6	Code	Numeric	3	The number dBASE 5 assigns to each database file that is used. Program files are assigned 0, and each new database file gets the next higher number. Index, format, label, query, report form, screen, and view files are assigned the same number as the database file with which they are used.
7	Tag	Character	4	Not used.

Example

```
* Set up new catalog
SET CATALOG TO CustCat.CAT
```

SET CENTURY

Syntax

```
SET CENTURY on/OFF
```

Purpose: Determines the display and input of the century prefixes of the years in dates. SET CENTURY ON shows all four digits of the year portion of the date—for example, 1994. SET CENTURY OFF (the default) shows only the last two digits of the year portion of a date—for example, 94. With SET CENTURY OFF, all dates are assumed to be in the 1900 to 1999 date range (the 20th century).

Example

```
SET CENTURY OFF
? {10/10/94}          && displays "10/10/94"
SET CENTURY ON
? {10/10/94}          && displays "10/10/1994"
```

SET CLOCK

Syntax

```
SET CLOCK on/OFF
```

Purpose: Turns the on-screen display of the time ON or OFF (default). The clock normally is displayed at row 0, column 68, unless you have used the SET CLOCK TO command. See SET CLOCK TO for an example. If the Desktop menu is open the normal display position is hidden.

SET CLOCK TO

Syntax

```
SET CLOCK TO [<row>, <column>]
```

Purpose: Determines the position of the time display. If you use SET CLOCK TO without the *<row>* and *<column>* parameters, the time is displayed at row 0, column 68. If the Desktop menu is open, the normal display position is hidden.

Example

```
* Display the clock at the bottom left corner of the screen
SET CLOCK TO 24,0
```

SET COLOR

Syntax

```
SET COLOR ON/off
```

Purpose: Switches between color and monochrome screen display on systems that have both types of monitors. SET COLOR ON enables color display; SET COLOR OFF enables monochrome display. Monochrome display adaptors default to OFF; all others default to ON.

Example

```
* Sets color on/off according to previously
* defined variable NEEDMONO
IF NeedMono
   SET COLOR OFF
ENDIF
```

SET COLOR OF

Syntax

```
SET COLOR OF NORMAL / MESSAGES / TITLES / BOX / HIGHLIGHT /
   INFORMATION / FIELDS TO [<color attribute>]
```

Purpose: Enables you to set the indicated area to the *<color attribute>* value. Tables 24.3 and 24.4 in the SET COLOR TO section show the colors and the attribute group names.

SET COLOR TO

Syntax

```
SET COLOR TO [<standard>][,[<enhanced>][,[<perimeter>]
   [,[<background>]]]]
```

Purpose: Enables you to set the color values used for each of the parameters. Each parameter can have a foreground/background color pair; for example, BG/B indicates cyan letters on a blue background. With some monitors (such as EGA-type displays), the *<perimeter>* parameter cannot be set. You can change only one of the color values by specifying that parameter only.
A color value of ",R" sets the *<enhanced>* color to red, leaving the *<standard>* color unchanged. If you don't specify one of the colors in a foreground/background pair, that color is set to black. A color pair of /N+ is the same as N/N+.

Use the plus sign (+) with the color value (for example, R+) to indicate a high-intensity color for the foreground color. An asterisk (*) added to the color value causes that color to blink; for example, R* indicates blinking red. Use a blank (X) as either the foreground or background color for times when you don't want to see the characters, as in password entry. Monochrome monitors can use the U color for underline and I for inverse video instead of color values. Other color values used on monochrome displays will be ignored.

Table 24.3 shows the various color values, and Table 24.4 shows the attribute groups available in dBASE 5.

Table 24.3 Color Table

Color	Letter Code	Color	Letter Code
Black	N or blank	Magenta	RB
Blue	B	Brown	GR
Green	G	Yellow	GR+
Cyan	BG	White	W
Blank	X	*<color>*+	Bright color
Gray	N+	*<color>**	Blinking color
Red	R	*<color>**+	Bright, blinking color

Table 24.4 Color Attribute Groups

Group Name	Partial Example
NORMAL	@...SAY output, unselected BROWSE fields
MESSAGES	Message line, error box interiors, prompt box interiors
TITLES	List headings, browse field names headings, ruler line
BOX	Menu borders, list borders, prompt box borders
HIGHLIGHT	Highlighted menu and list choices, selected box
INFORMATION	Clock, error box borders, status line
FIELDS	Editable fields in BROWSE or @...GET

A complete list of color values appears in the *dBASE 5 Language Reference*.

SET CONFIRM

Syntax

```
SET CONFIRM on/OFF
```

Purpose: Determines whether the cursor automatically moves to the next field (SET CONFIRM OFF) when the last character of the field has been entered, or whether the user must press Enter before the cursor moves to the next field (SET CONFIRM ON). Some users are accustomed to pressing Enter, as they would with an adding machine; use SET CONFIRM ON to make sure that the cursor is in the proper field when you enter a group of numbers.

Example

```
* Turn on confirm during data entry program
SET CONFIRM ON
DO Data_In                 && data input routine
SET CONFIRM OFF            && reset to default
```

SET CONSOLE

Syntax

```
SET CONSOLE ON/off
```

Purpose: SET CONSOLE OFF prevents reports and programs that are sent to the printer from being displayed on-screen. SET CONSOLE ON sends the reports and programs to the screen and to the printer. This command is available from within programs only, not at the Command window. SET CONSOLE affects only output from the ?, ??, LIST, or DISPLAY command, and not @...SAY commands.

Example

```
* Don't show the report while it's printing
@ 12,15 SAY "Report printing ..."
SET CONSOLE OFF
REPORT FORM CustList TO PRINT
SET CONSOLE ON
@ 13,15 SAY "Report finished!"
```

SET CUAENTER

Syntax

```
SET CUAENTER ON/off
```

Purpose: Determines whether the user can press the Enter key to select the default pushbutton on a dBASE 5 form. Set CUAENTER to OFF if you want the user to have to press Ctrl-Enter to select the default pushbutton. With CUAENTER set OFF, the Enter key functions like a Tab key, advancing the focus one object for each press. The SelectAll property of combo boxes, entry fields, and spin boxes is also set to false.

The default setting for SET CUAENTER is ON. This enables the Enter key to select the pushbutton selected, and the user presses the Tab key to advance the focus one object. The ON setting changes the default value of combo boxes, entry fields, and spin boxes to true.

SET CURRENCY

Syntax

```
SET CURRENCY LEFT/right
```

Purpose: Determines the position of the currency symbol. The default currency symbol is to the left (SET CURRENCY LEFT) but can be changed to the end of the currency string (SET CURRENCY RIGHT). If you change the position of the currency symbol, you also may need to change the thousands separator character (SET SEPARATOR) and the character used for the decimal point (SET POINT). See SET CURRENCY TO for an example.

SET CURRENCY TO

Syntax

```
SET CURRENCY TO [<currency unit character string>]
```

Purpose: Changes the symbol that is used in the display of currency values. The *<currency unit character string>* can be any alphabetic characters and defaults to the dollar sign ($). If you change the currency symbol, you also may need to change the thousands separator character (SET SEPARATOR) and the character used for the decimal point (SET POINT).

Example

```
* Use defaults
MTOT = 123456.78
@ 5,10 SAY MTOT PICTURE "@$"
* Displays as $123,456.78
* Use DM for currency displays
MTOT = 123456.78
SET CURRENCY TO "DM"
SET CURRENCY RIGHT
SET POINT TO ","        & Change decimal to comma
SET SEPARATOR TO " "    & Change comma to space
* Displays "123 456,78 DM"
@ 5,10 SAY MTOT PICTURE "@$"
```

SET CURSOR

Syntax

```
SET CURSOR ON/off
```

Purpose: Determines whether the cursor is displayed. SET CURSOR OFF hides the cursor; SET CURSOR ON redisplays the cursor. This command has no effect on UI objects.

Example

```
* Turn off cursor while getting the password
password = space(8)
SET CURSOR OFF
@ 12,15 SAY "Enter Password " ;
GET Password PICTURE "@!" COLOR N/N
READ
SET CURSOR ON
```

SET DATE

Syntax

```
SET DATE [TO]
   AMERICAN / ANSI / BRITISH / FRENCH / GERMAN /
   ITALIAN / JAPAN / USA / MDY / DMY / YMD
```

Purpose: Determines the displayed format of the date. The number of digits for the year value is determined by the SET CENTURY setting. The available formats are shown in Table 24.5.

Table 24.5 SET DATE Formats

Format Name	Result	Examples Using January 3, 1994	
		Set Century On	Set Century Off
AMERICAN	mm/dd/yy	01/03/94	01/03/1994
ANSI	yy.mm.dd	94.01.03	1994.01.03
BRITISH	dd/mm/yy	03/01/94	03/01/1994
FRENCH	dd/mm/yy	03/01/94	03/01/1994
GERMAN	dd.mm.yy	03.01.94	03.01.1994
ITALIAN	dd-mm-yy	03-01-94	03-01-1994
JAPAN	yy/mm/dd	94/01/03	1994/01/03
USA	mm-dd-yy	01-03-94	01-03-1994
MDY	mm/dd/yy	01-03-94	01-03-1994

Format Name	Result	Examples Using January 3, 1994	
		Set Century On	**Set Century Off**
DMY	dd/mm/yy	03/01/94	03/01/1994
YMD	yy/mm/dd	94/01/03	1994/01/03

SET DBTRAP

Syntax

```
SET DBTRAP ON/off
```

Purpose: Determines whether potentially unsafe operations are detected and the program halted if a dBASE command is interrupted when another command is executed. The default is ON.

Example

```
* Turn on error trapping
SET DBTRAP ON
```

SET DEBUG

Syntax

```
SET DEBUG on/OFF
```

Purpose: Determines whether output from the SET ECHO command is sent to the printer (SET DEBUG ON) or the screen (SET DEBUG OFF). This command is useful during program debugging because you can see the assignment of variables and other functions while the program is running. This command works in conjunction with SET ECHO.

Example

```
* Turn on debug for the CUSTEDIT program
SET ECHO ON
SET DEBUG ON
DO CustEdit
SET DEBUG OFF       && resets debug back to normal
SET ECHO OFF
```

SET DECIMALS TO

Syntax

```
SET DECIMALS TO <number of decimal places>
```

Purpose: Determines the number of decimal places displayed for numeric results. The *<number of decimal places>* can be from 0 to 18. Because any decimal number less than 1 includes a 0. before it, a numerical value can have as many as 20 digits.

Example

```
SET DECIMALS TO 2
? 3 / 5                && displays 0.60
SET DECIMALS TO 18     && maximum allowed
? 3 / 5                && displays 0.600000000000000000
```

SET DEFAULT TO

Syntax

```
SET DEFAULT TO <drive>[:]
```

Purpose: Specifies the default drive for all operations and file storage. The default is the drive that was in use when you started dBASE 5; the default can be changed with an entry in the CONFIG.DB file. The default directory is the one in use on the new default drive. Use the SET DIRECTORY command to change the default drive and directory in one step. See the example given for SET DIRECTORY TO.

Note

SET DEFAULT does not change the current DOS drive or directory; SET DIRECTORY may do either or both.

SET DELETED

Syntax

```
SET DELETED on/OFF
```

Purpose: Determines whether records marked for deletion are ignored by other dBASE 5 commands. If this command is set ON, marked records are not shown by commands such as LIST and DISPLAY. If this command is set OFF (the default), marked records are shown. The INDEX and REINDEX commands always include marked records, whether SET DELETED is on or off.

If you need to recall (unmark) records marked for deletion, use SET DELETED OFF so that the RECALL ALL command can access marked records.

Example

```
* Don't show deleted records during LIST
USE CustList
SET DELETED ON
BROWSE
SET DELETED OFF
```

SET DELIMITERS

Syntax

```
SET DELIMITERS on/OFF
```

Purpose: Determines whether the field delimiters (usually colons) are displayed around entry fields. SET DELIMITERS ON displays the entry field delimiters; SET DELIMITERS OFF (the default) does not display the delimiters. You can change the delimiter characters with the SET DELIMITERS TO command.

Example

```
* Don't want delimiters around input fields
SET DELIMITERS OFF
```

SET DELIMITERS TO

Syntax

```
SET DELIMITERS TO <delimiter characters> / DEFAULT
```

Purpose: Defines the characters used to delimit entry fields if SET DELIMITERS is set to ON. You can specify two characters; the first character is used for the beginning of the field, and the second character is used for the end of the field. You can change back to the default delimiters by issuing SET DELIMITERS TO without a value or by using SET DELIMITERS TO DEFAULT.

Example

```
* Set up field delimiters
SET DELIMITERS TO "<>"   && will show as "<entry area>"
SET DELIMITERS ON        && must be enabled to use delimiters
```

SET DESIGN

Syntax

```
SET DESIGN ON/off
```

Purpose: Controls access to the design mode, where the user can make changes to the database, report form, label, query, and applications from the Control Center. SET DESIGN OFF prevents design mode access; SET DESIGN ON enables design mode access.

Example

```
* Don't let user get into design screen
SET DESIGN OFF
```

SET DEVELOPMENT ON

Syntax

```
SET DEVELOPMENT ON/off
```

Purpose: Determines whether dBASE 5 checks the creation date and times of the compiled object file with the source code. If the program source is newer, the program is recompiled when SET DEVELOPMENT is ON and you use the DO <*program name*> command. SET DEVELOPMENT ON does the creation date and time checking (the default); SET DEVELOPMENT OFF does not check the creation date and times. The command normally is left ON to prevent the use of outdated object code files. If you used SET DEVELOPMENT OFF, you need to use COMPILE to compile the program files manually before you use the program.

Example

```
* Make sure source code has not changed since last COMPILE
SET DEVELOPMENT ON
```

SET DEVICE TO PRINTER

Syntax

```
SET DEVICE TO PRINTER
```

Purpose: Sends all @...SAY output to the printer rather than the screen. Any @...GET commands are ignored. If an @...SAY command specifies a row and column location that is above the current printer column and row, a page eject occurs. Output to the printer is cancelled with the SET DEVICE TO SCREEN/FILE command.

Example

```
* Ask whether user wants hard copy of current record
Answer = .F.
   @ 24,15 SAY "Print hard copy of this record? (Y/N) ";
      GET Answer PICTURE "Y"
   READ
IF Answer
   SET DEVICE TO PRINTER
   * Showdata routines displays screen data using @...SAYS
   DO ShowData
   SET DEVICE TO SCREEN
ENDIF
```

SET DEVICE TO SCREEN

Syntax

```
SET DEVICE TO SCREEN
```

Purpose: Sends @...SAY commands to the screen rather than to the printer (SET DEVICE TO PRINTER) or a file (SET DEVICE TO FILE <*filename*>). This command normally sends @...SAY commands back to the screen after a SET DEVICE TO PRINTER/FILE command.

Example

```
* Send a simple report to the printer
USE Orders
@ 11,35 SAY "Report printing"
SET DEVICE TO PRINTER
@ 2,35 SAY "BACK ORDER REPORT"   && report title
@ 3,35 SAY DATE(), TIME()
@ 5,0                            && skip to line 5
LIST Customer, PartNum, PartDesc, BackDate ;
   FOR BackDate < DATE()-30 TO PRINT
SET DEVICE TO SCREEN      && @...SAYs back to screen
EJECT                     && form feed
@ 12,35 SAY "REPORT FINISHED"
```

SET DIRECTORY TO

Syntax

```
SET DIRECTORY TO [[<drive>:][<path>]]
```

Purpose: Changes the current working drive and directory for all operations and storage of files. The <*drive*> parameter is optional, but if used it must include the colon (:). The <*drive*> and <*path*> parameters should have no spaces between them. SET DIRECTORY TO without parameters restores the drive and directory that were in use when you first started dBASE 5.

The SET DIRECTORY command is equivalent to a combination of the RUN<*drive*>: and RUN CD <*path*> commands. You can use the SET DIRECTORY command to change the default drive and directory in one command.

Example

```
* Change to the C:\CLIENT\DATA directory
SET DIRECTORY TO C:\CLIENT\DATA
```

SET DISPLAY TO

Syntax

```
SET DISPLAY TO MONO / COLOR / EGA25 / EGA43 / MONO43 /
    VGA25 / VGA43 / VGA50
```

Purpose: Selects a monochrome or color display, or sets the number of lines on EGA or VGA displays. If you SET DISPLAY to a display type not installed on your computer, an error message is shown on-screen.

Example

```
* Set up 43-line screen, then mono or color
* according to previously defined variable NeedMono
IF NeedMono
   SET DISPLAY TO MONO43
ELSE
   SET DISPLAY TO EGA43
ENDIF
```

SET ECHO

Syntax

```
SET ECHO on/OFF
```

Purpose: Determines whether commands from dBASE 5 programs are displayed on-screen (or sent to the printer, if SET DEBUG is ON) during execution. SET ECHO ON will display or print the commands; SET ECHO OFF (the default) will not display or print the commands. This command is useful during debugging, but can clutter the screen. Place SET ECHO ON and SET ECHO OFF around a block of program commands that are causing problems so that you see only those commands when program execution reaches that point in your code.

Example

```
* Check this area of the program for problems
SET DEBUG ON        && send commands to printer, not screen
SET ECHO ON         && start output
* Problem program block here
SET ECHO OFF        && stop output
SET DEBUG OFF       && reset debug status
```

SET EDITOR

Syntax

```
SET EDITOR TO [<full path name and suffix>]
```

Purpose: Allows you to use an external DOS text editor as the default editor. You can SET EDITOR from either the Command window or from within the CONFIG.DB file. This command does not change the way an editor object (created with the DEFINE EDITOR command) edits text.

SET ENCRYPTION

Syntax

```
SET ENCRYPTION ON/off
```

Purpose: Determines whether copied files—such as those created with COPY, JOIN, and TOTAL—are stored as encrypted files. Use SET ENCRYPTION OFF to copy a file to an unencrypted file. You must have logged on successfully with the PROTECT command to access an encrypted file.

Example

```
* Set encryption off for now
SET ENCRYPTION OFF
```

SET ESCAPE

Syntax

```
SET ESCAPE ON/off
```

Purpose: Determines whether pressing the Esc key halts the execution of a program or stops screen output. If SET ESCAPE is set to OFF, the Esc key is ignored, unless you are using Esc for INKEY( ) functions. The default ON setting enables the program to respond to Esc.

When Esc is pressed during a dBASE 5 program, you see an error box with three options: Cancel, Ignore, Suspend.

You then have the option of cancelling the current program, ignoring the pressing of Esc and resuming the program, or suspending the program. A suspended program can be continued with the RESUME command.

> **Caution**
>
> Make sure that the program is operating properly before you use the SET ESCAPE OFF command. With Esc disabled, you won't be able to stop programs stuck in endless loops. The only way to stop the program is to reboot your computer, which may cause data damage or loss. Test the program completely before using the SET ESCAPE OFF command.

SET EXACT

Syntax

```
SET EXACT on/OFF
```

Purpose: Determines whether the length of two compared character strings must be exactly the same. If SET EXACT is OFF, the second string is compared to the first string until the last character of the second string is reached. If the second string is longer than the first, the comparison will be false. If SET EXACT is ON, the strings must compare exactly, excluding trailing blanks. SET EXACT ON makes the equal sign (=) behave like the exact match operator (==).

Example

```
* Compare two strings
FirstOne = "Smithsonian"
SecondOne = "Smith"
SET EXACT OFF
? FirstOne = SecondOne          && returns .T.
? SecondOne = FirstOne          && returns .F.
SET EXACT ON
? FirstOne = SecondOne          && returns .F.
```

SET EXCLUSIVE

Syntax

```
SET EXCLUSIVE on/OFF
```

Purpose: Enables a user or program to open a database for exclusive use (SET EXCLUSIVE ON). This command prevents other users on a network from being able to access the database until SET EXCLUSIVE is set to OFF. If you use the CREATE and SAVE commands, EXCLUSIVE is set to ON.

Example

```
* Make sure that exclusive is ON
SET EXCLUSIVE ON
```

SET FIELDS

Syntax

```
SET FIELDS on/OFF
```

Purpose: Determines whether the fields list specified in the SET FIELDS TO command is used. If SET FIELDS is OFF, all fields in all databases are available for use. Using the SET FIELDS TO command turns SET FIELDS ON.

Example

```
USE Inventory
SET FIELDS TO Part,Desc
LIST TO PRINT    && only Part and Desc are listed
SET FIELDS OFF
LIST TO PRINT    && all fields are listed.
```

SET FIELDS TO

Syntax

```
SET FIELDS TO [<field> [/R] /<calculated field id>...]
   [,<field> [/R] /<calculated field id>...]
```

Purpose: Determines the fields used as defaults when you use commands such as LIST and DISPLAY. The /R parameter sets the read-only flag for database fields. You can specify calculated fields, such as QtyPrice = Qty_Ord * UnitPrice. Use SET FIELDS TO without parameters to clear the field list. The SET FIELDS TO command is additive; specifying additional commands adds to the field list.

Example

```
* Specify active fields
SET FIELDS TO ID_Code, ItemDesc, QtyPrice = Qty_Ord * UnitPrice
```

SET FIELDS TO ALL

Syntax

```
SET FIELDS TO ALL [LIKE/EXCEPT <skeleton>]
```

Purpose: Enables you to specify similarly named fields to the field list. The *<skeleton>* can include the ? wild card, which indicates any match in that character position, and the * wild card, which indicates any match for multiple character positions.

Example

```
* Add to the current field list
* Adds CustNum, CustName, CustAddr, CustCity, etc.
SET FIELDS TO ALL LIKE Cust*
```

SET FILTER TO

Syntax

```
SET FILTER TO [FILE <filename>/?] [<condition>]
```

Purpose: Causes only those records that meet the *<condition>* to be accessed by other dBASE 5 commands. The TO FILE *<filename>* option uses a dBASE III Plus-type query file. The FILE ? option displays a list of available query files.

This command applies only to the current work area. Use a GO TOP or SKIP command to initialize the action of the filter so that subsequent records will meet the filter *<condition>*.

Note

The SET FILTER command runs faster if you have indexed your data table on the same fields as the filter. As long as the index is created prior to applying the filter, the index does not need to be active. If a database has an index, a filter applied to a data table consisting of one million records will only take a couple of seconds to return the requested information.

Example

```
* Limit access to part numbers 14000 - 14999
USE Parts
SET FILTER TO PartNum >= 14000 .AND. PartNum < 15000
```

SET FIXED

Syntax

```
SET FIXED on/OFF
```

Purpose: This command is provided to maintain compatibility with dBASE III programs; it is ignored by later versions of dBASE. Use the SET DECIMALS command in dBASE IV and 5 programs.

SET FORMAT TO

Syntax

```
SET FORMAT TO [<format filename> / ? ]
```

Purpose: Enables a previously defined screen format (FMT) file to be used for data input with the READ, EDIT, APPEND, INSERT, CHANGE, or BROWSE commands. The format file is created with the CREATE/MODIFY SCREEN command or from the Control Center. If the compiled format file (FMO) is not found, the FMT file is compiled and used. Use the ? parameter to choose from a list of available format files. Close the format file with a CLOSE FORMAT command or by issuing SET FORMAT TO without parameters.

You can only use this command with non-UI screens and windows like those created in previous versions of dBASE. It is ignored by dBASE 5's UI objects.

Note

Use the MODIFY SCREEN command to change a format file. Using the MODIFY COMMAND command produces differences between the FMO and FMT files.

Example

```
* Use the format file for the entry screen
USE Clients
SET FORMAT TO Client
APPEND
```

SET FULLPATH

Syntax

```
SET FULLPATH on/OFF
```

Purpose: Determines whether the full drive and path names are returned with functions such as DBF( ) and NDX( ).

Example

```
SET DIRECTORY TO D:\CLIENT\DATA
USE Invoice
SET FULLPATH OFF
? DBF()        && returns "D:INVOICE.DBF"
SET FULLPATH ON
? DBF()        && returns "D:\CLIENT\DATA\INVOICE.DBF"
```

SET FUNCTION

Syntax

```
SET FUNCTION <key number> / <key name> / <key label>
   TO <command string>
```

Purpose: Assigns the *<command string>* to the function key. You can indicate the function key by its number (1 through 10), by its name (for example, Shift-F10), or by its key label (for example, F10). Use the semicolon (;) to indicate simulating the Enter key. You can assign commands to keys F2 through F10, Shift-F1 through Shift-F10, and Ctrl-F1 through Ctrl-F10. The Alt-F1 through Alt-F10 keys are available for macros only. The F11 and F12 keys are not available for programming.

Example

```
* Assign current date to F10
SET FUNCTION F10 TO DTOC(DATE())
* Assign current time to Shift-F10
SET FUNCTION SHIFT-F10 TO TIME()
* Assign "Newcastle", Enter key, "CA" to Ctrl-F3
SET FUNCTION CTRL-F3 TO "Newcastle;CA"
```

SET HEADINGS

Syntax

```
SET HEADINGS ON/off
```

Purpose: Controls whether field headings show when you use the DISPLAY, LIST, SUM, or AVERAGE command. If SET HEADINGS is ON (the default), field headings are shown. If SET HEADINGS is OFF, field headings are not shown. When SET HEADINGS is ON, the width of the column is set to the width of the field name or the width of the field, whichever is greater.

Note

The field headings appear in uppercase if you used uppercase field names in LIST or other commands. If the field names are in lowercase, the field name headings are displayed or printed in lowercase.

Example

```
* Turn on the headings for this quick list
SET HEADINGS ON
USE CustList
LIST CustName, Contact, Phone TO PRINT
SET HEADINGS OFF
```

SET HELP

Syntax

```
SET HELP ON/off
```

Purpose: Determines whether the dBASE 5 Help option is available if an incorrect command is entered at the Command window. The Error box contains three options: Cancel, to cancel the command; Edit, to edit the command and then re-execute it; and Help, to display the dBASE 5 help box for that command.

Example

```
* Disable help option at Command window
SET HELP OFF
```

SET HISTORY

Syntax

```
SET HISTORY ON/off
```

Purpose: dBASE 5 does not recognize this command, but does not return an error message if it is used.

Stores commands typed at the Command window in a history buffer. With SET HISTORY set to ON, you can use the up- and down-arrow keys to recall previous commands to the current Command window. The LIST HISTORY and DISPLAY HISTORY commands also show the contents of the history buffer, which normally contains the last 20 commands executed. The size of the history buffer is specified by the SET HISTORY TO command.

Example

See SET HISTORY TO for an example.

SET HISTORY TO

Syntax

```
SET HISTORY TO <number of commands>
```

Purpose: dBASE 5 does not recognize this command, but does not return an error message if it is used.

Sets the size of the history buffer, which can be from 0 to 16,000 commands. SET HISTORY TO 0 clears the contents of the history buffer.

Example

```
* Store 50 commands in history buffer
SET HISTORY TO 50
```

SET HOURS TO

Syntax

```
SET HOURS TO [12/24]
```

Purpose: Displays time clock (if SET CLOCK is ON) using a 12- or 24-hour clock; the default is a 12-hour clock. SET HOURS TO without a parameter changes the value to the default, which can be set to either value in the CONFIG.DB file.

Example

```
* Set up clock display in upper right corner
* Current time is 9:31:44 pm
SET CLOCK ON             && turns on clock display
SET CLOCK TO 12          && clock displays 9:31:44
SET CLOCK TO 24          && clock displays 21:31:44
```

SET IBLOCK TO

Syntax

```
SET IBLOCK TO <number of 512-byte blocks>
```

Purpose: Changes the default size of the indexing block allocated for new index files. Even though the default value of SET IBLOCK TO is 1, index blocks are always at least 1,024 bytes in size, so the default index block size is 1,024 bytes. Valid settings for SET IBLOCK TO range from 1 to 63 units, each unit being 512 bytes.

Example

```
* Set index block size to 2048 bytes
USE CustList
SET IBLOCK TO 4
```

SET INDEX TO

Syntax

```
SET INDEX TO ?/<filename list> [ORDER <NDX filename> /
   [TAG] <MDX tag> [OF <MDX filename>]]
```

Purpose: Opens index files for the current database. If NDX files are used, the first index file name in the *<filename list>* is the active or controlling index; the other index files are updated but do not control the movement through the file. Both index (NDX) and multiple-index (MDX) files are available. The command attempts first to open an MDX file; if the command cannot find one, it opens an NDX file.

The TAG *<MDX tag>* OF *<MDX filename>* option enables you to specify the tag name contained in the MDX file. The ORDER option enables you to specify a controlling index that is not the first index file in the *<filename list>*. You also can change the controlling index with the SET ORDER TO command. Use SET INDEX TO without any parameters to close the current indexes.

Note

You should keep all indexes up-to-date when you use a database. If the indexes are not current, the `Record not in index` error message may occur, or searching for a record with FIND or SEEK will be unsuccessful.

Example

```
* Order file by Names index
USE CustList
SET INDEX TO Names
```

SET INSTRUCT

Syntax

```
SET INSTRUCT ON/off
```

Purpose: Determines whether the prompt boxes are displayed or whether the dBASE 5 code is shown while reports, labels, and forms are being generated.

Example

```
* Turn off prompt boxes, etc.
SET INSTRUCT OFF
```

SET INTENSITY

Syntax

```
SET INTENSITY ON/off
```

Purpose: Determines whether the enhanced screen color is used for @...GET commands (@..SAY commands use the standard screen color). Screen colors are set with the SET COLOR TO command.

Example

```
* Turn on high intensity for this message
SET INTENSITY ON
Answer = .F.
@ 12,20 SAY "Are you sure? (Y/N) " ;
GET Answer PICTURE "Y"
READ
```

SET KEY TO

Syntax

```
SET KEY TO [<value> ¦ RANGE [<low value>[,<high value>]]]
EXCLUDE [HIGH ¦ LOW]
```

Purpose: Filters the database to permit the display of only records meeting the conditions specified. Because it operates on an index key, SET KEY requires that a database be in use with an active index. SET KEY TO issued without any of the optional arguments cancels the filtering specified in the previous SET KEY command. Data types for optional expressions should be the same. The EXCLUDE option allows you to ignore the high or low end point values of the range entered in RANGE. To change the range, you must give the SET KEY command again, entering new values for the range.

Example

```
USE Customer ORDER City
SET KEY TO "Chicago","Dallas"
```

SET LDCHECK

Syntax

```
SET LDCHECK ON/off
```

Purpose: dBASE IV Version 2.0 and dBASE 5 support language drivers that determine the character set and language tables used. SET LDCHECK enables or disables language driver ID checking, which is important when using files created with different international versions of dBASE. (See LANGTABLES and ASCIISORT in Chapter 29, "Using the System Configuration File.")

Example

```
SET LDCHECK ON      && Turn language driver checking on
USE MyFile
SET LDCHECK OFF     && Turn language driver checking off
```

SET LIBRARY TO

Syntax

```
SET LIBRARY TO [<filename>]
```

Purpose: Enables you to specify a library file that contains procedures and functions to be used throughout your dBASE programs.

Example

```
SET LIBRARY TO LibProc
```

SET LOCK

Syntax

```
SET LOCK ON/off
```

Purpose: Determines whether certain dBASE commands will automatically lock database files in a multiuser system. With SET LOCK ON, the commands listed in Table 24.5 will automatically try to lock a file. Automatic locking is disabled by SET LOCK OFF.

Table 24.5 Commands That Automatically Lock Files

Command	Action	Level	SET LOCK OFF Disables LOCK?
@GET/READ	Edit	Record	No
APPEND FROM	Update	File	No
APPEND [blank]	Update	Record	No

Command	Action	Level	SET LOCK OFF Disables LOCK?
AVERAGE	Read only	File	Yes
BROWSE	Edit	Record	No
CALCULATE	Read only	File	Yes
CHANGE/EDIT	Edit	Record	No
COPY TAG	Read/write	File	Yes on read/ No on write
COPY [STRUCTURE]	Read/write	File	Yes on read/ No on write
COUNT	Read only	File	Yes
DELETE/RECALL	Update	Record	No
DELETE/RECALL	Update	File	No
EDIT	Update	Record	No
INDEX	Read/write	File	Yes on read/ No on write
JOIN	Read/write	File	Yes on read/ No on write
LABEL	Read only	File	Yes
REPLACE	Update	Record	No
REPLACE [scope]	Update	File	No
REPORT	Read only	File	Yes
SET CATALOG ON	Catalog	File	No
SORT	Read/write	File	Yes on read/ No on write
SUM	Read only	File	Yes
TOTAL	Read/write	File	Yes on read/ No on write
UPDATE	Update	File	No

Example

```
* Enable automatic file locking
SET LOCK ON
* Disable automatic locking
SET LOCK OFF
```

SET MARGIN TO

Syntax

```
SET MARGIN TO <number of columns>
```

Purpose: Sets the left margin value for all printed output. You also can use the `_ploffset` system memory value to set the left margin. Both commands affect the left margin, but only the last command is used—the two are not additive. The system memory variable `_lmargin` is added to the SET MARGIN value when `_wrap` is true (.T.).

Example

```
* Set the left margin if not correct
IF _ploffset <> 10
   SET MARGIN TO 10
ENDIF
```

SET MARK TO

Syntax

```
SET MARK TO [<single character>]
```

Purpose: Changes the delimiter used in the date display of month/day/year. Any single character can be used. The default is the slash (/), but the delimiter also can be determined by the format selected with the SET DATE command. SET MARK overrides the character specified in SET DATE.

Example

```
* Change the date delimiter
* Current date is 06/15/92
SET CENTURY OFF
SET DATE TO USA
? DATE()            && displays "06-15-92"
SET DATE TO MDY
? DATE()            && displays "06/15/92"
SET MARK TO "."
? DATE()            && displays "06.15.92"
```

SET MBLOCK TO

Syntax

```
SET MBLOCK TO <number of 64-byte blocks>
```

Purpose: Changes the default size of the block allocated for new memo field files. The default value of SET MBLOCK TO is 8, which is equivalent to 512 bytes (8 x 64). By using 64-byte units, SET MBLOCK TO allows you to allocate blocks in smaller units than the SET BLOCKSIZE TO command, which can help save disk space if you are using small memo fields. SET MBLOCK TO also allows you to set the memo block size independent of the index block size.

Example

```
* Set the memo block size to 128 bytes
SET MBLOCK TO 2
CREATE CustList
```

SET MEMOWIDTH

Syntax

```
SET MEMOWIDTH TO <number of characters>
```

Purpose: Determines the width of memo fields when they are sent to the screen or printer. The default value is 50; the range can be from 8 to 255. Word wrap will occur if the system variable `_wrap` is set to true (.T.). (See Chapter 27, "Using System Memory Variables.")

Example

```
* Set up memo field width of 45
SET MEMOWIDTH TO 45
_wrap = .T.      && make sure that word wrap is enabled
```

SET MENU

Syntax

```
SET MENU ON/off
```

Purpose: This command is provided for compatibility with dBASE III programs; it is ignored by dBASE 5.

SET MESSAGE TO

Syntax

```
SET MESSAGE TO [<message text> [AT <row> [,<column>]]]
```

Purpose: Displays the *<message text>* at the *<row>*, *<column>* location. If the AT *<row>*, *<column>* parameter is not specified, the message is displayed at line 24 (on 25-line screens) or line 42 (on 43-line screens). If the *<column>* parameter is not specified, the message is centered on the *<row>*. If SET STATUS is ON, the message is displayed on the bottom line. If you want a message to appear on line 0 (the top line), first use SET SCOREBOARD OFF and turn off the clock display. The message may contain as many as 79 characters.

The SET MESSAGE location also is used for @...SAY...GET commands that have a MESSAGE parameter. Messages are not displayed inside window areas, and may overwrite them.

Example

```
* Put all data entry messages at the screen bottom
* They will be centered, because no <column> was specified
* The ScrnLines variable was previously set for the
* number of lines on the screen
SET MESSAGE TO "DATA ENTRY" AT ScrnLines
```

SET MOUSE

Syntax

```
SET MOUSE ON/off
```

Purpose: Enables the mouse pointer in dBASE 5. If SET MOUSE is ON, the mouse pointer is displayed. SET MOUSE OFF disables display of the mouse pointer. The default setting is ON if a mouse driver is installed when dBASE is started. If you issue SET MOUSE ON when no mouse driver is available, an error message is displayed. You can only use this command with non-UI screens and windows like those created in previous versions of dBASE. It is ignored by dBASE 5's UI objects.

Example

```
* Check to see if mouse installed, then turn on mouse
IF ISMOUSE( )
    SET MOUSE ON
ENDIF
```

SET NEAR

Syntax

```
SET NEAR on/OFF
```

Purpose: When SET NEAR is set to ON, a FIND or SEEK puts the record pointer just after the most likely location of the desired record, if the SEEK or FIND was unsuccessful. You therefore can get close to the desired record even if an exact match cannot be found. With SET NEAR OFF (the default), an unsuccessful FIND or SEEK will place the record pointer at the end of the file.

With SET NEAR ON, FOUND( ) is true for an exact match and false for a near match, and EOF( ) may be false with a near match. With SET NEAR OFF, FOUND( ) is false and EOF( ) is true if no exact match is found.

Example

```
* Set up near matches for the find routine
SET NEAR ON
DO FindCust          && find customer program
SET NEAR OFF
IF .NOT. FOUND()
   DO SHOW MISS      && Show near matches
ENDIF
```

SET ODOMETER TO

Syntax

```
SET ODOMETER TO <record count interval>
```

Purpose: Determines the update interval for functions that display a record counter. The default value is 1, and the maximum is 200. To remove the record counter from the screen for operations such as COPY, RECALL, and INDEX, use SET TALK OFF.

Note

A low odometer value can slightly degrade the performance of some commands.

Example

```
* Turn on the record counter for reindexing
USE Clients INDEX Clients
SET ODOMETER TO 20
SET TALK ON          && enable display of odometer
RINDEX
```

SET ORDER TO

Syntax

```
SET ORDER TO
SET ORDER TO <index number>
SET ORDER TO <filename> / [TAG] <MDX tagname> [OF <MDX filename>]
   [NOSAVE]
```

Purpose: The SET ORDER TO command offers three alternatives:

- The first alternative inactivates any index for the current database. Records are shown in their natural, record-number order.

- The second command determines the active NDX index, where *<index number>* is the relative position of the desired index as given in the index list. The *<index number>* can be from 0 to 10 (a value of 0 resets to natural order). This command maintains compatibility with dBASE III NDX index files when there are no open MDX files.

- The third alternative assigns the controlling dBASE 5 index files or tags; the order must be specified with the order file name, not its number. The [OF *<MDX filename>*] option is used if an identical tag name appears in two or more open MDX files or when you want to use an index file other than the production MDX file. The NOSAVE option tells dBASE not to save newly created indexes when the MDX file is closed.

Example

```
* Place the CUSTLIST file in
* Zip Code index order
USE CustList
SET ORDER TO TAG Zip
* Put file in natural order
SET ORDER TO
```

SET PATH TO

Syntax

```
SET PATH TO <path list>
```

Purpose: Like the DOS PATH command, SET PATH TO specifies the drive and directories that will be used by dBASE 5 to find files (normally program files) not in the current directory. The *<path list>* can contain as many as 60 characters, and each directory must be separated by a semicolon (;).

> **Note**
>
> If you specified a path with the DOS PATH command, dBASE 5 ignores it. To use a path, you must specify it from within dBASE. The Control Center does not use the SET PATH path specification. The DIR command uses only the current directory.

Example

```
SET PATH TO C:\DBASE4\PROGRAMS;C:\DBASE4
```

SET PAUSE

Syntax

```
SET PAUSE on/OFF
```

Purpose: Determines whether the screen output of SQL SELECT commands pauses with each screenful of data. SET PAUSE ON enables pausing of the display; SET PAUSE OFF (the default) causes the screen output to continue until the command is complete. The SET PAUSE setting is similar to the difference between the LIST and DISPLAY commands: SET PAUSE OFF is like LIST; SET PAUSE ON is like DISPLAY.

Example

```
* Pause after each screenful of SQL data
SET PAUSE ON
```

SET POINT TO

Syntax

```
SET POINT TO <decimal point character>
```

Purpose: Changes the character used as the decimal point in numbers. The default is a period (.), but this can be changed to a comma (,) for international users. Any single character can be used except a number or a space. To change back to the default value, use SET POINT TO without a parameter value.

Example

```
* Set up for normal decimal character
SET POINT TO "."
```

SET PRECISION TO

Syntax

```
SET PRECISION TO <number of decimal places>
```

Purpose: Determines the number of decimal places used internally by dBASE 5 in all mathematical calculations of type-N numbers. The default value is 16, but any value from 10 to 20 can be used.

Example

```
* Set up maximum precision
SET PRECISION TO 20
```

SET PRINTER

Syntax

```
SET PRINTER on/OFF
```

Purpose: Determines whether output (other than @...SAY output) is sent to the printer (SET PRINTER ON).

Example

```
* List system status to printer
* while showing screen message
SET PRINTER ON
CLEAR
@ 12,15 SAY "Printing system status"
LIST STATUS
EJECT
SET PRINTER OFF
```

SET PRINTER TO

Syntax

```
SET PRINTER TO <DOS device>
SET PRINTER TO \\<computer name>\<printer name> =
   <destination>
SET PRINTER TO FILE <filename>
```

Purpose: SET PRINTER TO offers three options:

- The first alternative determines the output port for all printed output. The *<DOS device>* normally is set to PRN, but you can change it to any of the three parallel ports (LPT1, LPT2, LPT3) or the serial ports (COM1, COM2, COM3, COM4).
- The second alternative sends output to a shared network printer and tells the network server to print the next print job. The *<computer name>* is the network-assigned name for the network file server. The *<printer name>* is the network-assigned name for the printer on the network. The *<destination>* is the installed shared printer, such as LPT1, LPT2, or LPT3.
- The third alternative sends printer output to the file specified in *<filename>*. The output includes the printer control commands used by the currently installed printer driver (as defined by the `_pdriver` system memory variable). After you use this command, you can use the DOS COPY command at any time to send the printer-formatted file to the printer. All printed output is sent to the *<filename>* until you use a SET PRINTER TO command without parameters.

Example

```
* Send output to LPT2:
SET PRINTER TO LPT2
* Send output to the network printer
SET PRINTER TO \\MAINCPU\PRINTER = LPT1
* Send printed output to a file
SET PRINTER TO FILE OUTPUT.TXT
```

SET PROCEDURE TO

Syntax

```
SET PROCEDURE TO [<procedure filename>]
```

Purpose: Opens a procedure file (*<procedure filename>*) that contains a number of routines used by a dBASE 5 program. You can have as many as 963 procedures in a procedure file, but you're limited to the number of procedures that fit in available memory (RAM). Most procedure files are short routines. You can close a procedure file with the CLOSE PROCEDURE command or by using SET PROCEDURE TO without a file name parameter.

When you use this command, dBASE assumes that the procedures have been compiled to an object code file with a DBO file extension. If the object code file cannot be found, the source file is compiled to a DBO file. Only one procedure file can be active at one time.

Caution

Make sure that your procedure program does not have the same file name as any other program. If it does, the compiled procedure will overwrite the other program's compiled file.

Example

```
* Open the procedure file
SET PROCEDURE TO ProgProc
```

SET REFRESH TO

Syntax

```
SET REFRESH TO <number of seconds>
```

Purpose: Sets the time interval in *<number of seconds>* when dBASE 5 checks a file to determine whether a record being browsed or edited has been changed. The default value is 0, and the value can range from 0 to 3,600 seconds (one hour). When the refresh value expires, dBASE 5 checks any files in a BROWSE or EDIT mode and updates the screens with any changes that are found.

Example

```
* Update screen every 15 seconds
SET REFRESH TO 15
```

SET RELATION TO

Syntax

```
SET RELATION TO [<key expression> INTO <alias>
   [, <key expression> INTO <alias>...]]
```

Purpose: Links two databases together, based on a common *<key expression>*. The *<key expression>* value must match the controlling index of the child database. You can set multiple relations by specifying additional key expressions into *<alias>* parameters. The INTO *<alias>* database must have been opened previously with a USE command. The active (parent) database is linked to the child database with the child database's INTO *<alias>* name. When you move through the active parent database, the child database follows the key expression of the parent database if SET SKIP TO is defined. If the child database doesn't have a matching record, the record pointer is positioned at EOF( ).

Example

```
* Link the Customer's State field with the SalesTax field
SELECT 2                      && child database
USE SalesTax ORDER State      && indexed on State field
SELECT 1                      && parent database
USE Customer
* set the parent-child relation
SET RELATION TO Customer->State INTO SalesTax
* show the Customer's State and Sales Tax Rate
LIST Customer->State, SalesTax->State, SalesTax->Rate
```

SET REPROCESS TO

Syntax

```
SET REPROCESS TO [<number of retries>]
```

Purpose: Determines the number of times that dBASE 5 tries a network record or file lock command before returning an error. The default is 0; if you don't specify the ON ERROR command, the message Please wait, another user has locked this record or file appears until the record or file is available. The command is retried until the record or file is available or until you press the Esc key. Allowable values are from –1 to 32,000. The –1 value sets up an infinite retry that cannot be canceled with the Esc key.

Example

```
* Set up 20 tries as maximum
* An err_trap routine will tell the user
* that the record is in use by another
SET REPROCESS TO 20
```

SET SAFETY

Syntax

```
SET SAFETY ON/off
```

Purpose: Prevents existing files from being overwritten accidentally. If SET SAFETY is ON, the message File already exists, Overwrite or Cancel appears when you try to overwrite an existing file. You then must select Overwrite to overwrite the file. Because SET SAFETY OFF assumes that you want to overwrite an existing file, the message is not displayed. UI editor objects do not recognize SET SAFETY commands, so be sure to provide protection against accidental overwriting or erasing of files by users.

Note

With SET SAFETY OFF, files will be overwritten or erased. Make sure that you are aware of the SET SAFETY status before you use commands that overwrite or erase files.

Example

```
* Reindex the file; automatically overwrite the old index
USE Students
SET SAFETY OFF
INDEX ON LastName + FirstName TO Students
* Make sure that user verifies zapping a database
SET SAFETY ON
USE TempData EXCLUSIVE
ZAP
```

SET SCOREBOARD

Syntax

```
SET SCOREBOARD ON/off
```

Purpose: Determines whether the keyboard indicators show on line 0 of the screen. This line is hidden by the Desktop menu in dBASE 5. SET SCOREBOARD ON (along with SET STATUS OFF) displays the keyboard indicators. (If SET STATUS is ON, the SET SCOREBOARD command is ignored.)

The indicators are: Del to indicate records marked for deletion (in BROWSE and EDIT), Ins for Insert mode, Caps for Caps Lock mode, and Num for Number Lock mode. SET SCOREBOARD OFF erases all data from the screen, providing an easy way to clear your screen during program execution by setting SCOREBOARD OFF then ON.

Example

```
* Don't need the scoreboard on
SET SCOREBOARD OFF
```

SET SEPARATOR TO

Syntax

```
SET SEPARATOR TO [<separator character>]
```

Purpose: Determines the character used as the thousands separator. The default is the comma, but this default can be changed to any character. This command is used most commonly with the SET POINT and SET CURRENCY commands. Only one character is allowed as the separator character. See SET CURRENCY TO for an example.

SET SKIP TO

Syntax

```
SET SKIP TO [<alias> [, <alias> ] ...]
```

Purpose: When this command is used with the SET RELATION command, it makes all records in the child database accessible as you move the record pointer through the parent database. The *<alias>* activates the SET SKIP command for those *<alias>* databases that you specify. The SKIP list is active until you use a SET SKIP TO command without any parameters.

Example

```
* Set up the grades and students relationship
* The Grades database is indexed on the StudentId field
* as is the Students database
USE Grades IN 2 ORDER StudentID   && work area 2
USE Students IN 1                 && work area 2
SELECT 1
* Sets up the relation
SET RELATION TO StudentId INTO Grades
* Make sure that all grade records are used
SET SKIP TO Grades
* List all the student's test scores
LIST Students->StudentId, Students->LastName,;
   Student->FirstName,;
Grades->TestDate, Grades->Score
```

SET SPACE

Syntax

```
SET SPACE ON/off
```

Purpose: Determines whether a space is printed between variables or data when the LIST, DISPLAY, ?, or ?? commands are used. If SET SPACE is ON, a space is printed between the characters; SET SPACE OFF prevents printing of the space.

Example

```
FirstName = "Erica"
LastName = "Jean"
SET SPACE ON
? FirstName, LastName    && results in "Erica Jean"
SET SPACE OFF
? FirstName, LastName    && results in "EricaJean"
```

SET SQL

Syntax

```
SET SQL on/OFF
```

Purpose: Enables the use of SQL commands at the Command window. SET SQL ON enables the use of SQL commands; SET SQL OFF disables the use of SQL commands. When the SQL commands are enabled, the SQL prompt is shown in place of the Command window. The SET SQL command cannot be used in programs.

Example

```
SET SQL ON   && Used only at Command window, not in programs
```

SET STATUS

Syntax

```
SET STATUS ON/off
```

Purpose: Determines whether the status bar is shown at the bottom of the screen. The status bar contains the current command name, the file in use, the current record number, the total number of records, the scoreboarded information (Del, Caps, Ins, Num), and whether dBASE is in SQL or Command mode.

Example

```
* Turn off status bar
SET STATUS OFF
```

SET STEP

Syntax

```
SET STEP on/OFF
```

Purpose: Performs one command at a time, halting between commands. When SET STEP is ON, the message Press SPACE to Step, S to Suspend, or Esc to Cancel... is displayed between the execution of each command. You can press the space bar to execute the next command, press S to suspend the program and display the Command window, or press Esc to cancel the currently executing program. SET STEP is used primarily during debugging. The default value is OFF.

Example

```
* Turn step on for problem code area
SET STEP ON
```

SET TALK

Syntax

```
SET TALK ON/off
```

Purpose: Determines whether the response to dBASE 5 commands is displayed after the command is entered. Programs normally contain a SET TALK OFF command to disable the dBASE 5 command response because responses would clutter the screen. Use SET TALK ON (the default) to show the responses.

Example

```
* Turn off dBASE 5 responses
* They just clutter the screen during the program
SET TALK OFF
```

SET TITLE

Syntax

```
SET TITLE ON/off
```

Purpose: Determines whether the catalog file title prompt is displayed. If SET TITLE is ON, creating or adding to a report, label, database, query, form, program, or application produces a prompt for the catalog title. (The catalog file title is shown as the description in these cases.) If SET TITLE is OFF, the catalog title prompt is not displayed.

Example

```
* Don't need to show the catalog title prompt
SET TITLE OFF
```

SET TRAP

Syntax

```
SET TRAP on/OFF
```

Purpose: Activates the dBASE 5 debugger when a program causes an error or when the Esc key is pressed. If SET TRAP is OFF (default), pressing the Esc key displays a message box with three options: Cancel, Ignore, and Suspend.

You have the option of canceling the current program, ignoring the pressing of the Esc key, or suspending the program. A suspended program can be continued with the RESUME command. When SET TRAP is ON, dBASE 5 brings up the debugger when an error occurs or when the Esc key is pressed (*see* DEBUG).

If an ON ERROR command is in effect, SET TRAP is ignored, and the ON ERROR statement is executed.

SET TYPEAHEAD TO

Syntax

```
SET TYPEAHEAD TO <number of characters>
```

Purpose: Specifies the size of the type-ahead buffer. The buffer normally holds 20 characters (keystrokes); allowable values are from 0 to 32,000. During full-screen editing or appending, the keyboard buffer stores 20 characters only, regardless of the SET TYPEAHEAD TO value. You can use the CLEAR TYPEAHEAD command to clear the keyboard buffer.

> **Note**
>
> If you have an error-handling procedure in your program, you may want to set the TYPEAHEAD buffer to 0 to disable the keyboard buffer. Doing so ensures that errors are trapped properly and that the error-handling procedure is not bypassed inadvertently by unprocessed keystrokes in the buffer.

Example

```
* Disable TYPEAHEAD because the ON ERROR command is used
ON ERROR DO err_trap     && error trapping procedure
SET TYPEAHEAD TO 0
* Clear out any characters in keyboard buffer
CLEAR TYPEAHEAD
```

SET UNIQUE

Syntax

```
SET UNIQUE on/OFF
```

Purpose: SET UNIQUE ON includes in an index only the first record of records having the same key value. To include all records in the index, use SET UNIQUE OFF.

Example

```
* Print a list of only the unique city names in the database
USE CustList
SET UNIQUE ON
INDEX ON City TAG CityUniq   && also activates the new index
LIST City TO PRINT
```

SET VIEW TO

Syntax

```
SET VIEW TO <query filename> / ?
```

Purpose: Executes a query (QBO or QBE) that was created with the Control Center or at the Command window (with CREATE/MODIFY VIEW). Use the ? parameter to choose from a list of available queries. If a catalog is open and SET CATALOG is ON, the catalog is updated to include the *<query filename>*. dBASE prompts you for a title only if SET TITLE is ON. dBASE III VUE files are reformated to QBE files and compiled if you use them in the SET VIEW TO command.

Example

```
* Set up the customer status query
USE Clients
SET VIEW TO CustStat
```

SET WINDOW OF MEMO TO

Syntax

```
SET WINDOW OF MEMO TO <window name>
```

Purpose: Determines the window specification (*<window name>*) that is used when you edit memo fields with the APPEND, BROWSE, CHANGE, EDIT, or READ command. The *<window name>* must have been specified previously with the DEFINE WINDOW command. You can override this window for an individual memo field by using the WINDOW parameter of an @...GET command.

You can only use this command with non-UI screens and windows like those created in previous versions of dBASE. It is ignored by dBASE 5's UI objects.

Example

```
USE Clients        && has a memo field called Notes
DEFINE WINDOW Memo_Wind FROM 15,0 TO 20,79
SET WINDOW OF MEMO TO Memo_Wind
@ 1,1 GET Notes
```

SET WP

Syntax

```
SET WP TO [<full path name and suffix>]
```

Purpose: Determines the editor to be used within memo fields. This can be useful if the memo field contains data of a type different from the editor objects—for instance, .PCX file, or a specialized word processing package. You can SET WP from the Command window or from the CONFIG.DB file. This setting does not cause any changes to occur to the settings issued by the DEFINE EDITOR or MODIFY COMMAND/FILE commands. The user presses Ctrl-Home to open the memo field and enter the editing window for the editor set by this command.

Chapter 25

Using SQL Commands

The SQL commands are similar to many of their dBASE 5 counterparts. SQL commands work on *tables* or *views*, which are selected records from a SQL database. Table 25.1 shows important SQL terms and their equivalent terms in dBASE 5.

It is important to note that dBASE 5's compiler does not support SQL commands. Thus, SQL commands only function in interactive SQL mode in dBASE. If the compiler finds a SET SQL command in a program it is attempting to compile, it returns an error and does not create the object defined.

Table 25.1 Comparing SQL and dBASE Terms

SQL	dBASE
Database	Database
Table	Data table
Row	Record
Column	Field

SQL Data Types

The SQL language supports eight *data types*, which are similar to the data types used in dBASE 5. Table 25.2 shows the different data types.

Table 25.2 SQL Data Types

Type	Description
SMALLINT	Whole numbers from –99,999 to 999,999.
INTEGER	Positive whole numbers up to 11 digits, negative whole numbers up to 10 digits.
FLOAT (*x*,*y*)	Exponential numbers from 0.1e–307 to 0.9e+308, where *x* = the total number of digits, maximum 20 *y* = number decimal places, maximum 18
DECIMAL (*x*,*y*)	Decimal numbers to 19 significant digits (with a negative sign as one digit in negative numbers), where *x* = the total number of digits, maximum 19 *y* = number decimal places, maximum 18
NUMERIC (*x*,*y*)	Numbers to 20 significant digits (with a negative sign as one digit in negative numbers), where *x* = the total number of digits + 1 for the decimal point, maximum 20 *y* = number decimal places, maximum 18
DATE	A date in the form mm/dd/yy.
CHAR(*n*)	A series of as many as 254 characters, enclosed in single or double quotation marks, where *n* represents the number of characters. You can compare character-type columns only to other character-type columns or string constants.
LOGICAL	True (.T. or .Y.) or false (.F. or .N.) values. You can compare LOGICAL columns only to other LOGICAL columns or constants.

Make sure you are comparing only compatible data types; you cannot, for example, compare character columns with float-type columns. INTEGER, SMALLINT, FLOAT, DECIMAL, and NUMERIC column types are compatible with each other.

SQL Functions Used in SELECT

The SQL functions that can be used in the SELECT command are shown in Table 25.3.

When you use SQL functions, the column name is placed within the parentheses, as in SUM(ord_qty), which sums the ORD_QTY column. You also can use the column number, as in SUM(3), which sums the values in column 3 of the table or view.

Table 25.3 SQL SELECT Functions

Function	Description
COUNT( )	Counts the number of selected rows.
SUM( )	Sums the values in a numeric column.
MIN( )	Determines the minimum value in the column. The column can be a character, date, or numeric column.
MAX( )	Determines the maximum value in the column. The column can be a character, date, or numeric column.
AVG( )	Determines the average value in a numeric column.

SQL Predicates

SQL predicates are the words BETWEEN, IN, and LIKE used in the WHERE clause. BETWEEN looks for values within the range, IN looks for values in a list, and LIKE compares a character column to a character string. Table 25.4 shows examples of each, and an equivalent dBASE 5 *<condition>*.

Table 25.4 Comparing SQL Predicates and dBASE 5 Conditions

SQL Predicate	dBASE 5 Condition
WHERE ord_qty BETWEEN 100 200;	FOR ord_qty >= 100 .AND. and ord_qty <= 200
WHERE unit_type IN ("EA", "CASE", "PALLET");	FOR unit_type + "/" $"EA/CASE/PALLET/"
WHERE custname LIKE "CH%";	FOR LEFT(custname,2) = "CH"

The LIKE command permits two wild cards: an underscore (_), which matches any single character, and the percent symbol (%), which matches any number of characters. You can combine the predicates with the AND, OR, and NOT logical operators.

dBASE 5 Functions and Commands in SQL

You can use some dBASE 5 functions and commands in SQL statements. You can, for example, use the DATE( ) function in a WHERE clause to limit the SQL command to rows with certain date values. Some functions, such as COL( ), can be used only in a SQL program, not at the SQL prompt. Many dBASE 5 commands can be used in *SQL mode* (entered at the SQL Command window or used in a SQL program).

Caution

Because all SQL commands end with a semicolon (;), make sure you enter the dBASE 5 command on one complete line *without* using a semicolon, whether entered at the SQL prompt or included in a SQL program.

SQL Security

The PROTECT command prevents unauthorized users from accessing specific databases. After a database has been protected, the user must log in with a password to use the database.

Note

The dBASE 5 PROTECT command also *encrypts* databases so that they can be used only by authorized users. See the PROTECT command in Chapter 22, "Using dBASE 5 Commands."

To assign privileges to SQL files, use the SQL commands GRANT and RE-VOKE. These commands grant or revoke various *privileges* that are used to limit access to SQL tables and views.

SQL Command Descriptions

SQL commands follow the same syntax rules that dBASE 5 commands ob-serve. See the introduction to this reference guide for information about dBASE 5 command syntax and the way it is diagrammed in this book.

SQL commands can be entered in the Command window by using the SET SQL ON command. Likewise, you turn off SQL with the SET SQL OFF command. Check the status bar of the Command window to be sure you are in the right mode before entering commands. If no status bar appears at the bottom of the screen, use the SET STATUS ON command to turn on the status bar.

Remember that all SQL statements end with a semicolon (;). Several of the examples on the following pages show a SQL statement broken into separate lines, for clarity. You can break your SQL statements into several lines, as well—as long as the SQL statement has the semicolon at the end of the command (and nowhere else). This is the opposite of the way dBASE commands work with semicolons. In dBASE commands, a semicolon indicates that the statement continues; in SQL, a semicolon indicates the end of the statement.

The SQL commands that follow are listed alphabetically.

ALTER TABLE

Syntax

```
ALTER TABLE <table name> ADD (<column name> <data type>
   [,<column name> <data type>...]);
```

Purpose: Adds new columns called *<column name>* to the existing *<table name>*. The new table can use any of the SQL data types.

Example

```
ALTER TABLE parts ADD (newnum CHAR(6));
```

CLOSE

Syntax

```
CLOSE <SQL cursor name>;
```

Purpose: Closes the SQL cursor, releasing the memory used by the cursor. You can reopen the cursor with an OPEN *<SQL cursor name>* command. This command is used only in SQL program files (PRS files).

Example

```
CLOSE partscur;
```

CREATE DATABASE

Syntax

```
CREATE DATABASE [<path>]<database name>;
```

Purpose: Creates a new database and the SQL catalog tables that will be used with the new database. The *<path>* can be as many as 64 characters long, but shouldn't include any space characters. If the *<path>* does not exist, the database is created as a subdirectory below the current directory. When the SQL database is created, it becomes the active SQL database.

Example

```
CREATE DATABASE parts;
```

CREATE INDEX

Syntax

```
CREATE [UNIQUE] INDEX <index name> ON <table name>
   (<column name> [ASC/DESC] [,<column name>
   [ASC/DESC]...]);
```

Purpose: Creates an index that is based on the columns specified in *<column name>*. The index helps the SELECT commands execute faster. Columns of any data type except logical can be used as the index column. The UNIQUE option creates an index made up of only the unique values in the *<column name>*, to prevent duplicate index key values. Use the ASC option to create ascending indexes; use DESC to create descending indexes. (ASC is the default.)

Example

```
CREATE INDEX partnum ON parts (partnumbr);
```

CREATE SYNONYM

Syntax

```
CREATE SYNONYM <synonym name> FOR <table/view>;
```

Purpose: Creates an alternative name for a view or table in the current database, enabling you to use a shortened table or view name.

Example

```
CREATE SYNONYM pn FOR partnumbr;
```

CREATE TABLE

Syntax

```
CREATE TABLE <table name> (<column name> <data type>
   [,<column name> <data type>...]);
```

Purpose: Creates a new SQL table for the current database. The *<table name>* is defined by the *<column name>* and the *<data type>* for each column. Any data type, except memo, can be used. Tables can contain up to 521 columns, with a maximum row width of 4,000 bytes.

Example

```
CREATE TABLE parts
(part_num char(8),
part_desc char (20),
unitcost decimal(5,2),
unitby char(3),
vendcode char(9));
```

CREATE VIEW

Syntax

```
CREATE VIEW <view name> [(<column name>, <column name>..)]
   AS <subselect> [WITH CHECK OPTION];
```

Purpose: Creates a table based on the columns defined in other tables or views. After using this command, you can add data to the view, which updates the underlying tables. You can define the *<column name>* for each column of the view; if you don't specify the *<column name>*, the view contains the column names of the underlying tables in the *<subselect>* predicate. Use the WITH CHECK OPTION parameter to make sure that inserted or updated rows meet the condition of the SELECT...WHERE command that defines the rows of the view.

Example

```
* Create a view containing back-ordered parts
CREATE VIEW backordr
AS SELECT partnum, partdesc, orddate
FROM orders WHERE shipdate = {};
```

DBCHECK

Syntax

```
DBCHECK [<table name>];
```

Purpose: Looks at the current catalog table for any SQL tables to make sure that the underlying DBF and MDX files are consistent with the catalog tables. If any differences are found, error messages are returned. DBCHECK will not work on encrypted files.

Example

```
* Make sure that the PARTS catalog table is consistent
* with the underlying databases and indexes
DBCHECK parts;
```

DBDEFINE

Syntax

```
DBDEFINE [<database file name>];
```

Purpose: Creates catalog table entries for the *<database file name>* and its associated indexes. If you want to create catalog entries for all databases and indexes in the current SQL database, use the DBDEFINE command without a *<database file name>*. Any memo fields in the database are ignored. If the MDX index was created with the INDEX...UNIQUE command, the table is added to the SQL catalog, but the TAG is not.

Example

```
* Create SQL catalog entries for all DBF tables
* in current directory
DBDEFINE;
```

DECLARE

Syntax

```
DECLARE <cursor name> CURSOR FOR <SELECT command>
   [FOR UPDATE OF<column list>/ORDER BY <clause>];
```

Purpose: Defines a SQL *cursor* that acts as a record pointer to SQL data. The cursor points to the rows of the result table. The cursor is associated with the *<SELECT command>*, and must be opened with the OPEN *<cursor>* command. Use the FOR UPDATE option if you want the cursor to enable updates. The ORDER BY option enables you to determine the order of the columns. This command is used only in SQL program files.

Example

```
* Table to show ordered parts
DECLARE partordr CURSOR FOR
SELECT partnum, partdesc, onhand, backqty, ordqty, ordate
FROM parts
WHERE ordqty > 0;
```

DELETE FROM

Syntax

```
DELETE FROM <table name> [<alias name>] [WHERE <clause>];
```

Purpose: Deletes rows from the *<table name>*. All rows are deleted unless you include the WHERE *<clause>*. After rows are deleted, they are erased permanently—there is no UNDELETE command. You can recall deleted rows only with a ROLLBACK if they are part of a BEGIN...END TRANSACTION command sequence.

> **Caution**
>
> You can use the SELECT...WHERE command to look at the rows that will be deleted. Doing so helps make sure you have used the proper WHERE clause.

Example

```
* Delete all inactive customers
DELETE FROM custnames WHERE lastdate < DATE() - 400;
```

DELETE FROM WHERE CURRENT OF

Syntax

```
DELETE FROM <table name> WHERE CURRENT OF <SQL cursor name>;
```

Purpose: Deletes the last row that has been fetched by the *<SQL cursor name>* on the *<table name>*. This command is used only in SQL program (PRS) files.

Example

```
DELETE FROM parts WHERE CURRENT OF partcurs;
```

DROP DATABASE

Syntax

```
DROP DATABASE <database name>;
```

Purpose: Deletes a database by deleting DBF and MDX files in the database directory for which there is a corresponding entry in the Systables and Sysidxs catalog tables. Use the STOP DATABASE command before you use DROP DATABASE.

Example

```
* Drop the temp database from the current SQL environment
DROP DATABASE temp;
```

DROP INDEX

Syntax

```
DROP INDEX <index name>;
```

Purpose: Removes the index specified in *<index name>*. Indexes are dropped automatically when the table that defined the index is dropped.

Example

```
* Drop the temp index but keep the temp database
DROP INDEX temp;
```

DROP SYNONYM

Syntax

```
DROP SYNONYM <synonym name>;
```

Purpose: Removes the *<synonym name>* from the current table or view. Synonyms are created with the CREATE SYNONYM command and are deleted automatically if their associated tables or views are deleted.

Example

```
* Drop the temp synonym
DROP SYNONYM temp;
```

DROP TABLE

Syntax

```
DROP TABLE <table name>;
```

Purpose: Deletes the *<table name>* from the current view or table. The table was created with the CREATE TABLE command. Any indexes, views, and synonyms that were created from the table also are deleted automatically.

Example

```
* Delete the temp table and all its related files
DROP TABLE temp;
```

DROP VIEW

Syntax

```
DROP VIEW <view name>;
```

Purpose: Deletes the *<view name>*. No underlying tables are deleted, but any synonyms and views based on the view are deleted.

Example

```
* Delete the temp view
DROP VIEW temp;
```

FETCH

Syntax

```
FETCH <cursor name> INTO <memvar list>;
```

Purpose: Moves the cursor to the next row of the result table and puts the values from that row into the *<memory variable list>*. The DECLARE...CURSOR and OPEN CURSOR commands must have been used before the FETCH command. This command is used only in SQL program files (PRS files).

Example

```
* Move the previously defined cursor to the next row
FETCH partcurs INTO mparts, mdesc, mqty, munitcost;
```

GRANT

Syntax

```
GRANT ALL [PRIVILEGES]/<privilege list>
    ON [TABLE] <table list>
    TO PUBLIC/<user list>
    [WITH GRANT OPTION];
```

Purpose: Gives the current user access to the current database tables and views. The database must have been protected with the dBASE 5 PROTECT command, and the user must have logged in to gain access to dBASE 5. Entries for the *<privilege list>* are described in Table 25.5.

The ALL option grants the user all privileges. The TO PUBLIC option grants all users access to the table and view. The GRANT OPTION parameter grants a user the power to grant privileges to other users.

Table 25.5 GRANT Privileges

Privilege	Effect
ALTER	User can add columns to a table (not allowed on a view).
DELETE	User can delete rows from a view or table.
INDEX	User can use CREATE INDEX.
INSERT	User can add rows to a view or table.
SELECT	User can display rows from a view or table.
UPDATE [(columns)]	User can update rows in a table or view, or update only specific columns.

Example

```
* Give the insert privilege to user "Jason"
GRANT INSERT ON TABLE custname TO Jason;
* Give all privileges to use Mike
GRANT ALL ON TABLE custname TO Mike;
```

INSERT INTO

Syntax

```
INSERT INTO <table name> [(<column list>)] VALUES
     (<value list>);
INSERT INTO <table name> [(<column list>)]
     <SELECT command>;
```

Purpose: These commands insert rows in a table or updatable view. The *<column list>* option enables you to specify the order of the columns that are used with the *<value list>*.

The INSERT INTO...VALUES command inserts the *<value list>* data into a new row. The *<value list>* can be constants, character strings, memory variables, dBASE 5 functions that return a value, or the SQL keyword USER. Separate the values in the *<value list>* with commas, and make sure each value matches the data type of the corresponding column.

The INSERT INTO...SELECT command inserts rows retrieved by a SELECT command.

Example

```
* Insert the memory variables into parts table
INSERT INTO parts VALUES (partnum, partdesc, cost, unitsize);
```

LOAD DATA FROM

Syntax

```
LOAD DATA FROM [<path>]<file name> INTO TABLE <table name>
   [[TYPE] SDF/DIF/WKS/SYLK/FW2/RPD/dBASEII/
   DELIMITED [WITH BLANK/WITH <delimiter>]];
```

Purpose: Imports data from another type of file (specified in *<file name>*) and adds it to the existing *<table name>*. Use the complete *<path>* and *<file name>* if the file is not in the current SQL directory. The allowable file *<types>* are listed in Table 25.6.

Table 25.6 File Types for LOAD DATA FROM

Type	Description
SDF	System data format ASCII files
DIF	VisiCalc files
WKS	Lotus 1-2-3 spreadsheet files
SYLK	MultiPlan spreadsheet files

Type	Description
FW2	Framework II database and spreadsheet files
RPD	RapidFile database files
dBASEII	dBASE II files

Files in dBASE III format, along with later versions, do not require a TYPE parameter. The DELIMITED option enables you to transfer data from a formatted ASCII text file. For more on importing files, see APPEND FROM in Chapter 22, "Using dBASE 5 Commands."

Example

```
* Append the data from the PARTS.DBF file into the PARTS
* SQL table
LOAD DATA FROM C:\DBASE4\DATA\PARTS.DBF INTO TABLE parts;
```

OPEN

Syntax

```
OPEN <cursor name>;
```

Purpose: Opens a cursor that was defined previously with the DECLARE CURSOR command. The SELECT command associated with the cursor is executed, and the cursor is placed before the first row in the result table. This command is valid only in PRS files.

Example

```
* Open the previously defined partcurs cursor
OPEN partcurs;
```

REVOKE

Syntax

```
REVOKE ALL [PRIVILEGES]/<privileges list>
   ON [TABLE] <table list> FROM PUBLIC/<user list>;
```

Purpose: Removes access privileges on the current TABLE or *<table list>*. The privileges were given with the GRANT command. You can revoke all privileges with ALL PRIVILEGES; to revoke just some of the privileges, use the *<privilege list>*. Entries for the *<privilege list>* are described in Table 25.7.

Table 25.7 REVOKE Privileges

Privilege	Effect
ALTER	User can add columns to a table (not allowed on a view).
DELETE	User can delete rows from a view or table.
INDEX	User can use CREATE INDEX.
INSERT	User can add rows to a view or table.
SELECT	User can display rows from a view or table.
UPDATE	User can update rows in a table or view, or update only specific columns.

You can revoke privileges from all users by using FROM PUBLIC or revoke privileges from specific users by using the FROM *<user list>* option. Only those privileges granted previously can be revoked. You can revoke privileges from the current table or from a *<table list>*.

Example

```
* Revoke the DELETE privilege from user Stacy
REVOKE DELETE ON parts FROM Stacy;
```

ROLLBACK

Syntax

```
ROLLBACK [WORK];
```

Purpose: Restores the contents of a view or table to the way they were before you started the BEGIN...END TRANSACTION command block. The WORK option is included to maintain compatibility with IBM's DB2 implementation of the SQL standard. ROLLBACK is most commonly used in programs, accompanied by the dBASE command ON ERROR.

Example

```
* Rollback the changes to the current custname table
ROLLBACK;
```

RUNSTATS

Syntax

```
RUNSTATS [<table name>];
```

Purpose: Updates the database statistics of the SQL system catalog tables. The statistics are used to help SQL determine the best way to execute the SQL database operations. RUNSTATS often is used after commands that make changes to a table or when data is added to more than 10 percent of the rows in a table. Use the optional *<table name>* to update statistics for a specific table. If you don't specify a table name, all table statistics are updated.

Example

```
* Update the statistics for the partsnum table
RUNSTATS partsnum;
```

SELECT

Syntax

```
SELECT [ALL/DISTINCT] <column list> /*
   [INTO <memory variable 1> [,<memory variable 2 >, ...]]
   FROM <table>/<view> [alias] [[, <table>/<view>
     [<alias>]] ...]
   [WHERE [NOT] <search condition 1>
     [AND/OR [NOT] <search condition 2> ...]]
   [GROUP BY <column>[,<column>...]]
   [HAVING [NOT] <search condition 1>
     [AND/OR [NOT] <search condition 2> ...]]
   [UNION <SELECT command>]
   [ORDER BY <column name>/<column number> [ASC/DESC]
     [, <column name>/<column number> [ASC/DESC]...]/
   FOR UPDATE OF <columns> [, <column> ...]]
   SAVE TO TEMP <table name> [(<column> [,<column>...])] [KEEP]
```

Purpose: Produces a result table by selecting rows and columns from a table or group. The result table is used by other SQL commands. Each clause syntax of the command is detailed in the following entries, along with an example for that clause.

The SELECT clause specifies the columns, SQL aggregate functions, or expressions that should be included in the result table. You can use the ALL option to select all rows or use the DISTINCT option to eliminate duplicate rows based on the column list. You can select all columns with the * option or specify a *<column list>*. (ALL is the default.)

The INTO clause is used when a SELECT statement would return only a single row. The result values are stored in the memory variables: column 1's result in *<memory variable 1>*, column 2's result in *<memory variable 2>*, and so on. If more than one row is in the result table, only the first row's data is placed in the memory variables. If you specify the INTO clause, you cannot also specify the GROUP BY, HAVING, UNION, ORDER BY, FOR UPDATE OF, or SAVE TO TEMP clause.

The required FROM clause specifies the tables or views that are used to create the result table. You can use an *alias,* which can be up to 10 characters long; it must start with a letter, and is used in the same manner as database aliases. Do not use single-letter aliases of A through J; they are reserved for database alias names.

The WHERE clause specifies the search condition used to determine the data that will appear in the result table. You can use any of the comparison operators. The search condition can use any valid expression. Include parentheses as needed to achieve the desired result.

The GROUP BY clause groups the rows in the result table by columns that have the same values so that each group is reduced to a single row. Each item is separated by a comma. You cannot use the GROUP BY clause if you use an INTO clause.

The HAVING clause restricts grouped rows that appear in the result table. Groups are specified with the GROUP BY clause. You can combine search conditions with the AND/OR NOT option.

The UNION clause combines the result tables of two or more *<subselect>* entries into a single result table. Duplicate rows are eliminated. Each *<subselect>* must produce the same number of columns, with compatible data types and widths. The ORDER BY option enables you to specify the order of the result union. The SAVE TO TEMP clause creates a temporary table that can be saved as a dBASE 5 DBF file if you use the KEEP option.

The ORDER BY clause determines the order of rows in the result table. Data is placed in the rows in ascending (ASC, the default) order or descending (DESC) order. The order of the columns in the result table is determined by the *<column names>* or *<column number>* values. You cannot use this clause if you use the FOR UPDATE OF clause.

The FOR UPDATE OF clause specifies which columns can be updated when you use the UPDATE WHERE CURRENT OF command. This command is used only in programs, and is ignored if entered from the Command window. The columns specified must be in the FROM clause of the SELECT command. You cannot use this clause with the ORDER BY, SAVE TO TEMP, or INTO clauses. If you wanted to use this clause, you could enter something like:

```
FOR UPDATE OF ORDDATE
```

The SAVE TO TEMP clause is a dBASE extension to the SQL SELECT command. The clause saves, as a temporary table or as a dBASE file, the result table generated by a SELECT statement. Unless you specify the optional KEEP keyword, the table is available only for the remainder of the SQL session. You cannot use this clause in a SELECT statement if you also use the INTO or FOR UPDATE OF clauses.

Example

```
* Select these columns, collect values by order date, sort by
* order date, vendor, parts, description, cost
SELECT ALL Parts, Desc, Cost, Vendor, OrdDate
   FROM Parts
   WHERE OrdQty >= 100
   GROUP BY OrdDate
   HAVING OrdQty*Cost > 1000
   ORDER BY OrdDate, Vendor, Parts, Desc, Cost;
```

SET SQL

Syntax

```
SET SQL ON

SET SQL OFF
```

Purpose: SET SQL ON enters SQL mode from the dBASE 5 Command window. There is no semicolon at the end. SET SQL is not allowed in a program file.

SET SQL OFF exits SQL mode and returns you to the dBASE 5 Command window. A semicolon at the end is not required.

Example

```
* Enter SQL mode from dBASE
SET SQL ON

* Return to the dBASE 5 Command window
SET SQL OFF
```

SHOW DATABASE

Syntax

```
SHOW DATABASE;
```

Purpose: Lists the SQL databases that are available for use. The database name, creator's user ID, creation date, and DOS directory name are shown.

Example

```
* Show current SQL database list
SHOW DATABASE;
```

START DATABASE

Syntax

```
START DATABASE <database name>;
```

Purpose: Activates a database for use by subsequent SQL commands. START DATABASE is normally the first command used when you enter SQL commands in the Command window in SQL mode. Only one database can be active at any one time. Use STOP DATABASE to finish using a database.

Example

```
* Start using the PARTS database
START DATABASE parts;
```

STOP DATABASE

Syntax

```
STOP DATABASE;
```

Purpose: Closes the current database. The database must be stopped (closed) before you can start (open) another database. Use this command before you use the DROP DATABASE command.

Example

```
* Stop using the currently active PARTS database
STOP DATABASE;
```

UNLOAD DATA TO

Syntax

```
UNLOAD DATA TO [path]<file name>
   FROM TABLE <table name>
   [[TYPE] SDF/DIF/WKS/SYLK/FW2/RPD/dBASEII/
   DELIMITED [WITH BLANK/WITH<delimiter>]];
```

Purpose: Exports the SQL table *<table name>* to the *<file name>*. The type of file created defaults to a dBASE 5 DBF file, unless you use the TYPE option. The available types are described in Table 25.8.

Table 25.8 File Types for UNLOAD DATA TO

Type	Description
SDF	System data format ASCII files
DIF	VisiCalc files
WKS	Lotus 1-2-3 spreadsheet files

Type	Description
SYLK	MultiPlan spreadsheet files
FW2	Framework II database and spreadsheet files
RPD	RapidFile database files
dBASEII	dBASE II files

Files in dBASE III format, and later versions, do not require a TYPE parameter. The DELIMITED option enables you to transfer data to a formatted ASCII text file.

Example

```
* Export the CURRORD table data to a Lotus spreadsheet file
UNLOAD DATA TO orders FROM TABLE currord TYPE WKS
```

UPDATE

Syntax

```
UPDATE <table name>/<view name>
SET <column name>=<new value>[,<column name>=<new value>...]
   [WHERE <clause>];
UPDATE <table name>
   SET <column name>=<new value>[,<column name>=<new value>...]
   WHERE CURRENT OF <SQL cursor name>;
```

Purpose: Changes the table or view data in columns for the specified rows. The new value for each column is specified by the SET... parameter.

UPDATE...WHERE is used to select the rows in the table or view that you want to update. The WHERE CURRENT OF clause is used to update only the row currently pointed to by the cursor.

Example

```
* Add 5 percent to all costs, update the last increase date
* field for all rows where the cost has not increased in
* the last 90 days
UPDATE parts SET cost = cost * 1.05, lastinc = DATE()
WHERE lastinc = DATE() - 90;
```

Chapter 26

Using UI Properties, Methods, and Commands

Working with event-driven programming tools makes the task of creating complex applications simpler and more user friendly. dBASE 5 gives you the tools necessary to create objects which are not automatically linked together but which are designed to call on each other to get the job done.

Properties control the way the object appears and operates. Methods act like functions, in that they return a value which can then be used to perform other operations. UI commands are used to create the various objects. If you do not specify a value for a property for a specific object, the default values are used by dBASE to set the appearance or function for that object.

This chapter is divided into three sections. The first section, "Properties," is an alphabetic list of all the properties you can use to customize the look of your objects. The second section, "Methods," describes the uses of these function-like routines that your object uses to do its job. The last section, "Commands," details the syntax and purpose of each UI command.

Other commands used by dBASE can be found in Chapter 22, "Using dBASE 5 Commands," Chapter 24, "Using SET Commands To Configure dBASE 5," and Chapter 25, "Using SQL Commands."

Using Dot Reference Notation

All properties and methods are accessible using dot reference notation, which has the format *<object name>.<member name>*. The *<object name>* is the name of the object selected. The *<member name>* is any property, method, or object that belongs to the selected object. Dot reference notation is necessary because not all properties can be set in the DEFINE statement of an object in your program. Each property and method in the following sections details how the property or method is used in relation to a specific object.

To set the value of a property using dot reference notation, such as changing the CurSel property of the combo box CMNAME7 on form ABC to 4, you would issue the statement:

```
ABC.CMNAME7.CurSel = 4
```

This moves the focus of the cursor to the fourth item in the combo box list.

To get the CurSel property of the combo box CMNAME7 on form ABC, issue the statement:

```
MYSELECT = ABC.CMNAME7.CurSel
```

This returns the current value of the CurSel property to a memory variable called MYSELECT. Note that you can nest dot notation to specify the selected *<object name>* (ABC.CMNAME7) and the desired *<member name>* reference (CurSel).

You use dot reference notation the same way you use any memory variable to return and use the values of individual properties and methods. Simply substitute the dot reference notation string into the usual memory variable place to set the value of a property, query the value of a property or method, or perform manipulations with the value of a property or method.

Properties

After

Syntax

```
After <object reference>
```

Applies To

BROWSE, CHECKBOX, COMBOBOX, EDITOR, ENTRYFIELD, FIELD, FORM, LISTBOX, MENU, MENUITEM, PUSHBUTTON, RADIOBUTTON, RECTANGLE, SPINBOX, TEXT

Default

If only one object is placed on the form, it returns the value of the current object since this property is circular. For example, the Editor Object returns the value EDITOR::_CmdWindow.

Purpose: Controls the tabbing order of multiple objects on a form. The default tabbing order is the order in which the objects are created. By assigning the After property of an object (object 1) to another object (object 2), you tell the program to tab from object 2 to object 1. The tabbing order automatically cycles to come back to the starting point. Pressing the Tab key advances the cursor one object, while pressing Shift-Tab causes the cursor to move back one object.

The After property can be set in the DEFINE statement for the object by using dot reference notation. This allows you to set the property's value, query the value of the property, and then use the returned value of the property in a variable. The value returned appears in the following format:

```
<object type>::<object reference>
```

Alias

Syntax

```
Alias <alias name expC>
```

Applies To

BROWSE

Default

The alias of the current database that was in effect when opened

Purpose: Indicates which database to display with the browse object. The database to be displayed does not have to be in the current directory for Alias to work. The *<alias name expC>* is the database name or the alias work area, and must be in either single or double quotation marks, or in brackets.

An alias is a second name assigned to refer to a database which has been opened. You can assign an alias name with the ALIAS clause of the USE command. Otherwise, dBASE assigns an alias for you using the file name with an underscore preceding it to indicate the alias.

The Alias property can be set in the DEFINE statement for the object by using dot reference notation. This allows you to set the property's value, query the value of the property, and then use the returned value of the property in a variable. The value returned appears in the following format:

```
<object type>::<object reference>
```

Append

Syntax

```
Append <expL>
```

Applies To

BROWSE

Default

True

Purpose: Enables the user to add records to the database that the browse object displays. Setting Append to false turns this ability off. The Append property can be set in the DEFINE statement for the object by using dot reference notation. This allows you to set the property's value, query the value of the property, and then use the returned value of the property in a variable. The value returned appears in the following format:

```
<object type>::<object reference>
```

AutoSize

Syntax

```
Autosize <expL>
```

Applies To

FORM

Default

False

Purpose: Ensures that the window opened is sized to display all controls on the form when set to true. If a user resizes the open window, for instance makes it smaller, when the window is closed and reopened, it resizes to display all the controls on the form. False forces the window to size to the default dimensions, which are determined by the form's height and Width properties, and the FROM...TO clause of the DEFINE FORM command for the form, and the size of the window when the user closed it. It is recommended that you set AutoSize to false after placing all the controls on the form, to enhance the performance of your form.

The AutoSize property can be set in the DEFINE statement for the object by using dot reference notation. This allows you to set the property's value, query the value of the property, and then use the returned value of the property in a variable. The value returned appears in the following format:

```
<object type>::<object reference>
```

Before

Syntax

```
Before <object reference>
```

Applies To

BROWSE, CHECKBOX, COMBOBOX, EDITOR, ENTRYFIELD, FIELD, FORM, LISTBOX, MENU, MENUITEM, PUSHBUTTON, RADIOBUTTON, RECTANGLE, SPINBOX, TEXT

Default

If only one control appears on the form, it points to itself since this property is circular. For example, the Editor object would return the value EDITOR::_Clipboard.

Purpose: Controls the tabbing order of multiple objects on a form. The default tabbing order is the order in which the objects were created. Before allows you to specify the order in which objects should receive focus. Assigning the Before property of an object (object 1) to another object (object 2) sets the tabbing order to be object 1 followed by object 2. To reverse this order, you assign the Before property of object 2 to object 1, then the tabbing order becomes object 2 followed by object 1. Pressing the Tab key advances the focus to the next object, while pressing Shift-Tab moves the focus back one object. The focus is cyclical, allowing the user to tab through all the choices and then back to the beginning object.

The Before property can be set in the DEFINE statement for the object by using dot reference notation. This allows you to set the property's value, query the value of the property, and then use the returned value of the property in a variable. The value returned appears in the following format:

```
<object type>::<object reference>
```

Border

Syntax

```
Border <expL>
```

Applies To

CHECKBOX, ENTRYFIELD, LISTBOX, PUSHBUTTON, RADIOBUTTON, RECTANGLE, SPINBOX, TEXT

Default

False

Purpose: Controls whether a border is placed around an object. The border width is not included in the Top and Left dimensions of the object, rather the border contains the object's dimensions within the border's Height and Width properties. To place a border around a group of controls, use the Group property. By using a Text object as the title of the group, you can position the title of the form on the border as long as the dimensions of the Height and Width properties overlap the dimensions of the border. To change the style of the border, you can use the BorderStyle property to create a border other than a single line, or to raise or lower the line. When creating a rectangular border, you can use the ColorCorderRaised property to modify the look of the border.

The Border property can be set in the DEFINE statement for the object by using dot reference notation. This allows you to set the property's value, query the value of the property, and then use the returned value of the property in a variable.

BorderStyle

Syntax

```
BorderStyle <border setting expN>
```

Applies To

CHECKBOX, ENTRYFIELD, PUSHBUTTON, RADIOBUTTON, RECTANGLE, SPINBOX, TEXT

Default

0 (Normal)

Purpose: Determines the way the border of an object appears. The *<border setting expN>* is a numeric value which is determined from the following choices:

BorderStyle	Result
0 (Normal)	Single line border
1 (Raised)	Raises the border line
2 (Lowered)	Lowers the border line

You can only use BorderStyle if the Border property in the DEFINE statement of the object is set to true. Setting Border to false turns off the border. You can change the colors of the border with the ColorBorderRaised property.

The BorderStyle property can be set in the DEFINE statement for the object by using dot reference notation. This allows you to set the property's value, query the value of the property, and then use the returned value of the property in a variable.

CalcField

Syntax

```
CalcField <expL>
```

Applies To

FIELD

Default

False

Purpose: Specifies whether a field is to be used to display the results of calculations (a read-only field). If the DataLink property of the field is an expression, set the CalcField property to true, which prevents the user from editing the field. Setting CalcField to false allows the user to edit the field.

The CalcField property can be set in the DEFINE statement for the object by using dot reference notation. This allows you to set the property's value, query the value of the property, and then use the returned value of the property in a variable. The value returned appears in the following format:

```
<object type>::<object reference>
```

Checked

Syntax

```
Checked <expL>
```

Applies To

MENU, MENUITEM

Default

False

Purpose: Indicates if a box on a menu is selected or if a box on a form has an X in it, indicating it is active. This property is used in conjunction with the OnClick event handler. When a user makes the choice active (checked), the OnClick property calls its routines or none if no routines are defined. When the choice is not active (not checked), the OnClick property may call its routine or do nothing.

The Checked property can be set in the DEFINE statement for the object. Dot reference notation allows you to set the property's value, query the value of the property, and then use the returned value of the property in a variable.

ClassName

Syntax

```
<object reference>.ClassName
```

Applies To

BROWSE, CHECKBOX, COMBOBOX, EDITOR, ENTRYFIELD, FIELD, FIELDLIST, FORM, LISTBOX, OBJECT, PUSHBUTTON, RADIOBUTTON, RECTANGLE, SPINBOX, TEXT

Default

Original type of the object

Purpose: Identifies the type of object which has been defined. This is useful for determining what the object type is at any given point in the program. The ClassName property may not be used in the DEFINE statement. To query the value of the property and assign the value to a variable, you must use dot reference notation. The value returned appears in the following format:

```
<object type>::<object reference>
```

ColorBorder

Syntax

```
ColorBorder <color setting expC>
```

Applies To

BROWSE, EDITOR, FORM, RECTANGLE

Default

Object	Setting
Browse	"W/B"
Editor	"W/B"
Form	"N/W"
Rectangle	"W+/W"

Purpose: Indicates an object's border color. The *<color setting expC>* consists of a character string within single or double quotations marks or within brackets. A forward slash (/) separates the color setting and color codes.

You can change the color of the border with the ColorBorder property from the DEFINE statement. You can use dot reference notation to set the property's value, query the value, and use the value in a variable.

See SET COLOR TO in Chapter 24, "Using SET Commands To Configure dBASE 5" for more information on the color codes.

ColorBorderHighlight

Syntax

```
ColorBorderHighlight <color setting expC>
```

Applies To

BROWSE, EDITOR, FORM

Default

Object	Setting
Browse	"W+/B"
Editor	"W+/B"
Form	"W+/W"

Purpose: Indicates the color to be used in the border of an object when it is selected. The *<color setting expC>* clause consists of a character string within single or double quotations marks or within brackets. A forward slash (/) separates the color setting and color codes.

An active object's border color can be changed with the ColorBorder-Highlight property from the DEFINE statement. You can use dot reference notation to set the property's value, query the value, and use the value in a variable.

See SET COLOR TO in Chapter 24, "Using SET Commands To Configure dBASE 5," for more information on the color codes.

ColorBorderLowered

Syntax

```
ColorBorderLowered <color setting expC>
```

Applies To

FORM, RECTANGLE

Default

Object	Setting
Form	"N/W"
Rectangle	"N/W"

Purpose: Determines the color of the lowered portion of the border which has been raised or lowered. You must have set the Border property to true to use this property to specify the color of an object's lowered border. Any objects appearing inside the associated form window when the Border is set to true will be the same color as the border. The *<color setting expC>* consists of a character string within single or double quotes, or within brackets. Color setting and color codes are separated with a forward slash (/).

ColorBorderLowered may be used from the DEFINE statement of the object. Dot reference notation enables you to set the property's value, query the value, and use the value of the property in a variable.

See SET COLOR TO in Chapter 24, "Using SET Commands To Configure dBASE 5," for more information on color settings and codes.

ColorBorderRaised

Syntax

```
ColorBorderRaised <color setting expC>
```

Applies To

FORM, RECTANGLE

Default

Object	Setting
Form	"W+/W"
Rectangle	"W+/W"

Purpose: Determines the border color of the raised portion of an object's border. The *<color setting expC>* consists of a character string within single or double quotes, or within brackets. Any objects appearing inside the associated form window when the Border is set to true will be the same color as the border. Color setting and color codes are separated with a forward slash (/).

ColorBorderRaised may be used from the DEFINE statement of the object. Dot reference notation enables you to set the property's value, query the value, and use the value of the property in a variable.

See SET COLOR TO in Chapter 24, "Using SET Commands To Configure dBASE 5," for more information on color settings and codes.

ColorDisabled

Syntax

```
ColorDisabled <color setting expC>
```

Applies To

BROWSE, CHECKBOX, COMBOBOX, EDITOR, ENTRYFIELD, FORM, LISTBOX, MENUBAR, PUSHBUTTON, RADIOBUTTON, SPINBOX, TEXT

Default

Object	Setting
Browse	"N+/W"
Check box	"N+/GB"
Combo box	"N+/B"
Editor	"N+/W"
Entry field	"N+/B"
Form	"N+/W"
List box	"N+/W"
Menu bar	"N+/W"
Pushbutton	"N+/W"
Radio button	"N+/GB"
Spin box	"N+/B"
Text	"N+/W"

Purpose: Determines the object's color when it does not have focus. The color selected only applies to a text object when the text object appears as a label on an object. The *<color setting expC>* consists of a character string within single or double quotes, or within brackets. Color setting and color codes are separated with a forward slash (/).

ColorDisabled may be used from the DEFINE statement of the object. Dot reference notation enables you to set the property's value, query the value, and use the value of the property in a variable.

See SET COLOR TO in Chapter 24, "Using SET Commands To Configure dBASE 5," for more information on color settings and codes.

ColorDisabledHighlight

Syntax

```
ColorDisabledHighlight <color setting expC>
```

Applies To

MENUBAR

Default

"N+/G"

Purpose: Indicates the color of a menu or menu item when it does not have focus. The *<color setting expC>* consists of a character string within single or double quotes, or within brackets. Color setting and color codes are separated with a forward slash (/).

ColorDisabledHighlight may be used from the DEFINE statement of the object. Dot reference notation enables you to set the property's value, query the value, and use the value of the property in a variable.

See SET COLOR TO in Chapter 24, "Using SET Commands To Configure dBASE 5," for more information on color settings and codes.

ColorEntryHighlight

Syntax

```
ColorEntryHighlight <color setting expC>
```

Applies To

BROWSE, COMBOBOX

Default

Object	Setting
Browse	"B/W"
Combo box	"W+/G"

Purpose: Determines the color that an entry field's text will appear in when it has focus. The *<color setting expC>* consists of a character string within single or double quotes, or within brackets. Color setting and color codes are separated with a forward slash (/).

ColorEntryHighlight may be used from the DEFINE statement of the object. Dot reference notation enables you to set the property's value, query the value, and use the value of the property in a variable.

See SET COLOR TO in Chapter 24, "Using SET Commands To Configure dBASE 5," for more information on color settings and codes.

ColorEntryNormal

Syntax

```
ColorEntryNormal <color setting expC>
```

Applies To

BROWSE, COMBOBOX

Default

Object	Setting
Browse	"W+/GB"
Combo box	"W+/B"

Purpose: Indicates the color of text in a browse object or a combo box. The *<color setting expC>* consists of a character string within single or double quotes, or within brackets. Color setting and color codes are separated with a forward slash (/).

ColorEntryNormal may be used from the DEFINE statement of the object. Dot reference notation enables you to set the property's value, query the value, and use the value of the property in a variable.

See SET COLOR TO in Chapter 24, "Using SET Commands To Configure dBASE 5," for more information on color settings and codes.

ColorEntryScrollBar

Syntax

```
ColorEntryScrollBar <color setting expC>
```

Applies To

COMBOBOX

Default

"G+/B"

Purpose: Indicates the color of arrows in scroll bars within an entry field of a combo box. The *<color setting expC>* consists of a character string within single or double quotes, or within brackets. Color setting and color codes are separated with a forward slash (/).

ColorEntryScrollBar may be used from the DEFINE statement of the object. Dot reference notation enables you to set the property's value, query the value, and use the value of the property in a variable.

See SET COLOR TO in Chapter 24, "Using SET Commands To Configure dBASE 5," for more information on color settings and codes.

ColorHighlight

Syntax

```
ColorHighlight <color setting expC>
```

Applies To

CHECKBOX, EDITOR, ENTRYFIELD, LISTBOX, MENUBAR, PUSHBUTTON, RADIOBUTTON, SPINBOX, TEXT

Default

Object	Setting
Check box	"W+/GB"
Editor	"B/W"
Entry field	"W+/G"
List box	"W+/G"
Menu bar	"N/G"
Pushbutton	"W+/G"

Object	Setting
Radio button	"W+/GB"
Spin box	"W+/G"
Text	"N+/W"

Purpose: Indicates colors of text in fields, entry fields, text areas, and list box options when it receives focus from the user. There are two settings involved in setting these colors: foreground and background. The *<color setting expC>* consists of a character string within single or double quotes, or within brackets. Color setting and color codes are separated with a forward slash (/).

ColorHighlight may be used from the DEFINE statement of the object. Dot reference notation enables you to set the property's value, query the value, and use the value of the property in a variable.

See SET COLOR TO in Chapter 24, "Using SET Commands To Configure dBASE 5," for more information on color settings and codes.

ColorIcon

Syntax

```
ColorIcon <colorsetting expC>
```

Applies To

BROWSE, COMBOBOX, EDITOR, FORM, SPINBOX

Default

Object	Setting
Browse	"GB+/B"
Combo box	"N/G"
Editor	"GB+/W"
Form	"GB+/W"
Spin box	"N/G"

Purpose: Determines the colors to be used on the Close icon, object borders, and on the navigation bar of a browse object. The *<color setting expC>* consists of a character string within single or double quotes, or within brackets. Color setting and color codes are separated with a forward slash (/).

ColorIcon may be used from the DEFINE statement of the object. Dot reference notation enables you to set the property's value, query the value, and use the value of the property in a variable.

See SET COLOR TO in Chapter 24, "Using SET Commands To Configure dBASE 5," for more information on color settings and codes.

ColorListHighlight

Syntax

```
ColorListHighlight <color setting expC>
```

Applies To

COMBOBOX

Default

"W+/BG"

Purpose: Determines the color to be used on selected text within a list box when the combo box receives focus from the user. The *<color setting expC>* consists of a character string within single or double quotes, or within brackets. Color setting and color codes are separated with a forward slash (/).

ColorListHighlight may be used from the DEFINE statement of the object. Dot reference notation enables you to set the property's value, query the value, and use the value of the property in a variable.

See SET COLOR TO in Chapter 24, "Using SET Commands To Configure dBASE 5," for more information on color settings and codes.

ColorListNormal

Syntax

```
ColorListNormal <color setting expC>
```

Applies To

COMBOBOX

Default

"RG+/B"

Purpose: Determines the color to be used for text in a combo box's list box which does not have focus. The *<color setting expC>* consists of a character string within single or double quotes, or within brackets. Color setting and color codes are separated with a forward slash (/).

ColorListSelected may be used from the DEFINE statement of the object. Dot reference notation enables you to set the property's value, query the value, and use the value of the property in a variable.

See SET COLOR TO in Chapter 24, "Using SET Commands To Configure dBASE 5," for more information on color settings and codes.

ColorListScrollBar

Syntax

```
ColorListScrollBar <color setting expC>
```

Applies To

COMBOBOX

Default

"B/GB"

Purpose: Determines the color to be used on the arrows of the scroll bars in a combo box's list box. The *<color setting expC>* consists of a character string within single or double quotes, or within brackets. Color setting and color codes are separated with a forward slash (/).

ColorListScrollBar may be used from the DEFINE statement of the object. Dot reference notation enables you to set the property's value, query the value, and use the value of the property in a variable.

See SET COLOR TO in Chapter 24, "Using SET Commands To Configure dBASE 5," for more information on color settings and codes.

ColorListSelected

Syntax

```
ColorListSelected <color setting expC>
```

Applies To

COMBOBOX

Default

"N/GB"

Purpose: Determines the color to be used on selected text within a combo box's list box when the combo box is not selected. The *<color setting expC>* consists of a character string within single or double quotes, or within brackets. Color setting and color codes are separated with a forward slash (/).

ColorListSelected may be used from the DEFINE statement of the object. Dot reference notation enables you to set the property's value, query the value, and use the value of the property in a variable.

See SET COLOR TO in Chapter 24, "Using SET Commands To Configure dBASE 5," for more information on color settings and codes.

ColorMenuBarNormal

Syntax

```
ColorMenuBarNormal <color setting expC>
```

Applies To

MENUBAR

Default

"N/W"

Purpose: Determines the color to be used on a menubar when it appears at the top of the screen or form window, which makes it easier to distinguish it from non-MDI menus that may appear on the screen. The *<color setting expC>* consists of a character string within single or double quotes, or within brackets. Color setting and color codes are separated with a forward slash (/).

ColorMenuBarNormal may be used from the DEFINE statement of the object. Dot reference notation enables you to set the property's value, query the value, and use the value of the property in a variable.

See SET COLOR TO in Chapter 24, "Using SET Commands To Configure dBASE 5," for more information on color settings and codes.

ColorMenuBarPick

Syntax

```
ColorMenuBarPick <color setting expC>
```

Applies To

MENUBAR

Default

"R/W"

Purpose: Determines the color to be used on a menubar pick character when it receives focus. The *<color setting expC>* consists of a character string within single or double quotes, or within brackets. Color setting and color codes are separated with a forward slash (/).

ColorMenuBarPick may be used from the DEFINE statement of the object. Dot reference notation enables you to set the property's value, query the value, and use the value of the property in a variable.

See SET COLOR TO in Chapter 24, "Using SET Commands To Configure dBASE 5," for more information on color settings and codes.

ColorNormal

Syntax

```
ColorNormal <color setting expC>
```

Applies To

BROWSE, CHECKBOX, EDITOR, ENTRYFIELD, FORM, LISTBOX, MENUBAR, PUSHBUTTON, RADIOBUTTON, RECTANGLE, SPINBOX, TEXT

Default

Object	Setting
Browse	"RG+/B"
Check box	"N/GB"
Editor	"RG+/B"
Entry field	"W+/B"
Form	"B/W"
List box	"N/BG"
Menu bar	"N/W"
Pushbutton	"N/G"
Radio button	"N/GB"
Rectangle	"N/W"
Spin box	"W+/B"
Text	"N/W"

Purpose: Indicates the color to be used for objects which do not have focus. You may specify two color options: one for foreground color and one for background color. The *<color setting expC>* consists of a character string within single or double quotes, or within brackets. Color setting and color codes are separated with a forward slash (/).

ColorNormal may be used from the DEFINE statement of the object. Dot reference notation enables you to set the property's value, query the value, and use the value of the property in a variable.

See SET COLOR TO in Chapter 24, "Using SET Commands To Configure dBASE 5," for more information on color settings and codes.

ColorPickHighlight

Syntax

```
ColorPickHighlight <color setting expC>
```

Applies To

CHECKBOX, MENUBAR, PUSHBUTTON, RADIOBUTTON, TEXT

Default

Object	Setting
Check box	"N/GB"
Menu bar	"R/G"
Pushbutton	"RG+/GB"
Radio button	"RG/GB"
Text	"RG+/W"

Purpose: Determines the color to use on a pick character when the object receives focus. The *<color setting expC>* consists of a character string within single or double quotes, or within brackets. Color setting and color codes are separated with a forward slash (/).

ColorPickHighlight may be used from the DEFINE statement of the object. Dot reference notation enables you to set the property's value, query the value, and use the value of the property in a variable.

See SET COLOR TO in Chapter 24, "Using SET Commands To Configure dBASE 5," for more information on color settings and codes.

ColorPickNormal

Syntax

```
ColorPickNormal <color setting expC>
```

Applies To

CHECKBOX, MENUBAR, PUSHBUTTON, RADIOBUTTON, TEXT

Default

Object	Setting
Check box	"RG+/GB"
Menu bar	"R/W"
Pushbutton	"RG+/G"
Radio button	"RG+/GB"
Text	"RG+/W"

Purpose: Determines the color to be used on a pick character when it is available for the user to select but has not been selected. The *<color setting expC>* consists of a character string within single or double quotes, or within brackets. Color setting and color codes are separated with a forward slash (/).

ColorPickNormal may be used from the DEFINE statement of the object. Dot reference notation enables you to set the property's value, query the value, and use the value of the property in a variable.

See SET COLOR TO in Chapter 24, "Using SET Commands To Configure dBASE 5," for more information on color settings and codes.

ColorScrollBar

Syntax

```
ColorScrollBar <color setting expC>
```

Applies To

BROWSE, EDITOR, ENTRYFIELD, FORM, LISTBOX, SPINBOX

Default

Object	Setting
Browse	"B+/GB"
Editor	"B+/GB"
Entry field	"G+/B"
Form	"GB/B"
List box	"B+/GB"
Spin box	"G+/B"

Purpose: Determines the color to use on an object's scroll bar. The *<color setting expC>* consists of a character string within single or double quotes, or within brackets. Color setting and color codes are separated with a forward slash (/).

ColorScrollBar may be used from the DEFINE statement of the object. Dot reference notation enables you to set the property's value, query the value, and use the value of the property in a variable.

See SET COLOR TO in Chapter 24, "Using SET Commands To Configure dBASE 5," for more information on color settings and codes.

ColorSelected

Syntax

```
ColorSelected <color setting expC>
```

Applies To

LISTBOX, PUSHBUTTON

Default

Object	Setting
List box	"RG+/BG"
Pushbutton	"BG+/G"

Purpose: Determines the color to be used on selected text when the associated list box or pushbutton is not selected. The *<color setting expC>* consists of a character string within single or double quotes, or within brackets. Color setting and color codes are separated with a forward slash (/).

ColorSelected may be used from the DEFINE statement of the object. Dot reference notation enables you to set the property's value, query the value, and use the value of the property in a variable.

See SET COLOR TO in Chapter 24, "Using SET Commands To Configure dBASE 5," for more information on color settings and codes.

ColorShadow

Syntax

```
ColorShadow <color setting expC>
```

Applies To
LISTBOX, MENU, PUSHBUTTON

Default
"G/N"

Purpose: Determines the color to be used for an object's shadow. The *<color setting expC>* consists of a character string within single or double quotes, or within brackets. Color setting and color codes are separated with a forward slash (/).

ColorShadow may be used from the DEFINE statement of the object. Dot reference notation enables you to set the property's value, query the value, and use the value of the property in a variable.

See SET COLOR TO in Chapter 24, "Using SET Commands To Configure dBASE 5," for more information on color settings and codes.

Column

Syntax

```
Column <column expN>
```

Applies To
EDITOR, LISTBOX

Default
1

Purpose: Sets the number of columns to be used within an editor or list box. You may choose from 1 to 80 columns for a list box. If the list box contains one column only a vertical scroll bar appears. If the list box contains multiple columns, a horizontal scroll bar appears, and the prompts will snake from the bottom of one column to the top of the list in the next column. An Editor object may contain 1 to 254 columns. The Column value moves the cursor from its present location to new value. Entering a value larger than the number of columns in the Editor object positions the cursor at the end of the line.

Column may be used in the DEFINE statement of the associated object. Dot reference notation enables you to set the property's value, query the value, and use the value of the property in a variable.

CurSel

Syntax

```
CurSel <prompt expN>
```

Applies To

COMBOBOX, LISTBOX

Default

1

Purpose: Indicates which prompt contained in a combo box or list box has focus. The *<prompt expN>* represents the order of the prompt in the list box, where the prompts are listed sequentially. Resetting the CurSel value moves the focus to the new prompt value. The first prompt in any list box is selected by default.

CurSel may be used in the DEFINE statement of the associated object. Dot reference notation enables you to set the property's value, query the value, and use the value of the property in a variable.

DataLink

Syntax

```
DataLink <expC>
```

Applies To

CHECKBOX, COMBOBOX, ENTRYFIELD, FIELD, RADIOBUTTON, SPINBOX

Default

The same control as given in the DEFINE statement of the object

Purpose: Creates a link between a control of a form and a field in an open database. The *<expC>* consists of a character string (naming a field in an open database) within single or double quotation marks, or within brackets. You use DataLink to reference a field in a database which is open; add new records to a database with a one-step process; provide record locking and unlocking for applications with file sharing abilities; maintain a position within the file; or to only browse the object while updating the value returned from the database. Maintaining your record position within the file requires using the Refresh( ) method to reset the field value in the browse object as the record pointer moves through the database.

Establish the file position prior to trying to open the file using the Open( ) method for the first time, or before you try to use Refresh( ) to obtain data via your DataLink reference. If you need to append data to your file, define the position of the file to the end of the file marker when you want to add the record.

If you choose not to assign the alias at the start of the routine, dBASE gets the data from the database and returns its own alias derived from the current work area name. You are not able to change this alias.

DataLink enables users to change the object's value. It also lets you modify the value of any control which also uses a DataLink reference, when the Event handler is activated. To modify the control, reset the Value property of the object, or use Refresh( ) to refresh the database's values.

The DataLink also lets you use the Submit( ) method to put values into the field of the database. Posting the values to the fields with Submit( ) causes dBASE to return to the record position where it had been before the last Refresh( ) was conducted, write the data into the databases that contain the field reference, release all locks, and set the value of ReadModal( ). ReadModal( ) returns a true value if the form had been opened with ReadModal( ). If Submit( ) was not executed, the value is false.

DataLink may be used in the DEFINE statement of the associated object. Dot reference notation enables you to set the property's value, query the value, and use the value of the property in a variable.

DataSource

Syntax

```
DataSource <expC>
```

Applies To

COMBOBOX, EDITOR, LISTBOX

Default

Empty String

Purpose: Specifies what prompts appear in a list box or combo box, or what text file or memo field appears in an editor object. The *<expC>* consists of a valid value character string within single or double quotations, or within brackets.

When used in a combo box or list box, the character string consists of one of the following statements:

```
"ARRAY <array name>"
"DIRECTORY <directory name skeleton>"
"DRIVE"
"FILEMASK <filename skeleton>"
"STRING <expC [, expC...]>"
"STRUCTURE"
```

To use the contents of an array as the prompts for your list box or combo box, use DataSource "ARRAY *<array name>*" where *<array name>* is the name of the source array. The elements may be of any type; however, DataSource only uses character strings as prompts. Therefore, any numerical values in the array would become text.

DataSource "DIRECTORY *<directory name skeleton>*" draws on all directory and subdirectory names within a specified drive and path for the prompts. DataSource "DRIVE" draws upon all local and network drive names and uses them as prompts. DataSource "FILEMASK *<filename skeleton>*" draws upon all valid filenames within a specified drive and path and uses them as prompts. DataSource "STRUCTURE" uses the fieldnames in an open active database as prompts. DataSource "STRING <expC1 [, expC...]] uses the character strings entered in the syntax as prompts.

When DataSource is used for an editor object, one of the following statements will be used in the *<expC>* statement of the property:

```
"MEMO <memo field name>"
"FILENAME <file name>"
```

DataSource "MEMO *<memo field name>*" displays the memo field in an editor object from an open active database currently being used. Information entered into the memo field may be saved to the memo file. DataSource "FILENAME *<file name>*" displays a text file in an editor object. You can use DataSource "FILENAME *<file name>*" with a file that has not been created, thus creating a new file, then save it with Ctrl-Enter or set the value of the SaveFile property to true.

DataSource may be used in the DEFINE statement of the associated object. Dot reference notation enables you to set the property's value, query the value, and use the value of the property in a variable.

Debug

Syntax

```
Debug <expC>
```

Applies To
BROWSE, CHECKBOX, COMBOBOX, ENTRYFIELD, FIELD, FORM, LISTBOX, MENU, MENUITEM PUSHBUTTON, RADIOBUTTON, SPINBOX

Default
False

Purpose: Evaluates the execution of a control's event handler code. Set the debugger to remember breakpoints if you don't want to have the Debug property start the debugger whenever an event handler executes its code.

Debug may be used in the DEFINE statement of the associated object. Dot reference notation enables you to set the property's value, query the value, and use the value of the property in a variable.

Default

Syntax

```
Default <expL>
```

Applies To
PUSHBUTTON

Default
False

Purpose: Determines which pushbutton is the one executed when the user pushes the Enter key. If no pushbuttons have their Default property set to true, then the first one created is executed when the Enter key is pressed. You can specify which pushbutton is the default by setting its Default property to true. If more than one pushbutton's Default property is set to true, only the last one set is recognized as the default pushbutton. Be careful that the default pushbutton's GrabFocus property is set to true, or it will not execute.

CUAENTER determines whether pressing Enter executes the default button of the form. If CUAENTER is ON and the Default property of a pushbutton is true, pressing Enter executes that pushbutton, unless another pushbutton has focus. This action triggers the OnClick event handlers for the pushbutton which had focus. The GrabFocus property activates the OnClick event handler, and selects the pushbutton if its value is true, or doesn't select the pushbutton if the value is false. If no default pushbutton has been defined on a given form, pressing Enter has no effect.

If CUAENTER is OFF, and focus is on anything other than the Editor object or a pushbutton, the Enter key merely tabs to the next pushbutton, giving that pushbutton focus. If the focus is on a pushbutton, the Enter activates the OnClick event handler.

Pressing Ctrl-Enter on a form that contains a default pushbutton, whether CUAENTER is ON or OFF, gives the default pushbutton the focus if GrabFocus is true, and executes the OnClick event handler.

Default may be used in the DEFINE statement of the associated object. Dot reference notation enables you to set the property's value, query the value, and use the value of the property in a variable.

Delete

Syntax

```
Delete <expL>
```

Applies To

BROWSE

Default

False

Purpose: Determines whether a user may mark records from a browse object for later deletion. This property can prevent unauthorized deletion of records by prohibiting marking of records from the browse object. Setting this property to true allows users to mark records for deletion and to recall records. The deletion will not occur until the PACK command is issued. This property has no effect on ON KEY, ON ERROR, OnSelChange, or EscExit.

Delete may be used in the DEFINE statement of the associated object. Dot reference notation enables you to set the property's value, query the value, and use the value of the property in a variable.

Design

Syntax

```
Design <expL>
```

Applies To

BROWSE, FORM, MENUBAR

Default

False

Purpose: Indicates whether the form window is in design mode. When true, the user is able to size and move the objects within the form window. This disables the event handlers during the design process. Set it back to false to prohibit changing the appearance of the form's objects. Design may be used in the DEFINE statement of the associated object. Dot reference notation enables you to set the property's value, query the value, and use the value of the property in a variable.

DesignSelect

Syntax

```
DesignSelect <expL>
```

Applies To

BROWSE, CHECKBOX, COMBOBOX, EDITOR, ENTRYFIELD, LISTBOX, PUSHBUTTON, RADIOBUTTON, RECTANGLE, SPINBOX, TEXT

Default

False

Purpose: Indicates that an object on a form window has been selected for modification through the Design property by displaying its colors in reverse video. When DesignSelect is set to false, the colors return to their normal appearance. DesignSelect may be used in the DEFINE statement of the associated object. Dot reference notation enables you to set the property's value, query the value, and use the value of the property in a variable.

Draw

Syntax

```
Draw <expL>
```

Applies To

EDITOR, FORM

Default

True

Purpose: Controls display and saving of defined objects. When true, any defined objects appear in the form window. When false, defined objects are saved without displaying them on the screen. Draw may be used with controls, text messages, and other objects. Draw may be used in the DEFINE statement of the associated object. Dot reference notation enables you to set the property's value, query the value, and use the value of the property in a variable.

Enabled

Syntax

```
Enabled <expL>
```

Applies To

BROWSE, CHECKBOX, COMBOBOX, EDITOR, ENTRYFIELD, FIELD, FORM, LISTBOX, MENU, MENUITEM, PUSHBUTTON, RADIOBUTTON, SPINBOX, TEXT

Default

True

Purpose: Determines the ability of an object to be selected and receive focus. When true, the object can be selected and receive focus. This allows the user to edit, view, or input data into the object. False disables the object's ability to gain focus. SetFocus( ) will return a value of false when Enabled is set to false. Some objects change appearance when disabled: check box, menu, menu item, pushbutton, radio button, and a text object if used as a label for another object. Enabled may be used in the DEFINE statement of the associated object. Dot reference notation enables you to set the property's value, query the value, and use the value of the property in a variable.

EscExit

Syntax

```
EscExit <expL>
```

Applies To

BROWSE, EDITOR, FORM

Default

True

Purpose: Controls the use of the Escape key as a means of closing a browse, editor, or form window. Setting EscExit to false disables the Escape key as a means of closing objects. ExcExit may be used in the DEFINE statement of the associated object. Dot reference notation enables you to set the property's value, query the value, and use the value of the property in a variable.

EventType

Syntax

```
EventType <expN>
```

Applies To

EVENT

Default

0 (zero)

Purpose: Passes information to the event handler procedures on how to respond to the keyboard or mouse. With EventType you can specify two types of events: evMouseDown (expN 0x0001) or evKeyDown (expN 0x0010). Additionally, several other event object properties pass information in a similar manner: KeyAlt, KeyCtrl, KeyNormal, KeyShift, KeyValue, MouseRow, MouseColumn, MouseLeft, MouseRight, and MouseMiddle. Refer to the individual property descriptions for more information on how each operates.

You may not use EventType from the DEFINE statement of the object. However, you may still use the dot reference notation to set the property's value, query the value, and use the value in a variable.

FieldArrange

Syntax

```
FieldArrange <expL>
```

Applies To

BROWSE

Default

False

Purpose: Determines whether the Field Arrange dialog box appears inside the browse object. The dialog box allows the user to add or remove, and rearrange the fields that are displayed in the browse object. The user calls the dialog box by double-clicking on the field heading. FieldArrange may be used in the DEFINE statement of the associated object. Dot reference notation enables you to set the property's value, query the value, and use the value of the property in a variable.

FieldList

Syntax

```
FieldList <object reference>
```

Applies To

BROWSE, FIELDLIST

Default

If none specified, all fields in the current database are displayed

Purpose: Sets the field list to display within a browse object, or creates a parent object for any fields objects that may be in the browse object. This property functions the same way that the SET FIELDS TO command worked in dBASE IV. FieldList may be used in the DEFINE statement of the associated object. Dot reference notation enables you to set the property's value, query the value, and use the value of the property in a variable.

First

Syntax

```
<object reference>.First
```

Applies To

FIELDLIST, FORM, MENU, MENUBAR

Default

First

Purpose: Determines which child objects receive focus upon the opening of a parent object. First operates as the opposite of the Parent property, as First returns the first child object of the parent object. In a menu bar object, First determines the first menu bar or item. In a menu object, First determines the first menu or menu item to be displayed.

First may not be used in the DEFINE statement of the object. However, you can use dot reference notation to set the property's value, query the value for the first child object, and use the value in a variable or parent form window. The value is returned *<object type>*::*<object reference>*. If the form window has no child objects, a value of false is returned.

Form

Syntax

```
<object reference>.Form
```

Applies To

MENU, MENUBAR, MENUITEM

Default

Returns a value of False if object is not a form window

Purpose: Returns the form window associated with a particular menu, menu bar, or menu item object. Form can be used to determine which form window is a child of a menu bar object by querying the parent object. The value is returned in the format FORM::*<object reference>*. You cannot use Form from the DEFINE statement, but you can still use the dot reference notation to query the value of the property and use the returned value in a variable.

Function

Syntax

```
Function <function symbol expC>
```

Applies To

COMBOBOX, ENTRYFIELD, FIELD, SPINBOX

Default

Empty string

Purpose: Specifies the way text appears in a control. Function specifies how text will be formatted the same way as the function parameter @...GET read command. The *<function symbol expC>* consists of a character string including one or more function symbols, and within single or double quotation marks, or within brackets. The function symbols (!, ^, $, A, D, E, L, M, R, S<*n*>, T) must begin with the @ symbol (which designates it as a function) and must not be separated by spaces, commas, or any other characters. For example, to restrict the data entry to alphabetic characters only, enter Function "@A". Text objects use the function symbols !, A, and T. Entry field and field objects use !, A, D, E, L, M, R, S<*n*>, and T. If you want to use some of the Picture symbols with the Function symbols, the Function symbols must be preceded by the @ symbol.

Function may be used in the DEFINE statement of the associated object. Dot reference notation enables you to set the property's value, query the value, and use the value of the property in a variable.

GrabFocus

Syntax

```
GrabFocus <expL>
```

Applies To

PUSHBUTTON

Default

True

Purpose: Defines what happens when a pushbutton is selected. GrabFocus combines with the TabStop property to create three styles for what occurs when a pushbutton is selected by the user.

Style	GrabFocus	TabStop
Normal	True	True
Cancel	False	True
Speedbar	False	False

The Normal style causes dBASE to execute the Valid event handler. Then the OnLostFocus event handler for the object which had focus is executed. Once that is accomplished, focus is transferred to the pushbutton. If the user selects the pushbutton again, a procedure is activated based on what action had been defined for a mouseclick or tabbed selection. If the user enters data into an entry field, the pushbutton becomes highlighted and only executes the associated action when the user selects the pushbutton.

The Cancel style ignores the Valid and OnLostFocus event handlers for the object selected previously, and goes right to putting focus on the pushbutton that the user selected. The OnGotFocus event handler is then executed. If the pushbutton is again selected, the OnClick event handler is executed. The pushbutton only appears highlighted when selected.

The Speedbar style also ignores the Valid and OnLostFocus event handlers for the object which was highlighted. However, the user cannot tab to any pushbuttons so no pushbuttons receive focus. The user may select the pushbutton by clicking on it, at which time dBASE will execute the OnClick event handler.

You may use dot reference notation to set the property's value, query the value, and then use the returned value in a variable. You may not use GrabFocus from the DEFINE statement of the object.

Grid

Syntax

```
Grid <expL>
```

Applies To

BROWSE

Default

True

Purpose: Determines whether grid lines will be visible in the browse object. The grid lines provide distinguishing lines between the various columns and rows of the browse object, which may make it easier to read the fields and records. Grid may be used in the DEFINE statement of the associated object. Dot reference notation enables you to set the property's value, query the value, and use the value of the property in a variable.

Group

Syntax

```
Group <expL>
```

Applies To

CHECKBOX, RADIOBUTTON

Default

True

Purpose: Determines whether the control being defined, the current control, and the controls defined next, are all part of the same group. The user may select only one control from within a group. Movement from control to control within a group is accomplished by pressing the arrow keys. To move to a different group press the Tab key. When you tab into a different group, dBASE returns focus to the last control which had focus. The tabbing order of a group determines the extent of any group. Only the first control in the group may have a true value; the rest must have a false Group property value.

Radio buttons within one group can only have one button's Value property set to true at one time. If no radio button in the group has its Value property set to true, focus is given to the first radio button in the group and its Value property is automatically set to true.

Group may be used in the DEFINE statement of the associated object. Dot reference notation enables you to set the property's value, query the value, and use the value of the property in a variable.

Heading

Syntax

```
Heading <expC>
```

Applies To

FIELD

Default

Field name

Purpose: Creates the heading (title) for the field contained in a field list of a browse object. The *<expC>* consists of any character string desired as a heading for the field. Heading may be used in the DEFINE statement of the associated object. Dot reference notation enables you to set the property's value, query the value, and use the value of the property in a variable.

Height

Syntax

```
Height <expN>
```

Applies To

BROWSE, CHECKBOX, COMBOBOX, EDITOR, ENTRYFIELD, FORM, LISTBOX, PUSHBUTTON, RADIOBUTTON, RECTANGLE, SPINBOX, TEXT

Default

Object	Height
Browse	10
Check box	1
Combo box	5
Editor	10

Object	Height
Entry field	1
Form	10
List box	5
Pushbutton	2
Radio button	1
Rectangle	5
Spin box	1
Text	1

Purpose: Sets the exact heigh of the object. The measurement, based on the character's size in the row, refers to the distance from the base of the object to the top of it. This property can be used in combination with the Width property to control the exact dimensions of an object. You can also set the Top, Left, Width, and Height properties from the DEFINE statement by using FROM *<row1>*,*<col1>* TO *<row2>*,*<col2>*. The height of the object does not include the border of the object if the Border property for the object is true. The default height settings depend on the type and contents of the object. See the DEFINE command for the individual object for more information.

Height may be used in the DEFINE statement of the associated object. Dot reference notation enables you to set the property's value, query the value, and use the value of the property in a variable.

HelpFile

Syntax

```
HelpFile <file name expC>
```

Applies To

BROWSE, CHECKBOX, COMBOBOX, EDITOR, ENTRYFIELD, FIELD, FORM, LISTBOX, MENU, MENUITEM, PUSHBUTTON, RADIOBUTTON, SPINBOX, TEXT

Default

Empty string

Purpose: Specifies a help file (DBF) which holds the information to be used for help topics tied to specific actions, fields, or events. This property, used together with the HelpId property, provides the helpful hints necessary to make the application user-friendly. The HelpId lists the topic for a specific context-sensitive help file; HelpFile contains the text for the field. Set up your help system by putting the name of the help file into the object's HelpFile property, then put the keyword (field name) of the help topic into the object's HelpId property. The keyword may consist of characters or numbers.

Before you can implement your help system, however, it is necessary to set up specific procedures for event handling when the OnHelp event handler is executed by the user selecting the object and pressing F1. The OnHelp event handler that you design functions by using the HelpId and HelpFile properties to find the help topic in the help file database.

HelpFile may be used in the DEFINE statement of the associated object. Dot reference notation enables you to set the property's value, query the value, and use the value of the property in a variable.

HelpId

Syntax

```
HelpId <context string exp>
```

Applies To

BROWSE, CHECKBOX, COMBOBOX, EDITOR, ENTRYFIELD, FIELD, FORM, LISTBOX, MENU, MENUITEM, PUSHBUTTON, RADIOBUTTON, SPINBOX, TEXT

Default

Empty String

Purpose: Provides the information specifying the help topic to be displayed from the HelpFile. See HelpFile.

InsertLine

Syntax

```
<object reference>.InsertLine<text expC>
```

Applies To

EDITOR

Default
Empty string

Purpose: Indicates a character string to be inserted in an editor object on the line following the one that the LineNo property points to. The *<text expC>* consists of text within single or double quotation marks, or within brackets. It is not necessary to add a CR/LF (carriage return/line feed) to the statement. You cannot use InsertLine from the DEFINE statement. Dot reference notation allows you to insert the text by using the following syntax: *<editor object reference>*.InsertLine = *<"character string">*.

Key

Syntax

```
Key <procedure>
```

Applies To
ENTRYFIELD, FIELD, FORM

Default
Empty string

Purpose: Calls a procedure when a user presses a key. This property allows you to change the character being entered by the user to a different character. A typical use is to protect the password being entered at the keyboard by displaying asterisks on the screen for each letter of the password typed. Two parameters are sent to the object's event handler by Key. The first consists of the ASCII decimal number of the character. The second relates the position of the character within the character string being typed by the user. Key may be used in the DEFINE statement of the associated object. Dot reference notation enables you to set the property's value, query the value, and use the value of the property in a variable.

KeyAlt

Syntax

```
KeyAlt <expL>
```

Applies To
EVENT

Default
Returns a true value if the Alt key was pressed

Purpose: Returns a value that specifies if the Alt key had been pressed by the user. This property is used by dBASE as a means for passing information from an event to an event handler. For instance, when an object is selected, the OnClick event calls a procedure based on the information relayed by the KeyAlt property. There are several properties that act as a go-between for events and event handlers: EventType, KeyCtrl, KeyNormal, KeyShift, KeyValue, MouseRow, MouseColumn, MouseLeft, MouseRight, and MouseMiddle.

KeyAlt cannot be used in the DEFINE statement of the associated object. Dot reference notation, however, enables you to query the property's value, and use the returned value of the property in a variable.

KeyCtrl

Syntax

```
KeyCtrl <expL>
```

Applies To

EVENT

Default

Returns a true value if the Control (Ctrl) key was pressed

Purpose: Returns a value that specifies if the Ctrl key had been pressed by the user. KeyCtrl works similar to KeyAlt.

KeyNormal

Syntax

```
KeyNormal <expL>
```

Applies To

EVENT

Default

Returns a true value if Shift, Alt, or Ctrl were not pressed

Purpose: Determines if the Shift, Alt, or Ctrl keys were not pressed during the last combination of keystrokes. This property works similar to KeyAlt and Key Ctrl.

KeyShift

Syntax

```
KeyShift <expL>
```

Applies To

EVENT

Default

Returns a true value if the Shift key was pressed

Purpose: Determines whether the Shift key was pressed during the last combination of keystrokes. KeyShift works the same way as KeyAlt.

KeyValue

Syntax

```
<object reference>.KeyValue<key value name>
```

Applies To

EVENT

Default

Empty string

Purpose: Determines what key or combination of keys were pressed on the keyboard. The value is determined from the codes listed in Table 26.1. The property passes information from the event to the event handler. You cannot use KeyValue from the DEFINE statement. However, you can use dot reference notation to set the property's value, query the value, and use the returned value in a variable.

Table 26.1 Key Value Properties

Key	Value
kbCtrlA	1
kbCtrlB	2
kbCtrlC	3
kbCtrlD	4
kbCtrlE	5

(continues)

Table 26.1 Continued

Key	Value
kbCtrlF	6
kbCtrlG	7
kbCtrlH	8
kbCtrlI	9
kbCtrlJ	10
kbCtrlK	11
kbCtrlL	12
kbCtrlM	13
kbCtrlN	14
kbCtrlO	15
kbCtrlP	16
kbCtrlQ	17
kbCtrlR	18
kbCtrlS	19
kbCtrlT	20
kbCtrlU	21
kbCtrlV	22
kbCtrlW	23
kbCtrlX	24
kbCtrlY	25
kbCtrlZ	26
Extended key codes	
kbEsc	283
kbAltSpace	512
kbCtrlIns	1024
kbShiftIns	1280

Key	Value
Extended key codes	
kbCtrlDel	1536
kbShiftDel	1792
kbBack	3592
kbCtrlBack	3711
kbShiftTab	3840
kbTab	3849
kbAltQ	4096
kbAltW	4352
kbAltE	4608
kbAltR	4864
kbAltT	5120
kbAltY	5376
kbAltU	5632
kbAltI	5888
kbAltO	6144
kbAltP	6400
kbCtrlEnter	7178
kbEnter	13
kbAltA	7680
kbAltS	7936
kbAltD	8192
kbAltF	8448
kbAltG	8704
kbAltH	8960
kbAltJ	9216
kbAltK	9472

(continues)

Table 26.1 Continued	
Key	**Value**
Extended key codes	
kbAltL	9728
kbAltZ	11264
kbAltX	11520
kbAltC	11776
kbAltV	12032
kbAltB	12288
kbAltN	12544
kbAltM	12800
kbF1	15104
kbF2	15360
kbF3	15616
kbF4	15872
kbF5	16128
kbF6	16384
kbF7	16640
kbF8	16896
kbF9	17152
kbF10	17408
kbHome	18176
kbUp	18432
kbPgUp	18688
kbGrayMinus	18989
kbLeft	19200
kbRight	19712
kbGrayPlus	20011

Key	Value
Extended key codes	
kbEnd	20224
kbDown	20480
kbPgDn	20736
kbIns	20992
kbDel	21248
kbShiftF1	21504
kbShiftF2	21760
kbShiftF3	22016
kbShiftF4	22272
kbShiftF5	22528
kbShiftF6	22784
kbShiftF7	23040
kbShiftF8	23296
kbShiftF9	23552
kbShiftF10	23808
kbCtrlF1	24064
kbCtrlF2	24320
kbCtrlF3	24576
kbCtrlF4	24832
kbCtrlF5	25088
kbCtrlF6	25344
kbCtrlF7	25600
kbCtrlF8	25856
kbCtrlF9	26112
kbCtrlF10	26368
kbAltF1	26624

(continues)

Table 26.1 Continued

Key	Value
Extended key codes	
kbAltF2	26880
kbAltF3	27136
kbAltF4	27392
kbAltF5	27648
kbAltF6	27904
kbAltF7	28160
kbAltF8	28416
kbAltF9	28672
kbAltF10	28928
kbCtrlPrtSc	29184
kbCtrlLeft	29440
kbCtrlRight	29696
kbCtrlEnd	29952
kbCtrlPgDn	30208
kbCtrlHome	30464
kbAlt1	30720
kbAlt2	30976
kbAlt3	31232
kbAlt4	31488
kbAlt5	31744
kbAlt6	32000
kbAlt7	32256
kbAlt8	32512
kbAlt9	32768
kbAlt0	33024

Key	Value
Extended key codes	
kbAltMinus	33280
kbAltEqual	33536
kbCtrlPgUp	33792
kbNoKey	0
kbRightShift	1
kbLeftShift	2
kbCtrlShift	4
kbAltShift	8
kbScrollState	16
kbNumState	32
kbCapsState	64
kbInsState	128
Standard keyboard keys	
kbAsterisk	42
kbDot	46
kbEquals	61
kbMinus	45
kbPlus	43
kbSlash	47
kbLC_c	99
kbLC_n	110
kbUC_C	67
kbUC_N	78
kb0	48
kb1	49
kb2	50

(continues)

Table 26.1 Continued

Key	Value
Standard keyboard keys	
kb3	51
kb4	52
kb5	53
kb6	54
kb7	55
kb8	56
kb9	57

Label

Syntax

```
Label <expL>
```

Applies To

TEXT

Default

True

Purpose: Sets the way that text is treated in an object that loses focus. If you want the text to remain highlighted when it has lost focus, set Label to true. dBASE will then ignore Picture and Function property settings. A pick character can be defined by placing an ampersand (&) in front of the character, or by using a tilde (~) both in front of and behind the character. Setting Label to false removes the highlighting when focus shifts to another object, and allows the tilde and ampersand symbols to appear alongside the text.

Label can be used from the DEFINE statement of the associated object. Dot reference notation can be used to set the property's value, query the value, and use the returned value in a variable.

Left

Syntax

```
Left <column expN>
```

Applies To

BROWSE, CHECKBOX, COMBOBOX, EDITOR, ENTRYFIELD, FORM, LISTBOX, PUSHBUTTON, RADIOBUTTON, RECTANGLE, SPINBOX, TEXT

Default

0

Purpose: Determines the location of an object's left border relative to the parent form window, or to the Desktop if no parent object was created. The location of the left border is measured in character columns. Entering a value of zero in the Left property causes the object's border to appear at the left border of the form window. Entering a value of the Width plus one character positions the border on the right border of the form window. While the zero column is set to the far left column on the screen, if the screen window has a border, then the first column inside of the window is called the zero column.

You can use the Top property to further control the location of the border on the form window. You can also use FROM...TO and the AT clause of the DEFINE statement to specify where the border shall appear. If you want the object to size itself, use the FROM...TO clause which sizes the border by requiring the location of the upper-left and lower-right corners. The AT clause only asks for the upper-left corner coordinates, and therefore provides no sizing capability.

You can use the Left property from the DEFINE statement. You may also use dot reference notation to set the property's value, query the value, and use the returned value.

LineNo

Syntax

```
LineNo <line number expN>
```

Applies To

EDITOR

Default

1

Purpose: Indicates the line number in an editor object which currently is active. You can use LineNo to perform a type of GoTo cursor movement. You cannot use LineNo from the DEFINE statement of the associated object. However, you may use dot reference notation to specify a line number, query the value and use that value in a variable.

Lines

Syntax

```
<object reference>.Lines
```

Applies To
EDITOR

Default
1

Purpose: Returns the value of the current line number within the editor object. Whenever LineNo is already set to be positioned on the last line of the edit buffer, you can add a line to the editor object with the InsertLine property. dBASE then increases the number of lines by one for each line added. Lines cannot be used from the DEFINE statement of the object. You can use dot reference notation to query the value of the property and use the returned value in a variable.

Lock

Syntax

```
Lock <fields expN>
```

Applies To
BROWSE

Default
0

Purpose: Sets the number of fields to lock into place as the user scrolls through a browse object. Setting Lock to zero allows all the fields to scroll. When a non-zero positive number is entered in the value of Lock, the locked fields appear to the left as the user scrolls right or left. Lock can be used from the DEFINE statement. Dot reference notation allows you to set the property's value, query that value, and use the returned value.

Maximize

Syntax

```
Maximize <expL>
```

Applies To

BROWSE, EDITOR, FORM

Default

False

Purpose: Determines whether a maximize button appears on the window to give the user the option for maximizing the form window. A form window normally contains both a Minimize button and a Maximize button. When the form is maximized it takes up the entire work area defined by the parent form window or windows, usually roughly equivalent to the screen size. (Minimizing the window shrinks the window down to a small icon.) If you want the user to have this option, set Maximize to true, or false if you don't want the form window maximized. If the MDI property has a true value set, the Maximize property is also set to true. However, if you decide to use the OF *<form>* clause to specify the form that the Maximize property affects, the default value of Maximize is set to false.

Maximize may be used from the DEFINE statement of the associated object. You may also use dot reference notation to set the property's value, query that value, and use the returned value.

MDI

Syntax

```
MDI <expL>
```

Applies To

FORM

Default

True

False if opened with ReadModal( )

Purpose: Toggles MDI compatibility on and off. MDI (Multiple Document Interface) gives the user the ability to open more than one form in a window. If the Moveable and Sizeable properties have been set to true, setting MDI to true allows the forms to be displayed in tiled or cascaded format. It also replaces the Desktop menu with the window's menu, and places a number in the upper-right corner of the MDI window. Setting the MDI property to false positions the menu inside the form window.

Pressing Alt-N (where N is the number of the window) jumps the focus to the desired window. To close the form window, press Ctrl-F4, or press Esc if the EscExit property has been set to true. If the form was opened with the ReadModal( ) method, pressing Alt-F4 closes the application window.
You can use Ctrl-F6 to move between the form's child windows.

MDI may be used from the DEFINE statement of the associated object. You may also use dot reference notation to set the property's value, query that value, and use the returned value.

Menu

Syntax

```
Menu <menu bar object reference>
```

Applies To

BROWSE, EDITOR, FORM

Default

False

Purpose: Determines which menu bar is to be displayed inside a browse, editor, or form object. Menu may be used from the DEFINE statement of the associated object. You may also use dot reference notation to set the property's value, query that value, and use the returned value.

Minimize

Syntax

```
Minimize <expL>
```

Applies To

BROWSE, EDITOR, FORM

Default

False

Purpose: Determines whether a minimize button appears on the window to give the user the option for reducing the form window. A form window normally contains both a Minimize button and a Maximize button. When the form is minimized it shrinks the window to an icon which appears at the bottom of the screen. (Maximizing the window normally causes the window to fill the entire screen.) If you want the user to have this option, set Minimize to true, or false if you don't want the form window minimized. If the MDI property has a true value set, the Minimize property is also set to true. However, if you decide to use the OF *<form>* clause to specify the form that the Minimize property affects, the default value of Minimize is set to false.

Minimize may be used from the DEFINE statement of the associated object. You may also use dot reference notation to set the property's value, query that value, and use the returned value.

Modify

Syntax

```
Modify <expL>
```

Applies To

BROWSE, EDITOR

Default

True

Purpose: Determines whether a user is allowed to edit the contents of a browse or editor object. If you don't want the user to be able to change records or text, set this property to false, which will also cause the object's Key event handler to be executed if one has been defined.

Modify may be used from the DEFINE statement of the associated object. You may also use dot reference notation to set the property's value, query that value, and use the returned value.

MouseColumn

Syntax

```
MouseColumn <column expN>
```

Applies To

EVENT

Default

0, if the mouse has not moved.

Purpose: Returns a value which indicates the column in which the mouse click occurred. This is used in conjunction with the OnClick and Key properties to pass relevant information to the event handlers associated with the object. See EventType, KeyAlt, KeyCtrl, KeyNormal, KeyShift, KeyValue, MouseLeft, MouseRight, MouseRow, and MouseMiddle.

You can use dot reference notation to query the value of the property and to use the returned value.

MouseLeft

Syntax

```
MouseLeft <expL>
```

Applies To

EVENT

Default

True, if the left mouse button has been pressed.

Purpose: Returns a logical value which indicates when the left mouse button was pressed by the user. This is used in conjunction with the OnClick and Key properties to pass relevant information to the event handlers associated with the object. See EventType, KeyAlt, KeyCtrl, KeyNormal, KeyShift, KeyValue, MouseRow, MouseColumn, MouseRight, and MouseMiddle.

You can use dot reference notation to query the value of the property and to use the returned value.

MouseMiddle

Syntax

```
MouseMiddle <expL>
```

Applies To

EVENT

Default

True, if the middle mouse button has been pressed.

Purpose: Returns a value which indicates if the middle mouse button was pressed. This is used in conjunction with the OnClick and Key properties to pass relevant information to the event handlers associated with the object. See EventType, KeyAlt, KeyCtrl, KeyNormal, KeyShift, KeyValue, MouseRow, MouseLeft, MouseRight, and MouseColumn.

You can use dot reference notation to query the value of the property and to use the returned value.

MouseRight

Syntax

```
MouseRight <expL>
```

Applies To

EVENT

Default

True, if the right mouse button has been pressed.

Purpose: Returns a value which indicates if the right mouse button was pressed by the user. This is used in conjunction with the OnClick and Key properties to pass relevant information to the event handlers associated with the object. See EventType, KeyAlt, KeyCtrl, KeyNormal, KeyShift, KeyValue, MouseRow, MouseLeft, MouseColumn, and MouseMiddle.

You can use dot reference notation to query the value of the property and to use the returned value.

MouseRow

Syntax

```
MouseRow <row expN>
```

Applies To

EVENT

Default

0

Purpose: Returns a value which represents the row position at which the mouse click occurred from within the current object. This is used in conjunction with the OnClick and Key properties to pass relevant information to the event handlers associated with the object. See EventType, KeyAlt, KeyCtrl, KeyNormal, KeyShift, KeyValue, MouseLeft, MouseColumn, and MouseMiddle.

You can use dot reference notation to query the value of the property and to use the returned value.

Moveable

Syntax

```
Moveable <expL>
```

Applies To

BROWSE, EDITOR, FORM

Default

True. Browse object default varies.

Purpose: Allows the user to reposition the object with the mouse, if set to true. If the Text property has been set to true, a title bar will appear in the window. This allows the object to be moved even if the Moveable property has been set to false. Using the option clause OF *<form>* resets the Moveable property to false.

Moveable may be used from the DEFINE statement of the associated object. You may also use dot reference notation to set the property's value, query that value, and use the returned value.

Name

Syntax

```
<object name expC>.Name
```

Applies To

BROWSE, CHECKBOX, COMBOBOX, EDITOR, ENTRYFIELD, FIELD, FIELDLIST, FORM, LISTBOX, OBJECT, PUSHBUTTON, RADIOBUTTON, RECTANGLE, SPINBOX, TEXT

Default

Name of object assigned when defined

Purpose: Retrieves the name of an object. When entering *<object name expC>* be sure to use single or double quotation marks, or brackets on either side of the object name. Name may not be used from the DEFINE statement. Use dot reference notation to query the value of the property and use the returned value.

NavBar

Syntax

```
NavBar <expL>
```

Applies To

BROWSE

Default

True

Purpose: Determines whether a navigation bar appears in a browse object, allowing the user to scroll through the contents of display. When set to true, the user may use the scroll arrows to step through the records, or the "#" symbol to return to the selected record, or the arrow and bar to move to the first or last record of the display. When set to false, the user may scroll through the display, but may not change the record pointer.

NavBar may be used from the DEFINE statement of the associated object. You may also use dot reference notation to set the property's value, query that value, and use the returned value.

OnAppend

Syntax

```
OnAppend <procedure>
```

Applies To

BROWSE

Default

Empty string

Purpose: Ensures that specified actions are performed before records are added to a data table. You specify an event handler which will be executed when the user wishes to add records. OnAppend may be used from the DEFINE statement of the associated object. You may also use dot reference notation to set the property's value, query that value, and use the returned value.

OnChange

Syntax

```
OnChange <procedure>
```

Applies To

BROWSE, CHECKBOX, COMBOBOX, RADIOBUTTON

Default

Empty string

Purpose: Specifies the actions to be performed when a user modifies an entry. These actions are accomplished automatically when the user changes a field's contents and moves to a new location in the browse object, changes a check box setting, moves between prompts in a combo box or spin box, clicks a different radio button, or moves from a previously modified record to a new record in the browse object. The OnChange event handler is only executed when the change is completed, which is indicated by the user moving to a different record.

OnChange may be used from the DEFINE statement of the associated object. You may also use dot reference notation to set the property's value, query that value, and use the returned value.

OnClick

Syntax

```
OnClick <procedure>
```

Applies To

FORM, MENU, MENUITEM, PUSHBUTTON, TEXT

Default

Empty string

Purpose: Indicates the name of an event handler to be executed upon selection of the object. These actions are then performed automatically. OnClick may be used from the DEFINE statement of the associated object. You may also use dot reference notation to set the property's value, query that value, and use the returned value.

OnClose

Syntax

```
OnClose <procedure>
```

Applies To

BROWSE, EDITOR, FORM

Default

Empty string

Purpose: Determines the procedures to be executed when the user clicks the Close icon, presses Ctrl-F4 or Esc, or when the form.Close( ) or form.Release( ) methods are executed. After one of these options has been executed, the OnClose event handler causes dBASE to execute the Valid event handler for the control on the form which currently has focus, if one has been defined. A false value returned from the Valid event handler leaves the form window open. The OnLostFocus event handler for that control is then executed, followed by the OnLostFocus event handler for the form window. Next the form window's OnClose event handler is activated, which in turn clears the form window from the screen and closes all controls and child windows.

OnClose may be used from the DEFINE statement of the associated object. You may also use dot reference notation to set the property's value, query that value, and use the returned value.

OnDelete

Syntax

```
OnDelete <procedure>
```

Applies To

BROWSE

Default

Empty string

Purpose: Indicates the actions to be performed after a user deletes a record from within a browse object. The *<procedure>* is the name of the event handler that should be run for deletion events. The user can either mark the records for deletion individually, or press Ctrl-U while the record has focus to have dBASE mark the record and activate the OnDelete event handler.

OnDelete may be used from the DEFINE statement of the associated object. You may also use dot reference notation to set the property's value, query that value, and use the returned value.

OnEdit

Syntax

```
OnEdit <procedure>
```

Applies To

BROWSE

Default

Empty string

Purpose: Activates a specified procedure that is triggered by any modifications performed on a field within a browse object. The OnEdit event handler is executed only after the user has moved the focus from the edited field to another field in the browse object. This calls the OnChange event handler, which in turn calls the OnSkip event handler to complete the edit process and change focus.

OnEdit may be used from the DEFINE statement of the associated object. You may also use dot reference notation to set the property's value, query that value, and use the returned value.

OnGotFocus

Syntax

```
OnGotFocus <procedure>
```

Applies To

BROWSE, CHECKBOX, COMBOBOX, EDITOR, ENTRYFIELD, FIELD, FORM, LISTBOX, PUSHBUTTON, RADIOBUTTON, SPINBOX

Default

Empty string

Purpose: Executes a set of actions when focus transfers to an object by means of the tab key, a mouse click, or by dBASE assigning focus. The *<procedure>* is the name of the procedure to be executed when the object receives focus. If no procedure is defined for OnGotFocus nothing happens when focus is received by the object.

OnGotFocus may be used from the DEFINE statement of the associated object. You may also use dot reference notation to set the property's value, query that value, and use the returned value.

OnHelp

Syntax

```
OnHelp <procedure>
```

Applies To

BROWSE, CHECKBOX, COMBOBOX, EDITOR, ENTRYFIELD, FIELD, FORM, LISTBOX, MENU, MENUITEM, PUSHBUTTON, RADIOBUTTON, SPINBOX

Default

Empty string

Purpose: Calls a given event handler when an object has focus and the user presses F1. The *this* object reference will retrieve all associated information for the object, rather than just the help context information for the object, thus providing more complete information for the user. You can also use the Form Designer to create help for objects. See Chapter 21, "Creating Objects with UI," for more information on the Form Designer.

OnHelp may be used from the DEFINE statement of the associated object. You may also use dot reference notation to set the property's value, query that value, and use the returned value.

OnLostFocus

Syntax

```
OnLostFocus <procedure>
```

Applies To

BROWSE, CHECKBOX, COMBOBOX, EDITOR, ENTRYFIELD, FIELD, FORM, LISTBOX, PUSHBUTTON, RADIOBUTTON, SPINBOX

Default

Empty string

Purpose: Executes a specified action or actions when an object loses focus due to the user choosing a different control, dBASE moving focus automatically, or your program shifting focus. When a control loses focus, the OnLostFocus event handler immediately executes the procedure named in

<procedure>. This works differently than the Valid property which insists on receiving a returned logical value of true before executing the procedure.

OnLostFocus may be used from the DEFINE statement of the associated object. You may also use dot reference notation to set the property's value, query that value, and use the returned value.

OnMouseDblClk

Syntax

```
OnMouseDblClk <procedure>
```

Applies To

FORM, TEXT

Default

Empty string

Purpose: Executes specified actions when a double-click is made within a form window, but not on a control. OnMouseDblClk may be used from the DEFINE statement of the associated object. You may also use dot reference notation to set the property's value, query that value, and use the returned value.

OnMove

Syntax

```
OnMove <procedure>
```

Applies To

FORM

Default

Empty string

Purpose: Indicates an event handler which contains a set of actions to be performed automatically when the form window is moved. OnMove may be used from the DEFINE statement of the associated object. You may also use dot reference notation to set the property's value, query that value, and use the returned value.

OnOpen

Syntax

```
OnOpen <procedure>
```

Applies To

BROWSE, EDITOR, FORM

Default

Empty string

Purpose: Calls an event handler (*<procedure>*) which contains specific actions to be performed before opening the associated window. A window may be opened by the user by entering a command at the Command window, using program files, or with the help of an event handler.

Before you can open the window, though, you must set up the links between the displayed fields and the window. You do this with the Value property, which assigns the original values of the window, or by using the DataLink property, which links the fields to be displayed to an alias or database name. Once the original values are set, use the Open( ) method to open the window or editor. Then when the user wants to open the window, the OnOpen property executes the appropriate event handler, allowing the user to work with the fields displayed in the form window.

OnOpen may be used from the DEFINE statement of the associated object. You may also use dot reference notation to set the property's value, query that value, and use the returned value.

OnSelChange

Syntax

```
OnSelChange <procedure>
```

Applies To

COMBOBOX, ENTRYFIELD, FIELD, LISTBOX, SPINBOX

Default

Empty string

Purpose: Activates an event handler when focus is changed from one control to another, a value is changed in an entry field or field via an @M list selection, or the value in a spin box is changed. OnSelChange may be used from the DEFINE statement of the associated object. You may also use dot reference notation to set the property's value, query that value, and use the returned value.

OnSize

Syntax

```
OnSize <procedure>
```

Applies To

FORM

Default

Empty string

Purpose: Calls an event handler (*<procedure>*) which contains specific actions to be performed if the user modifies the size of the window. The window can only be resized if the Sizeable property is set to true, and the OnGotFocus property event handlers have been executed. OnSize may be used from the DEFINE statement of the associated object. You may also use dot reference notation to set the property's value, query that value, and use the returned value.

OnSkip

Syntax

```
OnSkip <procedure>
```

Applies To

BROWSE

Default

Empty string

Purpose: Calls an event handler which contains specified actions to be executed if the record pointer moves within a browse object. The record pointer is moved by pressing the up- or down-arrow keys, Ctrl-PgDn, Ctrl-PgUp, or the arrows on the navigation bar. OnSkip is executed after the OnChange event handler completes its execution. OnSkip may be used from the DEFINE statement of the associated object. You may also use dot reference notation to set the property's value, query that value, and use the returned value.

Parent

Syntax

```
Parent <picture template expC>
```

Applies To

BROWSE, CHECKBOX, COMBOBOX, EDITOR, ENTRYFIELD, FIELD, FIELDLIST, FORM, LISTBOX, MENU, MENUBAR, MENUITEM, PUSHBUTTON, RADIOBUTTON, SPINBOX, TEXT

Default

False if object has no parent, or is not contained in an object

Purpose: Determines whether an object has a parent object by returning the name of the parent object. The inverse of Parent is First, which returns the name of the child object. Parent may be used from the DEFINE statement of the associated object. You may also use dot reference notation to set the property's value, query that value, and use the returned value. The returned value is either the name of the parent object or false if no parent object exists.

Picture

Syntax

```
Picture <picture template expC>
```

Applies To

COMBOBOX, ENTRYFIELD, FIELD, SPINBOX

Default

Empty string

Purpose: Determines how the characters in a text string are read by dBASE. *<picture template expC>* contains picture template characters within single or double quotation marks or brackets. This property works like the @...GET...READ command. The template consists of picture template characters (see Table 26.2), function symbols (see Function property) and individual alphanumeric characters in the text string. Function symbols may be incorporated into the *<picture template expC>* by preceding them with the @ symbol. When mixing picture and template functions in one expression, list the function symbols first, insert a space, then list the picture template characters.

Table 26.2 Picture Template Characters Used in the Picture Property

Template Character	Result
9	Only accepts numbers, the plus (+) and minus (–) signs as valid characters
#	Limits valid characters to number, spaces, periods, and signs
!	Turns input into uppercase characters
$	Replaces leading blanks with the dollar sign or whatever symbol is defined by the SET CURRENCY TO command
*	Leading blanks replaced by asterisks
.	Sets where the decimal point or other decimal indicator (set by SET SEPARATOR) is entered
,	Sets thousands separator with a comma, unless defined differently by SET SEPARATOR
A	Only accepts alphabetic characters
L	Only accepts logical operators (T, t, F, f, Y, y, N, n), which are then converted to uppercase
N	Only accepts alphanumeric characters and underscore characters. Does not allow spaces or punctuation
X	All characters are accepted
Y	Only accepts Y, y, N, or n.

Picture may be used from the DEFINE statement of the associated object. You may also use dot reference notation to set the property's value, query that value, and use the returned value.

ProcFile

Syntax

```
ProcFile <filename expC>[,] [<path>\]<object filename expC>
```

Applies To

BROWSE, CHECKBOX, COMBOBOX, EDITOR, ENTRYFIELD, FIELD, FORM, LISTBOX, MENU, MENUBAR, MENUITEM, PUSHBUTTON, RADIOBUTTON, SPINBOX, TEXT

Default
Parent object's ProcFile property value is used for an object whose ProcFile property is not defined. If no library or linked object file (DBO) is given, the parent's DBO file is used.

For form windows, browse objects, and editor objects, the ProcFile is the name of the source file (PRG) which contains the DEFINE statement of the object. The full path of the file containing the DBO file is included for files which are compiled and linked, however, if the source code file is given without specifying the DBO file, the full path of all linked files is included.

Purpose: Indicates the name and location of PRG and DBO files (if necessary) which hold the event handlers for the object in the DEFINE statement. Whenever possible use the default settings for this property.

There may be times when you will need to call PRG or DBO files from a different directory than the current one. You can use ProcFile to identify what files and where they are located by specifying the source file name in one of three ways: simply state the source filename; state the source filename with a comma after it, then the full path of the file; or state the filename with just the comma after it.

When you only state the filename, dBASE automatically attaches the linked DBO filename. For a program file that is located in the PROCS directory with a DBO file located in the subdirectory System1, dBASE takes the following statement:

```
form.Radiobutton.ProcFile = "close.prg"
```

and gives it a value of

```
CLOSE.PRG,C:\procs\System1
```

However, if you tell dBASE that the source file is CLOSE.PRG,C:\procs\System1 it knows that all the linked and compiled source code is located in that subdirectory.

Placing a comma after the filename and not specifying the path causes dBASE to look for the event handler procedures in an object file based on the string within the quotes used. For example, entering "close.prg" as the filename tells dBASE to use CLOSE.DBO to look for the compiled and linked object file source code.

Note

You must always give the full path and source filename when setting a value for ProcFile with a desktop object outside of the DEFINE statement.

You may also use ProcFile to use external functions from within an event handler. Remember that ProcFile can only name the filename and location of the function, so you may need to ensure that the source file and the function or procedure are in the same source file as the event handler. SYSPROC or CONFIG.DB's library values, or SET PROCEDURE can tell you if the function will be available at execution.

Another use for ProcFile is to use event handlers which have the same name but are located in different source code files. Anytime that a dBASE event handler uses an external function or procedure, it searches SYSPROC, then the current DBO file, SET PROCEDURE, any DBOs being called, SET LIBRARY, DBO, PRG, and PRS.

ProcFile may be used from the DEFINE statement of the associated object. You may also use dot reference notation to set the property's value, query that value, and use the returned value.

RangeMax

Syntax

```
RangeMax <expD ¦ expN>
```

Applies To

COMBOBOX, ENTRYFIELD, FIELD, SPINBOX

Default

False when multiple data types are used; 0 for single data type

Purpose: Determines the upper limit of a numeric or date value range to be used within an object. (RangeMin sets the lower limit.) This property specifies the range of valid possibilities that a user may enter into an entry field of an object. *<expD | expN>* consists of either a date within braces, or a numeric expression. See RangeRequired for setting restrictions to the entries being made.

RangeMax may be used from the DEFINE statement of the associated object. You may also use dot reference notation to set the property's value, query that value, and use the returned value.

RangeMin

Syntax

```
RangeMin <expD ¦ expN>
```

Applies To

COMBOBOX, ENTRYFIELD, FIELD, SPINBOX

Default

False when multiple data types are used; 0 for single data type

Purpose: Sets the lower limit of an entry field's date or numeric range within an object. (RangeMax sets the upper limit.) This property specifies the range of valid possibilities that a user may enter into an entry field of an object. *<expD | expN>* consists of either a date within braces, or a numeric expression. See RangeRequired for setting restrictions to the entries being made.

RangeMin may be used from the DEFINE statement of the associated object. You may also use dot reference notation to set the property's value, query that value, and use the returned value.

RangeRequired

Syntax

```
RangeRequired <expL>
```

Applies To

COMBOBOX, ENTRYFIELD, FIELD, SPINBOX

Default

False

Purpose: Defines a valid range of numeric or date entries that may be used within an object. RangeRequired enforces the specified range on existing entries as well any new entries made in the field. RangeRequired works in conjunction with RangeMin and RangeMax.

RangeRequired may be used from the DEFINE statement of the associated object. You may also use dot reference notation to set the property's value, query that value, and use the returned value.

SaveFile

Syntax

```
<object reference>.SaveFile <expL ¦ expC>
```

Applies To

EDITOR

Default

False

Purpose: Determines whether a file accessed from an editor object is to be saved. If you want to be able to save the file after performing manipulations or entries to it, set this property to true. If the file has a name, SaveFile saves the file to its existing name. If the file does not have a name, you can use a false value of the DataSource property to open the SaveAs dialog box in order to give the file a name before saving. Or if the file is different from the DataSource file, dBASE uses the new version to save it to a new filename, and reflects the change in DataSource. The last option is to use dot reference notation to assign a new file name to the file before saving it.

SaveFile may be used from the DEFINE statement of the associated object. You may also use dot reference notation to set the property's value, query that value, and use the returned value.

SelectAll

Syntax

```
SelectAll <expL>
```

Applies To

COMBOBOX, ENTRYFIELD, FIELD, SPINBOX

Default

False if CUAENTER has been set to OFF. True if CUAENTER has been set to ON.

Purpose: Indicates if the control becomes highlighted upon receiving focus. When set to true, this gives the user a way to quickly delete or type over the entry. Moving focus by pressing an arrow key removes the highlighting without affecting the entry. Use the DataLink or Value properties to set the initial value of a field.

SelectAll may be used from the DEFINE statement of the associated object. You may also use dot reference notation to set the property's value, query that value, and use the returned value.

Separator

Syntax

```
Separator <expL>
```

Applies To

MENUITEM

Default

False

Purpose: Determines if a menu item becomes a visual separator for a list of items on a menu. This property creates a blank line between items when the property value is set to true. (You can also use the Text property to create a blank line by setting the *<expC>* to an empty string.)

Separator may be used from the DEFINE statement of the associated object. You may also use dot reference notation to set the property's value, query that value, and use the returned value.

Shadow

Syntax

```
Shadow <expL>
```

Applies To

BROWSE, CHECKBOX, COMBOBOX, EDITOR, ENTRYFIELD, FORM, LISTBOX, MENUBAR, MENUITEM, RADIOBUTTON, RECTANGLE, SPINBOX, TEXT

Default

True for browse, editor, form, and menu bar objects.

False for check box, combo box, entry field, list box, menu item, radio button, rectangle, spin box, and text objects.

Purpose: Indicates whether a one row wide and two column high colored line appears on the bottom and right sides of an object. Setting Shadow to false removes the colored line. You can modify the color of the shadow for list boxes, menus, or pushbutton objects using the ColorShadow property.

The optional OF <*form*> clause in the DEFINE statement of the object defaults the value of Shadow to false.

Shadow may be used from the DEFINE statement of the associated object. You may also use dot reference notation to set the property's value, query that value, and use the returned value.

Shortcut

Syntax

```
Shortcut <keystroke expC>
```

Applies To

MENUITEM

Default

Empty string

Purpose: Defines a key combination to be used in place of the menu item's selection option. It is not recommended that you use a printable ASCII key as a shortcut. See Table 22.8 in the ON KEY command in Chapter 22, "Using dBASE 5 Commands," for a list of available non-printing ASCII keys. The <*keystroke expC*> must include the keystroke combination (CTRL-A) surrounded by single or double quotations marks, or within brackets.

The menu bar recognizes the keystroke combination only after the check box and radio buttons have executed any Alt-keys that may have been pressed. However, when the MDI property is set to false and the form window has focus, the Desktop menu bar acts on the keystrokes first.

Shortcut may be used from the DEFINE statement of the associated object. You may also use dot reference notation to set the property's value, query that value, and use the returned value.

ShowDeleted

Syntax

```
ShowDeleted <expL>
```

Applies To

BROWSE

Default

False

Purpose: Indicates whether deletion markers will display for items in a browse object which have been marked for deletion. Setting this to true allows the delete markers to be displayed, letting the user see which records have been flagged for removal. Leaving this set to false, hides the delete flags.

ShowDeleted may be used from the DEFINE statement of the associated object. You may also use dot reference notation to set the property's value, query that value, and use the returned value.

ShowRecNo

Syntax

```
ShowRecNo <expL>
```

Applies To

BROWSE

Default

False

Purpose: Determines if record numbers appear within the browse object as references for the user. Setting it to true turns the numbers on; false turns them off. ShowRecNo may be used from the DEFINE statement of the associated object. You may also use dot reference notation to set the property's value, query that value, and use the returned value.

Sizeable

Syntax

```
Sizeable <expL>
```

Applies To

BROWSE, EDITOR, FORM

Default

False

Purpose: Determines whether the user may resize the window by dragging the lower-right corner to a desired size. Setting this to true allows resizing; false prevents it. When the Sizeable property is set to true, the border of the object appears as a double line, with a single line displayed at the lower-right corner which allows the user to position the cursor on the line and drag it to the desired size. The user can also use the mouse to resize the object from the right side by dragging the border to the desired size. The false setting makes the border appear as a single line, which cannot be resized. The optional OF <*form*> clause of the DEFINE statement for the object sets this value to false.

Sizeable may be used from the DEFINE statement of the associated object. You may also use dot reference notation to set the property's value, query that value, and use the returned value.

Sorted

Syntax

```
Sorted <expL>
```

Applies To

COMBOBOX, LISTBOX

Default

False

Purpose: Determines whether prompts in the object are listed in alphabetical, numerical, or chronological order. The natural order is the order in which the prompts were created. Setting this property to true sorts the prompts; false leaves them in their natural order.

Sorted may be used from the DEFINE statement of the associated object. You may also use dot reference notation to set the property's value, query that value, and use the returned value.

SpinOnly

Syntax

```
SpinOnly <expL>
```

Applies To

SPINBOX

Default

False

Purpose: Determines if the user may manually enter values into a spin box entry field. Set this value to true to allow users to enter data into the entry field; false to force the user to use the arrows to increment or decrement the values.

SpinOnly may be used from the DEFINE statement of the associated object. You may also use dot reference notation to set the property's value, query that value, and use the returned value.

StatusMessage

Syntax

```
StatusMessage <message expC>
```

Applies To

BROWSE, CHECKBOX, COMBOBOX, EDITOR, ENTRYFIELD, FIELD, FORM, LISTBOX, MENU, MENUITEM, PUSHBUTTON, RADIOBUTTON, SPINBOX

Default

Empty string

Purpose: Provides a text string on the status bar once a control gains focus. This text string can be used to convey a message, a warning, or a caution to the user. The *<message expC>* must consist of a message that is surrounded by single or double quotation marks, or within brackets.

StatusMessage may be used from the DEFINE statement of the associated object. You may also use dot reference notation to set the property's value, query that value, and use the returned value.

Step

Syntax

```
Step <expN>
```

Applies To

SPINBOX

Default

1

Purpose: Defines the increment or decrement rate a user uses to step through the values of a spin box. Step may be used from the DEFINE statement of the associated object. You may also use dot reference notation to set the property's value, query that value, and use the returned value.

Style

Syntax

```
Style <expN>
```

Applies To

COMBOBOX

Default

1 (Drop Down)

Purpose: Defines the style of combo box created with the DEFINE statement. You may choose between 1 (drop down) or 2 (drop down list).The drop down (1) allows the user to type information into the entry field. The drop down list (2) does not. Neither style will display until the user has clicked the arrow located on the right side of the entry field.

Style may be used from the DEFINE statement of the associated object. You may also use dot reference notation to set the property's value, query that value, and use the returned value.

SysMenu

Syntax

```
SysMenu <expL>
```

Applies To

BROWSE, EDITOR, FORM

Default

True

Purpose: Indicates if the user will see a Close icon (a button at the top-left corner) on the window border that may be used to close the object. Setting SysMenu to false removes the Close icon, and prevents the user from using that button and from pressing Ctrl-F4 to close the object. The user must use either Window Close, Window Close All, or Esc to exit the window. However, when the MDI property has been set to true, the SysMenu value is ignored. The option OF *<form>* clause of the DEFINE statement sets this property to false.

SysMenu may be used from the DEFINE statement of the associated object. You may also use dot reference notation to set the property's value, query that value, and use the returned value.

TabPos

Syntax

```
TabPos <expN>
```

Applies To

EDITOR

Default

4

Purpose: Defines the spacing of columns in an editor object by indicating the number of character columns between them. TabPos may be used from the DEFINE statement of the associated object. You may also use dot reference notation to set the property's value, query that value, and use the returned value.

TabStop

Syntax

```
TabStop <expL>
```

Applies To

BROWSE, CHECKBOX, COMBOBOX, EDITOR, ENTRYFIELD, LISTBOX, PUSHBUTTON, RADIOBUTTON, SPINBOX

Default

True

Purpose: Allows the user to press either the Tab or Shift-Tab key to shift focus between controls in an object. Setting this property to false prevents the user from using these keys to select a control. TabStop is different from Enabled in that when Enabled is set to false the control is not available for selection. TabStop does not change the availability of the control when it is set to false. When setting up pushbuttons, you need to use TabStop with the GrabFocus property to determine how the pushbutton will gain focus.

TabStop may be used from the DEFINE statement of the associated object. You may also use dot reference notation to set the property's value, query that value, and use the returned value.

Text

Syntax

```
Text <expC>
```

Applies To

BROWSE, CHECKBOX, EDITOR, FORM, MENU, MENUITEM, PUSHBUTTON, RADIOBUTTON, TEXT

Default

Object	Setting
Browse	Full file path of the database file as title
Check Box	Character string entered
Pushbutton	Character string entered
Radio Button	Character string entered
Editor	Full file path name for DataSource
Menu	Character string entered
Form	Name of type of object
Menu Item	Name of type of object
Text	Name of type of object

Purpose: Used to specify the title of the object. Setting the Text property is as simple as typing the desired name, say Push This, in the *<expC>* parameter. You indicate letters of the title that the user can use to select the control by placing a tilde (~) before and after the characters, or simply placing an ampersand (&) before one letter. For example, you could enter Text "&Push This" or Text "~P~ush This" to designate the title of a pushbutton. The letter(s) appearing between the tildes or after the ampersand are underlined on-screen to let the user know which letters to use to select the pushbutton. The Text property defines the prompt for check boxes, pushbuttons, and radio buttons. Text objects use whatever character string is entered in the Text property as the text of the object. If you leave the Text property blank on a menu item, it acts as a separator line, similar to the way the Separator property functions.

Text may be used from the DEFINE statement of the associated object. You may also use dot reference notation to set the property's value, query that value, and use the returned value.

Top

Syntax

```
Top <expN>
```

Applies To

BROWSE, CHECKBOX, COMBOBOX, EDITOR, ENTRYFIELD, FORM, LISTBOX, PAGEBREAK, PUSHBUTTON, RADIOBUTTON, RECTANGLE, SPINBOX, TEXT

Default

0

Purpose: Defines where the top of the object appears on the screen, using a measurement in character rows relative to the form window or the Desktop. When used in combination with the Left property, Top allows exact placement of an object on a form window. The default value of 0 positions the object over the form window border; adding one to the form window's Height value repositions the object on top of the form window's bottom border. You can specify the location of the object with the FROM...TO clause of most DEFINE statements, using either FROM *<row>,<col>* TO *<row>,<col>* or AT *<row>,<col>*. The first clause specifies the dimensions of the object by defining the upper-left and lower-right coordinates. The second clause only defines the object's upper-left corner, without specifying the overall size of the object.

The Top property allows you to specify an exact location for where a pagebreak control scrolls the items of a scrollable form window. The pagebreak control will be displayed as the first column of a form window when used during design mode. However, it will not appear during execution. You may use any value between 0 and 32767 for the value of Top.

Top may be used from the DEFINE statement of the associated object. You may also use dot reference notation to set the property's value, query that value, and use the returned value.

Valid

Syntax

```
Valid <UDF>
```

Applies To

COMBOBOX, ENTRYFIELD, FIELD, SPINBOX

Default
Empty function

Purpose: Uses a UDF (User Defined Function) to evaluate entries in a field. The UDF must return a true value before the user may shift focus from one control to another on a form. This property can be used with ValidRequired to ensure that all entries in the field are valid, whether existing or entered during an editing session. If the UDF returns a false value, focus is not transferred to the next control, and the user is forced to correct the error.

Valid may be used from the DEFINE statement of the associated object. You may also use dot reference notation to set the property's value, query that value, and use the returned value.

ValidErrorMsg

Syntax
```
ValidErrorMsg <expC>
```

Applies To
COMBOBOX, ENTRYFIELD, FIELD, SPINBOX

Default
Empty string

Purpose: Displays a message or warning to the user when an invalid entry is made and the control's Valid property returns a value of false. The Valid property requires that a true value be returned by the UDF associated with it. If a false value is returned, focus is not shifted from the control, and the ValidErrorMsg text is displayed.

ValidErrorMsg may be used from the DEFINE statement of the associated object. You may also use dot reference notation to set the property's value, query that value, and use the returned value.

ValidRequired

Syntax
```
ValidRequired <expL>
```

Applies To
COMBOBOX, ENTRYFIELD, FIELD, SPINBOX

Default
False

Purpose: Used in conjunction with the Valid property to verify entries made and/or existing within an object's entry field before shifting focus to another control. The user cannot change the focus of a control unless the entry is valid, indicated by a true value being returned by the Valid UDF associated with the object. Both the Valid property and the ValidRequired property must return values of true before focus may be moved to the next control.

ValidRequired may be used from the DEFINE statement of the associated object. You may also use dot reference notation to set the property's value, query that value, and use the returned value.

Value

Syntax

```
Value <any value>
```

Applies To

CHECKBOX, COMBOBOX, EDITOR, ENTRYFIELD, FIELD, LISTBOX, RADIOBUTTON, SPINBOX

Default

Empty string, false, zero, or blank date

Purpose: Defines the initial value of a control, returns a value from an object, or retrieves the value that a user entered or selected. Setting the original values of an object may be done using Value or the DataLink property. You can also create a link to a database using DataLink, then use Value to set a new value to a field. After initial values are determined, open the form window or editor with the Open( ) or ReadModal( ) methods. The Refresh( ) method allows you to retrieve the newest values entered in the database and put them into the objects for the user to see. If the OnOpen event handler has been defined, it will execute so that new values may be entered, or existing values changed, by the user. Field values may be changed with dot reference notation from the program, or via the user's use of the control for that field. Changes in values do not affect the data table until the Submit( ) method is executed.

Value may be used from the DEFINE statement of all objects listed in the Default section, except the editor object. You may use dot reference notation to set the property's value, query that value, and use the returned value.

The editor object's Value property will return a character value that cannot exceed 255 characters. The character string is shortened by dBASE at the point that it finds an embedded CHR(0) within the string. Value may not be used in the DEFINE statement of an editor object.

Value either defines or returns the contents of either a field or expression which is given in the DataLink property of a field object. You may define the value of the calculated field. The data types must be the same for Value to work within a field object, unless it is connected to a browse object.

In a radio button object, if the button does not currently have focus the Value property returns a false. Only when the user has selected the radio button will the value be true. As soon as a radio button loses focus, the Value property resets to false.

Visible

Syntax

```
Visible <expL>
```

Applies To

BROWSE, CHECKBOX, COMBOBOX, EDITOR, ENTRYFIELD, FIELD, FORM, LISTBOX, PUSHBUTTON, RADIOBUTTON, RECTANGLE, SPINBOX, TEXT

Default

True

Purpose: Determines whether the user can see an object on the screen. Setting this to false hides the object or control from view. One use for this property is to hide the Command window during execution of your applications. Enter _CmdWindow.Visible = .F. in the command line to turn off the Command window while your program is running.

Visible may be used from the DEFINE statement of the associated object. You may also use dot reference notation to set the property's value, query that value, and use the returned value.

Width

Syntax

```
Width <expN>
```

Applies To

BROWSE, CHECKBOX, COMBOBOX, EDITOR, ENTRYFIELD, FIELD, FORM, LISTBOX, PUSHBUTTON, RADIOBUTTON, RECTANGLE, SPINBOX, TEXT

Default

Generally depends on length of the DataLink or Text properties of the object, and whether AutoSize is set to true or false.

Purpose: Used in combination with the Height property to specify the dimensions of an object. The Width is measured from the left border to right border using whole or rational numbers. Horizontal scroll bars will appear if the contents of an entry field are longer than the Width measurement.

Width may be used from the DEFINE statement of the associated object. You may also use dot reference notation to set the property's value, query that value, and use the returned value.

WindowState

Syntax

```
WindowState <state expN>
```

Applies To

BROWSE, EDITOR, FORM

Default

0 (Normal)

Purpose: Determines whether a window is minimized, maximized, or restored. If the Minimize or Maximize properties are set to false, the WindowState property value is ignored. The *<state expN>* is determined from the following choices:

Setting	Result
0 (Normal)	Restores form window to defined dimensions
1 (Minimized)	Shrinks window to an icon
2 (Maximized)	Blows up window to fill screen

WindowState may be used from the DEFINE statement of the associated object. You may also use dot reference notation to set the property's value, query that value, and use the returned value.

WordWrap

Syntax

```
WordWrap <expL>
```

Applies To

EDITOR

Default
False if memo field has no text lines.

True if DataSource value equals "MEMO" or false if DataSource value equals "FILENAME".

Purpose: Determines whether lines of text in an editor object are allowed to automatically wrap, as usually occurs within a memo field. WordWrap may be used from the DEFINE statement of the associated object. You may also use dot reference notation to set the property's value, query that value, and use the returned value.

Methods

Methods share some common restrictions. Methods may not be used in DEFINE statements. Dot reference notation is used to retrieve the object reference for each method and to find out what the returned value is, and then to use that returned value in another variable.

ActiveControl

Syntax

```
<object reference>.ActiveControl()
```

Applies To
BROWSE, FORM

Purpose: Returns a value that indicates which control currently has focus. The value is returned in the following format:

```
FORM::<form window reference>
```

If no control has focus, a false value is returned instead of the object reference.

ActiveField( )

Syntax

```
<object reference>.ActiveField()
```

Applies To
FIELDLIST

Purpose: Returns the value of the active field within a field list object of the associated browse list. You associate a field list object to a browse object with the FieldList property. ActiveField( ) returns the value of the field the user selected. ActiveField( ) returns the value in the following format:

```
<object type>::<object reference>
```

A value of false is returned if no field was selected by the user.

Close( )

Syntax

```
<object reference>.Close()
```

Applies To

BROWSE, EDITOR, FORM, MENUBAR

Purpose: Closes an object, clearing it off the Desktop and activating the OnClose event handler associated with the object. The OnLostFocus event handler is executed if the object had focus before the Close( ) method was executed. You can throw out any entries made to the object by not using the Submit( ) method before closing or releasing the window. This property does not affect the Value property of any associated objects. Record locks are also left alone by the Close( ) method. Close( ) returns true if it could close the window, or false if it was not able to do so.

Modified( )

Syntax

```
<object reference>.Modified()
```

Applies To

BROWSE, CHECKBOX, COMBOBOX, EDITOR, ENTRYFIELD, FIELD, FORM, RADIOBUTTON, SPINBOX

Purpose: Returns a value that tells if the user made changes to records or text. If the logical value is true, changes were made.

Open( )

Syntax

```
<object reference>.Open()
```

Applies To

BROWSE, EDITOR, FORM, MENUBAR

Purpose: Opens a modeless object, which allows the user to use other open objects on the screen while it is open. This feature is helpful when the user will need to access multiple windows to accomplish the tasks of the application. You must have set the initial values for the fields within the objects to be opened later by the Open( ) method. Use the Value or DataLink properties to set the initial values, then use the Open( ) method to access the fields in the appropriate objects. The Open( ) method calls the OnOpen event handler, if you've previously defined one, that tells dBASE what actions to take before placing the desired object on the screen.

Execute the Release( ) method prior to using the Close( ) method to exit the object. The Release( ) method clears the object from memory and frees the memory variables that were used with the object. When the Close( ) method is executed, dBASE clears the object off the screen, runs the OnLostFocus event handler if defined, and calls the OnClose event handler associated with the object. If you want to save whatever values may have been entered or changed during the session, execute the Submit( ) method prior to the Close( ) method. Otherwise, those values are lost.

ReadModal( )

Syntax

```
<object reference>.ReadModal()
```

Applies To

BROWSE, EDITOR, FORM

Purpose: Opens an object in modal mode, which prevents the user from exiting the object without closing it with the controls provided on the form window. A typical use for modal objects is a dialog box containing a warning or important message that requires the user to click OK before it clears from the screen and returns to the application. Modal windows are not able to work with MDI windows, so only non-MDI windows should be opened with this method. Opening a modal window leaves the current procedure running while the modal window appears on top of it. The OnOpen event handler for the form window is activated, and any variables that the procedure set are accessible by the modal window. However, any objects outside of the modal window cannot receive focus until the modal window is closed using the control buttons on the modal window.

To close the modal window, use the Close( ) method. This clears the object from the screen, calls the OnLostFocus event handler, and then the OnClose event handler. If you don't want to save any changes that may have been entered into fields on the object, simply do not execute the Submit( ) method. Otherwise, use the Submit( ) method to save the changes as long as the fields have been linked via the DataLink property.

The returned value for ReadModal( ) is in the following format:

```
FORM::<form window reference>
```

A true value indicates the data has been posted to the appropriate fields via the DataLink property. False indicates that the Submit( ) method was not activated prior to retrieving the value. To ensure that the windows are opened correctly without causing any problems to the application, query the value returned and have the program print an error message if the window cannot be opened.

Refresh( )

Syntax

```
<object reference>.Refresh()
```

Applies To

FORM

Purpose: Restores the original values of fields that are linked to a database which appear on a form window. This cancels any changes that may have been entered in controls on the form by the user. Refresh( ) cannot be used to restore the values linked to only one control, unless that control is the only one on the form window. dBASE uses the record position used by the Refresh( ) method to figure out which record of the database should be refreshed. Using Refresh( ) with an editor object lets you update the field if the record position of the edited file is moved during the session.

RefreshRecord( )

Syntax

```
<object reference>.RefreshRecord()
```

Applies To

BROWSE

Purpose: Works on a browse object to restore the original value of a field from the associated database record. This applies only to the current record in the browse object. The values are retrieved from records linked to a database by the DataLink property. Using RefreshRecord( ) releases the record locks created, and throws out all modifications made.

A true value is returned if the original value is restored, or false if it cannot restore the value.

Release( )

Syntax

```
<object reference>.Release()
```

Applies To

BROWSE, CHECKBOX, COMBOBOX, EDITOR, ENTRYFIELD, FIELD, FIELDLIST, FORM, LISTBOX, MENU, MENUBAR, MENUITEM, OBJECT, PAGEBREAK, PUSHBUTTON, RADIOBUTTON, RECTANGLE, SPINBOX, TEXT

Purpose: Clears an object from memory and frees the memory variables used in the object's procedures. You can close an object with Release( ) only if it was opened with the Open( ) method. Closing an object with the Close( ) method does not clear the object from memory. When Release( ) is executed, the OnClose event handler is run prior to the object's closure.

SetFocus( )

Syntax

```
<object reference>.SetFocus()
```

Applies To

BROWSE, CHECKBOX, COMBOBOX, EDITOR, ENTRYFIELD, FIELD, FORM, LISTBOX, PUSHBUTTON, RADIOBUTTON, SPINBOX

Purpose: Used by an application to give the focus to a specified form window or object, thus allowing the user to enter new data via a mouse click or from the keyboard. An object which is highlighted is selected and has focus. You can change the color of the highlighting with the ColorHighlight property. ColorNormal can be used to alter the color of an object which is not selected.

SetFocus( ) allows you to have more than one object on the screen at one time, with focus shifting between the objects and among the controls on each object. Any event handlers that may have been defined, such as Valid, OnLostFocus, and OnGotFocus, are executed as the focus changes from control to control or object to object. If the Enabled property has been set to false, SetFocus( ) will return a value of false.

Submit( )

Syntax

```
<object reference>.Submit()
```

Applies To

FORM

Purpose: Posts any changes made to data within an object to the associated database which is defined in the DataLink property for the object. Submit( ) only works with high-level objects such as form windows or browse objects, and not for controls. The Submit( ) method is executed after the Value property determines if the data entered is correct and after the ValidRequired property (if defined) has verified that the entry is within the specified ranges for the field. Including the Submit( ) method in the OnClose event handler forces changes to be saved each time the object is closed.

A true value will be returned if the data can be saved to the database, or false if the changes were not saved.

Commands

In this section, the commands used to create UI objects are explained, along with their complete syntax for their DEFINE statement. Properties listed in the DEFINE statement that operate differently from the default mode of operation are explained for each command. The individual properties are explained in detail in the Properties section of this chapter. Methods are explained in the Methods section.

The first step in creating UI objects is to create the high-level form that contains all the objects and controls necessary for the application. Use DEFINE FORM to name the form and set the properties. Only then can you associate the appropriate text boxes, spin boxes, browse objects, and so on, to the desired form.

For all DEFINE statements, the DEFINE command is followed by a unique name for the object. If the object being defined is the child object of a parent object, then you must enter the parent object's name in the OF <form name> clause.

The FROM...TO clause allows you to set the dimensions of the object. FROM *<row1>,<col1>* indicates the coordinates of the upper-left corner of the object, while TO *<row2>,<col2>* indicates the lower-right corner. When you use the optional OF clause the coordinates are relative to the parent object; without the OF clause the coordinates are relative to the screen area. In most cases, if you enter values for the Height and Width properties of an object (where they apply) those values take precedence over the FROM...TO values.

The AT clause specifies at what location to position the object when it is opened on the form. AT *<row>*, *<col>* indicates the position of the upper-left corner for the object. Entering values in the Top or Left properties for the object takes precedence over the AT clause values.

DEFINE BROWSE

Syntax

```
DEFINE BROWSE<browse name>[OF <form name>]
  [FROM <row1>,<col1>[TO <row2>,<col2>]] ¦ AT <row>,<col>]
  [PROPERTY
     [After <object name>]
     [, Alias <alias name>]
     [, Append <expL>]
     [, Before <object name>]
     [, ColorBorder <color expC>]
     [, ColorBorder HighLight <color expC>]
     [, ColorDisabled <color expC>]
     [, ColorEntryHighLight <color expC>]
     [, ColorEntryNormal <color expC>]
     [, ColorIcon <color expC>]
     [, ColorNormal <color expC>]
     [, ColorScrollBar <color expC>]
     [, Debug <expL>]
     [, Delete <expL>]
     [, Design <expL>]
     [, DesignSelect <expL>]
     [, Enabled <expL>]
     [, EscExit <expL>]
     [, FieldArrange <expL>]
     [, FieldList <object name>]
     [, Grid <expL>]
     [, Height <expN>]
     [, HelpFile <expC>]
     [, HelpId <help context exp>]
     [, Left <expN>]
     [, Lock <expN>]
     [, Maximize <expL>]
     [, Menu <menu name>]
     [, Minimize <expL>]
     [, Modify <expL>]
     [, Moveable <expL>]
     [, NavBar <expL>]
     [, OnAppend <procedure>]
     [, OnChange <procedure>]
     [, OnClose <procedure>]
     [, OnDelete <procedure>]
     [, OnEdit <procedure>]
     [, OnGotFocus <procedure>]
     [, OnHelp <procedure>]
     [, OnLostFocus <procedure>]
     [, OnOpen <procedure>]
     [, OnSkip <procedure>]
     [, Parent <object name>]
     [, ProcFile <filename>[,] [<path>\]<object filename>]
     [, Shadow <expL>]
     [, ShowDeleted <expL>]
     [, ShowRecNo <expL>]
     [, Sizeable <expL>]
     [, StatusMessage <expC>]
     [, SysMenu <expL>]
```

```
    [, TabStop <expL>]
    [, Text <expC>]
    [, Top <expN>]
    [, Visible <expL>]
    [, Width <expN>]
    [, WindowState <expN>]
 [CUSTOM
    <property name 1><value 1>[, <property name 2><value 2>,,,]]
```

Purpose: Creates an object that allows you to display data in rows and columns in a form object window. You may also edit records from the data table from within the browse object. This object is often used to display prompts generated from dBASE with the DataSource and DataLink properties. The prompts may consist of filenames from a specified directory, or the available drives on a system, or other specified list. The user may then select an item from the list with which to work. The user may mark files for deletion, open a file, or perform any action associated with the OnClick event handler.

Table 26.3 lists the read-only properties and methods associated with a browse object. These may only be changed via dot reference notation through the following syntax:

```
[<memvar>=] ¦ [<command>] <object reference>.[<read-only property>]¦ [<method>]
```

Table 28.3 Read-Only Properties and Methods for the Browse Object

Read-Only Property	Method
ClassName	ActiveControl( )
Name	Close( )
	Modified( )
	Open( )
	ReadModal( )
	RefreshRecord( )
	Release( )
	SetFocus( )

If the OF *<form name>*clause is used with a browse object, dBASE sets the default values of Maximize, Moveable, Sizeable, Shadow, and SysMenu to false.

To display a child browse object, you must open the parent object first. If you attempt to open a browse object while no data table is active, an Open File dialog box appears on the screen from which the user may select a data table to open. When you close a data table associated with a browse object, the object is closed as well.

Each row of the object lists one record from the active database file. Each column displays one field of the record. The FieldList property allows you to specify the fields to be displayed in the browse object. Otherwise, all fields in the database are listed in the object. Moving around in a browse object simply requires pressing the Tab or Shift-Tab keys to advance or reverse through the items presented. If the cursor is at the bottom of a record, pressing the Tab key takes you to the beginning. Similarly, pressing Shift-Tab while at the first record moves the cursor to the end of the record.

When you want to look at or edit a memo field, simply double-click the field or press Ctrl-Home to call up the dBASE text editor or other editor you may have specified using SET WP. Now you can perform the editing to the memo field. As long as the memo field is not a read-only field, pressing Ctrl-W or Ctrl-End saves your changes.

The user presses the arrow keys, PageUp, PageDown, or uses the mouse to move the cursor through the options shown in a browse object. As the cursor moves through the records of the browse object, the record pointer changes position. If the user scrolls through the displayed list with the scroll bars, the record pointer does not change position. Only when the cursor is moved does the record pointer move accordingly.

Table 26.4 lists the default property values for all properties associated with the browse object.

Table 26.4 Property and Default Values for the Browse Object

Property	Default
After	Varies
Alias	*<current alias>*
Append	.T.
Before	Varies
ClassName	BROWSE
ColorBorder	W/B

Property	Default
ColorBorderHighlight	W+/B
ColorDisabled	N+/W
ColorEntryHighlight	B/W
ColorEntryNormal	W+/GB
ColorIcon	GB+/B
ColorNormal	RG+/B
ColorScrollBar	B/GB
Debug	.F.
Delete	.F.
Design	.F.
DesignSelect	.F.
Enabled	.T.
EscExit	Varies
FieldArrange	Varies
FieldList	Empty string
Grid	.T.
Height	10
HelpFile	Empty string
HelpId	Empty string
Left	0
Lock	0
Maximize	Varies
Menu	.F.
Minimize	.F.
Modify	.T.
Moveable	Varies
Name	*<object name>*

(continues)

Table 26.4 Continued

Property	Default
NavBar	.T.
OnAppend	Empty string
OnChange	Empty string
OnClose	Empty string
OnDelete	Empty string
OnEdit	Empty string
OnGotFocus	Empty string
OnHelp	Empty string
OnLostFocus	Empty string
OnOpen	Empty string
OnSkip	Empty string
Parent	.F.
ProcFile	Empty string
Shadow	Varies
ShowDeleted	.F.
ShowRecNo	.F.
Sizeable	Varies
StatusMessage	Empty string
SysMenu	Varies
TabStop	.T.
Text	*<full path and file name of database>*
Top	0
Visible	.T.
Width	80
WindowState	0

The EscExit and FieldArrange properties default to false if they do not have a parent object, or true if a parent object exists.

When the NavBar property is true, the narrowest width measurement the browse object may have is 23. When NavBar is false, the narrowest is 12.

The Open( ) method can be used to open a browse object. However, each time the object receives focus or a memo field is selected, the OnGotFocus event handler is executed if the browse object was opened with Open( ). If this isn't the way you want the browse object to operate, open it with the ReadModal( ) method, which limits the execution of OnGotFocus to only the first opening of the object.

WindowState indicates whether the window is maximized or minimized. Setting either the Maximize or Minimize properties to false causes dBASE to ignore the WindowState property's value. The window may not be resized by the user unless the Sizeable property is set to true.

DEFINE CHECKBOX

Syntax

```
DEFINE CHECKBOX <check box name> OF <form name>
  [AT <row>,<col>]
  [PROPERTY
     [After <object name>]
     [, Before <object name>]
     [, Border <expL>]
     [, Border Style <expN>]
     [, ColorDisabled <color expC>]
     [, ColorHighLight <color expC>]
     [, ColorNormal <color expC>]
     [, ColorPickHighlight <color expC>]
     [, ColorPickNormal <color expC>]
     [, DataLink <expC>]
     [, Debug <expL>]
     [, DesignSelect <expL>]
     [, Enabled <expL>]
     [, Group <expL>]
     [, Height <expN>]
     [, HelpFile <expC>]
     [, HelpId <help context exp>]
     [, Left <expN>]
     [, OnChange <procedure>]
     [, OnGotFocus <procedure>]
     [, OnHelp <procedure>]
     [, OnLostFocus <procedure>]
     [, Parent <object name>]
     [, ProcFile <filename>[,] [<path>\]<object filename>]
     [, Shadow <expL>]
     [, StatusMessage <expC>]
     [, TabStop <expL>]
```

VI

Reference Guide

```
      [, Text <expC>]
      [, Top <expN>]
      [, Value <expL>]
      [, Visible <expL>]
      [, Width <expN>]
   [CUSTOM
      <property name 1><value 1>[, <property name 2>{value 2>..]]
```

Purpose: Creates an object which provides a box to be checked by the user depending on the user's desired choice. The check box is a toggle, which represents a logical value: a box marked with an X indicates a yes, on, or true; a box without an X is a no, off, or false. The user may select any number of options from the check boxes. Check boxes are different from radio buttons, because radio buttons may only have one button selected at a time. The user puts an X in the check box by either pressing the space bar while focus is on the desired box, or by using the mouse to click the box. When the box is checked, the Value property is true.

Table 26.5 lists the read-only properties and methods of the check box. These may only be changed via dot reference notation through the following syntax:

```
[<memvar>=] ¦ [<command>] <object reference>[,<read-only property>] ¦ [<method>]
```

Table 26.5 Read-Only Properties and Methods for the Check Box

Read-Only Property	Method
ClassName	Modified( )
Name	Release( )
	SetFocus( )

The Group property defaults to true to allow you to create a group of related check boxes that the user may select from. A typical use of check boxes may be seen in a font selection box in a word processing program, where the user can select the box for bold, italic, and underline simultaneously. To create a group, set the first group member's Group property to true, and the others in the group to false. Then set the first member of the second group to true, and remaining members of the second group to false.

Table 26.6 lists the properties and their default settings for a check box.

Table 26.6 Properties and Default Settings for the Check Box

Property	Default
After	Empty string
Before	Empty string
Border	.F.
BorderStyle	0
ClassName	CHECKBOX
ColorDisabled	N+/BG
ColorHighlight	W+/BG
ColorNormal	N/BG
ColorPickHighlight	RG+/BG
ColorPickNormal	RG+/BG
DataLink	Empty string
Debug	.F.
DesignSelect	.F.
Enabled	.T.
Group	.T.
Height	1
HelpFile	Empty string
HelpId	Empty string
Left	0
Name	*<object name>*
OnChange	Empty string
OnGotFocus	Empty string
OnHelp	Empty string
OnLostFocus	Empty string
Parent	*<form name>*
ProcFile	Empty string

(continues)

Table 26.6 Continued

Property	Default
Shadow	.F.
StatusMessage	Empty string
TabStop	.T.
Text	Empty string
Top	0
Value	.F.
Visible	.T.
Width	11

You can provide an informative prompt for the check box by entering a text string in the Text property for the check box. You may also want to assign a pickletter (keyboard shortcut) for the check box. See Shortcut for more information.

DEFINE COMBOBOX

Syntax

```
DEFINE COMBOBOX <combo box name> OF <form name>
  [FROM <row1>,<col1>[TO <row2>,<col2>]] ¦ [AT <row>,<col>]
  [PROPERTY
     [After <object name>]
     [, Before <object name>]
     [, ColorDisabled <color expC>]
     [, ColorEntryHighlight <color expC>]
     [, ColorEntryNormal <color expC>]
     [, ColorEntryScrollBar <color expC>]
     [, ColorIcon <color expC>]
     [, ColorListHighlight <color expC>]
     [, ColorListNormal <color expC>]
     [, ColorListScrollBar <color expC>]
     [, ColorListSelected <color expC>]
     [, CurSel <expN>]
     [, DataLink <expC>]
     [, DataSource <options>]
     [, Debug <expL>]
     [, DesignSelect <expL>]
     [, Enabled <expL>]
     [, Function <expC>]
     [, Height <expN>]
     [, HelpFile <expC>]
```

```
    [, HelpId <help context exp>]
    [, Left <expN>]
    [, OnChange <procedure>]
    [, OnGotFocus <procedure>]
    [, OnHelp <procedure>]
    [, OnLostFocus <procedure>]
    [, OnSelChange <procedure>]
    [, Parent <object name>]
    [, Picture <expC>]
    [, ProcFile <filename>[,] [<path>\]<object filename>]
    [, RangeMax <expN ¦ expD>]
    [, RangeMin <expN ¦ expD>]
    [, RangeRequired <expL>]
    [, SelectAll <expL>]
    [, Shadow <expL>]
    [, Sorted <expL>]
    [, StatusMessage <expC>]
    [, Style <expN>]
    [, TabStop <expL>]
    [, Top <expN>]
    [, Valid <UDF>]
    [, ValidErrorMsg <expC>]
    [, ValidRequired <expL>]
    [, Value <expC>]
    [, Visible <expL>]
    [, Width <expN>]
 [CUSTOM
    <property name 1><value 1> [, <property name 2><value 2>...]]
```

Purpose: Creates an object which allows for selection of desired information by accessing a scrolling list of choices, and by providing a space for text to be entered manually by the user. An example would be the Open dialog box used in Windows applications, where you can select a file from the list or enter the file name in the entry field.

The user can quickly jump to the desired item in the list by typing the first letter of the item name. If more than one item shares a common first letter, the first item with that letter appears at the top of the scroll list box. The user may also use the scroll bars at the side of the list box to quickly scroll through the options available. A horizontal scroll bar appears across the bottom of the screen if the text prompts cannot be contained in the defined combo box. You may want to assign a pickletter (keyboard shortcut) to the combo box. See Shortcut for more information.

Table 26.7 lists the read-only properties and methods of the combo box object. You may change these through dot reference notations through the following syntax:

```
[<memvar>=] ¦ [<command>] <object reference>.[<read-only property>] ¦ [<method>]
```

Table 26.7 Read-Only Properties and Methods of the Combo Box Object

Read-Only Property	Method
ClassName	Modified( )
Name	Release( )
	SetFocus( )

Table 26.8 lists the properties and their default settings for combo boxes.

Table 26.8 Properties and Default Settings for the Combo Box

Property	Default
After	Empty string
Before	Empty string
ClassName	COMBOBOX
ColorDisabled	N+/B
ColorEntryHighlight	W+/G
ColorEntryNormal	W+/B
ColorEntryScrollBar	G+/B
ColorIcon	N/G
ColorListHighlight	W+/BG
ColorListNormal	RG+/B
ColorListScrollBar	B/BG
ColorListSelected	N/BG
CurSel	1
DataLink	Empty string
DataSource	Empty string
Debug	.F.
DesignSelect	.F.
Enabled	.T.

Property	Default
Function	Empty string
Height	5
HelpFile	Empty string
HelpId	Empty string
Left	0
Name	*<object name>*
OnGotFocus	Empty string
OnChange	Empty string
OnHelp	Empty string
OnLostFocus	Empty string
OnSelChange	Empty string
Parent	*<form name>*
Picture	Empty string
ProcFile	Empty string
RangeMax	.F.
RangeMin	.F.
RangeRequired	.F.
SelectAll	Varies
Shadow	.F.
Sorted	.F.
StatusMessage	Empty string
Style	2
TabStop	.T.
Top	0
Valid	Empty string
ValidErrorMsg	Empty string
ValidRequired	.F.

(continues)

Table 26.8 Continued

Property	Default
Value	Empty string
Visible	.T.
Width	18

The Style property of a combo box determines the kind of combo box you wish to create. A style of 1 creates a drop-down combo box, which allows the user to either enter data manually or select the item from the list box. A style of 2 creates a drop-down list box, which prevents the user from manually entering data. The user must use the list box to select an item.

The Height property determines the list box's height, however it does not include a height value for the entry field. When you create a combo box, the drop-down list box is created as a modal object. The drop-down list box displays a minimum of five items if possible, but may shorten its height to fit on the screen.

A combo box which has a Style property set to 1 may use the Function and Picture properties to control how the entry field behaves. It accepts all the function templates (!, A, D, E, L, M, R, S<*n*>, T, and V<*n*>) and the picture templates except the $ and * options.

When SET CUAENTER is set to OFF SelectAll defaults to false. When SET CUAENTER is ON, SelectAll defaults to true. If SelectAll is true, when the user enters a valid character or control key in the entry fields, the numeric data value is set to zero and eliminates the other data type values.

Prompts for the combo box are created using the DataSource property. The prompts for a list box always consist of character strings.

DEFINE EDITOR

Syntax

```
DEFINE EDITOR <editor name> [OF <form name>]
  [FROM <row1>,<col1> [TO <row2>,<col2>]] ¦ [AT <row>,<col>]
  [PROPERTY
     [After <object name>]
     [, Before <object name>]
     [, ColorBorder <color expC>]
     [, ColorBorderHighLight <color expC>]
     [, ColorDisabled <color expC>]
     [, ColorHighlight <color expC>]
```

```
    [, ColorIcon <color expC>]
    [, ColorNormal <color expC>]
    [, ColorScrollBar <color expC>]
    [, Column <expN>]
    [, DataSource <options>]
    [, DesignSelect <expL>
    [, Draw <expL>]
    [, Enabled <expL>]
    [, EscExit <expL>]
    [, Height <expN>]
    [, HelpFile <expC>]
    [. HelpId <help context exp>]
    [, Left <expN>]
    [, Maximize <expL>]
    [, Menu <object name>]
    [, Minimize <expL>]
    [, Modify <expL>]
    [, Moveable <expL>]
    [, OnClose <procedure>]
    [, OnGotFocus <procedure>]
    [, OnHelp <procedure>]
    [, OnLostFocus <procedure>]
    [, OnOpen <procedure>]
    [, Parent <object name>]
    [, ProcFile <filename>]
    [, SaveFile <expC>]
    [, Shadow <expL>]
    [, Sizeable <expL>]
    [, Status Message <expC>]
    [, SysMenu <expL>]
    [, TabPos <expN>]
    [, TabStop <expL>]
    [, Top <expN>]
    [, Text <expC>]
    [, Visible <expL>]
    [, Width <expN>]
    [, WindowState <expC>]
    [, WordWrap <expL>]]
[CUSTOM
    <property name 1><value 1> [, <property name 2><value 2>...]]
```

Purpose: Creates an editor object that is scrollable in a form object window, which permits the user to change or peruse the existing text or memo field. *<Editor name>* lets you create the editor window, then you can use *<form name>* to specify the name of the editor object on which you wish to position the form.

The OF clause causes the window's coordinates to be relative to the upper-left corner of the parent form, and sets the logical value to false for Maximize, Moveable, Sizeable, Shadow, and SysMenu properties. Excluding the OF clause sets the coordinates to be relative to the upper-left corner of the video screen, and makes these same properties true.

The AT clause is used to create an entry field on the form. See DEFINE ENTRYFIELD for more information.

Table 26.9 lists the read-only and write-only properties, along with the methods associated with DEFINE EDITOR. Dot reference notation enables you to access the read-only properties and methods. The syntax for the dot reference notation is:

```
[<memvar>=] ¦ [<command>] <object reference>.[<read-only property>] ¦ [<methods>]
```

Table 26.9 Read-Only and Write-Only Properties and Methods for DEFINE EDITOR

Read-Only Properties	Write-Only Properties	Methods
ClassName	InsertLine	Close( )
LineNo		Modified( )
Lines		Open( )
Name		ReadModal( )
Value		Release( )
		SetFocus( )

Table 26.10 lists the default settings of the properties associated with the editor object.

Table 26.10 Properties and Default Settings for the Editor Object

Property	Default
After	Empty string
Before	Empty string
ClassName	EDITOR
ColorBorder	W/B
ColorBorderHighlight	W+/B
ColorBorderHighlight	W+/B
ColorDisabled	N+/B
ColorHighlight	B/W

Property	Default
ColorIcon	GB+/W
ColorNormal	RG+/B
ColorScrollBar	B/BG
Column	1
DataSource	Empty string
DesignSelect	.F.
Draw	.T.
Enabled	.T.
EscExit	Varies
Height	10
HelpFile	Empty string
HelpId	Empty string
InsertLine	Empty string
Left	0
LineNo	Read-only
Lines	Read-only
Maximize	Varies
Menu	Empty string
Minimize	.F.
Modify	.T.
Moveable	.T.
Name	*<object name>*
OnClose	Empty string
OnGotFocus	Empty string
OnHelp	Empty string
OnLostFocus	Empty string
OnOpen	Empty string

(continues)

Table 26.10 Continued

Property	Default
Parent	Empty string
ProcFile	Empty string
SaveFile	.F.
Shadow	Varies
Sizeable	Varies
StatusMessage	Empty string
SysMenu	.T.
TabPos	4
TabStop	.T.
Text	UNTITLED
Top	0
Value	Read-only
Visible	.T.
Width	80
WindowState	0
WordWrap	Varies

If you want to create a new, untitled editor object, leave the DataSource property blank. This property determines which text file or memo field the object will display. There are two options for displaying an existing file or field:

- "FILENAME *<filename>*" — Displays the text file *<filename>*. If this file does not currently exist, dBASE creates the file if you save it using Ctrl-End, or by setting the SaveFile property to true.
- "MEMO *<memo field name>*" — Displays the memo field indicated in *<memo field name>*.

To create a title for your editor object, use the Text property to enter the desired character string. The default for this property is the full path of the text file or database file being used.

Note

SET EDITOR and SET WP have no effect from the DEFINE EDITOR command.

Updates to memo fields are performed when the editor window is closed. The pointers used by dBASE to locate the record are also updated when you close the window.

DEFINE ENTRYFIELD

Syntax

```
DEFINE ENTRYFIELD <entry field name> OF <form name>
  [AT <row>,<col>]
  PROPERTY
     [After <object name>]
     [, Before <object name>]
     [, Border <expL>]
     [, BorderStyle <expN>]
     [, ColorDisabled <color expC>]
     [, ColorHighLight <color expC>]
     [, ColorNormal <color expC>]
     [, ColorScrollBar <color expC>]
     [, DataLink <expC>]
     [, Debug <expL>]
     [, DesignSelect <expL>]
     [, Enabled <expL>]
     [, Function <expC>]
     [, Height <expN>]
     [, HelpFile <expC>]
     [, HelpId <help context exp>]
     [, Key <procedure>]
     [, Left <expN>]
     [, OnGotFocus <procedure>]
     [, OnHelp <procedure>]
     [, OnLostFocus <procedure>]
     [, OnSelChange <procedure>]
     [, Parent <object name>]
     [, Picture <expC>]
     [, ProcFile <filename>[,] [<path>\]<object filename>]
     [, RangeMax <expN | expD>]
     [, RangeMin <expN | expD>]
     [, RangeRequired <expL>]
     [, SelectAll <expL>]
     [, Shadow <expL>]
     [, StatusMessage <expC>]
     [, TabStop <expL>]
     [, Top <expN>]
```

```
      [, Valid <UDF>]
      [, ValidErrorMsg <expC>]
      [, ValidRequired <expL>]
      [, Value <exp>]
      [, Visible <expL>]
      [, Width <expN>]
   [CUSTOM
      <property name 1><value 1>[, <property name 2><value 2>...]]
```

Purpose: Defines an entry field for viewing or accepting a user's changes. If you are familiar with using the @...SAY...GET commands in dBASE, using the entry field object for accepting user data will be easy. The Function property uses the familiar templates for functions (!, A, D, E, L, M, R, S<*n*>, T, and V<*n*>), while the Picture property uses the familiar templates for pictures except the $ and * options.

Table 26.11 lists the read-only properties and the methods associated with the field entry object. Dot reference notation gives you access to these read-only properties and methods, using the following syntax:

```
[<memvar>=] ¦ [<command>]<object reference>.[<read-only property>] ¦ [<method>]
```

Table 26.11 Read-Only Properties and Methods for the Field Entry Object

Read-Only Properties	Methods
ClassName	Modified( )
Name	Release( )
	SetFocus( )

Table 26.12 lists the defaults for the properties associated with an entryfield.

Table 26.12 Properties and Default Values for an Entryfield

Property	Default
After	Empty string
Before	Empty string
Border	.F.
BorderStyle	0
ClassName	ENTRYFIELD

Property	Default
ColorDisabled	N+/B
ColorHighlight	W+/G
ColorNormal	W+/B
ColorScrollBar	G+/B
DataLink	Empty string
Debug	.F.
DesignSelect	.F.
Enable	.T.
Function	Empty string
Height	1
HelpFile	Empty string
HelpId	Empty string
Key	Empty string
Left	0
Name	*<object name>*
OnGotFocus	Empty string
OnHelp	Empty string
OnLostFocus	Empty string
OnSelChange	Empty string
Parent	*<object name>*
Picture	Empty string
ProcFile	Empty string
RangeMax	.F.
RangeMin	.F.
RangeRequired	.F.
SelectAll	Varies
Shadow	.F.

(continues)

Table 26.12 Continued

Property	Default
StatusMessage	Empty string
TabStop	.T.
Top	0
Valid	Empty string
ValidErrorMsg	Empty string
ValidRequired	.F.
Value	Current value of DataLink property
Visible	.T.
Width	13

The DataLink property determines which field of the current database is affected by the entry field. The Value property determines which value is being inserted into the field by the entry field. The types of data in both the DataLink and Value properties must be the same, otherwise a Datatype mismatch error occurs.

To create pickletters and prompts for the entry field, see DEFINE TEXT for more information.

DEFINE FIELD

Syntax

```
DEFINE FIELD <field name> OF <field list name>
  [PROPERTY
     [After <object name>]
     [, Before <object name>]
     [, CalcField <expL>]
     [, DataLink <expC>]
     [, Debug <expC>]
     [, Enabled <expL>]
     [, Function <expC>]
     [, Heading <expC>]
     [, HelpFile <expC>]
     [, HelpId <help context exp>]
     [, Key <procedure>]
     [, OnGotFocus <procedure>]
     [, OnHelp <procedure>]
```

```
[, OnLostFocus <procedure>]
[, OnSelChange <procedure>]
[, Parent <object name>]
[, Picture <expC>]
[, ProcFile <filename>[,] [<path>\]<object filename>]
[, RangeMax <expN ¦ expD>]
[, RangeMin <expN ¦ exp D>]
[, RangeRequired <expL>]
[, SelectAll <expL>]
[, StatusMessage <expC>]
[, Valid <UDF>]
[, ValidErrorMsg <expC>]
[, ValidRequired <expL>]
[, Value <exp>]
[, Visible <expL>]
[, Width <expN>]
[CUSTOM
<property name 1><value 1> [, <property name 2><value 2>...]]
```

Purpose: Creates a field object which is used to control the interaction of a field list object with browse objects. You use this object to define which elements are to be included in the browse field list. You link the field objects, which are contained in field list objects, to browse objects by using the FieldList property in the DEFINE BROWSE syntax or by using dot reference notation, or with the DEFINE FIELDLIST command.

Before you can use the DEFINE FIELD command, you must have already created the field list objects using DEFINE FIELDLIST. Use the browse object that is linked with the field object to activate the objects contained by the field object. Field objects cannot be parent objects, thus they are always a child object with a field list object as parent, which in turn must be connected to a browse object.

If you are familiar with using the @...SAY...GET commands in dBASE, using the entry field object for accepting user data will be easy. The Function property uses the familiar templates for functions (!, A, D, E, L, M, R, S<*n*>, T, and V<*n*>), while the Picture property uses the familiar templates for pictures, except the $ and * options.

Table 26.13 lists the read-only properties and the methods associated with DEFINE FIELD. Dot reference notation gives you access to read-only properties and methods, using the following syntax:

```
[<memvar>=] ¦ [<command>]<object reference>.[<read-only property>] ¦ [<method>]
```

Table 26.13 Read-Only Properties and Methods for DEFINE FIELD

Read-Only Properties	Methods
ClassName	Modified( )
Name	Release( )
	SetFocus( )

Table 26.14 lists the properties and their default values for a field object.

Table 26.14 Properties and Default Values for a Field Object

Property	Default
After	*<object reference>*
Before	*<object reference>*
CalcField	.F.
ClassName	FIELD
DataLink	Empty string
Debug	.F.
Enabled	.T.
Function	Empty string
Heading	*<field name>*
HelpFile	Empty string
HelpId	Empty string
Key	Empty string
Name	*<object name>*
OnGotFocus	Empty string
OnHelp	Empty string
OnLostFocus	Empty string
OnSelChange	Empty string
Parent	*<field list name>*

Property	Default
Picture	Empty string
ProcFile	Empty string
RangeMax	0
RangeMin	0
RangeRequired	.F.
SelectAll	.F.
StatusMessage	Empty string
Valid	Empty string
ValidErrorMsg	Empty string
ValidRequired	.F.
Value	Varies
Visible	.T.
Width	Len(*<field name>*)

DEFINE FIELDLIST

Syntax

```
DEFINE FIELDLIST <field list name> [OF [<form name>.]<browse name>]
  [PROPERTY
     [, Parent <object name>]]
  [CUSTOM
     <property name 1><value 1>[, <property name 2><value 2>...]]
```

Purpose: Creates the parent object that field objects depend upon. These objects are used in connection with browse objects to perform viewing and editing tasks. The browse object must be created with DEFINE BROWSE before using the DEFINE FIELDLIST command.

The OF clause is optional, but can be used to link the field list to a browse object. You may also use the browse object's FieldList property or use the DEFINE BROWSE syntax, or dot reference notation to accomplish the link. *<form name>* indicates the parent form of the browse object. You must use dot reference notation to specify the *<form name>*.

Table 26.15 lists all properties and methods for DEFINE FIELDLIST. Dot reference notation gives you access to read-only properties and methods, using the following syntax:

```
[<memvar>=] ¦ [<command>]<object reference>.[<read-only property>] ¦ [<method>]
```

Table 26.15 Properties and Methods for DEFINE FIELDLIST

Property	Default	Method
ClassName	FIELDLIST	ActiveField( )
First	Empty String	Release( )
Name	*<object name>*	
Parent	Empty string	

DEFINE FORM

Syntax

```
DEFINE FORM <form name>
  [FROM <row1>,<col1>[TO <row2>,<col2>]] ¦ [AT <row>,<col>]
  [PROPERTY
     [After <object name>]
     [, AutoSize <expL>]
     [, Before <object name>]
     [, ColorBorder <color expC>]
     [, ColorBorderHighlight <expC>]
     [, ColorBorderLowered <color expC>]
     [, ColorBorderRaised <color expC>]
     [, ColorDisabled <color expC>]
     [, ColorIcon <color expC>]
     [, ColorNormal <color expC>]
     [, ColorScrollBar <color expC>]
     [, Debug <expL>]
     [, Design <expL>]
     [, Draw <expL>]
     [, Enabled <expL>]
     [, EscExit <expL>]
     [, Height, <expN>]
     [, HelpFile <expC}
     [, HelpId <help context exp>]
     [, Key <procedure>]
     [, Left <expN>]
     [, Maximize <expL>]
     [, MDI <expL>]
     [, Menu <object name> ¦ <expL>]
     [, Minimize <expL>]
     [, Moveable <expL>]
     [, OnClick <procedure>]
     [, OnClose <procedure>]
     [, OnGotFocus <procedure>]
```

```
        [, OnHelp <procedure>]
        [, OnLostFocus <procedure>]
        [, OnMouseDblClk <UDF>]
        [, OnMove <procedure>]
        [, OnOpen <procedure>]
        [, OnSize <procedure>]
        [, Parent <object name>]
        [, ProcFile <filename>[,] [<path>\]<object reference>]
        [, Shadow <expL>]
        [, Sizeable <expL>]
        [, StatusMessage <expC>]
        [, SysMenu <expL>]
        [, Text <expC>]
        [, Top <expN>]
        [, Visible <expL>]
        [, Width <expN>]
        [, WindowState <expN>]]
     [CUSTOM
        <property name 1><value 1> [, <property name 2><value 2>...]]
```

Purpose: Creates the rectangular area known as a *form*, which is used for data entry and retrieval and contains objects such as pushbuttons, entry fields, and spin boxes. A form is the workplace for your user. It provides entry fields for entering data, browse objects for editing and viewing records, and other objects that make your application easier to use.

Table 26.16 lists the read-only properties and the methods associated with DEFINE FORM. Dot reference notation gives you access to read-only properties and methods, using the following syntax:

```
[<memvar>=] ¦ [<command>]<object reference>.[<read-only property>] ¦ [<method>]
```

Table 26.16 Read-Only Properties and Methods for DEFINE FORM

Read-Only Properties	Methods
ClassName	ActiveControl( )
First	Close( )
Name	Modified( )
	Open( )
	ReadModal( )
	Refresh( )
	Release( )
	SetFocus( )
	Submit( )

Table 26.17 lists the properties and their default values for a form object.

Table 26.17 Properties and Default Values for a Form Object

Property	Default
After	*<object reference>*
AutoSize	.F.
Before	*<object reference>*
ClassName	FORM
ColorBorder	N/W
ColorBorderHighlight	W+/W
ColorBorderLowered	N/W
ColorBorderRaised	W+/W
ColorDisabled	N+/W
ColorIcon	GB+/W
ColorNormal	B/W
ColorScrollBar	BG/B
Debug	.F.
Design	.F.
Draw	.T.
Enabled	.T.
EscExit	.T.
First	.F.
Height	10
HelpFile	Empty string
HelpId	Empty string
Key	Empty string
Left	0
Maximize	.F.

Property	Default
MDI	.T.
Menu	Empty string
Minimize	.F.
Moveable	.T.
Name	*<object name>*
OnClick	Empty string
OnClose	Empty string
OnGotFocus	Empty string
OnHelp	Empty string
OnLostFocus	Empty string
OnMouseDblClk	Empty string
OnMove	Empty string
OnOpen	Empty string
OnSize	Empty string
Parent	Empty string
ProcFile	Empty string
Shadow	.T.
Sizeable	.F.
StatusMessage	Empty string
SysMenu	.T.
Text	*<object name>*
Top	0
Visible	.T.
Width	40
WindowState	0

Since you can use multiple forms at one time, avoid the use of public variables in the event handlers for each form. This helps keep the objects from conflicting with each other as they perform their tasks.

Use either the Refresh( ), Release( ), or Submit( ) method to unlock all records which were locked while the form was active. One or more of these methods must be issued prior to closing the form window.

DEFINE LISTBOX

Syntax

```
DEFINE LISTBOX <listbox name> OF <form name>
  [FROM <row1>,<col1> [TO <row2>,<col2>]] ¦ [AT <row>,<col>]
  [PROPERTY
     [After <object name>]
     [, Before <object name>]
     [, Border <expL>]
     [, ColorDisabled <color expC>]
     [, ColorGrid <color expC>]
     [, ColorHighlight <color expC>]
     [, Color Normal <color expC>]
     [, ColorScrollBar <color expC>]
     [, ColorSelected <color expC>]
     [, Column <expN>]
     [, CurSel <expN>]
     [, DataSource <expC>]
     [, Debug <expL>]
     [, DesignSelect <expL>]
     [, Enabled <expL>]
     [, Height <expN>]
     [, HelpFile <expC>]
     [, HelpId <help context exp>]
     [, Left <expN>]
     [, OnGotFocus <procedure>]
     [, OnHelp <procedure>]
     [, OnLostFocus <procedure>]
     [, OnSelChange <procedure>]
     [, Parent <object name>]
     [, ProcFile <filename>[,] [<path>\] <object filename>]
     [, Shadow <expL>]
     [, Sorted <expL>]
     [, StatusMessage <expC>]
     [, TabStop <expL>]
     [, Top <expN>]
     [, Value <expC>]
     [, Visible <expL>]
     [, Width <expN>]]
  [CUSTOM
     <property name 1><value 1> [, <property name 2><value 2>...]]
```

Purpose: An object used to allow your application's user to choose one or several options for entering into a field, either with scroll bars or via prompts generated by the data table being accessed by the list box. For instance, a list box may display a directory of files that a user could choose from to edit, delete, or copy.

Table 26.18 lists the read-only properties and the methods associated with DEFINE LISTBOX. These can be accessed by using the following syntax:

```
[<memvar>=] ¦ [<command>] <object reference>,[<read-only property>] ¦ [<method>]
```

Table 26.18 Read-Only Properties and Methods for DEFINE LISTBOX

Read-Only Property	Methods
ClassName	Release( )
Name	SetFocus( )

Table 26.19 contains the properties associated with DEFINE LISTBOX, along with the default values for each.

Table 26.19 Properties and Default Values for DEFINE LISTBOX

Property	Default
After	*<object reference>*
Before	*<object reference>*
Border	.F.
ClassName	LISTBOX
ColorDisabled	N+/W
ColorHighlight	W+/G
ColorNormal	N/BG
ColorScrollBar	B/BG
ColorSelected	RG+/BG
Column	1
CurSel	1
DataSource	Empty string
Debug	.F.
DesignSelect	.F.

(continues)

Table 26.19 Continued

Property	Default
Enabled	.T.
Height	5
HelpFile	Empty string
HelpId	Empty string
Left	0
Name	*<object name>*
OnGotFocus	Empty string
OnHelp	Empty string
OnSelChange	Empty string
Parent	*<form name>*
ProcFile	Empty string
Shadow	.F.
Sorted	.F.
StatusMessage	Empty string
TabStop	.T.
Top	0
Value	Empty string
Visible	.T.
Width	12

A vertical scroll bar appears on the list box if it is only one column wide and the contents are larger than the box. A horizontal scroll bar appears if there is more than one column of data. Prompts in a list box snake from the bottom of the first column to the top of the second. A list box may contain any of six types of prompts, all of which consist of character strings. You define the type of prompts to use with the DataSource property.

By pressing the first letter of the prompt, dBASE jumps the cursor to that prompt, or to the first prompt whose first letter matches the typed letter. This causes the prompt to be highlighted, waiting for the user to take an action on that prompt, or move to another prompt or control. Placing a text label on the list box allows you to assign a pickletter to the box, allowing the user to press the Alt key and the underlined letter (the pickletter) in the text label. See DEFINE TEXT for more information on how to define labels.

DEFINE MENUBAR

Syntax

```
DEFINE MENUBAR <menu bar name> [OF <form name>]
  [PROPERTY
     [ColorDisabled <expC>]
     [, ColorDisabledHighlight <expC>]
     [, ColorHighlight <expC>]
     [, ColorMenuBarNormal <expC>]
     [, ColorMenuBarPick <expC>]
     [, ColorNormal <expC>]
     [, ColorPickHighlight <expC>]
     [, ColorPickNormal <expC>]
     [, Design <expL>]
     [, Parent <object name>]
     [, ProcFile <filename>[,] [<path>\] <object filename>]
     [, Shadow <expL>]]
  [CUSTOM
     <property name 1><value 1> [, <property name 2><value 2>...]]
```

Purpose: One of three elements that comprise a pull-down menu structure, DEFINE MENUBAR creates a top-level object which contains the menu structure for the Desktop or a form. It may contain either the menu or menu item objects. Menu item objects are text strings that provide choices to the user. Choosing the item calls the OnClick event handler. Choosing a menu object, on the other hand, triggers the drop down action of the menu or menu item.

Where the menu bar is positioned is determined by the way you define it. If you set the MDI property of the form to false, then the menu bar is positioned on the form. If the MDI property is true, then the menu bar is displayed as a single gray line across the top of your screen.

Table 26.20 lists the read-only properties and the methods associated with DEFINE MENUBAR. You gain access to read-only properties and methods through the following dot reference notation syntax:

```
[<memvar>=] ¦ [<command>]<object reference>.[<read-only property>] ¦ [<method>]
```

Table 26.20 Read-Only Properties and Methods for DEFINE MENUBAR

Read-Only Property	Methods
First	Close( )
Form	Open( )
	Release( )

Table 26.21 lists the properties and their default settings.

Table 26.21 Properties and Default Settings for DEFINE MENUBAR

Property	Default
ColorDisabled	N+/W
ColorDisabledHighlight	N+/G
ColorHighlight	N/G
ColorMenuBarNormal	N/W
ColorMenuBarPick	R/W
ColorNormal	N/W
ColorPickHighlight	R/G
Design	.F.
First	Empty string
Form	Empty string
Parent	.F.
ProcFile	Empty string
Shadow	.T.

DEFINE MENU...OF

Syntax

```
DEFINE MENU <menu name 1>
  OF [[<form name>.][<menu bar name>.]]<menu name 2> ¦ [<form
  ➥name>.]<menu bar name>
  [PROPERTY
     [After <object name>]
     [, Before <object name>]
     [, Checked <expL>]
     [, Debug <expL>]
     [, Enabled <expL>]
     [, First <object name>]
     [, HelpFile <expC>]
     [, HelpId <expC>]
     [, OnClick <procedure>]
     [, OnHelp <procedure>]
     [, Parent <object name>]
     [, ProcFile <filename>[,] [<path>\]<object filename>]
     [, StatusMessage <expC>]
     [, Text <expC>]]
  [CUSTOM
     <property name 1><value 1> [, <property name 2><value 2>...]]
```

Purpose: Creates UI menus associated with a form. The menu is one of several elements available for creating a menu system: menu bars, menu items, pull-down menus, and cascading menus. Table 26.22 lists the read-only properties and methods accessible through dot reference notation in the following syntax:

```
[<memvar>=] ¦ [<command>]<object reference>.[<read-only property>] ¦ [<method>]
```

Table 26.22 Read-Only Properties and Methods for DEFINE MENU...OF

Read-Only Property	Method
First	Release( )
Form	

Table 26.23 lists the properties and their default values for a menu created with the DEFINE MENU...OF command.

Table 26.23 Properties and Default Values for Menu Created with DEFINE MENU...OF Command

Property	Default
After	*<object reference>*
Before	*<object reference>*
Check	.F.
Debug	.F.
Enabled	.T.
First	Empty string
Form	Empty string
HelpFile	Empty string
HelpId	Empty string
OnClick	Empty string
OnHelp	Empty string
Parent	*<object reference>*
ProcFile	Empty string
StatusMessage	Empty string
Text	Empty string

Enter a unique name of a menu to be created in the *<menu name1>* clause of the syntax. *<form name>* refers to the name of the form that the menu is associated with. *<menu bar name>* indicates the parent object for the new menu. *<menu name2>* refers to the name of the menu only if the menu has a parent menu. *<menu name1>* refers to the parent menu created with the DEFINE MENU command. This is how you create a pull-down menu or a cascading menu.

You need to connect three menu objects together to create a pull-down menu structure: menu item, menu bar, and menu. The first step is to create the parent menu object with the DEFINE MENU command. Then use DEFINE MENU *<menu name1>* OF *<menu bar name>* to place a title for the pull-down menu in the menu bar. To create the title for the menu, enter a character string in the Text property of the desired menu. Next, use the DEFINE

MENUITEM command to create the individual items displayed on the menu. Be sure to assign a procedure to each menu item by using the OnClick event handler to activate the desired action, say for opening a file, closing the file, or saving the file. Create any cascading menus using DEFINE MENU *<menu name 2>* OF [*<form name>*,]*<menu bar name>*,*<menu name1>*. Your system's memory capacity is the only factor limiting the number of cascading menus you can create.

You can make your user's job easier by assigning a pickletter to each menu item. This provides a shortcut keyboard method for selecting a menu item, which for some users is faster than the mouse. See Shortcut for more information.

DEFINE MENUITEM

Syntax

```
DEFINE MENUITEM <menu item name>
  OF [<form name>.][<menu bar name>.]<menu name> ¦ [<form
name>.]<menu bar name>
  [PROPERTY
     [After <object name>]
     [, Before <menu name>]
     [, Checked <expL>]
     [, Debug <expL>]
     [, Enabled <expL>]
     [, HelpFile <expC>]
     [, HelpId <expC>]
     [, OnClick <procedure>]
     [, OnHelp <procedure>]
     [, Parent <object name>]
     [, ProcFile <filename>[,] [<path>\]<object filename>]
     [, Separator <expL>]
     [, Shortcut <expC>]
     [, StatusMessage <expC>]
     [,.Text <expC>]
  [CUSTOM
     <property name 1><value 1> [, <property name 2><value 2>...]]
```

Purpose: Provides a text string which the user can select to activate an action from a menu which has been created with the DEFINE MENUBAR or DEFINE MENU...OF command. DEFINE MENUITEM defines one of three elements used to create a pull-down menu structure: menu bar, menu item, and menu. The menu item calls the OnClick event handler. Table 26.24 lists the read-only properties and methods of DEFINE MENUITEM which may be accessed via the following dot reference notation syntax:

```
[<memvar>=] ¦ [<command>] <object reference>,[<read-only property>] ¦ [<method>]
```

VI

Reference Guide

Table 26.24 Read-Only Properties and Methods for DEFINE MENUITEM

Read-Only Property	Method
First	Release( )
Form	

Use the default settings of the menu item command, shown in Table 26.25, to create standard menu item objects, or modify them to tailor the objects to fit your needs.

Table 26.25 Property and Default Values for MENUITEM

Property	Default
After	Empty string
Before	Empty string
Checked	.F.
Debug	.F.
Enabled	.T.
First	Empty string
Form	Empty string
HelpFile	Empty string
HelpId	Empty string
OnClick	Empty string
OnHelp	Empty string
Parent	Empty string
ProcFile	Empty string
Separator	.F.
Shortcut	Empty string
StatusMessage	Empty string
Text	Empty string

You cannot create cascading menus with the DEFINE MENUITEM command, but you can with the DEFINE MENU...OF command. Each menu item created with DEFINE MENUITEM is placed beneath the one before it, and will contain the same character string as the *<menu item name>* until you change the name with the Text property for the object. Defining a pickletter for the menu item speeds the user's access to the choices. See Shortcut for more information. The Shortcut property can be used to select a menu item and then call its OnClick event handler. See the ON KEY command in Chapter 22.

DEFINE OBJECT

Syntax

```
DEFINE OBJECT <object name>
  [CUSTOM
     <property name 1><value 1> [, <property name 2><value 2>...]]
```

Purpose: Creates a generic object that allows the user to define an individualized object for placement of functions, event handlers, or data. The read-only properties and methods are listed in Table 26.26 and can be accessed through the following dot reference notation:

```
[<memvar>=] ¦ [<command>]<object reference>.[<read-only property>] ¦ [<method>]
```

Table 26.26 Read-Only Properties and Methods for DEFINE OBJECT

Read-Only Property	Method
ClassName	Release( )
Name	

Objects that are created using the DEFINE OBJECT command may pass properties and conditions to other objects or procedures. Using the CUSTOM syntax defines user-defined properties and connects them to an object. Routines which create generic objects may access the variables in the objects, but no routines from outside of the originating routine may access the variables. When naming your customer objects, limit the length of the name to 11 characters.

DEFINE PAGEBREAK

Syntax

```
DEFINE PAGEBREAK <page break name> OF <form name>
  PROPERTY
     Top <expN>
```

Purpose: Places a division marker in a scrollable form to allow multiple pages of entry fields for extensive data entry tasks. You can insert the pagebreak command at any point in the sequence of DEFINE statements for a form's entry fields to create attractive and easily understood forms for input of data by the user. The user presses the Tab or PageDown key to advance to the next entry field or next page. PageUp returns the cursor to the previous page. The only property for the PAGEBREAK command is Top, which must be used to indicate at what position the upper-left corner of the form window will appear.

DEFINE PUSHBUTTON

Syntax

```
DEFINE PUSHBUTTON <pushbutton name> OF <form name>
  [AT <row>,<col>]
  [PROPERTY
     [After <object name>]
     [, Before <object name>]
     [, Border <expL>]
     [, BorderStyle <expN>]
     [, ColorDisabled <color expC>]
     [, ColorHighlight <color expC>]
     [, ColorNormal <color expC>]
     [, ColorPickHighlight <color expC>]
     [, ColorPickNormal <color expC>]
     [, ColorSelected <color expC>]
     [, ColorShadow <color expC>]
     [, Debug <expL>]
     [, Default <expL>]
     [, DesignSelect <expL>]
     [, Enabled <expL>]
     [, GrabFocus <expL>]
     [, Height <expN>]
     [, HelpFile <expC>]
     [, HelpId <help context exp>]
     [, Left <expN>]
     [, OnClick <procedure>]
     [, OnGotFocus <procedure>]
     [, OnHelp <procedure>]
     [, OnLostFocus <procedure>]
     [, Parent <object name>]
     [, ProcFile <filename>[,] [<path>\]<object filename>]
     [, StatusMessage <expC>]
     [, TabStop <expL>]
     [, Text <expC>]
     [, Top <expN>]
     [, Visible <expL>]
     [, Width <expN>]]
  [CUSTOM
     <property name 1><value 1> [, <property name 2><value 2>...]]
```

Purpose: Creates a pushbutton object which calls a specified procedure when selected by either a mouse click or by pressing the Enter key while the button is highlighted. *<pushbutton name>* is the relevant name you give to the object when you create it.

To remove the shadow from the pushbutton, set the Height property to 1. The label of the pushbutton is created by entering a character string in the Text property. Use the Width property to adjust the size of the pushbutton so that the label fits inside the object.

The read-only properties and the methods associated with this command are listed in Table 26.27. You can access the read-only properties and methods through the following dot reference notation:

```
[<memvar>=] ¦ [<command>] <object reference>.[<read-only property>] ¦ [<method>]
```

Table 26.27 Read-Only Properties and Methods for DEFINE PUSHBUTTON

Read-Only Property	Method
ClassName	Release( )
Name	SetFocus( )

Table 26.28 lists the properties and default values for a pushbutton.

Table 26.28 Properties and Default Values for PUSHBUTTON

Property	Default
After	*<object reference>*
Before	*<object reference>*
Border	.F.
BorderStyle	0
ClassName	PUSHBUTTON
ColorDisabled	N+/W
ColorHighlight	W+/G
ColorNormal	N/G

(continues)

Table 26.28 Continued

Property	Default
ColorPickHighlight	RG+/BG
ColorPickNormal	RG+/G
ColorSelected	BG+/G
ColorShadow	N/W
Debug	.F.
Default	.F.
DesignSelect	.F.
Enabled	.T.
GrabFocus	.T.
Height	2
HelpFile	Empty string
HelpId	Empty string
Left	0
Name	*<object name>*
OnClick	Empty string
OnGotFocus	Empty string
OnHelp	Empty string
OnLostFocus	Empty string
Parent	*<form name>*
ProcFile	Empty string
StatusMessage	Empty string
TabStop	.T.
Text	*<object name>*
Top	0
Visible	.T.
Width	7

You may want to add shortcut keys that consist of the Alt key and a pickletter. These keyboard shortcuts allow the user to use keystroke combinations to select the pushbutton. See Shortcut for more information.

No matter what else you want on your form, remember that each pushbutton must have some specific action or actions associated with it, whether that be to close a dialog box, cancel an action, or retrieve a file. Define the task for the pushbutton through the OnClick, OnHelp, or OnLostFocus property of the form. No changes are made to the data table until the Submit( ) method is executed. If no procedure is defined for the OnClick, OnHelp, or OnLostFocus property associated with the Submit( ), then Submit( ) merely closes the form. Be sure that your procedure identifies which pushbutton was selected, either by the user or by default, before executing the Submit( ) method.

DEFINE RADIOBUTTON

Syntax

```
DEFINE RADIOBUTTON <radio button name> OF <form name>
  [AT <row>,<col>
  [PROPERTY
     [After <object name>]
     [, Before <object name>]
     [, Border <expL>]
     [, BorderStyle <expN>]
     [, ColorDisabled <color expC>]
     [, ColorHighlight <color expC>]
     [, ColorNormal <color expC>]
     [, ColorPickHighlight <color expC>]
     [, ColorPickNormal <color expC>]
     [, DataLink <expC>]
     [, Debug <expL>]
     [, DesignSelect <expL>]
     [, Enabled <expL>]
     [, Group <expL>]
     [, Height <expN>]
     [, HelpFile <expC>]
     [, HelpId <help context exp>]
     [, Left <expN>]
     [, OnChange <procedure>]
     [, OnGotFocus <procedure>]
     [, OnHelp <procedure>]
     [, OnLostFocus <procedure>]
     [, Parent <object name>]
     [, ProcFile <filename>[,] [<path>\]<object filename>]
     [, Shadow <expL>]
     [, StatusMessage <expC>]
     [, TabStop <expL>]
     [, Text <expC>]
     [, Top <expN>]
     [, Value <exp>]
     [, Visible <expL>]
```

```
      [, Width <expN>]]
   [CUSTOM
      <property name 1><value 1> [, <property name 2><value 2>...]]
```

Purpose: Creates a radio button to be used in a series of options which allow the user to choose only one option. A radio button appears on the form as a circle, which is filled by a black dot when selected. The dot disappears when another radio button is selected, and reappears in the newly selected button. You must define the form that the radio button is to be placed on, prior to defining the radio button. Radio buttons typically appear in groups.

The read-only properties and the methods associated with this command are listed in Table 26.29. You can access the read-only properties and methods through the following dot reference notation:

```
[<memvar>=] ¦ [<command>] <object reference>.[<read-only property>] ¦ [<method>]
```

Table 26.29 Read-Only Properties and Methods for DEFINE RADIOBUTTON

Read-Only Property	Method
ClassName	Modified( )
Name	Release( )
	SetFocus( )

You can control how the radio button operates by changing the defaults listed in Table 26.30.

Table 26.30 Properties and Default Values for the Radio Button

Property	Default
After	*<object reference>*
Before	*<object reference>*
Border	.F.
BorderStyle	0
ClassName	RADIOBUTTON
ColorDisabled	N+/BG
ColorHighlight	W+/BG

Property	Default
ColorNormal	N/BG
ColorPickHighlight	RG+/BG
ColorPickNormal	RG+/BG
DataLink	Empty string
Debug	.F.
DesignSelect	.F.
Enabled	.T.
Group	.T.
Height	1
HelpFile	Empty string
HelpId	Empty string
Left	0
Name	*<object name>*
OnChange	Empty string
OnGotFocus	Empty string
OnHelp	Empty string
OnLostFocus	Empty string
Parent	*<form name>*
ProcFile	Empty string
Shadow	.F.
StatusMessage	Empty string
TabStop	.T.
Text	Empty string
Top	0
Value	.F.
Visible	.T.
Width	11

When the radio button has been selected, the Value property returns a true *value*.

To define the field of a current database as linked to the radio button, enter the appropriate value in the DataLink property of the radio button. The Value property may be used to be sure the data type matches the data type of the DataLink property prior to inserting the value into the field. A Datatype mismatch error appears if this is false.

To group radio buttons, set the Group property to true for the first item in the group, false for all others. Then you can start a second group by setting the first member of the second group's Group property to true, and all others to false. Repeat this for as many groups of radio buttons as you need to complete the task. This works because only one member of the group may be selected at any one time.

To provide text with your radio button, enter the appropriate character string in the radio button's Text property. You may wish to assign a pickletter for the button as well. See Shortcut for more information.

DEFINE RECTANGLE

Syntax

```
DEFINE RECTANGLE <rectangle name> OF <form name>
  [FROM <row1>,<col1> TO <row2>,<col2>] ¦ [AT <row>,<col>]
  [PROPERTY
     [After <object name>]
     [, Background <expC>]
     [, Before <object name>]
     [, Border <expL>]
     [, BorderStyle <expN>]
     [, ColorBorder <color expC>]
     [, ColorBorderLowered <color expC>]
     [, ColorBorderRaised <color expC>]
     [, ColorNormal <color expC>]
     [, DesignSelect <expL>]
     [, Height <expN>]
     [, Left <expN>]
     [, Shadow <expL>]
     [, Top <expN>]
     [, Visible <expL>]
     [, Width <expN>]]
  [CUSTOM
     <property name 1><value 1> [, <property name 2><value 2>...]]
```

Purpose: Creates a visual box that may be used for grouping objects, such as independent groups of radio buttons. Use the DEFINE FORM command to create the form, then create the rectangle for containing your objects. Be sure that no objects are placed underneath the rectangle, as any objects under the rectangle become invisible. The rectangle is a visual box, which means it cannot receive focus or contain data.

Table 26.31 lists the read-only properties and methods of DEFINE RECTANGLE. These properties and methods are accessed via dot reference notation using the following syntax:

```
[<memvar>=] ¦ [<command>] <object reference>.[<read-only property>] ¦ [<method>]
```

Table 26.31 Read-Only Properties and Methods for DEFINE RECTANGLE

Read-Only Property	Method
ClassName	Release( )
Name	

You may resize the rectangle, as long as DesignSelect is set to true, by dragging the lower right-hand corner with your mouse.

Modifying the defaults of the associated properties, listed in Table 26.32, allows you to customize the rectangle's appearance and actions.

Table 26.32 Properties and Defaults for DEFINE RECTANGLE

Property	Default
After	Empty string
Before	Empty string
Border	.T.
BorderStyle	0
ClassName	RECTANGLE
ColorBorder	W+/W
ColorBorderLowered	N/W
ColorBorderRaised	W+/W
ColorNormal	N/W
DesignSelect	.F.
Height	5

(continues)

Table 26.32 Continued

Property	Default
Left	0
Name	*<object name>*
Shadow	.F.
Top	0
Visible	.T.
Width	18

DEFINE SPINBOX

Syntax

```
DEFINE SPINBOX <spin box name> OF <form name>
  [AT <row>,<col>]
  [PROPERTY
     [After <object name>]
     [, Before <object name>]
     [, Border <expL>]
     [, BorderStyle <expN>]
     [, ColorDisabled <color expC>]
     [, ColorHighlight <color expC>]
     [, ColorIcon <color expC>]
     [, ColorNormal <color expC>]
     [, ColorScrollBar <color expC>]
     [, DataLink <expC>]
     [, Debug <expL>]
     [, DesignSelect <expL>]
     [, Enabled <expL>]
     [, Function <expC>]
     [, Height <expN>]
     [, HelpFile <expC>]
     [, HelpId <help context exp>]
     [, Left <expN>]
     [, OnChange <procedure>]
     [, OnGotFocus <procedure>]
     [, OnHelp <procedure>]
     [, OnLostFocus <procedure>]
     [, Parent <object name>]
     [, Picture <expC>]
     [, ProcFile <filename>[,] [<path>\]<object filename>]
     [, RangeMax <expN ¦ expD>]
     [, RangeMin <expN ¦ expD>]
     [, RangeRequired <expL>]
```

```
    [, Select All <expL>]
    [, Shadow <expL>]
    [, SpinOnly <expL>]
    [, StatusMessage <expC>]
    [, Step <expN>]
    [, TabStop <expL>]
    [, Top <expN>]
    [, Valid <UDF>]
    [, ValidErrorMsg <expC>]
    [, ValidRequired <expL>]
    [, Value <exp>]
    [, Visible <expL>]
    [, Width <expN>]]
  [CUSTOM
    <property name 1><value 1> [, <property name 2><value 2>...]]
```

Purpose: Creates a spin box, which consists of an entry field where the user may manually enter a numeric value or a date, and arrows that increment or decrement the default value of the entry field. Create the form first, then use DEFINE SPINBOX to create the spin box. To define the data table that the spin box affects, use the DataLink property. You can adjust the rate of increment or decrement by changing the value entered in the Step property. You will want to create prompts attached to the spin box entry area. Use the DEFINE TEXT command to create a text object and position it near the spin box.

Table 26.33 lists the read-only properties and methods associated with a spin box. These may only be changed via dot reference notation through the following syntax:

```
[<memvar>=] ¦ [<command>] <object reference>.[<read-only property>] ¦ [<method>]
```

Table 26.33 Read-Only Properties and Methods for a Spin Box

Read-Only Property	Method
ClassName	Modified( )
Name	Release( )
	SetFocus( )

Table 26.34 lists the properties and their default values for a spin box.

Table 26.34 Properties and Default Values for a Spin Box

Property	Default
After	*<object reference>*
Before	*<object reference>*
Border	.F.
BorderStyle	0
ClassName	SPINBOX
ColorDisabled	N+/B
ColorHighlight	W+/G
ColorIcon	N/G
ColorNormal	W+/B
ColorScrollBar	G+/B
DataLink	Empty string
Debug	.F.
DesignSelect	.F.
Enabled	.T.
Function	Empty string
Height	1
HelpFile	Empty string
HelpId	Empty string
Left	0
Name	*<object name>*
OnChange	Empty string
OnGotFocus	Empty string
OnHelp	Empty string
OnLostFocus	Empty string
OnSelChange	Empty string
Parent	*<form name>*

Property	Default
Picture	Empty string
ProcFile	Empty string
RangeMax	0
RangeMin	0
RangeRequired	.F.
SelectAll	Varies
Shadow	.F.
SpinOnly	.F.
StatusMessage	Empty string
Step	1
TabStop	.T.
Top	0
Valid	Empty string
ValidErrorMsg	Empty string
ValidRequired	.F.
Value	0
Visible	.T.
Width	11

You may want to assign shortcut keys for the keyboard. These key combinations allow the user to select the spin box label without using the mouse. See Shortcut for more information on assigning pickletters.

DEFINE TEXT

Syntax

```
DEFINE TEXT <text name> OF <form name>
  [AT <row>,<col>]
  [PROPERTY
     [After <object name>]
     [, Before <object name>]
     [, Border <expL>]
     [, BorderStyle <expN>]
```

```
    [, ColorDisabled <color expC>]
    [, ColorHighlight <color expC>]
    [, ColorNormal <color expC>]
    [, ColorPickHighlight <color expC>]
    [, ColorPickNormal <color expC>]
    [, DesignSelect <expL>]
    [, Enabled <expL>]
    [, Height <expN>]
    [, HelpFile <expC>]
    [, HelpId <help context exp>]
    [, Label <expL>]
    [, Left <expN>]
    [, OnClick <procedure>]
    [, OnMouseDblClk <UDF>]
    [, Parent <object name>]
    [, ProcFile <filename>[,] [<path>\]<object filename>]
    [, Shadow <expL>]
    [, Text <expC>]
    [, Top <expN>]
    [, Visible <expL>]
    [, Width <expN>]]
 [CUSTOM
    <property name 1><value 1> [, <property name 2><value 2>...]]
```

Purpose: Creates an object which contains a specified text string to be used as a label, title, prompts, or general information. By setting the Label property to true, the text object becomes a label for a combo box, entry field, list box, or spin box. You may also want to use pickletters in your text string to enable the user to select the object from the keyboard. The text object displays the text, underlining the special character(s) the user must type after pressing the Alt key. See Shortcut for information on assigning pickletters to an object. If you want to hide the text in an object, set the Visible property to false.

Table 26.35 lists the read-only properties and methods associated with a text object. These may only be changed via dot reference notation through the following syntax:

```
[<memvar>=] ¦ [<command>] <object reference>.[<read-only property>] ¦ [<method>]
```

Table 26.35 Read-Only Properties and Methods for a Text Object

Read-Only Property	Method
ClassName	Release( )
Name	

If the text object is not wide enough to display an entire character string, a horizontal scroll bar appears across the bottom of the form so that the user can scroll to the hidden text.

Table 26.36 lists the default properties of a text object.

Table 26.36 Properties and Default Values for a Text Object

Property	Default
After	*<object reference>*
Before	*<object reference>*
Border	.F.
BorderStyle	0
ClassName	TEXT
ColorDisabled	N+/W
ColorHighlight	W+/W
ColorNormal	N/W
ColorPickHighlight	RG+/W
ColorPickNormal	RG+/W
DesignSelect	.F.
Enabled	.T.
Height	1
HelpFile	Empty string
HelpId	Empty string
Label	.T.
Left	0
Name	*<object name>*
OnClick	Empty string
OnMouseDblClk	Empty string
Parent	*<form name>*

(continues)

Table 26.36 Continued

Property	Default
ProcFile	Empty string
Shadow	.F.
Text	*<object reference>*
Top	0
Visible	.T.
Width	Len(*<object name>*)

Chapter 27

Using System Memory Variables

System memory variables enable you to change various printer parameters to control the appearance of printed output. All system memory variables start with the underline character (_) and have default values when you start dBASE 5. You can change the system memory variables within your program, at the Command window, or from any dBASE print menu. The default values in this section are shown in uppercase letters, and alternative values are shown in lowercase letters. You can use upper- or lowercase characters when you use the system memory variables.

_Alignment

Syntax

```
_alignment = "LEFT"/"center"/"right"
```

Purpose: Determines the alignment of the text printed with the ?/?? commands. The text is normally placed at the left margin but can be centered or right-justified. The _ALIGNMENT command affects text within the margins, not text that is aligned with the PICTURE functions. The alignment setting is ignored if the _wrap variable is set to false (.F.).

Example

```
* Set up left text alignment
_alignment = "LEFT"
?"Left Side"
Left Side
_alignment = "Center"
?"Now Center"
                              Now Center
```

_Box

Syntax

```
_box = .T./.f.
```

Purpose: Determines whether the boxes that are defined with the DEFINE BOX command are printed. You can set the <*condition*> to true (.T.) or false (.F.), or to a statement that evaluates as true or false. The _box variable normally is set to true.

Example

```
* Turn off box printing
_box = .F.
```

_Clipboard

Syntax

```
_clipboard = <object reference>/CLIPBOARD::_clipboard
```

Purpose: Provides a temporary storage location for text. The Clipboard is a window object with the visible property set to false to hide it. It is normally used to hold the text from the Desktop that has been selected for cut or copy. You also can directly modify the contents in a program, using the dot reference notation (see Chapter 21, "Creating Objects with UI") to change the InsertLine, LineNo, or Value properties. Table 27.1 shows the properties and their settings.

Table 27.1 The Clipboard's Window Properties and Settings

Property	Default	Description
ColorBorder	W+/B	Indicates selected color of border
ColorNormal	GR+/B	Indicates color selected when object has focus
Enabled	.T.	Enables objects to be selected when true
Height	9	Determines height of window
InsertLine	Empty string	Shows a text string which is inserted in object
LineNo	Empty string	Shows line position in object where text string is to be inserted
Left	0	Indicates left border position
Maximize	.T.	Enables the form to be increased to full size when true

Property	Default	Description
MDI	.T.	Sets the form to follow MDI protocol when true
Minimize	.T.	Enables the form to follow MDI protocol when true
Moveable	.T.	Enables form to be moved with mouse when true
Modified	.F.	Sets logical for disenabling changes to the window when false
Sizeable	.T.	Enables resizing of window with mouse when true
SysMenu	.T.	Shows the close icon when true, hides it when false
Text	"Clipboard"	Denotes the form's title
Top	1	Determines location of the top border
Value	Empty string	Specifies text for current line
Visible	.F.	Sets object to not visible when false, visible when true
Width	80	Width of the object in characters
WindowState	0	Indicates the form's window state

Example

```
_Clipboard.Value= " "   && clear the clipboard
_Clipboard.LineNo=1     && set to first line
_Clipboard.InsertLine="Testing"     && store string to clipboard
MPurpose= _Clipboard.value          && use value from clipboard
```

_Cmdwindow

Syntax

```
_cmdwindow = <object reference>/COMMANDEDITOR::_cmdwindow
```

Purpose: Provides a reference to the window in which the new command line editor executes. By changing the properties of this object you can change the size and placement of the Command window. Setting the visible property to false removes the Command window from the screen while your program runs. Table 27.2 lists the properties of this memory variable.

Table 27.2 The Properties of the Command Window Variable

Property	Default	Description
ColorBorder	W+/B	Indicates the border color for the object
ColorNormal	GR+/B	Indicates color of test when the object gets focus
Height	9	Defines the height of the object
Left	0	Defines the location of the left border
Maximize	.T.	Enables the form to be increased to full size when true
Minimize	.T.	Enables the form to be reduced to an icon when true
Moveable	.T.	Enables form to be moved with mouse when true
Sizeable	.T.	Enables resizing of window with mouse when true
SysMenu	.T.	Shows the close icon when true, hides it when false
Text	"COMMAND"	Denotes the form's title
Top	1	Determines location of the top border
Visible	.T.	Sets object to not visible when false, visible when true
Width	50	Width of the object in characters
WindowState	0	Indicates the form's window state

Example

```
_cmdwindow.text = "Commands Go Here"
```

_Indent

Syntax

```
_indent = <number of columns>/0
```

Purpose: Determines the *<number of columns>* to indent the first paragraph of text printed with the ? command when the _wrap variable is set to true (.T.). The _indent value normally is 0. The lowest value is the negative of lmargin; if _lmargin is 15, the _indent can be as low as –15. The highest value is one less than the difference between _rmargin and _lmargin (_rmargin – _ lmargin –1). The sum of the _indent and _lmargin values must be less than the _rmargin value. The _indent value is used only if _wrap is set to true.

Note

The _ploffset (page left offset) value also can affect the actual printed position of the text.

Example

```
* Default indent is 0
?"Now is the time"
Now is the time
_indent = 5
?"Now is the time"
     Now is the time
```

_Lmargin

Syntax

```
_lmargin = <left margin column position>/0
```

Purpose: Defines the left margin used with the ? command if _wrap is set to true. The _lmargin value defaults to 0, but can be from 0 to 254. If _lmargin is set to 0, the first printed position will be at the left edge of the paper plus any _ploffset (page left offset) value (see _ploffset). The (_lmargin + _indent) value must be less than the _rmargin value.

Example

```
* Set up eight-character left margin
_lmargin = 8
```

_Padvance

Syntax

```
_padvance = "FORMFEED"/"linefeeds"
```

Purpose: Determines whether dBASE 5 advances the paper to the next top of form by using the form-feed character or by outputting line-feed commands. The _padvance variable set to LINEFEEDS is useful for printing short forms, such as checks, without having to set the form's length setting on the printer. The _plength variable then is used to set the length of the form.

Example

```
* Set up for check printing
_padvance = "LINEFEEDS"
```

_Pageno

Syntax

```
_pageno = <page number>/1
```

Purpose: Sets the current page number. The default value is 1, but it can be set to between 1 and 32,767. You also can use the _pageno value in your report to output the current page number (? _pageno).

Example

```
* Set up first page number
_pageno = 1
```

_Pbpage

Syntax

```
_pbpage = <beginning page number>/1
```

Purpose: Determines the beginning page number for a print job, as defined with the PRINTJOB command in a program. Any page number less than the _pbpage value will not be printed. The _pbpage value defaults to 1, but can be set to between 1 and 32,767. The _pbpage value must be less than or equal to _pepage (print job end page). This command is useful if you want to print just the remaining part of a report after a printer jam.

Example

```
* Start printing on page 1
_pbpage = 1
```

_Pcolno

Syntax

```
_pcolno = <column number>/0
```

Purpose: Determines the beginning column number for streaming output from the ?? command or returns the current column number. The _pcolno value can be from 0 to 255.

Example

```
* Set up column 0
_pcolno = 0
```

_Pcopies

Syntax

```
_pcopies = <number of copies>/1
```

Purpose: Determines the number of copies to be printed in a print job. The default is 1; you can use values from 1 to 32,767. This command can be used only in a program, because it requires a PRINTJOB/ENDPRINTJOB command.

Example

```
* Set up two copies of report
_pcopies = 2
```

_Pdriver

Syntax

```
_pdriver = "<printer driver file name>"/"GENERIC.PR2"
```

Purpose: Assigns the desired printer driver or returns the name of the currently active printer driver. The printer driver is assigned when dBASE 5 is installed, or you can set the default printer driver in the CONFIG.DB file. The *<printer driver file name>* must include the drive and directory name if the specified PR2 file doesn't exist in the current directory. An ASCII printer driver can be used to produce ASCII text files containing no printer commands.

Example

```
* Set up a custom printer driver
_pdriver = "CUSTOM3.PR2"
```

_Pecode

Syntax

```
_pecode = <control codes>/<EMPTY STRING>
```

Purpose: Determines the ending control codes for a print job. The pecode is sent at the ENDPRINTJOB command in your program. The *<control codes>* can be text or printer control commands, such as {27} for the `<escape>` character used by most printers. The Hewlett-Packard LaserJet printer reset code could be sent as "{ESC}E", "{27}{69}", or "{27}E" (because "E" = "{69}").

Example

```
* Set up HP LaserJet reset command
* at print job end
_pecode = "{ESC}E"
```

_Peject

Syntax

```
_peject = "BEFORE" / "after" / "both" / "none"
```

Purpose: Determines whether a page is ejected from the printer before and/or after the print job. Use the _peject command before the PRINTJOB command.

Example

```
* Set up page eject before next printjob
_peject = "BEFORE"
```

_Pepage

Syntax

```
_pepage = <ending page number>/32767
```

Purpose: Determines the ending page of a print job, with a default *<ending page number>* value of 32,767. The allowable values are 1 to 32,767. The _pepage variable should not be less than the _pbpage (print beginning page) value. This variable is useful in conjunction with the _pbpage system variable to print a portion of a print job within a PRINTJOB/ENDPRINTJOB block.

Example

```
* End print job at page 20
_pepage = 20
```

_Pform

Syntax

```
_pform = "<print form file name>"
```

Purpose: Activates the *<print form file name>* or returns the name of the currently active *<print form file name>*. Setting the _pform *<print form file name>* enables you to use the following settings from the print form, rather than the current settings: _padvance, _pageno, _pbpage, _pcopies, _pdriver, _pecode, _peject, _pepage, _plength, _ploffset, _ppitch, _pquality, _pscode, _pspacing, and _pwait.

> **Note**
>
> A print form (PRF) file can be created only by using the dBASE 5 Print menu.

Example

```
* Set up our custom print form
_pform = "CUSTOM12.PRF"
```

_Plength

Syntax

```
_plength = <paper length in lines>/66
```

Purpose: Sets the length of the output page; the default is 66 lines. This is the number of lines on the entire page from the top to bottom of the paper. A value from 1 to 32,767 can be assigned. The _plength value is then used to determine when a _peject and _padvance take place. You can use _plength to set up for short forms, such as checks or invoices.

> **Note**
>
> The number of lines on a page also is affected by the setting of the number of lines per inch. The lines per inch normally is set at 6, but you can set up 8 lines per inch or other values by using a printer control code sequence.

Example

```
* Set up for legal paper
_plength = 84
```

_Plineno

Syntax

```
_plineno = <line number>/0
```

Purpose: Assigns the *<line number>* for streaming output or returns the current *<line number>*. The _plineno value can range from 0 (the default) to the current _plength-1. This setting does not affect actual line positioning.

Example

```
* Set up line number 12
_plineno = 12
* Show current line number
? _plineno
```

_Ploffset

Syntax

```
_ploffset = <column number>/0
```

Purpose: Determines the page left offset for printed output. Use the _ploffset value to adjust text on the printed page. The _ploffset default is 0, but can range from 0 to 254.

Example

```
* Set up eight-character left margin
_ploffset = 8
```

_Ppitch

Syntax

```
_ppitch = "pica"/"elite"/"condensed"/"DEFAULT"
```

Purpose: Sets the printer pitch (number of characters per inch) or returns the string corresponding to the current printer pitch. The default for _ppitch is "DEFAULT". The current pitch is defined by the current setting on the printer. The _ppitch variable sends the appropriate escape code (defined by the currently active printer driver) to the printer. Pica is 10 characters per inch (cpi), elite is 12 cpi, and condensed is about 17.16 cpi (on most printers).

Example

```
* Set up condensed print
_ppitch = "condensed"
```

_Pquality

Syntax

```
_pquality = <condition>/.F.
```

Purpose: Enables you to select the print quality of the output on printers that can produce several levels of print quality. The default setting is false (.F.). If _pquality is set to false, the printer prints in draft mode. If this variable is set to true (.T.), the output is set to near-letter quality. This variable will cause an error if used with laser printers, because laser printers only generate letter-quality print. You also can use _pquality to return the current print quality setting as true (near-letter quality) or false (draft).

Examples

```
* Set printer to near-letter quality
_pquality = .T.
* Set printer to draft mode
_pquality = .F.
```

_Pscode

Syntax

```
_pscode = <control code>/<EMPTY STRING>
```

Purpose: Sends the *<control codes>* string to the printer at the beginning of a print job. (The _pecode is used for the ending control code of a print job.) You can set the _pscode variable at any time. It is sent to the printer by the PRINTJOB command. The *<control code>* can be ASCII text or values; values must be enclosed in braces ({ }). To send the landscape command code for a Hewlett-Packard LaserJet printer, you can use {27}&l10 or {27}{38}{108}{49}{79} or "{ESC}&l10" as the *<control code>*.

Example

```
* Set starting control code for print job
_pscode = "{ESC}&l10"
```

_Psize

Syntax

```
_psize = <expC>
```

Purpose: Enables you to use a standard paper size to set the page length. The current value of _plength determines the default page setting for this variable. Total line count from top to bottom of a page determines the page length. Table 27.3 lists the values that can be assigned to this variable.

Table 27.3 Values for plength memvar

Value	Lines Per Page
Default	Uses value currently in _plength
Letter	66
Legal	84
A4	70
B5	60
Executive	63

Example

```
_psize = "Legal"
```

_Pspacing

Syntax

```
_pspacing = 1 / 2 / 3
```

Purpose: Determines the line spacing for printed output. The default is single spacing (1).

> **Note**
>
> The _pspacing value affects the height of a box. If _pspacing is 3, then a box that has a defined height of 5 prints as 13 lines high.

Example

```
* Set up double spacing
_pspacing = 2
```

_Pwait

Syntax

```
_pwait = <condition>
```

Purpose: Determines whether the printer will pause after printing each page to enable you to insert paper. The default is false (.F.). The *<condition>* can be .T. or .F., or a condition that evaluates to true or false. Use a _pwait setting of .T. to print on single-sheet, manually fed paper.

Example

```
* Set up for continuous paper
_pwait = .F.
```

_Rmargin

Syntax

```
_rmargin = <right margin column position>/<EMPTY STRING>
```

Purpose: Defines the right margin position for ?/?? output when _wrap is true. The default value is 79. The minimum value is the greater of (_lmargin + 1) and (_lmargin + _indent + 1). The maximum value is 255. If _wrap is set to false, then _rmargin value is ignored.

Example

```
* Set for wide paper margin
_rmargin = 130
```

_Tabs

Syntax

```
_tabs = "<tab stop positions>"
```

Purpose: Sets the tab stops for screen, printer, or file output with the ?/?? commands. _tabs also sets the default tab stops used within memo fields when editing. The default value is a null string (" "), but the default tab stops are at every eight character positions within the memo editor (_tabs = "8,16,24,32...").

Example

```
* Set up tab stops every 10 columns
_tabs = "10,20,30,40,50,60,70,80"
```

_Wrap

Syntax

```
_wrap = <condition>
```

Purpose: Sets word wrapping between the margins on (if <*condition*> is true) or off (if <*condition*> is false). The _alignment, _indent, _lmargin, and _rmargin variables are used only when _wrap is on (true).

Example

```
* Make sure that word wrap is on
_wrap = .T.
```

Chapter 28

Using Preprocessor Directives

In an ever-changing world like the computer industry, it's good to know that you can write code today that allows for an anticipated change tomorrow. Preprocessor directives enable you to let the program decide how it executes based on what conditions are present at the time of compilation. In this chapter, you see how these directives can help your program make the decision.

Compiler Basics

In releases of dBASE through III+, dBASE acted as an interpreter of your code. With dBASE IV, a partial compiler was introduced that sped up execution of programs and allowed your programs to run without a complete copy of dBASE, although the RUNTIME program is still required. dBASE 5 introduces a full compiler and linker to allow you to generate stand-alone executables from your dBASE code.

The compiler goes through several steps when it is preparing your code for execution. The first step is to pass your code through a *preprocessor*. The preprocessor looks for special codes—preprocessor directives—that tell it what sections of code should be passed on to the compiler. Using the preprocessor directives you can create *macros*, or variable names, that mark the place in your code where a text string will be placed. Any place in the code that the preprocessor sees the macro name, it will replace the macro name with the text string that was defined for the macro. After a macro has been created, you can use other preprocessor directives to test for the existence or value of the macro. The preprocessor can use the tests to include or exclude entire blocks of code from the output that is sent to the next stage of the compiler. In the next stage the compiler reads all the lines of code passed to it and creates a list of all the variable names, called a symbol table.

Macros can be defined in your code using the #define preprocessor directive, or from the Desktop menus at compile time. You can use the Options, Advanced Compiler, Define preprocessor directives choice on the Desktop Menu to define macros prior to compiling your code. You can also use the Program, Arguments choice and use the –D to indicate macro definitions for the compilation of your program. Any macros that are defined in your code will override macros that are defined using the menu options without generating any warnings or errors.

There are several advantages to using preprocessor directives in your code. Because the preprocessor replaces the macro name with the defined string before the compiler creates the symbol table, the preprocessor macros are not counted against the maximum number of variable names. This leaves you more variables to use in the design and execution of your code. You don't have to use memory variables to switch between different versions of your code, you can use a macro instead.

Tests of the macro values using preprocessor directives are performed during the compile cycle, so excluded code is not included in the final executable. This makes your delivered executable program smaller. Also, because the code does not have to be tested for during execution, the program will run faster.

Using the preprocessor macros to create pseudo functions can make your code more readable. By defining a macro for a complex string of dBASE functions and operations, and then using that macro in your code, you reduce the length of your listing.

Caution

Although the macro reduces the length of the listing, the macro is expanded before being sent to the compiler. Make sure your line will be less than the maximum line length (4,096 characters) when the macros are expanded or the compiler will abort with `Line exceeds maximum of 4096 characters`.

Preprocessor Directives

#define

Syntax

```
#define <macro name>[(<parameter list>)]
[<macro expression>[(<parameter list>)]]
```

Purpose: Equates a name, *<macro name>*, to a value or set of instructions. When the compiler finds the *<macro name>* in your code, it will be replaced by the contents of <macro expression>. The name must begin with a nonnumeric character or an underscore. It can contain alphanumeric characters or underscores, but cannot use symbols (i.e., *, &&, =), or the words NOTE, or TEXT as the name.

The *<macro expression>* parameter contains a character string that is used to replace the contents of *<macro name>*. This can be a single character, logical, or numeric value, or any single line command.

The *<parameter list>* parameter enables you to pass values into the macro to be changed at compile time.

The macro can act as a procedure, executing a block of code, or a function, returning a single value from the block of code. Macros can be nested by first defining the macro to be used in the definition, then including that macro in a second macro definition.

> **Caution**
>
> Do not define macros in your code that you plan to change at compile time from the menus. The #define directive overrides any macro definitions done outside the program at compile time.

Example

```
#define ReleaseVer "1.0"
#define IdString "This is version "+ReleaseVer+" of the software"
#define DayMinute(ValueIn)
STR(VAL(SUBSTR(ValueIn,1,2))*60+VAL(SUBSTR(ValueIn,4,2)))
* The following statement displays the version statement:
*    This is version 1.0 of the software
?IdString
SET HOURS TO 24
* The following statement converts the current time into minutes
* since midnight. It is expanded by the preprocessor to read:
*STR(VAL(SUBSTR(TIME(),1,2))*60+VAL(SUBSTR(TIME(),4,2)))
?"There have been "+Day_Minute(TIME( ))+" minutes since midnight."
* For 9:00 am the output would look like:
There have been 540 minutes since midnight.
```

#if...#endif

Syntax

```
#if <condition>
     <commands>
[[#elif <condition>
     <commands>]/
[#else
     <commands>]]
#endif
```

Purpose: Conditionally compiles a block of code depending on the logical value of the stated condition. If the #if statement is true, the *associated block of commands*—commands after #if statement through the next #elif, #else, or #endif statement—is compiled; if false, the block is skipped.

A *<condition>* can be any combination of previously defined macros (see #define) and logical, mathematical, or relational operators that return a logical true or false. The *<condition>* cannot use .T., .F., $ (substring comparison operator), or ^ (exponential operator) in its definition. The *<commands>* parameter can include dBASE statements, preprocessor directives, or a combination of both.

The #elif statement is only evaluated if the #if statement is false. If the #elif statement is true, the preprocessor then acts on the block of commands associated with #elif; if false, the block is skipped. As with any if...then...else syntax, when the #if statement is followed by an #else statement, and the #if statement is false, the program skips to the #else statement and continues the program.

Only one #elif or #else statement can be included in a single #if...#endif clause; however, #if clauses can be nested as many as 64 levels deep.

Example

```
* If this version is for a 486, set the maximum array
* size to be 4000 and use the high precision math routine,
* otherwise set maximum array size to 2000 and use the
* low precision math routine to speed processing.
#if ReleaseVer="486"
     #define MaxArray 4000
     DO HighMath
  #else
     #define MaxArray 2000
     DO LowMath
#endif
DEFINE ARRAY clPhoneList[5,MaxArray]
```

If ReleaseVer is defined the code that is passed to the compiler from the preprocessor looks like this:

```
     DO HighMath
DEFINE ARRAY clPhoneList[5,4000]
```

#ifdef

Syntax

```
#ifdef <macro name>
     <commands>
[[#elif <condition>
     <commands>]/
[#else
     <commands>]]
#endif
```

Purpose: Determines whether *<macro name>* has been previously defined, and selects which specified block of code to compile. The #ifdef directive is true only if the macro has been previously defined. This is the inverse function of #ifndef. This statement follows programming conventions for if...endif syntax. When the #ifdef statement is true (the macro has been defined), the code is compiled; when false, the code is skipped. You can nest up to 64 levels of #ifdef statements, if desired.

The *<commands>* parameter includes any dBASE statements, preprocessor directives, or a combination of both. *<macro name>* indicates the name of a macro that was created using the #define directive in a source file, or by entering a macro name from Options Advanced Compiler Define preprocessor symbols from the Developer's Desktop, or by setting the –D command-line switch from the Program Argument Menu. A *<condition>* can be any logical expression that calls defined preprocessor macros and determines whether the logical return is true or false. The expression cannot use the substring comparison operator ($), the exponential operator (^), .T., or .F. in its definition.

You can use only one #elif or one #else statement with each #ifdef statement. If the #ifdef statement is followed by the #elif statement, and the #ifdef statement is false, then the program processes the code associated with the #elif statement. If the #ifdef statement is followed by an #else statement, and the macro has not been defined, the program only includes the block of commands associated with the #else statement.

Example

```
* Start a loop to process your data
FOR LoopCount = 1 to 50
   * If the DEBUG macro is defined, display the loop counter.
   #ifdef DEBUG
   ?The value of LoopCount is , LoopCount
   #endif
```

#ifndef

Syntax

```
#ifndef <macro name>
     <commands>
[[#elif <condition>
     <commands>]/
[#else
     <commands>]]
#endif
```

Purpose: The inverse function of #ifdef, returning a logical true only when the macro has *not* been defined. See #ifdef for complete description of how this directive functions.

Example

```
* Check the printer type. Define the macro if
* it hasn't been defined yet. Set the print control string.
#ifndef PrintType
    #define PrintType "HP LaserJet"
    #define PrintCtrl CHR(27) + "E"
#else
     #if PrintType = "HP LaserJet"
         #define PrintCtrl CHR(27) + "E"
     #elif PrintType = "Epson"
         #define PrintCtrl
     #endif
#endif
???PrintCtrl

* This block sends the appropriate print control string to the
* printer. If the PrintType macro was undefined prior to
* executing the block, the code sent to the compiler would be:
???CHR(27) + E
```

#include

Syntax

```
#include "<filename>"/<<filename>>
```

Purpose: Inserts an external file of dBASE code—an include file—into whatever file is current during compilation. The #include directive allows you to break up your code into smaller modules of dBASE commands or #define directives. These modules can be used as an include file which can be used in multiple program files. The *“<filename>”/ <<filename>>* indicates the full name of the file, followed by an optional description of the full path.

Depending on how you use the #include statement, the preprocessor looks for the include file in one of three ways:

- If you only give the file name in quotation marks, the current directory is searched, then the set of directories that were specified by the –I option of the **P**rogram, **A**rguments menu, or in the **O**ptions, **A**dvanced Compiler, **I**nclude directories menu.
- If you enter the file name in angle brackets, the search is performed on the –I or the specified path. If the –I option is not used, or the correct path is not given, the preprocessor returns an error message that it cannot find the file.
- If you enter an exact path using quotation marks (angle brackets won’t work here) for the include file, the preprocessor only searches that path. If the preprocessor can’t find the include file in the location specified, the compiler returns an error message to that effect.

Example

```
* Include three different files using each of the methods
#include "C:\DBASE\KEYVAL.INC"
#include "MYERRS.LST"
#include <FUNCDEF.H>

* You can combine the #if and #include to customize your code
* Check to see if developers menus should be used, otherwise
* use the standard menus.
#ifdef DevMenus
   #if DevMenus = "TRUE"
      #include "MenuDev.PRG"
   #else
      #include "MenuStd.PRG"
   #endif
#else
   #define DevMenus "FALSE"
   #include "MenuStd.PRG"
#endif
```

#undef

Syntax

```
#undef <macro name>
```

Purpose: Releases the name of a macro so that it may be redefined by using #define, or the **O**ptions, **A**dvanced Compiler, D**e**fine preprocessor symbols menus from the Desktop, or from the command line using the –D option.

You will get an error message if you try to define a macro that is already defined. It is often a good idea to check if a macro name is already defined before you define it. You can then release the macro name and redefine it for the value you need in your routine.

Example

```
#ifdef MaxArray
   #undef MaxArray
#endif
#define MaxArray 4000
```

Chapter 29

Using the System Configuration File

The CONFIG.DB file contains the default configuration of your installation of dBASE 5. Created during the installation process, the file contains configuration information, memory allocation parameters, function key definitions, SET command settings, and color settings. In this chapter you'll learn how you can work with this file to control how dBASE operates.

The entries for CONFIG.DB are broken into several sections in this chapter:

- General configuration commands
- Memory parameters
- Function keys
- SET commands
- Design surface

At the end of this chapter is a section that describes how to use a mouse in this DOS-based application. You'll find that working with a mouse in dBASE 5 for DOS is very similar to working with a mouse in the Windows environment or on a Macintosh.

You can change the CONFIG.DB file with a program editor, by using the DBSETUP program, or with the command MODIFY COMMAND CONFIG.DB. The default CONFIG.DB file normally is stored in the dBASE 5 program directory. You can create a custom CONFIG.DB file for each of your applications and store it in the directory with the application. If you start dBASE from the application directory, the CONFIG.DB for that application will be used.

Tip
To specify a configuration file other than CONFIG.DB, use the optional /C switch when starting dBASE 5.

Any of the configuration parameters that can be set in your program with the SET command (see Chapter 24, "Using SET Commands To Configure dBASE 5") can also be inserted into CONFIG.DB. The format for all commands in the CONFIG.DB is *<parameter>* = *<value>*. The command word SET is not used in the CONFIG.DB file. The only way to change some configuration parameters is to edit the CONFIG.DB file. See Table 29.1 for a list of the parameters you can change only by editing CONFIG.DB.

Table 29.1 Parameters Changed by Editing CONFIG.DB

Configuration Parameters	
ASCIISORT	PRINTER
BUCKET	PRINTER FONT
COMMAND	PROMPT (prior to dBASE 5)
EXPSIZE	REFRESH
FASTCRT	REPROCESS
FILES	RESETCRT
GETS	SQLDATABASE
INDEXBYTES	SQLHOME
LANGTABLES	SYSPROC
LDRIVER	TABS
LOCALSHARE	TEDIT/EDITOR
NOCLOCK	WP
PDRIVER	
Memory Parameters	
CTMAXSYMS	MVBLKSIZE
MVARSIZE	RTBLKSIZE
MVMAXBLKS	RTMAXBLKS
Miscellaneous	
<key label>	PRG*<surface>*

Configuration Commands

This series of commands is used in the CONFIG.DB file to control the default configuration of dBASE 5.

ASCIISORT

Syntax

```
ASCIISORT = ON/OFF
```

Default

```
ASCIISORT = ON
```

Purpose: Causes sorting to be performed in ASCII order. This option works only if LANGTABLES is set to ON.

BUCKET

Syntax

```
BUCKET = <number of 1K memory blocks>
```

Default

```
BUCKET = 2
```

Purpose: Specifies the number of 1K memory blocks. Use larger values if you have multiple screens or many PICTURE clauses in a format file. The range is from 1 to 31.

COMMAND

Syntax

```
COMMAND = <dBASE V command or program>
```

Default

```
COMMAND = ASSIST
```

Purpose: Specifies a *<dBASE V command or program>* to execute automatically when dBASE 5 is started. To automatically run a program called MAINPROG.PRG whenever you start up dBASE, for example, make sure that COMMAND = DO MAINPROG appears in your CONFIG.DB file. The default is COMMAND = ASSIST, which brings you immediately to the Control Center. Remove this line if you want to go straight to the Command window when you start dBASE 5.

> **Note**
>
> You also can start a program immediately as you start up dBASE by following the DBASE command with the program name. For example, typing **DBASE MAINPROG** at the DOS prompt is equivalent to using **COMMAND = DO MAINPROG** in the CONFIG.DB file.

EXPSIZE

Syntax

```
EXPSIZE = <number of 1K bytes>
```

Default

```
EXPSIZE = 100
```

Purpose: Specifies the size (in bytes) of the memory buffer that holds expressions during program compilation. If your program uses complex expressions, you may see the error message EVAL work area overflow. You can correct this problem by specifying a larger EXPSIZE value. The allowable range is from 100 to 2000.

FASTCRT

Syntax

```
FASTCRT = ON/OFF
```

Default

```
FASTCRT = ON
```

Purpose: Controls the use of a fast display option. The default ON setting enables dBASE to display information on color screens more quickly, but can cause a "snow" effect on CGA-type video/monitor setups. If you see "snow" on-screen during screen displays, set FASTCRT to OFF in your CONFIG.DB file.

FILES

Syntax

```
FILES = <number of files>
```

Default

```
FILES = 99
```

Purpose: Controls the number of files dBASE 5 can have open at any one time. The allowable range is from 15 to 99, and is limited by the FILES statement for DOS in the CONFIG.SYS file.

GETS

Syntax

```
GETS = <number of GET statements>
```

Default

```
GETS = 128
```

Purpose: Specifies the number of @...GET statements that can be active at any one time. Increase this value (the allowable range is from 35 to 1023) if your input screen has a large number of fields.

INDEXBYTES

Syntax

```
INDEXBYTES = <number of 1K index file nodes>
```

Default

```
INDEXBYTES = 63
```

Purpose: Specifies the number of 1K index blocks that can be cached in memory. To increase indexing speed, specify a higher setting if memory is available. The available range is 2 to 2048 (2 kilobytes to 2 megabytes).

LANGTABLES

Syntax

```
LANGTABLES = OFF/ON
```

Default

```
LANGTABLES = OFF
```

Purpose: Changes the setting for the language table, enabling foreign language characters and lower- and uppercase characters to be sorted together. LANGTABLES default is OFF if the country code is set to United States; otherwise, the default is ON. In dBASE 5, the SET LDCHECK command is used to check for conflicting language drivers.

LDRIVER

Syntax

```
LDRIVER = <string>
```

Default

```
LDRIVER = "DB437UK0"
```

Purpose: Specifies which language driver is used inside dBASE. LDRIVER maps the DOS code page into dBASE for translation of the ASCII characters above 127 into the foreign language characters with accents and other symbols.

LOCALSHARE

Syntax

```
LOCALSHARE = ON/OFF
```

Default

```
LOCALSHARE = ON
```

Purpose: When set to ON, LOCALSHARE enables file sharing protection on a single system when used with the DOS SHARE program and with EXCLUSIVE = OFF. With LOCALSHARE set to OFF, local file sharing is disabled.

NOCLOCK

Syntax

```
NOCLOCK = OFF/ON
```

Default

```
NOCLOCK = OFF
```

Purpose: If set to ON, the clock display is suppressed until a SET CLOCK command is issued.

PDRIVER

Syntax

```
PDRIVER = <printer driver file name>
```

Default

```
PDRIVER = GENERIC.PR2
```

Purpose: Specifies the default printer driver, which is selected during the installation of dBASE 5. The *<printer driver file name>* should exist in the dBASE 5 directory or in the currently set path. Use the _pdriver system memory variable to change the current printer driver temporarily.

Example

```
PDRIVER = HPDSK150.PR2
```

PRINTER

Syntax

```
PRINTER <printer number> = <filename>
   [NAME <printer name string>] [DEVICE <device>]
```

Default

The value varies, depending on the printer(s) you use.

Purpose: Enables you to configure up to four different printers. The *<printer number>* is a value of 1 to 4. The *<filename>* is the name of the printer driver file. The *<name string>* defines the printer name that is shown on the Printer Destination menus. The *<device>* specifies the DOS port to use, such as LPT1 or COM2.

Example

```
PRINTER 1 = HPDSK150.PR2 NAME "HP DeskJet (HP 2276)"   DEVICE LPT1
```

PRINTER FONT

Syntax

```
PRINTER <printer number> FONT <font number> =
   <begin font escape code>, <end font escape code>
   [NAME <font name string>]
```

Default

The value varies, depending upon the printer(s) you use.

Purpose: Installs or changes the fonts for the *<printer number>* set with the PRINTER command. The *<font number>* specifies a number from 1 to 5 that is used to identify the font. The *<begin font escape code>* is the printer escape code that is used to "turn on" the font. The *<end font escape code>* is the printer escape code that is used to "turn off" the font (normally the command that sets the font back to the printer's default). These escape codes can be found in your printer manual. The *<font name string>* is the text that is displayed on the Words Style menu to describe the font.

Example

```
PRINTER 1 FONT 1 = {27}(10U{27}(s0u0p10h12v0s0b3t2Q,{27}(3@,
   NAME "Courier 10/12 pt"
```

PROMPT

Syntax

```
PROMPT = "<dBASE IV dot prompt string>"
```

Default

In versions prior to dBASE 5, the dBASE dot prompt (.). Ignored in dBASE 5.

Purpose: The Command window made this command obsolete in dBASE 5. Defines a prompt string to replace the "dot" of the dot prompt in dBASE IV and earlier versions. The *<prompt string>* can be as many as 19 ASCII characters.

Example

```
PROMPT = "<Enter DB4 Command>"
```

REFRESH

Syntax

```
REFRESH = <number of seconds>
```

Default

```
REFRESH = 0
```

Purpose: Specifies the number of seconds between screen updates when dBASE is used on a network.

REPROCESS

Syntax

```
REPROCESS = <number of retries>
```

Default

```
REPROCESS = 0
```

Purpose: Specifies the number of retries for executing a command when dBASE is used on a network. A setting of –1 calls for infinite retries.

RESETCRT

Syntax

```
RESETCRT = ON/OFF
```

Default

```
RESETCRT = ON
```

Purpose: Resets the display screen to the mode in use before an external program was run.

SQLDATABASE

Syntax

```
SQLDATABASE = <SQL database name>
```

Default

```
SQLDATABASE = SAMPLES
```

Purpose: The name of the SQL database that is activated when you start SQL from inside dBASE. The default is set when you install dBASE 5.

SQLHOME

Syntax

```
SQLHOME = <path name>
```

Default

The DBASE\SQLHOME directory of the drive where you installed dBASE 5.

Purpose: Sets the drive and directory names that contain your SQL system files.

SYSPROC

Syntax

```
SYSPROC = <file name>
```

Purpose: Enables you to specify a file containing procedures to be used by your dBASE programs.

TABS

Syntax

```
TABS = <tab setting list>
```

Default

Every eight columns.

Purpose: Sets the initial tab stop settings. The default is every eight columns (8, 16, 24...), but can be set to any series of numbers separated by commas.

Example

```
TABS = 10,20,30,40,50,60,70,80
```

TEDIT/EDITOR

Syntax

```
TEDIT = <ASCII file editor program>
```

or

```
EDITOR = <ASCII file editor program>
```

Default

The built-in text editor.

Purpose: Specifies the program to be used as the text editor for the MODIFY COMMAND command. The text editor should be able to read and write ASCII text files. The command line must include the program name, drive, and directory.

> **Caution**
>
> You must have enough extra memory available to load the text editor program. Many word processing programs can read and write ASCII text files, but many of these require you to specify saving the file as a text file rather than as a normal word processing file that may contain non-ASCII characters.

Example

```
TEDIT = C:\DOS\EDIT
```

WP

Syntax

```
WP = <memo field editing program>
```

Default

The built-in memo editor.

Purpose: Specifies the name of the program to use for editing dBASE 5 memo fields. Include the drive and directory of the program.

> **Caution**
>
> You must have enough extra memory available to load the word processing program.

Example

```
WP = C:\WP51\WP
```

Memory Allocation Commands

This series of CONFIG.DB commands control the amount of memory used by dBASE 5 for memory variables, run-time symbols, and compile-time symbols. You can use the DISPLAY/LIST MEMORY command to get information about the current allocation of memory.

To conserve memory, use small values for MVBLKSIZE and RTBLKSIZE commands. If your system doesn't have enough dynamic memory to maintain the memory variables, you get an error message.

CTMAXSYMS

Syntax

```
CTMAXSYMS = <number of compile-time symbols,
   from 1 to 5000>
```

Default

```
CTMAXSYMS = 500
```

Purpose: The maximum number of compile-time symbols allocated to a program or procedure file. These are the names of the user-defined variables, fields, and procedures. Increase this value if you see the message `Exceeded maximum number of compile time symbols` when compiling a file.

MVARSIZE

This command has been retained from dBASE III for compatibility purposes. It is ignored by dBASE 5.

MVMAXBLKS/MVBLKSIZE

Syntax

```
MVMAXBLKS = <number of blocks, from 1 to 150>
MVBLKSIZE = <number of memory variables, from 25 to 100>
```

Default

```
MVMAXBLKS = 10
MVBLKSIZE = 50
```

Purpose: MVMAXBLKS sets the maximum number of blocks of dynamic memory available for memory variables. The MVBLKSIZE command sets the number of memory variables for each block. The default values enable up to

500 memory variables. Each memory variable in a block uses up to 56 bytes of memory, so the default can use a total of 28,000 bytes of memory.

RTMAXBLKS/RTBLKSIZE

Syntax

```
RTMAXBLKS = <number of blocks, from 1 to 150>
RTBLKSIZE = <number of memory variables, from 25 to 100>
```

Default

```
RTMAXBLKS = 10
RTBLKSIZE = 50
```

Purpose: RTMAXBLKS sets the maximum number of blocks of dynamic memory available for user-defined memory variables and run-time session symbols. RTBLKSIZE is the number symbol for each block. These function in the same way as the MVMAXBLKS and MVBLKSIZE variables.

Managing Memory and Temporary Files

To optimize the performance of dBASE 5, you can use certain methods to manage memory and disk usage. The options available to you depend on the version of dBASE you are using.

dBASE 5 for DOS uses 32-bit protected mode technology to provide full access to all RAM on the system. The use of this enhancement nearly doubles the speed and performance of dBASE 5 over dBASE IV. This also means that you cannot run dBASE 5 on any system with less than an 80386 processor. The built-in virtual memory manager also enables use of disk space to expand the apparent amount of available RAM. Use the following DOS command in your AUTOEXEC.BAT file to change the amount of space to allocate from the disk:

```
SET DOS4GVM=virtualsize#<kilobytes expN> maxmem#<kilobytes expN>
```

dBASE 5 often creates temporary files, and using another DOS environment variable, you can specify where these files will be stored. For optimal performance, you should have your temporary files stored in a directory on your fastest disk drive, or on a RAM drive if you have one. You can set either the DBTMP or TMP environment variables to the drive and path where you want to put temporary files. To specify a RAM disk which is drive D, for example, you can use the following command:

```
SET DBTMP=D:\
```

To place files in the \TEMP directory of your C drive, use the following command:

```
SET TMP=C:\temp
```

As a reminder, these commands must be issued from the DOS prompt before you run dBASE 5 for them to work, so you may want to include them in your AUTOEXEC.BAT file.

Function Key Assignment Commands

In the CONFIG.DB file, you can select the commands to be used when you press the function keys. (Current assignments are displayed by the DISPLAY/LIST STATUS command.) You can define F2 through F10, Shift-F1 through Shift-F9, and Ctrl-F1 through Ctrl-F10. The F1 and Shift-F10 keys, along with the Alt-function key combinations used for macros, are not assignable. These entries are equivalent to the SET FUNCTION command. The dBASE Desktop has its own assignments for many of the Alt and Ctrl key combinations that override your settings while working from the Desktop. The values you set are valid inside your programs.

<key label>

Syntax

```
<key label> = "<command string>"
```

Default

See Table 29.1.

Purpose

The *<key label>* is the name of the key, such as F2, Shift-F8, or Ctrl-F3. The *<command string>* is the command or text assigned to that key and must be enclosed in quotes. The semicolon is used to indicate the Enter key. Table 29.2 shows the default settings of the function keys.

Table 29.2 Default Function Key Settings

Function Key	Description
F1*	Help (Reserved)
F2	"ASSIST;"
F3	"LIST;"

(continues)

Table 29.2 Continued

Function Key	Description
F4	"DIR;"
F5	"DISPLAY STRUCTURE;"
F6	"DISPLAY STATUS;"
F7	"DISPLAY MEMORY;"
F8	"DISPLAY;"
F9	"APPEND;"
F10*	"EDIT;"

**F1 and SHIFT-F10 are not programmable.*

Example

```
F3 = "DO HELP;"
```

SET Commands in CONFIG.DB

The SET commands can be specified at the Command window or within the CONFIG.DB file. (See Chapter 24, "Using SET Commands To Configure dBASE 5," for information about each of the SET commands.) You also can change the various settings from the SET menu. The SET commands in the CONFIG.DB file are issued automatically when dBASE 5 is started, but the settings can be changed by issuing the SET commands during your dBASE 5 session at the Command window, within a program, or from the SET menu. The changes affect only the current dBASE 5 session.

Table 29.3 shows the default for each SET command in the CONFIG.DB file.

Table 29.3 Defaults for CONFIG.DB SET Commands

Command	Default
ALTERNATE	ON
ALTERNATE TO	*<empty string>*
AUTOSAVE	OFF
BELL	ON

Command	Default
BELL TO	550, 2
BLOCKSIZE	1
CARRY	OFF
CATALOG	*<empty string>*
CENTURY	OFF
CLOCK	OFF
CLOCK TO	0, 68
COLOR	ON for color, OFF for monochrome
COLOR TO	*<color settings>*
CONFIRM	OFF
CONSOLE	ON
CURRENCY	"$"
CURRENCY	LEFT
CURSOR	ON
DATE	AMERICAN
DBTRAP	OFF
DEBUG	OFF
DECIMALS	2
DEFAULT	*<current drive letter>*
DELETED	OFF
DELIMITERS TO	OFF
DELIMITERS	:
DESIGN	ON
DEVELOPMENT	ON
DEVICE	SCREEN
DIRECTORY	*<startup directory>*

(continues)

Table 29.3 Continued

Command	Default
DISPLAY	*<default set during installation>*
ECHO	OFF
ENCRYPTION	OFF
ESCAPE	ON
EXACT	OFF
EXCLUSIVE	OFF
FULLPATH	OFF
FUNCTION	See Table 29.2
HEADING	ON
HELP	ON
HISTORY	ON (ignored in dBASE 5)
HISTORY TO	20 (ignored in dBASE 5)
HOURS	12
IBLOCK	1
INSTRUCT	ON
INTENSITY	ON
LDCHECK	ON
LIBRARY	*<empty string>*
LOCK	ON
MARGIN	0
MARK	/
MBLOCK	8
MEMOWIDTH	50
MOUSE	ON
NEAR	OFF
ODOMETER	1

Command	Default
PATH	*<empty string>*
PAUSE	OFF
POINT	.
PRECISION	16
PRINTER	OFF
PROCEDURE	*<empty string>*
REFRESH	0
REPROCESS	0
SAFETY	ON
SCOREBOARD	ON
SEPARATOR	,
SPACE	ON
SQL	OFF
STATUS	OFF
STEP	OFF
TALK	ON
TRAP	OFF
TYPEAHEAD	20
UNIQUE	OFF
VIEW	*<empty string>*

Color Setting Commands

These CONFIG.DB settings enable you to specify screen colors. See SET COLOR in Chapter 24, "Using SET Commands To Configure dBASE 5" for further information and examples. The following color settings are available in the CONFIG.DB file:

```
COLOR OF NORMAL = <foreground color>/<background color>
COLOR OF TITLES = <foreground color>/<background color>
COLOR OF MESSAGES = <foreground color>/<background color>
COLOR OF BOX = <foreground color>/<background color>
COLOR OF INFORMATION = <foreground color>/<background color>
COLOR OF HIGHLIGHT = <foreground color>/<background color>
COLOR OF FIELDS = <foreground color>/<background color>
```

Table 29.4 shows the color letter codes for each color.

Table 29.4 Color Codes

Color	Letter Code
Black	N or blank
Blue	B
Green	G
Cyan	BG
Blank	X
Gray	N+
Red	R
Magenta	RB
Brown	GR
Yellow	GR+
While	W
<color code>+	Bright color
*<color code>**	Blinking color
*<color code>**+	Bright, blinking color

Design Surface Programs

dBASE 5 enables you to specify special programs that execute when entering, exiting, or using various design surfaces in the Control Center. The general syntax for these parameters is

```
PRG<surface> = <entry>,<exit>,<layout>,<field>,<execute>
```

The surface keywords are shown in Table 29.5.

Table 29.5 Control Center Surfaces

Keyword	Control Center Surface
PRGCC	Control Center
PRGDATA	Database design
PRGQUERY	Queries design
PRGFORM	Forms design
PRGREPORT	Reports design
PRGLABEL	Labels design
PRGAPPLIC	Applications
PRGBROWSE	Browse screen
PRGEDIT	Edit screen

Each argument can accept a file name of a program to run when the event occurs. If programs are not specified for a specific event, the option can be skipped if the commas are left to indicate the number of arguments. The program names are not set off by quotation marks.

```
PRGLABEL = C:\DOS\EDIT,,,,C:\DOS\EDIT
```

PRGAPPLIC

Syntax

```
PRGAPPLIC = <entry>
```

Purpose: Defines the program that will be run for the Applications Generator panel in the Control Center.

PRGBROWSE

Syntax

```
PRGBROWSE = <entry>
```

Purpose: Defines the program that will be run for browse of a data table in the Control Center.

PRGCC

Syntax

```
PRGCC = <entry>,<exit>,<layout>
```

Purpose: Defines the programs that will be run for the Control Center.

PRGDATA

Syntax

```
PRGDATA = <entry>,<exit>
```

Purpose: Defines the programs that will be run for the database design panel in the Control Center.

PRGEDIT

Syntax

```
PRGEDIT = <entry>
```

Purpose: Defines the programs that will be run for editing procedures in the Control Center.

PRGFORM

Syntax

```
PRGFORM = <entry>,<exit>,<layout>,<field>,<execute>
```

Purpose: Defines the programs that will be run for the form design panel in the Control Center.

PRGLABEL

Syntax

```
PRGLABEL = <entry>,<exit>,<layout>,<field>,<execute>
```

Purpose: Defines the programs that will be run for the label design panel in the Control Center.

PRGQUERY

Syntax

```
PRGQUERY = <entry>,<exit>,<layout>,<field>,<execute>
```

Purpose: Defines the programs that will be run for the query design panel in the Control Center.

PRGREPORT

Syntax

```
PRGREPORT = <entry>,<exit>,<layout>,<field>,<execute>
```

Purpose: Defines the programs that will be run for the report design panel in the Control Center.

Default File Extension Settings

In most cases, you can override the default file name extensions by specifying the full *<filename.extension>* as the file name. Table 29.6 shows the default file extensions, along with their purpose.

Table 29.6 Default File Name Extensions

Extension	Purpose
$$$	Temporary file
ACC	Multiuser access control file
APP	Application design object file
BAK	Command, procedure, or database backup file
BAR	Horizontal bar design object file from APGEN
BCH	Batch process design object file from APGEN
BIN	Binary file
CAT	Catalog file
CHT	Chartmaster file, used with dBASE/Chartmaster Bridge program
COD	Template source file
CPT	Encrypted memo file
CRP	Encrypted data file
CVT	Backup of database file before change detection field was added by CONVERT
DB	Configuration file
DB2	Renamed dBASE II file used for import and export

(continues)

Table 29.6 Continued

Extension	Purpose
DBF	Database file
DBK	Backup DBF created when structure was modified
DBO	Command and procedure object file
DBT	Database memo file
DEF	Selector definition file
DIF	Data Interchange Format (VisiCalc) file
DOC	Documentation file
FIL	Files list design object file from APGEN
FMO	Compiled screen form file
FMT	Generated screen form file
FNL	Report binary name list file
FR3	Renamed dBASE III report form file
FRG	Generated report form file
FRM	Report form file
FRO	Compiled report form file
FW2, FW3, FW4	Framework spreadsheet/database file
GEN	Template file
KEY	Keystroke macro file
LB3	Renamed dBASE III label form file
LBG	Generated label form file
LBL	Label form file
LBO	Compiled label form file
LNL	Label binary name list file
LOG	Transaction log file
MDK	Backup MDX from when DBF structure was modified
MDX	Multiple-index file

Extension	Purpose
MEM	Memory file
NDX	Single-index file
POP	Popup menu design object file from APGEN
PR2	Printer driver file
PRF	Print form file
PRG	dBASE 5 command or procedure file
PRS	dBASE/SQL command or procedure file
PRT	Printer output file
QBE	QBE query file
QBO	Compiled QBE query file
QRY	dBASE III Plus Query file
RES	Resource file
RPD	RapidFile database file
SC3	Renamed dBASE III screen file
SCR	Screen file
SNL	Screen binary name list file
STR	Structure list design file from APGEN
T44/W44	Intermediate work files used by SORT and INDEX which can be deleted
TBK	Database memo backup file
TXT	ASCII output text file
UPD	QBE Update query file
VAL	Values list design object file from APGEN
VUE	dBASE III Plus View file
WIN	Logical window save file
WKS	Lotus 1-2-3 worksheet file
WK1	Lotus 1-2-3 worksheet file

Using the Mouse with dBASE

The CONFIG.SYS file allows you to control if a mouse can be used from within dBASE 5. After you adjust to clicking instead of typing, the mouse is usually faster and easier than typing in commands. For your user's convenience, you will probably want to make sure he can operate the application with a mouse.

To use a mouse with dBASE 5, be sure that a mouse driver is loaded into your computer's memory. You normally load a mouse driver by including a DEVICE=MOUSE.SYS command in your CONFIG.SYS file, or by putting a MOUSE.COM command in your AUTOEXEC.BAT file. Consult the manual that came with your mouse for specific instructions on loading your mouse driver. (The mouse is supported in dBASE 5, and dBASE IV Versions 1.5 and 2.0. Previous versions of dBASE do not support the mouse.)

If a mouse driver is present in memory, dBASE automatically displays the mouse pointer, which is a small rectangle that looks like a cursor. If your mouse has more than one button, use the left button with dBASE in three ways:

- To *click* an item, press the button once and release it.
- To *double-click*, press the button twice in rapid succession.
- To *drag* an object, hold down the button while moving the mouse, then release the button when the dragging is complete.

In dBASE 5, the right mouse button brings up the HELP screen.

Using the Mouse in Work Surfaces

This section discusses ways the mouse can be used in various work areas of dBASE.

Control Center

To highlight a file, click the file name. To activate a file, double-click the file name. To create a new file, double-click the `<create>` marker.

Menus

To pull down a menu, click the menu name in the menu bar. To select an option from the menu, click that option. To cycle through or toggle available multiple-choice options, click the item until the desired choice appears. To close a menu, click outside the menu area.

Navigation Line

The navigation line at the bottom of the screen can display key labels, such as Data:F2 or Help:F1. To simulate the keypresses described, click the key label in the navigation line. For double labels, such as Prev/Next field:Shift-Tab/Tab, click the appropriate keystroke within the label (for example, Tab or Shift-Tab).

Lists

When dBASE presents a list, such as a files list box or the expression builder box, click an item to highlight it. Click it again to select it. If the item is not highlighted initially, you can double-click it to select it. To move up or down a list, click the top or bottom borders of the box. To close the list box, click outside the box.

Data-Entry Boxes

To open a data-entry box, click the related menu option. Relocate the cursor within the input area by clicking the new position. To zoom the box to provide a larger input area, double-click the entry box, then double-click in the zoomed area again to reduce it. To abort the data entry, click outside the box, or click inside the box but outside the input area to accept data.

Error and Warning Boxes

An error box can ask for a response, such as Cancel, Edit, or Help. Click the appropriate response word. To abandon an operation and close the box, click outside the box area.

Help Screens

When presented with help options, such as Contents or Related Topics, click the option button at the bottom of the Help screen. To select an item from a list, double-click the item. To scroll up and down a list, click the top or bottom border of the box, or double-click to move up or down a page at a time. To exit Help, click outside the Help box.

Browse Screen

To highlight a field, click the field. To reposition the cursor within a field, click the new position. To pan right or left, click the right or left borders of the browse table, or double-click to move to the extreme right or left field. To move the highlight up or down a row, click the top or bottom borders of the browse table, or double-click to move up or down a page at a time. To size a column, drag the right column border to the right or left. To edit a memo field, double-click the memo marker.

Edit and Form Screens

Click a field to highlight it, or click a position within a field to relocate the cursor. To edit a memo field, double-click the memo marker or in the memo window.

Database Design

Click a row or field to highlight it, or click a position within a field to relocate the cursor. Click the Field Type or Index input fields to cycle through available choices. To add a new field definition row, click below the last row.

Form, Label, and Report Design

In the design surface, double-click the position where you want to add a field. Double-click a field to modify it. To move or copy an item, click the item to select it, or drag the mouse across the area to be selected, and then click the Move:F7 or Copy:F8 labels. Move the mouse to position the item in the new location, then click to complete the operation. To create a box or line, select Box or Line from the Layout menu, click the position to start drawing the box or line, drag the mouse to draw it, and then release the button when finished. To size an item, click it, click Size:Shift-F7, move the mouse pointer to the size desired, and click. In the Report Design screen, double-click a band border to open or close the band.

The Program Editor

To reposition the cursor, click the new position. To select a block of text in the program editor, drag the mouse over the block.

Queries Design

To highlight a field, click the field in the file skeleton or the top border of a field in the view skeleton. To move right or left in the file skeleton, click the Tab or Shift-Tab labels in the navigation line. To pan to see fields that are off the screen, click the left or right arrowhead symbol in the view skeleton. To add or remove a field from the view skeleton, double-click the field name in the file skeleton. To reposition the cursor, click the new position within a field. To zoom a field to a larger input area, double-click the field or input area, then double-click the zoomed area to reduce it again.

Applications Generator

To select a design object on the work surface, click the object. The last menu used with the object is activated. To move an object, click the top or left border and drag the object to the new location. To size an object, click the right or bottom border and drag the object to the correct size.

Using the Mouse in Programs

dBASE provides commands and functions related to the mouse. You can have your programs detect the existence of a mouse and the screen location of the mouse pointer by using the ISMOUSE( ), MROW( ), and MCOL( ) functions, which are described in Chapter 23, "Using Functions."

The ON MOUSE command can be used to execute a command when the mouse button is clicked. See Chapter 22, "Using dBASE 5 Commands," for a description of this command.

You can use the SET MOUSE ON/off command, described in Chapter 24, "Using SET Commands To Configure dBASE 5," to activate or deactivate mouse usage in dBASE.

The mouse also is used to select options in various UI objects. See Chapter 26, "Using UI Properties, Methods, and Commands," for more information on these related commands.

Note

If your mouse is not working with dBASE 5, be sure that a mouse driver has been installed and that SET MOUSE is set to ON.

Index

Symbols

! (exclamation point)
picture template, 449
RUN command, 509
 # (pound sign)
logical operator, 640
not equal to relational operator, 201, 640
picture template, 449
$ (dollar sign)
included relational operator, 201
picture template, 449
& function, 751-752
&& (double ampersand), commenting programs, 409
( ) function, 752
*** (asterisk)**
multiplication operator, 639
picture template, 449
program code, 409
wild card, 153
queries, 203
***/&& command, 642-643**
+ (plus sign)
addition operator, 639
concatenating character fields, 168
string operator, 641
- (minus sign)
string operator, 641
subtraction operator, 639
. (period) picture template, 449
/ (slash) division operator, 639
< (less than) relational operator, 201, 640
<= (less than or equal to) relational operator, 201, 640
<> (not equal to)
logical operator, 640
relational operator, 201, 640
= (equal sign)
initializing memory variables, 424
logical operator, 640
relational operator, 201, 640
== (exactly equal to) relational operator, 201
> (greater than) relational operator, 201, 640
>= (greater than or equal to) relational operator, 201, 640
? (question mark) wild card, 153
queries, 203
? command, 519
?/?? command, 643-644
??? command, 645
@ command, 645-650
@...CLEAR command, 451, 650
@...FILL command, 452
@...FILL TO command, 650-651
@...SAY command, 519
@...SAY...GET command, 646
@...SAY...GET commands, 445-451
@...SCROLL command, 452, 651
@...TO command, 452, 651-652
^ (caret) exponentiation operator, 639
9 picture template, 449

A

A picture template, 449
Abandon Changes and Exit command (Exit menu), 120
ABS( ) function, 753
ACCEPT command, 444, 652
Accept Value When edit option (forms), 273
ACCESS( ) function, 753
ACOPY( ) function, 753-754
ACOS( ) function, 755
ACTIVATE MENU command, 491, 652
ACTIVATE POPUP command, 653
ACTIVATE SCREEN command, 653
ACTIVATE WINDOW command, 653-654
ACTIVATE WINDOW commands, 499
ActiveControl method, 982
ActiveField( ) method, 982-983
Add a Group Band command (Bands menu), 309
Add Condition Box command (Condition menu), 212
Add Field to View command (Fields menu), 192
Add File to Catalog command (Catalog menu), 77
Add File to Query command (Layout menu), 241
Add New Records command (Records menu), 128
adding, *see* inserting
addition sign (+), 639
ADEL( ) command, 755

ADIR( ) function, 756-757
Advanced Compiler Options dialog box, 414
AELEMENT( ) function, 757
AFIELDS( ) function, 757-758
AFILL( ) function, 758-759
After property, 900-901
AGROW( ) function, 759
AINS( ) function, 759-760
ALEN( ) function, 760
Alias property, 901
ALIAS( ) function, 761
_Alignment system memory variable, 1041
ALTER TABLE command (SQL), 569, 883
American Standard Code for Information Interchange (ASCII), 171
.AND. logical operator, 640
AND condition (summary calculations), 225
APPEND command, 654-655
APPEND FROM ARRAY command, 488, 656
APPEND FROM command, 655-656
APPEND MEMO command, 656-657
Append property, 902
Append to Macro command (Macros menu), 81
Application menu commands
  Display Sign-on Banner, 536
  Save Current Application Definition, 543
applications
  Applications Generator, 528
    batch process, 552
    designing main menu, 536-538
    distributing applications, 556-560
    documentation, 549-551
    editing, 555-556
    file list, 552
    generating code, 548-549
    mouse, 1088
    navigating, 536
    planning applications, 528-533
    pop-up menus, 539-547
    pull-down menus, 539-547
    running Mailer application, 551
    saving, 538
    starting, 533, 675
    structure list, 552
    troubleshooting, 533, 556
  defining files, 477-479
  designing, 479-486
  editing files, 485-486
  embedding SQL code, 594-599
  external programs, 508-511
  forms, 485
  help screens, 502-503
  inventory, 484-485
  invoices, 481-484
  keyboard macros, 511-512
  Mailer, 530-536, 551
  menus, 486-498
  procedure libraries, 504-508
  reports, 485, 513
    indexing data tables, 515
    sample program, 520-524
    searching data tables, 515-518
    sorting data tables, 513-515
    translating files, 524-525
    viewing results, 518-520
  troubleshooting, 503
  windows, 498-502
ARESIZE( ) function, 761
arrays (memory variables), 432-434, 488
  copying elements, 753-754
  declaring, 682
  deleting entries, 755
  DOS files, characteristics, 756-757
  field characteristics, 757-758
  inserting
    data in fields, 732
    elements, 759-760
    records, 656
  procedure libraries, 506
  retrieving, 734
  searching, 762
  sizing, 759-761
  sorting, 763
  storing values, 744
ASC( ) function, 762
ASCAN( ) function, 762
ascending sorts, 163
ASCII (American Standard Code for Information Interchange), 171
ASCII Chart, 59-60
ASCII Chart command (Tools menu), 59
ASCII files, viewing contents, 747
ASCII sorts (queries), 232
ASCIISORT command, 1065
ASIN( ) function, 763
ASORT( ) function, 763
ASSIST command, 657
asterisk (*)
  multiplication operator, 639
  picture template, 449
  program code, 409
  wild card, 153
    queries, 203
ASUBSCRIPT( ) function, 763-764
AT( ) function, 764
ATAN( ) function, 764
ATN2( ) function, 765
Attach Pull-Down Menus command (Menu menu), 541
attaching
  pop-up menus to menu bar, 540-543
  pull-down menus to menu bar, 543-545
  text files to memo fields, 140
attributes (fields)
  forms, 261
  reports, 297-302
AutoSize property, 902
AVERAGE command, 657
Average field, 307
AVG operator, 224
AVG( ) function, 662
  SQL, 881

B

Backward Search command (Go To menu), 139, 153
bands (reports)
  Detail, 293
  fields, 296-297
  Group, 294
  mailmerge reports, 324-326
  Page Footer, 294, 312-313
  Page Header, 293, 312-313
  Report Intro, 293
  Report Summary, 294
Bands menu commands, Add a Group Band, 309
BAR( ) function, 443, 492, 765
BARCOUNT( ) function, 765
BARPROMPT( ) function, 492, 766

batch process, 552
BCD (binary-coded decimal) numbers, 782
Before property, 903
Begin Generation command (Generate menu), 549
Begin Printing command
Print menu, 321
Quick Report menu, 179
Begin Recording command (Macros menu), 78
BEGIN TRANSACTION command, 589, 658
BETWEEN predicate (SELECT command), 578
binary files
executing, 663
importing, 656-657
loading, 709
Binary Named List (BNL) files, 690
BLANK command, 659
Blank Field command (Fields menu), 155
Blank Record command (Records menu), 156
blanking records, 156, 659
BNL (Binary Named List) files, 690
BOF( ) function, 766
Border property, 903-904
BorderStyle property, 904-905
_Box system memory variable, 1042
Box command (Layout menu), 276
boxes
@...TO command, 651
defining styles, 683
forms, 276-277
reports, 313-314
break points (debugging programs), 416
breaking SQL commands, 567
breakpoints (debugging code), 461
BROWSE command, 659-661
Browse screen, 127
records, 145-146
fields, 146-149
inserting, 130-131
Browse window (crosstabs), 349
BUCKET command, 1065
building SQL statements, 573-574

C

CalcField property, 905
CALCULATE command, 661-662
calculated fields, 216-217
deleting, 220-221
forms, 274-275
functions, 218-219
inserting, 220
mailmerge reports, 329-330
reports, 302-305
Calculator, 60-61
Calculator command (Tools menu), 60
Calendar, 61-62
Calendar command (Tools menu), 61
CALL command, 510-511, 663
CALL( ) function, 766-767
CANCEL command, 416, 663
caret (^) exponentiation operator, 639
Carry Forward edit option (forms), 272
Cascade command (Window menu), 49
Catalog menu commands
Add File to Catalog, 77
Edit Description of Catalog, 76
Modify Catalog Name, 73
Remove Highlighted File From Catalog, 78
Use a Different Catalog, 74
CATALOG( ) function, 767
catalogs
Control Center, 73-76
relational databases, 371
categories (Control Center), 68-72
CDOW( ) function, 767
CEILING( ) function, 767
Century command (Settings submenu), 134
CERROR( ) function, 768
Change Action command (Item menu), 543
Change Dir command (File menu), 55
Change Directory dialog box, 55
Change Drive:Directory command (File menu), 86
CHANGE( ) function, 768-769
CHANGE/EDIT command, 664-665
changing, *see* switching
CHAR data type (SQL), 571, 880
character fields, 110-111
concatenating, 168
embedded values, searching, 203-204
picture functions, 267
reports, 300-301
queries, 193-195
template symbols, 263-264
templates (reports), 299
character functions, 166-167
character strings (low-level files), 779
check boxes, 39-40, 993-996
Checked property, 905-906
CHR( ) function, 769
ClassName property, 906
CLEAR command, 666
Clear Deletion Mark command (Records menu), 157
Clipboard, 59
programming, 407-408
_Clipboard system memory variable, 1042-1043
Clipboard command (Edit menu), 407
CLOSE command, 666-667
SQL, 591, 883
Close command (Window menu), 51
Close( ) method, 983
closing
ASCII Chart, 59
cursors (SQL), 591-592
databases, 137
dialog boxes, 37
files, 58, 666
low-level files, 778
windows, 51
_Cmdwindow system memory variable, 1043-1044
CMONTH( ) function, 218, 769
CNT operator, 224
CNT( ) function, 662
code
Applications Generator, 548-549
compiling programs, 1055-1056
Customer Tracking system, 466-476
debugging programs, 460-465, 553-554

Desktop Editor, 398-403
embedding SQL code in applications, 594-599
environment variables, 434-438
loops, 699
memory variables, 424
arrays, 432-434
initializing, 424-428
private, 428-429
public, 428-429
user input, 444-445
uses, 429-431
menus, 441-444
Program Editor, 404-406
standards, 422-424
Text Editor, 406-408
word processing programs, 408-409
code display window, 460
COL( ) function, 769-770
color
@...FILL TO command, 650-651
forms, 279-281
settings, 1079-1080
color properties, 906-921
Column property, 921
columnar reports, 290
columns (SQL tables), 568-571
combo boxes, 996-1000
COMMAND command, 1065
command files, editing, 622-633
Command window, 43
entering commands, 43-44
reusing commands, 44-45
SQL mode, 567
commands
configuration commands, 1065-1073
flow control, 389
function key assignment commands, 1075-1076
memory allocation commands, 1073-1074
UI objects, 987-1040
see also individual command names
commenting programs, 409, 642, 713
compact executables, building, 558-559
COMPILE command, 413, 667
Compile Options dialog box, 413
Compiler command (Options menu), 413
compiling programs, 412-415, 667, 1055-1056
COMPLETED( ) function, 770
concatenating character fields, 168
condition box
deleted records, 212-213
memo fields, 213-214
Condition menu commands
Add Condition Box, 212
Remove Condition Box, 214
conditional indexing, 172-173
CONFIG.DB file, 1063-1064
color, 1079-1080
configuration commands, 1065-1073
function key assignment commands, 1075-1076
memory allocation commands, 1073-1074
SET commands, 1076-1079
CONFIG.SYS file
environment settings, 27-31
mouse settings, 1086-1089
CONTINUE command, 668
Control Center, 51-52
ASSIST command, 657
Browse screen, 128
catalogs, 73-78
categories, 68-72
design surface programs, 1080-1083
DOS utilities, 84-86
copying files, 92-93
deleting files, 92
editing files, 95
file list, changing, 88-91
moving files, 93-94
naming files, 94-104
switching directories, 86-88
viewing files, 94-95
Edit screen, 127
exiting, 102-103
exporting data, 83-84
files
creating, 69-70
modifying, 72
opening, 70-72
protecting, 96-101
forms, 253
importing data, 82-83
Labels, 331-339
macros, 78-82
mouse, 1086
Reports Design screen, 288
screen settings, 101-102
Control Center command (Window menu), 51
control objects (forms), 613
Control of Printer command (Print menu), 317-318
CONVERT command, 668-669
converting
character expressions to date variables, 770-771
databases to SQL tables, 587
date fields to strings, 168
date variables to string variables, 775-776
numeric expressions to character expressions, 769
numeric fields to strings, 168
COPY command, 524
Copy command
Edit menu, 59, 400
Operations menu, 92
COPY FILE command, 669
COPY INDEXES command, 669-670
COPY MEMO command, 670
COPY STRUCTURE command, 670
COPY TAG command, 671
COPY TO ARRAY command, 673-674
COPY TO command, 671-673
COPY TO...STRUCTURE EXTENDED command, 673
copying
array elements, 753-754
ASCII characters, 59
databases, 655-656, 671-673
files, 92-93, 669
form elements, 258
memo fields, 670
text
Desktop Editor, 400
Program Editor, 405
COS( ) function, 770
COUNT command, 674
Count field, 307
COUNT( ) function (SQL), 575, 881
Create Calculated Field command (Fields menu), 217
CREATE command, 119, 674
CREATE DATABASE command (SQL), 569, 883-884
CREATE FROM command, 675

CREATE INDEX command (SQL), 569, 884
Create Link by Pointing command (Layout menu), 245
Create New Index command (Organize menu), 164
CREATE STRUCTURE EXTENDED commands, 680
CREATE SYNONYM command (SQL), 569, 884
CREATE TABLE command (SQL), 569, 884-885
CREATE VIEW command (SQL), 569, 885
CREATE/MODIFY APPLICATION command, 675
CREATE/MODIFY LABEL command, 675-676
CREATE/MODIFY QUERY command, 676
CREATE/MODIFY REPORT command, 676-677
CREATE/MODIFY SCREEN command, 677
CREATE/MODIFY STRUCTURE command, 677-679
CREATE/MODIFY VIEW command, 679-680
Cross Tabulation command (Tools menu), 346
Cross Tabulation Expert dialog box, 19
Crosstab Expert dialog box, 346
crosstabs, 343-345
- Browse window, 349
- creating, 346-349
- fields, 348-349
- opening files, 348
- reports, 357-358
- saving, 350
- troubleshooting, 358

CTMAXSYMS command, 1073
CTOD( ) function, 427, 770-771
CurSel property, 922
cursors (SQL)
- closing, 591-592
- commands, 590
- declaring, 590-591
- DELETE command, 593-594
- fetching, 591
- opening, 591
- UPDATE command, 592-593

custom forms, 284-285
Customer Tracking system program code, 466-476
customizing
- label size, 333-335
- objects (forms), 614-618

Cut command (Edit menu), 400

D

data entry, 126-137
data tables (reports), 437-438
- indexing, 515
- searching, 515-518
- sorting, 513-515

data types
- character fields, 110-111
  - concatenating, 168
  - embedded values, searching, 203-204
  - picture functions, 267, 300-301
  - queries, 193-195
  - template symbols, 263-264
  - templates, 299
- date fields, 111
  - converting to strings, 168
  - editing, 134
  - queries, 195
- display fields, picture functions, 268
- float fields, 111
  - picture functions, 269
  - template symbols, 264
- logical fields, 112
  - queries, 196
  - templates, 264
- memo fields, 112-113, 123
  - attaching text files, 140
  - copying, 670
  - editing, 134-137
  - forms, 259-261
  - importing text, 656-657
  - memory variables, 429
  - printing, 141
  - queries, 197
  - reports, 295-296
  - saving, 141
  - searching, 213-214
  - SET commands, 829
  - troubleshooting, 141
- numeric fields, 111
  - converting to strings, 168
  - editing, 133
  - picture functions, 269
  - queries, 195
  - template symbols, 264
  - templates, 298
  - totalling, 746
- SQL (structured query language), 571-573, 879-880

database administrators, 585
databases
- closing, 137
- converting to SQL tables, 587
- copying, 655-656, 671-673
- creating, 678-680
- defining, 110-115
- designing, 107-108, 115-118
- editing, 121-123, 143-144
- encryption, 828
- fields, 109
  - data types, 110-113
  - deleting, 123
  - freezing, 149
  - indexing, 113-115, 150-152, 162-163
  - inserting, 123
  - locking, 146-147
  - naming, 110
  - sizing, 148-149
  - values, 109
  - width, 113
- joining, 706-707
- linking, 245-248
- locking, 782-783
- normalizing, 482
- packing, 157, 244, 721-722
- printing, 120
- records, 108
  - blanking, 156
  - data entry, 126-137
  - deleting, 156-157
  - editing, 131-132, 145-149, 155
  - inserting, 128-131
  - marking for deletion, 157
  - navigating, 154
  - searching, 149-154, 173-176
  - sorting, 161-173, 176-178
  - tracking, 132-133
- relational databases, 360-361
  - catalogs, 371
  - designing, 364-371
  - forms, 374-375
  - queries, 371-373
  - reports, 376-378
  - uses, 361-364

saving, 118-121
searching (queries), 188-189
SET commands, 828
structure
editing, 712
viewing, 694
DataLink property, 922-923, 931-932
DataSource property, 923-924
DATE data type (SQL), 571, 880
date fields, 111
converting to strings, 168
editing, 134
queries, 195
DATE( ) function, 391, 771
DAY( ) function, 771
DBA (database administrator), 585
dBASE 5
exiting, 31
starting, 25-27
dBASE IV menus, 442-444
dBASE Set command (Options menu), 407
DBCHECK command (SQL), 885
DBDEFINE command (SQL), 587, 886
DBF( ) function, 772
DEACTIVATE MENU command, 680
DEACTIVATE POPUP command, 680-681
DEACTIVATE WINDOW command, 499, 681
DEBUG command, 681
Debug property, 924-925
debugging programs, 415-417, 459, 553-554
breakpoints, 461
code display window, 460
example, 462-465
help, 460
starting debugger, 681
variables, 460
DECIMAL data type (SQL), 571, 880
DECLARE command, 433, 681-682
DECLARE command (SQL), 886
DECLARE CURSOR command (SQL), 590-591
declaring cursors (SQL), 590-591
default file extensions, 1083-1085
Default property, 925-926
Default Value edit option (forms), 272
#define preprocessor directive, 392-394, 1057
DEFINE BAR command, 682-683
DEFINE BOX FROM command, 683
DEFINE commands (UI objects)
BROWSE, 988-993
CHECKBOX, 993-996
COMBOBOX, 996-1000
EDITOR, 1000-1005
ENTRFIELD, 1005-1008
FIELD, 1008-1011
FIELDLIST, 1011-1012
FORM, 609-612, 1012-1016
LISTBOX, 1016-1019
MENU, 442, 490-491, 684
MENU...OF, 1021-1023
MENUBAR, 1019-1020
MENUITEM, 1023-1025
OBJECT, 1025
PAGEBREAK, 1025-1026
PUSHBUTTON, 1026-1029
RADIOBUTTON, 1029-1032
RECTANGLE, 1032-1034
SPINBOX, 1034-1037
TEXT, 1037-1040
DEFINE PAD command, 685
DEFINE POPUP, 686-687
DEFINE WINDOW command, 498, 687-688
defining
application files, 477-479
databases, 110-115
Delete a Line commands (Words menu), 139
Delete Calculated Field (Fields menu commands), 220
DELETE command, 524, 688
SQL, 583-584, 593-594
Delete command (Operations menu), 92
DELETE FILE command, 688-689
DELETE FROM command (SQL), 886-887
DELETE FROM WHERE CURRENT OF command (SQL), 887
Delete property, 926
DELETE TAG command, 689
DELETED( ) function, 772
deleting
array entries, 755
boxes
forms, 278
reports, 314
calculated fields, 220-221
data (SQL), 583-584
fields, 123
forms, 257
mailmerge reports, 330
queries, 191-192
reports, 297
files, 689
DOS utilities, 92
from catalogs, 78
index tags, 689
lines
forms, 278
reports, 314
memory variables, 729-730
records, 156-157
packing databases, 721-722
unmarking for deletion, 728
ZAP command, 750
text
Desktop Editor, 399
Program Editor, 404-405
text editor, 139
descending sorts, 163
DESCENDING( ) function, 772-773
Design menu commands
Horizontal Bar Menu, 537
Pop-up Menu, 539, 543
Design property, 926-927
design surface programs, 1080-1083
designing
applications, 479-486
databases, 107-108, 115-118
mailmerge reports, 324-331
relational databases, 364-371
DesignSelect property, 927
Desktop Editor (programming)
exiting, 403
navigating, 398
saving, 402-403
text
copying, 400
deleting, 399
inserting, 398
moving, 400

searching, 400-402
selecting, 399
Desktop Interface, *see* Developer's Desktop
Destination command (Print menu), 316-317
Detail band (reports), 293
Developer's Desktop, 12-13, 33-34
accessories, 19, 59-62
Crosstab Expert, 19, 346-347
dialog boxes, 18-19, 36-43
main menu bar, 13, 34-36
Project Manager, 19-20
windows, 14-15
DEXPORT command, 689-690
DGEN( ) function, 773
dialog boxes, 18-19, 36-38
Advanced Compiler Options, 414
Change Directory, 55
check boxes, 39-40
closing, 37
Compile Options, 413
Cross Tabulation Expert, 19
Crosstab Expert, 346
Find, 401
input boxes, 39
list boxes, 41-42
Open File, 21, 53
pushbuttons, 38
radio buttons, 40
Replace, 401
Save Crosstab Result As, 350
spin boxes, 42-43
UI Object Inspector, 790-791
dictionary sorts (queries), 232
DIFFERENCE( ) function, 773
DIPSLAY/LIST MEMORY command, 692-693
directives, 391-396, 458
directories, switching, 55-56
Control Center, 86-88
DIRECTORY/DIR command, 690
DISKSPACE( ) function, 774
DISPLAY command, 519
Display commands (Words menu), 279
display fields, picture functions, 268
Display First Duplicate Key Only command (Organize menu), 175
Display Sign-on Banner command (Application menu), 536
DISPLAY/LIST command, 690-691
DISPLAY/LIST FILES command, 691-692
DISPLAY/LIST HISTORY command, 692
DISPLAY/LIST STATUS command, 693
DISPLAY/LIST STRUCTURE command, 693-694
DISPLAY/LIST USERS command, 694
DISTINCT clause (SELECT command), 576
distributing applications, 556
compact executables, building, 558-559
gathering files, 557-558
preparing to link, 556-557
StandAlone executables, building, 559
troubleshooting, 560
division operator (/), 639
DMY( ) function, 774
DO CASE...ENDCASE command, 695-696
DO command, 388, 695
DO WHILE command, 456
DO WHILE...ENDDO command, 696-697
documenting applications, 409
Applications Generator, 549-551
dollar sign ($)
included relational operator, 201
picture template, 449
DOS menu commands, Set Default Drive:Directory, 86
DOS Shell command (File menu), 64-65
DOS utilities, 84-86
file list, changing, 88-91
files
copying, 92-93
deleting, 92
editing, 95
moving, 93-94
naming, 94-104
viewing, 94-95
switching directories, 86-88
dot reference notation, 899-900
DOW( ) function, 775
Draw property, 927
DROP DATABASE command (SQL), 569, 887
DROP INDEX command (SQL), 569, 887
DROP SYNONYM command (SQL), 569, 888
DROP TABLE command (SQL), 569, 888
DROP VIEW command (SQL), 569, 888
DTOC( ) function, 391, 775
DTOR( ) function, 775
DTOS( ) function, 168, 775-776

E

Edit command (Operations menu), 95
Edit Database Description command (Layout menu), 120
Edit Description of Catalog command (Catalog menu), 76
Edit Field Name command (Fields menu), 191
Edit menu commands
Clipboard, 407
Copy, 59, 400
Cut, 400
Maximize, 59
Paste, 400
edit options (forms), 269
Accept Value When, 273
Carry Forward, 272
Default Value, 272
Editing Allowed, 270
Largest Allowed Value, 272-273
Message, 271
Permit Edit If, 270-271
Range Must Always Be Met, 273
Smallest Allowed Value, 272-273
Unaccepted Message, 274
Value Must Always Be Valid, 273
Edit screen, 127
records
editing, 145
inserting, 128-130
Edit window, opening windows, 45

editing
Applications Generator, 555-556
command files (forms), 622-633
data (SQL), 582-583
databases, 143-144
structure, 121-123, 712
fields, 134-137
files, 95
forms, 283-284
indexes, 176
labels, 338
macros, 81
mailmerge reports, 330
menus (forms), 619-622
program files, 485-486
QBE files, 679-680
records, 131-132, 155
Browse screen, 145-149
CHANGE/EDIT command, 664-665
Edit screen, 145
text (forms), 255-256
text editor, 137-140
view skeletons (QBE), 191-193
Editing Allowed edit option (forms), 270
editor, 22-23
editor objects, 1000-1005
EJECT command, 697
EJECT PAGE command, 697
Eject Page Now command
Print menu, 141
Quick Report menu, 179
#elif preprocessor directive, 392
#else preprocessor directive, 392
ELSE clause, 455
embedded values, searching, 203-204
embedding SQL code in applications, 594-599
Enabled property, 928
encryption, 828
End Recording command (Macros menu), 79
END TRANSACTION command, 589, 658
#endif preprocessor directive, 392
entry fields, 1005-1008
environment settings, 27-31
environment variables, 434-435
data tables, 437-438
INDEX command, 438-441
saving current environment, 435-436
setting environment, 436-437
EOF( ) function, 776
equal sign (=)
initializing memory variables, 424
logical operator, 640
relational operator, 201, 640
Erase Marked Records command (Organize menu), 157, 244
error trapping (SQL), 601
ERROR( ) function, 776-777
EscExit property, 928
EVALUATE( ) function, 777
EventType property, 929
exactly equal to (==) relational operator, 201
exclamation point (!)
picture template, 449
RUN command, 509
executing
commands (pop-up menus), 713
queries, 198-200
Exit command (File menu), 31
Exit menu commands
Abandon Changes And Exit, 120
Exit to Command Window, 52
Save Changes And Exit, 120, 136
Transfer to Query Design, 198
Exit to Command Window command (Exit menu), 52
exiting
Control Center, 102-103
dBASE 5, 31
Desktop Editor, 403
Forms Design screen, 282
Labels Design screen, 338-339
mailmerge reports, 330
pads (menus), 716
pop-up menus, 716
Program Editor, 406
Reports Design screen, 314
EXP( ) function, 777
exponentiation operator (^), 639
EXPORT command, 524
Export command (Tools menu), 83
EXPORT TO command, 698
exporting
data from SQL tables, 588
files, 698
from Control Center, 83-84
expressions, 165-166
Expression Builder, 169
functions
calculated fields, 218-219
character functions, 166-167
conversion functions, 168-169
nesting functions, 169
numeric functions, 167-168
EXPSIZE command, 1066
external programs, 508-511

F

FASTCRT command, 1066
FCLOSE( ) function, 778
FCREATE( ) function, 778
FDATE( ) function, 778
FEOF( ) function, 779
FERROR( ) function, 779
FETCH command (SQL), 591, 595, 888-889
fetching cursors (SQL), 591
FFLUSH( ) function, 779
FGETS( ) function, 779
field entry objects (forms), 613
FIELD( ) function, 780
FieldArrange property, 929
FieldList property, 930
fields, 109
blanking, 659
calculated fields, 216-217
deleting, 220-221
functions, 218-219
inserting, 220
counting, 781
crosstabs, 348-349
data entry, 727
deleting, 123
forms
attributes, 261-274
calculated fields, 274-275
color, 279-280

deleting, 257
edit options, 269-274
inserting, 256
memo fields, 259-261
picture functions, 266-269
sizing, 259
templates, 261-265
freezing, 149
indexing, 150-152, 162-163
advantages, 113-115
ASCII sort order, 171-172
concatenating character fields, 168
conditional indexing, 172-173
converting data types, 168-169
COPY INDEX command, 669-670
COPY TAG command, 671
creating indexes, 163-169
deleting index tags, 689
dictionary sort order, 172
Expression Builder, 169
expressions, 165-166
functions, 166-168
INDEX ON command, 703-704
moving screen cursor, 151
multiple field indexes, 171
multiple fields, 115
nesting functions, 169
Organize menu commands, 175-176
queries, 230-231
searching records, 173-176
sorting records, 169-184
troubleshooting, 174
inserting, 123
labels, 335-337
mailmerge reports, 326-330
locking, 146-147
naming, 110
queries
deleting, 191-192
inserting, 192
moving, 192-193
naming, 191
reports
attributes, 297-302
bands, 296-297
calculated fields, 302-305
deleting, 297
inserting, 294-295
memo fields, 295-296
picture functions, 299-302
sizing, 297
Summary fields, 305-307
suppressing repeated values, 302
templates, 297-299
searching multiple fields, 207-208
sizing, 148-149
troubleshooting, 142, 150
values, 109
width, 113
see also data types
Fields menu commands
Add Field to View, 192
Blank Field, 155
Create Calculated Field, 217
Delete Calculated Field, 220
Edit Field Name, 191
Filter Method, 248
Freeze Field, 149
Include Indexes, 230
Lock Fields on Left, 147
Remove Field From View, 191
Size Field, 148
Sort on This Field, 231
file list (Application Generator), 552
File menu commands
Change Dir, 55
Change Drive:Directory, 86
DOS Shell, 64-65
Exit, 31
New, 45
Open, 53
Print, 57
Save, 56
Save All, 57
Save As, 57
file skeletons (QBE), 190
FILE( ) function, 780
files, 21-22
attaching to memo fields, 140
closing, 58, 666
CONFIG.DB, 1063-1064
color, 1079-1080
configuration commands, 1065-1073
function key assignment commands, 1075-1076
memory allocation commands, 1073-1074
SET commands, 1076-1079
CONFIG.SYS, mouse settings, 1086-1089
contents, viewing, 690-691
Control Center
adding to catalogs, 76-78
creating, 69-70
deleting from catalogs, 78
modifying, 72
opening, 70-72
protecting, 96-101
copying, 669
DOS utilities, 92-93
creating, 52-53
default file extensions, 1083-1085
deleting, 689
DOS utilities, 92
directories, switching, 55-56
editing, 95
exporting, 698
importing, 702-703
integrity tags, 733
listing, 690
low-level files, 778-779, 783
moving, 93-94
naming, 730
DOS utilities, 94-104
opening, 53-55, 748-749
printing, 57-58
saving, 56-57
translating, 524-525
viewing, 94-95
FILES command, 1066
Filter Method command (Fields menu), 248
filtering records (condition box), 212-214
FIND command, 516, 698-699
Find command (Search menu), 401
Find dialog box, 401
find operator (QBE), 215
finding, *see* searching
First property, 930
FIXED( ) function, 780-781
FKLABEL( ) function, 781
FKMAX( ) function, 781
FLDCOUNT( ) function, 781-782
FLDLIST( ) function, 782

FLOAT data type (SQL), 571, 880
float fields, 111
- picture functions, 269
- template symbols, 264

FLOAT( ) function, 782
FLOCK( ) function, 782-783
FLOOR( ) function, 783
flow control commands, 389
Follow Record To New Position command (Records menu), 151
FOPEN( ) function, 783
FOR clauses (indexes), 173
FOR UPDATE OF clause (SELECT command), 894
FOR( ) function, 783
FOR...ENDFOR/NEXT command, 699
Form Designer command (Tools menu), 606
Form property, 931
form reports, 290
forms, 1012-1016
- applications, 485
- boxes, 276-277
- color, 279-281
- command files, editing, 622-633
- copying elements, 258
- creating, 252-255, 605-612
- custom forms, 284-285
- DEFINE FORM command, 609-612
- editing, 283-284
- fields
  - attributes, 261-274
  - calculated fields, 274-275
  - color, 279-280
  - deleting, 257
  - edit options, 269-274
  - inserting, 256
  - memo fields, 259-261
  - picture functions, 266-269
  - sizing, 259
  - templates, 261-265
- Forms Design screen, 253, 606-607, 677
  - exiting, 282
  - mouse, 1088
  - navigating, 253-255
- lines, 277-278
- menus
  - default menus, 618-619
  - editing, 619-622
- moving elements, 258
- mulTiple-page forms, 282-283
- Object Inspector window, 608
- objects
  - commands, 987-1040
  - control, 613
  - customizing, 614-618
  - field entry, 613
  - methods, 982-987
  - properties, 900-982
- relational databases, 374-375
- running, 633-634
- saving, 281-282, 607
- selecting elements, 257
- text, editing, 255-256
- troubleshooting, 284
  - objects, 618
  - tab order, 634

Forward Search command (Go To menu), 139, 153
FOUND( ) function, 784
FPUTS( ) function, 784
FREAD( ) function, 784
Freeze Field command (Fields menu), 149
freezing fields, 149
FROM clause (SELECT command), 579, 894
FSEEK( ) function, 784-785
FSIZE( ) function, 785
FTIME( ) function, 785
FUNCTION command, 700
function key assignment commands, 1075-1076
Function property, 931
functions, 166
- calculated fields, 218-219
- character functions, 166-167
- conversion functions, 168-169
- *see also* individual function names

FV( ) function, 785-786
FWRITE( ) function, 786

G

Generate menu commands
- Begin Generation, 549
- Select Template, 548

Generate Sample Labels command (Print menu), 341
GETENV( ) function, 786
GETS command, 1067
GO command, 388
Go To Line Number command (Go To menu), 139-140
Go To menu commands
- Backward Search, 139, 153
- Forward Search, 139, 153
- Go To Line Number, 139-140
- Go To Record Number, 152
- Index Key Search, 154, 173
- Last Record, 152
- Match Capitalization, 154
- Replace, 140
- Skip, 152
- Top Record, 152

Go To Record Number command (Go To menu), 152
GO TOP command, 438
GO/GOTO command, 700-701
GrabFocus property, 932-933
GRANT command, 585
GRANT command (SQL), 586, 889
greater than (>) relational operator, 201, 640
greater than or equal to (>=) relational operator, 201, 640
Grid property, 933
Group band (reports), 294
GROUP BY clause (SELECT command), 576, 894
Group property, 933-934
grouping records, 227-228
- reports, 307-310

H

HAVING clause (SELECT command), 576, 894
Heading property, 934
Height property, 934-935
help, 20-21, 62-64
- debugging programs, 460
- SET commands, 829

HELP command, 701
help screens (applications), 502-503
HelpFile property, 935-936
HelpId property, 936
hidden calculated fields (reports), 304
hiding
- condition box, 214
- menu bar, 680

HOME( ) function, 787
Horizontal Bar Menu command (Design menu), 537

I

ID( ) function, 787
#if preprocessor directive, 392, 395
#if...#endif preprocessor directive, 1058-1059
IF command, 454-455
IF...ENDIF command, 701-702
#ifdef preprocessor directive, 392, 395, 1059-1060
#ifndef preprocessor directive, 392, 1060
IIF( ) function, 787
IMPORT command, 524
Import command (Tools menu), 83
IMPORT FROM command, 702-703
importing
  binary files, 656-657
  data to SQL tables, 587-588
  files, 702-703
  from Control Center, 82-83
IN predicate (SELECT command), 578
#include preprocessor directive, 392, 1060-1061
Include Indexes command (Fields menu), 230
included relational operator ($), 201
_Indent system memory variable, 1044-1045
INDEX command, 438-441, 515
Index Key Search command (Go To menu), 154, 173
INDEX ON command, 703-704
INDEX...FOR query method, 248
INDEXBYTES command, 1067
indexing
  data tables (reports), 515
  fields, 150-152, 162-163
    advantages, 113-115
    ASCII sort order, 171-172
    concatenating character fields, 168
    conditional indexing, 172-173
    converting data types, 168-169
    COPY INDEX command, 669-670
    COPY TAG command, 671
    creating indexes, 163-169
    deleting index tags, 689
    dictionary sort order, 172
    expressions, 165-169
    grouping records, 227
    INDEX ON command, 703-704
    moving screen cursor, 151
    multiple field indexes, 171
    multiple fields, 115
    Organize menu commands, 175-176
    queries, 230-231
    searching records, 173-176
    sorting records, 169-184
    troubleshooting, 174
indirect referencing, 752
initializing memory variables, 424-428
INKEY( ) function, 788-790
input (programs)
  @... commands, 445-452
  memory variables, 444-445, 704-705
  testing, 453-454
    IF command, 454-455
    WHILE loops, 455-456
input boxes, 39
INPUT command, 444, 704-705
INSERT command, 705-706
  SQL, 581-582, 596
INSERT INTO command (SQL), 890
Insert Page Break command (Words menu), 139, 330
inserting
  array elements, 759-760
  calculated fields, 220
  data (SQL), 581-582
  fields, 123
    forms, 256
    labels, 335-337
    mailmerge reports, 326-330
    queries, 192
    reports, 294-295
  Group bands (reports), 308-309
  objects on forms, 613
  page breaks (mailmerge reports), 330
  Page Footer bands (reports), 312-313
  Page Header bands (reports), 312-313
  records, 705-706
    APPEND command, 654-655
    Browse screen, 130-131
    Edit screen, 128-130
    memory variable arrays, 656
    update queries, 241-243
  text
    Desktop Editor, 398
    Program Editor, 404
    text editor, 139
InsertLine property, 936-937
INSPECT( ) function, 790-791
INT( ) function, 167, 791
INTEGER data type (SQL), 571, 880
integrity tags (files), 733
INTO clause (SELECT command), 575, 893
inventory applications, 484-485
invoice applications, 481-484
ISALPHA( ) function, 791
ISBLANK( ) function, 791
ISCOLOR( ) function, 792
ISLOWER( ) function, 792
ISMARKED( ) function, 792
ISMOUSE( ) function, 793
ISUPPER( ) function, 793
Item menu commands, Change Action, 543

J-K

JOIN WITH command, 706-707

key fields, 162
Key property, 937
KEY( ) function, 793
KeyAlt property, 937-938
KEYBOARD command, 707
keyboard macros, 511-512
keyboard shortcuts (Control Center), 72
KeyCtrl property, 938
KEYMATCH( ) function, 794
KeyNormal property, 938
KeyShift property, 939
KeyValue property, 939-946

L

L picture template, 449
LABEL FORM command, 708
Label property, 946
label reports, 675-676
- dimensions, 332-335
- editing, 338
- fields, 335-337
- files, editing, 711-712
- Labels Design screen, 331-332
  - mouse, 1088
- printing, 341
- queries, 340
- saving, 338-339
- troubleshooting, 339
- viewing, 340-341

LANGTABLES command, 1067
language enhancements, 23-24
Largest Allowed Value edit option (forms), 272-273
Last Record command (Go To menu), 152
LASTKEY( ) function, 794
Layout menu commands
- Add File to Query, 241
- Box, 276
- Create Link by Pointing, 245
- Edit Database Description, 120
- Line, 278
- Print database structure, 120
- Quick Layout, 253
- Save This Database File Structure, 119
- Save This Form, 281
- Save This Query, 221
- Save This Report, 314
- Write View as Database File, 200

LDRIVER command, 1068
LDRIVER( ) function, 794-795
Left property, 947
LEFT( ) function, 166, 795
LEN( ) function, 795
less than (<) relational operator, 201, 640
less than or equal to (<=) relational operator, 201, 640
libraries, macros, 80
LIKE predicate (SELECT command), 578, 881
like relational operator, 201
LIKE( ) function, 795-796
Line command (Layout menu), 278
LineNo property, 947-948
LINENO( ) function, 796
lines
- forms, 277-278
- reports, 313-314

Lines property, 948
linking databases, 245-248
List All command (Window menu), 47, 50
list boxes, 41-42, 1016-1019
LIST command, 520, 638
listings
- 21.1 Form Designer Saves Object Code, 609
- 21.2 dot reference notation, 610-612
- 21.3 PRG file, 622-624
- 21.4 DFM file, 625-628
- 21.5 MNU file, 629-632

LKSYS( ) function, 796-797
_Lmargin system memory variable, 1045
LOAD command, 709
- SQL, 587-588

LOAD DATA FROM command (SQL), 890-891
Load Library command (Macros menu), 81
loading macros, 734-735
local variables, naming, 722
LOCALSHARE command, 1068
LOCATE command, 515, 709-710
Lock Fields on Left command (Fields menu), 147
Lock property, 948
locking
- databases, 782-783
- fields, 146-147, 150
- records
  - CONVERT command, 668-669
  - RLOCK( ) function, 813
  - unlocking, 747

LOG( ) function, 797
LOG10( ) function, 797
LOGICAL data type (SQL), 571, 880
logical fields, 112
- queries, 196
- templates, 264

logical operators, 640
LOGOUT command, 710
LOOKUP( ) function, 797-798
LOOP command, 456
loops, 699
low-level files, 778-779, 783
LOWER( ) function, 167, 798
LTRIM( ) function, 431, 798
LUPDATE( ) function, 798-799

M

macros, 511-512
- & function, 751-752
- editing, 81
- libraries, 80
- loading, 734-735
- naming, 81
- playing, 79, 722-723
- recording, 78-79
- saving, 738-739
- slowing playback process, 80

Macros menu commands
- Append to Macro, 81
- Begin Recording, 78
- End Recording, 79
- Load Library, 81
- Name, 81
- Save Library, 80

Mailer application, 530-536, 551
mailmerge reports, 290-291
- bands, 324-326
- calculated fields, 329-330
- designing, 324-331
- editing, 330
- exiting, 330
- fields, 326-330
- page breaks, 330
- printing, 341
- queries, 340
- saving, 330
- troubleshooting, 339
- viewing, 340-341

main menu bar, 13, 34-36
managing memory, 1074-1075
manual databases, 107-108
many-to-many relationships, 247
margins (reports), 292
Mark Record For Deletion command (Records menu), 157
marking records for deletion, 157, 688
- update queries, 243-244

Match Capitalization command (Go To menu), 154
mathematical operators, 639
Max field, 307
MAX operator, 224
MAX( ) function, 662, 799
SQL, 881
Maximize command (Edit menu), 59
Maximize property, 949
MCOL( ) function, 799
MDI property, 949-950
MDX files, 439
MDX( ) function, 799-800
MDY( ) function, 800
MEMLINES( ) function, 800
memo fields, 112-113, 123
attaching text files, 140
copying, 670
editing, 134-137
forms, 259-261
importing text, 656-657
memory variables, 429
printing, 141
queries, 197
reports, 295-296
saving, 141
searching, 213-214
SET commands, 829
troubleshooting, 141
memory
managing, 1074-1075
SET commands, 830
memory allocation commands, 1073-1074
memory variables, 424
arrays, 432-434, 488
copying elements, 753-754
declaring, 682
deleting entries, 755
DOS files, characteristics, 756-757
field characteristics, 757-758
inserting data in fields, 732
inserting elements, 759-760
inserting records, 656
searching, 762
sizing, 759-761
sorting, 763
data entry, 727
deleting, 729-730
initializing, 424-428
listing, 692-693
private, 428-429, 724
procedure libraries, 506
public, 428-429, 726
retrieving, 734
storing values, 744
system memory variables, 1041-1053
user input, 444-445, 704-705
uses, 429-431
MEMORY( ) function, 800-801
menu bar, 34-36
hiding, 680
Menu menu commands
Attach Pull-Down Menus, 541
Put Away Current Menu, 540
Save Current Menu, 540
Menu property, 950
MENU( ) function, 801
menus
Application Generator, designing main menu, 536-538
applications, 486-489
customizing pop-up menus, 496-497
DEFINE MENU command, 490-491
lists (pop-up), 497-498
menu bars, 490
pop-up menus, 491-492
pull-down menus, 490
sample program, 492-496
dBASE IV menus, 442-444
executing commands, 717
forms, 618-622
menu bars, 1019-1020
creating, 684
mouse, 1086
object-oriented, 444
pads, 685
exiting, 716
pop-up
defining, 682-683, 686-687
executing commands, 713
exiting, 716
hiding, 680
text-based menus, 441-442
troubleshooting, 551
UI menus, 1021-1023
viewing, 546, 652
Message edit option (forms), 271
MESSAGE( ) function, 802
methods, 982-987
Min field, 307
MIN operator, 224
MIN( ) function, 662, 802
SQL, 881
Minimize property, 950-951
minus sign (-)
string operator, 641
subtraction operator, 639
MLINE( ) function, 802
MOD( ) function, 802-803
Modified( ) method, 983
Modify Catalog Name command (Catalog menu), 73
MODIFY COMMAND command, 710-711
Modify Existing Index command (Organize menu), 176
MODIFY FILE command, 711
MODIFY LABEL command, 711-712
Modify property, 951
MODIFY STRUCTURE command, 121, 712
MONTH( ) function, 803
mouse, 27
properties, 951-953
settings, 1086-1089
Move command
Operations menu, 93
Window menu, 48
MOVE WINDOW command, 712-713
Moveable property, 954
moving
fields
bands (reports), 296-297
mailmerge reports, 330
queries, 192-193
files, 93-94
form elements, 258
text
Desktop Editor, 400
Program Editor, 405
windows, 48, 712-713
MROW( ) function, 803
multiple search conditions
AND condition, 207-208
OR condition, 209
mulTiple-page forms, 282-283

multiplication operator (*), 639
MVARSIZE command, 1073
MVMAXBLKS/MVBLKSIZE command, 1073

N

N picture template, 449
Name command (Macros menu), 81
Name property, 954
naming
- default file extensions, 1083-1085
- fields, 110
  - queries, 191
- files, 94-104, 730
- macros, 81
- variables, 722

NavBar property, 955
navigating
- Applications Generator, 536
- Desktop Editor, 398
- Forms Design screen, 253-255
- Program Editor, 404
- records, 154
- Reports Design screen, 288-289
- text editor, 137-139

NDX( ) function, 803-804
nested queries (SQL), 579
nesting functions, 169
network programs, developing, 417-418
NETWORK( ) function, 804
networks
- SET commands, 830
- viewing user list, 694

New command (File menu), 45
Next command (Window menu), 46
NOCLOCK command, 1068
normalizing databases, 482
.NOT. logical operator, 640
not equal to (<>)
- logical operator, 640
- relational operator, 201, 640

NOTE command, 713
NPV( ) function, 662
NUMERIC data type (SQL), 571, 880
numeric fields, 111
- converting to strings, 168
- editing, 133
- picture functions, 269
- queries, 195
- template symbols, 264
- templates (reports), 298
- totalling, 746

numeric functions, 167-168

O

Object Inspector window, 608
object-oriented menus, 444
objects
- commands, 987-1040
- dot reference notation, 899-900
- methods, 982-987
- properties, 900-982
- forms, 613-618

ON BAR command, 713
ON ERROR/ESCAPE/KEY command, 713-715
ON EXIT BAR command, 716
ON EXIT MENU command, 716
ON EXIT PAD command, 716-717
ON EXIT POPUP command, 717
ON KEY command, 502
ON MENU command, 717
ON MOUSE command, 717-718
ON PAD command, 491, 718
ON PAGE command, 719
ON POPUP command, 719
ON READERROR command, 720
ON SELECTION BAR command, 720
ON SELECTION MENU command, 720
ON SELECTION PAD command, 491, 721
ON SELECTION POPUP command, 721
OnAppend property, 955
OnChange property, 956
OnClick property, 956
OnClose property, 957
OnDelete property, 957-958
OnEdit property, 958
OnGotFocus property, 958-959
OnHelp property, 959
OnLostFocus property, 959-960
OnMouseDblClk property, 960
OnMove property, 960
OnOpen property, 961
OnSelChange property, 961-962
OnSize property, 962
OnSkip property, 962
Open command (File menu), 53
OPEN command (SQL), 591, 891
Open File dialog box, 21, 53
Open( ) method, 983-984
opening
- cursors (SQL), 591
- files, 53-55, 748-749
  - Control Center, 70-72
  - cross tabulation, 348
  - low-level files, 783
- queries, 200
- windows, 45-47

operating systems, 804
Operations menu commands
- Copy, 92
- Delete, 92
- Edit, 95
- Move, 93
- Rename, 94
- View, 95

operators
- precedence, 641-642
- sort operators, 233
- summary operators, 224
- types, 639-641

Options menu commands
- Compiler, 413
- dBASE Set, 407

.OR. logical operator, 640
OR condition, 209
ORDER BY clause (SELECT command), 894
Order Records By Index command (Organize menu), 150, 169
ORDER( ) function, 804
Organize menu commands
- Create New Index, 164
- Display First Duplicate Key Only, 175
- Erase Marked Records, 157, 244
- Modify Existing Index, 176

Order Records By Index, 150, 169
Remove Unwanted Index Tag, 175
Sort Database On Field List, 177
OS( ) function, 804
output
programs, 457
SET commands, 830
Output Options command (Print menu), 318-319

P

PACK command, 524, 721-722
packing databases, 157, 244, 721-722
PAD( ) function, 442, 805
PADPROMPT( ) function, 805
pads (menus), 685
exiting, 716
_Padvance system memory variable, 1045-1046
page breaks, 1025-1026
mailmerge reports, 330
text editor, 139
Page Dimensions command (Print menu), 319-320
Page Footer bands (reports), 294, 312-313
Page Header bands (reports), 293, 312-313
_Pageno system memory variable, 1046
PARAMETERS command, 506, 722
Parent property, 963
passwords, 96-101
Paste command (Edit menu), 400
PAYMENT( ) function, 805-806
_Pbpage system memory variable, 1046
PCOL( ) function, 806
_Pcolno system memory variable, 1046
_Pcopies system memory variable, 1047
PCOUNT( ) function, 508, 806
_Pdriver system memory variable, 1047
PDRIVER command, 1068
_Pecode system memory variable, 1047
_Peject system memory variable, 1048
_Pepage system memory variable, 1048
Perform the Update command (Update menu), 237
period (.) picture template, 449
Permit Edit If edit option (forms), 270-271
_Pform system memory variable, 1048-1049
PI( ) function, 806-807
picture functions (fields)
forms, 266-269
reports, 299-302
Picture property, 963-964
picture templates, 449
PLAY MACRO command, 511, 722-723
playing macros, 79
_Plength system memory variable, 1049
_Plineno, 1049
_Ploffset system memory variable, 1049-1050
plus sign (+)
addition operator, 639
concatenating character fields, 168
string operator, 641
pop-up lists (applications), 497-498
Pop-up Menu command (Design menu), 539, 543
pop-up menus
activating, 653
applications, 491-492
Applications Generator, 539-547
creating, 442
customizing, 496-497
defining, 682-683, 686-687
executing commands, 713
exiting, 716
hiding, 680
POPUP( ) function, 807
pound sign (#)
logical operator, 640
not equal to relational operator, 201, 640
picture template, 449
_Ppitch system memory variable, 1050
_Pquality system memory variable, 1050
predefined label sizes, 332-333
predicates (SQL), 881
preprocessor directives, 391-396, 458, 1057-1062
Preset menu commands, 548
Print command (File menu), 57
Print database structure command (Layout menu), 120
Print Form command (Print menu), 320
PRINT JOB...ENDPRINT JOB command, 723-724
Print menu commands
Begin Printing, 321
Control of Printer, 317-318
Destination, 316-317
Eject Page Now, 141
Generate Sample Labels, 341
Output Options, 318-319
Page Dimensions, 319-320
Print Form, 320
View Report, 340
View Report On Screen, 315
PRINTER command, 1069
PRINTER FONT command, 1069
printing
databases, 120
files, 57-58
label reports, 341
mailmerge reports, 341
memo fields, 141
Quick Reports, 179-180
reports, 316-320, 733
SET commands, 831
without printer drivers, 645
PRINTSTATUS( ) function, 807
private memory variables, 428-429, 724
procedure libraries, 506
PRIVATE/PRIVATE ALL command, 724
PROCEDURE command, 724-725
procedure libraries, 504-508
ProcFile property, 964-966
Program Editor
MODIFY COMMAND command, 710-711
navigating window, 404
saving, 406
text
copying, 405
deleting, 404-405

inserting, 404
moving, 405
searching, 406
selecting, 404
PROGRAM( ) function, 807
programming, 384
applications
defining files, 477-479
designing, 479-486
editing files, 485-486
embedding SQL code, 594-599
external programs, 508-511
forms, 485
help screens, 502-503
inventory, 484-485
invoices, 481-484
keyboard macros, 511-512
Mailer, 530-536, 551
menus, 486-498
procedure libraries, 504-508
reports, 485, 512-525
windows, 498-502
Applications Generator, 528
batch process, 552
designing main menu, 536-538
distributing applications, 556-560
documentation, 549-551
editing, 555-556
file list, 552
generating code, 548-549
mouse, 1088
navigating, 536
planning applications, 528-533
pop-up menus, 539-547
pull-down menus, 539-547
running Mailer application, 551
saving, 538
starting, 533, 675
structure list, 552
commands, 388-390
comments, 642, 713
compiling programs, 412-415, 667, 1055-1056
Customer Tracking system, 466-476
debugging programs, 415-417, 459, 553-554
breakpoints, 461
code display window, 460
example, 462-465
help, 460
starting debugger, 681
variables, 460
Desktop Editor, 397-402
documenting programs, 409
environment variables, 434-438
functions, 390-391
BAR( ), 443, 492
BARPROMPT( ), 492
CTOD( ), 427
LTRIM( ), 431
PAD( ), 442
RIGHT( ), 431
RTRIM( ), 431
SPACE( ), 425
STR( ), 430
STUFF( ), 429
SUBSTR( ), 431
TRANSFORM( ), 449
VAL( ), 430
guidelines, 384-388
input, 445-456
loops, 699
memory variables, 424
arrays, 432-434
initializing, 424-428
private, 428-429
public, 428-429
user input, 444-445
uses, 429-431
menus
dBASE IV menus, 442-444
object-oriented, 444
text-based menus, 441-442
mouse, 1089
network programs, 417-418
output, 457
picture templates, 449
preprocessor directives, 391-396, 458, 1057-1062
Program Editor, 404-406
Project Manager
creating projects, 410-411
options, 411-412
running programs, 695
SET commands, 831
standards, 422-424
Text Editor, 406-408
troubleshooting, 396
applications, 503
Applications Generator, 533, 556
distributing applications, 560
indexing data tables, 441
menus, 551
printing, 453
reports, 525
word processing programs, 408-409
programs, design surface (Control Center), 1080-1083
Project Manager, 19-20
creating projects, 410-411
options, 411-412
Project Manager command (Window menu), 410
PROMPT command, 1070
PROMPT( ) function, 808
properties, 900-982
PROTECT command, 725-726
SQL, 585, 882
Protect Data command (Tools menu), 96
protecting files, 96-101
PROW( ) function, 808
_Pscode system memory variable, 1051
_Psize system memory variable, 1051-1052
_Pspacing system memory variable, 1052
PUBLIC command, 726
public memory variables, 428-429, 506, 726
pull-down menus
applications, 490
Applications Generator, 539-547
creating, 442
pushbutton objects, 1026-1029
pushbuttons, 38
Put Away Current Menu command (Menu menu), 540
PV( ) function, 808-809
_Pwait system memory variable, 1052

Q

QBE (query by example), 188-189
queries
calculated fields, 216-217
deleting, 220-221
functions, 218-219
inserting, 220
condition box, 212-214
files, creating, 679-680
creating, 189-197

embedded values, 203-204
executing, 198-200
fields, 191-193
file skeletons, 190
find operator, 215
grouping records, 227-228
indexes, 230-231
linking databases, 245-248
methods, 248-249
multiple conditions
AND condition, 207-208
OR condition, 209
opening, 200
ranges, 204-205
relational databases, 371-373
relational operators, 201-202
reports, 221-222, 315, 340
saving, 200, 221
search values, 193-197
sorting output, 231-235
multiple fields, 233-235
sounds like operator, 206
summary calculations, 223-227
troubleshooting
editing records, 248
executing queries, 199
grouping records, 235
ranges, 206
sorting output, 235
summary calculations, 227
view skeletons, 193
update queries, 236
inserting records, 241-243
marking records for deletion, 243-244
replacing values, 237-240
saving, 244
unmarking records, 244
variables, 229
view skeletons, 191-193
wild cards, 203

query by example, 188-189
question mark (?) wild card, 153, 203
Quick Layout command (Layout menu), 253
Quick Report menu commands
Begin Printing, 179
Eject Page Now, 179
Quick Reports, 178
columnar reports, 290
form reports, 290
mailmerge reports, 291
options, 182-183
printing, 179-180
troubleshooting, 183
types, 290
QUIT command, 416, 726-727

R

radio buttons, 40, 1029-1032
RAND( ) function, 809
Range Must Always Be Met edit option (forms), 273
RangeMax property, 966
RangeMin property, 967
RangeRequired property, 967
ranges, searching, 204-205
RAT( ) function, 809-810
RCUSTFOR.DFM program code, 469-472
RCUSTFOR.MNU program code, 472-476
RCUSTFOR.PRG program code, 466-469
READ command, 727
READKEY( ) function, 810-811
ReadModal( ) method, 984-985
RECALL command, 525, 728
RECCOUNT( ) function, 811
RECNO( ) function, 811
recording macros, 78-79
records, 108
blanking, 156, 659
counting, 674, 811
data entry, 126-137
deleting, 156-157
marking for deletion, 157, 243-244, 688
packing databases, 721-722
unmarking for deletion, 728
ZAP command, 750
editing, 131-132, 155
Browse screen, 145-149
CHANGE/EDIT command, 664-665
Edit screen, 145
fields
freezing, 149
indexing, 113-115
locking, 146-147
sizing, 148-149
filtering (condition box), 212-214
grouping, 227-228
reports, 307-310
inserting, 705-706
APPEND command, 654-655
Browse screen, 130-131
Edit screen, 128-130
memory variable arrays, 656
update queries, 241-243
locking
CONVERT command, 668-669
RLOCK( ) function, 813
unlocking, 747
navigating, 154
searching, 149-150
CONTINUE command, 668
FIND command, 698-699
Go To menu commands, 152-154
GO/GOTO command, 700-701
indexes, 150-152, 173-176
LOCATE command, 709-710
SEEK command, 741
sorting, 161-162, 176-178
indexes, 162-173
tracking, 132-133
troubleshooting, 132, 158, 248
viewing, 659-661
Records menu commands
Add New Records, 128
Blank Record, 156
Clear Deletion Mark, 157
Follow Record To New Position, 151
Mark Record For Deletion, 157
Undo Change To Record, 155
RECSIZE( ) function, 812
REFRESH command, 1070
Refresh( ) method, 985
RefreshRecord( ) method, 985
REINDEX command, 728-729
relational databases, 360-361
catalogs, 371
creating files, 370-371
designing, 364-371
forms, 374-375
queries, 371-373
relationships, 367-368

reports, 376-378
structure, 365-370
troubleshooting, 378
uses, 361-364
relational operators, 640
queries, 201-202
RELEASE command, 428, 729-730
RELEASE SCREENS command, 730
Release( ) method, 986
Remove Condition Box command (Condition menu), 214
Remove Field From View command (Field menu), 191
Remove Highlighted File From Catalog command (Catalog menu), 78
Remove Unwanted Index Tag command (Organize menu), 175
removing, *see* blanking; deleting
RENAME command, 730
Rename command (Operations menu), 94
renaming, *see* naming
Replace command
Go To menu, 140
Search menu, 401
Replace dialog box, 401
REPLACE FROM ARRAY command, 731-732
replacing
text
Desktop Editor, 400-402
Program Editor, 406
text editor, 139-140
update queries, 237-240
REPLICATE( ) function, 812
REPORT FORM command, 457, 732-733
Report Intro band, 293
Report Summary band (reports), 294
reports
applications, 485, 513
indexing data tables, 515
sample program, 520-524
searching data tables, 515-518
sorting data tables, 513-515
translating files, 524-525
viewing results, 518-520
bands
Detail, 293
Group, 294
Page Footer, 294, 312-313
Page Header, 293, 312-313
Report Intro, 293
Report Summary, 294
boxes, 313-314
crosstabs, 357-358
fields
attributes, 297-302
bands, 296-297
calculated fields, 302-305
deleting, 297
inserting, 294-295
memo fields, 295-296
picture functions, 299-302
sizing, 297
Summary fields, 305-307
suppressing repeated values, 302
templates, 297-299
grouping records, 307-310
label reports
dimensions, 332-335
editing, 338
fields, 335-337
printing, 341
queries, 340
saving, 338-339
viewing, 340-341
lines, 313-314
mailmerge reports
bands, 324-326
calculated fields, 329-330
designing, 324-331
editing, 330
exiting, 330
fields, 326-330
page breaks, 330
printing, 341
queries, 340
saving, 330
viewing, 340-341
margins, 292
printing, 316-320, 733
program output, 457
queries, 221-222, 315
Quick Reports, 178
columnar reports, 290
form reports, 290
mailmerge reports, 291
options, 182-183
printing, 179-180
troubleshooting, 183
types, 290
relational databases, 376-378
Reports Design screen, 288, 676-677
exiting, 314
mouse, 1088
navigating, 288-289
saving, 314
tabs, 292
text, 311-312
troubleshooting
calculated fields, 305
grouping records, 309
mailmerge reports, 339
titles, 313
viewing, 315
Reports menu commands, User Information, 99
REPROCESS command, 1070
RESET command, 733-734
RESETCRT command, 1070
RESTORE FROM command, 734
RESTORE MACRO command, 511, 734-735
RESTORE SCREEN FROM command, 735
RESTORE WINDOW command, 735
RESUME command, 735-736
retrieving data (SQL), 574-581
RETRY command, 736
RETURN command, 736-737
REVOKE command (SQL), 586, 891-892
RIGHT( ) function, 166, 431, 812-813
RLOCK( ) function, 813
_Rmargin system memory variable, 1052-1053
ROLLBACK command, 737-738
SQL, 588-589, 892
ROLLBACK( ) function, 813-814
rolling back transactions, 588-589
ROUND( ) function, 814
ROW( ) function, 814
rows (SQL tables), 568-571
RTMAXBLKS/RTBLKSIZE command, 1074
RTOD( ) function, 814
RTRIM( ) function, 431
RTRIM/TRIM( ) function, 815

RUN command, 508-509, 738
RUN( ) function, 509-510, 815
running
forms, 633-634
programs, 695
RUNSTATS command (SQL), 892-893

S

Save All command (File menu), 57
Save As command (File menu), 57
Save Changes And Exit command (Exit menu), 120, 136
SAVE command, 388
Save command (File menu), 56
Save Crosstab Result As dialog box, 350
Save Current Application Definition command (Application menu), 543
Save Current Menu command (Menu menu), 540
Save Library command (Macros menu), 80
SAVE MACRO command, 511
SAVE MACROS TO command, 738-739
SAVE SCREEN TO command, 739
Save This Database File Structure command (Layout menu), 119
Save This Form command (Layout menu), 281
Save This Query command (Layout menu), 221
Save This Report command (Layout menu), 314
SAVE TO command, 739
SAVE TO TEMP clause (SELECT command), 894
SAVE WINDOW command, 739-740
SaveFile property, 968
saving
Applications Generator, 538
crosstabs, 350
databases, 118-121
Desktop Editor, 402-403
environments, 435-436
files, 56-57
forms, 281-282, 607
labels, 338-339
macros, 738-739
mailmerge reports, 330
memo fields, 141
Program Editor, 406
queries, 200, 221
reports, 314
troubleshooting, 158
update queries, 244
user profiles, 100
SCAN command, 456, 499
SCAN...ENDSCAN command, 740
screen display, settings, 101-102, 831-832
screen output (programs), 457
Search menu commands
Find, 401
Replace, 401
searching
arrays (memory variables), 762
data tables (reports), 515-518
databases (queries), 188-189
memo fields, 213-214
records, 149-150
CONTINUE command, 668
FIND command, 698-699
Go To menu commands, 152-154
GO/GOTO command, 700-701
indexes, 173-176
indexing fields, 150-152
LOCATE command, 709-710
SEEK command, 741
text
Desktop Editor, 400-402
Program Editor, 406
text editor, 139-140
security (SQL), 584-587, 882
SEEK command, 516, 740-741
SEEK( ) function, 816
SELECT command (SQL), 574-581, 741-742, 880-881, 893-895
Select Template command (Generate menu), 548
SELECT( ) function, 816
SelectAll property, 968-969
selecting
form elements, 257
objects (forms), 614
text
Desktop Editor, 399
Program Editor, 404
Separator property, 969
SET commands
alphabetical listing, 832-877
CONFIG.DB file, 1076-1079
databases, 828
dates, 829
encryption, 828
general settings, 829
help, 829
memo fields, 829
memory, 830
networks, 830
number display, 830
output, 830
printing, 831
program files, 831
screen display, 831-832
sound, 832
SQL, 832
times, 829
Set Default Drive:Directory command (DOS menu), 86
SET ECHO command, 29, 436
SET ESCAPE OFF command, 444
SET FILTER query method, 248
SET KEY query method, 248
SET ORDER command, 518
SET PRINT OFF command, 437
SET PRINT ON command, 437
SET REPROCESS command (SQL), 602
SET SAFETY commands, 525
SET SCOREBOARD command, 30, 436
SET SQL command (SQL), 895
SET STATUS OFF command, 30, 436
SET TALK command, 29, 436
SET( ) function, 816-817
SetFocus( ) method, 986
Settings command, 133
Settings command (Tools menu), 101
Shadow property, 969-970
shortcut keys, 72
Shortcut property, 970
SHOW DATABASE command (SQL), 569, 895
SHOW MENU command, 742
SHOW POPUP command, 742-743
ShowDelete property, 970-971

ShowRecNo property, 971
SIGN( ) function, 817
SIN( ) function, 817
Size command (Window menu), 47
Size Field command (Fields menu), 148
Sizeable property, 971-972
sizing
  arrays (memory variables), 759, 761
  fields, 148-150
    forms, 259
    reports, 297
  windows, 47-48
SKIP command, 388, 443, 743
Skip command (Go To menu), 152
slash (/) division operator, 639
Smallest Allowed Value edit option (forms), 272-273
SMALLINT data type (SQL), 571, 880
SORT command, 513
Sort Database On Field List command (Organize menu), 177
Sort on This Field command (Fields menu), 231
SORT TO command, 743-744
Sorted property, 972
sorting
  arrays (memory variables), 763
  data tables (reports), 513-515
  file list, 89
  query output, 231-235
  records, 161-162, 176-178
    indexes, 162-173
sound, settings, 832
SOUNDEX( ) function, 817-818
sounds like relational operator, 201, 206
SPACE( ) function, 425, 818
Specify Update Operation command (Update menu), 236
spin boxes, 42-43, 1034-1037
SpinOnly property, 972-973
SQL (structured query language), 566
  building statements, 573-574
  Command window, 567
  commands
    breaking, 567
    dBASE commands, 882
    see also individual command names
  cursors, 590-594
  data
    deleting, 583-584
    editing, 582-583
    inserting, 581-582
    retrieving, 574-581
  data types, 879-880
  embedding code in applications, 594-599
  error trapping, 600-601
  functions, 575, 880-881
  predicates, 881
  security, 584-587, 882
  system files, 570
  tables, 568
    columns, 568-571
    converting databases, 587
    data types, 571-573
    exporting data, 588
    importing data, 587-588
    rows, 568-571
  transactions, 601-604, 658
    rolling back, 588-589
  troubleshooting, 584
SQLDATABASE command, 1071
SQLHOME command, 1071
SQRT( ) function, 819
StandAlone executables, building, 559
START DATABASE command (SQL), 569, 896
starting
  Applications Generator, 533, 675
  dBASE 5, 25-27
  debugger, 681
StatusMessage property, 973
Std field, 307
STD operator, 224
STD( ) function, 662
Step property, 973
STOP DATABASE command (SQL), 569, 896
STORE command, 388, 424, 744
STR( ) function, 168, 430, 819
string operators, 641
strings, converting, 168
structure list (Applications Generator), 552
structured query language, *see* SQL
STUFF( ) function, 429, 819
Style property, 974
styles (reports), 311-312
Submit( ) method, 986-987
subqueries, 579
SUBSTR( ) function, 167, 431, 820
subtraction operator (-), 639
SUM command, 745
Sum field, 307
SUM operator, 224
SUM( ) function, 662
  SQL, 881
summary calculations, 223-227
summary fields
  crosstabs, 349
  reports, 305-307, 310
suppressing repeated values (reports), 302
SUSPEND commands, 416, 745
switching
  catalogs (Control Center), 75
  directories, 55-56
    Control Center, 86-88
syntax (commands), 637-639
SysMenu property, 974
SYSPROC command, 1071
system memory variables, 1041-1053

T

tables (SQL)
  columns, 568-571
  converting databases, 587
  data types, 571-573
  exporting data, 588
  importing data, 587-588
  rows, 568-571
TabPos property, 975
_Tabs system memory variable, 1053
tabs (reports), 292
TABS command, 1071
TabStop property, 975
TAG( ) function, 820
TAGCOUNT( ) function, 820
TAGNO( ) function, 821
TAN( ) function, 821
TEDIT/EDITOR command, 1072
Template Language interpreter, 773
templates (fields)
  forms, 261-265
  reports, 297-299
testing input (programs), 453-456

text
blocks of text, 139
Desktop Editor
copying, 400
deleting, 399
inserting, 398
moving, 400
searching, 400-402
selecting, 399
Program Editor
copying, 405
deleting, 404-405
inserting, 404
moving, 405
searching, 406
selecting, 404
forms, editing, 255-256
inserting, 139
reports, 311-312
text editor
attaching text files to memo fields, 140
blocks of text, 139
Clipboard, 407-408
deleting text, 139
inserting text, 139
MODIFY FILE command, 711
navigating, 137-139
page breaks, 139
programming, 406-407
searching text, 139-140
Text property, 976
text-based menus, 441-442
TEXT...ENDTEXT command, 746
TIME( ) function, 821
Too many files are open error message, 28
Tools menu commands
ASCII Chart, 59
Calculator, 60
Calendar, 61
Cross Tabulation, 346
Export, 83
Form Designer, 606
Import, 83
Protect Data, 96
Settings, 101, 133
Top property, 977
Top Record command (Go To menu), 152
TOTAL ON command, 746
transactions (SQL), 601-604, 658
rolling back, 588-589, 737-738
Transfer to Query Design command (Exit menu), 198
TRANSFORM( ) function, 449, 822
translating files, 524-525
TRIM( ) function, 822
troubleshooting
Browse screen, 130
crosstabs, 358
database structure, 121, 123
Edit screen, 130
fields, 142, 150
forms, 284
objects, 618
tab order, 634
indexes, 174
labels, 339
memo fields, 141
programming, 396
applications, 503
Applications Generator, 533, 556
distributing applications, 560
indexing data tables, 441
menus, 551
printing, 453
reports, 525
word processing programs, 409
queries
editing records, 248
executing, 199
grouping records, 235
ranges, 206
sorting output, 235
summary calculations, 227
view skeletons, 193
Quick Reports, 183
records
blanking, 158
deleting, 158
editing, 132, 248
relational databases, 378
reports
calculated fields, 305
grouping records, 309
mailmerge reports, 339
titles, 313
saving, 158
SQL, 584, 594
TYPE command, 747
TYPE( ) function, 822-823

U

UDFs (user-defined functions), 596, 700
UI (user interface)
commands, 987-1040
dot reference notation, 899-900
methods, 982-987
properties, 900-982
see also forms
UI Object Inspector dialog box, 790-791
Unaccepted Message edit option (forms), 274
unary negative sign (-), 639
unary positive sign (+), 639
#undef preprocessor directive, 392, 1061-1062
Undo Change To Record command (Records menu), 155
UNION clause (SELECT command), 577, 894
UNIQUE( ) function, 823
UNLOAD command (SQL), 588
UNLOAD DATA TO command (SQL), 896-897
UNLOCK command, 747
unnamed calculated fields (reports), 304
UPDATE command (SQL), 582-583, 897
embedding in cursor commands, 592-593
Update menu commands
Perform the Update, 237
Specify Update Operation, 236
UPDATE ON command, 747-748
update queries, 236
inserting records, 241-243
marking records for deletion, 243-244
replacing values, 237-240
saving, 244
unmarking records, 244
upgrading to dBASE 5, 12
UPPER( ) function, 167, 823
Use a Different Catalog command (Catalog menu), 74
USE command, 388, 437, 748-749

USE EXCLUSIVE command, 122
user-defined functions (UDFs), 596, 700
User Information command (Reports menu), 99
user input
  memory variables, 444-445, 704-705
  programs
    @... commands, 445-452
    testing, 453-456
user interface, *see* UI
user profiles, 97
USER( ) function, 824
users, access levels, 753

V

VAL( ) function, 430, 824
Valid property, 977-978
ValidErrorMsg property, 978
ValidRequired property, 978-979
Value Must Always Be Valid edit option (forms), 273
Value property, 979-980
values, 109
Var field, 307
VAR operator, 224
VAR( ) function, 662
variables (queries), 229
VARREAD( ) function, 824-825
VERSION( ) function, 825
View command (Operations menu), 95
View Report command (Print menu), 340
View Report On Screen command (Print menu), 315
view skeletons (QBE), 191-193
viewing
  ASCII file contents, 747
  database structure, 694
  file contents, 690-691
  files, 94-95
  label reports, 340-341
  mailmerge reports, 340-341
  menus, 546, 652
  records, 659-661
  report results (applications), 518-520
  reports, 315
Visible property, 980

W

WAIT command, 388, 445, 750
WHERE clause (SELECT command), 575, 894
WHILE loops, 455-456
width (fields), 113
Width property, 980-981
wild cards
  queries, 203
  searching records, 153
Window menu commands
  Cascade, 49
  Close, 51
  Control Center, 51
  List All, 47, 50
  Move, 48
  Next, 46
  Project Manager, 410
  Size, 47
WINDOW( ) function, 825
Windows, starting dBASE 5, 26-27
windows, 14-15
  applications, 498-502
  closing, 51
  Command window
    entering commands, 43-44
    reusing commands, 44-45
  defining, 687-688
  Edit window, 45
  hiding, 681
  listing, 50
  moving, 48, 712-713
  multiple windows, displaying, 48-49
  opening, 45-47
  sizing, 47-48
  zoom box, 48
WindowState property, 981
word processing programs, 408-409
Words menu commands
  Delete a Line, 139
  Display, 279
  Insert Page Break, 139, 330
  Write, 141
  Write/Read Text File, 140
WordWrap property, 981-982
WP command, 1072
_Wrap system memory variable, 1053
Write command (Words menu), 141
Write View as Database File command (Layout menu), 200
Write/Read Text File command (Words menu), 140
writing help screens (applications), 502-503

X–Y–Z

X picture template, 449

Y picture template, 449
YEAR( ) function, 825

ZAP command, 525, 750
zoom box, 48